W9-ACB-655

art since 1900

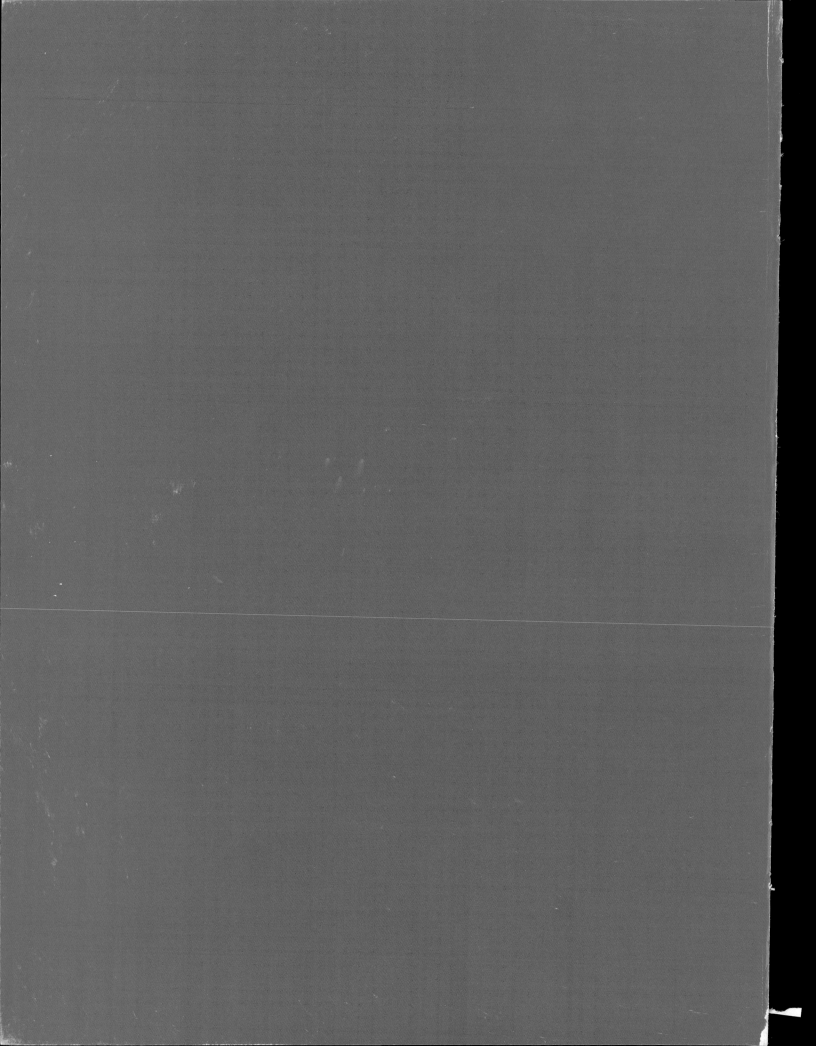

art since 1900

modernism
antimodernism
postmodernism

with 637 illustrations, 413 in color

hal foster
rosalind krauss
yve-alain bois
benjamin h. d. buchloh

Thames & Hudson

To Nikos Stangos (1936–2004), in memoriam

With love, admiration, and grief, we dedicate this book to Nikos Stangos, great editor, poet, and friend, whose belief in this project both instigated and sustained it through the course of its development.

We would like to thank Thomas Neurath and Peter Warner for their patient support, and Nikos Stangos and Andrew Brown for their editorial expertise. The book would not have been begun without Nikos; it would not have been completed without Andrew.

The publishers would like to thank Amy Dempsey for her assistance in the preparation of this book.

First published in hardcover in the United States of America by Thames & Hudson Inc., 500 Fifth Avenue, New York, New York 10110

thamesandhudsonusa.com

Library of Congress Catalog Card Number 2004102006
ISBN 0-500-23818-9

Printed and bound in Singapore by CS Graphics

Contents

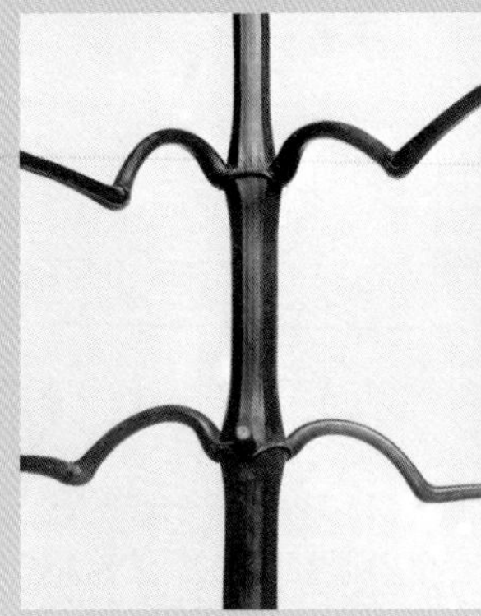

1920–1929

1930–1939

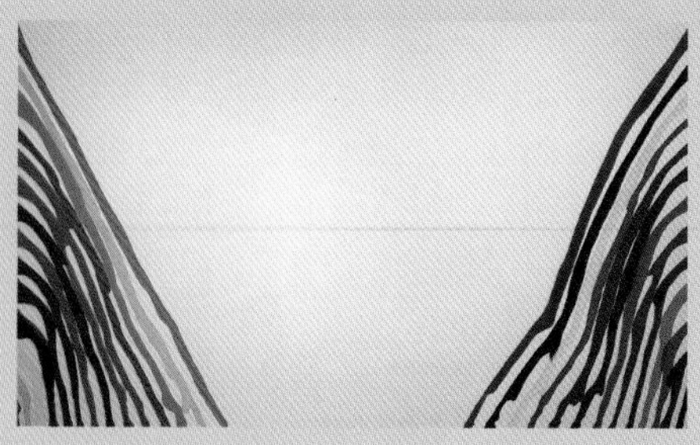

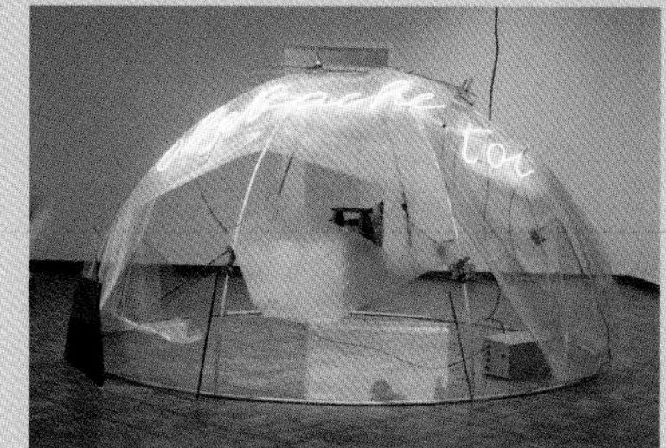

1960–1969

1970–1979

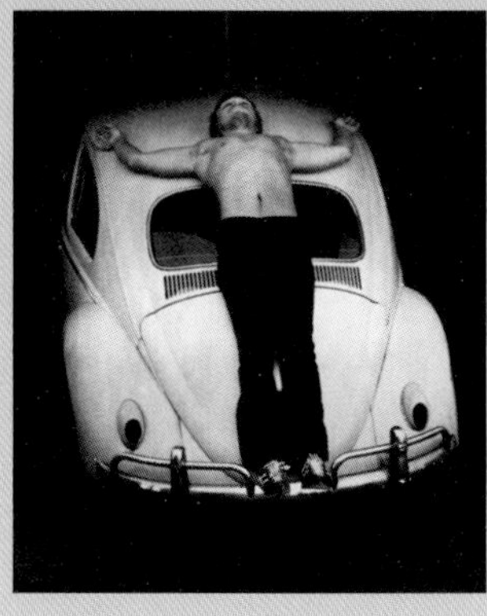

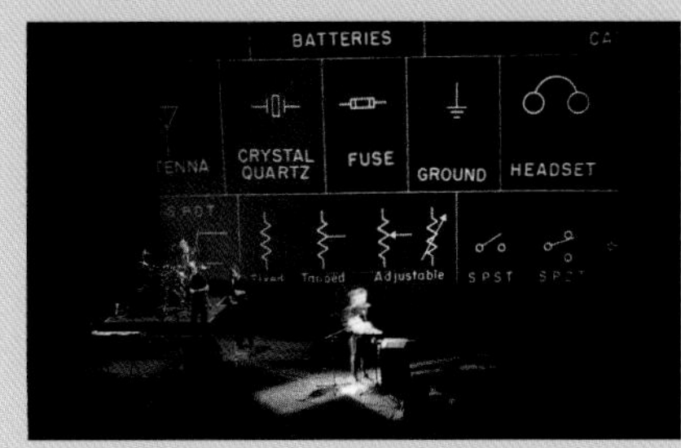
BATTERIES
CRYSTAL QUARTZ
FUSE
GROUND
HEADSET
Adjustable
SPST

How to use this book

Art Since 1900 has been designed to make it straightforward for you to follow the development of art through the twentieth century and up to the present day. Here are the features that will help you find your way through the book.

Each entry centers on a key moment in the history of twentieth-century art, indicated by the title at the head of the entry. It might be the creation of a groundbreaking work, the publication of a seminal text, the opening of a crucial exhibition, or another significant event. Where two or more entries appear in any one year, they are identified as 1900a, 1900b, and so on.

Picture references in the text direct you clearly to the illustration under discussion.

Symbols in the margin indicate that other related entries may be of interest. The corresponding cross-references at the foot of the page direct you to the relevant entries. These allow you to follow your own course through the book, to trace, for example, the history of photography or sculpture or the development of abstraction in its different forms.

1908

Wilhelm Worringer publishes *Abstraction and Empathy*, which contrasts abstract art with representational art as a withdrawal from the world versus an engagement with it: German Expressionism and English Vorticism elaborate this psychological polarity in distinctive ways.

"I caught a strange thought," the German Expressionist Franz Marc (1880–1916) wrote from the front during World War I (where he would soon be killed), "it had settled on my open hand like a butterfly—the thought that people once before, a long time ago, like alter egos, loved abstractions as we do now. Many an object hidden away in our museums of anthropology looks at us with strangely disturbing eyes. What made them possible, these products of a sheer will to abstraction?" However strange, this thought was not entirely new: Marc echoes French poet Charles Baudelaire on poetic "correspondences," and the notions of an affinity between abstract arts, of the tribal artist as alter ego of the modern artist, and of a primordial will to abstraction are all in keeping with a dissertation written in 1908 by the German art historian Wilhelm Worringer (1881–1965). The connection is not accidental, as another letter from Marc makes clear. In early 1912 he wrote his Russian colleague Wassily Kandinsky (1866–1944), with whom he had founded the association of artists Der Blaue Reiter (The Blue Rider) in Munich in 1911: "I am just reading Worringer's *Abstraktion und Einfühlung* [Abstraction and Empathy], a good mind, whom we need very much. Marvelously disciplined thinking, concise and cool, extremely cool."

Worringer was not an unambiguous advocate of the German Expressionists. When they were attacked by a jingoistic antimodernist in 1911, he defended them as harbingers of a new age marked by an embrace of elemental forms, an interest in tribal art, and, above all, a rejection of the "rationalized sight" that he deemed too dominant from the Renaissance through neo-Impressionist painting. Otherwise Worringer left the terms of his affiliation vague; for example, in a 1910 foreword to *Abstraction and Empathy*, he noted only a "parallelism" with "the new goals of expression." However, this parallelism did point to an "inner necessity" in the age, and this metaphysical bent was shared by the Blaue Reiter artists, who often wrote of their art in terms of a "spiritual awakening." This was most evident in the *Blaue Reiter Almanach* that Marc and Kandinsky published in 1912 with a cover image of a blue rider by Kandinsky inspired by folk images of Saint George [1]. Apart from Expressionist work, this influential collection of essays and illustrations featured tribal art from the Pacific Northwest, Oceania, and Africa, the art of children, Egyptian puppets, Japanese masks and prints, medieval German sculpture and woodcuts, Russian folk art, and Bavarian devotional glass paintings. Kandinsky was especially drawn to the

1 • Wassily Kandinsky, final study for the cover of the *Blaue Reiter Almanach*, 1911
Watercolor, india ink and pencil, 27.6 x 21.9 (10⅞ x 8⅝)

latter two forms, while his partner, Gabrielle Münter (1877–1962), was strongly attracted to the art of children, the emotive immediacy of which she sought to convey in her own painting.

A metaphysical approach to art was also practiced by Die Brücke (The Bridge), the other primary group of German Expressionists. ▲ Headed by Ernst Ludwig Kirchner, it was founded in Dresden in 1905, included Fritz Beyl (1880–1966), Erich Heckel, and Karl Schmitt-Rottluff (1884–1976), all of whom were once architectural students, and was disbanded in Berlin eight years later. The metaphysical bent is clear from the names of the two groups: the Blaue Reiter was titled after a traditional figure of Christian revelation ("one stands before the new works as in a dream,"

▲ 1903

1900–1909

German Expressionism, English Vorticism, and early abstraction | 1908 85

Boxes throughout provide background information on key personalities, important concepts, and some of the issues surrounding the art of the day. Further elaboration of terms is available in the glossary at the back of the book.

5 • Marcel Duchamp, *Sixteen Miles of String*, at "First Papers of Surrealism," 1942
Vintage silver-gelatin print, 19.4 x 25.4 (7⅝ x 10)

Sidney Janis and Arturo Schwartz), it was a figure of the difficulty of all modernist art; for others (like Marcel Jean), it was a trope of age like a cobweb, though whether this age was one of veneration or decay was not clear. Still others dismissed the entire show as a tedious tangle. Certainly the installation played on the Surrealist fascination with the labyrinth as a figure of the unconscious (with the man-beast Minotaur at its center), a figure that it seemed to transform into an allegory of contemporary history, or rather of a breach in this history marked by war and exile, a breach that distanced the Surrealist art on display, almost literally, from the present. From this angle, the exhibited artists were posed as contemporary Ariadnes with little hope of finding their way out of the maze. If such an allegorical account appears dubious, we can simply state that the string obscured both pictorial and architectural spaces in a way that at once underscored and interrupted the given frames of painting and gallery alike. In any case, it was a negative, almost nihilistic gesture, but typically Duchamp presented it as playful, for he asked a group of children to play ball in the gallery for the duration of the opening. Nonetheless, the installation was hardly the "fun house space" that John Cage recalled of "Art of This Century."

While Kiesler wanted to do away with frames in order to render Surrealist art somehow immediate, Duchamp worked to elaborate frames excessively into a literal maze, as if to resist the institutional acculturation of this art. This difference has led T. J. Demos to see Surrealism-in-exile as torn between a search for a "compensatory home," as represented by Kiesler, and an acceptance of a profound homelessness, as represented by Duchamp. This seems right; however, circumstances changed again with the end of the war. In 1947 the two friends collaborated on the design of yet another "International Exhibition of Surrealism," now back in Paris. Their installation returned to the model of a deranged narrative used in the 1938 exhibition in Paris: the viewer had to pass through a series of tests in a sequence of spaces before looking at the works on display. Here, then, the trope was neither a compensatory home nor an indefinite homelessness but a rite of return, and the narrative was one of ritual reincorporation. But at this point Surrealism had little left but such rituals, and few new initiates to go through them. In the postwar period it would dissolve into other movements altogether; it would disappear from the map.

Peggy Guggenheim (1898–1979)

Peggy Guggenheim was one of the greatest collectors and most passionate supporters of avant-garde art in the twentieth century. When she died, her collection included works by Kandinsky, Klee, Picabia, Braque, Gris, Severini, Balla, van Doesburg, Mondrian, Miró, Ernst, de Chirico, Tanguy, Dalí, Magritte, Pollock, Motherwell, Gorky, and Brauner. She also collected sculpture: by Brancusi, Calder, Lipchitz, Laurens, Pevsner, Giacometti, Moore, and Arp. In 1920, she moved from the United States to Paris, where the minor Surrealist painter Laurence Vail (whom she would marry) introduced her to a bohemian world that included Marcel Duchamp, Man Ray, Anaïs Nin, Max Ernst, and Samuel Beckett.

Her collecting began as a function of the first gallery she opened, in London in 1938 (modestly called Guggenheim Jeune), with Duchamp as her adviser. The opening exhibition was of the drawings of Jean Cocteau, and succeeding exhibitions featured Tanguy, Kandinsky, Arp, and Brancusi. After a year she decided to open a museum of modern art in London and convinced Herbert Read to be the museum's first director. By 1940 she had entered on a campaign to "buy a picture a day," and as the war worsened she worried about where to store her collection. The Louvre in Paris turned the works down as "not worth saving," but finally she found a château near Vichy with barns large enough to house them all. With her collection in storage for the war, Guggenheim went to Marseilles, where she contributed money to the effort to arrange passage out of Europe for a group of intellectuals and artists. She eventually left in 1942 in a plane that also carried Ernst and her two children from her abortive marriage to Vail.

In New York, she married Ernst and set to work on her new gallery, "Art of This Century." The gallery arranged the first solo exhibitions of some of the major figures of the developing school of Abstract Expressionism: Pollock in 1943, Baziotes in 1944, Rothko in 1945, and Clyfford Still in 1946. Believing Pollock to be "the greatest painter since Picasso," she arranged a contract to give him $150 a month. Lee Krasner later said:

> *"Art of This Century" was of the utmost importance as the first place where the New York School could be seen.... Her Gallery was the foundation, it's where it all started to happen.*

1940–1945

The decade is indicated at the side of each page.

FURTHER READING

Bruce Altshuler, *The Avant-Garde in Exhibition: New Art in the Twentieth Century* (New York: Harry N. Abrams, 1994)

T. J. Demos, "Duchamp's Labyrinth: 'First Papers of Surrealism,'" *October*, no. 97, Summer 2001

Lewis Kachur, *Displaying the Marvelous: Marcel Duchamp, Salvador Dali, and Surrealist Exhibition Installations* (Cambridge, Mass.: MIT Press, 2001)

Martica Sawin, *Surrealism in Exile: The Beginning of the New York School* (Cambridge, Mass.: MIT Press, 1994)

Further reading lists at the end of each entry enable you to continue your study by directing you to some of the key books and articles on the subject, including primary and secondary historical documents and recently published texts. A general bibliography and a list of useful websites at the back of the book provide additional resources for research.

The Surrealists in New York | 1942b **301**

The entry's date and name appears at the foot of each page.

Preface: a reader's guide

This book is organized as a succession of important events, each keyed to an appropriate date, and can thus be read as a chronological account of twentieth-century art. But, like the pieces of a puzzle that can be transformed into a great variety of images, its 107 entries can also be arranged in different ways to suit the particular needs of individual readers.

First, some narratives might be constructed along national lines. For example, within the prewar period alone, the story of French art unfolds via studies of figurative sculpture, Fauvist painting, Cubist collage, and Surrealist objects, while German practice is traced in terms of Expressionist painting, Dada photomontage, Bauhaus design, and Neue Sachlichkeit (New Objectivity) painting and photography. The Russian avant-garde is followed from its early experiments with new forms and materials, through its direct involvement in political transformation, to its eventual suppression under Stalin. Meanwhile, British and American artists are tracked in their ambivalent oscillation between the demands of national idioms and the attractions of international styles.

As an alternative to such national narratives, the reader might trace transnational developments. For example, within the prewar period alone one might focus on the fascination with tribal objects, the emergence of abstract painting, or the spread of a Constructivist language of forms. The different incarnations of Dada from Zurich to New York, or the various engagements of modernist artists with design, might be compared. More generally, one might cluster entries that treat the great experiment that is modernism as such, or that discuss the virulent reactions against this idea, especially in totalitarian regimes. Mini-histories of different media might be produced in terms not only of traditional forms of painting and sculpture, but also of new modes distinctive to twentieth-century art, such as collaged and montaged images and found and readymade objects. For the first time in any survey, a discussion of photography—both in terms of its own development and as a force that radically transforms the other media—is woven into the text.

A third approach might be to group entries according to thematic concerns, within the prewar or the postwar periods, or in ways that span both. For example, the impact of the mass media on modern art might be gauged from the first Futurist manifesto, published in a major newspaper, *Le Figaro*, in 1909, through the Situationist critique of consumer culture in France after World War II, to the rise of the artist as media celebrity in our own time. Similarly, the institutions that shaped twentieth-century art might also be explored, either in close focus or in broad overview. For instance, one can review the signal school of modernist design, the Bauhaus, from its interwar incarnations in Germany to its postwar afterlife in the United States. Or one can follow the history of the art exhibition, from the Paris Salons before World War I, through the propagandistic displays of 1937 (including the "Degenerate 'Art'" ["Entartete 'Kunst'"] show staged by the Nazis), to the postwar forms of blockbuster exhibition and international survey (such as "Documenta 5" in 1972 in Germany). The complicated relationship between art and politics in the twentieth century can be studied through any number of entries. One might also define an approach through readings in such topics as the relationships between prewar and postwar avant-gardes, or between modernist and postmodernist models of art.

Along with such narratives of form and theme, other subtexts in the history of twentieth-century art can be foregrounded. Especially important to the authors are the theoretical methods that have framed the manifold practices of this art. One such approach is psychoanalytic criticism, which focuses on the subjective effects of the work of art. Another method is the social history of art, which attends to social, political, and economic contexts. A third seeks to clarify the intrinsic structure of the work—not only how it is *made* (in the formalist version of this approach) but also how it *means* (in its structuralist version). Lastly, poststructuralist modes of criticism are deployed in order to address questions not only of signification but also of institution—of how works come to be designated as art and valued as such. Many entries present test cases of these four methods at work, especially when their own development is related to that of the art at issue. For each mode of criticism, an introduction that sketches its history and defines its terms is also provided.

As might be expected, these methods often clash: the subjective focus of psychoanalytic criticism, the contextual emphasis of the social history of art, the intrinsic concerns of formalist and structuralist accounts, and the poststructuralist attention to institutional framing cannot easily be reconciled. In this book, these tensions are not masked by an unbroken story unified by a single voice; rather, they are dramatized by the four authors, each of whom has a different allegiance to these methods. In this regard, *Art Since 1900* is "dialogical," in the sense given the term by Russian theorist Mikhail Bakhtin: each speech act is structured by the positions that it confronts, as a response to other speakers whom it moves to oppose or attempts to persuade. The marks of such dialogue are multiple in this book. They appear in the different types of perspective that one author might privilege, or in the different ways that a single subject—abstraction, say—might be treated by the various voices. This conversation is also carried on through the cross-references that act as signposts to the intersections between the entries. This "intertext" not only allows two different positions to coexist but also, perhaps in relation to the third perspective provided by the reader, dialectically binds them.

Of course, with new orientations come new omissions. Certain artists and movements, addressed in previous textbooks, are scanted here, and every reader will see grievous exclusions—this is the case for each of the authors as well. But we also have the conviction that the richness of the conversation, as it illuminates different facets of the debates, struggles, breakthroughs, and setbacks of twentieth-century art, compensates a little for the parts of the story that are left in ellipsis. Our use of the headline to introduce each entry acknowledges both the strengths and the weaknesses of our overall approach, for this telegraphic form can be seen either as a mere signal of a complex event—from which it is then severed—or as an emblematic marker of the very complexity of the history of which it is the evocative precipitate.

It is now common practice—in publishing, in teaching, and in curating—to break the art of the twentieth century into two halves separated by World War II. We acknowledge this tendency with the option of the two-volume format; at the same time we believe that a crucial subject for any history of this art is the complex dialogue between prewar and postwar avant-gardes. To tell this story it is necessary to produce the full sweep of the twentieth century at once. But then such a panorama is also essential for the many other stories to which the four of us have lent our voices here.

Hal Foster
Rosalind Krauss
Yve-Alain Bois
Benjamin H. D. Buchloh

Introductions

In these four introductions, the authors of *Art Since 1900* set out some of the theoretical methods of framing the art of the twentieth and twenty-first centuries. Each describes the historical development of a particular methodology and explains its relevance to the production and reception of the art of the period.

The last hundred years or so have witnessed several major shifts in both private and public debates about art, its nature, and its functions. These shifts need to be considered in terms of other histories, too: with the emergence of new academic disciplines, new ways of thinking and speaking about cultural production coexist with new modes of expression.

We have written the following methodological introductions in order to identify and analyze the different conventions, approaches, and intellectual projects that underpin our project as a whole. Our intention has been to present the diverse theoretical frameworks that can be found in the book and to explain their relationship to the works and practices discussed in the individual entries. For that reason, each introduction begins with an overview of the mode of criticism, setting it firmly in its historical and intellectual context, before proceeding to a brief discussion of its relevance to the production and interpretation of art. Whether these introductions are read as stand-alone essays or in conjunction with other texts dealing with the individual modes of criticism, they will inform and enhance understanding in ways that allow each reader to develop an individual approach to the book and to the art of the period.

1 Psychoanalysis in modernism and as method

1 • Hannah Höch, *The Sweet One, From an Ethnographic Museum*, c. 1926
Photomontage with watercolor, 30 x 15.5 (11 13/16 x 6 1/8)

In this collage—one of a series that combines found photographs of tribal sculpture and modern women—Höch plays on associations at work in psychoanalytic theory and modernist art: ideas of "the primitive" and the sexual, of racial others and unconscious desires. She exploits these associations to suggest the power of "the New Woman," but she also seems to mock them, literally cutting up the images, deconstructing and reconstructing them, exposing them as constructions.

Psychoanalysis was developed by Sigmund Freud (1856–1939) and his followers as a "science of the unconscious" in the early years of the twentieth century, at the same time that modernist art came into its own. As with the other interpretative methods presented in these introductions, psychoanalysis thus shares its historical ground with modernist art and intersects with it in various ways throughout the twentieth century. First, artists have drawn directly on psychoanalysis—sometimes to explore its ideas visually, as often in Surrealism in the twenties and thirties, and sometimes to critique them theoretically and politically, as often in ▲ feminism in the seventies and eighties. Second, psychoanalysis and modernist art share several interests—a fascination with origins, with dreams and fantasies, with "the primitive," the child, and the insane, and, more recently, with the workings of subjectivity and • sexuality, to name only a few [**1**]. Third, many psychoanalytic terms have entered the basic vocabulary of twentieth-century art and criticism (e.g., repression, sublimation, fetishism, the gaze). Here I will focus on historical connections and methodological applications, and, when appropriate, I will key them, along with critical terms, to entries in which they are discussed.

Historical connections with art

Psychoanalysis emerged in the Vienna of artists such as Gustav ■ Klimt, Egon Schiele, and Oskar Kokoschka, during the decline of the Austro-Hungarian Empire. With the secession of such artists from the Art Academy, this was a time of Oedipal revolt in advanced art, with subjective experiments in pictorial expression that drew on regressive dreams and erotic fantasies. Bourgeois Vienna did not usually tolerate these experiments, for they suggested a crisis in the stability of the ego and its social institutions—a crisis that Freud was prompted to analyze as well.

This crisis was hardly specific to Vienna; in terms of its relevance to psychoanalysis, it was perhaps most evident in the attraction to things "primitive" on the part of modernists in France and Germany. For some artists this "primitivism" involved ◆ a "going-native" of the sort play-acted by Paul Gauguin in the South Seas. For others it was focused on formal revisions of Western conventions of representation, as undertaken, with the

▲ 1924, 1930b, 1931, 1942b, 1975 • 1903, 1907, 1922, 1987, 1994a ■ 1900a ◆ 1903

2 • Meret Oppenheim, *Object* (also called *Fur-Lined Teacup* and *Déjeuner en fourrure*), 1936
Fur-covered teacup, saucer, and spoon, height 7.3 (2$\frac{7}{8}$)

To make this work, Meret Oppenheim simply lined a teacup, saucer, and spoon bought in Paris with the fur of a Chinese gazelle. Mixing attraction and repulsion, this dis/agreeable work is quintessentially Surrealist, for it adapts the device of the found thing to explore the idea of "the fetish," which psychoanalysis understands as an unlikely object invested with a powerful desire diverted from its proper aim. Here art appreciation is no longer a matter of disinterested teatime propriety: it is boldly interrupted through a smutty allusion to female genitalia that forces us to think about the relation between aesthetics and erotics.

3 • André Masson, *Figure*, 1927
Oil and sand, 46 x 33 (18$\frac{1}{8}$ x 13)

In the Surrealist practice of "automatic writing," the author, released from rational control, "took dictation" from his or her unconscious. André Masson's use of strange materials and gestural marks, sometimes almost dissolving the distinction between the figure and the ground, suggested one method to pursue "psychic automatism," opening up painting to new explorations not only of the unconscious but also of form and its opposite.

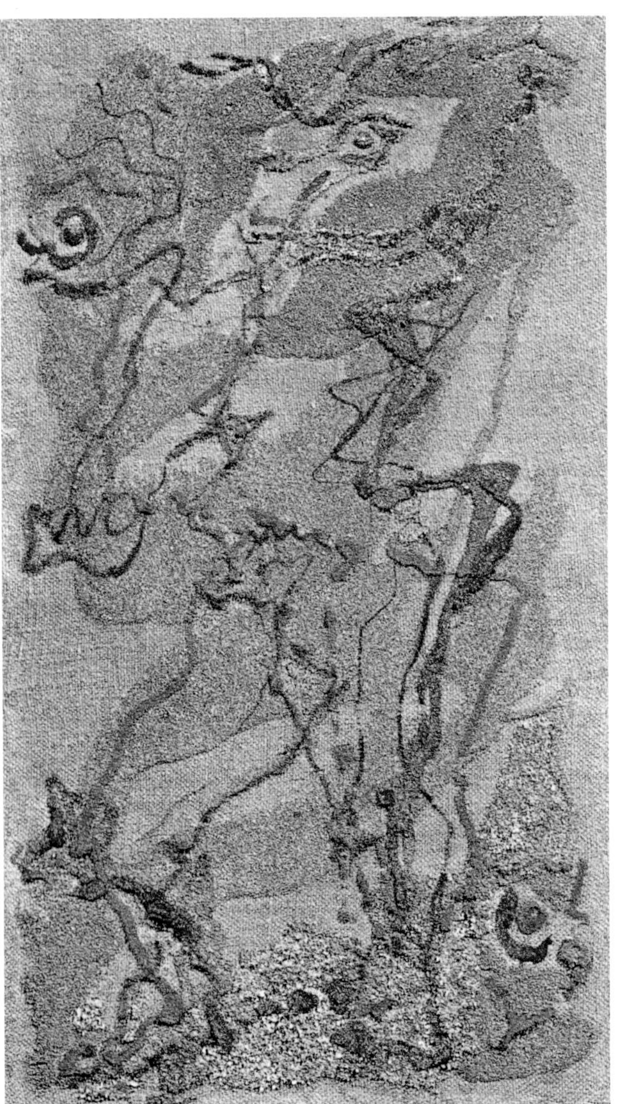

▲ aid of African objects, by Pablo Picasso and Henri Matisse in Paris. Yet almost all modernists projected onto tribal peoples a purity of artistic vision that was associated with the simplicity of instinctual life. This projection is the primitivist fantasy *par excellence* and psychoanalysis participated in it then even as it provides ways to question it now. (For example, Freud saw tribal peoples as somehow fixed in pre-Oedipal or infantile stages.)

Strange though it may seem today, for some modernists an interest in tribal objects shaded into involvement with the art of children and of the insane. In this regard, *Artistry of the Mentally Ill* (*Bildnerei der Geisteskranken*), a collection of works by psychotics ● presented in 1922 by Hans Prinzhorn (1886–1933), a German psychiatrist trained in psychoanalysis and art history alike, was of special importance to such artists as Paul Klee, Max Ernst, and ■ Jean Dubuffet. Most of these modernists (mis)read the art of the insane as though it were a secret part of the primitivist avant-garde, directly expressive of the unconscious and boldly defiant of all convention. Here psychoanalysts developed a more complicated understanding of paranoid representations as projections of desperate order, and of schizophrenic images as symptoms of radical self-dislocation. And yet such readings also have parallels in modernist art.

An important line of connection runs from the art of the insane, through the early collages of Ernst, to the definition of Surrealism as a disruptive "juxtaposition of two more or less disparate realities," as ◆ presented by its leader André Breton [**2**]. Psychoanalysis influenced Surrealism in its conceptions of the image as a kind of dream, understood by Freud as a distorted writing-in-pictures of a displaced wish, and of the object as a sort of symptom, understood by Freud as a bodily expression of a conflicted desire; but there are several other affinities as well. Among the first to study Freud, the Surrealists attempted to simulate the effects of madness in automatic writing and art alike [**3**]. In his first "Manifesto of Surrealism" (1924), Breton described Surrealism as a "psychic automatism," a liberatory inscription of unconscious impulses "in the absence of any control

▲ 1903, 1907 ● 1922 ■ 1946 ◆ 1924, 1930b, 1931, 1942b

4 • Karel Appel, *A Figure*, 1953
Oil and colored crayons on paper, 64.5 x 49 (25 3/8 x 19 1/4)

After World War II an interest in the unconscious persisted among artists such as the Dutch painter Karel Appel, a member of Cobra (an acronym for the home bases of the group—Copenhagen, Brussels, Amsterdam); at the same time the question of the psyche was reframed by the horrors of the death camps and the atomic bombs. Like other groups, Cobra came to reject the Freudian unconscious explored by the Surrealists as too individualistic: as part of a general turn to the notion of a "collective unconscious" developed by Carl Jung, they explored totemic figures, mythic subjects, and collaborative projects in an often anguished search not only for a "new man" but for a new society.

exercised by reason." Yet right here emerges a problem that has dogged the relation between psychoanalysis and art ever since: either the connection between psyche and art work is posited as too direct or immediate, with the result that the specificity of the work is lost, or as too conscious or calculated, as though the psyche could simply be illustrated by the work. (The other methods in this introduction face related problems of mediation and questions of causation; indeed, they vex all art criticism and history.) Although Freud knew little of modernist art (his taste was conservative, and his collection ran to ancient and Asian figurines), he knew enough to be suspicious of both tendencies. In his view, the unconscious was not liberatory—on the contrary—and to propose an art free of repression, or at least convention, was to risk psychopathology, or to pretend to do so in the name of a psychoanalytic art (this is why he once called the Surrealists "absolute cranks").

Nevertheless, by the early thirties the association of some modernist art with "primitives," children, and the insane was set, as was its affinity with psychoanalysis. At this time, however, these connections played into the hands of the enemies of this art, most catastrophically the Nazis, who in 1937 moved to rid the world ▲ of such "degenerate" abominations, which they also condemned as "Jewish" and "Bolshevik." Of course, Nazism was a horrific regression of its own, and it cast a pall over explorations of the unconscious well after World War II. Varieties of Surrealism lingered on in the postwar period, however, and an interest in the unconscious persisted among artists associated with *art informel*, • Abstract Expressionism, and Cobra **[4]**. Yet, rather than the difficult mechanisms of the individual psyche explored by Freud, the focus fell on the redemptive archetypes of a "collective unconscious" imagined by Swiss psychiatrist Carl Jung (1875–1961), an old apostate of psychoanalysis. (For example, Jackson Pollock was involved in Jungian analysis in ways that affected his painting.)

Partly in reaction against the subjective rhetoric of Abstract Expressionism, much art of the sixties was staunchly antipsychological, concerned instead with ready-made cultural images, as in ■ Pop art, or given geometric forms, as in Minimalism. At the same time, in the involvement of Minimalist, Process and Performance art with phenomenology there was a reopening to the bodily subject that prepared a reopening to the psychological subject in ◆ feminist art. This engagement was ambivalent, however, for even as feminists used psychoanalysis, they did so mostly in the register of critique, "as a weapon" (in the battle cry of filmmaker Laura Mulvey) directed at the patriarchal ideology that also riddled psychoanalysis. For Freud had associated femininity with passivity, and in his famous account of the Oedipus complex, a tangle of relations in which the little boy is said to desire the mother until threatened by the father, there is no parallel denouement for the little girl, as if in his scheme of things women cannot attain full subjecthood. And Jacques Lacan (1901–81), the French psychoanalyst who proposed an influential reading of Freud, identified woman as such with the lack represented by castration. Nonetheless, for many feminists Freud and Lacan provided the most telling account

▲ 1937a • 1946, 1947b, 1949, 1957a ■ 1960c, 1964b, 1965 ◆ 1969, 1974, 1975

5 • Barbara Kruger, *Your Gaze Hits the Side of My Face*, 1981
Photographic silkscreen on vinyl, 139.7 x 104.1 (55 x 41)

Psychoanalysis helped some feminist artists in the eighties to critique power structures not only in high art but in mass culture too: particular attention was drawn to how images in both spheres are structured for a male heterosexual spectatorship—for a "male gaze" empowered with the pleasures of looking, with women mostly figuring as passive objects of this look. In her pieces of the period, the American artist Barbara Kruger juxtaposed appropriated images and critical phrases (sometimes subverted clichés) in order to question this objectification, to welcome women into the place of spectatorship, and to open up space for other kinds of image-making and viewing.

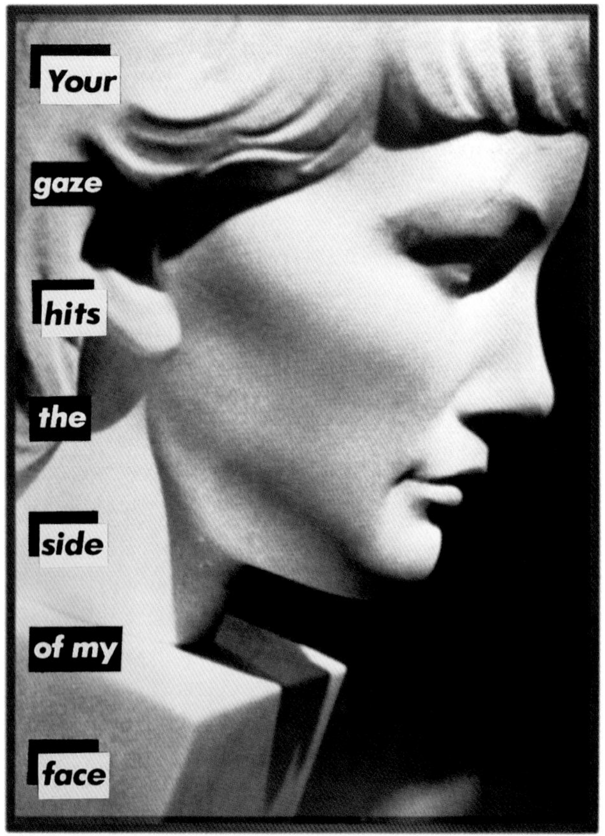

of the formation of the subject in the social order. If there is no natural femininity, these feminists argued, then there is also no natural patriarchy—only a historical culture fitted to the psychic structure, the desires and the fears, of the heterosexual male, and so vulnerable to feminist critique [**5, 6**]. Indeed, some feminists have insisted that the very marginality of women to the social order, as mapped by psychoanalysis, positions them as its most radical critics. By the nineties this critique was extended by gay and lesbian artists and critics concerned to expose the psychic workings of homophobia, as well by postcolonial practitioners concerned to ▲ mark the racialist projection of cultural others.

Approaches alternative to Freud

One can critique Freud and Lacan, of course, and still remain within the orbit of psychoanalysis. Artists and critics have had affinities with other schools, especially the "object-relations" psychoanalysis associated with Melanie Klein (1882–1960) and D. W. Winnicott (1896–1971) in England, which influenced such aestheticians as Adrian Stokes (1902–72) and Anton Ehrenzweig (1909–66) and, indirectly, the reception of such artists as Henry • Moore and Barbara Hepworth. Where Freud saw pre-Oedipal stages (oral, anal, phallic, genital) that the child passes through, Klein saw positions that remain open into adult life. In her account these positions are dominated by the original fantasies of the child, involving violent aggression toward the parents as well as depressive anxiety about this aggression, with an oscillation between visions of destruction and reparation.

For some critics this psychoanalysis spoke to a partial turn in nineties art—away from questions of sexual desire in relation to the social order, toward concerns with bodily drives in relation to ■ life and death. After the moratorium on images of women in some feminist art of the seventies and eighties, Kleinian notions suggested a way to understand this reappearance of the body often in damaged form. A fascination with trauma, both personal and collective, reinforced this interest in the "abject" body, which also led artists and critics to the later writings of the French psychoanalyst Julia Kristeva (born 1941). Of course, social factors—the AIDS epidemic above all—also drove this pervasive aesthetic of mourn- ◆ ing and melancholy. In the present, psychoanalysis remains a resource in art criticism and history, but its role in artmaking is far from clear.

Levels of Freudian criticism

Psychoanalysis emerged out of clinical work, out of the analysis of symptoms of actual patients (there is much controversy about how Freud manipulated this material, which included his own dreams), and its use in the interpretation of art carries the strengths as well as the weaknesses of this source. There is first the basic question of who or what is to occupy the position of the patient—the work, the artist, the viewer, the critic, or some combination or relay of all these. Then

▲ 1989, 1993c, 1994a • 1934b ■ 1994a ◆ 1987

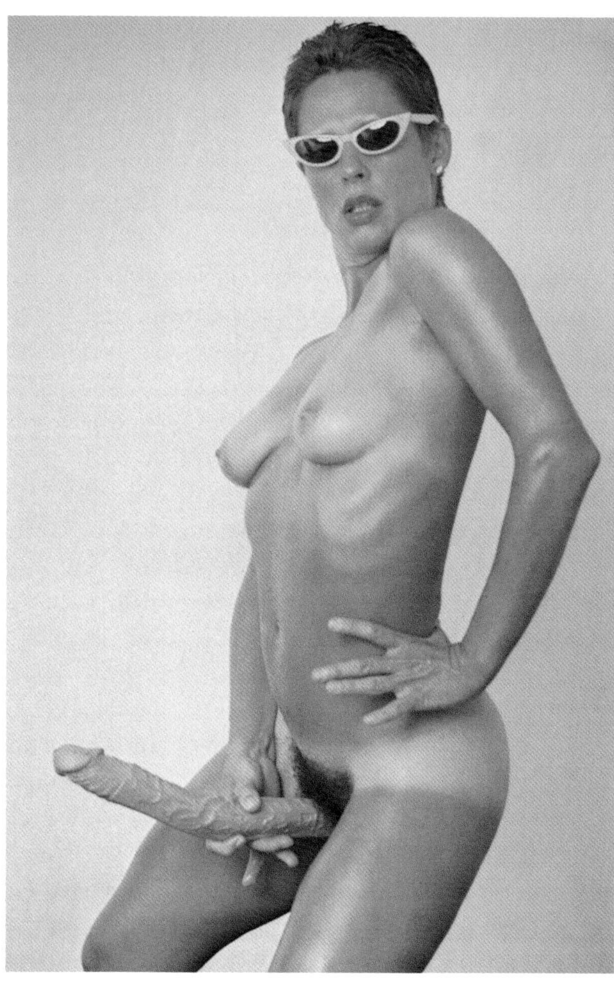

6 • Lynda Benglis, *Untitled*, 1974 (detail)
Color photograph, 25 x 26.5 (9⅞ x 10⅜)

With the rise of feminism in the sixties and seventies, some artists attacked patriarchal hierarchies not only in society in general but in the art world in particular: psychoanalysis figured as both weapon—because it offered profound insights into the relation between sexuality and subjectivity—and target—because it tended to associate women not only with passivity but also with lack. In this photograph, used in a notorious advertisement for a gallery show, the American artist Lynda Benglis mocked the macho posturing of some Minimalist and Postminimalist artists, as well as the increased marketing of contemporary art; at the same time, she seized "the phallus" in a way that both literalized its association with plenitude and power and parodied it.

there arises the complicated issue of the different levels of a Freudian interpretation of art, which I will here reduce to three: symbolic readings, accounts of process, and analogies in rhetoric.

Early attempts in Freudian criticism were governed by symbolic readings of the art work, as if it were a dream to be decoded in terms of a latent message hidden behind a manifest content: "This is not a pipe; it is really a penis." This sort of criticism complements the kind of art that translates a dream or a fantasy in pictorial terms: art then becomes the encoding of a riddle and criticism its decoding, and the whole exercise is illustrational and circular. Although Freud was quick to stress that cigars are often just cigars, he too practiced this kind of deciphering, which fits in all too well with the traditional method of art history known as "iconography"—a reading back of symbols in a picture to sources in other kinds of texts—a method that most modernist art worked to foil (through abstraction, techniques of chance, and so on). In this regard, the Italian historian Carlo Ginzburg has demonstrated an epistemological affinity between psychoanalysis and art history based in connoisseurship. For both discourses (which developed, in modern form, at roughly the same time) are concerned with the symptomatic trait or the telling detail (an idiosyncratic gesture of the hands, say) that might reveal, in psychoanalysis, a hidden conflict in the patient and, in connoisseurship, the proper attribution of the work to an artist.

In such readings the artist is the ultimate source to which the symbols point: the work is taken as his symptomatic expression, and it is used as such in the analysis. Thus in his 1910 study *Leonardo da Vinci and a Memory of his Childhood*, Freud leads us from the enigmatic smiles of his *Mona Lisa* and Virgin Marys to posit in the artist a memory regarding his long-lost mother. In this way Freud and his followers looked for signs of psychic disturbances in art (his predecessor Jean-Martin Charcot did the same). This is not to say that Freud sees the artist as psychopathological; in fact he implies that art is one way to avoid this condition. "Art frees the artist from his fantasies," the French philosopher Sarah Kofman comments, "just as 'artistic creation' circumvents neurosis and takes the place of psychoanalytic treatment." But it is true that such Freudian criticism tends to "psychobiography," that is, to a profiling of the artist in which art history is remodeled as psychoanalytic case study.

If symbolic readings and psychobiographical accounts can be reductive, this danger may be mitigated if we attend to other aspects of Freud. For most of the time Freud understands the sign less as symbolic, in the sense of directly expressive of a self, a meaning, or a reality, than as symptomatic, a kind of allegorical emblem in which desire and repression are intertwined. Moreover, he does not see art as a simple revision of preexisting memories or fantasies; apart from other things, it can also be, as Kofman suggests, an "originary 'substitute'" for such scenes, through which we come to know them *for the first time* (this is what Freud attempts in his Leonardo study). Finally, psychobiography is put into productive doubt by the very fact that the psychoanalytic account of the unconscious, of its disruptive effects, puts all intentionality—all authorship, all biography—into productive doubt too.

Freudian criticism is not only concerned with a symbolic decoding of hidden meanings, with the semantics of the psyche. Less obviously, it is also involved with the dynamics of these processes, with an understanding of the sexual energies and unconscious forces that operate in the making as well as the viewing of art. On this second level of psychoanalytic interpretation, Freud revises the old philosophical concept of "aesthetic play" in terms of his own notion of "the pleasure principle," which he defined, in "Two Principles of Mental Functioning" (1911), in opposition to "the reality principle":

> *The artist is originally a man [sic] who turns from reality because he cannot come to terms with the demand for the renunciation of instinctual satisfaction as it is first made, and who then in phantasy-life allows full play to his erotic and ambitious wishes. But he finds a way of return from this world of phantasy back to reality; with his special gifts he moulds his phantasies into a new kind of reality, and men concede them a justification as valuable reflections of actual life. Thus by a certain path he actually becomes the hero, king, creator, favorite he desired to be, without pursuing the circuitous path of creating real alterations in the outer world. But this he can only attain because other men feel the same dissatisfaction as he with the renunciation demanded by reality, and because this dissatisfaction, resulting from the displacement of the pleasure-principle by the reality-principle, is itself a part of reality.*

Three years before, in "Creative Writers and Day-Dreaming" (1908), Freud had speculated on how the artist overcomes our resistance to this performance, which we might otherwise deem solipsistic, if not simply inappropriate:

> *[H]e bribes us by the purely formal—that is, aesthetic—yield of pleasure which he offers us in the presentation of his phantasies. We give the name incentive bonus or fore-pleasure to a yield of pleasure such as this, which is offered to us so as to make possible the release of still greater pleasure arising from deeper psychical sources.... [O]ur actual enjoyment of an imaginative work proceeds from a liberation of tensions in our minds.*

Let us review some of the (pre)conceptions in these statements. First, the artist avoids some of the "renunciations" that the rest of us must accept, and indulges in some of the fantasies that we must forgo. But we do not resent him for this exemption for three reasons: his fictions reflect reality nonetheless; they are born of the same dissatisfactions that we feel; and we are bribed by the pleasure that we take in the resolution of the formal tensions of the work, a pleasure that opens us to a deeper sort of pleasure—in the resolution of the psychic tensions within us. Note that for Freud art originates in a turn from reality, which is to say that it is fundamentally conservative in relation to the social order, a small aesthetic compensation for our mighty instinctual renunciation. Perhaps this is another reason why he was suspicious of modernist art, concerned as much of it is not to "sublimate" instinctual energies, to divert them from sexual aims into cultural forms, but to go in the opposite direction, to "desublimate" cultural forms, to open them up to these disruptive forces.

Dreams and fantasies

While the semantics of symbolic interpretation can be too particular, this concern with the dynamics of aesthetic process can be too general. A third level of Freudian criticism may avoid both extremes: the analysis of the rhetoric of the art work in analogy with such visual productions of the psyche as dreams and fantasies. Again, Freud understood the dream as a compromise between a wish and its repression. This compromise is negotiated by the "dream-work," which disguises the wish, in order to fool further repression, through "condensation" of some of its aspects and "displacement" of others. The dream-work then turns the distorted fragments into visual images with an eye to "considerations of representability" in a dream, and finally revises the images to insure that they hang together as a narrative (this is called "secondary revision"). This rhetoric of operations might be brought to bear on the production of some pictures—again, the Surrealists thought so—but there are obvious dangers with such analogies as well. Even when Freud and his followers wrote only about art (or literature), they were concerned to demonstrate points of psychoanalytic theory first and to understand objects of artistic practice second, so that forced applications are built into the discourse, as it were.

Yet there is a more profound problem with analogies drawn between psychoanalysis and visual art. With his early associate Josef Breuer (1842–1925) Freud founded psychoanalysis as a "talking cure"—that is, as a turn away from the visual theater of his teacher, the French pathologist and neurologist Jean-Martin Charcot (1825–93), who staged the symptomatic bodies of female hysterics in a public display at the Salpêtrière Hospital in Paris. The technical innovation of psychoanalysis was to attend to symptomatic *language*—not only of the dream as a form of writing but also of slips of the tongue, the "free association" of words by the patient, and so on. Moreover, for Freud culture was essentially a working out of the conflicted desires rooted in the Oedipus complex, a working out that is primarily narrative, and it is not clear how such narrative might play out in static forms like painting, sculpture, and the rest. These emphases alone render psychoanalysis ill-suited to questions of visual art. Furthermore, the Lacanian reading of Freud is militantly linguistic; its celebrated axiom—"the unconscious is structured like a language"—means that the psychic processes of condensation and displacement are structurally one with the linguistic tropes of "metaphor" and ▲"metonymy." No analogy in rhetoric, therefore, would seem to bridge the categorical divide between psychoanalysis and art.

And yet, according to both Freud and Lacan, the crucial events in subject formation are *visual* scenes. For Freud the ego is first a bodily image, which, for Lacan in his famous paper on "The Mirror

▲ Introduction 3

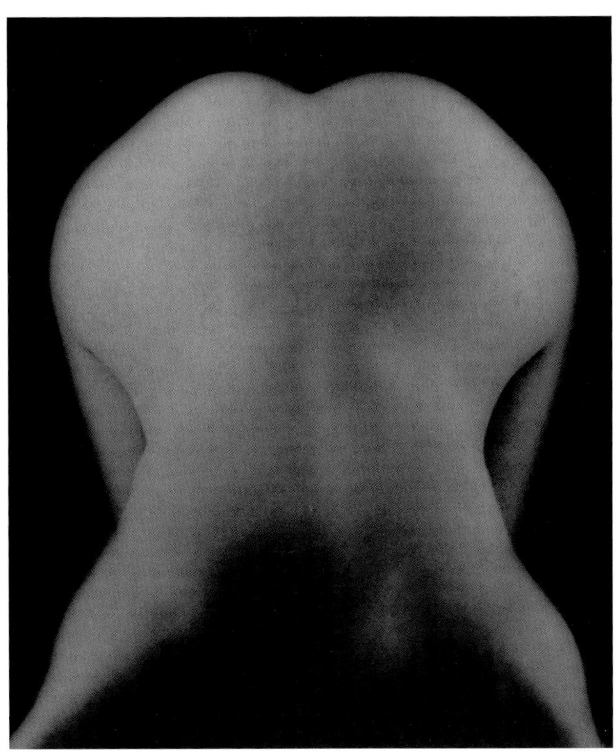

7 • Lee Miller, *Nude Bent Forward*, Paris, c. 1931

Psychoanalysis is concerned with traumatic scenes, whether actual or imagined, that mark the child profoundly—scenes where he or she discovers sexual difference, for example, scenes that are often visual but also often uncertain in nature. At different times in the twentieth century, artists, such as the Surrealists in the twenties and thirties and feminists in the seventies and eighties, have drawn on such images and scenarios as ways to trouble assumptions about seeing, expectations about gender, and so on. In this photograph by the American artist Lee Miller, a sometime associate of the Surrealists, it is not immediately clear what we see: A body? A male or a female? Or some other category of being, imaging, and feeling?

Stage" (1936/49), the infant initially encounters in a reflection that allows for a fragile coherence—a visual coherence as an image. The psychoanalytic critic Jacqueline Rose also alerts us to the "staging" of such events as "moments in which perception *founders* ... or in which pleasure in looking tips over into the register of *excess*." Her examples are two traumatic scenes that psychoanalysis posits for the little boy. In the first scene he discovers sexual difference—that girls do not have penises and hence that he may lose his—a perception that "founders" because it implies this grave threat. In the second scene he witnesses sexual intercourse between his parents, which fascinates him as a key to the riddle of his own origin. Freud called these scenes "primal fantasies"—primal both because they are fundamental and because they concern origins. As Rose suggests, such scenes "demonstrate the complexity of an essentially visual space" in ways that can be "used as theoretical prototypes to unsettle our certainties once again"—as indeed they were used, to different ends, in some Surrealist art of the twenties and thirties **[7]** and in ▲ some feminist art of the seventies and eighties. The important point to emphasize, though, is this: "Each time the stress falls on a problem of seeing. The sexuality lies less in the content of what is seen than in the subjectivity of the viewer." This is where psychoanalysis has the most to offer the interpretation of art, modernist or other. Its account of the effects of the work on the subject and the artist as well as on the viewer (including the critic) places the work, finally, in the position of the analyst as much as the analyzed.

In the end we do well to hold to a double focus: to view psychoanalysis historically, as an object in an ideological field often shared with modernist art, and to apply it theoretically, as a method to understand relevant aspects of this art, to map pertinent parts of the field. This double focus allows us to critique psychoanalysis even as we apply it. First and last, however, this project will be complicated—not only by the difficulties in psychoanalytic speculation, but also by the controversies that always swirl around it. Some of the clinical work of Freud and others was manipulated, to be sure, and some of the concepts are bound up with science that is no longer valid—but do these facts invalidate psychoanalysis as a mode of interpretation of art today? As with the other methods introduced here, the test will be in the fit and the yield of the arguments that we make. And here, as the psychoanalytic critic Leo Bersani reminds us, our "moments of theoretical collapse" may be inseparable from our moments of "psychoanalytic truth."

FURTHER READING

Leo Bersani, *The Freudian Body: Psychoanalysis and Art* (New York: Columbia University Press, 1986)

Sigmund Freud, *Art and Literature*, trans. James Strachey (London: Penguin, 1985)

Sarah Kofman, *The Childhood of Art: An Interpretation of Freud's Aesthetics*, trans. Winifred Woodhull (New York: Columbia University Press, 1988)

Jean Laplanche and J.-B. Pontalis, *The Language of Psychoanalysis*, trans. Donald Nicholson-Smith (New York: W. W. Norton, 1973)

Jacqueline Rose, *Sexuality in the Field of Vision* (London: Verso, 1986)

▲ 1924, 1930b, 1931, 1975

2 The social history of art: models and concepts

Recent histories of art comprise a number of distinct critical models (for example, formalism, structuralist semiotics, psychoanalysis, social art history, and feminism) that have been merged and integrated in various ways, in particular in the work of American and British art historians since the seventies. This situation sometimes makes it difficult, if not altogether pointless, to insist on methodological consistency, let alone on a singular methodological position. The complexity of these various individual strands and of their integrated forms points firstly to the problematic nature of any claim that one particular model should be accepted as exclusively valid or as dominant within the interpretative processes of art history. Our attempts to integrate a broad variety of methodological positions also efface the earlier theoretical rigor that had previously generated a degree of precision in the process of historical analysis and interpretation. That precision now seems to have been lost in an increasingly complex weave of methodological eclecticism.

The origins of the methodologies

All these models were initially formulated as attempts to displace earlier humanist (subjective) approaches to criticism and interpretation. They had been motivated by the desire to position the study of all types of cultural production (such as literature or the fine arts) on a more solidly scientific basis of method and insight, rather than have criticism remain dependent on the various more-or-less subjective approaches of the late nineteenth century, such as the biographistic, psychologistic, and historicist survey methods.

▲ Just as the early Russian Formalists made Ferdinand de Saussure's linguistic structure the matrix of their own efforts to understand the formation and functions of cultural representation, subsequent historians who attempted to interpret works of art in psychoanalytic terms tried to find a map of artistic subject • formation in the writings of Sigmund Freud. Proponents of both models argued that they could generate a verifiable understanding of the processes of aesthetic production and reception, and promised to anchor the "meaning" of the work of art solidly in the operations of either the conventions of language and/or the system of the unconscious, arguing that aesthetic or poetic meaning operated in a manner analogous to other linguistic conventions and narrative structures (e.g., the folktale), or, in terms of the unconscious, as in Freud's and Carl Jung's theories, analogous to the joke and the dream, the symptom and the trauma.

The social history of art, from its very beginning in the first decades of the twentieth century, had a similar ambition to make the analysis and interpretation of works of art more rigorous and verifiable. Most importantly, the early social historians of art (Marxist scholars like the Anglo-German Francis Klingender [1907–55] and the Anglo-Hungarian Frederick Antal [1887–1954]) tried to situate cultural representation within the existing communication structures of society, primarily within the field of ideological production under the rise of industrial capitalism. After all, social art history's philosophical inspiration was the scientificity of Marxism itself, a philosophy that had aimed from the very beginning not only to analyze and interpret economic, political, and ideological relations, but also to make the writing of history itself—its historicity—contribute to the larger project of social and political change.

This critical and analytical project of social art history formulated a number of key concepts that I will discuss further: I shall also try to give their original definitions, as well as subsequent modifications to these concepts, in order to acknowledge the increasing complexity of the terminology of social art history, which results partially from the growing differentiation of the philosophical concepts of Marxist thought itself. At the same time, it may become apparent that some of these key concepts are presented not because they are important in the early years of the twenty-first century, but, rather, because of their obsolescence, withering away in the present and in the recent past. This is because the methodological conviction of certain models of analysis has been just as overdetermined as that of all the other methodological models that have temporarily governed the interpretation and the writing of art history at different points in the twentieth century.

Autonomy

▲ German philosopher and sociologist Jürgen Habermas (born 1929) has defined the formation of the bourgeois public sphere in general and the development of cultural practices within that

▲ Introduction 3, 1915 • Introduction 1

▲ 1988

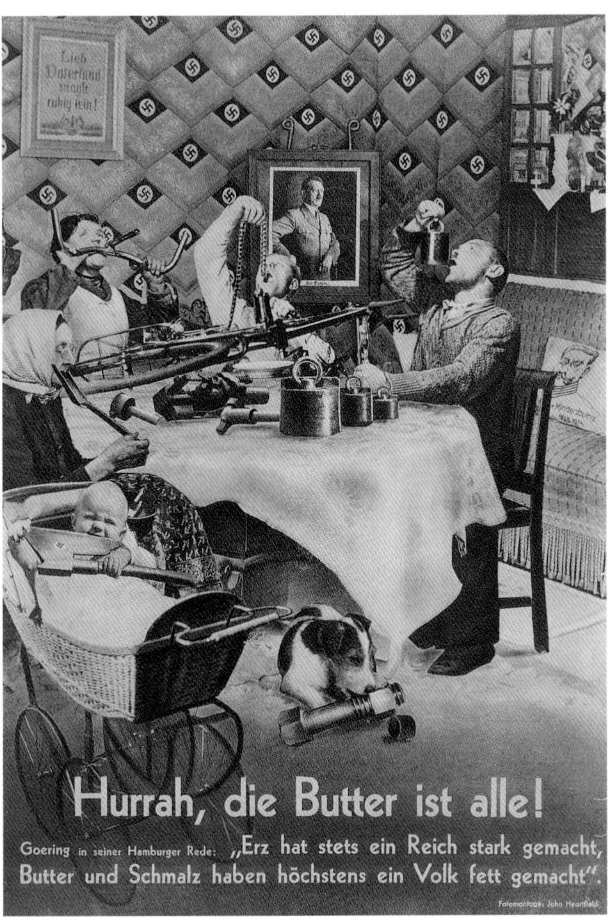

1 • John Heartfield, *"Hurray, the Butter is Finished!"*, cover for *AIZ*, December 19, 1935
Photomontage, 38 x 27 (15¼ x 10¾)

The work of John Heartfield, along with that of Marcel Duchamp and El Lissitzky, demarcates one of the most important paradigm shifts in the epistemology of twentieth-century modernism. Refiguring photomontage and constructing new textual narratives, it established the only model for artistic practice as communicative action in the age of mass-cultural propaganda. Denounced as such by the intrinsically conservative ideologies of formalists and modernists defending obsolete models of autonomy, it addressed in fact the historical need for a change of audiences and of the forms of distribution. Inevitably, it became the singular, most important example of counterpropaganda to the hegemonic media apparatus of the thirties, the only voice in the visual avant-garde to oppose the rise of fascism as a late form of imperialist capitalism.

sphere as social processes of subjective differentiation that lead to the historical construction of bourgeois individuality. These processes guarantee the individual's identity and historical status as a self-determining and self-governing subject. One of the necessary conditions of bourgeois identity was the subject's capacity to experience the autonomy of the aesthetic, to experience pleasure without interest.

This concept of aesthetic autonomy was as integral to the differentiation of bourgeois subjectivity as it was to the differentiation of cultural production according to its proper technical and procedural characteristics, eventually leading to the modernist orthodoxy of medium-specificity. Inevitably then, autonomy served as a foundational concept during the first five decades of European modernism. From Théophile Gautier's program of *l'art pour l'art* and Édouard Manet's conception of painting as a project of perceptual self-reflexivity, the aesthetics of autonomy culminate in the poetics of Stéphane Mallarmé in the 1880s. Aestheticism conceiving the work of art as a purely self-sufficient and self-reflexive ▲ experience—identified by Walter Benjamin as a nineteenth-century theology of art—generated, in early-twentieth-century formalist thought, similar conceptions that would later become the doxa of painterly self-reflexivity for formalist critics and historians. These ranged from Roger Fry's responses to Postimpressionism—in particular the work of Paul Cézanne—to Daniel-Henry Kahnweiler's neo-Kantian theories of Analytical Cubism, to the ● work of Clement Greenberg (1909–94) in the postwar period. Any attempt to transform autonomy into a transhistorical, if not ontological precondition of aesthetic experience, however, is profoundly problematic. It becomes evident upon closer historical inspection that the formation of the concept of aesthetic autonomy itself was far from autonomous. This is first of all because the aesthetics of autonomy had been determined by the overarching philosophical framework of Enlightenment philosophy (Immanuel Kant's [1724–1804] concept of disinterestedness) while it simultaneously operated in opposition to the rigorous instrumentalization of experience that emerged with the rise of the mercantile capitalist class.

Within the field of cultural representation, the cult of autonomy liberated linguistic and artistic practices from mythical and religious thought just as much as it emancipated them from the politically adulatory service and economic dependency under the auspices of a rigorously controlling feudal patronage. While the cult of autonomy might have originated with the emancipation of bourgeois subjectivity from aristocratic and religious hegemony, autonomy also saw the theocratic and hierarchical structures of that patronage as having their own reality. The modernist aesthetic of autonomy thus constituted the social and subjective sphere from within which an opposition against the totality of interested activities and instrumentalized forms of experience could be articulated in artistic acts of open negation and refusal. Paradoxically, however, these acts served as opposition and—in their ineluctable condition as extreme exceptions from the universal rule—they confirmed the regime of total instrumentalization. One might have

▲ 1935 ● 1906, 1911, 1942a, 1960b

2 • El Lissitzky and Sergei Senkin, *The Task of the Press is the Education of the Masses*, 1928
Photographic frieze for the international exhibition *Pressa*, Cologne

Like Heartfield, El Lissitzky transformed the legacies of collage and photomontage according to the needs of a newly industrialized collective. Especially in the new genre of exhibition design, which he developed in the twenties in works such as the Soviet Pavilion for the international exhibition *Pressa*, it became evident that Lissitzky was one of the first (and few) artists of the twenties and thirties to understand that the spaces of public architecture (that is, of simultaneous collective reception) and the space of public information had collapsed in the new spaces of the mass-cultural sphere. Therefore Lissitzky, an exemplary "artist-as-producer," as Walter Benjamin would identify the artist's new social role, would situate his practice within the very parameters and modes of production of a newly developing proletarian public sphere.

to formulate the paradox that an aesthetics of autonomy is thus the highly instrumentalized form of noninstrumentalized experience under liberal bourgeois capitalism.

Actual study of the critical phase of the aesthetic of autonomy in the nineteenth century (from Manet to Mallarmé) would recognize that this very paradox is the actual formative structure of their pictorial and poetic genius. Both define modernist representation as an advanced form of critical self-reflexivity and define their hermetic artifice in assimilation and in opposition to the emerging mass-cultural forms of instrumentalized representation. Typically, the concept of autonomy was both formed by and oppositional to the instrumental logic of bourgeois rationality, rigorously enforcing the requirements of that rationality within the sphere of cultural production through its commitment to empirical criticality. Thereby an aesthetics of autonomy contributed to one of the most fundamental transformations of the experience of the work of art, initiating the shift that Walter Benjamin in his essays of the thirties called the historical transition from cult-value to exhibition-value. These essays have come to be universally considered as the founding texts of a philosophical theory of the social history of art.

The concept of autonomy also served to idealize the new distribution form of the work of art, now that it had become a free-floating commodity on the bourgeois market of objects and luxury goods. Thus autonomy aesthetics was engendered by the capitalist logic of commodity production as much as it opposed that logic. In fact, the Marxist aesthetician Theodor W. Adorno (1903–69) still maintained in the late sixties that artistic independence and aesthetic autonomy could, paradoxically, be guaranteed only in the commodity structure of the work of art.

Antiaesthetic

Peter Bürger (born 1936), in his important—although problematic—essay, *Theory of the Avant-Garde* (1974), argued that the new spectrum of antiaesthetic practices in 1913 arose as a contestation of autonomy aesthetics. Thus—according to Bürger—the historical avant-gardes after Cubism universally attempted to "integrate art with life" and to challenge the autonomous "institution of art." Bürger perceives this project of the antiaesthetic to be at the center ▲ of the revolts of Dadaism, Russian Constructivism, and French Surrealism. Yet, rather than focusing on a nebulously conceived integration of art and life (an integration never satisfactorily defined at any point in history) or on a rather abstract debate on the nature of the institution of art, it seems more productive to focus here on the very strategies that these avant-garde practitioners themselves had propagated: in particular, strategies to initiate fundamental changes in the conception of audience and spectatorial agency, to reverse the bourgeois hierarchy of aesthetic exchange-value and use-value, and most importantly perhaps, to conceive of cultural practices for a newly emerging internationalist proletarian public sphere within the advanced industrial nation states.

Such an approach would not only allow us to differentiate these avant-garde projects more adequately, but would also help us understand that the rise of an aesthetic of technical reproduction (in diametrical opposition to an aesthetic of autonomy) emerges at that very moment of the twenties when the bourgeois public sphere begins to wither away. It is at first displaced by the progressive forces of an emerging proletarian public sphere (as was the case in the ● early phases of the Soviet Union and the Weimar Republic), only to be followed, of course, by the rise of the mass-cultural public sphere, either in its totalitarian fascist or state-socialist versions in ■ the thirties or by its postwar regimes of the culture industry and of spectacle, emerging with the hegemony of the United States and a largely dependent culture of European reconstruction.

The antiaesthetic dismantles the aesthetics of autonomy on all levels: it replaces originality with technical reproduction, it destroys a work's aura and the contemplative modes of aesthetic experience and replaces these with communicative action and aspirations toward simultaneous collective perception. The antiaesthetic (such ▲ as the work of John Heartfield [**1**]) defines its artistic practices as temporary and geopolitically specific (rather than as transhistorical), as participatory (rather than as a unique emanation of an exceptional form of knowledge). The antiaesthetic also operates as a ● utilitarian aesthetic (e.g., in the work of the Soviet Productivists [**2**]), situating the work of art in a social context where it assumes a variety of productive functions such as information and education or political enlightenment, serving the needs of a cultural self-constitution for the newly emerging audiences of the industrial proletariat who were previously excluded from cultural representation on the levels of both production and reception.

Class, agency, and activism

The central premises of Marxist political theory had been the concepts of class and class-consciousness—the most important factors to drive forward the historical process. Classes served in different moments of history as the agents of historical, social, and political change (e.g., the aristocracy, the bourgeoisie, the proletariat, and the most powerful class in the twentieth century, the *petite bourgeoisie*, paradoxically the most neglected by classical Marxist accounts). It had been Marx's argument that class itself was defined by one crucial condition: a subject's situation in relation to the means of production.

Thus, privileged access to (or, more decisively, controlling ownership of) the means of production was the constitutive condition of bourgeois class identity in the later eighteenth and the entire nineteenth centuries. In contrast, during the same period, the conditions of proletarianization identify those subjects who will remain forever economically, legally, and socially barred from access to the means of production (which would, of course, also include the means of education and the acquisition of improved professional skills).

Questions concerning the concept of class are central to the social history of art, ranging from the class identity of the artist to whether cultural solidarity or mimetic artistic identification with the struggles of the oppressed and exploited classes of modernity can actually amount to acts of political support for revolutionary or oppositional movements. Marxist political theorists have often regarded that kind of cultural class alliance with considerable skepticism. Yet this mode of class alliance determined practically all politically motivated artistic production of modernity, since very few, if any, artists and intellectuals had actually emerged from the conditions of proletarian existence at that time. Class identity becomes all the more complicated when considering how the consciousness of individual artists might well have become radicalized at certain points (e.g., the revolution of 1848, the revolutions of 1917, or the anti-imperialist struggles of 1968) and artists might then have assumed positions of solidarity with the oppressed classes of those historical moments [**3**]. Slightly later, however, in the wake of their cultural assimilation, the same artists might have assumed positions of complicit or active affirmation of the ruling order and simply served as the providers of cultural legitimation.

▲ 1916a, 1920, 1921, 1924, 1930b, 1931 ● 1921, 1923, 1925b, 1930a ■ 1934a, 1937a, 1957a, 1960c ▲ 1920 ● 1921

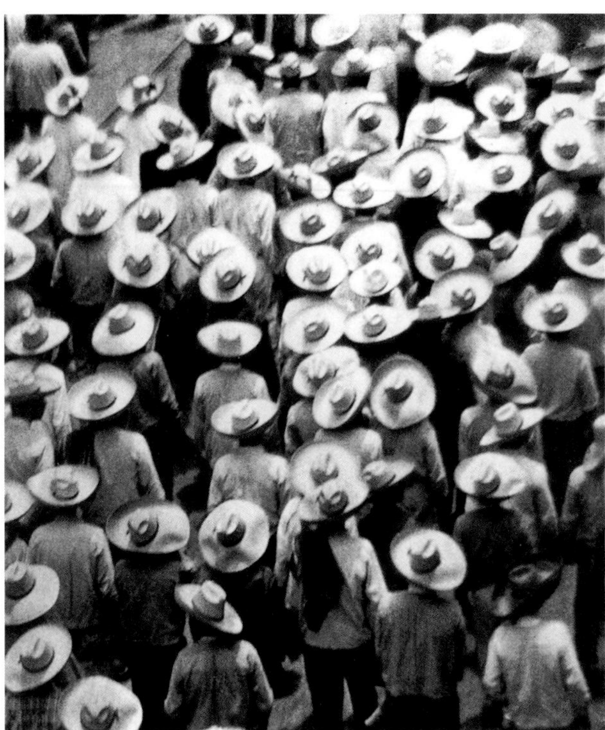

3 • Tina Modotti, *Workers' Demonstration, Mexico, May 1*, 1929
Platinum print, 20.5 x 18 (8⅛ x 7⅛)

The work of the Italian-American artist Modotti in Mexico gives evidence of the universality of the political and social commitment among radical artists of the twenties and thirties. Abandoning her training as a "straight" modernist photographer in the mold of Edward Weston, Modotti's work in Mexico would soon reorient itself to make photography a weapon in the political struggle of the Mexican peasant and working class against the eternal deferrals and deceptions of the country's oligarchic rulers. Expanding the tradition of the *Taller Grafico Popular* to address that class now with the means of photographic representation, she nevertheless understood the necessity of making the regionally specific and uneven development of forms of knowledge and artistic culture the basis of her work. Accordingly, Modotti never adopted the seemingly more advanced forms of political photomontage, but retained the bonds of realist depiction necessary for activist political messages in the geopolitical context in which she had situated herself. At the same time, as the image *Workers' Demonstration* signals, she was far from falling into the conciliatory and compensatory realisms of "straight" and "New Objective" photography. What would have been merely a modernist grid of serially repeated objects of industrial manufacture in the work of her historical peers (such as Alfred Renger-Patzsch) becomes one of the most convincing photographic attempts of the twenties and thirties to depict the social presence and political activism of the working and peasant class masses as the actual producers of a country's economic resources.

This also points to the necessary insight that the registers of artistic production and their latent or manifest relationships to political activism are infinitely more differentiated than arguments for the politicization of art might generally have assumed. We are not simply confronted with an alternative between a politically conscious or activist practice on the one hand, and a merely affirmative, hegemonic culture (as the Italian Marxist philosopher and aesthetician Antonio Gramsci [1891–1937] called it) on the other. Yet, the function of hegemonic culture is clearly to sustain power and legitimize the perceptual and behavioral forms of the ruling class through cultural representation, while oppositional cultural practices articulate resistance to hierarchical thought, subvert privileged forms of experience, and destabilize the ruling regimes of vision and perception just as they can also massively and manifestly destabilize governing notions of hegemonic power.

If we accept that some forms of cultural production can assume the role of agency (i.e., that of information and enlightenment, that of criticality and counterinformation), then the social history of art faces one of its most precarious insights, if not a condition of crisis: if it were to align its aesthetic judgment with the condition of political solidarity and class alliance, it would inevitably be left with only a few heroic figures in whom such a correlation between class-consciousness, agency, and revolutionary alliance could actually be ascertained. These examples would include Gustave Courbet and Honoré Daumier in the nineteenth century, Käthe Kollwitz and ▲ John Heartfield in the first half of the twentieth century, and artists ● such as Martha Rosler [**4**], Hans Haacke [**6**], and Allan Sekula in the second half of the twentieth century.

Thus, in recognizing that compliance with class interests and political revolutionary consciousness can at best be considered an exceptional rather than a necessary condition within the aesthetic practices of modernity, it leaves the social art historian with a difficult choice. That is, either to exclude from consideration most actual artistic practices of any particular moment of modernism, disregarding both the artists and their production because of their lack of commitment, class-consciousness, and political correctness, or to recognize the necessity for numerous other criteria (beyond political and social history) to enter the process of historical and critical analysis.

Since the proletarian's only means of survival is the sale of his or her own labor like any other commodity, producing a phenomenal accretion of surplus value to the entrepreneurial bourgeois or to the corporate enterprise by supplying the subject's labor power, it is, therefore, the very condition of labor and the laborer that radical artists from the nineteenth century onward, from Gustave Courbet ■ to the Productivists of the twenties, confront. For the most part, however, they confront it not on the level of iconography (in fact, the almost total absence of the representation of alienated labor is the rule of modernism) but rather with the perpetual question of whether the labor of industrial production and the labor of cultural production can and should be related, and, if so, how—as analogous? as dialectical opposites? as complementary? as mutually exclusive? Marxist attempts to theorize this relationship (and the

▲ 1920 ● 1971, 1972b, 1984a ■ 1921

4 • Martha Rosler, *Red Stripe Kitchen*, from the series *Bringing the War Home: House Beautiful*, 1967–72
Photomontage printed as color photograph, 61 x 50.8 (24 x 20)

Rosler is one of the very few artists in the postwar period to have taken up the legacies of the political photomontage work of the thirties. Her series *Bringing the War Back Home: House Beautiful*, begun in 1967, explicitly responds to both a historical and an artistic situation. First of all, the work participated in the growing cultural and political opposition against the imperialist American war in Vietnam. Rather than creating the works as individual photomontages, Rosler conceived them as a series for reproduction and dissemination in a number of antiwar and countercultural journals in order to increase the visibility and impact of the images. She had clearly understood Heartfield's legacy and the dialectics of distribution form and mass-cultural iconography. Second, Rosler explicitly countered the Conceptualist's claim that photography should merely serve as a neutral document of analytical self-criticality, or as an indexical trace of the spatio-temporal stagings of the subject. Rather, she identified photography as *one* of several discursive tools in the production of ideology in the mass-cultural arsenal. By inserting sudden documentary images of the war in Vietnam into the seemingly blissful and opulent world of American domesticity, Rosler not only reveals the intricate intertwinement of domestic and militaristic forms of advanced capitalist consumption, but also manifestly challenges the credibility of photography as a truthful carrier of authentic information.

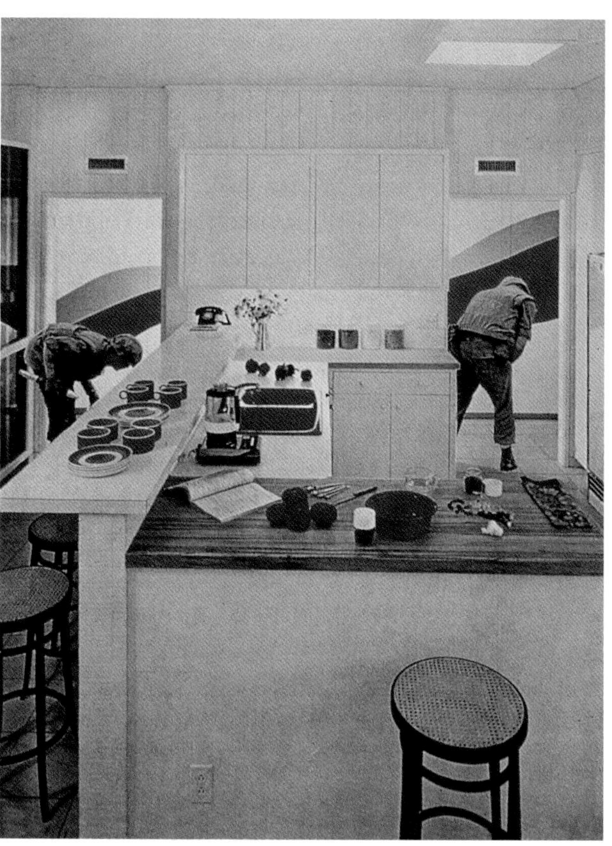

social art historian's attempts to come to terms with these theorizations) span an extreme range: from a productivist–utilitarian aesthetic that affirms the constitution of the subject as necessary in the production of use-value (as in the Soviet Productivists, the ▲ German Bauhaus, and the De Stijl movements) to an aesthetic of ludic counterproductivity (as in the simultaneous practices of Sur- • realism) which negates labor-as-value and denies it any purchase whatsoever on the territory of art. Such an aesthetic regards artistic practice as the one experience where the possibility of historically available forms of unalienated and uninstrumentalized existence shine forth, whether for the first time or as celebratory reminiscences of the bliss of rituals, games, and child's play.

It is no accident, then, that modernism has mostly avoided the actual representation of alienated labor, except for the work of great activist photographers such as Lewis Hine, where the abolition of child labor was the driving agenda of the project. In contrast, whenever painting or photography in the twentieth century celebrated the labor force or the forceful laborer, one could—and can—be sure of being in the company of totalitarian ideologies, whether fascist, Stalinist, or corporate. The heroicization of the body subjected to alienated physical labor serves to instill collective respect for intolerable conditions of subjectivation, and in a false celebration of that labor it also serves to naturalize that which should be critically analyzed in terms of its potential transformation, if not its final abolition. Conversely, the all-too-easy acceptance of artistic practices as mere playful opposition fails to recognize not only the pervasiveness of alienated labor as a governing form of collective experience, but also prematurely accepts the relegation of artistic practice to merely a pointless exemption from the reality principle altogether.

Ideology: reflection and mediation

The concept of ideology played an important role in the aesthetics of György Lukács (1885–1971), who wrote one of the most cohesive Marxist literary aesthetic theories of the twentieth century. Although rarely addressing artistic visual production, Lukács's theories had a tremendous impact on the formation of social art history in its second phase of the forties and fifties, in particular on the work of his fellow Hungarian Arnold Hauser (1892–1978) and the Austrian Marxist Ernst Fischer (1889–1972).

Lukács's key concept was that of reflection, establishing a rather mechanistic relationship between the forces of the economic and political base and the ideological and institutional superstructure. Ideology was defined as an inverted form of consciousness or—worse—as mere false consciousness. Furthermore, the concept of reflection argued that the phenomena of cultural representation were ultimately mere secondary phenomena of the class politics and ideological interests of a particular historical moment. Subsequently, though, the understanding of reflection would depart from these mechanistic assumptions. Lukács's analysis had in fact argued for an understanding of cultural production as dialectical historical operations, and he saw certain cultural practices (e.g., the

▲ 1917, 1921, 1923 • 1924, 1930b, 1931

Homes for America

Early 20th-Century Possessable House to the Quasi-Discrete Cell of '66

5 • Dan Graham, *Homes for America*, from *Arts Magazine*, 1967
Print, 74 x 93 (29⅛ x 36⅝)

Graham's publication of one of his earliest works in the layout and presentational format of an article in the pages of a rather prominent American art magazine demarcates one of the key moments of Conceptual art. First of all, modernism's (and Conceptualism's) supposedly radical quest for empirical and critical self-reflexivity is turned in on itself and onto the frames of presentation and distribution. Graham's magazine article anticipates the fact that crucial information on artistic practices is always already mediated by mass-cultural and commercial forms of dissemination. Accordingly, Graham integrates that dimension of distribution into the conception of the work itself. The artist's model of self-reflexivity dialectically shifts from tautology to discursive and institutional critique. What distinguishes his approach to the problems of audience and distribution from the earlier models of the historical avant-garde is the skepticism and the precision with which he positions his operations exclusively within the discursive and institutional sphere of the given conditions of artistic production (rather than the project of utopian social and political transformations). Yet the choice of prefabricated suburban tract-housing in New Jersey first of all expands the subject matter of Pop art from a mere citation of mass-cultural and media iconography to a new focus on social and architectural spaces. At the same time, Graham reveals that the spatial organization of the lowest level of everyday suburban experience and architectural consumption had already prefigured the principles of a serial or modular iterative structure that had defined the sculptural work of his predecessors, the Minimalists.

bourgeois novel and its project of realism) as the quintessential cultural achievement of the progressive forces of the bourgeoisie. When it came to the development of a proletarian aesthetic, however, Lukács became a stalwart of reactionary thought, arguing that the preservation of the legacies of bourgeois culture would have to be an integral force within an emerging proletarian realism. The task of Socialist realism in Lukács's account eventually came simultaneously to preserve the revolutionary potential of the progressive bourgeois moment that had been betrayed and to lay the foundations of a new proletarian culture that had truly taken possession of the bourgeois means of cultural production.

Since the theorizations of ideology in the sixties, aestheticians and art historians have not only differentiated general theories of ideology, but have also elaborated the questions of how cultural production relates to the apparatus of ideology at large. The question of whether artistic practice operates inside or outside ideological representations has especially preoccupied social art historians since the seventies, all of them arriving at very different answers, depending on the theory of ideology to which they subscribe. Thus, for example, those social art historians who followed the model of the early Marxist phase of American art historian Meyer Schapiro (1904–96) continued to operate under the assumption that cultural representation is the mirror reflection of the ideological interests of a ruling class (e.g., Schapiro's argument about Impressionism being the cultural expression of the leisured share-holding bourgeoisie). According to Schapiro, these cultural representations do not merely articulate the mental universe of the bourgeoisie: they also invest it with the cultural authority to claim and maintain its political legitimacy as a ruling class.

Others have taken Meyer Schapiro's Marxist social history of art as a point of departure, but have also adopted the complex ideas that he developed in his later work. He took the infinitely more complicated questions of mediation between art and ideology into account by recognizing that aesthetic formations are relatively autonomous, rather than fully dependent upon or congruent with ideological interests (a development that is evident, for example, in Schapiro's subsequent turn to an early semiology of abstraction). One result of a more complex theorization of ideology was the attempt to situate artistic representations as dialectical forces within their historically specific moment. That is, in certain cases a particular practice might very well articulate the rise of progressive consciousness not only within an individual artist, but also the progressivity of a patron class and its self-definition in terms of a project of bourgeois enlightenment and ever-expanding social and economic justice (see, for example, Thomas Crow's [born 1948] classic essay "Modernism and Mass Culture," concerning the dialectical conception of the idiom of neo-Impressionist divisionism in its drastic changes from affiliation with the politics of radical anarchism to an indulgent style).

Social art historians of the seventies, like Crow and T. J. Clark (born 1945), conceived of the production of cultural representation as both dependent upon class ideology and generative of counter-ideological models. Thus, the most comprehensive account of

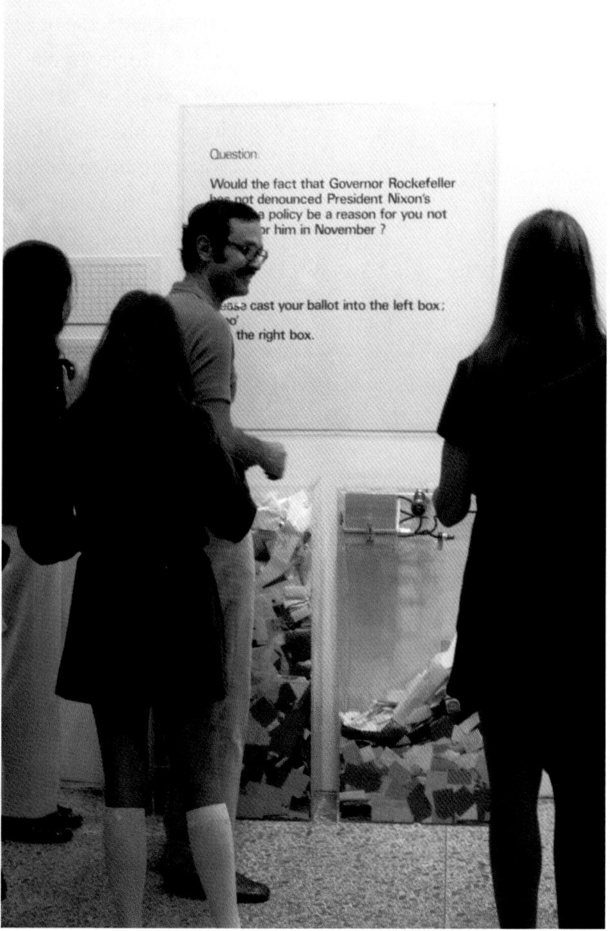

6 • Hans Haacke, *MOMA-Poll*, 1970
Audience participatory installation: two transparent acrylic ballot boxes, each 40 x 20 x 10 ($15\frac{3}{4} \times 7\frac{7}{8} \times 3\frac{7}{8}$), equipped with photoelectic counter, text

For the exhibition "Information" at New York's Museum of Modern Art in 1970, Haacke installed one of the first of his new works to deal with "social systems," called either *Polls* or as *Visitors' Profiles*. In these installations, traditionally passive spectators became active participants. Haacke's subjection of the processes of production and reception to elementary forms of statistical accounting and positivist information is a clear response to the actual principles governing experience in what Adorno had called the "society of administration." At the same time, Haacke's work, like Graham's, shifts attention from the critical analysis of the work's immanent structures of meaning to the external frames of institutions. Thus Haacke repositions Conceptual art in a new critical relation to the socioeconomic conditions determining access and availability of aesthetic experience, a practice later identified as "institutional critique." Haacke's *MOMA-Poll* is a striking example of this shift since it confronts the viewer with a sudden insight into the degree to which the museum as a supposedly neutral space guarding aesthetic autonomy and disinterestedness is imbricated with economic, ideological, and political interests. The work also reconstitutes a condition of responsibility and participation for the viewer that surpasses models of spectatorial involvement previously proposed by artists of the neo-avant-garde, while it recognizes the limitations of the spectators' political aspirations and their psychic range of experience and self-determination.

nineteenth-century modernist painting and its shifting fortunes within the larger apparatus of ideological production can still be found in the complex and increasingly differentiated approach to the question of ideology in the work of Clark, the leading social art historian of the late twentieth century. In Clark's accounts of the work of Daumier and Courbet, for example, ideology and painting are still conceived in the dialectical relations that Lukács had suggested in his accounts of the work of eighteenth and nineteenth-century literature: as an articulation of the progressive forces of the bourgeois class in a process of coming into its own mature identity to accomplish the promises of the French Revolution and of the culture of the Enlightenment at large.

Clark's later work *The Painting of Modern Life: Paris in the Art of Manet and his Followers* (1984), by contrast, does not discuss merely the extreme difficulty of situating the work of Manet and Seurat within such a clear and dynamic relationship to the progressive forces of a particular segment of society. Rather, Clark now faces the task of confronting the newfound complexity of the relationship between ideology and artistic production, and of integrating it with the methodology of social art history that he had developed up to this point. This theoretical crisis undoubtedly resulted in large part from Clark's discovery of the work of the Marxist Lacanian Louis Althusser (1918–90). Althusser's conception of ideology still remains the most productive one, in particular with regard to its capacity to situate aesthetic and art-historical phenomena in a position of relative autonomy with regard to the totality of ideology. This is not just because Althusser theorizes ideology as a totality of linguistic representations in which the subject is constituted in a politicized version of Lacan's account of the symbolic order. Perhaps even more important is Althusser's distinction between the totality of the ideological state apparatus (and its subspheres in all domains of representation) and the explicit exemption of artistic representations (as well as scientific knowledge) from that totality of ideological representations.

Popular culture versus mass culture

One of the most important debates among social art historians concerns the question of how so-called high art or avant-garde practices relate to the emerging mass-cultural formations of modernity. And while it is of course understood that these formations change continuously (as the interactions between the two halves of the systems of representation are continuously reconfigured), it has remained a difficult debate whose outcome is often indicative of the particular type of Marxism embraced by the critics of mass culture. It ranges from the most violent rejection of mass-cultural formations in the work of Adorno, whose infamous condemnation of jazz is now universally discredited as a form of eurocentric Alexandrianism that was—worst of all—largely dependent on the author's total lack of actual information about the musical phenomena he so disdained.

The opposite approach to mass-cultural phenomena was first developed in England, in the work of Raymond Williams (1921–88),

7 • Gerhard Richter and Konrad Lueg/Fischer, *Life with Pop—Demonstration for Capitalist Realism*, at Möbelhaus Berges, Düsseldorf, October 11, 1963

In 1963, Gerhard Richter and Konrad Lueg (who later, as Konrad Fischer, became one of Europe's most important dealers of the Minimal and Conceptual generation) staged a performance in a Düsseldorf department store. It initiated a German variation on the neo-avant-garde's international reorientation toward mass culture that—since the late fifties—had gradually displaced postwar forms of abstraction in England, France, and the United States. The neologism "capitalist realism," coined by Richter for this occasion, reverberates with realism's horrible "other," the Socialist variety that had defined Richter's educational background in the Communist part of Germany until 1961. The spectacle of boredom, affirmation, and passivity against the backdrop of a totalizing system of objects of consumption took the work of Piero Manzoni as *one* of its cues, namely the insight that artistic practice would have to be situated more than ever in the interstitial spaces between objects of consumption, sites of spectacle, and ostentatious acts of artistic annihilation. But its brooding melancholic passivity was also a specifically German contribution to the recognition that from now on advanced forms of consumer culture would not only determine behavior in a way that had been previously determined by religious or political belief systems, but that in this particular historical context of Germany they would also serve as the collective permit to repress and to forget the population's recent massive conversion to fascism.

whose crucial distinction between popular culture and mass culture became a productive one for subsequent attempts by cultural historians such as Stuart Hall (born 1932) to argue for an infinitely more differentiated approach when analyzing mass-cultural phenomena. Hall argued that the same dialectical movement that aestheticians and art historians had detected in the gradual shift of stylistic phenomena from revolutionary and emancipatory to regressive and politically reactionary could be detected in the production of mass culture as well: here a perpetual oscillation from initial contestation and transgression to eventual affirmation in the process of industrialized acculturation would take place. Hall also made it seem plausible that a fundamental first step in overcoming the eurocentric fixation on hegemonic culture (whether high bourgeois or avant-garde) was acceptance that different audiences communicate within different structures of tradition, linguistic convention, and behavioral forms of interaction. Therefore, according to the new cultural-studies approach, the specificity of audience address and experiences should be posited above all claims—as authoritarian as they are numinous—for universally valid criteria of aesthetic evaluation, that is, that hierarchical canonicity whose ultimate and latent goal would always remain the confirmation of the supremacy of white, male, bourgeois culture.

Sublimation and desublimation

The model of cultural studies that Williams and Hall elaborated, and that became known later as the Birmingham Centre for Contemporary Cultural Studies, laid the foundations for most of the work in cultural studies being done today. Even though he is not known ever to have engaged with the work of any of the British Marxists, Adorno's counterargument would undoubtedly have been to accuse their project of being one of extending desublimation into the very center of aesthetic experience, its conception and critical evaluation. Desublimation for Adorno internalizes the very destruction of subjectivity further; its agenda is to dismantle the processes of complex consciousness formation, the desire for political self-determination and resistance, and ultimately to annihilate experience itself in order to become totally controlled by the demands of late capitalism.

Another and rather different Marxist aesthetician, Herbert Marcuse (1898–1979), conceived of the concept of desublimation in almost the opposite way, arguing that the structure of aesthetic experience consisted of the desire to undermine the apparatus of libidinal repression and to generate an anticipatory moment of an existence liberated from needs and instrumentalizing demands. Marcuse's Freudo-Marxist aesthetic of libidinal liberation was situated at the absolute opposite pole of Adorno's ascetic aesthetics of a negative dialectics, and Adorno did not fail to chastize Marcuse publicly for what he perceived to be the horrifying effects of hedonistic American consumer culture on Marcuse's thoughts.

Whatever the ramifications of Marcuse's reconception of desublimation, it is certainly a term for which ample evidence could be found in avant-garde practices before and after World War II. Throughout modernity, artistic strategies resist and deny the established claims for technical virtuosity, for exceptional skills, and for conformity with the accepted standards of historical models. They deny the aesthetic any privileged status whatsoever ▲ and debase it with all the means of deskilling, by taking recourse to an abject or a low-cultural iconography, or by the emphatic foregrounding of procedures and materials that reinsert the disavowed dimensions of repressed somatic experience back into the space of artistic experience.

The neo-avant-garde

One of the major conflicts of writing social art history after World War II derives from an overarching condition of asynchronicity. On the one hand, American critics in particular were eager to establish the first hegemonic avant-garde culture of the twentieth century; however, in the course of that project they failed to recognize that the very fact of a reconstruction of a model of avant-garde culture would inevitably not only affect the status of the work being produced under these circumstances, but would also affect the critical and historical writing associated with it even more profoundly.

In Adorno's late-modernist *Aesthetic Theory* (1970), the concept • of autonomy retains a central role. Unlike Clement Greenberg's remobilization of the concept in favor of an American version of late-modernist aesthetics, Adorno's aesthetics operates within a principle of double negativity. On the one hand, Adorno's late modernism denies the possibility of a renewed access to an aesthetics of autonomy, a possibility annihilated by the final destruction of the bourgeois subject in the aftermath of fascism and the Holocaust. On the other hand, Adorno's aesthetics also deny the possibility of a politicization of artistic practices in the revolutionary perspective of Marxist aesthetics. According to Adorno, politicized art would only serve as an alibi and prohibit actual political change, since the political circumstances for a revolutionary politics are de facto not accessible in the moment of postwar reconstruction of culture.

By contrast, American neomodernism and the practices of what ■ Peter Bürger called the neo-avant-garde—most palpably advocated by Greenberg and his disciple Michael Fried (born 1939)—could uphold their claims only at the price of a systematic *geschichtsklitterung*, a manifest attempt at writing history from the perspective of victorious interests, systematically disavowing the major transformations that had occurred within the conception of high art and avant-garde culture discussed above (e.g., the legacies of Dada and the Russian and Soviet avant-gardes). But worse still, these critics failed to see that cultural production after the Holocaust could not simply attempt to establish a continuity of modernist painting and sculpture. Adorno's model of a negative dialectics (most notoriously formulated in his verdict on the impossibility of lyrical poetry after Auschwitz) and his aesthetic theory—in open opposition to Greenberg's neomodernism—suggested the ineluctable necessity of rethinking the very precarious condition of culture at large.

It appears that the strengths and successes of the social history of art are most evident in those historical situations where actual mediations between classes, political interests, and cultural forms of representation are solidly enacted and therefore relatively verifiable. Their unique capacity to reconstruct the narratives around those revolutionary or foundational situations of modernity makes the accounts of social art historians the most compelling interpretations of the first hundred years of modernism, from David in the work of Thomas Crow to the beginnings of Cubism in T. J. Clark's work.

However, when it comes to the historical emergence of avant-garde practices such as abstraction, collage, Dada, or the work of Duchamp, whose innermost *telos* it had been actively to destroy traditional subject–object relationships and to register the destruction of traditional forms of experience, both on the level of narrative and on that of pictorial representation, social art history's attempts to maintain cohesive narrative accounts often emerge at best as either incongruent or incompatible with the structures and morphologies at hand, or at worst, as falsely recuperative. Once the extreme forms of particularization and fragmentation have become the central formal concerns in which postbourgeois subjectivity finds its correlative remnants of figuration, the interpretative desire to reimpose totalizing visions onto historical phenomena sometimes appears reactionary and at other times paranoid in its enforcement of structures of meaning and experience. After all, the radicality of these artistic practices had involved not only their refusal to allow for such visions but also their formulation of syntax and structures where neither narrative nor figuration could still obtain. If meaning could still obtain at all, it would require accounts that would inevitably lead beyond the frameworks of those of deterministic causation.

FURTHER READING

Frederick Antal, *Classicism and Romanticism* (London: Routledge & Kegan Paul, 1966)

Frederick Antal, *Hogarth and His Place in European Art* (London: Routledge & Kegan Paul, 1962)

T. J. Clark, *Farewell to an Idea* (New Haven and London: Yale University Press, 1999)

T. J. Clark, *Image of the People: Gustave Courbet and the Second French Republic, 1848–1851* (London: Thames & Hudson, 1973)

T. J. Clark, *The Absolute Bourgeois: Artists and Politics in France, 1848–1851* (London: Thames & Hudson, 1973)

T. J. Clark, *The Painting of Modern Life: Paris in the Art of Manet and his Followers* (London: Thames & Hudson, 1984)

Thomas Crow, *Painters and Public Life in 18th-Century Paris* (New Haven and London: Yale University Press, 1985).

Thomas Crow, *The Intelligence of Art* (Chapel Hill, N.C.: University of North Carolina Press, 1999)

Serge Guilbaut, *How New York Stole the Idea of Modern Art: Abstract Expressionism, Freedom, and the Cold War* (Chicago and London: University of Chicago Press, 1983)

Nicos Hadjinicolaou, *Art History and Class Struggle* (London: Pluto Press, 1978)

Arnold Hauser, *The Social History of Art* (1951), four volumes (London: Routledge, 1999)

Fredric Jameson (ed.), *Aesthetics and Politics* (London: New Left Books, 1977)

Francis Klingender, *Art and the Industrial Revolution* (1947) (London: Paladin Press, 1975)

Meyer Schapiro, *Modern Art: 19th and 20th Century, Selected Papers, vol. 2* (New York: George Braziller, 1978)

Meyer Schapiro, *Romanesque Art, Selected Papers, vol. 1* (New York: George Braziller, 1977)

Meyer Schapiro, *Theory and Philosophy of Art: Style, Artist, and Society, Selected Papers, vol. 4* (New York: George Braziller, 1994)

▲ 1968b • 1942a, 1960b ■ 1960a

3 Formalism and structuralism

In 1971–2, the French literary theorist Roland Barthes (1915–80) held a year-long seminar devoted to the history of semiology, the "general science of signs" that had been conceived as an extension of linguistics by the Swiss Ferdinand de Saussure (1857–1913) in his *Course in General Linguistics* (posthumously published in 1916) and simultaneously, under the name of semiotics, by the American philosopher Charles Sanders Peirce (1839–1914) in his *Collected Papers* (also posthumously published, from 1931 to 1958). Barthes had been one of the leading voices of structuralism from the mid-fifties to the late sixties, together with the anthropologist Claude Lévi-Strauss (born 1908), the philosopher Michel Foucault (1926–84), and the psychoanalyst Jacques Lacan, and as such had greatly contributed to the resurrection of the semiological project, which he had clearly laid out in *Elements of Semiology* (1964) and "Structural Analysis of Narratives" (1966). But he had seriously undermined that very project in his most recent books, *S/Z*, *The Empire of Signs* (both 1970), and *Sade, Fourier, Loyola* (1971).

The curiosity of Barthes's auditors (myself among them) was immense: in this period of intellectual turmoil marked by a general Oedipal desire to kill the structuralist model, they expected him to ease their understanding of the shift underway from ▲ A (structuralism) to B (poststructuralism)—a term that neatly describes Barthes's work at the time, but which was never condoned by any of its participants. They anticipated a chronological summary. Logically, such a narrative, after a presentation of Saussure's and Peirce's concepts, would have discussed the work of the Russian Formalist school of literary criticism, active from around 1915 to the Stalinist blackout of 1932; then, after one of its ● members, Roman Jakobson (1896–1982), had left Russia, of the Prague Linguistic Circle grouped around him; then of French structuralism; and finally, in conclusion, it would have dealt with ■ Jacques Derrida's deconstruction.

Barthes's audience got the package they had hoped for, but not without a major surprise. Instead of beginning with Saussure, he initiated his survey with an examination of the ideological critique proposed, from the twenties on, by the German Marxist playwright Bertolt Brecht (1898–1956). Although Barthes, no less than his peers, had succumbed to the dream of scientific objectivity when the structuralist movement was at its peak, he now implicitly advocated a subjective approach. No longer interested in mapping a discipline, he endeavored instead to tell the story of his *own* semiological adventure, which had started with his discovery of Brecht's writings. Coming from someone whose assault on biographism (the reading of a literary piece through the life of its author) had always been scathing, the gesture was deliberately provocative. (The enormous polemic engendered by the antibiographism of Barthes's *On Racine* (1963), which had ended in *Criticism and Truth* (1966), Barthes's brilliant answer to his detractors, and which had done more than anything else to radically transform traditional literary studies in France, was still very much on everyone's mind.) But there was a strategic motive as well in this Brechtian beginning, a motive that becomes apparent when one turns to the essay in which Barthes had discussed Saussure for the first time.

"Myth Today" was a postscript to the collection of sociological vignettes Barthes had written between 1954 and 1956 and published under the title *Mythologies* (1957). The main body of the book had been written in the Brechtian mode: its stated purpose was to reveal, underneath the pretended "naturalness" of the *petit-bourgeois* ideology conveyed by the media, what was historically determined. But in "Myth Today" Barthes presented Saussure's work, which he had just discovered, as offering new tools for the kind of Brechtian ideological analysis he had so far been conducting. What is perhaps most striking, in retrospect, is that Barthes's exposition of Saussurean semiology begins with a plea in favor of formalism. Shortly ▲ after alluding to Andrei Zhdanov and his Stalinist condemnation of formalism and modernism as bourgeois decadence, Barthes writes: "Less terrorized by the specter of 'formalism,' historical criticism might have been less sterile; it would have understood that … the more a system is specifically defined in its forms, the more amenable it is to historical criticism. To parody a well-known saying, I shall say that a little formalism turns one away from History, but that a lot brings one back to it." In other words, right from the start Barthes conceived of what was soon to be named "structuralism" as part of a broader formalist current in twentieth-century thought. Furthermore, Barthes was denying the claims of the antiformalist champions that formalist critics, in bypassing "content" to scrutinize forms, were retreating from the world and its historical realities to the ivory tower of a humanistic "eternal present."

▲ Introduction 4 ● 1915 ■ Introduction 4 ▲ 1934a

"Semiology is a science of forms, since it studies significations apart from their content." Such is the definition that immediately precedes Barthes's passage quoted above. Its terminology is somewhat flawed, for Barthes was still a novice in structural linguistics, and he would soon know that the word "content" has to be replaced by "referent" in such a sentence. But the basic axioms are already there: signs are organized into sets of oppositions that shape their signification, independently of what the signs in question refer to; every human activity partakes of at least one system of signs (generally several at once), whose rules can be tracked down; and, as a producer of signs, man is forever condemned to signification, unable ▲ to flee the "prison-house of language," to use Fredric Jameson's formulation. Nothing that man utters is insignificant—even saying "nothing" carries a meaning (or rather multiple meanings, changing according to the context, which is itself structured).

Choosing in 1971 to present these axioms as derived from Brecht (rather than from Saussure, as he had done in 1957), Barthes had a polemical intention: he was pointing to the historical link between modernism and the awareness that language is a structure of signs. Indeed, although Brecht's star has somewhat faded in recent years, he was regarded in postwar Europe as one of the most powerful modernist writers. In his numerous theoretical statements, Brecht had always attacked the myth of the transparency of language that had governed the practice of theater since Aristotle; the self-reflective, anti-illusionistic montagelike devices that interrupted the flow of his plays aimed at aborting the identification of the spectator with any character and, as he phrased it, at producing an effect of "distanciation" or "estrangement."

The first example Barthes commented on in his 1971–2 seminar was a text in which the German writer patiently analyzed the 1934 Christmas speeches of two Nazi leaders (Hermann Goering and Rudolf Hess). What struck Barthes was Brecht's extreme attention to the form of the Nazi texts, which he had followed word for word in order to elaborate his counterdiscourse. Brecht pinpointed the efficacy of these speeches in the seamless flow of their rhetoric: the smokescreen with which Goering and Hess masked their faulty logic and heap of lies was the mellifluous continuity of their language, which functioned like a robust, gooey adhesive.

Brecht, in short, was a formalist, eager to demonstrate that language was not a neutral vehicle made to transparently convey concepts directly from mind to mind, but had a materiality of its own and that this materiality was always charged with significations. But he immensely resented the label of formalism when it was thrown at modern literature as a whole by the Marxist philosopher György Lukács, writing in the USSR at a time when calling anyone a formalist was equivalent to signing his or her death warrant. By then virulently opposed to modernism in general—but in particular to the technique of montage that Sergei Eisenstein invented in film and Brecht adapted to the theater, and to the kind of interior monologue that concludes James Joyce's *Ulysses*—Lukács had proposed nineteenth-century realist novels (those of Balzac in particular) as the model to be emulated, especially if one was to write from a "proletarian" point of view. Yet it was Lukács who was the "formalist," wrote Brecht in his rebuttal. In calling for a twentieth-century novel with a "revolutionary" content but penned in a form that dated from a century earlier, a form that belonged to the era before the self-reflexivity and anti-illusionism of modernism, Lukács was fetishizing form.

Thus the term "formalist" was an insult that Lukács and Brecht tossed at each other, but the word did not have the same sense for each. For Brecht, a formalist was anyone who could not see that form was inseparable from content, who believed that form was a mere carrier; for Lukács, it was anyone who believed that form even affected content. Brecht's uneasiness with the term, however, should give us pause, especially since the same uneasiness has mushroomed in art history and criticism since the early seventies. (It is particularly noteworthy in this context that the art critic whose name is most associated in America with formalism, Clement ▲ Greenberg, also had such misgivings: "Whatever its connotations in Russian, the term has acquired ineradicably vulgar ones in English," he wrote in 1967.) In order to understand the ambivalence, it is useful to recall Barthes's dictum: "a little formalism turns one away from History, but that a lot brings one back to it." For what Brecht resented in Lukács's "formalism" was its denial both of history and of what the Danish linguist Louis Hjelmslev would call the "form of content"—of the fact that the very structure of Balzac's novels was grounded upon the world view of a particular social class at a particular juncture in the history of Western Europe. In short, Lukács had practiced only a "restricted" formalism, whose analysis remains at the superficial level of form-as-shape, or morphology.

The antiformalism that was prevalent in the discourse of art criticism in the seventies can thus be explained in great part by a confusion between two kinds of formalism, one that concerns itself essentially with morphology (which I call "restricted" formalism), and one that envisions form as structural—the kind embraced by Brecht when he sorted out the "continuity" of Goering's and Hess's speeches as an essential part of their ideological machine. The confusion was compounded by Greenberg's gradual turnabout. While his analyses of the dialectical role of *trompe-l'oeil* devices in • Georges Braque's Cubist still lifes [1] or that of the alloverness of ■ Jackson Pollock's drippings) are to be counted on the structural ledger, by the late 1950s his discourse was more reminiscent of the morphological mode promulgated at the beginning of the twenti- ◆ eth century by the British writers Clive Bell and Roger Fry, whose concern was merely good design. The distinction between these two formalisms is essential to a retrieval of formalism (as structuralism) from the wastebasket of discarded ideas.

Structuralism and art history

Although the linguistic/semiological model provided by Saussure became the inspiration for the structuralist movement in the fifties and sixties, art history had already developed structural methods by the time this model became known in the twenties. Furthermore,

▲ 1984b

▲ 1942a, 1960b • 1911 ■ 1949, 1960b ◆ 1906

1 • Georges Braque, *Violin and Pitcher*, 1910
Oil on canvas, 117 x 73 (46 x 28¾)

One of the benchmarks of formalism is its attention to rhetorical devices, to the signification of the means of signification themselves. Examining this painting by Braque, Clement Greenberg singled out the device of the realistic nail and its shadow painted *on top* of the faceted volumes depicted on the picture's surface. Both flattening the rest of the image and pushing it back into depth, the *trompe-l'oeil* nail was for the artist a means of casting some doubt with regard to the traditional, illusionistic mode of representing space.

the first literary critics who can be called structuralists—the Russian ▲ Formalists—were particularly aware of their art-historical antecedents (much more than of Saussure, whom they discovered only after writing many of their groundbreaking works). Finally, it was • Cubism that first helped the Russian Formalists to develop their theories: in deliberately attacking the epistemology of representation, Cubism (and abstract art in its wake) underscored the gap separating reference and meaning and called for a more sophisticated understanding of the nature of signs.

The role played by art history and avant-garde art practice in the formation of a structuralist mode of thinking is little known today, but it is important for our purpose, especially with regard to the accusations of ahistoricism often thrown at structuralism. In fact, one could even say that the birth of art history as a discipline dates from the moment it was able to structure the vast amount of material it had neglected for purely ideological and aesthetic reasons. It might seem odd today that seventeenth-century Baroque art, for example, had fallen into oblivion during the eighteenth and early nineteenth centuries, until Heinrich Wölfflin (1864–1945) rehabilitated it in *Renaissance and Baroque* (1888). Resolutely opposed to the dominant normative aesthetic of Johann Joachim Winckelmann (1717–68), for whom Greek art was an unsurpassable yardstick for all subsequent artistic production, Wölfflin endeavored to show that Baroque art had to be judged by criteria that were not only different from but resolutely opposed to those of Classical art. This idea, that the historical signification of a stylistic language was manifested through its rejection of another one (in this case, a preceding one) would lead Wölfflin to posit "an art history without names" and to establish the set of binary oppositions that constitutes the core of his most famous book, *Principles of Art History*, which appeared in 1915 (linear/painterly, plane/recession, closed/open form; multiplicity/unity; clearness/unclearness).

Wölfflin's formalist taxonomy, however, was still part of a teleological and idealistic discourse, modeled on Hegel's view of history, according to which the unfolding of events is prescribed by a set of predetermined laws. (Within every "artistic epoch," Wölfflin always read the same smooth evolution from linear to painterly, from plane to recession, etc., which left him with little room to explain how one switched from one "epoch" to the next, particularly since he denied nonartistic historical factors much of a causative role in his scheme.) But if Wölfflin's idealism prevented him from developing his formalism into a structuralism, it is to Alois Riegl (1858–1905) that ones owes the first full elaboration of a meticulous analysis of forms as the best access to a social history of artistic production, signification, and reception.

Just as Wölfflin had done with the Baroque era, Riegl undertook the rehabilitation of artistic eras that had been marginalized as decadent, most notably the production of late antiquity (*Late Roman Art Industry*, 1901). But he did more than Wölfflin to advance the cause of an anonymous history of art, one that would trace the evolution of formal/structural systems rather than merely study the output of individual artists: if the well-known works of Rembrandt and Frans

▲ 1915 • 1911, 1912

Hals figure in his last book, *The Group Portraiture of Holland* (1902), they are as the end-products of a series whose features they inherit and transform. Riegl's historical relativism was radical and had far-reaching consequences, not only because it allowed him to disregard the distinction between high and low, major and minor, pure and applied art, but because it led him to understand every artistic *document* as a *monument* to be analyzed and posited in relationship with others belonging to the same series. In other words, Riegl demonstrated that it was only after the set of codes enacted (or altered) by an art object had been mapped in their utmost details that one could attempt to discuss that object's signification and the way it related to other series (for example to the history of social formations, of science, and so forth)—an idea that would be of importance for both the Russian Formalists and Michel Foucault. And it is because Riegl understood meaning as structured by a set of oppositions (and not as transparently conveyed) that he was able to challenge the overwhelming role usually given to the referent in the discourse about art since the Renaissance.

A crisis of reference

A similar crisis of reference provided the initial spark of Russian Formalism around 1915. The polemical target of the Russian Formalist critics was the Symbolist conception that poetry resided in the images it elicited, independent of its linguistic form. But it was through their confrontation with Cubism, then with the first ▲ abstract paintings of Kazimir Malevich and the poetic experiments of his friends Velemir Khlebnikov and Aleksei Kruchenikh—poems whose sounds referred to nothing but the phonetic nature of language itself—that the Russian Formalists discovered, before they ever heard of Saussure, what the Swiss scholar had called the "arbitrary nature of the sign."

Allusions to Cubism abound in Roman Jakobson's writings, particularly when he tries to define poetic language as opposed to the language of communication used in everyday life. In "What is Poetry?", a lecture delivered in 1933, he writes:

> *[Poeticity] can be separated out and made independent, like the various devices in say, a Cubist painting. But this is a special case.... Poeticity is present when the word is felt as a word and not a mere representation of the object being named or an outburst of emotion, when words and their composition, their meaning, their external and inner form, acquire a weight and value of their own instead of referring indifferently to reality.... Without contradiction [between sign and object] there is no mobility of concepts, no mobility of signs, and the relationship between concept and sign becomes automatized. Activity comes to a halt, and the awareness of reality dies out.*

These last lines refer to the device of *ostranenie*, or "making strange," as a rhetorical figure, whose conceptualization by Viktor Shklovsky (1893–1984) in "Art as Device" (1917) is the first theoretical landmark of Russian Formalism (the family resemblance of this notion with Brecht's "estrangement effect" is not fortuitous). According to Shklovsky, the main function of art is to defamiliarize our perception, which has become automatized, and although Jakobson would later dismiss this first theory of defamilarization, it is the way he interpreted Cubism at the time. And for good reason, ▲ as one could say that the first, so-called "African," phase of Cubism was rooted in a deliberate practice of estrangement. Witness this declaration of Pablo Picasso (1881–1973): "In those days people said that I made the noses crooked, even in the *Demoiselles d'Avignon*, but I had to make the nose crooked so they would see that it was a nose. I was sure later they would see that it wasn't crooked."

For Shklovsky, what characterized any work of art was the set of "devices" through which it was reorganizing the "material" (the referent), making it strange. (The notion of "device," never rigorously defined, was a blanket term by which he designated any stylistic feature or rhetoric construction, encompassing all levels of language—phonetic, syntactic, or semantic.) Later on, when he devoted particular attention to works such as the eighteenth-century "novel" *Tristram Shandy* by Laurence Sterne, where the writer pays more attention to mocking the codes of storytelling than to the plot itself, Shklovsky began to conceive not only our perception of the world but also the daily language of communication as the "material" that literary art rearranges—but the work of art remained for him a sum of devices through which the "material" was de-automatized. For Jakobson, though, the "devices" were not simply piled up in a work but were interdependent, constituting a system, and they had a constructive function, each contributing to the specificity and unity of the work, just as each bone has a role to play in our skeleton. Furthermore, each new artistic device, or each new system of devices, had to be understood either as breaking a previous one that had become deadened and automatized, or as revealing it (laying it bare), as if it had been there all along but unperceived: in short, any artistic device (and not just the world at large or the language of daily communication) could become the "material" made strange by a subsequent one. As a result, any device was always semantically charged for Jakobson, a complex sign bearing several layers of connotations.

It is this second notion of *ostranenie* that Jakobson had in mind when he spoke of the isolation of the various devices in a Cubist work as a "special case": in laying bare the traditional mechanisms of pictorial representation, Cubism performed for Jakobson and his colleagues the same function that neurosis had played for Freud's discovery of the unconscious. Much as the special (pathological) case of neurosis had led Freud to his general theory of the psychological development of man, the special (defamiliarizing) case of Cubism was seized by the Russian Formalists as support for their antimimetic, structural conception of poetic language.

In hindsight, however, we can see that bestowing a status of "normalcy" to the traditional means of pictorial representation that Cubism fought and whose devices it laid bare is not sustainable: it would posit such traditional means of representation as constituting a

▲ 1915 ▲ 1907

kind of ahistorical norm against which all pictorial enterprises would have to be measured (bringing us back, in effect, to Winckelmann). Perceiving the essentializing danger of this simple dualism (norm/exception), Jakobson grew more suspicious of the normative postulates upon which his early work had been based (the opposition between the language of daily use as norm, and of literature as exception). But he would always take advantage of the model offered by psychoanalysis, according to which *dysfunction* helps us understand *function*. In fact, one of his major contributions to the field of literary criticism—the dichotomy that he established between the metaphoric and metonymic poles of language—was the direct result of his investigation of aphasia, a disorder of the central nervous system characterized by the partial or total loss of the ability to communicate. He noted that for the most part aphasic disturbances concerned either "the selection of linguistic entities" (the choice of *that* sound rather than *this* one, of *that* word rather than *this* one) or "their combination into linguistic units of a higher degree of complexity." Patients suffering from the first kind of aphasia (which Jakobson terms "the similarity disorder") cannot substitute a linguistic unit for another one, and metaphor is inaccessible to them; patients suffering from the second kind of aphasia ("the contiguity disorder") cannot put any linguistic unit into its context, and metonymy (or synecdoche) is senseless for them. The poles of similarity and contiguity were directly borrowed from Saussure (they correspond in his *Course* to the terms *paradigm* and *syntagm*), but they were expressly linked by Jakobson to the Freudian concepts of displacement and condensation: just as the limit between these two activities of the unconscious remained porous for Freud, Jakobson's polar extremes do not preclude the existence of hybrid or intermediary forms. But once again it is the opposition of these two terms that structured for him the immense domain of world literature. And not only literature: he saw Surrealist art as essentially metaphoric, and Cubism as essentially metonymic.

The arbitrary nature of the sign

Before we examine a Cubist work from a structural point of view, let us at last turn to Saussure's famous *Course* and its groundbreaking exposition of what he called the arbitrariness of the sign. Saussure went far beyond the conventional notion of arbitrariness as the absence of any "natural" link between the sign (say, the word "tree") and its referent (any actual tree), even though he would have been the last to deny this absence, to which the simple existence of multiple languages attests. For Saussure, the arbitrariness involved not only the relation between the sign and its referent, but also that between the signifier (the sound we utter when we pronounce the word "tree" or the letters we trace when we write it down) and the signified (the concept of tree). His principal target was the Adamic conception of language (from Adam's performance in the Book of Genesis: language as an ensemble of names for things), which he called "chimeric" because it presupposes the existence of an invariable number of signifieds that receive in each particular language a different formal vestment.

This angle of attack led Saussure to separate the problem of referentiality from the problem of signification, understood as the enactment in the utterance (which he called *parole*, as opposed to *langue*, designating the language in which the sign is uttered) of an arbitrary but necessary link between a signifier and a "conceptual" signified. In the most celebrated passage of his *Course*, Saussure wrote:

> *In language there are only differences. Even more important, a difference generally implies positive terms between which the difference is set up; but in language there are only differences* without positive terms... *The idea [signified] or phonic substance [signifier] that a sign contains is of less importance than the other signs that surround it.*

This not only means that a linguistic sign does not signify by itself, but that language is a system of which all units are interdependent. "I eat" and "I ate" have different meanings (though only one letter has shifted its position), but the signified of a temporal present in "I eat" can exist only if it is opposed to the signified of a temporal past in "I ate": one would simply not be able to identify (and thus understand) a linguistic sign if our mind did not compute its competitors within the system to which it belongs, quickly eliminating the ill-suitors while gauging the context of the utterance (for "I eat" is opposed not only to "I ate," but to "I gorge," "I bite," or even—leaving the semantic realm of food—"I sing," "I walk," and so forth). In short, the essential characteristic of any sign is to be what other signs are not. But, Saussure adds,

> *the statement that everything in language is negative is true only if the signified and the signifier are considered separately; when we consider the sign in its totality, we have something that is positive in own class.*

In other words, the acoustic signifier and the "conceptual" signified are negatively differential (they define themselves by what they are not), but a positive fact results from their combination, "the sole type of facts that language has," namely, the sign. Such a caveat might seem strange, given that everywhere else Saussure insisted on the *oppositional* nature of the sign: is he not suddenly reintroducing a substantive quality here, when all his linguistics rests on the discovery that "language is form and not substance"?

Everything revolves around the concept of *value*, one of the most complex and controversial concepts in Saussure. The sign is positive because it has a value determined by what it can be compared with and exchanged with within its own system. This value is absolutely differential, like the value of a hundred-dollar bill in relation to a thousand-dollar bill, but it confers on the sign "something positive." Value is an economic concept for Saussure; it permits the exchange of signs within a system, but it is also what prevents their perfect exchangeability with signs belonging to another system (the French word *mouton*, for example, has a

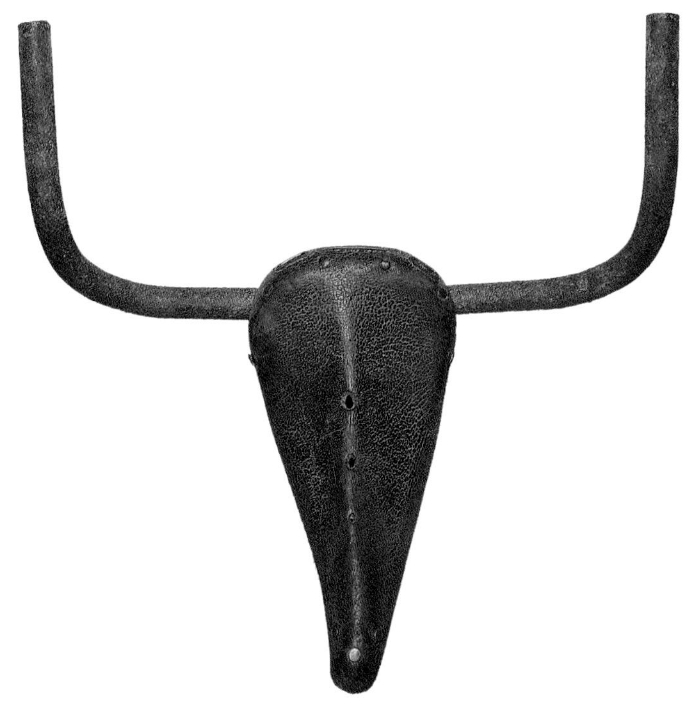

2 • Pablo Picasso, *Bull's Head*, 1942
Assemblage (bicycle seat and handlebars), 33.5 x 43.5 x 19 (13¼ x 17⅛ x 7½)

Although he never read Saussure, Picasso discovered in his own visual terms what the father of structural linguistics had labeled the "arbitrariness of the sign." Given that signs are defined by their opposition to other signs within a given system, anything can stand for anything else if it conforms to the rules of the system in question. Using the handlebar and seat of a bicycle, Picasso remains within the realm of representation, defining the minimum required for a combination of disparate elements to be read as the horned head of a bull, while at the same time demonstrating the metaphoric power of assemblage.

different value than the English *sheep* or *mutton*, because it means both the animal and its meat).

To explain his concept of value, Saussure invoked the metaphor of chess. If, during a game, a piece is lost, it does not matter what other piece replaces it provisionally; the players can arbitrarily choose any substitute they want, any object will do, and even, depending on their capacity to remember, the absence of an object. For it is the piece's function within a system that confers its value (just as it is the piece's position at each moment of the game that gives it its changing signification). "If you augment language by one sign," Saussure said, "you diminish in the same proportion the [value] of the others. Reciprocally, if only two signs had been chosen ... all the [possible] significations would have had to be divided between these two signs. One would have designated one half of the objects, the other, the other half." The value of each of these two inconceivable signs would have been enormous.

Reading such lines, it comes as no surprise that Jakobson and the
▲ Russian Formalists had arrived at similar conclusions through a examination of Cubism—that of Picasso, in particular, who almost maniacally demonstrated the interchangeability of signs within his pictorial system, and whose play on the minimal act required to transform a head into a guitar or a bottle, in a series of collages
● he realized in 1913, seem a direct illustration of Saussure's pronouncement. This metaphoric transformation indicates that, *contra* Jakobson, Picasso is not bound to the metonymic pole. Instead, he seems to particularly relish composite structures that are both metaphoric and metonymic. A case in point is the 1944 sculpture of the *Bull's Head* [**2**], where the conjunction (metonymy) of a bicycle handlebar and seat produced a metaphor (the sum of these two bicycle parts are like a bull's head), but such swift transformations based on the two structuralist operations of substitution and combination are legion in his oeuvre. Which is to say that Picasso's Cubism was a "structuralist activity," to use Barthes's phrase: it not only performed a structural analysis of the figurative tradition of Western art, but it also structurally engineered new objects.

An example is Picasso's invention of what one could call space as a new sculptural material. The fact that the Cubist constructions Picasso created in 1912–13 represent a key moment in the history of sculpture has long been recognized, but the means through which Picasso articulated space anew are not always understood. To make a story short: until Picasso's 1912 *Guitar* [**3**], Western sculpture, either carved or cast, had either consisted in a mass, a volume that detached itself from a surrounding space conceived as neutral, or retreated to the condition of bas-relief. Helped by his discovery of African art, Picasso realized that Western sculpture was paralyzed by a fear of being swallowed by the real space of objects (in the post-Renaissance system of representation, it was essential that art remained securely roped off from the world in an ethereal realm of illusions). Rather than attempting to discard the rope altogether, as Marcel Duchamp would soon do in his ready-
■ mades, Picasso answered the challenge by making space one of sculpture's materials. Part of the body of his *Guitar* is a virtual

▲ 1915 ● 1912 ■ 1914

3 • Pablo Picasso, *Guitar*, Fall 1912
Construction of sheet metal, string, and wire, 77.5 x 35 x 19.3 (30½ x 13¾ x 7⅝)

For structuralism, signs are oppositional and not substantial, which is to say that their shape and signification are solely defined by their difference from all other signs in the same system, and that they would mean nothing in isolation. By the sheer contrasting juxtaposition of void and surface in this sculpture, which marks the birth of what would be called "Synthetic Cubism," whose major formal invention would be collage, Picasso transforms a void into a sign for the skin of a guitar and a protruding cylinder into a sign for its hole. In doing so, he makes a nonsubstance—space—into a material for sculpture.

volume whose external surface we do not see (it is immaterial) but that we intuit through the position of other planes. Just as Saussure had discovered with regard to linguistic signs, Picasso found that sculptural signs did not have to be substantial. Empty space could easily be transformed into a differential mark, and as such combined with all kinds of other signs: no longer fear space, Picasso told his fellow sculptors, shape it.

As Jakobson has noted, however, Cubism is a "special case" in which devices can be separated out (in a Cubist painting shading is emphatically independent from contour, for example), and few artists in this century were as good structuralists as Picasso was during his Cubist years. Another candidate proposed by ▲structuralist critics was Piet Mondrian (1872–1944). Indeed, in deliberately reducing his pictorial vocabulary to very few elements, from 1920 on—black horizontal and vertical lines, planes of primary colors and of "noncolors" (white, black, or gray)—and in producing an extremely various oeuvre within such limited parameters [**4, 5**], Mondrian demonstrated the combinatory infinitude of any system. In Saussurean terminology, one could say that because the new pictorial *langue* that he created consisted in a handful of elements and rules ("no symmetry" was one of them), the range of possibilities proceeding from such a Spartan language (his *parole*) became all the more apparent. He had limited the corpus of possible pictorial marks within his system, but this very limitation immensely accrued their "value."

Despite the fact that Mondrian seems to be a structuralist *avant la lettre* it is not the structural type of formal analysis, but rather the morphological one, that was first proposed in the study of his art. This morphological formalism, mainly concerned with Mondrian's compositional schemes, remained impressionistic in nature, though it gave us excellent descriptions of the balance or imbalance of planes in his works, the vividness of the colors, the rhythmic staccato. In the end this approach remained tautological, especially in its blunt refusal to discuss "meaning," and it is not by chance that an iconographic, Symbolist interpretation was long thought preferable, even though it ran counter to what the artist himself had to say.

A structural reading of Mondrian's work began to emerge only in the seventies. It examines the semantic function played by various combinations of pictorial elements as Mondrian's work evolved and seeks to understand how a seemingly rigid formal system engendered diverse significations. Rather than assigning a fixed meaning to these elements, as the Symbolist interpretation had wanted to do, it is able to show, for example, that from the early thirties, the "Neoplastic" pictorial vocabulary that he had coined in 1920 and used ever since was transformed into a self-destructive machine destined to abolish not only the figure, as he had done before, but color planes, lines, surfaces, and by extension every possible identity—in other words, that Mondrian's art elicited an epistemological nihilism of ever-growing intensity. In short, if art critics and historians had been more acutely attentive to the formal development of his oeuvre, they might have earlier

▲ 1913, 1917, 1944a

on grasped the connection he felt more inclined to make in his writings, from 1930, between what he tried to achieve pictorially and the political views of anarchism. By the same token, however, they would have understood that if his classic Neoplastic work had been governed by a structural ethos, during the last decade of his life this ethos was geared toward the deconstruction of the set of binary oppositions upon which his art had been based: they would have perceived that, like Barthes, Mondrian had began as a practitioner of structuralism only to become one of its most formidable assailants. But they would have had to be versed in structuralism itself to diagnose his attack.

Two aspects of Mondrian's art after 1920 explain why his art became an ideal object for a structuralist approach: first, it was a closed corpus (not only was the total output small, but as noted above, the number of pictorial elements he used were in a finite number); second, his oeuvre was easily distributed into series. The two first methodological steps taken in any structural analysis are the definition of a closed corpus of objects from which a set of recurrent rules can be deduced, and, within this corpus, the taxonomic constitution of series—and it is indeed only after the multiple series scanning Mondrian's oeuvre had been properly mapped that a more elaborate study of the signification of his works became possible. But what a structural analysis can do with the production of a single artist, it can also do at the microlevel of the single work, as the Russian Formalists or Barthes have amply shown, or at the macrolevel of a whole field, as Claude Lévi-Strauss has demonstrated in his studies of vast ensembles of myths. The method remains the same, only the scale of the object of inquiry changes: in each case, discrete "units" have to be distinguished so that their interrelationship can be understood, and their oppositional signification emerge.

The method has indeed its limits, for it presupposes the internal coherence of the corpus of analysis, its unity—which is why it yields its best results when dealing with a single object or with a series that remains limited in range. Through a forceful critique of the very notions of internal coherence, closed corpus, and authorship, what is now called "poststructuralism," ▲ hand in hand with the literary and artistic practices labeled "postmodernist," • would efficiently blunt the preeminence that structuralism and formalism had enjoyed in the sixties. But, as numerous entries in this volume make clear, the heuristic power of structural and formalist analysis, especially with regard to the canonical moments of modernism, need not be discarded.

4 • Piet Mondrian, *Composition with Red, Blue, Black, Yellow, and Gray*, 1921
Oil on canvas, 39.4 x 35 (15½ x 13¾)

5 • Piet Mondrian, *Composition with Blue, Black, Yellow, and Red*, 1922
Oil on canvas, 39.5 x 34.7 (15⅜ x 13⅔)

Permutation and combination are the means by which any discourse is generated and as such they constitute the two main aspects of what Barthes called the "structuralist activity." In these two canvases, Mondrian checks, just as a scientist would do, if and how our perception of a central square changes according to the modifications of its surroundings.

FURTHER READING

Roland Barthes, *Mythologies* (1957), trans. Annette Lavers (New York: Noonday Press, 1972)

Roman Jakobson, "What is Poetry?" (1933) and "Two Aspects of Language and Two Types of Aphasic Disturbances" (1956), in Krystyna Pomorska and Stephen Rudy (eds.), *Language and Literature* (Cambridge, Mass.: Harvard University Press, 1987)

Fredric Jameson, *The Prison-House of Language: A Critical Account of Structuralism and Russian Formalism* (Princeton: Princeton University Press, 1972)

Thomas Levin, "Walter Benjamin and the Theory of Art History," *October*, no. 47, Winter 1988

Ferdinand de Saussure, *Course in General Linguistics*, trans. Wade Baskin (New York: McGraw-Hill, 1966)

▲ Introduction 4 • 1977, 1984b

4 Poststructuralism and deconstruction

Throughout the sixties, youthful ideals measured against official cynicism created a collision course that climaxed in the uprisings of 1968, when, in reaction to the Vietnam War, student movements throughout the world—in Berkeley, Berlin, Milan, Paris, Tokyo—erupted into action. A student leaflet circulating in Paris in May 1968 declared the nature of the conflict:

> *We refuse to become teachers serving a mechanism of social selection in an educational system operating at the expense of working-class children, to become sociologists drumming up slogans for governmental election campaigns, to become psychologists charged with getting "teams of workers" to "function" according to the best interests of the bosses, to become scientists whose research will be used according to the exclusive interests of the profit economy.*

Behind this refusal was the accusation that the university, long thought to be the precinct of an autonomous, disinterested, "free" search for knowledge, had itself become an interested party to the kind of social engineering the leaflet imputed to both government and industry.

The terms of this indictment and its denial that discrete social functions—whether intellectual research or artistic practice—could be either autonomous or disinterested could not fail to have repercussions beyond the boundaries of the university. They immediately affected the art world as well. In Brussels, for ▲ example, Marcel Broodthaers (1924–76) and other Belgian artists joined their student confreres by occupying the Salle de Marbre of the Palais des Beaux-Arts and temporarily "liberating" it from its former administration into their own control. Furthermore, in a gesture that was also patterned on the action of the student movements, Broodthaers coauthored statements that were released to the public in leaflet form. One of them announced, for example, that the Free Association (as the occupiers identified themselves) "condemns the commercialization of all forms of art considered as objects of consumption." This form of public address, which he had used since 1963, was then to become increasingly the basis of his work, which he was to carry out in the name of a fictitious museum, the "Musée d'Art Moderne," under the aegis of which he would mount a dozen sections—such as the "Section XIXème siècle ("Nineteenth-Century Section") and the "Département des Aigles" (Department of Eagles) [**1**]—and in the service of which he addressed the public through a series of "Open Letters." The former separations within the art world—between producers (artists) and distributors (museums or galleries), between critics and makers, between the ones who speak and the ones who are spoken for—were radically challenged by Broodthaers's museum, an operation that constantly performed a parodic but profound meditation on the vectors of "interest" that run through cultural institutions, as far-from-disinterested accessories of power.

This attitude of refusing the subordinate posture as the one who is spoken for by seizing the right to speak, and consequently of challenging the institutional and social divisions that support these separations of power, had other sources of entitlement besides student politics. There was also the reevaluation of the premises, the suppositions, of the various academic disciplines collectively called the human sciences that crystallized around the time of 1968 into what has been termed poststructuralism.

There is no "disinterest"

▲ Structuralism—the dominant French methodological position against which poststructuralism rebelled—had viewed any given human activity—language, for example, or kinship systems within a society—as a rule-governed system that is a more or less autonomous, self-maintaining structure, and whose laws operate according to certain formal principles of mutual opposition. This idea of a self-regulating structure, one whose ordering operations are formal and reflexive—that is, they derive from, even while they organize, the material givens of the system itself—can clearly be mapped onto the modernist conception of the different and separate artistic disciplines or mediums. And insofar as this parallel obtains, the intellectual and theoretical battles of 1968 are highly relevant to the developments in the world of art in the seventies and eighties.

Poststructuralism grew out of a refusal to grant structuralism its premise that each system is autonomous, with rules and operations that begin and end *within* the boundaries of that system.

▲ 1972a

▲ Introduction 3

1 • Marcel Broodthaers, "Musée d'Art Moderne, Département des Aigles, Section des Figures (The Eagle from the Oligocene to the Present)," 1972
Installation view

As director of his museum, Broodthaers organized its "Section Publicité" for Documenta, as well as exhibitions of particular richness for other museums, this one for the Städtische Kunsthalle, Düsseldorf, in 1972. A collection of diverse objects, the eagles included were drawn from mass-cultural material (for example, the stamps on champagne corks) as well as precious objects (such as Roman *fibulae*), all of them captioned "This is not a work of art." As Broodthaers explained in the catalogue, the caption marries the ideas of Duchamp (the readymade) to those of Magritte (his deconstructive "This is not a pipe," as in the inscription on *The Treachery of Images* of 1929). The museum department responsible for this exhibition was the "Section des Figures" (Illustrations Section).

In linguistics, this attitude expanded the limited study of linguistic structures to those modes through which language issues into action, the forms called *shifters* and *performatives*. Shifters are words like "I" and "you," where the referent of "I" (namely, the person who utters it) shifts back and forth in a conversation. Performatives are those verbal utterances that, by being uttered, literally enact their meaning, such as when a speaker announces "I do" at the moment of marriage. Language, it was argued, is not simply a matter of the transmission of messages or the communication of information; it also places the interlocutor under the obligation to reply. It therefore imposes a role, an attitude, a whole discursive system (rules of behavior and of power, as well as of coding and decoding) on the receiver of the linguistic act. Quite apart from the content of any given verbal exchange, then, its very enactment implies the acceptance (or rejection) of the whole institutional frame of that exchange—its "presuppositions," as linguistics student Oswald Ducrot, early in 1968, called them:

> *The rejection of presuppositions constitutes a polemical attitude very different from a critique of what is set forth: specifically, it always implies a large dose of aggressiveness that transforms the dialogue into a confrontation of persons. In rejecting the presuppositions of my interlocutor, I disqualify not only the utterance itself, but also the enunciative act from which it proceeds.*

One form of post-1968 rejection of presuppositions was that French university students now insisted on addressing their professors with the intimate form of the second person—"*tu*"—and by their first names. They based this on the university's own abrogation of presuppositions when it called in the police (which historically had no jurisdiction within the walls of the Sorbonne) to forcibly evict the student occupiers.

Unlike the idea of the autonomous academic discipline (or work of art) whose frame is thought to be necessarily external to it—a kind of nonessential appendage—the performative notion of language places the frame at the very heart of the speech act. For the verbal exchange, it was being argued, is from the very beginning the act of imposing (or failing to impose) a set of presuppositions on the receiver of that exchange. Speech is thus more than the simple (and neutral) transmission of a message. It is also the enactment of a relation of force, a move to modify the addressee's right to speak. The examples Ducrot used to illustrate the presuppositional imposition of power were a university exam and a police interrogation.

Challenging the frame

The French structural linguist Émile Benveniste (1902–76) had already done more than anyone else to bring about this transformation in the way language came to be viewed in the sixties. Dividing types of verbal exchange into *narrative* on the one hand and *discourse* on the other, he pointed out that each type has its

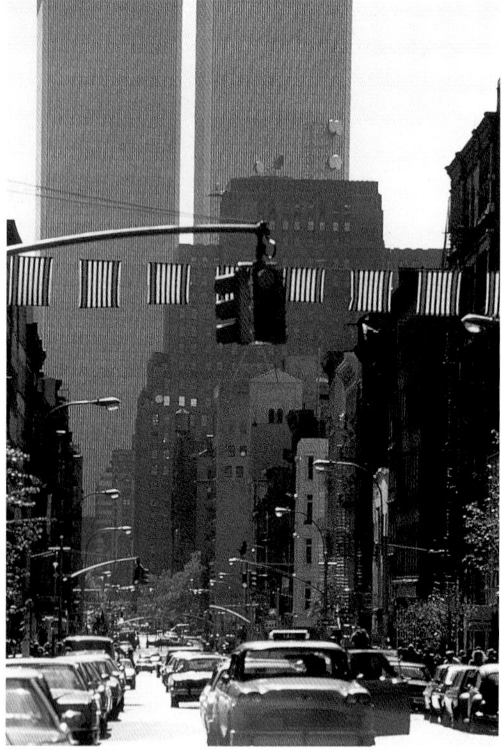

2 • Daniel Buren, Photo-souvenir: *"Within and beyond the frame,"* 1973 (detail)
Work in situ, John Weber Gallery, New York

By the early seventies Buren had reduced his painting practice to a type of readymade: canvases cut from commercially produced gray-and-white striped awning material (used for the awnings on French state office buildings) which he would "personalize" by hand-painting over one of the stripes at the edge of the swatch. For the John Weber installation, he ran the canvases through the gallery and out the window across the width of the street—as a kind of bannerlike advertisement for the exhibition.

own characteristic features: narrative (or the writing of history) typically engages the third person and confines itself to a form of the past tense; in contrast, discourse, Benveniste's term for live communication, typically engages the present tense and the first and second persons (the shifters "I" and "you"). Discourse is marked, then, by the existential facts of its active transmission, of the necessary presence within it of both sender and receiver.

The French historian and philosopher Michel Foucault, teaching at the Collège de France in 1969, developed this idea further. Applying Benveniste's term "discourse" to what had always been understood as the neutral communication of scholarly information contained within a given departmental discipline and—like narrative—confined to the transmission of "objective" information, Foucault took up the contrary position that "discourses" are always charged from within by power relations, and even by the exercise of force. Knowledge, according to this argument, ceases to be the autonomous contents of a discipline and now becomes *disciplinary*—that is, marked by the operations of power. Foucault's "discourse," then, like Ducrot's "presuppositions," is an acknowledgment of the discursive frame that shapes the speech event, institutionally, like the relations of power that operate in a classroom or a police station.

▲ Broodthaers's seizing of the right to speak, in his guise as "museum director," performed the kind of challenge to institutional frames that poststructuralists such as Foucault were then theorizing. Indeed, Broodthaers made his work out of those very frames, by enacting the rituals of administrative compartmentalization and by parodying the way those compartments in turn create collections of "knowledge." And as the frames were made to become apparent, not outside the work but at its very center, what indeed took place was the putting of "the very legitimacy of the given speech act at stake." Under each of the Museum's exhibits, the Department
● of Eagles affixed the Magrittean label: "This is not a work of art."

Broodthaers was not alone in this decision to make artistic practice out of the framing, as it were, of the institutional frames. Indeed, the whole practice of what came to be called "institutional critique" derived from such a practice—calling attention to the supposedly neutral containers of culture and questioning this
■ putative neutrality. The French artist Daniel Buren, for instance, adopted a strategy to challenge the power of the frames by refusing to leave their presuppositions alone, implicit, unremarked. Instead, his art, emerging in the seventies, was one of marking all those divisions through which power operates. In 1973 he exhibited *Within and beyond the frame* **[2]**. A work in nineteen sections, each a suspended gray-and-white-striped canvas (unstretched and unframed), Buren's "painting" extended almost two hundred feet, beginning at one end of the John Weber Gallery in New York and gaily continuing out the window to wend its way across the street, like so many flags hung out for a parade, finally attaching itself to the building opposite. The frame referred to in the title of the work was, obviously, the institutional frame of the gallery, a frame that functions to guarantee certain things about the objects it encloses.

▲ 1972a ● 1927a, 1972a ■ 1967c, 1971

3 • Robert Smithson, *A Non-site (Franklin, New Jersey)*, 1968
Painted wooden bins, limestone, silver-gelatin prints and typescript on paper with graphite and transfer letters, mounted on mat board. Bins installed 41.9 x 208.9 x 261.6 ($16\frac{1}{2}$ x $82\frac{1}{4}$ x 103); frames 103.5 x 78.1 ($40\frac{3}{4}$ x $30\frac{3}{4}$).

Smithson's *Non-sites* have been productively related to the dioramas in the Museum of Natural History in New York, in which samples of the natural world are imported into the Museum as exhibits that necessarily contaminate the "purity" of the aesthetic space. The bins or containers of his *Non-sites* comment ironically on Minimalism, accusing it of an aestheticism that Minimalist artists like Donald Judd and Robert Morris would have energetically denied.

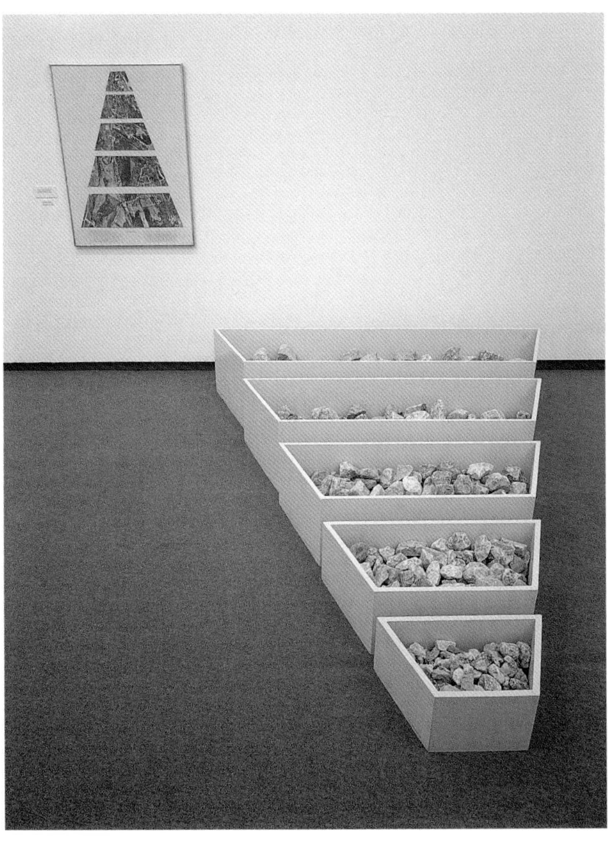

These things—like rarity, authenticity, originality, and uniqueness—are part of the value of the work implicitly asserted by the space of the gallery. These values, which are part of what separates art from other objects in our culture, objects that are neither rare, nor original, nor unique, operate then to declare art as an autonomous system within that culture.

Yet rarity, uniqueness, and so forth are also the values to which the gallery attaches a price, in an act that erases any fundamental difference between what it has to sell and the merchandise of any other commercial space. As the identically striped paintings (themselves barely distinguishable from commercially produced awnings) breached the frame of the gallery to pass beyond its confines and out the window, Buren seemed to be asking the viewer to determine at what point they ceased being "paintings" (objects of rarity, originality, etc.) and started being part of another system of objects: flags, sheets hung out to dry, advertisements for the artist's show, carnival bunting. He was probing, that is, the legitimacy of the system's power to bestow value on work.

▲ The question of frames was also at the heart of Robert Smithson's thinking about the relation between the landscape, or natural site, to its aesthetic container, which the artist labeled "non-site." In a series of works called *Non-sites*, Smithson imported mineral material—rocks, slag, slate—from specific locations into the space of the gallery by placing this material into geometrically shaped bins, each one visually connected, by means of its form, to a segment of a wall map indicating the area of the specimens' origin [**3**]. The obvious act of aestheticizing nature, and of turning the real into a representation of itself through the operations of the geometrical bin to construct the raw matter of the rocks into a sign—trapezoid—that comes to "stand for" the rocks' point of extraction, and thus for the rocks themselves, is what Smithson consigns to the system of the art world's spaces: its galleries, its museums, its magazines.

The ziggurat-like structures of Smithson's bins and maps might imply that it was only an ironic formal game that was at issue in this aspect of his art. But the graduated bins were also addressing a kind of natural history that could be read in the landscape, the successive stages of extracting the ore from the initial bounty, to the progressive barrenness, to a final exhaustion of supply. It was this natural history that could not be represented within the frames of the art world's discourse, concerted as it is to tell quite another story—one of form, of beauty, of *self*-reference. Therefore, part of Smithson's strategy was to smuggle another, foreign mode of representation into the frame of the gallery, a mode he took, in fact, from the natural history museum, where rocks and bins and maps are not freakish, aestheticized abstractions but the basis of an altogether different system of knowledge: a way of mapping and containing ideas about the "real."

The effort to escape from the aesthetic container, to break the chains of the institutional frame, to challenge the assumptions (and indeed the implicit power relations) established by the art world's presuppositions was thus carried out in the seventies in

▲ 1967a, 1970

4 • Richard Long, *A Circle in Ireland*, 1975

By going out into the landscape for the materials of his *Non-sites*, Smithson introduced the idea that the landscape itself might be a sculptural medium. Earthworks were a result of this suggestion, in which artists such as Long, Walter De Maria, Christo, or Michael Heizer operated directly on the earth, often making photographic records of their activities. This dependence on the photographic document was the confirmation of Walter Benjamin's predictions in the 1936 essay "The Work of Art in the Age of Mechanical Reproduction."

relation to specific sites—gallery, museum, rock quarry, Scottish Highlands, California coast—which the work of art functioned to *reframe*. This act of reframing was meant to perform a peculiar kind of reversal. The old aesthetic ideas that the sites used to frame (although invisibly, implicitly) now hovered over these real places like so many exorcised ghosts, while the site itself—its white walls, its neoclassical porticos, its picturesque moors, its rolling hills and rocky outcroppings **[4]**—became the material support (the way paint and canvas or marble and clay used to be) for a new kind of representation. This representation was the image of the institutional frames themselves, now forced into visibility as though some kind of powerful new developing fluid had unlocked previously secret information from an inert photographic negative.

Derrida's double session

Jacques Derrida (1930–2004), a philosopher teaching at the École Normale Supérieure in Paris, seized upon Benveniste's and Foucault's radicalization of structural linguistics to fashion his own brand of poststructuralism. He started out from the very terms of structuralism itself, in which language is marked by a fundamental ▲ bivalency at the heart of the linguistic sign. According to structuralist logic, while the sign is made up of the pairing of signifier

▲ Introduction 3

and signified, it is the signified (the referent or concept, such as a cat or the idea of "cat") that has privilege over the mere material form of the signifier (the spoken or written letters *c, a, t*). This is because the relationship between signifier and signified is arbitrary: there is no reason why *c, a, t* should signify "catness"; any other combination of letters could do the job just as well, as the existence of different words for "cat" in different languages demonstrates ("*chat*," "*gatto*," "*Katze*," etc.).

But this inequality between signifier and signified is not the only one at the heart of language. Another feature to emerge from the structuralist model is the unevenness of terms that make up opposing binary pairs such as "young/old" or "man/woman." This inequality is between a *marked* and an *unmarked* term. The marked half of the pair brings more information into the utterance than the unmarked half, as in the binary "young/old" and the statement "John is as young as Mary." "As young as" here implies youth, whereas "John is as old as Mary" implies neither youth nor advanced age. It is the unmarked term which opens itself to the higher order of synthesis most easily, a condition that becomes clear if we look at the binary "man/woman," in which it is "man" that is the unmarked half of the pair (as in "mankind," "chairman," "spokesman," etc.).

That the unmarked term slips past its partner into the position of greater generality gives that term implicit power, thus instituting a hierarchy within the seemingly neutral structure of the binary pairing. It was Derrida's determination not to continue to let this inequality go without saying, but rather to say it, to "mark" the unmarked term, by using "she" as the general pronoun indicating a person, and—in the theorization of "grammatology" (see below)—to put the signifier in the position of superiority over the signified. This marking of the unmarked Derrida called "*deconstruction*," an overturning that makes sense only within the very structuralist frame that it wants to place at the center of its activity by framing that frame.

Derrida's extremely influential book *Of Grammatology* (1967) proceeded from such a deconstructive operation to mark the unmarked, and thus to expose the invisible frame to view. If we compare the status of "he says" to that of "he writes," we see that "says" is unmarked, while "writes," as the specific term, is thus marked. Derrida's "grammatology" intends to mark speech (*logos*) and thus to overturn this hierarchy, as well as to analyze the sources of speech's preeminence over writing. This analysis had begun with Derrida's doctoral thesis, *Speech and Phenomenon*, in which he analyzed the phenomenologist Edmund Husserl's (1859–1938) dismissal of writing as an infection of the transparency and immediacy of thought's appearance to itself. And as he analyzed the privilege of *logos* over the dismissed sign of the memory trace (writing, *grammé*), Derrida developed the logic of what he called the *supplement*, an aid brought in to help or extend or supplement a human capacity—as writing extends memory or the reach of the human voice—but which, ironically, ends by supplanting it. Such a hierarchy is also behind the Derridean term *différance*, itself aurally indistinguishable from *différence*, the French word for that difference on which language is based. *Différance*, which can only be perceived in its written form, refers, precisely, to writing's operation of the trace and of the break or spacing that opens up the page to the articulation of one sign from another. This spacing allows not only for the play of difference between signifiers that is the basis of language ("cat," for example, can function as a sign and assume its value in the language system only because it *differs* from "bat" and from "car"), but also for the temporal unfolding of signifieds (meaning being elaborated in time through the gradual iteration of a sentence): *différance* not only differs, then, it also defers, or temporalizes.

If deconstruction is the marking of the unmarked, which Derrida sometimes called the *re-mark*, its striving to frame the frames took the analytical form of the essay "The Parergon," which attends to Immanuel Kant's major treatise "The Critique of Judgment" (1790), a treatise that not only founds the discipline of aesthetics but also powerfully supplies modernism with its conviction in the possibility of the autonomy of the arts—the art work's self-grounding and thus its independence from the conditions of its frame. For Kant argues that "Judgment," the outcome of aesthetic experience, must be separate from "Reason"; it is not dependent on cognitive judgment but must reveal, Kant argues, the paradoxical condition of "purposiveness without purpose." This is the source of art's autonomy, its disinterestedness, its escape from use or instrumentalization. Reason makes use of concepts in its purposive pursuit of knowledge; art, as self-grounding, must abjure concepts, reflecting instead on the sheer purposiveness of nature as a transcendental concept (and thus containing nothing empirical). Kant argues that the logic of the work (the *ergon*) is internal (or proper) to it, such that what is outside it (the *parergon*) is only extraneous ornament and, like the frame on a painting or the columns on a building, mere superfluity or decoration. Derrida's argument, however, is that Kant's analysis of aesthetic judgment as self-grounding is not itself self-grounding but imports a frame from the writer's earlier essay "The Critique of Pure Reason" (1781), a cognitive frame on which to build its transcendental logic. Thus the frame is not extrinsic to the work but comes from *outside* to constitute the inside as an inside. This is the parergonal function of the frame.

Derrida's own reframing of the frame was perhaps most eloquently carried out in his 1969 text "The Double Session," referring to a double lecture he gave on the work of the French poet Stéphane Mallarmé (1842–98). The first page of the essay shows Derrida's almost modernist sensitivity to the status of the signifier, a sensitivity that parallels the poststructuralist's canny assessment of the "truths" of structuralism [**5**]. Like a modernist monochrome, the page presents itself as a buzz of gray letters as it reproduces a page from the Platonic dialogue "Philebus," a dialogue devoted to the theory of mimesis (representation, imitation). Into the lower-right corner of this field of gray, however, Derrida inserts another text, also directed at the idea of mimesis: Mallarmé's "Mimique,"

SOCRATES: And if he had someone with him, he would put what he said to himself into actual speech addressed to his companion, audibly uttering those same thoughts, so that what before we called opinion (δόξαν) has now become assertion (λόγος).—PROTARCHUS: Of course.—SOCRATES: Whereas if he is alone he continues thinking the same thing by himself, going on his way maybe for a considerable time with the thought in his mind.—PROTARCHUS: Undoubtedly.—SOCRATES: Well now, I wonder whether you share my view on these matters.—PROTARCHUS: What is it?—SOCRATES: It seems to me that at such times our soul is like a book (Δοκεῖ μοι τότε ἡμῶν ἡ ψυχὴ βιβλίῳ τινὶ προσεοικέναι).—PROTARCHUS: How so?—SOCRATES: It appears to me that the conjunction of memory with sensations, together with the feelings consequent upon memory and sensation, may be said as it were to write words in our souls (γράφειν ἡμῶν ἐν ταῖς ψυχαῖς τότε λόγους). And when this experience writes what is true, the result is that true opinion and true assertions spring up in us, while when the internal scribe that I have suggested writes what is false (ψευδῆ δ' ὅταν ὁ τοιοῦτος παρ' ἡμῖν γραμματεὺς γράψῃ), we get the opposite sort of opinions and assertions. —PROTARCHUS: That certainly seems to me right, and I approve of the way you put it—SOCRATES: Then please give your approval to the presence of a second artist (δημιουργὸν) in our souls at such a time.—PROTARCHUS: Who is that?—SOCRATES: A painter (Ζωγράφον) who comes after the writer and paints in the soul pictures of these assertions that we make.—PROTARCHUS: How do we make out that he in his turn acts, and when?—SOCRATES: When we have got those opinions and assertions clear of the act of sight ('όψεως) or other sense, and as it were see in ourselves pictures or images (εἰκόνας) of what we previously opined or asserted. That does happen with us, doesn't it?—PROTARCHUS: Indeed it does.—SOCRATES: Then are the pictures of true opinions and assertions true, and the pictures of false ones false?—PROTARCHUS: Unquestionably.—SOCRATES: Well, if we are right so far, here is one more point in this connection for us to consider.—PROTARCHUS: What is that?—SOCRATES: Does all this necessarily befall us in respect of the present (τῶν ὄντων) and the past (τῶν γεγονότων), but not in respect of the future (τῶν μελλόντων)?—PROTARCHUS: On the contrary, it applies equally to them all.—SOCRATES: We said previously, did we not, that pleasures and pains felt in the soul alone might precede those that come through the body? That must mean that we have anticipatory pleasures and anticipatory pains in regard to the future.—PROTARCHUS: Very true.—SOCRATES: Now do those writings and paintings (γράμματά τε καὶ ζωγραφήματα), which a while ago we assumed to occur within ourselves, apply to past and present only, and not to the future?—PROTARCHUS: Indeed they do.—SOCRATES: When you say 'indeed they do', do you mean that the last sort are all expectations concerned with what is to come, and that we are full of expectations all our life long?—PROTARCHUS: Undoubtedly.—SOCRATES: Well now, as a supplement to all we have said, here is a further question for you to answer.

MIMIQUE

Silence, sole luxury after rhymes, an orchestra only marking with its gold, its brushes with thought and dusk, the detail of its signification on a par with a stilled ode and which it is up to the poet, roused by a dare, to translate! the silence of an afternoon of music; I find it, with contentment, also, before the ever original reappearance of Pierrot or of the poignant and elegant mime Paul Margueritte.

Such is this PIERROT MURDERER OF HIS WIFE composed and set down by himself, a mute soliloquy that the phantom, white as a yet unwritten page, holds in both face and gesture at full length to his soul. A whirlwind of naive or new reasons emanates, which it would be pleasing to seize upon with security: the esthetics of the genre situated closer to principles than any! (no)thing in this region of caprice foiling the direct simplifying instinct… This — "The scene illustrates but the idea, not any actual action, in a hymen (out of which flows Dream), tainted with vice yet sacred, between desire and fulfillment, perpetration and remembrance: here anticipating, there recalling, in the future, in the past, *under the false appearance of a present*. That is how the Mime operates, whose act is confined to a perpetual allusion without breaking the ice or the mirror: he thus sets up a medium, a pure medium, of fiction." Less than a thousand lines, the role, the one that reads, will instantly comprehend the rules as if placed before the stageboards, their humble depository. Surprise, accompanying the artifice of a notation of sentiments by unproffered sentences — that, in the sole case, perhaps, with authenticity, between the sheets and the eye there reigns a silence still, the condition and delight of reading.

175

5 • Jacques Derrida, *Dissemination*, trans. Barbara Johnson, page 175 ("The Double Session")

Derrida, whose deconstructive theory consisted of an assault on the visual—as a form of presence that his idea of spacing as an aspect of deferral (or *différance*) was meant to dismantle—often invented surprisingly effective visual metaphors for his concepts. Here, the insertion of Mallarmé's "Mimique" into a corner of Plato's "Philebus" suggests, visually, the idea of the fold, or redoubling, that Derrida produces as a new concept of mimesis, in which the double (or second-order copy) doubles no single (or original). Another example occurs in the essay "The Parergon," where a succession of graphic frames is interspersed throughout a text focused on the function of the frame of the work of art, a frame that attempts to essentialize the work as autonomous but which does nothing more than connect it to its context or nonwork.

the poet's account of a performance he saw carried out by a famous mime and based on the text "Pierrot, Murderer of His Wife." Behind Derrida, on the blackboard of the classroom, had appeared a three-fold introduction to the lecture, hanging above his words, he said, like a crystal chandelier:

l'antre de Mallarmé
l'"entre" de Mallarmé
l'entre-deux "Mallarmé"

Because in French there is no aural distinction between *antre* and *entre*, this textual ornament depends on its written form in order to make any sense, in the same way that *différance* must be written in order to register *its* signified. This homophonic condition is itself "between-two," as in Mallarmé's "*entre-deux*," a between-ness that Derrida will liken to the fold in a page, a fold which turns the singleness of the material support into an ambiguous doubleness (a fold materialized in turn by the insertion of "Mimique" into the "Philebus" at its corner).

In the text of "The Double Session" itself, Derrida plays, like any good modernist, with the material condition of the numbers that emerge from Plato's and Mallarmé's definitions of mimesis. Plato's definition turns on the number four, while the poet's turns on the double, or the number two. And like any good modernist, Derrida materializes the classical foursome, understanding it as a frame: Plato says that (1) the book imitates the soul's silent dialogue with the self; (2) the value of the book is not intrinsic but depends on the value of what it imitates; (3) the truth of the book can be decided, based on the truthfulness of its imitation; and (4) the book's imitation is constituted by the form of the double. Thus Platonic mimesis doubles what is single (or simple) and, being thus decidable, institutes itself within the operations of truth. Mallarmé's imitation, on the other hand, doubles what is already double or multiple and is, therefore, undecidable: between-two. The text of the mime-drama that Mallarmé recounts in "Mimique" tells of Pierrot's discovery of his wife Columbine's adultery, which he decides to avenge by killing her. Not wanting to be caught, however, he refuses the obvious possibilities of poison, strangling, or shooting, since all of them leave traces. After kicking a rock in frustration, he massages his foot to assuage the pain and inadvertently tickles himself. In his helpless laughter, the idea dawns on him that he will tickle Columbine to death and she will thus die laughing. In the performance, the actual murder is mimed with the actor playing both parts: the diabolical tickler and the convulsively struggling victim, writhing with pleasure. Since such a death is impossible, the imitation imitates not what is simple but rather a multiple, itself a pure function of the signifier, a turn of speech ("to die laughing"; "to be tickled to death"), rather than of actuality. As Mallarmé writes: "The scene illustrates only the idea, not a positive action, in a marriage that is lewd but sacred, a marriage between desire and its achievement, enactment and its memory: here, anticipating, recollecting, in the future, in the past, under a

6 • Louise Lawler, *Pollock and Soup Tureen*, 1984
Cibachrome, 40.6 x 50.8 (16 x 20)

Photographing works of art as they enter into the spaces arranged for them by collectors, Lawler produces the images as though they were illustrations of interiors in *Vogue* or any other luxury design periodical. Stressing the commodification of the work of art, Lawler's images also focus on the collector's incorporation of the work into his or her domestic space, thereby making it an extension of his subjectivity. The detail of Pollock's web of paint is thus related to the intricate design of the soup tureen, as a form of *interpretation* personal to the collector.

false appearance of the present. In this way the mime acts. His game ends in a perpetual allusion without breaking the mirror. In this way it sets up a pure condition of fiction."

Imitation that folds over what is already double, or ambiguous, does not, then, enter the realm of truth. It is a copy without a model and its condition is marked by the term *simulacrum*: a copy without an original—"a false appearance of the present." The fold through which the Platonic frame is transmuted into the Mallarméan double (or between-two) is likened by both poet and philosopher to the fold or gutter of a book, which in its crevice was always sexualized for Mallarmé, hence his term "lewd but sacred." This is the fold—"false appearance of the present"—that Derrida will call *hymen*, or will refer to at times as "invagination," by which the condition of the frame will be carried into the inside of an argument, which will, in turn, frame it.

Art in the age of the simulacrum

Terms like *parergon*, *supplement*, *différance*, and *re-mark* ground new artistic practice in the wake of modernism. All of these idea from the simulacrum to the framing of the frame—became staple not just of poststructuralism but of postmodernist pair David Salle, who is perhaps most representative of that pai developed in a context of young artists who were highly cri art's traditional claims to transcend mass-cultural cor This group—initially including figures like Robert Long ▲ Sherman, Barbara Kruger, Sherrie Levine, and Louise —was fascinated by the reversal between reality ar resentation that was being effected by a late-twenti culture of information.

Representations, it was argued, instead of comin in an imitation of it, now precede and construct rea emotions imitate those we see on film and reac romances; our "real" desires are structured for images; the "real" of our politics is prefabric news and Hollywood scenarios of leadership; c congeries and repetition of all these images, str ratives not of our own making. To analyze representation that precedes its referent (the it is supposed to copy) would cause this themselves probing questions about the r culture: its basis in mechanical reproduc repetition, its status as multiple without

"Pictures" was the name given to thi of it by the critic Douglas Crimp. Ther ● the way Cindy Sherman, posing for a portraits" in a variety of different co the look of a fifties movie still and stereotypical film heroine—care Southern belle, outdoor girl—ha mediated by, always constructed it, thus a copy without an origi

▲ 1975, 1977, 1980, 1984b ● 197

critics versed in theories of poststructuralism came to identify with such work involved a serious questioning of notions of authorship, originality, and uniqueness, the foundation stones of institutionalized aesthetic culture. Reflected in the facing mirrors of Sherman's photographs, creating as they did an endlessly retreating horizon of quotation from which the "real" author disappears, these critics saw what Michel Foucault and Roland Barthes had analyzed in the fifties and sixties as "the death of the author."

The work of Sherrie Levine was set in this same context, as she rephotographed photographs by Elliot Porter, Edward Weston, and Walker Evans and presented these as her "own" work, questioning by her act of piracy the status of these figures as authorial sources of the image. Folded into this challenge is an implicit reading of the "original" picture—whether Weston's photographs of the nude torso of his young son Neil, or Porter's wild technicolor landscapes—as itself always already a piracy, involved in an unconscious but inevitable borrowing from the great library of images—the Greek classical torso, the windswept picturesque countryside—that have already educated our eyes. To this kind of radical refusal of traditional conceptions of authorship and originality, a critical stance made unmistakable by its position at the margins of legality, the name "appropriation art" has come to be affixed. And this type of work, building a critique of forms of ownership and fictions of privacy and control came to be identified as postmodernism in its radical form.

The question of where to place this widely practiced, eighties actic of "appropriation" of the image—whether in a radical camp, s a critique of the power network that threads through reality, ways already structuring it, or in a conservative one, as an enthuastic return to figuration and the artist as image-giver—takes on other dimension when we view the strategy through the eyes of inist artists. Working with both photographic material approated from the mass-cultural image bank and the form of direct ress to which advertising often has recourse—as it cajoles, or ors, or preaches to its viewers and readers, addressing them as "—Barbara Kruger elaborates yet another of the presupposi- of the aesthetic discourse, another of its institutional frames. s the frame of gender, of the unspoken assumption set up n artist and viewer that both of them are male. Articulating sumption in a work like *Your gaze hits the side of my face* where the typeface of the message appears in staccato the image of a classicized female statue, Kruger fills in part of the presuppositional frame: the message transmiteen the two poles classical linguistics marks as "sender" iver," and assumes is neutral but presupposes as male, is a out in play by something we could call an always-silent amely, the symbolic form of Woman. Following a postst linguistic analysis of language and gender, Kruger's efore interested in woman as one of those subjects who k but is, instead, always spoken for. She is, as critic ey writes, structurally "tied to her place as bearer of t maker of meaning."

This is why Kruger, in this work, does not seize the right to speech the way that Broodthaers had in his open letters but turns instead to "appropriation." Woman, as the "bearer of meaning" is the locus of an endless series of abstractions—she is "nature," "beauty," "motherland," "liberty," "justice"—all of which form the cultural and patriarchal linguistic field; she is the reservoir of meanings from which statements are made. As a woman artist, Kruger acknowledges this position as the silent term through her act of "stealing" her speech, of never laying claim to having become the "maker of meaning."

This question of the woman's relation to the symbolic field of speech and the meaning of her structural dispossession within that field has become the medium of other major works by feminists. ▲ One of these, Mary Kelly's *Post-Partum Document* (1973–9), tracks the artist's own connection to her infant son through five years of his development and the 135 exhibits that record the mother–child relationship. This recording, however, is carried on explicitly along the fault line of the woman's experience of the developing autonomy of the male-child as he comes into possession of language. It wants to examine the way the child himself is fetishized by the mother through her own sense of lack.

Two kinds of absences structure the field of aesthetic experience at the end of the twentieth century and into the twenty-first. One of them we could describe as the absence of reality itself as it retreats behind the miragelike screen of the media, sucked up into the vacuum tube of a television monitor, read off like so many printouts from a multinational computer hook-up. The other is the invisibility of the presuppositions of language and of institutions, a seeming absence behind which power is at work, an absence which artists from Mary Kelly, Barbara Kruger, and Cindy Sherman to Hans • Haacke, Daniel Buren, and Richard Serra attempt to bring to light.

FURTHER READING

Roland Barthes, *Critical Essays*, trans. Richard Howard (Evanston: Northwestern University Press, 1972)

Roland Barthes, *Image, Music, Text*, trans. Stephen Heath (New York: Hill and Wang, 1977)

Douglas Crimp, "Pictures," *October*, no. 8, Spring 1979

Jacques Derrida, *Of Grammatology*, trans. Gayatri Spivak (Baltimore: The Johns Hopkins University Press, 1976)

Jacques Derrida, "Parergon," *The Truth in Painting*, trans. Geoff Bennington (Chicago and London: University of Chicago Press, 1987)

Jacques Derrida, "The Double Session," *Dissemination*, trans. Barbara Johnson (Chicago and London: University of Chicago Press, 1981)

Michel Foucault, *The Archaeology of Knowledge* (Paris: Gallimard, 1969; translation London: Tavistock Publications; and New York: Pantheon, 1972)

Michel Foucault, "What is an Author?", *Language, Counter-Memory, Practice*, trans. D. Bouchard and S. Simon (Ithaca, N.Y.: Cornell University Press, 1977)

Mary Kelly, *Post-Partum Document* (London: Routledge & Kegan Paul, 1983)

Laura Mulvey, "Visual Pleasure and Narrative Cinema," *Visual and Other Pleasures* (Bloomington: Indiana University Press, 1989)

Craig Owens, "The Allegorical Impulse: Towards a Theory of Postmodernism," *October*, nos 12 and 13, Spring and Summer 1980

Ann Reynolds, "Reproducing Nature: The Museum of Natural History as Nonsite," *October*, no. 45, Summer 1988

▲ 1975 • 1967c, 1969, 1970, 1971, 1972b, 1993a

1900–1909

52 1900a Sigmund Freud publishes *The Interpretation of Dreams*: in Vienna, the rise of the expressive art of Gustav Klimt, Egon Schiele, and Oskar Kokoschka coincides with the emergence of psychoanalysis. HF

57 1900b Henri Matisse visits Auguste Rodin in his Paris studio but rejects the elder artist's sculptural style. YAB

64 1903 Paul Gauguin dies in the Marquesas Islands in the South Pacific: the recourse to tribal art and primitivist fantasies in Gauguin influences the early work of André Derain, Henri Matisse, Pablo Picasso, and Ernst Ludwig Kirchner. HF
box • The exotic and the naive HF

70 1906 Paul Cézanne dies at Aix-en-Provence in southern France: following the retrospectives of Vincent van Gogh and Georges Seurat the preceding year, Cézanne's death casts Postimpressionism as the historical past, with Fauvism as its heir. YAB
box • Roger Fry and the Bloomsbury Group RK

78 1907 With the stylistic inconsistencies and primitivist impulses of *Les Demoiselles d'Avignon*, Pablo Picasso launches the most formidable attack ever on mimetic representation. RK
box • Gertrude Stein RK

85 1908 Wilhelm Worringer publishes *Abstraction and Empathy*, which contrasts abstract art with representational art as a withdrawal from the world versus an engagement with it: German Expressionism and English Vorticism elaborate this psychological polarity in distinctive ways. HF

90 1909 F. T. Marinetti publishes the first Futurist manifesto on the front page of *Le Figaro* in Paris: for the first time the avant-garde associates itself with media culture and positions itself in defiance of history and tradition. BB/RK
box • Eadweard Muybridge and Étienne-Jules Marey HF

1900a

Sigmund Freud publishes *The Interpretation of Dreams*: in Vienna the rise of the expressive art of Gustav Klimt, Egon Schiele, and Oskar Kokoschka coincides with the emergence of psychoanalysis.

Sigmund Freud declares in the epigraph to *The Interpretation of Dreams*, "If I cannot move the higher powers, I will stir up hell." With this passage, taken from *The Aeneid*, the Viennese founder of psychoanalysis "intended to picture the efforts of the repressed instinctual impulses." And right here, we might think, lies the connection between this intrepid explorer of the unconscious and such brazen innovators in Viennese art as Gustav Klimt (1862–1918), Egon Schiele (1890–1918), and Oskar Kokoschka (1886–1980). For they too seemed to stir up hell, in the early years of the century, through a liberatory expression of repressed instincts and unconscious desires.

These artists did stir up hell, but it was no simple liberation. Unfettered expression is rare in art, let alone in psychoanalysis, and Freud would not have supported it in any case: a conservative collector of ancient, Egyptian, and Asian artifacts, he was wary of modernist artists. The connection between these four Viennese contemporaries is better drawn through the notion of the "dream-work" developed by Freud in *The Interpretation of Dreams*. According to this epochal study, a dream is a "rebus," a broken narrative-in-images, a secret wish struggling to be expressed and an internal censor struggling to suppress it. Such a conflict is often suggested in the most provocative paintings by Klimt, Schiele, and Kokoschka, which are frequently portraits: a struggle between expression and repression in sitter and painter alike. Perhaps more than any other modernist style, this art places the viewer in the position of psychoanalytic interpreter.

Oedipal revolt

Although Paris is more celebrated as a capital of modernist art, Vienna witnessed several events that are paradigmatic of turn-of-the-century avant-gardes. First was the very act of "secession"—the withdrawal from the Academy of Fine Arts in 1897 of a group of nineteen artists (including Klimt) and architects (including Joseph Maria Olbrich [1867–1908] and Josef Hoffmann [1870–1956]) into an order of its own, replete in this case with its own building [**1**]. In opposition to the old academic guard, the Secession advocated the new and the youthful in the very names of the international style that it adopted, which was called *art nouveau* in French and *Jugendstil* in German (literally, "youth style"). Also typical of avant-gardes was that this advocacy provoked great scandal. First, in 1901, the University of Vienna rejected a grim painting on the subject of philosophy that it had commissioned from Klimt, who responded with a second painting on the subject of medicine that was even more outrageous. Then, in 1908, the School of Arts and Crafts expelled Kokoschka after a performance of his lurid drama of passion and violence, *Murderer, the Hope of Woman*—the first banishment in his long, nomadic life. And finally, in 1912, the authorities charged Schiele with kidnapping and corrupting a minor, jailed him for twenty-four days, and burned many of his sexually explicit drawings.

1 • Joseph Maria Olbrich, *House of the Vienna Secession*, 1898
A view of the main entrance

These controversies were not staged for bourgeois titillation; they pointed to genuine rifts between private reality and public morality in Vienna at the time. For the new art emerged as the Austro-Hungarian Empire was collapsing; it was symptomatic, the historian Carl E. Schorske has suggested, of "the crisis of the liberal ego" in the old order. Here lies a further connection with Freud: more than a liberation of the self, this art attests to a conflict within the individual subject regarding its threatened authorities, the academy and the state—in Freudian terms the superego that surveys us all—"a crisis of culture characterized by an ambiguous combination of collective oedipal revolt and narcissistic search for a new self" (Schorske).

This crisis was hardly punctual or uniform. Differences existed not only between the Secession and the Academy but also between the Expressionist aesthetic of young painters such as Schiele and Kokoschka and the Art Nouveau ethos of Secession artists such as Klimt, who advocated a "total work of the arts." (This *Gesamtkunstwerk* was exemplified by the Palais Stoclet in Brussels, designed by Hoffmann in 1905–11 with arboreal mosaic murals created by Klimt [**2**]). The Secession was divided internally as well. In its craft studios (or *Werkstätte*), it promoted the decorative ▲ arts, which other modernist styles often suppressed ("the decorative" became a term of anxious embarrassment for many proponents of abstract art); for example, Klimt used such archaic media as tempera and gold-leaf as well as mosaic. On the other hand, in its expressive use of line and color, the Secession also encouraged modernist experiments in abstract form. In this way, it was caught up in contradiction: in style between figuration and abstraction; in mood between fin-de-siècle malaise and early-twentieth-century *joie de vivre*. And this conflict tended to be evoked in the edgy, almost neurasthenic line that Klimt passed on to Schiele and Kokoschka.

In these tensions with the Art Nouveau style of the Secession, the great German critic Walter Benjamin (1892–1940) later glimpsed a basic contradiction between the individual basis of crafted art and the collective basis of industrial production:

> *The transfiguration of the lone soul was [the] apparent aim [of Art Nouveau]. Individualism was its theory. With [the Belgian designer Henry] van de Velde, there appeared the house as expression of the personality. Ornament was to such a house what the signature is to a painting. The real significance of Art Nouveau was not expressed in this ideology. It represented the last attempt at a sortie on the part of Art imprisoned by technical advance within her ivory tower. It mobilized all the reserve forces of interiority. They found their expression in the mediumistic language of line, in the flower as symbol of the naked, vegetable Nature that confronted the technologically armed environment.*

If Art Nouveau represented a last sortie on the part of Art, the Secession signaled its full embrace of the Ivory Tower, as exemplified by its white building, replete with floral facade ornament and grill dome, intended by its designer Olbrich as "a temple of art which would offer the art-lover a quiet, elegant place of refuge." Thus, even as the Secession broke with the Academy, it did so only to retreat to a more pristine space of aesthetic autonomy. And yet, in a further contradiction, the Secession took this autonomy to be expressive of the spirit of its time, as announced by the motto inscribed beneath the dome: "TO EACH AGE ITS ART, TO ART ITS FREEDOM." Here is, as art historians in Vienna might have said at the time, the very "artistic will" (or *Kunstwollen*) of this new movement.

2 • Josef Hoffmann, Palais Stoclet, Brussels, 1905–11
Dining room murals by Gustav Klimt, furniture by Josef Hoffmann

Defiance tinctured by impotence

The first president of the Vienna Secession was Gustav Klimt, whose career passed from the historical culture of the Austro-Hungarian Empire, through the antitraditional revolt of the avant-garde at the turn of the century, to an ornamental portraiture of Viennese high society after this modernist revolt appeared, to him at least, to be routed. His father, an engraver, had sent him to the School of Arts and Crafts, from which he emerged as an architectural decorator in 1883, just as the monumental buildings of the central Ringstrasse of remodeled Vienna came to completion. His early works included allegorical paintings for two new Ringstrasse buildings—a painting of dramatic figures (including Hamlet) for the ceiling of the City Theater (1886–8) and a painting of cultural representatives (including Athena) for the lobby of the Museum of Art History (1891). In 1894, on the basis of these successes, the new University of Vienna commissioned him to produce three ceiling paintings—representing Philosophy, Medicine, and Jurisprudence, respectively—on the Enlightenment theme of the "Triumph of Light over Darkness." Klimt worked intermittently on the project for the next ten years, exhibiting the first painting, *Philosophy*, in 1900. By this time, however, he was caught up in the Secession, and the finished painting was hardly what the University had in mind. Rather than a pantheon of philosophers, Klimt presented an anguished passage of commingled bodies through an amorphous space overseen by an obscure sphinx in the center and a luminous head (which evoked Medusa more than Athena) at the bottom. In this world, Darkness seemed to triumph over Light.

If Klimt questioned rationalist philosophy in this commission for the University, he mocked therapeutic medicine in the next,

▲ 1910

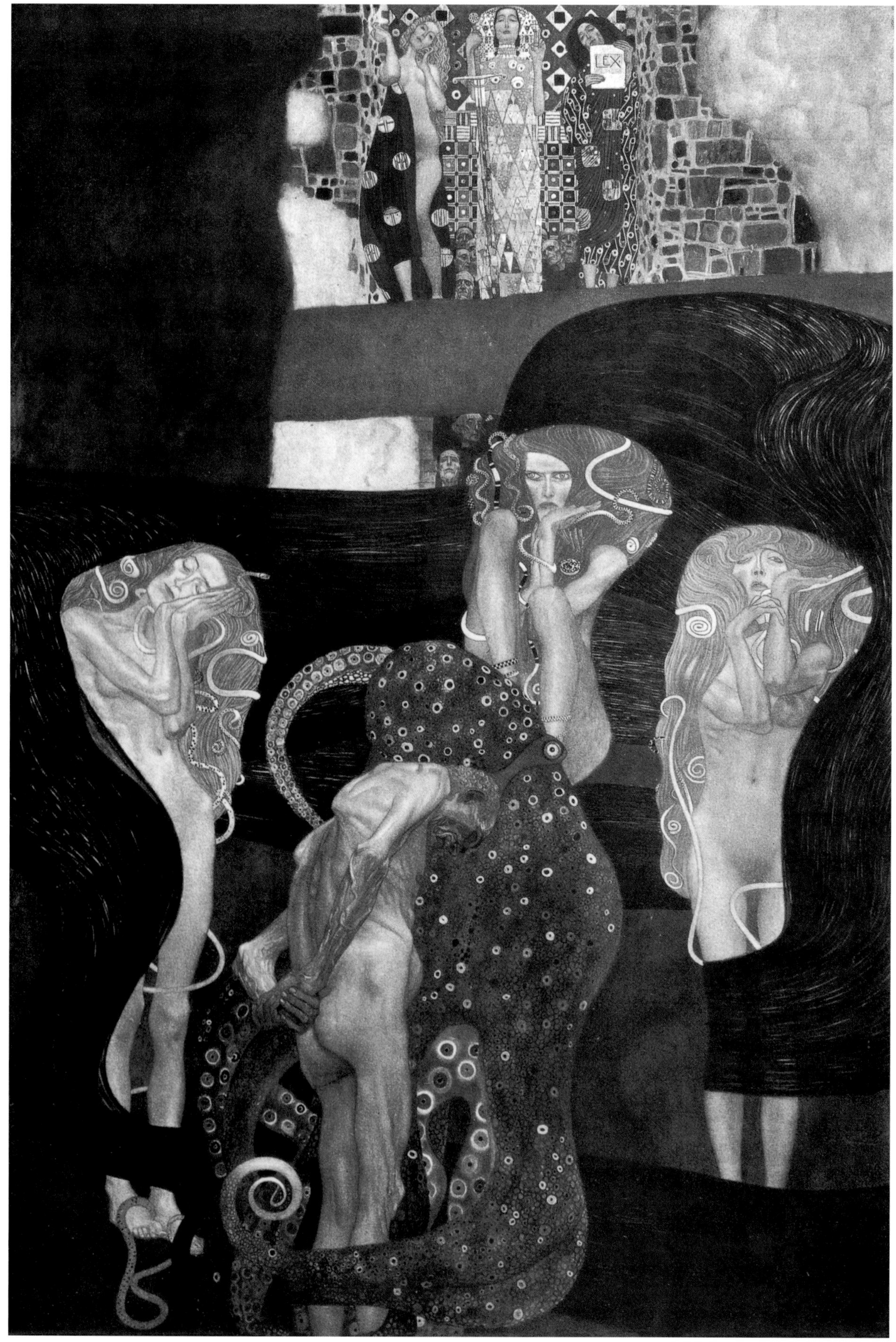

3 • Gustav Klimt, *Jurisprudence*, 1903–7
Oil on canvas, dimensions unknown (destroyed 1945)

unveiled in 1901. Here Medicine is represented as yet another hell, with even more bodies, some slung in sensuous slumber, others massed with cadavers and skeletons—a grotesque phantasmagoria of "the unity of life and death, the interpenetration of instinctual vitality and personal dissolution" (Schorske). An even stronger slap in the face of the University, the painting was again rejected and Klimt rebuked. His rejoinder was to rework the final representation of Jurisprudence **[3]** into one last hell of criminal punishment, with three large, intense furies around an emaciated man, all naked in a dark space below, and three small, impassive graces gowned in a hieratic space above. These allegorical figures of Truth, Justice, and Law hardly assist the male victim, who, surrounded by octopus tentacles, is at the mercy of the three furies of punishment (one sleeps obliviously, one stares vengefully, one winks as if on the take). Here punishment appears psychologized as castration: the man is gaunt, his head bowed, his penis near the maw of the octopus. In a sense, it is this constricted man whom Schiele and Kokoschka will attempt to liberate, though in their art too he will remain broken. "His very defiance was tinctured by the spirit of impotence," Schorske writes of Klimt. This is true of Schiele and Kokoschka as well.

These failed commissions signaled a general crisis in public art at this time: clearly, public taste and advanced painting had parted company. For the most part, Klimt then withdrew from the avant-garde in order to paint realistic portraits of stylish socialites, ornamental people set against ornamental backgrounds. His withdrawal left it to Schiele and Kokoschka to probe "repressed instinctual impulses," and they did so in the guise of often anguished figures stripped of historical reference and social context. (To look at his figures, Schiele once remarked, is "to look inside.") Skeptical of the decorative refinements of Art Nouveau, both Schiele and Kokoschka turned to Postimpressionist and Symbolist painters for expressive precedents. (As in other capitals, retrospective exhibi-▲tions of Vincent van Gogh and Paul Gauguin were influential, as were Secession shows of the Norwegian Edvard Munch [1863–1944] and the Swiss Ferdinand Hodler [1853–1918].)

Symptomatic portraiture

Having grown up in a bourgeois family of railway officials, Egon Schiele met Klimt in 1907 and soon adapted the sinuous, sensuous line of his mentor into his own angular, anxious mode of drawing; in the ten years before his death (Schiele died in the Spanish Flu epidemic of 1918) he produced some three hundred paintings and three thousand works on paper. In bloody reds and earthy browns, pale yellows and bleak blacks, Schiele attempted to paint pathos directly in melancholic landscapes with blighted trees, as well as desperate pictures of aggrieved mothers and children. More notorious are his drawings of adolescent girls, often sexually exposed, and his self-portraits, sometimes in similarly explicit positions. If Klimt and Kokoschka explored the reciprocal relation between sadistic and masochistic drives, so Schiele probed another Freudian pair of perverse pleasures—voyeurism and exhibitionism. Often he stares so intently—into the mirror, at us—that the difference between his gaze and ours threatens to dissolve, and he seems to become his only viewer, the solitary voyeur of his own display. But for the most part, Schiele does not seem defiantly proud of his self-image so much as pathetically exposed by its damage.

Consider his *Nude Self-Portrait in Gray with Open Mouth* **[4]**. The figure recalls the emaciated victim of *Jurisprudence* turned round and made younger. He has broken free; yet free, he is broken: his arms are no longer bound—they are amputated. Less an angel in flight, he is a scarecrow pinioned and cut at the knees. His slight asymmetry skews other oppositions as well: although male, his penis is retracted, and his torso is more feminine than not. With rings around his eyes, his face resembles a death-mask, and his open mouth could be interpreted equally as a vital scream or as a deathly gaping. This self-portrait seems to capture the moment when vitality and mortality meet in neurotic morbidity.

This transformation of the figure is the primary legacy of Viennese art at this time. It might seem conservative in relation to other

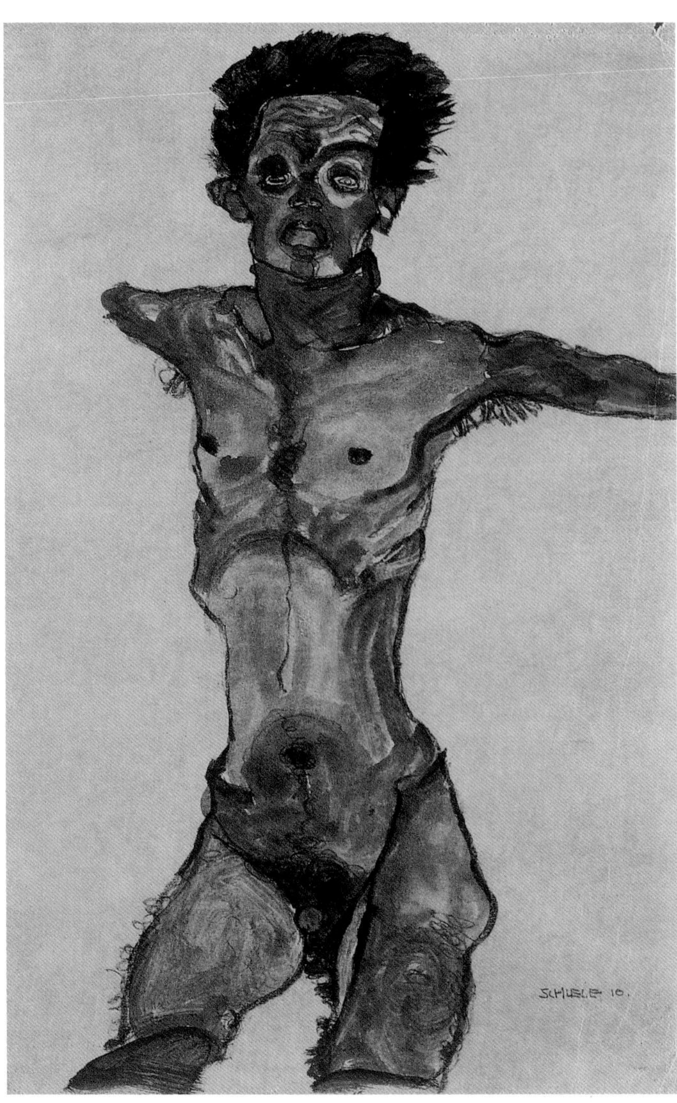

4 • Egon Schiele, *Nude Self-Portrait in Gray with Open Mouth*, 1910
Gouache and black crayon on paper, 44.8 x 31.5 ($17\frac{5}{8}$ x $12\frac{3}{8}$)

▲ 1903, 1906

modernist art, but it provoked the Nazis to condemn it as "degen- ▲ erate" thirty years later. Well past its service as classical ideal (the academic nude) and a social type (the proper portrait), the figure here becomes a cipher of psychosexual disturbance. Without direct influence from Freud, these artists developed a sort of symptomatic portraiture that extended van Gogh's expressive renderings of people, a portraiture that evokes less the desires of the artist than the repressions of the sitter—indirectly, through tics and tensions of the body. Here, what the attenuated, often emaciated line is in Klimt and Schiele, the agitated, often scratched line is in Kokoschka: a sign of a tortuous surfacing of subjective conflict.

Also influenced by Klimt, Oskar Kokoschka developed this symptomatic portraiture further than Schiele, and he probed its disruptive dimension further too—to the point where he was forced to leave Vienna altogether. During his troubles, Kokoschka was supported by the modernist architect and critic Adolf Loos (1870–1933), already notorious for his austere designs and fierce polemics, and the 1909 Kokoschka portrait of this great purist could be said to capture their "partnership of opposites" **[5]**. Similar to the Schiele self-portrait in stylistic respects (down to the ringed eyes), the painting evokes a subjectivity that is nonetheless quite different. The clothed Loos gazes inward: he is composed, but one senses he is under great pressure. Indeed, rather than *ex*pressed, or pressed outward, his being seems *com*pressed, or pressed inward. Self-possessed in both senses of the term, he reins in his energies with an intensity that seems to deform his wrung hands.

A year before the portrait was painted, Loos had published his diatribe against the Art Nouveau of the Secession; titled "Orna- • ment and Crime" (1908), it might as well have read "Ornament *is* Crime." Loos deemed ornament not only erotic in origin but excremental as well, and though he excused such amorality in ■ children and "savages," "the man of our day who, in response to an inner urge, smears the walls with erotic symbols is a criminal or a degenerate." Not coincidentally, in this land given the excremental nickname "Kakania" by the novelist Robert Musil, Freud published his first paper on "character and anal eroticism" in 1908 as well. Yet, whereas Freud wanted merely to *understand* the civilized purposes of this repression of anal-erotic drives, Loos wanted to *enforce* them: "A country's culture can be assessed by the extent to which its lavatory walls are smeared," he wrote. "The evolution of culture is synonymous with the removal of ornament from utilitarian objects." Loos was not sympathetic to psychoanalysis; his friend and compatriot the critic Karl Kraus (1874–1936) once called it "the disease of which it thinks it is the cure." But like Freud, Loos did imagine the anal as a messy zone of indistinctness, and this is why he implied that the applied arts of the Secession and the violent outbursts of Expressionism were excremental. Against such confusion, Loos and Kraus demanded a self-critical practice in which each art, language, and discipline would be made ever more distinct, proper, and pure. We do well to remember that Vienna was the home not only of such disruptive painters as Klimt, Schiele, and Kokoschka, but also of such disciplinary voices as Loos in architecture, Kraus in journalism, Arnold Schoenberg ▲ (1874–1951) in music, and Ludwig Wittgenstein (1889–1951) in philosophy (who once wrote that "all philosophy is the critique of language"). Already at the beginning of the century, then, we find in Vienna an opposition fundamental to much modernism that followed: an opposition between expressive freedoms and rigorous constraints.

5 • Oskar Kokoschka, *Portrait of the Architect Adolf Loos*, 1909
Oil on canvas, 73.7 x 92.7 (29 x 36½)

FURTHER READING

Walter Benjamin, "The Paris of the Second Empire in Baudelaire," in *Charles Baudelaire: A Lyric Poet in the Era of High Capitalism* (London: New Left Books, 1973)

Allan Janik and Stephen Toulmin, *Wittgenstein's Vienna* (New York: Simon and Schuster, 1973)

Adolf Loos, "Ornament and Crime," in Ulrich Conrads (ed.), *Programs and Manifestoes on 20th-Century Architecture* (Cambridge, Mass.: MIT Press, 1975)

Carl E. Schorske, *Fin-de-Siècle Vienna: Politics and Culture* (New York: Vintage Books, 1980)

Kirk Varnedoe, *Vienna 1900: Art, Architecture, and Design* (New York: Museum of Modern Art, 1985)

▲ 1937a • 1962b ■ 1903, 1922 ▲ 1958

1900b

Henri Matisse visits Auguste Rodin in his Paris studio but rejects the elder artist's sculptural style.

When Henri Matisse (1869–1954) visited Auguste Rodin (1840–1917) in his studio in 1900, the sixty-year-old artist was a towering figure. Rodin had long enjoyed a considerable reputation as the lone sculptor who had been able to rejuvenate a moribund medium after a full century of tedious academic monuments and predictable kitsch statues. But his sculptural production was split, as American art historian Leo Steinberg has noted, between a public and a private one: while his reputation had been largely based on his marble works, which in some ways continued rather than overturned the academic tradition, the larger and more innovative part of his output (in numerous plasters rarely cast in bronze) was kept in the secrecy of his studio. His *Monument to Balzac*, with its thick column of a body cloaked in an overcoat depriving it of any traditional expressive attribute, was perhaps the first public sculpture in which Rodin revealed his preferred, private style: its unveiling in 1898, which created an enormous scandal, may be considered the birth of modern sculpture. Rodin had worked assiduously on the monument for seven years and was wounded (though perhaps not entirely surprised) when it was dismissed as a "crude sketch" by the members of the Société des Gens de Lettres who had commissioned it and was recklessly caricatured by the press (it would not be installed in its present public location in Paris until 1939). Rodin responded to the criticism by erecting a pavilion at the 1900 Universal Exhibition, held at various sites across Paris from April to November of that year, to house a retrospective of his works: for Matisse and many others at this point, Rodin represented the romantic ideal of the uncompromising artist, refusing to yield to the pressures of a bourgeois society.

Legend has it that when Matisse, encouraged by an admiring friend who was one of Rodin's many assistants, visited the elder sculptor, he brought with him a selection of his rapid sketches after the model in order to obtain feedback, and that Rodin did not much like what he saw. The advice he gave—that Matisse should "fuss" more over his drawing and add details—met a resolutely deaf ear: there was not much difference between this precept and the École des Beaux-Arts instruction that Matisse had already definitively rejected (and which he would have expected Rodin to scorn as well).

In the footsteps of the master

But whatever guidance Matisse had sought from Rodin concerning his drawing method, his visit must have been prompted above all by a curiosity with regard to Rodin's sculptural practice. It is uncertain if Matisse was already working on *The Serf* [**1**] at that point; but, whether as the underlying cause of the visit or as its immediate effect, this sculpture marks both Matisse's first serious

1900–1909

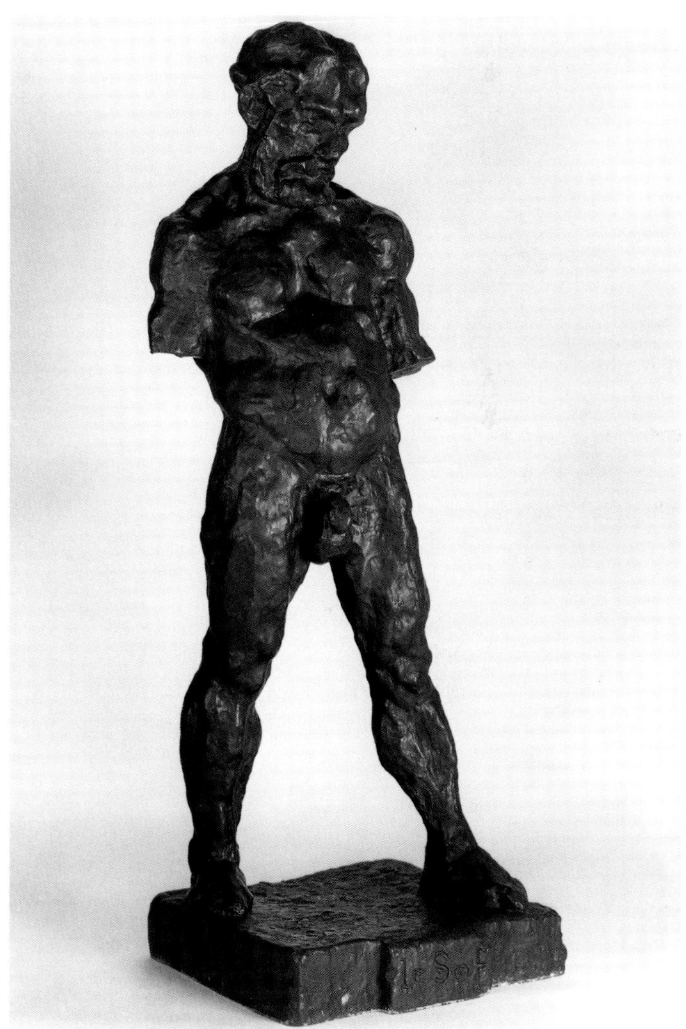

1 • Henri Matisse, *The Serf*, 1900–3 (1908 cast)
Bronze, height 92.4 (36⅜)

engagement with Rodin's art and his definitive departure from it, for it is a direct answer to Rodin's armless *The Walking Man* [**2**], which was exhibited as a study for *Saint John the Baptist*, along with the much tamer, anatomically whole *Saint John* itself, in the 1900 pavilion. By using the same model—a man nicknamed Bevilaqua, long known to be a favorite of Rodin's—in approximately the same pose, Matisse underlined both his debt to Rodin and their differences, a dialectic later sharpened by the amputation of *The Serf*'s arms at the time of its casting, in 1908.

Even though Rodin's *Walking Man* is not really walking—as Leo Steinberg pointed out, both his feet are anchored onto the ground, much like those of a "prizefighter in a delivery of a blow"—the illusion is that of bound energy: the movement is arrested, but the figure is ready to spring. Matisse's *Serf*, by contrast, is irremediably static, self-contained. The spectator is never tempted to imagine the figure moving, never tempted to animate it in his or her mind. The body itself seems malleable: the ungracious proportions of the model are accentuated by the sinuous curve traced in space by the whole figure, a general undulation stemming from the prominent belly and spanning the height of the whole body, up through the recessed thorax and the hunched back to the tilted head in one direction, and down to the right shin functioning as a break under the inward-bent knee in the other. It suggests no extension of any kind, into neither mental nor physical space: one of the first resolutely modernist antimonuments, the sculpture asserts its autonomy as an object.

This is not to say that *The Serf* owes nothing to Rodin's craft. The sculpture's very impression of malleability comes in great part from the surface agitation of the work, a stylistic feature essential to Rodin's "private" art and signaling one of the greatest upheavals of the Western sculptural tradition since antiquity—a tradition that demanded of the sculptor that he "give life" to the marble (the myth of Pygmalion), that he make one believe (or rather *pretend* to make one believe, since nobody is ever fooled) that his statue is endowed with organic life. While the public Rodin is wholly heir to this tradition, the private Rodin is a master of "process art," his sculpture being a catalog of the procedures, accidental or not, that make up the art of modeling or casting. The gaping wound in the back of *The Walking Man*, the great scrape across that of *Flying Figure* (1890–1), the excrescences on the forehead of his 1898 *Baudelaire*, and many other "anomalies" set into the bronze testify to Rodin's determination to treat sculptural processes as a language whose signs are manipulable. In other words, the public Rodin champions the transparency of sculpture as a language, whereas the private Rodin insists on its opacity, on its materiality.

Matisse, no doubt stimulated by these examples, accentuates the agitation of *The Serf*'s surface; he amasses muscular discontinuities, conceiving all his sculpture as an accumulation of more or less even, small round shapes, or of knife-strokes on which light falters. But in doing so, he goes too far and approaches the style of Medardo Rosso (1858–1928), the Italian self-proclaimed rival of Rodin who labeled himself an Impressionist and indeed aspired to imitate Impressionist brush-strokes in his wax sculptures. Unlike Rodin's, Rosso's sculpture is pictorial, and it is strictly frontal. The dematerializing effect of light on Rosso's surfaces, the way the contours of his figures are eaten up by shadow and can only be experienced from a single point of view—these are features that Matisse comes to reject at the very moment he is flirting with their possibility.

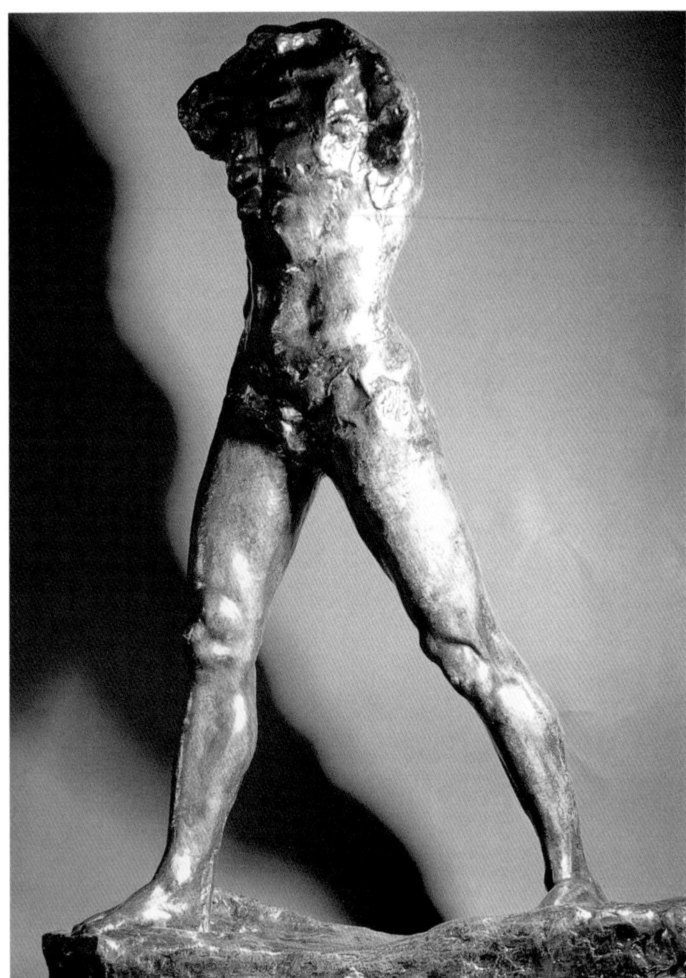

2 • Auguste Rodin, *The Walking Man*, 1900
Bronze, 84 x 51.5 x 50.8 (33 x 20¼ x 20)

The Serf, one of the two pieces through which Matisse learned the art of sculpture (it necessitated between three and five hundred sessions with the model!), is thus a paradoxical work: in his uncontrolled imitation of Rodin's "processual" marks, Matisse is more royalist than the king. The surface agitation itself comes dangerously close to destroying the integrity of the figure and its overall arabesque, and to transforming it, as Rosso would have it, into an ersatz picture. From then on, Matisse would understand better the principle of Rodin's materiality, and never abuse it again in this way. Almost all of his future bronzes would continue to bear the marks of his manipulation of the clay, but without endangering the physicality of the sculpture. Perhaps the most striking example of this effect is the exaggeration of the forehead of *Jeannette V* [**3**], which had such a vivid impact on Picasso when he discovered it in 1930 that he set out to emulate it in a series of heads or busts he modeled shortly thereafter.

Matisse breaks away

But during his visit to Rodin's studio Matisse also learned what fundamentally differentiated his aesthetic from that of the master: "I could not understand how Rodin could work on his *Saint John*, cutting off the hand and holding it on a peg; he worked on the details holding it in his left hand, it seems, anyhow keeping it detached from the whole, then replacing it on the end of the arm; then he tried to find its direction in accord with his general movement. Already, for myself I could only envisage the general architecture, replacing explanatory details by a living and suggestive synthesis." Matisse had already realized that he was not a "realist" when he modeled a jaguar after a work by the nineteenth-century French sculptor Antoine-Louis Barye and failed to understand the anatomy of a flayed cat he had secured for the occasion (*Jaguar Devouring a Hare* [1899–1901], the other sculpture through which he learned this art and bid farewell to anatomic verisimilitude). So it was not the bare artificiality of Rodin's method that Matisse resented but his combination of grafted fragments and his endless fascination with the partial figure.

4 • Aristide Maillol, *La Méditerranée* (The Mediterranean), 1902–5
Bronze, 104.1 x 114.3 x 75.6 (41 x 45 x 29¾) including base

Which is to say that Matisse ignored one of the most modern ▲ aspects of Rodin's practice, one that Constantin Brancusi, on the contrary, would emulate and refine (it is not by chance that Brancusi, after a brief apprenticeship in Rodin's studio, had fled under the spell of a veritable "anxiety of influence," claiming that "nothing grows under the shadows of the great trees"). One could even say that the cut-and-paste aspect of Rodin's sculpture, by which the cast of the same figure or fragment of figure is reused in different groups and different orientations in space, represents the ▲ first bout of what would become, with Picasso's Cubist constructions, one of the main tropes of twentieth-century art.

3 • Henri Matisse, *Jeannette V*, 1916
Bronze, height 58 (22⅞)

Matisse resisted Rodin's metonymic fragmentation, and in some ways his sculpture represents the opposite approach. With other sculptors, such a desire to think the figure as an indivisible whole developed into an academic fashion, especially since it went along with an entrenched attachment to the traditional motif of the female nude. It brought about, for instance, the plump nudes of Aristide Maillol (1861–1944) [**4**], or the much leaner silhouettes, on the other side of the Rhine, of Wilhelm Lehmbruck (1881–1919)—both sculptors strongly leaning on the Greco-Roman tradition and opting, against Rodin and Matisse, for resolutely smooth surfaces by which the bronze is required to imitate marble. This reaffirmation of the whole even engendered a kind of hybrid sculpture that one could call pseudo-Cubist, or proto-Art Deco: Jacques Lipchitz, Raymond Duchamp-Villon, and Henri Laurens in Paris and, to a certain extent, Jacob Epstein • and Henri Gaudier-Brzeska in England all produced works that seem to rely upon a Cubist mode of articulation but in effect magnify the solidity of the mass, their planar discontinuity remaining at the superficial level of a stylistic wrapping and never fully engaging the volume in space.

The fundamental trait that distinguishes their works from Matisse's is that they are fully frontal—made to be seen from a single point of view (or sometimes four distinct ones, in the case of Maillol

▲ 1927b

▲ Introduction 3 • 1925a, 1934b

5 • Henri Matisse, *The Back (I)*, c. 1909
Bronze, 188.9 x 113 x 16.5 ($74\frac{3}{8}$ x $44\frac{1}{2}$ x $6\frac{1}{2}$)

6 • Henri Matisse, *The Back (II)*, 1916
Bronze, 188.5 x 121 x 15.2 ($74\frac{1}{4}$ x $47\frac{5}{8}$ x 6)

or Laurens)—while Matisse's are eloquently not. To understand this point, it would be helpful to consider what German-American art historian Rudolf Wittkower proposed, along with the example of Rodin, as one of only two avenues offered to Matisse's generation by the sculpture of the nineteenth century, that is, the theories of German sculptor Adolf von Hildebrand (1847–1921)—unlikely as it may be that Matisse ever knew of Hildebrand except by hearsay. Hildebrand held that all sculpture should be a disguised relief, made of three planes staggered in depth, whose legibility must be immediately accessible from a set point of view. (In his eyes, the greatness of Michelangelo is that he always allows us to discern the virtual presence of the block of marble: his figures are "sandwiched" between the front and back of the original stone mass.) An actual relief is even better, Hildebrand wrote, since, in this, the (framed) figures are virtually freed from having to deal with the anxieties of the infinite surrounding space. In short, Hildebrand thought in terms of planes (and held modeling in contempt as too physical).

Even in the series of four *Back* reliefs that he produced from 1909 to 1930, Matisse disobeyed Hildebrand's instructions (he was in fact closer here than ever to Rodin, whose other famous "failed" monument, *The Gates of Hell*, is an opaque confusion of forms against which the eye, allowed no progression in depth, can only come to an abrupt halt). As conceived by Hildebrand and by the entire academic tradition, the relief presupposes a background representing an imaginary space from which the figures emerge, with the anatomical knowledge of the beholder providing all the necessary information concerning what is concealed from view. The relief's background functions like the picture plane in the system elaborated during the Renaissance by Leon Battista Alberti: it is a virtual plane, assumed to be transparent. In some respects, in fact, the *Backs* could be seen as an ironic response to Hildebrand in that the figure gradually becomes identified with the wall bearing it: in *The Back (I)* [**5**], the figure is leaning on the wall (there is a realist justification for this strange pose that so willfully ignores the conventions of the genre);

7 • Henri Matisse, *The Back (III)*, 1916
Bronze, 189.2 x 111.8 x 15.2 (74½ x 44 x 6)

8 • Henri Matisse, *The Back (IV)*, 1931
Bronze, 188 x 112.4 x 15.2 (74 x 44¼ x 6)

in *The Back (II)* [**6**], the differentiation between the modeling of the back and the treatment of the background begins to blur (in certain light conditions, the vertebral column disappears almost entirely); in *The Back (III)* [**7**], the figure is almost completely aligned with the limits of the "support"; in *The Back (IV)* [**8**], it has become a simple modulation of the support (there is no difference between the braid of hair and the space that continues it between the legs—simply a difference in degree of protrusion). In short, if for once Matisse actually did sculpt as a painter here (as he wrongly claimed he always did), he in no sense forgot the pictorial revolution he had carried out beforehand: he borrowed from his painting the anti-illusionism and ▲ the "decorative" effect (Matisse's name for the *allover*) that characterizes it. Needless to say, this is a far cry from Hildebrand.

But the *Backs*, being reliefs, are an exception. Most of Matisse's bronzes command the beholder to move round them. A case in point is *The Serpentine* [**9**]. If the critics have long since noted that the title refers to the "S" traced by the figure in space and to the reduction of its anatomy to mere ropes, the allusion to the *figura serpentinata*—a principle established by Michelangelo and taken to extremes by Mannerism—has often escaped them. Matisse, however, was fully conscious of his historical borrowing ("Maillol worked through mass like the Ancients, while I work through the arabesque, like the Renaissance artist," he used to say). Right at the end of his life, noting that the model of *The Serpentine* (taken from a photograph) was "a small plump woman," he explained that he had ended up "doing her that way so that everything was visible, regardless of the point of view." He also talked of "transparency," even going as far to suggest that the work anticipates the Cubist revolution. But Matisse was mistaken on this point, for at least two reasons.

The inaccessible "thing-in-itself"

We have seen that Matisse rejected (with Rodin) the ideal of the imaginary transparency of the material cherished by both the

▲ 1910

9 • Henri Matisse, *The Serpentine*, 1909
Bronze, 56.5 x 28 x 19 (22¼ x 11 x 7½)

academic tradition and by Hildebrand, but when he speaks of transparency here he has two other meanings of the word in mind. One encapsulates the related dream of an *ideational* transparency, that of a full and immediate grasp of the work of art's signification; and the other designates, in studio parlance, the use of empty space by modern sculptors. To start with the latter, *The Serpentine*'s "transparency" has nothing to do with the way in which empty ▲ space—in the wake of Picasso's famous *Guitar* from the fall of 1912—is transformed in Cubist sculpture into one of the major constitutive elements in a system of oppositional signs. In *The Serpentine*, empty space is only a secondary effect of the pose, and Matisse never used it again. The other issue is more important, for what actually happens is the opposite of what Matisse claims: you can *never* see everything at once; whatever your point of view, you can *never* fully grasp the work's signification. As one moves around *The Serpentine*, one sees a kind of spatial accordion, constantly expanding and contracting (or, to employ another metaphor, the negative spaces open and close like butterfly wings). One is constantly surprised by the multiplicity of aspects that are each time absolutely unforeseeable. From the back, its minuscule insect-head (that of a praying mantis?) reveals a massive head of hair that comes as a complete shock; the joins of the arabesques formed by the torso, the arms, and the left leg ceaselessly break the body without ever negating its plumb line (the right leg is rigorously parallel to the vertical pillar on which the elbow rests). In short, you can circle *The Serpentine* a hundred times, but you will never finally manage to possess it; its curvilinear dance in space ensures its wholeness but also its distance: this wholeness, that of the thing-in-itself, is made inaccessible to us.

And it is precisely here that one pinpoints the major difference between Matisse's sculpture and the art of Michelangelo, for example, or of Giambologna, to which it has been compared. For Giambologna also forces you to move around his sculptures, but there always comes a moment when your journey around a piece reaches a discernible endpoint, always a moment when you realize what is going on. The reason is simple: on the one hand, the distortions produced by the *contrapposto* always remain within the limits of anatomical knowledge (thanks to which we "overlook" a certain conspicuously elongated leg or an impossibly foreshortened knee, and read the figure as a continuous form); on the other hand, the gestures represented always have some kind of justification, either realist or rhetorical (like a kneeling bather drying herself, or the *Sabine* whose pathetic gesture, calling on heaven to rescue her from the colossus who is carrying her off, completes the spiral of the sculptor's most famous group). Matisse cares little for all of this—for anatomy (he simply ignores it, once again driving home the lesson learned from the private Rodin) or for evocative gestures.

The fact that there is no climax to our circumnavigation around a sculpture by Matisse, nor any privileged view afforded at any time, and, moreover, that the different aspects are unpredictable from one point of view to the next, explains the difficulty one experiences when trying to photograph it: only a film, perhaps, would do justice

10 • Henri Matisse, *Reclining Nude I (Aurora)*, 1907
Bronze, height 34.5 (13½)

to the absence of arris—sharp planar edges—that characterizes Matisse's flow. Conscious of this difficulty, Matisse offered to help photographers charged with publicizing his sculptures. Not surprisingly, he rarely chose a frontal view (he showed the five *Jeannettes* in profile, for example, or from behind). Or if he did, it is when the axis of the figure itself was not organized frontally. It seems that what mattered most to him was to find the most eccentric, least expected point of view, which is often the one where the arabesques close the sculpture in on itself (and which therefore provides the least information on its contortions). Matisse often had several photographs taken of the same work, and seemed to take pleasure in the sharp discordances from one to the next. He chose three points of view for *Reclining Nude I* [**10**]: frontal (as it appears in the background of the painting *The Music Lesson* [1916/17] at the Barnes Foundation); in three-quarter profile angled toward the back, which folds in on itself the arm raised in a simple vertical and reveals the "helmet" of hair; but also in full profile (facing the feet), from an angle that enlarges the whole figure, crushes the torso and the bulge of the thigh, fills out the shoulders and, above all, blocks all access to the length of the belly. It is as if he were playing a game with cognition, teasing our desire for its fullness, and declaring its necessary incompleteness—the very condition of modernity.

FURTHER READING

Adolf von Hildebrand, "The Problem of Form in the Visual Arts" (1893), translated in Harry Mallgrave and Eleftherios Ikonomou (eds), *Empathy, Form, and Space: Problems in German Aesthetics, 1873–1893* (Los Angeles: Getty Institute, 1994)

Rosalind Krauss, *Passages in Modern Sculpture* (New York: Viking Press, 1977; reprint Cambridge, Mass.: MIT Press, 1981)

Isabelle Monod-Fontaine, *The Sculpture of Henri Matisse* (London: Thames & Hudson, 1984)

Leo Steinberg, "Rodin," *Other Criteria: Confrontations with Twentieth-Century Art* (London, Oxford, and New York: Oxford University Press, 1972)

Rudolf Wittkower, *Sculpture* (London: Allen Lane, 1977)

▲ Introduction 3

1903

Paul Gauguin dies in the Marquesas Islands in the South Pacific: the recourse to tribal art and primitivist fantasies in Gauguin influences the early work of André Derain, Henri Matisse, Pablo Picasso, and Ernst Ludwig Kirchner.

Four painters of the late nineteenth century influenced modernists in the early twentieth century more than all others: Georges Seurat (1859–91), Paul Cézanne (1839–1906), Vincent van Gogh (1853–90), and Paul Gauguin (1848–1903). Each proposed a new purity in painting, but each did so according to a different priority: Seurat stressed optical effects; Cézanne, pictorial structure; van Gogh privileged the expressive dimension of painting; Gauguin, its visionary potential. Although not as generative in terms of style, Gauguin was more influential as a persona: the father of modernist "primitivism," he reformulated the vocation of the Romantic artist as a kind of vision-quest among tribal cultures. Inspired by his example, some modernist artists attempted to go native, or at least to play at it. Two German Expressionists, Emil Nolde (1867–1956) and Max Pechstein (1881–1955), traveled to the South Pacific in emulation of ▲ Gauguin, while two others, Ernst Ludwig Kirchner (1880–1938) and Erich Heckel (1883–1970), restaged primitive life in their studio decor or on nature outings. But many modernists drew on tribal art for forms and motifs: some, like Henri Matisse and Pablo Picasso, did so in profound, structural ways; others, in superficial, illustrational ways.

All of these artists sought to challenge European conventions that they felt to be repressive, and all imagined the primitive as an exotic world where style and self might be refashioned dramatically. Here primitivism extends well beyond art: it is a fantasy, indeed a whole cluster of fantasies, concerning return to origin, escape into nature, liberation of instinct, and the like, all of which were projected onto the tribal cultures of racial others, especially in Oceania and Africa. But even as a fantasy-construction, primitivism had real effects: it was not only part of the global project of European imperialism (on which the very passageways to the colonies, the very appearance of tribal objects in the metropolises, depended), but also part of the local maneuverings of the avant-garde. Like prior returns *inside* Western art (e.g., the Romantic recovery of medieval art in the nineteenth century by artists such as the Pre-Raphaelites), these primitivist sojourns *outside* Western art were strategic: they appeared to offer a way not only to exceed old academic conventions of art but also to trump recent avant-garde styles (e.g., Realism, Impressionism, neo-Impressionism) that were deemed to be too concerned with strictly modern subjects or purely perceptual problems.

Primitivist pastiche

Gauguin came to his primitivist quest late, only after he had lost a lucrative position on the Paris Stock Exchange in 1883, at the age of thirty-five. Initially, he worked in Brittany in western France, still a folkloric region then, along with other Symbolist artists such as Émile Bernard (1868–1941), first in 1886 and, after a failed trip to Panama and Martinique in 1887, again in 1888. Gauguin was inspired to go to Tahiti in part by the "native villages" that were set up like zoo displays of indigenous peoples at the 1889 Universal Exhibition in Paris; he was also very taken by Buffalo Bill's Wild West show. For all its rhetoric of purity, primitivism was often just such a mix of kitsch and cliché (legend has it that Gauguin arrived in Tahiti wearing a cowboy hat). Apart from an eighteen-month return to Paris in late 1893 to manage the market for his art, he lived in Tahiti from 1891 until his final move to the Marquesas Islands in 1901. In effect, Gauguin pushed beyond the folk culture of Brittany to the tropical paradise of Tahiti (such was its legendary status, at least since Denis Diderot's *Supplement to the Voyage of Bougainville* was published in 1796), and then on to the Marquesas, which he saw as a place of sacrifice and cannibalism, dark complement to light Tahiti. As he did so, Gauguin understood his voyage out in space as a voyage back in time: "Civilization is falling from me little by little," he wrote in his Tahitian memoir *Noa-Noa* (1893). This conflation, as if *farther away* from Europe equaled *farther back* in civilization, is characteristic of primitivism, indeed of the racialist ideology of cultural evolution still pervasive at the time.

Yet Gauguin also proposed a partial revaluation of this ideology. For in his paintings and writings the primitive became the pure term and the European, the corrupt. In "the kingdom of gold," he wrote of Europe just prior to his first departure for Tahiti, "everything is putrefied, even men, even the arts." This is the source of both his stylistic rejection of Realism and his Romantic critique of capitalism, two positions that his Expressionist followers held as well. Of course, to reverse this opposition of primitive and European was not to undo or to deconstruct it. The two terms

▲ 1908

1 • André Derain, *The Dance*, 1905–6
Oil and distemper on canvas, 179.5 x 228.6 (70¾ x 90)

remained very much in place, and his revision of this binarism only forced Gauguin into an ambivalent position. "I am the Indian and the man of sensitivity [in one]," he once wrote to his abandoned wife Mette, with a special emphasis on his partial Peruvian ancestry. His myth of Tahitian purity also flew in the face of the social facts. In 1891, after ten years as a French colony, Tahiti was hardly the "unknown paradise" where "to live is to sing and to love," and the Tahitians hardly a new race after the biblical Flood, as Gauguin presented them in the pages of *Noa-Noa.*

If Polynesia was polyglot, so was his art. Less purist than eclectic, Gauguin drew on the courtly art of Peru, Cambodia, Java, and Egypt more than on the tribal art of Oceania or Africa. ("Courtly" and "tribal" suggest different sociopolitical orders, though both terms are now almost as disputed as "primitive.") Often motifs from these various cultures appear in strange ensembles; the Tahitian women in his *Market Day* (1892), for example, sit in poses derived from a tomb painting of Eighteenth-Dynasty Egypt. Nor did his arrival in Tahiti transform his style dramatically: the bold contours Gauguin derived from the stone sculptures of Breton churches, as well as the strong colors he developed from Japanese prints, persisted. So did many of his subjects: the visionary spirituality of the Breton womenfolk in *Vision after the Sermon* (1888), for example, becomes the saintly simplicity of the native Tahitian women in *We Hail Thee, Mary* (1891), only here pagan innocence rather than folk belief redefines Christian grace. Such syncretism of style and subject matter might suggest a primordial sharing of aesthetic and religious impulses across cultures (this possibility interested other primitivists, like Nolde, too), but it also points to a paradox of much primitivist art: that it often pursues purity and primacy through hybridity and pastiche. Indeed, primitivism is often as mixed stylistically as it is contradictory ideologically, and it is this eclectic construction that Gauguin passed on to his legatees.

Avant-garde gambits

A large Gauguin retrospective was held at the Salon d'Automne in Paris in 1906, yet artists such as Picasso had begun to study him as early as 1901. Already in a painting such as *The Dance* [**1**]—

The exotic and the naive

Primitivism was hardly the first exoticism in modern Europe: phantasmatic versions of the East abounded in art and literature alike. The eighteenth century saw a fashion for Chinese porcelain (*chinoiserie*), and nineteenth-century artists were drawn first to North Africa and the Middle East (Orientalism) and then to Japan (*japonisme*). These fascinations often followed historic conquests (e.g., the Napoleonic campaign in Egypt in 1798, and the forced opening of Japan to foreign trade in 1853) and imperial byways (e.g., French artists tended to head to French colonies, German artists to German, and so on). But these places were "imaginary geographies" (in the words of Edward Said in his 1978 book *Orientalism*); that is, they were space–time maps onto which psychological ambivalence and political ambition could be projected.

Thus Orientalist art often depicted the Middle East as ancient, a cradle of civilization, but also as decrepit, corrupt, feminine, in need of imperial rule. Japan was known to be an ancient culture too, but *japonistes* perceived its past as innocent, with a pure vision that, retained in Japanese prints, fans, and screens, might be accessed by Europeans clouded by Western conventions of representation. Primitivism projected an even more primordial origin, but here too the primitive was divided into a pastoral or noble savage (in the sensuous paradise of the tropics, often associated with Oceania) and a bloody or ignoble savage (in the sexual heart of darkness, usually connected to Africa). Each of these exotic theaters persists to this day, however muted or inflected, and others have joined them, propagated, as was the case then, by mass media. Avant-gardists appealed to these imaginary geographies for tactical reasons. The Impressionists and Postimpressionists had already occupied Japan, Picasso once suggested, so his generation grabbed up Africa instead, though some like Matisse and Paul Klee retained Orientalist settings as well. By the same token, the Surrealists turned to Oceania, Mexico, and the Pacific Northwest because the arts there were more surrealistic, so they said, but it was also in order to circumvent the Cubists and the Expressionists. The rule that a step outside a tradition is also a strategy within it holds for the frequent turn to folk art as well—whether it is Gauguin and Breton crucifixes, Wassily Kandinsky and Bavarian glass painting, or Kazimir Malevich and Vladimir Tatlin and Byzantine icons.

A special case is the modernist celebration of the "naive" artist, such as Henri Rousseau (1844–1910), also known as Le Douanier (customs officer), so named after his day job for fifteen years. Naive art was often associated with child, tribal, and folk art as untutored and intuitive. And yet Rousseau was a Parisian, not a peasant, who, far from oblivious to academic art, attempted a realist representation based on studio photographs and Salon compositions. In part his painting seemed surreal to his avant-garde contemporaries simply because it was technically awkward. Guillaume Apollinaire tells us that Rousseau measured the features of his portrait sitters, then transferred the lengths directly to the canvas, only to produce, in the pursuit of a realist effect, a surreal one. His jungle pictures also have an anxious intensity, as everyday house plants are transformed, with each vine and leaf meticulously contoured and flattened whole to the canvas, into an eerily animate forest. Rousseau was sincere, as was the appreciation of his modernist friends—among them Picasso, who hosted a banquet in his honor in 1908. Sincere, but, again, these identifications were often tactical and temporary. Here the last word might be given to the sociologist Pierre Bourdieu: "The artist agrees with the 'bourgeois' in one respect: he prefers naïveté to 'pretentiousness.' The essential merit of the 'common people' is that they have none of the pretensions to art (or power) which inspire the ambitions of the 'petit bourgeois.' Their indifference tacitly acknowledges the monopoly. That is why, in the mythology of artist and intellectuals, whose outflanking and double-negating strategies sometimes lead them back to 'popular' tastes and opinions, the 'people' so often play a role not unlike that of the peasantry in the conservative ideologies of the declining aristocracy."

a rhythmic arrangement of ornamental women set in an imaginary tropical scene replete with parrot and snake—André Derain (1880–1954) treated the primitivism of Gauguin as if it were a Fauvist theme park of decorative freedom and feminine sensuality. Matisse also painted such idylls in *Luxe, calme et volupté* (1904–5) ▲ and *Le Bonheur de vivre* (1905–6), but his scenes are more pastoral than primitivist, and, like Picasso, when he engaged tribal art directly in 1906, his interest was more formal than thematic. Ironically, this formal interest led both Matisse and Picasso away from Gauguin around the time of his retrospective. Concerned to strengthen the structural basis of their art, both turned from Gauguin and Oceanic motifs to Cézanne and African objects, which they read in terms of each other—partly to defend against the excessive influence of either term. Indeed, Picasso later insisted • that the African objects—which he, like Matisse, collected—were "witnesses" to the development of his art rather than "models" for it—a defensive recognition of the importance of tribal art that other primitivists would also make.

The primitivist trajectories of Matisse and Picasso were divergent. Initially, both were interested in the Egyptian sculpture they ▲ saw at the Louvre. But Picasso soon turned to Iberian reliefs, whose broad contours influenced his portraits of 1906–7, while Matisse, who was always more involved in the Orientalist dimension of French painting, traveled to North Africa. From late 1906, however, both artists were prepared to learn from African masks and figures. "Van Gogh had Japanese prints," Picasso once remarked succinctly, "we had Africa." But, again, they developed different lessons from its art. Whereas African sculpture was • crucial to Cubist collage and construction in particular, Matisse used it to stake out a plastic alternative to Cubism. Above all, he admired its "invented planes and proportions." This is apparent in his sculptures of the time, such as *Two Negresses* (1908), which

▲ 1906 • 1907 ▲ 1907, 1911 • Introduction 3, 1912

possesses the large heads, round breasts, and prominent buttocks of some African figures. But "invented planes and proportions" are also evident in his contemporaneous paintings, where they helped Matisse to simplify his drawing and to free his color from descriptive functions. This is evident in his foremost primitivist canvas, *The Blue Nude: Souvenir of Biskra*, which, like its sculptural ▲ counterpart, *Reclining Nude I* (1907), is a radical revision of the academic nude.

Ever since Édouard Manet (1832–83) cast the academic nude—from the Venuses of Titian to the *Odalisques* of Ingres—onto the lowly divan of a Parisian prostitute in *Olympia* (1863), avant-garde painting staked its transgressive claims on the subversion of this genre more than any other. Gauguin copied *Olympia* on canvas [**2**] as well as in a photograph, which he took to Tahiti as a kind of talisman, and he painted his adolescent Tahitian wife Teha'amana in a scene that cites Manet's painting. But *The Spirit of the Dead Watching* [**3**] recalls *Olympia* mostly in order to trump it. For the art historian Griselda Pollock this is an "avant-garde gambit" of three moves in one: Gauguin makes *reference* to a tradition, here not only the tradition of the academic nude but also its avant-garde

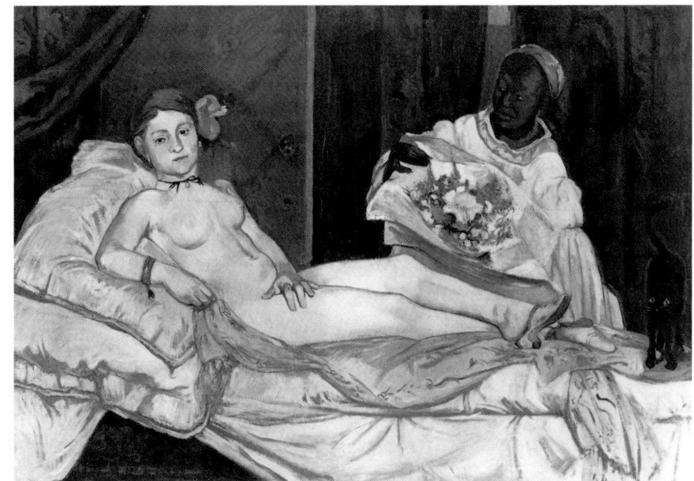

2 • Paul Gauguin, *Copy of Manet's Olympia*, 1890–1
Oil on canvas, 89 x 130 (35 x 51¾)

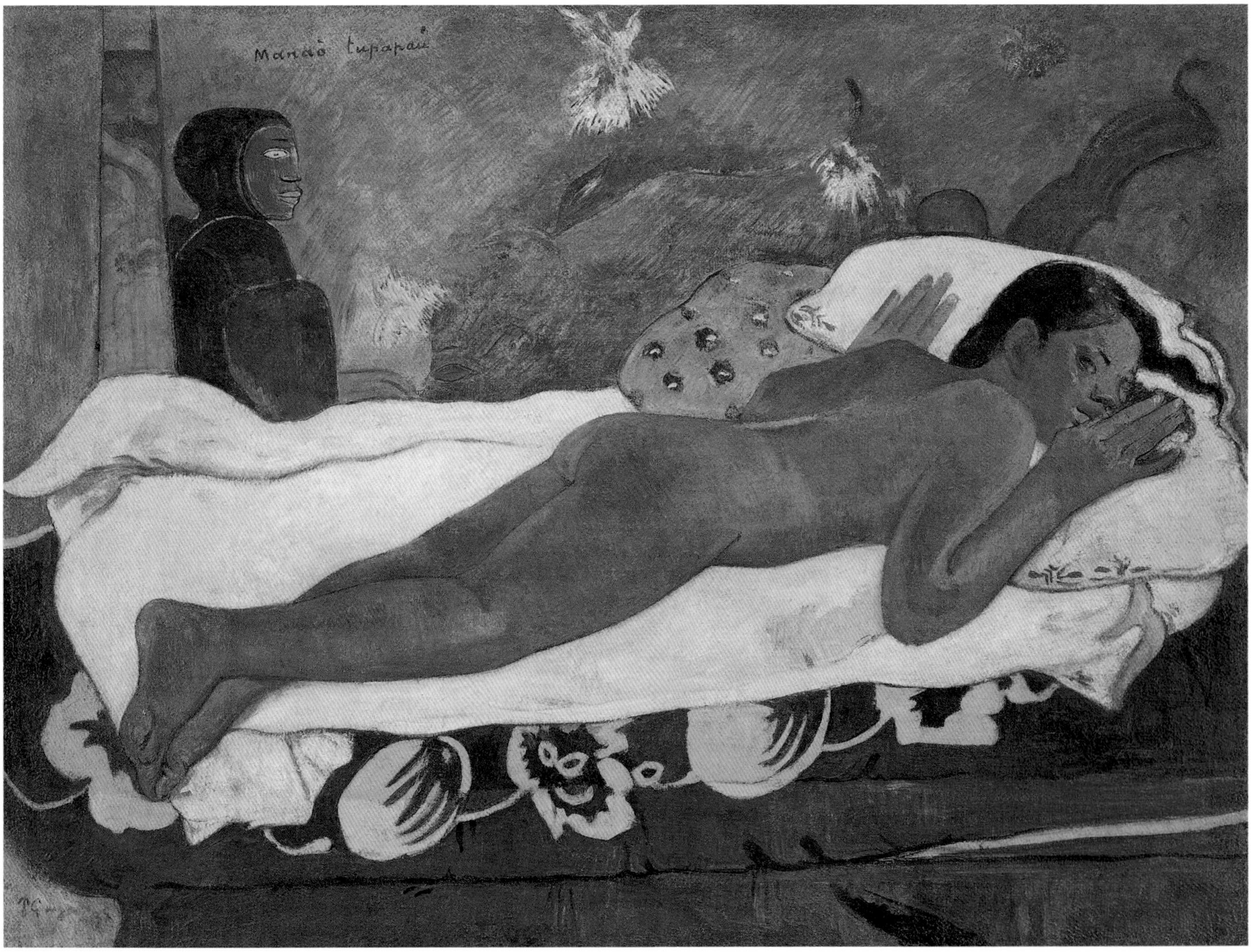

3 • Paul Gauguin, *The Spirit of the Dead Watching* (*Manao Tupapau*), 1892
Oil on burlap mounted on canvas, 73 x 92 (28½ x 36⅜)

▲ 1900b

subversion; he also shows *deference* to its masters, here not only Titian and Ingres but also Manet; and finally, he proposes his own *difference*, an Oedipal challenge to all these paternal precedents, a claiming of master status alongside them. Clearly, Matisse with ▲ *The Blue Nude*, Picasso with *Les Demoiselles d'Avignon* (1907), and Kirchner with *Girl under a Japanese Umbrella* [**4**] are also involved in a pictorial competition with artistic forebears and with each other, one staged, as it were, on the bodies of women. Each artist looks outside the Western tradition—in a turn to tribal art, in a fantasy of a primitive body—as a way to advance inside the Western tradition. In retrospect, this outside, this other, is then incorporated into the formal dialectic of modernist art.

First Gauguin revises Manet, reworks his blunt scene of a Paris prostitute into an imaginary vision of a Tahitian "spirit of the dead." He inverts the figures, substitutes a black spirit for the black maid in *Olympia*, and replaces the white body of the prostitute with the black body of the primitive girl. Gauguin also averts her gaze (this is crucial: Olympia returns our gaze, stares the male viewer down as if he were a customer), and rotates her body so as to expose her buttocks (this, too, is crucial: it is a sexual pose that Teha'amana, unlike Olympia, does not control—the implied male viewer does). It is with this double precedent of *Olympia* and *Spirit* that, in quick succession after the Gauguin retrospective, Matisse, Picasso, and Kirchner all wrestle. In *The Blue Nude: Souvenir of Biskra* [**5**], Matisse moves the newly forged figure of the prostitute/primitive to an Orientalist site, the oasis of Biskra in North Africa (which he had visited in 1906), whose ground lines and palm fronds echo the contours of the bent elbow and prominent buttocks of his nude. In doing so, he recalls the odalisque term in this particular dialectic of the primitive body (an odalisque was a female slave, usually a concubine, in the Near East, a fantasy figure for many nineteenth-century artists); and yet, as noted above, his figure is more Africanist than Orientalist (as if to underscore this point, Matisse added the subtitle in 1931). So, even as Matisse recovers the pose of *Olympia*, he also deepens the primitivizing of feminine sexuality begun in *Spirit*, the principal sign of which is the prominent buttocks (made so by the violent rotation of her left leg across her pubic area). In this way *The Blue Nude* trumps both Manet and Gauguin—another modernist victory won on the battleground of the prostitute/primitive nude.

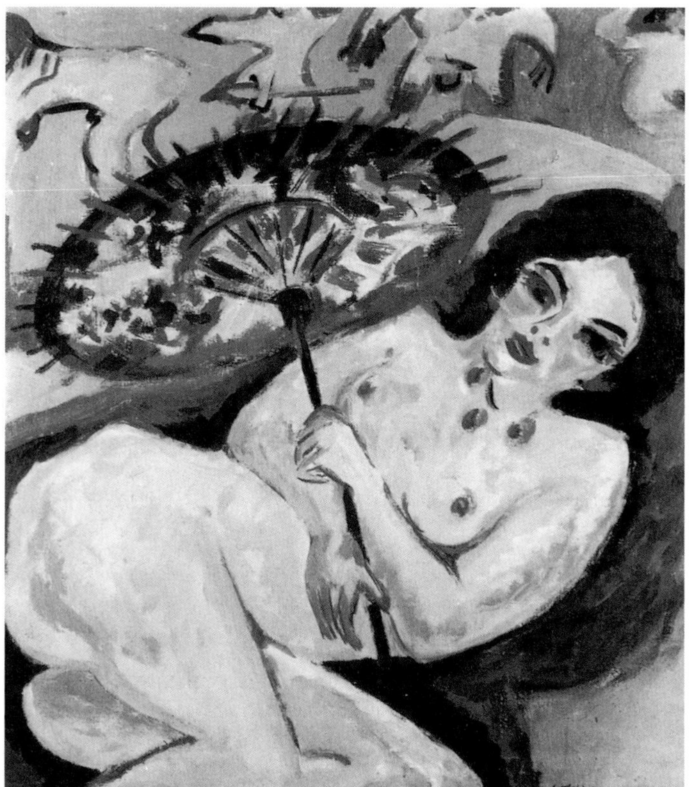

4 • Ernst Ludwig Kirchner, *Girl under a Japanese Umbrella*, 1909
Oil on canvas, 92.5 x 80.5 (36½ x 31½)

Primitivist ambivalence

Shown to great uproar in the Salon des Indépendants of 1907, *The Blue Nude* then provokes Picasso to an extreme of rivalry with *Les Demoiselles d'Avignon*, which returns the primitive body to a brothel, and so "resolves" prostitute and primitive in one figure. Moreover, Picasso multiplies this figure by five—three visaged in his Iberian manner, two in his African—and pushes them vertically to the frontal plane of the canvas where they gaze at the viewer with a sexual threat that exceeds not only the Gauguin and the Matisse but also the Manet. In *Girl under a Japanese Umbrella*, Kirchner, too, responds to *The Blue Nude* (he could not have seen *Les Demoiselles*); he inverts the pose but retains the signal rotation of the body that raises the buttocks. Kirchner also replaces the Orientalist setting of *The Blue Nude* with *japoniste* props like the parasol. But the telling element of the decor is the frieze of sketchy figures above the nude. This recalls the wall hangings that decorated his studio with sexually explicit images, some inspired by house beams from the German colony of Palau that Kirchner had studied in the ethnographic museum in Dresden. In this frieze, Kirchner points to a fantasy of anal eroticism only implied by *Spirit* and *The Blue Nude*, and so points as well to a narcissistic dimension of modernist primitivism that is not simply formal—and perhaps not as masterful as it first seems. For the prostitute/primitive is such a fraught image not only because it disrupts an academic genre but also because it provokes great ambivalence concerning sexual and racial differences.

Although subordinated as a prostitute, Olympia commands her sex, which she covers with her hand, and this partial power is crucial to the provocation of the painting. In *Spirit*, Gauguin takes this female power away: Teha'amana is prone, subordinate to the gaze of the viewer. Yet the tradition of the primitive body is not simply about voyeuristic mastery. Gauguin concocted a story of religious dread to accompany his painting, but this diverts us from its sexual significance: *Spirit* is a dream of sexual mastery, but this mastery is not actual; its pictorial performance may even compensate for a felt lack of such mastery in real life. This suggests that the painting works on an anxiety or an ambivalence that Gauguin

▲ 1907

5 • Henri Matisse, *The Blue Nude: Souvenir of Biskra*, 1907
Oil on canvas, 92.1 x 142.5 (36¼ x 56⅛)

secretly, maybe unconsciously, presumed. This ambivalence—perhaps a simultaneous desire and dread of feminine sexuality—is more active in *The Blue Nude*, and Matisse defended against it more actively, too. "If I met such a woman in the street," he stated unequivocally after his painting was attacked, "I should run away in terror. Above all I do not create a human, I make a picture." Kirchner seems not to have needed such a defense; at least in *Girl under a Japanese Umbrella* he paraded an erotic fantasy without much anxiety—but also without much force.

It was the problematic genius of Picasso that led him to work his sexual and racial ambivalences into thematic and formal experiments. In effect, *Les Demoiselles* maps two memory-scenes onto one another: a distant visit to a bordello in Barcelona (his student home) and a recent visit to the Musée d'Ethnographie du Trocadéro in Paris (now the Musée de l'Homme), both apparently traumatic for Picasso—the first sexually, the second racially, in ways that the painting conflates. The encounter in the ethnographic museum was momentous: among other effects, Picasso transformed *Les Demoiselles* in its wake. Such visits—to tribal exhibits at museums, fairs, circuses, and the like—were important to many primitivists, and a few were later narrated precisely as traumatic encounters in accounts in which the full significance of tribal art is revealed in retrospect, only to be denied in part (again, the claim that such objects are "witnesses," not "models"). In one version of the tale of his visit to the Trocadéro, Picasso called *Les Demoiselles* his "first exorcism painting." This term is suggestive in ways that he did not suspect, for much modernist primitivism engages tribal art and primitive bodies only at times to exorcise them formally, just as it recognizes sexual, racial, and cultural differences only at times to disavow them fetishistically.

FURTHER READING

Stephen F. Eisenman, *Gauguin's Skirt* (London and New York: Thames & Hudson, 1997)
Hal Foster, *Prosthetic Gods* (Cambridge, Mass.: MIT Press, 2004)
Sander L. Gilman, *Difference and Pathology: Stereotypes of Sexuality, Race and Madness* (Ithaca, N.Y.: Cornell University Press, 1985)
Robert Goldwater, *Primitivism in Modern Art* (New York: Vintage Books, 1967 [originally published 1938])
Jill Lloyd, *German Expressionism: Primitivism and Modernity* (New Haven and London: Yale University Press, 1991)
Griselda Pollock, *Avant-Garde Gambits 1883–1893: Gender and the Colour of Art History* (London and New York: Thames & Hudson, 1992)
William Rubin (ed.), *"Primitivism" in 20th Century Art: Affinity of the Tribal and the Modern* (New York: Museum of Modern Art, 1984)

1906

Paul Cézanne dies at Aix-en-Provence in southern France: following the retrospectives of Vincent van Gogh and Georges Seurat the preceding year, Cézanne's death casts Postimpressionism as the historical past, with Fauvism as its heir.

Henri Matisse was very fond of a particular Cézanne dictum: "Beware of the influential master!" He often quoted it when addressing the issue of inheritance and tradition. Noting that Cézanne had revisited Poussin in order to escape from the spell of Courbet, he would take pride in the fact that he, Matisse, had "never avoided the influence of others," emphasizing the importance of Cézanne in his own formation (he is "a sort of god of painting," "the master of us all"; "if Cézanne is right, I am right," and so on). But Matisse's claim that he was strong enough to assimilate the example of a master without succumbing to it is disingenuous when it comes to Cézanne. Unlike his friend, and future fellow Fauve, Charles Camoin (1879–1965), who jauntily visited the aging painter in Aix several times, Matisse was acutely aware of the potential danger that Cézanne represented for young admirers like himself. Looking at Matisse's *Still Life with a Purro I*, or his *Place des Lices, Saint-Tropez*, both painted in the summer of 1904, one cannot help but think of a statement he made half a century later (it was one of his last): "When one imitates a master, the technique of the master strangles the imitator and forms around him a barrier that paralyzes him."

The four evangelists of Postimpressionism

The year 1904 was when Cézanne, cut off from a world that had ridiculed him all his life, finally attained celebrity. Imposing articles were published about him (notably an essay by Émile Bernard [1868–1941]); dealers other than Ambroise Vollard, his lone official supporter since 1895, started gambling on him (he had a one-man show in Berlin); and in the fall, a mini-retrospective of his work (with thirty-one paintings) was presented at the Salon d'Automne, one of the two annual Parisian art fairs of the time (three years later, in 1907, its spring equivalent, the Salon des Indépendants, would top this event with an exhibition double in size).

A document from 1905 provides a window onto the atmosphere of the Parisian art world at the time. The poet-critic Charles Morice's "Enquête sur les tendances actuelles des arts plastiques" (Investigation of Current Trends in the Plastic Arts) presented the answers to a questionnaire that its author had sent to artists of various persuasions. The question that received the longest and most passionate replies was "What do you think of Cézanne?" (Matisse did not bother to give his obvious answer). The rise of Cézanne's reputation was then unstoppable: by the time he died, in October 1906, his appeal was so pervasive that his foremost champion, the painter-theoretician Maurice Denis (1870–1943)—who had paradoxically seen him as the savior of the moribund tradition of French classicism—cried foul and berated the work of his many followers as either too derivative or, in the case of Matisse, nothing less than a betrayal.

Morice's "Investigation" helps us to put this sudden hype surrounding Cézanne into context. He had bluntly asked: "Is Impressionism finished?" Then, more diplomatically: "Are we on the eve of something?" and "Must the painter expect everything from nature, or must he only ask from it the plastic means to realize the thought that is in him?" These questions were followed by a request for an evaluation of the work of Whistler, Fantin-Latour, and Gauguin, as well as that of Cézanne. If the query about Gauguin was to be expected, since Morice had long been a close ▲ ally of the painter's (he had coauthored *Noa-Noa* with him), those concerning Whistler and Fantin-Latour, testifying to Morice's active participation in the Symbolist movement twenty years earlier, were incongruous (as the answers confirmed). A more savvy critic would have juxtaposed the names of van Gogh and Seurat with those of Cézanne and Gauguin in such a questionnaire, for by then it had become obvious that the new generation's loud "Yes" to Morice's sequence of anti-Impressionism questions was a cumulative effect of this quartet's coeval work.

It should be noted that van Gogh and Seurat were long dead—the first in 1890, the second, the following year—and that Gauguin, who died in 1903, had been abroad for more than a decade. It comes as no surprise, therefore, that, among the four evangelists of Postimpressionism, Cézanne should be the most present at this point. Yet, for Matisse and his peers, it was urgent to reckon with them all. Between 1903 and Cézanne's death in 1906, van Gogh, Gauguin, and Seurat had each been celebrated by several retrospective exhibitions (with their attendant string of publications), sometimes with the direct involvement of Matisse. And while the personal relationships between these four father-figures of modernist painting had been marred by hostile

▲ 1903

ignorance, if not outright conflict, it now seemed possible to grasp what they had in common.

Their direct epigones had already done some of the groundwork as far as art theory was concerned. Both Denis and Bernard had advocated a synthesis between the art of Gauguin and that of Cézanne; but the most important event for Matisse and his cohorts was the serialization of Paul Signac's *D'Eugène Delacroix au néo-impressionnisme* (From Eugène Delacroix to neo-Impressionism) in *La Revue blanche* in 1898. Not only did this treatise present Seurat's method (indifferently labeled "divisionism" or "neo-impressionism") in an orderly, accessible fashion, but, as its title made clear, it was conceived as a teleological account, as a genealogy of the "new" in art from the early nineteenth century on. There was surprisingly little emphasis on Seurat's dream or on the optical physiology theories on which it was based—the idea that the human eye could perform something like the prismatic decomposition of light in reverse, that the "divided" colors would resynthesize on the retina in order to attain the luminosity of the sun—perhaps because Signac had already admitted to himself that this was a chimera. Rather, Signac insisted on the successive "contributions" of Delacroix and of the Impressionists, understood as having paved the way for the total emancipation of pure color performed by neo-Impressionism. Within such a context, Cézanne's idiosyncratic, atomistic brush-strokes (one color per stroke, each kept conspicuously discrete) were deemed a congruent contribution consolidating the ban on the mixing of colors that had still been standard practice during Impressionism.

Matisse's first encounter with Signac's gospel was premature. After a trip to London in order to see Turner's paintings (on the advice of Cézanne's mentor, the old Camille Pissarro), he had headed for Corsica, where his art—then a murky and not-so-competent form of Impressionism—turned "epileptic," as he wrote in a panic to a friend, upon his sudden discovery of southern light. In the numerous paintings he completed in Corsica and then in Toulouse in 1898 and 1899, the feverish brush-strokes are thick with impasto, and the colors ineluctably lose their intended incandescence as the pastes mix directly on the canvas. The cardinal axiom of Postimpressionism (of whatever persuasion), that one had to "organize one's sensation," to use Cézanne's celebrated phrase, came to Matisse via Signac precisely at this point. But his attempt at following the minute procedures required by the divisionist system, during the next few months, remained frustrating. Yet this failure exacerbated his desire to comprehend the whole of Postimpressionism (he notably purchased several works by its masters—then a considerable financial sacrifice for him—including a small painting by Gauguin and, above all, Cézanne's *Three Bathers*, a painting from the mid- to late 1870s that he would treasure like a talisman until he donated it to the city of Paris in 1936).

Cohabiting with these few works and never missing a Postimpressionist show constituted the major part of Matisse's modernist education prior to his second bout of divisionism. He gradually understood that despite major differences in their art, the four major Postimpressionists had all stressed that if color and line were to be celebrated, if their expressive function were to be enhanced, they had to become independent from the objects they depicted. Further, these artists showed Matisse that the only way to assert this autonomy of the basic elements of painting was first to isolate them (as a chemist would do) and then to recombine them into a new synthetic whole. Although Seurat had erred when he sought to apply this experimental method to the immateriality of light, that unreachable Holy Grail of painters, his analysis/synthesis process resulted in the apotheosis of the physical, nonmimetic components of painting, and it was such a return to basics, Matisse was now ready to see, that governed Postimpressionism in general. Because divisionism was the only Postimpressionist branch that came with an explicit method, it was a good place from which to start again. When Signac invited Matisse to spend the summer of 1904 in Saint-Tropez, Matisse was still trying out the various Postimpressionist dialects, but he was a far more seasoned modernist than he had been in 1898. Even though it was now harder for Matisse to play the apprentice, the timing was right.

Matisse comes of age to lead the Fauves

As far as Signac was concerned, the anxious and reluctant Matisse was finally turning out to be his best pupil: Signac purchased *Luxe, calme et volupté* **[1]**, the major canvas that Matisse completed in Paris upon his return from Saint-Tropez and exhibited at the 1905 Salon des Indépendants (where both van Gogh and Seurat had a retrospective). Was it the idyllic subject matter that particularly seduced Signac—five naked nymphs picnicking by the seashore under the eyes of a crouched, dressed Madame Matisse and those of a standing child wrapped in a towel? Or was it the title derived from Charles Baudelaire (1821–67), a rare direct literary allusion in Matisse's oeuvre? Whatever the case, Signac chose not to notice the heavy colored contours wriggling all over the composition in defiance of his system. But when Matisse sent *Le Bonheur de vivre* to the Salon des Indépendants of the subsequent year, Signac was incensed by precisely such elements in this canvas, and by the undivided flat planes of color. Between these two events, the Fauve scandal had taken place at the infamous 1905 Salon d'Automne.

As the British critic, painter, and teacher Lawrence Gowing remarked, "Fauvism was the best prepared of all the twentieth-century revolutions." But one should add that it was also one of the shortest: it lasted but a season. True, most of the Fauves had known each other for years and had long considered the older Matisse as their leader (between 1895 and 1896, Albert Marquet [1875–1947], Henri Manguin [1874–1949], and Charles Camoin were his colleagues in the studio of Gustave Moreau, the only oasis of freedom at the École des Beaux-Arts, and when he switched to the Académie Carrière after Moreau's death in 1898, he met André Derain, who soon introduced him to Maurice de Vlaminck [1876–1958]). But the initial spark can be traced to Matisse's visit to Vlaminck's studio, at Derain's urging, in February 1905. Matisse had then just

1 • Henri Matisse, *Luxe, calme et volupté*, 1904–5
Oil on canvas, 98.3 x 118.5 ($38\frac{3}{4}$ x $46\frac{5}{8}$)

finished *Luxe, calme et volupté*, of which he was rightfully proud, but now he felt unsettled by the coloristic violence of Vlaminck's production. It would take him the whole summer, which he spent with Derain in Collioure, close to the Spanish border, to get over Vlaminck's jejune audacity. Spurred by Derain's presence, and by the visit they paid together to a trove of Gauguin's works, he painted nonstop for four consecutive months. The results of this strikingly productive campaign were the key works of what was soon to be called Fauvism.

Upon seeing the academic marbles of a now long-forgotten sculptor in the middle of the room where the work of Matisse and his friends Derain, Vlaminck, Camoin, Manguin, and Marquet was exhibited at the 1905 Salon d'Automne, a critic exclaimed "Donatello chez les fauves!" ("Donatello among the wild beasts!"). The label stuck—perhaps the most celebrated baptismal episode of twentieth-century art—in large part because the uproar was considerable. Matisse's Fauve canvases—*The Woman with the Hat* [**2**] in particular, painted shortly after his return from Collioure—provoked the crowd's hilarity as no work had done since the public display of Manet's *Olympia* in 1863, and news that this infamous painting had ▲ been purchased (by Gertrude and Leo Stein) did not calm the sarcasm of the press. Not only did Matisse's associates benefit from his sudden fame, but the idea that he was the head of a new school of painting crystallized, and indeed his art was emulated (the initial Fauves were soon joined by others such as Raoul Dufy [1877–1953], Othon Friesz [1879–1949], Kees van Dongen [1877–1968] and, • momentarily, Georges Braque [1882–1963]). But while his acolytes, with the exception of Braque, got forever stuck in the exploitation (and banalization) of the pictorial language invented during the summer of 1905, for Matisse the Collioure explosion had been only a beginning: it marked the moment when he finally achieved the synthesis of the four trends of Postimpressionism that had captivated him, and laid the ground for his own system, whose first fully fledged pictorial manifestation would be *Le Bonheur de vivre*.

▲ 1907 • 1911, 1912

Roger Fry (1866–1934) and the Bloomsbury Group

Undoubtedly the most passionate supporter of advanced French painting in the English-speaking world at the beginning of the twentieth century was the British artist and critic Roger Fry. It was he who, with his 1910 exhibition "Manet and the Post-Impressionists" at the Grafton Gallery, first introduced the work of Cézanne, van Gogh, Gauguin, Seurat, Matisse, and others to an incredulous London public, in the process coining the now-familiar term "Postimpressionism." He followed the show with a second in 1912, again at the Grafton Gallery, "The Second Post-Impressionist Exhibition."

Fry was one of the most prominent members of the Bloomsbury Group, a shifting community of artists and writers in London during the opening decades of the twentieth century that included the novelist Virginia Woolf and her husband Leonard; her sister, the painter Vanessa Bell, and Bell's lover Duncan Grant; the Strachey brothers, James and Lytton, both writers; and the economist John Maynard Keynes.

Fry's aestheticism and passion for avant-garde French art formed part of the Group's model for a life devoted to the minute analysis of sensation and of consciousness. As the poet Stephen Spender described it: "Not to regard the French Impressionist and Post-Impressionist painters as sacrosanct, not to be an agnostic and in politics a Liberal with Socialist leanings, was to put oneself outside Bloomsbury." In his 1938 essay "My Early Beliefs," Keynes tried to convey the sensibility of the Group:

> *Nothing mattered except states of mind, our own and other people's of course, but chiefly our own. These states of mind were not associated with action or achievement or with consequences. They consisted in timeless, passionate states of contemplation and communion, largely unattached to "before" and "after." Their value depended, in accordance with the principle of organic unity, on the state of affairs as a whole which could not be usefully analyzed into parts."*

The example Keynes gives of such a state is of being in love:

> *The appropriate subjects of passionate contemplation and communion were a beloved person, beauty and truth, and one's prime objects in life were love, the creation and enjoyment of aesthetic experience and the pursuit of knowledge.*

Virginia Woolf's recollection of Fry illustrates many of Keynes's characterizations of Bloomsbury, such as the pursuit of "timeless, passionate states of contemplation and communion, largely unattached to 'before' and 'after'" whose "value depended, in accordance with the principle of organic unity, on the state of affairs as a whole which could not be usefully analyzed into parts." Accordingly, she describes Fry's inaugural Slade lectures at the Queen's Hall of Cambridge University in 1933, and the effect they had on their audience:

> *He had only to point to a passage in a picture and to murmur the word "plasticity" and a magical atmosphere was created. He looked like a fasting friar with a rope round his waist in spite of his evening dress: the religion of his convictions. "Slide, please," he said. And there was the picture—Rembrandt, Chardin, Poussin, Cézanne—in black and white upon the screen. And the lecturer pointed. His long wand, trembling like the antenna of some miraculously sensitive insect, settled upon some "rhythmical phrase," some sequence; some diagonal. And then he went on to make the audience see—"the gem-like notes; the aquamarines; and topazes that lie in the hollow of his satin gowns; bleaching the lights to evanescent pallors." Somehow the black-and-white slide on the screen became radiant through the mist, and took on the grain and texture of the actual canvas.*
>
> *He added on the spur of the moment what he had just seen as if for the first time. That, perhaps, was the secret of his hold over his audience. They could see the sensation strike and form; he could lay bare the very moment of perception. So with pauses and spurts the world of spiritual reality emerged in slide after slide—in Poussin, in Chardin, in Rembrandt, in Cézanne—in its uplands and its lowlands, all connected, all somehow made whole and entire, upon the great screen in the Queen's Hall.*

Fry's conviction that aesthetic experience could be communicated by bringing another to perceive a work's organic unity, and its accompanying feature of "plasticity," led to a style of verbal exposition focused exclusively on the formal character of a given work. Consequently, his writing has been labeled "formalist." Trying to convey Fry's pursuit of perceptual immediacy, Woolf recounts his words about looking at pictures: "I spent the afternoon in the Louvre. I tried to forget all my ideas and theories and to look at everything as though I'd never seen it before.... It's only so that one can make discoveries.... Each work must be a new and a nameless experience." It is possible to discover Fry's capture of this "new and nameless experience" in the essays he wrote, some of which are collected in *Vision and Design* (1920) and *Transformations* (1926).

2 • Henri Matisse, *The Woman with the Hat*, 1905
Oil on canvas, 81.3 x 60.3 (32 x $23\frac{3}{4}$)

Matisse's system

What one witnesses first in Matisse's Fauve output is the progressive abandonment of the divisionist brush-stroke: Matisse retains from Signac's tutoring the use of pure color and the organization of the picture plane through contrasts of complementary pairs (this is what ensures the picture's coloristic tension), but he relinquishes the most easily recognizable common denominator of Cézanne and Seurat: their search for a unitary mode of notation (the pointillist dot, the constructive stroke) that could be used indifferently for the figures and the ground. And other major traits of Postimpressionism are summoned: from Gauguin and van Gogh, flat, unmodulated planes of nonmimetic color and thick contours with a rhythm of their own; from van Gogh's drawings, a differentiation of the effect of linear marks through variations in their thickness and their closeness to one another; from Cézanne, a conception of the pictorial surface as a totalizing field where everything, even the unpainted white areas, plays a constructive role in bolstering the energy of the picture.

The moment when Matisse "gets" Cézanne—and stops merely trying to imitate him, as he had done in the past—is also his farewell to the tedium of pointillism: while Signac had advocated filling the composition outward from any area (or more precisely, from any line of demarcation) chosen as a point of departure, the myriad dots being patiently added in a sequence preordained by the "law of contrasts," Matisse found out that he could not follow this myopic, incremental procedure. As is made clear by one of the few unfinished canvases from the Fauve season, *Portrait of Madame Matisse* [**3**], Matisse, like Cézanne, works on all areas of his picture at once and distributes his color contrasts so that they echo all over the surface (note, for example, the way the triad orange/green-ocher/red-pink is disseminated and calls in turn for various neighboring greens). There is a gradual process, to be sure, but it concerns the level of color saturation: a color harmony is determined at first in a subdued mode (it was at this point that *Portrait of Madame Matisse* was interrupted), then it is heated up, all parts of the canvas being simultaneously brought to a higher pitch. Would the public of the Salon d'Automne have found *The Woman with the Hat* less offensive if Matisse had shown with it this abandoned work? Would the piercing dabs of vermilion, the palettelike fan, the rainbow mask of the face, the harlequin background, the dissolution of the very hat's unity into a shapeless bouquet, the telescoped anatomy, as seen through a zoom lens—would all this have seemed less arbitrary to the laughing crowd if Matisse had allowed them a glimpse at his working method? Nothing is less certain. *The Open Window* [**4**], now perhaps the most celebrated of the Fauve canvases, was no less decried at the

3 • Henri Matisse, *Portrait of Madame Matisse (The Green Line)*, 1905
Oil on canvas, 40.6 x 32.4 (16 x $12\frac{3}{4}$)

4 • Henri Matisse,
***The Open Window*, 1905**
Oil on canvas, 55.2 x 46.4
(21¾ x 18¼)

Salon, and yet it is less aggressive than the others, and more transparent about its procedures: it is easy to sort out the pairs of complementary colors that structure it, make it vibrate and visually expand, and that order our gaze never to stop at any given point.

Shortly after the Fauve salon, Matisse, reflecting upon his achievement of the past few months, stumbled upon an axiom that would remain one his guidelines all his life. It can be summarized by the statement, "One square centimeter of any blue is not as blue as a square meter of the same blue," and indeed, speaking about the red planes of his *Interior at Collioure (The Siesta)* from c. 1905–6, Matisse would marvel at the fact that, although they looked to be of a different hue, they had all been painted straight out of the same tube. Discovering that color relations are above all surface-quantity relations was a major step. Struck by a statement Cézanne had made about the foundational unity of color and drawing, he had been complaining to Signac that in his work, and particularly in *Luxe, calme et volupté*, so cherished by the older artist, the two components were split and even contradicting each other. Now, through his equation "quality = quantity," as he often put it, he understood why for Cézanne the traditional opposition between color and drawing was necessarily annulled: since any single color can be modulated by a mere change of proportion, any division of a plain surface is in itself a coloristic procedure. "What counts most with colors are relationships. Thanks to them and them alone a drawing can be intensely colored without there being any need for actual color," wrote Matisse. In fact, it is very probable that Matisse made this discovery about color while working on a series of black-and-white woodcuts in the beginning of 1906, and then set himself up to apply or to verify it in *Le Bonheur de vivre* [**5**].

5 • Henri Matisse, *Le Bonheur de vivre* (The Joy of Life), 1906
Oil on canvas, 174 x 240 (68½ x 94⅞)

A parricide in paint

The largest and most ambitious work he had painted so far, *Le Bonheur de vivre* constituted his sole entry at the 1906 Salon des Indépendants. Six months after the Fauve scandal, the stakes were high: it was all or nothing, and Matisse carefully planned his composition in the most academic fashion, establishing first the decor from sketches made at Collioure and then planting, one by one, the figures or groups of figures that he had studied separately. But if the elaboration of this vast machine had been academic, the result was not. Never had flat planes of unmodulated pure color been used on such a scale, with such violent clashes of primary hues; never had contours so thick, also painted in bright hues, danced such free arabesques; never had anatomies been so "deformed," bodies melting together as if made of mercury—except perhaps in Gauguin's prints, which Matisse had revisited during the summer. With this bombshell, he wanted definitively to turn over a page of the Western tradition of painting. And to make sure that one got the message, he reinforced it by means of a cannibalistic attack at the iconographic level.

Scholars have painstakingly pursued the vast array of sources that Matisse convoked in this canvas. Ingres is predominant (he had a retrospective at the 1905 Salon d'Automne, with his *The Turkish Bath* and *The Golden Age* prominently displayed), as is the Postimpressionist quartet; but Pollaiuolo, Titian, Giorgione, Agostino Carracci, Cranach, Poussin, Watteau, Puvis de Chavannes, Maurice Denis, and many more painters are also invited to this ecumenical banquet. New guests keep being discovered; the whole pantheon of Western painting seems to be quoted—back to the very origin, since even prehistoric cave painting can be traced in the contours of the goats on the right. This medley of sources goes hand in hand with the stylistic disunity of the canvas and the discrepancies of scale—yet further rules of the pictorial tradition that Matisse deliberately upsets.

And that is not all: behind the paradisiacal imagery of the frolicking nymphs, behind the happy theme (the Joy of Life), the painting has a somber ring to it. For if the pastoral genre to which the canvas refers established a direct connection between physical beauty, visual pleasure, and the origin of desire, it was also based on a solid anchoring of sexual difference—something that, as Margaret Werth has shown, Matisse perturbs here in countless ways. Werth starts by observing that the shepherd flutist, the only male figure in the painting, had initially been conceived as a female nude; she then notes that the sexual attributes of the other flutist, the large nude in the foreground, also clearly female in a study, were suppressed; that all the figures either have counterparts or form couples, but that all of them—apart from the shepherd and the "Ingresque" nude standing on the left, gazing at the spectator—are de-anatomized. (The culmination of this sadistic assault on the body is provided by the couple kissing in the foreground, two bodies—one of indeterminate sex—virtually melded with a single head.) The montagelike nature of the composition, with "disjunctive transitions" that are "characteristic of dream images or hallucination," leads Werth to construct a psychoanalytic interpretation of the painting as a phantasmatic screen, a polysemic image conjuring up a series of contradictory sexual drives corresponding to the polymorphous infantile sexuality that Freud uncovered (narcissism, auto-eroticism, sadism, exhibitionism)—a catalog that revolves around the Oedipus complex and the concomitant castration anxiety.

At all levels (formal, stylistic, thematic), the painting is parricidal. The dancers of *Le Bonheur de vivre* celebrate the definite toppling of a dreaded authority—that of the academic canon legislated by the École des Beaux-Arts. But Matisse let us know that the resulting freedom is not without risks, for whoever kills the symbolic father is left without guidance and must endlessly reinvent his own art in order to keep it alive. As such, this canvas opens the gates of twentieth-century art.

FURTHER READING

Roger Benjamin, *Matisse's "Notes of a Painter": Criticism, Theory, and Context, 1891–1908*, (Ann Arbor: UMI Research Press, 1987)

Catherine C. Bock, *Henri Matisse and Neo-Impressionism 1898–1908* (Ann Arbor: UMI Research Press, 1981)

Yve-Alain Bois, "Matisse and Arche-drawing," *Painting as Model* (Cambridge, Mass.: MIT Press, 1990) and "On Matisse: The Blinding," *October*, no. 68, Spring 1994

Judi Freeman (ed.), *The Fauve Landscape* (New York: Abbeville Press, 1990)

Richard Shiff, "Mark, Motif, Materiality: The Cézanne Effect in the Twentieth Century," in Felix Baumann et al., *Cézanne: Finished/Unfinished* (Ostfildern-Ruit: Hatje Cantz Verlag, 2000)

Margaret Werth, "Engendering Imaginary Modernism: Henri Matisse's *Bonheur de vivre*," *Genders*, no. 9, Autumn 1990

1907

With the stylistic inconsistencies and primitivist impulses of *Les Demoiselles d'Avignon,* Pablo Picasso launches the most formidable attack ever on mimetic representation.

Picasso's *Les Demoiselles d'Avignon* **[1]** has acquired a mythical status: it is a manifesto, a battlefield, a herald of modern art. Fully conscious that he was producing a major work, Picasso threw everything into its elaboration: all his ideas, all his energy, all his knowledge. We now know *Les Demoiselles d'Avignon* as one of the "most worked-upon" canvases ever, and due attention is paid to the sixteen sketchbooks and numerous studies in various media that Picasso devoted to its making—not counting the drawings and paintings produced in the picture's immediate wake, in which Picasso further explored a whole range of avenues opened up by the painting during its fast-paced genesis.

But if no modern picture has been as much discussed during the last quarter of a century—with book-length essays and even an entire exhibition with a two-volume catalogue glorifying it—this plethora of commentary follows a striking dearth of discussion. Indeed, the painting long remained in quasi obscurity—one could even say that it was *resisted.* (A telling anecdote of this resistance: it seems that at the end of the twenties, two decades after *Les Demoiselles*'s completion, the collector Jacques Doucet intended to bequeath the picture to the Musée du Louvre, but the museum refused the offer, as it had done with the Cézannes of the Gustave Caillebotte bequest in 1894). Late recognition is the stuff of which legends are made, but what is so particular in this case is that the painting's deferred reception is not just linked to but also commanded by its subject matter and formal structure: *Les Demoiselles* is above all a work about beholding, about the trauma engendered by a visual summons.

Circumstances played a role in this spectacular delay. To begin with the painting had almost no public life for thirty years. Until Doucet bought it from Picasso for a song in 1924—at the urging of André Breton and to the immediate regret of the artist—*Les Demoiselles* had moved out of the artist's studio only once or twice, and then only during World War I: for two weeks in July 1916, in a semiprivate exhibition organized by the critic André Salmon at the Salon d'Antin (during which the painting acquired its present title), and possibly in the joint exhibition of Matisse's and Picasso's work in January–February 1918, organized by the dealer ▲ Paul Guillaume and with a catalogue prefaced by Guillaume Apollinaire. In the fall and winter of 1907, friends and visitors had seen the painting in Picasso's studio immediately after its completion, but access to it had rapidly dwindled (because of Picasso's numerous moves, often to cramped quarters, and his understandable desire always to show the latest crop of his protean and ever-changing production, the canvas was rarely on view even for the circle of the artist's intimates, which accounts for the paucity of their comments). Once in Doucet's possession, the painting was visible only by appointment, until it was sold by his widow to a dealer in the fall of 1937. Immediately shipped to New York, it was then bought by the Museum of Modern Art, where it became the museum's most precious fixture—the end of *Les Demoiselles*'s private life.

The literature roughly follows a similar pattern. The painting was not even specifically named in the rare early articles that devoted a passage to it (by Gelett Burgess in 1910, André Salmon in 1912, and Daniel-Henry Kahnweiler in 1916 and 1920). Furthermore, it was only very rarely reproduced before its landing in New York: after Burgess's journalistic piece ("The Wild Men in Paris," in the May 1910 issue of the *Architectural Record*), its reproduction was not published until 1925, in the journal *La Révolution surréaliste* (by no means a bestseller), and to appear in a monograph on the artist it had to await Gertrude Stein's **[2]** *Picasso* of 1938. Shortly thereafter, ▲ Alfred H. Barr's *Picasso: Forty Years of His Art*, which functioned as the catalogue of the Museum of Modern Art's 1939 Picasso retrospective, began the process of *Les Demoiselles*'s canonization. But Barr's seminal account, which received its definitive touch in 1951, when his text was revised for the publication of *Picasso: Fifty Years of His Art*, and which became the standard view of the painting, consolidated rather than broke down the walls of resistance that had encircled the work since its inception. Barr's view was not • fundamentally challenged until Leo Steinberg's (born 1920) groundbreaking essay "The Philosophical Brothel" appeared in 1972. No previous text had done as much to transform the status of *Les Demoiselles*, and all subsequent studies are appendages to it.

A "transitional picture"?

Before the publication of Steinberg's study, the consensus was that *Les Demoiselles* was the "first Cubist painting" (and thus, as Barr puts it, a "transitional picture," perhaps more important for what it

▲ 1911, 1912 ▲ 1927c ● 1960b

1 • Pablo Picasso, *Les Demoiselles d'Avignon*, June–July 1907
Oil on canvas, 243.8 x 233.7 (80 x 78)

announced than as a work in itself). Barr had ignored the corollary of this notion in Kahnweiler's account, namely that the picture had been left unfinished, but this idea was nevertheless accepted by everyone else, and most authors marked it by criticizing the picture's "lack of unity." The stylistic discrepancy between the canvas's left and right sides was seen as a function of Picasso's rapid shift of interest from the archaic Iberian sculpture that had helped him finish his *Portrait of Gertrude Stein* [**2**] in the late summer of 1906 to African art, which he had finally encountered with a new impact and coherence during a visit to the Musée d'Ethnographie du Trocadéro midway through the elaboration of *Les Demoiselles.* The quest for sources did not stop there: Barr had named Cézanne, Matisse, and El Greco; others would add Gauguin, Ingres, and Manet.

Though Barr had published three of Picasso's preliminary studies for *Les Demoiselles,* he had merely paid lip service to them and no attention at all to the many others already made available in

2 • Pablo Picasso, *Portrait of Gertrude Stein*, late summer 1906
Oil on canvas, 100 x 81.3 (39⅜ x 32)

Gertrude Stein (1874–1946)

The youngest child of an upper-middle-class, American-Jewish family, the writer Gertrude Stein spent her first years in Europe, her youth in Oakland, and her university time at Harvard and The Johns Hopkins Medical School, before joining her older brother Leo in Paris in the winter of 1904–5. Buying Matisse's *The Woman with a Hat* from the 1905 Salon des Indépendants, she and Leo began avidly to collect advanced painting and to entertain artists and writers at their home on the rue de Fleurus. Deeply influenced by her sense of modernist composition, which, following her understanding of Cézanne, she saw as creating a uniform emphasis, without internal hierarchy, center, or "frame," she determined to capture the "object as object" with each aspect of it equally compelling and alive: "Always and always, Must write the hymn of repetition." Between 1906 and 1911, corresponding to the development of Cubism, she put this formal principle to work in her massive novel *The Making of Americans*. By 1910, Leo had turned against Picasso and his Cubist "funny business," and by 1913 he had separated his half of their collection to move to Florence. Gertrude continued to live on the rue de Fleurus with her lifelong companion Alice B. Toklas. Her accounts of her special friendship with Picasso are found in *Matisse, Picasso and Gertrude Stein* (1933), *Picasso* (1938), and *The Autobiography of Alice B. Toklas* (1933).

Christian Zervos's *catalogue raisonné* of Picasso's work, then in progress. In its early state, the composition consisted of seven figures in a theatrical arrangement derived from the Baroque tradition, replete with the usual curtains opening onto a stage [**3**]. In the center, a clothed sailor was seated among five prostitutes, each of whom was turning her head toward an intruder, a medical student entering at the left holding a skull in his hand (replaced by a book in some studies). For Barr, this morbid scenario, which he saw as "a kind of *memento mori* [reminder of death] allegory or charade" on the wages of sin, could be all the more easily dispensed with since Picasso himself had quickly dropped it. In the final version, Barr wrote, "all implications of a moralistic contrast between virtue (the man with the skull) and vice (the man surrounded by food and woman) have been eliminated in favour of a purely formal figure composition, which as it develops becomes more and more dehumanized and abstract."

In his essay, Steinberg dismissed most of these views, which by then had turned into clichés. The picture could not be reduced to a "purely formal figure composition" that would make it (according to the rather unsophisticated view offered of Cubism at the time) a mere forerunner of things to come. Picasso had indeed abandoned the "*memento mori* allegory," but not the sexual thematics of the painting (which is undoubtedly why Steinberg borrowed as the title of his piece one of the first names given to the picture by Picasso's friends, "Le Bordel philosophique" [The Philosophical Brothel]). Furthermore, *Les Demoiselles*'s lack of stylistic unity was not an effect of haste but a deliberate strategy: it was a late decision, to be sure, but in keeping with the elimination of the two male figures and the adoption of an almost square, vertical format, less "scenic" than that of all the studies for the general composition of ▲ the picture. And the primitivizing appeal to African art was not just happenstance (Picasso had been introduced to African art by Matisse in 1906 [**4**], months before his decision to shift the mask-like faces of the two *demoiselles* on the right from an "Iberian" to an "African" model [**5**]): it shared in the thematic organization of the painting, even if Picasso later denied its significance.

Rejecting Barr's "*memento mori*," Steinberg changed the terms of the allegory put aside by Picasso from those of "death versus hedonism" to those of "cool, detached learning versus the demands of sex." Both the book and the skull present in Picasso's studies indicate that the medical student is the one who does not participate; he does not even look at the *demoiselles*. As for the timid sailor, he is there to be initiated by the fearsome females. His androgyny in many sketches sharply contrasts with his phallic attribute: the *porron* (a wine flask with an erect spout) on the table. Soon the sailor disappeared and the student underwent a gender switch. In the completed canvas he is replaced by the standing nude opening the curtain on the left. Conversely, the bodies of several

▲ 1903

Below left
4 • Photograph of Picasso in his studio in the Bateau-Lavoir, Paris, 1908

Below
5 • Pablo Picasso, *Study for the Head of the Crouching Demoiselle*, June–July 1907
Gouache on paper, 63 x 48 (24⅘ x 18⅞)

3 • Pablo Picasso, *Medical Student, Sailor, and Five Nudes in a Bordello* (composition study for *Les Demoiselles d'Avignon*), March–April 1907. Crayon drawing, 47.6 x 76.2 (18¾ x 30)

demoiselles were masculine in many drawings. There is enough cumulative evidence, then, to determine that while he was working on the picture Picasso's thematic concern revolved around the primordial question of sexual difference, and that of the fear of sex. So his problem seems to have been how to hold onto this theme while relinquishing the allegory.

This is where the stylistic disjunction of the final canvas comes into play, and not only that but also the utter isolation of the five prostitutes vis-à-vis one another, and the suppression of clear spatial coordinates. (On close inspection, the discrepancies are even stronger than Barr had noted, and they do not concern only the right-hand "African" side of the picture: the hand of the standing *demoiselle* who replaced the student at the far left seems severed from her body, and the sketchbooks reveal, as Steinberg notes, that her immediate neighbor, most often read as standing, is in fact lying down even though she has been verticalized and made parallel to the picture's surface.) Whereas in the first scenario the characters react to the student's entrance and the spectator looks on from outside, in the finished painting "this rule of traditional narrative art yields to an anti-narrative counter-principle: neighboring figures share neither a common space nor a common action, do not communicate or interact, but relate singly, directly, to the spectator.... The event, the epiphany, the sudden entrance, is still the theme—but rotated through 90 degrees towards a viewer conceived as the picture's opposite pole." In other words, it is the work's lack of stylistic and scenic unity that binds the painting to the spectator: the core of the picture is the frightful gaze of the *demoiselles*, particularly those with the deliberately monstrous faces on the right. Their "Africanism," according to the ideology of the time that made Africa the "dark continent," is a device designed to fend off the beholder. (An old word derived from the Greek and meaning "having the power to avert evil" describes the intimidating glare of Picasso's nudes particularly well: it is *apotropaïc*.) The picture's complex structure, as William Rubin showed in the longest study ever devoted to the work (which emphasized Picasso's deep-seated death anxiety), concerns the link that ties Eros to Thanatos, that is, sex to death.

The trauma of the gaze

▲ We are now moving into Freudian territory, a fairly recent step in the literature devoted to the painting. Several psychoanalytic scenarios dealing with the "primal scene" and the "castration complex" apply amazingly well to *Les Demoiselles d'Avignon*. They help us understand both the suppression of the allegory and the brutality of the finished picture. One thinks, here, either of the remembered childhood dream of Freud's most famous patient, Sergei Pankejeff (1887–1979)—the "Wolf-Man" **[6]**—in which the boy found himself petrified as his window opened and he was stared at by motionless wolves (the dream being the aftereffect of the shock of the primal scene [his witnessing parental intercourse])—or of Freud's short text on the head of the Medusa, with all its multitude of meanings. These include the notion that the Medusa's head is the female sex organ—the sight of which arouses castration anxiety in the young male; the image of castration itself (decapitation); and the denial of castration, on the one hand by a multiplication of penises (her hair consists of snakes) and, on the other, by its power to turn the spectator to stone, in other words, into an erect, albeit dead, phallus.

In front of Picasso's painting, too, the beholder is nailed to the floor by the whores who address him more violently, as Steinberg points out, than by any picture since Velázquez's *Las Meninas*. In switching from the "narrative" (allegory) to the "iconic" mode, to use the terms employed by Rubin, that is, from the historical tone of stories ("Once upon a time") to the personal threat ("Look at me; I'm watching you"), Picasso both revealed the fixity of the viewer's position as established by the monocular perspective on which Western painting had been based and, by recasting it as petrification, demonized it. The undiminished power of *Les Demoiselles d'Avignon* lies in this very operation, called the "return of the repressed": in it, Picasso highlighted the contradictory libidinal forces at work in the very act of beholding, making of his whole picture the Medusa's head. Bordello pictures are part of a long tradition within the genre of erotic art (a tradition that Picasso knew well: he had long admired Degas's monotypes and for years had yearned to collect them—a dream he could fulfill only late in life). These soft-porn scenes are meant to gratify the voyeurism of male, heterosexual, art lovers. Picasso overthrows this tradition: interrupting the story, the gaze of his *demoiselles* challenges the (male) spectator by signifying to him that his comfortable position, outside the narrative scene, is not as secure as he might think. No wonder the painting was resisted for so long.

One of its early adversaries no doubt understood, at least partially, what was going on. Matisse was furious when he saw the painting (some accounts say he was in stitches, but this amounts to

6 • Sergei C. Pankejeff's sketch of his remembered childhood dream (c. 1910), published in Sigmund Freud's "From the History of an Infantile Neurosis," 1918

▲ Introduction 1, 1900a

7 • Pablo Picasso, *Three Women*, 1908
Oil on canvas, 200 x 178 (78¾ x 70⅛)

the same thing). He was a bit like Poussin saying of Caravaggio (to whom we owe the best representation of Medusa's head, and who was criticized in his time for being unable to "compose a real story") that he had been "born to destroy painting." Undoubtedly, rivalry was a sting that sharpened Matisse's perception (just as it had stimulated Picasso's), for just a year and a half earlier Matisse ▲ had completed his breakthrough canvas *Le Bonheur de vivre*, whose thematic is in many ways very close to that of Picasso's picture (one detects in it the same conflictual imagery revolving around the castration complex). Matisse knew that this canvas (which Picasso saw every time he went to dinner at the house of Gertrude and Leo Stein) had strongly impressed the younger artist, notably for its syncretic cannibalizing of a whole array of historical sources. For Picasso, one of the most devastating challenges must have been the forceful way in which Matisse had co-opted Ingres's *The Turkish Bath*, which had struck both artists at the 1905 Salon d'Automne: how tame was the Ingrisme of his own Rose period, by comparison, particularly of *The Harem*, painted in Gosol in the summer of 1906, just a few months before he tackled *Les Demoiselles d'Avignon* and only a few weeks before he "painted in" the face of Gertrude Stein's portrait! Meanwhile, Matisse had also thrown in another challenge: shortly after introducing Picasso to African art he had • painted his *Blue Nude*, the first canvas ever to de-aestheticize the traditional motif of the female nude explicitly by way of "primitivism." And now Picasso was combining both acts of parricide against the Western tradition: juxtaposing contradictory sources into a medley that annulled their decorum and their historical significance, and at the same time borrowing from other cultures. In both *Le Bonheur de vivre* and *Les Demoiselles d'Avignon*, the parricide was astutely linked to an Oedipal thematics, but Picasso, in focusing his attack on the very condition of beholding, had carried the struggle against mimesis much further.

The crisis of representation

We can now return to the standard, pre-Steinberg assumption that *Les Demoiselles* was the "first" Cubist painting. While certainly wrong if one reads early Cubism as a kind of geometric stylization of volumes, this assumption makes sense if Cubism is understood as a radical questioning of the rules of representation. In grafting an Iberian masklike face onto the bust of Gertrude Stein, in conceiving of a face as a given sign that could be borrowed from a vast repertory, Picasso had called the illusionistic conventions of depiction into question. But in *Les Demoiselles* he pushed the idea that signs are migratory and combinatory, and that their signification depends upon their context, even further, though he did not fully explore it. This would be the work of Cubism as a whole, whose origin can then be located in *Three Women* of 1908 [**7**], in which Picasso strove to display a single signlike unit (the triangle) for every element of the painting, whatever it was supposed to depict. But several studies for the face of the crouching *demoiselle* at the lower right—the site of the most startling attack on the very idea of beauty in relation to woman—reveal that he had sensed the endless metaphoric possibilities of the sign system he was inventing: in these studies, we can see that face is in the process of being transformed into a torso [**5**]. Yet these amorphic experiments were put aside and one had to wait for Picasso's second examination ▲ of African art in his collages, in 1912, for the full implication of his semiological impulse to be reached. Thus *Les Demoiselles d'Avignon* was a traumatic event; and its profound effect was deferred for Picasso as well: it took him the whole adventure of Cubism to be able to account for what he had done.

FURTHER READING

William Rubin, "From 'Narrative' to 'Iconic' in Picasso: The Buried Allegory in *Bread and Fruitdish on a Table* and the Role of *Les Demoiselles d'Avignon*," *The Art Bulletin*, vol. 65, no. 4, December 1983

William Rubin, "The Genesis of *Les Demoiselles d'Avignon*," *Studies in Modern Art* (special *Les Demoiselles d'Avignon* issue), Museum of Modern Art, New York, no. 3, 1994 (chronology by Judith Cousins and Hélène Seckel, critical anthology of early commentaries by Hélène Seckel)

Hélène Seckel (ed.), *Les Demoiselles d'Avignon*, two volumes (Paris: Réunion des Musées Nationaux, 1988)

Leo Steinberg, "The Philosophical Brothel" (1972), second edition *October*, no. 44, Spring 1988

▲ 1906 • 1903 ▲ 1912

1908

Wilhelm Worringer publishes *Abstraction and Empathy*, which contrasts abstract art with representational art as a withdrawal from the world versus an engagement with it: German Expressionism and English Vorticism elaborate this psychological polarity in distinctive ways.

"I caught a strange thought," the German Expressionist Franz Marc (1880–1916) wrote from the front during World War I (where he would soon be killed), "it had settled on my open hand like a butterfly—the thought that people once before, a long time ago, like alter egos, loved abstractions as we do now. Many an object hidden away in our museums of anthropology looks at us with strangely disturbing eyes. What made them possible, these products of a sheer will to abstraction?" However strange, this thought was not entirely new: Marc echoes French poet Charles Baudelaire on poetic "correspondences," and the notions of an affinity between abstract arts, of the tribal artist as alter ego of the modern artist, and of a primordial will to abstraction are all in keeping with a dissertation written in 1908 by the German art historian Wilhelm Worringer (1881–1965). The connection is not accidental, as another letter from Marc makes clear. In early 1912 he wrote his Russian colleague Wassily Kandinsky (1866–1944), with whom he had founded the association of artists Der Blaue Reiter (The Blue Rider) in Munich in 1911: "I am just reading Worringer's *Abstraktion und Einfühlung* [Abstraction and Empathy], a good mind, whom we need very much. Marvelously disciplined thinking, concise and cool, extremely cool."

Worringer was not an unambiguous advocate of the German Expressionists. When they were attacked by a jingoistic antimodernist in 1911, he defended them as harbingers of a new age marked by an embrace of elemental forms, an interest in tribal art, and, above all, a rejection of the "rationalized sight" that he deemed too dominant from the Renaissance through neo-Impressionist painting. Otherwise Worringer left the terms of his affiliation vague; for example, in a 1910 foreword to *Abstraction and Empathy*, he noted only a "parallelism" with "the new goals of expression." However, this parallelism did point to an "inner necessity" in the age, and this metaphysical bent was shared by the Blaue Reiter artists, who often wrote of their art in terms of a "spiritual awakening." This was most evident in the *Blaue Reiter Almanach* that Marc and Kandinsky published in 1912 with a cover image of a blue rider by Kandinsky inspired by folk images of Saint George [**1**]. Apart from Expressionist work, this influential collection of essays and illustrations featured tribal art from the Pacific Northwest, Oceania, and Africa, the art of children, Egyptian puppets, Japanese masks and prints, medieval German sculpture and woodcuts, Russian folk art, and Bavarian devotional glass paintings. Kandinsky was especially drawn to the latter two forms, while his partner, Gabrielle Münter (1877–1962), was strongly attracted to the art of children, the emotive immediacy of which she sought to convey in her own painting.

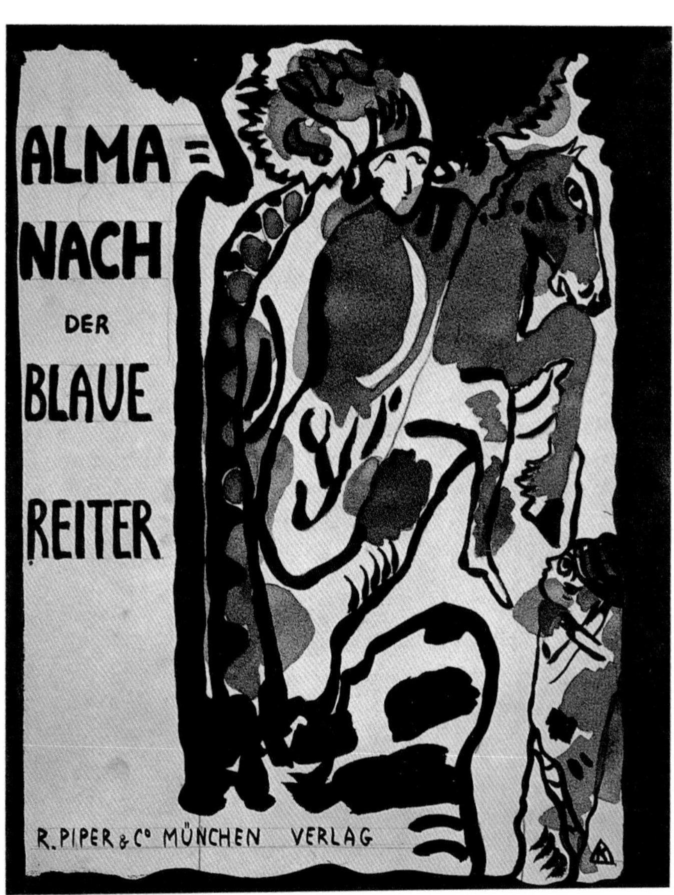

1 • Wassily Kandinsky, final study for the cover of the *Blaue Reiter Almanach*, 1911
Watercolor, india ink and pencil, 27.6 x 21.9 (10⅞ x 8⅝)

A metaphysical approach to art was also practiced by Die Brücke (The Bridge), the other primary group of German Expressionists. ▲ Headed by Ernst Ludwig Kirchner, it was founded in Dresden in 1905, included Fritz Beyl (1880–1966), Erich Heckel, and Karl Schmitt-Rottluff (1884–1976), all of whom were once architectural students, and was disbanded in Berlin eight years later. The metaphysical bent is clear from the names of the two groups:

▲ 1903

the Blaue Reiter was titled after a traditional figure of Christian revelation ("one stands before the new works as in a dream," Marc wrote in a prospectus for the *Almanach*, "and hears the horsemen of the Apocalypse"), while Die Brücke derived its name from Friedrich Nietzsche, who stated in *Thus Spoke Zarathustra* (1883–92) that "man is a rope, fastened between animal and Superman—a rope over an abyss ... he is a bridge and not an end." German Expressionism echoed the metaphysical concerns of *Abstraction and Empathy* in other ways too. Like Worringer, Marc expressed the natural world as a place of primal flux, while Kirchner expressed the urban world as a place of primitive vitality. However, this very insistence on *expression* did not fully correspond with the Worringerian conception of abstraction.

Opposed styles

Abstraction and Empathy develops two notions—*Einfühlung* or "empathy," derived from the German psychologist and philosopher Theodor Lipps (1851–1914), and *Kunstwollen* or "artistic will," derived from the Viennese art historian Alois Riegl—in order to relate different artistic styles to different "psychic states." Across history and culture, Worringer argues, two opposed styles—naturalistic representation and geometric abstraction—have expressed two opposed attitudes—an empathic engagement with the world and a shocked withdrawal from it. "Whereas the precondition for the urge to empathy is a happy pantheistic relationship of confidence between man and the phenomena of the external world," Worringer writes, "the urge to abstraction is the outcome of a great inner unrest inspired in man by the phenomena of the outside world ... We might describe this state as an immense spiritual dread of space." This condition of dread before nature (Worringer was influenced here by Georg Simmel [1858–1918], the great German sociologist of alienation) is very different from the state of intimacy with nature that Gauguin, for example, pro- ▲ jected onto the primitive. According to Worringer, primitive man sees nature as a hostile chaos: "dominated by an immense need for tranquility," the tribal artist turns to abstraction as "a refuge from appearances." This notion led Worringer to construct a problematic hierarchy of culture (as outlined in *Form in Gothic* [1910], his sequel to *Abstraction and Empathy*), with the primitive at the bottom. The modern, however, was not placed at the top: on the contrary, "slipped down from the pride of knowledge, [modern] man is now just as lost and helpless vis-à-vis the world-picture as primitive man." As a consequence, according to Worringer, the modern artist also struggles to arrest and separate the flux of phenomena, to abstract and preserve the stability of forms: driven once more by "inner unrest" and "spatial dread," he too turns to abstraction. This account is very different from later celebrations of abstract art, the triumphal humanism of which Worringer challenges before the fact.

But does this account of abstraction really suit the Blaue Reiter, as Marc and Kandinsky **[2]** hoped it might? It might be more relevant to Die Brücke, for it could be argued that Kirchner and colleagues used abstract elements—unreal colors, uneasy perspec-

2 • Wassily Kandinsky, *With Three Riders*, 1911
Ink and watercolor on paper, 25 x 32 (9⅞ x 12⅝)

▲ 1903

tives—in order to register "inner unrest" and "spiritual dread." Like Worringer, Kirchner often pictured modernity as primitive, not only in the figure of the primitive prostitute that he inherited ▲ from Manet and Gauguin by way of Matisse and Picasso, but also in the streets of the modern city where, for observers such as Simmel, the prostitute was only emblematic of a general regression. Just as, according to Worringer, the natural world appeared chaotic to primitives, so, too, according to Kirchner, did the urban world appear chaotic to moderns (German industrialization was fast and furious during the first two decades of the century). In *The Street, Dresden* [**3**], Kirchner evokes Dresden as a vital but nervous confrontation: huddled masses border the picture and block its expanse, while several figures, mostly women with faces that resemble masks, bear down on us (the little girl here is especially bizarre). With its distorted space and lurid orange-red, the picture is tinged with the anxiety often associated with the painting of Edvard Munch, the Norwegian forerunner of the Expressionists. At the same time the figures also suggest the "blasé attitude" that Simmel ascribed to "the mental life" of the modern city. "The metropolitan type," Simmel argued in a famous essay of 1903, "develops an organ protecting him against the threatening currents and discrepancies of his external environment." *The Street* might evoke such a current in the electric line that courses around the figures and through the avenue in orange, green, and blue. Part nervous stimulation, part protective shield, this line isolates these urban dwellers even as it also connects them: it suggests a paradoxical kind of alienation that unites. This effect becomes more extreme in "The Street" paintings that Kirchner produced in Berlin after his move there, with other Die Brücke members, in 1911: the colors of these pictures are more acrid, the perspectives are more • perverse (he adapted Cubism and Futurism for this effect), and the figures (often prostitutes and clients) are more anxious-blasé. If there is a new kind of modern beauty here, as art historian Charles Haxthausen has argued, it is also, at least in part, a terrible beauty.

Again, for Worringer, abstraction served to ease the stimulation provoked by the chaos of the world. Kirchner, on the other hand, approached abstraction in order to register this stimulation, indeed to heighten it. The abstraction of the Blaue Reiter is different again: Marc moved toward abstraction in pursuit of a connection with the natural world, while Kandinsky did so in search of a communion with the spiritual realm. For both artists, the isolation of human beings was a problem to overcome, not a condition to deepen. "We search," Kandinsky wrote in 1909, "for artistic forms that reveal the penetration of these collected forces." Rather than abstraction *versus* empathy, then, the Blaue Reiter proposed an aesthetic of abstraction *as* empathy—empathy with nature and/or spirit. (In this respect they were in line with the "abstract empathy" already suggested in the *Jugendstil* or Art Nouveau style in Munich that influenced Kandinsky.) The Blaue Reiter artists sought an equation of feeling and form, a reconciliation between "inner necessity" and outer world; Kandinsky insisted that the very "contents" of his art are "what the spectator *lives* or

3 • Ernst Ludwig Kirchner, *The Street, Dresden*, 1908
Oil on canvas, 150.5 x 200 (59¼ x 78⅞)

feels while under the effect of the *form and color combinations* of the picture." And this is one reason why they took music, which featured prominently in the *Almanach*, as an aesthetic paragon. Again, this was not to reverse the Worringerian poles of abstraction and empathy but to force them together: as Kandinsky states in the *Almanach*, "Realism = Abstraction; Abstraction = Realism."

Pantheistic penetration

If Kandinsky aspired to a transcendental world of spirit, Marc delved into the immanent world of nature. Guided at first by Gauguin, Marc defined his project in 1910 as "a pantheistic penetration into the pulsating flow of blood in nature, in trees, in animals, in the atmosphere." To trace this flow he elaborated two kinds of drawing: first, a fluent, organic, and airy line influenced by Matisse and Kandinsky; then, a more constricted, geometric, and anxious line ▲ influenced by Picasso and Robert Delaunay (like Kirchner, Marc adapted Cubism to his own ends). Marc also devised a color symbolism to modulate the moods of this flow: blue was "severe" and "spiritual"; yellow, "gentle" and "sensual"; red, "brutal" and "heavy." Although this intuitive system was gendered reductively (blue as masculine, yellow as feminine), it led Marc, in the few years left to him, to produce a number of animal paintings that are among the finest in the Western tradition. Finally, however, these pictures do not convey an "animalization of art" (Marc) so much as a humanization of nature: less than empathic communion with nature, they suggest an expressive projection on the part of the artist. In 1853 the English aesthetician John Ruskin critiqued this projection as "the pathetic fallacy"; some time after 1913 Marc also came to question it:

> *Is there a more mysterious idea for an artist than to imagine how nature is reflected in the eyes of an animal? How does a horse see the world, how does an eagle, a doe, or a dog?... Who says the doe feels the world to be Cubistic? It's the doe that feels, therefore*

▲ 1903, 1907 • 1909, 1911 ▲ 1913

the landscape must be "doelike." The artistic logic of Picasso, Kandinsky, Delaunay, Burliuk [a Russian associate of the Blaue Reiter], etc., is perfect. They don't "see" the doe and they don't care. They project their inner world—which is the noun of the sentence. Naturalism contributes the object. The predicate ... is rendered but rarely.

Rather than an imposed expression, Marc sought an empathic abstraction that might resolve self and other pictorially. No doubt this is an impossible ideal, but a painting such as *The Fate of Animals* **[4]** does evoke one kind of "pantheistic penetration." Here, however, the common point between human and animal seems to be pain or agony—even the trees appear to be butchered. Indeed, on the back of the canvas Marc scrawled "and all being is flaming suffering," as if, like urban tension in Kirchner, natural suffering in Marc was the one thing that united all creatures. And yet, the very desperation of this work points to the ultimate *separation* between beings: after all, suffering is singular and solitary in its effects. In his pursuit of empathy, Marc touches its limit: the animal other is revealed as precisely other, inhuman, beyond empathy. This is still not abstraction versus empathy, but it is no longer abstraction as empathy. Empathy has failed, and here abstraction becomes the sign of this limit.

Dehumanization as diagnostic

In the end, the model of abstraction versus empathy might pertain less to German Expressionism than to English Vorticism, a movement—named by the poet-critic Ezra Pound (1885–1972) and directed by the prolific painter-novelist-critic Wyndham Lewis ▲ (1882–1957)—that included the sculptors Jacob Epstein (1880–1959) and Henri Gaudier-Brzeska (1891–1915) and the painter David Bomberg (1890–1957), among others. The connection here to Worringer is not as attenuated as it might seem. In January 1914, the poet-critic T. E. Hulme (1883–1917), an associate of the Vorticists, delivered a lecture in London on "Modern Art and its Philosophy" that adapted *Abstraction and Empathy* toward an advocacy of Vorticism. Here Hulme—who, like Gaudier-Brzeska and Marc, would soon die in the war that effectively ended both Vorticism and Expressionism—divided modern art into two

4 • Franz Marc, *The Fate of the Animals*, 1913
Oil on canvas, 194.3 x 261.6 (76½ x 103)

▲ 1934b

opposed styles—the organic (his version of the empathic) and the geometric (his version of the abstract). Like Worringer, he then argued that these styles correspond to two opposed "attitudes"—an "insipid optimism," dominant since the Renaissance, that placed man at the center of nature, and a steely antihumanism, emergent in Vorticist art, that valued "a feeling of separation in the face of outside nature."

"What he said," Lewis remarked of Hulme, "I *did*"—though, again, it was Worringer who set the aesthetic terms for both men. In "The New Egos," a text published in *Blast* (1914), his vitriolic journal of Vorticism, Lewis presented his own Worringerian parable. It concerns two complementary figures, "a civilized savage" and a "modern town-dweller"; neither is "secure" as both live in a "vagueness of space." Yet the civilized savage is able to ease his insecurity with an art of the figure abstracted to a "simple black human bullet," whereas the modern town-dweller only senses that "the old form of egotism is no longer fit for such conditions as now prevail." Lewis concludes his parable with a Worringerian credo: "All clean, clear-cut emotions depend on the element of strangeness, and surprise, and primitive detachment. Dehumanization is the chief diagnostic of the World." The Expressionists agreed with this diagnosis, but Lewis saw dehumanization as a solution as much as a problem: if the modern age is to survive its own dehumanization, it must dehumanize further; it must take "strangeness, and surprise, and primitive detachment" to the limit.

Lewis rarely forgoes the human figure altogether. His early "designs" often manifest a tension between figure and surround, as if the body, never secure, were caught between definition, about to break free as an autonomous form, and dispersal, about to be invaded by space. Slowly, however, Lewis abstracts the figure, as if to harden it into a "simple black human bullet." Sometimes this hardening appears to come from without—outside in—as in *The Vorticist* (1912), in which the body seems to be shocked into abstraction by a hostile world. Sometimes it appears to come from within—inside out—as in *Vorticist Design* (c. 1914), in which the body seems to be driven to abstraction by some innate will. In one especially concentrated figure, *The Enemy of the Stars* [**5**], the two kinds of armorings appear to converge. On the one hand, with a head like a receiver, the figure looks reified from without, its skin turned into a shield; on the other hand, stripped of organs and arms, it also looks reified from within, its bone structure turned into a "few abstract mechanical relations" (as Hulme once remarked of these figures). In either case, this "enemy of the stars" is the opposite of the Blue Rider whom Kandinsky evokes on an ascent toward the heavens: here Lewis suggests an abstraction of the figure that is indeed antiempathic.

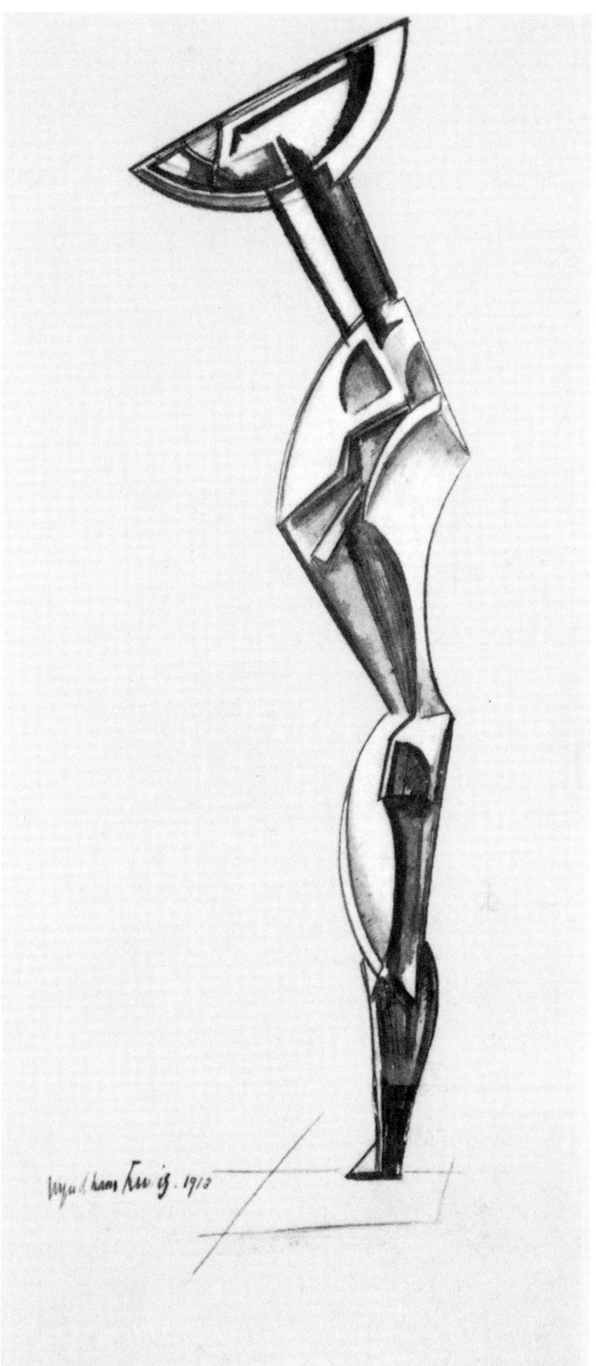

5 • Wyndham Lewis, *The Enemy of the Stars*, 1913
Pen and ink, ink wash, 44 x 20 (17¼ x 7⅞)

FURTHER READING

Charles W. Haxthausen (ed.), *Berlin: Culture and Metropolis* (Minneapolis: University of Minnesota Press, 1990)

T. E. Hulme, *Speculations: Essays on Humanism and the Philosophy of Art*, ed. Herbert Read (London: Routledge & Kegan Paul, 1987 [first published 1924])

Fredric Jameson, *Fables of Aggression: Wyndham Lewis, the Modernist as Fascist* (Berkeley and Los Angeles: University of California Press, 1979)

Wassily Kandinsky and Franz Marc (eds), *The Blaue Reiter Almanac* (London: Thames & Hudson, 1974)

Jill Lloyd, *German Expressionism: Primitivism and Modernity* (New Haven and London: Yale University Press, 1991)

Rose-Carol Washton Long (ed.), *German Expressionism: Documents from the End of the Wilhelmine Empire to the Rise of the National Socialism* (Berkeley and Los Angeles: University of California Press, 1995)

Wilhelm Worringer, *Abstraction and Empathy*, trans. Michael Bullock (Cleveland: Meridian Books, 1967)

1909

F. T. Marinetti publishes the first Futurist manifesto on the front page of *Le Figaro* in Paris: for the first time the avant-garde associates itself with media culture and positions itself in defiance of history and tradition.

On February 20, 1909, Filippo Tommaso Marinetti (1876–1944) published his "Manifeste de fondation du Futurisme," the first Futurist manifesto, on the front page of the French newspaper *Le Figaro* [**1**]. This event signaled the public arrival of Futurism, and pointed in multiple ways to its specific project.

First of all, it showed that, from its very outset, Futurism wished to establish the avant-garde's liaison with mass culture. Second, it demonstrated a conviction that all techniques and strategies operative in mass-cultural production would henceforth be essential for the propagation of avant-garde practices as well; the mere decision to publish the manifesto in the widest-circulation newspaper in France demonstrated the triple embrace of advertising, journalism, and forms of mass distribution. Third, it indicated that, from its initial stages, Futurism was committed to a fusion of artistic practices with advanced forms of technology in a way that Cubism, ▲ while confronting this question in the development of collage, would never wholly embrace. The slogans of Futurism that celebrated "congenital dynamism," "the break-up of the object," and "light as a destroyer of forms," while also lauding the mechanical, famously declared that a speeding automobile is "more beautiful than the Victory of Samothrace": this was to prefer the industrialized object to the unique rarity of the cult statue. And last, although not yet visible in 1909, it prepared the way for Futurism to overturn traditional assumptions about the avant-garde's innate tendency toward, and association with, progressivist, leftist—if not Marxist—politics. For Futurism was to become, in Italy in 1919, the first avant-garde movement of the twentieth century to have its own political and ideological project assimilated into the formation of fascist ideology.

From backwater to frontrunner

In terms of its artists' models, the background of Futurism is complex. Its sources are to be found in nineteenth-century French Symbolism, in French neo-Impressionist or divisionist painting, • and in early-twentieth-century Cubism, which was evolving contemporaneously with Futurism and was clearly known to the majority of the artists in the Italian movement. What was specifically Italian in Futurism's formation, however, was the very belatedness of this modernist avant-garde. Thus, at the moment of the manifesto's first publication, the key figures of Futurist painting, such as Umberto Boccioni (1882–1916), Giacomo Balla (1871–1958), and Carlo Carrà (1881–1966), were still working in the rather *retardataire* manner of 1880s divisionism. None of the strategies that had emerged in Paris in the wake of Cézanne's dis- ▲ coveries, or in the development of Fauvism or early Cubism, entered Futurist painting at its earliest moment, that is to say, prior to 1910. Furthermore, Futurism was typified by the eclecticism with which these belatedly discovered avant-garde strategies were adapted. Indeed, the speed with which they were then patched together in order to reformulate a new Futurist pictorial and sculptural aesthetic is indicative of that very eclecticism.

In the wake of Marinetti's manifesto, several other Futurist manifestos followed, written by artists who had joined the group. Among them were *Futurist Painting: Technical Manifesto*, published in 1910 and signed by Boccioni, Balla, Carrà, Luigi Russolo (1885–1947), and Gino Severini (1883–1966); the *Technical Manifesto of Futurist Sculpture*, published in 1912 by Boccioni; *Fotodinamismo futurista*, also published in 1912, by the photographer Anton Giulio Bragaglia; a 1912 manifesto of Futurist music by Ballila Pratella (1880–1955); Russolo's "The Art of Noises" in 1913; and a manifesto of Futurist architecture by Antonio Sant'Elia (1888–1916) in 1914.

As pronounced in these documents, the strategies of Futurism revolved around three central issues. First, there was an emphasis on synesthesia (the breaking down of the boundaries between the different senses, for instance, between sight, sound, and touch) and kinesthesia (the breaking down of the distinction between the body at rest and the body in motion). Second, Futurism tried to construct an analogue between pictorial signification and existing technologies of vision and representation, such as those being developed by photography—particularly in its extended forms, such as chronophotography—and by early cinema. Third, Futurism's rigorous condemnation of the culture of the past, its violent attack on the legacies of bourgeois tradition, organized an equally passionate affirmation of the need to integrate art with advanced technology, even the technology of warfare, opening up the movement to fascism.

▲ 1912 • 1907, 1911 ▲ 1906, 1907

1 • Front page of *Le Figaro*, February 20, 1909

1900–1909

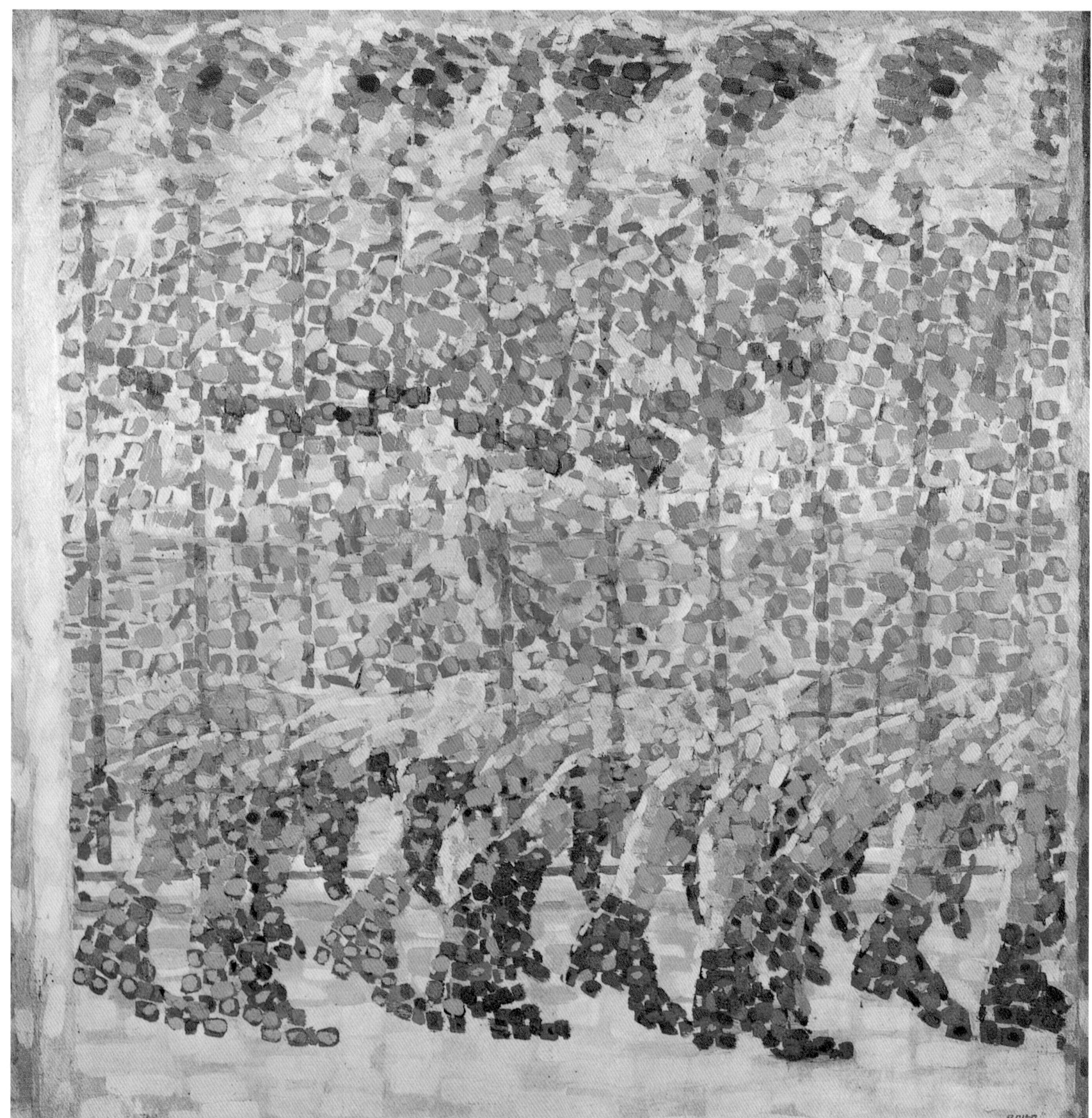

2 • Giacomo Balla, *Girl Running on a Balcony*, 1912
Oil on canvas, 125 x 125 (49¼ x 49¼)

Futurism's stress on synesthesia and kinesthesia followed directly from its critique of the bourgeois aesthetic according to which painting and sculpture were traditionally understood as static arts. It was in contradistinction to this that Futurism strove to incorporate the experience of simultaneity, temporality, and bodily movement within the boundaries of the art object. Such an attempt to make the perception of movement an integral element of the representation of the body in space was informed by Futurism's discovery of the French scientist Étienne-Jules Marey's "chronophotography," an early form of stroboscopic work. Paradoxically, however, it was the literalness with which Balla and Boccioni used a divisionist pictorial idiom to interpret Marey's scientific device that marked their work as strangely delayed and limited, since the very status of the painting as a singular static object was something the Futurist painters never challenged. Further, in trying to adopt chronophotography to their own art, the Futurists bound the pictorial signifier into a purely *mimetic* relationship with the technological field—picturing movement by blurring outlines, for example—rather than into a *structural* one, such as adopting the serial forms of industrial production.

Futures without a past

Balla was undoubtedly the most interesting painter in the movement, even though at the time of the first manifesto in 1909 he was still working in a very traditional way, as he literally applied divisionist methods to the perception of light and public urban space. This is most evident in his painting *Street Light* (1909–10), where the juxtaposition between nature and culture is programmatically stated in the opposition between a street lantern and the moon, and where the dynamism of light waves is executed in a painfully literal manner by swallowlike wedges that surge away from the luminous source, which are transformed chromatically as they move from the iridescence at the picture's center toward the complete absence of chroma at its margins, a representation of darkness and night.

4 • Giacomo Balla, *Dynamism of a Dog on a Leash*, 1912
Oil on canvas, 89.9 x 109.9 (35⅜ x 43¼)

3 • Umberto Boccioni, *Unique Forms of Continuity in Space*, 1913 (1931 cast)
Bronze, 111.2 x 88.5 x 40 (43⅞ x 34⅞ x 15¾)

By 1912 Balla had redefined his pictorial syntax by folding the repetitive contours characteristic of chronophotography into his own representation of objects. Paintings such as *Girl Running on a Balcony* [**2**] or *Dynamism of a Dog on a Leash* [**4**], both from 1912, are significant for the literal way they inscribe the simultaneity of the perception of movement onto the spatial organization of the painting. In 1913, Balla's step to abandon representation altogether in order to find a more adequate way to depict speed, temporality, movement, and visual transformation led to one of the first valid models of nonrepresentational painting. With all figuration deleted, these works were devoted both to the repetition of a structural armature in order to articulate sequence and speed and to a nonrepresentational chromatic idiom that abandoned all references to local color. The compositional and coloristic matrix thus formed no longer participates in what could be called ▲ Cubism's transformation of Renaissance perspective into a new phenomenological space; rather, Balla attempts a transformation of pictorial space into a mechanical, optical, or a temporal space by means of fully nonrepresentational strategies.

Two examples of Boccioni's sculpture clarify the Futurist relationship to the kinesthetic perception of objects in space. The first, *Unique Forms of Continuity in Space* [**3**], in its peculiar ambiguity between a robot and an amphibious figure, once again attempts to incorporate the traces visible in Marey's chronophotography into the sculptural body. Yet, at the same time as it inserts the fluidity of perception into a static representation, it generates the peculiar hybrid between spatial contiguity and the singular, holistic, sculptural object. In Boccioni's *Dynamism of a Speeding Horse and House* [**5**], Futurism's susceptibility to the illusionistic adaptation of motion photography is rejected, however, in favor of a static object in which the effects of simultaneity and kinesthesia are produced by the mere juxtaposition of different materials and the degree of fragmentation to which they are presented. Unlike

▲ 1911

Eadweard Muybridge (1830–1904) and Étienne-Jules Marey (1830–1904)

The Englishman Eadweard Muybridge and the Frenchman Étienne-Jules Marey are yoked in time and by work: not only do they share the same birth and death dates, but also together they pioneered the photographic study of movement in ways that influenced not only the development of Futurist art but also the modern rationalization of labor and, it could be argued, of space–time in general.

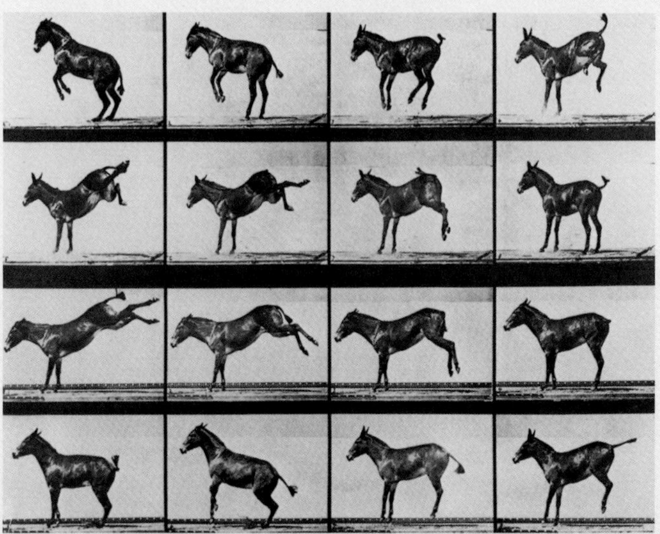

First known as a photographer of American West and Central American landscapes, Muybridge was enlisted in 1872 by Leland Stanford, the millionaire ex-governor of California, in a racing dispute about the gait of horses. In Palo Alto, Muybridge photographed horses with a battery of cameras; typically, he arranged the images in rows and reshot them in a grid that could be scanned both horizontally and vertically. A book, *The Horse in Motion*, which Stanford bowdlerized, appeared in 1882, the same year that Muybridge sailed to Europe for a lecture tour. In Paris he was welcomed by Marey, the famous photographer Nadar, the Salon painter Ernest Meissonier, and the great physiologist Hermann von Helmholtz—some indication of the range of interest in this work that registered perceptual units beyond the limits of human vision.

Unlike Muybridge, who considered himself an artist, Marey was a physiologist by training who had previously worked on graphic methods to record motion. When he first saw work by Muybridge in the science journal *La Nature* in 1878, he turned to photography as a more precise and neutral way to register discrete movement. Marey first devised a photographic gun with a circular plate that yielded near-instantaneous serial photographs from a singular viewpoint. He then used a slotted disk in front of the camera to break up movement in set intervals that could be registered on a single photographic plate; it was this work that he first described as "chronophotography." In order to avoid superimposition, Marey clad his subjects entirely in black, with metal-studded strips along arms and legs (bits of paper were used for animals). Along with the singular viewpoint, this device effectively restored a spatio-temporal coherence to the very perceptual field that was otherwise fragmented. It was more scientific than the Muybridge approach, which did not have a consistent point of view or interval between images, but it was also less radical in its disruption of the apparent continuum of vision.

It was this disruption that most intrigued the modernists—the Futurists in their pursuit of a subversive speed, and artists like Marcel Duchamp in their search for spatio-temporal dimensions not previously perceived. But could it be that, like Muybridge and Marey, these artists were also involved in a historical dialectic that far exceeded their work as individuals—a modern dialectic of a ceaseless renovation of perception, of a perpetual liberating and redisciplining of vision that would persist throughout the twentieth century?

5 • Umberto Boccioni, *Dynamism of a Speeding Horse and House*, 1914–15
Gouache, oil, wood, paste-board, copper, and painted iron, 112.9 x 115 (44½ x 45¼)

Unique Forms of Continuity in Space, which retains the traditional sculptural methods of modeling and bronze-casting, the work incorporates industrially produced materials as called for in Boccioni's own manifesto: leather, found fragments of glass, shards of metal, preformed elements of wood. One of the first fully nonrepresentational sculptures of the twentieth century, it compares most adequately with the abstract sculpture produced in ▲ Russia at that time by Vladimir Tatlin.

Insofar as collage surfaced as the key technique in the contradictory range of Futurism's attempts to fuse avant-garde sensibilities with mass culture, Carrà's *Interventionist Demonstration* **[6]** is a central example of the Futurist aesthetic as it came to a climax just before World War I. Indeed, the work incorporates all of the devices with which Futurism was most engaged: the legacy of divisionist painting; the Cubist fragmentation of traditional perceptual ● space; the insertion of clippings from newspapers and found materials from advertising; the suggestion of kinesthesia through a visual dynamic set up by the collage's construction as both a vortex and a matrix of crisscrossing power lines set as mutually counteractive diagonals; and last, but not least, the juxtaposition of the separate phonetic dimension of language with its graphic signifiers.

Typically enough, the phonetic performance of language in *Interventionist Demonstration* is in almost all instances onomatopoeic. In directly imitating the sounds of sirens (the wail evoked by "HU-HU-HU-HU"), the screeches of engines and machine guns ("TRrrrrrrrr" or "traaak tatatraak"), the screams of people ("EVVIVAAA"), it is distinctly different from the structural analysis of the phonetic, the textual, and the graphic components of language in Russian Cubo-Futurist poetry or the *calligrammes* of ▲ Apollinaire. The juxtaposition of anti-German war slogans ("Down with Austro-Hungary") with found advertising material, or the concatenation of Italian patriotic declarations ("Italia Italia") with musical fragments, continues the technique of Cubist collage but turns this aesthetic into a new model of mass-cultural instigation and propaganda. Its glorification of war is further registered in the drum beats evoked by the words "ZANG TUMB TUUM."

A liberation of language: *parole in libertà*

Zang Tumb Tuum of 1914, the first collection of Marinetti's "free word poetry" was prefaced by his slightly earlier manifesto of Futurist poetry, *Destruction of Syntax—Imagination without Strings—Words-in-Freedom*. Using a set of expressive typographic and orthographic variations and an unstructured spatial organization, *Zang Tumb Tuum* tries to express the sights, sounds, and smells of the poet's experience in Tripoli. This assertion of "words-in-freedom" emerged from a long and complicated dialogue with late-nineteenth-century Symbolist poetry and its early-twentieth-century legacy in France. Although deeply influenced by, and dependent upon, the example of Mallarmé, Marinetti publicly declared his opposition to the French poet's project. Insisting that

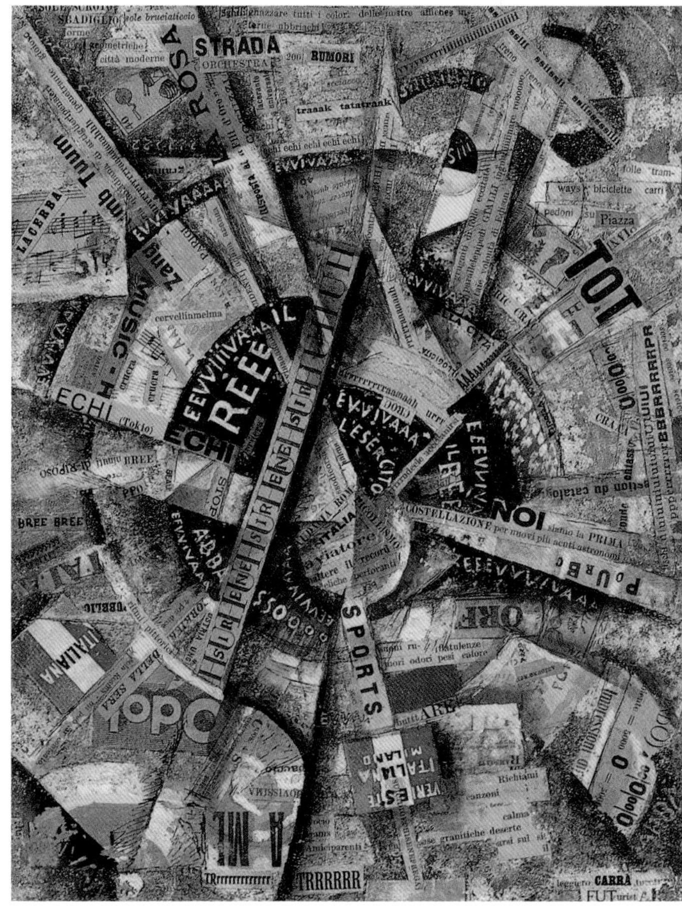

6 • Carlo Carrà, *Interventionist Demonstration*, 1914
Tempera and collage on cardboard, 38.5 x 30 (15⅛ x 11¾)

▲ 1914 ● 1911, 1912 ▲ 1912

words must be liberated from the static and esoteric models of language with which Mallarmé had been engaged, Marinetti promoted a new dynamic of "wireless imagination" intended to assimilate the simultaneity of perception to the new sounds of advertising and technological experience. *Words-in-Freedom* is the programmatic declaration by Marinetti in which all of the traditional fetters to which language had been subjected—lexicality, the production of meaning, syntax, grammar—are supposedly ruptured in favor of a purely phonetic, purely textual, purely graphic performance. But in fact, against Marinetti's will, the mimetic relationship to the technological apparatus binds this model of poetry all the more into the traditional determinants of linguistic representation.

This was the source of one of the conflicts that arose between ▲ Marinetti and the Russian avant-garde when in 1914 the Italian poet went to Moscow in an attempt to proselytize for Futurism. What the Russian Cubo-Futurist poets criticized Marinetti for was the relationship manifested in his work between poetry and the mimetic operations of language, particularly his use of onomatopoeia—the formation of words imitating sounds associated with the act or objects to be denoted. At that time, the Russian Futurists had already moved to a structuralist understanding of the • arbitrary logic of language, which meant that they enforced a strict separation of both the phonetics and the graphics of signs—the way language sounds and the way it looks—from the natural world to which those signs might refer. So insistent were the Russian Futurists on making this separation the subject of their own writing that they carried it to the point of constructing a new anti- ■ semantic and antilexical poetry.

Fascism and Futurism

The rise of fascism in Italy at the end of World War I brought the ideological and political orientation of Futurism into focus. The celebration of technology, the anti-*passatista* (antitraditionalist) position, the rigorous condemnation of the culture of the past, the violent deformation of the legacies of bourgeois culture, were all essential elements of Futurism from its inception. But these were now linked with an equally passionate affirmation of the necessity to integrate art and warfare as the most advanced instance of the technological. If in the first manifesto Marinetti had constructed a myth of origin for the Futurist movement—he recounts the moment of his awakening when, racing in his sports car, he overturned in the muddy waters of a suburban ditch thereupon to emerge, reborn, as a post-Symbolist artist and Futurist poet—this had already announced a deep commitment to the irrationality of violence and power.

Marinetti's espousal of advanced industrial technology and the aesthetic of the machine led him to welcome the outbreak of war as a great purification in line with his overall hatred of tradition and bourgeois cultural subjectivity. As the first avant-gardist to set out deliberately to destroy tradition, Marinetti declared his own war by calling for the destruction of cultural institutions—opera houses, theaters, libraries, museums. In doing so, he positioned Futurist culture at the forefront of a newly emerging rupture between the avant-garde and tradition by organizing the avant-garde as the stage for the annihilation of historical continuity and historical memory. Further, Marinetti's subsequent, postwar attempt to synchronize art and advanced technology with fascist ideology was to be the only occasion in the history of twentieth-century avant-gardes where a link between these elements was positioned explicitly in the perspective of reactionary right-wing politics.

In the embrace of fascism by Marinetti—who unsuccessfully stood for parliament as a Fascist Party candidate in 1919, and who eventually became Mussolini's cultural adviser—one of the key problems facing twentieth-century avant-gardes thus emerged. This is the question of whether avant-garde practices are still to be situated within the bourgeois public sphere or whether they should aim to contribute to the formation of different mass-cultural public spheres, be they fascist public spheres (if there could ever be such a ▲ thing) or proletarian public spheres, the goal of Russian and Soviet • artists working at that time. Alternatively, as in the case of Dada, the avant-garde could rally for the destruction of the bourgeois public sphere, including its institutions and discursive formations.

With the accidental death of Boccioni in 1916, the death in battle of Sant'Elia in the same year, and the radical change in political and aesthetic orientation on the parts of Severini and Carrà around the same time, Futurism lost its way as an avant-garde movement (although Marinetti would continue to pursue a Futurist agenda in art, literature, and politics throughout the twenties and thirties). Severini, living in Paris, abandoned his Cubo-divisionist pictorial strategies in 1916 and adopted pure, classical forms inspired by the ■ art of the Italian Renaissance. By returning to tradition in this way, and by using quattrocento painting as the matrix of *italianità*, he was a harbinger of the later, gradual secession of fascist ideology ◆ from modernist practices. This ideology of the nation state would undertake to connect itself instead to the roots of local cultures, whose origins it would seek to recover.

The encounter between Carrà and Giorgio de Chirico in a military hospital in Ferrara in 1917 triggered a further instance of counterreaction within the avant-garde. Carrà had already become restless under the yoke of Futurism and had written that he no longer cared for "emotional electricians' games." Now, he absorbed de Chirico's attention to form [**7**]. Practically overnight, Carrà abandoned all the Futurist projects with which he had been involved to practice the older man's *pittura metafisica*. In this sense, the discovery of de Chirico has to be recognized as an integral element of Italian avant-garde thinking at that time. Turning to the geometric solidity of "primitivist" painters such as Le Douanier Rousseau and the early Renaissance artists Giotto and Uccello, Carrà spoke of them as the creators of "plastic worlds," or better, "plastic tragedies." His article on Giotto in the newspaper *La Voce* (1915) addressed Giotto as a man devoted to "pure plasticity," the "fourteenth-century visionary" who brought the "magic silence of forms" back to life. Giotto, he wrote, was dedicated to "the original

▲ 1915 • Introduction 3 ■ 1915 ▲ 1921 • 1916a, 1920 ■ 1919 ◆ 1937a

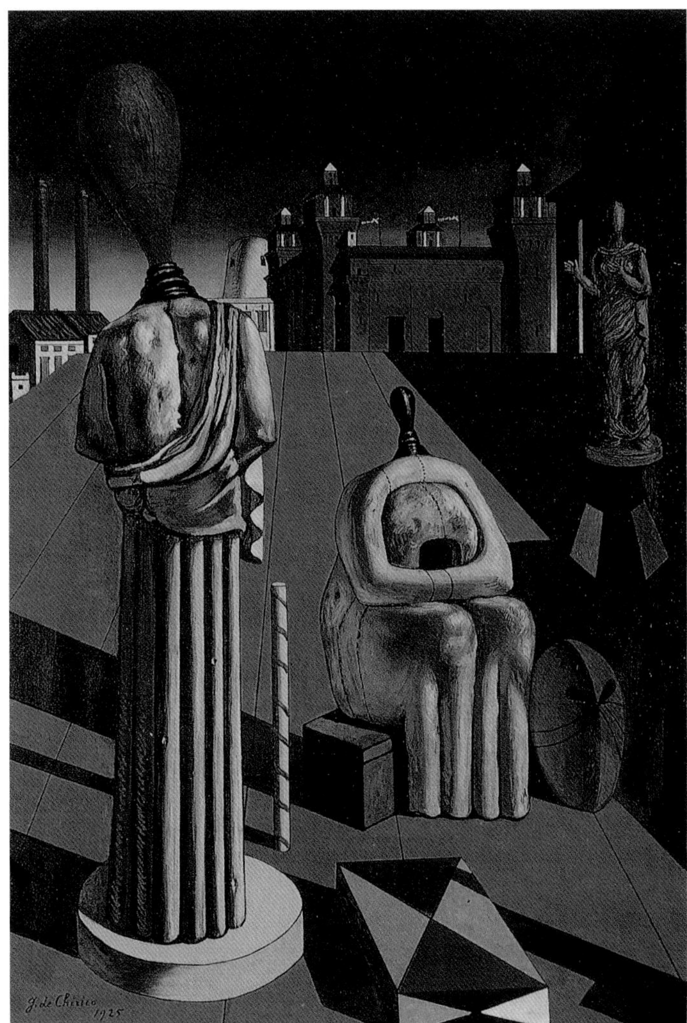

7 • Giorgio de Chirico, *The Disquieting Muses*, 1925
Oil on canvas, 97 x 67 (38¼ x 26½)

8 • Carlo Carrà, *Metaphysical Muse*, 1917
Oil on canvas, 90 x 66 (35⅜ x 26)

solidity of things." Carrà's celebration of formal solidity as the antidote to Futurist disintegration repeats the terms through which modernist painting had originally developed pictorial stability in reaction against a pursuit of the evanescence of light. "We, who feel that we are the nondegenerate offspring of a great race of builders," Carrà wrote in the catalogue of his 1917 exhibition in Milan, "have always sought precise, substantial figures and terms, and the ideal atmosphere without which a painting does not go beyond elaborate technicalism and episodic analysis of external reality." Thus does Carrà reject Impressionism and the Futurist imitation of its effects. In 1918, Carrà theorized the method that he and de Chirico had developed in the essay "Contributo a un nuove arte metafisica."

Carrà's *Metaphysical Muse* [**8**] demonstrates his absorption of de Chirico's visual repertory. On the slanting floorboards of a shallow stage, he places the plaster mannequin of a tennis player, in combination with geometrical solids and painted stage sets of maps and buildings. In fact, all the paintings he showed in the Milan exhibition shared the nocturnal silence of de Chirico's palace courtyards and city squares, interrupted by nothing except long, isolated shadows.

After noise, silence; after the celebration of the mass displacements imposed by war, praise for the patrician sensibilities of tradition. Carrà's and Severini's emergence from the very ranks of Futurism to become key followers of de Chirico was the first and perhaps the most intense example of the antimodernism or countermodernism that subsequently spread throughout Europe in various parallel movements, to which the collective name ▲"*rappel à l'ordre*" was given. Paradoxically, it was within the art of de Chirico and Carrà that the dimension of historical memory so vituperatively prosecuted and eroded within the first four years of Futurist activity returned with a vengeance, to become the central issue within which these artists would continue to operate.

FURTHER READING

Umbro Apollonio (ed.), *Futurist Manifestos* (London: Thames & Hudson, 1973)

Anne Coffin Hanson (ed.), *The Futurist Imagination* (New Haven: Yale University Art Gallery, 1983)

Pontus Hulten (ed.), *Futurism and Futurisms* (New York: Abbeville Press; and London: Thames & Hudson, 1986)

Marianne Martin, *Futurist Art and Theory 1909–1915* (Oxford: Clarendon Press, 1968)

Christine Poggi, *In Defiance of Painting* (New Haven and London: Yale University Press, 1992)

▲ 1919

1910–1919

100 1910 Henri Matisse's *Dance II* and *Music* are condemned at the Salon d'Automne in Paris: in these pictures, Matisse pushes his concept of the "decorative" to an extreme, creating an expansive visual field of color that is difficult to behold. YAB

106 1911 Pablo Picasso returns his "borrowed" Iberian stone heads to the Louvre Museum in Paris from which they had been stolen: he transforms his primitivist style and with Georges Braque begins to develop Analytical Cubism. RK
box • Guillaume Apollinaire RK

112 1912 Cubist collage is invented amid a set of conflicting circumstances and events: the continuing inspiration of Symbolist poetry, the rise of popular culture, and Socialist protests against the war in the Balkans. RK

118 1913 Robert Delaunay exhibits his "Windows" paintings in Berlin: the initial problems and paradigms of abstraction are elaborated across Europe. HF

125 1914 Vladimir Tatlin develops his constructions and Marcel Duchamp proposes his readymades, the first as a transformation of Cubism, the second as a break with it; in doing so, they offer complementary critiques of the traditional mediums of art. HF
box • The "Peau de l'Ours" RK

130 1915 Kazimir Malevich shows his Suprematist canvases at the "0.10" exhibition in Petrograd, thus bringing the Russian Formalist concepts of art and literature into alignment. YAB

135 1916a In Zurich, the international movement of Dada is launched in a double reaction to the catastrophe of World War I and the provocations of Futurism and Expressionism. HF/RK
box • Dada journals RK

142 1916b Paul Strand enters the pages of Alfred Stieglitz's magazine *Camera Work*: the American avant-garde forms itself around a complex relationship between photography and the other arts. RK
box • The Armory Show RK

148 1917 After two years of intense research, Piet Mondrian breaks through to abstraction, an event immediately followed by the launching of *De Stijl*, the earliest avant-garde journal devoted to the cause of abstraction in art and architecture. YAB

154 1918 Marcel Duchamp paints *Tu m'*: his last ever painting summarizes the departures undertaken in his work, such as the use of chance, the promotion of the readymade, and photography's status as an "index." RK
box • Rrose Sélavy RK

160 1919 Pablo Picasso has his first solo exhibition in Paris in thirteen years: the onset of pastiche in his work coincides with a widespread antimodernist reaction. RK
box • Sergei Diaghilev and the Ballets Russes RK
box • *Rappel à l'ordre* RK

1910

Henri Matisse's *Dance II and Music* are condemned at the Salon d'Automne in Paris: in these pictures, Matisse pushes his concept of the "decorative" to an extreme, creating an expansive visual field of color that is difficult to behold.

"My picture threw me out onto the streets!" Matisse declared to a friend who was surprised by his impromptu visit. Two days earlier this friend had left him carefully preparing his material and, stockpiling groceries, vowing to lock himself up for a month in order to realize an important commission he had just received—and now Matisse felt he could not add a single stroke to his hastily brushed canvas. The picture in question was either *Seville Still Life* or *Spanish Still Life* **[1]**, both painted "in a fever" in December 1910 while the artist was resting in Spain. "This is the work of a nervous man," Matisse would later say of the pair, and indeed there is perhaps no more agitated painting in his entire production than these two still lifes.

The circumstances of their making are worth recalling. Coming back to Paris elated from a trip to Munich, where he had gone to see the first major exhibition ever devoted to Islamic art, Matisse was confronted with an almost unanimously negative critical response to *Dance II* **[2]** and *Music* **[3]**, the canvases he had sent to the 1910 Salon d'Automne, the annual showcase for contemporary art established seven years earlier (his sole supporter was the poet Guillaume ▲ Apollinaire, for whom he felt no sympathy). By then he was used to such turmoil surrounding his work, to some extent even thriving on it; but this time the hostile consensus hit him hard. Not only did it catch Matisse at a moment when he was particularly fragile (his father had died a day after his return to Paris), it also had an immediate effect on his most courageous and faithful patron, the Russian collector Sergei Shchukin, who had commissioned the two large paintings and had been enthusiastically following their progress from afar. Shchukin arrived in Paris in the midst of this public uproar, and, balking, decided at the eleventh hour not to accept them. (Adding to Matisse's injury, his dealers borrowed his studio to display the work they had convinced Shchukin to purchase instead, the large *grisaille* sketch for a mural by Puvis de Chavannes.)

Feeling guilty on his way back to Moscow, Shchukin sent a telegram rescinding his decision and asking for *Dance II* and *Music* to be shipped at great speed, followed by a letter canceling the purchase of the Puvis and apologizing for his momentary weakness. The immediate danger of the end of Shchukin's support was averted, but Matisse was shaken by these about-faces. Mulling over the fickleness of collectors and the treachery of art dealers, he left for Spain, where for a whole month he was unable to sleep or work. There, he received Shchukin's latest commission for two still lifes (which would be very handsomely paid), as well as the news that *Dance II* and *Music* had arrived safely in Moscow ("I hope to come to like them one day," Shchukin wrote).

1 • Henri Matisse, *Spanish Still Life*, 1910–11
Oil on canvas, 89 x 116 (35 x 45⅝)

Rather than taming his style for the new commission, Matisse took a huge gamble—a true "all or nothing"—in carrying one of its features to the extreme, namely the decorative profusion that had characterized many of his works from the previous years, such as the 1908 *Harmony in Red*, which already belonged to Shchukin. As if he had nothing to lose (which was very far from being the case), Matisse refused to retreat toward the neoclassical conception of the decorative represented by Puvis: it is as if he were warning his patron—who had suddenly become worried about the nudity of the figures in *Dance II* and *Music*, and about what was called at the time their "Dionysian" character—that a still life could be just as visually disquieting. One could even argue that, in proposing *Seville Still Life* and *Spanish Still Life* to Shchukin immediately after the two panels the Russian collector had found so hard to swallow, Matisse was deliberately alternating between two modes—one austere, one swarming—as if to demonstrate that they were two sides of the

▲ 1911, 1912

2 • Henri Matisse, *Dance II*, 1910
Oil on canvas, 260 x 391 (101⅝ x 153½)

same coin. The prior holdings of the Shchukin Collection suggest that this might have been a consistent strategy on the part of Matisse (compare the sparse 1908 *Game of Bowls* and the 1909 *Nymph and Satyr* with *Harmony in Red*, bought shortly before the still-life commission); and Shchukin's subsequent purchases followed the same pattern (compare the austere 1912 *Conversation* with *The Painter's Family* or *The Pink Studio* of 1911, bought at the same time).

An "aesthetic of blinding"

Both *Seville Still Life* and *Spanish Still Life* are difficult to behold—that is, the viewer cannot gaze at their pullulating arabesques and color flashes for very long. As had already happened in *Le Bonheur* ▲ *de vivre*, but now much more so, these paintings appear to spin before the eye; nothing there ever seems to come to rest. Flowers, fruits, and pots pop up like bubbles that dissolve into their busy, swirling background as quickly as one manages to isolate them. The centrality of the figure is dismantled: the viewer feels compelled to look at everything at once, at the whole visual field, but at the same time feels forced to rely on peripheral vision to do so, at the expense of control over that very field.

Now, compare this turbulence with *Music* [**3**]. At first sight nothing could be more dissimilar to the frantic still lifes than the sobriety of this large composition. But this difference dwindles once actual scale is taken into consideration. For when confronted with *Music*'s one hundred-plus square feet of saturated color, and its frieze of five musicians evenly distributed on the surface, once again one stumbles upon an aporia of perception: either one tries to contemplate the figures one by one but cannot do so because of the sheer coloristic summons of the rest of the canvas; or, conversely, one attempts to take in the vast surface at a glance but cannot prevent the optical vibrations that are caused by the figures' vermilion forms as they clash with the blue-and-green ground from deflecting our grasp of the visual field. Figure and ground constantly annul each other in a crescendo of energies—that is, the very opposition upon which human perception is based is deliberately destabilized—and our vision ends up blurred, blinded by excess.

This "aesthetic of blinding" was already in place in 1906—it was the result of Matisse's complex negotiations, during the heyday of ▲ Fauvism, with the legacy of Postimpressionism. But it assumed a new urgency around 1908, at which time Matisse reflected upon it in his famous "Notes of a Painter," one of the most articulate artistic manifestos of the twentieth century. There, among other things, Matisse defined the diffraction of the gaze that he was aiming for as the core of his concept of expression: "Expression, for me, does not

▲ 1906

▲ 1906

3 • Henri Matisse, *Music*, 1910
Oil on canvas, 260 x 389 (101⅝ x 153¼)

reside in passions glowing in a human face or manifested by a violent movement. The entire arrangement of my picture is expressive: the place occupied by the figures, the empty spaces around them, the proportions, everything has its share." In other words, as he would keep saying all his life, "expression and decoration are one and the same thing."

Matisse answers the younger Picasso

Many factors contributed to the sudden acceleration of Matisse's art and theoretical sophistication in 1908. One of them, perhaps the most important, was his competition with Picasso. In the fall ▲ of 1907 he had seen *Les Demoiselles d'Avignon*, Picasso's direct • answer to both his *Le Bonheur de vivre* and his *Blue Nude*. The painting had made Matisse uneasy, in part because it had carried primitivism further than any of his own previous attempts, and he had to respond.

His first reply was the large *Bathers with a Turtle* [**4**], one of his barest and eeriest canvases (the primitivism of the central, standing nude has been noted by all commentators). Countering Picasso's "Medusa effect," Matisse turned the glare of his giant nudes away from the beholder—but not without signaling that a simple retreat to the traditional regime of mimetic identification was no longer an available option (on this point he was concurring with Picasso). The picture is not the depiction of a bucolic scene, nor is it an allegory. What are these huge creatures doing, feeding a turtle they do not even look at? We cannot understand the motive of their action any more than they seem able to communicate it among themselves. The spectator is left to ponder over the enigmatic "expression" of the standing nude or that of her seated neighbor. But no clue is given by their surroundings. For the first time in Matisse's work the decor is reduced to modulated bands of plain color, as in Byzantine mosaics: green for the grass, blue for the water, blue-green for the somber sky—a cipher of a landscape, frontally facing us. This is an uninhabitable world, into which we are not invited.

Shchukin had perceived the profound melancholy of this work and, saddened that it had been sold to another collector, he asked Matisse for a substitute. That was to be *Game of Bowls*, a far less powerful painting, but indicative of the direction Matisse's work was to take. The "landscape" is as bare as in *Bathers with a Turtle* (though the color spectrum is much lighter), but now formal rhythms set the composition in motion (the three dark-haired heads of the players being ironically echoed by their three green bowls). There are no mysterious expressions here: the distorted

▲ 1907 • 1903, 1906

faces of Picasso's *Les Demoiselles* are no longer Matisse's concern; the features of the bowlers are written in shorthand. The visual rhythm, whose function was still embryonic in *Bathers with a Turtle*, is now what unifies the canvas.

The next step was *Harmony in Red* [**5**], Matisse's first fully successful realization of what would be his lifelong pictorial program: a surface so tense that our gaze rebounds from it; a composition so dispersed, so rippled with echoes in all directions, that we cannot gaze at it selectively; a maze so energetic that it always seems to expand laterally. Matisse made one last attempt at painting in Picasso's centripetal mode in his *Nymph and Satyr* of late 1908 (again for Shchukin), one of his very few paintings with a violent theme. But this was to remain an exception (matched only by a series of drawings and unfinished canvases on the same theme from 1935, and by the studies for *The Stations of the Cross* ceramic panel in the Vence Chapel from 1949): after it, we will not be asked to look at an action from a distance; instead, we will be confronted with a wall of painting forcing its color saturation onto us.

A certain form of violence is implied by this kind of address. Today, after so many pages praising Matisse as the painter of "happiness" (or, conversely, berating his "hedonism"), the particular type of aggressiveness embedded in his art is somewhat veiled. But the fiercely negative response that he received at the time—which ▲ kept accelerating from the reception of *Luxe, calme et volupté* at the 1905 Salon des Indépendants, through the Fauve scandal of 1905 and the cries that greeted *Le Bonheur de vivre* in 1906 and *Blue Nude* in 1907, to the nearly universal condemnation of *Dance II* and *Music* in 1910—is a clear indication that he was touching a sensitive nerve. What became obvious in the case of the reception of these last two works is that it was precisely Matisse's conception of the "decorative" that was perceived as a slap in the face of tradition—the tradition of painting as well as the tradition of beholding.

4 • Henri Matisse, *Bathers with a Turtle*, 1908
Oil on canvas 179.1 x 220.3 (70½ x 87¾)

▲ 1906

5 • Henri Matisse, *Harmony in Red*, 1908
Oil on canvas, 180 x 220 (70⅞ x 86⅝)

Hypnotic "decorations"

It was not by chance that Matisse's dealers had been quick to offer Shchukin a Puvis in replacement for his two panels. High expectations were vested in the notion of the "decorative" at that very moment, the 1910 Salon marking the climax of the numerous debates that had been raging on the issue since the turn of the century (it was deemed capable of restoring the greatness of French art after the crisis of representation engendered by Postimpressionism and further deepened by Fauvism and Cubism). A return to Puvis—"decorative" compositions draped in a neoclassical rhetoric—was called for, but this is exactly what Matisse refused to condone. He labeled *Dance II* and *Music* "decorative panels" when sending them to the Salon, and this enraged the critics: the paintings were not made to soothe the eye, to gently adorn a wall; they were the crude product of a madman, posterlike bacchanals that threatened to swirl out of their frame.

The high-pitched color was obviously a major cause of this resistance, but it would not have had such an impact if it had not been for the ample scale of the works (not only are they large but also the number of elements they display are reduced: in each canvas there are only five figures of the same "lobster" color, as was said at the time, and two background zones—blue for the sky and green for the land). In fact, the coloristic impact of *Dance II* and *Music*, which remained unequaled in painting until the large canvases of Mark ▲ Rothko and Barnett Newman in the late forties, provided the clearest confirmation of Matisse's principle according to which "a square centimeter of blue is less blue than a square meter of the same blue."

But if the anticlassical decenteredness of these works was perceived as a threat, and criticized in *Music* even more than in *Dance II*, it is also because with them Matisse finally found a means to emulate properly, though with different means, Picasso's ● apotropaïc stance in *Les Demoiselles d'Avignon*. Although it is just as bare as *Music*, *Dance II* partakes in the profuse mode of Matisse's notion of the "decorative." Looking at it, we are condemned to endless motion, forbidden to let our gaze ever break the circling round of its feverish arabesque. The only escape from this hypnotic frenzy is to recoil, just as Matisse had done, panicked in front of his own Spanish still lifes. Yet *Music* is more powerful, though in a subtler fashion, in this interdiction to join in peacefully.

Like Picasso's *Les Demoiselles*, this painting had begun as a genre scene, the five musicians (among them a woman) looking at each other, interacting. In the final canvas, the figures, now all male, have undergone the same ninety-degree rotation that Leo Steinberg discussed in Picasso's painting: stilted in their pose, ignoring each other, they stare terrifyingly at us. Matisse himself is said to have been afraid by what he called the "silence" of this canvas: in contrast with the sweeping movement of *Dance II*, in *Music* everything is arrested. The black holes of the three singers' mouths are unequivocally morbid (closer to signaling death than sound); the violinist's bow poised before the downstroke is nothing but ominous. In his review of the Salon, Yakov Tugenhold, one of the most gifted Russian critics of the time (Shchukin paid careful attention to his prose), described the figures of *Music* as "boy werewolves hypnotized by the first-ever strains of the first instruments." No critical metaphor could better indicate that in this canvas Matisse is charting the same Freudian territory as Picasso had done in his brothel scene, for, even more than *Les Demoiselles*, *Music* is akin to the ▲ image of the Wolf-Man's dream. We have to add a proviso to Tugenhold's metaphor, however: it is not the musicians but the spectators who are hypnotized.

This hypnosis is based on a pendulum in our perception that makes us switch from our incapacity to focus on the figures to that of seizing the whole visual field at once, an oscillation that defines the very invention of Matisse's concept of the "decorative," and which is particularly difficult to obtain in a sparse composition. It is thus not surprising that Matisse should have preferred the overcrowded mode as a surefire means to keep the beholder's gaze moving. It should be noted, however, that he never totally relinquished the barren version of the decorative, that it played a major role in his production at several key moments of his career, most notably when his rivalry with Picasso was at stake. One such moment was when he was trying to learn the language of Cubism, from 1913 to 1917 (after which he retreated to Nice and into Impressionism until 1931, when the conjoined commissions of an illustrated Mallarmé book and that of a mural on the theme of Dance for the Barnes Foundation led him back to the aesthetics of his youth). From Matisse's "Cubist" years date works such as *French Window in Collioure* (1914) or *The Yellow Curtain* (c. 1915), so strikingly similar, once again, to works by Rothko or Newman, or *The Blue Window* (1913) and *The Piano Lesson* (1916), whose oneiric ● atmosphere the Surrealist poet André Breton found so appealing.

The works immediately following *Dance II* and *Music*, however, swung in the other direction. After the two "nervous" Spanish still lifes came the famous large interiors of 1911, *The Red Studio*, *Interior with Eggplants* [**6**], *The Pink Studio*, and *The Painter's Family*

▲ 1947b, 1951 ● 1907

▲ 1907 ● 1924

6 • Henri Matisse, *Interior with Eggplants*, 1911
Oil on canvas, 212 x 246 (82⅜ x 96⅞)

(the last two immediately purchased by Shchukin). Less frenetic than the pictures done at Seville, and considerably larger, they explore the same isotropic universe in expansion. In *The Red Studio*, a monochrome bath of redness floods the field, annulling even the possibility of contour (which exists only negatively, as unpainted, reserved areas of the canvas); in *The Painter's Family*, the multiplication of decorative patterns that surround the figure makes us oblivious to the most violent color contrasts, such as the opposition between the unmitigated black dress of the standing figure and the lemon-yellow book she holds; in *Interior with Eggplants*, the most underrated but most radical work of the series, everything cooperates in leading us astray: the pulsating repetition of the flower motif that invades floor and walls and blurs their demarcation; the reflection in the mirror that coloristically matches the landscape outside the window and confuses levels of reality; the syncopated rhythm and different scales of the ornamental fabrics; the gestures of the two sculptures (one on the table, the other on the mantelpiece) that rhyme with the arabesques of the folded screen. The three eggplants that give the painting its title are right in the middle of the canvas, but Matisse has blinded us to them and it is only through a conscious effort that we manage, only fleetingly, to locate them.

FURTHER READING

Alfred H. Barr, Jr., *Matisse: His Art and His Public* (New York: Museum of Modern Art, 1951)
Yve-Alain Bois, "Matisse's Bathers with a Turtle," *Bulletin of the Saint Louis Art Museum*, vol. 22, no. 3, Summer 1998
Yve-Alain Bois, "On Matisse: The Blinding," *October*, no. 68, Spring 1994
John Elderfield, "Describing Matisse," *Henri Matisse: A Retrospective* (New York: Museum of Modern Art, 1992)
Jack D. Flam, *Matisse: The Man and His Art, 1869–1918* (Ithaca, N.Y. and London: Cornell University Press, 1986)
Alastair Wright, "Arche-tectures: Matisse and the End of (Art) History," *October*, no. 84, Spring 1998

1911

Pablo Picasso returns his "borrowed" Iberian stone heads to the Louvre Museum in Paris from which they had been stolen: he transforms his primitivist style and with Georges Braque begins to develop Analytical Cubism.

During 1907, the year in which the poet-critic Guillaume Apollinaire employed him as a secretary, the young rascal Géry Pieret would regularly ask Apollinaire's artist- and writer-friends if they would like anything from the Louvre. They assumed, of course, that he meant the Louvre Department Store. In fact, he meant the Louvre Museum, from which he had taken to stealing various items displayed in undervisited galleries.

It was on his return from one of these pilfering trips that Pieret offered two archaic Iberian stone heads to Picasso, who had discovered this type of sculpture in 1906 in Spain and had used it for ▲ his portrait of the American writer Gertrude Stein. Substituting the prismatic physiognomy of its carving—the heavily lidded, staring eyes; the continuous plane that runs the forehead into the bridge of the nose; the parallel ridges that form the mouth—for the sitter's face, Picasso was convinced that this impassive mask was "truer" to Stein's likeness than any faithfulness to her actual features could be. He was thus only too happy to acquire these talismanic objects; and "Pieret's heads" went on to serve as the basis for the features of • the three left-hand nudes in *Les Demoiselles d'Avignon.*

But in 1911, when Pieret disastrously popped back up in the lives ■ of both Apollinaire and Picasso, primitivism had been left behind in the artist's development of Cubism, and thus the heads had long since vanished from his pictorial concerns, if not from the back of his cupboard. Picasso's sudden problem was that at the end of August 1911 Pieret had taken his latest Louvre "acquisition" to the offices of *Paris Journal*, selling the newspaper his story about how easy it was to filch from the museum. Since the Louvre had just suffered, one week earlier, the theft of its most precious object, Leonardo's *Mona Lisa*, and a dragnet was being set up by the Paris police, Apollinaire panicked, alerted Picasso, and the two of them handed Picasso's Iberian heads over to the newspaper, which, publishing this turn of events as well, led the authorities to both poet and painter. They were taken in for questioning, Apollinaire being held far longer than Picasso, but were eventually released without charge.

The rise of analysis

The artistic distance that separated Picasso in late 1911 from the primitivism for which the heads had served him earlier was enormous. The Iberian heads and African masks that Picasso had used as models in 1907 and 1908 had been a means of "distortion," to ▲ use the term of art historian Carl Einstein when, in 1929, he tried to understand the development of Cubism. But this "simplistic" distortion, Einstein wrote, gave way "to a period of analysis and fragmentation and finally to a period of synthesis." *Analysis* was also the word applied to the shattering of the surfaces of objects and their amalgamation to the space around them when Daniel-Henry Kahnweiler, Picasso's dealer during Cubism's development, sat down to write the most serious early account of the movement, *The Rise of Cubism* (1920). And so the term *analytical* got appended to Cubism, and "Analytical Cubism" became the rubric under which to contemplate the transformation Picasso and Georges Braque had achieved in 1911. For by that time, they had swept away the unified perspective of centuries of naturalistic painting and had invented instead a pictorial language that would translate coffee cups and wine bottles, faces and torsos, guitars and pedestal tables into so many tiny, slightly tilted planes.

To look at any work from this "analytical" phase of Cubism, Picasso's *Daniel-Henry Kahnweiler* of 1910 [**1**], for instance, or Braque's *The Portuguese (The Emigrant)* from 1911–12 [**2**], is to observe several consistent characteristics. First, there is a strange contraction of the painters' palettes, from the full color spectrum to an abstemious monochrome—Braque's picture is all ochers and umbers like a sepia-toned photograph; Picasso's, mainly pewter and silver with a few glints of copper. Second, there is an extreme flattening of the visual space as though a roller had pressed all the volume out of the bodies, bursting their contours open in the process so that what little surrounding space remains could flow effortlessly inside their eroded boundaries. Third, there is the visual vocabulary used to describe the physical remains of this explosive process.

This, given its proclivity for the geometrical, supports the "Cubist" appellation. It consists, on the one hand, of shallow planes set more or less parallel to the picture surface, their slight tilt a matter of the patches of light and shade that flicker over the entire field, darkening one edge of a given plane only to illuminate the other but not doing this in any way consistent with a single light source. On the other, it establishes a linear network that

▲ 1907 • 1907 ■ 1903 ▲ 1930b

scores the entire surface with an intermittent grid: at certain points, identifiable as the edges of described objects—Kahnweiler's jacket lapels or his jawline, for instance, or the Portuguese sitter's sleeve or the neck of his guitar; at others, the edges of planes that, scaffoldlike, seem merely to be structuring the space; and at still others, a vertical or horizontal trace that attaches to nothing at all but continues the grid's repetitive network. Finally, there are the small grace-notes of naturalistic details, such as the single arc of Kahnweiler's mustache or the double one of his watch-chain.

Given the exceedingly slight information we can gain from this about either the figures or their settings, the explanations that grew up around Picasso's and Braque's Cubism at this time are extremely curious. For whether it was Apollinaire in his essays collected as *The Cubist Painters* (1913), or the artists Albert Gleizes (1881–1953) and Jean Metzinger (1883–1956) in their book *On Cubism* (1912), or any of the critics and poets gathered around the movement, such as André Salmon (1881–1969) or Maurice Raynal (1884–1954), all the writers attempted to justify this swerve away from realism by arguing that what was being delivered to the viewer was *more* not less knowledge of the depicted object. Stating that natural vision is impoverished since we can never see the whole of a three-dimensional object from any single vantage point—the most we see of a cube, for example, is three of its faces—they argued that Cubism overcomes this handicap by breaking with a single perspective to show the sides and back simultaneously with the front, so that we apprehend the thing from everywhere, grasping it conceptually as a composite of the views we would have if we actually moved around it. Positing the superiority of conceptual knowledge over merely perceptual realism, these writers inevitably gravitated toward the language of science, describing the break with perspective as a move toward non-Euclidean geometry, or the simultaneity of distinct spatial positions as a function of the fourth dimension.

Guillaume Apollinaire (1880–1918)

Born the illegitimate son of a member of the lesser Polish nobility, Guillaume Albert Apollinaire de Kostrowitzky grew up on the French Riviera among the cosmopolitan *demi-monde*. At seventeen, deeply affected by the poets Paul Verlaine and Stéphane Mallarmé, he composed a handwritten anarcho-symbolist "newspaper" filled with his own poems and articles. Apollinaire soon became an active figure in a Parisian avant-garde that included Alfred Jarry and André Salmon, and he met Picasso in 1903. Together with Salmon and Max Jacob, he formed the group known as the *bande à Picasso* (the Picasso gang). Having started to write art criticism in 1905, he steadily campaigned for advanced painting, publishing *The Cubist Painters* in 1913, the same year in which he published the major collection of his poems *Alcools*. At the outbreak of World War I, Apollinaire enlisted in the French Army and was sent to the front in early 1915. From there, he mailed a stream of postcards to his friends containing his notes and *calligrammes*, the typographically experimental poems he published in 1918.

Hit by shrapnel in the trenches in early 1916, Apollinaire was trepanned and returned to Paris. In 1917, he delivered the lecture "L'esprit nouveau et les poètes," and in 1918 he staged the play *Les Mamelles de Tirésias*, both of them anticipating the aesthetics of Surrealism. Weakened by his wounds, he succumbed to an influenza epidemic that swept Paris in November 1918.

The laws of painting as such

Kahnweiler, who had exhibited the 1908 Braque landscapes that gave Cubism its name (the journalist-critic Louis Vauxcelles wrote that Braque had reduced "everything to geometric schemas, to cubes"), and who had been active as Picasso's dealer since 1909, had a very different argument to make about the inner workings of Cubism, one far easier to reconcile with how the paintings actually look. Cut off by the outbreak of World War I from his Paris gallery and the pictorial movement he had followed so closely, Kahnweiler used his time in Switzerland to reflect on the meaning of Cubism, composing his explanation in 1915–16.

Arguing that Cubism was exclusively concerned with bringing about the unity of the pictorial object, *The Rise of Cubism* defines this unity as the necessary fusion of two seemingly irreconcilable opposites: the depicted volumes of "real" objects and the flatness of the painter's own physical object (just as "real" as anything in the world before the artist), which is the canvas plane of the picture. Reasoning that the pictorial tool to represent volume had always been the shading that brings forms into illusionistic relief, and that shading was a matter of the gray- or tonal-scale alone, Kahnweiler saw the logic of banishing color from the Cubist "analysis" and of solving the problem in part by using the shading tool against its own grain: creating the lowest possible relief so that depicted volume would be far more reconcilable with the flat surface. Further, he explained the logic of piercing the envelopes of closed volumes in order to override the gaps opened up between the edges of objects and thus to be able to declare the unbroken continuity of the canvas plane. If he ended by declaring that "this new language has given painting an unprecedented freedom," this was not as an argument about conceptual mastery over the world's empirical data—as in Apollinaire's notion of Cubism keeping up with

1 • Pablo Picasso, *Daniel-Henry Kahnweiler*, Fall–Winter 1910
Oil on canvas, 100.6 x 72.8 ($39\frac{1}{2}$ x $28\frac{5}{8}$)

modern science—but one of securing the autonomy and internal logic of the picture object.

This explanation, dismissing extra-pictorial motivations for Cubism, accorded with the understanding of those who used the ▲ new style, as Piet Mondrian would, as the basis for developing a purely abstract art. Not that Mondrian was disengaged from the world of modernity, such as developments in science and industry, but he believed that for a painter to be modern he needed first and foremost to understand the logic of his own domain and to make this understanding evident in his work. Such a theory would later emerge as the doctrine of "modernism" (as opposed to modernity) • that the American critic Clement Greenberg would enunciate in the early sixties by arguing that modernist painting had adopted the approach of scientific rationalism and of Enlightenment logic by limiting its practice to the area of "its own competence" and thus—exhibiting "what was unique and irreducible in each particular art"—to demonstrating the laws of painting rather than those of nature.

It is not surprising, then, that Greenberg's discussion of how Cubism developed would reinforce Kahnweiler's. Tracing an unbroken progression toward the compression of pictorial space, beginning with *Les Demoiselles d'Avignon* and ending with the 1912 ■ invention of collage, Greenberg saw Analytical Cubism as the increasing fusion of two types of flatness: the "depicted flatness" by which the tilted planes shoved the fragmented objects closer and closer to the surface; and the "literal flatness" of that surface itself. If by 1911 in a picture such as Braque's *The Portuguese* [**2**], Greenberg said, these two types of flatness threatened to have become indistinguishable, so that the grid would seem to be articulating only one surface and one flatness, the Cubists responded by adding illusionistic devices, only now ones that would "undeceive the eye," rather than, as in traditional practice, continuing to fool it. Such devices consisted of things like a depicted "nail" seeming to pierce the top of a canvas so as fictively to cast its shadow onto the surface "beneath" it; or they are to be found in the stenciled lettering of *The Portuguese*, which, by demonstrably sitting on top of the canvas surface (the result of the letters' semimechanical application), pushes the little patches of shading and the barely tilted geometric shapes back into the field of depicted relief just "below" that surface.

A mountain to climb

In pointing to the fact that Braque adopted these devices earlier than Picasso—not only the stenciled lettering and the nails illusionistically tacking the whole canvas to the studio wall but also the wood-graining patterns employed by house painters—Greenberg set up an internal competition between the two artists, thereby rupturing their "*cordée*," or self-proclaimed posture of having been roped together like mountaineers as they explored their new pictorial terrain (their collaboration was so shared that they often did not sign their own paintings). This vision of a race toward flatness was further enhanced by the question of which of the two first

2 • Georges Braque, *The Portuguese (The Emigrant)*, Fall 1911–early 1912
Oil on canvas, 114.6 x 81.6 (45⅛ x 32⅛)

internalized the lessons of late Cézanne by adopting the practice of visual slippage between adjacent elements (called *passage*, in French) that was an early version of the Cubist piercing of the spatial envelopes of objects.

Yet as our eyes become increasingly accustomed to this group of paintings, we realize that the works of the two men are consistently differentiated by the greater concern for transparency in Braque's and the denser, more tactile quality of Picasso's—something underscored by the latter's interest in exploring the possibilities of Cubism for sculpture. This compressed sense of density, this inter- ▲ est in the experience of touch, made art historian Leo Steinberg protest against the merging of the two artists' concerns and thus the blurring of our vision of individual pictures.

Indeed, Picasso's overwhelming concern with a vestigial kind of depth—manifested most dramatically in the landscapes he painted in Spain at Horta de Ebro in 1909 [**3**]—makes the whole schema of Cubism's development by a progressive flattening of pictorial space seem peculiarly incomplete. For in these works, where we seem to be looking upward—houses ascending a hill toward the top of a mountain, for example, their splayed-apart roof and wall planes

▲ 1913, 1917, 1944a • 1942a, 1960b ■ 1907, 1912 ▲ 1907, 1960b

3 • Pablo Picasso, *Houses on the Hill, Horta de Ebro*, Summer 1909
Oil on canvas, 65 x 81.5 (25⅝ x 31⅞)

4 • Pablo Picasso, *Girl with a Mandolin (Fanny Tellier)*, Spring 1910
Oil on canvas, 100.3 x 73.6 (39½ x 29)

allying them with the frontal picture surface—and yet, in total contradiction, to be precipitously plunging downward through the full-blown spatial chasm opened between the houses, it is not flatness that is at issue but quite another matter. This could be called the rupture between visual and tactile experience, something that had obsessed nineteenth-century psychology with the problem of how the separate pieces of sensory information could be unified into a single perceptual manifold.

This problem enters the writing on Cubism as well, as when Gleizes and Metzinger say in *On Cubism* that "the convergence which perspective teaches us to represent cannot evoke the idea of depth," so that "to establish pictorial space, we must have recourse to tactile and motor sensations." However, the idea of a simultaneous spatial composite, the solution they thought Cubism had reached, was very far from Picasso's results at Horta, where, as ▲ Gertrude Stein insisted, the style was born. For the Horta paintings tear the composite apart. They make depth something tactile, a matter of bodily sensation, a vertiginous plunge down through the center of the work. And they make vision something veil-like (and thus strangely compressed to the flatness of a screen): the array of shapes hung always parallel to our plane of vision to form that shimmering, curtainlike veil that James Joyce called the "diaphane."

Thus, if for his part Picasso *was* interested in late Cézanne, his focus was on something different from Braque's interest in the reconciliatory effect of *passage*. It was, instead, on the effect of divisiveness to be found in Cézanne's late paintings, as when in many still lifes the objects on the table hang decorously in visual space but, as the floor on which that table sits approaches the position of the painter/viewer, the boards seem to give way beneath our feet. In doing so, the works dramatize the separation of sensory channels of experience—visual versus tactile—thereby bringing the painter up against the problem of visual skepticism, namely that the only tool at his or her command is vision, but that depth is something vision can never directly *see*. The poet and critic Maurice Raynal had touched on this skepticism in 1912 when he referred to "Berkeley's idealism" and spoke of the "inadequacy" and "error" of painting dependent on vision. As we have seen, the consistent position of such a critic was to substitute "conception" for vision, and thus "to fill in a gap in our seeing." Picasso, however, seemed not to be interested in filling in this gap, but instead, in exacerbating it, like a sore that will not heal.

Unlike Braque's attention to still life, Picasso therefore returned again and again to the subject of portraiture. There he pursued the logic of the way his sitters—his lovers and closest friends—were fated to vanish from his tactile connection to them behind the visual veil of the "diaphane" with its frontalized shapes; but at the same time he expressed his dismay at this fact by the display of gratuitously "helpless" pockets of shading, a velvety voluptuousness increasingly detached from the volumes they would formerly have described. This is to be found behind the right arm and breast of Fanny Tellier (the sitter for *Girl with a Mandolin* [**4**]) or in the area around Kahnweiler's chin and ear.

▲ 1907

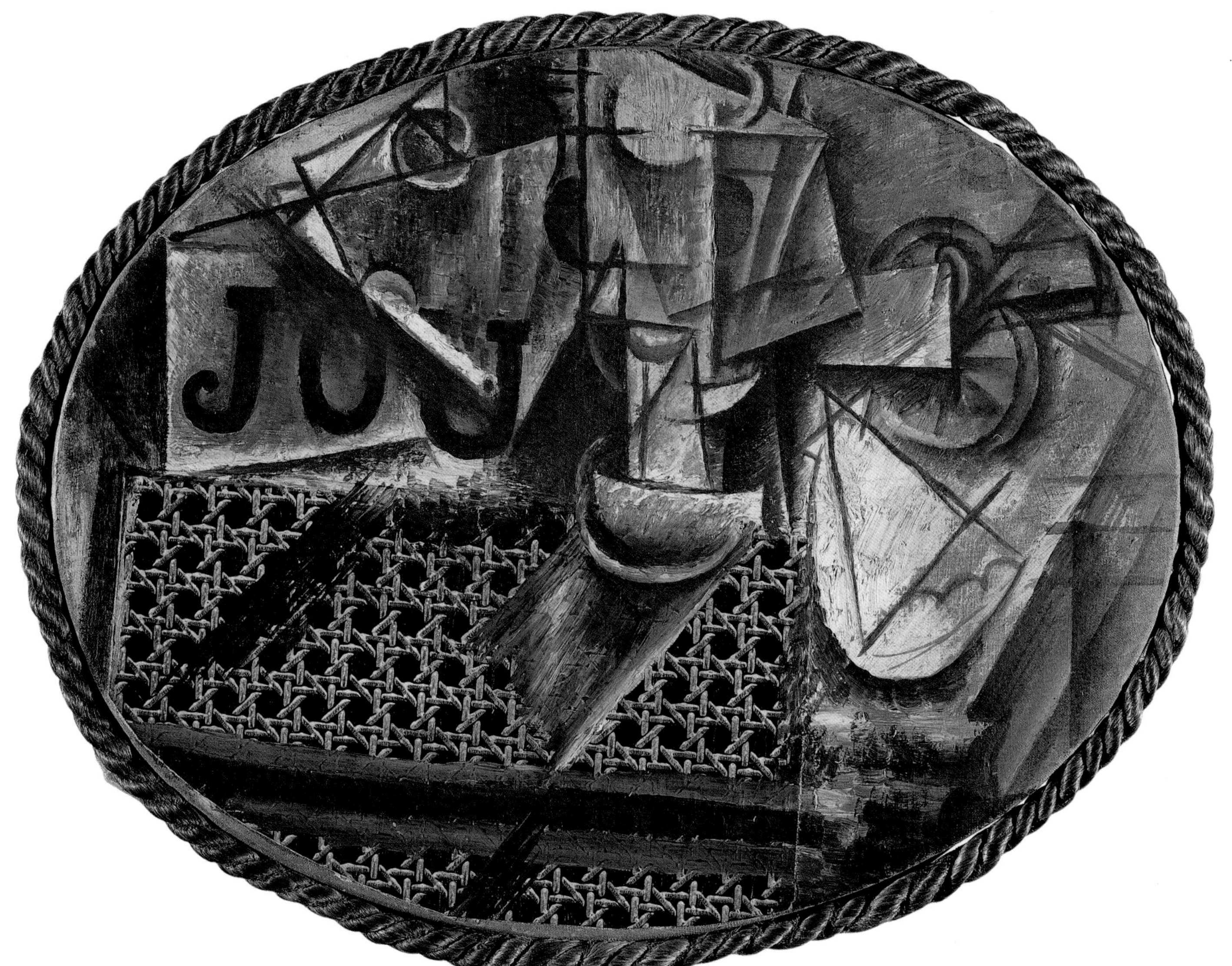

5 • Pablo Picasso, *Still Life with Chair Caning*, 1912
Oil and pasted oilcloth on canvas, surrounded with rope, 27 x 34.9 (10⅝ x 13¾)

And nowhere is this disjunction between the visual and the tactile as absolute *and* as economically stated than in the *Still Life with Chair Caning* [**5**] that Picasso painted in the spring of 1912, near the very end of Analytical Cubism. Affixing a length of rope around the edge of an oval canvas, Picasso creates a little still life that appears both to be set within the carved frame of a normal painting, and thus arranged in relation to the vertical field of our plane of vision, and to be laid out on the surface of an oval table, the carved edge of which is presented by the same rope and the covering for which is given literally by a glued-on section of printed oilcloth. Like the downward plunge at Horta, the table-top view is presented as one alternative here, a horizontal in direct opposition to the "diaphane's" vertical, a bodily perspective declaring the tactile as separate from the visual.

Braque's commitment to transparency declares his fidelity to the visuality of the visual arts, his obedience to the tradition of painting-as-diaphane. His *Homage to J. S. Bach* (1911–12) places a violin (signaled by the telltale "f"-holes and the scroll of its neck) on a table behind a music-stand holding the score titled "J. S. BACH" (a slant rhyme on Braque's name). Because of the patchy shading, each object reads clearly behind the other and the still life falls before our eyes like a lacy curtain.

FURTHER READING

Yve-Alain Bois, "The Semiology of Cubism," in Lynn Zelevansky (ed.), *Picasso and Braque: A Symposium* (New York: Museum of Modern Art, 1992)

Clement Greenberg, "The Pasted-Paper Revolution," *The Collected Essays and Criticism, Vol. 4: Modernism with a Vengeance, 1957–1969*, ed. John O'Brian (Chicago: University of Chicago Press, 1993)

Daniel-Henry Kahnweiler, *The Rise of Cubism*, trans. Henry Aronson (New York: Wittenborn, Schultz, 1949)

Rosalind Krauss, "The Motivation of the Sign," in Lynn Zelevansky (ed.), *Picasso and Braque: A Symposium* (New York: Museum of Modern Art, 1992)

Christine Poggi, *In Defiance of Painting* (New Haven and London: Yale University Press, 1992)

Robert Rosenblum, *Cubism and Twentieth-Century Art* (New York: Harry N. Abrams, 1960, revised 1977)

William Rubin, "Cézannisme and the Beginnings of Cubism," in William Rubin (ed.), *Cézanne: The Late Work* (New York: Museum of Modern Art, 1977)

Leo Steinberg, "Resisting Cézanne: Picasso's *Three Women*," *Art in America*, vol. 66, no. 6, November–December 1978

1912

Cubist collage is invented amid a set of conflicting circumstances and events: the continuing inspiration of Symbolist poetry, the rise of popular culture, and Socialist protests against the war in the Balkans.

If modernism consistently allied itself with "the shock of the new," the form this took in poetry was expressed by Guillaume ▲ Apollinaire in the summer of 1912 as he abruptly changed the title of his forthcoming book of poems from the Symbolist-sounding *Eau de vie* to the more popularly jazzy *Alcools* and hastily wrote a new work to add to the collection. This poem, "Zone," registered the jolt that modernity had delivered to Apollinaire by celebrating the linguistic pleasures of billboards and street signs.

Apollinaire's announcement came at the very moment when a former literary avant-garde was transforming itself into the establishment through the newly formed magazine *La Nouvelle Revue Française* (*N. R. F.*) and its championing of writers such as André Gide, Paul Valéry, and most importantly—with Albert Thibaudet's scholarly study now devoted to him—Stéphane Mallarmé. But what Apollinaire was signaling was that the barricade that Symbolism—and Mallarmé in particular—had tried to erect between newspaper journalism and poetry had now broken open. One had only to look at "Zone" to see this. "The handbills, catalogs, posters that sing out loud and clear," it proclaims, "that's the morning's poetry, and for prose there are the newspapers ... tabloids lurid with police reports."

Newspapers, which "Zone" celebrated as a source for literature, proved the turning-point for Cubism as well, particularly Picasso's, as, in the fall of 1912, he transformed Analytical Cubism into the new medium of collage. If collage literally means "gluing," Picasso had, of course, already begun this process earlier in the year ● with his *Still Life with Chair Caning*, an Analytical Cubist painting onto which he had glued a swathe of mechanically printed oilcloth. But the mere attachment of foreign matter to an unchanged ■ pictorial conception—as in the case of the Futurist painter Gino Severini, who, in 1912, fixed real sequins onto his frenetic depictions of dancers—was quite distinct from the path Cubism was to follow once Braque introduced [**1**], and Picasso took up, the integration of relatively large-scale paper shapes onto the surfaces of Cubist drawings.

With this development—called *papier collé*—the entire vocabulary of Cubism suddenly changed. Gone were the little canted planes with fractured patches of modeling, sometimes attached at their corners, sometimes floating freely or gravitating toward a section of the picture's gridded surface. In their place now were papers of various shapes and descriptions: wallpapers, newspapers, bottle labels, musical scores, even bits of the artist's old, discarded drawings. Overlaying each other the way papers would on a desk or work table, these sheets align themselves with the frontality of the supporting surface; and beyond signaling the surface's frontal condition, they also declare it to be paper-thin, only as deep as the distance from the topmost sheet to the ones below it.

Visually, however, the operations of *papier collé* work against this simple literalism, as when, for instance, several papers combine to force the background sheet to read as the frontmost element by defining it—against the grain of its material position—as the surface of the leading object on the still life's table, a wine bottle, perhaps, or a musical instrument [**2**]. The visual play of such a "figure–ground reversal" had also been a staple of much of Analytical Cubism. But collage now went beyond this into the declaration of a rupture with what could be called—using the semiological term for it—the "iconic" itself.

Visual representation had always presumed that its domain was the "iconic," in the sense of the image's possessing some level of resemblance to the thing it portrayed. A matter of "looking like," resemblance could survive many levels of stylization and remain intact as a coherent system of representation: that square attached to that inverted triangle joined to those zigzag shapes producing, say, the visual identities of head, torso, and legs. What seemed to have nothing to do with the iconic was the domain the semiologists call "symbolic," by which they mean the wholly arbitrary signs (because in no way resembling the referent) that make up, for example, language: the words *dog* and *cat* bearing no visible or audible connection to the meanings they represent or to the objects to which those meanings refer.

Swept away

It was by adopting just this arbitrary form of the "symbolic" that Picasso's collage declared its break with a whole system of representation based on "looking like." The clearest example brings this about by deploying two newspaper shapes in such a way as to declare that they were cut, jigsaw-puzzle fashion, from a single

▲ 1911 ● 1911 ■ 1909

original sheet [**2**]. One of these fragments sits within a passage of charcoal drawing to establish the solid face of a violin, the paper's lines of type functioning as a stand-in for the grained wood of the instrument. The other, however, gravitating to the upper right of the collage, declares itself not the continuation of its "twin" but, instead, the contradictory opposite, since *this* fragment's lines of type now appear to assume the kind of broken or scumbled color through which painters have traditionally indicated light-filled atmosphere, thereby organizing the newsprint piece as a sign for "background" in relation to the violin's "figure."

▲ Using what semiologists would call a "paradigm"—a binary opposition through which each half of the pair gains its meaning by *not* signifying the other—the collage's manipulation of this pair declares that what any element in the work will mean will be entirely a function of a set of negative contrasts rather than the positive identification of "looking like." For even if the two elements are literally cut from the same cloth, the oppositional system into which they are now bound contrasts the meaning of one—opaque, frontal, objective—with that of the other—transparent, luminous, amorphous. Picasso's collage thus makes the elements of the work function according to the structural-linguistic definition of the sign itself as "relative, oppositive, and negative." In doing so, collage seems not only to have taken on the visually arbitrary condition of linguistic signs but also to be participating in (or, according ▲ to the Russian-born linguist Roman Jakobson, even initiating) a revolution in Western representation that goes beyond the visual to extend to the literary, and past that into the political economy.

1 • Georges Braque, *Fruit Dish and Glass*, 1912
Charcoal and pasted paper, 62 x 44.5 (24⅜ x 17½)

2 • Pablo Picasso, *Violin*, 1912
Pasted paper and charcoal, 62 x 47 (24⅜ x 18½)

Off the gold standard

For if the meaning of the arbitrary sign is established by convention rather than what might seem the natural truth of "looking like," it can, in turn, be likened to the token money of modern banking systems, the value of which is a function of law rather than a coin's "real" worth as a given measure of gold or silver or a note's redeemable relation to precious metal. Literary scholars have thus set up a parallel between naturalism as an aesthetic condition and the gold standard as an economic system in which monetary signs, like literary ones, were understood to be transparent to the reality that underwrote them.

If the point of this parallel is to prepare the literary critic for the modernist departure from the gold standard and its adoption of "token" signs—arbitrary in themselves and thus convertible to any value set by a signifying matrix or set of laws—no one effected this break with linguistic naturalism as radically or as early as did Stéphane Mallarmé, within whose poetry and prose the linguistic

▲ Introduction 3

▲ Introduction 3, 1915

sign was treated as wildly "polysemic," or productive of multiple—and often opposed—meanings.

Just to stay with the term *gold*, Mallarmé used it not only to explore the phenomenon of the metal and its related concepts of richness or luminosity but also to take advantage of the fact that the word in French for gold ("*or*") is identical to the conjunction translated as "now"; it is thus productive of the kind of temporal or logical deflection of the flow of language that the poet went on to exploit, not just at the level of meaning (that is, the signified) but also at that of the material support for the sign (the signifier). Thus in the poem titled "Or" this element appears everywhere, both freestanding and embedded within larger signs, a signifier that sometimes folds over onto its signified—"*trésOR*"—but more often one that does not—"*dehOR*," "*fantasmagORique*," "*hORizon*," "*majORe*," "*hORs*"—seeming thereby to demonstrate that it is the very uncontrollability of the physical spread of *or* that makes it a signifier truly cut free of the gold standard of even its most shifting signified.

There is of course a paradox in using this example within the larger account of modernity—including that of Picasso's collage—as something established by the arbitrariness of the token-money economy. For Mallarmé deploys the very marker of what token-money set out to replace, namely (outmoded) gold, to celebrate the freely circulating meaning of the new system. Yet the value he continues to accord to gold is not that of the old naturalism but rather that of the sensuous material of poetic language in which nothing is transparent to meaning without passing through the carnality of the signifier's flesh, its visual outline, its music: /gold/ = sound; *or* = son*or*e. This was the poetic gold that Mallarmé explicitly contrasted with what he called the *numéraire*, or empty cash value, of newspaper journalism in which, in his eyes, language had reached its zero point of being a mere instrument of reporting.

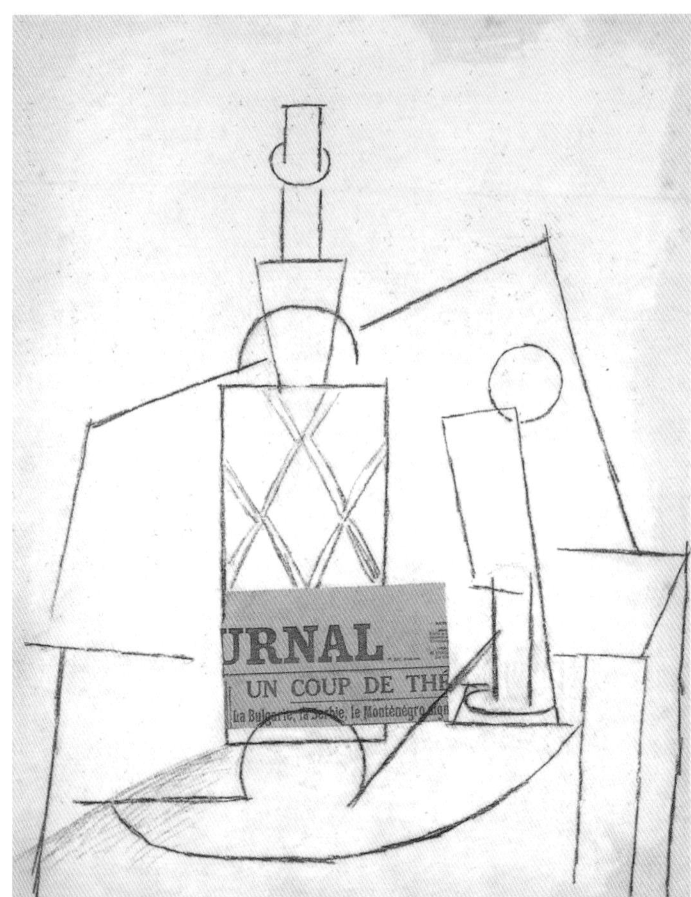

3 • Pablo Picasso, *Table with Bottle, Wine Glass, and Newspaper*, Fall–Winter 1912
Pasted paper, charcoal, and gouache, 62 x 48 (24⅜ x 18⅞)

Prospecting on the fringes

The interpretation of Picasso's collage is, within art-historical scholarship, a battleground in which various parts of the foregoing discussion are pitted against one another. For on the one hand there is the bond between Picasso and Apollinaire, the painter's great friend and most active apologist, which would support the model of Picasso's having a "make it new" (or, as Apollinaire called it, an *esprit nouveau*) attitude toward journalism and the newspaper—almost, as it were, throwing "the morning's poetry" in Mallarmé's face. Emphasizing Apollinaire's exultation in what was modern, both in the sense of what was most ephemeral and what was most at odds with traditional forms of experience, this position would ally Picasso's use of newsprint and other cheap papers with a willful attack on the fine-arts medium of oil painting and its drive for both permanence and compositional unity. The highly unstable condition of newsprint condemns collage from the outset to the transitory; while the procedures for laying out, pinning, and gluing *papiers collés* resemble commercial design strategies more than they do the protocols of the fine arts.

This position would also see Picasso, like Apollinaire, as being caught up in a drive to find aesthetic experience at the margins of what was socially regulated, since it was only from that place that the advanced artist could construct an image of freedom. As the art historian Thomas Crow has argued, this drive has consistently led the avant-garde toward "low" forms of entertainment and unregimented spaces (for Henri de Toulouse-Lautrec [1864–1901] this had been the twilight-zone nightclub; for Picasso, it was the working man's café), even though, ironically, such prospecting has always ended by opening up such spaces for further socialization and commodification by the very forces the advanced artist sought to escape.

If these arguments posit Picasso's embrace of both the "low" and the "modern" values of the newspaper, there are also those commentators who picture his reasons for exploiting this material as primarily political. Picasso, they say, cut the columns of newsprint so that we can read the articles he selected, many of which in the fall of 1912 reported on the war then raging in the Balkans. This is true, of course, at the level of the headlines—an early collage [**3**] presents us with "*Un Coup de Thé*[*âtre*], *La Bulgarie*, *La Serbie*, *Le Monténégra sign*[*ent*]" ("A Turn of Events, Bulgaria, Serbia, Montenegro Sign")—but also in the small type where battlefield reports are grouped around a café table that faces accounts of a social antiwar rally in Paris [**4**]. In giving what she sees as Picasso's reasons for

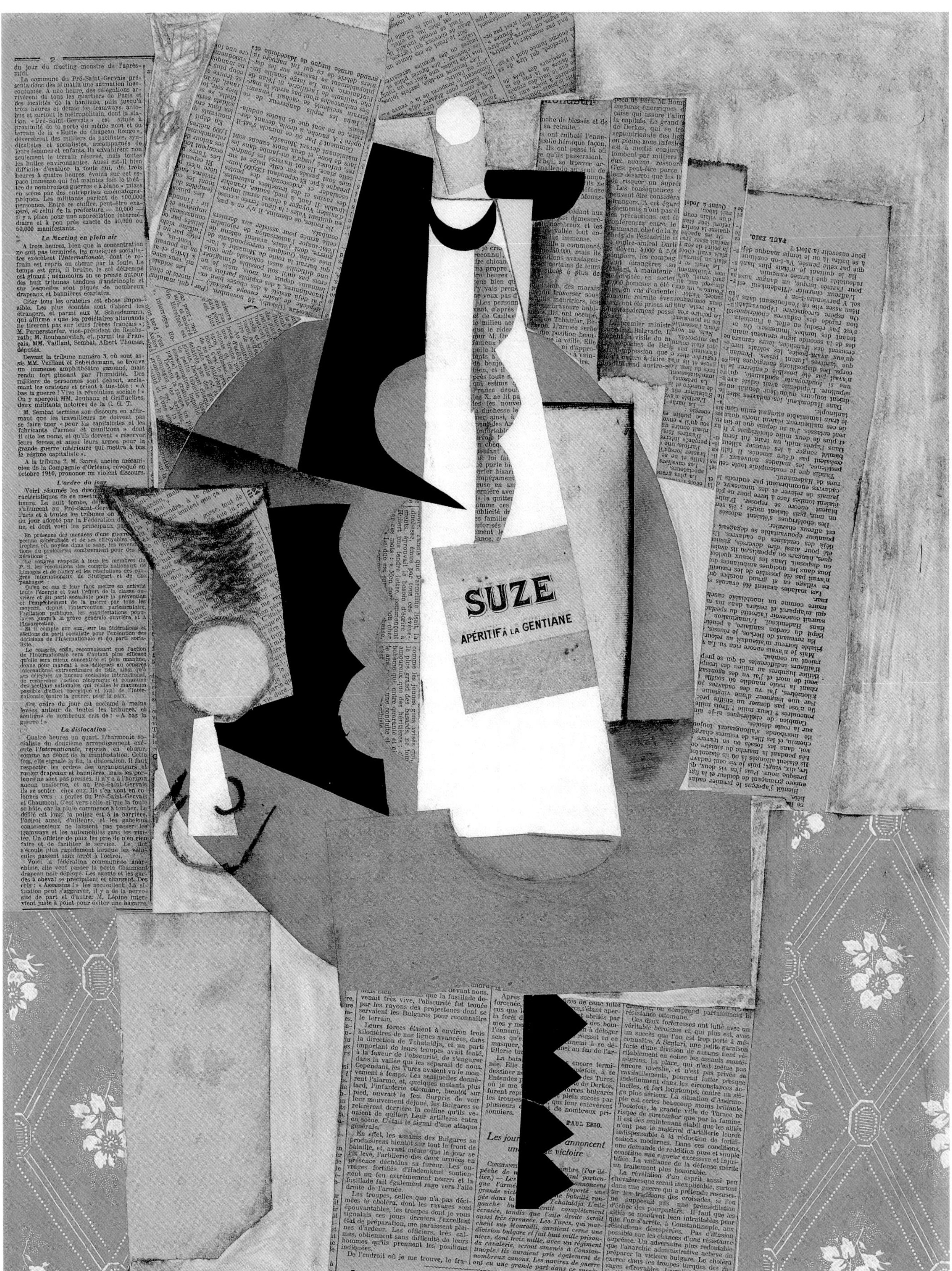

4 • Pablo Picasso, *Glass and Bottle of Suze*, 1912
Pasted paper, gouache, and charcoal, 65.4 x 50.2 (25¾ x 19¾)

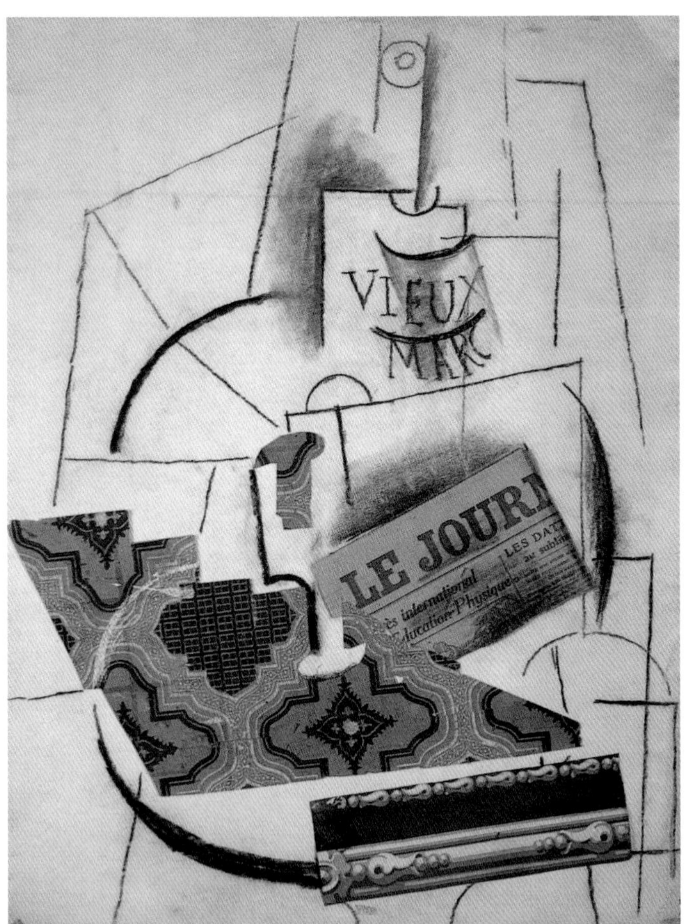

5 • Pablo Picasso, *Bottle of Vieux Marc, Glass, and Newspaper*, 1913
Charcoal and pasted and pinned paper, 63 x 49 (24¾ x 19¼)

this, art historian Patricia Leighten has argued, variously, that he is bringing the reader/viewer into contact with a politically charged reality in the Balkans; or that he is presenting the reader/viewer with the kind of heated discussion that would be going on in a Parisian café where workers, unable to afford a newspaper subscription, would go for their daily news; or again, that Picasso is taking apart the managed cacophony of the newspaper—with its interests in serving up news as so many disjointed entertainments—and is using collage as a means of "counterdiscourse" that will have the power to rearrange the separate stories into a coherent account of capital's manipulation of the social field.

With these propositions we have come progressively further away from the idea of collage as performing a rupture with an older naturalistic, "iconic" system of representation. For whether we imagine Picasso deploying newspaper reports to picture a faraway reality, or using them to depict people conversing in a café, or making them into a coherent ideological picture where previously there had been nothing but confusion, we still think of visual signs as connecting directly to the things in the world they are supposed to be depicting. Picasso's only innovation would be, then, to replace his disputants with speech-balloons for their arguments as he seats them with perfect representational decorum around a more or less conventionally drawn café table. We have, that is, an example of the politically committed artist (although Picasso's politics during this period are themselves open to dispute), but we have lost Picasso as the artistic innovator at the level of importance to the whole history of representation with whom we were engaging at the outset.

This is where the claims of Mallarmé begin to challenge those of Apollinaire, even the Apollinaire who seemed to respond to Picasso's collage by inventing his own fusion of the verbal and the visual in the *calligrammes* he began to fashion in 1914. For constellating written signs into graphic images, the *calligrammes* become doubly "iconic": the letters forming the graphic shape of a pocket watch, for example, merely reinforce at the level of the visual what they express in textual form: "It's five to noon, at last!" And if they thereby take on the graphic excitement of advertisements or product logos, the *calligrammes* nonetheless betray what is most radical in Picasso's challenge to representation: his refusal of the unambiguous "icon" in favor of the endlessly mutational play of the "symbol."

Like Mallarmé's mutational play, where nothing is ever just one thing—as when signifiers divide, doubling "*son or*" (his or her gold) with "*son or*" (the sound "or" and by implication the *sono*rity of poetry)—Picasso's signs mutate visually by folding over onto one another to produce the oppositional pair of the paradigm. As in the earlier *Violin*, this is apparent in the *Bottle of Vieux Marc, Glass, and Newspaper* [**5**], where a toquelike shape, cut from a sheet of wallpaper, reads as *transparency* by articulating both the lip of the wine glass and its liquid contents, while below, the upside-down silhouette left by the "toque's" excision from the sheet registers the *opacity* of the stem and base of the object, declaring itself a figure (no matter how ghostly) against the wallpaper's tablecloth ground. The paradigm is perfectly expressed, as the signifiers—identical in shape—produce each other's meaning, their opposition in space (right side up/upside down) echoing their semantic reversal.

If the play of visual meaning in the collages is thus mutational, the textual play mobilized by Picasso's use of newsprint is also cut free from the fixity of any one "speaker" to whose voice, or opinion, or ideological position we might attribute it. For no sooner do we decide that Picasso has cut an item from the financial pages to denounce the exploitation of the worker, and thereby to "speak" through the means of this clipping, than we have to remember that Apollinaire, from his perch as writer for a half-fraudulent financial magazine, was famous for handing out spurious advice about the stock market and that the voice the collage plants here could just as easily be "his."

Picasso had, indeed, let Mallarmé himself speak from the surfaces of various of these collages, as when "*Au Bon Marché*" doubles a voice like Fernande Olivier's (Picasso's ex-mistress)—speaking of white sales and a trousseau—with the various voices that Mallarmé used as pen-names in his elegant fashion magazine *La Dernière Mode*, or when the headline *Un coup de thé* sounds the title of Mallarmé's most radical poem: "Un coup de dés."

Much has been made of Picasso's recourse to the models of distortion and simplification offered by African tribal art. ▲ Kahnweiler

▲ 1907

insisted, however, that it was a particular mask in Picasso's collection that "opened these painters' eyes." This mask from the Ivory Coast tribe called Grebo is a collection of "paradigms."

Picasso's own venture into constructed sculpture shows the effect of the Grebo example. Made of sheet metal, string, and wire, ▲ his *Guitar* of 1912 **[6]** establishes the instrument's shape through a single plane of metal from which the sound-hole projects, much like the eyes of the Grebo mask. Each plane hovers against the relief-plane as figure against ground, a form of paradigm which the earlier *Violin* had so brilliantly explored. The earliest collage to reflect the lesson of the Grebo mask is *Guitar, Sheet Music, and Glass* **[7]**, in which each collage piece reads as hovering against the flat sheet of the background, the black crescent of the guitar's lowest edge doubling as its shadow cast on the supporting table; its sound-hole seeming to project as a solid tube in front of the instrument's body.

FURTHER READING

Yve-Alain Bois, "Kahnweiler's Lesson", *Painting as Model* (Cambridge, Mass.: MIT Press, 1990)

Yve-Alain Bois, "The Semiology of Cubism," in Lynn Zelevansky (ed.), *Picasso and Braque: A Symposium* (New York: Museum of Modern Art, 1992)

Thomas Crow, "Modernism and Mass Culture," in Serge Guilbaut, Benjamin H. D. Buchloh, and David Solkin (eds), *Modernism and Modernity* (Halifax: The Press of the Nova Scotia College of Art and Design, 1983)

Rosalind Krauss, *The Picasso Papers* (New York: Farrar, Straus & Giroux, 1998)

Patricia Leighten, *Re-Ordering the Universe: Picasso and Anarchism, 1897–1914* (Princeton: Princeton University Press, 1989)

Robert Rosenblum, *Cubism and Twentieth-Century Art* (New York: Harry N. Abrams, 1960, revised 1977)

7 • Pablo Picasso, *Guitar, Sheet Music, and Glass*, Fall 1912
Pasted paper, gouache, and charcoal, 47.9 x 36.5 (18⅞ x 14¾)

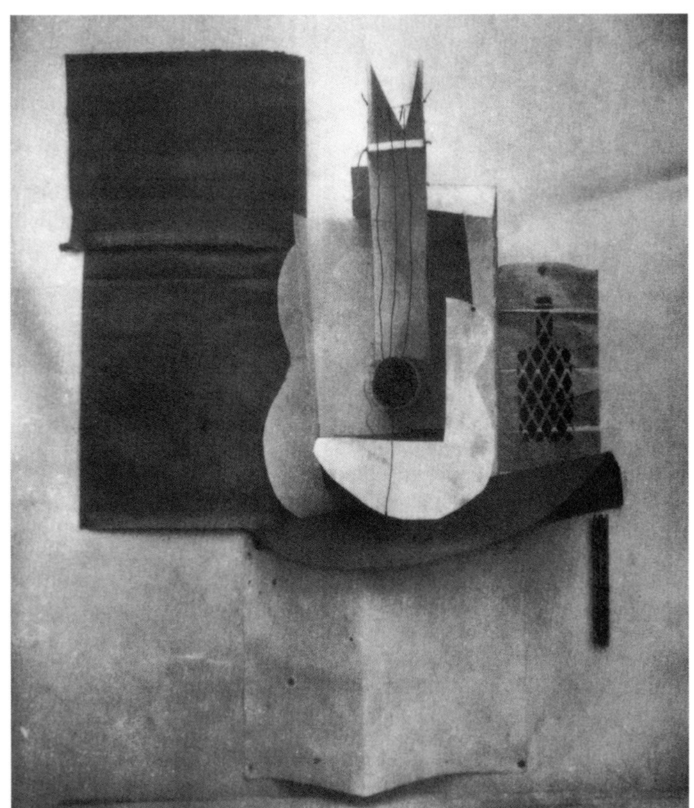

6 • Construction mounted in Picasso's studio at 5 bis, rue Schoelcher, 1913
Includes cardboard maquette for *Guitar* (destroyed)

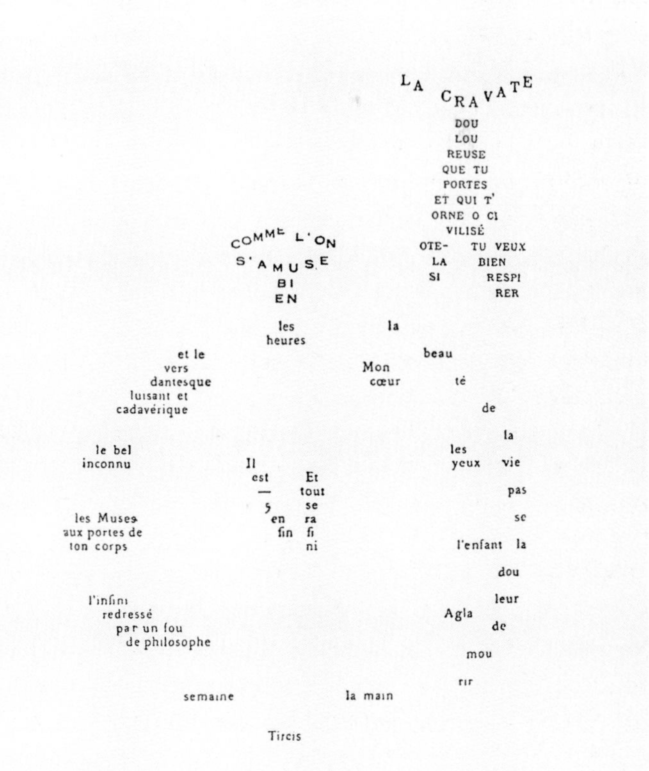

8 • Guillaume Apollinaire, "La Cravate et la montre," 1914
From *Calligrammes: Poèmes de la paix et de la guerre, 1913–16, Part I: Ondes*, 1925

▲ Introduction 3

1913

Robert Delaunay exhibits his "Windows" paintings in Berlin: the initial problems and paradigms of abstraction are elaborated across Europe.

"Cézanne broke the fruit dish," Robert Delaunay (1895–1941) once remarked, "and we should not glue it together again, as the Cubists do." This call for abstraction is clear enough, yet its actual development was complicated: centered on painting, abstraction was driven by diverse motivations, methods, and models. Some artists deepened the painterly aspect of Impressionism; others, the expressive dimension of ▲ Postimpressionism; still others, the linear design of Art Nouveau. The fragmented "fruit dish" of Cézanne and Picasso was influential to many painters on the verge of nonrepresentational art; the broad color fields of Matisse were inspirational to others; and the bold geometric forms of African sculpture also served as an important provocation, sometimes replaced or supplemented by folk art (and, in Russia, by religious icons). In 1912–13 such precedents and provocations converged to allow the recognition of abstraction as a value, even a necessity, in its own right. Since abstraction is primordial to the arts of several cultures, there is no question of a single origin or a first abstraction: in this sense, abstraction was found as much as it was invented. In a famous ● anecdote Wassily Kandinsky told how, when he returned one night to his studio in Murnau, Germany (he dated the event to 1910), he failed to recognize one of his paintings upside down in the dim light—only to discover the expressive potential of abstract forms through this experience.

If there was no one parent of abstraction, there were several midwives, in particular the Frenchman Delaunay, the Russian Sonia Terk (1885–1979; she married Delaunay in 1910), the Dutchman ■ Piet Mondrian, and the Russians Kandinsky and Kazimir Malevich (1878–1935). The last three are often given pride of place as the most committed, but other early abstractionists include the Czech František Kupka (1871–1957), the Frenchman Fernand Léger (1881–1955), the Russian Rayonists Mikhail Larionov (1881–1964) and Natalia Goncharova (1881–1962), the English Vorticist Wyndham Lewis, the Italian Futurists Giacomo Balla and Gino Severini, the German-Swiss Paul Klee (1879–1940), the Alsatian Hans ◆ Arp (1888–1966), the Swiss Sophie Taeuber (1889–1943; she married Arp in 1921), the American Synchromists Morgan Russell (1886–1953) and Stanton Macdonald-Wright (1890–1973), and still others like the American Arthur Dove (1880–1946), who called his near-abstractions "extractions." This list makes two points obvious at once: abstraction was international, and many of its innovators were not formed in avant-garde Paris. Why would this ▲ be so? Although Matisse and Picasso opened the way to abstraction, they were too invested in the world of objects—or, more precisely, in the visual play of figures and signs that this world afforded—to enter into abstraction fully. On the other hand, Kandinsky, Malevich, Mondrian, Klee, and Kupka were formed in cultures (Russian, Dutch, German, Czech) whose metaphysical imperatives and/or iconoclastic impulses might have made abstraction less alien.

In this respect Russia was especially important as a crucible for abstraction. There were important collections of avant-garde painting (the Shchukin Collection alone boasted thirty-seven ● Matisses and forty Picassos), vigorous exhibitions of international art not only in St. Petersburg and Moscow but in provincial cities too, and a range of groups eager to assimilate the lessons of Symbolism, Fauvism, Futurism, and Cubism, as well as to elaborate on folk art, children's drawings, and medieval icons (an exhibition of restored icons was staged in Moscow in 1913). The latter interests were strong in Larionov, who was drawn to the popular woodcarvings known as *lubki*, and Goncharova, whose early paintings of peasant life also reflect the simple forms and strong outlines of peasant carvings, embroidery, and enamels. Larionov and Goncharova were very active in exhibition-making too ("Knave of Diamonds" in 1910 and "The Donkey's Tail" in 1912 were the ■ most important); and inspired by Cubist and Futurist works, they moved away from primitivist experiments toward a form of abstraction marked by fractured lines and luminous colors—a style that Larionov dubbed Rayonism for the manner in which the surface of the painting seems to be struck by multiple rays of light that cross, crystallize, and sometimes dissolve there. The structure of these paintings owes much to Cubism, but the dynamism is Futurist (as is the rhetoric that supported them), and this combination of Cubist faceting and Futurist movement resulted in paintings that are among the earliest abstractions anywhere. Only a few such works were made, however, before Larionov and Goncharova fled the war for Paris (where they were often commissioned to design sets and costumes for the Ballets Russes produced ◆ by Sergei Diaghilev).

▲ 1903, 1906 ● 1908 ■ 1908, 1915, 1917, 1944a ◆ 1908, 1909, 1916a, 1918 ▲ 1906, 1910, 1911, 1912 ● 1910 ■ 1909, 1911 ◆ 1919

Even as abstraction moved away from a mimetic relation to the world, it did not necessarily embrace the "arbitrary" nature of the ▲ visual sign as explored in Cubist collage and construction. Abstract artists might have declined to depict worldly things, but they often aspired to evoke transcendental concepts—such as "feeling," "spirit," or "purity"—and in this way they replaced one type of grounding, one form of authority, with another. (In such influential texts as "Concerning the Spiritual in Art" [1911], Kandinsky called this new authority "internal necessity," and others came up with similar coinages.) Such insistence on transcendental truths betrays an anxiety that abstraction might be arbitrary in two additional senses. First, arbitrary in the sense of *decorative*: in a 1914 lecture in Cologne, Kandinsky cautioned that "ornamental" abstraction might impede rather than produce the requisite transcendental effect of art. And, second, arbitrary in the sense of *meaningless*: faced with the charge, actual or anticipated, that abstraction had no meaning at all, its proponents often overcompensated with tendentious claims of absolute meanings—transcendental for Kandinsky, revelatory for • Malevich, utopian for Mondrian, and so on. When not defined in such grandiose terms, abstraction was often framed negatively—against art based in mimesis (which was regarded as academic) and against design intended as decoration (which was regarded as a low or applied form). But many exceptions qualify this rule. For example, how are we to categorize the grids of Sophie Taeuber [**1**], who sometimes based these works (which predate the first modular abstractions by Mondrian) on the quasi-spontaneous arrangements ■ of collaged squares of Hans Arp? For his part, Arp called them "probably the first examples of 'concrete art'," at once "pure and independent" and "elementary and spontaneous." Are they high art? Low? Transcendental in ambition? Decorative? Programmatic? Aleatory? These works complicated such hierarchical oppositions almost before they were in place.

1 • Sophie Taeuber, *Horizontal Vertical*, 1917
Watercolor, 23 x 15.5 (9 x 6⅛)

Definitions and debates

Standard definitions favor the idea of abstraction as idealization. The *Oxford English Dictionary* offers "separated from matter," "ideal," and "theoretical" for the adjective *abstract*, and "deduct," "remove," and "disengage" for the verb. Appropriate for some artists who evoked ideal states through disengagement from the world, these meanings did not suit others who privileged the opposite terms—the materiality of paint on canvas, or the worldliness of utilitarian designs. This tension between idealist and materialist imperatives runs throughout modernist abstraction, and it is not solved by related terms such as "nonobjective" or "pure." Abstraction approaches the nonobjective by definition; on the other hand, many artists sought "objectivity" above all—to make an art as "concrete" and as "real" as an object in the world. Indeed, Delaunay, Léger, Arp, Malevich, and Mondrian all declared abstraction the most *realist* of modes for this very reason. So, too, abstraction was often promoted as "pure," the final refinement of art for its own sake; on the other hand, purity was often associated with reduction to the constituent materials of a medium, the stuff of paint and canvas, which are difficult to see as pure. In the end, these tensions are integral to abstraction, which is best defined as a category that manages such contradictions—holds them in suspension, or puts them into dialectical play.

The materialist/idealist opposition governed discourses around abstraction as well. Some artists were guided by Platonic, Hegelian, or spiritualist philosophies. For instance, Malevich, Kandinsky, ▲ Mondrian, and Kupka were all influenced by Theosophy, which held (among other beliefs) that man evolved from physical to spiritual states in a series of stages that could be evoked by geometric forms; in *Evolution* (1911), Mondrian imaged the geometric sublimation of a female figure in this way. Perhaps paradoxically, some artists also looked to science to support the idealist version of abstraction. "Why should we continue to follow nature," Mondrian asked around 1919, "when many other fields have left nature behind?" In this regard non-Euclidean geometry interested artists • as diverse as Malevich and Marcel Duchamp for its nonperspectival conception of space and its antimaterialist idea of form. In addition, analogies were made to other arts, especially music.

▲ 1912 • 1908, 1915, 1917, 1944a ■ 1918
▲ 1908, 1915, 1917 • 1914, 1915, 1918, 1935, 1966a, 1993a

"All art," the English aesthetician Walter Pater famously remarked, "constantly aspires towards the condition of music"; so it was still for some artists in the first generation of abstractionists. (This points to a further paradox: can the essence of one art, painting, be found via another art, such as music?) Klee and Kupka were drawn to Baroque and classical music, Johann Sebastian Bach in particu-▲lar; Kandinsky, to late-Romantic and modern music, especially Richard Wagner and Arnold Schoenberg. Indeed, Kandinsky patterned the categories of his early abstractions—"Improvisations," "Impressions," "Compositions"—on music, which also influenced his emphasis on color tone, linear rhythm, "thorough-bass" (a notion derived from Goethe), and immediacy to feeling. Kupka, too, stressed the Symbolist analogy between pure music and pure painting, with the attendant implication that such art could act directly "on the soul" without the distraction of content or subject matter; his large canvas *Amorpha, Fugue in Two Colors* [**2**] is often claimed as the first nonfigurative painting to be exhibited publicly in Paris, at the Salon d'Automne in 1912, though it was inspired in part by the mundane movements of a multicolored ball (a plaything of his stepdaughter), as well as by the celestial motions of the planets (which had also informed his previous *Disks of Newton* paintings). ● For his part, Mondrian adored jazz: he found its syncopated rhythm analogous to his asymmetrical equilibrium of color planes, and its resistance to melodic narratives parallel to his resistance to temporal readings of visual art.

Other abstract artists were driven by materialist concerns. Some looked to abstraction as the only mode adequate to the becoming-abstract of the object-world in a world transfigured by new modes of commodity production, public transportation, and image reproduction. The project to capture the increased mobility of products, people, and images in the modern city was not strictly ■ Futurist; it also provoked artists such as Léger to a paradoxical type of realist abstraction. In his *Contrast of Forms* [**3**], we see a symbiosis of human and mechanical forms abstracted as if to the geometric specifications of the canvas. Indeed, by the end of the decade Léger would conceive painting, in analogy with the machine, as a device of interrelated parts. Yet already in 1913 he referred the abstraction of his painting, as well as the separation of all modernist arts, to a capitalist division of labor—a modern condition that he sought to make a modernist virtue:

> *Each art is isolating itself and limiting itself to its own domain. Specialization is a modern characteristic, and pictorial art, like all other manifestations of human genius, must submit to its law; it is logical, for by limiting each discipline to its own purpose, it enables achievements to be intensified. In this way pictorial art gains in realism. The modern conception is not simply a passing abstraction, valid only for a few initiates; it is the total expression of a new generation whose needs it shares and whose aspirations it answers.*

◆ Cubism was the first style to perform this paradox of an art that appears both abstract and realist, and it remained the crucible for most abstract artists. Yet "Cubism did not accept the logical conse-

2 • František Kupka, *Amorpha, Fugue in Two Colors*, 1912
Oil on canvas, 211.8 x 220 (83⅜ x 86⅝)

3 • Fernand Léger, *Contrast of Forms*, 1913
Oil on canvas, 55 x 46 (21⅝ x 18)

▲ 1908 ● 1917, 1944a ■ 1909 ◆ 1911, 1912

4 • Piet Mondrian, *Tableau No. 2/Composition VII*, 1913
Oil on canvas, 104.5 x 111.1 (41⅛ x 43¾)

quences of its own discoveries," Mondrian remarked in a retrospect shared by others, "it was not developing towards its own goals, the expression of pure plastics." Thus in 1912–13 some artists pushed ▲ the "analytical" aspect of Cubism to dissolve the motif altogether. They did so either in linear coordination with the implicit grid of the canvas, as with Mondrian in a work such as *Tableau No. 2/Composition VII* [**4**], or through prismatic effects of color seen as light, as with Delaunay in a work such as *Fenêtres simultanés sur la ville* (*Simultaneous Windows on the City*) [**5**]. If Mondrian explicated the grid in a way that exceeded the faceted planes of Cubism, Delaunay intensified color in a manner that was alien to its muted palette. Meanwhile, other artists pushed the "synthetic" aspect of Cubism: the flat shapes ▲ of Cubist collage were the immediate precedent for the abstract color planes of Malevich, while the factual elements of Cubist construction, which Picasso showed Vladimir Tatlin in Paris in the spring of • 1914, were one provocation of his Constructivist "analysis of materials." Some kind of passage through Cubism became almost a prerequisite for followers: "From a [Cubist] analysis of the volume and space of objects to the [Constructivist] organization of elements," the Russian Liubov Popova (1889–1924) wrote in a 1922 studio note, as if this development were already a catechism.

In most instances one element of painting was made dominant, even turned into a medium of meaning in its own right: thus the privileging of verticals and horizontals in Mondrian, of color as

▲ 1911 ▲ 1912 ● 1914, 1921

light in Delaunay, of monochrome geometries in Malevich. Soon these elements were refined further into two relatively stable para- ▲ digms of abstract painting: the grid and the monochrome. To a great extent they became fixed because the grid worked to undo the primordial oppositions of line and color, figure and ground, motif and frame (it was the genius of Mondrian to explore these possibilities), and the monochrome worked to negate the two dominant paradigms of Western painting since the Renaissance: the window and the mirror (it was the hubris of Malevich to announce the end of these old orders).

In 1913, as they advanced toward the grid and the monochrome respectively, Delaunay and Malevich provide an instructive contrast. Delaunay mostly scoffed at models extrinsic to painting: "I never speak of mathematics and never bother with spirit"; "I am horrified by music and noise." Concerned with "pictorial realities" alone, he looked to color to carry all aspects of painting: "color gives depth (not perspective, nonsequential but simultaneous) and form and movement." To this end, Delaunay developed "the law of simultaneous contrasts," which French artists from Delacroix to Seurat had adapted from an 1839 treatise by the chemist Michel-Eugène Chevreul, into his own notion of *simultanéisme.* Besides color contrasts, this "simultaneity" pertains to the immediacy of pictorial image to retinal image, indeed to the transcendental simultaneity of the visual arts as opposed to the mundane temporality of the verbal arts (this opposition is a persistent one in modern aesthetics from the German Enlightenment philosopher Gotthold Ephraim Lessing [1729–81] to the late-modernist critics ▲ Clement Greenberg and Michael Fried). In some of these interests Delaunay was joined by Morgan Russell and Stanton Macdonald-Wright, who were also active in Paris in these years. They too treated light in terms of prismatic color, though they allowed for effects of spatial projection and even temporal duration that Delaunay tended to resist; they also pursued musical analogies for abstraction that Delaunay tended to dismiss.

5 • Robert Delaunay, *Fenêtres simultanées sur la ville*, 1911–12
Oil on canvas and wood, 46 60 (18 1/8 x 23 5/8)

Delaunay made his breakthrough in his "Windows" series, some twenty-three paintings and drawings executed in 1912, thirteen of which were shown to great effect in Berlin in January 1913 (he had ● previously exhibited with the Blaue Reiter in Munich). To coincide with the show, Klee translated a text by Delaunay titled "Light" that presented a series of equations among color, light, eye, brain, and soul. In his aesthetic the painting is the "window" of all these "transparencies"—a medium abstracted into *im*mediacy, dissolved into what it mediates. In this way Delaunay hardly rejected the old paradigm of painting-as-window; on the contrary, he *purified* it: the reality of vision is delivered in the abstraction of painting. Consider *Simultaneous Windows on the City*, which set the compositional type for the series. The Eiffel Tower, the central motif of his entire oeuvre, is now vestigial, its green arcs caught up in a play of opaque and transparent color planes pushed beyond Cubist faceting toward a post-Cubist grid (which, in the neo-Impressionist fashion of Seurat, Delaunay extended to the frame). The windows are thus referential, pictorial, and objective all at once; they reconcile the "sublime subject" of Paris with the "self-evident structure" of painting, as the ■ poet-critic Guillaume Apollinaire, a great Delaunay supporter, once remarked. Delaunay rendered the medium opaque, only to make it disappear again in the interests of transparent immediacy. In effect, *Simultaneous Windows on the City* are windows without curtains, almost eyes without lids: color as light is nearly blinding here. The next step was to do away altogether with the windows in order to present the painting in direct analogy with the retina. This is what Delaunay did in *Disk* **[6]**, the purest of abstractions at this time, a circular painting of seven concentric bands of solid colors divided into quarters, with the more intense primaries and complementaries closer to the center. Although sometimes dismissed as a mere demonstration of color theory—a color chart in fact—*Disk* contains resources for abstraction (utter nonreferentiality and opticality, structured canvas and composition) that would not be developed fully for another fifty years or more. The year 1913 was also a significant one for Sonia Terk Delaunay, who, already active in design (primarily books and embroidery), illustrated *The Prose of the Transsiberian and of the Little Jeanne of France* by the avant-garde poet Blaise Cendrars **[7]**. Published on a single sheet of paper two meters long folded into twelve panels, this object-book combined avant-garde abstraction and typography (the same text was set in ten typefaces, and a railroad map was included) in order to evoke the prismatic simultaneity of modern life. Often exhibited and reproduced, the book cover was widely influential (Terk may have affected German modernists almost as much as her husband did), and its success encouraged her to apply the same "simultaneist"

▲ 1957b

▲ 1942a, 1960b ● 1908 ■ 1911, 1912

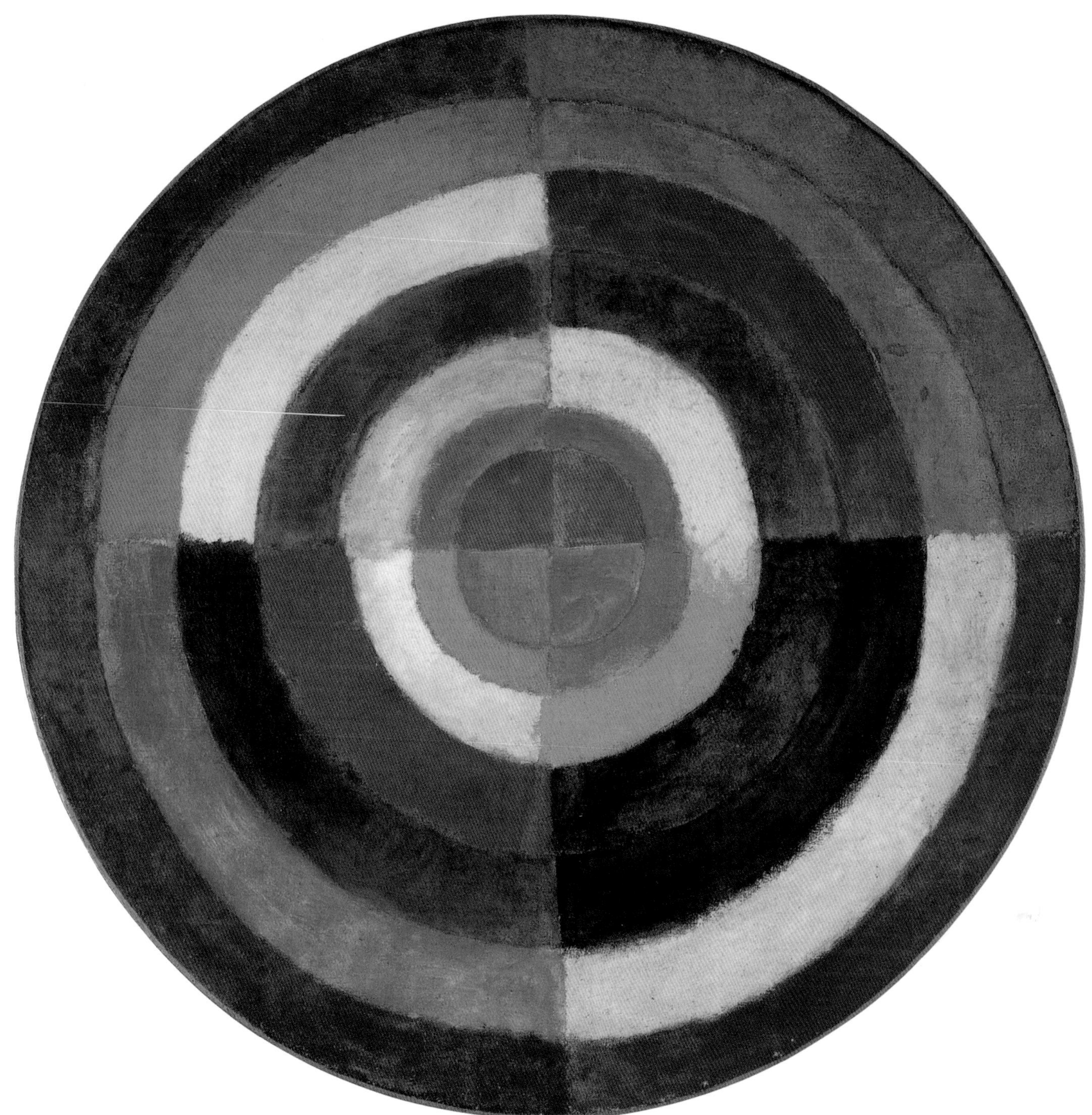

6 • Robert Delaunay, *Premier disque simultané* (Disk [The First Disk]), 1913–14
Oil on canvas, diameter 135 (52¾)

rhythms of abstract colors to other designs—clothes, posters, even electric lamps devised to diffuse light into color on Paris streets.

Malevich took a different course: not to purify painting-as-window but to paint it out. He referred his first total abstraction, ▲ *Black Square* (1915), to a sketch for a backdrop that he designed for a Futurist opera, *Victory over the Sun* (1913), an opera opposed to Symbolist art ("the old, accepted concept of the beautiful sun," its composer V. N. Matiushin once scoffed) as well as to naturalist theater. Here Malevich places, in a perspectival box, a square divided diagonally into a black triangle above and a white triangle below in order to evoke the "victory over the sun," the eclipse of light by dark, perhaps the overcoming of empirical vision and perspectival space by transcendental vision and modernist infinity [**8**]. In this sketch the countdown to his own private *tabula rasa* begins: on the other side of this "zero of form," Malevich announced, lies "the supremacy of pure feeling in creative art"—hence his term for his abstract style, Suprematism.

Thus Delaunay and Malevich appear to be opposed: the first proclaims the transparency of the window to color as light; the second, the victory over the sun in the triumph of the black square. But both

▲ 1915

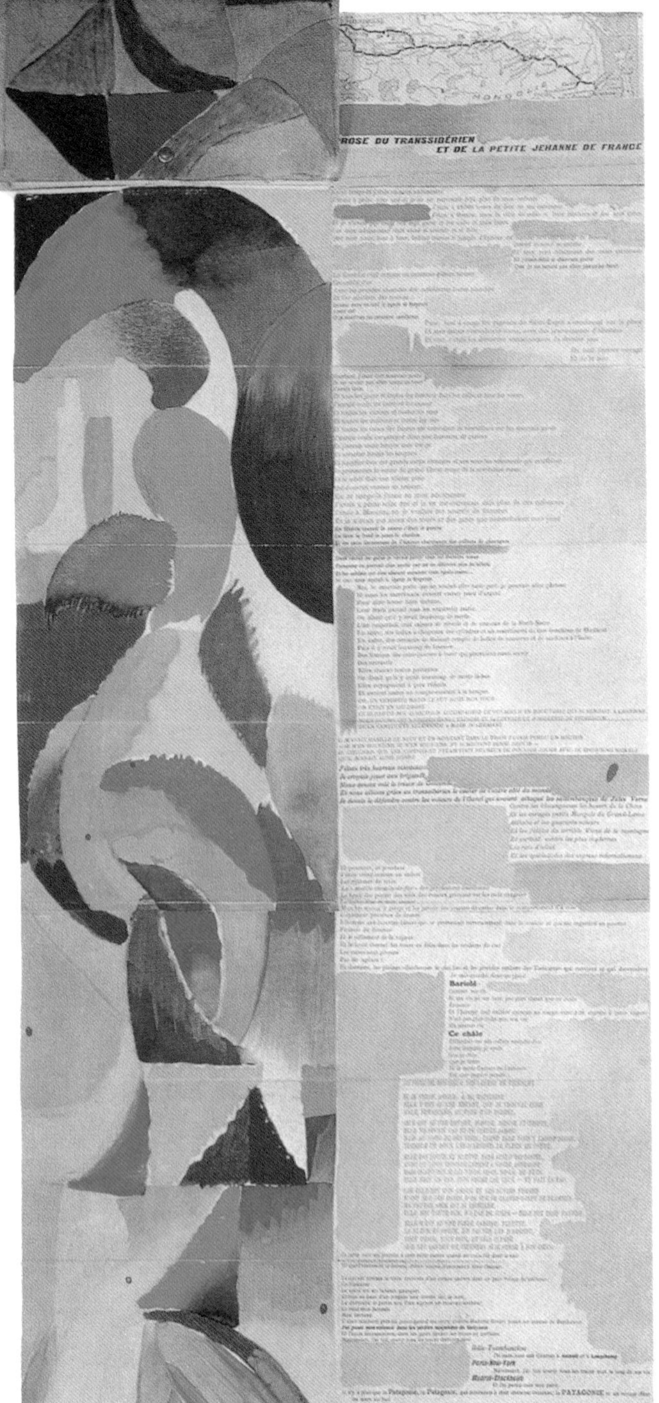

7 • Sonia Terk Delaunay, *La Prose du Transsiberian et de la Petite Jehanne de France* (The Prose of the Transsiberian and of the Little Jeanne of France), 1913
Watercolor on paper, 193.5 x 37 (76⅛ x 14⅝)

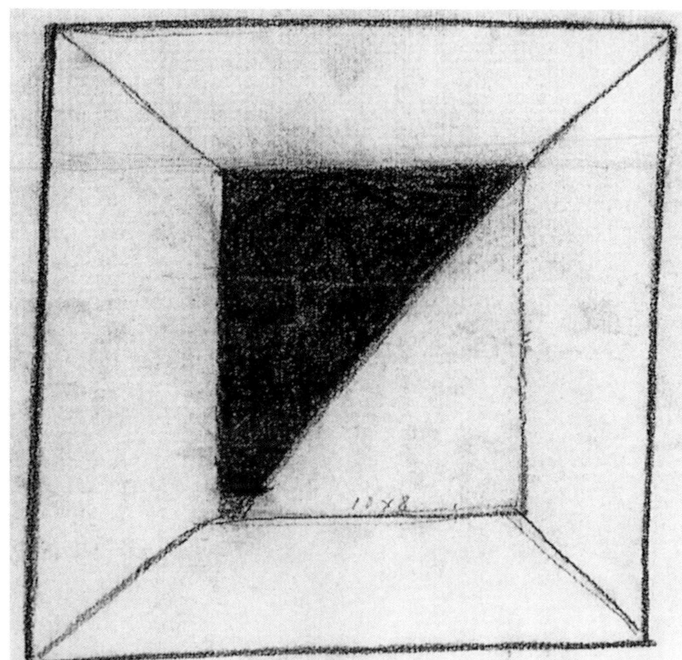

8 • Kazimir Malevich, sketch for *Victory over the Sun*, Act 2, Scene I, 1913
Graphite pencil on paper, 21 x 27 (8¼ x 10⅝)

are high priests of pure vision, and this renders them opposites that belong together. Even as Delaunay atomizes the motif in his color as light, while Malevich darkens it through his eclipse of the sun, both cancel one relation to reality only to affirm another, higher relation, and in this transformation they are joined by others such as Kandinsky and Mondrian for whom abstraction is the apotheosis of the real, not its downfall. They may render the medium opaque, self-evidently material as canvas and paint, but they do so in order to render it transparent again—to feeling, spirit, or purity, all of which these abstractions are asked to signify at one time or another.

In the end abstraction is a paradoxical mode that suspends such oppositions—between spiritual effect and decorative design, between material surface and ideal window, between singular work and serial repetition (bereft of external referents, abstract paintings tend to be read internally, in terms of one another, in sets, and they are often designated in this manner too: "*Untitled # 1, 2, 3 ...*"). The materialist/idealist contradiction might be the most profound of all: painting as a plane covered with paint, the medium disclosed in its empirical materiality, versus painting as a map of a transcendental order, a window to a world of spirit. For the French ▲ philosopher Michel Foucault, however, this relation is less contradictory than complementary: modern thought, he argues, often comprehends both kinds of investigations, empirical and transcendental, and both kinds of dispositions, materialist and idealist. Nonetheless, this tension is *experienced* as a contradiction not only in modernist art but also in modern culture at large, and it suggests one reason why this culture has privileged artists who, like Mondrian, are able to hold on to both poles at once, who offer aesthetic resolutions to this apparent contradiction.

FURTHER READING

Yve-Alain Bois, "Malevitch: le carré, le degré zero," *Macula*, no. 1, 1978

Arthur A. Cohen (ed.), *The New Art of Color: The Writings of Robert and Sonia Delaunay* (New York: Viking Press, 1978)

Michael Compton (ed.), *Towards a New Art: Essays on the Background of Abstract Art 1910–1920* (London: Tate Gallery, 1980)

Gordon Hughes, "The Structure of Vision in Robert Delaunay's 'Windows'," *October*, no. 102, Fall 2002

Rosalind Krauss, "Grids," *The Originality of the Avant-Garde and Other Modernist Myths* (Cambridge, Mass.: MIT Press, 1985)

Fernand Léger, *Functions of Painting*, trans. Alexandra Anderson (New York: Viking Press, 1973)

Kazimir Malevich, *Essays on Art 1915–1933*, ed. Troels Andersen (London: Rapp and Whiting, 1969)

▲ 1971

1914

Vladimir Tatlin develops his constructions and Marcel Duchamp proposes his readymades, the first as a transformation of Cubism, the second as a break with it; in doing so, they offer complementary critiques of the traditional mediums of art.

▲ The years 1912–14 were momentous ones in the avant-garde. New forms of picture-making such as abstraction and collage broke with representational painting, and new forms of object-making such as the construction and the readymade challenged figurative sculpture, as the old focus on the human body was displaced by new explorations of industrial materials and commercial products. These developments were internal to modernist art, but they were also influenced by external events, such as the increased industrialization and commodification of everyday life, which was far more advanced in the Paris of Marcel Duchamp (1887–1968) than in the Moscow and St. Petersburg of Vladimir Tatlin (1885–1953). At the same time, these new objects seemed almost to anticipate such worldly transformations. The first Tatlin constructions preceded the Russian Revolution in 1917, while the first Duchamp readymades predated the commodity culture of the twenties. "What happened from the social aspect in 1917," Tatlin wrote, "was realized in our work as pictorial artists in 1914, when 'materials, volume, and construction' were accepted as our foundations." Such materialist foundations were achieved • in Constructivist art, Tatlin implies, *before* they were established in Communist society.

Yet the breaks marked by the construction and the readymade were not as punctual or as final as we often like to think. Art historians favor the dramatic convenience of the signal event: Duchamp, pressed by his own brothers to withdraw his Cubist painting *Nude Descending a Staircase No. 2* [**1**] from the Salon des Indépendants in the spring of 1912, abandons painting altogether; or Tatlin, on a visit to Paris in the spring of 1914, encounters the Cubist constructions of Picasso and proceeds directly to his own reliefs. These events did occur, but they were not simple causes; indeed, the readymade and the construction must be seen as complementary responses to two overdetermined developments. First, Duchamp and Tatlin were responding in different ways to a crisis in representation signaled by Cubism. Second, that crisis had revealed a truth about "bourgeois" art, both academic and avant-garde, to which the two artists were also responding—that it was presumed to be autonomous, separate from social life, an institution in its own right. "The category *art as institution* was not invented by the avant-garde movements," the German critic Peter

1 • Marcel Duchamp, *Nude Descending a Staircase No. 2*, 1912
Oil on canvas, 147 x 89.2 (57⅞ x 35⅛)

▲ 1912, 1913 • 1921

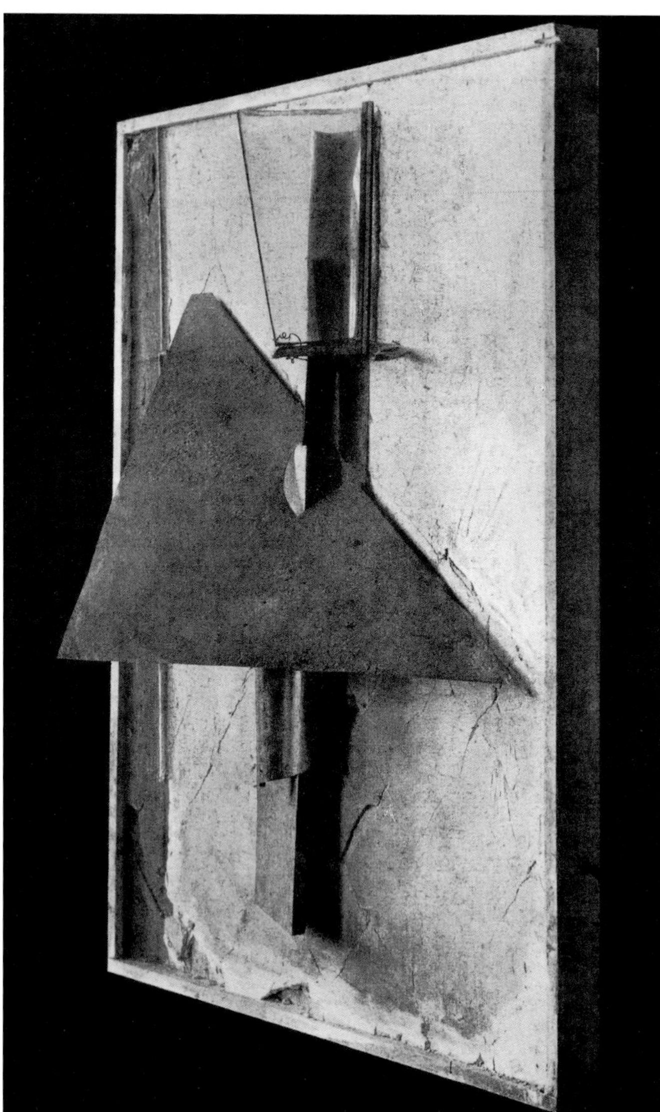

2 • Vladimir Tatlin, *Selection of Materials: Iron, Stucco, Glass, Asphalt*, 1914
Dimensions unknown

▲ Bürger writes in *Theory of the Avant-Garde* (1974). "But it only became recognizable after the avant-garde movements had criticized the autonomy status of art in developed bourgeois society." Once valued as the sign of artistic freedom, according to Bürger, this autonomy had become the mark of its "social ineffectuality," and this in turn prompted "the self-critique of art" advanced paradigmatically by Duchamp and Tatlin.

The material dictates the form

Tatlin was born in the Ukrainian city of Khar'kov to a poet-mother and an engineer-father who was an expert on American railroads. Although active in the Cubo-Futurist avant-garde by 1907–8, Tatlin remained a sometime sailor (likely a ship's carpenter) until 1914–15. These facts are more than anecdotal: his work was oriented by the parental poles of poetics and engineering, and directed by his keen sense of crafted materials. His 1914 sojourn to Paris was epiphanic— ● he probably saw such Picasso constructions as *Guitar* (1912) —although he was already acquainted with Cubism from the great ▲ Shchukin Collection in Moscow. This is evident from such early paintings as *The Sailor: A Self-Portrait* (1911–12), which shows some quasi-Cubist faceting. Yet his first monumental figures are pushed toward the picture plane in a way more suggestive of archaic Russian pictures than contemporary Cubist ones—not only the folkloric woodprints that were popular in his Cubo-Futurist milieu but also religious icons, whose muted palette of colors, flat application of paint, and sheer materiality appealed to Tatlin. Sculptor and critic Vladimir Markov suggested why as early as 1914: "Let us remember icons; they are embellished with metal halos, metal casings on the shoulders, fringes and incrustations; the painting itself is decorated with precious stones and metals, etc. All of this destroys our contemporary conception of painting." In this modernist rereading of the medieval icon, its very materiality disallows any illusion of the real world and instead conducts "the people to beauty, to religion, to God." In his constructions Tatlin reversed the thrust of this anti-illusionism in order to direct the viewer not to a transcendental realm of God but to an immanent reality of materials. In effect, he ● used the Russian icon as Picasso had used the African mask: as a "witness" to his own analytical development of modernist precedents, as a guide to an art no longer governed by resemblance.

His first known relief, *The Bottle* (1913, now lost), remains a Cubist still life, with different materials used to signify different objects (e.g., glass for bottle). Set within a frame, it is still more pictorial composition than material construction, though his basic repertoire of wood, metal, and glass is in place. In *Selection of Materials: Iron, Stucco, Glass, Asphalt* [**2**], Tatlin is already on the threshold of Constructivism. The frame remains, but the materials are no longer composed pictorially. An iron triangle projects into space, in contrast with a wooden rod set at an angle in the stucco surface; below and above are two further juxtapositions of curved metal and cut glass. *Selection* has the character of a demonstration: it first lists its materials, then allows intrinsic properties to suggest appropriate forms. "The material dictates the forms, and not the opposite," critic Nikolai Tarabukin wrote in a 1916 definition of Constructivism based on such works. "Wood, metal, glass, etc. impose different constructions." For Tatlin, machined wood was square and planar, and so suggested rectilinear forms; metal could be cut and bent, and so suggested curvilinear forms; glass was somewhere in between, with a transparency that might also mediate between interior and exterior surfaces. How different this materialism is from the ambiguity of Cubist constructions! Far from the "arbitrary," Tatlin sought to make his constructions "necessary" through this "truth to materials," an ur-modernist aesthetic that tended also to be an ethics and, after the Russian Revolution, a politics as well.

Yet this was not merely a positivistic reduction to materials, as would often be the case in postwar versions of the aesthetic. For along with Cubist constructions and Russian icons, a third model was in play here—the contemporaneous language experiments of ■ "transrational" poets such as Aleksei Kruchenikh and Velemir

▲ 1960a ● Introduction 3 ▲ 1910 ● 1903, 1907 ■ Introduction 3, 1915

Khlebnikov, whose play *Zangezi* Tatlin directed and designed in 1923. Khlebnikov not only shattered syntax but also broke language down into phonemes, the basic units of speech. He did so, however, ▲ not with a Futurist or Dadaist delight in destruction but in order to reassemble these pieces of sound and script into new "word-constructions" suggestive of new meanings. It was this constructive act that Tatlin affirmed: "Parallel to his word-constructions, I decided to make material constructions."

After 1914 Tatlin adopted the term "counter-relief," as if to signal a dialectical advance in his constructions: just as the first "painterly reliefs" exceeded painting, so the new "counter-reliefs," which extended from the wall, exceeded the painterly reliefs. Sometimes these counter-reliefs were suspended across corners with axial wires and rods [**3**]. These "corner counter-reliefs" were complex constructions of metal planes, squared and curved, perpendicular and angular. Not painting, sculpture, or architecture, they were "counters" to all three arts that activated materials, spaces, and viewers in new ways. First shown in December 1915 at • "0.10: The Last Futurist Exhibition of Paintings" in Petrograd (once St. Petersburg, soon to be Leningrad), where Tatlin vied with Kazimir Malevich for leadership of the Russian avant-garde, the counter-reliefs drew young artists into the experimental ■ ("laboratory") phase of Constructivism. If the painterly reliefs advanced the Constructivist notion of *faktura*, which, in contradistinction to Western "facture," stressed the mechanical aspect of the painterly mark rather than its subjective side, the counter-reliefs advanced the Constructivist notion of *construction*, which, in opposition to Western "composition," stressed active engagement with art rather than contemplative reflection of it. Yet to be developed was the third notion of Constructivism, *tectonics*, the dialectical connection of Constructivist formal experimentation with Communist principles of socioeconomic organization, but this most difficult step in the Constructivist program had to await the Revolution.

Works of art without the artist

Son of a supportive notary-father, Duchamp had three siblings who were also artists. His two older brothers, Jacques Villon (1875–1963) and Raymond Duchamp-Villon (1876–1918), drew Marcel into the "Puteaux Group" of Cubists around Albert Gleizes and Jean Metzinger. This circle had begun to turn Cubism into a doctrine by 1912, and Duchamp withdrew over its rejection of his *Nude Descending a Staircase No. 2.* Stung by the controversy, Duchamp would never again be its victim; on the contrary, he became a master of the art of provocation—one of his more ambiguous legacies to twentieth-century art. The mysterious move from his Cubist paintings, which are mostly "nudes," "virgins," and "brides" tinctured with personal eroticism, to his readymades, which are mostly banal products distanced from subjectivity, remains a provocation in its own right. We have only a few pieces of this puzzle. In the summer of 1912 Duchamp lived in Munich,

3 • Vladimir Tatlin, *Corner Counter-Relief*, 1915
Iron, aluminum, primer, dimensions unknown

which he later called "the scene of my complete liberation"—perhaps from the strictly "retinal" concerns of the Parisian avant-garde ("retinal" was his term for painting that did not engage the "gray matter" of the mind). Earlier, in 1911, he had befriended ▲ the wealthy Francis Picabia (1879–1953), who had introduced him to the idea of the artist as dandyish "negator," an attitude that Duchamp would later adopt and develop. Also in 1911 he had attended a play by Raymond Roussel (1877–1933) based on his novel *Impressions of Africa* (1910). Extremely eccentric, Roussel made a method out of the arbitrary: he would select a phrase, construct a homophone of it (that is, a phrase similar in sound but not in sense), use one of the phrases to begin the story and the other to end it, and then concoct a narrative to connect the two. Writing here became a dysfunctional kind of machine. "Roussel showed me the way," Duchamp insisted, not only to the homophonic puns and • dysfunctional machines of his "rotoreliefs," but more generally to his various stratagems that combined chance and choice, the arbitrary and the given. These stratagems, such as his mechanical drawings and readymade objects, put conventional notions of art and artist alike into radical doubt; they were "works of art without an artist to make them," he once remarked.

Two further anecdotes are telling in this regard. In 1911 Duchamp painted an "exploded" coffee grinder; in its "diagrammatic aspect," he commented later, "I began to think I could avoid all contact with traditional pictorial painting." Then, in 1912, at the Salon de la locomotion aérienne, he remarked to his friend, the ■ sculptor Constantin Brancusi: "Painting is over. Who'd do better than this propeller? Tell me, could you do that?" This was not an endorsement of machine art before the fact—again, the machines that interested Duchamp were dysfunctional figures of frustrated desire (like the ones that populate his *The Bride Stripped Bare by her* ◆ *Bachelors, Even*, also known as the *Large Glass*, 1915–23). But the question does point to the queries soon posed in his own work: What is the relation of utilitarian objects to aesthetic objects, of

▲ 1909, 1916a • 1915 ■ 1921

▲ 1916b, 1919 • 1918, 1993a ■ 1927b ◆ 1918

The "Peau de l'Ours"

The readymade, perhaps more than other art form, exposes the complicated relationship between art and the market. On the one hand, endowing an object (even, as Duchamp showed, a mass-produced one such as a urinal) with aesthetic value, could inflate its price from lowly work to masterpiece. On the other, the buying and selling of these expensive works has the same structure as the marketing of any other luxury item, thus lowering the object (aesthetically speaking) to the level of any other commodity. Hence the avant-garde found itself trapped within a structural condition in which it was in an endless race with the very capital logic it wished to expose.

That the avant-garde would prove to be an excellent investment was the bet that businessman André Level made in 1904 when, with twelve other speculators, he founded the "Peau de l'Ours" [Skin of the Bear], a consortium to buy avant-garde works, hold them for ten years, and then sell them off at auction. By 1907, Level's group had already been buying Matisse and Picasso heavily, and in that year it acquired Picasso's *Family of Saltimbanques* directly from the artist for 1,000 francs (expending the whole of its budget for the year). When it came to the time for the sale, held at the Hôtel Drouot in Paris on March 2, 1914, their collection of 145 items, consisting primarily of Fauvist and Cubist works, went under the hammer. Level advertised the event heavily, drawing large crowds to the presale exhibition and the auction itself, making it a kind of verdict on avant-garde art. In the event, the *Family of Saltimbanques*—the success of the evening—was sold for 12,650 francs, while the whole collection had increased its price fourfold, the initial investment of 27,500 francs now returning an impressive total of 116,545 francs.

commodities to art? Can a picture be made as anonymous, as non-subjective, as "perfect" as a propeller? From this point on he did prefer objects that were given, not made, and images that were scripted, not invented (not "retinal" at all), such as his two *Chocolate Grinders* diagrammed in projection in 1913 and 1914. Sly allusions to sex and scatology, these grinders of colored substances also parodied painting, reduced it to the status of an industrial diagram—which, as art historian Molly Nesbit has shown, informed the teaching of drawing in French schools when Duchamp was a child.

He chose it

Duchamp used chance to decenter authorship, but his quintessential device in this respect was the readymade, an appropriated product positioned as art. This device allowed him to leap past old aesthetic questions of craft, medium, and taste ("is it good or bad painting or sculpture?") to new questions that were potentially ontological ("what is art?"), epistemological ("how do we know it?"), and institutional ("who determines it?"). Two of his notes are especially important here. The first, written in 1913, is a programmatic question: "Can one make works that are not 'works' of art?" The second, from 1914, is an obscure fragment: "A kind of pictorial Nominalism." Both notes suggest that Duchamp had begun to construe *naming* art—that is, nominating a given image or object as art—as tantamount to *making* art. Although the term was not yet in place, the first "readymade" was a bicycle wheel set upside down on a stool **[4]**. He would find the name for his new technique, precisely readymade, only when he moved to New York in 1915 for the war, as a label for clothing bought off the rack, potentially mass produced and consumed. How are we to read this wheel? As "art" at all? Indeed, as a "work" at all (for it involved almost no labor of his own)? Or is this wheel that spins freely nothing but work, nothing but function? *Bottlerack* (1914) pushed the question of use further. Although it might suggest an abstract sculpture, this bottle-dryer remains both a utilitarian object and a simple commodity, and so compels us to consider the complex relationships between aesthetic value, use-value, and exchange-value.

4 • Marcel Duchamp, *Bicycle Wheel*, 1913 (1964 replica, original lost)
Readymade: bicycle wheel fixed to a stool, height 126 (49 5/8)

The most notorious readymade was a urinal named *Fountain* [**5**], which compounded the provocative questions of the other readymades with a scandalous evocation of the bathroom. Duchamp chose the urinal from a New York showroom of J. L. Mott Iron Works, a manufacturer of such fixtures, rotated it ninety degrees, signed it R. Mutt ("R" for Richard, slang for a rich man, and "Mutt" to refer both to Mott and to Mutt, a popular cartoon character of the time), set it on a pedestal, and submitted it to the American Society of Independent Artists for its first exhibition in April 1917. Duchamp was the chair of the hanging committee, but the show was unjuried, that is, it accepted all 2,125 works by 1,235 artists that were offered ... except for *Fountain* by the unknown R. Mutt. It was rejected on grounds that Duchamp rebutted, through his proxy Beatrice Wood, in a defense titled "The Richard Mutt Case," published in the May issue of their short-lived magazine *The Blind Man*. It reads in full:

> *They say any artist paying six dollars may exhibit.*
>
> *Mr Richard Mutt sent in a fountain. Without discussion this article disappeared and never was exhibited.*
>
> *What were the grounds for refusing Mr Mutt's fountain:-*
>
> *1 Some contended it was immoral, vulgar.*
>
> *2 Others, it was plagiarism, a plain piece of plumbing.*
>
> *Now Mr Mutt's fountain is not immoral, that is absurd, no more than a bathtub is immoral. It is a fixture that you see every day in plumbers' show windows.*
>
> *Whether Mr Mutt with his own hands made the fountain or not has no importance. He* CHOSE *it. He took an ordinary article of life, placed it so that its useful significance disappeared under the new title and point of view—created a new thought for that object.*
>
> *As for plumbing, that is absurd. The only works of art America has given are her plumbing and her bridges.*

The principal questions here—of immorality and utility, of originality and intentionality—are contested in art to this day. So, too, are the related problems of "choice," that is, of art as a process of nomination by the authority of the artist. Were the readymades art because Duchamp declared them to be, or were they "based on a reaction of visual indifference, a total absence of good or bad taste, a complete anaesthesia," as he argued much later, and so a challenge to such authority? Never shown in its initial guise, *Fountain* was suspended in time, its questions deferred to later moments. In this way it became one of the most influential objects in twentieth-century art well after the fact.

In the dominant tradition of bourgeois aesthetics from the Enlightenment to the present, art cannot be utilitarian because its value depends on its autonomy, on its "purposiveness without ▲ purpose" (in the famous phrase of the philosopher Immanuel Kant), precisely on its uselessness. In this tradition, to use art is almost nihilistic—a point that Duchamp dramatized in another note from 1913 where he proposed to "use a Rembrandt as an

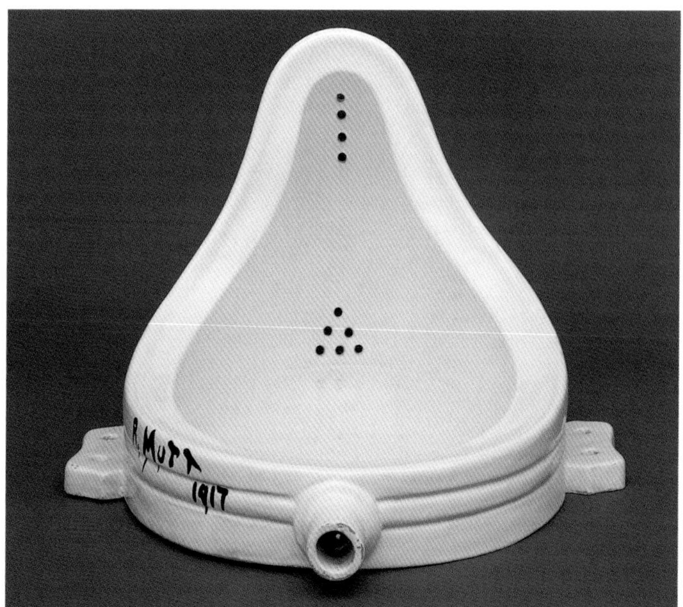

5 • Marcel Duchamp, *Fountain*, 1917 (1964 replica)
Readymade: porcelain, 36 x 48 x 61 (14⅛ x 18⅞ x 24)

ironing-board." In this regard the readymade may be only a gesture of bourgeois radicality; as the German critic Theodor Adorno once remarked (as though he had the Rembrandt ironing-board in mind): "It would border on anarchism to revoke the reification of a great work of art in the spirit of immediate use-values." This is the great difference between the critiques of the institution of art advanced by Duchamp and Tatlin, which is also to say, the great difference between the contexts in which they worked. In bourgeois Paris and New York, Duchamp could only attack the institution of autonomous art, sometimes dandyishly, sometimes nihilistically, while in revolutionary Russia, Tatlin could hope, at least for a time, to see this institution transformed. Like the dandy Charles Baudelaire and the engaged Gustave Courbet in mid-nineteenth-century France, Duchamp and Tatlin posed two complementary models of the artist: the ambivalent consumer who seeks to rename art within a horizon of a commodity culture versus the active producer who seeks to reposition art vis-à-vis industrial production within a horizon of Communist revolution. What others would make of these possibilities, within their own historical limits, is a most important story in twentieth-century art.

FURTHER READING

John Bowlt (ed.), *Russian Art of the Avant-Garde: Theory and Criticism 1902–1934* (London: Thames & Hudson, 1976)

Pierre Cabanne, *Dialogues with Marcel Duchamp* (London: Thames & Hudson, 1971)

Marcel Duchamp, *The Essential Writings of Marcel Duchamp* (London: Thames & Hudson, 1975)

Thierry de Duve, *Pictorial Nominalism: On Duchamp's Passage from Painting to the Readymade*, trans. Dana Polan (Minneapolis: University of Minnesota Press, 1991)

Thierry de Duve (ed.), *The Definitively Unfinished Marcel Duchamp* (Cambridge, Mass.: MIT Press, 1991)

Christina Lodder, *Russian Constructivism* (New Haven and London: Yale University Press, 1983)

Molly Nesbit, *Their Common Sense* (London: Black Dog Publishing, 2001)

▲ Introduction 2

1915

Kazimir Malevich shows his Suprematist canvases at the "0.10" exhibition in Petrograd, thus bringing the Russian Formalist concepts of art and literature into alignment.

When Aleksei Kruchenikh's (1886–1968) *Zaumnaya gniga* appeared in Moscow in 1915, little distinguished its content from that of a dozen previous books of his poems illustrated by one of his avant-garde artist-friends, including Kazimir Malevich and, from 1913, his own wife Olga Rozanova (1886–1918). Although Rozanova was already one of the most inventive participants in the Suprematist movement launched by Malevich in 1915, her illustrations for *Zaumnaya gniga* belonged to an earlier phase of the Russian avant-garde, called "neo-primitivist," during which the idiom of early Cubism was grafted onto the Russian *lubki* (popular broadsides, usually woodprints, whose folkloric tradition goes back to the early seventeenth century).

The title itself, *Zaumnaya gniga*, would not have surprised any follower of Kruchenikh's activity, or that of any other "Cubo-Futurist" poet (as he and his friends called themselves at the time): one could translate it as *Transrational Boog* (*boog*, not *book*—the typo is intended, as the neologism *gniga* is an obvious deformation of *kniga* [book]). In the "transrational" tongue invented by Kruchenikh and his peers, which was aimed at "defying reason" and at freeing the word from the common rules of language, it was indeed appropriate that a boo*k* should become just a boog, a combination of letters whose indeterminate meaning would be the sheer product of associations in the mind of the reader. Kruchenikh's phonetic verses, devoid of any direct connection to a referent ("*Dyr bul shchyl/ubeshchur/skum/vy so bu/ r l ez*"), had been one of the rallying points of the Russian avant-garde ever since he had officially launched the "concept" of *zaum* ("beyond reason") in 1913 (and even before that, in 1912, with the deliberately outrageous publication of *Slap in the Face of Public Taste*, a collective poetic almanac coauthored with David Burliuk, Vladimir Mayakovsky, and Velemir Khlebnikov).

Rozanova's illustration for the cover of *Zaumnaya gniga*, however, was not typical in this context (it could easily be mistaken ▲ for a product of the not-yet-born Dada): it is a collage consisting of the silhouette of a heart (cut out of red paper) onto which a real button has been glued. Besides those of the artist and her husband, a third name adorns the cover, that of an apprentice *zaum* poet, Alyagrov, who contributed two texts to the volume, his first (and last) publication under this pseudonym.

The fact that Alyagrov was none other than the very young Roman Jakobson, who, fresh out of high school, had just founded the Moscow Linguistic Circle (he was later to become one of the ▲ founders of structuralism), may come as a surprise. But even more is in store: even though Jakobson's lifelong passion for language stemmed from his early interest in poetry (notably that of Stéphane Mallarmé, whom he was translating at the age of twelve), his real inspiration had come from painters—and particularly from Malevich, with whom he had planned a trip to Paris just before World War I. The trip was canceled, but weekly visits with Malevich to the Shchukin Collection, host of so many Cubist masterpieces, buttressed Jakobson's firm belief that the relationships between signs are more significant than their potential connection to a referent. It is necessary to underline the nonidentity of the sign and the object, as Jakobson kept repeating all his life, because "without contradiction there is no mobility of concepts, no mobility of signs, and the relationship between concept and sign becomes automatized."

The concepts of Russian Formalism

Along with Opoyaz (the Society of Poetical Language), established in Petrograd in 1916 (of which Jakobson was also a member), the Moscow Linguistic Circle became one of the two birthplaces of the school of literary criticism known as Russian Formalism (the label was coined by enemies, as is often the case: it presupposes a dichotomy between form and content, the very opposition that the Russian Formalists wanted most to annul, as did their fellow *zaum* poets). Right from the start, the issue at stake seems to have been: "What is it that makes a work literary; what is literariness as such?"

The question was polemical, directed against almost any trend of literary studies at the time: against the Symbolists, for whom the text was a transparent vehicle for a transcendent image; against the positivists and the psychologists, for whom the biography of the writer or his putative intention were the determining factors; and against the sociologists, for whom the truth of a literary text was to be found in the historical context of its formation and the political-ideological content it conveyed. For the Formalists, the literariness of a text was a product of its structure, from the phonetical level to the syntactic, from the microsemantic unit of the word to that of

▲ 1916a, 1920

▲ Introduction 3

the plot. The text for them was an organized whole, whose elements and devices had first to be analyzed, almost in a chemical fashion ("isolated and laid bare just as they are in a Cubist painting," as Jakobson wrote) before anything could be said of its signification.

In his "Art as Device" (1917), Viktor Shklovsky, an important member of Opoyaz, formulated one of the first concepts of Formalist literary analysis: *ostranenie*, or "making strange." Long exploited by *zaum* poets, *ostranenie* best marks the early convergence of views between Formalist critics and avant-garde poets and painters, most particularly their common opposition to a conception of language that reduces it to its pure value as instrument: for communication, for narration, for teaching, and so on. It is to be noted that their shared credo yielded unprecedented collaborations: not only were the Formalist critics the strongest defenders of *zaum* poetry, but also both Jakobson and Shklovsky were ardent apologists of Malevich's Suprematism; and if Malevich designed the set and costumes for Kruchenikh's opera *Victory* ▲ *over the Sun*, he also wrote *zaum* poems throughout his life. The real source of this parallel was the belief on the part of painter and critic alike in the power of art to renew perception. For the Formalist critic this meant showing how an author's use of language differs from our ordinary use, how commonsense language is "made strange" within the text; Shklovsky called such a critical move one of laying bare the aesthetic "device." For the painter this meant "de-automatizing" vision so as to confront the viewer with the fact that pictorial signs are not transparent to their referents but have an existence of their own, that they are "palpable," as Jakobson would say.

Malevich's Suprematism: the zero of painting

After a quick-paced autodidact education through all the previous "isms" of modern art—from Symbolism to Impressionism, Postimpressionism, Cubism, and Futurism—Malevich attempted to create a *zaum* brand of painting. He first focused on a particular • aspect that had been overlooked in the collage aesthetic of Synthetic Cubism, the discrepancy of scale and style it allows. Thus, in *Cow and Violin* (1913), a small and realistic profile of a cow, as if lifted from a children's encyclopedia, is painted over the much larger image of a violin, itself superimposed over a concatenation of geometric color planes. Soon after, Malevich deemed the "transrational" absurdity of these juxtapositions insufficient if he were to attain, in a Formalist fashion, the "pictorial" as such—which he called "the zero of painting."

He ended up his *zaum* phase with two types of experiments (later pursued by his numerous followers) that were destined to push the very notion against which he was struggling—that of the transparency of the pictorial language, essential in any mimetic conception of painting—to its limit. One of these experiments consisted of the simple inscription of a sentence, or a title, in place of the representation of the objects it named. There are several of these nominalist propositions that never went beyond the stage of drawing, such as the notation "Fight on the Boulevard" hastily jotted down and framed on a piece of paper. The second of these last *zaum* attempts consisted in the collage of actual whole objects, such as a thermometer or a postage stamp, transforming the picture itself into an envelope, as in *Warrior of the First Division, Moscow* from 1914 [**1**]. In both cases (nominalist inscription or readymade objects), the ironical emphasis is on the tautology: the only purely transparent sign is that which refers to itself word for word, object for object. The shirt button in Rozanova's cover for *Zaumnaya gniga* probably refers to Malevich's assemblage, but also to reliefs by Ivan Puni (1892–1956), another of Malevich's followers (for example, *Relief with Plate* of 1919). Puni's painting *Baths* (1915), even combines assemblage and nominalism, being at once the sign-board for a public bathhouse (thus an object) and the inscription of the word "bath."

But rather than the aesthetic disjunctions of collage, it is the large, undivided planes of color that are most striking in Malevich's works such as *Warrior of the First Division, Moscow* or *Composition with Mona Lisa* (1914), in which the only figurative element, a reproduction of Leonardo's painting, is blocked out in red. And it is these color planes that Malevich will "isolate" in giving birth to his own version of abstraction, which he called Suprematism. The founding moment of Suprematism occurred in December 1915, at the "0.10" exhibition in Petrograd (subtitled "The Last Futurist Exhibition of Paintings," the show owes its name to the fact that its ten participants—including Vladimir

1 • Kazimir Malevich, *Warrior of the First Division, Moscow*, 1914
Oil and collage on canvas, 53.6 x 44.8 (21⅛ x 17⅝)

▲ 1913 • 1912

▲ Tatlin, who showed his first corner counter-relief there—were all seeking to determine the "zero degree," the irreducible core, the essential minimum of painting or of sculpture).

● Thus, almost half a century before Clement Greenberg, Malevich posited that the "zero" condition of painting in the culture of his time is that it is flat and delimited. From this critical reduction there stems Malevich's emphasis on the textural quality of his surfaces, his attention to painterly facture, but also his predilection for the figure of the square, a form long conceived, as its Latin name attests, as the result of one of the simplest geometrical acts of delimitation (*quadrum* means both "square" and "frame"). And from this identification of the figure of the square with the ground of the picture itself—in Malevich's *Black Square*, for example, which hovered over his other works at "0.10," parodying the placement of icons in traditional Russian houses [**2**]—there developed in Malevich's work the very inquiry into what Michael Fried,
■ writing in 1965 about Frank Stella's black paintings, would call "deductive structure" (in which the internal organization of the picture—the placement and morphology of its figures—is deducted from, and thus an indexical sign of, the shape and proportions of its support). Malevich's 1915 *Black Cross*, his *Four Squares* (one of the first regular grids of twentieth-century art), and many other "noncompositions" presented at "0.10" are indexical paintings; that is, the division of the picture's surface, the marks it received, are not determined by the artist's "inner life" or mood (as
▲ was the case for Kandinsky's abstract paintings), but by the logic of the "zero"—they refer directly to the material ground of the picture itself, which they map.

Making strange with color

Malevich was not a positivist (he always stuck to an antirationalist point of view that brought him, especially in his late, postrevolutionary texts, close to a mystical position). Even in the most "deductive" of his canvases, he always made sure that his squares were slightly skewed so that (by virtue of the *ostranenie*) one would notice their stark simplicity and read them as stubbornly "one" (both unique and whole) rather than identifying them as geometric figures. For what mattered most to him, as he kept repeating, was "intuition."

One of the surest routes to attain this nonverbal, nonarticulate mode of communication in painting was color, the sheer expanse of undivided planes of saturated pigment. Malevich's passion for

2 • A view of the "0.10" exhibition in Petrograd, 1915
Malevich's *Black Square* can be seen in the corner of the room above his other paintings.

▲ 1914, 1921 ● 1942a, 1960b ■ 1958 ▲ 1908, 1913

color played a major role in his rapid evolution from Cubism to abstraction, as did the works of Matisse, also discovered in the ▲ Shchukin Collection. But despite his enthusiasm for the French master's *ostranenie* tactics of using arbitrary color, Malevich quickly came to the conclusion (via his apprenticeship in the "analytical" mode of thinking pertaining to Cubism) that color would never be "isolated" and perceived as such (that is, it would never reign "supreme") without first being freed from any determination of a subject matter other than its own radiance.

And this desire to explore "color" as such, to expose the "zero" of color, also led Malevich to take leave of the deductive structure. For next to the *Black Square* or the *Red Square* [**3**], which was exhibited under the ironic, *zaum* title of *Peasant Woman: Suprematism* (it is now subtitled *Painterly Realism of a Peasant Woman in Two Dimensions*), one could see many pictures on the walls of "0.10" in which rectangles of all sizes and of various colors floated on a white background. For a brief period, these paintings led to what Malevich would later call "aerial suprematism," works he would himself severely criticize for their return to illusionism and their quite direct allusion to a cosmic imagery as though one were viewing Earth from outer space [**4**].

● It was the sixties American artist Donald Judd, one of the harshest critics of illusionism in painting, and always ready to point out how much of it still remained in the works of the pioneers of abstraction and their followers of the twenties and thirties, who was the first to reinscribe these agitated paintings into the theoretical framework of the Formalist (*ostranenie*) logic. Reviewing a Malevich retrospective exhibition in 1974, Judd noted that in these canvases colors do not "combine; they can only make a set of three or any two in the way that three bricks make a set." Those sets, writes Judd, "are not harmonic, do not make a further overall color or tone." In other words, the color relationships are not compositional. The allusion to bricks, to the "one thing next to the other" of Minimalism, is very much to the point. But colors are not random either: they assert their independence from the whole via their fragmentary groupings into clusters, preventing any perceptual organization of the shapes into a gestaltist order (and allowing for clashing, almost "kitsch" juxtapositions, such as red and pink).

After zero ...

By 1917–18, as the ideological directions of the October Revolution were making increasing demands on the artists of the Russian avant-garde—the only artistic group to have given it support from the start—Malevich found it increasingly difficult to justify his pictorial activity ideologically. His own political inclinations, close to anarchism, which he saw as perfectly congruent with his aesthetics, were not of great help after the Bolsheviks' repression of an anarchist revolt at Kronstadt in 1918. His momentary farewell to painting constitutes one of the borderline experiences of twentieth-century art, the moment when the "zero" is almost tangible —there, on the canvas. The works in question are several pictures

3 • Kazimir Malevich, *Red Square (Painterly Realism of a Peasant Woman in Two Dimensions)*, 1915
Oil on canvas, 53 x 53 (20⅞ x 20⅞)

4 • Kazimir Malevich, *Suprematist Construction*, 1915–16
Oil on canvas, 88 x 70 (34⅝ x 27⅝)

▲ 1910 ● 1965

in which a "white" form (slightly off-white, to be more precise) glides, at the threshold of visibility, on the white expanse of the canvas [**5**]. Displaying almost nothing but the smallest differentiation of tone, and the sensual marks of the brush-stroke, sometimes these "white-on-white" pictures were even exhibited on a white ceiling, thus emphasizing their own potential dissolution, as white squares themselves, into the architectural space.

Malevich was enlisted in several cultural and agitprop tasks after the Revolution (from planning new museum collections to designing posters), but his most sustained activity was as a pedagogue. In 1919, having dislodged Chagall as head of the Popular Art Institute in Vitebsk, and having secured the help of the much younger El ▲ Lissitzky (1890–1941), he founded the Unovis school (the Russian acronym for "Affirmers of the New Art"). The pictorial production of his pupils, most of them in their teens, was derivative at best. How odd it is to imagine the unheated Unovis classrooms full of paintings of bouncing red squares, in the midst of a huge economic crisis, civil war, and famine! But it was there that Malevich began to develop, with his students, his conception of architecture, which he would actively pursue at the Institute for the Study of the Culture of Contemporary Art of Leningrad (or Ginkhuk), of which he was appointed director in 1922. As there was no question of actual building, architecture was approached as a language, much as Malevich had analyzed the constituents of painting: What would be the zero in architecture? Where would architecture go if it were devoid of function? The results of his inquiry, models of ideal cities and dwellings called *arkhitektoniki*, with their multiplication of cantilevers and their questioning of the classical opposition of post and lintel, were to have an immediate impact on the emerging International Style in architecture and town-planning (particularly after their publication, through El Lissitzky, in several European publications in the mid-twenties).

5 • Kazimir Malevich, *Suprematist Painting (White on White)*, 1918
Oil on canvas, 79.3 x 79.3 (31 x 31)

While abstract painting, *zaum* poetry, and Formalist criticism, now deemed bourgeois and elitist, increasingly became the target of ▲ political censorship in Soviet Russia, architectural research, even as utopian as that of Malevich and his followers, remained relatively free. But soon after the death of Lenin (in 1924) cultural repression began to close down on all spheres of cultural activity, and even Malevich's *arkhitektoniki* had to pay tribute to the heroic, neoclassical proportions demanded by Stalin's watchdogs. Malevich, still teaching (to a thinning student body) and devoting vast energy to writing (most of it unpublished at that time), started painting again in the late twenties. But because abstraction was now almost a political crime, he became engaged in the very strange activity of running through his own pictorial evolution in reverse, going back not only to Cubo-Futurism but also as far as Impressionism, yet consistently antedating this belated production as if it were from his youth. This manifest fraud, puzzling to the historians, is in keeping • with the modernist creed of his quest for the zero: like Mondrian, Malevich thought that each art had to define its own essence by eliminating those conventions deemed unnecessary and, in this evolutionary march, each work of art was to be a step beyond the preceding one—which means that each was assigned a proper date on this progression. A flashback is always possible within this logic, but it would have been morally wrong to present something which could (and should) have been done in 1912 as dating from 1928. (Similarly, when around 1920 Mondrian was forced to paint flowers for economic reasons, he made sure to adorn these "commercial" works with his signature of around the turn of the century.)

The last works by Malevich, however, from the early thirties, are not antedated. Crude pastiches of Renaissance portraits in harsh colors, but often bearing a tiny Suprematist emblem (the geometric ornaments of a belt or a hat), these paintings are replete with irony. Unlike, say, a de Chirico, Malevich is not welcoming ■ here the "return to order." But condemned to figuration and to a mimetic conception of painting against which he had fought all his life, he is "making strange" the very practice of portraiture by giving a sense of the historical distance denied by his censors between the epoch of genuine portrait-making and his own.

FURTHER READING

Troels Andersen, *Malevich* (Amsterdam: Stedelijk Museum, 1970)
Victor Erlich, *Russian Formalism* (New Haven and London: Yale University Press, 1981)
Paul Galvez, "Avance rapide," *Cahiers du Musée National d'Art Moderne*, no. 79, Spring 2002
Roman Jakobson, *My Futurist Years*, ed. Bengt Jangfeldt and Stephen Rudy (New York: Marsilio Publishers, 1997)
Gerald Janecek, *The Look of Russian Literature: Avant-Garde Visual Experiments, 1900–1930* (Princeton: Princeton University Press, 1984)
Anna Lawton (ed.), *Russian Futurism Through its Manifestoes 1912–1928* (Ithaca, N.Y. and London: Cornell University Press, 1988)
Kazimir Malevich, *Essays on Art*, ed. Troels Andersen, four volumes (Copenhagen: Borgen Verlag, 1968–78)
Krystyna Pomorska, *Russian Formalist Theory and Its Poetic Ambiance* (The Hague and Paris: Mouton, 1968)
Angelica Rudenstine (ed.), *Kazimir Malevich 1878–1935* (Washington, D.C.: National Gallery of Art, 1990)

▲ 1926, 1928
▲ 1934a
● 1913, 1917, 1944a
■ 1909, 1919, 1924

1916a

In Zurich, the international movement of Dada is launched in a double reaction to the catastrophe of World War I and the provocations of Futurism and Expressionism.

Dada encompassed a wide range of practices, politics, and places, so it could hardly be coherent even if it wanted to be, which it did not: most of its participants viewed any coherence, any order, with derisive laughter (legend has it that the word "Dada" was picked at random from a German–French dictionary). The Dadaist idea of an anarchic assault on all artistic convention quickly caught fire. Despite its short life—by the early twenties it was mostly burned out or variously subsumed into ▲ Surrealism in France and Neue Sachlichkeit in Germany—it had no fewer than six major bases of operation: Zurich, New York, Paris, Berlin, Cologne, and Hanover, some of which were connected intermittently by various journals, nomadic artists, and ▲ ambitious impresarios (such as Tristan Tzara and Francis Picabia). Born in double reaction to the catastrophe of World War I and the • provocations of Futurism and Expressionism, Dada took direct aim at bourgeois culture, which it blamed for the butchery of the war; yet in many ways this culture was already dead for Dada, and Dada arose to dance on its grave (Hugo Ball, a principal figure in the Zurich group, once called Dada a "requiem mass" of the most ribald sort). In short, the Dadaists pledged to attack all norms, even

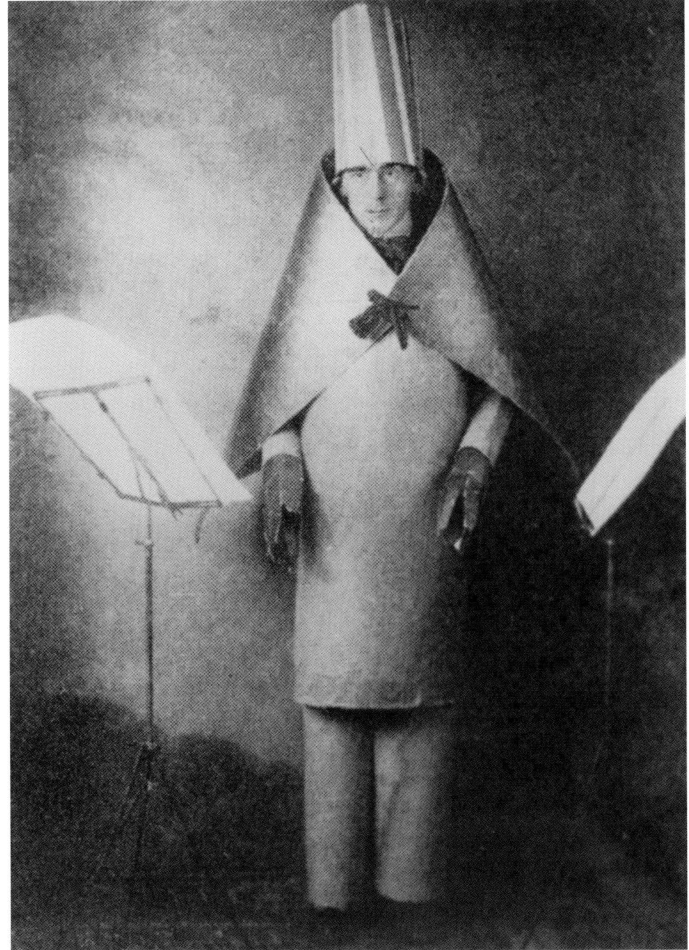

1 • Hugo Ball in his "Magical Bishop" costume, at the Cabaret Voltaire, Zurich, June 1916

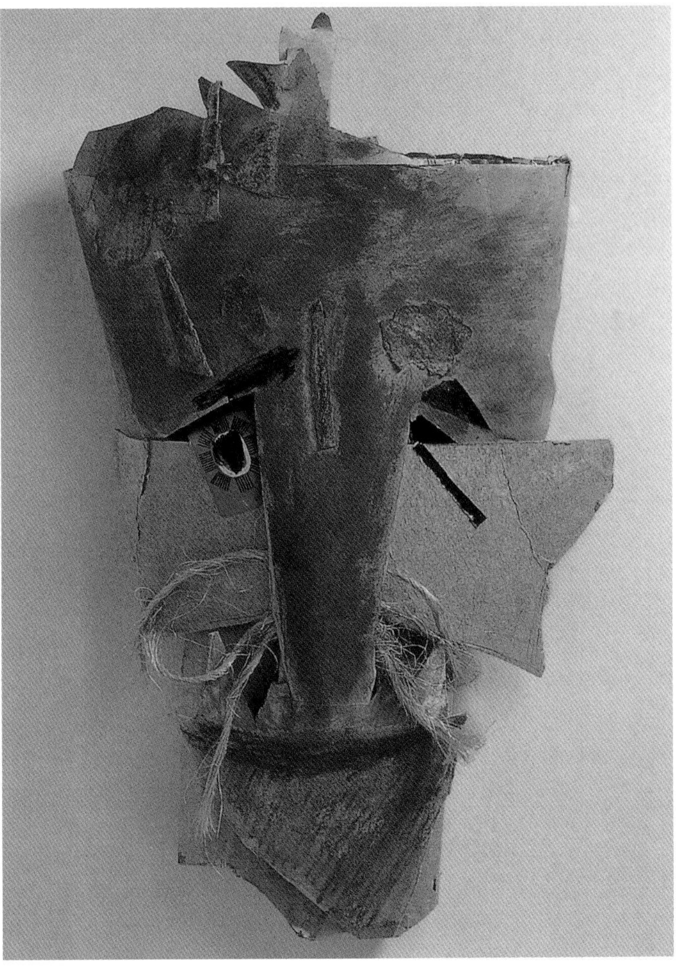

2 • Marcel Janco, *Mask*, c. 1919
Paper, cardboard, string, gouache, and pastel, 45 x 22 x 5 (17¾ x 8⅝ x 2)

▲ 1924, 1925b, 1929, 1930b, 1931

▲ 1916b, 1919 • 1908, 1909

incipient ones of their own ("Dada is Anti-Dada" was a favorite refrain), and they did so, in Zurich, through outlandish performances, exhibitions, and publications.

A farce of nothingness

The international group of poets, painters, and filmmakers drawn to neutral Switzerland before or during the war included the Germans Ball (1886–1927), Emmy Hennings (1885–1948), Richard Huelsenbeck (1892–1974), and Hans Richter (1888–1976), the Romanians Tzara (1896–1963) and Marcel Janco (1895–1984), the ▲ Alsatian Hans Arp, the Swiss Sophie Taeuber, and the Swede Viking Eggeling (1880–1925). Zurich was a principal refuge for other vanguards too: James Joyce lived there for a time, as did Vladimir Lenin—indeed diagonally across the street from the Cabaret Voltaire that served as Dada headquarters. Named after the great French satirist of the eighteenth century (author of *Candide*, an attack on the idiocies of his age), the Cabaret was founded on February 5, 1916, as a vaudevillian mockery of "the ideals of culture and of art"—"that is our *Candide* against the times," Ball wrote in his extraordinary diary, *Flight Out of Time*. "People act as if nothing had happened, [as if] all this civilized carnage [were] a triumph." The Dadaists aimed to act out this crisis in hysterical fashion, but also, amid this performed chaos, "to draw attention, across the barriers of war and nationalism, to the few independent spirits who live for other ideals" (Ball). Surrounded by Expressionist posters and primitivist pictures by Janco and Richter, these provocateurs recited contradictory manifestos (both Futurist and Expressionist), poems in French, German, and Russian (that is, in languages on different sides of the war), and quasi-African chants; they also contrived concerts with typewriters, kettledrums, rakes, and pot covers. "Total pandemonium," Arp described it in retrospect. "The people around us are shouting, laughing, and gesticulating. Our replies are sighs of love, volleys of hiccups, poems, moos, and miaowing of medieval Bruitists [literally noise-makers]. Tzara is wiggling his behind like the belly of an Oriental dancer. Janco is playing an invisible violin and bowing and scraping. Madam Hennings, with a Madonna face, is doing the splits. Huelsenbeck is banging away nonstop on the great drum, with Ball accompanying him on the piano pale as a chalky ghost. We were given the honorary title of Nihilists."

Yet they were not nihilists alone. The Dadaists acted out the dislocations of exile in almost solipsistic ways ("Tristan Tzara," the pseudonym of Sami Rosenstock, suggests "sad in country"), but they also formed a community of artists committed to internationalist politics and universal languages (which Richter and Eggeling, for example, sought in abstract film). They were destructive in spirit, but also often affirmative; regressive in posture, but also sometimes redemptive; and for Ball the term "Dada" held all these associations together: "In Romanian Dada means yes yes, in French a hobby horse. To Germans it is an indication of idiotic naivete and of a preoccupation with procreation and the baby carriage." If some Dadaists were nihilistic, others like Ball had mystical leanings, and this paradoxical position was pronounced ▲ in their relation to language. Like Futurists such as Marinetti, Dadaists such as Ball worked to release language from conventional syntax and semantics into raw sound (the Hanover Dadaist ● Kurt Schwitters figures prominently here as well). Yet the Dadaist interest in sound poetry diverged greatly from the Futurist embrace of nonrational expression: in his "words-in-freedom" the jingoistic Marinetti worked to plunge language into a bodily matrix of all the senses, in a production of meaning understood as force, while the pacifist Ball sought to empty language not only of conventional sense but also of the instrumental reason that had underwritten the mass carnage of the war. "A line of poetry is a chance to get rid of all the filth that clings to this accursed language," Ball wrote. "Every word that is spoken and sung here says at least this one thing: that this humiliated age has not succeeded in winning our respect." Even as Ball worked to shatter language, however, he also sought to recover the word as "*logos*," to transform language into "magical complex images."

The short life of the Cabaret Voltaire ended abruptly on June 23, 1916, with a legendary performance by Ball [**1**], recounted here in *Flight Out of Time*:

> *My legs were in a cylinder of shiny blue cardboard, which came up to my hips so that I looked like an obelisk. Over it I wore a huge coat collar cut out of cardboard, scarlet inside and gold outside.... I also wore a high, blue-and-white-striped witch doctor's hat.... I was carried onto the stage in the dark and began slowly and solemnly: "gadji beri bimba/ glandridi lauli lonni cadori/ gadjama bim beri glassala/ glandridi glassala tuffm i zimbrabim/ blassa galassasa tuffm i zimbrabim...."... Then I noticed that my voice had no choice but to take on the ancient cadence of priestly lamentation, that style of liturgical singing that wails in all the Catholic churches of East and West.... For a moment it seemed as if there were a pale, bewildered face in my Cubist mask, that half-frightened, half-curious face of a ten-year-old boy, trembling and hanging avidly on the priest's words in the requiems and high masses in his home parish.... Bathed in sweat, I was carried down off the stage like a magical bishop.*

In the performance Ball is part shaman, part priest, but he is also a child once again entranced by ritual magic. This "playground for crazy emotions" witnessed other such performances with fantastic costumes and bizarre masks, often contrived for the occasion by Janco [**2**]; Sophie Taueber contributed theatrical props and dance pieces as well. "The motive power of these masks was irresistibly conveyed to us," Ball remarked of the masks, which he regarded as modern equivalents of those in ancient Greek and Japanese theater. "[They] simply demanded that their wearers start to move in a tragic-absurd dance."

Clearly Ball saw Dada as an avant-garde rite of possession and exorcism. The Dadaist "suffers from the dissonances [of the world] to the point of self-disintegration.... [He] fights against the agony

▲ 1913, 1918

▲ 1909 ● 1926

and the death throes of this age." In effect Ball regarded the Dadaist as a traumatic mime who assumes the dire conditions of war, revolt, and exile, and inflates them into a buffoonish parody. "What we call Dada is a farce of nothingness in which all the higher questions are involved," he remarked less than two weeks before his Magical Bishop performance, "a gladiator's gesture, a play with shabby leftovers." Here Dada mimes dissonance and destruction in order to purge them somehow, or at least to transform such shock into a kind of protection that nonetheless retains a strong dose of terror and agony. "The horror of our time, the paralyzing background of events, is made visible," Ball once commented of the Janco masks; and of the poetry of Huelsenbeck he had this to say: "The Gorgon's head of a boundless terror smiles out of the fantastic destruction."

Exhausted, Ball left Zurich soon after his performance (eventually to return to the Church), and Tzara took over as instigator of Zurich Dada. Tzara was the "natural antithesis of Ball," Richter once remarked, as dandyish in his stance of disgust as Ball was desperate. His model as avant-garde impresario was Marinetti: Tzara not only stressed the Futurist aspects of Dada but also orchestrated Dada much as Marinetti had Futurism—with manifestos, a journal, even a gallery. In a self-contradictory development, Zurich Dada thus became less a chaotic mix of other styles than an artistic movement of its own. In the third issue of *Dada* (1918), Tzara published the "Dada Manifesto," which put Dada on the map of European avant-gardes; it also attracted Picabia from New York, and together he and Tzara prepared the Dadaist campaign in Paris that was to follow the war. When the war did end, so, effectively, did Zurich Dada, as refugees were free to move once again.

A juxtaposition of avant-garde devices

The key figure of the second phase of Zurich Dada was Hans Arp. Active in the Paris avant-garde before Dada, Arp adapted Cubist ▲ collage to Dadaist ends: it became a medium less of semiotic analysis than of chance composition. In his *Collage of Squares Arranged* • *According to the Laws of Chance* (1916–17), Arp tore rough squares, irregular in size, out of sheets of commercial paper of different colors, let them fall, and then glued them where they landed on the support. Over the years he did many other such collages, sometimes with the paper neatly cut and composed, sometimes roughly torn and arrayed. Probably also inspired by Duchamp, in such ■ experiments in chance as his *Three Standard Stoppages* (1913–14), Arp worked "against the bombast of the gods of painting (the Expressionists)," as Ball once remarked—that is, against the authority of the expressive artist. Arp regarded his collages as "a denial of human egotism"; but they are more as well—indeed they enact a brilliant juxtaposition of avant-garde devices only recently invented. For active here are not only collage and chance, but also the readymade (in the commercial paper) and the abstract grid, which many of the early collages evoke, only to defy. As the critic T. J. Demos has commented, "The grid indicates the logic of scientific rationality, the use of chance represents its total rejection. Surely Arp invoked the former only to attack it with the latter."

For Arp these devices served to displace the "volition" of the artist toward a condition of "anonymity," an interest he also explored in early experiments with automatic drawing (some date ▲ to 1916), a device later elaborated by the Surrealists—with whom Arp came to be associated—to access the unconscious. He also produced many extraordinary reliefs, mostly in painted wood: these are abstract compositions that are also suggestive of biomorphic shapes of the body (human and animal) and other natural forms [**3**]. Such works attest to a metamorphic impulse in Zurich Dada that qualifies its destructive drive (it is also pronounced in the films of Richter), but their beauty might make them seem atypical of Dada; with titles like *Torso*, *Bird Forms*, and the like, they are also vaguely referential. On this score Arp was most adventurous in the gridded • "duo-collages" that he produced with his wife Sophie Taueber. Taueber was teaching textile design in Zurich when she met Arp in 1915, and almost immediately they began to collaborate on paintings, collages, and woven works—"probably the first examples of 'concrete art'," Arp later remarked, at once "pure and independent" and "elementary and spontaneous." Here Arp and Taueber added collaboration to the other techniques that helped to loosen art from

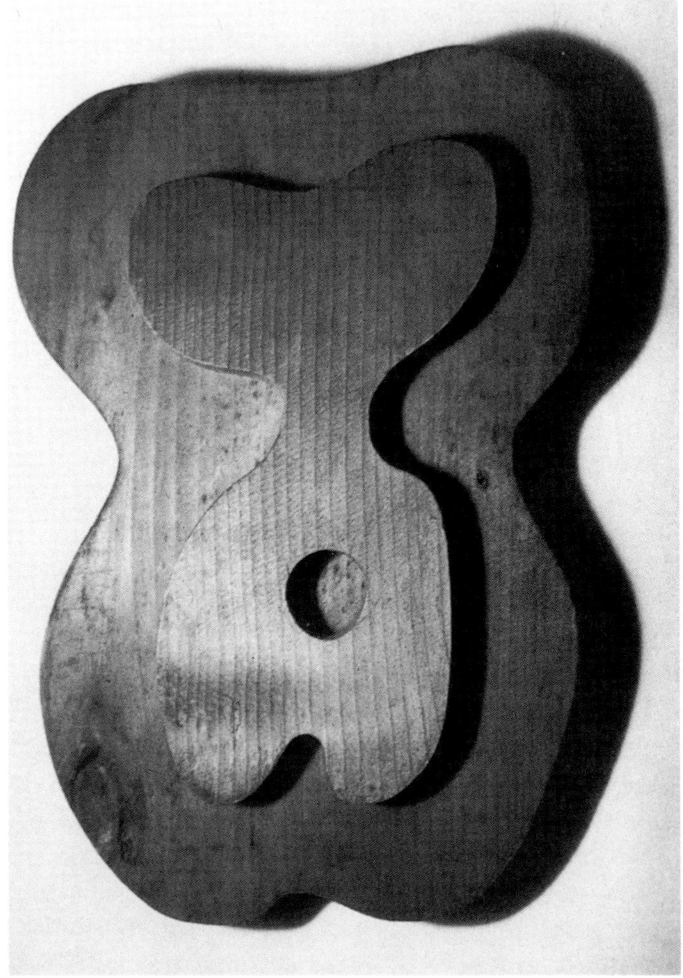

3 • Hans Arp, *Torso, Navel*, 1915
Wood, 66 x 43.2 x 10.2 (26 x 17 x 4)

▲ 1912 • 1918 ■ 1918 ▲ 1924, 1930b, 1931, 1942b • 1913

Dada journals

The group of artists and poets who gravitated toward Zurich at the outbreak of World War I immediately started *Cabaret Voltaire* (1916), the journal through which Dada was able to spread throughout Europe and into North America. If art is understood by psychoanalysis as sublimatory—a way of rising above the animal instincts that form the underbelly of the psyche—Dada saw itself as desublimatory—scoffing at the spiritual ambitions of poetry and painting. In his short history of the movement, Richard Huelsenbeck wrote, "The German *dichter* [poet] is the typical dope.... He does not understand what a gigantic humbug the world has made of the 'spirit'."

By 1917, *Dada*, edited by Tristan Tzara, was also being published in Zurich. *Dadaco*, an anthology with Dada works of art, such as photomontages by George Grosz, soon followed. That the very word "*dada*" was provocative is heralded by an article in *Dadaco* which begins: "Was ist dada? Eine Kunst? Eine Philosophie? Eine Politick? Eine Feuerversicherung? Oder: Staatsreligion. Ist dada wirkliche Energie? Oder ist es Garnichts, d.h. alles?" (What is dada? An art? A philosophy? A politics? A fire insurance policy Or: Official religion? Is dada truly energy? Or is it nothing at all, i.e., everything?")

The Dada movement in the United States soon resulted in Man Ray's *Ridgefield Gazook*, published from 1915, as well as *New York Dada*, the periodical he produced with Marcel Duchamp. The international character of Dada journals is further illustrated by Kurt Schwitters's *Merz* in Hanover and Francis Picabia's *391*, the latter published out of Barcelona. But in France, *La Nouvelle Revue Française* resumed publication in 1919 (after having been suppressed during the war) by accusing the "new school" of nonsense symptomatized by the "indefinite repetition of the mystical syllables 'dada dadada dada da.'" The French novelist André Gide joined the debate with an article announcing: "The day the word Dada was found, there was nothing left to do. Everything written subsequently seemed to me a bit beside the point.... Nothing was up to it: DADA. These two syllables had accomplished that 'sonorous inanity,' an absolute of meaninglessness."

Indeed, in Gide's novel *The Counterfeiters* (1926), the villain Strouvilhou imagines what a Dada journal should be when he says, "If I edit a review, it will be in order to prick bladders—in order to demonetize fine feelings, and those promissory notes which go by the name of *words*." In the first issue, he announces (with the Duchamp collage *L.H.O.O.Q.* in mind), there will be "a reproduction of the *Mona Lisa*, with a pair of mustaches stuck on to her face." It is this linking of abstraction and nonsense that is associated, in Gide's narrative, with the emptying out of the sign's meaning: "If we manage our affairs well," says Strouvilhou, "I don't ask for more than two years before a future poet will think himself dishonored if anyone can understand a word of what he says. All sense, all meaning will be considered anti-poetical. Illogicality shall be our guiding star."

traditional strictures of authorship and composition (Arp would ▲ soon collaborate with Max Ernst in Cologne as well): made just ● prior to the first modular abstractions of Piet Mondrian, the duo-collages eliminate autographic elements just as radically.

A miniature sublime

The genius of the term Dada lay in the force with which it radiated a contemptuous meaninglessness, and the Zurich Dadaists used this confusion strategically to stage the work of very different artists—not only Futurists like Marinetti and Expressionists like ■ Wassily Kandinsky, but also the German-Swiss painter Paul Klee, whose art was shown at the Galerie Dada in 1917. Again, Marinetti sought to glorify the war: his 1914 collection *Zang Tumb Tuum* extolled the Italian campaign in Libya, and in 1915, at the front near Lake Garda, under the Alps, he threw himself into capturing the dynamics of this huge battlefield, certain that his pictographic medium would be equal to the task. Marinetti not only viewed the war as representable but sought to aestheticize it as well. "We Futurists," he would become notorious for declaring, "have rebelled against the branding of war as anti-aesthetic.... War is beautiful because it initiates the dreamt-of metallization of the human body. War is beautiful because it enriches a flowering meadow with the fiery orchids of machine guns. War is beautiful because it combines the gunfire, the cannonades, the cease-fire, the scents, and the stench of putrefaction into a symphony."

Klee represents a position antipodal to Marinetti's. Still mobilized in the German army in 1918, Klee continued to practice his art during the waning days of the war, with the agonizing immobility of trench combat exacerbated by aerial bombing and systematic gassing. In its opening weeks the war had taken the life of Auguste Macke, Klee's closest collaborator in the Blaue Reiter; and two years later it would claim another Expressionist colleague, Franz Marc, killed near Verdun. During his momentous trip to Tunis with Macke in early 1914, Klee had bathed himself in the sensuous immediacy of light and exotic color, expressing his impressions of this world in a vibrant grid patterned in part on Delaunay's ◆ "Windows"; now he felt sickened by the very thought of reality. "I dally in that shattered world only in occasional memories," he wrote in 1915. "The more horrifying this world becomes (as it is these days) the more art becomes abstract."

It is this impulse toward abstraction that powers a work like *"Einst dem Grau der Nacht enttaucht ..."* ("Once Emerged from the Gray of Night ..." **[4]**. In his Tunis pictures Klee had used blocks of juxtaposed pink and ocher wash to evoke the forms of the Casbah or the geometries of sunstruck walls. Here he refused to use anything like visual resemblance to summon an experience of the real world. If the colored grid remains, it has been evacuated of the airy mobility and spatial expansiveness that it formerly possessed. Instead the wiry edges of printed letters grip the colored patches, flattening and tightening them as though they were the panes of stained-glass windows and the writing were its leading. The work's

▲ 1922, 1924 ● 1917 ■ 1908, 1909, 1913 ◆ 1908, 1913

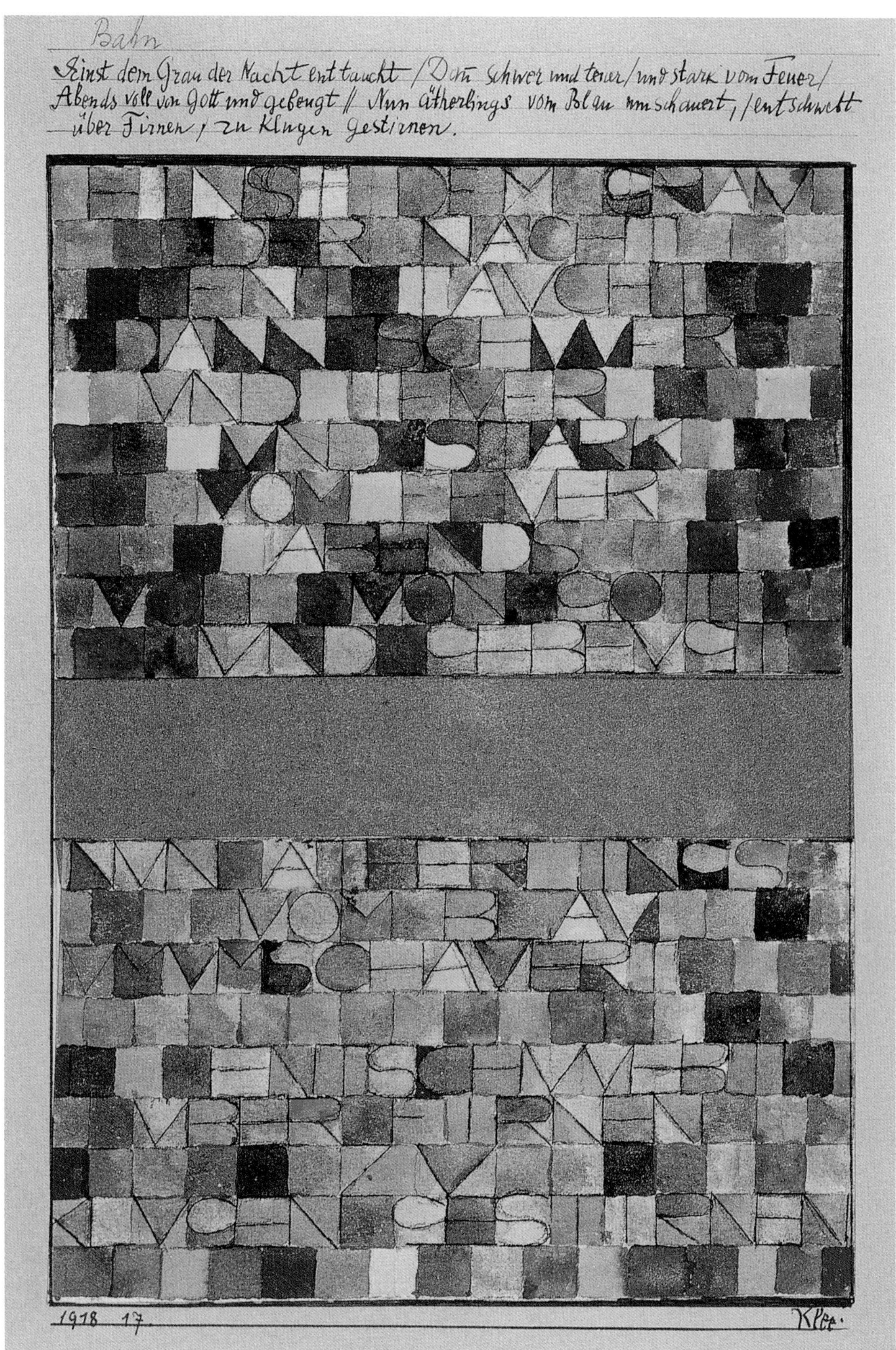

4 • Paul Klee, “*Einst dem Grau der Nacht enttaucht ...*” (“Once Emerged from the Gray of Night ...”), 1918
Watercolor and pen drawing, 22.5 x 15.9 (8⅞ x 6¼)

5 • Paul Klee, *Angelus Novus*, 1920
India ink, colored chalks, and brown wash on paper, 31.8 x 24.2 (12½ x 9½)

tiny size and the band of silver paper that separates the grid's upper and lower registers also evoke a page of manuscript illumination on which is inscribed a poem. Although one can barely make out the verse, one is nonetheless compelled to read: "Once emerged from the gray of night / that hard and costly / and thick with fire / the God-filled evening emerged and arches over." And after the silver break it continues: "Now toward the ether, showering in blue / vanishing over glaciers / toward the wisdom of stars."

Modernist art's drive toward abstraction might not signal its withdrawal from reality so much as reality's withdrawal from it—that is, from art's capacity to represent a reality transformed by technology and war. The turn toward the written sign executed by Klee in *"Once Emerged from the Gray of Night ..."* suggests the truth of this position. What he termed "the cold romanticism of abstraction" captures his own understanding of the requirements of representing the fundamentally unrepresentable—what Enlightenment thinkers and Romantic artists had called "the Sublime." These authors had used the term to describe a combination of oppressive fear and exalted release, folded into an intimation of an immensity beyond human comprehension. In this regard the Sublime entered into the opening years of the twentieth century through two new forms of the fearfully unrepresentable: the millions of dead as a result of modern warfare and the unappeasable drives of the unconscious mind.

Klee's script painting addressed the first of these conditions in a kind of miniature sublime. Unlike the German Expressionist poet Christian Morgenstern (1871–1914), who had suspended linguistic marks between verbal and visual images, Klee refused this sort of calligrammatic embrace, in which the visual depiction is folded ▲ over the verbal naming (as in Guillaume Apollinaire's practice of the form). In Morgenstern's "Fishes' Serenade," lines of what look like the indications of poetic meter—the little iambic curves of the unstressed syllables—constellate into an oval shape, thus transforming the written dashes of the poem into the visual form of a fish replete with scales, or alternatively, the wavy surface of a pool of water. Despite his admiration for Morgenstern, Klee withdrew from the calligram's excess of representation, its determination to throw a double net over reality. Instead he used an elusive statement about emerging from chaos into clarity to summon the idea of immensity; at the same time this statement insists on the impossibility of directly portraying its own terrible contents.

Klee also evoked this programmatic indirection in a lapidary remark that became his credo: "Art does not represent the visible; rather, it makes visible." This conceptual approach was not limited to "abstract things like numbers and letters," which characterize other paintings such as *Villa R* (1919) and *The Vocal Fabric of Rosa Silber* (1922); it also extended to his belief that the movement of a line in the process of its execution could be conveyed to the viewer, for whom the image would unfold in time more than in space. This narrativization of his work, captured visually in what Klee called a "line going on a walk" and verbally in his suggestive captions and titles (often inscribed in the margins of his pictures), led some of his admirers to project their own interpretative accounts. One ▲ such admirer was Walter Benjamin, who had purchased Klee's *Angelus Novus* **[5]** at the time of its initial exhibition. In "Theses on the Philosophy of History" (1940), the last essay completed before his death, Benjamin uses the picture as the basis for a parable about the destructive effects of capitalist technology's vaunted "progress," a parable that is also in keeping with Klee's *"Once Emerged from the Gray of Night ..."*:

> *A Klee painting named Angelus Novus shows an angel looking as though he is about to move away from something he is fixedly contemplating. His eyes are staring, his mouth is open, his wings are spread. This is how one pictures the angel of history. His face is turned toward the past. Where we perceive a chain of events, he sees one single catastrophe which keeps piling wreckage upon wreckage and hurls it in front of his feet. The angel would like to stay, awaken the dead, and make whole what has been smashed. But a storm is blowing from Paradise; it has got caught in his wings with such violence that the angel can no longer close them. This storm irresistibly propels him into the future to which his back is turned, while the pile of debris before him grows skyward. This storm is what we call progress.*

FURTHER READING

Jean Arp, *Arp on Arp: Poems, Essays, Memories*, ed. Marcel Jean, trans. Joachim Neugroschel (New York: Viking Press, 1972)

Hugo Ball, *Flight Out of Time: A Dada Diary* (1927), ed. John Elderfield, trans. Ann Raimes (New York: Viking Press, 1974)

Leah Dickerman (ed.), "Dada," special issue, *October*, no. 105, Summer 2003

Richard Huelsenbeck, *Memoirs of a Dada Drummer*, ed. Hans J. Kleinschmidt, trans. Joachim Neugroschel (New York: Viking Press, 1974)

Robert Motherwell (ed.), *The Dada Painters and Poets* (1951) (Cambridge, Mass.: Harvard University Press, 1989)

Hans Richter, *Dada: Art and Anti-Art* (London: Thames & Hudson, 1978)

▲ 1912

▲ 1935

1916b

Paul Strand enters the pages of Alfred Stieglitz's magazine *Camera Work*: the American avant-garde forms itself around a complex relationship between photography and the other arts.

That Alfred Stieglitz (1864–1946) should have been portrayed ▲ by Francis Picabia in 1915 in the form of a camera [**1**] would have surprised no one in the world of avant-garde art, certainly not in New York, but not in Paris either. For by 1915, Stieglitz's magazine *Camera Work* (published from 1903) was famous on both sides of the Atlantic, and his gallery at 291 Fifth Avenue in Manhattan, having changed its name in 1908 from the Little Galleries of the Photo-Secession to simply 291, had mounted major exhibitions of Matisse (1908, 1910, and 1912), Picasso (1911, 1914, and 1915), Brancusi (1914), and Picabia (1915).

Nonetheless, several contradictions crisscross the "face" of Stieglitz's portrait. For one thing, the Dada spirit of the mechanomorphic form has nothing to do with Stieglitz's own aesthetic convictions; his belief in American values such as sincerity, honesty, and innocence clash as much as possible with Picabia's ironic rendering of the human subject as a machine. And as a continuation of this, Stieglitz's commitment to authenticity, taking the form, as it did, of truth to the nature of a given medium, had placed him at direct odds with the photographic practice of his day. The result was that from 1911, 291 no longer exhibited camera-based work (the one exception being Stieglitz's own exhibition in 1913 to coincide with the Armory Show). In Stieglitz's eyes, that is, modernism and photography had, distressingly, become antithetical.

It was only when the young Paul Strand (1890–1976) presented Stieglitz with the photographs he had made in 1916 that the elder man could see the vindication of his own position. For he viewed Strand's work as a demonstration that the values of modernism and those of "straight photography" *could* utterly fuse on the surface of a single print. Accordingly, Stieglitz decided to hold an exhibition of Strand's photographs at 291 and to revive *Camera Work*, which had been languishing since January 1915. In October 1916, he brought out issue number 48, and in June 1917 he ended the project with number 49/50. Both issues were intended as monuments to Strand and to a renewed sense of photography's having definitively joined an authentic modernism. With this assessment in place, Stieglitz ended his entrepreneurship on behalf of the avant-garde and redevoted himself to his own practice of photography.

The peculiar zigzag of this trajectory had begun in Berlin, where Stieglitz had enrolled as an engineering student in 1882. A course in photochemistry introduced the young American to photography, a medium he took to immediately, although he had had no previous training in art. "I went to photography really a free soul," he later explained. "There was no short cut, no foolproof photographing—no 'art world' in photography. I started with the real A.B.C."

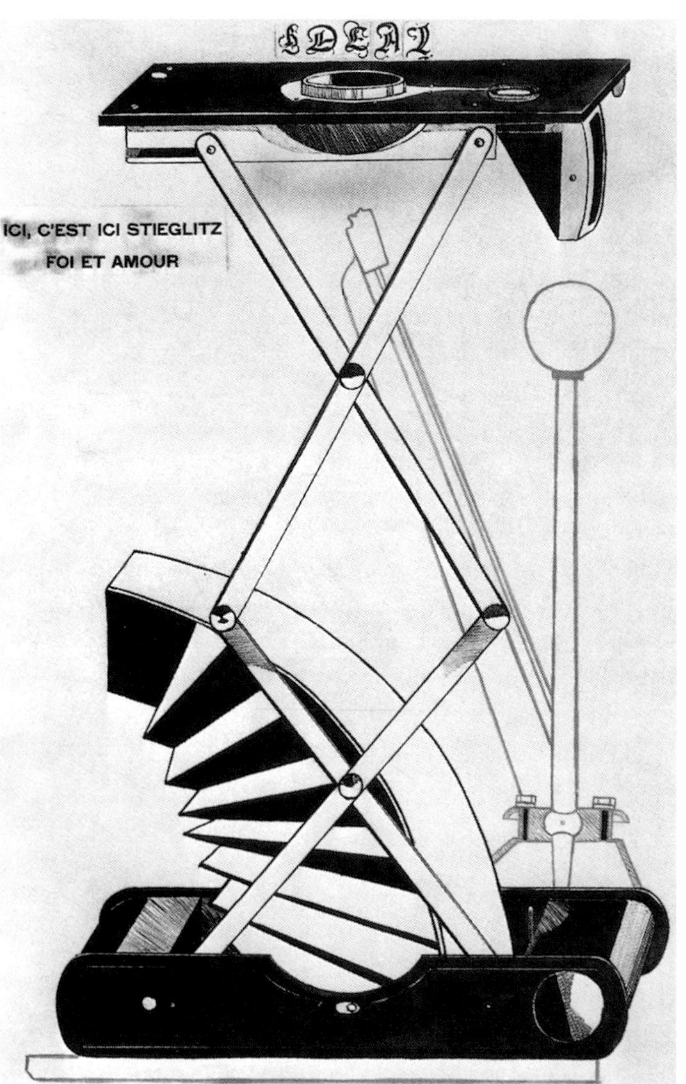

1 • Francis Picabia, *Ici, c'est ici Stieglitz*, 1915
Pen and red ink on paper, 75.9 x 50.8 (29⅞ x 20)

▲ 1914, 1916a, 1919

By 1889, Stieglitz had made *Sun Rays—Paula—Berlin* **[2]**, a work that in its sharpness of detail was far away from the idiom that had settled over all aesthetically ambitious photography in the late nineteenth century and into the first decade of the twentieth. Called "Pictorialist," this photography had bet the future of the medium on aping the features of painting and was thus involved in various effects of blurring (soft focus, greased lenses) and even handwork ("drawing" on the negatives with gum bichromate) to manipulate the final image as much as possible.

Focusing instead on "the real A.B.C." of photography, *Sun Rays—Paula—Berlin* not only mobilizes a strict realism to separate itself from Pictorialism's simulation of "art," but also produces something of an inventory of the values and mechanisms inherent to the medium itself. One of these mechanisms is the brute fact of the photomechanical, by which light enters the camera through a shutter to make a permanent trace on the sensitive emulsion of the negative. Bodying forth this light as a sequence of rays falling across the field in a striated pattern of dark and light, *Sun Rays* also identifies the opened windows through which sunlight streams into the darkened room (or *camera*) with the camera's shutter.

None of this would be remarkably different from the various Impressionist attempts to present the light on which their technique depended as the very subject of a given painting were it not for the concatenation of images pictured inside the room itself. For there the photomechanical's relation to mechanical reproduction—to the multiple duplication and serialization of the image—is dramatized, as the young woman writing at the table bends her head toward a framed portrait (possibly of herself) that we identify as a photograph, since above her on the wall we see its exact duplicate flanked by two landscapes betraying their own identity as photographs in their similar condition as identical twins. And this fact of reproducibility set up inside the image of *Paula* rebounds, by implication, onto *Paula* itself, so that at some later point in the series it, too, could take up residence on that same wall. In this sense, *Paula* is a display of Chinese boxes, a demonstration of the reproducible as a potentially infinite series of the same.

Stieglitz forms the Photo-Secession

Nothing could be further from the values Stieglitz encountered in the photographic magazines and exhibitions occurring both in Europe and in the America to which he returned in 1890. Joining the New York Camera Club, Stieglitz had no choice but to take up arms *for* Pictorialism rather than against it, since it was only in the hands of certain of its practitioners (such as Clarence White ▲ [1871–1925] and Edward J. Steichen [1879–1973]) that photography was being taken seriously as a valid means of artistic expression. From 1897 Stieglitz began to edit *Camera Notes* as a forum for the Pictorialist group he supported against the vigorous opposition of the more conservative members of the New York Camera Club, which had recently merged with the Society of Amateur Photographers to form the Camera Club of New York, the magazine's sponsor. In 1902, on the pattern of other avant- ▲ garde "secessions," this group resigned from the Club and constituted itself as "The Photo-Secession," led by Stieglitz, who inaugurated *Camera Work* as its editorial arm in 1903 and, with the encouragement and assistance of Steichen, opened "The Little Galleries of the Photo-Secession" in 1905.

Soon, however, Stieglitz's natural antipathy to Pictorialist manipulation and his belief instead that photographic excellence must arise from a "straight" approach to the medium, opened a rift

The Armory Show

On February 15, 1913, an exhibition sponsored by the Association of American Painters and Sculptors opened at the armory quartering the 69th Regiment of the National Guard in New York City. Baptized "The Armory Show," the intention of its organizers was to bring the most advanced European art to the consciousness of American artists, who would be tested by showing alongside the work of their counterparts from across the Atlantic. The effort to find such work took the show's impresarios, Arthur B. Davies and Walt Kuhn, associates of the most noticeable wing of the American avant-garde—a group of realist painters called The Eight (Stieglitz's more radical 291 operation was known mostly to insiders)—all around Europe. For the developing international avant-garde exhibition circuit now included the "Sonderbund International" in Cologne, Roger Fry's "Second Post-Impressionist Exhibition" in London, as well as shows at The Hague, Amsterdam, Berlin, Munich, and Paris, where Gertrude Stein and other Americans-in-residence gave Davies and Kuhn access to dealers such as Daniel-Henry Kahnweiler and Ambroise Vollard, or artists like Constantin Brancusi, Marcel Duchamp, and Odilon Redon.

Outrage against the exhibition's 420 works, expressed by the press, mounted quickly during the month of the show's duration, bringing record crowds (a total of 88,000) to the Armory. Famous sneers at Brancusi's *Mlle Pogany* ("a hard-boiled egg balanced on a cube of sugar"), at Duchamp's *Nude Descending a Staircase* ("explosion in a shingle factory"), at Henri Matisse's *Blue Nude* ("leering effrontery") set part of the tone. But the other part was fixed by the leap in taste among American artists and collectors who experienced the assembled work as a revelation. Thus, while the newspaper headline in the *Sun* ironically signaled the exhibition's departure as good riddance—"Cubists Migrate, Thousands Mourn"—the success of the show, which had also toured Chicago and Boston, inaugurated a clamor for advanced art, which would now be hosted at department stores, art societies, and private galleries (between 1913 and 1918 there were almost 250 such exhibitions). Another immediate effect was the repeal of the fifteen percent import duty on art less than twenty years old, a legal battle led by lawyer and collector John Quinn. It was this that permitted European art to enter the States, but it also set the stage for the notorious customs case over the entry of Brancusi's *Bird in Space* in 1927, in which modernism's very status as art became a legal issue.

▲ 1959d

▲ 1900a

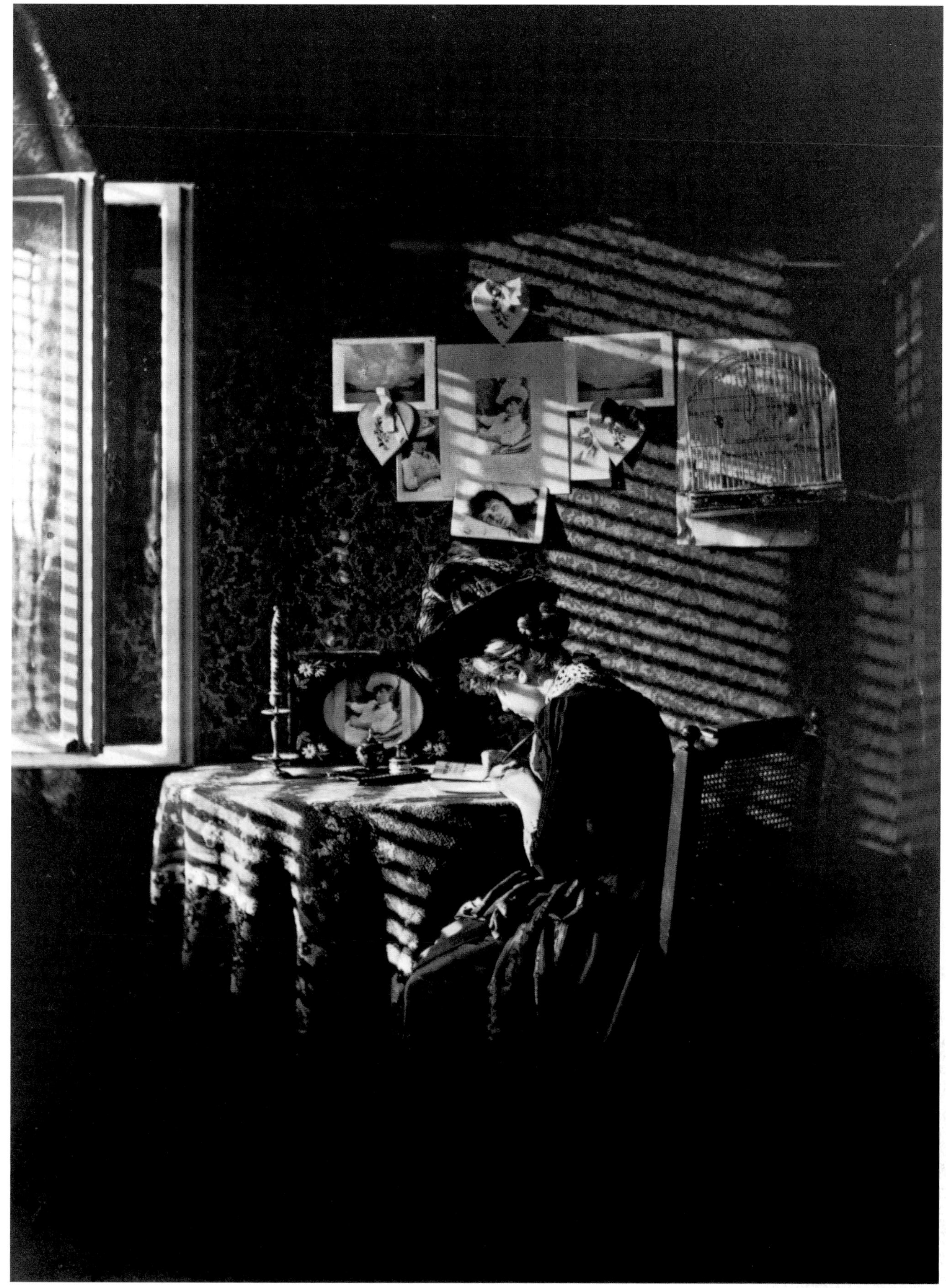

2 • Alfred Stieglitz, *Sun Rays—Paula—Berlin*, 1889
Silver-gelatin print, 22 x 16.2 (8⅝ x 6⅜)

between himself and his Photo-Secession confreres. Confessing to Steichen that he could not see enough strong work coming from photographic quarters to fill the gallery, Stieglitz relied on the younger man, by now installed in Paris, to supply the gallery with serious work, by which the two agreed that the choice must necessarily shift from photography to modernist painting and sculpture. ▲ Beginning with the Rodin drawings that Steichen picked out in 1908, the selections came to be increasingly influenced by far more adventurous tastes, whether they were those of Leo and Gertrude • Stein or those of the American organizers of the 1913 Armory Show who had been scouring Europe for examples of the most advanced work. Thus Stieglitz's commitment to straight photography progressively synchronized itself with a belief in Cubism and African art rather than with the late Symbolist values of Pictorialism celebrated by and through Steichen's portrait of Rodin.

Indeed, nothing could offer a greater contrast than Steichen's *Rodin and The Thinker* **[3]** and Stieglitz's *The Steerage* **[4]**: the former, a willing sacrifice of detail to the dramatic conflation of silhouetted profiles (the sculptor's confronting the hunched contour of his own *Thinker*) against the blurred features of Rodin's *Victor Hugo*, which, godlike, constitutes the enigmatic background; the latter, a devastatingly sharp play of forms. Captured from the upper deck of an ocean liner, *The Steerage* peers down into the jumble of human forms separated visually from the parade of bourgeois passengers above it by the bright diagonal of a gangplank. The separation of classes could not, thus, be more forcefully maintained even while the photograph's even-handed mechanical viewing, which holds everything in the same focus, produces a redistribution of "wealth" over the surface of the image, such redistribution given a formal translation in the rhyming of ovals (the straw hats, the sunlit caps, the boat's funnels) over the surface of the print.

It would be this principle of rhyming, but now emptied of its social content and, almost, of any recognizable content whatsoever, that Stieglitz would find in the work that Strand produced in the summer of 1916, after having experimented with Pictorialism for a number of years. Whether it was *Abstraction, Bowls* or *Abstraction, Porch Shadows, Twin Lakes, Connecticut* **[5]**, Strand so controlled the play of light that a deep ambiguity settled over the image—as concave confused itself with convex, or vertical field with horizontal—without yielding anything of the relentless sharpness of the photographic as such. Indeed Strand's photographic "abstraction" did not seem to depend on pushing toward the unrecognizability of the objects photographed. The experience of being startled by a kind of hyper-vision—vision ratcheted into a focus beyond any normal type of seeing—that outdistanced the mere registration of this or that object could be found in Strand's presentation of lowly things such as *The White Fence* (1916), a line of pickets seen against a darkened yard.

3 • Edward Steichen, *Rodin and The Thinker*, 1902
Gum-bichromate print

4 • Alfred Stieglitz, *The Steerage*, 1907
Photogravure, 33.5 x 26.5 (13¼ x 10⅜)

The jolt delivered to Stieglitz by Strand's photography was reinforced by his growing sense of conviction that modernism itself was no longer the exclusive property of Europe. And, indeed, at the same moment when he encountered Strand's new work he had another revelation, in the form of the series of drawings by Georgia ▲ O'Keeffe (1887–1986) called *Lines and Spaces in Charcoal*, which had been passed to him by a friend, and which he exhibited in 1916 as well. The abstract watercolors that O'Keeffe went on to make in 1917, flooded as they were with a kind of pure luminosity, constituted the final exhibition at 291.

▲ 1900b • 1907 ▲ 1927c

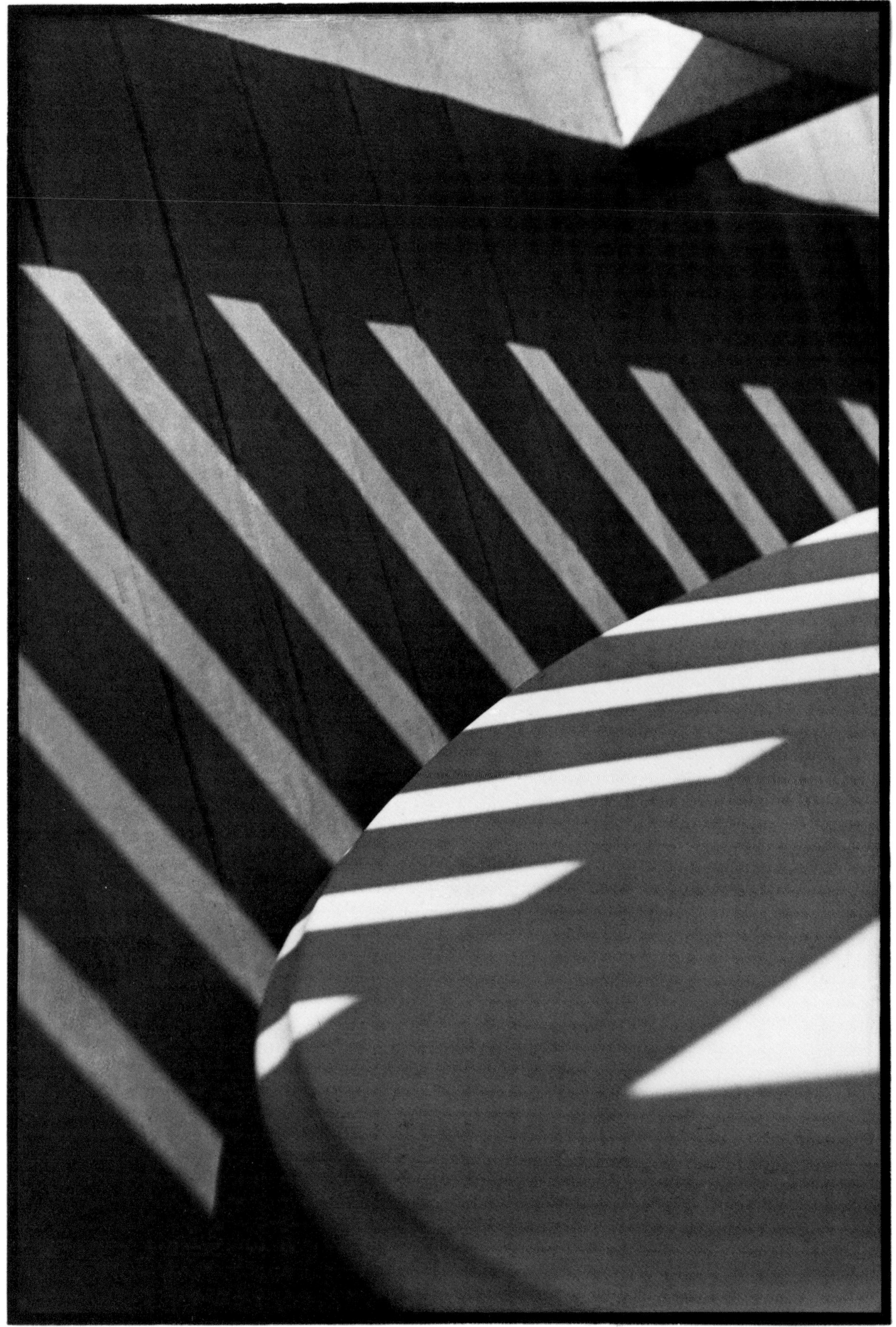

5 • Paul Strand, *Abstraction, Porch Shadows, Twin Lakes, Connecticut*, 1916
Silver-platinum print, 32.8 x 24.4 (12⅞ x 9⅝)

By 1918 Stieglitz had set off on a new phase of his life and his art. Living now with O'Keeffe and spending his summers with her at Lake George, New York, he turned with a new intensity to photography. In certain instances he seemed bent on outdoing Strand in the dazzling purity of a photographic kind of "hyper-vision." But in other parts of his work he returned to the kind of investigation he had opened in *Sun Rays—Paula—Berlin*, namely the naked answer to the question "What is a photograph?"

The abstraction of the cut

Coming most radically in the form of a series of cloud pictures that Stieglitz made between 1923 and 1931, called *Equivalents* **[6]**, the answer to this question was now struck by the drive toward unity that one finds in many modernist responses to the same kind of ontological question—"What is ___________?"—responses, when posed for the medium of painting, for instance, that take the form of the monochrome, the grid, the image placed serially, etc. Stieglitz's answer now focuses on the nature of the cut or the crop: the photograph is something necessarily cut away from a larger whole. In being punched out of the continuous fabric of the heavens, any *Equivalent* displays itself as a naked function of the cut, not simply because the sky is vast and the photograph is only a tiny part of it, but also because the sky is essentially not composed. Like Duchamp's ▲ readymades, these pictures do not attempt to discover fortuitous compositional relationships in an otherwise indifferent object; rather, the cut operates holistically on every part of the image at once, resonating within it the single message that it has been radically moved from one context to another through the single act of being cut away, dislocated, detached.

This detachment of cutting the image away from its ground (in this case, the sky) is then redoubled within the photograph as its resultant image produces a sense in us as viewers that we have been vertiginously cut away from our own "grounds." For the disorientation caused by the verticality of the clouds as they rise upward along the image in sharp slivers results in our not understanding what is up and what is down, or why this photograph that seems to be so much *of* the world should not contain the most primitive element of our relationship to that world, namely our sense of orientation, our rootedness to the Earth.

In unmooring, or ungrounding, these photographs, Stieglitz naturally enough omits any indication of Earth or horizon from the image. Thus, on a literal level, the *Equivalents* float free. But what they lose literally, they parody formally, since many of the images are strongly vectored (that is, given a sense of direction), light zones abruptly bordering dark ones, producing an axis, like the separation of light and dark achieved by the horizon line that organizes our own relation to the Earth. Yet this formal echo of our natural horizon is taken up in the work only to be denied by being transformed into the uninhabitable verticality of the clouds.

At this moment, then, the cut or crop became Stieglitz's way of emphasizing photography's absolute and essential transposition of reality; essential not because the photographic image is unlike reality in being flat, or black and white, or small, but because as a set of marks on paper traced by light, it is shown to have no more "natural" an orientation to the axial directions of the real world than do those marks in a book we know as writing. It is in this "equivalence" that "straight" photography and modernism effortlessly join hands.

6 • Alfred Stieglitz, *Equivalent*, c. 1927
Silver-gelatin print, 9.2 x 11.7 (3⅝ x 4⅝)

▲ 1914

FURTHER READING

Jonathan Green (ed.), *Camera Work: A Critical Anthology* (New York: Aperture, 1973)

Maria Morris Hambourg, *Paul Strand, Circa 1916* (New York: Metropolitan Museum of Art, 1998)

William Innes Homer, *Alfred Stieglitz and the American Avant-Garde* (Boston: N.Y. Graphic Society, 1977)

Dickran Tashjian, *Skyscraper Primitives: Dada and the American Avant-Garde, 1910–1925* (Middletown, Conn.: Wesleyan University Press, 1975)

Allan Trachtenberg, "From *Camera Work* to Social Work," *Reading American Photographs* (New York: Hill and Wang, 1989)

1917

After two years of intense research, Piet Mondrian breaks through to abstraction, an event immediately followed by the launching of *De Stijl*, the earliest avant-garde journal devoted to the cause of abstraction in art and architecture.

When, in July 1914, Piet Mondrian returned to Holland for a family visit, his sojourn was caught up in the events of World War I, keeping him away from Paris for five long years. If he had originally moved to the French capital in early 1912 with one goal in mind, it was that of mastering Cubism. Unaware, however, of the movement's recent redirection ▲ in relation to its innovative use of collage, with all its consequences for the status of the representational sign, Mondrian wound the clock back to the summer of 1910. At that particular moment in Cubism's history, both Picasso and Braque, having found themselves on the verge of painting totally abstract grids, had recoiled. First reintroducing snippets of referentiality into their pictures (such as the tie and mustache in Picasso's *Portrait of* ● *Daniel-Henry Kahnweiler*, they soon added lettering, flush with the picture plane, that aimed to make everything else in the painting look three-dimensional by comparison, thus ensuring that the representational character of the picture be at least hinted at.

Reading this Analytical Cubism through the lens of fin de siècle Symbolism mixed with Theosophy (an occultist and syncretic doctrine that combined various Eastern and Western religions and philosophies, highly popular in Europe at the turn of the century), Mondrian quickly became aware that just what Picasso and Braque feared most (abstraction and flatness) was precisely what he was searching for, since that would accord with the category of "the universal" that was central to his own belief system. Adopting a frontal point of view, Mondrian found a way of translating his favorite motifs (first trees and then architecture—most notably, in 1914, blank walls uncovered by the demolition of adjacent build- ■ ings) into a more orthogonally rigorous version of the Cubist grid. Through this means, what he called an image's *particularity* is overcome and spatial illusion is replaced by "truth," by the opposition of vertical and horizontal that is the "immutable" essence of all things. The method is infallible, Mondrian thought at the time: everything can be reduced to a common denominator; every figure can be digitalized into a pattern of horizontal versus vertical units and thus disseminated across the surface; and all hierarchy (thus all centrality) can be abolished. The picture's function now becomes the revelation of the world's underlying structure, understood as a reservoir of binary oppositions; but further, and more important,

1 • Piet Mondrian, *Composition No. 10 in Black and White (Pier and Ocean)*, 1915
Oil on canvas, 85 x 108 (33½ x 42½)

it is also to show how these oppositions can neutralize one another into a timeless equilibrium.

It was at this juncture, in 1914, that Mondrian went back to Holland, where, unlike his isolated situation in France, he had a considerable following; for beginning in 1908 he had turned away from Dutch naturalism, embraced modernism, and immediately risen to the head of the local avant-garde. Joining his old Theosophist friends in his usual summer haunt—the artists' colony of Domburg—he attempted to apply his digitalizing technique to the motifs he had painted in various Postimpressionist styles—the small Gothic church, the sea, the piers—before having left for Paris. Only two paintings would result from this group of studies (one in 1915, *Composition No. 10 in Black and White* [1], better known by its nickname *Pier and Ocean*; the other, *Composition 1916*), but together they mark a sea change.

One of the most important factors in this shift was Mondrian's exposure to the philosophy of Hegel, which helped him break away from the inherently static character of digitalization and the neo-Platonic notion of essential truths to be disclosed behind a world of illusions. For if Hegel's Theory of Dialectics is grounded in opposi-

▲ 1912 ● 1911 ■ 1913

2 • Piet Mondrian, *Composition in Line*, 1917
Oil on canvas, 108 x 108 (42 9/16 x 42 9/16)

tions, it does not seek their neutralization. On the contrary, it is a dynamic system moved by tensions, by contradiction. Mondrian's lifelong motto coined at that time—"each element is determined by its contrary"—stems directly from Hegel. The issue is no longer the translating (or, since it is a matter of establishing a set of arbitrary signs that will turn the real world into a form of code, a better term would be *transcoding*) of the visible world into a geometric pattern, but rather the enactment on canvas of the laws of dialectics that govern the world, visible or not.

Though both *Composition No. 10 in Black and White* and *Composition 1916* were based on drawings that had refined the digitalizing method, these canvases now forsook it, abandoning as well the overall symmetry that had resulted from the process (from now on symmetry would be banned from Mondrian's work). In the "plus/minus" drawings that led to the first of these two paintings, Mondrian explored the cruciform structure resulting from the vertical intrusion of the pier as seen from above into the horizontality of reflections on the sea. But rather than the cruciform itself, what we see in the painting is its simultaneous gestation and dissolution—▲ something perfectly caught by Theo van Doesburg (1883–1931) when he wrote about the work in a review that its "methodical construction embodies 'becoming' rather than 'being'." And although almost immediately after completing it, Mondrian would judge *Composition 1916* severely for its too-strong emphasis on one direction in particular (the vertical), all references to the church facade have been suppressed in the work: it is no longer the spectacle of the world that is transcoded but the elements of the art of painting itself that are digitalized—line, color, plane, each reduced to a basic cipher. Though Mondrian would never entirely forgo his original spiritualist position, his art now became, and would remain, one of the most elaborate explorations of the materiality of painting itself, an analysis of its signifiers. This dialectical jump from extreme idealism to extreme materialism is a common feature in the evolution of • many early pioneers of abstraction.

Mondrian's principle of reduction is that of maximal tension: a straight line is but a "tensed curve." The same argument goes for surfaces (the flatter, the tenser) and was soon to apply to color. That Mondrian would wait four more years (until 1920) before adopting the triad of the pure primaries (red, yellow, and blue, used alongside black, gray, and white) should not mask the fact that he already knew at this point that it was the inevitable consequence of his logic. He had first to purge himself entirely of the idea, derived from Goethe, of color as the matter that sullies the purity (read spirituality) of light—this was the last vestige of representation to go, perhaps because its mimetic character, coated in symbolism, was harder to detect. But this delay did not prevent Mondrian, when he started work on *Composition in Line* **[2]** in mid-1916, from taking the plunge into pure abstraction.

Once freed from any referential obligation, Mondrian's work evolved at breakneck speed. *Composition in Line*, finished in early 1917, radicalizes the dynamism of the two previous works, accentuating the tension between an originary randomness and a purported nonhierarchical order. But with it Mondrian realized that a major component of the pictorial language still remained somewhat passive in his work. For, though the figure itself, utterly dispersed by and absorbed within the grid, is now so thoroughly atomized that it is bound to remain a virtuality—each cluster of linear units competing for attention—the white ground behind these black or dark-gray lines is not yet fully "tensed." It is optically activated by the geometrical relations that virtually interconnect the discrete elements of the picture, but in itself it remains an empty space waiting to be filled with a figure—and this, Mondrian now understood, would stop only if the ground ceases to exist as ground. Which is to say that the opposition between figure and ground—the very condition of representation—had to be abolished if an aesthetic program of pure abstraction were to be fulfilled. It was to finding means of achieving this that Mondrian devoted the years from 1917 to 1920.

In a series of canvases immediately following *Composition in Line*, Mondrian eliminated all superimposition of planes. In the first of these paintings, lateral extension is conceived as an antidote to atmospheric illusion, but soon Mondrian realized that floating color planes, appearing as though they were going to glide sideways out of the picture, still presuppose the neutrality of the ground. Gradually aligning the colored rectangles, and, most importantly, ending up this series by dividing the interstitial space itself into rectangles of various shades of white, he thereby eliminated the very notion of passive interstice.

The final step in this rapid march toward the abolition of the ground as ground would be the modular grid, which Mondrian explored in nine canvases dating from 1918 and 1919. In using the proportions of the canvas as the basis of its division into regular units, Mondrian came to terms with a deductive structure that suppresses, in principle, any projection of an a priori image onto the surface. There is no difference between ground and nonground (or, to put it another way, the ground is the figure, the field is the image). The whole surface of the canvas has again become a grid, but this grid is no longer a Cubist scaffolding built up in empty space, since every zone of the canvas is now transformed into a commensurable rectangular unit.

This does not mean, however, that every unit is of equal weight: throughout this series of modular canvases, which comprises his first four so-called "diamond" paintings, Mondrian never abandoned an opposition between marked (through a greater thickness of the "contour," or through color) and unmarked units. This may come as a surprise were it not for Mondrian's Hegelianism: a dynamic tension must lie at the core of any work, which is what an even grid would automatically disallow. (It is precisely because the allover continuity of a regular grid annuls the pathos of tension that ▲ a painter such as Ad Reinhardt, and scores of Minimalist artists after him, had such a predilection for this form.) So in Mondrian's least compositional works, the poorly nicknamed *Checkerboard with Dark Colors* and *Checkerboard with Light Colors* **[3]**, there is a clear sense of struggle between the "objective" data of the operating module and the "subjective" play of the color distribution. In order for the "universal" to manifest itself, a zest of "particularity" must still be factored in—at least for the time being.

These two paintings are the last of the kind. As soon as he finished them, in the spring of 1919, Mondrian returned to Paris, utterly confident that with his modular grids he had just discovered the ultimate answer to most pictorial problems facing artists in the wake of Cubism. But the atmosphere had changed in the • French capital, as exemplified by Picasso's exhibition of neoclassical works. This surely helped Mondrian realize that the absolute "elimination of the particular" was a utopian dream, and thus that the solution of the modular grid, for all its radicality, was, if not a red herring, at least ahead of its time—something for the distant future perhaps, when conditions of perception would have changed, but something that no one would be able to grasp in the present situation. Furthermore, Mondrian began to realize that the modular grid did not accord with his own theories and beliefs: in that such grids are based on repetition (for Mondrian, there was no

▲ 1928, 1937b • 1913 ▲ 1957b • 1919

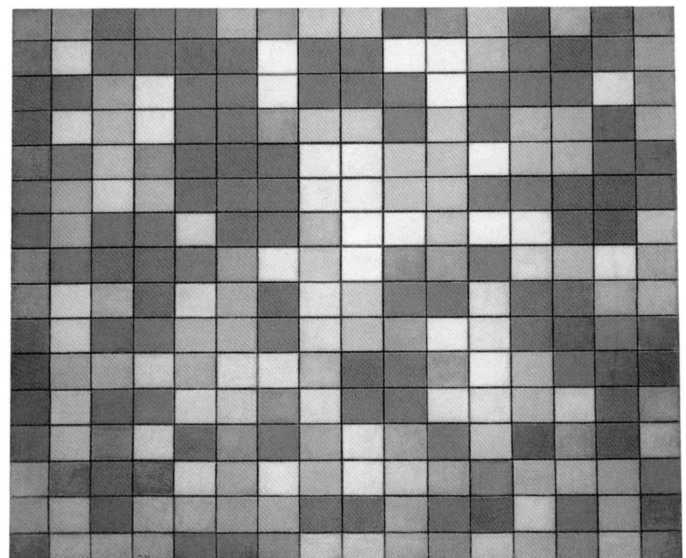

3 • Piet Mondrian, *Composition with Grid 9 (Checkerboard with Light Colors)*, 1919
Oil on canvas, 86 x 106 (33⅞ x 41¾)

difference between the repetitive rhythm of a machine and that of the seasons), and because reticulation (division into a network of squares) engenders illusionistic optical effect (all illusions are feats of nature), he felt that they doubly contradicted his theoretical ban on the "natural."

The invention of Neoplasticism

By the end of 1920, Mondrian's mature style, which he called "Neoplasticism," was in place. Its invention was the result of an intense period of work during which Mondrian gradually eradicated modularity. The difficult goal he now set himself was to reintroduce composition without restoring the hierarchical opposition of figure and ground. The path he chose drew from the same logic that had given birth to his regular grids, but now in reverse. The new equilibrium would not be based on the promise of an equalization of all units but on their dissonance. Optical illusions would now be eliminated entirely, not only the effects of visual flicker induced by the clustering of black lines at the intersections of the grids but even, in the end, the very possibility of color contrasts: color planes cease to be adjacent and, from now on, they are more often than not displaced to the painting's periphery. There is no more opposition between figure and ground here than in the modular grids, but now each unit, clearly differentiated (it is at this point that the primary colors appear), aims at destroying the centrality of all others.

Composition with Yellow, Red, Black, Blue, and Gray [**4**], the first Neoplastic painting proper, demonstrates the efficiency of Mondrian's new method. Although the balancing logic of the painting had called for a large central square, we do not perceive it as such. In this pictorial language, with its hostility to the idea of the gestalt (or form understood as the separation of figure from its background), nothing, not even an easily recognized shape (rectangle, square) placed on the axis of symmetry, must get the lion's share of attention. From now on, each Neoplastic painting would be a microcosmic model, a practico-theoretical object in which the destructive powers of dialectical thought are tested each time anew. Using a vocabulary that is fixed once and for all (there would be no ▲ major change until Mondrian's last years in New York), Mondrian would patiently spend the next two decades applying himself to combating the idea of identity as a form of self-sufficiency unthreatened by its opposite or its negation. After the figure and the ground, he would tackle the plane and the line: one after the other, these elements of painting, and their secular functions, would be questioned.

Most pioneers of abstraction were staunch evolutionists, but Mondrian seems to be the only one to have matched his words with his deeds. It does not diminish the messianic strength of his convictions, bolstered by his Hegelianism, to note that he was not working in a vacuum. Help and adulation from younger colleagues came at the right moment with the birth of *De Stijl*, a journal founded in October 1917 by van Doesburg, around whom gathered a nucleus of painters (Bart van der Leck and Vilmos Huszar) and architects (J. J. P. Oud, Jan Wils, and Robert van't Hoff), plus a sculptor (Georges Vantongerloo) and a poet (Antony Kok), all of whom were focused on modernism as a utopian integration of the arts into the space of living.

Van Doesburg was the coordinator, but Mondrian was the mentor: his theory of art was the basis for the collective activity of the group—even if dissensions caused several members to drift away very early on (such as van der Leck, reluctant to forgo figuration in his paintings entirely, or Jan Wils, too attached to symmetry in his buildings). In their analysis of the figure–ground opposition, none of the painters would propose anything more radical than did Mondrian, but the very fact that van Doesburg and Huszar were concerned with the same problem certainly encouraged him. It was in its collaborative program, however, that the De Stijl group proved the most inventive.

● The movement's agenda was typically modernist. Like Kazimir Malevich's Suprematism, De Stijl conceived of its production as the logical culmination of the art of the past, and saw as the motor of this "inevitable" evolution the ontological quest of each individual art for its own "essence," and the elimination of any superfluous convention (countless texts by Mondrian and his peers reflect upon these principles with regard not only to painting, sculpture, and architecture, but also to music, dance, and literature). What is specific to De Stijl is the way its members considered the articulation between the individual arts: nothing can be gained from the sheer confusion of distinctive fields (the medley of Art Nouveau is sharply criticized by van Doesburg); nothing is more reprehensible than the very idea of "applied" arts; each art has to determine its own irreducible elements before attempting a fusion with any other art. Different arts can unite only if they share such "irreducible elements," which explains the centrality for De Stijl of the relationship between painting and

▲ 1944a ● 1915

4 • Piet Mondrian, *Composition with Yellow, Red, Black, Blue, and Gray*, 1920
Oil on canvas, 51.5 x 61 (20¼ x 24)

architecture, two mediums available for such fusion because of their common use of planar units.

In the end, however, the collaboration between architects and painters proved extremely difficult and led to the progressive dismantling of the original group, the practitioners of each art being reluctant to relinquish any prerogative to those of the other. The main stumbling block was theoretical. For Mondrian, architecture, by its very nature, could not perform the abolition of hierarchy, centrality, and "particularity" that lay at the core of his aesthetics. Architecture was doomed by anatomy (the post-and-lintel structure), and thus—paradoxically, since it is nonmimetic—could never become abstract. The De Stijl painters thus conceived their art as a Trojan horse entering architectural space in order to destroy its anatomical structure visually, but at the cost of reintroducing a form of illusion. For example, in Huszar's and Gerrit Rietveld's experimental project of 1923, *Spatial Color Composition for an Exhibition, Berlin* [**5**], the physical shape of the room, especially its corners, is negated optically by wandering planes of color. Thus, even if Mondrian retained a lifelong interest in the possibility of the "abstract interior" (the hybrid form invented by De Stijl members as a result of their collective analysis), transforming his successive studios, first in Paris and then in New York, into paintings that deploy their planar elements throughout the real space of the room, he knew that the "future dissolution of art into the environment" that he had envisioned early on as a logical consequence of his Hegelian program was not to be realized during his lifetime, if ever. Though he kept writing on all the arts and imagining how his Neoplastic theory, once transferred to their domain, would affect them, painting remained the only uncompromising field of experimentation for him. De Stijl had given him some important feedback, but retrospectively it is obvious that he could not have condoned for long the devolution of his highly elaborate pictorial language into principles of good design.

5 • **Vilmos Huszar and Gerrit Rietveld, *Spatial Color Composition for an Exhibition, Berlin*, 1923, from *L'Architecture vivante*, Autumn 1924**

FURTHER READING

Carel Blotkamp, *Mondrian: The Art of Destruction* (New York: Harry N. Abrams, 1994)

Carel Blotkamp et al., *De Stijl: The Formative Years* (Cambridge, Mass.: MIT Press, 1986)

Yve-Alain Bois, "The De Stijl Idea," *Painting as Model* (Cambridge, Mass.: MIT Press, 1990)

Piet Mondrian, *The New Art—The New Life* (Boston: G. K. Hall & Co, 1986)

Angelica Rudenstine (ed.), *Piet Mondrian* (The Hague: Gemeentemuseum; Washington, D.C.: National Gallery of Art; and New York: Museum of Modern Art, 1994)

Nancy Troy, *The De Stijl Environment* (Cambridge, Mass.: MIT Press, 1983)

1918

Marcel Duchamp paints *Tu m'*: his last ever painting summarizes the departures undertaken in his work, such as the use of chance, the promotion of the readymade, and photography's status as an "index."

Marcel Duchamp had landed in New York in 1915 still awash in the celebrity of his *Nude Descending a Staircase No. 2* 1912, the most notorious painting of the 1913 ▲ Armory Show. Whether it was as "A Rude Descending a Staircase," or as "An Explosion in a Shingle Factory" (to echo the popular press), this Cubist picture, having set up a beachhead for avant-gardism in the New World, had secured a welcome for its author among the art patrons and collectors in and around Manhattan—figures such as Walter Arensberg, the Stettheimer sisters, and Katherine Dreier. It is not surprising, then, that Dreier should have asked Duchamp, in 1918, to make a long, friezelike painting to go over the bookcases in her library, something like the commission for decorative panels that Hamilton Easter Field had given to Picasso in 1910. What *is* surprising is that Duchamp should have accepted it.

For by the time of his arrival in America, Duchamp had abandoned working in oils; and the ambitious picture over which he was to begin laboring in 1915, *The Bride Stripped Bare by her Bachelors, Even* (also known as the *Large Glass*), was not, technically speaking, a painting [**1**]. Supported on trestles in the tiny apartment that Arensberg lent to Duchamp, it was in fact two very large panes of glass to which designs of a highly enigmatic kind were applied by a variety of curious means: dust that had settled on the work during months of inactivity was carefully "fixed" in certain places; or shapes of lead and stretches of wire were glued to its surface; or again, silvering was adhered in a given area and then carefully scratched away so as to leave a tracery of mirrored line. Although the execution was meticulous when actually carried out, Duchamp worked on it only sporadically—the piece was completed in 1923. Indeed, he spent as much time creating the conceptual climate for the work through the mass of notes he jotted down, some as early as 1911, others dating to 1915, which he later published collectively as *The Green Box* (1934).

The note labeled "Preface," and thus accorded some sort of authority over the various ideas generated for the *Large Glass*, is written as a strange syllogism. "Given," it starts, "[1] the waterfall, [2] the illuminating gas, we shall determine the conditions of the instantaneous State of Rest ... of a succession of different facts ..."; such "instantaneous State of Rest" being equivalent, it tells us in an appendix to the note, to "the expression extra-rapid." Now, if this "Preface" gives us any clues to what Duchamp thought he was doing *in the place* of painting, they are in the terms *instantaneous* (in French *instantané*—the word, if used as a noun, for snapshot) and *extra-rapid*. For in 1914 Duchamp had "published" a group of fifteen notes dealing with his ideas about art by placing the replicated scraps of paper in boxes normally containing photographic glass plates, the advanced technical capacities of which were indicated by the boxes' labels "extra-rapid" or "extra-rapid exposure."

If at first it might seem counterintuitive to think of *The Bride Stripped Bare* as a photograph—so imposing, intricate, and, to use Duchamp's own expression, "allegorical appearing" is it relative to the tiny scale and documentary straightforwardness of a snapshot—we have nonetheless to keep two things in mind. The first is the intense "realism" of the objects suspended within the glass, not only because of their sense of solidity but also because of the strong single-point perspective used to delineate them (and by implication, the space that contains them). The second is the impenetrability of the "allegory" itself, expressed on the one hand by the mechanical contraption housing the bachelors and, on the other, by the metallic shells and amorphous cloud of the bride.

You push the button ...

In the years before Duchamp's "Notes" were published the only key to this mysterious narrative was the work's long but somehow noncommittal title, more a statement of fact—a bride is stripped by her (?) bachelors—than an explanation of meaning. Even after their publication, however, the mystery has not lifted but only burgeoned into more and more elaborate decipherings: "the stripping of the bride is an allegory of courtly love"; "the stripping is a kind of alchemical purification—base matter turning into spirit"; "the stripping is our access to the fourth dimension"; etc. As each of these explanations leads to no definitive "solution" but only back to the brute fact of the objects' sitting in the solidity of their "realistic" presentation, we encounter a feature of photography that connects the two aspects of the glass: its verism and its mute resistance to interpretation. For photographs do not bind their interpretive text into themselves the way paintings with their compositional protocols are

▲ 1914, 1916b

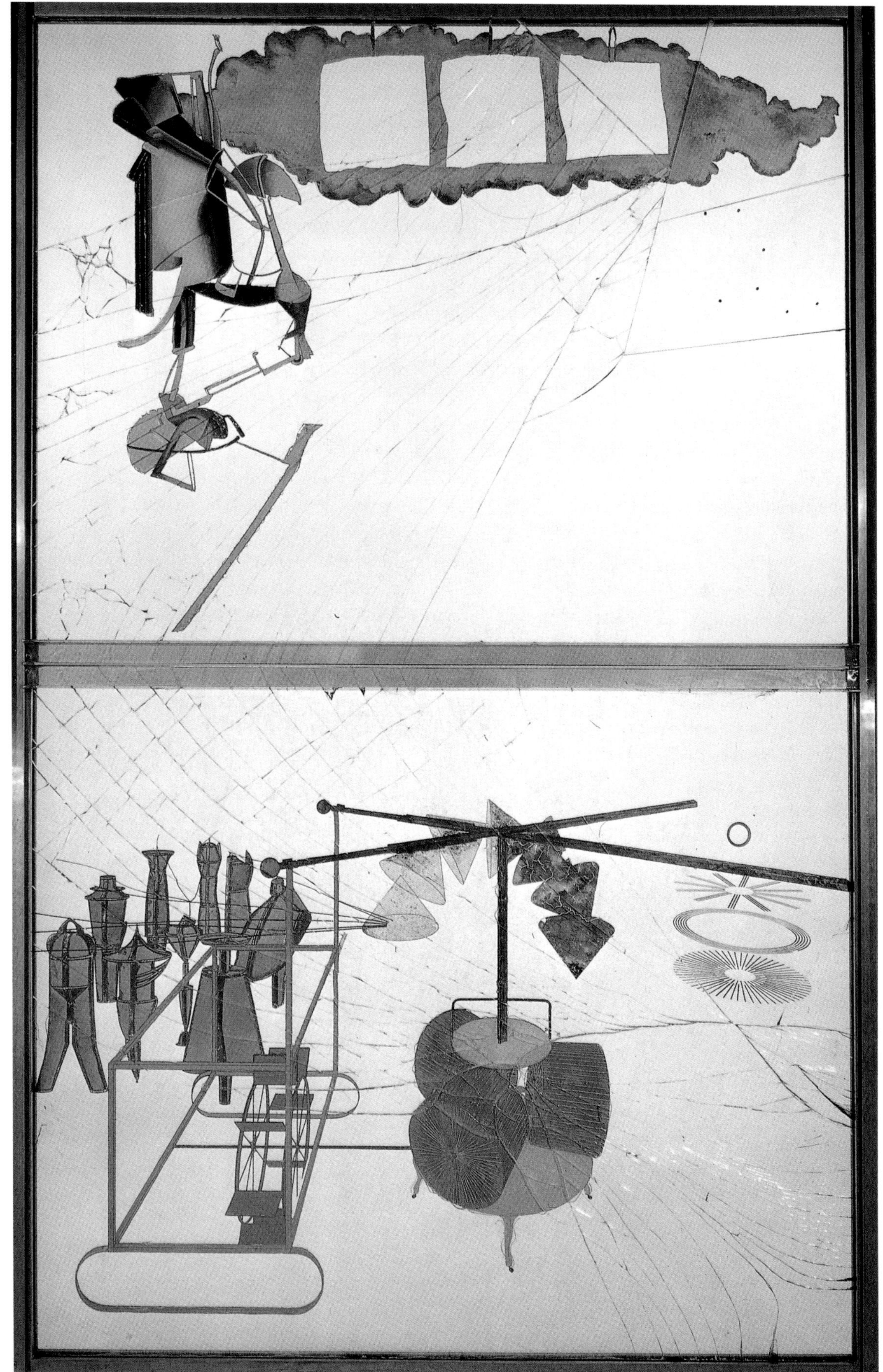

1 • Marcel Duchamp, *The Bride Stripped Bare by Her Bachelors, Even (The Large Glass)*, 1915–23
Oil, varnish, lead foil, lead wire, and dust on two sheets on glass panels, 276.9 x 175.9 (109¼ x 69¼)

able to do. Rather, stenciled directly off reality, the photograph is a manifestation of fact which often depends on an added text—such as the newspaper caption—for its explanation.

Addressing photography itself as a structural problem, in the ▲ early sixties the French critic and semiologist Roland Barthes called this basic feature of photography its condition of being "a message without a code." Barthes thereby contrasted the nature of the photographic sign with signs of different types: pictures or maps, say, or words. Insofar as words emerge from a background of systematized language with its own grammatical rules and its own lexical compendium, these particular signs belong to a highly coded system. Moreover, it is only from within that system that meaning attaches to them, since they neither look like the thing to which they refer (the way pictures do) nor are literally caused by it (the way footprints are), and so their relationship to meaning is purely arbitrary and thus conventional; and to mark their distinction from other types of signs, semiologists call them *symbols*.

Pictures, on the other hand, are given the name *icon*, since they relate to their referents not by convention but through the axis of resemblance. Nonetheless, they, too, are able to be composed or manipulated so as to incorporate coded meanings: national colors, for example, or the seating arrangement through which we recognize the Last Supper.

It is the last of the three types of sign, the *index*, that resists coding altogether, since it cannot be internally reorganized or rearranged. This is because the index is literally *caused* by its referent and thus has a blocklike connection to it: like the weather vane pushed into a certain direction by the wind, or the fever induced in the body by microbes, or the circles left on tables by cold glasses, or the patterns etched in the sand by the outgoing tide. Thus, if photography is a message without a code, this puts it in a class with footprints and medical symptoms, and distances it from the Sistine Chapel ceiling, no matter how resemblant (or iconic) a photograph might also be. The fact that it is a photochemically produced trace—the index of the object to which the light-sensitive medium was exposed—is what counts for the semiologist.

It seems also to have been what counted for Duchamp. For across the field of *The Bride Stripped Bare* the index finds multiple repetitions. Not only are the seven conical forms of the "sieves" (that part of the bachelor machine in which male desire is condensed) corporealized by fixing the amount of dust that fell on the glass over the course of several months (an index of time passing), but the nine "shots" (the rays of desire that actually penetrate into the bride's realm) are traces of where matches fired from a toy cannon hit the surface. Or again, the three "draft pistons" (openings in the cloudlike shape appended to the bride) are shapes obtained by suspending a square of fabric in front of an open window, thrice photographing its deformations caused by the wind, and then using the profiles registered on the resultant prints as stencils from which to transfer the shapes to the glass.

Procedurally, the execution of the "pistons" follows that of the *Three Standard Stoppages* [**2**], an earlier work Duchamp made by dropping three meter-long strings from the height of one meter onto a surface on which the entirely chance configuration of each was fixed, all three then being used to cut stencils that would serve as very curious "yardsticks" indeed, since each one has a different profile and results in a different length. To this artisanally wrought operation of chance, the "pistons" merely added the more mechanical intervention of the camera's shutter and the photographic print.

But the *Three Standard Stoppages* underscore the sense in which the index—the unique trace or precipitate of an event or, in this case, of a chance occurrence—in being "a message without a code," is resistant to language. For language depends on its signs (for example, its words) remaining stable over the many instances of their repetition. Even though a given context may reconfigure the connotation or even the *meaning* (or signified) of a word, its form (or signifier) must be the same for each iteration of it. This is even more nakedly true for units of measure—such as feet and inches—in which both signifier and signified must remain constant from one context to another. Duchamp's ironically non-"standard" yardstick, which changes its length from instance to instance, thus defies the coding that gives measurement its precision and its meaning.

A note from *The Green Box* explicitly connects the two systems—linguistic and numerical—by imagining what Duchamp calls "prime words": "Conditions of a language: the search for 'prime words' ('divisible' only by themselves and by unity)." The

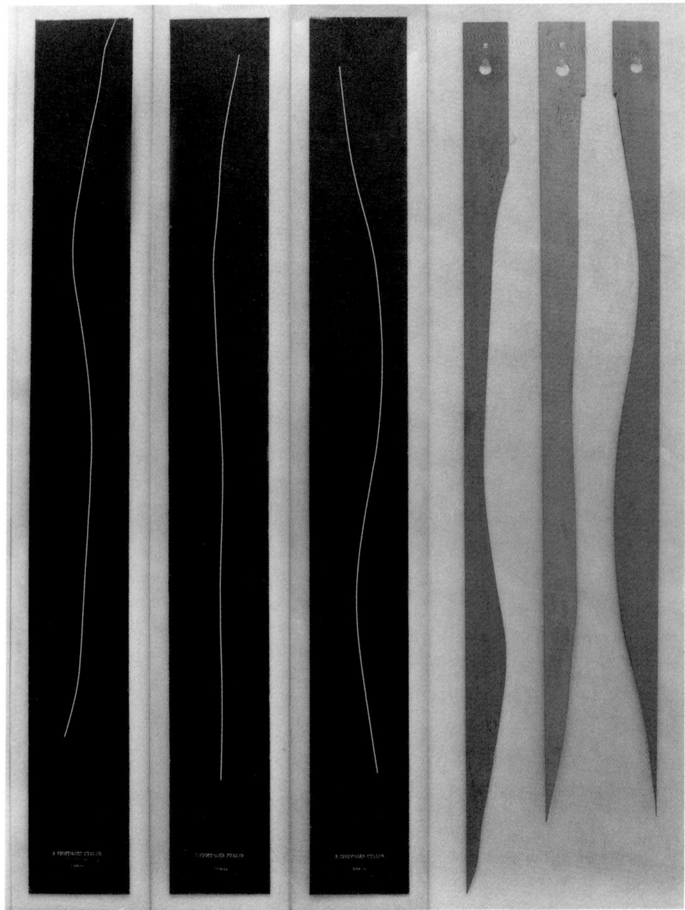

2 • Marcel Duchamp, *Three Standard Stoppages*, 1913–14
Thread, glue, and paint on glass panels fitted in a wooden box, 28.2 x 129.2 x 22.7 (11⅛ x 50⅞ x 9)

▲ Introduction 3

impossibility of the prime number's entering into numerical relations with the rest of the arithmetic system—being divisible by other numbers or dividing itself into them—is thus explicitly related to a kind of linguistic sign that resists the "combinatory function of language"—the rules that allow either a small set of sounds to be recombined into the huge set of words that make up a vocabulary, or that permit the combination of these words into infinite numbers of sentences. The "prime word" can be thought of, rather, as an index lodged inside the system of language, a marker of a specific event, as when a child is baptized with a proper name—which thus belongs uniquely to that child—or when I point my finger toward something and say "this," thus naming (but only for the specific instance of my pointing) a particular object: this book, this apple, this chair.

Panorama of the index

If we started out, then, by seeing the *Large Glass* through the model of the photograph, what we quickly begin to realize is that for Duchamp the photographic category is, in turn, folded into the far more generalized model of the index, which can be visual (snapshots, for instance, but also smoke, fingerprints, etc.) or verbal ("this," "here," "today"). Further, we also realize that the index implies not just a shift in the traditional type of sign employed by the visual artist (from iconic to indexical) but also a deep change in artistic procedure. For the index, insofar as it marks the trace of an event, can be the precipitate of a chance occurrence, as in the deformations recorded by the *Large Glass*'s "draft pistons." Indeed, Duchamp explicitly referred to the *Three Standard Stoppages* as "canned chance." But chance, of course, rules out the traditional artist's desire to compose his or her work, to prepare it step by step. And in abrogating composition, the use of chance also nullifies the idea of skill that had always been associated with the very definition of the artist. Embracing something far more like (and even more radical than) Kodak's photographic slogan "You push the button, we do the rest," Duchamp's use of chance both mechanizes the making of the work (the artist is like a camera, thus depersonalized) and deskills it (nothing, not even a camera, is needed).

The possibilities of Duchamp's recourse to chance were quickly seized on by others who were also interested in strategies for undoing the role of composition in the making of the work. One of ▲ these was Hans Arp, the Dada artist, who some time around 1915 began to make collages by tearing up pieces of paper and dropping • them onto a waiting surface [**3**]. Another was Francis Picabia, who threw ink at a page to make a formless splotch which he called *The Blessed Virgin* (1920). In producing this blasphemous conjunction of meaningless sign and sacred formula, however, Picabia was going beyond Arp's procedural implementation of chance to participate in Duchamp's extension of it into the realm of meaning—or rather a short circuit in the field of meaning.

Another of Duchamp's notes from *The Green Box* pulls chance, photography, and linguistic emptiness all together. Called "Specification for Readymades," it declares that the readymade will be whatever object the artist stumbles on at a moment he or she predetermines. Calling this a kind of rendezvous or encounter, the note compares it with a snapshot (the indexical recording of the event) but also says that it is "like a speech pronounced on no matter what occasion but at such and such an hour," which is to say, a linguistic event whose mechanized inappropriateness renders it meaningless.

3 • Hans Arp, *Collage of Squares Arranged According to the Laws of Chance*, 1916–17
Collage of colored papers, 48.6 x 34.6 (19⅛ x 13⅝)

If we have seen that Duchamp's notes often pull together various strands of the index's implications, this tendency to synthesize is nowhere more in evidence than in his valedictory painting made for Katherine Dreier. For *Tu m'* [**4**], a kind of résumé of Duchamp's post-Cubist production, is a panorama of the index in its many ▲ forms. Several of his readymades—the *Bicycle Wheel* (1913) and the *Hat Rack* (1916)—themselves the index or trace of the rendezvous through which Duchamp encountered them, are projected onto the canvas as cast shadows (another form of index). The *Three Standard Stoppages* appear both in depicted form and as a series of profiles traced from their stencils. The finicky representation of a pointing hand, its *index* finger extended toward the right side of the work as if to designate the hat rack with the gesture "this," opens onto the verbal form of the index that is finally invoked in the work's title: *Tu m'* ("You __________ [to] me").

▲ 1913, 1916a • 1916b, 1919 ▲ 1914

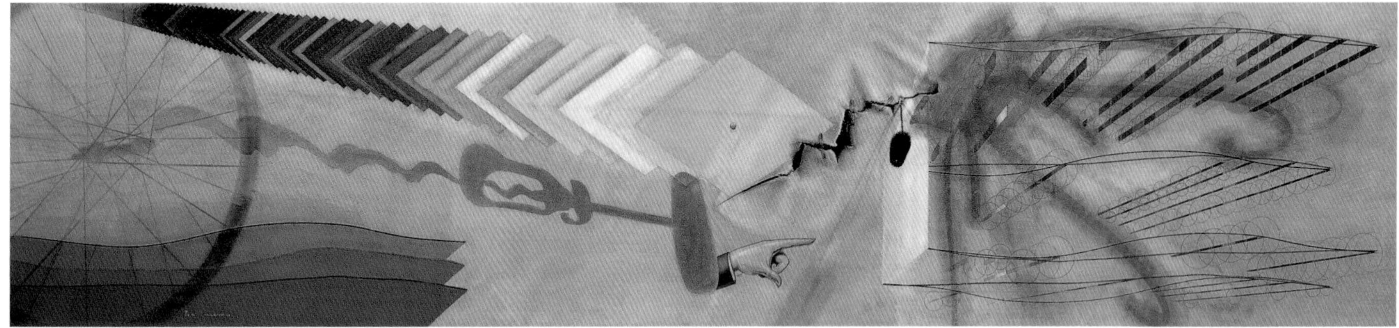

4 • Marcel Duchamp, *Tu m'*, 1918
Oil and graphite on canvas, with bottle-washing brush, safety pins, nut and bolt, 69.9 x 311.8 (27½ x 122¾)

Just as *this* or *that* are indexical words connected with a referent only within the temporary context of a given act of pointing, so the personal pronouns *you* and *I* are similarly indexical, connecting to their referent in the shifting context of a given speech event. For it is only the one who says "I" who fills the pronoun at the moment of saying it, during which time his or her interlocutor is named as "you," although becoming "I" in turn, by taking up the other side of the conversation. It is because the signified of the personal pronouns shifts in this way—naming now one participant in a colloquy, now the other—that linguists have called these indexical kinds of words "shifters."

What does it mean, however, that in *Tu m'* Duchamp invokes the two sides of the colloquy at once, as though he were mixing up linguistic decorum by occupying both poles himself: "You ___________ [to] me"? Could this relate to yet another note from *The Green Box* which consists of a little sketch for the *Large Glass* with the feminine bride in the upper register labeled MAR (for *mariée*) and the masculine bachelors in the lower one labeled CEL (for *célibataires*). Put together, of course, these two syllables produce the "Marcel" by which Duchamp names himself, although strangely split and doubled as would be the case with *Tu m'*.

If the iconic mode of representation had significantly changed in the move from naturalism to modernist forms such as Cubism or Fauvism, and if the single-point perspective of the earlier system had been under attack by the destruction of perspective involved in modernism, nonetheless within iconic representation certain things remain constant. One of these is the assumption of a unified subject or viewer as the one who makes contact with the image.

5 • Marcel Duchamp and Man Ray, *Belle Haleine, Eau de Voilette* (Beautiful Breath, Veil Water), 1921
Perfume bottle with collage label inside oval violet cardboard box, 16.3 x 11.2 (6⅜ x 4⅜)

Rrose Sélavy

One of the sketches Duchamp drew for the *Large Glass* and published in the *Green Box* shows the double field of the work with the upper area labeled "MAR" (short for *mariée* [bride]) and the lower one "CEL" (short for *célibataires* [bachelors]). With this personal identification with the protagonists of the *Glass*, (MAR + CEL = Marcel) Duchamp thought about assuming a feminine persona. As he told his interviewer, Pierre Cabanne:

> Cabanne: *Rrose Sélavy was born in 1920, I think.*
> Duchamp: *In effect, I wanted to change my identity, and the first idea that came to me was to take a Jewish name ... I didn't find a Jewish name that I especially liked, or that tempted me, and suddenly I had an idea: why not change sex? It was much simpler. So the name Rrose Sélavy came from that ...*
> Cabanne: *You went so far in your sex change as to have yourself photographed dressed a a woman.*
> Duchamp: *It was Man Ray who did the photograph ...*

Having stopped work on the *Glass* in 1923, Duchamp transferred his artistic enterprise to this new character and had business cards printed up giving his name and profession as "Rrose Sélavy, Precision Oculist." The works he went on to make as "oculist" were machines with turning optical disks—the *Rotary Demisphere* and the *Rotoreliefs*—as well as films, such as *Anemic Cinema.*

There is a way to understand Rrose Sélavy's enterprise as the undermining of the Kantian aesthetic system in which the work of art opens onto a collective visual space acknowledging, in effect, the simultaneity of points of view of all the spectators who are gathered to see it, a multiplicity whose appreciation for the work speaks with, as Kant would say, the universal voice. On the contrary, Duchamp's "precision optics" were, like the holes in the door of his installation *Etant données,* available to only one viewer at a time. Organized as optical illusions, they were clearly the solitary visual projection of the viewer placed in the right vector to experience them. As the *Rotoreliefs*—a set of printed cards—revolved like visual records on a phonograph turntable, their designs of slightly skewed concentric circles spiral to burgeon outward like a balloon inflating and then to reverse themselves into an inward, sucking movement. Some appeared like eyes or breasts, trembling in a phantom space; another sported a goldfish that seemed to be swimming in a basin whose plug had been pulled, so that the fish was being sucked down the drain. In this sense, Duchamp's switch to Rrose and her activities marks a turn from an interest in the mechanical (the Bachelor Machine, the Chocolate Grinder) to a concern for the optical.

Perspective had specifically located this viewer in its plotting of a ▲ precise vantage point. But both Cubism and Fauvism, by finding other means to unify the pictorial space, also address themselves to a unified human subject: the viewer/interpreter of the work.

The final implication of Duchamp's removal of his field of operations from the iconic to the indexical sign becomes clear in this context. For beyond its marking a break with "picturing" and a rejection of "skill," beyond its displacement of meaning from repeatable code to unique event, the index's aspect as shifter has implications for the status of the subject, of the one who says "I," in this case Duchamp "himself." For as the subject of the vast self-portrait assembled by *Tu m',* Duchamp declares himself a disjunctive, fractured subject, split axially into the two facing poles of pronominal space, even as he would split himself sexually into the two opposite poles of gender in the many photographic self-portraits he would make while in drag and sign "Rrose Sélavy" **[5]**. Taking up Rimbaud's "je est un autre" ("I is an other"), Duchamp's shattering of subjectivity was perhaps his most radical act.

FURTHER READING

Roland Barthes, "The Photographic Message" and "The Rhetoric of the Image," *Image/Music/Text* (New York: Hill and Wang, 1977)

Marcel Duchamp, *Salt Seller: The Writings of Marcel Duchamp (Marchand du Sel)*, eds Michel Sanouillet and Elmer Peterson (New York: Oxford University Press, 1973)

Thierry de Duve, *Pictorial Nominalism: On Duchamp's Passage from Painting to the Readymade*, trans. Dana Polan (Minneapolis: University of Minnesota Press, 1991)

Thierry de Duve (ed.), *The Definitively Unfinished Marcel Duchamp* (Cambridge, Mass.: MIT Press, 1991)

Rosalind Krauss, "Notes on the Index," *The Originality of the Avant-Garde and Other Modernist Myths* (Cambridge, Mass.: MIT Press, 1985)

Robert Lebel, *Marcel Duchamp* (New York: Grove Press, 1959)

▲ 1906, 1907, 1911, 1912

1919

Pablo Picasso has his first solo exhibition in Paris in thirteen years: the onset of pastiche in his work coincides with a widespread antimodernist reaction.

When Wilhelm Uhde, the German collector and dealer of French avant-garde art, entered the Paul Rosenberg Gallery in 1919, he was stunned. Instead of the powerful style he had witnessed Picasso developing in the years leading ▲ up to the outbreak of World War I—first Analytical Cubism, a major example of which was Picasso's 1910 portrait of Uhde • himself, then collage, and finally "Synthetic Cubism" (the form that collage took when rendered in oil paint on canvas)—Uhde was confronted with a strange mixture.

On the one hand there were neoclassical portraits, redolent of the manner of Ingres, Corot, late Renoir, indeed the whole panoply of nineteenth-century French artists influenced by the classical tradition, all the way from Greek and Roman antiquity up through the Renaissance and into the work of seventeenth-century French painters such as Poussin [**1**]. On the other hand there were Cubist still lifes, but now of a compromised form: impregnated with vistas of deep space, prettified by a decorative palette of pinks and cerulean blues. Uhde remembers:

> *I found myself in the presence of a huge portrait in what is known as the Ingres manner; the conventionality, the sobriety of the attitude seemed studied, and it seemed to be repressing some pathetic secret.... What was the meaning of this and the other pictures I saw on that occasion? Were they but an interlude, a gesture—splendid but without significance ...?*

Wanting to see what he viewed as Picasso's self-betrayal as merely a parenthesis, the momentary flagging of his true creative energies, Uhde nonetheless had suspicions that the artist had capitulated to something more sinister, to the fear inspired by the xenophobia unleashed by French nationalism during the war, a hatred of everything foreign that had already manifested itself in a prewar cultural campaign in which Cubism was linked with the approaching enemy and affixed with the label "*boche*" ("kraut"). Accordingly, Uhde continues his speculations on the cause of what he has seen:

> *Or was it that at this time when men were ruled by hate ... [Picasso] felt that innumerable people were pointing their fingers at him, reproaching him with having strong German sympathies and accusing him of being secretly in connivance with the enemy?... Was he trying definitely to range himself on the French side, and did these pictures attest to the torment of his soul?*

Among the many things that emerge from this scene, the two most obvious concern the enormity of the break that Uhde sensed in Picasso's art and, given this, his conviction that its explanation had to be found in a cause outside the inner logic of the work itself.

Uhde has since been joined by many historians in seeking this explanation, even though not all of them agree with him about the nature of this external cause. Yet for the ones who side with Uhde in looking to politics for an answer, that explanation is linked to the *rappel à l'ordre* (return to order), a widespread postwar reaction against what was seen as the avant-garde's promotion of anarchic and antihumanist expressive means and an embrace instead of a classicism worthy of the French ("Mediterranean") tradition.

Was Picasso, the avant-garde leader, now following in the wake of this massive "return," his ship unable to hold its own against the flood tide of historical reaction? To some scholars the actual date of Picasso's conversion makes the postwar *rappel à l'ordre* dubious as an explanation. For Picasso had already begun to embrace a classical style *during* the war, as, for example, in his 1915 portrait drawings of Max Jacob [**2**] and Ambroise Vollard. So, instead, these scholars look to the circumstances of Picasso's personal life. They cite his isolation, ▲ with close artistic allies like Braque and Apollinaire away at the front, and Eva Gouel, the companion of his prewar years, dying of cancer; they mention his growing restlessness with a Cubist style that had become increasingly formulaic and, in the hands of lesser followers, banal; they see his excitement at being swept up in the glamour of the Ballets Russes, with its eccentric personnel such as Sergei Diaghilev, its elegant ballerinas, and its glittering clientele; finally, they see his succumbing to the charms of Olga Koklova, the dancer in the corps of the Ballets Russes whom Picasso would marry in 1918 and whom he would allow to integrate him into that world of wealth and pleasure for which the avant-garde was just another form of *chic*.

But if these two explanations—one sociopolitical, the other biographical—are at odds with each other, they agree about looking for the reason for this change *outside* the limits of Picasso's actual work. In this they share a common understanding about the nature of causal explanation. As a consequence they are opposed to another

▲ 1911 • 1912 ▲ 1911, 1912

1 • Pablo Picasso, *Olga Picasso in an Armchair*, 1917 (detail)
Oil on canvas, 130 x 88.8 (51⅛ x 35)

position, which insists that the postwar manner can be logically deduced from Cubism itself and thus, like the growth of an organism, its genetic coding is entirely internal to it and more or less impervious to external factors. The principle that this side sees at work—internal to Cubism itself—is collage: the grafting of heterogeneous material onto the formerly homogeneous surface of the work of art. If collage could paste matchbooks and calling cards, wallpaper swatches, and newsprint onto the field of Cubism, they reason, why cannot this practice be extended to the grafting of a whole range of "extraneous" styles onto the unfolding oeuvre, so that Poussin will be redone in the manner of archaic Greek sculpture, or the realist compositions of the seventeenth-century painter Le Nain will be presented through the gay confetti of Seurat's pointillism? Ultimately, the defenders of this position argue, there is no need to explain the change in Picasso, since nothing in fact changes; the collage principle remains the same—only the "extraneous" matter shifts a little.

Contextualists versus internalists

The radical division between these two camps of scholars brings us face to face with the issue of historical method. The contextual explanation sets itself against the theory of the internally determined growth of the creative individual, each position feeling the other is blind to certain facts. The contextualists, for example, see the other side as refusing to face up to the reactionary content unleashed by neoclassicism and the need to find the source of such

Sergei Diaghilev (1872–1929) and the Ballets Russes

In the late nineteenth century, German composer Richard Wagner theorized the achievement he hoped his operatic theatre would realize under the term *Gesamtkunstwerk.* This idea of a "total work of the arts" meant the coordination of all the senses—sound, spectacle, narrative—into a single continuity. The antimodernism of Wagner's position lay in its negation of the idea of a given work's obligation to reveal the boundaries of its own medium and to seek its own possibility of meaning within those boundaries. Wagner never achieved a true *Gesamtkunstwerk,* however; it was left to another form of musical theater and another impresario from another country to do so. During the first half of the twentieth century, Sergei Diaghilev, Russian director of the Ballets Russes, wove together the full range of avant-garde talent into a sumptuous fabric of visual spectacle: his composers ranged from Igor Stravinsky and Erik Satie to Darius Milhaud and Georges Auric; his choreographers were Massine and Nijinsky; his set and costume designers were Picasso, Georges Braque, and Fernand Léger, among others.

Writer Jean Cocteau describes the meeting he arranged in 1919 between Diaghilev and Picasso in order to convince the latter to collaborate on Cocteau's own ballet *Parade*:

> *I understood that there existed in Paris an artistic Right and an artistic Left, which were ignorant or disdainful of each other for no valid reasons and which it was perfectly possible to bring together. It was a question of converting Diaghilev to modern painting, and the modern painters, especially Picasso, to the sumptuous, decorative esthetic of the ballet: of coaxing the Cubists out of their isolation, persuading them to abandon their hermetic Montmartre folklore of pipes, packages of tobacco, guitars, and old newspapers ... the discovery of a middle-of-the-road solution attuned to the taste for luxury and pleasure, of the revived cult of French "clarity" that was springing up in Paris even before the war ... such was the history of* Parade.

The "sumptuous, decorative aesthetic," to which Cocteau refers was a gorgeous Art Nouveau texture, as bejeweled and gilded as any Tiffany lamp or oriental interior. For *Parade,* Picasso and Satie were to defy the Ballets Russes's usual designer Léon Bakst's drive toward Orientalist splendor, substituting the ascetic drabness of Cubist sets and costumes and unleashing the sounds of typewriters and popular ditties on the appalled audience, which responded by hurling insults at the stage: "*métèques,*" [half-breeds] and "*boches*" [krauts]. Cocteau, who prided himself on his fashionableness and his understanding of the high cultural taste for occasional slumming, had as his motto: "You have to know just how far you can go too far." But in *Parade* he and Diaghilev had apparently gone too far and the audience, along with the ballet's sponsors—the Comtesse de Chabrillon, the Comtesse de Chavigné, and the Comtesse de Beaumont—could not wait to tell them so.

Ballet companies now considered themselves heir to the ambitions of the artistic avant-garde. One in particular was the Ballet Suedois, whose director, Rolf de Maré, turned to Francis Picabia for the design of the set for *Relâche* (1924), a title that was itself a snub to its audience since it meant "performance canceled." Picabia's set consisted of over three hundred automobile headlights trained out toward the audience and turned on in unison at the end of one of the acts in a blinding, bedazzling, sadistic fury.

reaction; the internalists see themselves vindicated by the early date of Picasso's move, showing that it must be motivated by something native to his creative will and unproblematically continuous with his previous concerns with Cubism.

The positivist historians among us (or the positivist impulses within each of us) would like to cut the knot of this argument by coming up with a document that will solve the debate: a letter by Picasso, for example, or a statement in an interview in which he says what this change in style meant to him or what he intended by it. However, there rarely is such a thing in relation to Picasso (or to most other artists for that matter), and even in the few instances where it does exist, we *still* have to interpret it. In this case, for example, Picasso seems to have sided with the internalists when in response to the Swiss conductor Ernest Ansermet's question, put to him in Rome in 1917, about why he engaged simultaneously in two totally opposite styles (Cubism and neoclassicism), Picasso merely quipped: "Can't you see? The results are the same!"

But there are art historians who cannot accept this answer, seeming as it does to act out its own blindness to the difference between modernism and pastiche, or between authenticity and fraudulence. Modernist art, of which Cubism was a fundamental example, stakes its claim to authenticity on its progressive uncovering of the structural and material (and thus objectively demonstrable) realities of a given artistic medium; while pastiche—the flagrant imitation by one artist of the style of another—shrugs off this notion of an inner pictorial logic to be revealed, one that puts certain options out of bounds, and maintains instead that every option is open to the creative spirit. Thus Cubism and the pastiche of neoclassicism cannot be "the same," and we should rephrase our historical problem by asking what could have made Picasso, as early as 1915, imagine that they were?

2 • Pablo Picasso, *Max Jacob*, 1915
Pencil on paper, 33 x 25 (13 x 9⅞)

At this point it is important to realize that a fight had already begun, just before the war, over the legacy of Cubism, which is to say, over the future that Cubism itself had made possible. On the one hand there were artists—such as Piet Mondrian, or Robert Delaunay, ▲ or František Kupka (or in Russia, Kazimir Malevich)—who believed that this legacy was pure abstraction, the next logical move after the ascetically reduced grid of the Analytical Cubism of 1911–12. On the • other, there were those, such as Marcel Duchamp and (briefly) Francis Picabia, who saw Cubism opening up to the mechanization of art in an obvious extension of collage into the readymade. Picabia's own development of Cubism in this latter direction took the form of what he called "mechanomorphs," industrial objects (such as spark plugs or turbine parts or cameras) coldly rendered by means of mechanical drawing and declared to be portraits (whether of the pho- ■ tographer Alfred Stieglitz, the critic Marius de Zayas, or "a young American girl in a state of nudity" [**3**]). The date of most of this output, interestingly enough, was 1915, and it appeared in the magazine *291*, which Picasso would certainly have seen.

Now, if these two options were what the avant-garde saw as the logical next step of Cubism, they were not the possibilities that Picasso himself found acceptable as the fate of "his" brainchild. Always vociferously against abstraction, he was also opposed to any mechanization of seeing (as in, according to some, photography) or of making (as in the readymade).

Thus, if the precise onset of Picasso's embrace of classicism—1915—argues against the externalist notion of cause and for the idea of something internal to the work, that same date opens up an internalist explanation that, far from repressing the antimodernist, reactionary form of his pastiche, will explain both its continuousness with Cubism *and* its total break with it. For the summer of 1915 confronted Picasso with Cubism's own logical consequences in the form of Picabia's published, mechanomorphic portraits: mechanically drawn, coldly impersonal, readymade. But in styling his own rejection of such consequences as neoclassicism, Picasso embarked on a strange campaign of portraiture of his own, in which he began to churn out image after image, each startlingly like the other in pose, lighting, treatment, scale, and, in particular, the handling of line, which, bizarrely invariant and graphically insensitive, seemed to be produced more as an act of tracing than as a record of seeing [**4**].

It is possible, even preferable, then, to describe Picasso's neoclassicism with the exact same words as were used for Picabia's mechanomorphs: mechanically drawn, coldly impersonal, readymade. There is no reason why classicism might not be adopted as a strategy to rise above the industrial level of the mass-produced object, which the readymade extolled and in which abstract painting and sculpture participated in their own way by adopting the principle of

▲ 1913, 1915, 1917 • 1914, 1918 ■ 1916b

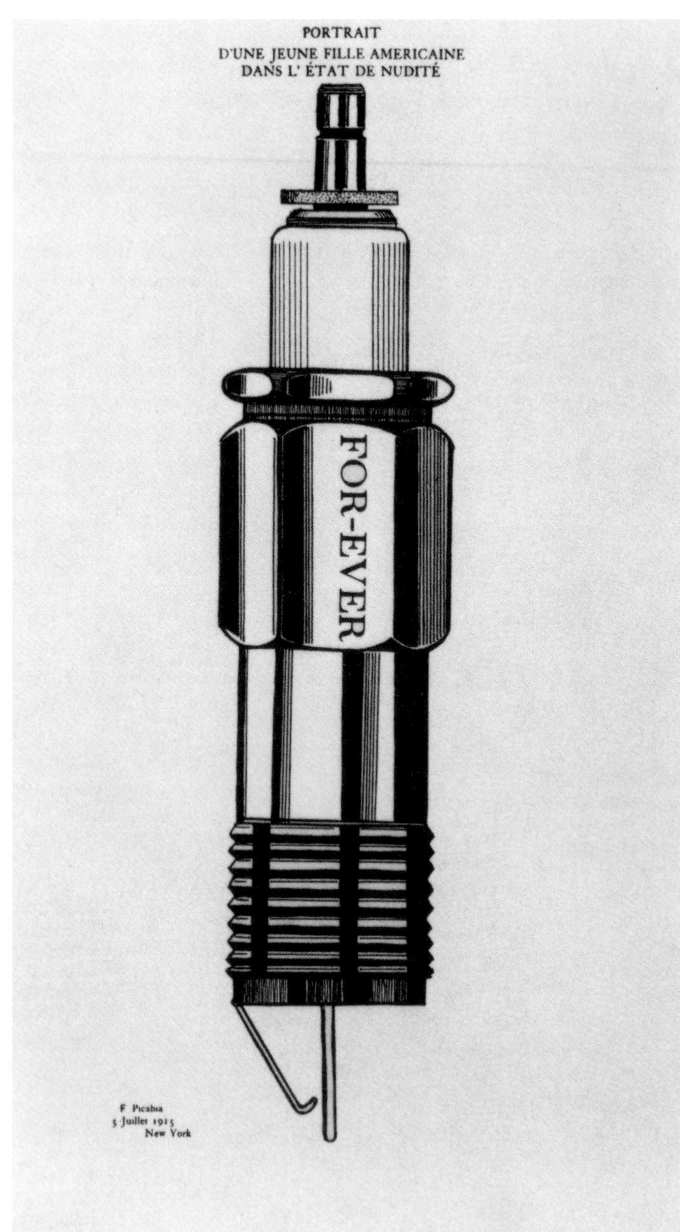

3 • Francis Picabia, *Portrait d'une jeune fille américaine dans l'état de nudité* (Portrait of a Young American Girl in the State of Nudity), 1915
Reproduced in *291*, nos 5/6, July/August 1915

serial production, for example, or by lowering the level of technical skill needed to execute the forms. But in Picasso's deployment of it the strategy backfires. For in his hands classicism ends by repeating those very same features of the position he despised, a position—we have to repeat—that was being claimed as continuous with Cubism, *inside* it as it were, rather than coming from the outside.

Other models of history

There is a naive belief that historical explanations are simply a record of the facts that the historian extracts from the archive. But facts need to be organized, analyzed, weighted, interrogated; and to do this all historians (consciously or not) have recourse to an underlying model that gives shape to the facts. We have seen the contextualists' model assuming, with greater or lesser sophistication, that cultural expression will be the effect of causes external to what the aesthetic sphere (erroneously) promotes as the "autonomy" of its own site of production. We have also seen the internalists cutting their model to the shape of an independent organism—whether that be the creative will of the artist or the coherent development of an artistic tradition.

The case we might call "Picasso-pastiche" suggests the usefulness of another model, one most clearly outlined by Freud in the psychoanalytic theories he was developing right at this moment. This model, which Freud called "reaction-formation," was meant to describe a curious transformation of repressed urges, a transformation that seemed to deny those low, libidinally charged impulses by substituting for them something that was their exact opposite: behavior that was "high," laudable, upright, proper. But this opposite, Freud points out, is in fact a way of continuing the prohibited behavior by smuggling it in under its cleaned-up, sublimated guise. The anal personality transforms the explosive urge toward dirtiness into the retentive features of obsessive thrift or conscientiousness; the infantile masturbator ends by being a compulsive hand-washer, whose gestures of stroking and rubbing carry on the earlier desires under a newly acceptable (albeit out-of-control) form. Further, says Freud, reaction-formation carries with it a "secondary gain." Not only is the subject able, furtively, to carry on his or her impulses, but now this behavior becomes socially commendable.

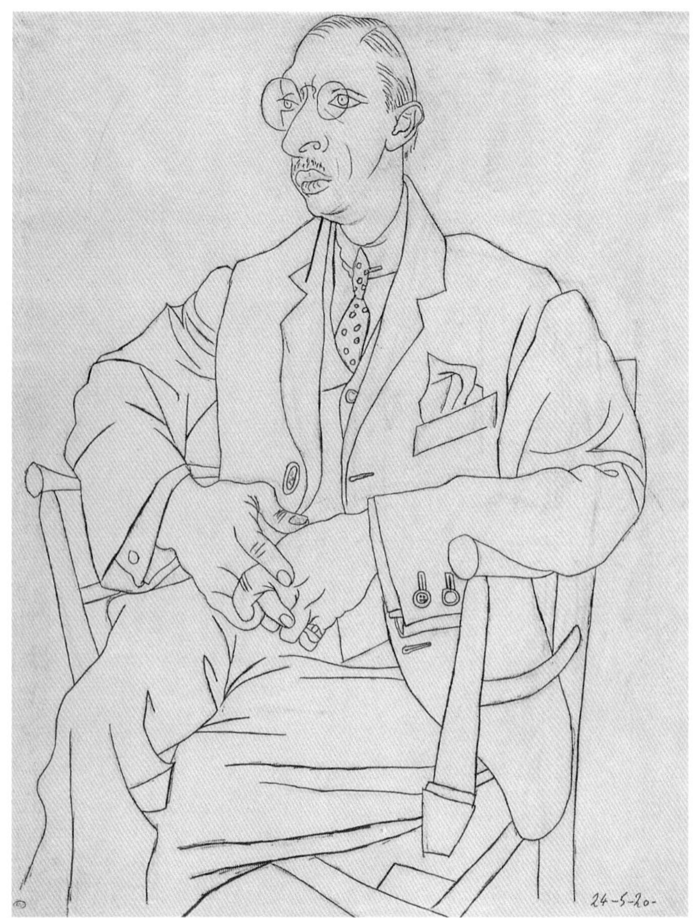

4 • Pablo Picasso, *Igor Stravinsky*, 1920
Lead pencil, charcoal, 61.5 x 48.2 (24¼ x 19)

There are two advantages of using reaction-formation as a model for Picasso-pastiche. First, it explains the dialectical connection—which is to say, the togetherness in opposition—between Cubism and its neoclassical "other." Second, it produces a structure that helps to account for the shape of many other antimodernist practices throughout the century, including the *rappel à l'ordre* ▲ production, but also reactionary painting from Giorgio de Chirico to later Picabia. It shows, that is, the degree to which those antimodernisms are themselves conditioned by exactly those features in the modernist work they wish to repudiate and repress.

To the cases of de Chirico and Picabia (as well as that of *pittura metafisica*), one must add that of Juan Gris, Picasso's fellow Spaniard, who emigrated to Paris in 1907, encountered Picasso, and soon devoted himself to Cubism. His *Portrait of Picasso* (1912) manifests his understanding of the new style as a matter of imposing a geometric grid over a relatively realistic representation so as to splinter its • contours and fragment its volumes. Instead of the orthogonal grid favored by Picasso and Braque, Gris adopted a diagonal one, which implied the receding lines of the perspective Cubism had abandoned.

5 • Juan Gris, *Newspaper and Fruit Dish*, 1916
Oil on canvas, 92 x 60 (36¼ x 23⅝)

Rappel à l'ordre

The *rappel à l'ordre* issued a call for a return to the presumed classical roots of French art, in the course of which its proponents opened an attack on Cubism. The beginnings of this return are assigned various dates, a late one being the 1923 essay by Jean Cocteau "Le Rappel à l'Ordre," a much earlier one being *Après le Cubisme*, published in 1918 by the painter Amédée Ozenfant and the architect Charles-Édouard Jeanneret. But what all these calls to order have in common is the idea that the prewar period was defined by chaos, by a decadent sensuality that needed to be replaced by the purity of classical rationalism, and by the barbarization of French culture by German influences. In fact, Ozenfant and Jeanneret called on artists to focus on the golden section and other ideas of classical proportion, making it possible for there to be a "new Pythagoras." "Science and great Art have the common ideal of generalizing," they wrote. Arguing that if "The Greeks triumphed over the Barbarians" it was because they sought intellectual beauty beneath sensory beauty.

Two versions of this classicism are represented by these two tracts, however. The first, Purism, has a modern, streamlined look, and speaks the language of science and of general laws, such as proportion. It argues that the artist-designer should dedicate himself to industry, producing for it the generalized types associated with classical forms. The second has a reactionary, Old Master character and recycles the themes and genres of the neoclassical art it wishes to revive. The mother-and-child theme became a preferred one—taken up by former Cubists such as Gino Severini as well as modified ones such as Albert Gleizes—as did the tradition of the *commedia del'arte.* Severini's clowns and harlequins, painted in the early twenties in the hard outlines and licked surfaces of the most academicized classicism, are determined examples of the latter.

The broken strokes of paint that Gris employs in his portrait reflects Analytical Cubism's own stippled surfaces, as does Gris's palette, which is limited to the muted colors of the painter's modeling and shading of volume. This stippled surface soon yielded to a far more enameled one paralleling metallic forms. The hardened surfaces of Gris's style during the teens echo Picabia's concern with the mechanomorph, the world seen as a collection of industrially wrought mechanical parts. And Gris's style gravitated to the industrially wrought aesthetic surface as well. In his *Newspaper and Fruit Dish* [**5**], textures such as wood-graining and reflected light are translated into the repetitive, mechanical language of commercial illustration. Gris himself thought of this hardened, aloof manner as a form of classicism, and it was in this way that Daniel-Henry Kahnweiler, the greatest contemporary interpreter of Cubism, also read his work.

FURTHER READING

Benjamin H. D. Buchloh, "Figures of Authority, Ciphers of Regression," *October*, no. 16, Spring 1981
Rosalind Krauss, *The Picasso Papers* (New York: Farrar, Straus & Giroux, 1998)
Kenneth Silver, *Esprit de Corps* (Princeton: Princeton University Press, 1989)

▲ 1909, 1924 ● 1911

1920–1929

1920

The Dada Fair is held in Berlin: the polarization of avant-garde culture and cultural traditions leads to a politicization of artistic practices and the emergence of photomontage as a new medium.

The Dada Fair held in June 1920 at Dr. Otto Burchard's gallery in Berlin was the first public appearance of the group of artists—diverse in both project and origin—who came to constitute the official Berlin Dada movement. The fact that the event was announced as a fair rather than as an exhibition signals that from the very outset its parody of the display of commodities, whether at the level of window design or of large commercial presentations, emphasized the Dadaists' intention to radically transform both the structure of exhibitions and the art objects within them [**1**].

Some of the central objects of the fair—specifically Hannah Höch's (1889–1978) *Cut with the Kitchen Knife through the Beer Belly of the Weimar Republic* [**2**], Raoul Hausmann's (1886–1971) *Tatlin at Home* (1920) and *Mechanical Head (Spirit of the Age)* [**3**], and the collaborative contributions of George Grosz (1893–1959) and John Heartfield (Helmut Herzfelde) (1891–1968)—indicate the diversity of strategies employed by the newly defined group. In contact with ▲ the work of both the Italian Futurists and the Soviet avant-garde, Berlin Dada situated itself at the intersection of a critical revision of traditional modernism, on the one hand, and a manifest embracing of the new synthesis of avant-garde art with technology on the other. But more specifically, Berlin Dada also stood in radical opposition to the local avant-garde, namely the hegemonic model of German • Expressionism. It was Expressionism's ethos, with its universalizing humanitarian aims, and its practice, with its fervent attempt to fuse spirituality and abstraction, that came under scrutiny and devastating critique at the hands of the Dadaists.

1 • First International Dada Fair at Kunstsalon Dr. Otto Burchard, Berlin, June 1920

Dada: distraction and destruction

Under the impact of World War I, in which Expressionism had played the fateful and ultimately failed role of trying to appeal to the supposedly universal terms of human existence, Dada explicitly positioned itself against this aspiration for artistic practice. This stance has erroneously appeared to many to be a form of nihilism, but what needs to be stressed instead is the positive nature of Dada's critique. Against Expressionism's effort to fuse the aesthetic and the spiritual, Dada constructed a model of antiaesthetics; against the attempt to claim universality for human experience by assimilating the aesthetic to the mystical, Dada emphasized extreme forms of political secularization of artistic practice.

Several of the Berlin Dada group rallied to the left, identifying with the aims of the Communist Party to the degree, in the cases of Heartfield and Grosz, of becoming members of the Party when it was founded in Germany in 1919. From that perspective it is important to recognize that Berlin Dada is an explicitly politicized avant-garde project previously unknown in the German context. However, this project's axis ranges from a critique of bourgeois concepts of high art to a model for activist propaganda and from embracing French examples of earlier proto-Dada practices—such ▲ as Duchamp's and Picabia's—to the systematic development of montage techniques intended to undermine the emerging mass-cultural power of the Weimar publication industry.

The simultaneity of objects, textures, printed matter, and surfaces to which Heartfield and Grosz relate in their initial work from 1918 (no longer extant) clearly has a precursor in Cubism. But this earliest photomontage work to come out of Berlin is explicitly conceived of as a mockery of Cubism's aestheticized, apolitical approach to the emerging power of mass-cultural imagery. In 1919, immediately following this parody of Picasso's form of

▲ 1909, 1915, 1921 ● 1908
▲ 1914, 1916b, 1918, 1919

2 • Hannah Höch, *Cut with the Kitchen Knife through the Beer Belly of the Weimar Republic*, c. 1919
Collage, 114 x 89.8 (44⅞ x 35⅜)

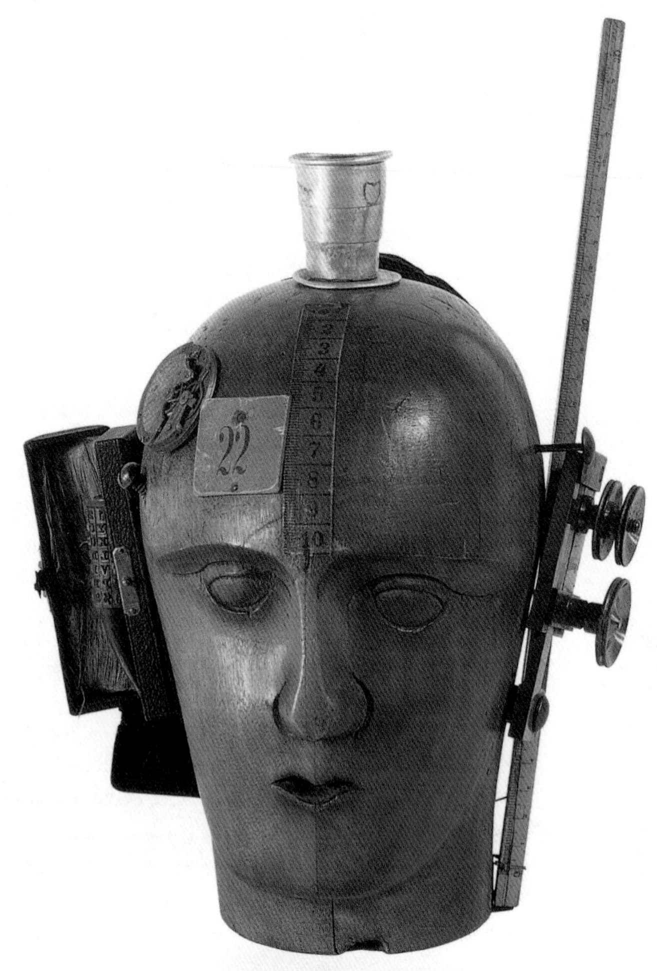

3 • Raoul Hausmann, *Mechanical Head (Spirit of The Age)*, c. 1920
Wood, leather, aluminum, brass, and board, 32.5 x 21 x 20 (12¾ x 8¼ x 7⅞)

collage, Heartfield, Hausmann, Höch, and Grosz—jointly and collaboratively—developed their first photomontage projects [**4**].

These were paralleled in the Soviet Union by the simultaneous development of photomontage by Gustav Klutsis and Aleksandr ▲ Rodchenko. Although both sides claim to have invented the medium, photomontage had been developed as early as the 1890s as a commercial technique for the design of advertising. In fact, in their first text on the montage, Hausmann and Höch refer to populist models for combining and transforming images as their inspiration, and identify the picture postcards soldiers sent home from the Front as the examples from which they took their cues.

One of the key works of 1919 is Höch's *Cut with the Kitchen Knife* ... in which the full range of technical and strategic ambiguities that would form the project of photomontage is apparent. From an iconically rendered narrative to a purely structural deployment of textual material, the possibilities established in Höch's work would become the axis of a dialectic operation within photomontage itself. In *Cut with the Kitchen Knife* ... the iconic narrative consists of a detailed inventory of key figures from the public world of the Weimar Republic. These move from political figures such as Friedrich Ebert, the Social Democratic President who had been responsible for the murders of members of the Spartakist Bund, specifically Rosa Luxemburg (1870–1919) and Karl Liebknecht (1871–1919), at the hands of his Minister of the Interior, Gustav Noske (who is depicted by Heartfield in a later photomontage as well), to figures of the cultural world such as Albert Einstein, Käthe Kollwitz (1867–1945), and the dancer Niddy Impekoven. All of these are disseminated across the field of the work according to a nonhierarchical, noncompositional, and aleatory principle of distribution, mingled with a variety of textual fragments that often invoke the nonsensical syllables "da-da." According to Huelsenbeck's claim, "*dada*" was found by inserting a knife into the pages of a dictionary; other origin stories for the term "dada" have been ▲ given, for example by the Cabaret Voltaire Dadaists.

But whether in the context of the Weimar Republic or in that of the Soviet Union, what links Heartfield, Grosz, Höch, and Hausmann on the one hand, and Rodchenko and Klutsis on the other, is first of all, the discovery of the photographic permeation of the visual world as a result of the emergence of the mass-cultural distribution of photographic images. Secondly, both groups participate in a nonsemantic production of meaning intended to destroy visual and textual homogeneity, to emphasize the materiality of the signifier over a presumed universal legibility of either the textual or iconic signified, and to stress the rupture and discontinuity of temporal and spatial forms of experience. The critical impulse behind this alogical attack on the very fabric of legibility was the intention to dismantle the mythical representations promoted by the mass-cultural production of commodity imagery and advertising. Lastly, photomontage represents the shared desire to construct a new type of art object, one that is ephemeral, one that has no claim either to innate worth or transhistorical value, one that is instead located within the perspective of intervention and rupture. This defines the political dimension of the photomontage practitioners' decision to stage artistic practice within the very medium of mass-cultural representation rather than outside or in opposition to it,

4 • George Grosz and John Heartfield, *Life and Activity in Universal City at 12.05 midday*, 1919
Photomontage, dimensions unknown

▲ 1921, 1935

▲ 1916a

as was the case in abstract art's attempt to retreat into the values specific to the mediums of painting or sculpture. These strategies link both groups' activities around 1919.

From photomontage to new narratives

As photomontage developed in Weimar Germany its range of options led its practitioners in various directions. In Hausmann's case the emphasis was increasingly textual with the verbal sign dismantled into graphic and phonetic fragments [**5**], whereas in Höch's work the focus on photographic imagery eventually displaced the structural separations that characterize the disjunction of textual elements. This was in favor of an increasingly homogeneous type of photomontage in which only two or three fragments are used to form peculiarly enigmatic figures.

John Heartfield, a third member of the original Berlin Dada group, quickly moved away from what he came to criticize as the "avant-gardist" dimension of the aestheticizing photomontage model, whose nonsensical or anomic qualities he rejected in favor of a new type of photomontage of communicative action. In this new form, photomontage was meant to reach an emerging working-class audience within what the Left hoped would become a proletarian public sphere. Those audiences are directly addressed through a strategy in which all former montage techniques are inverted: disjunction is replaced by narrative; the discontinuity of textures, surfaces, and materials is replaced by an artificially constructed homogeneity that is the result of Heartfield's careful airbrushing techniques; extreme forms of the fragmentation of language that isolated the grapheme or the phoneme are abandoned in favor of the insertion of captions whose function is to construct a revelation that will take a dialectical form. This type of commentary, which operates through the sudden juxtaposition of different types of historical and ▲ political information, is similar to what Bertolt Brecht subsequently developed in his own theatrical montage technique which, like Heartfield's work, was intended as an initiation to dialectics.

Heartfield's work also implicitly criticized early Berlin photomontage for having resulted in a set of singular objects that in the end possessed the status of traditional works of art just like any other individual work on paper or on canvas. Heartfield's attempt to create a work within the emerging proletarian public sphere, however, was specifically meant to alter the distribution form of photomontage by making it the vehicle of a printed medium and thus a mass-cultural tool.

The triggering moment in Heartfield's development was his encounter with Willi Münzenberg, who hired Heartfield to become the major designer of the *Arbeiter Illustrierte Zeitung*, the Communist Party organ founded in opposition to the old-style illustrated ▲ press. The *AIZ*, as it came to be called, specifically aimed to challenge the *Berliner Illustrierte Zeitung*, which had achieved a circulation ranging in the hundreds of thousands and could legitimately be called one of the first examples of mass media, serving as the model for subsequent magazines such as *Life* or *Paris Match*. The *AIZ* was thus conceived as a mass-cultural countertool.

Until his departure from Berlin after the Nazis' takeover of the government in 1933, Heartfield did most of his work for the *AIZ*, or as covers for books published by his brother Weiland Herzfelde and his Malik-Verlag publishing company. A typical example of his shift from the Berlin Dada photomontage aesthetic, as represented by Höch and Hausmann, would be Heartfield's *The Face of Fascism*, his cover illustration for *Italy in Chains*, published in 1928 by the Communist Party. Although juxtaposition, rupture, fracturing, and fragmentation are still operative here, they are so forged into a new coherence as to be able to serve different purposes altogether. Mussolini's head is fused with a skull that penetrates it from within and the vignettes that surround it work, on the right-hand side, to fuse images of victims of violence with the representation of dignitaries of the Pope and the Catholic Church and on the left, to fuse the top-hatted bourgeois capitalist with the armed Fascist street gangs. This technique of fusion was the alternative to what Heartfield criticized as the construction of

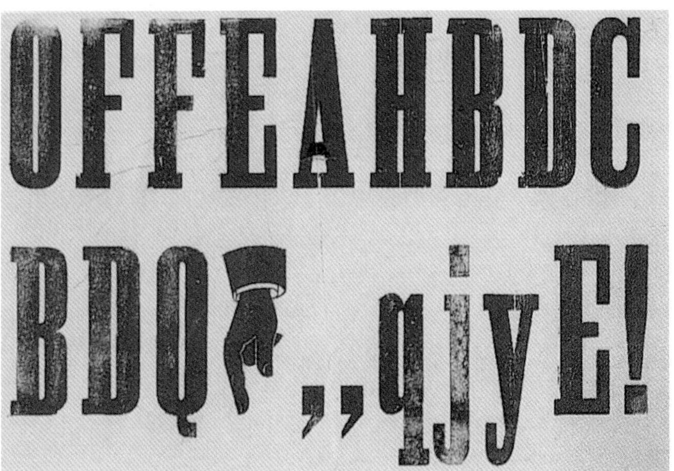

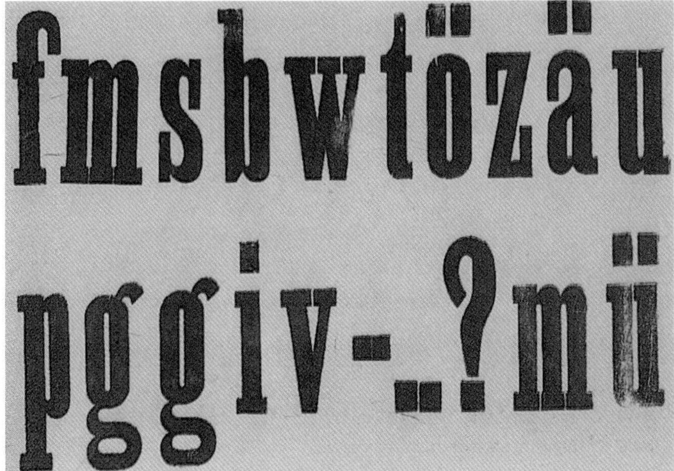

5 • Raoul Hausmann, *Off* and *fmsbw*, 1918
Two phonetic poem posters,
32.5 x 47.5 (12¾ x 18¾)

▲ Introduction 3

▲ 1930a

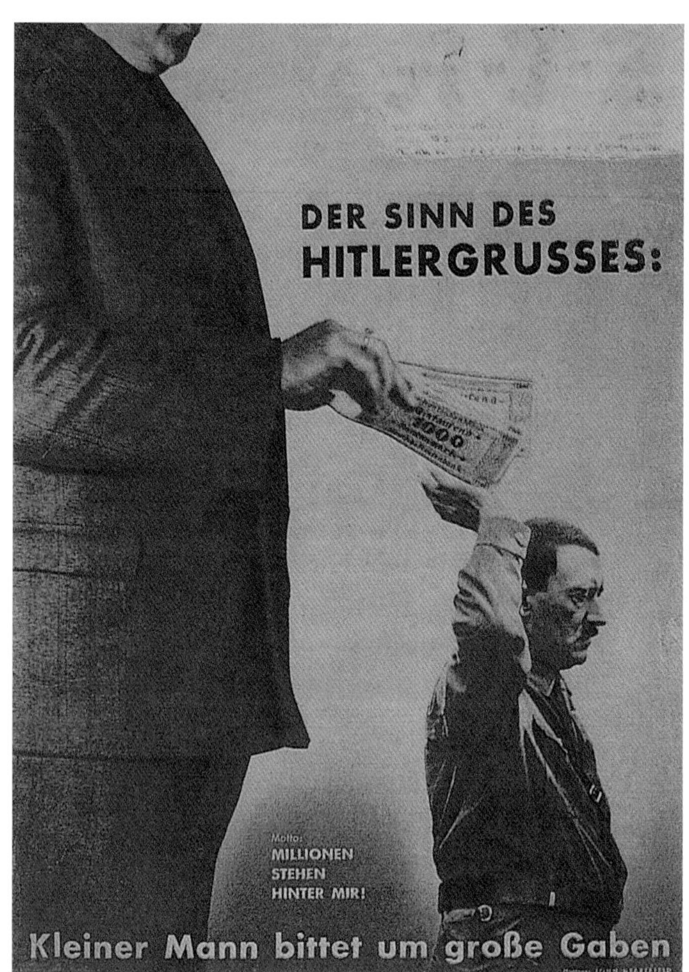

6 • John Heartfield, *The Meaning of the Hitler Salute: Little Man Asks for Big Gifts. Motto: Millions Stand Behind Me!*, 1932
Photomontage, 38 x 27 (15 x 10⅝)

mere nonsensical juxtapositions that generated rupture and shock but carried no political orientation, no countertruth, no moment of sudden revelation.

The fusion of opposites in Heartfield's work in 1928, five years before the rise of the Nazi Party, is particularly astonishing since it indicates the degree to which certain intellectuals were fully aware of the increasing threat to bourgeois institutions and democratic politics and were fully apprised of the need to locate cultural projects within strategies of opposition and resistance. This is even more evident in two of the images that Heartfield designed for the *AIZ* in 1932, portraying the Chairman of the German National Socialist Party, Adolf Hitler, a year before his election to become Chancellor in 1933. In each image, Hitler is depicted as a puppet, a hollow, artificial figure who executes the interests of capital. In the first, *Adolf—the Superman. Swallows Gold and Spouts Junk*, Hitler's body is shown in X-ray with a swastika in place of his heart, an Iron Cross instead of a liver, and his vertebrae made of gold coins, clearly framing the political argument that it was the German entrepreneurial class that was financing the Nazi Party in order to avert and eventually liquidate a proletarian revolution that had been initiated by the formation of the first Communist Party on German territory in 1919. The second, *The Meaning of the Hitler Salute: Little Man Asks for Big Gifts. Motto: Millions Stand Behind Me!* **[6]**, makes this point even more manifest in that Hitler is presented as a miniature figure standing in front of a huge, anonymous "fat cat" figure of a man passing a bundle of bank notes into the little man's raised arm and hand, thereby producing an ironic rereading of the "Hitler salute." Extremely simplified, grotesque, comical, and therefore all the more stunning, this form of argument was meant to clarify the otherwise inscrutable political and economic links that attracted big business to the leader of German fascism, seen as a counterforce and as a violent form of oppressing Socialist and Communist tendencies within the Weimar Republic. The assumption that *AIZ*, whose circulation at that time reached 350,000, would have a propagandistic effect turned out to be false since large numbers of the working class who had formerly voted Communist would vote for the Nazi Party in 1933, thereby dealing a final blow to the leftist aspirations of the Weimar Republic.

Unsurprisingly, Heartfield was one of the first artists to be prosecuted by the Gestapo after Hitler's rise to power. In 1933 he left for Prague, where his polemical, didactic, and propagandistic efforts against Hitler's regime were so widespread that Hitler intervened with the Czech government to order the closure of Heartfield's exhibitions in Prague.

From semiosis to communicative action

In the parallel evolution of photomontage within the Weimar and Soviet contexts, the changes that emerged around 1925 were aimed at transforming the original strategies. The techniques of alogical shock, of the nonsensical destruction of meaning, of the self-referential foregrounding of the graphic and phonetic dimension of language through an emphasis on fragmentation were now recast so as to be repositioned within the radical project of creating a proletarian public sphere. If by the mid-twenties a key cultural project of the avant-gardes was the transformation of audiences, this in turn required a return to the instrumentalized forms of language and image, where visual recognition and readability are paramount. The type of photomontage that Heartfield and Klutsis went on to produce now focused on the values of information and communication. The alogism, the shock, and the rupture of the previous work were discarded as so many bourgeois, avant-gardist jokes; its antiart position was seen as simply performing an act of shadow-boxing with the bourgeois public sphere and a model of culture that had long since been surpassed. The specific task that was now assigned to photomontage was no longer the destruction of painting and sculpture or culture as a separate, autonomous sphere; its task now was to provide mass audiences with images of didactic information and politicization.

One such example comes from a series of photomontages and posters Klutsis made between 1928 and 1930 **[7]**, in which the metonymy of a raised hand is used as an emblem of political participation and a key image of the actual representation of the masses in the voting process. Substituting a part of the body for the whole, the hand clearly "stands for" the subject who raises it, just as the single hand, within the boundaries of which a multitude of other such hands can be seen, "stands for" the unity of purpose produced by a single representative who can speak for a massive electorate. Variations on the image with different textual inscriptions were used for several purposes: one for a call to participate in the election of the Soviets; in another version for an appeal to women to become active in the Soviets through their own vote. The metonymy of the hand as a sign of physical, perceptual, and political participation in the collective process is a central example of how photomontage's initial strategy of cropping and fragmentation had been transformed by this time.

With the means of photomontage, Heartfield and Klutsis therefore became the first members of the avant-garde to invoke propaganda as an artistic model. Almost all discussions of twentieth-century art have shunned this term, since it is seen as being in direct opposition to the modernist definition of the work of art. The term *propaganda* implies manipulation, politicization, and a pure instrumentality that heralds the destruction of subjectivity. Yet Heartfield's and Klutsis's practice intervened in the very institutions and forms of distribution that had heretofore defined what artistic practice can be. By contrast, they sought the transformation of an aesthetic of the single object into one lodged in the mass-cultural distribution of the printed magazine, and a shift from the privileged spectator to the participatory masses then emerging through the industrial revolution of the Soviet Union or the changing industrial conditions in Weimar Germany. It was those aspirations that formed the actual structures and historical framework within which the formation of an aesthetic of a proletarian public sphere should be addressed. Propaganda as a counterform to the existing forms of ever-intensifying mass-cultural propaganda, namely advertising, clearly has to be recognized as a deliberate project undertaken by the Dada and Soviet avant-gardes to abolish the contradictions still maintained by the bourgeois vanguardist model of a pure, abstract opposition to the existing forms of mass culture.

FURTHER READING

Hanne Bergius, *Das Lachen Dadas (The Dada Laughter)* (Giessen: Anabas Verlag, 1989)
Hanne Bergius, *Montage und Metamechanik: Dada Berlin* (Berlin: Gebrüder Mann Verlag, 2000)
Brigid Doherty, "The Work of Art and the Problem of Politics in Berlin Dada," in Leah Dickerman (ed.), "Dada," special issue, *October*, no. 105, Summer 2003
Brigid Doherty, "We are all Neurasthenics, or the trauma of Dada Montage," *Critical Inquiry*, vol. 24, no. 1, Fall 1997

7 • Gustav Klutsis, *Let us Fulfill the Plan of the Great Projects*, 1930
Lithograph poster, dimensions unknown

1921

The members of the Moscow Institute of Artistic Culture define Constructivism as a logical practice responding to the demands of a new collective society.

1920–1929

On December 22, 1921, Varvara Stepanova (1894–1958) presented a paper entitled "On Constructivism" to her colleagues at the Inkhuk—the Moscow Institute of Artistic Culture, a state research institution founded in May 1920 under the auspices of the Department of Fine Arts (IZO) of the People's Commissariat of Enlightenment (Narkompros). It had been almost a year since the first director of the Institute, Wassily ▲ Kandinsky, had resigned, his psychology-based program being rejected as obsolete (if not plain counterrevolutionary) by a swarming group of newcomers marching behind Aleksandr Rodchenko (1891–1956).

As salaried employees of the state, the avant-garde artists and theoreticians who made up Stepanova's audience had to follow bureaucratic routine and keep a stenographic record of the animated discussion that followed the talk. From this we can discern that what was at stake that evening in December 1921 was less the retrospective account of Constructivism offered by Stepanova than the anxious question it prompted about the future: how will the Soviet artist justify his or her existence once he or she has voluntarily abandoned any artistic activity but is yet without the technical knowledge essential for industrial production? (Note the gender qualifiers here: there was perhaps no other artistic movement in the first half of the century where women exerted such a powerful role.)

The Marxist critic Boris Arvatov (1896–1940), soon to become one of the most vocal hard-liners of Productivism, aptly summed up the historical weight of the moment. The artist will not be of any use to industry until he acquires some education in a polytechnic institute, he remarked, but his work nevertheless has a function at the ideological level:

> *It's Utopia, but we have to say it. And every time we say it we will be avoiding dogmatism and will not be shading our eyes and we'll be saying that this is real, and necessary, and nobody will reproach us for it. We have to explain the great thing that this doctrine [Constructivism] has brought. It's true that the situation is tragic, like any revolutionary situation. This is the situation of a man on a riverbank who needs to cross over to the other side. You have to lay a foundation and build a bridge. Then the historical role will be fulfilled.*

At the end of 1921, the Constructivists were at a crossroads. Since the spring of that year, Lenin's New Economic Policy (NEP), characterized by a partial return to a free market, had been gradually replacing the centralized planning that had presided over Russia during the civil war, a system that had directly benefited members of the artistic avant-garde as a reward for their early and enthusiastic support of the Revolution. The Constructivists knew that the days of the Inkhuk as they had shaped it—as a place where they could freely conduct their "laboratory experiments"—were over, and they embraced the changes to come. The bridge mentioned by Arvatov (that between "art" and "production") had long been on everyone's mind (its necessity had already been advocated with great rhetorical flourish in the pages of *Iskusstvo Kommuny* [Art of the Commune], the official journal of IZO published from December 1918 to April 1919), but one could now feel a distinct acceleration. A month before Stepanova's talk, following a call by Osip Brik, a former ▲ member of Opoyaz, for them to transfer out of the jurisdiction of Narkompros into that of the Ministry of the Economy, the Inkhuk Constructivists had collectively decided to abandon "easelism" and to shift to "production." (The word "easelism" derives, of course, from "easel painting" but it was used to describe any kind of autonomous art object, including sculpture). Among the group, the most radical proponents of the Productivist program were even predicting the end of art altogether: Arvatov's bridge had to be built to reach the other side, but it would have to be destroyed as useless once this heaven had been attained. To a large extent, this remained wishful thinking, and the concerns that were vented during the December 1921 evening would eventually be proven to be well founded. But if the glee with which the Constructivists had endorsed their resignation as artists now rings of something like a manic denial, it certainly could not have looked in any way suicidal at the time. There was a logic to their self-immolation which constituted the climax of a whole year of experimentation.

"The first monument without a beard"

The birth of Constructivism came as a direct response to Vladimir Tatlin's model for the *Monument to the Third International*, often simply called his *Tower* **[1]**. Commissioned in early 1919, the

▲ 1908, 1913

▲ 1915

model was unveiled in Petrograd on November 8, 1920 (the third anniversary of the October Revolution), before being shipped to Moscow, where it was re-erected in the building hosting the VIIIth Congress of the Soviets at the very moment when Lenin's plan for the electrification of Russia was being debated. From the detailed pamphlet written by the critic and art historian Nikolai Punin and published on the occasion of the work's presentation, and from numerous declarations by the artist himself, we know that, while the model was a large wooden sculpture of between 18 and 21 feet high, the finished monument was to have been a huge metal-and-glass construction some 1,300 feet high—a third taller than the Eiffel Tower, at the time the tallest building in the world and a feat ▲ of engineering Tatlin had greatly admired during his trip to Paris before World War I. The most striking element of Tatlin's celebrated design was its tilted structure consisting of two dovetailing conical spirals and a complex web of oblique and vertical slats that framed four geometric glass volumes suspended on top of each other within its slanting core. Each of these volumes was supposed to be an independent building housing a different branch of the Comintern (the Soviet organization in charge of "spreading the revolution" to other countries), and each would rotate at a specific pace. The revolution of the lowest and largest volume, a cylinder destined to house the International's "legislative assemblies," was to take a year; that of the second volume, an oblique pyramid for the executive branch, would have lasted a month; that of the next

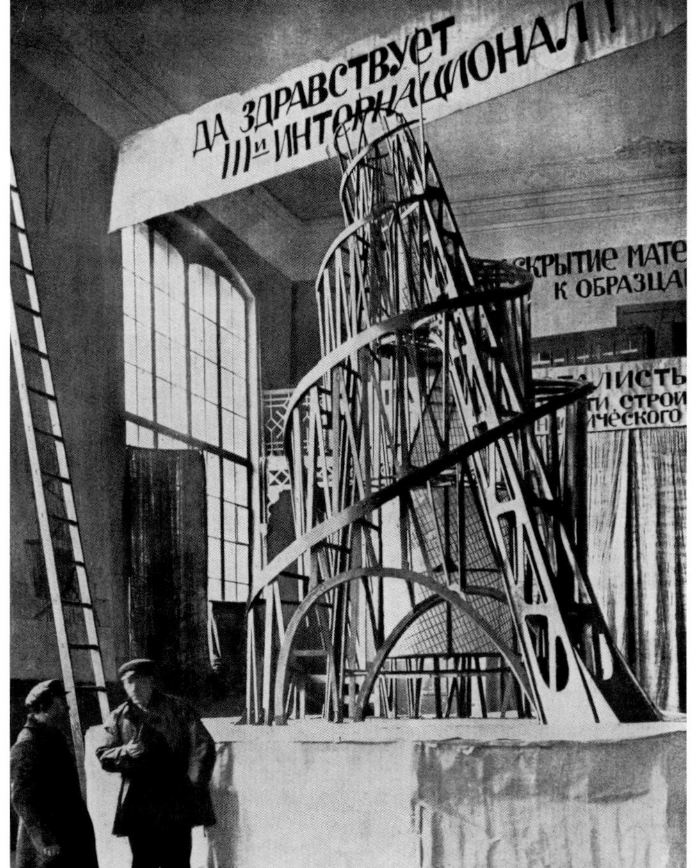

1 • Vladimir Tatlin, First model of the *Monument to the Third International* in the former Academy of Arts, Petrograd, 1920. Wood, height c. 548.6–640 (216–252)

Soviet institutions

As had been the case during the French Revolution in the eighteenth century, finding a name for a new institution, or renaming an old one, became highly charged political acts in revolutionary Russia, from the very first days of the February 1917 insurrection to Lenin's rise to power in October 1917 and well into the Stalinist era that followed his death in 1924. And the baptismal frenzy of the young Soviet state did not only affect official organizations, but also the many avant-garde groups that had multiplied in the teens, during the heyday of Cubo-Futurism. The absurdist monikers of these prerevolutionary groups (such as Knave of Diamonds, The Donkey's Tail, Tramway V) still smacked too much of the Symbolist past they had been intended to mock. A new linguistic form had to be devised to signify that a radically new era was beginning, and for both the Bolshevik power and that small fringe of the intelligentsia that immediately put itself at its service, the acronym became the prime signifier of such a *tabula rasa*. It was both economical and "poetically" unfamiliar.

The political nature of this linguistic device was established early with the coinage of Proletkult (for "Proletarian Culture") in 1906. Although this organization worried Lenin to the point that by 1909 he had excluded its leader Aleksandr Bogdanov from the Bolshevik party, it was only after the "ten days that shook the world" that it took real stride. But the new government countered its rise by founding an umbrella department, the Narkompros (for "People's Commissariat of Enlightenment"), headed by the liberal Anatoly Lunacharsky, whose domain encompassed cultural affairs, propaganda, and education, and under which all artistic groups—including the recently created Komfuts (for "Communist Futurists")—had to be subsumed. In January 1918, IZO, the visual arts section of Narkompros, was created and placed in Petrograd under the supervision of David Shterenberg, a well-traveled, francophile, eclectic modernist painter who did his best to satisfy the diverse tendencies of the Soviet avant-garde as well as reorganize all art museums of the USSR. His deputy in Moscow was Tatlin.

Among the many new institutions launched by Narkompros were the Svomas (for "Free State Studios"), founded in 1918 and replaced in 1920 by the Vkhutemas ("Higher State Artistic and Technical Workshops"), which can be characterized as the Soviet equivalents to the Bauhaus, the design school that had recently opened in Germany; the Inkhuk (for "Institute of Artistic Culture"), founded in Moscow in 1920 (its first director was Kandinsky, soon evicted by Rodchenko) and its pendant in Petrograd, the Ginkhuk, where Malevich took refuge after the close of his own school in Vitebsk, Unovis ("Affirmers of the New Art") in 1922. Even after the restoration of private business by the NEP in 1921, the government's hold on cultural affairs did not falter, neither did its penchant for acronyms: in 1922, the Inkhuk became part of the Rakhn ("Russian Academy of the Sciences of Art"), where it quickly lost its edge, and the AKhRR ("Association of Artists of Revolutionary Russia") began its steady ascent, which would end up ten years later in the brutal establishment of "Socialist Realism" as the official line in all the arts.

▲ 1914

volume, a cylinder for the propaganda services, would have taken a day; and that of the uppermost volume, a small hemisphere added late in the elaboration of the project, would have presumably lasted an hour.

Tatlin and his friends (most notably Punin as his official spokesman) developed three lines of argument in favor of the actual construction of the monument on its projected, vast scale. First, as opposed to the eyesores erected in various places to commemorate the Revolution, it would definitively be "modern" (the poet Vladimir Mayakovsky celebrated the project as "the first monument without a beard"), which meant for Tatlin that it was in strict obedience to the principle of the "culture of materials" (that is, of "truth to materials") he had been developing in his sculptural ▲ reliefs of 1914–17. Second, it was to be an entirely functional, productivist object (Mayakovsky also called it "the first object of October"), surpassing, in yet another sense, the Eiffel Tower, whose principal use was as a radio antenna. Third, like all public monuments, it was conceived as a symbolic beacon: it spelled out "dynamism" as the ethos of the Revolution.

At the Inkhuk, the formation by Rodchenko and his friends of the Working Group of Objective Analysis, which precipitated Kandinsky's demise as director, had preceded by just a few weeks the unveiling of Tatlin's monument. Given the enormous attention that this project received in Moscow at the time, it is not surprising that the Working Group focused on the issues it raised. The fact that it was an experimental design unlikely ever to be built (although it was declared technically possible by a team of Soviet engineers) did not deter them—on the contrary, the very fact that a project could have such an impact was an encouragement to pursue "laboratory work." Bracketing for the moment the concern for production and functionality, the members of the Working Group concentrated on the model's two other aspects, its "truth to materials" (or *faktura*) and its symbolic dynamism (or *tectonics*), which were seen by Rodchenko and the others as being contradictory in Tatlin's project. They felt that at the material level, and contrary to Tatlin's argument, nothing justified the formal use of a spiral and the appeal to an age-old iconography. The *Monument* was a romantic affair, they argued, elaborated by a lone artist in the secrecy of his studio and with the traditional tools of his craft; its formal organization remained an indecipherable secret that reeked of "bourgeois individualism": it was not a construction but an authorial composition.

The construction/composition debate

But those terms were too loose and had to be properly defined: from January 1, 1921, to the end of April, the Working Group conducted a lengthy debate centering upon the very notions of construction and composition. Each participant had to demonstrate, by means of a pair of drawings, what they understood of these two opposing words. Except for the drawings of Nikolai Ladovsky (1881–1941) and Karl Ioganson (c. 1890–1929)—both proposing as "construction" what would be labeled much later a "deductive structure," that is, a formal division of the surface that is predicated by the material properties (shape, proportion, dimension) of that very surface—the resulting portfolio is somewhat disappointing. Either the opposition was confused by a change of technique (*sfumato* for composition, sharp edge for construction) or by the evocation of a change in medium (a sketch of a painting versus that of a sculpture); or, especially in the case of Vladimir Stenberg (1899–1982), construction was simply understood as anything with a machine look. But the written statements

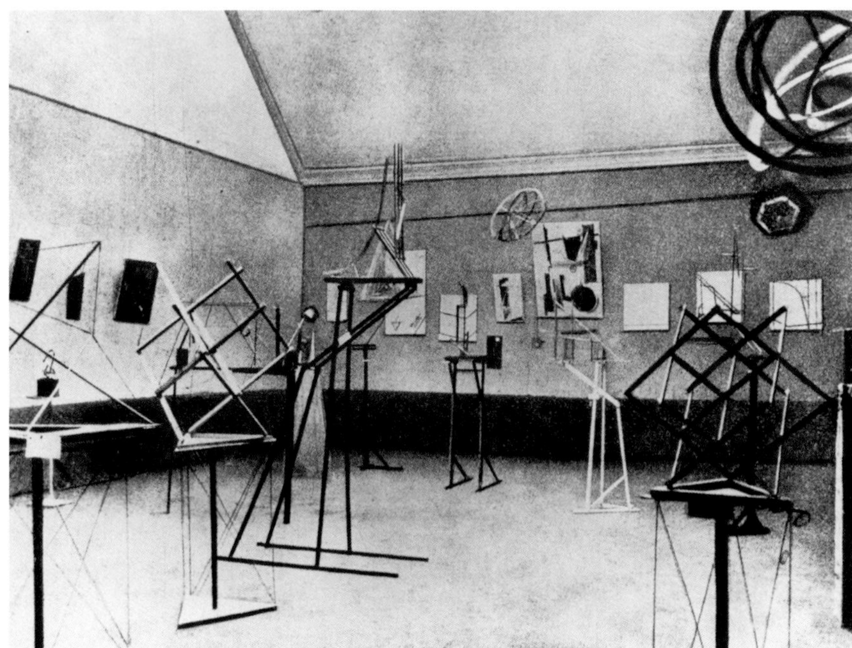

2 • The Obmokhu group exhibition, Moscow, May 1921
Karl Ioganson's *Study in Balance* can be seen on the extreme left.

3 • Karl Ioganson, *Study in Balance*, c. 1921
Medium and dimensions unknown (destroyed)

▲ 1914

and the many discussions that accompanied the production of these drawings are most enlightening. After much polemicizing, sometimes very harsh, a consensus was reached: construction was said to be based on a "scientific" mode or organization in which "no excess materials or elements" were involved. Or to put it in semiological terms, a construction was a "motivated" sign, that is, its arbitrariness is limited, its form and meaning being determined (motivated) by the relationship between its various materials (which is why it cannot borrow iconographical elements, for example), whereas a composition was "arbitrary."

This conclusion seems at first a rather meager result for four months of intense discussion, and the rhetoric of the debate was undoubtedly naive ("excess" = "waste" = "bourgeois epicureanism" = "morally condemnable"), but it is nevertheless from this lengthy forum that Constructivism as a movement arose: the term itself emerged during the debate, and Rodchenko quickly monopolized it, in March 1921, by forging with his closest allies the Working Group of Constructivists (it consisted of five sculptors or, rather, creators of "spatial constructions"—himself, Ioganson, Konstantin Medunetsky [1899–c. 1935], Vladimir Stenberg, and his brother Georgy [1900–33]—who were joined by Stepanova and, from outside the Inkhuk, the cultural agitator Aleksei Gan [1889–1940]). Gan, who had just been expelled from Narkompros for his extremism, was immediately put in charge of writing a Constructivist program, and a lot of debating among the Group evolved around his obscure terminology. Gan's confused and polemical prose (his book *Constructivism* appeared in 1922) is of no great help in assessing the thinking of the Group, and it is most unfortunate that this peripheral figure should have been assigned the central position of spokesman (it would prove particularly damaging, much later, when Stalin's commissars were on a repressive rampage, but it would also long distort the view of historians of the movement). Much more to the point is the artistic activity of the other founding members in the immediate aftermath of the construction/composition debate.

One farewell to art

A key event is their participation in the second group show of Obmokhu (Society of Young Artists), in May 1921, which consisted mainly of "spatial constructions" [**2**]. Even though only two of these sculptures survive, this legendary exhibition is well documented. Neither the works of the Stenberg brothers, which resemble metallic bridges, nor the polychrome sculptures of

4 • Aleksandr Rodchenko, *Oval Hanging Construction No. 12*, c. 1920
Plywood, open construction partially painted with aluminum paint, and wire, 61 x 84 x 47 (24 x 35 15/16 x 18 1/2)

Medunetsky (one of which was bought by Katherine Dreier at the "First Russian Exhibition" in Berlin in 1922, and is today at the Yale University Art Gallery in New Haven) abide by the strict definition of construction proposed during the debate. The first do not go beyond Tatlin's conception of the "truth to materials"; the ▲ second are clearly indebted to Malevich's painting. But Rodchenko's suspended sculptures and Ioganson's "Spatial Cross Series" testify to the major step accomplished in a very short time. Both series of works were conceived as demonstrations of a "scientific" (which meant at this time dialectic, materialist, Communist) method: there was no a priori conception (no borrowed image); every aspect of the work was determined by its material conditions.

In the case of Rodchenko's suspended sculptures, a single sheet of plywood coated with aluminum paint was cut out into concentric shapes (either a circle, a hexagon, a rectangle, or an ellipse—the latter being the only surviving example of the series [**4**]). These were then rotated in depth to create various three-dimensional geometric volumes: the sculpture could easily be folded back into its original planar condition, thereby laying bare the process of its production. Ioganson's works exhibited the same pedagogical directness. In one of them in particular [**3**], set on a triangular base and consisting of three rods maintained in space through the tension of a connecting string, Ioganson attempted to give a visual and measurable form to the "excess" that every construction should aim to eradicate: the string was longer than required, but this "excess," clamped at the end of the tense loop and hanging limp, also had a demonstrative function (to lower the three pointed rods and thus transform the sculpture, one had only to release more of the string's slack). In other words, in contrast with the bourgeois artist's studio secrets, the sculpture's "logical" mode of production and deductive structure were heralded as a means of opposing the fetishization of artistic inspiration.

The same could be said of the modular sculptures that Rodchenko realized soon after the Obmokhu exhibition (each of which is made of equal-sized woodblocks, the plan sometimes being equal to the elevation). The formal logic that presides over these works, once again a deductive structure, is close to that enacted by the ● Minimalists forty years later (Carl Andre would sing their praises when photographs of them appeared in the West). And it is not by chance either that such a logic should have had similar effects in both historical periods, no matter how dissimilar were the contexts of revolutionary Russia and late-fifties New York Bohemia as far as the status of painting was concerned. Carried to the extreme in this medium, the reductive direction upon which the Inkhuk Constructivist had embarked could only result in either the pure grid or the pure monochrome: within the parameters of abstraction, any other pictorial possibility would involve an opposition between figure and ground, thus giving rise to imaginary space, composition, ■ "excess." And just as Donald Judd would condemn painting for its incapacity to entirely shed illusionism, Rodchenko said farewell to this art after having shown his famous monochrome triptych at the exhibition "5 x 5 = 25" in September 1921 [**5**]: "I reduced painting

5 • Aleksandr Rodchenko, *Pure Red Color, Pure Yellow Color, Pure Blue Color*, 1921
Oil on canvas, 62.5 x 52.5 (24⅝ x 20⅝)

to its logical conclusion and exhibited three canvases: red, blue, and yellow," he later wrote. "I affirmed: It's all over. Basic colors. Every plane is a plane, and there is to be no more representation."

Rodchenko's iconoclastic gesture quickly became a legendary landmark (nicknamed "the last picture," it is described as a ▲ turning-point by Nikolai Tarabukin, a former Formalist critic who had become the most astute ideologue of the Inkhuk group, in his 1923 treatise *From the Easel to the Machine*): with it a page of history had been turned, a point of no return had been reached. Analysis was no longer the order of the day: there was now no other possible path than to "enter production." Stepanova's December 1921 paper was a memorial service. The elaboration of a Productivist platform would be the central preoccupation of Rodchenko and his friends during the early months of 1922.

The move to propaganda

But despite their enthusiasm and their willingness to "work in the factory," the Constructivists-turned-Productivists were to meet a depressing reality: in the New Economic Policy of Lenin they could no longer count on the blanket support of the state. To their great chagrin, their services were not welcome: they were either seen as an interfering nuisance by the new entrepreneurial cast of production managers, or derided as intellectual parasites by the workers. Stepanova and Liubov Popova successfully created a line of textile designs that were mass produced (these constitute perhaps the only

▲ 1915 ● 1962c, 1965 ■ 1965 ▲ 1914, 1915

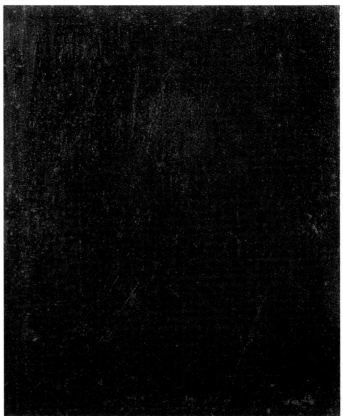

success story of the Productivist utopia, but it remains a minor achievement); Tatlin, too, managed to work in a factory, but he could not endure for long the task he was asked to perform (merely that of decorating objects), and none of the utilitarian objects he designed once he had returned to his studio was ever realized industrially (most notably a hideous stove destined to minimize the use of fuel; a bentwood chair that is, paradoxically, one of his most elegant sculptures; and a Leonardesque flying machine, a kind of winged bicycle that he called *Letatlin*, from the contraction of his name with the verb "*letat*," to fly). Division of labor, which the Constructivists, as good Marxists, had first chided as being conducive to alienated labor, but then paradoxically endorsed when Lenin had declared it essential to the reconstruction of Russia, had turned against them. Only Ioganson, who had been the most technically creative of the Constructivists (although he was, at most, in his very early twenties), managed to participate actively in the production of objects: he was hired as an inventor. In another context his talents would have thrived (his Obmokhu sculptures were similar to the tensile structures proposed by Kenneth Snelson and Buckminster Fuller in the late forties and early fifties, now called "tensegrity systems" and considered today a major step in the history of building technology). But no one was there at the time to recognize that for once the bridge called for by Arvatov had been crossed: all in all, the output of hard-core Productivism is pretty slim.

However, the new ethos devised in early 1922 bore important fruits: not in the production of everyday functional objects, but in the field of propaganda. If usefulness was the motto, and even if industry could not see a way to put artists to use, then they could at least be enlisted in advertising the Revolution (or even the objects produced, without their help, in state-owned factories). From the early twenties on, the creation of posters, theater sets, agitational stands, exhibition, and book designs became the chosen domain of the Constructivists, and with continuing success. As Tarabukin had predicted, their realizations in the ideological realm (that of imaging the Revolution) became their most important legacy. Rather than presiding over the production of objects, they had shaped the ideology of Production: they had found a niche, at last, within Soviet Russia's ever-intensifying division of labor.

FURTHER READING

Richard Andrews and Milena Kalinovska (eds), *Art Into Life: Russian Constructivism 1914–1932* (Seattle: Henry Art Gallery, University of Washington; and New York: Rizzoli, 1990)

Maria Gough, "In the Laboratory of Constructivism: Karl Ioganson's Cold Structures," *October*, no. 84, Spring 1998

Selim Khan-Magomedov, *Rodchenko: The Complete Work*, ed. Vieri Quilici (Cambridge, Mass.: MIT Press, 1987)

Christina Lodder, *Russian Constructivism* (New Haven and London: Yale University Press, 1983)

1922

Hans Prinzhorn publishes *Artistry of the Mentally Ill*: the "art of the insane" is explored in the work of Paul Klee and Max Ernst.

In the first decades of the century, many modernists drew on "primitive" art, while some also mimicked the art of children (e.g., the Blaue Reiter Expressionists). By the early twenties a third interest—the art of the insane—completed the set of exotic models. Today, these three might strike us as odd, but for modernists like Paul Klee they were natural, even necessary guides in the search for "primal beginnings in art." This points to a persistent paradox of the modernist search: that expressive *immediacy* would be pursued through the *mediation* of artistic forms as complex as tribal objects and schizophrenic images.

The reassessment of the art of the insane followed that of primitive art. Either dismissed out of hand or viewed in diagnostic terms, such art was ready for reevaluation. Yet most modernists saw it only according to their own ends: as intrinsically expressive, boldly defiant of convention, or directly revelatory of the unconscious, which for the most part it was not. The Romantics had also viewed the primitive, the child, and the insane as figures of creative genius unfettered by civilization. But in the modernist version of this trio the medium shifted from the verbal (poetry) to the visual (painting and sculpture), and the recovery of the art of the insane was complicated by its denigration after Romanticism. For by the middle of the nineteenth century this art was viewed less as a model of poetic inspiration than as a sign of psycho-physical "degeneration." A key figure here is the Italian psychiatrist Cesare Lombroso, who, along with his Hungarian follower Max Nordau, spread this ideological notion to several discourses. Lombroso understood madness as a regression to a primitive stage of psycho-physical development—a model that prepared a phobic association of primitive, child, and insane, which persisted in the twentieth century alongside the idyllic association of the three as creative innocents. In *Genius and Madness* (1877), a study of 107 patients, half of whom drew or painted, Lombroso detected this degeneration in "absurd" and "obscene" forms of representation.

Schizophrenic masters

This discourse of degeneration continued through psychiatry into psychoanalysis as it emerged in the late nineteenth century; and the diagnostic reading of the art of the insane persisted too. Like his French predecessor Jean-Martin Charcot, Sigmund Freud extended this approach through reversal, as he looked for signs of neurosis or psychosis in the work of "sane" masters like Leonardo or Michelangelo. By the turn of the century, with the clinical work of the German Emil Kraepelin and the Swiss Eugen Bleuler, focus fell on schizophrenia, which was understood as a broken relation to the self, as manifested in a dissociation of thought or a loss of affect—in any case, in a disruption of subjectivity marked by a disruption of image-making. This diagnostic approach was challenged only gradually, first with *L'Art chez fous* (1907) by Marcel Réja, the pseudonym of the French psychiatrist Paul Meunier, who examined the art of the insane for insight into the nature of artistic activity per se, and then with *Artistry of the Mentally Ill: A Contribution to the Psychology and Psychopathology of Configuration* (1922) by Hans Prinzhorn, who pursued this line of inquiry in a way that was provocative to several modernists.

Significantly, Prinzhorn studied art history (at the University of Vienna) before he turned to psychiatry and eventually to psychoanalysis. This unique training led the Heidelberg Psychiatric Clinic to appoint him in 1918; there he studied and extended its collection of art to some 4,500 works by 435 patients, most of them schizophrenics, from various institutions. With 187 images from this collection, his book included a "theoretical part," ten case-studies of "schizophrenic masters," and a summary of "results and problems." It was thus very selective; it was also often contradictory. On the one hand, Prinzhorn aimed not to be diagnostic; he saw six "drives" active in schizophrenic representation, but present in all artistic composition as well. On the other hand, Prinzhorn did not seek to be aesthetic; indeed, he cautioned against any direct equation with "sane" art, and, even as he called his ten favorites "masters," he used the archaic term *Bildnerei* ("artistry" or "image-making") in his title, in contradistinction to *Kunst* or "art." Nevertheless, Prinzhorn did refer to van Gogh, Henri Rousseau, James Ensor, Erich Heckel, Oskar Kokoschka, Alfred Kubin (who studied the art of the insane), Emil Nolde, and Max Pechstein. And further connections were made first by modernists, then by enemies of modernism—most infamously in the 1937 Nazi exhibition "Entartete 'Kunst'" ("Degenerate 'Art'") which attacked modernists like Klee through this association with the mad [**1**].

▲ 1903, 1907 ● 1908 ■ 1913, 1916a
▲ Introduction 1, 1900a ● 1900a, 1903, 1908 ■ 1937a

Zwei „Heilige"!!

Die obere heißt „Die Heilige vom inneren Licht" und stammt von Paul Klee. Die untere stammt von einem Schizophrenen aus einer Irrenanstalt. Daß diese „Heilige Magdalena mit Kind" immer noch menschenähnlicher aussieht als das Machwerk von Paul Klee, das durchaus ernst genommen werden wollte, ist sehr aufschlußreich.

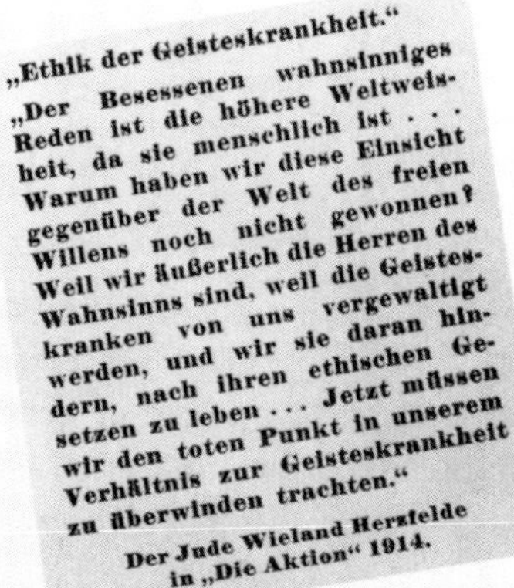

„Ethik der Geisteskrankheit."

„Der Besessenen wahnsinniges Reden ist die höhere Weltweisheit, da sie menschlich ist . . . Warum haben wir diese Einsicht gegenüber der Welt des freien Willens noch nicht gewonnen? Weil wir äußerlich die Herren des Wahnsinns sind, weil die Geisteskranken von uns vergewaltigt werden, und wir sie daran hindern, nach ihren ethischen Gesetzen zu leben ... Jetzt müssen wir den toten Punkt in unserem Verhältnis zur Geisteskrankheit zu überwinden trachten."

Der Jude Wieland Herzfelde in „Die Aktion" 1914.

1 • Paul Klee, *The Saint of Inner Light*, 1921, juxtaposed with a work by an unknown schizophrenic, in the brochure for the Nazi exhibition "Degenerate 'Art'," 1937 (texts translated below)

Two "Saints"!!

The one above is called "The Saint of Inner Light" and is by Paul Klee.

The one below is by a schizophrenic from a lunatic asylum. That this "Saint Mary Magdalen and Child" nevertheless looks more human than Paul Klee's botched effort, which was intended to be taken entirely seriously, is highly revealing.

"Ethics of Mental Illness"

"The crazy talk of obsessives is the higher wisdom, for it is human.... Why have we yet to gain this insight into the world of the free will? Because, superficially, we are in command of insanity, because we do violence to the mentally ill and prevent them from living in accordance with their own ethical laws.... Now we must seek to overcome the blind spot in our relationship with mental illness."

The Jew Wieland Herzfelde in "Action" 1914.

2 • Paul Klee, *Room Perspective with Inhabitants*, 1921
Watercolor and oil drawing, 48.4 x 31.5 (19 x 12½)

As his allusions suggest, Prinzhorn was interested in Expressionist art; his art-historical and philosophical models also inclined him toward a psychology of expression. Hence the six "drives" that govern the "artistry of the mentally ill": drives toward expression, play, ornamental elaboration, patterned order, obsessive copying, and symbolic systems, the interaction of which was said to determine each image. But here, too, Prinzhorn risked contradiction. For drives toward expression and play suggest a subject open to the world in a way that the other drives do not; on the contrary, compulsive ornamenting, ordering, copying, and system-building suggest a subject in rigid defense against the ▲ world (whether internal or external), not in empathic engagement with it. Even as Prinzhorn posed the former drives as correctives to the latter, he came to admit this essential difference between artist and schizophrenic:

> *The loneliest artist still remains in contact with reality.... The schizophrenic, on the other hand, is detached from humanity, and by definition is neither willing nor able to reestablish contact with it.... We sense in our pictures the complete autistic isolation*

▲ 1908

and the gruesome solipsism which far exceeds the limits of psychopathic alienations, and believe that in it we have found the essence of schizophrenic configuration.

The modernists most engaged by the art of the insane were Klee, the German Dadaist-turned-Surrealist Max Ernst (1891–1976), ▲ and Jean Dubuffet (1901–85), the French founder of *art brut*; all knew *Artistry of the Mentally Ill* well. Klee and Ernst often contrived fantastic systems that sometimes mixed forms of writing and drawing—what Kraepelin once disparaged as the "word and picture salad" of schizophrenic representation. They also often experimented with bodily distortions that evoke psychic disturbance more than formal play. Klee sometimes enlarged the eyes or heads of figures (a common trait in the art of children, too), or extended other features into ornamental patterns (a tendency of schizophrenic representation noted by Prinzhorn), as in the scrolled wreaths and wings of his *Angelus Novus*, a drawing owned ● by Walter Benjamin, for whom it was an allegorical angel of history-as-catastrophe. Even more disruptively, Klee sometimes repeated certain parts of the body (like the face) in other parts, as if to literalize a schizophrenic sense of self-dislocation; Dubuffet did much the same thing.

This apparent anxiety about body images could prompt a paradoxical treatment of boundaries in Klee and Ernst as in schizophrenic art. Sometimes boundaries are effaced, or exaggerated, and sometimes they are exaggerated to the point of effacement again—as if, in the attempt to underscore the lines between self and world necessary to a sense of autonomy, these distinctions were undone. Klee evokes a collapsing of figure and ground, a merging of subject and space, in *Room Perspective with Inhabitants* **[2]**. The anxiety about boundaries could also prompt a counter to this collapse—a paranoid vision of the world as estranged, and hostile in its estrangement. Ernst evokes this alienation in *The Master's Bedroom* **[3]**, where both the odd occupants and the skewed space seem to gaze back at the artist-viewer in threat, as if a traumatic fantasy, long repressed, had suddenly returned to possess its "master."

In-between worlds

In 1920, in the midst of his involvement with the art of the insane, Klee wrote his famous "Creative Credo," which begins: "Art does not reproduce the visible; rather, it makes visible." This principle points to the special status of the primitive, the child, and the insane for Klee: as inhabitants of an "in-between world" that "exists between the worlds our senses perceive," they "all still have—or have rediscovered—the power to see." This power is visionary for Klee, and as early as 1912, in a review of the Blaue Reiter, he deemed it necessary to any "reform" of art. And yet, just as Prinzhorn wanted to see schizophrenic art as expressive, only to discover that it is often radically *in*expressive, that is, expressive only of withdrawal, so Klee wanted to see an innocence of vision there, only to discover an intensity that often bordered on terror—the terror of the subject lost in space, as in *Room*

3 • Max Ernst, *The Master's Bedroom*, c. 1920
Collage, gouache, and pencil over a page from a schoolbook, 16.3 x 22 (6⅜ x 8⅝)

▲ 1924, 1946, 1959c ● 1916a, 1935

Perspective with Inhabitants, or of visible objects become viewing subjects, as in *The Master's Bedroom*.

▲ According to Oskar Schlemmer, his colleague at the Bauhaus school of art and design, Klee knew of the Heidelberg collection before Prinzhorn lectured near Stuttgart in July 1920; and according to another colleague, Lothar Shreyer, Klee identified with work represented in *Artistry of the Mentally Ill* upon its publication in 1922—and this at an institution, the Bauhaus, renowned for its rationalism. "You know this excellent piece of work by Prinzhorn, don't you?" Shreyer has Klee remark. "This is a fine Klee. So is this, and this one, too. Look at these religious paintings. There's a depth and power of expression that I never achieve in religious subjects. Really sublime art. Direct spiritual vision." When Klee simply illustrates "religious subjects," as in his "angels," "ghosts," and "seers," he often does not achieve this "power of expression." However, when he evokes "direct spiritual vision," he often approaches it—an expression that "makes visible." Yet precisely here Klee runs the risk of a primal vision that, far from innocent, is hallucinatory—the risk of an image that possesses the artist. This state, too "direct," too "sublime," is evoked in some schizophrenic representation, such as *Monstrance Figure* by Johann Knüpfer [**4**], one of the ten Prinzhorn "masters" whose work Klee would have known. A "monstrance" is a "making visible"; in the Roman Catholic Church it is an open or transparent vessel in which the Host is displayed for veneration. But this "monstrance figure" is monstrous—an image that, however obscure to us, appears too transparent to the "religious vision" of its schizophrenic maker, the intensity of which shines through untamed. Some Klees catch a glimmer of this same intensity, and it burns away his innocent idea of the art of the insane.

4 • Johann Knüpfer, *Monstrance Figure*, 1903–10
Pencil and ink on writing paper, 20.9 x 16.4 ($8\frac{1}{4}$ x $6\frac{1}{2}$)

Ernst had no illusions about the innocence of schizophrenic representation; on the contrary, he exploited its disturbances for his own antifoundational ends—to disrupt "the principle of identity" in art and self alike. Even before World War I he had encountered the art of the insane during his studies at the University of Bonn (which included psychology); at one point, he planned a book on such images. "They profoundly moved the young man," Ernst wrote in his art-treatise-cum-auto-analysis *Beyond Painting* (1948). "Only later, however, was he to discover certain 'procedures' that helped him penetrate into this 'no man's land.'" Already in his early Dadaist collages made in Cologne, Ernst not only assumed a quasi-autistic persona, "Dadamax," but also imaged the body in quasi-schizophrenic guise as a disjunctive, dysfunctional machine. These estranged schematic images are more caustic than the ironic mechanomorphic portraits of fellow • Dadaists Duchamp and Picabia, for they point to the narcissistic damage produced by the war (in which Ernst was wounded). In one collage based on a found printer's proof, *Self-Constructed Small Machine* [**5**], the body is a bizarre broken apparatus. On the left is a drum figure with numbered slots, on the right, a tripod personage, suggestive of a camera and a gun, as if the subject of military-industrial modernity were reduced to two functions: those of recording machine and killing machine. Below runs a confused account of this armored "anatomy," in German and in French, that conflates sex and scatology, as a child or a schizophrenic might. This "self-constructed small machine" is indeed reminiscent of a mechanical substitute for a damaged ego, as found in some schizophrenic representations, but it is a substitute that only debilitates this ego further. In his alienated self-portrait, then, Ernst evokes the *development* of the military-industrial subject as a *regression* to broken functions and disordered drives.

Traumatic fantasies

These early collages (which include, as in *The Master's Bedroom*, "overpaintings" on found representations from old schoolbooks) ▲ were crucial to the definition of the Surrealist image. They "introduced an entirely original scheme of visual structure," André Breton wrote when they were first shown in Paris in 1921, "yet at the same time [they] corresponded exactly to the intentions of

▲ 1923 ● 1916b, 1919 ▲ 1924

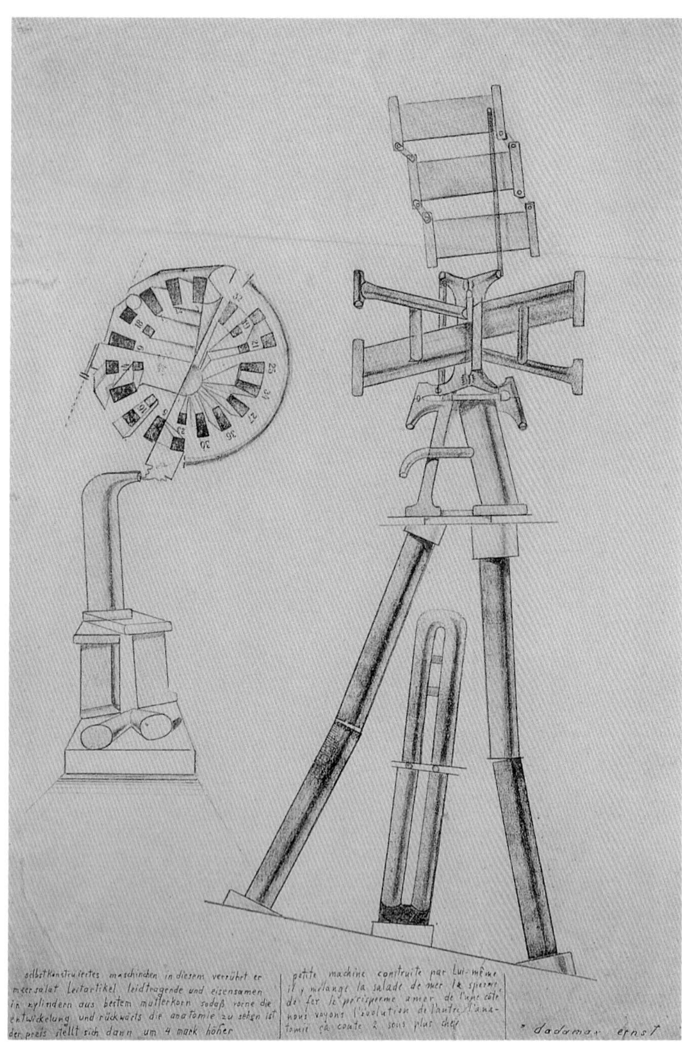

5 • Max Ernst, *Self-Constructed Small Machine*, c. 1920
Stamp and pencil rubbings of printer's block with ink on paper, 46 x 30.5 (18⅛ x 12)

Lautréamont and Rimbaud in poetry." Lautréamont was the nineteenth-century poet-hero of Surrealism whose enigmatic line—"beautiful as the chance encounter of a sewing machine and an umbrella on a dissecting table"—was adopted as its aesthetic motto. Already the French poet Pierre Reverdy had defined Surrealist poetics as "two realities, more or less distant, brought together." Now, with the example of the Ernst collages, Breton could also define Surrealist art as "the juxtaposition of two more or less disparate realities." Such juxtaposition is a principle of collage, but, as Ernst once remarked, "Ce n'est pas la colle qui fait le collage" (It's not the glue that makes the collage); other "procedures" might produce this catalytic effect as well. Key here is the connection between a disruption in representation and a disruption in subjectivity, and it is difficult to imagine this aesthetics of dis/connection without the model of schizophrenic art. Indeed, when Ernst moved to Paris in 1922 to join the Surrealists-to-be, he brought a copy of *Artistry of the Mentally Ill*—as a gift for Paul Éluard, who in the same year collaborated with Breton on a poetic simulation of madness titled *Immaculate Conception.*

Ernst connects disruptions of image and self in *Beyond Painting.* The book opens with a "vision of half-sleep" dated "from 5 to 7 years," in which little Max watches his roguish father make "joyously obscene" marks on a panel. This first encounter with painting is cast in terms of a "primal scene," which Freud defined as the fantasy of parental intercourse through which children tease out the riddle of their origins. Ernst uses this trope of the primal scene in the origin stories of all the procedures "beyond painting" that he introduced into the Surrealist repertoire—collage, *frottage* (an image produced through rubbing), *grattage* (an image produced through scraping), and so on. Through such procedures he sought to "desublimate" art—to open it up to psychosexual drives and disturbances. Again, his hallucinatory ideal seems underwritten by schizophrenic representation: "I was surprised," Ernst writes of these experiments, "by the sudden intensification of my visionary capacities and by the hallucinatory succession of contradictory images superimposed, one upon the other, with the persistence and rapidity characteristic of amorous memories."

In this way Ernst worked not only to deploy traumatic fantasy in art, but also to develop it as a general theory of aesthetic practice: "It is as a spectator that the author assists ... at the birth of his work.... The role of the painter is to ... *project that which sees itself in him.*" Here again, with the primal scene in mind, Ernst positions the artist as both a participant inside and a voyeur outside the scene of his art, as both an active creator of his fantasy and a passive receiver of his image. The visual fascinations and sexual confusions of the primal scene govern not only his definition of collage—"the coupling of two realities, irreconcilable in appearance, upon a plane which apparently does not suit them"—but also his description of its purpose—to disturb "the principle of identity," to "abolish" the fiction of "the author" as unitary and sovereign. His provocative images effect this disruption formally more than thematically. For example, even as *The Master's Bedroom* alludes to a primal scene, it is in the formal dis/connection of the image—its contradictory scale, anxious perspective, mad juxtaposition (table, bed, cabinet, tree; whale, sheep, bear, fish, snake)—that traumatic fantasy is evoked, paranoid affect produced. Such are the " 'procedures' that helped him penetrate this no man's land" of schizophrenic representation.

FURTHER READING

Max Ernst, *Beyond Painting* (New York: Wittenborn & Schultz, 1948)
Hal Foster, *Prosthetic Gods* (Cambridge, Mass.: MIT Press, 2004)
Sander L. Gilman, *Difference and Pathology: Stereotypes of Sexuality, Race, and Madness* (Ithaca, N.Y.: Cornell University Press, 1985)
Felix Klee, *Paul Klee: His Life and Work in Documents* (New York: George Braziller, 1962)
Hans Prinzhorn, *Artistry of the Mentally Ill*, trans. Eric von Brockdorff (New York: Springer-Verlag, 1972)
Werner Spies, *Max Ernst Collages: The Invention of the Surrealist Universe*, trans. John William Gabriel (New York: Harry N. Abrams, 1991)

1923

The Bauhaus, the most influential school of modernist art and design in the twentieth century, holds its first public exhibition in Weimar, Germany.

The Bauhaus was born with the Weimar Republic in 1919, and died with it at the hands of the Nazis in 1933. It developed out of the Arts and Crafts movement as the merger of the Weimar School of Arts and Crafts, begun in 1904 by the Belgian Art Nouveau artist-architect Henry van de Velde (1863–1957), and the Weimar Academy of Fine Arts, which seceded from the Bauhaus a year later in 1920. As the first director of the Bauhaus, the German architect Walter Gropius (1883–1969), wrote in 1923, "[John] Ruskin and [William] Morris in England, van de Velde ▲ in Belgium, [Joseph Maria] Olbrich, [Peter] Behrens and others in Germany, and, finally, the German Werkbund discovered the basis of a reunion between creative arts and the industrial world." But this "reunion" was the project of the Bauhaus much more than that of its Arts and Crafts and Art Nouveau antecedents; indeed, the eventual embrace of "the industrial world" signaled the effective end of these prior movements.

This embrace began in 1922–3. The Dutch De Stijl leader Theo • van Doesburg had visited the school in 1921–2, and the Russian Constructivist El Lissitzky also came to Weimar in 1922 for the ■ "Constructivist-Dadaist Congress" (organized by van Doesburg). But the turn toward industrial design was only clinched by the ◆ hiring of the Hungarian artist László Moholy-Nagy (1895–1946) as a teacher in 1923. In 1925, after a conservative change in the regional government of Weimar, the Bauhaus moved north to the industrial city of Dessau, where its involvement in industrial design deepened. In 1928 Gropius was replaced as director by the Swiss architect Hannes Meyer (1889–1954), a staunch Marxist under whom, ironically, the school achieved its only commercial success. Due to political problems, however, Meyer was replaced in 1930 by the German architect Ludwig Mies van der Rohe (1886–1969), who in 1932, after another conservative change in the regional government, moved the Bauhaus to Berlin. A year later, shortly after Hitler came to power, the Nazis shut it down. That the closure was among the first of the Nazi suppressions is testament to the force of the Bauhaus idea, which did not end there. Indeed, this idea spread with the emigration of teachers and students alike (Gropius, for example, was chairman of the architecture department at Harvard University from 1938 to 1952). Postwar reincarnations were attempted in the United States under Moholy-Nagy, as well as in ▲ Europe, and the Bauhaus continues to have a posthumous life throughout the West, not only in many art and architecture schools, but also in countless copies of its furniture and fixtures, appliances and accessories, typefaces and layouts.

Fundaments of material and form

On its founding, Gropius defined the Bauhaus as a "comprehensive system" with "the theoretical activity of an art academy combined with the practical activity of an arts and craft school." The Bauhaus idea was thus to unite the disciplines of fine and applied arts under that of building in a new *Gesamtkunstwerk* or "total work of the arts"—despite the fact that the school did not have a proper architecture department until 1927. Its initial curriculum consisted of two basic parts [**1**]. The first was instruction in craft workshops: sculpture, carpentry, metal, pottery, stained glass, mural painting, and weaving—the last headed by a rare female instructor, the gifted Gunta Stölzl (1897–1983). The second

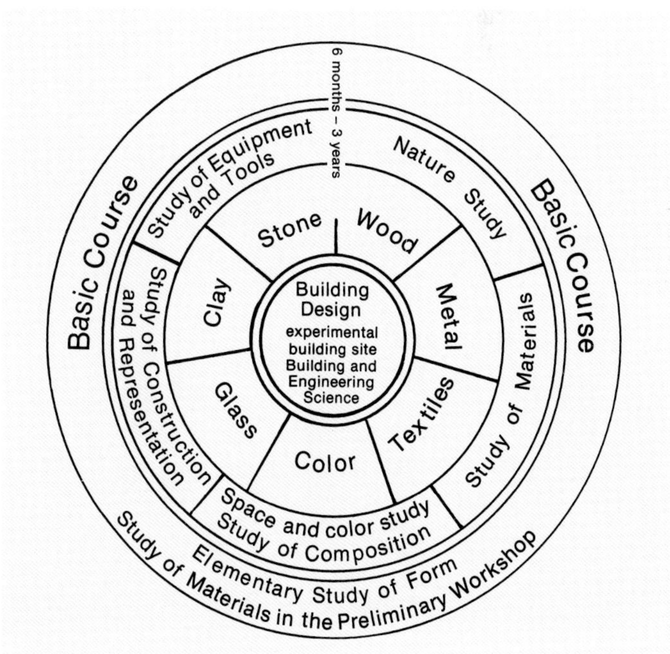

1 • Curriculum of the Weimar Bauhaus, 1923

▲ 1900a • 1917, 1928, 1937b ■ 1926, 1928 ◆ 1929, 1947a ▲ 1947a, 1957a was instruction in artistic "form problems": study of nature and materials; teaching in materials, tools, construction, and representation; and theory of space, color, and composition. "Workshop masters"—craftsmen—led the first instruction, while "form masters"—artists—led the second, although several of the latter also participated in the workshops. Despite attempts at equality, the workshop masters have remained obscure, while the form masters include such renowned twentieth-century artists as ▲ Wassily Kandinsky and Paul Klee.

In 1919 Gropius could afford only three appointments: the mystical Swiss painter Johannes Itten (1888–1967), who developed the first preliminary course required of all students; the German-American painter Lyonel Feininger (1871–1956), who developed a Cubist style with angular, quasi-Gothic lines [**2**]; and the German sculptor Gerhard Marcks (1889–1981), who became master of pottery. The next wave of recruits brought the best-known Bauhausians. Oskar Schlemmer (1888–1943), who arrived in late 1920, became master of sculpture and, after 1923, master of theater as well; he also did murals (several within the Bauhaus), for which his abstracted marionette figures in shallow geometric relief were well suited. Klee came in late 1920, too, followed by Kandinsky in early 1922. Although the Expressionist beginnings of the Bauhaus conflicted with its Constructivist leanings after the arrival of Moholy-Nagy, most of its artists were modernist in the sense that they all sought to reveal the fundamentals of materials, forms, and processes. It was this inquiry that drove the core curriculum of the Bauhaus—and all the later institutions that it inspired. This is true of the craft workshops as well: "We did not found our [weaving] workshop on a sentimental romanticism nor in protests against machine weaving," Stölzl remarked in retrospect. "Rather, we wanted to develop the greatest variety of fabrics by the simplest means, and thus to make it possible for the students to realize their own ideas."

2 • Lyonel Feininger, *Cathedral of the Future*, 1919
Woodcut for the 1919 Program of the Bauhaus, dimensions unknown

The variety of this inquiry can be evoked through the courses offered by its most celebrated figures. Klee and Kandinsky taught a design course in tandem. Both had metaphysical tendencies, but they could also be analytical. For Klee, theory had to emerge from practice; "intuition joined to research" was the credo of his teaching as well as his art. He encouraged students to develop artistic techniques analogous to natural processes—to find "the becoming of forms," "the antecedents of the visible." Like Kandinsky, he began with the basics of point and line, which he saw as either active, passive, or neutral. Even as he valued affective variety in line (his famous definition of a drawing is "a line going for a walk"), he prized compositional harmony above all. So did Kandinsky, and in this regard both men took music as the paragon of abstract art (Klee was also a gifted violinist).

▲ Like Klee, Kandinsky developed a psychology of pictorial elements, but his pedagogy was more dogmatic, in part because he was well established as artist and professor alike (he had set up the • program for the Moscow Institute of Art and Culture—Inkhuk—in 1920). His teaching focused on the analytical aspects of drawing and the emotive effects of color. In the first course, Kandinsky required students to abstract from a given object: first to reduce a still life to a simple form, then to render this form in a drawing, and finally to mark the tensions in this drawing as the basis for an abstract composition. In the second course, Kandinsky taught a theory of color structured on such opposites as yellow and blue (he saw yellow as warm and expansive, blue as cold and recessive), with the idea that a visual language could be developed that was more immediate than any verbal communication. He posited a similar psychology of line (for instance, verticals as warm, horizontals as cold) and combined these notions of color and line in a general theory of composition. A questionnaire circulated by Kandinsky suggests its flavor: he asked fellow Bauhausians to fill in a blank triangle, square, and circle with the colors that each form elicited; his own (correct) answer was yellow, red, and blue respectively. For all its claim to system, then, his theory remained subjective, not to say arbitrary, as did the painting that evolved from it. Indeed, what both system and painting bespeak, more than an "inner necessity" of spirit or a universal law of composition, as

▲ 1908, 1913, 1916a, 1922

▲ 1908, 1913 • 1921

he claimed, is an anxiety about the arbitrariness of abstraction, and an attempt to reground it in apodictic meaning.

From craft to industry

The real battle of the Bauhaus occurred not in these design classes but in the *Vorkurs*, a six-month probationary course required of all new students. Its first instructor was Itten, who, influenced by Kandinsky before his arrival, also investigated the psychological effects of line and color, which Itten understood in almost mystical terms. Even as his students investigated natural materials and drew diagrams of Old Master paintings, they were asked to capture the spirit of these things. When Moholy-Nagy replaced Itten as head of the *Vorkurs* in 1923, everything seemed to change—except perhaps the ethical basis of the instruction. Where Itten had dressed like a monk and abhorred machines, Moholy-Nagy looked like an engineer and declared the machine "the spirit of this century." Out went the meditative exercises with natural materials and Old Masters; in came a Constructivist analysis of new media and industrial techniques. Self-taught, Moholy-Nagy was protean in his production. ▲ He made collages and photomontages, photographs and photograms (cameraless photographs in which various objects are placed on coated paper and exposed to light), metal constructions and "light-space modulators" **[3]** (kinetic constructions with lights), and so on. Whereas Itten had diagrammed masterpieces, legend has it that Moholy-Nagy once ordered geometric paintings from a sign factory—he literally phoned the order in. Yet in all these experiments Moholy-Nagy was fiercely analytical and logical, committed to understanding "the new culture of light." If the students had tired of the cultish behavior of Itten by the time of his resignation in October 1922, they were shocked by the rationalist rigor of Moholy-Nagy. But when he resigned in 1928, this rigor had become synonymous with the Bauhaus idea, and it was carried on by Josef Albers, his collaborator in the *Vorkurs* and fellow promoter of ● Bauhaus principles in the United States after World War II.

All histories of the Bauhaus remark on its pedagogical shift from preindustrial craft to industrial design. The first stance was manifested in the 1919 program written by Gropius to announce the school ("Architects, sculptors, painters, we must all return to the crafts!"); while the second is dated to 1923, when Gropius delivered a new position paper, "Art and Technology: A New Unity," at the first Bauhaus exhibition, which was intended to demonstrate the new approach. Specific studies only nuance the shift as a progression from an early medievalist notion of craft to a later industrialist idea of craft. The first was advanced immediately after World War I in order to escape the "dilletantism" of academic art, to reunite artistic disciplines and artisanal practices under the *Gesamtkunstwerk* of building, and so to reconnect not only artists to craftsmen but both of these groups to workers and the *Völk* (the people) as well. The second was advanced in the mid-twenties as a necessary preparation for the new artist-as-designer now that industrial production had recovered somewhat after the war.

3 • László Moholy-Nagy, *Light-Space Modulator*, 1930
Kinetic sculpture of steel, plastic, wood, and other materials with electric motor, 151 x 70 x 70 (59½ x 27½ x 27½)

4 • Joost Schmidt, poster for the Bauhaus Exhibition, held in Weimar, July–September 1923

▲ 1929 ● 1947a

Evidence of this transformation is extensive. The original seal of the Bauhaus was an Expressionist stick figure with craft emblems under a wood frame designed by Karl Peter Röhl (1890–1969); in 1921 it was replaced by a confident Constructivist profile with Bauhaus lettering designed by Schlemmer. In 1919 the Bauhaus proclamation was illustrated with a Gothic-Cubist woodcut of "the cathedral of the future" by Feininger [**2**]; in 1923 the Bauhaus exhibition was announced by a rationalist lithograph poster by Joost Schmidt (1893–1948) that extended the Constructivist visage of Schlemmer into a figure that is at once human, machine, and architectural plan [**4**]. Until this time the emblematic building of the Bauhaus was an Arts and Crafts loghouse built in Berlin by Gropius and Adolf Meyer (1881–1929) for the timber merchant Adolf Sommerfeld; in 1923, for the Bauhaus exhibition, Georg Muche (1895–1987), who had arrived at the Bauhaus as much a mystic as Itten, modeled a steel-and-concrete "machine for living in." But the real mark of the pedagogical shift was the replacement of the mystical Itten and his core course based on meditative exercise with the technophilic Moholy-Nagy and his course based on structural analysis. The transformation was made institutional in 1925, when the Bauhaus moved to a modernist plant designed by Gropius in Dessau [**5**], and was renamed an "institute of design" replete with a new program, and established a limited company for trade and patents.

The transformation, then, is not in dispute; the question is how to understand it. Neither an overnight coup nor an orderly transition, the shift from "craft" to "industry" was driven by contradictory forces that preexisted the Bauhaus. (These forces were ▲ also active, for example, in the Deutscher Werkbund, an association of artists and industrialists founded by the architect Hermann Muthesius in 1907, in which Henry van de Velde argued for a craft basis for design, while Muthesius insisted on industrial prototypes.) Thus, more than a personal opposition, Itten and Moholy-Nagy registered a historical contradiction, as did the discrepancy between the early craft advocacy of Gropius and the technological commitment of his architecture, both early and late (as in his great Fagus shoe factory of 1911). In principle, the Bauhaus was always socialist, but its socialism changed as this socioeconomic contradiction developed. In its first moment, even as the Bauhaus looked to past models like medieval guilds, it also proclaimed a future utopia of artist-craftsmen united under building. In its second moment, however, this futuristic alliance became one of fellow producers in industrial design. In a sense, its historical contradiction is captured in the very term "Bauhaus": even as it invokes modernist design for us today—rationalist architecture, tubular furniture, sans-serif typography, and so on—the name actually derives from the medieval *Bauhütte*, or lodge for masons.

5 • Walter Gropius, the Bauhaus buildings, Dessau, c. 1925

Crisis and closure

"Originally the Bauhaus was founded with visions of the cathedral of socialism, and the workshops were established in the manner of the cathedral building lodges," Schlemmer wrote in November 1922. "Today we must think at best in terms of the house.... In the face of the economic plight, it is our task to become pioneers of simplicity." As Schlemmer sensed at the time, the two basic positions of the Bauhaus responded to two different Germanys: an anarchic country of 1919 that, torn by a lost war, an abdicated kaiser, and a failed revolution, was desperate to restore cultural community; and a fragile republic of 1923 that, wracked by inflation, was equally desperate to modernize industrially. Far from dead in 1919, the Art and Crafts movement was revived as a salve to the labor divisions and class conflicts exposed by the war. Such artist-architect associations as the Novembergruppe (named in honor of the failed November 1918 revolution in Germany) and the Arbeitsrat für Kunst (Workers' Council for Art) kept a "romantic anticapitalism" in the foreground of debate when the Bauhaus was founded. "For all its evils," Gropius, who belonged to both groups, wrote in 1919, "Bolshevism is probably the only way to create the preconditions for a new culture." What happened by 1923 to make him ditch his craft romanticism, propose a "new unity" of art and technology, advocate industrial design, and seek capitalist partnership?

More tactician than opportunist, Gropius had to struggle to keep the Bauhaus open through crisis and controversy, both internal and external. Before 1923, as inflation crippled the German economy (the Bauhaus student/teacher Herbert Bayer [1900–85] designed a one-million-mark note for general circulation in 1923), a craft program made perfect sense. By late 1923, however, the currency was reformed, and in early 1924 the Dawes loan plan from the United States began; German industry slowly recovered and soon boomed with foreign investments and new technologies. It was in this brief period of relative prosperity, which continued until the Wall Street Crash in 1929, that the Bauhaus shifted toward industrial design. The paradoxical position of Germany in between East and West helped its reorientation: the cultural experiments of Russian Constructivism inspired great interest (witness

▲ 1929

6 • Marcel Breuer, *Slat Chair*, 1922
Pearwood

7 • Marianne Brandt and Hein Briedendiek, bedside lamp, 1928
Designed for Körting and Mathiesen

▲ again the repeated presence of El Lissitzky in Germany), but so did the industrial techniques of American Fordism (the autobiography of Henry Ford was a bestseller in Germany in 1923). In effect, the Bauhaus adapted the ideological look of the former to moderate the economic logic of the latter—but then what could it do after a failed revolution in a state controlled by capitalists? In any case, upon its move to Dessau, "masters" became "instructors," workshops centered on the experience of material became technical laboratories based on the principle of function, and training was soon divided into two types—work on building techniques and work on industrial prototypes. Practices like woodcarving, stained glass, and pottery were dropped, metal and carpentry shops were combined, and the print shop was given over to design (in which Bayer in particular excelled).

Nevertheless, actual interaction with industry was limited, though not as limited as in Russian Constructivism, which dealt with an industry starved of raw materials and suspended between • rigid Communist and reformist capitalist policies. As of 1924 the Bauhaus had only twenty contracts with German firms, much of which was publicity work. This is not to deny the sheer brilliance of Bauhaus design or its great influence on subsequent production. Besides the famous fixtures of Moholy-Nagy and chairs of Marcel Breuer (1902–81) [**6**], the work of Marianne Brandt (1893–1983) is extraordinary in quality and variety; though best known for her tableware, her greatest successes were her lighting fixtures (with its wedge base and bell shade to focus light, her reading lamp [**7**] set the standard for decades to come, and she also innovated with other task lamps, as well as ceiling lights set in opaque globes and frosted glass). It is only to suggest that the new goal of industrial participation was no more realized than the old goal of craft rehabilitation. For both were responses to a historical problem that the Bauhaus alone could not solve: how to address the division of labor between artistic disciplines and artisanal practices on the one hand, and to adapt both of these to the capitalist modernization of Germany, which was intensive because it was tardy, on the other. The Nazis had a different solution, in which the polar forces that the Bauhaus attempted to moderate—the atavism toward a mythical Teutonic past and the acceleration toward a capitalist industrialist future—were forced together in a deadly compound.

▲ 1926 ● 1921

FURTHER READING

Herbert Bayer et al., *Bauhaus 1919–1928* (New York: Museum of Modern Art, 1938)
Eva Forgács, *The Bauhaus Idea and Bauhaus Politics* (Budapest: Central European University Press, 1995)
Marcel Franciscono, *Walter Gropius and the Creation of the Bauhaus in Weimar* (Urbana: University of Illinois Press, 1971)
László Moholy-Nagy, *Painting, Photography, Film* (1927), trans. Janet Seligman (Cambridge, Mass.: MIT Press, 1969)
Frank Whitford, *Bauhaus* (London and New York: Thames & Hudson, 1984)
Hans Wingler (ed.), *The Bauhaus: Weimar, Dessau, Berlin, Chicago* (Cambridge, Mass.: MIT Press, 1969)

1924

André Breton publishes the first issue of *La Révolution surréaliste*, establishing the terms of Surrealist aesthetics.

Developing as a young poet under the inauspicious conditions of World War I France, André Breton (1896–1966) was profoundly marked by two, mutually reinforcing phenomena. The first was his service as a medical orderly on a ward of shell-shock patients at the Val de Grâce Hospital in Paris; the second was his encounter with the sensibility of Dada in the person of Jacques Vaché, a permanent *révolté* and subscriber to the utter absurdity of life.

Breton's ardent acceptance of the ideas of psychoanalysis—the unconscious, the pleasure principle, the expressive power of the symptom and of dreams, castration anxiety, even the death drive—derived from his experience with profoundly disturbed trauma victims. And the very nature of their trauma—that something could happen for which there was no way to prepare ahead of time—fits, furthermore, into Vaché's absurdist views. The idea of life as a series of unpredictable and uncontrollable shocks was enacted by Breton and Vaché in a type of movie-going in which they entered and exited from screenings in rapid succession and without any regard for the program, thereby producing a random collage of visual and narrative experiences wholly out of their control. A few years later Breton would put this attitude of openness to whatever might happen—or *disponibilité*—to work poetically in *Les Champs magnétiques* (*Magnetic Fields*; 1920), which he wrote with Philippe Soupault as an exercise in stream-of-consciousness, and which he composed, in this sense, "automatically."

When it was time for Breton to separate himself from the Dada activities that had been mounted in Paris by the Romanian poet ▲Tristan Tzara after the ending of the war and the Cabaret Voltaire Dadaists had been able to move from Zurich to France, he used the avant-garde form of the manifesto to set out the terms of what he was announcing as a new movement. "SURREALISM, *n.*," his definition ran, "Psychic automism in its pure state ... Dictated by thought, in the absence of any control exercised by reason, exempt from any aesthetic or moral concern." And the two avenues the manifesto laid out for capturing the products of psychic automatism were (1) the kind of automatic writing *Magnetic Fields* had already explored and (2) the irrational narratives provided by dreams. Indeed, the new movement's very first act was to set up a central office in which to collect such narratives (offered by its young members) and to establish a magazine, *La Révolution surréaliste*, in which to publish them.

The interpretation of dreams

None of this was very promising, one might say, from the point of view of the visual arts, and indeed the magazine's first editor, Pierre Naville (who left the movement in 1927 to become Leon Trotsky's secretary), opened fire on the idea of any traffic with the fine arts or the refinements of style: "We have no taste," he wrote in the magazine's third issue (1925), "but distaste.... No one can still be in the dark about the fact that there isn't any *surrealist painting*. Neither pencil marks deposited by aleatory gestures, nor the image retracing dream figures.... But there are *spectacles*.... The street, the kiosques, cars, streetlamps bursting against the sky." And in accordance with his call for mass-cultural phenomena in place of "art," Naville illustrated the magazine mainly with photographs, many of them anonymous.

But Breton, who was an aesthete through and through—it was ▲he who had brokered the sale of Pablo Picasso's *Les Demoiselles d'Avignon* to the fashion designer Jacques Doucet; it was he who had purchased heavily from Daniel-Henry Kahnweiler's wartime sequestered stock of Cubist paintings at government auctions in 1921 and 1922; it was he who was amassing an extraordinary collection of tribal art—struck back, taking the magazine away from Naville in late 1925. Thereupon he began publishing the serialized treatise "Surrealism and Painting," in which he laid claim to a variety of older artists as Surrealists-without-knowing-it (Picasso ●and Giorgio de Chirico [**1**]), a group of Dada figures as threshold ■Surrealists (Max Ernst and Man Ray [1870–1976]), and a group of younger artists as burgeoning Surrealists (André Masson ◆[1896–1987] and Joan Miró [1893–1983]).

Insisting that psychic automatism could indeed issue from brush or pencil, Breton welcomed the uncontrolled production of Masson's automatic drawings and dribbled sand paintings, Miró's dripped and spattered "dream pictures," Ernst's trancelike rubbings (or *frottages*). The transfer of collectively written "poems" that would "automatically" generate surprising imagery (called *exquisite corpse* after the first result: "the exquisite corpse drinks

▲1916a

▲1907 ●1909 ■1922, 1930b, 1931 ◆1930b, 1942a, 1942b

the new wine") to games of collective drawing seemed to him an obvious move. But at the same time Breton also insisted on the importance of the idea of the symptom or trace or index as giving unimpeachable evidence of what lies behind reality by registering a disturbance on its surface. In practice this meant that he continued Naville's reliance on photography, not only in subsequent issues of the magazine but in the pages of his three autobiographical "novels," the first of which, *Nadja*, was published in 1928.

From the automatic text to the photograph seems a great leap indeed. The first is irrational and chaotic, while the second is mechanical and organized according to the very world the unconscious strives to disrupt. Yet in Breton's survey in "Surrealism and Painting" both of these poles are represented: automatism by the liquid spills and mists of Miró's open color paintings or the meanders of Masson's automatic drawings; the photographic by Man Ray's silver prints, often reproduced in *La Révolution surréaliste*, or the veristic dream paintings by Ernst, such as *Two Children Menaced by a Nightingale* [**2**].

It is this stylistic schizophrenia that has made Surrealism so elusive for many art historians. On the one hand, an iconographic bias has exploited the movement's formal heterogeneity to push for a thematic reading of its output, gathering works under various categories. Some of these reflect psychoanalytic concerns, such as castration anxiety (which produces a fear of female genitalia and imagery cycling around the idea of the *vagina dentata*) and fetishism; others relate to the searing experience of World War I, such as the disorienting wasteland of the trenches or the grotesque physiognomies of the wounded or a desire to regress toward a primitive state of humanity. On the other hand, a certain type of modernism wants to claim those parts of Surrealism's visual production that seem acceptably abstract—Miró and the half of Ernst that confines itself to *frottage*—while disencumbering itself of everything that seems retrograde and antimodernist because too suavely realistic—other parts of Ernst, late (and repetitious) ▲de Chirico and René Magritte, and, after 1930, Salvador Dalí's photographically rendered dream pictures [**3**].

2 • Max Ernst, *Two Children Menaced by a Nightingale*, 1924
Oil on wood in original frame, 69.9 x 57.2 x 11.4 (27½ x 22½ x 4½)

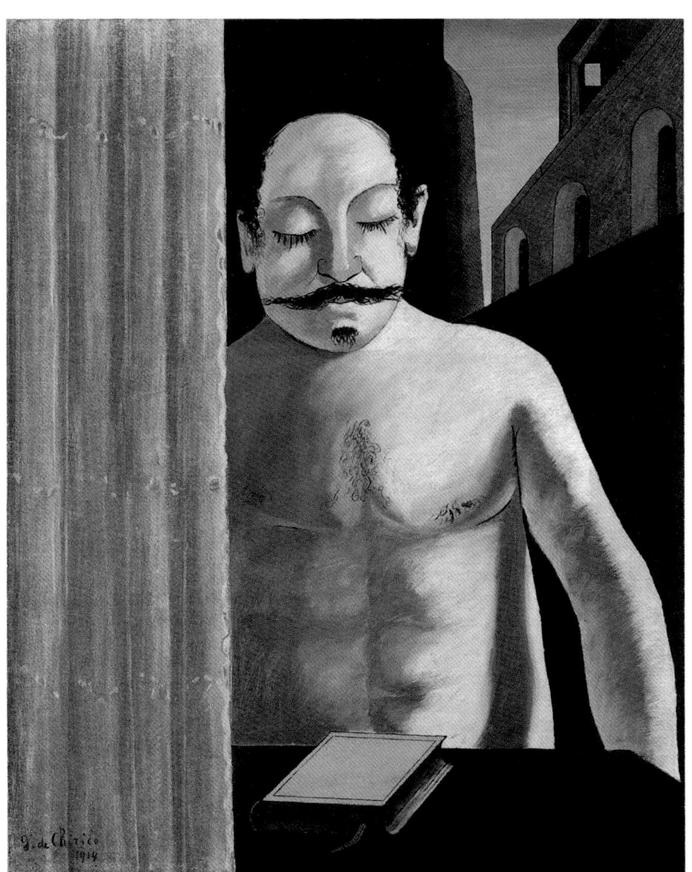

1 • Giorgio de Chirico, *The Child's Brain*, 1914
Oil on canvas, 80 x 65 (31⅛ x 25⅝)

That Miró lends himself to this modernist tendency is easy enough to see. Having begun in the late teens in Barcelona as a Fauve-derived painter, and having subsequently absorbed the lessons of Cubism, he arrived in Paris in the early twenties and by 1923 was assimilated to the circle of poets and artists around Breton. The "dream paintings" he was making by 1925 were erotic recodings of Matisse's work from around 1911, in that fields of intense color were allowed to spread uninterruptedly over the surface, so disembodied was the drawing within them. If in Matisse's case drawing had been carried out by means of negative lines or "reserves" (as in *The Red Studio* [1911]), in Miró's it was now performed as a kind of calligraphy that converted all bodies to the transparency and weightlessness of the written sign. These waves of blue, in which space is devoid of limits and objects float like wisps of smoke, and in which bodies turn into question marks

▲ 1927a

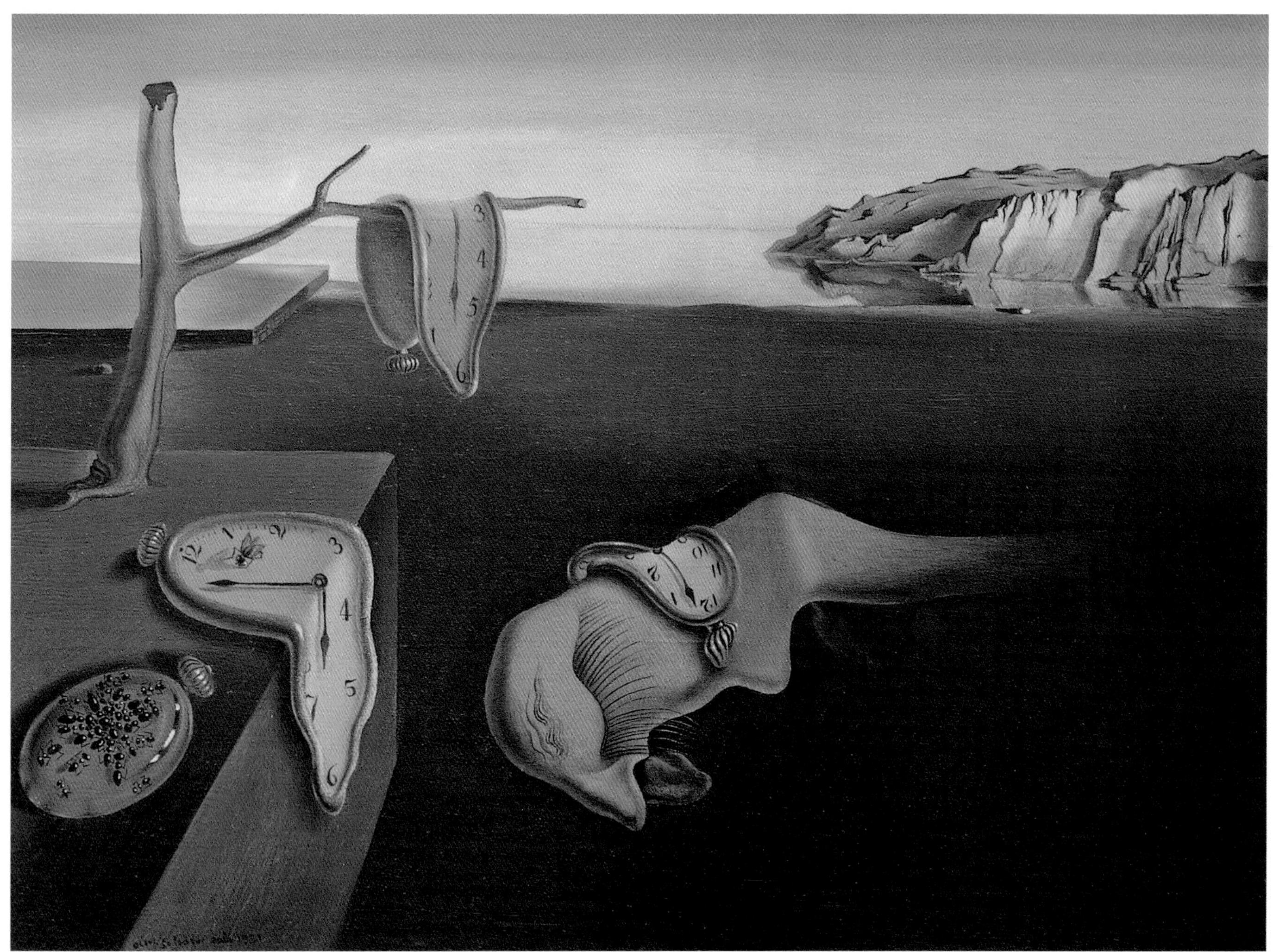

3 • Salvador Dalí, *The Persistence of Memory*, 1931
Oil on canvas, 24.1 x 33 (9½ x 13)

or signs for infinity—only the little red bar at the nexus of the figure eight indicating that the content of this graphic mark is the joining of two cells in erotic contact [**4**]—fit nicely with a modernist narrative of formal "progress."

But if the iconographic treatment of Surrealism seems insufficient, remaining blind as it does to something like the formal brilliance of Miró's art, the modernist account seems equally impoverished. It can neither produce a reading that would relate ▲ Miró to his colleagues in the movement—from Masson to Dalí to Surrealist photographers like Raoul Ubac (1910–85) and Hans Bellmer (1902–75)—nor can it address the structural issue of whether, on the level of the signifier (the form of expression), there is anything coherent in all the rich diversity of Surrealist activity.

The third alternative is to use the actual categories that Breton developed to theorize Surrealism and to mine them for their *structure*, thereby generating on the one hand a set of formal principles (the technique of *doubling* would be one of them) that can be permuted through a whole range of visual styles and, on the other, an understanding of the way such categories recode psychoanalytic or sociohistorical problems. As just one example we could take "objective chance," a variant on "psychic automatism" and a vehicle of the end result that Breton aspired to as a Surrealist, namely, "the marvelous."

Breton describes objective chance as the crossing-point of two causal chains, the first subjective, interior to the human psyche, and the second objective, a function of real world events. In this conjunction, so seemingly unprepared for, it is discovered that on each side there was a kind of determinism at work. On the side of the real, the subject seems to have been expected, since what the world proffers at this moment is a "sign" specifically addressed to him or her. While on the side of the subject, there is an unconscious desire driving him or her unwittingly toward this sign, even constituting it as such, and allowing the sign to be deciphered after the fact.

The semiosis of Surrealism

While *Nadja* is constructed as a tissue of objective chance, the clearest illustration of how it works is presented at the beginning of another autobiographical novel, *L'Amour fou* (Mad Love; 1937). There Breton tells of going to the Marché aux Puces flea market in Paris and bringing home a wooden spoon with a little carved shoe projecting from the underside of its handle [**5**]. Not even liking this

▲ 1930b, 1942a

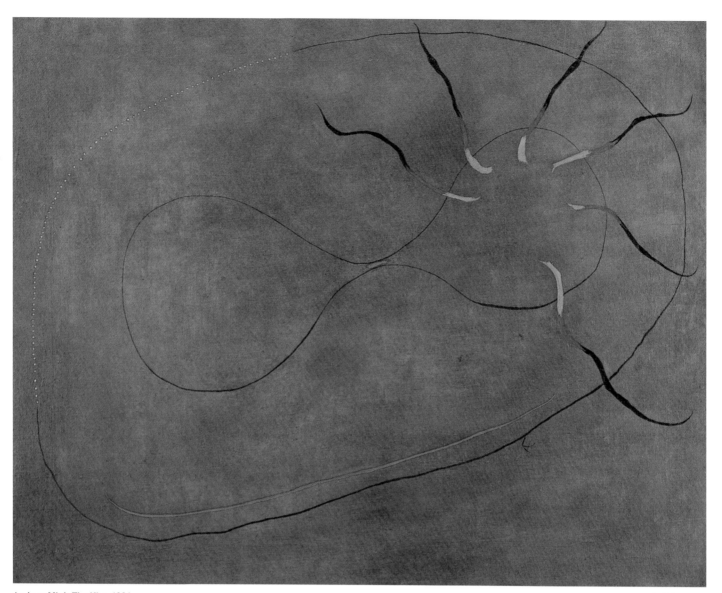

4 • Joan Miró, *The Kiss*, 1924
Oil on canvas, 73 x 92 (28$\frac{3}{4}$ x 36$\frac{1}{4}$)

object, he nonetheless sets it on his desk whereupon it reminds ▲ him of another object he had fruitlessly asked Alberto Giacometti to sculpt for him some time earlier. This object, an ashtray in the shape of a glass slipper, had been meant to exorcise the nonsense phrase that had been running through Breton's head like a persistent tune: "*cendrier-Cendrillon*," or "Cinderella ashtray." Now suddenly, he says, he begins to see the newly purchased spoon as a series of nested slippers, each the representational double of the preceding one (the bowl of the spoon as the front of the slipper, the handle as the middle section, and the shoe beneath as the heel; then the shoe itself as the front, the middle section, and the heel; and then—imaginatively—*its* heel as containing another such slipper; and so on). This structure in which an object is mirrored by another, the double functioning as the representation of the first, Breton understands semiotically—he sees it as constituting a sign.

In this, Breton is completely orthodox, since signs are always pictured as ghostly doubles of the things they represent. More

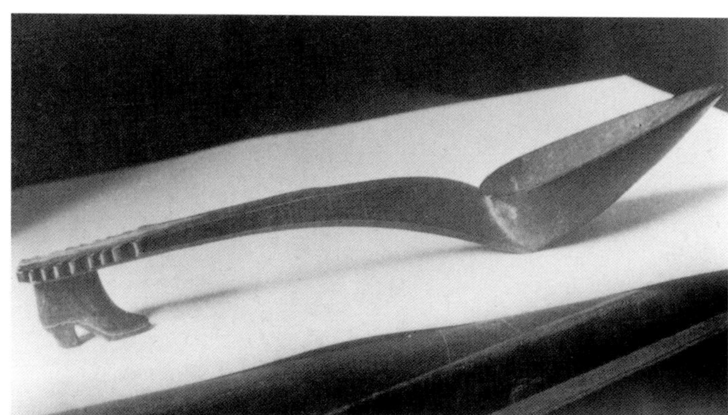

5 • Man Ray, André Breton's slipper-spoon, 1934
Reproduced in Breton's *L'Amour fou* (1937)

▲ 1931, 1959c

importantly this condition of doubling is itself at the very beginning of language, as when a baby, repeating a sound—"ma-ma" or "pa-pa" or "ca-ca"—suddenly understands that the second sound, in redoubling the first, both reaches back to mark the initial one as a signifier (which is to say, not just a random sound but a meaningful utterance) and sets it up as a carrier of intentional meaning.

The slipper-spoon is, then, the world convulsed into a sign. But crucially this sign was not only addressed *to* Breton; it was willed *by* him through the power of his own unconscious desire. For he associated this sign-material with his unconscious thoughts, which, unknown to him, were driving him to assume the role of a prince setting out to seek his mate. What immediately follows is the story of Breton's encounter with the subject of this "mad love," an encounter all of the details of which he discovers, to his amazement, were "predicted" by an automatic poem he had written a decade earlier and which he is now unconsciously repeating in the present. Thus if the world's "sign" is structured through the condition of the double, the unconscious operates on the same principle. Freud had described this as the compulsion to repeat; in the sixties, French psychoanalyst Jacques Lacan would recode this semiotically by saying that the unconscious is structured like a language. Redoubling, then, is the formal condition of the unconscious drives.

That photography is a function of doubling—not only does it "mirror" its object but, technically, its prints exist as multiples—

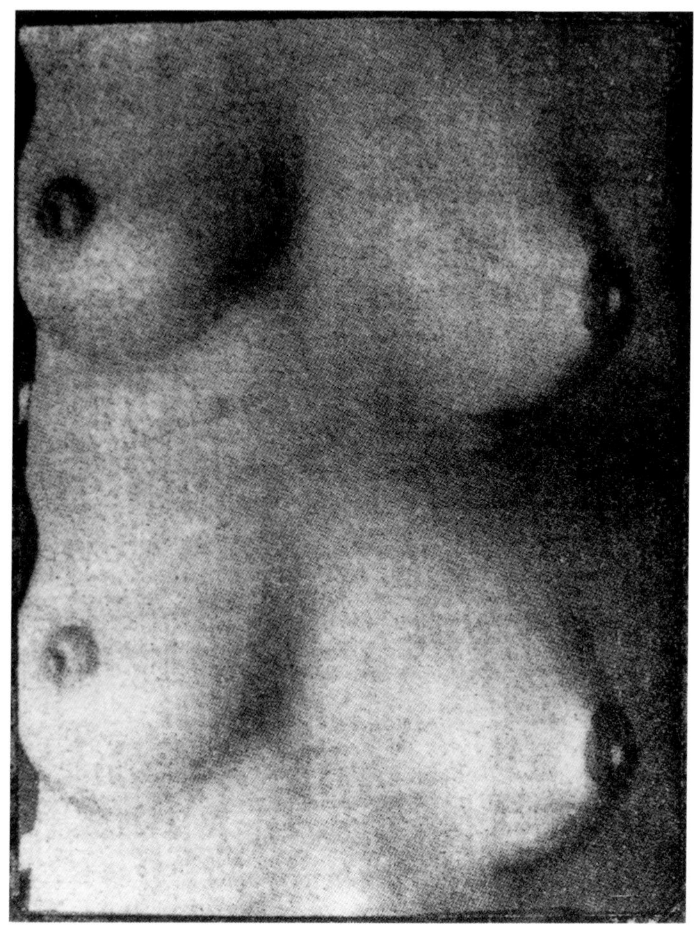

6 • Man Ray, *Untitled*, 1924
Published in *La Révolution surréaliste*

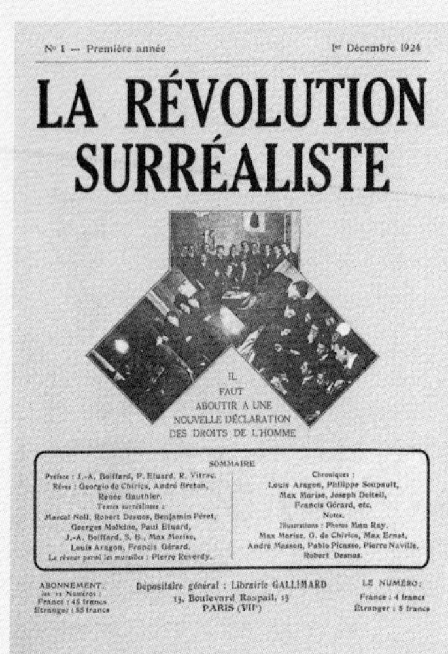

N° 1 — Première année — 1er Décembre 1924

LA RÉVOLUTION SURRÉALISTE

IL FAUT ABOUTIR A UNE NOUVELLE DÉCLARATION DES DROITS DE L'HOMME

SOMMAIRE

Préface : J.-A. Boiffard, P. Eluard, R. Vitrac.
Rêves : Georgio de Chirico, André Breton, Renée Gauthier.
Textes surréalistes : Marcel Noll, Robert Desnos, Benjamin Péret, Georges Malkine, Paul Eluard, J.-A. Boiffard, S. B., Max Morise, Louis Aragon, Francis Gérard.
Le rêveur parmi les murailles : Pierre Reverdy.

Chroniques : Louis Aragon, Philippe Soupault, Max Morise, Joseph Delteil, Francis Gérard, etc.
Notes.
Illustrations : Photos Man Ray. Max Morise, G. de Chirico, Max Ernst, André Masson, Pablo Picasso, Pierre Naville, Robert Desnos.

ABONNEMENT, les 12 Numéros : France : 45 francs, Étranger : 55 francs

Dépositaire général : Librairie GALLIMARD, 15, Boulevard Raspail, 15, PARIS (VIIe)

LE NUMÉRO : France : 4 francs, Étranger : 5 francs

Surrealist journals

La Révolution surréaliste, the journal that formed the backbone of the Surrealist movement, lasted ten years, from 1924 until, after issue no. 12, in 1929 it yielded to *Le Surréalisme au service de la révolution*, which in turn was outshone by the more lavish and aesthetically more ambitious *Minotaure*. The initial journal was riven by an internal debate between André Breton and the journal's first editor, Pierre Naville. Naville proudly modeled the cover of *LRS* on the nineteenth-century magazine of popular science *La Nature*, since the "positivist nature" of the latter stood for the status of the documentary material the Surrealist journal would publish—accounts of dreams, and answers to questionnaires around such problems as "Is suicide a solution?" In addition, Naville called the offices of the review the Surrealist "*centrale*," imitating the headquarters of Communist Party cells. A collage of three photographs of the members of the movement gathered in the *centrale* ornamented the first issue of *LRS* (December 1924). The place of photography was secured both inside the journal's covers and on its outside, since Naville was interested in anonymous, popular imagery and was programmatically hostile to art. But when Breton took over the editorship of the journal he began to publish his four-part text "Surrealism and Painting," in which the genesis of Surrealist visual production (in the work of Picasso) is shown to have yielded such contemporary practitioners as Miró, Arp, Ernst, and Masson.

The documentary focus of the journal was not abandoned altogether, however. Breton celebrated the "50th Anniversary of the Discovery of Hysteria" with the publication of photographs taken of Charcot's patients in the Salpetrière Asylum. The threshold between *LRS* and its successor *LSASDLR* was constructed by Breton's second manifesto of Surrealism, in which he exiled many of the original members of the movement, particularly those who had left the *centrale* to join with Georges Bataille and his radical journal *Documents*. Announcing on its cover that the areas of its concern would be ethnography, archaeology, and popular culture in addition to fine arts, *Documents* celebrated Bataille's own version of Naville's "distaste," in his exploration of the *informe* or formlessness.

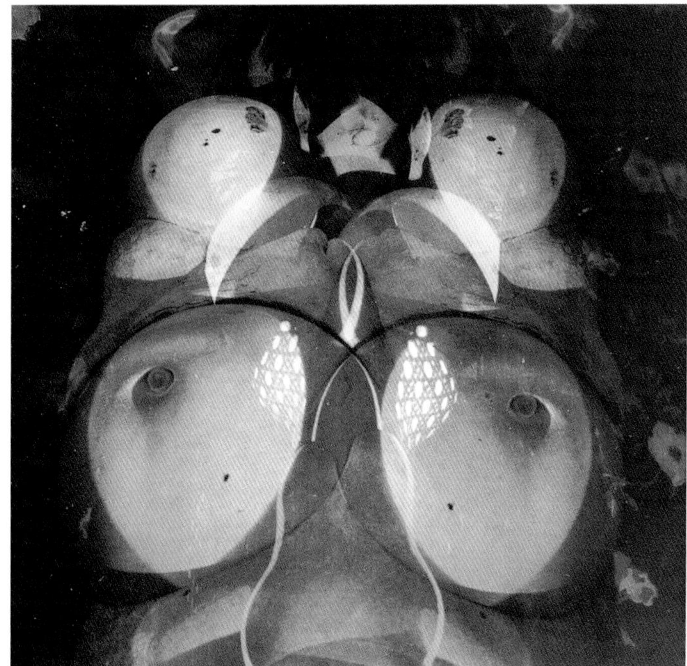

7 • Hans Bellmer, *La Poupée* (Doll), 1938
Published in *La Révolution surréaliste*

made it a perfect vehicle for Surrealism, which exploited this aspect in its use of double exposures, sandwich printing, juxtapositions of negative and positive prints of the same image, and montaged doubles to produce this sense of the world redoubled as sign. The first issue of *La Révolution surréaliste* carried several photographs by Man Ray in which doubling was at work [**6**].

But doubling, as was pointed out, has a certain psychoanalytic content, one aspect of which Freud discusses in his essay "The Uncanny" (1919). Ghosts, the very stuff of uncanniness, are doubles of the living; and it is when live bodies are redoubled by lifeless ones—as in the case of automata or robots, or sometimes with dolls, or with people in states of seizure—that they take on the uncanniness of ghosts. That doubles should produce this condition is due, Freud explains, to the return of early states of dread. One of these derives from infantile feelings of omnipotence, in which the child believes itself able to project its control into the surrounding world only to find, however, these doubles of itself turning round to threaten and attack it. Another is castration anxiety, in which, similarly, the threat takes the form of one's phallic double. More generally, Freud says, anything that reminds us of our inner compulsion to repeat will strike us as uncanny.

That Hans Bellmer would build his early artistic practice entirely around a specially constructed doll, which he would arrange in various situations and then photograph, engages with this operation of the uncanny. Not only is the doll itself connected to this experience but Bellmer's treatment both exploits the sense of the way the doll's appearance to the viewer is dependent on either the operations of dream or on those of objective chance, and, by means of photomechanical doubling, projects the doll as the emblem of castration anxiety: tumescent female redoubled as male organ [**7**].

Uncanny doubling, although unrelated to the figure of the doll, ▲ was also exploited by the Belgian Surrealist René Magritte. Interestingly, Freud's description of the experience of the uncanny maps directly onto Breton's recipe for objective chance. "Involuntary repetition," Freud wrote, "surrounds with an uncanny atmosphere what would otherwise be innocent enough, and forces upon us the idea of something fateful and unescapable where otherwise we should have spoken of 'chance' only." And in relation to objective chance in *Nadja*, where Breton's attraction to Nadja herself is partly due to her being able to predict when these chance occurrences would take place, Freud recalls the tendency of his neurotic patients to have "presentiments" that "usually come true," a phenomenon he links to the recurrence of primitive omnipotence of thoughts. To the common example of objective chance occurring in most people's lives through "uncanny" repetitions of the same number (our birthday, our street address, and, say, our new friend's telephone number), Freud responds: "Unless a man is utterly hardened and proof against the lure of superstition he will be tempted to ascribe a secret meaning to this obstinate recurrence of a number, taking it, perhaps, as an indication of the span of life allotted to him."

Objective chance indeed provides a common ground between Surrealist photographic practice and Miró's "dream paintings," since, like the former, the latter are focused on the waves of color yielding up a sign of the dreamer's desire. Miró himself acknowledged as much in an extraordinary painting of this period in which, on a white ground, he deposited a splotch of intense cerulean blue. Over it, he wrote "this is the color of my dreams"; but in the upper left corner of the work, in much larger letters, he inscribed "Photo." Somewhere on the painting's material surface the chain of the real and the chain of the unconscious will meet.

FURTHER READING

Hal Foster, *Compulsive Beauty* (Cambridge, Mass.: MIT Press, 1993)
Roman Jakobson, "Why 'Mama' and 'Papa'" (1959), *Selected Writings* (The Hague: Mouton, 1962)
Rosalind Krauss and Jane Livingston, *L'Amour fou: Surrealism and Photography* (New York: Abbeville Press, 1986)
William Rubin, *Dada and Surrealist Art* (New York: Harry N. Abrams, 1968)
Sidra Stich (ed.), *Anxious Visions: Surrealist Art* (New York: Abbeville Press, 1990)

▲ 1927a

1925a

While the Art Deco exhibition in Paris makes official the birth of modern kitsch, Le Corbusier's machine aesthetics becomes the bad dream of modernism and Aleksandr Rodchenko's Workers' Club advocates a new relationship between men and objects.

"As for this famous *Exposition*, it's probably not worth seeing it. They built such pavilions! Even from afar they are ugly and from close it's an horror." In the letters he wrote from Paris to his wife (the artist Varvara Stepanova), the Russian Constructivist Aleksandr Rodchenko did not mince his words about the Exposition Internationale des Arts Décoratifs of 1925—from which the label Art Deco derives. Siding with French workers who commented that the glitzy display of luxury goods was nothing short of immoral in such times of financial duress, the major exception for his utter contempt was Konstantin Melnikhov's Soviet Pavilion to which he had contributed the white, black, gray, and red color scheme: "Our pavilion will be the most beautiful for its newness," he beamed. Even if padded with national pride, Rodchenko's assessment of the fair was not unique. Calling the Exposition a "total failure," from both the social and the aesthetic point of view, the French critic Waldemar George singled out only five buildings that could "be properly called modern" at the Exposition: besides Melnikhov's pavilion, he named Gustave Perret's Théâtre, Robert Mallet-Stevens's Hall d'Entrée pour une Ambassade and Pavillon du Tourisme, and Le Corbusier's landmark manifesto, the Pavillon de l'Esprit Nouveau, named after the journal that the Swiss architect had been editing since 1920.

Department-store modernism

The project of the Exposition had been discussed since 1907 in French political circles—as the success of several international fairs, notably in Turin in 1902 and Milan in 1906, was quickly erasing the memory of the grand 1900 celebration in Paris. But it was the formidable participation of the Deutscher Werkbund at the 1910 Salon d'Automne in Paris, highlighting the thriving collaboration between designers and industry in Germany, that provided the definitive sting. French decorative art was in decline, a 1911 official report of the Société des Artistes Décorateurs asserted, its downfall clearly due to lack of imagination and servile dependence upon a glorious past, and it was soon to be smothered by foreign competition. An international contest, the report went on to say, would provide an incentive for the much needed reform of production, and it would force designers and industrialists alike to think about, rather than deliberately dodge, the new conditions brought about by the fast-developing machine age; the traditional association between decorative arts and luxury would be dissipated; a veritable "democratization of art" would follow, and art would at last regain its "true social function," which it had lost since the Middle Ages. Planned for 1915, the fair was postponed several times (first because of the war, then because of the financial and political crises that resulted from it), and ended up opening a decade later. In the meantime, the control of the enterprise had passed from the professional designers' organizations to leaders of commerce, with the four major Parisian department stores at the helm. Each had their own lavish pavilion, all built on the same model—a symmetrical temple one entered through a monumental door to discover an interior space divided into overstuffed living rooms around a central hall.

Designers were not the only constituents to be defeated by the massive onslaught of commercial interests. The choice of the fair's site—in the same area as its 1900 predecessor at the center of Paris—signaled the failure of social reformers (among them several architects such as Le Corbusier) to persuade the French government that the fair should be conceived as a testing ground for the burning issue of mass housing in postwar France. Rather than staging an architectural competition for a model housing complex in a vacant area, something that could be inhabited after the close of the exhibition—a strategy favored by the Deutscher Werkbund in the twenties—the exhibition's committee decided to allow the construction of temporary pavilions as showcases for foreign products or those of French provinces and national guilds, and also of any private company able to afford the considerable rent.

The immense touristic success of the fair was in direct proportion to its artistic mediocrity. For the most part, its architecture consisted of streamlined or slightly geometrized versions of past styles, and nearly all the luxury objects it contained could have been designed a quarter of a century earlier. Indeed, while the innovative furniture proposed by De Stijl or the Bauhaus had been utterly banned, the only foreign products to be welcome (and widely imitated) were those issued by the Wiener Werkstätte, founded in 1903. Amazingly, many of the best designers we now associate with Art Deco (such as Eileen Gray or Pierre Chareau) either did not participate or contributed very traditional interiors. "In fact," as Nancy Troy suggests, "the exposi-

▲ 1921 ● 1929 ▲ 1917, 1923

tion as a whole might well be described as an attempt to link contemporary life in France with a lost or rapidly vanishing past. The long vistas bordered by manicured lawns separating symmetrically positioned buildings created a sense of stability and order that France had not yet recovered almost seven years after the end of World War I, and the unabashed opulence of the majority of pavilions was in manifest contrast to the financial situation in which the exposition had been planned." One should add that even though the majority of visitors were from the middle class, which accounted for only a little less than a third of the French population at the time, few would have been able to afford much of its content. The fair was a fantasy land, where one dreamed about the way the affluent live before rushing to the department stores nearby in search of cheaper imitations of the saucer, teapot, or side table one had fancied. The commercial strategy was that of *haute couture*, not surprisingly given the spectacular participation of major couturiers such as Paul Poiret, whose three pavilions were floating extravaganzas on the Seine.

Le Corbusier's machine age

The most vociferous critic of the Exposition was Le Corbusier. After a long bureaucratic struggle he had been allowed to build his Pavillon de l'Esprit Nouveau, at the periphery of the fair **[1]**. It consisted of two parts. The first, airy and drenched in light, was presented as a two-storey unit excerpted from the (nonbuilt) Immeubles-Villas, an apartment-cum-garden complex which he had conceived in 1922 and whose design he had been refining ever since; the second part was a windowless rotunda off the patio, devoted to the Swiss architect's ideas on urbanism, notably his scandalous plan for Paris, the Plan Voisin (named after the pavilion's main sponsor, the Voisin aeroplane and car manufacturer) in which he was proposing to raze the center of Paris, save a few important historical monuments, and replace its chaotic urban palimpsest with a vast green area interrupted by high-rise towers placed at regular intervals. The Plan Voisin was pure provocation, and it produced the expected reaction in the press, but while the dwelling section of the pavilion was less harshly criticized, it also had a very conspicuous polemical intent.

Since the beginning of World War I, Le Corbusier had lambasted architects and designers for their refusal to take into consideration the new conditions of production created by the machine, a denial made particularly conspicuous by the rapid evolution of mechanical processes in all industrialized nations as a result of the war effort. Even when new modes of construction were involved and new materials used, this had no bearing on the design's formal aspect, almost invariably conceived as a superficial mask hiding the architectonic structure, in whatever historical style was favored by the client. For Le Corbusier, Art Deco represented the triumph of such fraudulence. Not only was the claim of its designers (that their goal was an aestheticization of mass products) a lie, but even had it been true, its premises would still have been wrong. His Pavillon de l'Esprit Nouveau was intended above all to demonstrate that by the sheer action of what he called "mechanical evolution" (a concept modeled after Darwin), industry was, by itself, able to engender a new kind of beauty: to tamper with it was a sure way to destroy it.

The pavilion was thus built using standard elements of the newest materials available, including the experimental wall paneling made of straw onto which concrete was projected. In the absence of any ornament, the modular regularity of the distribution of the vertical posts underscored the variations allowed by the structure (here a wall, there an opening) while, according to Le Corbusier, subliminally satisfying the visitor's "natural longing for order." But the most telling paean to industry was in the choice of furnishings that somewhat sparsely populated the pavilion: from the shelves and cabinets (industrial storage units labeled "*casiers standards*") to the chairs (notably, the famous Thonet bentwood café chairs, whose design dates from the nineteenth century) to the glass vases (laboratory glass vessels), most were objects already available in the marketplace and directly referring to public spheres of daily life, either work (office, laboratory), or leisure (cafés). In truth, some of these objects were slightly modified for the occasion—the Thonet chairs among them—but not in any way that would soften Le Corbusier's fundamental attack against his Art Deco colleagues reigning at the fair and their ideal of the bourgeois private home as an overall ensemble for which everything had to be custom made.

Le Corbusier's fascination with industrial standardization dates back to 1917, when he read Frederick W. Taylor's *Principles of Scientific Management*. In this book, published in 1911 and translated into French a year later, Taylor singles out efficiency in labor organization as the best way of maximizing profits and generating growth, even if it meant treating workers like machines. Henry Ford would soon follow suit (in 1913) with his invention of the assembly line, masterfully presenting this new form of slavery as a promise of more leisure time for the masses. Until the late twenties, with an amazing political naivety, Le Corbusier firmly believed that if industrial

1 • Le Corbusier, interior of the Pavillon de L'Esprit Nouveau, 1925
In the background is Fernand Léger's *The Baluster* next to a still life by Le Corbusier.

production were to be reformed according to Taylor's and Ford's principles, all the ills of postwar Europe would vanish by themselves. He saw modern architecture, situated at a midpoint between art (functionless) and industry, as an essential component of such a reform. And even though in his diatribes against decorative arts he had always insisted on the necessity to safeguard the autonomy of art—an autonomy consciously staged in his pavilion by the juxtaposition of a few modern paintings and sculptures and of an eclectic variety of objects whose use-value was highlighted—his theory and practice of painting rested for a good part on a fetishized notion of standardization. Indeed, his first homage to Taylorism appeared in *Après le cubisme* (1918) the book he wrote with Amédée Ozenfant to launch their pictorial movement, which they called Purism.

The taming of Cubism

Contrary to the claims made by Charles-Édouard Jeanneret (that is, Le Corbusier, who had not yet adopted his pseudonym) and Ozenfant in their tract, Purism is by no means a "post-Cubism." Rather, it consists of a mere academicization of Cubism which, paradoxically, ▲ was based on a complete misunderstanding of Braque and Picasso's enterprise. For the two Purist painters, Cubism was pure decoration— "if a cubist painting is beautiful," they write, "it is in the same way a carpet is beautiful." Although Cubism made ample use of geometrical forms, Ozenfant and Jeanneret claimed, it did so without recourse to any laws—its compositions were arbitrary, they were not controlled by any "standard." Braque and Picasso's extraordinary investigation of pictorial representation as indeed an arbitrary system of signs completely escaped the Purists, who saw in Cubism only an incompetent geometrization of reality that needed to be "corrected," just as the strictures of the assembly line prevented any erratic behavior on the part of workers.

This was not new by any means. As early as October 1912 a group of artists had organized the Salon de la Section d'Or (Golden Section) with the explicit program of presenting to the public a version of Cubism that would be tamed by "universal" principles of "geometric harmony" going back to classical Greece and well established in the tradition of French painting, from Poussin to Ingres to Cézanne and Seurat. Simultaneously, one of the participants—Raymond Duchamp-Villon—was presenting at the Salon d'Automne his facade of the Maison Cubiste, a project which is perhaps the seed of the Art Deco phenomenon. Conceived by André Mare, one of the most established designers in the future 1925 fair, and replete with works of Duchamp-Villon's co-exhibitors at the Section d'Or, such as his brothers Marcel Duchamp and Jacques Villon, but also Albert Gleizes and Jean Metzinger, the authors of *Du Cubisme* (1912) (a book long held as the theoretical basis of Cubism despite Picasso's and Braque's scorn), the decoration of the Maison Cubiste's three interior rooms is not particularly memorable. Its patent eclecticism was intended as the definitive blow against Art Nouveau design (deemed "international," which meant "German" at the time), and it was successful at that, but only by espousing the nationalist tenet of a Louis-Philippe revival (not quite a return to the *ancien régime*, since it had developed under a bourgeois monarchy, this style was heralded as the last true French style). Duchamp-Villon's facade partook of this revivalist mode, and it revealed even more clearly that the modernism of the Maison Cubiste was only cosmetic: this decor was not much more of a pastiche of a nineteenth-century version of a seventeenth-century *hôtel particulier*'s facade, powdered with specks of angular faceting.

In the postwar context, the nationalistic current of this academic Cubism flourished under the aegis of what has been called the ▲ "return to order": the "righting" of Cubism was part of the reconstruction ideology, together with a renewed interest in France's *latinità* or a public policy favoring a surge in birthrate. Given his horrified response when discovering Picasso's first Ingres pastiches in 1915, which arguably mark the beginning of the "return to order," it might come as a surprise that Juan Gris would have so definitively ● joined its ranks. Yet even though Gris's prewar collages are no less feats of spatial ambiguity and plastic wit than those of his Spanish friend and mentor, his artistic creed reveals a latent rationalism that could not have been further from Picasso's attack against the tradition of mimetic representation: "Cézanne transforms a bottle into a cylinder," he wrote, and "I begin with a cylinder in order to create a bottle." In other words, geometry comes first: objects, to be included at all in the composition, have to fit an a priori grid.

Ozenfant's and Jeanneret's paintings follow the same logic (though their justification, unlike Gris's, was an appeal to Taylorist organization)—and it is not by chance that Le Corbusier included one of Gris's canvases in his Pavillon. Indeed, for all their paintings—inevitably still lifes **[2]**, and most of them in a format determined by the golden section—Ozenfant and Jeanneret first established a grid of regulating lines ("*tracés régulateurs*") establishing the placement of "object-types" (supposedly the lucky survivors of "mechanical evolution"), often depicted both in plan

2 • Charles-Édouard Jeanneret (Le Corbusier), *Purist Still Life*, 1922
Oil on canvas, 65 x 81 ($25\frac{5}{8}$ x $31\frac{7}{8}$)

▲ 1911, 1912

▲ 1919 ● 1919

3 • Fernand Léger, *Three Women (Le Grand Déjeuner)*, 1921
Oil on canvas, 183.5 x 251.5 (72¼ x 99)

and elevation and alluding directly to architectural forms (a carafe becoming a doric column, the neck of a bottle, a chimney). Volumes are reduced to simple prisms, with an occasional accentuation of the modeling all the more perceptible now that most objects are rendered by planes of color as flat as the background; orthogonals dominate; colors are never strident: the overall tone is one of tasteful, but somewhat vapid, restraint.

Another painter whose work was included in Le Corbusier's 1925 pavilion needs to be mentioned here, namely Fernand Léger—for although his work too was inflected by the "return to order" ideology, he was the only French artist who shared, and even exceeded, the architect's adulation for the machine. Although Léger had never emulated Picasso's art, he borrowed from Analytical Cubism one of its main strategies (using a single notational element for every object represented in a painting) in order to realize in 1913 his first ▲ mature works, a series of canvases entitled *Contrasts of Forms.* On the verge of abstraction, these paintings were conceived as accretions of tubular volumes of bright color whose metallic rotundity is signified by white highlights. When he was drafted to World War I's battlefield, Léger's mechanistic enthusiasm did not abate, almost inexplicably, given the horrors he witnessed and profusely sketched, all due to the sheer force of modern armament. But he came back from the war with a blind desire to divest the machine of the destructive image it had in the eyes of his contemporaries. The tubular elements were gradually replaced by more recognizable segments of human anatomy [**3**]; the figures, almost all monochrome, schematically modeled, and striking poses that signify leisure, stood in more dramatic contrast to the colorful and dynamic background, most often cityscapes made of geometric shapes populated here and there by diagrammatic billboards.

The Baluster [**4**] is perhaps one of Léger's most legible canvases of the period, and, save for the brash color, stylistically the closest to the Purist aesthetic, which is undoubtedly why Le Corbusier chose it for his pavilion. As Carol Eliel notes, the central element can be read both as a baluster and a bottle; the red form that echoes it on the left, with its upended white circular opening, resembles the vents of factories or ocean liners illustrated in *L'Esprit Nouveau* and common in Léger's cityscapes of the period; the vertical edge of the book suggests a classical column; the "four verticals in the top half of the baluster, highlighted on a light ground, can be read as four smokestacks or grain silos, while the dashed horizontal form at the left edge of the canvas suggests the motions and movement of an assembly line as

▲ 1913

4 • Fernand Léger, *The Baluster*, 1925
Oil on canvas, 129.5 x 97.2 (51 x 38¼)

Black Deco

The association of negritude with abandon animated the artistic life of the Left Bank, particularly in the nightclub district, Montparnasse, where jazz filled the air with delicious dissonances, and frenzied music became the support for drunken dancing until late into the night. Floorshows such as those by Josephine Baker, who danced half-nude, underscored this relationship, which nonetheless soon gave way to a very different experience of black form. This could be called "Black Deco," or the aestheticized use of tribal shapes and motifs within the decorative arts. For the costumes and sets of the ballet *La Création du Monde* (1923), Fernand Léger exploited the strong silhouettes and repeated patterns of primitive sculpture. The entire panoply of Art Deco furniture and accessories followed this lead as silver patterns were combined with the sheen of ebony woods and leopard skins were juxtaposed with crocodile hides. Where this luxury trade led, artists soon followed and the influence of Black Deco on sculptors such as Constantin Brancusi and Jacques Lipchitz could be seen, as well as on designers like Le Corbusier and Jean Prouvé. For all these figures, Black Deco was a powerful cocktail mixing "primitive" Africa with machine-age America.

well as film sprockets." This last allusion is particularly significant, coming soon after Léger had finished his film *Ballet Mécanique* [**5**], which was, if not the very first, at least one of the most self-conscious attacks ever launched against narrative cinema. With its absurd repetition of found footage (a woman climbs a flight of steps twenty-three times), its kaleidoscopic multiplication of eyes, balls, hats, and other circular shapes within the same frame, its pulsatile celebration of linear motion, its decomposition and recomposition of bodies and faces, its dance of triangles, circles, and machine parts, *Ballet Mécanique* is Léger's most remarkable foray into abstraction. By contrast, and even though it was taken off the wall at the request of the government, the mural painting that he exhibited in Mallet-Stevens's Hall d'Entrée pour une Ambassade seems subdued. ▲ Inspired by De Stijl (in particular by van Doesburg's *Rhythm of a Russian Dance* of 1918), it belongs to a handful of works, all dating from 1924 to 1925, that Léger conceived as mural decoration—for him the only possible venue of pictorial abstraction.

Architecture or revolution/architecture as revolution

Had he been as distant from bourgeois culture as he thought he was, Léger might have reflected upon the very different proposal made by the Soviet entry at the Exposition, conceived as propaganda for the Soviet regime (which had just finally been recognized by the French government) and destined to prove that the Revolution was better equipped than the capitalist West to respond to the demands of postwar reconstruction. This entry consisted of two parts: Konstantin Melnikhov's Soviet Pavilion [**6**], and Rodchenko's Workers' Club built within that monument of 1900 kitsch, the Grand Palais.

Melnikhov's pavilion was by far the most daring building of the fair—Rodchenko was right on this point. In plan, it consisted of an oblong rectangle diagonally bisected by an exterior double staircase that functioned like a street one had walk through before entering any of the two enclosed triangular volumes on each of its sides. Triangles and ascending oblique lines were omnipresent (even lending

5 • Fernand Léger and Dudley Murphy, still from *Ballet Mécanique*, 1924

▲ 1917

a new meaning to a traditional feature such as the slant roof). Melnikhov had created in architectural forms a homage to the "red ▲ wedge" of the Revolution that was as dynamic as El Lissitzky's famous 1918 poster *Beat the Whites with the Red Wedge.* The red, white, and gray colors of the exterior walls and interlocking (oblique) canopies above the staircase made a stark contrast with the transparency of the main glass facades; the deliberately unluxurious material (painted wood) and the elemental, almost ludic, mode of assembly, in record time, of all the parts, which were shipped from Moscow, was a clear jab at the massive pomp of most pavilions in the fair and their decorative skin of enameled tiles or marble.

Though less ebullient, Rodchenko's interior was no less a critique of capitalist luxury and, above all, of capitalism's veneration of the private sphere, for it was relentlessly marked as a collective space [**7**]. The workers' club was a recent invention of the nascent Soviet regime. In exporting this concept—and in making sure it would not escape notice by commissioning one of the most active Constructivist artists for its design—the new Socialist Republic wanted to demonstrate that the Soviet Revolution, far from being barbarian, had engendered a new culture, and that, in its care, the workers had access to leisure, unlike those in capitalist countries. Faithful to the princi- • ples of his 1921 abstract sculptures, Rodchenko emphasized two aspects of his wood furniture (painted in the same colors as the Melnikhov building): the transparency of their mode of construction (without upholstery, all the joints were revealed) and their transformability. "Emphatically mobile," writes Leah Dickerman, "the Club's objects were to be adjustable by the user, both for convenience and for different functional requirements. The reading table had leaves that could be moved from an inclined position, for supporting reading matter, to a flat one, creating an expanded work surface; cylinders holding photographs allowed for a rotating display of many images in a small space; and the gaming surface of the chess table spun to the vertical to allow the players access to the built-in seats." The true star of this hymn to polyfunctionality was the collapsible orator rostrum/movie screen, with its lattice unfolding at will in all directions of space, and the care that Rodchenko devoted to its design reveals that he conceived of his club as a media space, in which workers would process information and act upon it.

6 • Konstantin Melnikhov's Soviet Pavilion at the Exposition Internationale des Arts Décoratifs in Paris, 1925

7 • Interior of Aleksandr Rodchenko's Workers' Club, built for the Exposition Internationale des Arts Décoratifs and installed in the Grand Palais, Paris, 1925

The assembly-line disposition of the two rows of chairs around the Club's table was no less informed by Taylor's principles than was Le Corbusier's raiding of the marketplace for "standard objects" with which to furnish his pavilion, but Rodchenko did not share the architect's blind faith in the machine as a guarantee of mankind's future well-being. At the same time as his Club showed (*contra* Léger) that the future of abstraction was not necessarily in decoration, it proposed a new relationship between men and objects, in which we would no longer be consumers but coplayers in the chess game of life. While Le Corbusier's *Towards a New Architecture* ended with this alternative: "architecture or revolution," Rodchenko, true to his Constructivist program, articulated the slogan "architecture *as* revolution" with every square inch of his Club. Both dreams, the subsequent history of the century tells us, ended up as nightmares.

FURTHER READING

Carol S. Eliel, "Purism in Paris, 1918–1925," *L'Esprit Nouveau: Purism in Paris, 1918–1925* (Los Angeles: Los Angeles County Museum of Art, 2001)

Leah Dickerman, "The Propagandizing of Things," *Aleksandr Rodchenko* (New York: Museum of Modern Art, 1998)

Christina Kiaer, "Rodchenko in Paris," *October*, no. 75, Winter 1996

Mary McLeod, "Architecture or Revolution: Taylorism, Technocracy, and Social Change," *Art Journal*, vol. 42, no. 2, Summer 1983

Nancy Troy, *Modernism and the Decorative Arts in France: Art Nouveau to Le Corbusier* (New Haven and London: Yale University Press, 1991)

▲ 1926, 1928 • 1921

1925b

Curator Gustav F. Hartlaub organizes the first exhibition of Neue Sachlichkeit painting at the Kunsthalle, Mannheim: a variation of the international tendencies of the *rappel à l'ordre*, this new "magic realism" signals the end of Expressionism and Dada practices in Germany.

The short life of the Weimar Republic (1919–33) qualifies more than any other period in the twentieth century for Antonio Gramsci's diagnosis that "the crisis consists precisely in the fact that the old is dying and the new cannot be born. In this interregnum, a great variety of morbid symptoms appears." The first five years of the newly founded republic were marked by perpetual economic and political turmoil, by social disorganization and disillusion. Not until 1924 did a relative stabilization of the economy give an elementary (and illusionary) sense of solidity to the democratic culture of the Republic, only for it to be shattered again in 1929 with the world economic crisis, and to be decisively destroyed in 1933 with Germany's embrace of fascism and the rise of Hitler. Even during these "sober" years from 1924 to 1929, comprising the crucial period of Neue Sachlichkeit, most members of the cultural intelligentsia, if not the population at large, perceived themselves as being part of what literary historian Helmut Lethen has called an experimental existence "between two wars."

The term "Neue Sachlichkeit," somewhat inadequately translated as "New Objectivity" or "New Sobriety," was coined by Gustav Friedrich Hartlaub, the director of the Kunsthalle in Mannheim, when he announced a forthcoming exhibition of new figurative work by a group of German painters. Initially planned for 1923, the show eventually took place between June 14 and September 13, 1925, and included works by Max Beckmann (1884–1950), Otto Dix (1891–1969), George Grosz, Alexander Kanoldt (1881–1939), Carlo Mense (1886–1965), Kay H. Nebel (1888–1953), Georg Scholz (1890–1945), and Georg Schrimpf (1889–1938). In his announcement of the project, Hartlaub defined Neue Sachlichkeit somewhat lapidarily as work governed by the "loyalty to a positively tangible reality." He was not alone in discerning this new tendency toward realism in German painting. In the same year as "Neue Sachlichkeit" opened, critic and art historian Franz Roh published *Nach-Expressionismus: Magischer Realismus* (Post-Expressionism: Magic Realism), thereby providing his own label—magic realism—to describe the emerging style. (The success of the Mannheim exhibition meant that Hartlaub's term prevailed.)

From its very inception, Hartlaub, Roh, and other critics such as Paul Westheim recognized that Neue Sachlichkeit was deeply divided: the rift was identified, as Hartlaub wrote, by the opposi▲tion between "the right wing of the neoclassicists like Picasso and the left wing of *veristic* painters like Beckmann, Grosz, Dix," that is, by the opposition between *Ingrismus* (named for the early nineteenth-century French painter Ingres) and *Verismus* (realism). These critics also recognized the extent to which the German artists' return to figuration (and its ostentatious departure from • Expressionism and Dada) was due, at least in part, to their recent encounters with French and Italian antimodernist precedents. As early as 1919 Westheim had stated in his *Das Kunstblatt*: "Characteristic of Carlo Carrà's work ... as indeed of a whole group of young artists, is an idiosyncratic, uncompromising realism (*verismo*), seeking a meticulous hard line which suppresses every trace of the individual artist's manner. In Germany, as is known, Grosz and Davringhausen are following a similar path." And in 1921 Westheim commented on the reverberations of Picasso's "Ingresque" style in Germany, addressing the topic again in September 1922 with a special issue of *Das Kunstblatt* that featured a questionnaire on the "New Realism."

From *manichino* to *machino*

The time and place of the Germans' encounter with *pittura metafisica* are firmly established, being, as is so often the case in the twentieth century, primarily in the pages of a journal. In this instance, it was the Italian publication *Valori plastici*, edited since 1918 by the critic and collector Mario Broglio. The third issue of the journal in 1919 was devoted in its entirety to the work of ■ Giorgio de Chirico, Carlo Carrà, and Giorgio Morandi. It was admired at once by Max Ernst, George Grosz, Georg Schrimpf, and Heinrich Maria Davringhausen (1894–1970) in the Munich gallery and bookshop of Hans Goltz, *Valori plastici*'s German distributor. This encounter led not only to Max Ernst's instant publication of a *metafisica* portfolio of lithographs entitled *Fiat Modes, Pereat Ars* (1919), but also to the first exhibitions of Davringhausen in 1919 and Grosz in 1920 at Goltz's gallery.

The iconography of the metaphysical *manichino* (mannequin) would be dramatically recoded in the hands of the German Neue Sachlichkeit artists to become a *machino*. What had appeared in de Chirico as an allegory of painting's lost capacity to engender

▲ 1919 • 1908, 1916a, 1920 ■ 1909, 1924, 1944b

figuration, reappeared now in Grosz's work as the "Republican Automaton," that peculiar hybrid between a tailor's dummy and the office robot in which the new identity of the *"civil servant,"* the white-collar authoritarian personality, appeared to be best captured [**1**]. Walter Benjamin's critique of *neusachlich* literature in the essay "Left Wing Melancholia" describes such types thus:

> *These puppets heavy with sadness that will walk over corpses if necessary. With their rigid body armor, their slowly advancing movements, and the blindness of their actions, they embody the human fusion of insect and tank.*

But even in its Neue Sachlichkeit adaptation, the *manichino/machino* morphology remains fluid, shifting easily from victor to victim. What is an authoritarian automaton in one image, becomes the industrially mechanized or armored body in the next. Or, after 1918, with six million soldiers returning from the war, in image after image we encounter the machinic body as the prosthetic body, the war cripple (as for example in the work of the Cologne Progressives group, like Heinrich Hoerle's *Cripple Portfolio* of 1920 or in Dix's *The War Cripples* [1920]).

The exclusion of photographers from Hartlaub's exhibition and from Roh's study (even though, four years later, Roh would publish the famous anthology of modernist photography *Foto-Auge*) indicates that the discoverers of a "new objectivity" wanted to see its truth-value established first of all with the traditional means of painting. Thus Hartlaub concluded his introduction to the exhibition by stating that:

> *What we are showing is that art is still there ... that it is alive, despite a cultural situation that seems hostile to the essence of art as other epochs have rarely been. Thus artists disillusioned, sobered, often resigned to the point of cynicism having nearly given up on themselves after a moment of unbounded, nearly apocalyptic hope—that artists in the midst of the catastrophe, have begun to ponder what is most immediate, certain, and durable:* truth and craft.

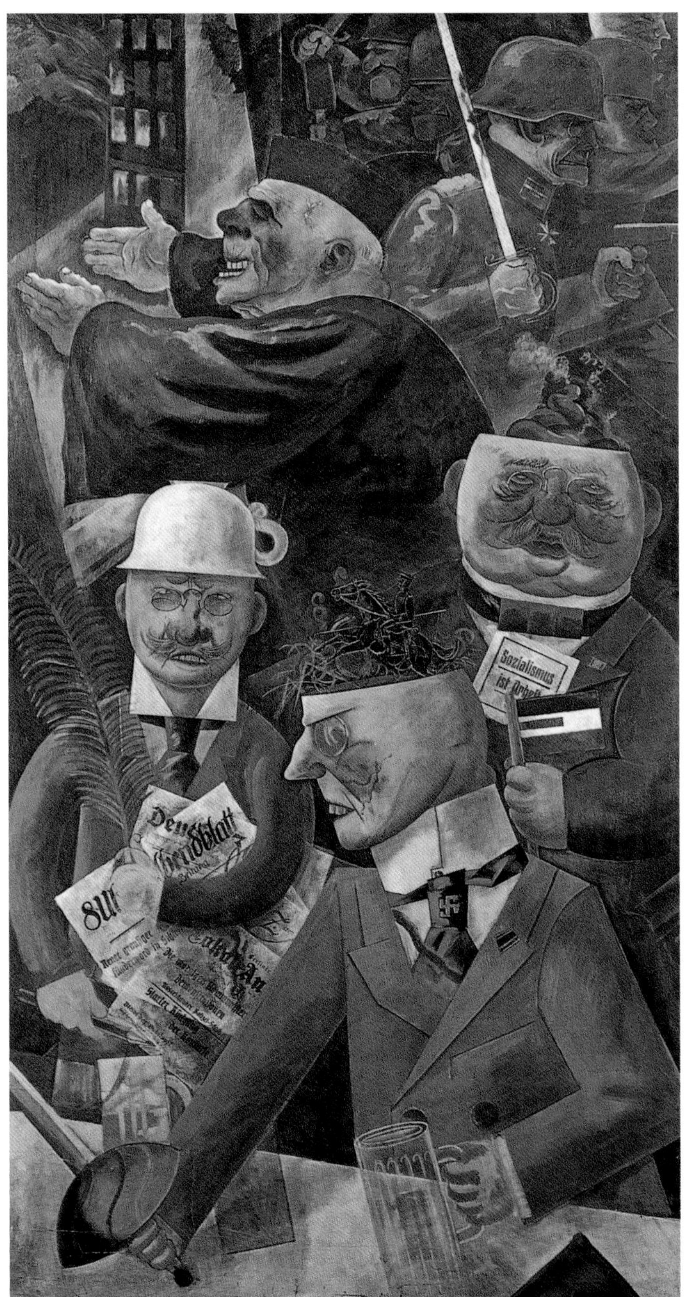

1 • George Grosz, *Pillars of Society*, 1926
Oil on canvas, 200 x 108 ($78\frac{3}{4}$ x $42\frac{1}{2}$)

That desperate desire for the objectivity of transhistorical truth could also be found in statements by other critics. Writing in *Der Cicerone* in 1923, Willi Wolfradt—once again opposing *Ingrismus* and *Verismus*—argued that both shared "the concept of clarity, the former in a more formal sense, and the latter in a more objective sense. In *Ingrismus* the definition of clarity is derived from antiquity, in *Verismus* it is derived from the machine. And while both might be incompatible worlds, in both worlds it is *objective truth that dominates.*" This opposition between the truth of craft and antiquity, on the one hand, and the truth of the machine on the other, originated, however, in a set of much more fundamental conflicts. First of all in the social schism between an enthusiastic embrace of industrial modernization along the lines of the much vaunted "Americanism" and "Fordism" (the source of endless fashions and cults in Weimar Germany) and a violent and pessimistic reaction against these processes of industrial mechanization and rationalization. This reaction was primarily to be found among the increasingly unemployed and proletarianized middle class, leading to the rise of antimodernist and eventually ethnic and racist ideologies of "returns" to phantasms of pure origins and uncontaminated authenticity. Invoking German sociologist Ferdinand Tönnies's (1855–1936) famous distinction between *Gemeinschaft* (community) and *Gesellschaft* (society), the new ideologues of the conservative right promised a return to preindustrial belief systems, mythical forms of social organization, and artisanal production, thereby laying the foundations for the fascism of 1933.

This conflict was exacerbated by the opposition between bourgeois concepts of high art and the proletarian needs for a progressive emancipatory mass culture. Not only was the sphere of a supposedly autonomous high culture increasingly precarious (and therefore all the more fetishized), but all the earlier forms of social relations and popular culture had been replaced by a protototalitarian mass culture and media apparatus. Unlike the ▲ Soviet avant-garde, however, which was simultaneously undergoing a very similar transformation from a radical experimental modernist aesthetic to a systematic exploration of what a new postrevolutionary avant-garde culture in a developing proletarian public sphere might mean, the artists of the Neue Sachlichkeit did not face a similarly homogeneous revolutionary society. First of all, the Weimar Republic, as novelist Alfred Döblin (1878–1957) famously stated, came without an instruction manual, indicating that the new democratic culture of the "belated nation" had to be acquired through trial and error. Second, unlike the Soviet Union, the Weimar Republic after 1919—despite its revolutionary aspirations—had been structured as a class society, albeit one in which previously oppressed social strata suddenly found themselves with more economic and political power than they might have ever imagined under the previous regime of Kaiser Wilhelm. Thus Weimar, politically organized around the principles of social democracy, became the democracy not only of a newly empowered oligarchic bourgeoisie, but also of an economically powerless but rabid *petite bourgeoisie* and a proletariat that was perpetually oscillating between revolutionary radicalization and fascist *embourgeoisement*. Ernst Bloch, in his 1935 book *Erbschaft dieser Zeit* (Heritage of our Times), was the first to argue that Neue Sachlichkeit, rather than revealing a new face of the collective, actually camouflaged an evolved capitalism that had adopted socialist principles, such as a planned economy, collective housing, and an overall sense of equality, but without reneging the primacy of an economy of profit. These universally governing conditions of reification—according to Bloch—generated Neue Sachlichkeit's seduction as much as the vacuity of its representations.

From fragments to figures

The peculiar fact that Neue Sachlichkeit had both former Expressionists (Beckmann and Dix) and former Dadaists (Grosz and Schad) among its key members deserves attention. After all, ● Expressionism had been the moment in which the humanist and pacifist subject staged itself in a histrionics of finality, whereas the ■ Dada artists accelerated and celebrated the demise of bourgeois subjectivity in a grotesque travesty of cultural practices and pretenses. Thus, one might well ask what the motivations of these artists might have been to abandon either the Expressionist aspirations or the Dadaist derisions in favor of a peculiar hybrid of putative objectivity. These extreme ambiguities of transition are particularly evident in a number of key works around 1919–20, such as Beckmann's *The Night* [**2**], Dix's crucial paintings from the same year such as *The War Cripples*, or Grosz's slightly later *Pillars of Society* from 1926 [**1**].

The Night is not only a classic example of Expressionism turning *neusachlich*, but even more so of the liberal inability (or refusal) to conduct an analysis of the political situation. Instead, it invokes and essentializes—in an act of humanist deflection—the universal catastrophe of the "human condition." While Beckmann's work had clearly acknowledged the tragic experiences of the failed German revolution of 1919, with its brutal murders of Marxist leaders Rosa Luxemburg and Karl Liebknecht among many others, this depiction of a cryptic scene of sado-masochistic mayhem positions the revolutionary worker (possibly a clandestine portrait of Lenin) on the same level of violent perpetration as the fascist *petit bourgeois*. Typically, Beckmann's humanist lament of universal bestiality fails to reflect on the painting's own heavily repressed but fully exposed indulgence in the sadistic scenes it pretends to reveal.

These ambiguities are keyed differently in Dix's most important paintings from the same moment, such as *The War Cripples*, *The Card Players*, and *Prager Strasse* (1920), or in Grosz's *Pillars of Society*. Here the subject is either depicted as the cripple, the physically annihilated victim of the imperialist war, or as the menacing impostor who inflicts the very conditions of physiological laceration and psychic trauma. Both the victor and the victim are mediated through similar iconographic, morphological, or formal devices of deformation, fragmentation, and literal bodily cuts. We witness therefore a dual dismissal in Neue Sachlichkeit's shift toward the fully closed contours and the fully modeled bodies. The first abandons Expressionist angularity, and its radiating ruptures in favor of the figure's newly enforced wholeness. The second literalizes the semiology of cuts and fragmentation from Dada photomontage and collage and redeploys these devices as surgical instruments: either, as in Dix, to lay bare the traumatized prosthetic body and the subject's threadbare existence; or, as in Grosz, to literally slice the lid from the heads of the representatives of the ruling powers of the state, the Church, and the military, revealing their skull's innermost recesses as stuffed with newspapers or grotesque steaming piles of feces. These travesties of the semiological radicality of Cubism articulate the simultaneous bankruptcy of the bourgeois subject as figuration, as much as they recognize that the proletarian subject can not yet be presented as the unified agent of a new history.

The Neue Sachlichkeit artists' inability to assume a position of class identity and agency became the third fundamental reason for the movement's internal rifts. It is not surprising then that they occupied the full spectrum of these contradictions. These ranged from the German adaptations of the Italian antimodernist *pittura* ▲ *metafisica* or the French *rappel à l'ordre* (such as Schrimpf, Mense, Kanoldt) to the radical extensions of Grosz's and John Heartfield's Dada aesthetic toward a new culture of the proletarian public sphere. Or they ranged from the cynical and melancholic attempts by the ex-Dadaist Christian Schad to pose as an Old Master of

▲ 1921 ● 1908 ■ 1916a, 1920 ▲ 1909, 1919

2 • Max Beckmann, *The Night*, 1918–19
Oil on canvas, 133 x 154 (52⅜ x 60⅝)

portrait painting (even if his portraits for the most part depicted bohemians and aristocrats situated at the margins of the newly established social hierarchy), to the printed typologies of the proletariat produced by Franz Wilhelm Seiwert (1894–1933) and Gerd Arntz (born 1900) in the context of the Cologne Progressives group (Seiwert, writing in the group's journal *A-Z* suggested in 1928 that New Objectivity was neither new nor objective, but rather, the opposite of both). In 1928 Arntz would codesign the pictograms for Isotype, the collectively accessible sign language analyzing the current conditions of social, political, and economic relations in the publications of the radical Viennese sociologist Otto Neurath.

It appears then that these conflicts between high art and mass culture, those of class identity and social relations, were literally acted out in the opposition between a renewed emphasis on the artisanal foundations of artistic production on the one hand and a commitment to the newly emerging apparatus of technical (that is, photographic) reproduction and mass cultural distribution on the other. Not surprisingly, the site where this battle was fought most actively was the portrait, seemingly one of the most venerable pictorial genres (even though it had been decisively ▲ deconstructed at the high moment of Analytical Cubism).

The "objective" portrait, the "human" subject

We find an enormously complex (and numerous) typology of portrait conceptions at the center of Neue Sachlichkeit. Starting with the post-Expressionist portraits of Beckmann, who remained committed throughout his entire oeuvre to the superannuated probing of the self, the artist seems to have been unable to relinquish not only the idea of a humanistically defined, self-motivated

▲ 1911

subjectivity, but also the conviction that his was a function to provide privileged forms of knowledge and insight. Schad's *Self-Portrait with Model* **[3]** brings these tropes of portraiture to a level of ostentatious self-consciousness where they become almost grotesque. In a cold confrontation, he depicts himself in the dress and pose of a Renaissance master (such as the transparent shirt in Bartolomeo Veneto's *Allegorical Portrait* [1507]). But the photographic realism in the depiction of his urbane physiognomy, and the mannered play on the fabric's transparency and the skin's opacity, manifestly contradict all claims to any historical continuity that either the genre and iconography of the self-portrait or the recitation of the most skillful traditions of painting could establish. His dubious female companion (as so often in Schad, she oscillates between prostitute and aristocratic bohemian, transvestite and *femme fatale*) is adorned in this instance with a sadistic cut to her face, undoubtedly inflicted by male property claims, clearly demarcating modernity.

At the other extreme of the spectrum of Neue Sachlichkeit portraiture one would find Dix's almost obsessive derision of the genre. Galvanizing his Expressionist legacy with the acid of caricature, Dix stripped his sitters of all pretenses and staged their subjecthood as either victim or prop of social construction. In his portrait of the journalist Sylvia von Harden **[4]**, the attributes of the New Woman (bobbed hair, cigarette, highly fashionable flapper dress, and drink) are both celebrated and derided simultaneously, most manifestly in the gesticulation of the hypertrophic

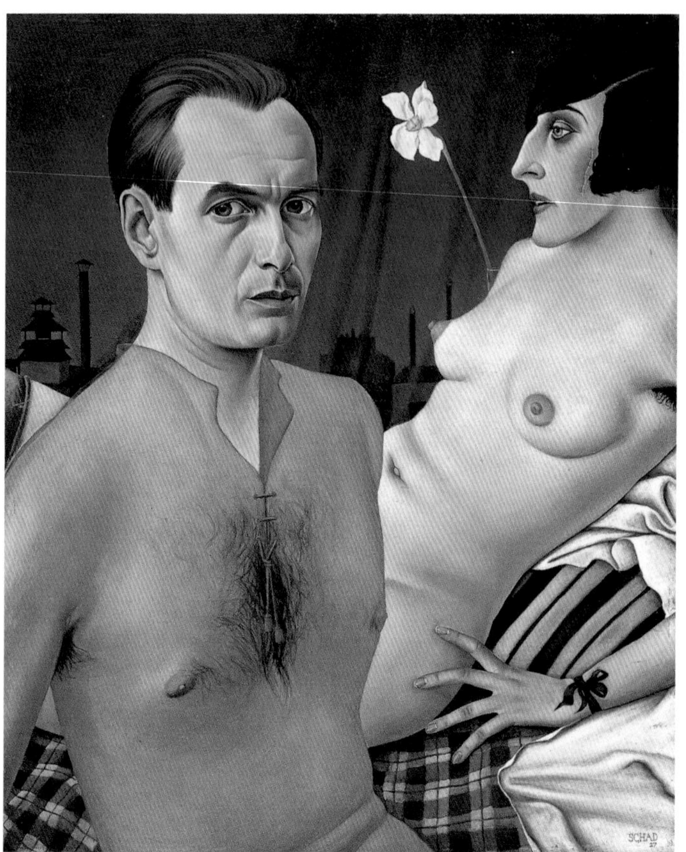

3 • Christian Schad, *Self-Portrait with Model*, 1927
Oil on canvas, 76 x 61.5 (29⅞ x 24¼)

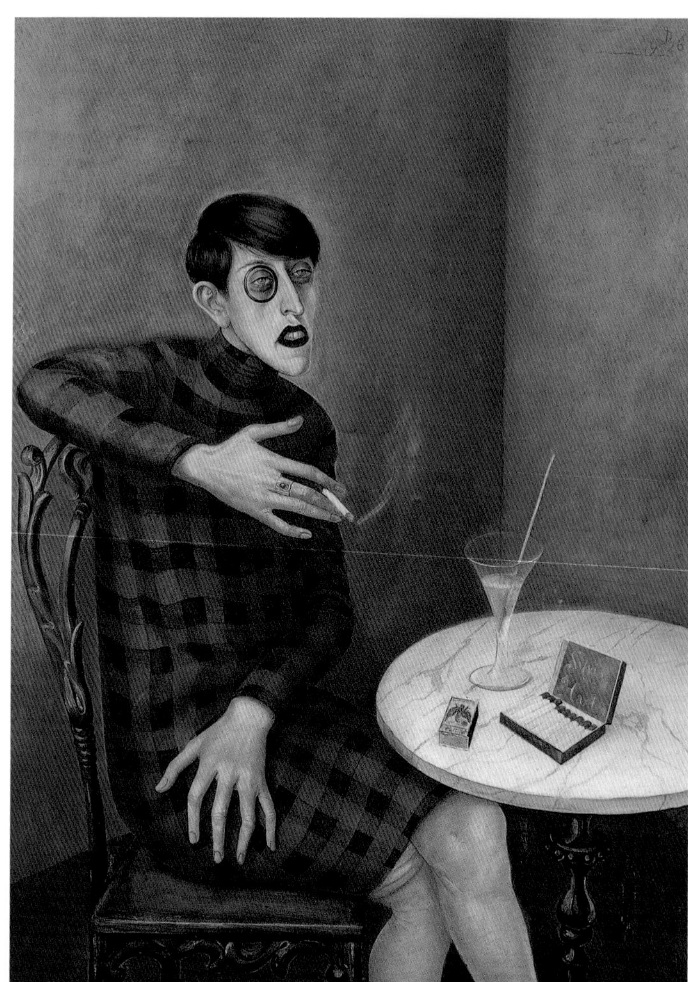

4 • Otto Dix, *Portrait of the Journalist Sylvia von Harden*, 1926
Mixed media on wood, 120 x 88 (47¼ x 34¾)

hands. This attitude of extreme ambiguity also governs one of the relatively rare portraits painted by George Grosz at the height of his Neue Sachlichkeit phase, the portrait of the writer and critic Max Hermann Neisse **[5]**. In distinction to Dix's caricaturesque hyperbole, Grosz by that time seems to have cooled his passion for caricature as modernism's countermodel, to which his friend, the historian of the medium Eduard Fuchs, had introduced him earlier in the decade. This intensified ambiguity, however, in which photography and caricature seem to recount their joint historical origins, could not be more appropriate to a quintessential *neusachlich* sitter like the critic Max Hermann Neisse, whose writings would soon thereafter shift from supporting Communist Party poets like Johannes R. Becher to championing the conservative Expressionist, and eventually fascist, Gottfried Benn.

Grosz, who had referred to himself as having "the character of an icepack" had been programmatic in his changing approach to the subject and its representation. Thus he wrote in an essay entitled "On some of my recent paintings" in *Das Kunstblatt* of 1921:

> *I am trying once again to draw a totally realistic picture of the world.... If one makes an effort to develop a totally lucid and limpid style, one comes inevitably close to Carrà. Nevertheless,*

5 • George Grosz, *The Poet, Max Hermann Neisse*, 1927
Oil on canvas, 59.4 x 74 (23⅜ x 29⅛)

everything separates me from him, who wants to be appreciated in metaphysical terms and whose problematic is totally bourgeois.... Man *in my paintings is no longer represented with a deep exploration of his confused psyche, but as a collectivist concept, almost mechanical. Individual destiny has no longer any importance whatsoever.*

It has become evident, even if only fairly recently, that in the battle between photography and painting, between the machine and antiquity, the latter lost out. It is most certainly true on the territory of the portrait, where the true genius of Neue Sachlichkeit ▲ is August Sander, whose systematic archive of the multiplicity of possible social subject positions was recorded on the verge of the fascism that would annihilate them all. Here the photographic archive is infinitely more relevant to the history of the portrait than any of the above-mentioned painterly attempts to come to terms with the crisis of subjectivity in the twenties. Helmut Lethen has called photography during that period "an instrument of definition," that has generated the "photographic physiognomies of Modernity in which the signatures of the individual have become assimilated to the conditions of technical reproduction."

FURTHER READING

Anton Kaes et al., *The Weimar Republic Sourcebook* (Berkeley and Los Angeles: University of California Press, 1994)

Helmut Lethen, *Cool Conduct: The Culture of Distance in Weimar Germany* (Berkeley: University of California, 2002)

Detlev Peukert, *The Weimar Republic* (New York: Hill and Wang, 1989)

Wieland Schmied, "L'histoire d'une influence: Pittura Metafisica et Nouvelle Objectivité," in Jean Clair (ed.), *Les Réalismes 1919–1939* (Paris: Musée National d'Art Moderne, 1981)

Wieland Schmied, "Neue Sachlichkeit and the Realism of the Twenties," in Catherine Lampert (ed.), *Neue Sachlichkeit and German Realism of the Twenties* (London: Hayward Gallery, 1978)

▲ 1929, 1935, 1968a

1926

El Lissitzky's *Demonstration Room* and Kurt Schwitters's *Merzbau* are installed in Hanover, Germany: the architecture of the museum as archive and the allegory of modernist space as melancholia are dialectically conceived by the Constructivist and the Dadaist.

In July 1919 Kurt Schwitters (1887–1948) jettisoned both his formation as an academically trained landscape and portrait painter and his recent past as a member of the German Expressionist avant-garde by publicly declaring his discovery of a new type of picture-making. The name he gave this new project was "Merz," a syllable fragmented from a larger word, *Kommerz*, which he had accidentally found on a torn advertisement for the Hannover Kommerzbank when wandering round his native Hanover. It was on the grounds of that fragment that Schwitters developed an aesthetic both of collage and of phonetic, textual, and graphic segmentation that became one of the key contributions to German Dada.

In his initial practice of Merz, however, Schwitters maintained all the idioms of the Expressionist and Futurist aesthetic that had been so influential for the German avant-garde during the late teens. In early Merz works, such as *Welten Kreise* (1919), one can trace both the dynamic vectors and force-lines of Cubo-Futurism and the chromatic scheme of Expressionist painting. Yet what radically alters works from this period is Schwitters's insertion of found metallic, wooden, or other debris collected in the streets [**1**]. Morphologically and formally, one could even go so far as to sense a distant echo of ▲ Francis Picabia's mechanomorphic works in these paintings. Yet, as with all responses that Schwitters makes, in each instance, the • legacy—whether of Expressionism, Cubism, Futurism, or Picabia's Dadaism—is transformed into what one could call a specific mode of "melancholic" response. In his reaction to the total transformation of painting into a technological object, or in his response to the assimilation of mechanomorphic forms to the shapes of the composition, or in his response to Expressionism's high-flown humanitarian ideals, Schwitters situates himself as an artist who returns to an allegorical reading of techno-scientific utopianism by countering it with a position of melancholic contemplation.

The debris in Schwitters's work was, quite logically, not accepted as a credible commitment to Dada practices; and already in early ■ 1919, the leader of the Berlin Dada circle Richard Huelsenbeck had denounced Schwitters as "the Biedermeier" of German Dada (a reference to an early-nineteenth-century style in German art and life, and a term often used pejoratively to describe something as conventional or bourgeois), thereby calling attention to Schwitters's manifest concern for a continuation of painting as a space of contemplative experience. As Schwitters himself never tired of saying, the technological objects, the found materials in his work, only functioned in order to conceive of a new type of *painting*. They were never theorized as readymades that would displace painting, or as morphologies that deny the validity of drawing, or as chromatic objects that dismantle the legacy of visual intensity in Expressionist art. In all instances, Schwitters's ultimate goal remained one of conceiving what he called a "painting for contemporary experience."

A similar change took place in Schwitters's drawings at this time. Here the Expressionist idiom of angular, jagged profiles was suddenly juxtaposed with the mechanized imprint of found office stamps that Schwitters had collected and now deployed as elements of mechanical drawing. Yet, as in the collages, the emphasis stays focused on the construction of an object that is primarily

1 • Kurt Schwitters, *Merzbild Rossfett (Horse Fat)*, c. 1919
Assemblage, 20.4 x 17.4 (8 x 6⅞)

▲ 1916b, 1919 • 1908, 1909, 1911, 1912, 1916a ■ 1916a, 1920

legible as poetic or pictorial, never reducing the compositional structure or the reading order to a fully homogenized, mechani- ▲ cally produced image such as in Picabia's mechanomorphic portraits. Rather, the drawings operate within the tension between manual inscription and technologically based textual production.

A corresponding ambiguity can be traced in Schwitters's practice of abstract sound poetry. This lifelong project began most notoriously with *An Anna Blume*, a masterpiece of German alogical verse in the tradition of early-twentieth-century writers such as Christian Morgenstern. But if, in its shrill and ludicrous exclamation and its florid homage, Schwitters's writing is first of all a Dada derision of both the bathos of Expressionism and the sentimentality of turn-of-the-century German writing, its position nonetheless remains ambiguous. For once again, rather than focusing on the linguistic self-referentiality that Russian Cubo-Futurist poetry forges in the context of a Formalist theorization ● of language, Schwitters's poetry positions itself in an ambivalent relationship to the most radical dismantling of narrative and representation. Similarly, it occupies the same position with regard to the dismemberment of the poetic texts that Dada figures such as Raoul Hausmann were producing at that same moment in Berlin ■ as they foregrounded the grapheme over the phoneme, exclusively making the poem the subject of a totally nonlexical structure.

Schwitters's declaration from the outset that he had no political ambitions whatever, that he wanted his work to be situated within the tradition of painting, that his goals were utterly aesthetic and aimed at a new plastic formal order, set him at a further remove from Berlin Dada. Remaining in Hanover, with brief interruptions, and developing his own project, Schwitters soon became the center of a separate avant-garde scene, with friends and collaborators forming around him. The museum director Alexander Dorner, especially, became a crucial organizer and curator in bringing international avant-garde activities to the provincial city.

Schwitters and Lissitzky in collaboration

In 1925, Dorner invited the Russian Constructivist El Lissitzky to return to Germany to produce a major installation for the Landesgalerie Hannover (Lissitzky had studied architecture and engineering in Darmstadt from 1909 to 1914 and had stayed in Germany for long periods in the early twenties while collaborating on a number of projects). Schwitters first came into contact with Lissitzky and Russian Constructivism and Productivism in 1922, and the two artists became friends and collaborators. In 1923 Schwitters invited Lissitzky to become the designer and coeditor of issue 8/9 of his magazine *Merz* [**2**], published in April 1924 and called "Nasci" ("being born" or "becoming"), which was an explicitly programmatic alliance of Constructivist and Dadaist ideals. While in historical hindsight it seems unlikely that these two models would have provided the basis of fruitful exchange, it is precisely in the collaboration between Lissitzky and Schwitters at the moment of 1926 that the productivity of such an encounter can be most adequately traced.

2 • El Lissitzky, cover design for Kurt Schwitters's *Merz*, no. 8/9, April–July 1924

By then both artists had been increasingly transforming their projects from pictorial or sculptural work into the investigation of architectural space. In his *Proun Room* for the Great Berlin Art Exhibition of 1923, for example, Lissitzky had transformed his ideas into three-dimensional form for the first time, designing the walls and ceilings with geometric shapes and reliefs [**3**]. An additional element was Dorner's intensifying attempt to theorize the new forms of display, the redesign of traditional museum spaces in favor of an adequate representation and display of avant-garde practices in painting and sculpture. Lissitzky had already designed a space for the 1926 International Exhibition in Dresden in which to show international, avant-garde, abstract art. For his first model, he rigorously emphasized walls on which the works would be hung by installing vertical wooden battens, spaced equidistant all across the display surfaces and painted white, gray, and black, and by placing the paintings on those surfaces. Ironically, the eventual master design of the 1926 Dresden exhibition was placed in the hands of the reactionary German architect Heinrich Tessenow, who would soon become known for his staunch advocacy of the return of architecture to an antimodernist regionalism.

It was Lissitzky's preliminary design for Dresden that made Dorner decide to invite the Russian to Hanover, and it was there that Lissitzky produced a second version of the cabinet for the display of abstract art, called the *Demonstration Room* [**4**]. During

▲ 1916b, 1919 ● 1915 ■ 1920

3 • El Lissitzky, *Proun Room*, 1923 (1965 reconstruction)
3,000 x 300 x 260 (1181½ x 118⅛ x 102⅜)

this extended stay in Hanover, Schwitters and Lissitzky further developed their friendship. Schwitters had by now also moved away from painting and collage to his own first architectural project, which came to be known as the *Merzbau* [**5**]. Beginning in his studio on the ground floor of his own private house, he gradually transformed all aspects of the traditional cubic space of the domestic room into an increasingly distorted, multiperspectival spatial structure, installing wooden, painted reliefs and loading various objects and additional forms into the spaces created.

The opposition between the *Merzbau* and the *Demonstration Room* and the close bond between their two authors produce one of the most puzzling moments of mid-twenties German avant-garde history. Yet one bridge that links the two is their focus on the issue of tactility and bodily experience in relation to the work of art. For Lissitzky's project to accommodate avant-garde painting and sculpture within the museum now focused primarily on Dorner's call for a new participatory mode of reading and perceiving. Dorner's project was to reconceive the museum as a space of author/object/spectator collaboration mediated through an increased experience of tactility. In the installation that Lissitzky designed, with its emphasis on drawers and cabinets and shelves that the spectator could open and move, thereby being directly involved in the repositioning of him- or herself as a spectator or in the positioning of the object in a new relationship, tactility and tangibility were clearly elements of a radically altered mode of perceptual interaction, changing the contemplative space of the museum into an archive.

But what Dorner's vision had not anticipated was the specific contribution that Lissitzky was to introduce into the design of the *Demonstration Room*. The transformation of the exhibition space and its display devices and conventions led him to articulate the actual historical transformation of the institution of the museum,

4 • El Lissitzky, *The Abstract Cabinet: Demonstration Room* in the Landesgalerie, Hanover, 1927–8 (1935 installation view)

as well as the actual status of the object displayed within it. The new situation moved the art work, that is, from being an object of cultic origins to one of pure exhibition-value, from being an object of transhistorical intelligibility to one of historical specificity, of the kind necessary to archival purposes. Those ideas about the need to transform the museum in terms of its functions, its audience, and its institutional definition had emerged in the Soviet Union as early as 1919, when artists discussed the reorientation of the aesthetic object from cult to exhibition and the transformation of viewing spaces from ones of ritual to ones of archival dimensions.

Apart from this shared interest in tactility, however, Schwitters's *Merzbau* inverted every single aspect of Lissitzky's approach, which we could call the rationalist transformation of the last residual ritualistic element in the display and reading of the work of art. In contrast, the *Merzbau*'s space was reconceived as specifically ritualistic, with the object and its display welded into an almost Wagnerian drive toward the condition of the *Gesamtkunstwerk*, in which all the senses, all perceptual elements, would be unified in an overall intensified form of visual, cognitive, and somatic—that is, physical—interaction with the objects, structures, and materials on display. Schwitters's attempt to construct a grotto, or a *Bau*, carried all the connotations that word has in German: from an animal burrow (the original ▲ meaning of *Bau*) to the famous Bauhaus declaration in which the medieval guilds of community and communality building cathedrals

▲ 1923

in a preindustrial society and the structure of the collective could be invoked. These sources came together in his perpetual insertions into the overall display of objects, textures, and materials that emphasize the somatic dimension of perception. Thus he brought the solicited residues of bodily secretions into the building (bottles of urine, for instance, or snippets of friends' hair), which he stored and inserted into the various layers of the structure. He thereby fabricated a manifestly nonrational, nonarchival, noninstitutional space, in which a certain regression into the totality of an unconscious architectural space was conceived, and called it *The Cathedral of Erotic Misery.*

Two extremes of avant-garde design

Schwitters's *Merzbau* and Lissitzky's *Demonstration Room* could therefore be theorized as the two extreme opposites of the possibilities of avant-garde design in the twenties. Clearly, compared with the ideology of the Bauhaus, neither Schwitters nor Lissitzky belongs to the utopianism of a Bauhaus spirit that was attempting at the same moment to transform everyday life and domestic architecture through a mode of rationalization and a form of democratized consumption. Specifically in the *Merzbau*, which would be continued throughout Schwitters's life (after the *Merzbau* in Hanover was destroyed by Allied bombing in 1943, Schwitters installed a second version in Norway, to where he had emigrated in 1937 after his work ▲ had appeared in the "Degenerate 'Art'" exhibition in Munich, and a third—the *Merzbarn*—near Ambleside in northern England, just before his death in 1948), the idea of a space of radical rationalization was refused on every single level. This project of instrumentalizing or rationalizing space was intended to reach right down to the most intimate sphere of everyday life, where function reigned supreme, as daily activities were submitted to planning, control, and the principle of greater efficiency. In the light of this, Schwitters's *Merzbau* proposed a space of total inefficiency, utter dysfunction, a complete refusal to subject spatial experience to rationality, transparency, and instrumentalization. By emphasizing the space as the ground, the grotto, and a home of a different kind, Schwitters created a secularized but at the same time ritualized space of bodily function, one of bodily retrieval outside and in opposition to a rigorously controlled public sphere.

Despite its appearance, Lissitzky's space is also dramatically different from the functional realm of Bauhaus design, specifically because of its theoretical accommodation of the radically transformed conditions of perception of the work of art. That is, Lissitzky's space is in a sense a program for the retheorization of the institution of the museum. If it has been misread as a dynamic display of abstract, avant-garde art, to which it supposedly lends support through its streamlined design, that false interpretation should be counteracted by emphasizing the degree to which Lissitzky saw the museum as being increasingly transformed into the mere institution of historicization and archival order. Thus, inasmuch as Lissitzky recognized that the cognitive and perceptual modes still embedded in easel painting were no longer to be rescued or redeemed by even the most advanced forms of abstraction, he had already subjected the avant-

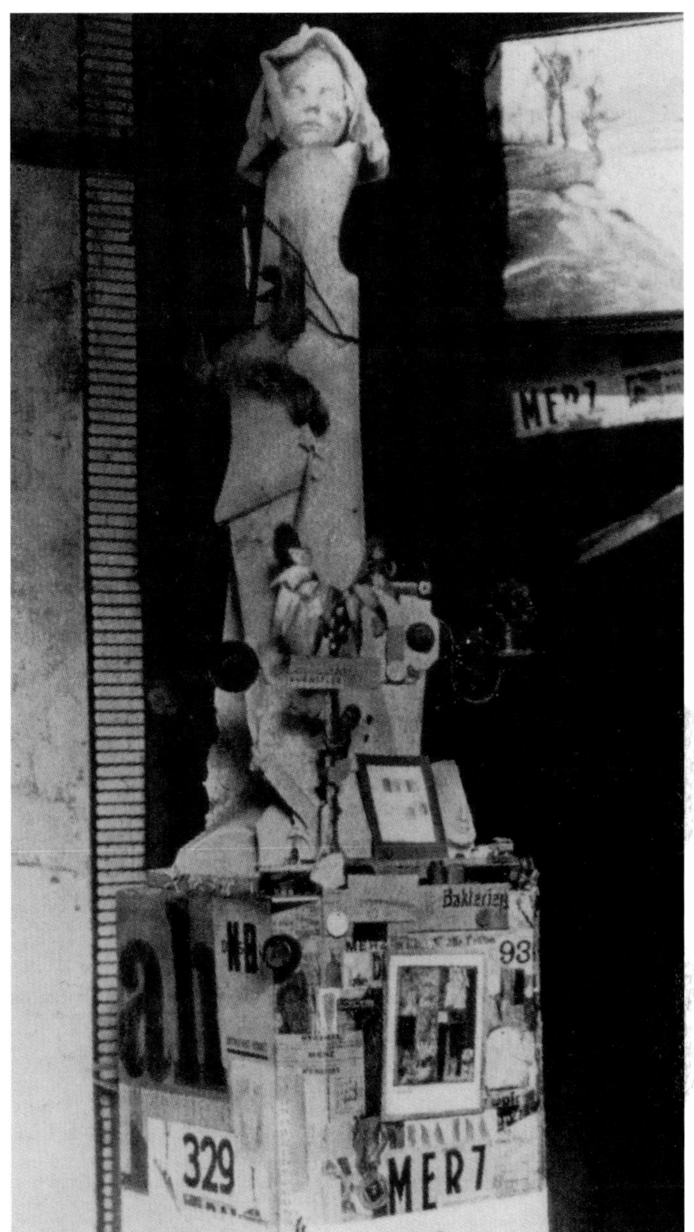

5 • Kurt Schwitters, *The Hanover Merzbau: The Merz Column*, 1923.
Mixed media, dimensions unknown (destroyed)

garde promise of abstraction to an internal critique. Looking at the display of the specimens of abstraction in the *Demonstration Room*, one can—with hindsight of course—recognize that even in the way these objects are displayed there is already a certain critical operation taking place. This is because Lissitzky's reliefs—wall structures, cabinets, drawers, movable panels—become the ultimate work of art, while the abstract paintings, in all their radicality, become mere illustrations of an aesthetic that had already been superseded.

FURTHER READING

Elizabeth Burns Gamard, *Kurt Schwitters' Merzbau* (Princeton: Princeton Architectural Press, 2000)
John Elderfield, *Kurt Schwitters* (London: Thames & Hudson, 1985)
Joan Ockman, "The road not taken: Alexander Dorner's way beyond art," in R. E. Somol (ed.), *Autonomy and Ideology: Positioning an Avant-Garde in America* (New York: The Monacelli Press, 1997)
Nancy Perloff and Brian Reed (eds), *Situating El Lissitzky: Issues and Debates* (Los Angeles: Getty Research Institute, 2003)
Henning Rischbieter (ed.), *Die Zwanziger Jahre in Hannover* (Hanover: Kunstverein Hannover, 1962)

▲ 1937a

1927a

After working as a commercial artist in Brussels, René Magritte joins the Surrealist movement in Paris, where his art plays on the idioms of advertising and the ambiguities of language and representation.

While still in Brussels, René Magritte (1898–1967) operated a studio specializing in commercial art from a garage behind his house; thereafter in Paris he often turned to book design and advertising work to support himself. For some critics, his deadpan representational style was always distressingly close to that of commercial art, but his experience in this field might also account for his abiding interest in the relation between figurative and verbal forms of representation, and the interaction—often the interference—between these ways of evoking an object or suggesting an idea. It might also explain his later willingness to issue the most important of his paintings in multiple copies. His most famous painting, *The Treachery of Images* [**1**], in which the picture of a pipe is captioned "This is not a pipe" ("Ceci n'est pas une pipe"), was issued at least five times, once as a large sign. Another, *Dominion of Light* (1952), in which a darkened house illuminated by streetlamps stands in a night landscape but is seen against a daytime sky, was reproduced in sixteen oil and seven gouache versions (the first in 1949, the last in 1964). In 1965 he would plagiarize his own *The Great Family* (1963)—an image in which the silhouette of an object (in this case, a bird; in *The Seducer*, a ship) is "fleshed out" by the substance of its milieu (here, clouds; there, waves)—to produce *Skybird* for Sabena Airlines, with the understanding that it would be used for publicity campaigns.

1920–1929

The potential complementarity of fine and commercial arts depended on the nature of mass culture. Stimulated by advertising, desire for a commodity became a craving less for a unique object than for one of many copies. As Walter Benjamin argued in ▲ "The Work of Art in the Age of Mechanical Reproduction" (1936), such desire aims to extract a sense of equivalence "even from a unique object by way of reproduction." Sucking the very idea of uniqueness and distance (or what Benjamin called "aura") out of lived experience, the culture of the commodity prepares simultaneously for the seductions of media imagery and the spectacle of an artist pirating his own work.

Everything in the Surrealist position, however, would seem to shun the prefabricated and the mass-produced. Everything would seem to be geared, instead, to the unrepeatable moment of shock in which the most banal object of everyday life would be reinfused • with wonder and revelatory power—what André Breton called "the marvelous" and theorized as "objective chance." As Surrealist artists lent themselves to jewelry design, department-store display, and Hollywood set design during the thirties and after the war, the commercialization of the movement struck a postwar generation of artists as a travesty of the Surrealist mission to transform reality in order to create a revolutionary consciousness. In 1962, on the occasion of Magritte's retrospective at Knokke-le-Zoute, Belgium, Marcel Mariën (1920–93), a second-generation Belgian Surrealist and editor of *Naked Lips*, circulated a leaflet to the magazine's subscribers titled "Big Reductions" and fraudulently signed "Magritte." At the top of the sheet a Belgian banknote was reproduced with Magritte's head montaged over that of King Leopold I. Below, Magritte is made to complain that his paintings are being used for sordid speculation, being bought like land, fur coats, or jewels. "I have decided to put an end to this shameful exploitation of mystery," the text goes on, "by bringing it within reach of every purse. Below will be found the necessary details [a mail-order form] which, I hope, will bring rich and poor together at the feet of genuine mystery. (The frame is not included in the price.)"

Repetition compulsion

It is possible to argue, however, that Magritte's fascination with and practice of the multiple was not a function of a slackening of his Surrealist "purity." Many of his earliest paintings are internally composed through recourse to the multiple. His 1928 portrait of Paul Nougé (1895–1967) doubles a single image of the Belgian poet, while *The Murderous Sky* [**2**] suspends the same bloody corpse of a bird four times against the background of a rocky cliff. Indeed, it could be said that what allows one to identify Magritte as a Surrealist is the sense that a form of doubling grips his work from the very start, infusing it with a version of just that Surrealist ▲ practice of the double that was connected to the Freudian concept of the uncanny and the compulsion to repeat.

Freud had identified the feeling of uncanniness as a sense of the return of something archaic, and had analyzed the accompanying anxiety as related to the death drive's compulsion to repeat; the uncanny could thus be said to be a kind of eruption of the nonliving in the midst of life: a return of the living dead. It is this

▲ 1935 • 1924 ▲ Introduction 1, 1924

1 • René Magritte, *The Treachery of Images*, 1929
Oil on canvas, 60 x 81 (23½ x 31½)

character that suffuses Magrittean imagery such as the whole series related to *The Human Condition* [**3**], in which the painting shows a landscape against which is superimposed a painting of the same landscape, the edges of the nested representation nearly fusing with what must now be recognized as the "merely" representational status of the master image, formerly understood as transparently real. Thus the dead double (the representation) erupts among the living reality to threaten its solidity, to suck out its substance, like the vampires that return by means of mirrors.

Within the context of Surrealism, Roger Caillois had offered an alternative example for the spookiness of the living dead. With the case of animal mimicry, in which a dizzying perspective is offered by the praying mantis of death imitating life imitating death, there ▲ opens a vertiginous hall of mirrors that would come to be identified during the sixties with the term *simulacrum*. Like the dead animal "playing dead," the simulacrum offers a case of resemblance in which a crucial internal thread between similar things is cut: "life" in the example of the mantis; "the absence of sin" in the instance of post-Fall humanity (man was originally made in the image of God; after the Fall he no longer resembles Him). In the two examples just given, however, there is an ultimate court of appeal that will allow one to distinguish the living insect from its dead copy or the innocent from the sinner. The ultimate simulacral state, however, is where there is no way to differentiate copy from original, dead from living. This is a state of multiples *without* ▲ originals. Michel Foucault would invoke that state at the very end of "Ceci n'est pas une pipe," his 1968 essay on Magritte and the simulacral: "A day will come when, by means of similitude relayed indefinitely along the length of a series, the image itself, along with the name it bears, will lose its identity. Campbell, Campbell, Campbell, Campbell [a reference to Andy Warhol's soup cans]."

It was during the very period of the early sixties, when Magritte was appearing to his fellow artists in Belgium to have sold out to the enemy, that Foucault was developing a theory of literature positively based on the idea of the simulacrum (although in a way unrelated to Surrealism). One example of this work, his book *Death and the Labyrinth* (1963) dealing with the writer Raymond Roussel, was known to Magritte, himself interested in Roussel's

▲ 1930b

▲ 1971

2 • René Magritte, *The Murderous Sky*, 1927
Oil on canvas, 73 x 100 (28½ x 39)

procedures for draining the meaning out of words (like the dead sucking life out of the living). In 1966 Magritte's attention was also drawn to Foucault's recently published *The Order of Things*, the title of which coincided with the name of Magritte's own current exhibition. He and Foucault exchanged letters during 1966; Foucault's interest led him in 1968 to address Magritte's work directly.

Using Magritte's *The Treachery of Images* as his essay's object lesson, Foucault's analysis turned on (what in French is called) "the object-lesson" itself. This is the grammar-school session in which, say, a teacher draws a picture on the blackboard and underneath it writes its name. Such a combination of picture and name Foucault calls a *lieu commun*, a "commonplace," or in the literal sense of the page, a "common ground," referring to the convention we experience from our very first A.B.C. book ("A is for apple; B is for baby; C is for ...") through to textbook explanations, dictionary entries, or scientific manuals of all kinds. It is a convention in which the channel of white space separating the domain of the illustration from the realm of the text in fact binds them together with all the ▲ powerful glue of what the philosopher Ludwig Wittgenstein would sometimes call a "language game" and at other times "a form of life."

The power of this convention is first that the fact of representation disappears within the object-lesson. Thus Foucault writes: "No matter that it is the material deposit, on a sheet of paper or a blackboard, of a little graphite or a thin dust of chalk. It does not 'aim' like an arrow or a pointer toward a particular [object] in the distance or elsewhere. It *is* [that object]." Second, the relationship encoded in the picture–caption couple is that of truth—between the image (as copy) and the model in the world to which it is transparent; for this reason, "the commonplace" serves as the basis for knowledge: "It is there," Foucault writes, referring to the channel linking image and caption, "on these few millimeters of white, the calm sand of the page, that are established all the relations of designation, nomination, description, classification."

Apparently challenging the banality of the commonplace, the modernist tradition of "the calligram" is only, Foucault argues, a ▲ covert attempt to reinforce it. When Guillaume Apollinaire writes a poem about rain in vertical lines of type that imitate rain, he assumes that he has collapsed the two-part structure of the commonplace into a higher order of synthesis in which *rain* (the word) disappears into its object made newly present on the page. Commenting that this transparency is futile, since to read the poem we have to disregard the image it forms, and to see the image we have to ignore the words, Foucault argues that the problematic of the calligram nonetheless serves as Magritte's point of departure, since what is happening in *The Treachery of Images* is a form of "unraveled calligram."

The work is calligrammatic in that the substance of the writing—"this is not a pipe"—and that of the image are so manifestly a matter of the same laborious hand (here the banality of Magritte's style of rendering serves this outcome). But this calligram is unrav-

▲ 1958

▲ 1911, 1912

3 • René Magritte, *The Human Condition*, 1933
Oil on canvas, 100 x 81 (39⅜ x 31⅞)

eled because it ironically undoes both the tautological urgency of the picture-poem and the truth content of the object-lesson at one and the same time. Such undoing turns on the operation of the *this* in the work, which functions in at least three ways at once, finally producing a confusion that aborts its operation completely. Does *this* in "This is not a pipe" point to the word "pipe" and thus the nonresemblance between word and picture? Does it point to itself, the word *this*, and thus the nonresemblance between this form of language and representation? Does it point to the object-lesson as a whole, and thus the nonresemblance between it and the real-world model to which it is supposed to be transparent? All of these nonresemblances being true, what falls apart within this ironic maneuver is the "truth" that language tries to encode in what it takes to be the primal force of the indexical aspect of language crystallized in the term *this*.

Returning to the channel of white that binds object and caption, Foucault concludes that if "the calligram absorbed that interstice," Magritte's calligram-against-the-grain reopens "the trap the calligram had sprung on the thing it described. But in the act, the object itself escaped.... The trap shattered on emptiness: image and text fall each to its own side, of their own weight. No longer do they have a *common ground*." And if the object (the real-world model) disappears from the place of knowledge, as the guarantee of its truth-value lying behind it but always transparent to it, what is left is the simulacral condition, a world of multiples without originals.

The unraveled museum

Developing as a young poet in the forties within the orbit of Magritte and other Belgian Surrealists such as Paul Nougé, as well ▲ as Marcel Mariën and Christian Dotrement, Marcel Broodthaers initially shared the ambivalence toward Magritte expressed in "Big Reductions." But in the course of establishing his "Musée d'Art Moderne" after 1968, Broodthaers began to draw close to the idea of a simulacral operation of language, and Magritte, mediated by Foucault's text, became strategically important to him. Thus in "The Eagle from the Oligocene to the Present," the exhibition his "Musée d'Art Moderne, Département des Aigles" mounted in 1972 in Düsseldorf, he displayed hundreds of objects each accompanied by a label stating "This is not a work of art." Explaining this caption by saying that "This is not a work of art'" is a formula obtained by the contraction of a concept by Marcel Duchamp and an antithetical • concept by Magritte, Broodthaers reproduced Duchamp's *Fountain* and Magritte's *The Treachery of Images* in the exhibition catalogue on facing pages and advised the reader to read Foucault's "Ceci n'est pas une pipe."

One way of understanding such a "contraction" is first, to see the object-lesson performed by Duchamp's readymade as pointing to the entire institutional context in which the work of art occurs, since it is that context that folds onto the ordinary object—urinal, curry comb, hat rack—to confer artistic status on it; and second, to feel the way that lesson is confounded by the multiple arrows of Magritte's "unraveled calligram"—pointing now to the label itself (as not being a work of art), now to the objects on display, many of which, like stuffed eagles or corks with eagles printed on them, are nonaesthetic in status (and thus not works of art), and now to the whole of the exhibition in its condition as "fictitious." For if Duchamp had wanted to expose the institution of the museum as conventional, Broodthaers is now displaying it as simulacral.

FURTHER READING

Thierry de Duve, "Echoes of the Readymade: Critique of Pure Modernism," *October*, no. 70, Fall 1994

Michel Foucault, "Ceci n'est pas une pipe," *Les Cahiers du Chemin* (1968), expanded as *Ceci n'est pas une pipe* (1973), and translated as "This Is Not a Pipe," trans. James Harkness (Berkeley: Quantum, 1983)

Denis Hollier, "The Word of God: 'I am dead'," *October*, no. 44, Spring 1988

David Sylvester and Sarah Whitfield, *René Magritte: Catalogue Raisonné*, five volumes (Houston: Menil Foundation; and London: Philip Wilson Publishers, 1992–7)

▲ Introduction 4, 1972a • 1914

1927b

Constantin Brancusi produces a stainless-steel cast of *The Newborn*: his sculpture unleashes a battle between models of high art and industrial production, brought to a head in the US trial over his *Bird in Space*.

▲ During the four weeks in 1907 when Constantin Brancusi (1876–1957) was one of the fifty assistants working for France's most famous sculptor, Auguste Rodin, he would have been exposed to two, antithetical phenomena. First, as one of a contingent of "pointers"—operators of caliper-like devices used to transfer a sculptural idea from its plaster model to the marble block (often to make enlargements or reductions)—he would have seen the travesty of the aesthetic "original" wrought by a kind of assembly-line production. Second, as the talented graduate hired by Rodin fresh from the École des Beaux-Arts, he would have experienced the other side of the master's practice in which, as though by magic, Rodin caught the most ephemeral gestures of a troupe of Balinese dancers weaving before him, suggesting the delicacy of their movements out of simple rolls of clay.

This latter output, the very opposite of the former, contained the • quintessence of what Walter Benjamin would call "aura," namely the uniqueness of something captured at a particular moment and in a particular place, this never-to-be-repeated quality resonating in the uniqueness of the medium, itself the result of a personalized touch. Relating this aura back to art's earliest sources in religious ritual, Benjamin pointed to the necessity that the cult object be an original in order to work its effect, for which substitutes or copies would be powerless. Secularization did nothing to diminish this importance of the aura-filled, aesthetic original, and from the Renaissance to Romanticism an ever higher premium was paid not only for the originality of a given artist's conception but also for the sense that the line or brush-stroke that delivered that idea was inimitable. Rodin's dancers, caught on the wing in a pinch of clay that bears the imprint of the master, could be said to be the supreme example of this desire. His marbles and bronzes in multiple copies, on the other hand, point instead to the type of art industry—with its traffic in replicas—that characterizes the decorative, rather than the fine, arts.

The birth of the world

Fleeing Rodin's studio after just one month, Brancusi adopted an approach to sculpture that could be said to be the exact opposite of this industrialization. For on the wood or stone he was able to salvage (being too poor then to buy his materials), he began to work without the intermediary of the clay or plaster model, carving directly into the block instead. The aesthetic honesty of such "direct carving" operates on two levels. First, it responds to the specific nature of the material in which it is fashioned, involving none of the transfers from modeled clay to stone or plaster and bronze through which traditional sculpture was conceived. Second, the immediacy of this response resists replication, ruling out the production of the multiple.

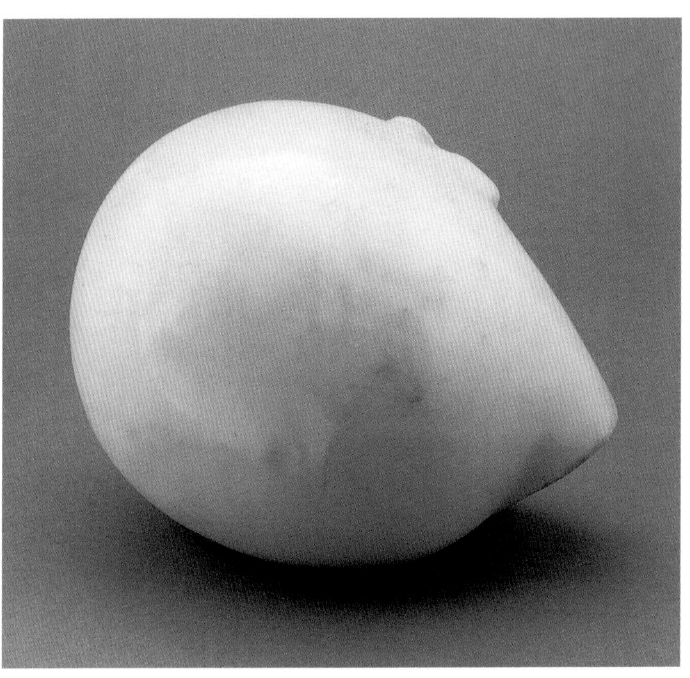

1 • Constantin Brancusi, *Prometheus*, 1911
Marble, 13.8 x 17.8 x 13.7 (5⅜ x 7 x 5⅜)

The ethos of direct carving brought other associations, all of which were welcomed by Brancusi, who began increasingly to affect the bearing of a Romanian peasant, wearing a long beard, worker's smock, and sandals. The rural wood-carving traditions of his native land were a reinforcement to his antiestablishment position, supporting as they did the influence of African and other primitive sculpture evident in his work by 1914. That in succumbing to such an influence he was merely following the rest of the Parisian avant-garde, first in its enthusiasm for Paul Gauguin (who had initiated ▲ direct carving within this milieu) and then for a wider primitivism, was something Brancusi did not like to admit, so adamant was he

▲ 1900a • 1935 ▲ 1903, 1907

that he stood outside the historical drive of modernism, so focused was he on the presumed timelessness and universality of his work.

Indeed it is this search for the historically unmediated that seems to underlie the course of Brancusi's art as it pursued forms of increasing simplification and purity. The trajectory of a single idea, as it moves from a realistic child's torso, its head bent in a caress of shoulder and cheek (*The Supplicant II*, 1907), to the suddenly isolated head as simplified oval lying on its side (*Head of a Sleeping Child*, 1908), to a sphere whose teardroplike appendage produces neck and shoulder with breathtaking economy and barely breaks the spherical surface with a whisper of the facial features [**1**], to an egglike form creased longitudinally and beveled at one end [**2**] to suggest at one and the same time the ovum and its moment of splitting into multiple cells, to a prone, entirely featureless ovoid, demonstrates this rage for reduction. Many of Brancusi's admirers saw this as a kind of Platonism, as when Ezra Pound wrote an early appreciation of the works as the "master-keys to the world of form," typically viewing Brancusi's sculptural gift as a genius for releasing the eidetic form—the pure "idea"—from the physical matter of the initial block.

The high finishes that Brancusi applied to his works, beginning with the bronze version of *Prometheus* in 1911, in which meticulous (and arduous) hand polishing brings the surface to a mirrorlike shine, only reinforce this sense of perfection. Thus, when a polished bronze version of *Sculpture for the Blind*, now titled *The Beginning of the World* [**3**], is set on an equally polished steel plate, the facing mirror surfaces concentrate the effect of the encapsulation of the "idea" behind its glittering surface.

The same finish was applied to Brancusi's *Bird in Space*, first rendered in sleek marble in 1923 and then in highly polished bronze in 1924 (to be repeated in bronze in 1927 [**4**], 1931, and 1941). This sculpture, delicately elongated and plumelike, is part bird's body, part outstretched wing, and part vision of the effortless rise into flight. In its condensation of gesture it seems to hark back to that aspect of Rodin's work that had not compromised its aura: those matchless dancers that had emanated from his fingers.

With this mention of Rodin, however, something quite contrary enters the discussion of Brancusi. For, like the master, this rustic "peasant" needed his own band of assistants to rub the marbles and bronzes into a perfect state of polish and, like Rodin, he was in the habit of issuing many of his pieces in small "editions"; furthermore, these gleaming objects with their slightly Africanized shapes and their mixture of svelte metallic contours and crenellated wooden bases, could easily slip over into a family resemblance with ▲ the most fashionable of decorative idioms, namely Art Deco, the twenties marriage of chrome and stainless steel, ebony and zebra skin, primitivism and industrialization. Far from being timeless and universal, Brancusi's work thus participates in the entirely historical phenomenon of stylistic change and, more "degradingly,"

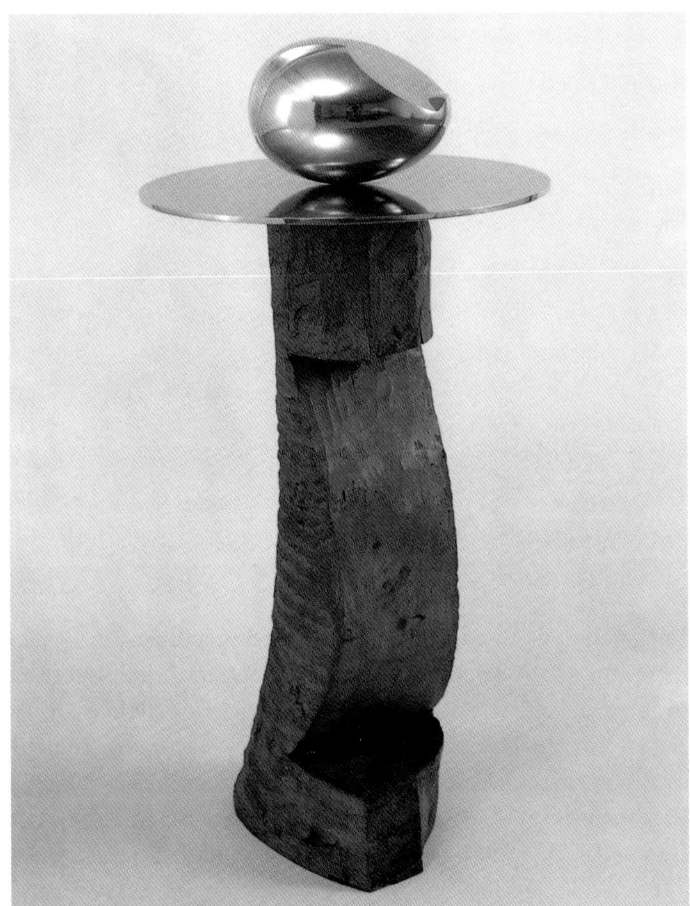

2 • Constantin Brancusi, *The Newborn II*, 1927
Stainless steel 17.2 x 24.5 x 17 (6¾ x 9⅝ x 6¾)

3 • Constantin Brancusi, *The Beginning of the World*, 1924
Bronze, 17.8 x 28.5 x 17.6 (7 x 11¼ x 6⅞)

▲ 1925a

in the revolving door of style known as fashion—a version of the "art industry" even more compromised than Rodin's.

Nothing could betray this connection more directly than the commission Brancusi undertook for the Vicomte de Noailles, who wanted a large version of the *Bird in Space* for the garden of his opulent country house. Designed by the fashionable architect Robert Mallet-Stevens, the 1923 mansion is pure Art Deco, a mixture of concrete, glass, and chrome; Brancusi's 150-feet-tall sculpture, it was decided, should be executed in stainless steel. Jean Prouvé, an architect who had pioneered in this medium, took charge of the project, and the two men embarked on a trial cast of *The Newborn* **[2]** before attempting the monumental version of the other work.

The result of their trial is pure paradox: part platonic solid, part ball bearing. On the surface there is no difference between this 1927 cast and the 1923 bronze, except one is "silver" and the other is "gold." But that is just the point. By allowing his "idea" to be submitted to industrialization—by using a material developed for mass production, one whose gleam has nothing to do with aura and everything to do with multiplicity—Brancusi produced a retroactive critique of his own aesthetic posture. Not only are his surfaces compromised by being twinned with high-end decoration, but his deep involvement with serialization is itself a version of industrial method. As he set the restricted number of his themes on their paths toward ever greater formal reduction, he was working serially. And then, once his repertory of forms had been established (by 1923), he repeated these over and over, with minor variations, until his death in 1957.

At the same time as Brancusi was working with Prouvé, a commotion was stirring the art world on the other side of the Atlantic. ▲When Edward Steichen tried to bring his recently purchased version of *Bird in Space* into New York for a large retrospective of Brancusi's work, US Customs officials classed the sculpture as a kitchen utensil, and thus as mass-produced, unoriginal, ready made, and requiring the payment of import duty, rather than as a work of art, which would have been duty free. Their decision was repeated a few weeks later when Marcel Duchamp entered the Port of New York with the large Brancusi he owned. Numerous protests, in which powerful American art collectors weighed in, were to no avail. The headline "Brancusi's Art Is Not Art, Federal Customs Men Rule" made front-page news in January 1927. It was not until these patrons, armed with prominent lawyers and art experts, took the case to trial in October 1927 that the decision was overturned, the courts admitting that something had changed in art to make Brancusi's work eligible for duty-free status. Accordingly, the judgment read:

> *There has been developing a so-called new school of art, whose exponents attempt to portray abstract ideas rather than to imitate natural objects.... The object is made of harmonious and symmetrical lines and while some difficulty might be encountered in associating it with a bird, it is nevertheless pleasing to look at and highly ornamental, and as we hold under the evidence that it is the original production of a professional sculptor ... we sustain the protest and find that it is entitled to free entry.*

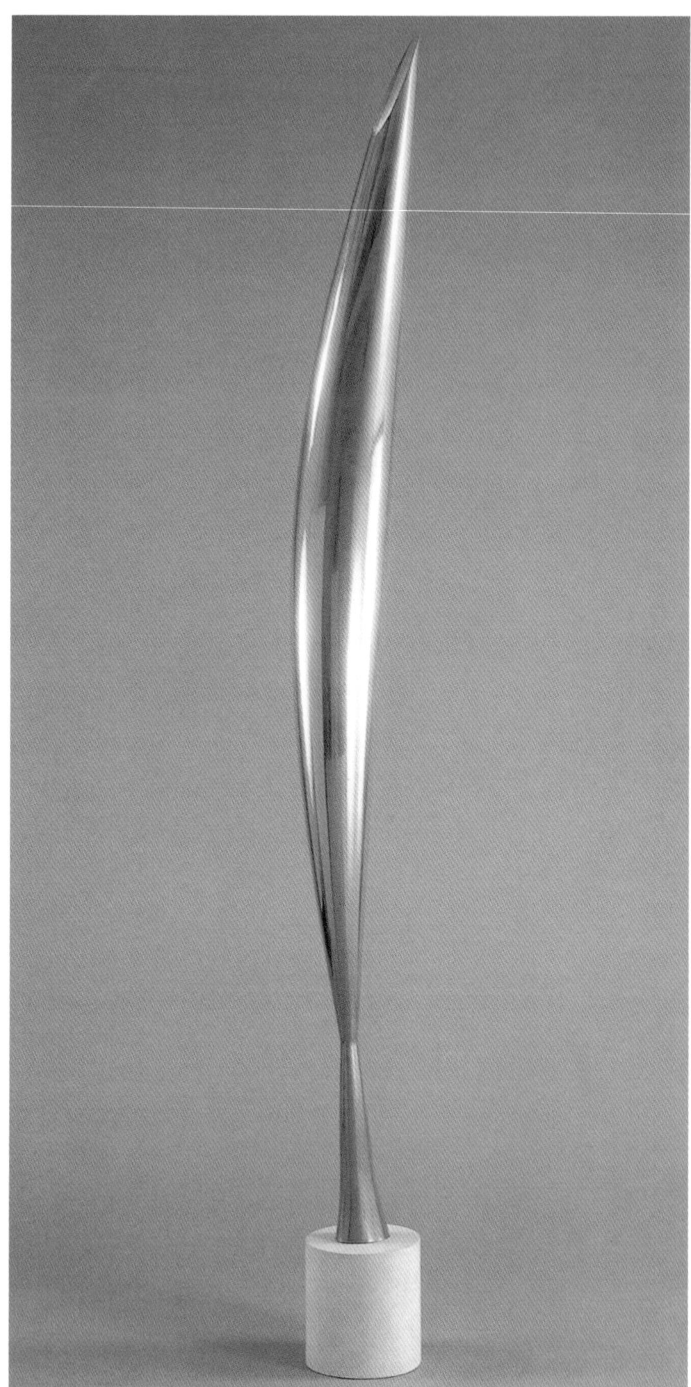

4 • Constantin Brancusi, *Bird in Space*, 1927
Bronze, height 184.1 ($72\frac{1}{2}$), circumference 44.8 ($17\frac{5}{8}$)

Buying the arguments of the critics, collectors, and museum directors ranged on its behalf, the judge accepted the idea that Brancusi's work was redeemed by its abstraction and its formal purity. The philistines working in the Customs Office were thereby seen as beneath contempt. Yet history often has exquisite jokes up its sleeve, one of them being the strange relationship between this Romanian "peasant" purist and the father of the readymade. Brancusi first met Duchamp in Fernand Léger's presence, so the story goes, at an aeronautics fair in Paris in 1912. Marveling at a propeller on display, Duchamp asked his new friend if he could do any

▲ 1916b, 1959d

better. His own conviction that no artist could led him the following year to present *Bicycle Wheel* as the first readymade, while Brancusi's response, it could be argued, was not only the *Bird in Space*—part propeller, part Mallarméan suggestion—but the whole ambivalence of his work's development, one aspect of which the men at Customs unerringly grasped.

The links between Duchamp and Brancusi do not stop at this peculiar double helix in which the industrial readymade crosses with a notion of "art" as inviolate concept. The two are also connected via a shared ambiguity between pure and impure at the level of carnality, since Duchamp's marriage between the industrially impersonal and ▲ the erotic—his *Fountain, Female Fig Leaf*, the entire scenario of the *Large Glass*, etc.—is echoed in Brancusi's mystic union between the abstract and the libidinal. Nowhere is this more obvious than in *Princesse X* [**5**], which was censored from the 1920 Salon des Indépendants on the grounds of obscenity, the purity of the artist's reduction of female torso to the double ovoids of the breasts connected by the curving tube of the neck to the ovoid of the head being redescribed—by Picasso, among others—as simply phallic. Although Brancusi protested any such connection, he continued to photograph the work from the angle that underscored this association. And indeed the kinds of reductions to which he submitted the human body seemed inevitably to participate in the logic of the part object, in which the whole body, in being metonymically rendered by a purified fragment, increasingly takes on the character of a sexual organ. This is particularly true of Brancusi's series of elegantly simplified male torsos (1917–24), which come to be suspended between a phallic representation and the "elbow" of a plumbing connection.

It is possible to take this opening onto the sexual and to recode it in terms of an iconography of the self-creating (male) body. Here it becomes important that what is male in Brancusi's *Torso* is its overall phallic shape, since the lithe body itself, without a penis, is to all intents and purposes female. This bi-gendering, so prominent in *Princesse X*, is read by such an interpretive strategy as a fantasy of male primacy involving the circumvention of the female body in a dream of omnipotent self-regeneration, a regeneration that can then be carried into the whole of Brancusi's work, with the *Bird in Space* now seen as a version of the immortal phoenix, and the *Newborns* as a way of bypassing the female in an act of parthenogenesis.

This strategy marries the eroticism of Brancusi's sculpture with the modernist drive toward autonomy, so that biological self-creation becomes the "unconscious" analogue for the formal desire to make an object that is self-contained. This, however, is to cut the eroticism of Brancusi's sculptures off from the industrial logic that functions as their (very different) "unconscious." A final story of Brancusi's connection to Duchamp makes clear the strange workings of this logic.

The story begins with the 1924 death of John Quinn, one of Brancusi's most enthusiastic American collectors. To save Brancusi's prices from the catastrophe of having many works dumped on the market at one time, Duchamp stepped in and, with the novelist Henri-Pierre Roché, bought the twenty-nine pieces in Quinn's collection at the fire-sale price of $8,500 for the lot. If Duchamp had stopped making art for sale in the early twenties, he had nonetheless now acquired a huge body of work by another artist, from the sale of which he was able to live. Brancusi was thus a participant in Duchamp's playing at every role within the institutional structure of art, from artist to critic to museum director to publisher and now to dealer. In 1933 when asked if he thought painters should be less professional, Duchamp replied that they should be more so, but that among dealers a bit of amateurishness would be welcome. It was Duchamp who was the perfect amateur "dealer" with just one artist in his stable; and Brancusi was, apparently, perfectly content with this situation: the unconscious of art presented as pure commerce.

FURTHER READING

Friedrich Teja Bach, Margit Rowell, and Ann Temkin, *Brancusi* (Philadelphia: Philadelphia Museum of Art, 1995)

Anna Chave, *Constantin Brancusi: Shifting the Bases of Art* (New Haven and London: Yale University Press, 1994)

Sidney Geist, *Brancusi: A Study of the Sculpture* (New York: Grossman, 1968) and "Rodin/Brancusi," in Albert E. Elsen (ed.), *Rodin Rediscovered* (Washington, D.C.: National Gallery of Art, 1981)

Carola Giedion-Welcker, *Constantin Brancusi* (New York: George Braziller, 1959)

Rosalind Krauss, *Passages in Modern Sculpture* (New York: Viking Press, 1977)

5 • Constantin Brancusi, *Princesse X*, 1915–16
Polished bronze, 61.7 x 40.5 x 22.2 ($24\frac{1}{4}$ x 16 x $8\frac{3}{4}$)

▲ 1914, 1918

1927c

Charles Sheeler is commissioned by Ford to document its new River Rouge plant: North American modernists develop a lyrical relation to the machine age, which Georgia O'Keeffe extends to the natural world.

When in *The Bridge* (1930) the American poet Hart Crane (1899–1932) saluted the Brooklyn Bridge as "harp and altar" on which to celebrate a new "myth to God," his encomium harked back to the ecstatic vision of his hero, nineteenth-century poet Walt Whitman. But for avant-gardists in New York the celebration of this feat of engineering, already under way in Cubist and Cubo-Futurist renderings of the bridge by John Marin (1870–1953) and Joseph Stella (1877–1946), might also have recalled the ironic defense made by Marcel Duchamp after his urinal ▲ *Fountain* was rejected by the Society of Independent Artists in 1917: that America's two greatest contributions to civilization were its plumbing and its bridges. This was as much compliment as insult. • Even as Dadaists like Duchamp and Francis Picabia used the machine sarcastically, in a manner opposite to the lyrical exaltations of Crane, Stella, and other North American machine-age artists, they also believed that such icons of modernity as industrial machines, suspension bridges, and skyscrapers made the United States "the country of the art of the future" (Duchamp) and New York "the futurist, the cubist city." And these are indeed the icons, extended to the factory and the city, that became the staples of North American machine-age art. So when Morton Schamberg (1881–1918) titled a cluster of pipe joints *God* (1916), some in his milieu may have taken it less as a Dadaist satire on the religion of art than as a modern fetish of American practicality not unworthy of a little worship.

The machine as modernist shrine

The United States might have possessed the prized icons of modernity, but its artists lacked the privileged styles of modernism. As a result they felt at once benighted and belated in relation to European modernists, a condition that complicated the transatlantic travel of artists in the teens and twenties. (The ocean-liner, celebrated by ■ Le Corbusier as a model of functional design in his famous manifesto *Vers une architecture* [1923] and detailed by Charles Demuth [1883–1935] in *Paquebot "Paris"* [1921–2] and Charles Sheeler [1883–1965] in *Upper Deck* [1929], was the vehicle of this passage.) Discontent with the messy realism of their elder compatriots, some American artists voyaged to Europe to seek out modernist art, while others had already seen such work in New York at the controversial

1 • Marsden Hartley, *The Iron Cross*, 1915
Oil on canvas, 121 x 121 (47⅝ x 47⅝)

Armory Show in 1913 or in the various exhibitions at the 291 Gallery, ▲ run by Alfred Stieglitz, and the de Zayas and Modern galleries, run by Marius de Zayas. Indeed, the North American encounter with modernism occurred mostly in the States, where Duchamp, Picabia, and others had fled during World War I. At the time New York was the interim capital of the avant-garde, which gravitated to two salons above all: one around Stieglitz (which Picabia favored), the other around the collectors Walter and Louise Arensberg (where • Duchamp met Man Ray, the American who was soon to be central to both Dada and Surrealism). In these settings Americans like Marin, Stella, Arthur Dove, and Marsden Hartley (1877–1943), who had already adapted different modernist idioms [1], mixed with Europeans involved in Dada. And this milieu provided the contradictory mix that artists like Demuth and Sheeler attempted to resolve: a diagrammatic draftsmanship validated by Dada but stripped of its irony, and a lyrical semiabstraction developed in different ways by Dove, Hartley, Marin, and Stella. To this combination was added a

▲ 1914 • 1916b, 1918, 1919 ■ 1925a ▲ 1916b • 1918, 1930b, 1931

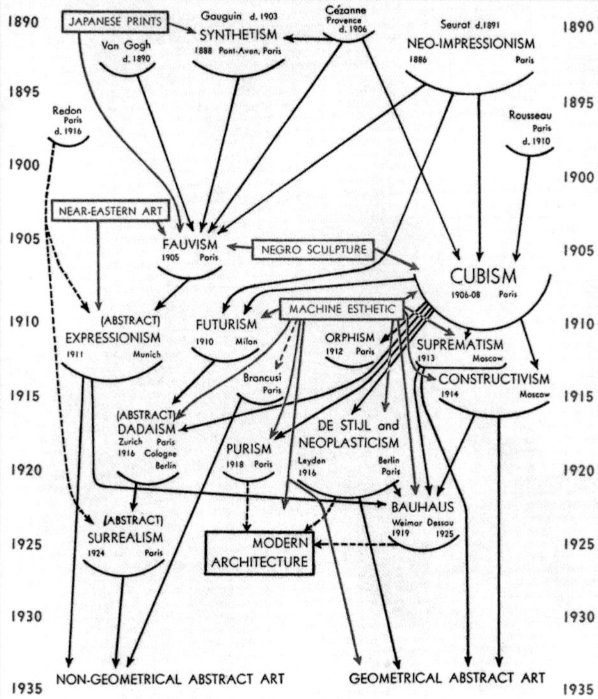

MoMA and Alfred H. Barr, Jr.

On November 7, 1929, only days after the Stock Market crash, the Museum of Modern Art opened a show of Postimpressionist masters (Cézanne, van Gogh, Gauguin) in six small rooms at 730 5th Avenue in New York. The brainchild of three collectors, Abby Aldrich Rockefeller (wife of John D. Jr.), Lillie P. Bliss (sister of the Secretary of the Interior), and Mary Quinn Sullivan, MoMA was inaugurated in the same period as the Whitney Museum of American Art (begun by Gertrude Vanderbilt Whitney in 1931), The Museum of Non-Objective Painting (the first incarnation of the Guggenheim Museum, opened by Solomon R. Guggenheim and Baroness Hilla Rebay von Ehrenweisen in 1939), and the Barnes Foundation (established by Albert C. Barnes near Philadelphia in 1922, though not opened to the public in his lifetime)—all cultural projects of rich Americans inspired in part by the 1913 Armory Show and such early advocates of modernist art as Alfred Stieglitz and Walter Arensberg. With A. Conger Goodyear as chairman of the board, the Modern pledged to exhibit "the great modern masters—American and European—from Cézanne to the present day" and "to establish a permanent public museum" of such work. (An agenda of design and education was also urged on the fledgling institution by the regents of the State University of New York.)

A persistent paradox of advanced art in the United States is located right here: its very reception often occurred within museum settings, and in this sense it was often already institutional. On the other hand, the museological field of modern art was brand new, so much so that MoMA turned to a twenty-seven-year old professor of art from Wellesley College named Alfred H. Barr, Jr. (1902–81) as director. Barr had taught the first course on twentieth-century art in the United States in 1927; in the winter of 1927–8 in Europe he encountered such radical experiments in art, architecture, and design as De Stijl in Holland, Constructivism in the Soviet Union, and the Bauhaus in Germany. Barr seems to have absorbed and rejected these models in almost equal measure. He proposed a broad framework for MoMA with departments not only of painting and sculpture, prints and drawings, but also of commercial art, industrial art, design, film, and photography (which were more widely exhibited than many at the museum might think today). However, the trustees scaled this plan back on the grounds that it would confuse the public, and Barr seems to have acquiesced in large part.

A similar compromise was reached regarding exhibition display. Barr did away with the traditional decorative grouping of cluttered art works, but he was not nearly as experimental as El Lissitzky and others in Europe. Instead he practiced a well-spaced positioning of objects arranged by subject and style on open walls and floors. The effect was to create an aesthetic dimension that appeared both autonomous and historical: the works were "isolated," in his own words, with "no effort ... made to suggest a period atmosphere"; at the same time they suggested an "almost perfect chronological sequence." For Barr style was the principal medium of meaning in modern art, and influence was its main motor. He was likely guided here by his Princeton professor, Charles Rufus Morey, who used a similar evolutionary scheme to narrate medieval art, but Barr made this system effectual for twentieth-century art in a way that was widely adopted by other institutions.

The first epitome of this MoMA museology was the 1936 show "Cubism and Abstract Art." On the one hand, Barr introduced a vast range of European avant-garde practices to an American audience—photographs, constructions, architectural models, posters, film stills, and furniture as well as paintings and sculptures. On the other hand, the signature element of the exhibition was the cover image of its scholarly catalogue, which consisted of a flowchart of the many avant-gardes first channeled into a few mainstream movements—Surrealism, Purism, Neoplasticism, Bauhaus, Constructivism—then further reduced to "Non-Geometrical Abstract Art" and "Geometrical Abstract Art."

By 1939, when MoMA moved to a new building on 53rd Street, it had begun to establish a proprietary right over these movements, and its history of style-influence was soon interpreted as a projection of future artmaking as well. Although the initial plan was to transfer or to sell works as they aged to other institutions, MoMA decided to keep its acquisitions, and in 1958 it opened a permanent installation of its collection. Barr was relieved of the directorship of the museum in 1943, but he retained a research position, and in 1947 he was reinstated as head of collections, in which position he remained until his retirement in 1967.

2 • Joseph Stella, *New York Interpreted: The Voice of the City*, 1920–2
Oil and tempera on canvas, four panels 224.8 x 137.2 (88½ x 54), central panel 252.1 x 137.2 (99¼ x 54)

photographic criterion of precision stipulated by Stieglitz and exemplified by Paul Strand. In fact, several of these young Americans, who came to be called "Precisionists," worked as photographers as well, and Sheeler collaborated with Strand on a short filmic celebration of New York called *Manahatta* in 1919.

Stylistically, Joseph Stella was more Cubo-Futurist than Precisionist, but no account of machine-age art can omit such works as his *New York Interpreted: The Voice of the City* [**2**], a painting of five panels, each over seven feet high, that evokes the city through massive scale, nighttime luster, and linear force. Here Stella conceives New York as a circuit of movement, with each panel devoted to a site of transportation. The two panels on the left are "The Port (The Harbor, The Battery)" and "The White Way I" (the great avenues of Manhattan as a modern Milky Way); on the right are "The White Way II" (a specific ode to Broadway) and "The Bridge" (as in Brooklyn Bridge, his favorite motif); and in the center, slightly higher than the other panels, is "The Skyscrapers (The Prow)," which evokes the island of Manhattan as a ship's prow, a mobile vessel of light in a sea of night. This is a pictorial version of the poetic trope of personification, used to excess by Hart Crane, in which a thing is addressed as a person. As the Expressionist Franz Marc had done with nature, Stella uses a Cubo-Futurist line to vitalize the city—to give it a "voice," to render it more than human. Like Crane, Stella saw New York as an "apotheosis" of "the new civilization," with the bridge as its "shrine," and his painting is a kind of modern altarpiece in which the city appears as a cathedral, with its skyscrapers, bridges, and avenues as so many columns, vaults, and naves.

In the Bauhaus the machine was opposed to the Church; in *The Biography of Henry Adams* (1900), Adams contrasted the dynamo to the Virgin as emblems of very different epochs. Here, however, such opposites are fused. This is the wager that machine-age art makes: that a spiritual (or at least lyrical) subjectivity can be achieved not in opposition to the machine or the city (as the Expressionists had thought) but by means of them. This American image of the metropolis diverges from the European account of the German sociologist Georg Simmel, for whom urban shocks are parried by a "blasé" subject. Like Crane, Stella urges a "gusto" embrace of the city instead. But this embrace, which, again like Crane, Stella saw in sexual as well as religious terms, was impossible to sustain, as the overwrought nature of both *The Bridge* and *New York Interpreted* might suggest.

The task of the modern poet, Crane once wrote, is "to acclimatize" the machine—an ambiguous formulation that points to a persistent problem of machine-age art. Does it "technologize" traditional forms (as *The Bridge* does to the epic, or *New York Interpreted* does to the altarpiece), or does it "traditionalize" technological developments through such forms, which are thereby updated? At the 1912 Salon de la locomotion aérienne in Paris, Duchamp remarked to Brancusi: "Painting is over. Who'd do better than this propeller? Tell me, could you do that?" The Precisionists attempted to do so through a monumental style that combined a precision associated with photography with an abstraction derived from Cubism—ingredients that chastened and transformed one another. For example, the "Cubism" of Demuth and Sheeler is not "analytical" in the sense that the object is not fragmented. On the contrary, the planar projections of the ship vents in *Upper Deck* by Sheeler and the grain elevators in *My Egypt* by Demuth [**3**] solidify the object, simplify its structure, and define its contour, and so clarify rather than complicate our vision. At the same time, these images are hardly photographic. Forms are reduced and spaces flattened, shadows emboldened and tonalities transformed—more so in Demuth, who is more lyrical than Sheeler. Architecture, then, is not only a prime motif of this art; it also influenced its way of seeing. *Upper Deck*, Sheeler once remarked, was painted "much as the architect completes his plans before the work," with a thorough study of structure and a clear presentation of perspective.

On this matter of architecture the European–American exchange became deliriously circular. With its bridges and factories, industrial America was not just a giant readymade for Dadaists like Duchamp

▲ 1916b ● 1908 ■ 1923 ▲ 1914, 1927b

and Picabia; it was also a polemical model of functional design for ▲ modernist architects like Walter Gropius and Le Corbusier. In the 1913 *Deutscher Werkbund Yearbook* Gropius published seven pages of photographs of American factories and grain elevators, one of which Le Corbusier retouched (to remove its nonmodernist details) in his Purist journal *L'Esprit Nouveau* in 1919 and again in *Vers une architecture*. Neither designer had visited the United States, but they needed this "Concrete Atlantis," as the architectural historian Reyner Banham called it, for its "factories and grain elevators were an available iconography, a language of forms, whereby promises could be made, adherence to the modernist credo could be asserted, and the way pointed to some kind of technological utopia." How better to argue for a functionalist architecture than to point to its "primitive" preexistence in utilitarian structures in the States? In this European allegory, industrial America was not only futuristic but also almost prehistoric. It was sometimes associated, through black culture, with ● exotic Africa, especially in France, where Le Corbusier participated in a "techno-primitive" cult of jazz, dancing, and boxing, and sometimes with ancient Egypt, especially in Germany, where Gropius made the connection to America via monumental architecture (for instance, the grain elevators as modern pyramids). The art historian Wilhelm Worringer pointed to this Egyptian association implicitly ■ in *Abstraction and Empathy* in 1908, which Gropius knew in 1913, and explicitly in *Egyptian Art* in 1927, which borrowed an American illustration from Gropius. This association was also adopted in the same year by Demuth in *My Egypt*, an exemplary Precisionist painting of grain elevators in his native town of Lancaster, Pennsylvania (other Precisionists like Ralston Crawford [1906–78] painted the elevators in Buffalo favored by Gropius et al.). The title *My Egypt* might seem ironic, but the elevators are imaged proudly, viewed from below with geometric masses raked by precise spotlights. It is as if Demuth wanted to claim that these elevators are also monuments for the ages, even to suggest another myth of modernity, not one of mobility (as with so many other modernists) but one of monumentality. Yet there is a catch to this myth. For Worringer, ancient Egypt represented an "artistic will" to abstraction that expressed an anxious withdrawal from a chaotic world, and he saw a similar anxiety behind modernist abstraction. Might the monumentality of Precisionist work point to a related ambivalence about a machinic world so dynamic as to be disintegrative, to a related turn to compositions of stasis and stability, as if in defense against modern chaos? As Strand once remarked, "spiritual control over the machine" was the primary struggle of this generation of artists.

The Precisionists represented modern icons, but were these artists modern*ist*? They never broached pure abstraction; on the contrary, they used its simplifications to represent the world all the more precisely. It was for this reason that Precisionism was sometimes called "Cubist Realism." "It was Sheeler," de Zayas remarked, perhaps with Strand also in mind, "who proved that Cubism exists in nature and that photography can record it," and that painting based on photography, as often with Sheeler, might do so as well. This return to clarity and stability, this reconciliation of representation and

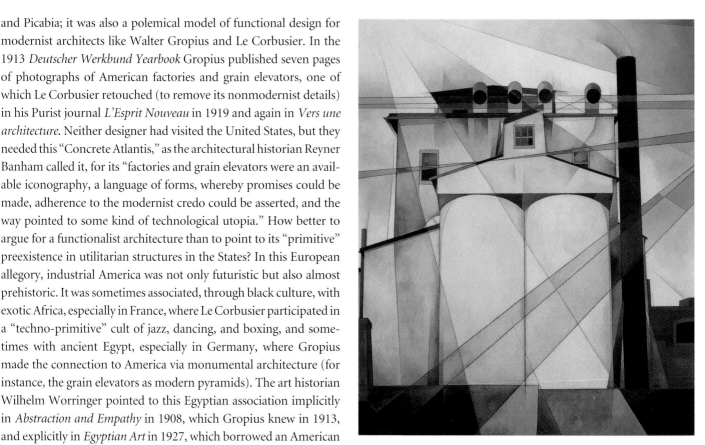

3 • Charles Demuth, *My Egypt*, 1927
Oil on board, 90.8 x 76.2 (35¾ x 30)

abstraction, aligns Precisionism with the mostly antimodernist ▲ "return to order" in much European art of the twenties. In fact it has more in common with the style known as Neue Sachlichkeit (New ● Objectivity) in Germany of the same time, yet without its critique of the military-industrial complex that produced World War I. Indeed, Precisionism was gung ho about capitalist modernity even after the Stock Market crash of 1929, and this aligns it more closely still with another ambiguous movement, the Purism of Le Corbusier and ■ Amedée Ozenfant. This style also sought to rationalize art and to classicize the machine—to aestheticize not only machined products but a mechanistic way of seeing as well, which is to say that the Purists also valued the "precisionism" of mass production. In this ◆ regard both movements were poles apart from Russian Constructivism, for rather than transform art vis-à-vis industry, they worked to recoup industry as an image for art. Precisionism also resisted the aesthetic implications of mechanical reproduction, for rather than transform painting vis-à-vis photography, it worked to assimilate photography into painting—to use its apparent transparency to the object in order to render painting as immediate, as illusionistic, as possible. (The Precisionists were also called "the Immaculates"—immaculate as in "immaculate conception," pure, without stain.) Whereas other modernists foregrounded the medium of painting, Sheeler admitted "his effort ... to eliminate the interception of the medium between the eyes of the spectator and the creation of the artist," to "set forth [the object] with the utmost clarity by means of craftsmanship so adequate as to be unobtrusive."

▲ 1923, 1925a ● 1925a ■ 1908

▲ 1919 ● 1925b ■ 1925a ◆ 1921

4 • Charles Sheeler,
***American Landscape*, 1931**
Oil on canvas, 61 x 78.7 (24 x 31)

5 • Stuart Davis,
***House and Street*, 1931**
Oil on canvas, 66 x 107.3 (26 x 42¼)

The epitome of this "capitalist illusionism" is the work done by Sheeler for the Ford Motor Company. By the mid-twenties Ford had outgrown its Highland Park factory where the Model T was assembled, so River Rouge was built ten miles from Detroit in order to produce the Model A. The largest industrial complex in the world, with twenty-three buildings, ninety-three miles of track, 53,000 machines, and 75,000 employees, it was a site of total automobile production, from the smelting of steel to the painting of cars. In 1927 Sheeler was commissioned to photograph the new factory. In six weeks he completed thirty-two official photographs, nine of which were published in magazines. (*Vanity Fair* printed one, *Criss-Crossed Conveyors*, with the caption "By Their Works Ye Shall Know Them," and referred to River Rouge as "an American altar of the God-Objective of Mass Production.") Sheeler showed some photographs as art works and used others for paintings, in which very few workers appear, and no drudgery, let alone exploitation, is shown. In short, he identified artistic perspective with technocratic surveillance, and he reconciled landscape composition with Taylorist and Fordist principles of work-management. In his compositions the fragmentation and reification of work and worker alike, which the Marxist critic György Lukács defined in 1923 as the prime effects of assembly-line production, are magically smoothed over. Sheeler even titled a few panoramas of River Rouge *Classic Landscape*, as if the plant were an idyll, and he continued to produce such paintings well into the worst years of the Depression.

The climax of this work is *American Landscape* **[4]**, where landscape is remapped as industrial production, America as the rationalization of labor, and nature as the transporting and processing of raw materials into Model As. In the foreground, at the start of production, is a vacant ladder, sign of the obsolescence of preindustrial man (the sole worker is a tiny figure on the tracks in the middle ground). In the background, at the end of production, stands a stack where smoke mixes with clouds. Here the world culminates in a factory, where it is a question no longer of the invasive machine in the "Edenic garden of America" (in the phrase of historian Leo Marx) but of the machine *as* this garden. This is the ideological effect of such machine-age art: it represents capitalist industry, but only to obscure its exploitation of labor behind an "occult mechanism"—a monumental structure, a beautiful image (this particular painting was purchased by a member of the Rockefeller family). Such art spiritualizes, monumentalizes, and naturalizes a historical moment as a "machine age": New York as glorious cathedral, grain elevators as Egyptian pyramids, a factory as a classical landscape.

Some artists did not subscribe to this monumentalist agenda. Although Stuart Davis (1894–1964) also evoked the urban life of the machine age, he did so through symbols of consumption rather than through icons of production. In a colorful style derived from ▲ Synthetic Cubism Davis painted the city as a street poster of jazzy rhythms, surfaces, and signs **[5]**. But he did so in a way that reclaims collage for painting and is neither disruptive of high art nor critical of mass culture. In effect, Davis displaced the machine, only to highlight the commodity in an artistic solution that foreshadows Pop art. •

6 • Georgia O'Keeffe, *Black Iris III*, 1926
Oil on canvas, 91.4 x 75.9 (36 x 29⅞)

1920–1929

It was left to Georgia O'Keeffe to salvage the lyrical subjectivity that some artists hoped to wrest from the machine age, but in order to do so she abandoned images of production and consumption altogether. After a decade of intermittent paintings of New York, she turned away from the city, and eventually rediscovered, in the desert landscape of the American Southwest, a relation to objects and images that reasserted rather than overwhelmed the body **[6]**. A male fantasy of self-creation—of men "born without a mother" (Picabia)—hovers over machine-age art from the mechanomorphic portraits of the Dadaists to the production pastorals of the Precisionists. With her abstracted flowers and landscapes, O'Keeffe, an artist who appears without progenitors, recaptures self-creation for her own art of nature and troubles the male gendering of this fantasy as well. In doing so, she charts an alternative identity for American artists, especially for women, one that departs from the machine age and its myths of modernity.

FURTHER READING

Reyner Banham, *A Concrete Atlantis: U.S. Industrial Building and European Modern Architecture 1900–1925* (Cambridge, Mass.: MIT Press, 1986)

Leo Marx, *The Machine in the Garden: Technology and the Pastoral Ideal in America* (New York: Oxford University Press, 1964)

Terry Smith, *Making the Modern: Industry, Art, and Design in America* (Chicago: University of Chicago Press, 1993)

Gail Stavitsky et al., *Precisionism in America: 1915–1941* (Montclair, N.J.: Montclair Art Museum, 1994)

Karen Tsujimoto, *Images of America: Precisionist Painting and Modern Photography* (Seattle: San Francisco Museum of Art/University of Washington Press, 1982)

Anne M. Wagner, *Three Artists (Three Women): Modernism and the Art of Hesse, Krasner, and O'Keeffe* (Berkeley: University of California Press, 1996)

▲ 1912 • 1960c, 1964b

1928

The publication of "Unism in Painting" by Wladyslaw Stzreminski, followed in 1931 by a book on sculpture he coauthored with Katarzyna Kobro, *The Composition of Space*, marks the apogee of the internationalization of Constructivism.

"The Blockade of Russia is Coming to an End": such is the title of the editorial launching the first issue of *Veshch'/Gegenstand/Objet*, a short-lived trilingual "international journal of modern art" published in 1922 by two members of the Russian avant-garde living in Berlin at the time: the Constructivist artist ▲ El Lissitzky and the writer Ilya Ehrenburg (1891–1967). The end of the blockade imposed by Western nations at the outbreak of the October Revolution of 1917 was still only a wish when the manifesto was penned (*Veshch's* inaugural double issue is dated March–April), but this wish was granted a few weeks later. On April 16, 1922, angering most other Western countries forced to swallow its diplomatic coup and, sooner or later, to follow suit, Germany signed the Treaty of Rapello, recognizing the Soviet government in Moscow. Neither El Lissitzky nor Ehrenburg was a political pundit, but no particular expertise was needed to sense that the wall of isolation behind which Soviet Russia had been kept ever since 1917 was about to topple and that Germany, the great loser of World War I, would be the first country to lend a hand to this pariah of the international community.

Russians in Berlin

Unlike Ehrenburg, who had traveled throughout Europe for a few months (allegedly to study) before settling in Berlin in the fall of 1921, Lissitzky arrived there straight from Moscow via Warsaw on New Year's Eve, 1921. Ehrenburg was more of a fellow traveler than an ardent Bolshevik, whereas Lissitzky considered it his duty to propagate the new developments of Soviet art in the West. It has never been proven that the Russian artist had received an official mandate, but at the very least he had the tacit support of Anatoly Lunacharsky's Soviet ministry of culture and education (Narkom- • pros, or People's Commissariat of Enlightenment) set up in 1917: he would be chosen to design the catalogue of the groundbreaking "Erste Russische Kunstausstellung" ("First Russian Art Exhibition") financed by the Soviet government and held at the van Diemen Galerie in October and November 1922 [**1**]. Both Ehrenburg and Lissitzky were immediately seduced by Berlin, then a formidable cultural and ideological melting-pot, vibrant with a multiplicity of pacifist and left-wing groups, some still hoping to revive the January 1919 uprising that had upset the city for a season before being brutally crushed with the assassinations of the Marxist leaders Karl Liebknecht and Rosa Luxemburg. In a matter of weeks the Russian artists established contacts with all the major players of the Berlin avant-garde, particularly with the highly politicized ▲ Berlin Dadaists but also with many artists from the countries artificially created by the Treaty of Versailles, which officialized the fall of the Austro-Hungarian Empire at the close of World War I. But

1 • El Lissitzky, preliminary sketch for the cover of the catalogue of "Erste Russische Kunstausstellung," 1922
Tracing paper, gouache, Indian ink, graphite, 27 x 19 (10⅔ x 7½)

▲ 1926 ● 1921 ▲ 1920

the largest group of immigrants was the Russians—and, contrary to what one might expect, relatively few of them were faithful to the deposed Czarist regime (those who were White Russians, as they were called, preferred Paris); many had been disenchanted by Lenin's politics or had fled the terrible famine and the civil war of 1918 to 1921, but they still hoped that one day they could go back to their country and contribute to its development.

There was perhaps no form of artistic production that piqued the curiosity of the cosmopolitan intelligentsia gathered in Berlin more than that of the Russian avant-garde. Communications with the rest of Europe had ceased at the beginning of 1914; although some information had begun to filter in from 1920 on (notably through the first book on the topic ever published in the West, *Neue Kunst in Russland 1914–1919* (New Art in Russia 1914–1919), written by the young, Vienna-based Soviet journalist Konstantin Umansky), and this had fueled the already vast interest in "the new Russian art."

The editors of *Veshch'* were fully aware that the timing was perfect, as the first paragraph of "The Blockade of Russia is Coming to an End" testifies:

> *The appearance of* Veshch' *is another sign that the exchange of practical knowledge, realizations, and "objects" between young Russian and West European artists has begun. Seven years of separate existence have shown that the common ground of artistic aims and undertakings that exists in various countries is not simply an effect of change, a dogma, or a passing fashion, but an inevitable accompaniment of the maturing of humanity. Art is today international, though retaining all its local symptoms and particularity. The founders of the new artistic community are strengthening ties between Russia, in the aftermath of the mighty Revolution, and the West, in its wretched postwar Black Monday frame of mind; in so doing they are bypassing all artistic distinctions whether psychological, economic, or racial.* Veshch' *is the meeting point of two adjacent lines of communication.*

The program that followed, forcefully laid out by Lissitzky in three parallel columns (one for each language: German, French, and Russian) punctuated by the repetition of the title of the journal in bold type, contained a condemnation of the "negative tactics of the Dadaists" (compared to those of the prewar Futurists) as well ▲ as those of the Russian Productivists:

> *We have nothing in common with those poets who propose in verse that verse should no longer be written, or with those painters who use painting as a means of propaganda for the abandonment of painting. Primitive utilitarianism is far from being our doctrine.* Veshch' *considers poetry, plastic form, theater as "objects" that cannot be dispensed with.*

This did not mean that *Veshch'* was advocating a return to art for art's sake, continued the editors: for them, "every organized work—whether it be a house, a poem, or a picture—is an "object" directed toward a particular end, which is calculated not to turn people away from life, but to summon them to make their contribution toward life's organization." Thus *Veshch'* vowed to "investigate examples of industrial products, new inventions, the language of everyday speech and the language of newspapers, the gesture of sports, etc.—in short, everything that is suitable as material for the conscious creative artist of our times." The key words were "organization" and "construction": contrary to what the Productivists believed, art would abdicate its ideological power if it was entirely subsumed into industrial production, but both art and industrial production could function as a model for each other. What the latter has to gain from this interrelation remains vague in the editorial, but according to its authors the recent developments of artistic production provide a clear lesson: its strength derives in great part from the fact that it is a collective enterprise and that each work is conceived according to a plan, following certain rules defined by the material, and not the mere result of subjective inspiration.

Although *Veshch'* played a major role in publicizing the art of the Russian avant-garde, it should be noted that most of the contributions appeared in Russian (a major exception is Lissitzky's long overall review of "exhibitions in Russia," illustrated by an ▲ installation photograph of the 1921 Obmokhu show, published in German). The editors' dream was to act as an intermediary between East and West and in so doing give ammunition to their colleagues at home, who were already fearing that Lenin's New Economic Policy, drafted in 1921 and advocating the return of "bourgeois specialists," was going to seal their fate. To inform the Soviet avant-garde of projects similar to its own in various countries of Europe was to encourage its members to hold fast: they were not alone. Thus, among the mass of information printed in the first issue of *Veshch'* one reads an announcement for an international exhibition of "Progressive Art" to be held in Düsseldorf.

The editors of *Veshch'* took an active part in the "Congress of International Progressive Artists" that coincided with the Düsseldorf exhibition (May 29–31, 1922), during which they solidified • their link with the Dutch movement De Stijl as well as with other groups working on similar premises in countries such as Romania, Switzerland, Sweden, and Germany [**2**]. With Hans Richter (an ex-Dadaist turned Constructivist filmmaker) and Theo van Doesburg, the mastermind behind De Stijl (who had just published his manifesto on "Monumental art" in the first issue of *Veshch'*), Lissitzky formed the "International Faction of Constructivists." In a "minority" statement conceived as a direct counterproposal to the humanist creed of the Congress's resolution, the three coauthors protested against the lack of definition of the term "progressive artist": "We define the progressive artist as one who fights and rejects the tyranny of the subjective in art, as one whose work is not based on lyrical arbitrariness, as one who accepts the new principles of artistic creation—the systematization of the means of expression to produce results that are universally comprehensible." Furthermore, they lambasted the corporatist ideology that fueled the Congress's ambition to create what they saw as "an international trade for the exhibition of painting." Against such a

▲ 1909, 1921

▲ 1921 • 1917

2 • El Lissitzky (fourth from right) and Theo van Doesburg (third from right) at the "Congress of International Progressive Artists" in Düsseldorf, 1922

"bourgeois colonial policy," they stated: "We reject the present conception of an exhibition: a warehouse stuffed with unrelated objects, all for sale. Today we stand between a society that does not need us and one that does not yet exist; the only purpose of exhibitions is to demonstrate what we wish to achieve (illustrated with plans, sketches, and models) or what we have already achieved." The definition of art that concludes this declaration confirms the constitution of a lingua franca of Constructivism: "Art is, in just the same way as science and technology, a method of organization which applies to the whole of life."

The "Erste Russische Kunstausstellung" at the van Diemen Galerie was not exactly a Constructivist exhibition—all trends of Russian art were represented, including the nascent "Socialist ▲ Realism"—but it provided the first occasion for an avid public to discover the prodigious activity of the Russian avant-garde in all media, from the Suprematist canvases of Malevich and his pupils to the theater design of Rodchenko's friends and the sculptures of Obmokhu, not to forget Lissitzky's own abstract paintings, which he called *prouns* (an acronym based on the Russian phrase "for the affirmation of the new"), and which made quite a sensation [**4**]. The exhibition was an immense success, with its Constructivist section receiving the lion's share of the press's attention. Lissitzky contributed in no small way to this triumph, taking an active part in all the public debates surrounding the exhibition and embarking on a lecture tour through several Dutch and German cities. His enthusiastic lecture on the "New Russian Art" still remains today one of the most lucid analyses of the development of the Russian avant-garde from 1910 to 1922.

The impact of the van Diemen show was immediate. Not only did commercial art galleries in Berlin (such as Der Sturm), till then clinging to Expressionism as a genuinely Germanic form of expression, rush to open their walls to the new avant-garde, but also there was the creation (or the conversion to Constructivism) of a myriad of avant-garde periodicals in Eastern European countries, all clearly indebted to the Russian model about which most of them were gathering information from correspondents in Berlin. Among many others, these publications included *Zenit* in Zagreb (now in Croatia) and then Belgrade (now in Serbia), *Revue Devetsilu*, *Zivot*, and *Pasmo* in Prague, *Zwrotnica* and *Blok* in Warsaw, *Contimporanul* in Bucharest—not to speak of architectural journals such as *G-Material zur elementaren Gestaltung* (based in Berlin) and *ABC* (based in Basel), which Lissitzky helped launch. (A case in point was Lajos Kassák's *MA* [also the name of a group of artists and writers], which had began its publication in 1916 in Budapest and moved to Vienna during the repression that followed the aborted Hungarian proletarian republic: as soon as László Moholy-Nagy, who left Vienna for Berlin in November 1919, became its editor there, *MA* turned into one of the most ardent advocates of the Constructivist position.)

This is not to say that the artists grouped around these little magazines suddenly woke up from a long sleep when touched by the magic wand of Russian Constructivism—as a matter of fact, many had been trying for several years to revive an avant-garde culture that had been all but eliminated in their countries by the events of World War I—but for the most part their post-Cubist production lacked direction, which is exactly what their encounter with Russian ▲ art provided them with. Malevich's brilliant interpretation of Cubism had nourished a whole generation of Russian artists, even if they had come to reject his aesthetic position; without necessarily being aware of this, the young turks of this emerging "internationale" were fed a coherent narrative (from Cubism to Suprematism to Constructivism) that laid down the principles of action they most needed. Few of these new converts produced highly original works. A major exception is that of the Hungarian László Peri (1899–1967), whose paintings of various geometric shapes on shaped wood, canvas, or occasionally concrete slabs are particularly striking [**3**]. Another exception is constituted by the paintings of Wladyslaw Strzeminski (1893–1952) and the sculptures of his wife, Katarzyna Kobro (1898–1951), a partnership that was the main force behind the Polish avant-garde of the twenties and early thirties.

To call Kobro and Strzeminski "new converts" would actually be misleading: firstly, born respectively in Moscow and Minsk

3 • László Peri, *Three-Part Space Construction*, 1923
Painted concrete, part 1: 60 x 68 (23⅝ x 26¾); part 2: 55.5 x 70 (21⅞ x 27½); part 3: 58 x 68 (22¾ x 26¾)

▲ 1934a

▲ 1915

4 • El Lissitzky, *Proun R.V.N.2*, 1923
Mixed media on canvas, 99 x 99 (39 x 39)

(Bielorussia, now Belarus), they had a direct knowledge of the Russian avant-garde, particularly of the art of Malevich with whom ▲ they had studied in the Svomas and later kept in close contact, often participating in artistic events held at Unovis, Malevich's school (where they most probably met Lissitzky); secondly, newly arrived in Poland in 1922, they did not share their fellow citizens' enthusiasm for the recent hardening of Constructivism into Productivism. The first major essay written by Strzeminski, "Notes on Russian Art," published in Kraków in 1922 shortly before Lissitzky's lecture, should be read as its pendant. Offering a rigorous analysis of the art of Malevich, Strzeminski warns against any instrumentalization of art, a danger he sees as a major threat not only in the Productivist but already present in the Constructivist position. Adhering to the statement of the International Faction of Constructivists, according to which the work of art is an object whose construction has to obey a certain number of rules in order to evacuate the "tyranny of the subjective," he soon conceived of his task as that of articulating such rules.

▲ 1921

Unism

By the end of the twenties, having rapidly ascended the ranks of the Polish avant-garde, Strzeminski proposed a full-blown theory, which he called Unism (published in 1928 as *Unizm w malarstwie* [Unism in Painting]) and which constitutes one of the most sophisticated discourses concerning abstract art. A brief summary of this theory is in order. In each medium, and differently in each medium, according to the theory of Unism, the artist must strive toward creating a "real" work of art (a work having a "real" existence, a work not relying upon any kind of transcendence). Any work of art whose formal configuration is not motivated by its physical condition (format, materials, and so on) is arbitrary, in the sense that the composition originates in an a priori vision conceived by the artist prior to its actual embodiment in matter, prior to the physical existence of the work. Such arbitrary compositions (which Strzeminski calls "baroque") are always enacting a drama (thesis, antithesis) whose resolution (synthesis) must convince. (Strzeminski was remarkably aware of the fact that the pictorial ordering we call composition, first theorized during the Italian Renaissance, had been borrowed from the art of rhetoric.) But, he continues, any "baroque" synthesis is necessarily a false solution because the problem it solves is grounded in metaphysical oppositions that are artificially superimposed upon matter (the figure–ground opposition, for example) and are, therefore, not "real." Any trace of dualism must be evacuated if one is to escape the idealism of composition so as to achieve a true construction (needless to say, Mondrian's dialectics was rejected by Strzeminski).

Pictorial flatness, formal deduction from the frame, and abolition of the figure–ground opposition are thus the three main conditions of Unism in painting. As soon as a shape is not motivated by the format of the canvas, it floats, creating a figure–ground dualism and thus entering the realm of the "baroque" (even if Malevich was praised for his *Black Square*, most of his overtly dynamic compositions were severely criticized).

Understandably, Strzeminski had a hard time putting his extremist theory into practice. His wish to suppress all contrasts, formulated as early as 1924, should have given rise to a monochromatic type of painting; yet this did not occur until 1932 (more than ▲ ten years after Rodchenko's *Red, Yellow, and Blue* triptych, and then for only a few canvases). But because he was keeping the monochrome at bay, Strzeminski had to find a means to "divide" the surface of his paintings, a means that would not be "arbitrary" and subjective. His invention, formulated in 1928—which would reap● pear in Frank Stella's black paintings of 1959, though without any awareness of this historical precedent—was the "deductive structure," to use the phrase coined by Michael Fried in 1965 with regard to Stella's work: the proportions of all of the canvas's formal divisions are determined by the ratio of its actual length and breadth.

In the extraordinary series of paintings deriving from this principle, the surface is divided in two or three planes (whose colors were supposed to be of equal intensity) and the negative–positive articulation suspends the figure–ground hierarchy [**5**]. The division is indeed proportional to the format of the painting, but the occasional use of curves, which would seem impossible in a deductivist structure (within an orthogonal format), shows that Strzeminski had to mellow his program and reintroduce a certain dose of "arbitrariness" for the sake of variety. This would lead to a major crisis which only emerged, paradoxically, after he had attempted with Kobro's help to transpose the theory of Unism into the domain of sculpture.

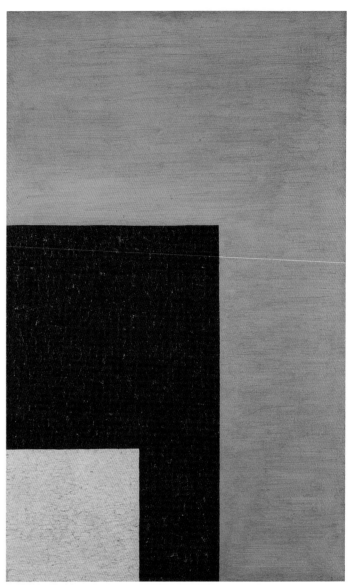

5 • Wladyslaw Strzeminski, *Architectonic Composition 9c*, c. 1929
Oil on canvas, 96 x 60 (37¾ x 23⅝)

He began, faithful to the modernist notion of the specificity of each medium, by positing the radical difference between the pictorial and the sculptural object: the first has "natural limits" beyond which it cannot go (the actual dimensions of the canvas), the second does not have such luck and the "unity" it must establish is with the "totality of space." To achieve this, the sculptural object must not stand out as a figure in an empty background (it cannot be a monument) but must incorporate space as one of its materials.

▲ 1921 ● 1958

6 • Katarzyna Kobro, *Spatial Composition #4*, 1929
Painted steel, 40 x 64 x 40 (15¾ x 25$\frac{3}{16}$ x 15¾)

In order not to be "a foreign body in space," it must "create the prolongation of space" that it materializes through its axes. Easier said than done—but Kobro was up to the task. The real inventiveness of Kobro's works after 1925, all made of intersecting planes, orthogonal or curved, lies in the two methods she employed to prevent her sculptures from being perceived as figures in space or rather as figures separated from space—two methods based on what could be called an extreme syntactic disjunctiveness. The first method was polychromy: the harsh contrast of primary colors makes the sculpture explode in three dimensions, preventing it from becoming a unified silhouette because each side of each plane is painted differently. The second method involved the temporal perception of the sculpture as the viewer turns around it, Kobro being particularly careful to make sure that it would look utterly different from each successive point of view and that no elevation could be inferred from any other. The combination of these two disjunctive methods is remarkably efficient in the works Kobro produced from 1929 to 1930, such as *Spatial Composition #4* [**6**], which, similar in that sense to Strzeminski's Unist canvases, could easily be misdated to 1960.

Strzeminski was rigorous enough to realize that, in positing the absence of any "natural limits" for the sculptural object, he had raised a major issue in his theory of painting. He asked himself: "If the division of the picture is determined by its dimensions, what then is the motivation of these particular dimensions?" The answer he provided created a vicious circle, while ignoring the Unist principle of the specificity of each medium: drawing from the "nature"of architecture, about which Strzeminski wrote that "the homogeneous rhythm of its movement must be a function of the dimensions of man," he established and proposed for every art a kind of ideal proportions (8/5). Demonstrating, despite himself, that it is impossible completely to eradicate the arbitrary in artistic production, Strzeminski reached back to a humanist ideal that Unism had precisely sought to destroy. The monochrome was his next way out, but by then the social metaphor that had been at the core of Strzeminski's enterprise—his conception of the nonhierarchical, "homogeneous" pictorial object in which all parts are equal and interdependent as a model for the society to come—was wearing thin. Condemning artistic redundancy, Strzeminski preferred to abort Unism rather than repeat himself. The rise of Hitler in Germany and of Stalin in Russia were the last straws that silenced his utopian impulse. He spent the final twenty years of his life teaching, drawing biomorphic landscapes as a hobby. He died a year after Kobro, in 1952, without having renounced the principles of Unism but with the full knowledge that they were just as idealist as anything against which he had struggled.

FURTHER READING

Stephen Bann, *The Tradition of Constructivism* (London: Thames & Hudson, 1971)
Yve-Alain Bois, "Strzeminski and Kobro: In Search of Motivation," *Painting as Model* (Cambridge, Mass.: MIT Press, 1990)
El Lissitzky, "New Russian Art," in Sophie Lissitzky-Kuppers, *El Lissitzky: Life, Letters, Texts* (London: Thames & Hudson, 1968)
Krisztina Passuth, *Les avant-gardes de l'Europe centrale* (Paris: Flammarion, 1988)
Ryszard Stanislawski, *Constructivism in Poland* (Essen: Folkwang Museum; and Otterlo: Kröller-Müller Museum, 1973)
Manfredo Tafuri, *The Sphere and the Labyrinth: Avant-Garde and Architecture from Piranesi to the 1970s* (Cambridge, Mass.: MIT Press, 1987)

1929

The "Film und Foto" exhibition, organized by the Deutscher Werkbund and held in Stuttgart from May 18 to July 7, displays a spectrum of international photographic practices and debates: the exhibition demarcates a climax in twentieth-century photography and marks the emergence of a new critical theory and historiography of the medium.

Partially motivated by the impact of World War I, the visual culture of Weimar Germany had increasingly focused on the photographic and the filmic image in all its variations: some authors have argued that this was in order to turn away from the traditional models of cultural production that still prevailed in France, England, and Italy even in the late twenties. Organized by Gustav Stotz (assisted by the architect Bernhard Pankok, the typographic designer Jan Tschichold, and others) on behalf of the Deutscher Werkbund (founded in 1907 to reconnect industry, artisanal, and artistic production), "Film und Foto" [**1**] displayed a tremendous diversity of international photographic practices. More than 200 photographers showed 1,200 photographs, and each national section had its individual curator. Edward Weston and Edward Steichen served for the United States section, which included works by Weston himself, his son Brett Weston, ▲ Charles Sheeler [**2**], and Imogen Cunningham; Christian Zervos ● presented Eugène Atget and Man Ray for France; Dutch designer and typographer Piet Zwart was in charge of the Dutch and Belgian ■ section; El Lissitzky selected the work to represent the Soviet ◆ Union; while László Moholy-Nagy and Stotz curated the German section, with works by, among others, Aenne Mosbacher [**3**], Aenne Biermann [**4**], Erhard Dorner, and Willi Ruge. Moholy-Nagy also conceived and designed the first room introducing the history and techniques of photography, and in a third, his own separate exhibition space, he displayed the principles and materials of his *Malerei, Photographie, Film* (Painting, Photography, Film) published as a Bauhaus book in 1925.

Not surprisingly, it was at this point that the professional identities of the new photographers, as suppliers of images of daily life, of political activities, of current events, of tourism, of fashion and consumption, were formed. By contrast, the artistic and functional "identities" of photography became increasingly fractured. It is important to recognize that "Film und Foto" succeeded because it summarized all of these tendencies of photography in the twenties. First of all, since the rise of the illustrated magazines, photography had emerged as the new medium of political and historical information (rivaled only by the weekly newsreels), integral to the formation of Weimar culture. As contributors to illustrated weeklies in Germany such as the *Berliner Illustrierte Zeitung* (*BIZ*) or the Ullstein *UHU*, which were the precursors of *Paris Match* in France ▲ and *Life* in the US, photographers opened up immensely important new information resources. Secondly, photography had achieved a central role in the design, development, and expansion of the advertising and fashion industries, aimed at the new lower-middle-class of (often female) white-collar workers in Berlin and other large industrialized urban centers. Thirdly, a new, antithetical model emerged—a type of counterformation to paid photojournalism, photographic advertisement, and product propaganda.

1 • Unknown designer, *Film und Foto*, 1929
Poster, lithograph on paper, 84.1 x 58.4 (33⅛ x 23)

▲ 1916b, 1927c, 1959d ● 1924, 1930b, 1931, 1935 ■ 1926, 1928 ◆ 1923, 1947a ▲ 1930a

2 • Charles Sheeler, *Pennsylvania Barn*, c. 1915
Silver-gelatin print, 19.1 x 23.9 (7½ x 9⅜)

Product propaganda and the proletarian public sphere

This model was developed as the result of attempts to abolish the professional specialization of ideological image production, and to make the tools of photography directly available to the working class. Organized to a considerable degree by the German Communist Party, the Workers' Photography Movement enabled the anonymous worker to participate in the emergent process of political and cultural self-representation. It organized its educational and agitational functions in the Workers' Photography Clubs and in Willi Münzenberg's journal *Der Arbeiter Fotograf*, published from 1926 onward. "Photography as a weapon" became the slogan that was coined in opposition to photography's increasing importance in the indoctrination of the mass public sphere with the ideologies of total consumption and the commercialization of the visual language of everyday life. Appropriately then, the "Film und Foto" exhibition expanded photography's traditional artistic parameters by including photojournalism, advertisement and amateur photography, as well ▲ as the political photomontage work of John Heartfield, yet it was primarily defined by the aesthetic contrast between Moholy-Nagy's concept of "New Vision" photography and Albert Renger-Patzsch's (1897–1966) project of "photographic photography," the techni- • cally masterful images of Neue Sachlichkeit. Moholy-Nagy and Renger-Patzsch had first pronounced their oppositional views of the "new" medium and the specificity of its aesthetic conventions in 1927, in the first issue of the new magazine *Das Deutsche Lichtbild* (The German Photograph). While Moholy-Nagy had prioritized the technical, optical and chemical dimensions in order to foreground photography's experimental and constructive qualities, Renger-Patzsch had insisted on its almost ontological realism: "In photography one should surely proceed from the essence of the object and one should try to represent it with photographic means alone, regardless of whether it is a human being, landscape, architecture, or something else" **[5]**. And later Renger-Patzsch stated that "the secret of good photography is that it can obtain artistic qualities just like a work of art, through its realism. Therefore let us leave art to the artists, and let us attempt to create photography with the means of photography, that can hold its own because of its photographic qualities, without having to borrow from art."

Moholy-Nagy's self-reflexive deployment of the medium, featuring photograms, superimpositions, the scientific devices of macrophotography and X-rays, as well as the cinematic devices of rapidly alternating close-up and long-distance shots, was matched by his emphasis on the diversity of photographic procedures, be they chemical, optical, or technical. He foregrounded cameraless photography as one of his "inventions." Even though

▲ 1920 • 1925b

3 • Aenne Mosbacher, *Koralle*, 1928

4 • Aenne Biermann, *Aschenschale*, c. 1928

the photogram had been deployed shortly before by artists such as ▲ Christian Schad and Man Ray (and cameraless photography of course had been known since the times of Anna Atkins and William Fox Talbot in the nineteenth century), it was Moholy-Nagy who now redefined the photogram practically, theoretically, and philosophically. Associating the photogram not only with a perfectly aperspectival space, he also saw it as the concrete embodiment of his project to use "light instead of pigment," to articulate "space through light," and to provide photographic evidence of a "time–space continuum."

All of these strategies originated in an optimism about the medium that considered camera vision as a powerful expansion of natural eyesight, even its technical prosthesis. Moholy-Nagy had stated in *Malerei, Photographie, Film* that "the photographic apparatus can complement our optical instruments, the eyes, and even make them perfect. This principle has already been deployed during scientific experiments of motion studies (striding, jumping and galloping) as well as in images of zoological, botanical and mineralogical forms (microscopic enlargements).... This becomes equally evident in the so-called mistaken, but all the more astonishing photographic images, taken from a bird's-eye or worm's-eye perspective, or from below or from a tilted angle that surprise us all the more today." **[6]** Clearly, Moholy-Nagy's experimental book and his display at "Film ▲ und Foto" inspired Walter Benjamin to write in 1931 (in his crucial review of some of the above-mentioned photography books, entitled "A Short History of Photography") that "it is a different nature that speaks to the camera than that speaking to the eye."

Naturalizing technology

The modernist abolition of central perspectival space in Cubist painting had led to a form of photography that aestheticized modernity's angularity and spatial discontinuities. Pictorial overviews of the landscape or the figure were displaced by the diagrammatic and the detail. In their compulsion to assimilate all forms of experience into the governing principles of technocratic order, photographers discovered that even the principles of modernist construction were ontologically prefigured in the natural orders of plants and petrifications. These photographic comparisons between natural and technological structures led to the discovery of the work of Karl Blossfeldt (1865–1932) and to the publication in 1928 of his collection of photographs, *Urformen der Kunst* (Prototypes of Art), which came to be seen as precursors to the photography of Neue Sachlichkeit.

Blossfeldt, initially trained as a sculptor, had been working as an instructor of drawing and mold casting at the Institute for Higher Education in Arts and Crafts (*Kunstgewerbeschule*) in Berlin since 1898. Increasingly he used photographs rather than plaster casts of plants as the models from which students were to learn the fundamental skills of naturalist drawing and functionalist design (in the traditions established by architect, teacher, and theorist Gottfried Semper and by Theodor Haeckel in the mid-nineteenth century). His first photographs of plants were published in 1896 and, maintaining the exact or similar technical tools, standards, and photographic principles for the next thirty years, Blossfeldt produced an enormous archive of glass plates recording the extreme differentiations of individual plant formations **[7]**, intending them to be used primarily as teaching supplements in his drawing classes. It was not until 1928, when the art dealer Karl Nierendorf initiated the publication of *Urformen der Kunst* with Ernst Wasmuth in

▲ 1918, 1925b, 1930b, 1931

▲ 1935

5 • Albert Renger-Patzsch, *Natterkopf*, 1925

Berlin, that Blossfeldt was discovered as the great pioneering photographer of the emerging aesthetic of Neue Sachlichkeit; Moholy-Nagy thus included him in the entrance room of the "Film und Foto" exhibition the following year.

Making macroscopic detail and scientific series the epistemic structures of photographic observation, Blossfeldt developed the format of a photographic typology that would reverberate all the ▲ way into the sixties in the work of Bernd and Hilla Becher. At the time of Neue Sachlichkeit in the twenties, Blossfeldt's photographs were celebrated as evidence that modernist technical construction and the identity of function and ornament had a foundation in nature. More importantly, Blossfeldt's magical imagery of plant details responded to the desire to reconcile the fragmented experience of time and space under the conditions of industrialized labor with an ontological experience of natural rhythms and evolution. If the visual contemplation of the machine could serve to eventually ban its menacing and alienating presence by naturalizing it using photographic means, then the detailed detection of a serially and structurally produced nature would comfort the spectator in the discovery of the profound unity of manmade and natural orders and structures. Franz Roh, the critic who would publish the crucial book *Foto-Auge* (Photo-Eye) in 1929 to accompany the "Film und Foto" exhibition, had already stated in an essay on post-Expressionist art in 1927 that "while expression had been detected until recently in the movement of life, we now discover the power of expression already in the stillness of being itself, while listening carefully to the *ursounds* of a mere entity that has come fully into being." Walter Benjamin in his essay in 1931 associated Blossfeldt with Atget's sobriety and singled out his photographs not only as early examples of photography's emancipation from Pictorialism, but also as evidence of its privileged access to the optical unconscious.

From now on, nature would be assimilated into technology, and technology had to be naturalized, or as Thomas Mann famously wrote in his review of Renger-Patzsch's 1928 book *Die Welt ist schön* (The World is Beautiful): "But what if now that psychic experience falls prey to the technological, the technological itself becomes soulful?" Renger-Patzsch's book, decorated with an emblem that combines the structures of an agave cactus with that of a telegraph mast, in a perplexing claim to correspondence, was initially meant to be called *Die Dinge* (The Things). It was Carl Georg Heise, the author of the preface, and the curator who had given Renger-Patzsch his first museum exhibition in 1927, who suggested the more emphatic title, involuntarily signaling to its critics the essentially affirmative character of Neue Sachlichkeit.

Walter Benjamin's response was the most devastating, identifying the problems of Renger-Patzsch's Neue Sachlichkeit photography more lucidly than anybody, when he stated: "What is creative in photography is its submission to fashion, and, not surprisingly, its motto is 'The World is Beautiful.' In that title, a tendency reveals itself that can position the montage of a soup can in cosmic space, but it cannot grasp any of the most elementary human contexts. Even in its most oneiric subjects, it still initiates more of the object's saleability rather than its cognition. Since the true visage of this type of photography is advertisement, (de-) construction would of course be its rightful counterpart."

The serial subject

But the photography of Neue Sachlichkeit was of course determined by a larger spectrum of contradictory promises and social interests, and its definition as a new type of "technological vision" lent itself in an ideal fashion to all of these tasks. First of all, the photographic aesthetic of Weimar articulated an anti-Expressionist restraint that began in Weimar Germany around 1925 as a response to the general political and economic stabilization of the period. Secondly, as a technologically formed aesthetic, it was part of a larger process of modernization in which the photographic practices themselves adjusted to a rapidly changing social environment, that is, the creation of a mass public sphere and rapidly advancing forms of industrialization.

Traditional German aesthetic thought, grounded in the subject's dialectical relationship to nature, was shifting to an aesthetic in which the primacy of nature would be displaced by the desire to associate the work of the artist with the advancement of industry and technology. And lastly, and most importantly perhaps, only photography, with its capacity to select, stage, and present objects as utterly authentic, could provide the images for a process of total commodification: only photography, with its intrinsically fetishistic structure, could record the impact of commodity fetishism on the subject's ▲ daily experience (which would become the project of Surrealism more than that of Neue Sachlichkeit). As Herbert Molderings has poignantly observed, the photographers of the Neue Sachlichkeit discovered their aesthetic project only "when it became evident that the serial principle and the intensification of repetition defined industrial production in general. Henceforth the rhythm of standardization and the ornamental accumulation of eternally identical objects would determine all the images of the new photographer."

▲ 1968a

▲ 1931

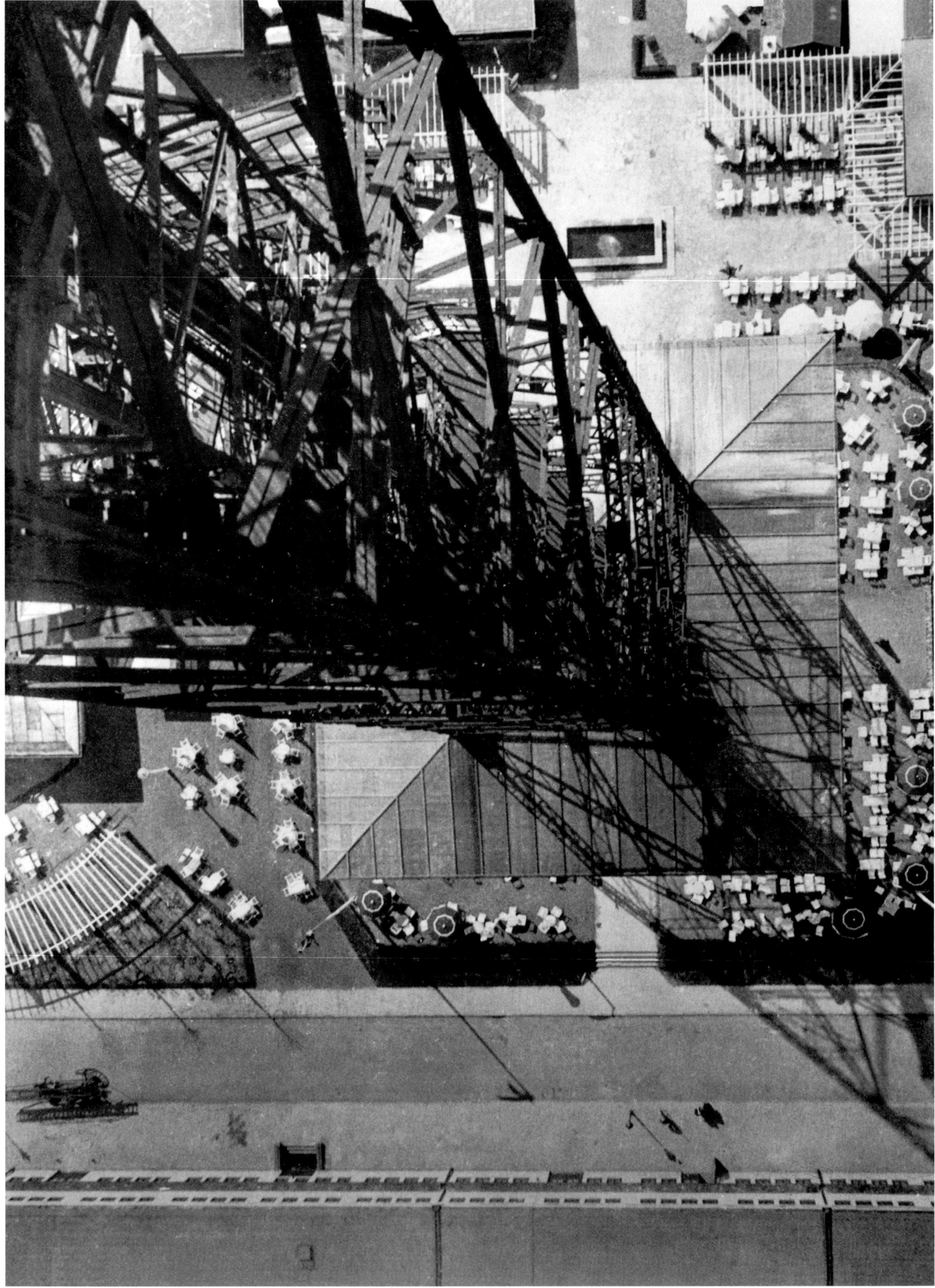

6 • László Moholy-Nagy, *Berlin*, 1928

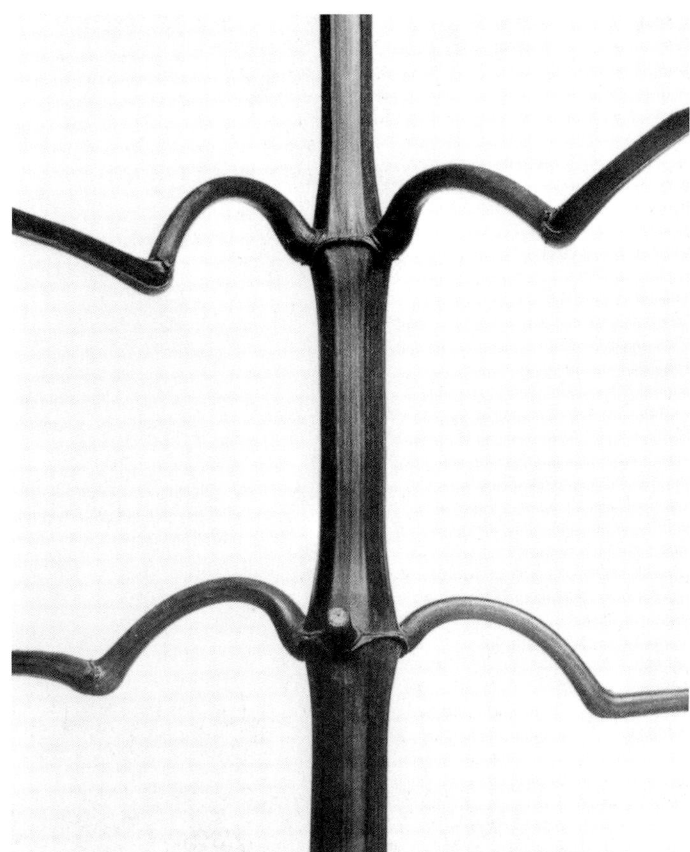

7 • Karl Blossfeldt, *Impatiens Glandulifera; Balsamine, Springkraut*, 1927
Silver salts print, dimensions unknown

▲ Paradoxically, August Sander (1867–1964), undoubtedly the greatest photographer of Neue Sachlichkeit, and one of the outstanding figures in the history of photography, was not included in the "Film und Foto" exhibition. Sander, who had been running a portrait studio since the beginning of the first decade of the twentieth century, had emphasized all along that photography had to be purged of its Pictorialist kitsch in favor of what he called "exact photography." In the early twenties, Sander had initiated a long-term project which attempted to construct an exhaustive documentation, entitled *Menschen des 20. Jahrhunderts* (Citizens of the Twentieth Century). His project—not unlike that of Atget's • disappearing Paris—resulted in an archive of tens of thousands of negatives (large parts of which were destroyed first by the Nazi government and subsequently by Allied bombs). Sander envisaged the eventual publication as consisting of forty-five portfolios of twelve images each that would represent and classify members of Weimar society according to their professional and class identities.

The ends of an archive

When a preliminary selection from the work was published in 1929, under the title *Antlitz der Zeit* (Face of Our Time), with an introduction by the novelist Alfred Döblin, it became instantly evident that Sander's was neither an ordinary portrait project nor a photographic enterprise that could be summoned for the aesthetics of Neue Sachlichkeit. Once again, it was Walter Benjamin's acumen that situated Sander's project in the most poignant historical context. Calling it an "atlas in physiognomic exercise," or a training manual (an *Übungsatlas*), Benjamin positioned Sander's *Antlitz der Zeit* in an astonishing, but historically precise comparison to the new (anti)portraits of the photographic and filmic culture of the Soviet Union. In both instances, Benjamin argued, the need for a new portrait form was articulated, one in which not only would a new social class find its proper representation (as in Soviet film), but one in which concern for a scientific understanding of social collectivity would displace the bourgeois subject's false claims for autonomy.

Sander was closely affiliated with the Cologne Progressives group, whose engagement in formulating a radically different conception of the subject and of a new proletarian public sphere had led them to an increased interest in social typology. One of the group's founders, Cologne artist Franz Wilhelm Seiwert had published a series of typological woodcuts called *Sieben Antlitze der Zeit* (Seven Portraits of our Time) in 1921, inspiring Sander's title.

While historians of photography have wondered why Sander's *Antlitz der Zeit* was confiscated and destroyed by the Nazi government in 1934, the answer seems relatively clear. First of all, Sander's project of a scientific typology of the social collective deconstructed the traditional safeguard of the singular bourgeois portrait. It replaced it with a collectivist photographic archive, unacceptable to an emerging totalitarian regime that was based on the destruction of the political identity of class and collectivity. Secondly, Sander's *Übungsatlas* delivered the last glance at an extraordinarily differentiated society, and the asynchronous diversity of the subject positions that Germany's first liberal democracy had allowed for. With the destruction of Sander's book and its photographic plates, the fascists attempted not only to eradicate the memory of that democracy, but—most significantly of all—to liquidate any possibility of a photographic analysis of social relations and their impact on the formation of the subject right from the very beginning.

FURTHER READING

George Baker, "August Sander: Photography between Narrativity and Stasis," *October*, no. 76, Spring 1996

Ute Eskildsen and Jan-Christopher Horak (eds), *Film und Foto der Zwanziger Jahre* (Stuttgart: Verlag Gerd Hatje, 1979)

Heinz Fuchs, "Die Dinge, die Sachen, die Welt der Technik," *Fotografie 1919–1979 Made in Germany* (Frankfurt: Umschau, 1979)

Gert Mattenklott, "Karl Blossfeldt: Fotografischer Naturalismus um 1900 und 1930," *Karl Blossfeldt* (Munich: Schirmer/Mosel, 1994)

Herbert Molderings, "Uberlegungen zur Fotografie der Neuen Sachlichkeit und des Bauhauses," in Molderings, Keller, and Ranke (eds), *Beitraege zur Geschichte und Aesthetik der Fotografie* (Giessen: Anabas Verlag, 1979)

Karl Steinorth (ed.), *Internationale Ausstellung des Deutschen Werkbundes "Film und Foto, 1929"* (Stuttgart: Deutsche Verlags-Anstalt, 1979)

▲ 1935 ● 1935

1930–1939

240 1930a The introduction of mass consumer and fashion magazines in twenties and thirties Weimar Germany generates new frameworks for the production and distribution of photographic imagery and helps foster the emergence of a group of important women photographers. BB

245 1930b Georges Bataille reviews *L'Art primitif* in *Documents*, making apparent a rift within the avant-garde's relation to primitivism and a deep split within Surrealism. RK

box • Carl Einstein YAB

250 1931 Alberto Giacometti, Salvador Dalí, and André Breton publish texts on "the object of symbolic function" in the magazine *Le Surréalisme au service de la révolution*: Surrealism extends its aesthetic of fetishism and fantasy into the realm of object-making. HF

255 1933 Scandal breaks out over the portrait of Lenin by Diego Rivera in the murals for the Rockefeller Center: the Mexican mural movement produces public political mural work in various American locations and establishes a precedent for political avant-garde art in the United States. AD

260 1934a At the First All Union Congress of Writers, Andrei Zhdanov lays down the doctrine of Soviet Socialist Realism. BB

266 1934b In "The Sculptor's Aims," Henry Moore articulates a British aesthetic of direct carving in sculpture that mediates between figuration and abstraction, between Surrealism and Constructivism. HF

271 1935 Walter Benjamin drafts "The Work of Art in the Age of Mechanical Reproduction," André Malraux initiates "The Museum without Walls," and Marcel Duchamp begins the *Boîte-en-Valise*: the impact of mechanical reproduction, surfacing into art through photography, is felt within aesthetic theory, art history, and art practice. RK

276 1936 As part of Franklin D. Roosevelt's New Deal, Walker Evans, Dorothea Lange, and other photographers are commissioned to document rural America in the grip of the Great Depression. RK

box • Works Progress Administration RK

281 1937a The European powers contest one another in national pavilions of art, trade, and propaganda at the International Exhibition in Paris, while the Nazis open the "Degenerate 'Art'" exhibition, a vast condemnation of modernist art, in Munich. HF

286 1937b Naum Gabo, Ben Nicholson, and Leslie Martin publish *Circle* in London, solidifying the institutionalization of geometric abstraction. YAB

1930a

The introduction of mass consumer and fashion magazines in twenties and thirties Weimar Germany generates new frameworks for the production and distribution of photographic imagery and helps foster the emergence of a group of important women photographers.

It is no accident that an astonishingly large number of women were among the key photographers of European and American photographic culture in the twenties and thirties. The famous question posed by Linda Nochlin in an essay in 1972 entitled "Why have there been no great women artists?" would have to be reversed for this period with the question being "Why were there so many great women photographers in the twenties and thirties?" In introducing the work of some of these photographers, and in order to explain this phenomenon, numerous and contradictory factors have to be considered. Generally speaking, one could argue that photography provided access to a technical and scientific apparatus of image production that displaced, once and for all, the exclusionist patriarchal rule that had declared exceptional manual skill, if not virtuosity, to be the single valid criterion of art. Photography—the techno-scientific reorganization of images—was causally intertwined with a general reformulation of the concepts of male sublimation that lay at the root of artistic identity. This is evident, for example, in the paradigm shift occurring in the work of Florence Henri (1893–1982) after she had taken courses with ▲ László Moholy-Nagy at the Bauhaus in Dessau in 1927 (as well as with Wassily Kandinsky and Paul Klee).

Recognizing that photography had become the central instrument of image production within the industrialization of everyday life, Henri adopted the principles and practices of Moholy-Nagy's "New Vision" photography. Returning to Paris in 1928, she wrote to her friend Lou Scheper :

> *Paris makes an incredibly old fashioned impression after the Bauhaus. I am no longer under its spell.... I am photographing.... I am fed up with painting and getting nowhere, and I have got an incredible number of ideas for photography.*

The tensions and tendencies embodied in the photography of Weimar women became apparent in a comparison of self-portraits by two of the most important protagonists of photography in the twenties. Germaine Krull's (1897–1985) *Self-Portrait with Ikarette* from 1925 **[1]** constructs the photographer's image within a complex amalgam of tropes of modernity: firstly, the fragmentation of the body and the metonymic foregrounding of the indexical hands that self-reflexively perform the act of photographic recording; secondly, the superimposition, if not the substitution, of the camera for the photographer's physiognomy, causes the photographer's eye and the optical device (the camera's viewfinder) to collapse in a mechanomorphic symbiosis. And lastly, the tropes of the emancipated "New Woman," in which the display of the technical apparatus is matched by an equally ostentatious display of the cigarette—offers yet another universal emblem of independence.

By contrast, Lotte Jacobi's (1896–1990) *Self-Portrait* of c. 1930 **[2]** emerges not only from a dramatic painterly chiaroscuro, but also from a far more traditional concept of the portrait and the photograph. The probing introspection with which Jacobi faces the camera seems to be driven by both *desires* for and *doubts* about the very feasibility of portraiture and the credibility of that genre, in which the representation of the subject had been anchored for centuries. In Jacobi's portrait the protagonist is not yet the camera itself, but is, rather, an artistic subject, albeit a struggling and desperate one. And yet, Jacobi's attempt to maintain a hierarchical relation between the subject and a (presumably subservient) technological apparatus is uncannily contested by the camera's glistening eye with its typographic inscription emerging from the dark of the studio space, and even more so by the ostentatiously lit remote-control cable that links machine and maker like an umbilical cord.

The "New Woman" as photographer

More concrete explanations for the increased numbers of women photographers can be found in the historical transformations of professional and educational institutions. Until the turn of the century, the traditional route to photographic education had been to work as an apprentice in the studio of a professional photographer (as did Jacobi, for example, who learned the profession in the workshop of her father and grandfather). Yet two institutions in Wilhelminian Germany offered photographic education within the curriculum when most of the traditional beaux-arts academies still barred female students. The first was the Institute for Photographic Education of the Lette Verein (founded in 1890 for the professional education of female photographers, it had begun with thirteen students and had 337 by 1919). The second major institution was the Teaching Institute for Photography *(Lehr- und*

▲ 1923

1 • Germaine Krull, *Self-Portrait with Ikarette*, 1925
Silver-gelatin print, 20 x 15.1 (7⅞ x 6)

2 • Lotte Jacobi, *Self-Portrait*, Berlin, c. 1930
Silver print, 32.1 x 25.1 (12⅝ x 9⅞)

Versuchsanstalt für Photographie), founded in Munich in 1900, which admitted women as of 1905; Krull, for example, studied with the American Pictorialist Frank Eugene Smith, who taught at the Munich Institute from 1907 to 1913. Nevertheless, it was not until 1921 that women could become full members of the German Professional Guild of Photographers. By the mid-twenties, photography was introduced in most German arts and crafts schools as a new medium within the curriculum of the applied arts. It had become more and more evident that the rapidly expanding need for advertisement and graphic design would benefit immensely from an increase in technical and artistic competence in photography. Thus, as of 1925 the Munich Institute for example, replaced its Pictorialist faculty and appointed younger photographers who ▲were familiar with the aesthetics of "New Objectivity." Other private institutions, such as the Reimann Schule appointed the young "New Vision" photographer Lucia Moholy to its faculty, where she remained from 1930 to 1933. The Bauhaus made its first faculty appointment in photography only under the directorship of Hannes Meyer, who nominated Walter Peterhans in 1929 to direct the new photographic curriculum that was aligned with the courses for advertising and design. Until 1933, when the Bauhaus was closed by the Nazi government, eleven women had successfully completed the photography class, among them several who went on to find considerable professional recognition, such as Ellen Auerbach (born 1906), Grete Stern (1904–99), Elsa Franke (1910–1981) and Irena Blühova (born 1904) (not to mention those who—like Henri—had studied with Moholy-Nagy).

But of equal, if not greater importance, were the newly arising professional opportunities offered to women. Statistics from 1925 record that 11.5 million women were professionals (35.8 percent of the total working population), making up the majority of low-level workers at the conveyor belts of industrial mass production, of white-collar workers in offices, and of sales personnel in department stores and retail industries. The social role model of the "New Woman" not only provided access to forms of emancipated experience. It also constructed women as producers and consumers and as objects within the overall process of the industrialization of new desires. Photographic mass culture generated and responded to these new behavioral forms and needs.

The new culture of illustrated magazines first emerged in Berlin (there were 200 registered magazines devoted to women, fashion, and domestic culture alone), ranging from Ullstein's conservative middle-class *BIZ*, the *Berliner Illustrierte Zeitung* (circulation 1.7 million copies), to a counterpublication for the working class, ▲Willi Münzenberg's *AIZ*, the *Arbeiter Illustrierte Zeitung*, sometimes reaching a print run of 350,000. Their equivalents in

▲ 1925b, 1929

▲ 1920

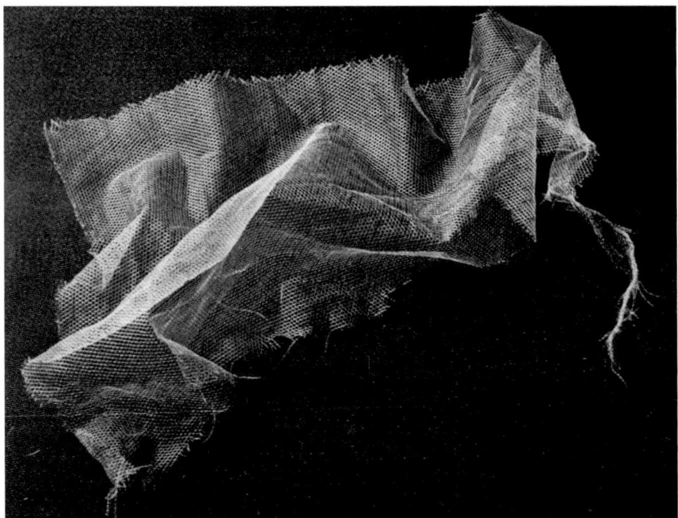

3 • Ringl + Pit (Ellen Auerbach and Grete Stern), *Fragment of a Bride*, 1930
Silver print, 16.5 x 22 (6 4/8 x 8 5/8)

Paris—for which many of the Weimar photographers supplied images—ranged from Lucien Vogel's liberal *VU* and Florent Fels's *VOILA* to the left-wing *Regards* (where Lisette Model's first photographs were published.)

These were soon followed by the American *Life* (whose first issue in 1936 had a cover photograph by Margaret Bourke White) and *Picture Post*, and the equivalent propaganda magazine in the Soviet Union, *USSR in Construction*. These photographic magazines would radically alter the image world of the bourgeois public sphere, either by constructing the earliest cohesive and totalizing forms of the new societies of spectacle and consumption, or by attempting to transform that sphere according to the needs of a newly emerging industrial proletariat and *its* public sphere.

The primary tasks of the illustrated magazines were achieved via four photographic genres. The first, visual reportage and photojournalism, had to simplify the complex narratives of history and politics by reducing them to a merely specular apprehension (the work of Alfred Eisenstaedt, Erich Salomon, or Felix Man, for example). The second, advertising photography, had to accelerate cycles of artificial actuality and immediate obsolescence. As product propaganda, photography had to modernize the objects and architectural spaces of everyday life according to the laws of an emerging consumer culture, while fashion photography had to initiate, sustain, and control the construction of new identities (such as the "New Woman").

The photographic work of Ringl + Pit (Ellen Auerbach and Grete Stern) is of exceptional significance in Weimar advertising photography. In images such as *Fragment of a Bride* [**3**] or *Polski Monopol* (1930), the two former Bauhaus students implemented the functions of advertising photography while simultaneously putting them on display with a supremely ironical self-reflexivity (unlike ▲ Albert Renger-Patzsch, their major rival in the field of Neue Sachlichkeit advertising photography). Both images concretize the two most important functions of the photograph as advertising: first, to serve as a deictic tool of ostentatious presentation (to render details with the highest exactitude, for example, to dramatize the play of light and shadow, and to exaggerate the transparency or the reflexivity of the surfaces of seduction), and second, to suspend the object in a condition of extreme fragmentation and spatial isolation so that it became the irresistible commodity fetish.

Travel photography was a third type of image production that women photographers developed in Europe in the prewar period (for example, Lotte Rosenberg-Errell's book *Kleine Reise zu Schwarzen Menschen* [Short Visit to Black People], published in 1931). Yet the genre of travel reportage became even more important after 1933 and in the immediate postwar period, more often than not as the result of exile. As with the previous genres, the motivations that defined and sustained it were manifold, ranging from the new medium's engagement in amateur—and professional—anthropology and ethnography to the instigation of new forms of mass and global tourism, or originating in the political desire to report on people's progress under radically changed historical and sociopolitical circumstances.

This stance is best exemplified in Jacobi's extensive documentation of the newly developing social relations in the Asian states of the Soviet Union, the formerly theocratic Islamic nations of Uzbekistan and Tajikistan that had been recently secularized. Travel photography would also fulfill the opposite need, that is, to document the urgent need for political change under conditions of political repression, as recorded in Germaine Krull's projects in Africa and Asia, or in Gisèle Freund's (1912–2000) work produced during her emigration to Argentina, and in Mexico in the fifties, when, as a suspected leftist, she was barred from entering the United States.

Travel photography in the guise of social documentary or political reporting would inevitably deteriorate in the postwar period, even in the hands of the greatest photographers (e.g., Henri Cartier-Bresson). Photographers could no longer match the excess of exotic visuality (the result of an increased access to geopolitical and ethnic diversities in the process of an expanding global tourism for which these photographers often served as unwitting pioneers) with the level of analysis necessary to grasp the political and economic links between the hunger for photographic images in the urban centers and the profoundly different conditions of experience that governed colonized and postcolonial societies. All too often, therefore, postwar travel photography served the continuously intensifying spectacle of exoticization and "othering," which found a first ▲ epochal climax in Edward Steichen's "The Family of Man" exhibition at the Museum of Modern Art in New York in 1955.

Three portrait positions

Lastly, and perhaps most importantly in the history of Weimar photography, we encounter the portrait in its most differentiated and dialectical forms. While still serving as *the* economic foundation of the photographic studio (the Berlin *Yellow Pages* for 1931 lists 600 photographic studios, of which at least 100 were owned and directed by women), the portrait also became the site where photography in

▲ 1929
▲ 1959d

4 • Gisèle Freund, *Demonstration in Frankfurt*, 1932

the thirties worked through its most profound contradictions. These ranged from the iterative production and distribution of images of the star, the new public persona whose function it was to compensate for the loss of subjective experience in the masses, to the contemplation of the precarious status—if not the final demise—of the representation of the bourgeois subject. The photograph's essential duality as both an exact indexical record and an artificial simulacrum (its most extreme form being the montage of photographs) lent itself to both the ideology of a physiognomically anchored identity and to the conception of subjectivity as pure construction.

At one extreme we find Erna Lendvai-Dircksen (1883–1962). Admitted as one of the first women members of the German Guild of Photographers in 1924, she ran one of the most successful portrait studios in Berlin. Lendvai-Dircksen claimed that a subject's identity was grounded in ethnicity and race, homeland and religion, and that therefore the portrait could best map that identity by tracing the physiognomy of the sitter as accurately as only photography would allow. In her lecture in 1933, "On German Photography," she polemicized against the "internationalist dissolution of the photograph by New Objectivity" and promised that her project would "save the German and the Germanic people's faces" and would follow the "inner obligation to participate in the restoration of the decaying German physiognomy." Not surprisingly, Lendvai-Dircksen not only became an ardent fascist herself in 1933, but her work would soon be published and distributed by the Nazi rulers as the photographic corroboration of their racist ideologies.

We find the dialectical opposite in portrait photographs by Freund and Jacobi, Annelise Kretschmer (1903–87), and in Helmar Lerski's (1871–1956) project *Köpfe des Alltags* (Everyday Heads), published in 1931. In 1932 Freund had still been attempting to construct the image of the new proletarian and collective subject in her photographs of mass demonstrations **[4]** and Jacobi had produced portraits of the Communist candidate Ernst Thälmann for the cover of *AIZ* in a desperate attempt to prevent the Nazi Party from coming to power in the fatal elections of 1933. In these images—as in the photographs by ▲ Aleksandr Rodchenko and the Soviet avant-garde photographers working at that time—the subject is anonymous, and ostentatiously presented as constructed by class, social relations, and professional identities. In some of the most radical work of the time, the subject is constituted in the process of labor itself, as in the extraordinary series of images of street workers, taken by Ella Bergmann-Michel between 1928 and 1932 from a bird's-eye view, in which the ground of labor (the grid of cubic basalt blocks making up a street) and the laboring figure itself are fused in an inseparable unity.

We find, however, a third model of Weimar portrait photography in the extraordinary portraits that Krull and Freund produced in the late twenties in Germany and when exiled in France in the thirties, and in particular in the work of Jacobi, one of the greatest portraitists of the twentieth century, during her years in Berlin and New York. These images are defined by an innate sense of the subject's fragility, its historically determined transitional status. Their almost exhaustive account of the intellectuals and artists of the interwar period (such as Krull's portrait of Walter Benjamin in 1926) reminds us of Nadar's astonishing pantheon of portraits of the Republican intellectuals and artists in France after 1848. These images seem to hold on to the last moment of European subjectivity

▲ 1935

before the concept of the subject and its social reality were annihilated by the joint onslaughts of fascist politics and engulfment by the image technologies of mass culture.

The subject in exile

As evident in her numerous portraits of actors of the period, for example *Lotte Lenya Weill* [**5**], Jacobi already seems to have recognized that the modern specular subject of the "star" would be constituted at the very intersection of fashion design, makeup, lighting techniques, and iterative distribution, in outright opposition to the traditional conception of unique subjectivity, that assumed "naturally" available markers of distinction (by class privilege) and the inevitable emanation of individual psychic presence. Photographs now appeared to be uniquely qualified to record images of that new type of constructed subjectivity. But Jacobi and Freund—like their ▲ great Viennese colleague Lisette Model— would also record subjectivity as suspended, in transition between Weimar culture and exile.

Freund had been a member of the Communist Student Organization at the University of Frankfurt, where she had been working on her doctoral dissertation under the tutelage of Karl Mannheim, Norbert Elias, and Theodor Adorno. Forced to emigrate to Paris in 1933, she saved her manuscript and subsequently completed it at the Sorbonne in Paris in 1936, where it was published in 1937 as the first social history of photography under the title *La Photographie en France au XIXème Siècle.*

Jacobi emigrated to New York in 1935. While stark chiaroscuro had been a hallmark of her portraits throughout the twenties, signifying dramatic specular modernity with its attributes of theatricality, fashion, and film (such as the portrait of the actor *Francis Lederer* or *Russian Dancer* in 1929), it acquired a distinctly melancholic dimension after her arrival in the United States. Jacobi's portraits recorded the danger of the historical moment and the tragic experiences of her sitters (the portraits of Erich Reiss, Karen Horney, and Max Reinhardt, for example) who found themselves not only biographically and professionally suspended in the geopolitical chasm of exile, but equally, as did Jacobi herself, in the historical shift from the radical bourgeois public sphere of Weimar culture to that of the culture industry of the United States.

While Jacobi's melancholic chiaroscuro attempted to rescue the subject's contemplative dimension, Freund's decision to employ color photography from 1938 onward (the portraits of James Joyce and of French interwar intellectual and artistic "celebrities," for example) situated the portrait within an altogether different set of relations, signaling the inevitable shift toward the spectacularization of subjectivity. Freund's color photographs seem involuntarily intertwined with the imminent influx of American technicolor movies and with the full-color advertisements of the *Saturday Evening Post* or *Life* magazine whose chromatic "naturalism" would simulate immediacy, presence and life, promising unlimited access to the universe of dead objects that consumer culture was soon to foist on its postwar subjects.

5 • Lotte Jacobi, *Portrait of Lotte Lenya Weill*, c. 1928
Silver print, 27.6 x 35.6 (10⅞ x 14)

It is particularly important to trace the development of the Weimar photographers after their emigration either to France (as was the case with Freund and Krull), to the United States (as was the case with Jacobi, Auerbach, and many others), or to Argentina (as in the case of Grete Stern). Bereft not only of their language and culture, but also of the progressive social and political contexts from within which they had emerged (for instance, the context of the Weimar avant-garde—such as the Bauhaus—the emergence of an emancipatory feminist consciousness evident in the radical enactment of the rights of the "New Woman," and the horizon of an actually existing socialist politics), they now found themselves confronted with totally different definitions of the social functions of photography. On the one hand was an outright and intensified commercialism in the rapidly accelerating consumer culture of the United States where "photography as a weapon" was more thoroughly discredited and censored than one might be able to recollect at this point. On the other hand was a general cultural backlash and a return to the patriarchal supremacy of painting as the centrally governing practice of visual culture (as in Abstract Expressionism), against which photography, shunted from its position at the radical forefront of Weimar culture, could now be relegated to its earlier role as the minor "sister art."

FURTHER READING

Ellen Auerbach, *Berlin, Tel Aviv, London, New York* (Munich and New York: Prestel Verlag, 1998)
Marion Beckers and Elisabeth Moortgat, *Atelier Lotte Jacobi: Berlin—New York* (Berlin: Nicolai Verlag, 1997)
Christian Caujolle (ed.), *Gisèle Freund: Photographer* (New York: Harry N. Abrams, 1985)
Ute Eskildsen (ed.), *Fotografieren hiess teilnehmen: Fotografinnen der Weimarer Republik*, (Essen: Museum Folkwang; and Düsseldorf: Richter Verlag, 1994)
Naomi Rosenblum, *A History of Women's Photographers* (New York: Abbeville Press, 1994)
Kim Sichel, *Germaine Krull: Photographer of Modernity* (Cambridge, Mass.: MIT Press, 1999)
Kelly Wise, *Lotte Jacobi* (Danbury: Addison House, 1978)

▲ 1959d

1930b

Georges Bataille reviews *L'Art primitif* in *Documents*, making apparent a rift within the avant-garde's relation to primitivism and a deep split within Surrealism.

By the time Georges Bataille (1897–1962)—philosopher, librarian, pornographer, critic, and editor of the dissident Surrealist magazine *Documents* (whom André Breton called Surrealism's "enemy from within")—decided to address the recently published *L'Art primitif* (Primitive Art) by French psychologist Georges Luquet, "primitivism" was no longer just the private enthusiasm of the avant-garde. In Paris especially, "primitivism" had emerged as spectacle—both at the level of high culture, as in the opera *The Creation of the World* (1923), with tribal costuming and sets by Fernand Léger and music by Darius Milhaud, and (given that the tribal could be updated in the contemporary imagination to include anything "African") at the lower end of the scale, as in the nightclub performances of Josephine Baker and in the eruption of jazz in Montparnasse bars and clubs. The newfound chic of "primitivism" also meant that tribal motifs were now a part of the world of expensive ornament, with the Art Deco palette of chrome and plastic ▲ expanded to accommodate a taste for ivory, ebony, and zebra skin.

Further, "primitivism," a term that encompassed both paleolithic and tribal art, was now understood in terms of the development of the human species ontogenetically as well as ethnically. It was the category through which to address the birth of art itself, whether in the caves at the dawn of human creativity or in the modern nursery at the onset of every child's urge to draw. This is why "primitivism" was now the province of psychologists as well as aestheticians (in his 1928 *Foundations of Art*, the French painter Amédée Ozenfant tried to operate as both). No longer a state of degeneracy or deviance, the • "primitive" was not now restricted to psychiatry but had also become the concern of developmental psychology. It was "Exhibit A" in the study of the evolution of human cognitive thought.

Bringing things down

In his review of *L'Art primitif*, Bataille summarized Luquet's developmental schema. Motor enthusiasm drives both contemporary child and earliest caveman to produce a random scrawl on paper or wall; empowered by the need to find "form" in the world, the scribbler starts to "recognize" the shapes of objects within this marking; recognition leads to the intention to produce such shapes at will and a primitive mimetic drive thus begins, first conveying natural objects in a schematic way, finally (at the end of the process) rendering them in a realistic manner.

But Bataille did not agree with Luquet. According to him, it was not Narcissus bending over a pool of water who was to be found in the caves 25,000 years ago but the Minotaur, a raging beast patrolling the dark, vertiginous space of the labyrinth. The child begins to mark, Bataille argues, not out of constructive impulses but from the joy of destruction, the pleasure of dirtying. Far from disappearing, this destructive drive continues into the representational phase, and as it does so it is consistently turned against the draftsman himself as a form of self-mutilation; for, Bataille points out, in the paleolithic caves the human effigy is consistently defaced and deformed, even while animal depictions become more and more assured. Auto-mutilation, the drive toward lowering or debasing the human form, is, then, at the core of art; it is not the law of form (or gestalt) that reveals what took place at art's beginnings but rather the sway of what Bataille calls the *informe*, the "formless."

"Informe," Bataille's little text on formlessness, appeared early on in the short life of *Documents*. It was part of the "Dictionary" written collectively by members of the *Documents* group over the two-year span of the magazine. Reflexive in nature, the text addressed the very definitions of words. A dictionary, it argued, should give words *jobs* rather than meanings, with the job of the word "formless" being that of undoing the whole system of meaning, itself a matter of form or classification. By declassifying, *formless* would also "de-class" or bring things down in the world (*déclasser*). It would break the back of resemblance—in which a categorical ideal or model is copied, the one always capable of being distinguished from the other—so necessary to the possibility of gathering things together in classes: "To assert that the universe does not resemble anything and is merely formless," Bataille concludes, "amounts to saying that the universe is something like a spider or spit."

The license to shock

Bankrolled by the art dealer Georges Wildenstein, *Documents* was supposed to have been an art magazine. But from the first issue the rubric "Fine Arts" was joined on its cover by those of "Doctrines,"

▲ 1925a • 1903, 1922

"Archaeology," and "Ethnography" (a fifth section, "Variétés," promising texts on popular culture, replaced "Doctrines" from issue five). In counterdistinction to the aestheticized ethnography that gripped the Surrealist movement by the end of the twenties, the *Documents* notion of the tribal was violently antiaesthetic. The premises of the ethnographers who published in the magazine—Marcel Griaule, Michel Leiris, Paul Rivet, Georges-Henri Rivière, André Schaeffner—were antimuseum; they believed that tribal material was meaningless when taken out of context and that, far from being a matter of arresting visual forms, such material concerned a pattern of ritual and daily experience (Griaule wrote on "spitting" as a form of hygiene) that could not be frozen into the world of the vitrine and the gallery.

In adding "spit" to the catalogue of their concerns, the ethnographers could be seen as announcing an affinity with Surrealism's own defiant posture, its decision to carry a "license to shock." Indeed, with many former members of the movement having ▲ abandoned André Breton for the *Documents* circle—the painter • André Masson, the poet Robert Desnos, the photographer Jacques-André Boiffard, to name three—Bataille's group was itself an alternative form of Surrealism, which the historian James Clifford has called "ethnographic surrealism." Like the Surrealists with their practice of automatic writing, and like the psychoanalyst in his use of free association, the *Documents* ethnographers demanded that everything should be allowed to surface. Their investigations, scientific in nature, should operate according to the law of no exclusions; they should concern everything in a culture from its highest to its lowest expressions; everything—"even the most formless"—should enter the world of ethnographic classification.

It is exactly at this point, the French critic Denis Hollier has argued, that a rift opens within *Documents* itself. For if its ethnographers thought of themselves as being shocking by attending equally to low and to high, their very act of attention strips the low of its power to shock. This is because theirs is precisely the work of *classification*, submitting "even the most formless" to the work of resemblance. Yet for Bataille, as we have seen, the "formless" resembles nothing. Lower than low, totally without example, and thus "impossible," it is that which declassifies. Bataille's concept of formless thus parts company with that of the ethnographers. "On the one hand," writes Hollier, "the law of 'no exception'; on the other, that of an absolute exception, of that which is unique but without properties."

Although he was an ethnographer, the writer Michel Leiris was closer to Bataille in many respects than to Marcel Griaule. His *Phantom Africa* (1934), the account of his participation in Griaule's 1933 expedition from Dakar to Djibouti (to study the Dogon people), was as much an exercise in personal introspection—dreams, fantasies—as it was objective reportage. Leiris was ■ also close to artists such as Joan Miró and Alberto Giacometti, writing the very first account of the latter's work for a review in *Documents*. Drawing these artists into Bataille's orbit, this connection (documented in Miró's 1927 painting *Michel [Leiris], Bataille, et moi*) was to prove fateful for both.

Taking Miró at his word when he claimed in 1927 that he wanted to "assassinate" painting, Leiris switched the discourse on ▲ Miró's dream pictures from Surrealist to formless. Accordingly, in his 1929 essay in *Documents*, he spoke of these works as being "not so much painted as dirtied," their calligrammatic drawing recoded in his eyes as graffiti. They are, he wrote, "troubling like destroyed buildings, tantalizing like faded walls on which generations of poster-hangers, allied over centuries of drizzle, have inscribed mysterious poems, long smears taking louche shapes, uncertain like alluvial deposits."

"Like a spider or spit"

When Bataille also addressed Miró's art in *Documents*, in 1930, he spoke of it as *informe*. And indeed, during the two years of Miró's entry into this orbit his rage against painting took the guise of making little constructions of objects picked out of garbage cans, or of working on collages with nails projecting from them [1]. Writing of the few canvases that Miró produced, which the artist termed "antipainting," Bataille related: "the decomposition was pushed to the point where nothing remained but some formless blotches on the cover (or, if you prefer, on the gravestone) of

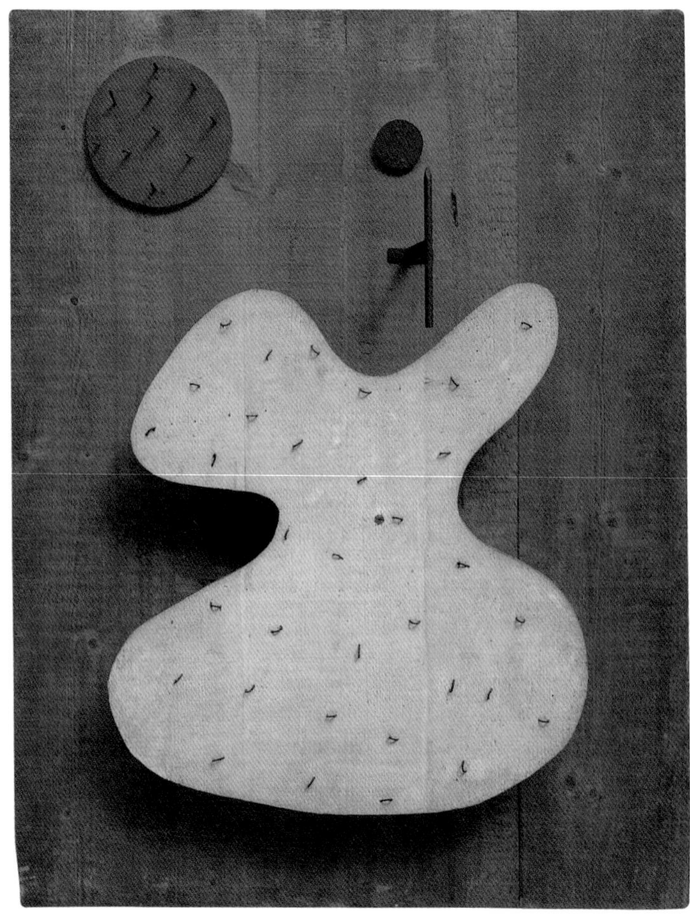

1 • Joan Miró, *Relief Construction*, Montroig, August–November 1930
Wood and metal, 91.1 x 70.2 x 16.2 ($35\frac{7}{8}$ x $27\frac{5}{8}$ x $6\frac{3}{8}$)

▲ 1924 • 1942a ■ 1924, 1931, 1959c ▲ 1924

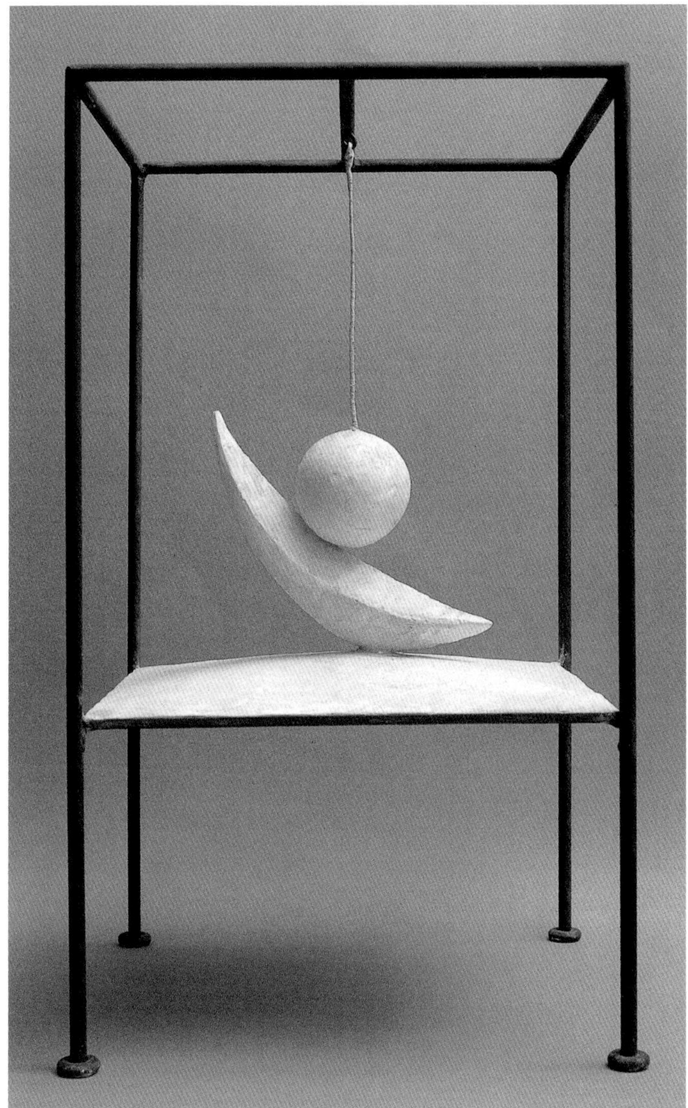

2 • Alberto Giacometti, *Suspended Ball*, 1930–1 (1965 reconstruction)
Plaster and metal, 61 x 36 x 33.5 (24 x 14⅛ x 13¼)

Carl Einstein (1885–1940)

Carl Einstein is best remembered today for being the first author to have discussed African sculptures in aesthetic terms rather than as ethnographic artifacts, in his profusely illustrated and groundbreaking *Negerplastik* (Negro Sculpture) of 1915, which was widely circulated among avant-garde artists of the day. He is also credited with writing the first extensive survey of twentieth-century art—in 1926, when only a quarter of the century in question had passed! But that is just the tip of a large iceberg. An accomplished writer whose modernist novel *Bebuquin* was celebrated in many avant-garde journals soon after its publication in 1912, Einstein was also a cultural critic whose positions were often akin to that of the Frankfurt School, particularly of its most famous members Theodor Adorno and Walter Benjamin. Reacting against the traditional formalism of his professor Heinrich Wölfflin, he proposed early on an interpretation of Cubism that, resolutely opposed to its then current apology as an art of synthesis and ideation, stressed instead its heterogeneous nature and its discontinuity. Soon after his arrival in Paris in 1928, he became one of the founders and major contributors of *Documents*, and sided with Georges Bataille in the elaboration of a view of Surrealism that radically dissented from André Breton's official line. A lifelong anarchist militant, he enlisted in the Spanish Civil War in 1936 and returned to France at the victory of General Franco, where he was arrested and interned by the French government until he committed suicide to escape Nazi persecutions.

painting's box of tricks." But one cannot kill off art *and* remain an artist; by 1930–1, Miró, who had practically stopped working, had to choose. His decision was to return to painting, but in a corrosive style that carried over a *Documents* sensibility in its attack on the human body and on "good form."

Giacometti's case is even more telling in regard to the issue of primitivism, since, as a developing sculptor, his attraction to the ▲ work of Brancusi led him at first to the kind of aestheticizing primitivism that Bataille and the *Documents* ethnographers abhorred. But through Masson and Leiris he, too, entered the pages of the magazine and soon thereafter into the sensibility of the formless. The first direction this took was an attraction to the theme of the praying mantis, itself an important incarnation of the attack on form. His most achieved production of formlessness was, however, the sculpture called *Suspended Ball*, which, ironically, caused great excitement • among the Surrealists when it was first exhibited in 1930 [**2**].

There, two caged forms—a recumbent wedge and a cloven ball hung, pendulum-like, from a strut at the cage's top—seem to make contact, as the ball appears to swing, caressingly, over the crescent shape below. This contact seems manifestly sexual since the forms are so genital in appearance. But the deep ambiguity that descends on them makes their gender identification a matter of constant indecision. Vulvalike, the wedge is also coded male, like the phallic knife that slices across the heroine's eye in Salvador Dalí and Luis Buñuel's film *Un Chien d'Andalou* (Andalusian Dog; 1929). Masculine in its active role, the ball's cleft also pronounces it as feminine. And the continual crisscross of this play of identification, itself imitating the metronomic swing of the structure's pendulum, results in just that act of declassifying that Bataille had termed the job of formlessness. The "impossible" condition that emerges in *Suspended Ball* is Hollier's "absolute exception," or what Roland Barthes would call, referring to a similar crossing of gender identifications in Bataille's pornographic novel *The Story of the Eye*, a "round phallicism."

The important lesson that *Suspended Ball* delivers is that the formless is not simply mess or slime. Its cancellation of boundaries is more structural than that since it involves a voiding of categories. Such a voiding is operational, active, like the swing of Giacometti's pendulum, or like the lowering from vertical to horizontal that Bataille invokes in his "Dictionary" definition when he says that the formless will "knock form off its pedestal and bring it down in

▲ 1927 • 1931

the world." Another example of such a lowering or cancellation of the difference between these spatial coordinates is the labyrinthine space of caves, where the axes of reason and of architecture no longer apply. It is from this that Bataille's love of the cave's denizen, the Minotaur, derives. Giacometti's decision in 1930 to orient his sculpture to the horizontal, making it out of nothing but what had formerly been the mere base of sculpture, emerged from this thought of the formless. The breakthrough in the history of modernist sculpture represented by a work like *No More Play* (1933), however, would be understood only in the sixties with a movement ▲ such as Earthworks.

That formlessness results from a blurring of categories, rather than from a literal clouding of shape, is once more apparent in two works reproduced in the magazine *Minotaure* (named by Bataille but controlled for the most part by Breton) in the early thirties. One of these, made as a frontispiece for the magazine, displays the Minotaur photographically, with Man Ray lighting his model so as to produce a headless torso whose arms and chest now double as the horns and brow of a bull [**3**]. Thus collapsing human and animal into a single "impossible" category, the seeming headlessness of the human model further implies the downward pull that goes with a loss of form. The other work, from *Minotaure*'s first issue, is also a photograph, again produced with a great precision that nonetheless yields up categorical blur. This is Brassaï's *Nude* [**4**], in which the female body is transgressively shot so as to project itself unmistakably as phallic, once more collapsing gender distinctions in the manner of *Suspended Ball.*

Minotaure was the site of a sequence of photoconceptual works made in a partnership between Salvador Dalí and Brassaï, all of which circle around the formless. *The Phenomenon of Ecstasy* [**5**], even while organizing the units of the images into a grid (that is, into the structure that announces form's drive toward order and logic), exploits the idea of a fall from vertical to horizontal and a (hysterical) collapse of upper organs (mouth, ear) onto lower ones (vagina, anus). *Involuntary Sculptures* (1933) displays the tiny results of unconscious, masturbatory gestures: bus tickets obsessively rolled in one's pockets, erasers or crusts of bread distractedly kneaded, etc. In the third work, Dalí discusses Hector Guimard's Art Nouveau metro entrances, photographed by Brassaï to demonstrate the presence within these forms of the silhouette of the praying mantis.

An embodiment of formlessness as fascinating as the Minotaur itself, the praying mantis received its most brilliant theorization from the pen of Roger Caillois, an ally of Bataille's, who wrote on the creature in the fifth issue of *Minotaure* (1934). Here formlessness moves through the channel of animal mimicry, in which insects camouflage themselves in a form of identification with their surrounding space. In the case of the mantis this takes the guise of "playing dead" as, stock still, it turns itself into a blade of grass. Although blending with the background produces its own type of categorical cancellation, as the difference between figure and ground or that between the interior and the exterior of the organism seems to be erased, the mantis's "playing dead" ratchets this up yet another notch on the scale of the "impossible." For the mantis, often decapitated in its fights with others, is an insect that carries on its living duties regardless—hunting, laying eggs, building nests. Dead, it plays at life. But since among its activities when alive was the defense of playing dead, it is assumed that a dead mantis would do this, too. Thus dead, it plays at life playing at death.

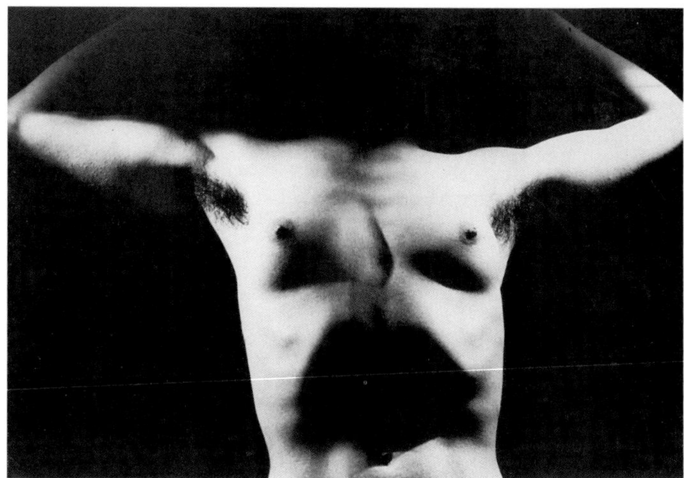

3 • Man Ray, *Minotaur*, 1934
Silver-gelatin print

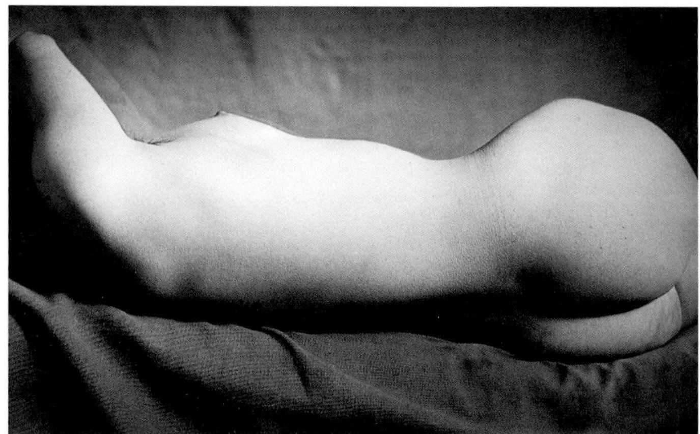

4 • Brassaï, *Nude*, 1933
Silver-gelatin print

The cancellation of resemblance produces the impossible instance of death playing dead. In another, later lexicon this would ▲ be called the *simulacrum*; Bataille called it the formless.

FURTHER READING

Dawn Ades (ed.), *Dada and Surrealism Reviewed* (London: Hayward Gallery, 1978)

Roland Barthes, "The Metaphor of the Eye," *Critical Essays* (Evanston: Northwestern University Press, 1972)

Yve-Alain Bois and Rosalind Krauss, *Formless: A User's Guide* (New York: Zone Books, 1997)

Roger Caillois, "La mante réligieuse," *Minotaure*, no. 5 (1934), translated in *October*, no. 44, Spring 1988

▲ 1967a, 1970

▲ Introduction 4, 1977, 1980

5 • Salvador Dalí, *The Phenomenon of Ecstasy*, 1933
Photomontage, dimensions unknown

1931

Alberto Giacometti, Salvador Dalí, and André Breton publish texts on "the object of symbolic function" in the magazine *Le Surréalisme au service de la révolution*: Surrealism extends its aesthetic of fetishism and fantasy into the realm of object-making.

Two challenges to traditional sculpture came in the form of ▲ the tribal artifact, as used by primitivist artists, and the • everyday commodity, as used in the Duchampian readymade. Although they are obviously different, each object seemed to possess or play on a kind of fetishistic power. The tribal artifact evoked the fetish as a ritual object, with a special life or cultic force of its own, while the readymade evoked the fetish as commercial product, the commodity fetish. According to the classic analysis of Karl Marx, capitalist production leads us to forget that commodities are made by human labor, and so we tend to endow these things with an autonomous life or power, to fetishize them in this sense as well. Part of the attraction of the tribal artifact was its very difference from a capitalist economy of commodity exchange, while part of the provocation of the readymade was its implicit demonstration that, despite its often transcendental pretenses, modern art was bound to this same economy—that like any other product it was made primarily for display and sale. With the advent of the Surrealist object, this partial typology of modernist object-making may be extended, for it involves a third kind of fetish, the sexual fetish, and part of its effect was also due to its juxtaposition of different economies of the object.

Ambivalent objects

Consider an object already cited in this book, the little slipper-spoon ■ found by André Breton in a Paris flea market. In his 1937 novel *L'Amour fou* (Mad Love), the object reminds Breton of a phrase, "Cinderella ashtray," that represents his desire for love—no doubt because of its conjoining of a spoon, a classic Surrealist emblem of woman, with a slipper, a classic sexual fetish. But this wooden spoon, Breton tells us in *L'Amour fou*, was also an object of "peasant fabrication," a crafted thing made for personal use that was outmoded, literally pushed to the flea market, by the industrial production of mass goods. Thus its service as a sign of a repressed wish or desire may be related to its status as a vestige of a displaced social formation or economic mode. That is, the Surrealist concern with "the uncanny" in subjective life, with familiar images, objects, or events made strange by repression, may be connected to the Marxist concern with "the nonsynchronous" in historical life—with the uneven development of social relations and productive modes. The very force of Surrealist objects like the slipper-spoon may depend on this connection between subjective and social histories.

"What prepares these products to receive the investment of psychic energy characteristic of their use by Surrealism," the American critic Fredric Jameson has argued, "is precisely the half-sketched, uneffaced mark of human labor, of the human gestures, on them; they are still frozen gesture, not yet completely separated from subjectivity, and remain therefore potentially as mysterious and expressive as the human body itself." Here Jameson elaborates on an insight of the German critic Walter Benjamin, who, in his essay "Surrealism: The Last Snapshot of the European Intelligentsia" (1929), celebrated the Surrealists as "the first to perceive the revolutionary energies in the 'outmoded,' in the first iron construction, the first factory buildings, the earliest photos, the objects that have begun to be extinct." To recover such "wish-symbols of the previous century" was, for Benjamin, to redeem these "ruins of the bourgeoisie" as talismans of "dialectical thinking" or "historical awakening." This "profane illumination" was sometimes sparked by the way that a particular object might set different economies of the object into contradiction.

The first Surrealist object proposed by Breton, in his essay "Introduction to the Discourse on the Paucity of Reality" (1924), was also seen in a flea market, but only in a dream. This object was a fantastic book, with pages made of black cloth and a wooden spine carved in the form of a gnome—a remainder from an even more exotic time than that of the slipper-spoon. In this early essay, Breton stressed the *unreality* of the Surrealist object, its challenge to "creatures and things of 'reason'" and use, a definition that he likely extrapolated from a reading of the readymade. But soon Breton shifted to stress the *reality* of the Surrealist object as a sign of desire, which points to an important difference from the readymade. For though the readymade is a found object, it is rarely outmoded and never uncanny in the Surrealist sense; and though it may pun sexually, it is not invested with psychic energy in the same sense either. On the contrary, Duchamp aimed at "visual indifference," even "complete anaesthesia," in the readymade, which, unlike the Surrealist object, is "separated from subjectivity" in order that it might challenge this deepest of bourgeois beliefs about the subjective origin of all art.

▲ 1903, 1907 • 1914 ■ 1924

Nonetheless, the Surrealist object derived from the Duchampian readymade, just as the Surrealist image derived from the Dadaist collage. Indeed, this development was an inaugural act of Surrealism, defined in the first issue of its first magazine *La Révolution surréaliste* (1924) as "any discovery that changes the nature or the destination of an object or a phenomenon." This transformation is best traced in the work of the American photographer and painter ▲ Man Ray, whose *Enigma of Isidore Ducasse* (1920), a photograph of an object said to be a sewing machine, blanketed with burlap and bound in rope, accompanied this definition in the magazine. (Ducasse, known as Lautréamont, was a nineteenth-century poet-hero of the Surrealists, who took his line—"beautiful as the chance encounter of a sewing machine and an umbrella on a dissecting table"—as an aesthetic motto.) In his days as a New York Dadaist, Man Ray produced and/or photographed several readymades, some pure, some "assisted"; respective examples of each kind are a simple eggbeater titled *Man* and its counterpart, two hemispherical reflectors divided by a glass pane pinched by six laundry pins, titled *Woman* (both 1918). The sexual puns are intended here, and they point to a transitional work titled *Gift* [1] made during his first Paris show in December 1921 (Man Ray lived in Paris until 1940). On a whim, accompanied by the composer Erik Satie, he purchased a flatiron used on coal stoves, glued a row of fourteen tacks to its bottom (most replicas show nails), and added the object to the exhibition. The sadistic charge, only implicit in the eggbeater and pins of *Man* and *Woman*, is explicit here, as the tacks turn the readymade iron into a proto-Surrealist object. "You can tear a dress to ribbons with it," Man Ray once remarked of this work, as if to acknowledge that its sadism was directed at women. "I did it once, and asked a beautiful eighteen-year-old colored girl to wear it as she danced," he added, in a way that suggests how racial fetishism can compound sexual fetishism (as it often does in his work). "Her body showed through as she danced around; it was like a bronze in movement. It was really beautiful." But if *Gift* were only sadistic, it would not be as effective as it is; what makes it so is its ambivalence, which is twofold. In terms of its address to the viewer, the object is aggressive, but it is designated a gift; as such it literalizes the ambivalence of any present—as both an offering made and a debt incurred—an ambivalence detailed by the French anthropologist Marcel Mauss in his *Essai sur le don* (Essay on the Gift) of 1925. So, too, *Gift* is ambiguous in terms of function (most irons smooth and press; this one gouges and tears) and in terms of gender (most irons are associated with female labor; this one has penile tacks). Placed in contradiction, these aims turn the iron into the artistic equivalent of a symptom or, more exactly, of a fetish, which Freud defined as an object in which conflicted desires converge.

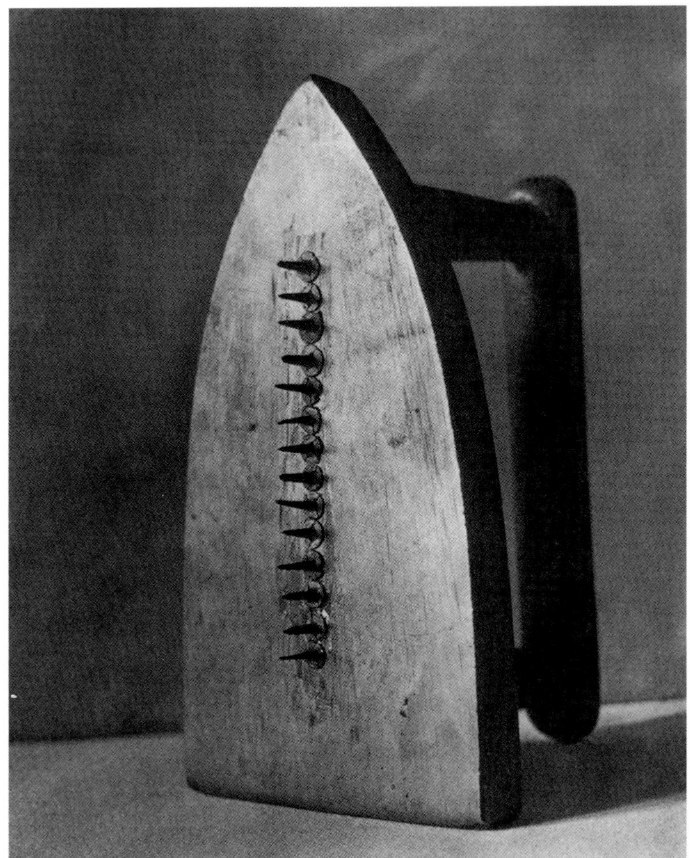

1 • Man Ray, *Gift*, 1921
Iron, nails, 17 x 10 x 11 (6⅝ x 3⅞ x 4⅓)

Objects mobile and mute

The Surrealists were among the first modernists to study Freud closely, but they also developed parallel insights, and it is not clear how much they knew of texts such as his 1927 essay on fetishism. For Freud the fetish is a substitute for the penis that the mother lacks. This lack is said to horrify the little boy who discovers it (the ambiguous case of the little girl is scanted), for it threatens him with this "castration" too, and so he turns to penile surrogates, that is, to fetishes, to maintain his fantasy of bodily wholeness, of phallic power. Thus fetishism is a practice of ambivalence in which the male subject both recognizes and disavows castration or any such traumatic loss. This ambivalence may split the subject, to be sure, but it may also split the fetish into an ambivalent object—both "memorial" to castration and "protection" against it. This is why, according to Freud, the fetish often registers both "hostility" and "affection," and why, apart from all the sexual desire displaced onto it, it is such a fraught thing.

The Surrealists were intrigued by this scenario, which they put into play in images and objects alike. For example, Surrealist photographs of nudes often oscillate between fragmentary parts and fetishistic wholes, in which the female body appears castrated and castrative one moment, only to appear integral and phallic the ▲ next. But castration anxiety and fetishistic defense are most focused in Surrealist objects—those by Alberto Giacometti above all others. It is as though some of his objects aim to suspend the castration that defines sexual difference in Freudian theory, or at • least to render sexual reference ambiguous (as in *Suspended Ball*); Others seem to disavow this castration fetishistically (such as the two *Disagreeable Objects* [1930–1]), while still others appear to

▲ 1918, 1924, 1930b

▲ Introduction 1, 1930b • 1930b

punish its female representative sadistically (such as the insectoid *Woman with Her Throat Cut* [1932]), with "horror at the mutilated creature or triumphant contempt for her" (Freud). At least for a few years Giacometti was able to turn the psychic ambivalence in fetishism into a symbolic ambiguity in object-making.

For the December 1931 issue of *Le Surréalisme au service de la révolution*, Giacometti sketched seven objects under the rubric *objets mobiles and muets*. This is a strange designation: it evokes things uncannily alive, mobile with desire but mute with repression. At least five of the objects were subsequently executed, while the other two evoke scenarios of sex and/or sacrifice also characteristic of Giacometti. In the drawing, a hand nearly touches the phallic form, as if to test the taboo against touching the desired thing (whether this be a totem animal, a sexual object, or an art work), that is, as if to point to the complementary relation between desire and prohibition, transgression and law, that structures the ambivalence of these works. Giacometti titled this object "disagreeable," as he did another one, also pictured in the drawing, in which the phallic form is cut by a plane; but it is difficult not to hear the word "agreeable" here as well. For both objects are at once "agreeable" as fetishes and "disagreeable" as shapes that nonetheless evoke castration. In its executed form, the first *Disagreeable Object* seems almost animate, an embryonic body with eyes, an object that suggests its own series of ambivalent associations (penis, feces, baby ...) analyzed elsewhere by Freud in terms of objects of feared loss. And recognition of castration does appear to be inscribed here in the form of the spikes: "hostility" for the fetish is indeed mixed with "affection."

This mixing of the agreeable and the disagreeable, the fetishistic and the castrative, is also at work in the most famous Surrealist ▲ object of all, the fur-lined teacup, saucer, and spoon made by the young German-Swiss Surrealist Meret Oppenheim (1913–85) in 1936. Such objects have stories—they are the precipitates of charged narratives—and the story here is this: one day at the Café de Flore in Paris, Oppenheim happened to show Picasso her design for a bracelet lined with fur, to which he replied that anything,

2 • The Galerie Charles Ratton, Paris, at the time of the "Exposition surréaliste d'objets," in May 1936

▲ Introduction 1

"even this cup and saucer," could be so covered (it is telling that by the mid-thirties such objects had already become not merely a genre of art but a style of jewelry). When Breton invited Oppenheim to exhibit in the 1936 "Exposition surréaliste d'objets" at the Galerie Charles Ratton **[2]**, she bought a tea set at a department store and lined each object (including a spoon for good measure) with the fur of a Chinese gazelle. Breton then titled the work *Déjeuner en fourrure* (*Luncheon in Fur*), a fitting homage to the painting by Édouard Manet *Déjeuner sur l'herbe* (Luncheon on the Grass) of 1862–3, as well as to the novel by Leopold von Sacher-Masoch *Venus in Furs* (1870; it was Sacher-Masoch who lent his name to the term "masochism"). For *Déjeuner en fourrure* is a still life-cum-nude, a witty disturbance of teatime propriety through a smutty allusion to female genitalia that plays ambivalently on oral eroticism as well. It also sends up the Freudian fetish, mocks it through excess, as if to fling its masculinist bias in the face of the male viewer. One senses the joy of power reversed in this well-played joke, a Venus in Furs who delights in her sadistic ploy. But the sadistic position, Freud tells us, can quickly turn into its masochistic double, and this reversal is suggested by another fetish contrived by Oppenheim in 1936, *Ma gouvernante—My Nurse—Mein Kindermädchen* **[3]** (her title implies that fetishism is not specific to gender or language). In his 1927 essay, Freud uses the bound feet of aristocratic women in old China as an example of the mixing of contempt and reverence in the fetish. Here Oppenheim offers us bound white high heels, a classic fetish in any case, turned over and cuffed in twine, an apparent trophy-testimonial of the sadism of men and the masochism of women. But this woman has garnished these heels with tassels and served them up on a silver platter, as if to subvert the sadistic position through sheer delight in the masochistic one; and indeed, in the sadomasochistic contract, the masochist is the person in control.

3 • Meret Oppenheim, *Ma gouvernante—My Nurse—Mein Kindermädchen*, 1936
Metal, paper, shoes, and string, 14 x 21 x 33 (5½ x 8¼ x 13)

Lost objects

By 1936 the fetish had begun to be a cliché in the hands of Surrealists who seemed to script objects after Freud. Salvador Dalí in particular was chastised by Breton for "the voluntary incorporation" of psychoanalytic interpretation into art in a way that weakened its effect. For Breton this scripting immobilized desire rather than motivated ambivalence, and yet he sought such a fixing, too. For he also held that every desire has a distinctive object, which chance would deliver as punctually as it had his slipper-spoon in the flea market. But the French psychoanalyst Jacques Lacan, who was a young associate of the Surrealists, has shown this idea of satisfied desire to be wishful thinking. In his account, need (the need of the infant, say, for maternal milk) can be satisfied, but desire (the desire of the infant, say, for the absent breast) cannot be satisfied, for its object is precisely lost (desire would not arise otherwise) and can only be re-created in fantasy. On the one hand, then, as Freud remarked, "the finding of a [sexual] object is in fact a refinding of it." On the other hand, as Lacan suggested, this refinding is forever a seeking: the object cannot be regained because it is phantasmatic, and desire cannot be satisfied because it is defined in lack. From this perspective, the Surrealist object is impossible in a way that most Surrealists never grasped, for they continued to insist on its discovery—on an object adequate to desire.

This confusion also comes into focus in the flea-market episode ▲ of the slipper-spoon, where Breton recounts how Giacometti made *Invisible Object* (*Hands Holding the Void*), otherwise known as *Feminine Personage* **[4]**. This figure was born of a romantic crisis, Breton tells us, and Giacometti had trouble with the hands, the head, and, implicitly, the breasts, which he resolved only when he discovered a strange helmet-mask at the market. For Breton this is a textbook case of a perfect match between desire and object. But in fact *Invisible Object* evokes the opposite condition, the *impossibility* of the lost object regained. With its cupped hands and blank stare, this feminine personage shapes "the invisible object" in its very absence; such is the eerie pathos of this alienated supplicant. In this way the Surrealist object is not only a fetish that covers

▲ 1924

4 • Alberto Giacometti, *Invisible Object (Hands Holding the Void)*, 1934
Bronze, 153 x 32 x 29 (60 2/8 x 12 5/8 x 11 3/8)

5 • Joseph Cornell, *Soap Bubble Set*, 1947–8
Construction, 32.4 x 47.3 x 7.6 (12 3/4 x 18 5/8 x 3)

up a lack; it is also a figure of this lack, an analogue of the lost object keyed to the maternal breast, as the invisible object is keyed here. We arrive, then, at this paradoxical formula of the found object in Surrealism: a lost object, it is never recovered but forever sought; always a substitute, it drives on its own search.

Faced with this difficulty, Giacometti turned back from traumatic fantasy to mimetic representation as the source of his art: "I worked ▲ with the model all day from 1935 to 1940." Yet, charged by fetishistic ambivalence, his Surrealist objects of the early thirties remain the high point of this practice. Too often in other hands these tableaux of "mobile and mute objects" became tabulations of inert and talky things. For example, in the same issue of *Le Surréalisme au service de la révolution* Dalí presented a tabulation of Surrealist objects that attempts to be absurd (he lists objects as "transubstantiated," "projected," "wrapped," and so on), to derange any order of things. But a "table" remains beneath such tabulations to arrange them, just as a table remains to support the "chance encounter of a sewing machine and the umbrella" in the line from Lautréamont. Often this table is one of display—many Surrealist objects appear in boxes or vitrines—and this display is not so alien to modes of exhibition in a gallery or indeed in a store. The objects in the celebrated 1936 show of Surrealist objects have circled back in this way to a setting like a flea market: these once-strange fetishes have once again become bric-à-brac for sale.

The Surrealist theater of fantasy was developed most effectively by the American Joseph Cornell (1903–72). Modeled on old dove-cotes, slot machines, and the like, his boxes adapt the cage and gameboard models of Giacometti, and they often mix the uncanny and the outmoded in Surrealist fashion. But even as these "philosophical toys" create an aesthetics of wonder—dream spaces where sand and stars, or soap bubbles and moon maps, seem to touch [**5**]—they amuse more than amaze. So too, even as they deal with loss, they smooth it over nostalgically more than activate it traumatically. Thus, however disparate his objects, Cornell allows subjectivity to cohere through the medium of memory. And although desire courses through some of his boxes (several are titled "hotel," and a few are posted with glamorous stars), in other boxes this desire often seems solitary and onanistic, and sometimes disconnected and dead (several are titled "museum," and a few hold stuffed birds). Here the Surrealist object arrives at another destination—not a display where disagreeable objects have become agreeable knickknacks, but a reliquary where the subject haunts its desire like a ghost.

FURTHER READING

Walter Benjamin, "Surrealism: The Last Snapshot of the European Intelligentsia" (1929), *Reflections*, trans. Edmund Jephcott (New York: Harcourt Brace Jovanovich, 1978)

André Breton, *Mad Love* (1937), trans. Mary Ann Caws (Lincoln, N.E.: University of Nebraska-Lincoln, 1987)

Hal Foster, *Compulsive Beauty* (Cambridge, Mass.: MIT Press, 1993)

Rosalind Krauss, *The Optical Unconscious* (Cambridge, Mass.: MIT Press, 1993)

Rosalind Krauss and Jane Livingston, *L'Amour fou: Surrealism and Photography* (New York: Abbeville Press, 1987)

▲ 1959c

1933

Scandal breaks out over the portrait of Lenin by Diego Rivera in the murals for the Rockefeller Center: the Mexican mural movement produces public political mural work in various American locations and establishes a precedent for political avant-garde art in the United States.

The Mexican mural movement was a state-sponsored, ideologically driven avant-garde of the twenties and thirties whose primary goal was to reclaim and re-create a Mexican identity based on Mexico's precolonial past. Diego Maria Rivera (1886–1957), David Alfaro Siqueiros (1896–1974), and José Clemente Orozco (1883–1949) exerted an enormous influence not only in their native Mexico but also internationally, especially in the United States.

The movement emerged at the end of the Agrarian Revolution of 1910–20, which pitted peasants, intellectuals, and artists against dictator Porfirio Díaz and the big landowners and foreign investors he supported. After ten years of civil war, the inauguration in 1920 of President Alvaro Obregón, a former revolutionary leader, reformist, and art lover, ushered in a period of hope and optimism. This Mexican renaissance was greatly assisted by the philosophical idealism of the Minister of Education, José Vasconcelos, who believed passionately that public art could be a vital component in his mission to educate and enthuse the public and garner support for the new government. It was Vasconcelos who initiated the government's mural program, making him, in a very real sense, the founder of the movement. Vasconcelos and the postrevolutionary government hoped that by collaborating with artists on cultural reforms, the Mexican people would be empowered to participate in the development of the nation and the creation of a new national, cultural and intellectual identity. Vasconcelos and most of the artists involved in the mural movement believed that this could be best achieved by drawing on their shared heritage rather than on the colonial past which had divided them.

Artists thrilled to the challenge of creating a new national art and cultural identity, and many returned to, or visited, Mexico to take part. One of the first was French-born part-Mexican Jean Charlot (1898–1979), who explained how the choice of style and subject all had social and political significance for Mexican artists:

> *Divergent points of view in aesthetic matters contribute substantially to the pulling apart of Mexico's social classes. The Indian preserves and practices pre-Hispanic art. The middle class preserves and practices a European art qualified by the pre-Hispanic or Indian. The so-called aristocratic class claims its art to be pure European.... When native and middle class share one criterion where art is concerned, we shall be culturally redeemed, and national art, one of the solid bases of national consciousness, will become a fact.*

Vasconcelos did not stipulate any particular style or subject matter, but most of the muralists adopted a mode of nationalist social realism, which drew on pre-Hispanic art forms and featured Mexican heroes and people. A respect for native traditions and popular history informed their art, as did an exploration of their Indian background. This did not, however, preclude an engagement with European modernism, for the new generation wanted to create a new, national art that was at once independent, socially committed, populist, and avant-garde. The quest also involved being able to communicate these revolutionary ideals to a largely illiterate audience in order to carry them along.

Important precursors of the mural movement included the painters Francisco Goitía (1882–1960) and Saturnino Herrán (1887–1918), who early in the century were beginning to develop a specifically Mexican art through their powerful, often tragic, scenes of the indigenous Indian population and events in Mexican history. The satirical caricatures and often harsh propagandist images for newspapers and prints of engraver José Guadalupe Posada (1852–1913) were a major influence on many of the future muralists, including Rivera and Orozco, for their style and content and their existence as a genuinely popular art form [**1**]. Another important figure was the artist Dr. Atl (Gerardo Murillo Cornado, 1875–1964). As a teacher at the Academy of San Carlos, he inflamed his students with his revolutionary ideals, his anticolonialism, and his fervent belief in the necessity of creating a national, modern art in Mexico that incorporated the "spiritual" qualities of Renaissance frescoes.

To these Mexican influences were added those of the Italian Renaissance and an awareness of Cubism, Futurism, Expressionism, Postimpressionism, Surrealism, the neoclassicism then ▲ sweeping through Europe, and the ideas of Marx and Lenin. Rivera, for instance, spent the years of the revolution in Europe, mostly in Paris, absorbing the various avant-garde developments. Siqueiros met up with Rivera in Paris in 1919: they discussed the revolution, modern art and the need to transform Mexican art with a social art movement.

▲ 1903, 1906, 1907, 1908, 1909, 1911, 1912, 1919, 1924, 1934a

In 1920, Vasconcelos, then Rector of the University of Mexico, suggested to Rivera that he go to Italy to study the art of the Renaissance, hoping that this might provide the genesis of an art suitable for postrevolutionary Mexico. Rivera spent the next seventeen months studying the work of Giotto, Uccello, Mantegna, Piero della Francesca, and Michelangelo, among others. The epic scale of Italian Renaissance religious art and its power to educate and awe illiterate masses was to be an important example for those who would shortly become the Mexican muralists.

Vasconcelos's mural program was launched in 1921, and at his request, Rivera returned to Mexico to take part. In the same year, Siqueiros published his "Manifesto to the Artists of America" in the sole issue of *Vida Americana.* In it he proclaimed that they should "create a monumental and heroic art, a human and public art, with the direct and living example of our great masters and the extraordinary cultures of pre-Hispanic America." Early in 1922, Rivera began work on his first mural commission at the Amphitheater Bolivar of the National Preparatory School in Mexico City and joined the Communist Party. In September, Siqueiros returned to Mexico, joined the Communist Party, and with the support of Orozco, he and Rivera helped found the Union of Technical Workers, Painters, and Sculptors. In 1923, Siqueiros and Orozco received their first mural commissions, also for the National Preparatory School [**1**].

1 • José Clemente Orozco, *The Trench*, 1926
Fresco, National Preparatory School, Mexico City

Under the auspices of the new Union, Siqueiros formulated a new manifesto which outlined the revolutionary ideology of the fledgling mural movement. Signed by a majority of the mural artists, it was published in 1924. Echoing the language of the Soviet ▲ Constructivists, "A Declaration of Social, Political, and Aesthetic Principles" proclaimed:

> *We repudiate so-called easel painting ... because it is aristocratic, and we praise monumental art in all its forms, because it is public property ... art must no longer be the expression of individual satisfaction which it is today, but should aim to become a fighting, educative art for all.*

This manifesto crystallized the principles of the mural movement and helped define it as a public, ideologically driven, didactic art. Although broadly speaking, the muralists worked in a figurative social realist style, this did not prevent them from developing highly individualistic forms of expression. By the mid-twenties, "The Big Three" had developed their distinctive revolutionary styles and subject matter.

Rivera created figure- and event-packed compositions dealing with both traditional and modern subject matter intended to inspire a sense of pride in his audience's Mexican heritage and proclaim a better future through socialism. He worked in a flat, decorative style with simplified forms, using both stylized figures as well as realistic, identifiable characters to tell his stories. His most ambitious project was *History of Mexico* for the Palacio Nacional in Mexico City, begun in 1929 and left unfinished at his death [**2**]. In two parts, "From the Pre-Hispanic Civilization to the Conquest" and "From the Conquest to the Future," he told the tale of Mexico's history beginning with the fall of Teotihuacán (around AD 900) and ending with Karl Marx leading the way to an ideal future.

Throughout his career, Siqueiros experimented with a variety of techniques and materials in his bold, turbulent, dynamic murals. His work has strongly Surrealist elements, using multiple perspectives, distortion, vibrant colors, and a mixture of realism and fantasy to express the raw power of the workers' universal struggle [**3**]. For his part, Orozco chose to convey the horrible human suffering of the downtrodden in a heartfelt, and often harrowing Expressionistic social realism, as seen in his murals for the National Preparatory School.

The Mexican muralists in the United States

The work of the three, particularly Rivera, was also beginning to attract attention from across the border. From the mid-twenties on, their work began to be featured in newspapers and the art press, and artists and intellectuals began to make the journey to Mexico to see them at work. They also began to be exhibited in New York, and in 1929 *The Frescoes of Diego Rivera* by Ernestine Evans was published, the first book on his work in English.

This attention soon led to commissions for all three in the United States, which brought their work to an even greater audience. Orozco painted frescoes at the New School for Social Research in New York from 1930–1, at Dartmouth College in Hanover, New Hampshire from 1932–4, where he also taught the techniques of

▲ 1921

2 • Diego Rivera, *History of Mexico: From the Conquest to the Future*, 1929–35
Fresco, south wall, National Palace, Mexico City

3 • David Alfaro Siqueiros, *Portrait of the Bourgeoisie*, 1939–40
Pyroxaline on cement, Mexican Electricians' Syndicate, Mexico City

fresco painting, and at Pomona College in Claremont, California in 1939. In 1932, Siqueiros accepted an invitation to teach at the Chouinard School of Art in Los Angeles and while there completed murals for the school and the Plaza Art Center. In 1935–6 he opened an experimental workshop in New York. Announcing it as "a laboratory of modern techniques," he taught the use of innovative materials, tools, and techniques, such as throwing, dripping, and spraying. Significantly, the future Abstract Expressionist ▲ painter Jackson Pollock was a member of the workshop.

While Orozco and Siqueiros made an impact through their work and teaching, it was Rivera's work in the United States that was most noticed. In 1930 and 1931 he had exhibitions in San Francisco and Detroit and executed murals for the California Stock Exchange and the California School of Fine Arts, also receiving a commission to paint murals for the Detroit Institute of Arts. More spectacularly, in December 1931 Rivera was given the second ● retrospective in the new Museum of Modern Art in New York (the first, earlier in the year, had been devoted to Matisse). The exhibition was a critical and popular success, with record attendance figures: almost 57,000 people were exposed to his Mexican-themed work and introduced to the new subject he was exploring—the modern industrial landscape of twentieth-century North America.

Rivera also turned his gaze onto the contemporary American scene in his murals for Detroit (*Detroit Industry*, 1932–3). The introduction of American themes and social commentary in his work provided an important catalyst for American Regionalists such as Thomas Hart Benton (1889–1975), and social realists, such as Ben Shahn (1898–1969). As Benton commented later:

> *I saw in the Mexican effort a profound and much-needed redirection of art towards its ancient humanistic functions. The Mexican concern with publicly significant meanings and with the pageant of Mexican national life corresponded perfectly with what I had in mind for art in the United States. I also looked with envy on the opportunities given Mexican painters for public mural work.*

In October of 1932 Rivera, Catalan muralist José María Sert (1876–1945) and the English artist Frank Brangwyn (1867–1956) were commissioned by the Rockefeller family to produce nine murals for the lobby of the RCA Building in the Rockefeller Center in New York. The oil family was one of the richest in the world, and John D. Rockefeller, Jr. was seen by many as the ultimate manifestation of American capitalism. Rockefeller's wife, Abby Aldrich Rockefeller was one of the founders of the Museum of Modern Art and they were already collectors of Rivera's work, having bought his sketchbook of the 1928 May Day parade in Moscow in 1931.

The title of Rivera's mural was *Man at the Crossroads Looking with Hope and High Vision to the Choosing of a Better Future* and he began work on it in March 1933 [**4**]. Some time in April the unmistakable head of Lenin appeared in the mural, leading to criticism in the press, such as the headline in the *World Telegraph*: "Rivera Perpetrates Scenes of Communist Activity for RCA Walls—and Rockefeller, Jr. Foots the Bill."

While the Rockefellers were aware of Rivera's politics, and not unduly concerned about them, this new twist and the negative publicity it was receiving placed them in an untenable position, jeopardizing the relationship with their partners in the Rockefeller Center venture. Nelson Rockefeller, son of the family and Rivera's principal contact and liaison, wrote to the artist:

> *Viewing the progress of your thrilling mural, I noticed that in the most recent portion of the painting you had included a portrait of Lenin.*
>
> *This piece is beautifully painted, but it seems to me that his portrait appearing in this mural might very easily offend a great many people... As much as I dislike to do so I am afraid we must ask you to substitute the face of some man where Lenin's head now appears.*

Rivera had literally painted himself into a corner—he was acutely aware of accusations from the Communist Party that he had sold out by working for the archcapitalist in the first place, and that he had become a figurehead for his assistants, who threatened to strike if he yielded to the request. After careful consideration, and with the aid of Shahn, then one of his assistants, Rivera replied that Lenin must stay, but as a compromise he would add some American heroes to the composition. He added, prophetically, "rather than mutilate the conception I should prefer the physical destruction of the composition in its entirety."

A few days later, on May 9, Rivera was dismissed, paid in full, and escorted from the premises. The "Battle of Rockefeller Center" was on: the mural was covered up, and the national and international press covered the story and the political protests that accompanied the forced stoppage. On February 10 and 11, 1934, the mural was destroyed. The scandal and the publicity made Rivera the most famous muralist in the Americas and a hero to left-wing artists in the United States who, after the Depression and the rise of fascism in Europe, had tried to distance themselves from the perceived decadence of Europe and European abstraction. They aspired to a native American art that addressed the plight of the common man and those aspects that defined America and differentiated it from Europe.

As American artists during the thirties searched for a unique "American" art that was not based on French models, they looked to the Mexican muralists, whose creation of an epic national style that was not antimodern provided a powerful model. As American artist Mitchell Siporin (1910–76), put it: "Through the lessons of our Mexican teachers, we have been made aware of the scope and fullness of the 'soul' of our own environment. We have been made aware of the application of modernism toward a socially moving epic art of our time and place."

Another American artist who was profoundly moved by the Mexicans and what they had achieved was George Biddle (1885–1973). In May 1933 he wrote to President Franklin D. Roosevelt suggesting that he initiate a government-sponsored mural program in the United States:

▲ 1949, 1960b ● 1927c

4 • Photograph of Diego Rivera's unfinished RCA Building mural, taken by Lucienne Bloch just before all work was stopped in May 1933

> *The Mexican artists have produced the greatest national school of mural painting since the Italian Renaissance. Diego Rivera tells me that it was only possible because Obregon allowed Mexican artists to work to plumber's wages in order to express on the walls of the government buildings the social ideals of the Mexican revolution.*
>
> *The younger artists of America are conscious as they never have been of the social revolution that our country and civilization are going through; and they would be eager to express these ideals in a permanent art form if they were given the government's cooperation. They would be contributing to and expressing in living monuments the social ideals that you are struggling to achieve.*

Aware of the "Battle of Rockefeller Center," Roosevelt commented that he did not want "a lot of young enthusiasts painting Lenin's head on the Justice Building," but he took the suggestion on board ▲ and the New Deal's cultural support programs were born.

After their time in the United States, "The Big Three" continued to work in Latin America, attracting numerous followers. They left behind a powerful example of a type of public, national avant-garde art that could be at once critical, satirical, inspirational, and celebratory. Its genuine popularity with critics, patrons, and collectors as well as with the people marked a convergence of tastes ● not seen again in the United States until the advent of Pop art.

The sheer size and bravado of the Mexicans' murals were also influential for American artists such as Ben Shahn, as was their creation of a popular figurative art with social content. While the Mexican muralists' influence on artists of the thirties was profound, their influence can also be detected in the work of later generations of artists producing political issue-driven art, and they can also be ▲ seen as prefiguring later movements negotiating issues of identity, such as the community mural movement of the late sixties and seventies in the United States and Latin America and the more recent urban community mural movement in postcolonial Africa.

FURTHER READING

Alejandro Anreus, *Orozco in Gringoland: The Years in New York* (Albuquerque: University of New Mexico Press, 2001)

Jacqueline Barnitz, *Twentieth-Century Art of Latin America* (Austin, Texas: University of Texas Press, 2001)

Linda Downs, *Diego Rivera: A Retrospective* (New York and London: Founders Society, Detroit Institute of Arts in association with W. W. Norton & Company, 1986)

Desmond Rochfort, *Mexican Muralists* (London: Laurence King Publishing, 1993)

Antonio Rodriguez, *A History of Mexican Mural Painting* (London: Thames & Hudson, 1969)

▲ 1936 ● 1960c, 1964b ▲ 1993c

1934a

At the First All Union Congress of Writers, Andrei Zhdanov lays down the doctrine of Soviet Socialist Realism.

Soviet Socialist Realism emerged as a historically and geopolitically specific variant of the universally prevailing antimodernist tendencies of the late twenties and thirties: the *rappel à l'ordre* in France, Neue Sachlichkeit in Germany, Nazi painting in the Third Reich, fascist neoclassicism in Mussolini's ▲ Italy, and the various forms of social realism in the United States. The terror regime of Joseph Stalin (1879–1953) not only provided the ideological and political framework, but also the pragmatic demands, for extraordinary propagandistic efforts by the ideological state apparatus. Accordingly, Stalin's hagiographers even credited him with having invented the term "Socialist Realism," claiming that during a secret meeting of writers in Maksim Gorky's (1868–1936) flat on October 26, 1932, Stalin supposedly stated the following:

> *If the artist is going to depict life correctly, he cannot fail to observe and point out what is leading towards Socialism. So this will be Socialist art. It will be Socialist Realism.*

The first documented *public* usage of the term "Socialist Realism," however, had already appeared in an article in the *Literaturnaya Gazeta* (Literary Gazette), for May 25, 1932, defining it—in the tautological language typical of ideology—as an art of "honesty, truthfulness, and as revolutionary in the representation of the proletarian revolution."

Andrei Zhdanov (1896–1948), Stalin's chief cultural commissar and Secretary of the Central Committee of the Communist Party, gave a programmatic definition of Socialist Realism at the First All Union Congress of Writers in August 1934. Quoting Stalin's (in)famous exhortation that artists and writers should become "the engineers of human souls," Zhdanov (and Stalin) actually echoed the theory of the prerevolutionary aesthetician Aleksandr Bogdanov, who had spoken of literature as a practice that should "organize workers and the oppressed in the struggle for the final destruction of all kinds of exploitation."

Zhdanov's normative aesthetics was paradoxical, requesting that Socialist Realism should engage in "revolutionary romanticism," but also that it should also stand with "both feet on the ground of real life and its materialist foundation." It stated that artists should "depict reality in its revolutionary development" but that they should also educate the worker in the utopian spirit of Communism. From January to March 1936—the year of the show trials and of the final elimination of the last remnants of modernism in the Soviet Union—Zhdanov published a series of articles in the Party's newspaper *Pravda* (The Truth) which denounced formalism in all of the arts. These publications, acquiring the status of prescriptions and prohibitions, introduced the period known as the *zhdanovschchina*, not only establishing the Party's total control of culture, but also the hegemony of Socialist Realism as the exclusive and official culture of authoritarian State Socialism.

Socialist Realism attempted to fuse the legacies of agitprop and ▲ the documentary projects of the twenties with heroicizing narratives that now—in the era of an intensely centralized Party control and its correlative ideology of authoritarian populism—had to be delivered in the manner of premodernist, nineteenth-century genre painting. This emphasis on narrative and figurative representation not only conflicted profoundly with the already existing practices of the • Soviet avant-garde, from the Constructivists to the artists of the *proletkult* and the LEF group (all of whose practices would soon be eliminated), but it proved to be incompatible even with the crucial legacies of nineteenth-century modernism. While the art of Jacques-Louis David and Eugène Delacroix, or of Honoré Daumier, François Millet, Gustave Courbet, and Adolph Menzel, would be celebrated either as art of revolutionary fervor or as art of the people, Impressionism and Postimpressionism—notably the work of Paul ■ Cézanne—now became the subject of endless debates, since they threatened Socialist Realism's fraudulent iconography and its false stylistic homogeneity. The notion of painting as a self-reflexive critical project had to be dismantled: Socialist Realism was to enforce the most banal forms of illusionistic depiction, foregrounding its purely mimetic functions and artisanal skills while claiming access to painting's putative transhistorical monumentality.

Reflection as a process

Georgy Plekhanov (1856–1918), one of the founders of Russian Marxism, was among the first to criticize the Impressionists, juxtaposing their work with that of a group of Russian nineteenth-century artists who were now presented as the really autochthonous predecessors of Socialist Realism, namely the Peredvizhniki ("Wanderers"

▲ 1919, 1925b, 1927c, 1936, 1937a
▲ 1920 • 1921 ■ 1906

or "Itinerants"). This group had been founded in 1870 to break away from the St. Petersburg Academy, to diversify patronage by organizing traveling exhibitions throughout Russia (and by charging entrance fees), and to provide a realistic—sometimes politically critical—picture of Russia. On the occasion of the forty-seventh exhibition of the Wanderers in 1922, they published a declaration which reads like an early definition of the tasks of Socialist Realism:

> *We want to reflect with documentary truthfulness in genre, portrait, and landscape the life of contemporary Russia and the full range of its diverse ethnicities and their lives deeply devoted to labor.... While remaining faithful to Realistic painting, we want to seek those devices that are closest to the masses of people ... to help the masses, in formally finished works of painting, become aware of and remember the great historic process taking place.*

Vladimir I. Lenin (1870–1924) and Leon Trotsky (1879–1940), but most importantly Joseph Stalin, disliked modernism intensely, in particular its recent Soviet avant-garde incarnations, and all three men favored the Peredvizhniki. Lenin's *Materialism and Empirico-Criticism* argued against the prevailing nineteenth-century theories of perception (by implication, against Impressionism and Post-impressionism) by stating that optical sensations were not—as the Russian followers of Austrian physiologist Ernst Mach (including Aleksandr Bogdanov [1873–1928] and, in his early writings, ▲ the aesthetic theorist Anatoly Lunacharsky) had suggested—real elements within the experience of the world, but rather that they were mere *reflections* of the real things.

Thus Lenin [**1**] referred back to German socialist Friedrich Engels's (1820–95) famous statement that "copies, photographs, images are mirror reflections of things." Yet Lenin defined *reflection* as no longer a mere mirror-image but rather as a *process* by which consciousness actively appropriates and transforms the world; this condition of *praxis* would now become the criterion of philosophical truth. Consequently, a *Theory of Reflection* emerges as one of the foundational theoretical programs of Socialist Realism, developed most notably in the early thirties during the Moscow sojourn of György Lukács, the Hungarian-German philosopher who was Marxism's foremost literary theoretician at the time.

Among painters, Impressionism remained a subject of continuous discussion. As late as 1939, Aleksandr Gerasimov (1881–1963) and his artistic colleagues in power (such as Boris Ioganson [1893–1973] and Igor Grabar [1871–1960]) could still call for the "all-sided illumination of Impressionism which was a very great contribution to the treasury of art." But less than ten years later, he would be among those condemning Impressionism in favor of a highly finished painterly style. As Matthew Cullerne Bown argues:

> *The Impressionist concentration on light, color and freedom of brushmark were all viewed negatively as tending towards the dissolution of solid, academically modelled forms in painting ... (Impressionism) was felt to be antagonistic to Socialist Realist painting which was intent on revealing the essences of events from the point of view of the party, the working class and the "laws" of historical development.*

1 • Moïsei Nappelbaum, *Photograph of V. I. Lenin*, 1918
Vintage silver-gelatin print

From the mid-twenties onward, it became increasingly evident that the Constructivist avant-garde had failed to produce a culture for the new industrial and rural proletarian masses. There continued to be fervent debates about the renewed or remaining functions of painting in this historical moment, ranging from calls for the return to representational traditionalism and narratives in the manner of the Peredvizhniki (such as the emerging program of AKhRR) to the more complex models incorporating revolutionary poster design and the cinematic forms of montage and temporality, such as the paintings of the OST (the Society of Easel Painters.) Anatoly Lunacharsky, whom Lenin had reluctantly appointed in 1917 as the first head of Narkompros (People's Commissariat for Enlightenment), initially remained loyal to the avant-garde artists whom he had championed and endowed with institutional power. But now, presumably under Party pressure, he too argued for an urgent revival of narrative and figuration in painting, stating in a speech on May 9, 1923, entitled "Art and the Working Class" that "the main thing is to conquer the aversion to subject matter." Not surprisingly, in 1925 Lunacharsky claimed the Peredvizhniki as the equally true historical predecessors of a populist Socialist art of the present, and he reintroduced one of their key concepts, the *kartina*—the Russian for "picture"—into artistic debates. However, the term would now define not only the obligatory pictorial *narrative* (preferably a

▲ 1921

dramatic scene that "realism" had to enact on the stage of painting) but also more specifically the cheap mass reproduction and distribution of that image in the tradition of the *lubki* woodcuts. In a speech of that year, Lunacharsky explicitly associated the concept of the *kartina* with the needs of the proletariat: "The proletariat needs the *kartina*. The *kartina* is understood as a social act."

▲ Thus, AKhRR (the Association of Artists of Revolutionary Russia), the group that considered itself to be the legitimate heir of the Peredvizhniki, laid the foundations of Socialist Realism, claiming that its members isolated "ideological content as the sign of the truthfulness of a work of art." AKhRR was officially founded at a meeting on March 1, 1922, and Yevgeny Katsman (1890–1976), one of the founders—ironically the brother-in-law of Kazimir Malevich—initially defined their project as "heroic realism."

Two major figures of Soviet Socialist Realism

By the end of 1925, AKhRR's membership numbered about one thousand artists, between them representing a broad range of the painterly positions that would soon define Socialist Realism: from the neoclassical academicism of Katsman and the sharp-focus photographic realism of Isaak Izraelevich Brodsky (1884–1939) to the more painterly approaches of the Moscow artists Ioganson, Gerasimov **[2]**, and Il'ya Mashkov (1881–1944). To others, though, it was evident that the task of constructing representations for a newly industrialized society could not be achieved by the deployment of those conventional painting practices that suggested that reality and its objects were merely emerging from the unchanging, originary forces of nature. Rather, the new society required a new type of painting, if any, in which contradictory social relations and their transformation could be articulated. Thus, the critique of the AKhRR painters was already formulated by the late twenties, most vociferously by the exiled German theoretician Alfred Kurella, who had become director of the Fine Arts Division (IZO) at Narkompros:

> *If one hears the definition of art voiced by AKhRR, and if one sees their works (especially the paintings by Brodski, Jakolev, Kacman, et al.) one cannot help but ask the question: why don't they just take photographs?... The artists of AKhRR have totally forgotten the difference between painting and photography.... In our century of artistic photography the purely documentary side of art is bound to perish.*

Partially in opposition to the reactionary ideas of AKhRR, the OST was formed in 1924, counting among its members Aleksandr Deineka (1899–1969), Yury Pimenov (1903–77), Kilment Redko (1881–1948), David Shterenberg (1881–1948; its chairman), and Aleksandr Tyshler (1898–1980). Some of these painters were former students of the avant-garde institutes Inkhuk and • Vkhutemas that had become the center of discussions between the Constructivists, the Productivists, and the Stankovists, that is, those painters who now closed ranks to maintain painting as a space of relative autonomy from either agitprop propaganda (such as photomontage and poster projects) or the production of utilitarian objects as advocated by the Productivists.

2 • Aleksandr Gerasimov, *Lenin on the Tribune*, 1929
Oil on canvas, 288 x 177 (113 x 70)

The central figure of OST—and undoubtedly the most important artist of the historical chapter of Socialist Realism—Aleksandr Deineka attempted to fuse the legacies of the Soviet poster and film culture with the traditions of easel painting, emphasizing that temporality had to become an integral element of painting if it was to attempt to articulate the historico-political processes of change and dialectical transformation. Conceiving a model of painterly montage, Deineka wanted to translate the dynamics of revolution and industrialization into a painterly and compositional dynamics by using rapidly altering spatial perspectives, cinematic points of view and shifting modes of painterly execution.

Both AKhRR artists and OST artists (along with members of other groups) contributed to an exhibition organized in 1928, celebrating the tenth anniversary of the Red Army (which had by now become the most important patron of portraits of its own heroic warriors and scenes of its victories). Deineka's painting *The Defense of Petrograd* was widely praised by the critics, partly because it opposed not only the model of nineteenth-century war paintings that served as the point of departure for most AKhRR painters, but also the photonaturalism of paintings such as Brodsky's *The Session of the Revolutionary War Council* (1928) and *Lenin in the Smolny Palace* **[4]**. Deineka's painting, by contrast, depicted the civil war not as a heroic episode of the past but as a process of collective transformation continuing in

▲ 1921 ● 1921

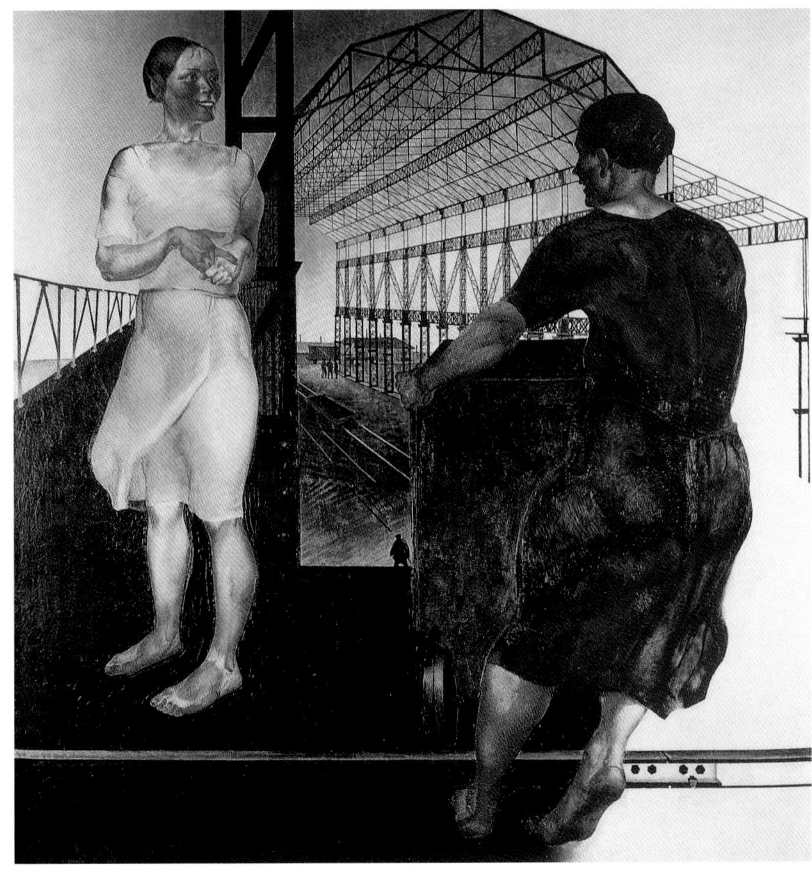

3 • Aleksandr Deineka, *Building New Factories*, 1926
Oil on canvas, 209 x 200 (82 x 79)

the present. As the critic Chvojnik stated in his review of the exhibition, "The simplicity of the painting's well-articulated rhythm gives a clear account of the endless stream and indefatigable will of the revolutionary proletariat." Deineka's compositional conception followed a pictorial principle that Ferdinand Hodler had developed earlier, in the first decade, with correlating positive figures and negative ground in a frieze of almost temporally structured alternating shapes passing across the surface of the painting. While Deineka's peculiar and masterly synthesis of Soviet modernism and a more traditional definition of public and monumental mural painting could be called one of the most successful projects inside the perimeters of Socialist Realism, his work also bears clear resemblances to the dilemma of ▲ Neue Sachlichkeit in Germany, which had equally attempted to fuse the reality of new industrial technologies with the apparent obsolescence of pictorial means and subject matter. His painting *Building New Factories* [**3**] embodies all these contradictions. While Deineka equates the new industrial architecture with the modular picture grid, he repositions the latter within receding perspectival space. And in the construction of the figures, he gives us the most detailed modeling of the female bodies, yet their faces follow the rules of typecasting the anonymous Socialist subject.

The second major figure of Socialist Realism—and in many ways Deineka's opposite—was Isaak Brodsky, who had joined AKhRR in 1923. His work and his biography exemplify the contradictions that governed the politics and the aesthetics of Socialist Realism. Brodsky had met Lunacharsky in Petrograd in the company of Maksim Gorky in late 1917 or early 1918, and Lunacharsky had endorsed him in a letter to Lenin: "From an ethical and political point of view the artist Brodsky merits complete trust." Before Stalin's final consolidation of power, however, Brodsky was subjected to severe criticism within the Association by the younger generation of artists and was excluded from AKhRR at its conference in May 1928 for his "extreme photonaturalism"—his *Brodskyism*, as the edict of exclusion called his sharp-focus neoclassical realism.

But the calls of the early plan years for a new, revolutionary, nonacademically based proletarian art that had denied the continuing validity of the realist easel picture, were soon to be extinguished. Brodsky reemerged, to become Stalin's favorite artist and a personal friend of Marshal Voroshilov, Stalin's commissar for defence. In 1934 he was appointed as rector of the Leningrad Academy of Art, where he enforced a return to the strictest rules of traditional academic art education, subsequently becoming the first artist to be awarded the Order of Lenin. Apparently Brodsky met Stalin on at least one occasion in 1933, when—in the company of Gerasimov and Katsman—Stalin advocated that they should paint "pictures that were comprehensible to the masses, and portraits that did not require you to guess who was portrayed."

One of Brodsky's most successful paintings—among his industrious production of portraits of Soviet heroes in oil and lithographs—was *Lenin in the Smolny Palace* [**4**]. Although it was

▲ 1925b

manifestly the result of a photographic projection after a photograph by Moïsei Nappelbaum, Brodsky nevertheless tried to disavow his photomechanical sources. In fact, he claimed to have produced this astonishing likeness from a number of sketches of Lenin that he made at the Third Comintern Congress; Brodsky even staged photographs that showed him producing these preparatory sketches. Thus, Leah Dickerman convincingly argues that:

> *The simultaneous dependence on and masking of photography that lies at the heart of socialist realist practice offer a structure of ambivalence. On the one hand, socialist realism's use of (and even more its insistent fidelity to) a photographic source speaks of desire for the photographic. On the other, the erasure of the image's mechanical origins speaks of fear of the photographic.*

Brodsky's portrait of Marshal Voroshilov [**5**], one of the most avid patrons of Socialist Realism, is a masterpiece of naturalizing ideology. It situates the chief of the most powerful military state apparatus, the Red Army, in a perfect fusion of peaceful leisure and the most detailed nature of a Russian landscape. That naturalist account, however, results from the concealed technical apparatus of photographic reproduction.

While the last major retrospective of "Artists of the Russian Federation over Fifteen Years" could still include a significant segment of works by the Soviet avant-garde when first exhibited at the Russian Museum in Leningrad in 1932, that proportion had already had to be excised in favor of Socialist Realism when the exhibition traveled to Moscow in June 1933. Ossip Beskin, editor of *Iskusstvo* (Art)—the Union's newly founded official journal

4 • Isaak Brodsky, *Lenin in the Smolny Palace*, 1930
Oil on canvas, 190 x 287 (74¾ x 113)

5 • Isaak Brodsky, *The People's Commissar for Defense, Marshal of the Soviet Union, K. E. Voroshilov, out skiing*, 1937
Oil on canvas, 210 x 365 (83 x 144)

(all other magazines having been abolished)—announced the final battle against the avant-garde with the publication of his book *Formalism in Painting* (1932).

This battle against modernism would culminate in the total liquidation of Soviet avant-garde culture during 1932 and 1933. A decree from the Central Committee of the Communist Party abolished all independent artistic groupings and established a nationwide Union of Soviet Artists, the *orgkomitet.* MOSSKh, the Moscow section of this envisaged union, was formed in 1932 and became the leading organization in the country, displacing or absorbing all the other groups (AKhRR, OST, OMKh, RAPHk, etc.).

Aleksandr Gerasimov had now emerged as the third key figure of Socialist Realism. He typically moved from one powerful position to the next, regardless of the fact that the political situation in general had become increasingly unmanageable for most intellectuals and artists after 1936. Thus, Gerasimov came to be elected chair of MOSSKh, and in a speech in 1939 he defined Socialist Realism as "an art realist in form and socialist in content," an art that would celebrate the construction of Socialism and heroicize those who toiled on its behalf. Fashioning himself as a man of the Russian people, he enjoyed the company and support of the party elite, devoting much of his energy to official commissions of portraits of Lenin, Stalin, and Voroshilov, executed in a glazed style that imbued the faces of authoritarian state socialism with a double sheen: that of an affirmation of their authenticity through photographic presence and that of a transposition to their heroic status within a timeless past of neoclassicism.

While Socialist Realism would continue to be constantly embattled from 1934 to the beginning of the Kruschev thaw in 1953 and onward, it was basically defined by the following key concepts:

1. *Narodnost'* (*narod* meaning "people," "nation"). Coined by the former member of the World of Art group, the Symbolist painter Aleksandr Benua (1870–1960), *narodnost'* insisted on the relationship of art to the *people.* Initially conceived as a multicultural model, which yet allowed for the specificity of each ethnic group within the newly formed Union, it became a monolithic and ethnocentric norm to produce a chauvinist Soviet (that is, a fictitious Russian) culture. *Narodnost'* required that painting should first appeal to popular sentiments and ideas, but the concept also addressed the artist's task to document the current work of the population, to communicate with the working masses and to recognize and dignify the structures of their daily lives. The concept of *narodnost'* also served to support a Soviet version of a return to tradition. The theorists of Socialist Realism—just like their French and Italian counterparts of the *rappel* ▲ *à l'ordre*—embraced the art of classical Greece, of the Italian Renaissance, and of the Dutch and Flemish Old Masters of genre painting. Nikolai Bukharin, for example, argued that artists should "combine the spirit of the Renaissance with the huge ideological baggage of our age of Socialist revolution." Ivan Gronsky, the editor of *Novy Mir* (The New World), stated in 1933 that "Socialist Realism is Rubens, Rembrandt, and Repin put to serve the working class."

2. *Klassovost'* insisted that Socialist Realism should clearly articulate the class consciousness of the artist as much as that of the depicted subjects, a consciousness that had been heightened during the Cultural Revolution.

3. *Partiynost'* required that representations and their artistic execution should publicly confirm that the Communist Party had the leading role in all aspects of Soviet life. The concept was first defined in Lenin's essay "Party Literature and Party Propaganda" (1905).

4. *Ideynost'* demanded the introduction of new forms as central to the work of art. These new forms and attitudes had to be approved by the Party. The concept also aimed to make evident that every Socialist Realist work of art would enact the project of Socialism and articulate the glorious future promised by Stalin and the Party.

5. *Tipichnost'* requested that portraits and figure painting should depict typical characters in typical circumstances as heroes and heroines, drawn from recognizable and familiar circumstances. As Cullerne Bown states, "*tipichnost'* was a double-edged sword in Socialist Realism: on the one hand it helped the creation of accessible and eloquent works of social art, on the other it was a pretext to criticize (as 'untypical') paintings which failed to present a rosy enough image of the Soviet reality."

Gerasimov's staying power exceeded that of all his colleagues. Thus, when the USSR Academy of Arts was created on August 5, 1947, as the Party's institution of total control, Gerasimov rose to yet another position of supreme power to become the Academy's first president. In this role, Gerasimov would be traveling through the Soviet satellite states—East Germany, Hungary, Poland, and Czechoslovakia—to inspect the successful enforcement of the Socialist Realist programs in the art academies of those countries. His decrees now defined the tasks of Socialist Realism with an ever-increasing authoritarian animus and antimodernist aggression:

> *To fight formalism, naturalism, and other manifestations of contemporary bourgeois decadent art, lack of ideology and political commitment in creative work, falsely scientific and idealistic theories in the area of aesthetics.*

FURTHER READING

Matthew Cullerne Bown, *Socialist Realist Painting* (London and New Haven:Yale University Press, 1998)

Leah Dickerman, "Camera Obscura: Socialist Realism in the Shadow of Photography," *October*, no. 93, Summer 2000

David Elliott (ed.), *Engineers of the Human Soul: Soviet Socialist Realist Painting 1930s–1960s* (Oxford: Museum of Modern Art, 1992)

Hans Guenther (ed.), *The Culture of the Stalin Period* (New York and London: St. Martin's Press, 1990)

Thomas Lahusen and Evgeny Dobrenko (eds), *Socialist Realism without Shores* (Durham, N.C. and London: Duke University Press, 1997)

Brandon Taylor, "Photo Power: Painting and Iconicity in the First Five Year Plan," in Dawn Ades and Tim Benton (eds), *Art and Power: Europe Under the Dictators 1939–1945* (London: Thames & Hudson, 1995)

Andrei Zhdanov, "Speech to the Congress of Soviet Writers" (1934), translated and reprinted in Charles Harrison and Paul Wood (eds), *Art in Theory 1900–1990* (Oxford and Cambridge, Mass.: Blackwell, 1992)

▲ 1919

1934b

In "The Sculptor's Aims," Henry Moore articulates a British aesthetic of direct carving in sculpture that mediates between figuration and abstraction, between Surrealism and Constructivism.

What counted as a tradition was never as well established in sculpture as in painting, so when the academic modeling of ideal figures based on (neo)classical precedents had lost all validity by the turn of the century, it was not clear what could replace it as a basic way of working. In Britain matters were complicated by the fact that modernist responses to this sculptural decay on the Continent were not yet well known in this early ▲ period: some news of the fragmented figures of Auguste Rodin had crossed the Channel, but little report of the semiabstract carving • practiced by Constantin Brancusi, let alone of the radically different models of the object, the construction, and the readymade, ■ proposed by Picasso, Tatlin, and Duchamp.

Nonetheless, before World War I, the British group of artists ◆ known as the Vorticists had already rejected the humanist tradition of academic art as "flat and insipid" (as the critic T. E. Hulme put it), and they looked primarily to Jacob Epstein to show the way in this new sculptural wilderness. Born to Polish Orthodox Jews in the United States, Epstein had moved to London in 1905 after three years of study in Paris. Although trained in the traditional modeling of the figure, he immediately looked for alternative models in the carved forms of preclassical and primitive arts at the British Museum, the Louvre, and elsewhere—especially ancient Greek, Egyptian, Assyrian, and American. The influence of these sources was already apparent in his first major commission in London, in 1908—a set of huge nudes bluntly carved in stone to represent different stages of human life for the new building of the British Medical Association on the Strand. Despite the time-honored theme of the male nude, these archaistic giants provoked great controversy, which is some indication of British conservatism in art at the time. Yet this furor was nothing compared with the one that greeted his next major work, *The Tomb of Oscar Wilde* in the Père Lachaise cemetery in Paris [**1**], which remains startling to this day. In high relief Epstein carved out of a great block of limestone an entity that can only be called alien—an implacable sphinx that is equal parts Mayan god and Assyrian winged bull (based on such a figure in the British Museum, it was likely inspired by Wilde's poem "The Sphinx"). Frozen in horizontal flight, this strange angel guards the great Irish writer who had been exiled to an early death for his homosexuality ("for his mourners will be outcast men," the inscription on the tomb reads in part, "and outcasts always mourn"). But the tomb, too, needed guarding, for the genitals of the sphinx were soon smashed—a gesture in which aesthetic and sexual reaction seem to have converged.

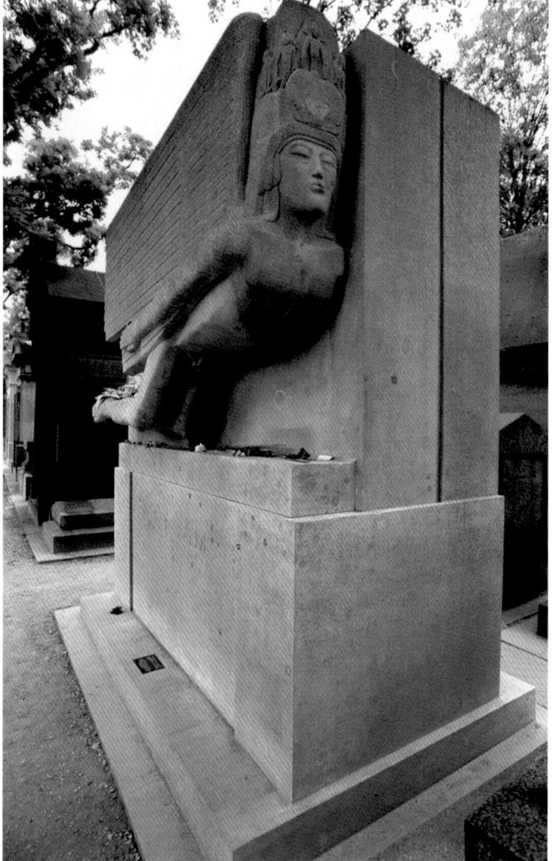

1 • Jacob Epstein, *The Tomb of Oscar Wilde*, 1912
Père Lachaise cemetery, Paris

Where all energy is concentrated

Drawn into the Vorticist circle in the years prior to World War I, Epstein moved away from allusions to the primitive, which his close friend Hulme could not abide, toward a different evocation of the primordial—of modern man as atavistic, aggressively mechanistic, even murderous. His long-lost *Rock Drill* [**2**],

▲ 1900b • 1927b ■ Introduction 3, 1914 ◆ 1908

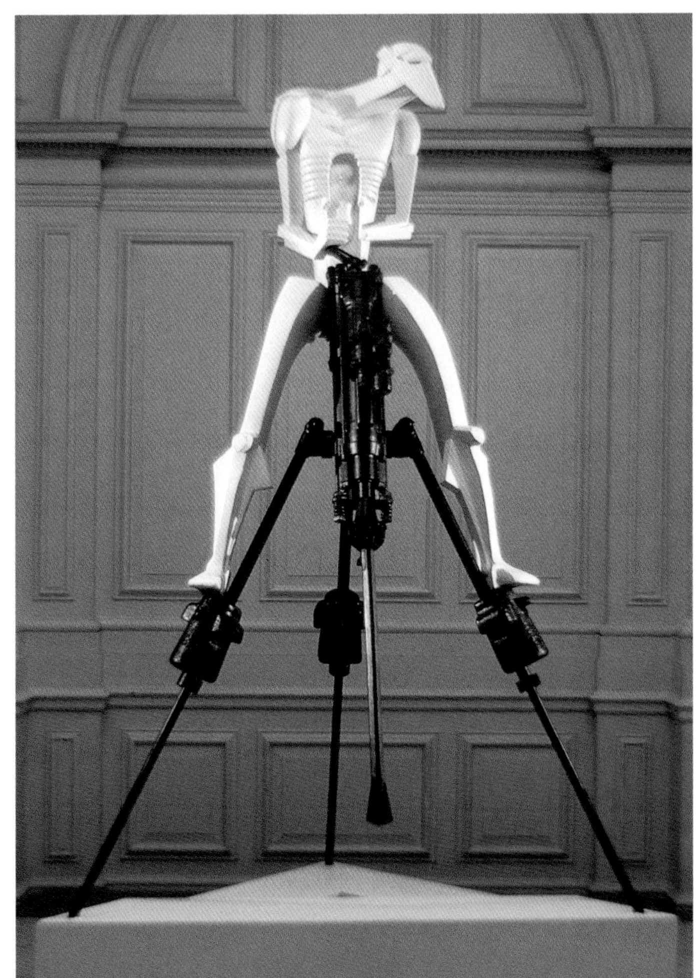

2 • Jacob Epstein, *Rock Drill*, 1913–15 (1973 reconstruction)
Polyester resin, metal, and wood, 205 x 141.5 (80¾ x 55¾)

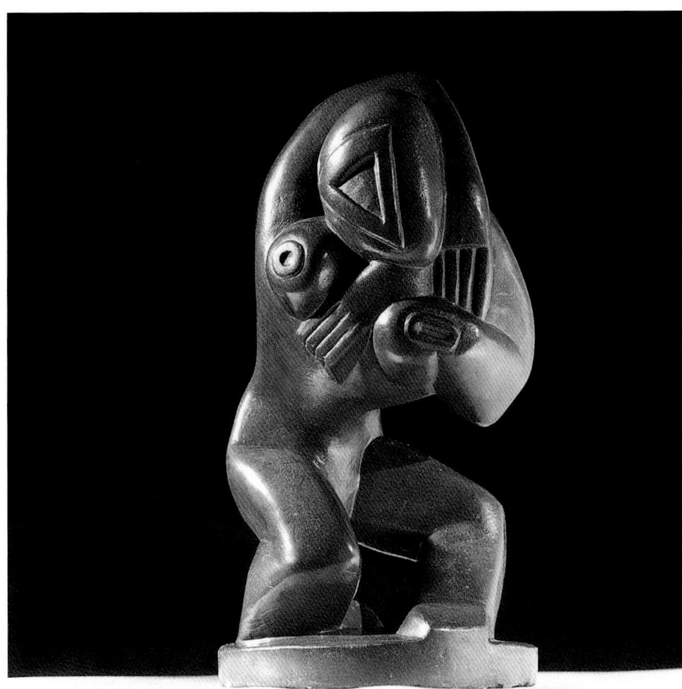

3 • Henri Gaudier-Brzeska, *Red Stone Dancer*, c. 1913
Red Mansfield stone, 43.2 x 22.9 x 22.9 (17 x 9 x 9)

a large conjunction of plaster creature and actual drill, is even more alien than his angel for Wilde, and without the redemption nominally promised by the latter. With a head that is half helmet and half snout, this machine-man with slatted ribs captures the Vorticist ethos of a "new ego" (as Vorticist leader Wyndham Lewis put it), hardened against the shocks of the modern world, more effectively than any other work. "Here is the armed, sinister figure of today and tomorrow," Epstein remarked in retrospect, after he had turned away from this kind of work. "No humanity, only the terrible Frankenstein's monster we have made ourselves into." This monster is not sterile, however, as it carries its amorphous progeny within its exposed midsection, as if to literalize the male fantasy of reproduction without women. This fantasy is common enough among modernists, but here this creation seems to occur outside of humanity altogether. (The opposite number of this belligerent robot is the ▲ supplicant *The Invisible Object* of Alberto Giacometti.)

Epstein produced nothing again so radical in its antihumanism as *Rock Drill*, and it was, in fact, his compressed fragments of carved figures in stone that were more influential on other Vorticists like Henri Gaudier-Brzeska, as well as on subsequent sculptors like Henry Moore (1898–1986) and Barbara Hepworth (1903–75). In Paris during the winter of 1912–13 Epstein had met Brancusi and befriended the Italian Amedeo Modigliani (1884–1920); perhaps this confirmation of direct carving furthered the practice in Britain. In any case, even as Epstein turned back to modeling after the war, Gaudier-Brzeska took up carving prior to it.

Although only twenty-four in 1914, this son of a French carpenter helped Lewis and Ezra Pound shape the Vorticist journal *Blast*. (Gaudier-Brzeska carved his *Hieratic Head of Ezra Pound* in the same year—the title captures this fierce evocation of Pound as high priest of modernist English poetry—and Pound published a book on Gaudier-Brzeska in 1916 that kept his work alive for Moore, Hepworth, and others.) "At the heart of the whirlpool ... where all energy is concentrated" is how Lewis defined "the vortex" in *Blast*, and Gaudier-Brzeska took this concentration of energy in the compression of mass as his goal. To achieve such vitalistic density he often interlocked forms in a way that partook of both Cubist and African models. Thus Gaudier-Brzeska gave his *Red Stone Dancer* **[3]** a ● savage *contrapposto* à la Matisse's *The Blue Nude*; at the same time its schematic signs—inscribed triangles for a face, ellipses for a hand (or is it a breast?)—possess some of the semiotic ambiguity of Picasso's ■ work of this time. Yet *Red Stone Dancer* also manifests a tension peculiar to Gaudier-Brzeska—a tension between an expressive kind of vitalism and an antinatural notion of abstraction that Hulme had elaborated from the 1908 thesis *Abstraction and Empathy* by the ◆ German art historian Wilhelm Worringer. Sometimes Gaudier-Brzeska was able to turn this tension to his advantage: for example, the interlocked forms of his carved plaster *Bird Swallowing a Fish* (1914) literalize a Vorticist conception of nature as eat-or-be-eaten. However dark, this vitalism appealed to Moore and Hepworth more than the mechanicity of other Vorticist work, for it retained nature as a primary reference for sculptural practice.

▲ 1931 ● 1903 ■ 1912 ◆ 1908

▲ Like some Futurists, some Vorticists were swallowed by the very war that they welcomed as "a great remedy": Gaudier-Brzeska was killed on the front in 1915 aged twenty-three, Hulme in 1917 (with an unfinished book on Epstein left behind). "Vorticism was not so much the harbinger of a new order as a symptom of the terminal disease of the old," Lewis later wrote. "The brave new world was a mirage—a snare and a delusion." Sculptors like Moore and Hepworth who were formed in the twenties turned away from the antihumanist swagger of the Vorticists (only, as we will see, to move toward a humanist sentimentality of their own). They were also less defensive regarding modernist developments on the Continent: whereas the Vorticists had a rivalrous relationship with Cubism and Futurism, the next generation advanced through a negotiation of such different avant-gardes as Surrealism and Constructivism. At the same time, Moore and Hepworth did not abandon the prewar principles of Gaudier-Brzeska and Epstein: in opposition to the academic tradition, they, too, looked to preclassical and primitive sources for "a world view" of sculpture (as Moore remarked in 1930), and in the process renewed the commitment to direct carving as an almost ethical value. Finally, like Gaudier-Brzeska and Epstein, Moore and Hepworth were initially outsiders to the British art establishment—Moore as the son of a Yorkshire miner; Hepworth, who was also from northern England, as a woman as well.

An intense life of its own

In his early carvings of the twenties Moore all but replicated prehistoric models in wood and stone—a small rounded horse, a smooth schematic head, a mother-and-child ensemble reminiscent of a fertility figure, and so on. By 1930 semiabstract figures predominated, both maternal and recumbent ones. Hepworth worked with these sympathetic types as well—all in stark contrast to the mechanistic Frankensteins and fragments of Vorticism. In opposition to relief (which Epstein sometimes still practiced), these carvers insisted on "the full three-dimensional realization" of sculpture in the round. To this end they also began to bore through the figure, and to rotate it around this hollow core, in order to make the sculpture whole through this very hole, as it were, with a fluent reciprocity of inside and outside that invited an almost tactile viewing of the finished work.

The next step was to extend this abstracted body, even to break it up in unequal parts on an elongated base. These parts were made to cohere as a kind of landscape (which could also reverse into landscape as a sort of body), as in Moore's *Four-Piece Composition: Reclining Figure* [**4**]. Or they came together as a kind of mother–child ensemble (that might also evoke a sort of landscape), as in Hepworth's *Large and Small Form* [**5**]. Her *Pictorial Biography* illustrates this piece opposite a photograph of Hepworth with one of her infant triplets on her knees in a composition that the sculpture seems to reproduce abstractly. This arrangement intimates that her biomorphic forms intend a psychological condition or emotional relationship in a way that points in turn to the influence of Surrealism, and Hepworth did acknowledge the impact of Hans Arp on her ▲ work, especially "the way Arp had fused landscape with the body."

Moore also touched on this influence in a 1934 publication by Unit One, a group of British artists that, according to its leader, the painter Paul Nash (1889–1946), had "two definite objects": "the pursuit of form," as in abstract art, and "the attempt to trace

4 • Henry Moore, *Four-Piece Composition: Reclining Figure*, 1934
Cumberland alabaster, length 51 (20⅛)

▲ 1909

▲ 1916a

5 • Barbara Hepworth, *Large and Small Form*, 1934
Alabaster, 23 x 37 x 18 (9 x 14 x 7)

the 'psyche'," as in Surrealism. In this short text (now known as "The Sculptor's Aims"), Moore articulates his aesthetic of direct carving in five points. First, there is *truth to material*: "the sculptor works direct" so that "the material can take its part in the shaping of an idea"; thus, for example, the very graining of the wood in the diminutive *Figure* (1931) seems to guide the sweep of its shoulders, neck, head, and hair (or cape). Second, *full three-dimensional realization*: here Moore champions sculpture in the round for its "dynamic tension between parts" and multiple "points of view," as in *Four-Piece Composition*. Third, *observation of natural objects*: different "principles of form and rhythm" are to be drawn from such things as pebbles, bones, trees, and shells. Fourth, *vision and expression*: here, in keeping with the plan of Unit One, Moore urges sculptors to attend to both "abstract qualities of design" and "the psychological human element." And, finally, *vitality*: the ultimate goal of sculpture is "an intense life of its own, independent of the object it may represent."

Despite its confidence, this program points to a basic tension in Moore, as well as in Hepworth: both were ambivalent about total abstraction, at least until this time. They were almost too ready to find a trace of the figure in their materials, as if it were somehow immanent in the wood or the stone, latent in its grains or veins, its curves or cracks. Thus projected in the material, this liminal figure grounds the sculpture in turn, keeps it away from the very abstraction that it otherwise appears to embrace. Sometimes Moore and Hepworth even inscribed partial profiles on the surface (as in *Four-Piece Composition*), as if to pull the sculpture back into a semifigurative reading.

Hepworth overcame this ambivalence more fully than did Moore, especially as she became involved with Ben Nicholson (they married in 1932), who had just moved from post-Cubist paintings ▲ to the geometric reliefs in white for which he is best known. "The experience," Hepworth later remarked, "helped to release all my energies for an exploration of free sculptural form." This move into abstraction deepened about the time that her triplets were born (in October 1934). At this point Hepworth became "absorbed in the relationships in space, in size and texture and weight, as well as in the tension between the forms." In this tension she hoped "to discover some absolute essence in sculptural terms"—an "absolute essence" that nonetheless had to convey "the quality of human relationships." This last condition is telling, for even as her sculpture became abstract, often geometrically so, it remained implicitly figurative in the very relationality of its forms. In this way, the figure was not canceled so much as elevated to the general; it was made to appear universal through abstraction, not despite it.

This is key to this British aesthetic, and central to its great acclaim (at least in the Anglo-American context). For in effect this sculpture served as a kind of compromise, as an aesthetic resolution to troublesome tensions. In the first instance these tensions were technical: Moore and Hepworth advocated direct carving in

▲ 1937b

opposition to the traditional practice of modeling and casting, yet all the natural references and maternal allusions made this carving seem like molding—on the analogy of erosion or gestation—and so pointed to an undoing of this old opposition in technique. In a related way, Moore and Hepworth eased the tension between the opacity of the sculptural material and the clarity of the sculptural idea, for the second seemed to arise naturally from the first in the kind of transformation that modern aesthetics had long privileged. Finally, they also appeared to overcome the more recent opposition between sculpture-as-fragment (associated with Rodin) and sculpture-as-totality (associated with Brancusi).

At the same time, Moore and Hepworth managed stylistic contradictions. With others in the Unit One milieu, they worked to reconcile Surrealist and Constructivist tendencies—"the psychological element" and "abstract principles" (Moore). This reconciliation was prepared by the watering-down of Surrealism on its crossing of the Channel, and by the reducing of Constructivism to abstract ▲ design in the *Circle* group around Naum Gabo. But Moore and Hepworth also contributed to this blurring of the two movements. • For example, for Russian Constructivists "truth to materials" meant a treatment of industrial materials in a way that might render the constructive process of art not only physically transparent but also socially relevant. For Moore and Hepworth, on the other hand, it was a means to allow the traditional materials of sculpture to guide its semifigurative working. The ideological service of this work was to humanize abstraction, and to keep it within the realm of art. It provided a similar service vis-à-vis Surrealism. Although the British art critic Adrian Stokes related this sculpture to the aggressive ■ drives foregrounded in the psychoanalysis of Melanie Klein, the "psychological human element" in Moore and Hepworth was too nonspecific to be very disruptive, much less perverse. In effect they offered a Surrealism without the uncanny, in which natural analogies were favored over psychological provocations.

A world view of sculpture

There was further conciliation offered in this work. As suggested above, rather than overthrow the figure, as in the construction and the readymade, Moore and Hepworth tended to generalize it through abstraction. In this way, the old regime of art persisted in the very appearance of the new, which again is part of the great appeal of this work—and part of its ideological service too. As the British art critic Charles Harrison has argued, Moore and Hepworth worked to generalize "sculpture" as "an innate category of experience—the response to 'significant form,' wherever it might be found," in bones or stones, bodies or landscapes ("significant form" was the phrase of the early-twentieth-century British formalist critic Clive Bell). Perhaps, as Harrison suggests, this "all-inclusiveness of sculpture" was "a radical and progressive idea" in Britain at the time, but it was still achieved through a softening of aesthetic differences and political edges. Clearly this "universalization" of sculpture was also a "rehumanization" of art, undertaken in reaction against the "dehumanization" preached by the Vorticists and made all too real in World War I. But just as clearly this rehumanization was no cure for "the terminal disease of the old" (Lewis). As Harrison has also suggested, it was a liberal response to what was already a crisis in liberalism—a liberalism about to be overwhelmed by various fascisms and another world war.

In large part this sculpture appears so human, almost natural, even universal, through its confection of modern and primitive allusions. In a short text from 1930 (now known as "A View of Sculpture"), Moore intimated that this primordial effect is, paradoxically, a mediated one:

> *The world has been producing sculpture for at least some thirty thousand years. Through modern development of communication much of this we now know and the few sculptors of a hundred years or so of Greece no longer blot our eyes to the sculptural achievements of the rest of mankind. Paleolithic and Neolithic sculpture, Sumerian, Babylonian and Egyptian, Early Greek, Chinese, Etruscan, Indian, Mayan, Mexican and Peruvian, Romanesque, Byzantine and Gothic, Negro, South Sea Island and North American Indian sculpture; actual examples of photographs of all are available, giving us a world view of sculpture never previously possible.*

This statement anticipates the notion advanced by André ▲ Malraux a few years later of a *musée imaginaire* of world art. This idea of a "museum without walls" was founded equally on the empire of the West (its appropriation of cultural artifacts from around the world) and the empire of photography (its ability to turn these disparate artifacts into similar examples of "style"). In their own way, Moore and Hepworth produced a kind of *sculpture imaginaire*, "a world view of sculpture" elaborated into a practice of modern sculpture. Why was this "world view of sculpture" so attractive at the time? To what needs did it respond? And how did it come to count as a primary kind of modern sculpture (alongside the abstract design of Gabo and company)? Greatly acclaimed in the forties and fifties, this sculpture was later punished for its very • success, as advanced artists in the sixties scorned its recipe of Surrealism and Constructivism and turned to the models that it seemed to occlude: the readymades of Duchamp and the constructions of ■ Rodchenko. And still today, after its great inflation and equally great deflation, it is difficult to see this sculpture clearly.

FURTHER READING

Charles Harrison, *English Art and Modernism 1900–1939* (New Haven and London: Yale University Press, 1981)

Barbara Hepworth, *A Pictorial Autobiography* (London: Tate Gallery, 1970)

Alex Potts, *The Sculptural Imagination: Figurative, Modernist, Minimalist* (New Haven and London: Yale University Press, 2000)

Ezra Pound, *Gaudier-Brzeska: A Memoir* (1916) (New York: New Directions, 1961)

Herbert Read, *Henry Moore: A Study of His Life and Work* (London: Thames & Hudson, 1965)

David Thistlewood (ed.), *Barbara Hepworth Reconsidered* (Liverpool: Tate Gallery, 1996)

▲ 1937b • 1914, 1921 ■ 1966b, 1994a ▲ 1935 • 1962c ■ 1914, 1921

1935

Walter Benjamin drafts "The Work of Art in the Age of Mechanical Reproduction," André Malraux initiates "The Museum without Walls," and Marcel Duchamp begins the *Boîte-en-Valise*: the impact of mechanical reproduction, surfacing into art through photography, is felt within aesthetic theory, art history, and art practice.

In 1931 Walter Benjamin wrote "A Short History of Photography," in which, as a critic and theorist increasingly shaped by Marxist thought, he analyzed the medium's relationship to social class. Sharing something of a historical berth with the nineteenth-century novel, photography began (in the 1840s and 1850s) by participating in the heyday of bourgeois culture, so Benjamin related. An amateur pastime, it commemorated the frank exchange of intimacy between friends, as its early practitioners—writers or painters—made each other's portraits, images whose long exposure time (around five minutes) imposed a kind of open gaze and physiognomic authenticity.

By the end of the century, the commercialization that had rapidly overtaken photography had overtaken the class that supported it as well. The clarity and strength with which the new lenses and emulsions had initially captured the captains of industry had yielded to an uncertainty that expressed itself in the hothouse settings for middle-class portraits with their aspirations toward "art"—the sitter posed amid the flowers of a winter garden, or greenhouse, dappled in light and shade. This was the bourgeoisie losing its proprietorship as a class, wrote Benjamin, and the only authentic way to photograph what had happened to it within the urban setting that housed it was to show its class extinction. This is what Eugène Atget did when, in image after image, he shot the streets of Paris emptied of people, as though one were at "the scene of a crime."

1 • Aleksandr Rodchenko, *Woman at the Telephone*, 1928
Silver-gelatin print, 39.5 x 29.2 (15½ x 11½)

The face of time

Photography's reinvention of "portraiture" awaited the twenties, so Benjamin argued. Here bourgeois individualism gave way to the kind of depersonalization that belongs to a different structure of society: a more collective one, as in the masses of faces passionately rendered in the films of Russian director Sergei Eisenstein; or a more anonymous one, as in Aleksandr Rodchenko's *Woman at the Telephone* [**1**]; or a more sociologized one, as in the social "types" catalogued by the ▲ German photographer August Sander in the late twenties, in his *Antlitz der Zeit* (1929) for instance, and early thirties [**2, 3**].

Returning four years later to the problem of photography and film in his essay "The Work of Art in the Age of Mechanical Reproduction," Benjamin exchanged the earlier analysis based on class for one now grounded in modes of production. The use-value of a work, he reasoned, cannot be separated from the conditions under which it is produced. Within primitive societies these conditions inevitably involve hand fabrication, whether by craft procedures or by a simple transfer of magical properties to an object through the touch of shaman or priest. This "cult-value," often operating out of sight of the community, depends on the authenticity of the sacred object, the healing or other properties of which will not inhere in mere replicas or reproductions. The culture of engraved copies of original works of art that begins to develop in the Renaissance adds "exhibition-value" to cult-value and clearly imposes a new use on

▲ 1929

2 • August Sander, *Farming Couple*, c. 1932
Silver-gelatin print, 26 x 18.2 (10¼ x 7⅛)

the art object, one involving its propaganda impact as its image circulates through papal or diplomatic channels. But this form of the copy makes a clear distinction between itself and the artistic original whose status *as original* is undiminished. Benjamin terms this status the work's "aura," by which he means its untransferable uniqueness. The handcraft that produces the etched copy participates in the mode of production of the original; both bear the touch of their maker.

With industrialization, conditions of production radically change, as a matrix or "die" is now fashioned from which to mass-produce objects. Mass production entered the world of the image initially via lithography, which, though hand-drawn, is mechanically printed. But photography soon took over as mechanical reproduction through and through. Hand work does not intervene in taking the picture nor in its printing and, in line with other industrial forms, its matrix—the negative—is not its "original" since it does not fully resemble the finished image. Rather the photograph is a multiple *without* an original. "From a photographic negative," as Benjamin wrote, "one can make any number of prints; to ask for the 'authentic' print makes no sense."

Authenticity and the aura connected to the original are thus *structurally* removed from the mechanically produced object, which, as Benjamin pointed out, "substitutes a plurality of copies for a unique existence." If such an existence could be characterized as tied to the place and time of its origin and thus psychologically distant from its viewer, the mechanical reproduction vaults over that distance. It satisfies "the urge to get hold of an object at very close range by way of its likeness." Mechanical reproduction thus develops a corresponding psychological drive, with its own way of seeing: "To pry an object from its shell, to destroy its aura, is the mark of a perception whose 'sense of the universal equality of things' has increased to such a degree that it extracts it even from a unique object by means of reproduction." Thus a serialization of production (base) begins to effect a serialization of vision, which drives in turn a taste for serialization in the work of art itself (superstructure). Going from the mode of production to the "use-value," Benjamin now writes: "To an ever greater degree the work of art reproduced becomes the work of art designed for reproducibility." The number of artists whose work has been "designed for reproducibility" either unconsciously or consciously (from Duchamp to ▲ Warhol and beyond) bears out Benjamin's prediction that the change in the mode of production would sweep all aesthetic values before it. "Earlier much futile thought had been devoted to the question of whether photography is an art," he wrote. "The primary

3 • August Sander, *Gentleman Farmer and Wife*, 1924
Silver-gelatin print, 26 x 18.3 (10¼ x 7¼)

▲ 1914, 1918, 1960c, 1964b, 1966a

4 • André Malraux with the photographic plates for the *Museum without Walls*, c. 1950

1930–1939

question—whether the very invention of photography had not transformed the entire nature of art—was not raised."

The off-the-wall museum

In 1935 Walter Benjamin was not the only one raising "the primary question" with regard to photography. The French novelist and left-wing political figure André Malraux (1901–76) also saw the medium as transforming "the entire nature of art," but with conclusions diametrically opposed to those of his German counterpart. Where they agreed was on the fact that the photograph wrenched the original away from the site for which it was made and relocated it in an entirely new place, closer to its viewer and reorganized for a new set of uses. They also agreed that this extraction somehow denatures the original works, since in the process of being folded into the photograph that reproduces such works, "they have," as Malraux argued, "lost their properties as *objects*." But where the two men disagreed was in the interpretation of this loss, since for Malraux, "by the same token, they have gained something: the utmost significance as to *style* that they can possibly acquire."

This stylization enabled by photography was a function of the kinds of close-ups and eccentric camera angles that began to be ▲ linked in the twenties to what was called the photographic "new vision." Photography's capacity for massive disruptions of original scale (tiny cylinder seals enlarged to become the same visual size as monumental bas-reliefs, for instance), its ability to use strange camera angles or theatrical lighting to effect stunning reinventions (with ancient Sumerian terracotta figures thereby emerging as the cousins of twentieth-century sculptures by Joan Miró), and its possibilities for wresting a dramatically framed fragment from a larger work by means of cutting or cropping: all of this surgically intervenes in the aesthetic unity of the original to enable new and startling grafts. The conclusion Malraux draws from this is a salute to the medium that makes it possible: "Classical aesthetics proceeded from the part to the whole; ours, often proceeding from the whole to the fragment, finds a precious ally in photographic reproduction."

Photography, then, is the great leveler, the means of submitting objects from every period and every place to a kind of stylistic homogeneity, so that they take on the features of "our aesthetics." And the payoff of this procedure is a compendium of total information about the world's art that is made possible by the new tool. This compendium, the art book, is what Malraux began to call "the museum without walls" [**4**]. The original French for this—

▲ 1929

the "*musée imaginaire*" (the imaginary museum)—brings out the antimateriality of the operation, its drive to reduce the physicality of the object to the virtuality of the image, a drive that will only be reinforced later in the century when the imaginary museum *really* reaches for global coverage and its virtual home will not be the art book but the internet.

If for Malraux the value of the art book is that it democratizes the experience of art by bringing it into the lives of vastly more people than the elitist museums had done (a value that is exponentially increased by the web, in the eyes of enthusiasts of the "information superhighway"), this was not its primary function. Rather, it was that, by means of its concatenation of photographic reproductions, the book recodes works of art from "objects" into "meanings"—as he had said, the works gain "the utmost *significance* as to style that they can possibly acquire." The art book is a semiotic machine, then; and the photograph is what gives it leverage. For the photograph is the great facilitator of *comparison*, of moving past the contemplation of a work in isolation to the *differential* experience ▲ of it, its meaning emerging—as linguist Ferdinand de Saussure had assured us it would—in relation to what it is *not*.

One of Malraux's very first texts, a 1922 preface to an exhibition catalogue, already presents this notion of art as a vast semiotic system, a multiple chorus of meaning. In it Malraux had written: "We can feel only by comparison. He who knows *Andromaque* or *Phèdre* will gain a better idea of the French genius by reading *A Midsummer Night's Dream* than by reading all the other tragedies by Racine. The Greek genius will be better understood by comparing a Greek statue to an Egyptian or Asiatic one than by acquaintance with a hundred Greek statues."

Malraux, at the age of twenty, did not stumble by himself onto this conception of the aesthetic as comparative and therefore as fundamentally semiotic. Apprenticed to the art dealer Daniel-Henry Kahnweiler, Malraux was indoctrinated into an experience of the visual arts that was informed by both German art history and Cubist aesthetics, which is to say a way of seeing that had dispensed with the idea of form as beauty in favor of a conception of it as "linguistic." Classical art, as an aesthetic absolute for Western taste, had instituted beauty as the ideal of artistic practice and experience. In the late nineteenth century the Swiss art historian • Heinrich Wölfflin had relativized this absolute by arguing that Classicism can only be "read" within a comparative system through which it can be contrasted with the Baroque. Setting up a group of formal vectors through which to make such comparative readings—the tactile versus the optical, the planar versus the recessive, closed form versus open form—Wölfflin transmuted form into the condition of the linguistic sign: oppositive, relative, and negative. Form no longer had value in itself, but only within a system, and in contrast to another set of forms. The aesthetic component was no longer beautiful; it was significant.

Kahnweiler's connection to this early, structuralizing art history in Germany influenced his own understanding of Cubism. For ■ Picasso's dealer saw the Cubist exploitation of African art, for example, as a breakthrough to the production of forms that would ▲ function as signs. Malraux took this dictum, and never forgot it. Art produces signs that can be read comparatively. Comparison decentralizes and dehierarchizes art, for the comparison works on the juxtaposition of systems—*all* systems: east versus west, high versus low, courtly versus popular, north versus south. And photography, by fragmenting and isolating the signifying elements from within a work's complexity, is the ultimate aid to this reading.

If the massive study that finally emerged from Malraux's contemplation of this problem was called *The Voices of Silence* (1951), this was because the "texts"—which he called "fictions"—that such readings can produce would release a new power from the mute work of art. It is this transformation into a system of meaning that makes up for what reproduction takes away, leaving no room for regret that these figures have lost "both their original significance as objects and their function (religious or other); we see them," he declared, "only as works of art and they bring home to us only their makers' talent."

Benjamin had said "That which withers in the age of mechanical reproduction is the aura of the work of art"; Malraux was insisting on retaining a notion of aura no matter how transformed. The "fiction" created by the art book transmits what he calls "the spirit of art." And it is this spirit that reproduction liberates to tell its story, no matter how silently: "Thus it is that, thanks to the rather specious unity imposed by photographic reproduction on a multiplicity of objects, ranging from the statue to the bas-relief, from bas-reliefs to seal-impressions, and from these to the plaques of the nomads, a 'Babylonian style' seems to emerge as a real entity, not a mere classification—as something resembling, rather, the life-story of a great creator."

The "original" copy

Dates seem to have their own center of gravity: 1935 was not just the moment for both Benjamin and Malraux to contemplate art's fate at the hands of reproduction, it was also the year when Duchamp began to create his own museum without walls, although whether it was to tell "the life-story of a great creator" (Duchamp himself) or not is, as always with Duchamp, held hostage to the artist's extreme sense of irony. The *Boîte-en-valise* [**5**] was begun in 1935 as a massive retrospective of Duchamp's work to date carried out through sixty-nine • reproductions, including tiny replicas of several of the readymades. Miniaturizing the museum exhibition to the size of a carrying case, this "art book" unmistakably strikes up a family resemblance to a salesman's sample case. It is thus that Malraux's eloquent "voices of silence" are rescored for advertising jingles and the "spirit of art" is retooled in the light of the commodity.

Yet nothing is simple with Duchamp. Over the course of the next five years he painstakingly produced his reproductions by the labor-intensive method of collotype printing, in which color is applied by hand with the use of stencils, on average thirty such for each proof. Executing them himself, these became *coloriages originaux* (original

▲ Introduction 3 • Introduction 3 ■ 1907 ▲ 1912 • 1914, 1918

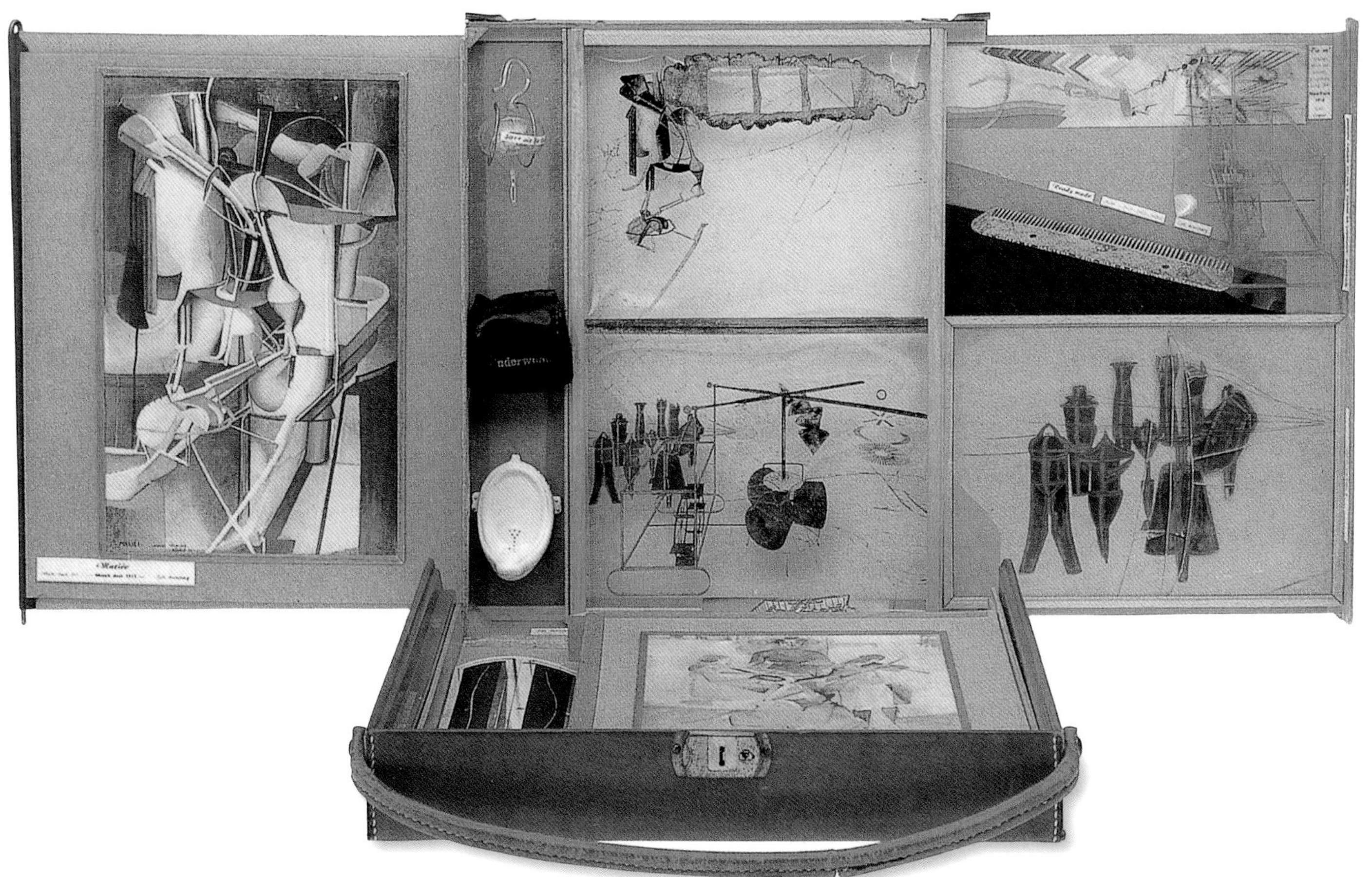

5 • Marcel Duchamp, *Boîte-en-valise*, 1935–41 (1941 version)
Assemblage, dimensions variable

colorings-in), which issued into the extreme aesthetic mutation of authorized "original" copies (some of them even signed and notarized) of original works, some of which (the readymades) were themselves unredeemably multiples. In this endless perspective of facing mirrors, original and reproduction thus continue to change places, with Duchamp now defying Benjamin's dicta by returning to the authenticating touch of the artist, and now thumbing his nose at Malraux's "great creator" by shackling this spirit to the compulsive performance of serialized repetition.

Summarizing the effect of the *Boîte*, David Joselit has written that it may appear to be about shoring up "Duchamp's artistic identity through a coherent summary of his oeuvre, but as an elaborate performance of compulsive repetition—the same form of repetition that Freud associated with the unconscious instinctual drive of death *and* Eros—Duchamp represented a self that is alternately organic and inorganic, masculine and feminine. The act of copying both *constitutes and destroys* the self.... He had found himself—*readymade*."

FURTHER READING

Walter Benjamin, *Illuminations* (New York: Schocken Books, 1969) and *One Way Street* (London: New Left Books, 1979)

Ecke Bonk, *Marcel Duchamp: The Box in a Valise* (New York: Rizzoli; and London: Thames & Hudson, 1989)

David Joselit, *Infinite Regress: Marcel Duchamp 1910–1941* (Cambridge, Mass: MIT Press, 1998)

André Malraux, *Museum without Walls*, trans. Stuart Gilbert and Francis Price (New York: Doubleday, 1967) and *The Voices of Silence*, trans. Stuart Gilbert (Princeton: Princeton University Press, 1978)

1936

As part of Franklin D. Roosevelt's New Deal, Walker Evans, Dorothea Lange, and other photographers are commissioned to document rural America in the grip of the Great Depression.

Two unforgettable films by the American documentary filmmaker Pare Lorentz (1905–92)—*The Plow That Broke the Plains* (1936) and *The River* (1937)—emerged from the many produced by the Information Division of the Farm Securities Administration (FSA), a US government agency established in 1936 as part of President Franklin D. Roosevelt's New Deal. Both films were documentaries of the crisis conditions of rural America in the grip of the Great Depression, the first depicting the Oklahoma Dust Bowl, the second, the catastrophic flooding of the Mississippi River system.

Beyond merely documenting the plight of the victims of these natural disasters, however, Lorentz was intent on achieving at least two other things: to articulate the human cause of these events in the persistent misuse of the land by its owners, and to propagandize for specific government programs to address this situation, such as the Tennessee Valley Authority (TVA) and its projects for building dams along the Mississippi River system. And for this latter goal to be effective, Lorentz needed to seize the imagination of the public, first, by acquainting the citizens of a huge country with parts of it they had never seen before or known much about; and, second, by giving his factual film the emotional drive of a fictional narrative. Only in this way could he overcome the characterization emanating from parts of the US Congress that Roosevelt's programs were a form of the "socialism" that many Americans dreaded, while at the same time countering this demonization by advocating a version of that very same socialism (that is, the centralization of authority necessary to the TVA, or the use of farm cooperatives in order to restructure the prospects of the tenant farmer).

To amber waves of grain ...

On the eve of moving into the FSA to head its Historical Section, Roy Emerson Stryker (1893–1975), had long meetings with the sociologist Robert Lynd to refine his own sense of mission with regard to documentary. He emerged from these sessions with the idea of coordinating the Section's efforts by preparing "shooting scripts" that he would issue to the team of photographers working under him. An early version of part of such a script goes:

HOME IN THE EVENING

Photographs showing the various ways that different income groups spend their evenings, for example:

Informal clothes
Listening to the radio
Bridge
More precise dress
Guests

The static character of this "script" obviously sets it apart from the grand flow of cinematic narrative, which can control its own temporal momentum, moving in a few dramatic seconds, for instance, from droplets melting from branches in the Wisconsin springtime to the vast sweep of the Mississippi reaching the Delta, as Lorentz did in *The River*. And indeed, Stryker's idea of how to collate the results of the images that his photographers would amass over the nine years of their collective efforts (consisting of more than 100,000 prints) was not a sequential narrative but a spatial container: an encyclopedic file or archive, organized, by categories and subcategories and subdivisions of these.

The immediate use to which the FSA photographs were put was the supply of visual information to the public, whether through the government's own books and exhibitions or, more effectively, through the mass media, in such newly founded illustrated weeklies as *Life* (begun in 1936) or *Look* (begun in 1937). For Stryker, the FSA material was, however, substantially different from the photojournalism on which these magazines thrived, since he viewed news photography as "dramatic, all subject and action"; while on the other hand, he said, "Ours shows what's in [the] back of the action." Against the news photo's subject and verb, Stryker characterized the FSA work as adjective and adverb.

This is probably as good a characterization as any of Dorothea Lange's *Migrant Mother* [**1**], the photograph that perhaps more than any other came to stand for the emotional appeal, effectiveness, and memory-searing quality of the FSA's work. For there is no action connected with this image, unless its sitter's staring into an utterly uncertain future could be called action. And as for the adjective and adverb connection, in its shuttling back and forth between the universal—the reading it invites of a timeless "human

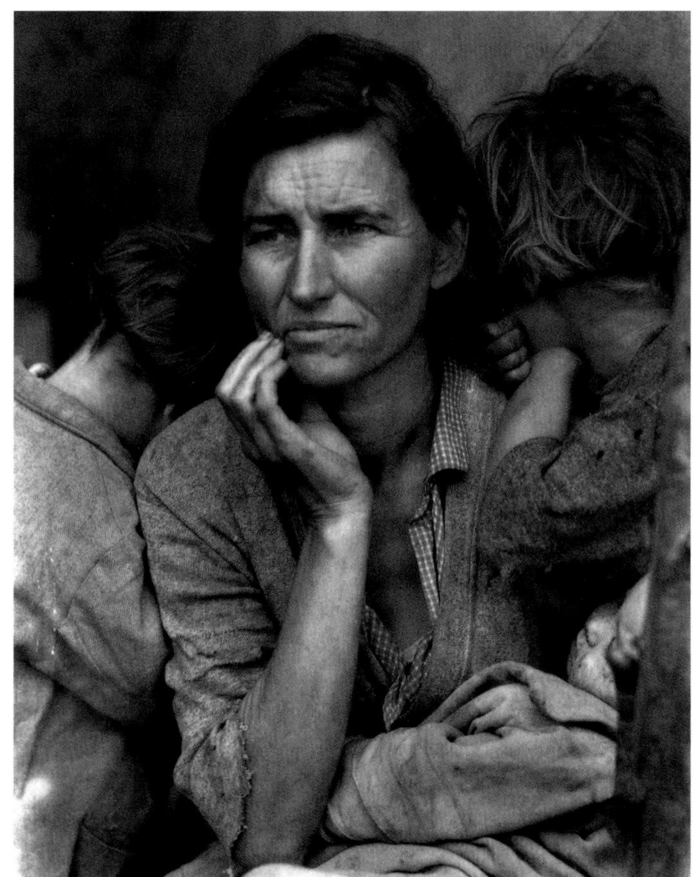

1 • Dorothea Lange, *Migrant Mother*, 1936

dignity" emerging from within a situation of despair—and the particularity of the woman the camera captures, this image constitutes an example of the kind of "humanitarian realism" that Stryker supported. Indeed, Lange's picture, which came to be called "Madonna of the Migrants," sets up certain echoes with religious paintings, whether these be the seventeenth-century Italian painter Caravaggio's projection of the mother of Christ into the lowliest of Roman peasant women, or a work like Rosso Fiorentino's *Dead Christ* (1525–6) which, like Lange's image, wedges the figure of the Man of Sorrows between two flanking angels.

The redemptive tenor suggested for Lange's work by such comparisons is not out of keeping with an overall concern of the survey. As a contemporary of Stryker's wrote: "You could feel the Depression deepen but you could not look out of the window and see it. Men who lost their jobs dropped out of sight. They were quiet, and you had to know just when and where to find them." Stryker saw the mission of his survey, with its search for the details of rural life and small-town poverty, as a project "to find them." And he gloried in the photographs of an entire range of human types, the faces of whom, he felt, proclaimed the will and the ability to survive the utmost hardship. As Stryker would later say: "The faces to me were the most significant part of the file."

But if Stryker read a message of survival and redemption in the photographs, others have seen them as globally projecting an entirely different message. The historian Alan Trachtenberg has

Works Progress Administration

From the time between Franklin Delano Roosevelt's inauguration as President of the United States in January 1933 and the summer of 1935, the federal government ran a series of work-relief projects in an attempt to aid the vast numbers of unemployed created by the Great Depression. At the urging of Henry Hopkins, the director of the Civil Works Administration, a small allocation was made to artists through the Public Works of Art Project. Typical of the early phase of federal relief, this program was both short-lived (its funding ran out after four months) and the target of political controversy. In New York, those lucky enough to be signed onto it spent their time cleaning and repairing the city's statues and monuments; with its demise they were forced back onto the relief rolls.

By the summer of 1935 Hopkins had managed to persuade Roosevelt to set up the Works Progress Administration, a mammoth program of work-relief that would "take America off the dole and put it back to work." As Hopkins expressed it: "Those who are forced to accept charity, no matter how unwillingly, are first pitied, then disdained." During its six years, the WPA employed an average of 2,100,000 workers and spent $2 billion. Its nearly quarter of a million projects ranged from raking leaves to building airfields. As he had in the Civil Works Administration, Hopkins made sure that money would be channeled to artists. Accordingly, over this same period five percent of WPA funds ($46 million) and two percent of its employees (38,000) were allotted to the creative and performing arts. For the visual arts this meant the Federal Arts Project, directed by Holger Cahill, in addition to which there was a Federal Music Project, Theater Project, and Writers' Project.

In New York City, about 1,000 artists joined the FAP payroll in its first four months. The guidelines that required painters to be divided up between the mural and easel divisions also mandated a screening procedure according to which artists would be classified as "unskilled, intermediate, skilled, or professional," with their payscale regulated by these grades. Traditionalists and modernists competed fiercely for administrative power and control of this and other processes. Although the traditionalists were dominant for the most part, a small group of abstract artists led by Burgoyne Diller and Harry Holtzman—disciples of Piet Mondrian—were able to gain enough power to assign murals to young abstract painters such as Arshile Gorky, Stuart Davis, Byron Browne, Jan Matulka, and Ilya Bolotowsky.

The effect of the Federal Arts Project was an overwhelming one of bringing artists together in a new way: artists not only helped each other get around bureaucratic rules, but also the WPA offices to which they went to get their checks and their assignments became meeting places along with the bars and coffee houses of the Village. No longer obliged to work at part-time jobs, these full-time artists now saw themselves as a single community.

written, for example: "If there is a great overarching theme of the FSA file, it is surely the end of rural America and its displacement by a commercial, urban culture with its marketplace relationships. Automobiles, movies, telephone poles, billboards, canned food, ready-made clothing: these familiar icons from the file bespeak a vast upheaval … a profound breach in the relation of American society to its "nature" and to the production of sustenance from the land."

In this reading, in which the file's images of trains sliding past grain silos can be seen as representations of the machine as the agent of the further impoverishment of the dispossessed, or the repeated pictures of billboards announce the replacement of handmade signs by printed ones, an important shift away from the human face is announced. And in such a shift, Stryker's disagreement with the most famous of his photographers can be felt. For Walker Evans (1903–75) had a predilection for just those building facades and posters that projected a land emptied of its "human" content that Stryker resisted [**2**].

The FSA style

Joining Stryker's project in 1935, when the FSA was still called the Resettlement Administration, Walker Evans worked for Stryker for eighteen months. Their differences were expressed as the split between Evans's demand for a "pure record" and Stryker's desire for pictures that would promote social or political change, a desire that led the decidedly nonsurvey photographer Ansel Adams (1902–84) to complain to Stryker: "What you've got are not photographers. They're a bunch of sociologists with cameras." Indeed, Evans was careful to separate himself from real documentary, a term he did not want applied to his work, saying: "The term should be *documentary style*. You see, a document has use, whereas art is really useless. Therefore art is never a document, although it can adopt that style."

Contained within Evans's seemingly paradoxical statement—that documentary could be just another "style," albeit the style in which photography "as such" is essentialized—is a whole aesthetic that developed around the medium in the thirties, slowly building into the postwar years and fully blossoming in the sixties to become the official stance of such arbiters of photographic taste and photographic history as the Museum of Modern Art's Department of Photography. ▲ Although the museum was an enthusiastic supporter of Evans's work, the documentary photographer who came to be seen as the most perfect representative of photography's essence was a Frenchman working in the opening decades of the century, Eugène Atget (1856–1927).

Like Evans's work, Atget's documentary pictures were commissioned in the context of various surveys: by the Library of the City of Paris, by French antiquarian societies, by builders' guilds, and so forth. But like Evans again, Atget's work made strong connections to aesthetic sensibilities that went beyond the sociological to lodge firmly in the tastes of contemporary art. Pictures like Evans's *Penny Picture Display, Savannah* [**3**], with its rows of contact sheets pressed against a shop window made synonymous with the surface of the print itself, the window's lettering—STUDIO—as compressive

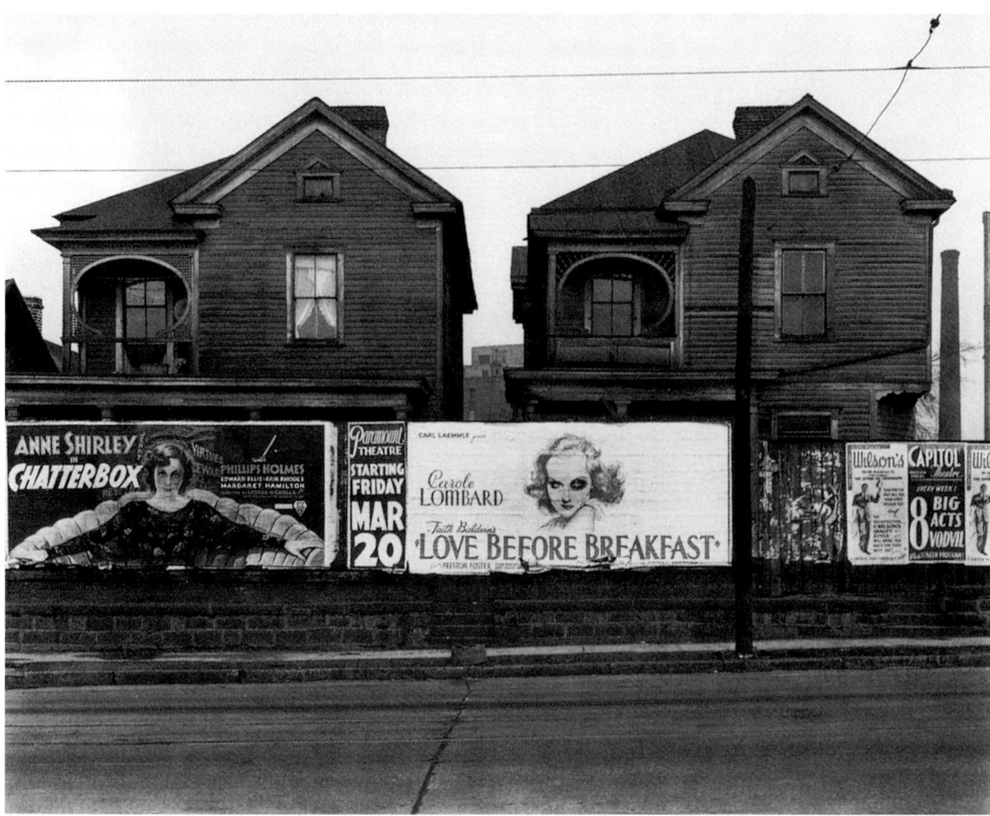

2 • Walker Evans, *Houses. Atlanta, Georgia*, 1936
Silver-gelatin print

▲ 1959d

3 • Walker Evans, *Penny Picture Display, Savannah*, 1936
Silver-gelatin print

a force as anything in Cubist collage, were seen as self-reflexively modernist rather than documentary. And if such a self-referential stance could be found in Evans, this same position was just as easy to spot in Atget. His facades of Parisian cafés come across as brilliant modernist exercises, photographed as they are head on, in such a way that the reflection of Atget's own body standing next to his shrouded stand-camera is deposited on the doorway's window at just the point at which the café-owner's curious face pierces the same mirrorlike surface from within to perch, magically, atop the cameraman's body, collapsing the space both before and behind the image's surface onto a single, flat plane [**4**].

Indeed, Atget was adopted by every variety of modernist sensibility from the twenties on. His "found" montages of shop-window reflection were Surrealist for the Surrealists; his flea-market "accumulations" were images of the serial life of the ▲ commodity for the German Neue Sachlichkeit; his limpid French gardens were sublime landscapes for the American styles that developed out of Precisionism as a form of "straight photography" • that included Paul Strand, Edward Weston (1886–1958), and the Ansel Adams who had accused Stryker of sociologism. In fact, there were so many different "Atgets" to be found among the eight thousand negatives he left that it might be hard to focus all of these into the kind of oeuvre that we associate with a specific author—with its coherence reflecting the organic unity of a single person and the focused intentionality of an individual consciousness.

But if the Museum of Modern Art was determined to do so, it was because the very idea of a photographic "author" had, by the sixties and seventies, come to be projected through Evans's formula of "documentary style," now proclaimed as the essence of photographic *art*. To understand this we have to hold two (contradictory) notions in our head at once: the idea of the total transparency of the documentary photograph to its real world referent, or content, a content with which it does not interfere in any way; and the idea of style as the registration of the artist's own temperament, his or her vision, his or her shaping consciousness. Yet we also have to consider that there is a plane on which these two contradictions can be resolved. This is that of the camera itself, or rather the plate-glass surface on which, in a reflex camera, the image on the lens is mirrored for the photographer's view; it is there that the picture is previsualized on its way to leaving the real world from which it is "peeled" to enter the other, flattened reality of the "image." It is this difference between the world of matter and the world of the image that the photographer sees in the reflex camera's mirror, a difference that gives to that photographer an ironic distance, a "second degree" relation to reality that he or she can register in the results themselves. And it is this registration, be it ever so subtle, that enters the work as style.

Evans's style is built from just this second degree. The roadside billboard held absolutely parallel to the picture surface so that

4 • Eugène Atget, *Café "Au Tambour," Quai de la Tournelle*, 1908
Silver-gelatin print (sepia-toned)

▲ 1929 • 1916b

5 • Walker Evans, *Steel Mill and Company Houses, Birmingham*, 1936
Silver-gelatin print

only a tiny bit of landscape peeps out from behind its edges, pits the billboard's own illusionistic rendering of a house interior against the camera's now flattened data of the real world so that the collapse between the two produces a sense of reality and illusion switching sides, with reality itself become simulacral. Or in his deadpan, twinned house facades, flattened by the stark lighting that seems to render them into drawings of themselves, the sense of their existence as "duplicates" or mere copies not only repeats this simulacral sensibility but ties it to the very duplicative and serial nature of photography as well. This frontality and flattening so consistent within Evans finally renders even the steel mills and workers' housing of a company town into merely a "picture" of themselves, unreal and uncanny [**5**].

But if these are features of Evans's *style*—personal, unmistakable, original—they are also dispersed throughout the full range of the FSA's photographic material. They are to be found, for instance, in the rhythmic, blank facades of Arthur Rothstein's photographs of sharecroppers' shanties, their hapless boarding etched into elegant patterns by light, or in the parallel rows of magazines in John Vachon's *Newsstand*, with their ranged repetitions of the same covers. Indeed, if Alan Trachtenberg called attention to such a displacement of the natural by the mechanical as the "overarching theme" of the FSA file, it was not to make Walker Evans the file's "author." But neither was it to make Stryker that "author," as some scholars are now doing. Instead it was an attempt to scatter authorship as such, making the survey's reach and the camera's machinic specificity intersect at a certain moment in historical time.

The death of the author

This depersonalization of the very idea of the author is, as we would imagine, at work in a certain branch of the critical assessment of Atget's work as well. If the Museum of Modern Art's desire to unify the vastness of his production around a single, authorial intention coincided, historically, with the sudden emergence in the mid-sixties of photography as a rarefied, collectible type of work of art, it also coincided with structuralism's proclamation of "the death of the author." The institution of the "author-function" or the "author-effect" in the place of an originary subject, the dispersion of such a subject into the labyrinth of a textual space whose myriad, already-written, already-heard voices any purported author merely quotes—all of this views authorship as nothing but an effect of the space of a multiplicity of archives or, as Michel Foucault put it, of discourses. For the structuralist critic, then, Atget "himself" is simply an author-effect, the fractured source of which is the multiplicity of the many archives for which he worked.

FURTHER READING

James Agee and Walker Evans, *Let Us Now Praise Famous Men* (Boston: Houghton Mifflin, 1941)
Lawrence W. Levine and Alan Trachtenberg, *Documenting America, 1935–1943* (Berkeley and Los Angeles: University of California Press, 1988)
Maria Morris Hambourg et al., *Walker Evans* (Princeton: Princeton University Press, 2004)
Molly Nesbit, *Atget's Seven Albums* (New Haven and London: Yale University Press, 1992)
John Szarkowski, *Atget* (New York: Museum of Modern Art, 2000)
Roy E. Stryker and Nancy Wood, *In This Proud Land: America 1935–1943 As Seen in the FSA Photographs* (Greenwich, Conn.: New York Graphic Society, 1973)

▲ 1977, 1980

1937a

The European powers contest one another in national pavilions of art, trade, and propaganda at the International Exhibition in Paris, while the Nazis open the "Degenerate 'Art'" exhibition, a vast condemnation of modernist art, in Munich.

On July 19, 1937, "Degenerate 'Art'" opened in the Nazi homeground of Munich, a day after Hitler inaugurated the "Great German Art" exhibition in the massive new House of German Art across the street. The Nazis intended the two shows as complementary demonstrations of racial types and political motives in art. The first was intended to expose the degeneration of modernist art as intrinsically Jewish and Bolshevik; the second, to display the purity of German art as self-evidently Aryan and National Socialist (ironically, only six of the 112 artists in "Degenerate 'Art'" were Jews). According to Minister of Propaganda Joseph Goebbels, degenerate art "insults German feeling, or destroys or confuses natural form, or simply reveals an absence of adequate manual and artistic skill." Nazi art was presented as its antithesis: archnationalist in subject, it exalted "German feeling," and archtraditionalist in style, it armored "natural form" in neoclassical cladding, as in the pumped-up figures of its foremost sculptors Arno Breker (1900–91) and Josef Thorak (1889–1952). To a great extent, then, Nazi aesthetics projected a paranoid image of modernist art, and reacted against this image in its own art. To this end, it abjected the art of "primitives," children, and ▲ the insane, the primary affiliations used to condemn modernist art in "Degenerate 'Art'," which also charged this art with "disrespect" for religion, femininity, and the military [**1**].

The two exhibitions were not complementary, however, in attendance: "Degenerate 'Art'" attracted five times as many visitors

1 • Room 3 of the "Degenerate 'Art'" exhibition, 1937, Munich
Showing the projection along the south wall, including the Dada wall

▲ 1903, 1922

as "Great German Art"—two million in Munich alone, nearly another million in its tour of thirteen other cities in Germany and Austria over the next three years. It remains the most visited show of modernist art ever. This is a highly ambiguous statistic: if the work was so repulsive, why did it attract so many? Is scorn born of resentment the most "popular" response to modernist art? Were there alternative, even subversive, kinds of spectatorship, one that secretly appreciated the art on view (there is some evidence of this)? The show was only one event among many other antimodernist exhibitions, anti-Semitic films, book burnings, and so on. Moreover, "Degenerate 'Art'" displayed just 650 of the 16,000 modernist works confiscated from thirty-two public art museums in 1937 alone, most of which were burned, "lost," or sold for cash—a provenance with which collections around the world are still coming to terms. However infamous, then, the exhibition was only a single episode in a long war on modernist culture, a total purge of progressive institutions. In 1933 the Nazis shut down the ▲ Bauhaus; in 1935 Hitler ordered the eradication of modernist art altogether; in 1936 Goebbels banned non-Nazi art criticism; and so on. Such is the cultural penetration of a totalitarian state, and the political importance of antimodernism to the Nazi regime.

Body politics

For the Russian art historian Igor Golomstock, several principles governed the art policies of totalitarian regimes of the interwar • period (he includes Stalinist Soviet Union and Fascist Italy equally): art was treated as an ideological weapon; the state assumed a monopoly over cultural institutions; the most conservative art movement was made official; and all other styles were condemned. There are exceptions to these rules, particularly the last two, especially under Mussolini. Modernism was anathema in many ways, but not always because it was antitraditional or antibourgeois. At first Mussolini embraced Futurism for its ideology of destruction, and all these regimes sought to replace old affiliations of culture and class with new identifications with leader, party, and state. However, no regime could tolerate modernist deformations of the body. Thus the Nazis condemned Expressionism, even though it was "German," more violently than abstraction, which they deemed "Bolshevik"—much to the chagrin of the Expressionist Emil Nolde, a Nazi Party member who was well represented in "Degenerate 'Art'." In general, modernist art was dangerous because it privileged the individual in terms of original vision, singular style, personal redemption, and so on. Even more than its deformations, this "subjectivism" ran counter to the corporate imperative of totalitarian regimes—the need to bind the masses psychically and almost physically to the leader, party, and state [**2**]. In this scheme the individual body could only figure the body politic, and it was often imaged as phobically intact, even phallicly aggressive, as in *Readiness* by Breker [**3**], an allegorical figure of Nazi militarism.

On the one hand, each totalitarian culture had to represent its political regime with its specific symbols—the Teutonic swastika

2 • Xanti Schawinsky, *1934—Year XII of the Fascist Era*, 1934
Letterpress poster, 95.7 x 71.8 (37⅝ x 28¼)

recovered by Hitler for his Nazi flag, or the ancient *fasces* of Roman lawmakers (an ax projecting from a bundle of rods bound with a red strap) recovered by the Italian Fascists for their party logo. On the other hand, it had to represent this regime as *non*specific, suprahistorical, even transcendental: thus the general use of a monumental neoclassicism. (Another highly ambiguous phenomenon is that other governments, not considered totalitarian, have also resorted to this idiom for similar reasons.) In this reversion to neoclassicism, Golomstock notes, the old hierarchy of academic genres was revived and recast. The royal portrait became the portrait of the party leader, and retained its "tendency to deify." The history painting became the "historico-revolutionary theme," and retained its tendency to mythify, with leaders, party martyrs (if Nazi or Fascist) or worker-heroes (if Stalinist) depicted as "creators of history." Genre painting became renderings of labor either as a "fierce struggle or a joyful festival." And landscape painting was treated "either as an image of the Fatherland … or as an arena of social transformations—the so-called 'industrial landscape'." The "historico-revolutionary" paintings were especially burdened, for they had another contradiction to face as well: the story of the nation had to be told, but its greatest epoch only began with the totalitarian regime. In this restrictive scenario, the best heroes, that is to say the safest ones, were either allegorical or dead or both. This mode of allegory and cult of death pervaded totalitarian architecture too.

However, the term "totalitarian" obscures as much as it illuminates. Politically, it elides the fundamental fact that Nazism and

▲ 1923 • 1909, 1934a

3 • Arno Breker, *Readiness*, Berlin, 1939
Bronze, height 320 (126)

Fascism (which are hardly identical) struggled bitterly against Communism. On the artistic front alone, the neoclassicisms of the three regimes were as different as the nationalist myths that they served. The Nazis contrived a massive neoclassicism in order to posit an Aryan Germany as the warrior-heir to ancient Greece, while the Fascists produced a sleek neoclassicism in order to present a Fascist Italy as the modern revival of ancient Rome. The kitschy academicism of the Soviet Union was different still: not bound up with antique origin myths, its "Socialist Realism" was focused on present ideology—in the words of culture commissar Andrei ▲ Zhdanov, "to educate workers in the spirit of Communism."

The intensity of antimodernism also varied from regime to regime. Mussolini allowed some modernist forms (from Futurist art to Rationalist architecture) to coexist, indeed to combine, with some reactionary forms. In this way, as the American critic Jeffrey Schnapp has suggested, Fascism used "aesthetic overproduction" to cover for its ideological instability. And although Stalin suppressed Constructivism, he also employed some of its leaders, such as Alek- ▲ sandr Rodchenko and El Lissitzky. (The recent argument, advanced by the Russian critic Boris Groys, that Stalin was the epitome of the Constructivist engineer of culture is reductive, indeed antimodernist in its own right.) The antimodernism of the Nazis was most thorough, but they too compounded atavistic forms of ritual (for instance, the party rallies at the Nuremberg Zeppenfeld designed by Albert Speer [1905–81]) with advanced forms of media (for instance, *Triumph of the Will*, the 1935 film by Leni Riefenstahl [1902–2003] of the 1934 party rally, the Nazi "Birth of a Nation"). In different ways, then, all three regimes mixed the modernist and the reactionary. Even when they were attracted to modernism for its transgression of bourgeois culture, they were repelled by its alienation of the masses; and even though they were eager to exploit the manipulative effects of media spectacle, they were reluctant to sacrifice the communal bases of archaic culture.

Some of these conflicts and contradictions surfaced at the International Exhibition in Paris, which opened in May 1937 under the government of Léon Blum, a Popular Front alliance of Socialists and Communists against Fascism. With several art shows (both traditional and modern) and many national pavilions, the vast site extended from the Hôtel des Invalides across the Seine to the Trocadéro, with the Eiffel Tower (emblem of past exhibitions) at its center. Some pavilions featured displays of art and trade, others foregrounded photomontage narratives of nation; still others combined the two kinds of exhibit. Although intended as an international fair pledged to peace (replete with a Peace Tower at its north end), the International Exhibition was dominated by a cultural war that soon became an actual military one. Indeed, the Spanish Civil War, which further pressured the confrontations here, was already under way.

The central confrontation occurred on the right bank of the Seine just above the Pont d'Iena [**4**]. There the Soviet pavilion, designed by Boris Iofan (1891–1976), a primary architect of Stalinist monoliths, faced the German pavilion, designed by Albert Speer, the chief architect to Hitlerian hubris. (In the continuum between culture and war at issue here, this master-builder of the Nazis became minister of armaments during World War II.) In his memoir *Inside the Third Reich* (1970), Speer revealed that a secret sketch of the Soviet pavilion influenced his own design: "A sculpted pair of figures thirty-three [meters] tall, on a high platform, were striding triumphantly towards the German Pavilion. I therefore designed a cubic mass, also elevated on stout pillars, which seemed to be checking this onslaught, while from the cornice of my tower an eagle with a swastika in its claws looked down on the Russian sculptures. I received a gold medal for the building; so did my Soviet colleague."

▲ 1934a

▲ 1921, 1926, 1928

Photographies Schall et « L'Illustration »
LES MOTIFS DE SCULPTURE QUI COURONNENT TROIS DES PRINCIPAUX PAVILLONS ÉTRANGERS
L'Allemagne (Aigle, professeur Schmidt-Ehmen) - L'U.R.S.S. (l'industrie et l'agriculture, groupe en acier de Mme Mouchina)
L'Italie (les diverses corporations, par les sculpteurs Servettaz, Mascherini, Fontana, Minguzzi et Bortolotti).

4 • Details of the Nazi (top left), Soviet (top right), and Italian (bottom) pavilions at the International Exhibition in Paris, 1937

As Speer suggests, the two pavilions were seen as equal instances of effective propaganda, but the similarity ends there. The Soviet structure served as a kinetic pedestal that thrust the steel-clad *Industrial Worker and Collective Farm Girl* sculpted by Vera Mukhina (1889–1953) forward, as if into world-historical prominence; they are sculptural embodiments of the proletariat as new heroes of history. No one could mistake this ensemble for the *Monument to the Third International* (1920) proposed by the ▲ Russian Constructivist Vladimir Tatlin: these allegorical figures represented the Soviet Union of Stalin, specifically his brutal Five-Year Plans to industrialize production and to collectivize agriculture. But, like the *Monument*, the Soviet pavilion did ascend dynamically, here to the union of hammer and sickle, Communist emblems of factory and farm. And as Speer also suggests, this advance was indeed arrested by the German pavilion, an oppressive temple to imperial power that announced a very different notion of nation and history; to note only the obvious, it culminated in emblems of party, not figures of labor.

Although its steel construction may seem modern, this pavilion was clad with German limestone, not to mention the swastika tiles in gold and red recessed between its piers. And although its stripped facade may also seem modern, this only "purified" the classical reference of the columns and the entablature. In fact, the pavilion was a typological pastiche in the guise of a pure monument, for even as its tower alluded to a classical temple, its exhibition hall alluded to a medieval church, in whose "apse" stood a model of the mausolean House of German Art designed by Paul Troost (1878–1934), the recently deceased predecessor to Speer as chief Nazi architect—an appropriate "altarpiece" in this architecture of death. For what is at stake in these historical allusions is the hubristic ambition to subsume history, indeed to transcend it. And this ambition was programmatic. Speer and Hitler, a failed artist and amateur architect in his own right, devised a "ruin theory" of architecture, whereby Nazi structures (such as the gargantuan Great Hall conceived by Speer for the new Berlin ordained by Hitler) would be built to last *beyond* the millennium of the Thousand-Year Reich—to subject all posterity to a sublime awe before its glorious ruins. Already "dead" in its neoclassicism, this aesthetic thus sought to dominate time posthumously—to turn time into a spectacle of domination. Perhaps this is what Walter ▲ Benjamin had in mind at the close of his famous essay on the new "mankind" fashioned by such spectacles: "its self-alienation has reached such a degree that it can experience its own destruction as an aesthetic pleasure of the first order."

A modernist retort

Within this war of pavilions there was also a battle of figures. Expunged from most modernist art for the first two decades of the century, the human figure returned with a vengeance in the ● *rappel à l'ordre* (return to order) of the twenties and thirties—not only in reactionary art but also in antidemocratic politics, in which, again, identification with the body of leader, party, and state became imperative. Such figures as the Soviet Worker and Farm Girl were hardly realist: they were allegorical types not only of comradeship but of equality in Communist labor. No less allegorical, the *Monumental Groups* by Thorak that flanked the German pavilion stressed the opposite: these trios of one nude man and two nude women insisted on sexual difference. This insistence accorded with the strict divisions in Nazi society as a whole, but one senses a psychic import here too, as if the phallic body-ego of the Nazi masculine ideal required a "feminine" other against whom to aggress—an other represented in different ways by Jews, Bolsheviks, homosexuals, gypsies, and so on.

The Italian figures across the Seine were different again. These robed representations of various corporations were intended to connect the Fascist state to ancient Rome (the same association was advanced within the Italian pavilion). But rather than enliven the past, they petrified the present, and turned this mythical history of Italy into a kitschy kind of costume ball. Different still were the two photographs of two women (the change in medium is significant) that stood out from the photomontage displays at the Spanish pavilion, which was under the control of the Republican

▲ 1914, 1921

▲ 1935 ● 1919

5 • Pablo Picasso, *Guernica*, 1937
Oil on canvas, 349 x 777 (137⅜ x 305⅞)

Popular Front government. The woman on the left, wrapped in the traditional costume of Salamanca, stands mute and grim, as if burdened by her status as a folklorish fetish, while the woman on the right strides toward us in a militia uniform, larger than life, with her mouth open in song or shout. The metaphor here is one of metamorphosis: the militant butterfly of Republican resistance bursts from the cocoon of Nationalist tradition, as her caption states: "Freeing herself from her wrapping of superstition and misery, from the immemorial slave is born THE WOMAN, capable of taking an active part in the development of the future." Unlike the Fascist figures, she sheds the past in the name of a liberated future; yet, unlike the Soviet figures, she does so with a photographic specificity that makes her fight real.

And it was real. In February 1936, the Popular Front won elections in Spain; in July, General Francisco Franco led an army revolt; and three years of civil war ensued between his Nationalists (mostly army, Church, and industrialists) and the Republicans (mostly Socialists, Communists, anarchists, and liberals, supported by Basques and Catalans). Hitler and Mussolini aided the Nationalists actively, while Stalin supported the Republicans weakly. This, then, was the battleground behind the militant woman in the pavilion—a pavilion that connected democratic resistance and modernist art at several levels. The building, a Corbusian structure designed by Josep Lluis Sert (1902–83), was modernist, as were its principal contents, two protest-paintings made on behalf of the Republican cause: *The Catalan Peasant in Revolt* by Miró and *Guernica* by Picasso, the centerpiece of the exhibit **[5]**.

On April 26, 1937, the German Condor Legion had bombed the Basque town of Guernica. Picasso, who had become the symbolic director of the Prado Museum in Madrid a year before, painted *Guernica* in six weeks, with motifs and forms drawn from his hybrid Cubist-Surrealist work of the period. The huge painting shows four women in terror: one falls from a house in flames; two others flee distorted by fear; the fourth cradles her dead child and screams. A dismembered soldier lies on the ground, while a horse cries out in agony and a bull stares us in the eye. These animals attest to the bestiality of the bombing, but in this world turned upside down they also possess a humanity that seems stripped from the humans here. Picasso holds all this debris together by a pyramidal massing of figures and a muted range of blacks, whites, and grays. But his genius is to transform his own modernist inventions of Cubist fragmentation and Surrealist distortion into an expression of outrage: this is modernist art in the service of political actuality. A response to the Nazi bombing, a riposte to the Nationalist accusation that the Republicans had defiled "the artistic treasures" of Spain, *Guernica* also defies the mythical histories of totalitarian regimes, and rebuts the reactionary beliefs that political art can only be social realist and that modernist art can never be public. Here modernism is reconciled with referentiality, responsibility, and resistance. "Did you do that?" a Nazi officer asked Picasso in front of *Guernica*. "No," Picasso is said to have replied, "you did."

FURTHER READING

Dawn Ades and Tim Benton (eds), *Art and Power: Europe Under the Dictators 1939–1945* (London: Thames & Hudson, 1995)

Stephanie Barron (ed.), *"Degenerate Art": The Fate of the Avant-Garde in Nazi Germany* (Los Angeles: Los Angeles County Museum of Art, 1991)

Igor Golomstock, *Totalitarian Art* (London: Icon, 1990)

Boris Groys, *The Total Art of Stalinism*, trans. Charles Rougle (Princeton: Princeton University Press, 1992)

Eric Michaud, *The Cult of Art in Nazi Germany*, trans. Janet Lloyd (Palo Alto: Stanford University Press, 2004)

Jeffrey Schnapp, *Staging Fascism* (Palo Alto: Stanford University Press, 1996)

1937b

Naum Gabo, Ben Nicholson, and Leslie Martin publish *Circle* in London, solidifying the institutionalization of geometric abstraction.

Circle: International Survey of Constructive Art, edited by the Russian sculptor Naum Gabo (1890–1977) and the British painter Ben Nicholson (1894–1982) and architect Leslie Martin (1908–2000) and published to coincide with the exhibition "Constructive Art" at the London Gallery in July 1937, is an extraordinary document. It can be read in two opposed ways: as the last gasp of the utopianism that characterized the historical avant-gardes of the twenties or as the first step into what could be called their cooptation and institutionalized devolution. The content and composition of this volume—first intended as a journal but produced, in the end, as a hefty one-time almanac—are worth examining in detail.

The design is resolutely inconspicuous, with its traditional grouping of plates off-text and its conventional typography. This clear demarcation between text and image echoes the strict adherence, in the organization of the volume, to the beaux-arts division of artistic practices by medium: the first three sections are devoted to painting, sculpture, and architecture respectively, and illustrated with an emphasis on historical continuity within each discipline, blending the works of the first generation of pioneers of "constructive art" with those of current (mostly British) artists and architects.

Only the fourth and last section, entitled "Art and Life," conveys the sense of open interdisciplinarity that had been the lingua franca of the small avant-garde publications that *Circle* was emulating or to which it was responding, though the paucity of illustrations in this section seems to indicate that the editors deemed it was less important than the first three. It consists of texts on unconnected topics: on ▲ art education (by ex-Bauhaus director Walter Gropius); on choreog- • raphy (by Ballets Russes star Leonide Massine); on "Light painting" (by László Moholy-Nagy, who had been living London since 1935 but ■ was to be appointed director of the New Bauhaus in Chicago within weeks after the publication of *Circle*); on typography (by Jan Tschi- ◆ chold, then still an ardent partisan of El Lissitzky's Constructivist book design but very soon to become one of the most powerful proponents, as typography director of Penguin Books, of a return to neoclassicism in this field); on "biotechnics" (by the Czech architect Karel Honzik, who proposed under such a title a fairly innocuous comparison between the geometric forms encountered in nature and the structural principles of architectural functionalism—a pale imitation of Karl Blossfeldt's successful *Urformen der Kunst*, whose first English edition dates from 1929); and, finally, on "the death of the monument" (by the American historian Lewis Mumford). If no attempt was made to stress a common denominator between the various contributions to this pot-pourri section, it is perhaps because *Circle's* editors felt that the task had already been performed by the brief unsigned editorial and by Gabo's lengthy essay, "The Constructive Idea in Art," at the beginning of the volume.

Given the dangers looming on the political horizon—made clear by the competitive stand-off between the Soviet and German pavil- ▲ ions at the 1937 Universal Exhibition, which had just opened in Paris when *Circle* appeared—the book's unsigned editorial seems, with hindsight, amazingly naive in its utter optimism. "A new cultural unity is slowly emerging out of the fundamental changes which are taking place in our present-day civilization," begins the short text. *Circle* is not a manifesto, we are told: its goal is to help the information circulate among practitioners of "the constructive trend in the art of today" who are working simultaneously in several countries, and to bypass all "dependence upon private enterprise" in order to directly reach the public. The editorial concludes with this sentence: "We hope to make clear a common basis and to demonstrate, not only the relationship of one work to the other but of this form of art to the whole social order." Gabo's essay, which immediately follows, sings the same tune. Acknowledging that *Circle's* efforts come after a century of revolutions that "have spared nothing in the edifice of culture which had been built up by the past ages," Gabo nevertheless affirms: "However long and however deep this process may go in its material destruction, it cannot deprive us any more of our optimism about the final outcome, since we see that in the realm of ideas we are now entering on the period of reconstruction."

"Social order," "period of reconstruction": the language is that of • the "return to order" that had blossomed in the aftermath of World War I, particularly in its modernist version as advocated by Le Cor- ■ busier in *L'Esprit Nouveau*. As if to underline this heritage, *Circle* contains the architect's intervention in a famous public symposium, at the Maison de la Culture in Paris, under the aegis of the Communist Party ("The Quarrel with Realism"), where he is as rhapsodic as ever in his praise of the Machine, a stance echoed in Leslie Martin's "The State of Transition" in the volume's architectural section. And, just as Le Corbusier's Purism was a reaction against the analytic

▲ 1923 • 1919 ■ 1929, 1947a ◆ 1926, 1928 ▲ 1937a • 1919 ■ 1925a

"excesses" of Cubism, Gabo sees the task of the "constructive" artist as that of building anew upon the *tabula rasa* created by the Cubist "revolutionary explosion." For him, the critical function of avant-garde art (Dada is specifically targeted) is a thing of the past:

> *The logic of life does not tolerate permanent revolutions.... The Constructive idea does not expect from Art the performance of critical functions even when they are directed against the negative side of life. What is the use of showing us what is bad without revealing what is good?*

Finally, like Le Corbusier before him in *Après le cubisme* of 1918, Gabo draws upon a parallelism between art and science in order to buttress his position. "We can find efficient support for our optimism in those two domains of our culture where the revolution has been the most thorough, namely, in Science and in Art." Critical of a cliché of the literature on Cubism according to which this new art represented an "illustration" of Einstein's Theory of Relativity, Gabo warns against any pseudomorphic analogies between the productions of art and those of science (curiously, the sole scientist who contributed to *Circle*, J. D. Bernal, precisely fell into that trap in his essay "Art and the Scientist"). Art and science are not to be directly linked, but they partake of a common "vision of the world," of a common search for "universal laws." The main difference between Gabo's stand and that of Le Corbusier on this matter concerns the style which they respectively consider as best suited to the task of expressing these "universal laws." Both Le Corbusier and Gabo argue for a new humanism that would be coded in geometric forms, but while the former demands anthropomorphism in art, Gabo conceives of geometric abstraction as the "cornerstone" of his program: "[The Constructive idea] has revealed an universal law that the elements of a visual art such as lines, colours, shapes, possess their own forces of expression independent of any association with the external aspects of the world [and] that their life and their action are self-conditioned psychological phenomena rooted in human nature."

The vagueness of this program is nowhere more apparent than in the choice of contemporary paintings and sculptures reproduced in *Circle*. Besides the anthology of works by early pioneers, mentioned above (Arp, Brancusi, Braque, Mondrian, Duchamp, El Lissitzky, Gabo, Gris, Léger, Kandinsky, Klee, Malevich, Medunetsky, Moholy-Nagy, Pevsner, Picasso, Taeuber-Arp, and Tatlin), *Circle* offers an eclectic panorama of the current production of a second generation of abstract artists, all working within the parameters set by their predecessors. As in the case of *Cercle et Carré* and of *Abstraction-Création*, which appeared in Paris in 1930 and 1932 and which, like *Circle*, were used as platforms to organize exhibitions, most of the recent art reproduced by Gabo and his acolytes represents a middle-brow, academicized version of geometric abstraction that has no programmatic characteristic other than that of being "non-objective," to use the vocabulary of the period.

The paintings are quite diverse—the post-Malevichean compositions of the German Friedrich Vordemberge-Gildewart (1899–1962) have little to do with the ovoids of the Swiss Hans Erni (born 1909); the jazzy, interlocking volumes of the British John Piper (1903–92) bear no resemblance to the calm opposition, in Ben Nicholson's white reliefs, of square and circle [**1**], nor to the floating shapes of

1 • Ben Nicholson, *1934 (relief)*, 1934
Oil on carved board, 71.8 x 96.5 (28¼ x 38)

the French Jean Hélion (1904–87) [2]. However, they are all figurative (in the sense that the duality of figure and ground is nowhere called into question, and that in each of them several figures are set upon a neutral background). Furthermore, they all seem based on the assumption that achieving a state of equilibrium between competing figures is what is requested from art, if art is indeed to express the kind of "universal law" called forth by Gabo. The recipe sometimes makes for elegant compositions, but it can also yield facile, decorative work. Heralded by *Circle* as evidence of a transnational "new cultural unity," this post-Cubist style, in which the main formal decision consists of a balancing act, was indeed fast becoming an international style, the rapidity of its spread being largely due to the fact that, with it, abstraction had lost its edge.

The section devoted to contemporary sculpture, though less eclectic in choice of works, had similar problems. Except for Calder's mobiles, the majority of the works presented are carved (in wood or marble) and presented on pedestals, Barbara Hepworth and Henry Moore having no qualms about that very traditional concept of the "monument" lambasted by Lewis Mumford in his contribution to the volume. The most telling position with regard to this issue is perhaps that of Gabo, whose essay, "Sculpture: Carving and Construction in Space" represents an about-face. While he reproduces some of his early works such as the *Kinetic Sculpture* of 1920, it is to denigrate them as experiments ("more an explanation of the idea of a kinetic sculpture than a kinetic sculpture itself"); while he nearly appropriates the theory of his ex-rival Tatlin, according to which each form has to be determined according to the properties of its material, he ends up advocating the notion of "absolute" form (absolute, thus not contingent upon its material); he repeats the plea of his 1920 "Realist Manifesto" for the constitution of space as a sculptural material, yet he defends the opposite possibility of the translation of his virtual volumes of the preceding years, done in Plexiglas, into massive stone carvings. His text ends with an apology for sculpture as the most efficient symbol of power—he praises this art for having given the "masses of Egypt confidence and certainty in the truth and the omnipotence of their King of Kings, the Sun"—that could have been written by Aristide Maillol or Arno Breker. Predictably, most of Gabo's subsequent work was miniature models of monuments. As Benjamin Buchloh noted, when Gabo finally realized one of these models on a large scale (the sculpture placed in front of the Bijenkorf in Rotterdam, completed in 1957), the "discrepancy between the structural and material elements," most conspicuous in "its bronze-wire network faking tension and structural function," would spectacularly betray Tatlin's legacy.

"Constructive" art versus Constructivism

In fact, Gabo is not a Constructivist (even if he labels his art "constructive"), though he successfully persuaded generations of art historians that he was a legitimate spokesman for the movement (including Alfred Barr, who legitimated the claim). He conceives of sculpture as the embodiment of a rational idea that could appeal directly to the mind of the spectator and be read as an image of consciousness: through material transparency (Plexiglas) of formal simplicity (symmetry, parabola), one would have access to the central core of the sculpture out of which volumes and surfaces project. This fundamentally figurative conception of sculpture is a far cry from the Constructivism of Rodchenko and the Obmokhu group, whom he opposed, as much as it is from that of Katarzyna Kobro, whose antimonumental stance constitutes the best rebuttal of Gabo's position (as well as a critique of most modernist sculpture).

There are two other serious differences between the Constructivist program and that of *Circle*. The first is that there is almost no trace of the political realm in the English publication. Reading Gabo's admonition that the Constructive idea should not compel "art to an immediate construction of material values in life," one could even say that it is resolutely apolitical. The immense question of new modes of production and distribution of art, so fervently discussed by the Soviet avant-garde, is completely ignored in the pages of *Circle*, where the only allusion to the life of works once they leave the artist's studio is a meek reference to the evils of "dependence upon private enterprise," mentioned above—a clear indication that the journal's editors, probably with the Art Deco phenomenon in mind, feared that their art would become mere decoration for bourgeois homes.

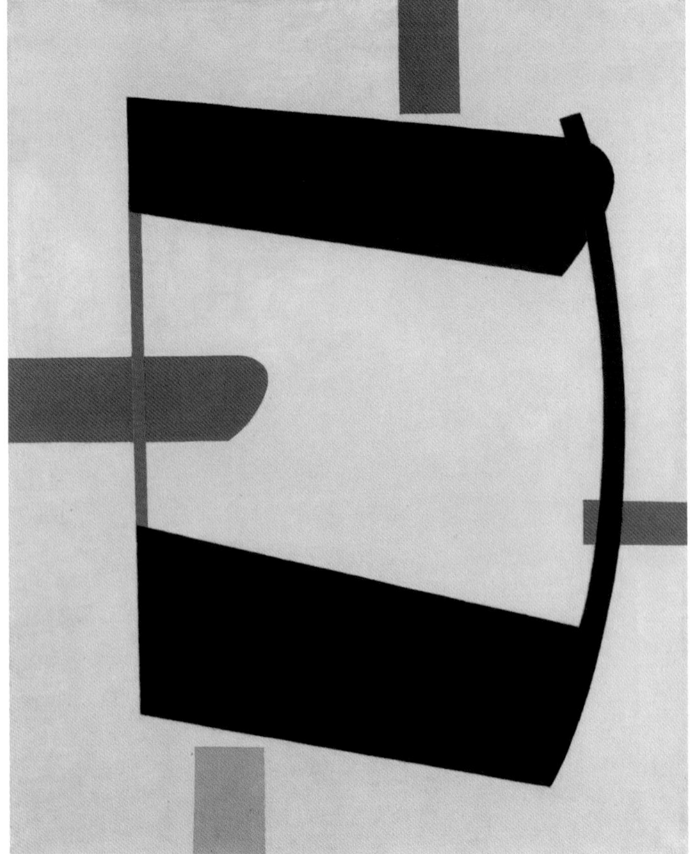

2 • Jean Hélion, *Equilibre*, 1933
Oil on canvas, 81 x 100 (31⅞ x 39⅜)

▲ 1934b ● 1955b ■ 1914, 1921 ◆ 1900b, 1937a ▲ 1921 ● 1928 ■ 1925a

The second major difference between a "constructive" and a Constructivist art concerns the issue of composition. For the Constructivists, the traditional order of composition was what had to be destroyed—because both the subjective arbitrariness of the aesthetic choices it elicited, and the age-old conventions of its formal devices (balance, hierarchy), were for them ciphers of the authoritarian social order of the Czarist regime and had no place in a revolutionary society. They went to great lengths to find ways in which one could motivate the organization of a work of art according to the properties of its material and the process in use: it is this motivated, "objective" organization (as opposed to the subjective, arbitrary composition) that they called a construction. Had Gabo ▲ participated in the 1921 debate at the Inkhuk (Moscow) at which such issues were discussed, he would undoubtedly have found himself a member of the losing minority.

In his defense, however, one should recall that by 1937 the strict opposition cast between composition and construction by Rodchenko and his peers was entirely forgotten. Furthermore, outside of Russia the very possibility of a noncompositional art had very few proponents (and the most articulate of them, Wladyslaw ● Strzeminski, was little known in the West, although reproductions of his works regularly appeared in *Abstraction-Création*). Yet, one emerging trend should have appealed to the *Circle* editors, especially to Gabo, given his recurrent fantasy about a convergence of ■ interests between art and science: Max Bill's Concrete Art which had just been launched in Zurich (either *Circle* did not know about it, which is rather improbable, since Bill was very well connected, or they deliberately censored it.)

The term "Concrete Art" is not Bill's own but Theo van ◆ Doesburg's. Better known for his steering of the De Stijl movement, the Dutch artist, then based in Paris, had in 1930 published a small journal called *Art Concret* (it had only one issue), around which he intended to found a new artists' group. In its pages, he advocated an art that would be programmed entirely by mathematic calculations before it was realized ("We reject artistic handwriting," he wrote, adding: "Painting which is done in the manner of Jack the Ripper can interest only detectives, criminologists, psychologists and psychiatrists.") The publication had no effect whatsoever and the group never coalesced, in great part because van Doesburg died only a few months later in a Swiss sanatorium. Bill, however, had been enormously impressed, as much as by van Doesburg's manifestos as by his *Arithmetic Drawing*, a variation on the black, gray, and white *Arithmetic Composition* [**3**], in which the "Russian doll" logic of a figure within a figure transforms a simple *opposition*—between a black square placed on its tip within a white square that is four times as large—into a deductive structure that exactly determines the placement of each element. Bill's art would never achieve the stark simplicity of van Doesburg's late canvas—one could say that he never could dispense with "good taste," ruining his very idea of a programmed, a priori art by his purely subjective introjection of aesthetic factors that could not be quantified, such as color.

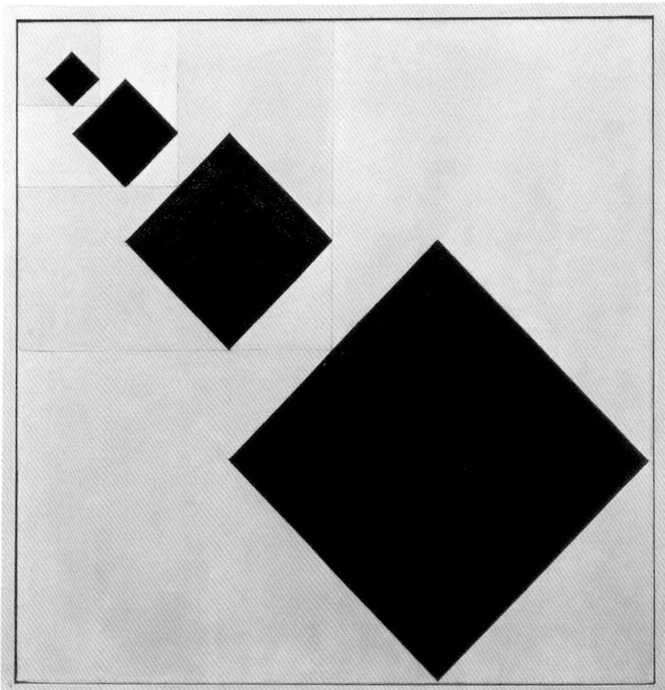

3 • Theo van Doesburg, *Arithmetic Composition*, 1930
Oil on canvas, 101 x 101 (39¾ x 39¾)

Yet theoretically at least, Bill's conception could have provided a way out for abstract artists who did not feel compelled by the post-Cubist, compositional model provided by *Circle*. Or they could ▲ have turned to Mondrian, and many thought they actually did, but at the cost of a gross misunderstanding due, in part, to his benevolent contribution to *Circle* and other publications of the sort. Had anyone then attentively read "Plastic Art and Pure Plastic Art," the long essay by Mondrian that accompanies the reproduction of his recent paintings in *Circle*, one would have been struck by this statement: "Neo-Plastic is as destructive as it is constructive," and one might have realized that his ultimate goal was to destroy all figures, a goal diametrically opposed to that of the artists supported by *Circle*. But no one paid attention, and figurative abstract art became a cottage industry of the cultural elite—notably in the United States, where for a decade it filled the Museum of Non-Objective Painting (later called the Guggenheim Museum) and Albert Eugene Gallatin's Museum of Living Art, as well as the exhibitions of the American Abstract Artists Association, giving abstraction a bad name until Abstract Expressionism—whose participants loathed the AAA—would cast it aside.

FURTHER READING

J. Leslie Martin, Ben Nicholson, and Naum Gabo (eds), *Circle* (1937; reprint London: Faber and Faber, 1971)

Benjamin H. D. Buchloh, "Cold War Constructivism," in Serge Guilbaut (ed.), *Reconstructing Modernism* (Cambridge, Mass.: MIT Press, 1990)

Jeremy Lewinson (ed.), *Circle: Constructive Art in Britain 1934–40* (Cambridge: Kettle's Yard Gallery, 1982)

▲ 1921 ● 1928 ■ 1955a, 1967c ◆ 1917, 1928 ▲ 1913, 1917, 1944a

1940–1944

1942a

The depoliticization of the American avant-garde reaches the point of no return when Clement Greenberg and the editors of *Partisan Review* bid farewell to Marxism.

In July 1942, an "Inquiry on Dialectic Materialism" appeared in the second issue of the international journal *Dyn*, founded and edited in Mexico from 1942–4 by the Austrian artist Wolfgang Paalen (1907–59). It consisted of a set of three questions that Paalen had sent to two dozen "distinguished scholars and writers," and of the answers (not everyone replied). The questions were: (1) Is Dialectic Materialism (the philosophy of Marx and Engels) "the science of a veritable 'dialectic' process"?; (2) Is the dialectic method elaborated by Hegel itself scientific (independently of its appropriation by Marxism), and if so, "does science owe important discoveries to this method"?; and (3) Are the laws established by Hegel in his *Logic*, laws which form the ground of his dialectic method, universally valid and useful?

Breton's spiteful silence

The addressees—a complete list of whom was provided—had been chosen both because they had not yet, or not recently enough, expressed their view on the matter and for their lack of direct involvement in "practical politics." Half of them responded. The ▲ most conspicuous among those who did *not* was André Breton, the founder of Surrealism, until then a fervent and efficient supporter of Paalen's art. The artist had been one of the scenographers of the famous "Exposition Internationale du Surréalisme" in Paris ● in January–February 1938, and in June of the same year Breton had prefaced an exhibition of his *fumages*, paintings realized by quickly grazing a smoking candle over a freshly prepared surface, and then editing the results—as always when the Surrealist conception of automatism is involved [**1**].

Had he answered, Breton would have disagreed with the majority of the respondents, who answered "No" to all three questions. Breton's admiration for Marx and Hegel never diminished, and Stalin's regime, of which he had been one of the harshest critics ever since the beginning of the Moscow trials in 1936, was for him doubly criminal in that its barbaric acts were committed in the name of dialectical materialism. But Breton's silence was motivated by spite: in the first issue of *Dyn*, published in April 1942 and which he had received in New York, where he had been living for less than a year, he had stumbled upon his protégé's treason, that is, Paalen's short but abrasive "Farewell to Surrealism." "In 1942,

1 • Wolfgang Paalen, *Ciel de Pieuvre*, 1938
Fumage and oil on canvas, 97 x 130 (38¼ x 51⅛)

after all the bloody failures of Dialectic Materialism and the progressive disintegration of all isms," Paalen claimed, one could no longer turn a blind eye to Surrealism's summary endorsement of certain of Marx's and Hegel's "too simplistic conceptions." Similarly discarding the movement's adherence to Freud's axiomatic principles concerning the fundamental role of unconscious desires in all human conduct, particularly the creative act, Paalen advocated greater familiarity with "the conquests and methods" of physical sciences on the part of artists, but dismissed allegiance to any one system of thought as dogmatic and constricting.

Breton did reply to Paalen, albeit indirectly, in the "Prolegomena to a Third Manifesto of Surrealism or Else," which appeared in June 1942 in the first issue of *VVV: Poetry, Plastic Arts, Anthropology, Sociology, Psychology,* a new Surrealist journal that he had launched in New York in 1940 (though the official editor was the sculptor David Hare [1917–91]). Reaffirming the spirit of rebellion that had always animated Surrealism, Breton rejected blind faith in any theoretical system, and, alluding to both Marxism and psychoanalysis, directly echoing Paalen's essay, he underlined how easily an "instrument of liberation" can be transformed into an "instrument of oppression," noting in passing that even science and mathematics are not immune to such a fate. Neither is Surrealism, implied Breton when denouncing what he called "a certain

▲ 1924 ● 1942b

Surrealist conformity," by which he meant the academicization of Surrealist practices in the American art world and their commercialization in the fashion and movie industries. (This seems to have been when Breton coined the anagram "Avida Dollars" to disparage Salvador Dalí, who epitomized this trend in his mind). The oddest pique, illustrating Breton's point that "man might not be the center of the universe," was reserved for the anthropomorphic (and thus nonmaterialist) conception of the animal kingdom manifested by an "exceptional" (materialist) thinker whose hand "had presided over some of the greatest events of our time," when speaking to him four years before, in Mexico, about the "natural" devotion of his dog. The brilliant thinker in question was Leon Trotsky, who, as a political refugee, Breton felt he could not publicly name—if anything, however, the strange allusion rightly points to the centrality of Trotsky (whose assassination by Stalin in 1940 had deeply affected Breton) for anyone concerned with the role of culture at this dire moment of history.

The American Artists' Congress

The Russian leader was certainly on the mind of several respondents to *Dyn's* inquiry who were actively involved, as editors or regular contributors, with the anti-Stalinist, New York-based literary journal *Partisan Review*, founded in 1934. These included Meyer Schapiro, Dwight Macdonald (1906–82), Philip Rahv (1908–73), and Clement Greenberg—the latter offering at least some explanation for his triple negative answers and adding that he "wished he could say yes." Most of them had espoused radical politics in the early thirties, as had the artists whom their journal was beginning to celebrate (soon to become the heroes of Abstract Expressionism, these had formed several unions and leftist organizations during their tenure at the WPA). When in the summer of 1935 Moscow had initiated the strategy of the Popular Front, intended to create an international alliance of intellectuals against fascism, these young men had volunteered their help and even embraced, momentarily, the cause of a "proletarian" art and culture, whereas Breton had been quick to detect the Stalinist trap, and immediately responded with a violent attack on the cultural politics of the USSR and a defense of artistic freedom.

A highlight of their growing involvement had been the first meeting of the American Artists' Congress, held in New York in February 1936, at which Schapiro read his paper, "The Social Bases of Art," where he harshly criticized the individualism of the modern (abstract) artist as political escapism that pandered to a new class of wealthy, dilettante patrons. (In the same breath, Stuart Davis, one of the organizers of the Congress, definitively broke with his longtime friend Arshile Gorky for his refusal to join in.)

The three show trials held in Moscow between August 1936 and March 1938 made the first serious dent in this youthful enthusiasm (though certain individuals, such as Davis, stubbornly stayed the course for several more years). Schapiro recanted his earlier antiformalist sermon in "The Nature of Abstract Art," a brilliant review of Alfred H. Barr, Jr.'s exhibition "Cubism and Abstract Art" at the Museum of Modern Art. (The review appeared in the short-lived journal *Marxist Quarterly* in January 1937.) Abstract art, Schapiro now claimed, was interacting with its historical context no less than any other art form, and was thus perfectly able to play an active role in it. Meanwhile *Partisan Review*, which had merged with a journal published by the Communist Party at the time of the first American Artists' Congress, had suspended publication in October 1936, to reappear only in December 1937, this time with a position closely allied to that of Trotsky whom a "commission of inquiry" chaired by John Dewey in April of that year had declared innocent of the crimes of which Stalin had accused him.

As early as July 1937, the editors of the future reincarnation of *Partisan Review* had courted Trotsky, then exiled in Mexico, hoping to obtain his contribution. Although appreciating their devotion, Trotsky delayed his decision until he had received some issues of the journal. His verdict was devastating: writing to Macdonald in January 1938, he snarled that for all their intelligence and education, the editors of *Partisan Review* basically had "nothing to say." Instead of "searching for themes that would not hurt anyone," the journal should follow the example of the artistic avant-garde movements ("naturalism, symbolism, futurism, cubism, expressionism and so on") which had always advanced their position by using the shock tactics of polemic and scandal. Trotsky's reluctance had not lessened two months later when he sent a letter to Rahv, but his insistence that the journal should keep an "eclectic" openness in aesthetic matters and support any "young and promising artistic movement" that came along indicates that for him cultural policy had become an important element in his struggle against Stalin. Trotsky finally gave in: the decisive factor was André Breton's arrival in Mexico in May 1938, of which Trotsky immediately informed the journal, even recommending the French poet as a contributor! (Ironically, it was Meyer Schapiro who had been instructed by Trotsky's secretary to send the Russian exile any of Breton's writing that he could find in New York.)

Breton had been in Mexico for less than a month and was in almost daily contact with him when Trotsky wrote an open letter dated June 17 to the editors of *Partisan Review*, published in its August–September 1938 issue as "Art and Politics." Its conclusion was particularly energizing: "Art, like science, not only does not seek orders, but by its very essence, cannot tolerate them.... Art can become a strong ally of revolution only insofar as it remains faithful to itself." The principal result of Breton's visit, however, was the manifesto "Towards a Free Revolutionary Art" calling for the formation of an International Federation of Independent Revolutionary Art, which he coauthored with Trotsky. The name of Diego Rivera replaced Trotsky's as cosignatory of the text when it was published worldwide, including in *Partisan Review* during the late fall of 1938 (even though Rivera, in whose house Trotsky was then living, had not taken the slightest part in its writing), because the Russian thought the manifesto would have more weight—especially as it condemned any enslavement of art by political

▲ 1924, 1930b ● Introduction 2, 1960b ■ 1936 ◆ 1927c ▲ 1927c ● 1933

forces—if it came from two creators, especially if they were from different persuasions. Just in case people had any doubt about his stance, Trotsky sent for publication in the following issue of *Partisan Review* a letter congratulating Breton—who by then had long since returned to Paris—on having joined forces with Rivera, and once again affirming that "the struggle for revolutionary ideas in art must begin with the struggle for artistic *truth*, not in terms of any single school, but in terms of *the immutable faith of the artist in his own inner self*."

The manifesto itself remains one of the most extraordinary documents of the period, notably for its appeal to both Marx and Freud, thus anticipating the Freudo-Marxism of Herbert Marcuse thirty years later. Its immediate effect on the art world was great. Greenberg quipped—in 1961, in a retrospective essay about the thirties—that "some day it will have to be told how 'anti-Stalinism,' which started out more or less as 'Trotskyism,' turned into 'art for art's sake,' and thereby cleared the way, heroically, for what was to come." In his first major essay, "Avant-Garde and Kitsch," published in *Partisan Review* in the fall of 1939, his analysis of the role of modernist art as a Trojan horse in a bourgeois society, and as the last rampart against barbarity, owes a lot to Breton and Trotsky's tract. For left-wing artists who had militated in Communist-infiltrated organization and had then been devastated by the Moscow trials, this signaled the end of a desiccating paralysis: not only was it all right not to follow the party line, but one did not have to think about one's art as primarily a mere instrument of the Revolution—Trotsky himself was saying so. Furthermore, despite his refusal to endorse any aesthetic program ▲ officially, Trotsky was singling out not only Mexican muralism (unsurprisingly, given the long history of political commitment by its artists) but also Surrealism!

By the time Stalin and Hitler signed a pact of nonaggression (August 23, 1939) and Soviet Russia invaded Finland (November 1939), any idea of a Popular Front had lost all credibility. Even Stuart Davis, who had long behaved like a Communist Party henchman, could no longer kid himself. He publicly resigned from the American Artists' Congress (the Popular Front's institutional voice in the US art scene), as did Schapiro, with Mark • Rothko, Adolph Gottlieb, and many other young artists in his wake. Meanwhile, in March 1939, Rivera's wife, Frida Kahlo (1907–54), had attended the exhibition "Mexique" organized and prefaced by Breton (obviously nostalgic about his recent trip to that country) at the exclusive Parisian art gallery Renou & Colle. There she met Paalen and invited him to come to Mexico: not even waiting for the outbreak of war, which many predicted though hoping for a miracle, he arrived in Mexico City via New York, where he stayed a few months, in September 1939. Two years later, the beginner American artist Robert Motherwell (1915–91) had joined Paalen, having gone from New York to Mexico with the Chilean Roberto Matta (born 1911), another of Breton's young recruits. He remained in Mexico further to perfect his Surrealist education under Paalen's guidance.

The Surrealists regroup in New York

The outbreak of the war and the influx of immigrants from Europe radically changed the situation of Surrealism in New York. The vociferous attacks against the movement as "escapist" had more or less died down (except from the discredited Stalinist wing), and its presence on the literary and artistic scene, as well as its attraction for young American artists, had grown at a spectacular pace. The first Surrealist painters to emigrate had been Kurt Seligman (1900–62), Yves Tanguy (1900–55), and Matta, in November 1939. A few months later, they helped prepare the escape from occupied France of those who had not been prescient (or fortunate) enough to leave before, most notably rallying American support for the Emergency Rescue Committee that Varian Fry, an editor and classicist from New York, had courageously set up in Marseilles without help from (and even in defiance of) the US government. The Committee first secured André Masson's and Breton's exit (they finally arrived in New York in May 1941, after a stressful stay in Martinique, which was administered by the collaborationist French government), then ▲ that of Max Ernst, who finally rejoined his friends in July.

This regrouping of the Surrealist troops in New York could only further stimulate the interest of a young generation of artists already aroused by a series of lectures on the movement delivered, at Schapiro's invitation, by Matta's and Paalen's friend, the painter Gordon Onslow Ford (1912–2003) at the New School of Social Research in January–February 1941. An exhibition of Surrealist art, curated by Howard Putzel, accompanied the lecture series, which • was attended by Motherwell and Gorky, but also Jackson Pollock, William Baziotes (1912–63), and Gerome Kamrowski (1914–2004), the latter three convening in Kamrowski's studio, quite possibly immediately after one of Ford's talks, and pouring oil and enamel on a "collective painting" [**2**]. Galleries and museums were playing their part too. A month after their immigration to the United States, Tanguy was offered a one-man show at the Pierre Matisse Gallery,

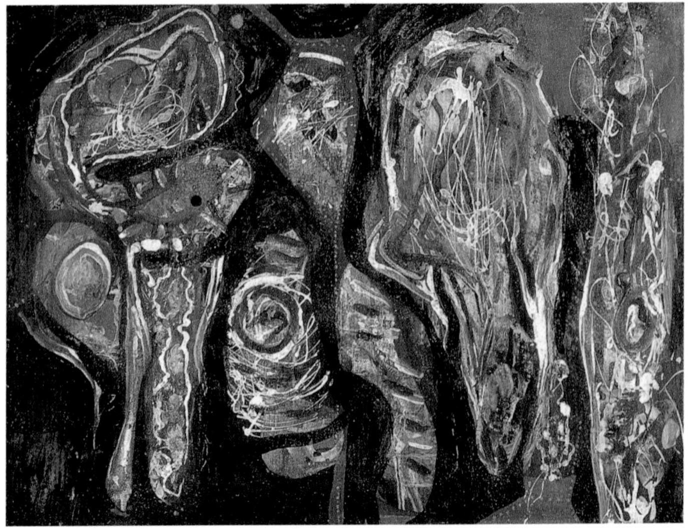

2 • Collective painting by Baziotes, Kamrowski, and Pollock, 1940–1
Oil and enamel on canvas, 48.9 x 64.8 ($19\frac{1}{4}$ x $25\frac{1}{2}$)

▲ 1933 • 1947b ▲ 1924 • 1949, 1960b

3 • André Masson, *Paysage Iroquois*, 1941
Indian ink on paper, 21 x 38 (8¼ x 15)

where he would exhibit again in 1942 and 1943, and Seligman at Nierendorf's (where he would show again in 1941, before moving to another gallery). Paalen's April 1940 exhibition at the Julien Levy Gallery, which quickly became something of an official gallery of Surrealist art, was immediately followed by Matta's, his work being shown together with Walt Disney's sketches for *Pinocchio*! Masson's retrospective opened at the Baltimore Museum of Art in October 1941, and in the following month the Museum of Modern Art presented a large retrospective of Miró (who had refused to leave Europe) in tandem with one of Dalí's art, though by then his Surrealist credentials had vanished, thanks to his profascist pronouncements. Ernst, too, was celebrated, not only through exhibitions but also by the special issue devoted to his work by the Surrealist-friendly journal *View*, directed by Charles Henri Ford. The culmination of this public exposure took place in the fall of ▲ 1942, soon after the arrival of Marcel Duchamp in New York. In "First Papers of Surrealism," scenographed by Duchamp, young American artists such as Baziotes, Hare, and Motherwell were invited for the first time to show their work side by side with veterans of the movement such as Seligman, Masson [**3**], Ernst, and Tanguy (not to mention Matta); its opening was followed a week later, on • October 20, 1942, by that of Peggy Guggenheim's gallery, "Art of This Century," where her important collection of Surrealist art was presented in a curved space specially designed by Frederick Kiesler.

Despite all this activity, however, there was a certain *ennui* around the Surrealist movement as a whole. At least, Breton felt it, though he would have been the last to admit it: the art presented by the younger generation was clearly derivative, showing a particular fondness for the imaginary landscapes of Tanguy and the "automatic" gesturality of Masson, and these old-timers, in turn, were mainly resting on their laurels. The only exception was Matta, who in 1937, then a twenty-six-year-old student of architecture, had been the youngest recruit of the Surrealist movement and hailed by Breton as its bright new hope. By 1940, he had learned how to translate, in large and colorful paintings, his drawings of bio/mechanomorphic creatures floating in fantastic sci-fi decors that had seduced Breton [**4**]. The clash between a rational, perspectival space and the oneiric irrationality of the figures that populate it had been at the core of much ▲ Surrealist painting, and Matta was not fundamentally departing from this model. But he was leaving aside the finicky *trompe-l'oeil* technique upon which the riveting effect of Tanguy's or Dalí's art mostly depended. In freeing his painting from the constraints of this academic studio practice and in welcoming sweeping gestures and automatism within the highly controlled stage of his cosmic landscapes, he had, almost despite himself, been led to a dramatic change of scale which struck his young American colleagues. Furthermore, his energy seemed boundless, his missionary zeal remarkably efficient. Soon after the "First Papers of Surrealism" exhibition, he set up a workshop where for a few months he "taught" pictorial automatism to Baziotes, Motherwell, Pollock, and a few others.

Breton had always been an authoritarian leader unwilling to share his power. He was wary of Matta's growing ascendancy in the New York art world, feeling that, despite Matta's allegiance and his orthodox discourse on the marvelous and the necessity of elaborating new myths (principles which Breton's "Prolegomena" had recently reaffirmed), these were not what was attracting Matta's young devotees. If Breton did not watch out, a new school, over which he would have no control whatsoever, was going to emerge from the ashes of Surrealism. Coincidentally, Breton stumbled upon the work of Armenian-born Arshile Gorky (1904–48)—whom he met in the winter of 1943–4 while Gorky was working on his formidable *The Liver is the Cock's Comb* [**5**]—and decided to champion his art.

Gorky's Surrealism becomes Abstract Expressionism

Paradoxically, however, Matta had been determinant in Gorky's development. Until around 1942–3, "among the painters in New York, Gorky stood out for years as the masterly apprentice," writes Meyer Schapiro. Until 1938 he was learning the language of Picasso, then he switched his attention to Miró. "In Matta," pursues

4 • Roberto Matta, *Years of Fear*, 1941–2
Oil on canvas, 111.7 x 142.2 (44 x 56)

▲ 1914, 1918, 1936, 1942b, 1966a • 1942b ▲ 1924

5 • Arshile Gorky, *The Liver is the Cock's Comb*, 1944
Oil on canvas, 186 x 249 (73¼ x 98)

Schapiro, "[Gorky] found for the first time a painter whose language, once mastered, he could use as freely himself. From Matta came the idea of the canvas as a field of prodigious excitement, unloosed energies, bright red and yellows opposed to cold greys, a new futurism of the organic as well as of mechanical forces. Gorky could draw his own conclusions from Matta's art without waiting for the inventor." **[6]** Liberated from copying by this "younger brother" who, among other things, encouraged him to paint more thinly (until then his canvases had been crusted with heavy impasto), Gorky took flight. Without discarding all the lessons of his long schooling, he added all the marks of an exuberant gesturality, including multiple run-offs of paint, to what he had learned from Picasso (dissociation of form and contour), Miró (biomorphic figures), Kandinsky (saturated color), Matisse (transparency of the paint layer, which allows for an active role of the underlayers), Matta (sci-fi landscape, amoebic decor), and even Duchamp (whose *Large Glass* he greatly admired). Until his suicide in 1948, he produced at top speed works that could only be called Surrealist because Breton acclaimed them, but which Pollock, ▲ Newman, and other Abstract Expressionist painters immediately regarded as the seed of their own movement.

6 • Arshile Gorky, *How My Mother's Embroidered Apron Unfolds in My Life*, 1944
Oil on canvas, 101.6 x 114.3 (40 x 45)

Always a loner, Gorky had been flattered by Breton's praise, and he flattered the French poet in return by letting him give titles to his canvases, but he steadfastly refused to play the part of a faithful member of the Surrealist group. In 1947, like Picasso before him, when Breton's demands became too pressing, he bade him farewell. Unlike Paalen's departure five years earlier, however, Gorky's defection signaled the end of Surrealism.

FURTHER READING

T. J. Clark, "More on the Differences between Comrade Greenberg and Ourselves," in Serge Guilbaut, Benjamin H. D. Buchloh, and David Solkin (eds), *Modernism and Modernity* (Halifax: The Press of the Nova Scotia College of Art and Design, 1983)

Serge Guilbaut, *How New York Stole the Idea of Modern Art: Abstract Expressionism, Freedom, and the Cold War* (Chicago and London: University of Chicago Press, 1983)

Martica Sawin, *Surrealism in Exile and the Beginning of the New York School* (Cambridge, Mass.: MIT Press, 1995)

Meyer Schapiro, "Arshile Gorky" (1957), *Modern Art: 19th and 20th Century, Selected Papers, vol. 2* (New York: George Braziller, 1978)

Dickran Tashjian, *A Boatload of Madmen: Surrealism and the American Avant-Garde 1920–1950* (London and New York: Thames & Hudson, 1995)

▲ 1947b

1942b

As World War II forces many Surrealists to emigrate from France to the United States, two shows in New York reflect on this condition of exile in different ways.

In 1929 the Surrealists published a map of the world in the Belgian journal *Variétés* [**1**]. It shows just two capitals, Paris and Constantinople, and redistributes land mass according to the artistic sympathies of the group. As the homes of the more "fantastic" tribal art favored by the Surrealists, Alaska and Oceania (the South Pacific) are vast, while Africa, the home of the more "formal" art already ▲ exploited by the Cubists and the Expressionists, is shrunken. Political affiliations also play a major role: Russia remains large, while the United States does not exist, and Germany and Austria have subsumed Europe entirely—though not yet ominously. Now flash forward nine years to 1938, to the first "International Exhibition of Surrealism" in Paris, only months after the Nazi condemnation ● of modernist art, the "Degenerate 'Art'" show, had opened in Munich. Among the works in Paris was a Surrealist object by Marcel Jean (born 1900) titled *Horoscope* [**2**], a dressmaker's dummy with plaster ornaments for its base and arms and a watch inset at its headless top. Jean painted the dummy a glossy blue, on which appears a gold-and-gray figure that is gradually disclosed to be both a map (some continents encircle the hips of the dummy) and a skeleton (we can make out its ribs). The two works convey the different moods of the two moments: the 1929 map bespeaks an imaginative appropriation of the world that wittily rewrites it according to Surrealist interests, while the 1937 horoscope-hourglass forecasts a deathly world, with its time running out. The first shows a Surrealism on the creative march; the second suggests a Surrealism that, however international, is on the political run.

The exhibition as "exquisite corpse"

By the thirties the exhibition had become a principal form of Surrealist activity. It could articulate political protest, as it did in "The Truth about the Colonies," a small counterexhibition to the official jingoistic Colonial Exhibition held in Paris in 1931; or it could announce an aesthetic shift, as it did in the "Surrealist Exhi■bition of Objects" at Galerie Charles Ratton in Paris in 1936, which showed radically diverse things—tribal art, Picasso constructions, mathematical objects, as well as such Surrealist objects as Meret ◆ Oppenheim's famous *Fur-Lined Teacup* (*Déjeuner en fourrure*). The exhibition could also promote the international acculturation

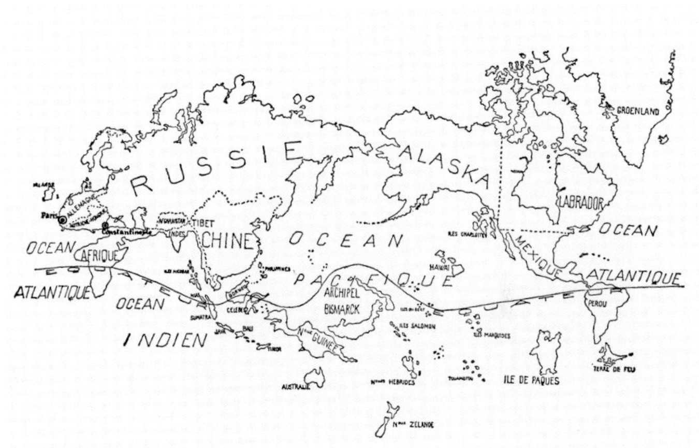

1 • *The World in the Time of the Surrealists*, first published in *Variétés*, 1929
Offset, printed in black, page size 24 x 17 (9½ x 6¾)

of Surrealism, as in the "International Surrealist Exhibition" at the New Burlington Galleries in London in the summer of 1936, and in "Fantastic Art, Dada, Surrealism" curated by Alfred H. Barr, Jr. at the Museum of Modern Art in December of the same year.

The objects in these shows were often bizarre, but the installations remained rather conventional. This changed dramatically with the "International Exhibition of Surrealism" in Paris in 1938, for here the narrative quality of the typical Surrealist object was extended into the actual space of the exhibition. No precedents existed for this sort of show: it was opposed to the rationalist displays proposed by various Constructivists in the twenties, such as ▲ the Demonstration Room of El Lissitzky, but it was also distinct from the anarchistic manifestations of the Dadaists, such as the ● 1920 Berlin Dada Fair. At the same time, to the extent that the Surrealist exhibition proposed an active, participatory viewer, it was closer in spirit to these other avant-gardist experiments than to any traditional form of exhibition with its passive, contemplative spectatorship. It should come as no surprise that, along with ■ André Breton and Paul Eluard, the "*générateur-arbitre*" (producer-referee) of the show was none other than Marcel Duchamp, already the veteran of several exhibition controversies and recently ◆ the curator of his own miniature museum, the *Boîte-en-valise*. "All exhibitions of painting and sculpture make me ill," Duchamp wrote his patron Jacques Doucet in 1925, two years after he seemed

▲ 1903, 1906, 1907 ● 1937a ■ 1931 ◆ Introduction 1 ▲ 1926 ● 1920 ■ 1924 ◆ 1914, 1918, 1935

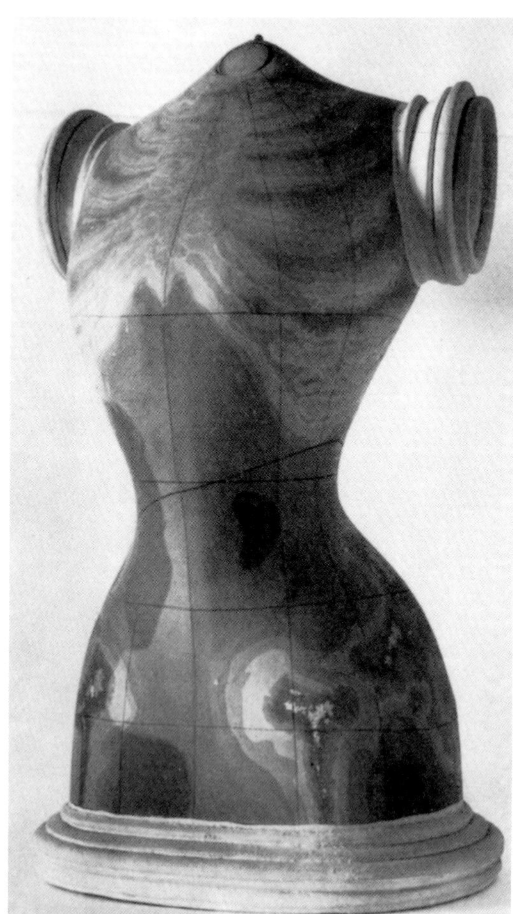

2 • Marcel Jean, *Horoscope*, 1937
Painted dressmaker's dummy, plaster, and watch, height 71.1 (28)

to withdraw from all forms of artmaking. "And I'd rather not be involved in them." Apparently this inhibition did not extend to the orchestration of such events.

The first "International Exhibition of Surrealism"—and it was international, with sixty artists from fourteen countries—opened on January 17, 1938, at the Galerie Beaux-Arts. Owned by Georges Wildenstein, who also published the magazine *Beaux-Arts*, this upscale gallery was located in the rue du Faubourg Saint-Honoré, a high-bourgeois venue that led to charges that the Surrealists had sold out, politically as well as economically. Yet Duchamp did all he could to refashion its elegant eighteenth-century interior into a dim urban underground that undercut its high-art ambience. (Moreover, as if to underscore the commercialism of the context, he hung graphic work on revolving doors redolent of department stores.) The exhibition appeared to be a deranged narrative along the lines of the Surrealist game "exquisite corpse," in which different players drew different parts of a figure or wrote different parts of a sentence, each unbeknownst to the other; but in fact its layout was quite calculated. As soon as one stepped indoors, one seemed to be outdoors again, for in the lobby stood *Rainy Taxi* by Salvador Dalí, an old cab entwined with vines, drenched by rain, and occupied by two mannequins—a driver with a shark's head and dark goggles, and a female passenger covered with live Burgundian snails, a kind of "Birth of Venus" as Lady of the Night. Already at this point Dalí played to a degraded notion of "Surrealism"—*Rainy Taxi* was so popular that it was re-created for the 1939 World's Fair in New York—and he was soon purged from the Surrealist ranks as much for his blatant commercialism (Breton renamed him, anagrammatically, "Avida Dollars") as for his outrageous expression of Nazi sympathies.

The theme of prostitution continued in the passageway that led from the lobby to the two galleries; it was decorated as a "Rue Surréaliste" with street signs (mostly fictitious, such as "Rue de la Transfusion de Sang") and sixteen female mannequins bizarrely dressed (or undressed) by Dalí, Miró, Ernst, Masson, Tanguy, Man Ray, and others. (Typically, Duchamp cross-dressed his mannequin with shirt, coat, tie, and hat, but no pants.) This passageway, which again confused interior and exterior, opened onto the main space, which combined other versions of indoors and outdoors. On the floor were dead leaves, moss and dirt, a small pond encircled by reeds and ferns, and, in each corner, a double bed with silk sheets. *Horoscope* stood at the foot of one bed, while various Surrealist pictures, such as *The Death of Ophelia* by Masson, hung on the walls. In short, the gallery was made up as a dream space, one with its own contrived logic. It was very dark: Duchamp had wanted the paintings on the walls to be illuminated by the approach of viewers, as in a peep show; when this could not be rigged, Man Ray, in his capacity as "master of lighting," handed out flashlights during the opening, with much the same effect of semi-lewd peering. (Duchamp would return ▲ to this positioning of the spectator in his diorama *Etant donnés*.) Attached to the ceiling were "1,200" coal bags, emptied of coal (due to insurance precautions) but dirty with dust nonetheless, while in the center of the floor stood a charcoal brazier [**3**]. (Almost thirty ● years later Andy Warhol "would play with a Pop, postindustrial version of these sacks—helium-filled pillows that he let float as "silver clouds" through a gallery show.) Here was another conflation of spaces—of industrial work and artistic entertainment—further complicated, with the coal sacks on the ceiling, by an inversion of up and down. To top off this mélange of signifiers of art and prostitution, commerce and industry, Dalí hired a dancer, Hélène Vanel, to perform a simulation of hysteria titled "The Unconsummated Act"; and by some accounts, insane-asylum laughter and German military music were also piped into the galleries.

This last note must have struck a grim chord, for during the week of the opening Nazi bombs fell on Barcelona and Valencia. Perhaps the political frame of the Spanish Civil War made the changed social status of Surrealism all the more obvious. For many of the Surrealist gestures in the show were almost conventional by the late thirties: once a figure of the uncanny, the mannequin had ■ become a Surrealist cliché, difficult to distinguish from its use in fashion, which had adopted such Surrealist devices as the dreamlike invocation of desire, sometimes with the assistance of the Surrealists. At the same time, Surrealism was embraced by high society, which was out in full force and evening dress for the opening of the 1938 show: once provocative politically, Surrealism had become chic in an *outré* sort of way. Yet had the Surrealists

▲ 1966a ● 1960c, 1964b ■ 1924, 1930b, 1931

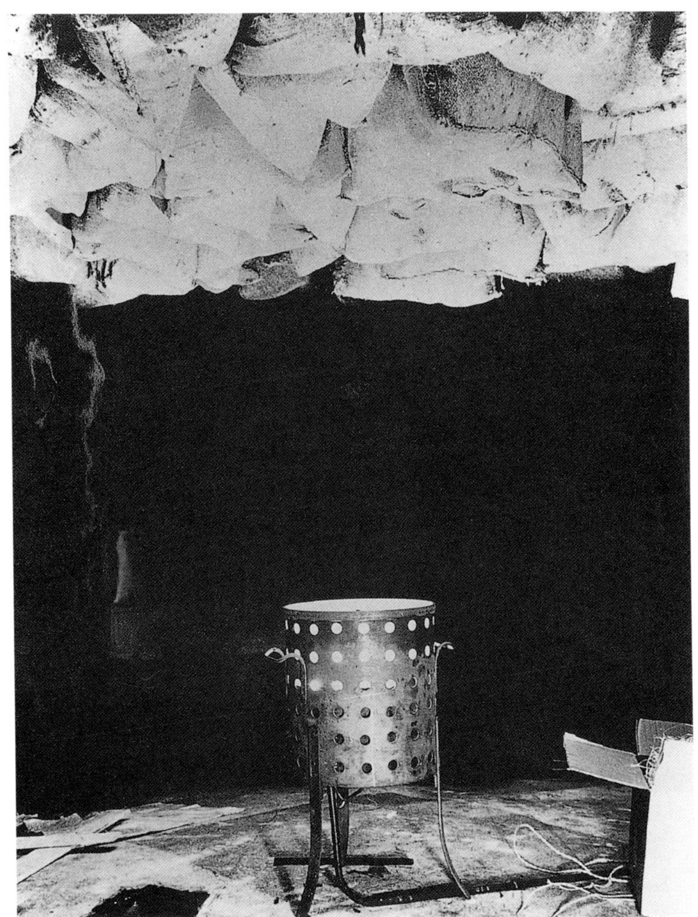

3 • Marcel Duchamp, *1,200 Coal Bags Suspended from the Ceiling Over a Stove*, 1938
Environment for the "International Exhibition of Surrealism," Galerie Beaux-Arts, Paris

simply withdrawn from the street to the salon, from political engagement to artistic spectacle (as some have charged)? Or did the 1938 show not disrupt accepted oppositions of interior and exterior, private and public, subjective and social? Perhaps the two developments are not mutually exclusive.

In any case, as Man Ray once remarked, the installation did "destroy that clinical atmosphere that reigned in the most modern of exhibition spaces," and here again we must place it in the context of its moment, for the year 1937 witnessed two very different models of museum display. On the one hand, there was a quasi-objective ideal of display put forward by the state-sponsored exhibition of ▲ museology at the 1937 International Exhibition in Paris, in which the proper techniques of "judgment, presentation, and protection of patrimony" were laid out ("noiseless rooms, evenly distributed lighting, studied floor and ceilings, appropriately sober surfaces, standardized labels, effusive wall text about the artists and works"), all designed to reassure viewers that "the exhibition space was neutral, the work of art autonomous, aesthetic appreciation disinterested." Obviously the Surrealist show flew in the face of this putatively scientific program. On the other hand, there was the opening just five months before of the twin Nazi demonstrations in Munich: the "Great German Art" exhibition, which laid out the reactionary aesthetic of Nazi kitsch, and the "Degenerate 'Art'" • show, which equated modernist art (including Surrealism) with moral depravity and mental illness in a large display of pilloried works. The Surrealist show also mocked this fiercely ideological use of museum display. (Might Duchamp have sought to echo—that is, to exacerbate—this riotous installation in his own?)

The exhibition as labyrinth

A year later, with the fall of France to the Nazis in 1939, the condition of the Surrealists changed utterly—from international expansion to escape and emigration, mostly to the country that did not exist on their 1929 map, the United States. In New York, along with such ▲ magazines as *VVV* (guided by Breton) and *View* (edited by the American poet Charles Henri Ford), the exhibition remained a primary medium of Surrealist activity, and it now had the additional function of a banding-together of exiles. A pair of near-simultaneous exhibitions in New York in 1942—"Art of This Century" and "First Papers of Surrealism"—dramatized these changed circumstances.

Exiles and émigrés

Ironically, the claim of New York to be "the capital of modern art" by mid-century depended in no small measure on the flight of many European artists and intellectuals from the rise of Hitler and the outbreak of World War II. Hitler came to power in January 1933; by September his Minister of Propaganda Joseph Goebbels had formed the Reich Chamber of Culture to administer all artistic production according to Nazi criteria. Outspoken critics of Nazism like Georg Grosz and John Heartfield had to leave Germany immediately—Grosz for the States, Heartfield first for Prague, then for London. Other avant-gardists, such as Kurt Schwitters, also found haven in England. If there were any doubts about Nazi policy concerning modernism, the "Degenerate 'Art'" show laid them to rest in 1937.

One of the first acts of the Nazis was to close the Bauhaus. The Russian-born Wassily Kandinsky fled to France, the Swiss-born Paul Klee returned to Switzerland; many others, such as the American-born Lyonel Feininger, came to the States. The American reception of Bauhaus architects, such as Walter Gropius and Mies van der Rohe, was already prepared by a landmark show on the "International Style" at the Museum of Modern Art in 1932. Six years later MoMA produced the exhibition "Bauhaus: 1919–1928," which also advanced the reputation of these émigrés. By this time László Moholy-Nagy and Marcel Breuer had joined Gropius and Mies, as well as Josef and Anni Albers, in the US.

The exodus of French artists came mostly after France fell to the Nazis in 1939. By 1941 André Breton and Fernand Léger had arrived in New York, along with other celebrated modernists such as the Dutch Piet Mondrian, the German Max Ernst, and the Russian Marc Chagall; Marcel Duchamp followed the next year. Even as some French artists disdained American culture, they also helped translate European modernism for young American artists—not only the immediate group of Abstract Expressionists but also the subsequent circle of John Cage, Merce Cunningham, Robert Rauschenberg, Jasper Johns, and others.

▲ 1937a • 1937a ▲ 1942a, 1968b

4 • Installation view of the Surrealist Gallery designed by Frederick Kiesler in "Art of This Century," New York, 1942

One thing had not changed, however: the embrace of socialites, such as the American Peggy Guggenheim, an heir to a copper-mining fortune, who had left Europe with her husband Max Ernst on July 14, 1941. To exhibit her collection of modernist art amassed in Europe, Guggenheim opened a gallery-museum called "Art of This Century" on October 20, 1942, in two converted tailor shops at 28–30 West 57th Street. The architect was Frederick ▲ Kiesler (1890–1965), a young associate of the De Stijl group, once active in Vienna but now resident in New York, who was already known for his avant-garde theater designs (in 1929 he had designed the first theater in United States specifically for film, the Film Guild Cinema on West 8th Street). Kiesler divided "Art of This Century" into four spaces: one for temporary shows and three for fixed exhibitions of the collection, each of which was styled after the art on display. With blue walls and turquoise floor decided by Guggenheim, the Abstract Gallery suspended its unframed paintings on wires that ran from ceiling to floor in giant Vs both parallel and perpendicular to the walls. The Kinetic Gallery displayed several • paintings by Paul Klee on a conveyor belt, while another device ■ showed the *Boîte-en-valise*, one work at a time, through a peephole. More unusual still was the Surrealist Gallery [**4**]. Here Kiesler called for bowed walls made of gum-wood, from which he projected Surrealist paintings supported by batlike struts at different angles; meanwhile his biomorphic chairs doubled as sculpture stands. Like Duchamp before him, Kiesler wanted to control the lighting—to illuminate one side at a time for two minutes each, to have the gallery pulse "like your blood."

This last ambition aligns Kiesler with the Surrealist vision of an "intrauterine" architecture that Dalí, Tristan Tzara, and Roberto Matta had proposed in articles of the thirties, and Kiesler elaborated in his "Endless House" project of 1950. Here is Tzara on such ◆ architecture in 1933, from the magazine *Minotaure*: "When it is understood that comfort resides in the half-light of the soft tactile depths of the one and only possible hygiene, that of prenatal desire, then circular, spherical, and irregular houses will be built again, which man kept from cave to cradle and to tomb in his vision of an intrauterine life, and which the aesthetics of castration, called modern, ignore." And here is Matta (who once worked for Le ▲ Corbusier) in 1938, also from *Minotaure*: "We must have walls like wet sheets that get out of shape and fit our psychological fears." Kiesler designed out of a similar fantasy of return to a primordial space of creation: in his Surrealist Gallery he sought to "dissolve the barrier and artificial duality of 'vision' and 'reality,' 'image' and 'environment'... [where] there are no frames or borders between art, space, life. In eliminating the frame, the spectator recognizes his act of seeing, or receiving, as a participation in the creative process no less essential and direct than the artist's own." In effect Kiesler wanted to disguise the mediation of the gallery in order to simulate the immediacy of psychic space—hence the removal of conventional supports like frames, partitions, and bases.

The American critic T. J. Demos has interpreted this "fusional installation design" as "a response to the anomie of exile"—more specifically, as an attempt to move away from the old Surrealist exploration of the uncanny (in German *Unheimlich* or unhomelike) toward a new Surrealist myth of "a habitable and conceivable world" (as Breton described it at the time). Duchamp, in his own 1942 installation of Surrealist art, "First Papers of Surrealism," which opened a week before "Art of This Century," projected a different kind of world again—more alien than uncanny but certainly not homelike. "[The Surrealists] had a lot of confidence in the ideas I could bring them," Duchamp later remarked to Pierre Cabanne, "ideas which weren't anti-Surrealist, but which weren't always Surrealist, either." "First Papers of Surrealism" was a benefit exhibition for war prisoners, sponsored by the Coordinating Council of French Relief Societies at the Whitelaw Reid Mansion (451 Madison Avenue). The designer Elsa Schiaparelli asked Duchamp to install the exhibition and, along with Breton and Ernst, he chose works by roughly fifty artists—mostly old Surrealist • warriors, but also some new American associates, such as Joseph ■ Cornell, Kay Sage, David Hare, William Baziotes, and Robert Motherwell. The title, "First Papers," refers to application forms for US citizenship, and it could be read either as an optimistic statement of a new life or a bitter mockery of all official identification at the height of World War II. Also ambiguous was the most celebrated gesture of the show—the tangle of string a mile in length that Duchamp wound all around the main gallery in a way that not only obscured the paintings but also obstructed entry to the space [**5**].

Duchamp had used string before: only three meters' worth in his ◆ 1913 experiment in "canned chance," *Three Standard Stoppages*, and different lengths in his 1918 *Sculpture for Traveling*, made up of strips of shower caps of various colors attached by string and stretched to the four corners of his studio at 33 West 67th Street. This work, which Duchamp took with him on a 1918 sojourn to Buenos Aires, bespeaks both a sense of displacement (in the traveling of the title) and a strategy of occupation (in the installation of the piece). The string in "First Papers" exacerbates the displacement, and turns the occupation into its near-opposite—obstruction—for again the tangle impeded access to the gallery. Several readings were offered of this tangle: for some witnesses (like

▲ 1917 • 1916a, 1922 ■ 1935 ◆ 1924, 1930b ▲ 1925a • 1931 ■ 1942a, 1947a ◆ 1918

5 • Marcel Duchamp, *Sixteen Miles of String*, at "First Papers of Surrealism," 1942
Vintage silver-gelatin print, 19.4 x 25.4 (7⅝ x 10)

Sidney Janis and Arturo Schwartz), it was a figure of the difficulty of all modernist art; for others (like Marcel Jean), it was a trope of age like a cobweb, though whether this age was one of veneration or decay was not clear. Still others dismissed the entire show as a tedious tangle. Certainly the installation played on the Surrealist fascination with the labyrinth as a figure of the unconscious (with the man-beast Minotaur at its center), a figure that it seemed to transform into an allegory of contemporary history, or rather of a breach in this history marked by war and exile, a breach that distanced the Surrealist art on display, almost literally, from the present. From this angle, the exhibited artists were posed as contemporary Ariadnes with little hope of finding their way out of the maze. If such an allegorical account appears dubious, we can simply state that the string obscured both pictorial and architectural spaces in a way that at once underscored and interrupted the given frames of painting and gallery alike. In any case, it was a negative, almost nihilistic gesture, but typically Duchamp presented it as playful, for he asked a group of children to play ball in the gallery for the duration of the opening. Nonetheless, the installation was hardly the "fun house space" that John Cage recalled of "Art of This Century."

While Kiesler wanted to do away with frames in order to render Surrealist art somehow immediate, Duchamp worked to elaborate frames excessively into a literal maze, as if to resist the institutional acculturation of this art. This difference has led T. J. Demos to see Surrealism-in-exile as torn between a search for a "compensatory home," as represented by Kiesler, and an acceptance of a profound homelessness, as represented by Duchamp. This seems right; however, circumstances changed again with the end of the war. In 1947 the two friends collaborated on the design of yet another "International Exhibition of Surrealism," now back in Paris. Their installation returned to the model of a deranged narrative used in the 1938 exhibition in Paris: the viewer had to pass through a series of tests in a sequence of spaces before looking at the works on display. Here, then, the trope was neither a compensatory home nor an indefinite homelessness but a rite of return, and the narrative was one of ritual reincorporation. But at this point Surrealism had little left but such rituals, and few new initiates to go through them. In the postwar period it would dissolve into other movements altogether; it would disappear from the map.

Peggy Guggenheim (1898–1979)

Peggy Guggenheim was one of the greatest collectors and most passionate supporters of avant-garde art in the twentieth century. When she died, her collection included works by Kandinsky, Klee, Picabia, Braque, Gris, Severini, Balla, van Doesburg, Mondrian, Miró, Ernst, de Chirico, Tanguy, Dalí, Magritte, Pollock, Motherwell, Gorky, and Brauner. She also collected sculpture: by Brancusi, Calder, Lipchitz, Laurens, Pevsner, Giacometti, Moore, and Arp. In 1920, she moved from the United States to Paris, where the minor Surrealist painter Laurence Vail (whom she would marry) introduced her to a bohemian world that included Marcel Duchamp, Man Ray, Anaïs Nin, Max Ernst, and Samuel Beckett.

Her collecting began as a function of the first gallery she opened, in London in 1938 (modestly called Guggenheim Jeune), with Duchamp as her adviser. The opening exhibition was of the drawings of Jean Cocteau, and succeeding exhibitions featured Tanguy, Kandinsky, Arp, and Brancusi. After a year she decided to open a museum of modern art in London and convinced Herbert Read to be the museum's first director. By 1940 she had entered on a campaign to "buy a picture a day," and as the war worsened she worried about where to store her collection. The Louvre in Paris turned the works down as "not worth saving," but finally she found a château near Vichy with barns large enough to house them all. With her collection in storage for the war, Guggenheim went to Marseilles, where she contributed money to the effort to arrange passage out of Europe for a group of intellectuals and artists. She eventually left in 1942 in a plane that also carried Ernst and her two children from her abortive marriage to Vail.

In New York, she married Ernst and set to work on her new gallery, "Art of This Century." The gallery arranged the first solo exhibitions of some of the major figures of the developing school of Abstract Expressionism: Pollock in 1943, Baziotes in 1944, Rothko in 1945, and Clyfford Still in 1946. Believing Pollock to be "the greatest painter since Picasso," she arranged a contract to give him $150 a month. Lee Krasner later said:

> *"Art of This Century" was of the utmost importance as the first place where the New York School could be seen.... Her Gallery was the foundation, it's where it all started to happen.*

FURTHER READING

Bruce Altshuler, *The Avant-Garde in Exhibition: New Art in the Twentieth Century* (New York: Harry N. Abrams, 1994)

T. J. Demos, "Duchamp's Labyrinth: 'First Papers of Surrealism'," *October*, no. 97, Summer 2001

Lewis Kachur, *Displaying the Marvelous: Marcel Duchamp, Salvador Dalí, and Surrealist Exhibition Installations* (Cambridge, Mass.: MIT Press, 2001)

Martica Sawin, *Surrealism in Exile: The Beginning of the New York School* (Cambridge, Mass.: MIT Press, 1994)

1943

James A. Porter's *Modern Negro Art*, the first scholarly study of African-American art, is published in New York as the Harlem Renaissance promotes race awareness and heritage.

Called the "father of African-American art history," James A. Porter (1905–70) was not only a distinguished art historian but also a successful painter in his own right. His groundbreaking survey *Modern Negro Art* (1943) was the result of ten years of collecting and collating documents about the history of African-American art, from its inception to the early forties. This seminal work made visible many little-known artists, especially Porter's contemporaries associated with the Harlem Renaissance, the African-American social, literary, and artistic movement that had been gathering force since the end of World War I.

The early flowering of the Harlem Renaissance

Although its spiritual home was in Harlem, New York, the Harlem Renaissance's ideas and ideals helped it blossom into a transnational movement. Several factors led to its flowering as it promoted and celebrated the black experience in a variety of art forms. One was the "Great Migration" between the two world wars, during which more than two million black Americans migrated to northern urban centers from the rural South. This was mainly because life in the South became increasingly difficult and dangerous after the passing of the racist and segregationist "Jim Crow" laws (so called after a black minstrel show character) and the growth of the white supremacist Ku Klux Klan. This mass migration in pursuit of a new life in the more liberal North led to a growing black urban population that included academics, intellectuals, and artists, many of whom settled in Harlem.

Earlier in the century, many black people were calling for better conditions, ranging from Booker T. Washington's (1856–1915) philosophy that unskilled black Americans should focus on economic advancement to the radical activism of Harlem-based Jamaican Marcus Garvey (1887–1940) and his Universal Negro Improvement Association (UNIA), formed in 1914. Garvey's worldwide movement was both ennobling—encouraging black people everywhere to consider themselves, and to take pride in themselves, as Africans—and separatist. Believing that the rift between black communities and their white oppressors was too great, he advocated a "back to Africa" agenda, a campaign to repatriate colonial blacks and African-Americans in order to "uplift the race."

The Pan-Africanist philosophy of African-American civil rights activist and author W. E. B. Du Bois (1868–1963), who helped to create the National Association for the Advancement of Colored People in 1909, was articulated early in the century. It emphasized the shared African heritage of black Americans, which was furthered by the birth in the twenties of the literary and ideological movement known as Negritude. Created by French-speaking African and Caribbean poets, it sustained interest in the black civilizations of Africa and promoted the idea of the beauty of the race and the concept of unity between Africa's descendants.

Such thinking encouraged racial pride, a sense of nationhood and international solidarity among those of African descent. Du Bois's ideas, however, were the most important for the Harlem Renaissance: unlike Washington and Garvey, he believed that African-Americans could achieve full economic, civil, and political parity with white Americans in America. He was also passionate in his view that art, the greatest achievement of civilized man, could play a conciliatory role, and that supporting and empowering black artists would enable them to make valid and important contributions to American society as a whole.

Other factors that nurtured the Harlem Renaissance included ▲ the European modernists' interest in "primitive" African art and their appreciation of African-American dance and music, particularly spirituals and jazz—encompassing both folk and avant-garde art from the New World. Black American intellectuals, such as philosopher Alain Locke (1886–1954) realized that this fashion for all things African and African-American could, and should, be capitalized on to work for social change.

Sociopolitical, economic, ideological, cultural, and aesthetic concerns all informed the search to define the "New Negro" and to encourage a cultural renewal that acknowledged the black American's African ancestry, life and history in America, and transformation into a modern urban persona. The New Negro Movement epitomized this need: as sociologist Charles S. Johnson (1893–1956) commented in 1925: "A new type of Negro is evolving—a city Negro." This new black urbanite required a new identity that would leave behind that of ex-slave.

Sculptor Meta Vaux Warrick Fuller (1877–1968) is acknowledged as one of the most important precursors of the Harlem

▲ 1903, 1906, 1907

Van Der Zee (1886–1983), Harlem's premier chronicler of the years 1920 to 1940, provided some of the most enduring, iconic images of the era [**2**]. In helping to create the image of the New Negro, styling and retouching the photographs to create uplifting images of black Americans, Van Der Zee produced photographs of Harlem's residents that capture the optimism, style, pride, and sophistication associated with this new urban identity.

The leaders of the New Negro Movement—black and white American philosophers, sociologists, critics, gallery owners, and patrons—believed that through culture, rather than politics, they could achieve their shared goal of equal rights and freedoms for black Americans. They reasoned that increased exposure through black arts and literature would help mainstream society see black Americans and their experience as *part of*, rather than *apart from*, the American experience.

They also thought that black American culture could, and should, be appreciated for more than just dance and music: the academics turned to those in the arts and letters to help them. The most responsive was Locke; he wanted to found a "Negro School of Art" in Harlem to increase black Americans' visibility and awareness of their African heritage and history. Some of his thinking was informed by ▲ his experiences in Berlin during the early days of German Expressionism, when he absorbed the idealistic belief that through art the world could be made a better place. This coalesced with Du Bois's introduction and advancement of the concept of a "talented

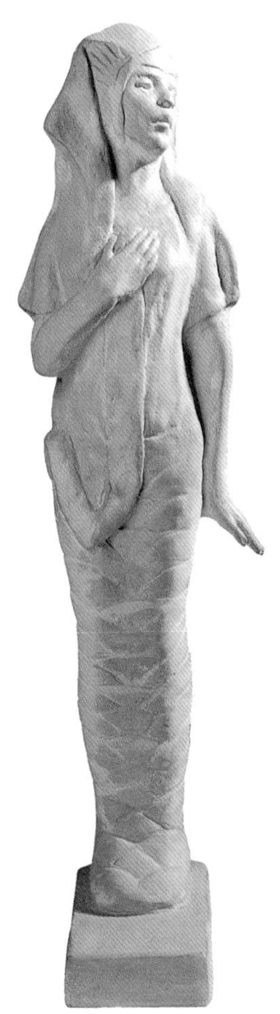

1 • Meta Warrick Fuller, *The Awakening of Ethiopia*, 1914
Bronze, 170.2 x 40.6 x 50.8 (67 x 16 x 20)

Renaissance. She took classes at the Pennsylvania Museum School of Industrial Art before going for several years to Paris, where she ▲ studied with Auguste Rodin. After her return to the United States in 1903 her work was exhibited regularly on the East Coast, where it came to the attention of the spokesmen for the Harlem Renaissance, who were drawn to her aesthetic based on the example of African sculpture and her use of black African and American subject matter.

Fuller was inspired by Du Bois's Pan-Africanist philosophy, which is evident in her best-known work, *The Awakening of Ethiopia* [**1**]. Drawing on an Egyptian sculptural tradition, the bronze figure of a woman awakening from a deep sleep could be read as a call to her fellow African-Americans for a rebirth of black culture after centuries of slavery and repression. Her use of black subject matter and of explicit links between Africa and black America provided a potent example for Locke and his followers as they tried to formulate an aesthetic for the New Negro.

The New Negro

The twenties were a time of optimism, pride, and excitement for African-Americans who hoped that their time for a respectable place in American society had finally arrived. Photographer James

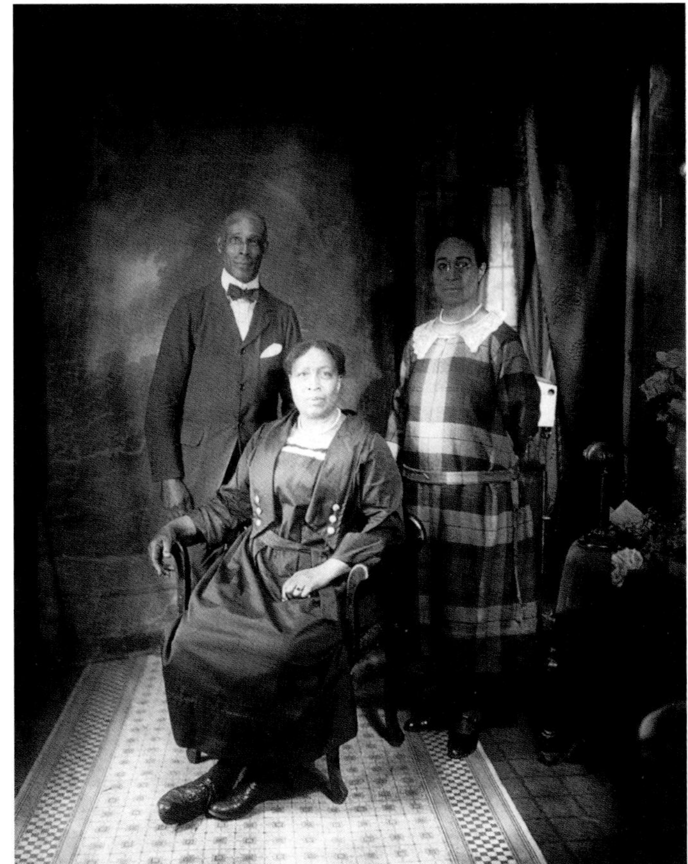

2 • James Van Der Zee, *Family Portrait*, 1926

▲ 1900a

▲ 1908

tenth"—the creation of an educated black elite whose mission it would be to better the lives of the less fortunate of their race.

White fascination with black America had been growing since around 1917, with the production of a number of plays and musicals featuring black themes and actors. While some were wary of this new interest, most leaders of the Harlem Renaissance saw it as the perfect opportunity to launch their black arts movement. In March 1921, Johnson organized a literary gala to celebrate young black writers at Manhattan's Civic Club, hosted by Locke with Du Bois as principal speaker, and attended by 110 literati, both black and white. Johnson's plan worked: Paul Kellogg, the white editor of *Survey Graphic*, a magazine of social and cultural issues, pitched to him the idea of a special issue dedicated to the black artists who had just been presented. The result was the March 1925 issue, "Harlem: Mecca of the New Negro," edited by Locke, which opened with a mission statement:

> *The* Survey *is seeking out month by month and year by year to follow the subtle traces of race growth and interaction through the shifting outline of social organization and by the flickering light of individual achievement.... If the* Survey *reads the signs aright, such a dramatic flowering of a new racespirit is taking place close at home among American Negroes, and the stage of that new episode is Harlem.*

It featured social essays, poetry, and fiction by and about the Harlem Renaissance and was illustrated throughout by German-born artist Winold Reiss (1886–1953). His dignified and realistic black-and-white pastel portraits included both Harlem personalities and ordinary residents—teachers, lawyers, schoolchildren, and Boy Scouts. Also included were Reiss's striking black-and-white Art Deco graphics of Harlem life, portraying an exciting, vibrant, modern city. The people and the work of the Harlem Renaissance were thus introduced to a largely white literary audience via the most popular issue in the magazine's history, selling out two printings.

Its success led to an expanded book version, published later in the same year by Albert and Charles Boni. *The New Negro: An Interpretation* was a 446-page anthology of essays, short fiction, poetry, and illustrations, edited and with contributions by Locke. In a manifesto-like form, he showcased new work and called for a celebration of black history and culture, imploring artists to rediscover and appreciate their African heritage and equally to reference and build on those traditions—such as folklore, blues, spirituals, and jazz—specific to their lives as African-Americans. The book was illustrated with color pastels by Weiss, stylish caricatures by New York-based Mexican Miguel Covarrubias (1904–57) and black-and-white Egyptian-style geometric woodcuts by African-American Aaron Douglas (1899–1979).

Although Reiss rarely features in discussions of the Harlem Renaissance, he was an influential figure: his worldwide studies of native populations, which respected and drew on their folk traditions, were an important example, as were his modernist graphic images. Thus, he was an important conduit for introducing many modernist European tendencies into American culture. Douglas, whom Locke would soon be calling a "pioneering Africanist," moved to Harlem (where he studied under Reiss) in 1924. Reiss encouraged him to move away from his strictly realist practice and to develop a style that respected his African ancestral heritage, his experience as an African-American, and modernist developments in art. He soon created an original modern black art in which the New Negro is an Art Deco silhouette. The American Precisionists' sharp angles and exuberance for the industrial landscape were harnessed toward his goal of expressing black pride and history [**3**]. His work quickly came to the attention of the Harlem Renaissance writers and he illustrated many of their books. Together with his illustrations in numerous magazines, this soon brought about his position as the Renaissance's "official" artist.

Individual and organizational support

With the publication of *The New Negro*, Locke became the main strategist and theoretician of the Harlem Renaissance, serving as mentor or, as he put it, "philosophical midwife," to many of its writers and artists. Existing support structures such as the National Association for the Advancement of Colored People (NAACP),

3 • Aaron Douglas, *The Creation*, 1935
Oil on masonite, 121.9 x 91.4 (48 x 36)

founded in 1909 to work for equal rights, and the Urban League, founded in 1910 to help new arrivals adjust to city life, championed the movement through their magazines: *The Crisis* (NAACP), edited by Du Bois and *Opportunity* (Urban League), edited by Johnson.

Further support and exposure came from wealthy white real-estate developer and philanthropist William Harmon (1862–1928). In 1926, achievement awards for African-Americans' contributions in music, the visual arts, literature, industry, education, race relations, and science were established under the auspices of the Harmon Foundation, which was a major patron of Harlem Renaissance artists: its annual national competition for black artists, the accompanying show and touring exhibition introduced their work to a national audience.

Artists from around the country responded enthusiastically to the Harlem Renaissance leaders' call to develop a visual vocabulary for black America. Writing to Langston Hughes in December 1925, Douglas expressed his thoughts on the matter:

> *Our problem is to conceive, develop, establish an art era.... Let's bare our arms and plunge them deep deep through the laughter, through pain, through sorrow, through hope, through disappointment, into the very depths of the souls of our people and drag forth material crude, rough neglected. Then let's sing it, dance it, write it, paint it.... Let's create something transcendentally material, mystically objective, Earthy. Spiritually earthy. Dynamic.*

The challenge was accepted and a number of different black representational possibilities were explored. A prominent strain explored by Fuller, Douglas, and others engaged heavily with the artists' African ancestry, while artists such as Archibald J. Motley (1891–1980) and Palmer C. Hayden (1893–1973) turned their attention to black folklore, history, and the minutiae of everyday life. Whether accessing a distant mythical past or nostalgia for a more recent rural past or celebrating progress and modernity, all the work of the Harlem Renaissance is involved in race consciousness and cultural identity for African-Americans.

The legacy of the first decade of the Harlem Renaissance ▲ included nationalism, primitivism, and atavism. The animated African mask in African-American Lois Mailou Jones's (1905–98) *Les Fétiches* [**4**], painted while she was in Paris, presents these ideas • seen through a Surrealist lens. She seems both to acknowledge the Surrealists' fetishizing of the "dehumanizing" mask and to reclaim it as part of her legacy, bringing it to life as a valid ingredient in the search to define a modern black identity.

The thirties

The Stock Market crash of October 23, 1929, brought the "roaring twenties" to an end and ushered in the Great Depression. This tempered much of the idealism and optimism of the early Harlem Renaissance; in many, it strengthened their sense of racial pride and social responsibility. As private support dried up, artists turned to the Public Works of Art Project and the Federal Art

4 • Lois Mailou Jones, *Les Fétiches*, 1938
Oil on canvas, 78.7 x 67.3 (31 x 26½)

▲ Project of the Works Progress Administration (WPA), which were organized in 1933 to employ artists at craftsmen's wages to decorate public property. Artists were assigned to either easel painting or mural painting; the subject matter was all aspects of the American scene and although no specific approach was stipulated, most were working in a social realist style at the time.

A considerable number of Harlem Renaissance artists were among those who received support from the WPA. Douglas, for example, painted a mural series, *Aspects of Negro Life*, for the WPA in 1934. Mounted in the 135th Street branch of the New York Public Library (now the Schomburg Center for Research in Black Culture), it brought Douglas's work to a larger audience, its monumental scale and epic quality furthering the Harlem Renaissance mission of promoting race awareness and pride and making a profound impression on the next generation of Harlem-based artists, among them Jacob Lawrence (1917–2000).

Lawrence moved to Harlem with his family during the thirties. He studied at the Harlem Art Center and spent many hours at the Schomburg Center absorbing Douglas's work and researching the struggles of the heroes of the black community. He soon developed his distinctive colorful, stylized figurative style and his central concern with the social issues and historical events effecting black Americans. Much of Lawrence's work of the late thirties was in series format, chronicling the lives of black heroes such as Toussaint Louverture (c. 1743–1803) (who was born into slavery, became a military leader and revolutionary, and established Haiti

▲ 1903, 1906, 1907 • 1924, 1930b, 1931 ▲ 1936

5 • Jacob Lawrence, *Pool Parlor*, 1942
Gouache and watercolor on paper, 18.7 x 57.8 (31 x 22¾)

as the first black Western republic) and the abolitionists Frederick Douglass, Harriet Tubman, and John Brown. His best-known work, painted while working in the easel division of the WPA, is *The Migration of the American Negro* (1940–1). This landmark narrative series of sixty small paintings captures the struggles of the "Great Migration" earlier in the century. The work was a critical success: part of it was published in the November 1941 issue of *Fortune* magazine, bringing Lawrence's work to a national audience. This early recognition led to numerous exhibitions, major museum purchases, and prizes, such as the one he won for *Pool Parlor* [**5**] in the "Artists for Victory" exhibition held at the Metropolitan Museum of Art in New York in 1942.

Norman W. Lewis (1909–79) was another young artist who began painting during the thirties in Harlem, where he absorbed Locke's ideas. *The Lady in the Yellow Hat* [**6**], an early work in an abstracted figurative mode, reflects this influence as well as that of social realism, but it also points to the future, for Lewis soon began to question the effectiveness of Locke's theories, abandoning realistic imagery to ▲ become the only African-American Abstract Expressionist.

Lewis was not alone in questioning the Harlem Renaissance ethos. James A. Porter, who encouraged black artists to pursue personal expression rather than a separatist agenda, took Locke to task in 1937 in the pages of *Art Front* for advancing what he saw as Locke's "defeatist philosophy of the Segregationist." In *Modern Negro Art*, he made his stance clear, discussing African-American artists' work not only in relation to black culture but also in the contexts of both American art history and the history of modern art.

The end of an era

After the horrors of World War II, many African-American artists felt that race-oriented, isolationist ideologies were no longer desirable or appropriate. One such artist was Romare Bearden (1912–88) who, while using black content or Africanesque symbols

▲ 1947a

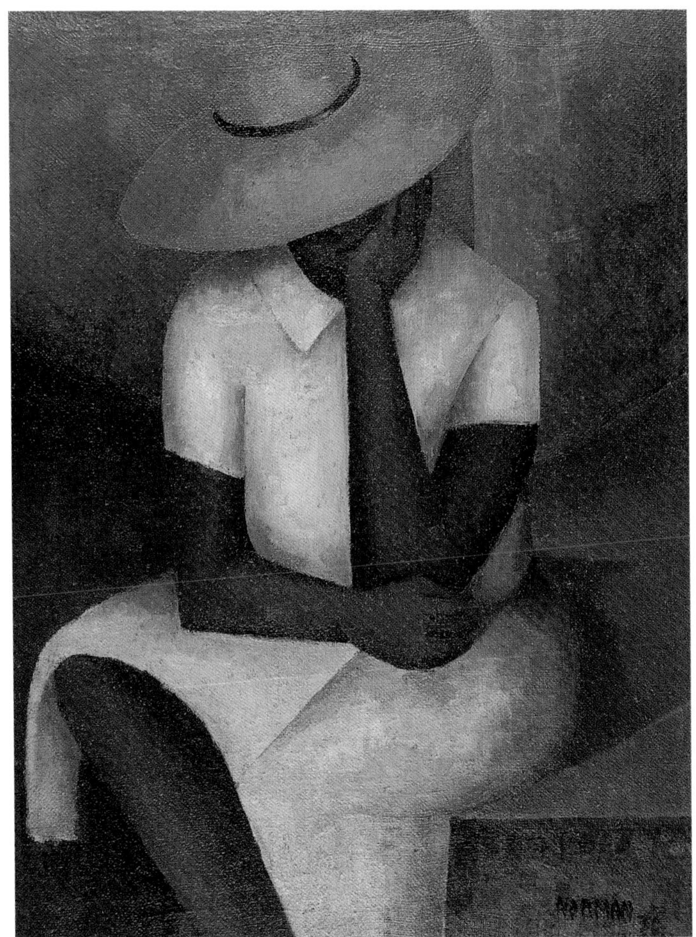

6 • Norman W. Lewis, *The Lady in the Yellow Hat*, 1936
Oil on burlap, 92.7 x 66 (36½ x 26)

7 • Elizabeth Catlett, *Tired*, 1946
Terracotta, 39.4 x 15.2 x 19.1 (15½ x 6 x 7½)

in his work, always strove to project something about the universal condition. In 1946 he wrote:

> *It would be highly artificial for the Negro artist to attempt a resurrection of African culture in America. The period between the generations is much too great, and whatever creations the Negro has fashioned in this country have been in relation to his American environment.... Modigliani, Picasso, Epstein and other* ▲ *modern artists studied African sculpture to reinforce their own design concepts. This would be perfectly appropriate for any Negro artist who cared to do the same ... the true artist feels that there is only one art—and it belongs to all mankind.*

Elizabeth Catlett's (born 1915) *Tired* of the same year shows an exhausted African-American woman worn out from the struggle but with the inner strength to carry on [**7**]. American born, but a Mexican citizen, Catlett always used the black figure as a symbol of racial and cultural pride. Her words echo the ideals championed by the Harlem Renaissance:

> *Art should come from the people and be for the people. Art for now must develop from a necessity within my people. It must answer a question, or wake somebody up, or give a shove in the right direction—our liberation.*

The innovative energy of the Harlem Renaissance declined with World War II, although the careers and ideas of its practitioners did not. The issues that Locke and Porter raised—what constitutes a black aesthetic; whether one should be a 'black artist' who creates black art or an American artist who is black—were not resolved during the Harlem Renaissance: rather, they continue to inform ▲artmaking and criticism whenever issues of identity arise.

FURTHER READING

M. S. Campbell et al., *Harlem Renaissance: Art of Black America* (New York: Studio Museum in Harlem and Harry N. Abrams, 1987)

David C. Driskell, *Two Centuries of Black American Art* (New York: Alfred A. Knopf and Los Angeles County Museum of Art, 1976)

Alain Locke (ed.), *The New Negro: An Interpretation* (first published 1925; New York: Atheneum, 1968)

Guy C. McElroy, Richard J. Powell, and Sharon F. Patton, *African-American Artists 1880–1987: Selections from the Evans-Tibbs Collection* (Washington, D.C.: Smithsonian Institution Traveling Exhibition Service, 1989)

James A. Porter, *Modern Negro Art* (first published 1943; Washington, D.C.: Howard University Press, 1992)

Joanna Skipworth (ed.), *Rhapsodies in Black: Art of the Harlem Renaissance* (London: Hayward Gallery, 1997)

▲ 1907

▲ 1993c

1944a

Piet Mondrian dies, leaving unfinished *Victory Boogie-Woogie*, a work that exemplifies his conception of painting as a destructive enterprise.

Piet Mondrian died in New York on February 1, 1944. Shortly thereafter his executor and heir—the young painter Harry Holtzman, who had helped organize Mondrian's immigration to the United States—opened his studio, left untouched, to the public. The threadbare yet extraordinarily dynamic space, with its white walls transformed into screens of optical flickers by the many rectangles of pure colors that were pinned onto them, and its makeshift all-white furniture designed by Mondrian from wooden crates (again, adorned with colored rectangles), were already well known to several visitors. But very few had previously seen the unfinished *Victory Boogie-Woogie* [**1**], even though the painter had worked on it since June 1942. It escaped none of these onlookers that there was a direct continuity between the pulsating surfaces of the walls and the staccato beat of Mondrian's last "lozangique" painting, as he called his series of square canvases rotated through forty-five degrees to stand on one corner (most commonly labeled his "diamond paintings").

This continuity was particularly enforced by the fact that not ▲ only had the black lines of classic Neoplasticism entirely vanished from the exceptionally large picture hovering on the easel, but so had *any* kind of line. One could speak only of "alignments" of tiny rectangles of color, most of them pieces of paper somewhat clumsily glued onto the canvas. But even these alignments are clearly on the verge of collapsing: they can be read only subliminally, inferred rather than seen, in most areas of the composition. Thus, to the visitors, the major difference between the walls and the painting must have seemed one of scale. Entering the box-car studio and being pulled toward *Victory Boogie-Woogie* at the very end of this long pristine space, one must have had the exhilarating feeling of walking into a painting.

But for those who had seen this ultimate canvas before Mondrian's death, their posthumous encounter with it was a horrifying shock—in fact, among the small circle of Mondrian's acquaintances who had witnessed the painter struggling over it during the last eighteen months of his life, many shared dealer and writer Sidney Janis's verdict: it was now a ruined masterpiece.

Mondrian had several times brought the painting to a conclusion (in a photograph dating from the winter of 1942–3, one can see him putting the "finishing" brush-stroke to it). But each time he had undone what he had achieved and, to the stupefaction of his friends, had started anew. He most certainly knew that his own end was coming, and his lifelong teleological bent had led him to assume that, if this painting were to be his swan song, it had to go further than anything he had done before. He was not interested in producing just one more painting in the electrifying style of his New York period. When a friend asked him why he kept repainting *Victory Boogie-Woogie*, instead of making several pictures from the different solutions that had been superimposed on this same canvas, Mondrian replied: "I don't want pictures. I just want to find things out." During the week of January 17–23, 1944, three days before entering the hospital to be treated for his fatal pneumonia, he had "unfinished" his masterwork one more time, covering its painted surface with a myriad tiny bits of colored tape and paper—to the great sorrow of Janis et al.

But negative criticism is often more perceptive than unconditional praise. The admirers of Mondrian's classic Neoplasticism saw only destruction in this collage of the eleventh hour. In many ways they were right, and they would have been surprised to hear Mondrian agree, and agree with glee. For destruction was precisely what he had endlessly sought during the long gestation of *Victory Boogie-Woogie*. The "finished" state that Janis and others had seen in his studio before the last frantic, week-long campaign was just not "destructive" enough for Mondrian: witnessing the panic of his most ardent supporters, he would have finally declared victory.

In fact, destruction had been at the very core of Mondrian's program all along. Since, right from his very first texts, he had written about the destruction of form, of the "particular," of individuality, his New York admirers should not have been so dismayed. They were not entirely at fault, however, for Mondrian had sent ambiguous signals with regard to his utopian dream of the "dissolution of art into the environment" (which he understood as a possibility for the "far distant future"): even though as early as 1922 he had determined that painting was the only vehicle within which his aesthetic principles could be truly tested by experiment, he had not gone out of his way to dissuade his early defenders from praising his art for its usefulness as a blueprint for modern architecture. By 1944, notwithstanding Mondrian's ever more aggressive statements about the fundamental role of negativity in his work

▲ 1917

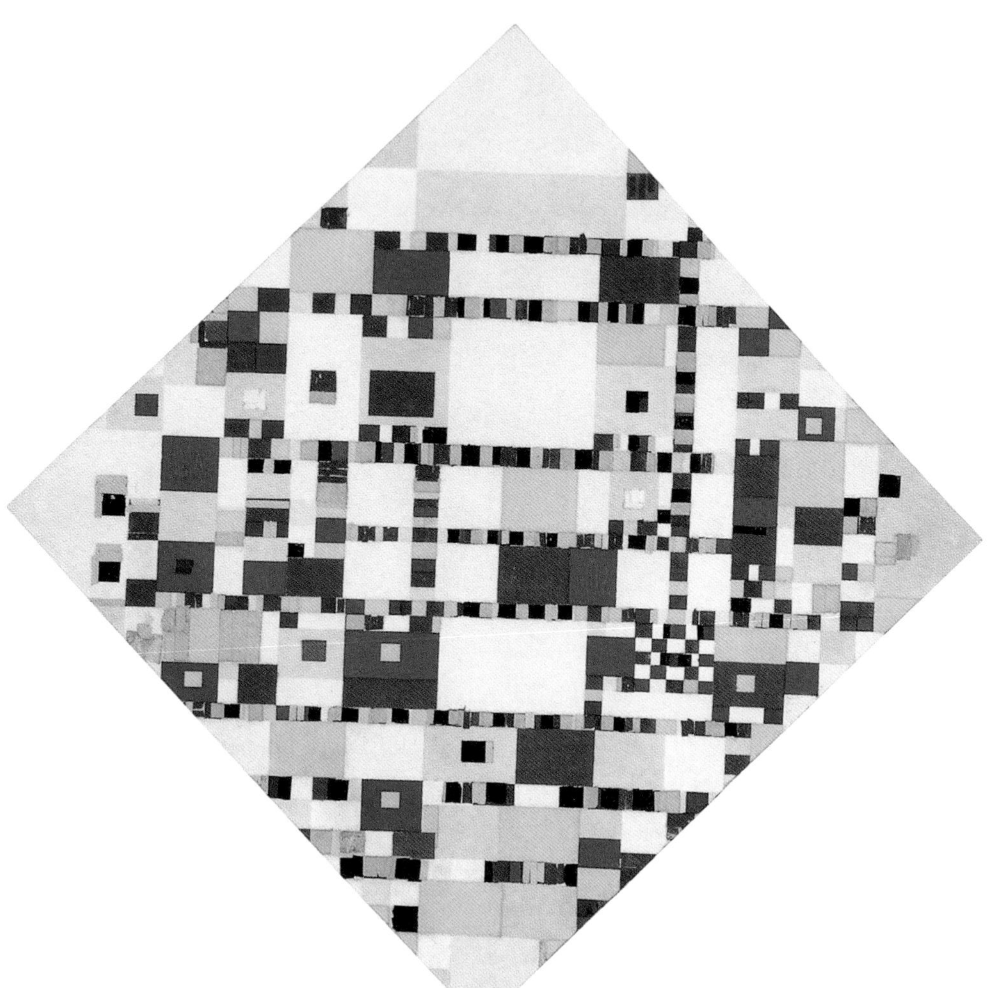

1 • Piet Mondrian, *Victory Boogie-Woogie*, 1942–4 (unfinished)
Oil and paper on canvas, 126 x 126 (49⅝ x 49⅝) diagonal

(such as "I think the destructive element is too much neglected in art"), it had become a cliché to think of him as the champion of a ▲ "constructive" aesthetic (already in 1937 Naum Gabo had been utterly baffled by Mondrian's refusal of this label.

It was in the thirties that Mondrian understood that he was not getting his message across. The posthumous publication, in the • last issue of *De Stijl* (in January 1932), of fragments of Theo van Doesburg's diary must have been a severe blow. There, Mondrian's former friend compared his work to the classical painting of the seventeenth-century French artist Nicolas Poussin. At that time, indeed, through a very long process of trial and error, Mondrian's dialectical system of composition had reached a peak, a perfect pitch where nothing could go wrong. The "negation" of one element by the other had led his paintings to be absolutely decentralized (thus achieving the destruction of the "particular" he was looking for), but they were also flawlessly balanced. Mondrian celebrated this climax in a series of eight paintings, from 1930 to 1932, all based on the same general organization. Yet such a self-satisfied rehashing (unique in his production, contrary to what one might think) soon gave way to the realization that he was "stuck."

Never indulgent with himself, he came to the conclusion that if he had indeed reached a serene equilibrium in his compositions, this was at a terrible cost, since it hardly conveyed the sense of dynamic evolution, of everlasting perfectibility in art and life, that was so essential to his dialectical thinking. Courageously (at the age of sixty), he concluded that, in order to better enact the destruction he had always been advocating, he had above all to shatter the language of painting itself, including his own. One by one, the elements of Neoplasticism, which he had conceived as the culmination of all the art of the past, were annihilated as entities.

The first thing to be "dissolved," as he said, was the plane. To this effect, Mondrian reintroduced a feature that he had banned from his painting since 1919 and that would utterly undermine the "classical" look of his works—that is, repetition. If until then he had conceived of repetition only as a natural (and therefore prohibited) phenomenon, it now became a favorite weapon in his struggle against identity: he multiplied the lines delimiting and linking the planes together so that "rhythm alone emerges, leaving the planes [themselves] as 'nothing'." Lines, which had been a secondary element in "classical" Neoplasticism, thus became the most active element, the main destructive agent, and their sheer multiplication

▲ 1937b • 1917

ensured not only that planes lost their "individuality" (as one cannot securely grasp a plane with multiple contours), but also that the same "depersonalization" would happen to the lines themselves.

Aesthetic sabotage

Mondrian's first attempt at such a radicalization of his pictorial program was *Composition B* of 1932 **[2]**, based on the same compositional schema as the climactic series of the previous two years. With this work he inaugurated what he called his "double line"—two parallel black lines and their white interstice, itself perceived as a line. But while in this canvas the white gap of the double line is narrow (it is of the same thickness as the intersecting—"single"—black line), it will soon widen and (as Mondrian would write, bemused, to a friend) "head toward the plane." And where there is no fundamental difference between lines and planes, since the line has given up its subordinate position, should there not be colored lines as well? Though Mondrian answered this question in the affirmative as early as 1933 (with the "diamond" composition of that year, *Composition with Yellow Lines*, now in the Gemeentemuseum in The Hague, which bears only four "lines/planes" on a white background), it would not be until after his arrival in New York, in October 1940, that he would fully explore this possibility.

During the three years following *Composition B*, Mondrian continued to use the classical type of 1930–2 as a solid platform on which to test the sabotage of his past pictorial language. In the only two paintings completed in 1934 (one of them destroyed as "degenerate" by the Nazis), he doubled *all* the lines; in 1935, he tripled the horizontal axis of *Composition Gris-Rouge* (Chicago Art Institute) and quadrupled that of *Composition No. II with Blue and Yellow* (Hirshhorn Museum, Washington, D.C.); in *Composition C* of the same year (Tate Modern, London), this horizontal division is a "double line" whose white interstice has become wider than two of the "planes" in the picture; in the last painting of the series, *Composition with Yellow* (1936, Philadelphia Museum of Art), it is no longer really a question of double lines: instead we find a "plurality" of lines that bisect the canvas.

Mondrian's next move, during the second half of the thirties, was to transform this "plurality" of lines (ever more numerous) into a sheer scansion, an irregular pulsation of the whole surface of the canvas. Two unexpected changes resulted from this gradual filling-in of his paintings (which had once been so bare as to contain only two black lines on a white ground, as in the *Lozenge Composition with Two Black Lines* of 1931), and in both cases we witness Mondrian transgressing a taboo of his Neoplastic system: first, effects of superimposition, banned since 1917, begin to reappear (effects that Mondrian then accentuated by varying the width of his black lines); second, one notices a return of the optical flickering caused by multiple linear intersections (something he had carefully avoided since 1919). It is as if the fear of illusionism that had engendered these past proscriptions was now far less an issue than that of making sure that nothing ever remains stable. To the

2 • Piet Mondrian, *Composition B, with Double Line and Yellow and Gray*, 1932
Oil on canvas, 50 x 50 (19⅝ x 19⅝)

variable thickness of the lines, to their multiplication and the discomforting retinal afterimage it creates, Mondrian then added a partial interruption of certain lines, which thereby cease to bisect the surface—rather, they interact to define fictive planes of a fugitive existence, forming and dissolving before our very eyes.

Mondrian's work was evolving at a rapid rate, his compositions becoming ever more complex, when, after a short interlude in Britain, he left Europe for America (he had fled Paris in 1938, mistakenly thinking that the French capital would be bombed by the Nazis—instead a bomb fell yards away from his London studio). There, after a few weeks of adjustment in New York, he took it upon himself to revise all the canvases he had brought with him (indeed all but four of the works completed in New York were begun in Europe). The myth of Mondrian's suddenly marveling at the Manhattan skyline at night is greatly exaggerated, since the changes in his art that occurred in America were more a direct consequence of an internal development than anything else. Yet there is no doubt that the urban vitality of New York (and specially the most recent jazz music that he suddenly discovered) hit Mondrian full in the face. He felt rejuvenated by the city; for the first time in his life he was acclaimed as a master and his advice was sought (it is ▲ thanks to his interest in Jackson Pollock's *Stenographic Picture* of ● 1942, for example, that Peggy Guggenheim gave this work a second look and ended up taking the American painter into her stable).

The first canvases to be reworked belong to a series of vertical compositions that Mondrian had initiated in Paris (in 1936), characterized by an "empty" bay in the center. In *Composition No. 9* **[3]**, we can clearly isolate all the features of his late European period (superimposition of bisecting lines, moderate flicker effect [on the right], unequal length of black lines that determine fictively

▲ 1949, 1960b ● 1942b

3 • Piet Mondrian, *Composition No. 9*, 1939–42
Oil on canvas, 79.7 x 74 (31¼ x 29)

overlapping rectangles of uncertain identity). To this vocabulary, Mondrian has added tiny dashes of color that seem to be unbounded by any restriction—one of them even crossing the stack of horizontal bars (in another canvas of the same batch, a red block cuts through a yellow plane, bringing the first color juxtaposition since 1917 into his art). Those dashes multiply and elongate in *Place de la Concorde* (1938–43), a picture titled in homage to the city in which Mondrian had started working on it, just as in the cases of *Trafalgar Square* (1939–43) and *New York* (1941–2). In this last painting, bisecting colored lines (briefly tried in 1933) reappear along with the dashes. The next step, with *New York City*, was the total elimination of black.

This work evolved from a series of paintings, once again initiated in Europe, where the sheer number of black lines crossing the canvas formed a grid, irregular, to be sure, but as optically active as that of the first two modular "diamond" paintings of 1918 and 1919. Mondrian had accepted the retinal afterimage as an inevitable by-product of the beat of lines scanning his canvases—but he was nevertheless wary of this. In *New York City*, he arrived at a solution to bypass this illusion, and he found it by pushing his enterprise of destruction of the language of painting further. During the early thirties, the plane as shape (the rectangle) had been "dissolved" by the multiple crossing of lines; then, in the late thirties, the identity of the line itself had

4 • Piet Mondrian, *New York City I*, c. 1941 (unfinished)
Oil and painted paper strips on canvas, 119 x 115 (47 x 45)

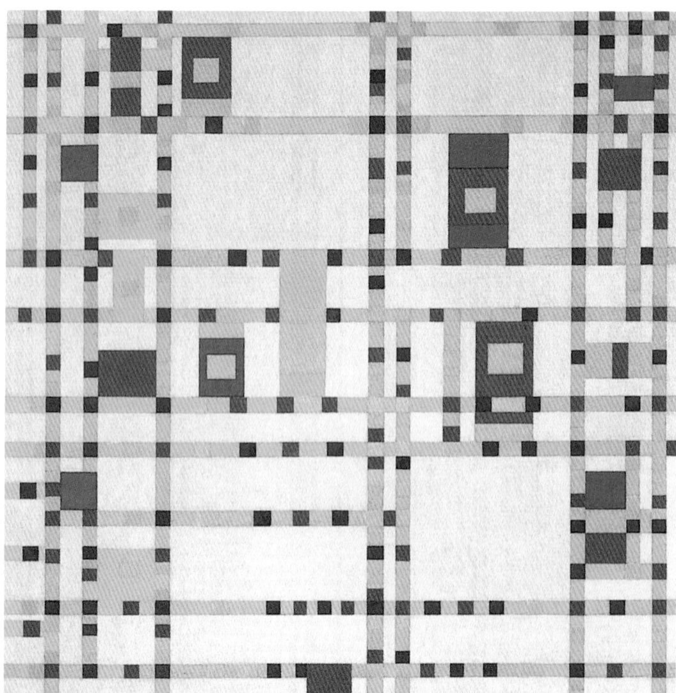

5 • Piet Mondrian, *Broadway Boogie-Woogie*, 1942–3
Oil on canvas 127 x 127 (50 x 50)

been abolished with the accelerated pulse of repetition, but what had remained untouched during this battle fought against the fundamentals was the ground on which lines and plane rest. It was now the negation of the ground as a geometric and physical entity to which Mondrian aspired. Thus *New York City* was conceived as a weave of colored lines that one can never reconfigure into independent virtual planes (as a red, a yellow, and a blue web) since no line of any given color behaves in a constant fashion (a red line will be above a blue one at an extremity and under at the other). But this deliberate loss of geometric identity is based on the physical unevenness of the ground: the painting is ostensibly layered, Mondrian having carefully imitated, via impasto and emphatic brush-strokes, the above-and-underneath of the braid that he had created with colored tapes while drafting the composition, as can be witnessed in the other canvases of the same series that were left unfinished **[4]**.

The logic behind this new turn was typical of Mondrian's reduction of all phenomena to their foundational dialectic: illusionism is what happens when the ground is being optically hollowed out, but if the ground did not exist as such to begin with, if there were no geometrically continuous surface, nothing of the sort would be possible. Yet it is probably only with his penultimate work that Mondrian fully grasped this particular point. Hailed as a masterpiece (and acquired by the Museum of Modern Art when it was exhibited, freshly painted, in 1943), *Broadway Boogie-Woogie* **[5]** was deemed a failure by Mondrian. "There is too much of the old in it," he would say. For although no previous picture of his had so efficiently captured the syncopated rhythm that he loved so much in jazz—with its colored lines divided into long beats of yellow (the base) and short beats of red, gray, and blue, and its rare larger planes that had become chords of three colors—this vibrant painting is devoid of the type of material weave he had created in *New York City*. In that canvas an unexpected effect of simultaneous contrast (illusionistic apparition of complementary colors) had resulted from the multiple crossing of colored lines; in *Broadway Boogie-Woogie*, he had tried not to correct this effect but to give it a form by marking each crossing of the predominantly yellow lines as a square of a different color, thus furthering the atomization of these lines. But the integrity of the ground had returned in full force.

This is probably what troubled him as well in the "finished" state of *Victory Boogie-Woogie*, and why he furiously appended all the bits of colored paper one can see pasted onto it today, ending up with a collage where the relative position of all elements, woven in thickness in a shallow cut of actual (not illusionary) space, is in a perpetual state of flux—where the ground has become a ghost whose only possible existence, a fleeting one, is that of appearing *above* the figure.

FURTHER READING

Yve-Alain Bois, "Piet Mondrian, *New York City*," *Painting as Model* (Cambridge, Mass.: MIT Press, 1990)

Yve-Alain Bois, Joop Joosten, and Angelica Rudenstine, *Piet Mondrian* (Washington, D.C.: National Gallery of Art, 1994)

Harry Cooper, "Mondrian, Hegel, Boogie," *October*, no. 84, Spring 1998

Harry Cooper and Ron Spronk, *Mondrian: The Transatlantic Paintings* (New Haven and London: Yale University Press, 2001)

1944b

At the outbreak of World War II, the "Old Masters" of modern art—Matisse, Picasso, Braque, and Bonnard—consider their refusal to flee occupied France as an act of resistance against barbarity: discovered at the Liberation, the style they had developed during the war years presents a challenge to the new generation of artists.

In 1950, the Grand Prize for Painting at the Venice Biennale was awarded to Henri Matisse (better late than never: he was 81). He had more works included in the show than any other artist that year. Not only had the French government selected him for its pavilion (along with Pierre Bonnard, Maurice Utrillo, and Jacques Villon), but his paintings easily dominated the historical exhibition devoted to Fauvism (including, besides Matisse, works by Braque, Derain, van Dongen, Dufy, Marquet, and Vlaminck). Matisse's presence at the 1950 Biennale amounted to a mini-retrospective, with twelve paintings in the Fauvism show and twenty-three in the French pavilion, which also included three sculptures and six drawings. With hindsight, it seems that the dice had been somewhat loaded, as though the Biennale's organizers had worried that it could be their jury's last chance to crown the modern Old Master, or old modern master. (In fact there would have been two more opportunities: Matisse did not die until the end of 1954.) As was often the case with Matisse's several postwar retrospective exhibitions, a deliberate emphasis was put both on the artist's early work and on his most recent work (done during or immediately after the war), which he was eager to present to the public. Altogether there were at least twenty-two paintings dating from 1896 to 1917 and seven from 1940 to 1948, while only six paintings covered the intervening period.

Bridging the hiatus

This time, however, Matisse hardly had to pull any strings for his strategy of "early/late and nothing in between" to be adopted: for reasons entirely different from his own assessment of his forte, the postwar strategy of the Biennale (which had closed in 1942 and reopened in 1948) was devoted to bridging the postwar present and the pre-Fascist past. The obvious goal was to erase memories of the twenties and thirties as a bad dream, and to atone for the hypernationalism (and growing antimodernism) of the Mussolini years. Nothing was better for this purpose than a latter-day version of "Sleeping Beauty." Matisse's evolution provided the perfect prop for the manufacture of such a collective amnesia, since it paralleled almost perfectly the life of the Biennale: the only times he had sent works to Venice were in 1920 and in 1928 during his

1 • Henri Matisse, *Still Life with Magnolia*, 1941
Oil on canvas, 74 x 101 (29⅛ x 39¾)

so-called 1917 to 1930 "Nice period"; that is, when Matisse himself had turned his back on the modernism of his youth and was participating in his own way in the conservative backlash called the ▲"return to order," a reactionary trend that the Biennale was backing with all its institutional might. However, as soon as Matisse rekindled in his work the flame of his avant-gardism of the pre-World War I years—this happened in 1931 to 1933, while he was working on the large "decoration" of *The Dance* for the Barnes Foundation in Philadelphia—he was no longer welcome in Venice, and he no longer cared to send works either. But the reopening of the Biennale after World War II was carefully designed as the turning of a new page, and Matisse, who had gone through his own *aggiornamento* in the interim years, was delighted to take part in this healing event. The message it allowed him to convey to a large audience—that in his recent art he had not only gone back to the roots of his aesthetic innovation but that new shoots had sprung from these roots—was remarkably in sympathy with the politics of reconstruction common to all Europe in the immediate postwar period, an ideological program for which the Venice Biennale was the most conspicuous flagship in the sphere of artistic consumption.

It was at Matisse's request that the Musée National d'Art Moderne in Paris sent to Venice *Still Life with Magnolia* of 1941 [1]

▲ 1919

2 • Henri Matisse, *Large Red Interior*, 1948
Oil on canvas, 146 x 97 (57½ x 38¼)

and *Large Red Interior* of 1948 [**2**], two works it had recently acquired. *Large Red Interior* is the painter's last major canvas and one could even call it his pictorial testament: it both concludes the great series of *interiors* realized in Vence after the war, of which four others were also presented in Venice, and it inevitably recalls the *Red Studio* of 1912 in that, like this recapitulative landmark of Matisse's early career, it represents among other things some of the artist's own creations tacked on the wall amidst an ocean of pulsatile red (a large brush-and-ink drawing of 1948 and *The Pineapple*, yet another canvas of the Vence series). *Still Life with Magnolia*, similarly bathed in red, remained Matisse's favorite painting until he had completed the Vence series: it is the first important canvas done in what could be called his "old-age style," just as *Large Red Interior*, seven years later, would be the last.

The close link between the *Red Studio* and *Large Red Interior* is not merely thematic. In purely formal terms, there is no fundamental difference between Matisse's "early" mature style (that is, ▲ post-*Le Bonheur de vivre* but prior to the Nice period) and the "old-age" style just mentioned. There are more similarities than differences, to take another example, between *Still Life with* ▲ *Magnolia* and the 1910 *Music*, or the 1913 *Blue Window*—these are all purely frontal arrangements of figures floating in a field of saturated color. Yet if what distinguishes the second batch of work from the first is tenuous—the unpainted white areas that surround the objects even as these figures are traced in heavy black contours; the light of the blank canvas that shows through the brushwork—the new air of freedom these conspicuous marks of spontaneity lend to the late paintings is the direct result of a philosophy of art that Matisse had began to develop around 1935.

The word that Matisse chose to characterize his new approach was "unconscious." This was perhaps infelicitous since his notion of the unconscious had little to do with the Freudian concept and its underpinning of repressed desires. Matisse's "unconscious" was more of a "reflex," as he also said at times. In practical terms, to "rely upon one's unconscious" meant for him to adopt a two-tier working process, a technique that he initially developed in drawing. He would first patiently "take possession of his model" and learn from it everything he needed to know through what he called an "analytical study" (more often than not realized in charcoal, and with many *pentimenti*); then, only when he felt that this cumulative storing of information had reached saturation, there would be the explosive relief of the line drawing, or rather drawings, done almost as if in a trance and without any possibility of correction, his hand guided by sheer instinct, just like the acrobat or the high-wire artist who will fall if he starts thinking about what he is currently doing and its dangers. By 1941 Matisse had fully mastered this dual temporality in the graphic realm (he was understandably proud of his accomplishment and started to compile a facsimile album of drawings illustrating his method, published in 1943 under the title *Thèmes et Variations*), but he was not certain of how to implement it in painting. *Still Life with Magnolia*, one of the canvases he worked on most intensely, represents the turning-point. On the one hand, there are countless preparatory drawings for this painting (which is unusual for him); on the other hand, he erased it several times to start it each time anew until he could paint it without thinking. While the mood of this work is ominous, its frontal address to the viewer no less petrifying than that of *Music* (and, like this early painting, which • was in part a response to Picasso's *Les Demoiselles d'Avignon*, no less recalling Freud's myth of Medusa's head), the technique Matisse employed there is responsible for the striking openness of all the Vence interiors. All appear to have been done in a matter of hours—and they were, if one considers only their final state; however, an unknown quantity of solvent had been used in effacing their previous incarnations, day after day. With this Penelopean process, Matisse had invented a new kind of pictorial automatism through which he felt that his lifelong goal of annihilating the gap between conception and realization could be achieved.

Matisse was seventy-nine when he painted *Large Red Interior*. Soon afterward he was definitively confined to bed. This was when he turned to another language of fusion, his paper cutouts [**3**]. This medium was not new in Matisse's repertoire—he had already used paper cutouts when working on the Barnes *Dance* in 1931 to 1933,

▲ 1906 ▲ 1910 • 1907

3 • Henri Matisse, *La Gerbe* (The Sheaf), 1953
Model for ceramic picture, cutout gouache, 2.9 x 3.4 (1⅛ x 1⅜)

then intermittently throughout the thirties for various decorative projects; his first major paper cutout opus, the album *Jazz*, was realized during the war, while he was temporarily bedridden (it was published in silkscreen form in 1947)—yet it is only during the last five years of his life that he had almost exclusive recourse to this means. It was particularly suitable, as was another medium he employed at the time (ceramic tiles), for working on large-scale decorative projects such as his Chapel of the Rosary in Vence, which was inaugurated in 1951. Like pictorial automatism, the paper cutouts represented a solution to a dilemma Matisse had sought to solve since the beginning of his career, this time not the split between conception and realization, but an effect of such a split, "the eternal conflict between [his] drawing and [his] color," about which he repeatedly complained and which the coloristic outburst of ▲ Fauvism—in particular *Le Bonheur de vivre*—had been intended to address. By "drawing directly into color," Matisse was able to maximize two sources of energy he had been employing with mastery for decades: the modulation of the intervals of white ground that animates his line drawings, and the electrifying saturation of his color.

"Old-age" style of modernist masters

Although Matisse's career provides the best example of the "old-age" style phenomenon among modernist masters, his case is not unique. Another artist similarly celebrated by the Venice Biennale, • this time in 1948, was Georges Braque (perhaps as a substitute for Picasso, whose political allegiance to the Communist Party, trumpeted shortly after the Liberation, compounded by his staunch opposition to General Franco's fascist Spanish government, made him an unlikely laureate). Pierre Bonnard would not have been an absurd choice either. The particulars are different each time, but the core issue remains the same: the art of those painters who had already become famous before World War I and who had long been venerated as pioneers of modern art betrays an unexpected renewal after World War II; younger artists emerging around 1945 had to cope with the fact that their heroes, of whom they had entirely lost sight for several years, were not only still alive but were also producing amazing new work.

Picasso was the most significant stumbling-block for the new generation (Pollock often lamented that the Spanish artist had invented everything, and he began to feel free from the senior artist's spell only after he had come up with the drip technique in ▲ 1947). There is no massive change between Picasso's pre- and postwar style (or rather multiplicity of styles) until the mid-sixties. But despite this surprising stylistic continuity in an oeuvre marked by discontinuities of all kinds, Picasso's work of the late forties and fifties is colored by a general approach that is antithetical to the structuralist method, based on the oppositional nature of pictorial • signs, that he had elaborated during the heyday of Cubism. It is not by chance that this later mode, which could be termed "phenomenological" (in that it presupposes a kind of empathy by which the artist attempts to know his model as if from within) is most efficiently deployed in works that are in direct but posthumous dialogue with Matisse, the perennial rival he finally felt free to honor. In the two series of paintings Picasso made with his old friend, who had just died, explicitly in mind—the *Women of Algiers* of 1955 [**4**], and the *Studio at "La Californie"* of 1955—the model that Picasso strives to know from within is as much the represented motif (Delacroix's courtesans in one case; the kitsch Art Nouveau/neo-rococo mirror-filled space of his new studio in Cannes in the other) as it is Matisse's art (the odalisques that Picasso claimed had been bequeathed to him, and the airiness of the Vence interiors). This was not the first time that Picasso had expressly launched a pictorial colloquy with a dead master, for he had explored Grünewald's *Crucifixion* in the early thirties; Poussin's *The Triumph of Pan* during the Liberation of Paris; and Cranach, Courbet, and El Greco in the late forties and early fifties. In Matisse, however, he was mourning a contemporary rather than playfully toying with a distant past. This endowed these works with

4 • Pablo Picasso, *Women of Algiers* (version H), 1955
Oil on canvas, 130.2 x 162.3 (51¼ x 63⅞)

▲ 1906 • 1911, 1912

▲ 1949, 1960b • Introduction 3, 1907, 1911, 1912

5 • Georges Braque, *The Billiard Table*, 1944
Oil on canvas, 130.5 x 95.5 (51$\frac{3}{8}$ x 37$\frac{5}{8}$)

an unusual gravity that he retained for the subsequent series in which he investigated the Western tradition of painting (forty-five canvases directly based on Velázquez's *Las Meninas* in 1957; twenty-seven canvases and around two hundred works in various media after Manet's *Le Déjeuner sur l'herbe* in 1959 to 1962). With Matisse's death, Picasso's world had received a blow that never quite healed. Musing on his own mortality, he would spend the rest of his long life arguing, more and more desperately, that painting as he had known it was still a game worth playing, but by the ▲ early sixties the phenomenon of the neo-avant-garde had clearly shifted the paradigm of expectations and young artists no longer deemed him relevant.

1940–1944

Braque's remarkable series of interiors revealed in Venice (including the first he painted, *The Billiard Table* [**5**]) bears signs of a liberation whose mechanism is not dissimilar from that experienced by Picasso in his "Matissean" paintings of 1955 to 1956, even if the cause is entirely different. Just as for the canvases of 1919 to 1921 (done when Braque was recovering in seclusion from the wound he had received at the front, and for once did not feel Picasso breathing down his neck) these late works magnify the artist's extraordinary technical know-how, the whole culinary aspect of painting of which he was a master without equal but that he had always tended to devalue under the peer-pressure of his sarcastic alter ego. In itself, the composition of these interior scenes is nothing but standard, one could even say academicized, Cubism, involving disjunction between color and form, multiple points of view, transparency, decomposition of the object into planes, etc., but their unusually large size underscores the materiality of the mixture of paint and sand Braque used to signify their obdurate reality as objects. Late in life, Braque was often praised for having restored a French tradition of still life that went back to Chardin in the eighteenth century, but if his interiors of the forties made an enormous impact, it is because in them he had unexpectedly switched from the intimate scale of the easel painting to the public scale of the mural.

One does not find a similar shift in scale in late Bonnard. In his *Studio with Mimosas* [**6**], there is nothing that was not already present in his work from the mid-thirties onward (the subtle chromatic interplay of accumulated paint layers of various colors—a stylistic feature emulated by Mark Rothko in his mature work; the zoom effect by which Bonnard crops the visual field and propels the beholder into the luminous thicket of things). Furthermore, the size of his canvases did not augment in the postwar period. What did, though, is the looseness of his brush-strokes. Outlines became ever less defined, as if perceived in a haze, and this general diffusion of form further reverberated Bonnard's coloristic high pitch, transforming the domestic world he had been depicting for decades into a full-blown oneiric space.

▲ Léger's postwar work, by contrast, constitutes a retreat. While he was in America during the war, Léger had explored the possibility of an isotropic pictorial space with his series of *Divers* and *Acrobats*: jumping from all sides, their floating figures move in defiance of gravity. Theoretically, these canvases could be hung in four different positions—this was Léger's hypothetical claim at least, although he undermined it by applying a sole signature in one elected corner. Léger's many versions of his *Divers* and *Acrobats* all convey a sense of directionlessness akin to that of Joan Miró's *Constellations* of 1940 to 1941, and although this debt is rarely acknowledged, the 1944 exhibition of Léger's works in New York might have played no less significant a role in the elaboration of Pollock's concept of the allover than Miró's 1945 show at the Pierre Matisse Gallery. However, while Miró retained this resolutely open-ended sense of indirection in his art for years to come, Léger opted for the heroic-monumental genre. Even though he had been one of the few modernist painters to think seriously, as early as the mid-twenties, about what would much ● later be coined (by Clement Greenberg) the "crisis of the easel painting," even though he had clearly stated that this medium as such was doomed to wither and that the survival of painting was predicated upon its ability to fuse with other media (including architecture) and develop a new sense of scale, he was himself bound by his ideological allegiance. Léger joined the Communist Party shortly after Picasso, but while the Spanish painter fluctuated between cynical endorsement of Stalinist politics through minor propaganda work (for example, his assembly-line production of dove "peace" designs) and utter indifference to the Party line, Léger believed in the credo and wished to "educate the masses" through his art. As a result, his postwar art, while still having recourse to all the stylistic devices he had developed since the early thirties (thick contours enclosing the figures; schematic modeling by degradation of black superimposed on flat planes of pure colors), becomes increasingly stiff. His figures end up mimicking, without the harsh rudeness and convincing naivety ■ one finds in the work of an Aleksandr Deineka, for example, the postures found in Soviet "Socialist Realist" painting. Unlike that of Matisse, Picasso, Braque, or Bonnard, Léger's art did not grow in the postwar Reconstruction period—which nevertheless did not prevent him from being a force with which the coming generation had to reckon.

▲ 1960a

▲ 1913, 1925a ● 1960b ■ 1934a

6 • Pierre Bonnard, *Studio with Mimosas*, 1939–46
Oil on canvas, 126 x 126 (49⅝ X 49⅝)

7 • Giorgio Morandi, *Still Life*, c. 1946
Oil on canvas, 28.7 x 39.4 (11⅜ x 15½)

A new generation comes into its own

Léger was passed over by the Venice Biennale. Having celebrated several figurative Old Masters of the School of Paris, the Biennale moved to Surrealism, another movement that had been deliberately ignored during the Fascist years (in 1954 Max Ernst received the ▲ Grand Prize for painting, and Hans Arp for sculpture), then, finally, it moved to the new generation—which meant at that time, for this old institution not particularly attuned to the most recent developments in art, postwar abstraction (Mark Tobey [1890–1976] and Eduardo Chillida [1924–2002] in 1958, Hans Hartung [1904–1989] • and Jean Fautrier [1898–1964] in 1960). But the attribution of Grand Prizes to international masters was not sufficient as a means for the Biennale to attend to its political campaign of redemptive amnesia: it also needed to address the troubled Italian context. The most daring move was its celebration in 1950 of "The Signers of the ▲ First Futurist Manifesto": in what amounted to a total travesty of history, it entirely omitted Marinetti, who as the uncontested leader of Futurism, had not only written the said manifesto but had also been the most famous official "bard" of Mussolini's regime. That his reluctant colleagues had not been reluctant enough—and had basically gone along with Marinetti's antics—was in no way addressed.

Not all of the Biennale's revisionist attempts were as ill-conceived or hypocritical. In 1948, two years before it tried to absolve Futurism of its past political crimes, it paid homage to *pittura metafisica* in a • group show featuring Carlo Carrà, Giorgio de Chirico, and Giorgio Morandi (1890–1964). The exhibition failed to convince many critics that de Chirico's late work was anything but a total renunciation of his early stance (which had been so important for the birth of Surrealism), and Carrà's dimly lit star did not get any brighter either, but Morandi, a secluded man, until then barely known outside Italy, was suddenly put on the map. This outburst of recognition did not change anything for him—neither in his art, whose very strict parameters had been established since the early twenties, nor in his monastic life. For years until he died, Morandi painted similar compositions: mainly small still-life arrangements of several empty vessels (bottles, glass, cups, vases) seen slightly from above and disposed frontally on a barren plane (the table is never more than a horizon line) and against a no-less-barren wall **[7]**; the whole always in tonal color schemes (he became of master of gray) and in sharp light (either zenithal and thus without shadows, or oblique, with accentuated shadows reminiscent of de Chirico's first manner). Morandi's art is one of reticence, of whisper—it is at odds with the buoyant claims of the many avant-garde movements that succeeded one another at growing pace during the twentieth-century. Like ■ Ad Reinhardt in his abstract "black," "ultimate" paintings, Morandi opted for what one would be tempted to call a minor mode—if this term did not necessarily carry negative connotations—a mode in which pathos and the agonistic rhetoric of high contrasts are abolished and where the work requires a long contemplation before it can begin to take hold. Unsurprisingly, beholders were slow to grasp Morandi's quiet stance—but, in the end, the hermit of Bologna did more to convince younger artists that the game of painting was still worth playing than did Picasso in his postwar grandstanding.

FURTHER READING

Lawrence Alloway, *The Venice Biennale 1895–1968: From Salon to Goldfish Bowl* (New York: New York Graphic Society, 1968)

Yve-Alain Bois, *Matisse and Picasso* (Paris: Flammarion, 1998)

John Golding et al., *Braque: The Late Works* (New Haven and London: Yale University Press, 1997)

Nicholas Serota (ed.), *Fernand Léger: The Later Years* (Munich: Prestel Verlag, 1987)

Leo Steinberg, "The Algerian Women and Picasso At Large," *Other Criteria: Confrontations with Twentieth-Century Art* (London, Oxford, and New York: Oxford University Press, 1972) and "Picasso's Endgame," *October*, no. 74, Fall 1995

Sarah Whitfield and John Elderfield, *Bonnard* (London: Tate Gallery; and New York: Museum of Modern Art, 1998)

▲ 1913, 1916a, 1918, 1922, 1924 • 1946 ▲ 1909 • 1909, 1924 ■ 1957b

roundtable

Art at mid-century

HF: First, let's address a few of the important narratives of prewar art that emerge in the postwar period, and clarify our historical differences from them. Second, we might take up the problem of antimodernism, and why this was long a difficult topic to discuss adequately. And third, we should grapple with the question of World War II as a caesura, and how different histories of twentieth-century art negotiate this break, either marking it as definitive, denying it in the interest of continuity, or bridging it in the name of reconstruction. No doubt we will stray from this itinerary—but let's begin with the account of prewar modernism developed by ▲ Alfred H. Barr, Jr., the first director of the Museum of Modern Art.

YAB: One thing that strikes us now is the difference between Barr's enthusiastic encounter with the Russian avant-garde on his trip to ● the Soviet Union in 1927–8 and the way Russian Constructivism was later melted down at MoMA to a production of abstract paintings and sculptures. Even if Barr was specifically searching for painters and sculptors on his visit ("I must find more painters," he noted in his diary after a visit to Rodchenko, who told him he had stopped painting in 1922), he was impressed by all the work done by Constructivist artists in what we could call the realm of propaganda or the "ideological front" (theater design, film sets, typography, exhibition design, etc.). Even if he was critical of the antiart concept of "factography" in the end, he spent a considerable amount of time with its theoretician, the writer Sergei Tretyakov, trying to understand it. Barr admired the "brilliant" Konstantin ■ Umansky, who "at the age of 19" had written the book *Neue Kunst in Russland* (it long remained the only synthetic study of Soviet art), and he was particularly struck by Umansky's comment that "a proletarian style was emerging from the wall newspaper with its combined text, poster, and photomontage": "an interesting and acute suggestion," Barr noted. In short, he was extremely curious about the transformations made in the aesthetic realm by the Soviet avant-garde, trying to gauge their consequences for the future. But then he seems to have "forgotten" all this almost as soon as he left Russia: he couldn't take it into consideration in the history of modern art he was constructing.

HF: Yet there are residues of his encounter with art in relation to industrial production in his interest in *design*, though that interest was ◆ mostly read through the Bauhaus, which Barr also visited—that is, through a more capitalist-friendly version of art into production.... When does he do his flowchart of modernist movements?

BB: 1936.

HF: Right, for his "Cubism and Abstract Art" show of that year.

YAB: And his Bauhaus show comes soon after, in 1938.

BB: I wouldn't dismiss his interest in the Bauhaus simply as the capitalist version of the art-into-production project. I think it indicates a more complex comprehension of the transformation of avant-garde practices in the twenties toward production, architecture, and design, and utilitarian definitions of art in general that are very significant for Barr's position. And it is accompanied ▲ by an equally strong interest in the legacy of Dada, which was another set of operations that opened up the traditional model of art in a radical way. All of these positions are present in his 1936 account. The question is: How do these extraordinary historical chapters get edited out in the reception of MoMA's exhibitions and in the work of the first generation of American artists and critics after Barr?

HF: Of course there are other chapters, other movements, in his chart, yet they are also streamlined: they are all made to flow into successors according to a historicist model of consecutive influence and formal progress, and this sets up the further editing ● of modernism that occurs down the line with Clement Greenberg and others. Granted, it is a pedagogical chart, an introductory one, and the lines are more complicated, not to say convoluted, than we usually recall ...

RK: Yet Barr does present a basic kind of bifurcation into, on the one hand, mechanicist models of form and, on the other, organicist models. And he emphasizes the organicist because he feels that ■ the most important phenomenon at the time is Surrealism. He wants to welcome Surrealism into the family of modernist forms.

HF: But those impulses are still formalized into "geometrical" and "nongeometrical" abstraction. True, the mechanicist is a force in the geometrical lineage, but it is removed from industrial production, indeed from social, economic, and political context altogether. Similarly, the organicist is a dimension of the nongeometrical lineage, but it is detached from the body and the

▲ 1927c ● 1921 ■ 1928 ◆ 1923 ▲ 1916a, 1920 ● 1960b ■ 1924, 1930b, 1931

drives, from all psychoanalytic associations. Barr has these terms in play, but in a formal sense only.

BB: The teleology of his view of modernist art would also have to be associated with the overall teleology of American liberal democracy in which the actual integration of artistic practices into the sphere of everyday life is not at issue. What is at issue is their institutional containment, not their practical deployment and realization—neither the politics of Dada and Surrealism nor the politics of ▲ Constructivism and Productivism.

HF: This also speaks to the unique situation in the United States in which the initial encounter with the avant-garde is quickly followed by its partial institutionalization. There is the Armory Show in 1913, of course—the legendary shock of the first encounter— the Alfred • Stieglitz circle in the teens, the New York Dada salons, and several gallery shows—but then there follows the Museum of Modern Art in 1929, "Art of This Century" in 1942, and so on, in which the reception of modernism all but occurs within the setting of the museum.

YAB: And the reception of the avant-garde in these museums, until very late, was only in regard to Europe. That was the complaint of many American artists: "They show the most advanced European art, and they don't even look at us." For the museums the source had to be from far away; it had to be Europe: that was the land, grand and strange, where these bizarre new objects were produced, and their foreignness is what allowed American museums to present them favorably and give them form institutionally. It's a new kind of exoticism, in a way.

roundtable

HF: So what happens to Surrealism in this story, if it's so important to the first generation of abstract artists in the United States? It is very present in the form of exiled artists in New York during the war. We should talk a little about how it gets assimilated or occluded.

■ **RK**: In 1940 Clement Greenberg writes "Towards a Newer Laocoon" in which he attacks Surrealism, among other things, for being narrative, and Lessing's *Laocoön* becomes a kind of master model (though it was published in 1766!) of how to separate the visual and spatial arts from the verbal and temporal arts in modernism. For Greenberg the literary is temporal, Surrealism is literary, and so it must be condemned as impure.

HF: It is improper to visual art, and so not a modernist art, in his sense, at all. I never quite understood how "Towards a Newer Laocoon" could follow so closely on his "Avant-Garde and Kitsch" essay (1939), with its framing of the avant-garde still in terms of a social struggle in a historical field. In one year he seems to go from an almost dialectical account of the avant-garde to a rather static analysis of the decorum of the arts.

BB: The story of the elision of Surrealism in early accounts of Abstract Expressionism is more complicated than the resistance of Greenberg alone. Take the rejection of Surrealism by Barnett ◆ Newman: it's clearly a process of a programmatic disidentification after an initial embrace. The embrace had to do with the radicality of automatist procedures of mark-making and even, possibly, with psychoanalytic models of the unconscious. Then, in the transition from the moment of Surrealist reception to the moment of the ▲ constitution of an Abstract Expressionist identity, Surrealism had to be rejected. This rejection was not a rejection of psychoanalysis—

YAB: —on the part of Newman it was.

BB: Nor did it mean the rejection of automatism. It was driven by a need to redefine aesthetic identity within the parameters of a new historical moment, and that entailed, for Newman too, a realization that the Surrealist indulgence in the unconscious was no longer valid after the trauma of World War II and the Holocaust. That is one rift, a major chasm, whether explicitly or only latently expressed. Another is the realization that this historical situation needed redefinition, not only in geopolitical terms or in terms of a new national identity, but also in terms that were specifically *tragic*. That's why Serge Guilbaut's account of the ideological functions of Abstract Expressionism and T. J. Clark's view of it as an art of middle-class vulgarity don't work for me: they don't understand the radicality of the point of departure of those artists.[1] There was a sense of loss, of destruction, of utter inaccessibility to prewar • culture that rivals Theodor Adorno's in its decisiveness—though, of course, it couldn't be articulated in his terms at the time. The fundamental difference between the postwar aesthetics of Adorno and of Greenberg might be defined as follows. On the one hand, Adorno was a Marxist philosopher and an avant-garde composer-musician formed in the most differentiated culture of the European bourgeoisie who witnessed the actual destruction by the Nazis not only of his own context but of European bourgeois culture at large. On the other hand, Greenberg was a member of a New York ■ Trotskyite circle around the journal *Partisan Review*, which was then aspiring to lay the foundation of a new democratic culture in the United States; the historical condition of the Holocaust and World War I could not be easily integrated into his progressivist model of the future.

YAB: Paradoxically, the difference between European and American perspectives was deepened by the presence of many Surrealists in New York—André Breton above all, but also Salvador Dalí, Max Ernst, André Masson, Roberto Matta, Kurt Seligman, Yves Tanguy, among others. Suddenly people who had been constructed at the level of myth were just *there*, and they didn't correspond to the legends. Some of them were living comfortable lives (Ernst was married to Peggy Guggenheim), and had a steady market. One shouldn't underestimate the shock of young admirers, such as ◆ Jackson Pollock and Arshile Gorky, who had worked in the Works Progress Administration, on seeing how little their heroes resembled *artistes maudits* or *enfants terribles*.

HF: Of course, the sense of the tragic and the traumatic could not be the basis of an affirmative story of modernism, a story of renewed continuity of the sort that Greenberg and others wanted to tell, and that institutions in this period of reconstruction needed to be told. So that dimension had to be occluded. The same goes for aspects of modernism contaminated by fascism—like late Futurism—or, especially in the McCarthy period, implicated in

▲ 1916a, 1920, 1921, 1924, 1928, 1930b, 1931 • 1916b, 1942b ■ 1960b ◆ 1951 ▲ 1947b • Introduction 2 ■ 1942a ◆ 1936, 1942a, 1949, 1960b

Communism. Hence, in part, the blind eye turned to most Russian ▲ Constructivism and some German Dada.

BB: Absolutely.

YAB: There is one mantra that Newman repeats in his early essays: "After the monstrosity of the war, what do we do? What is there to paint? We have to start all over again." You never find this discourse in Greenberg—as if the trauma didn't exist.

HF: This might be too speculative, but I wonder if it reappears in displaced form in the discourse about Abstract Expressionism, with a traumatic sense of the war and the Holocaust sublimated and subjectivized in the reception of such work in terms of the Sublime. The experience of "the abyss" or "the void" in a Pollock, a Newman, a Rothko, or a Gottlieb might register this kind of historical sublime, but writ small—in fact small enough so that the viewer can feel the traumatic frisson but also recoup it, even be empowered by it, along the lines of the Sublime as classically understood by Kant or Burke. Perhaps there is a trace of this recouping in the response that the viewer of the late-modernist work is supposed to have: the epiphanic bolt of insight, the sudden sense of transcendence, what Michael Fried later famously called "grace."

RK: Shedding the dross of one's own body becomes the figure of transcending—

HF: —the historical in general—

RK: —and the physical as well.

BB: And recent history in particular. That was one of the precarious questions being asked by intellectuals in the forties around *Partisan Review*: "Are you confronting the Holocaust? Are you making it the key topic of every moment of your daily thinking? Or are you turning away from it in order to make a new culture?" If you read *Partisan Review* from that time it is amazing how the two positions appear side by side from issue to issue: Hannah Arendt in 1946 speaking about the concentration camps, for example, and Clement Greenberg two years later speaking about the rise of a pure modernism. Either you confront that history or you don't. And if you don't, it's easier to claim access to a new identity-formation in relation to American liberal-democratic culture: that lies at the foundation of the new painting in New York as well, and it's one of the bases of American formalism as well. I'm not polemicizing; I'm trying to describe the etiology of that compulsion to purify, to disidentify with that historical body.

YAB: There were several attempts from the early fifties to the mid-sixties to speak about Jewishness, art, and their relationship to the trauma of the Holocaust, but every time the issue is raised it is hushed up: people don't want to hear about it. Two of the critics at issue here write seriously about this—Greenberg in "Self-Hatred and Jewish Chauvinism: Some Reflections on 'Positive Jewishness'" (in *Commentary* in November 1950) and Harold Rosenberg in "Is There a Jewish Art?" (in the same magazine in July 1966)—but only once each, I believe, and mostly to explain the silence. They try to theorize the post-traumatic silence with regard to the Holocaust on the part of artists.

HF: The early sixties is also the moment when New York intellectuals break apart over "the banality of evil" thesis developed by Arendt in her *New Yorker* coverage of the Eichmann trial in Jerusalem. (I've always wondered about the connection to another ▲ provocative "banality" at this time, that of Pop art, and the outraged response to its emergence by some of the same intellectuals—as if Pop also threatened the value of profundity, or whatever the opposite of banality is, in culture, morality, and politics.) After *Eichmann in Jerusalem* the traumatic silence gives way to a torrent of enraged speech. But, to return to that silence for a moment, one can imagine how oppressive it was for artists and writers to be asked, all but compelled, to think about the tragic and the traumatic in this way. One can understand the impulse to turn away, to begin again—even though that impulse is oppressive in its own way too, of course.

● **BB**: The figure of Meyer Schapiro should be brought into the conversation in this regard. There's another dimension here—Hal ■ just alluded to it—it's the dismantling of the Left. This is also the moment—to return to the comment about the shift in Greenberg from "Avant-Garde and Kitsch" in 1939 to "Towards a Newer Laocoon" in 1940—when the Marxist tradition is all but liquidated, sometimes auto-liquidated, self-exorcised.

HF: What's the famous line in Greenberg looking back on the thirties from the early fifties? "Some day it will have to be told how 'anti-Stalinism,' which started out more or less as 'Trotskyism,' turned into 'art for art's sake,' and thereby cleared the way, heroically, for what was to come."

RK: "Eliotic Trotskyism," T. J. Clark called it once.

YAB: The first traumatic event for the American Left was, of course, the Moscow show trials in 1936. And the Hitler–Stalin pact in 1939 was the last straw.

HF: Right. And Greenberg can't believe that some artists stick to the Party line. He later says of Pollock: "He was a damned Stalinist from start to finish." However misguided that position might have been, it also points to some resistance, political not only aesthetic, to Greenberg's reading of their art.

YAB: We have discussed what American artists faced immediately after the war, but not what French artists did. What was their situation? How different was it? There was the same trauma ...

BB: There was more: after all it was European culture that had been ruined in the war, and a central European nation state whose fascist takeover had wrought that destruction—a nation state that, like its ally Italy, had once represented the highest achievements of European humanism.

◆ **YAB**: The case of Jean Fautrier, an artist who was always suppressed in the States, is interesting in this regard. No one paid attention when he exhibited in New York in 1952, '56, and '57 (the

▲ 1920, 1921

▲ 1960c, 1964b ● Introduction 2 ■ 1942a ◆ 1946

last of these shows at Sidney Janis's), even though he was an abstract artist—not even Greenberg. But he has become more prominent lately, perhaps in part because we now recognize that he was one of the first avant-garde artists to take into account the trauma of the war and the Holocaust. It started during the war with his "Otages" paintings, but their exhibition in Paris in the immediate postwar moment was a great bomb. His attempt was immediately transformed by Jean Dubuffet, and also taken in a different direction ▲ by Lucio Fontana, so the "repression" of his work is not only an American phenomenon—it just took a different form in Europe, that of sanitization. It's always puzzled me that Fautrier's attempt to take the trauma into consideration disappeared so quickly.

BB: There is an even more deliberate desire to disavow the trauma, at least on the part of the next generation. If you look at Fontana, Piero Manzoni, and especially Yves Klein, you see the most important efforts in art to define European reconstruction culture. Perhaps paradoxically, the link—and it is particularly important for Fontana and Klein—that connects all these practices is spectacularization. At that moment two major theoreticians of postwar European aesthetics emerge: one is Adorno, and the ● other is Guy Debord. They represent the polarity through which an aesthetics of traumatization and the impossibility of renewing modernist continuity is articulated. That polarity reflects on the legacy of the Holocaust on the one hand and, on the other, on the apparatus of spectacle that will inevitably take over even the last remnants of opposition and exemption, resistance and subversion, that the avant-garde had previously claimed for itself. And that's where Fontana and Klein position themselves from the very beginning, even more so than Pollock—within the registers of spectacle culture.

HF: Some previous practices speak to both necessities. For example, the primordial and the primitive, the child and the insane, are old modernist interests, to be sure, but they return with special ■ force in the immediate postwar period with *art brut* and Cobra. Perhaps they provided a way at once to register the trauma of the Holocaust and to disavow it. To seek radical beginnings registers the horror of the past, but it is also an escapist flight from recent history—perhaps the Abstract Expressionist motto of "the First Man" functioned in a similar way.

BB: To dehistoricize the trauma. Also in play here is the sudden interest in sites like Lascaux: prehistoric caves in lieu of contemporary camps.

HF: Yes. But also evident there is an attempt to counter, perhaps even to recover, a primordialism that the Nazis had contaminated. It's not simply an either/or: either represent or disavow the trauma. There are aesthetic constructs that are almost compromise-formations—that acknowledge historical reality but in a bracketed, abstracted, or otherwise dehistoricized way. Again, the point is to describe these moves, to understand them, not to pathologize them.

BB: In addition to the first two complexes—namely, the trauma of World War II and the Holocaust and the destruction of the American Left and Left culture at large—a third question confronts the New York School in its formative stages: how does the mass-cultural sphere reemerge, and how should the avant-garde relate to that sphere? After all, that had been one of the central questions of the twenties that had affected the constitution of all avant-garde practices. Paradoxically, in the postwar moment, as the mass-cultural sphere in its American version reemerges with even greater power than in the twenties, the avant-garde withdraws into a mode of total denial of its existence: it adopts a completely entrenched, hermetic model of modernist refusal. It takes at least ten years, ▲ with the rise of Jasper Johns and proto-Pop art, before the mass-cultural sphere reenters artistic awareness explicitly.

● **HF**: There is also the Independent Group in Britain slightly earlier. But, yes, before then, there is this talk of "we unhappy few" against the world. And yet at the same time Pollock appears in—

YAB: *Vogue*.

HF: Yes, in 1951 his drip paintings are used as backdrops to fashion pictures by Cecil Beaton, but also, earlier, in *Life*, in the famous article that serves as the heading for our "1949" Pollock ■ entry: "Is he the greatest living painter in the United States?"

BB: That's not a confrontation; that's an erosion, and an indication that the isolation is delusory, or that the claim to it is delusory.

HF: Yes. Modernist refusal gets "mediated" at that point, literally: it begins to be circulated on a mass level as a bohemian pose. The Situationists see this problem clearly by the late fifties.

BB: And the disavowal of psychoanalysis—

YAB: —occurs at the same time that it's taken up in Hollywood.

HF: Dalí doing the dream-sequence sets for Hitchcock's *Spellbound* in 1945.

BB: More important is that it's being institutionalized at a mass level in the United States. That's when psychoanalysis is raised to its highest level of everyday, pragmatic practice.

HF: But it's only a particular version of psychoanalysis—ego ◆ psychology—that gets taken up, and which Jacques Lacan, a young associate of the Surrealists (of Dalí's in fact!), always railed against.

YAB: Its Jungian version also gets taken up, earlier even with Pollock. It all becomes a common kind of do-it-yourself psychotherapy around that time.

HF: So again it's not a case of outright repression. One can understand why these discourses are shirked: their terms get corrupted, their appropriation renders them invalid.

YAB: They become consumables: you consume this or that brand of psychoanalysis the same way you consume this or that fridge.

BB: As Walter Benjamin said, "Neurosis is the equivalent of the commodity on the psychic level."

▲ 1959a ● 1957a ■ 1946, 1957a ▲ 1958 ● 1956 ■ 1949 ◆ Introduction 1

RK: Can we understand the success of Greenberg's story, then, partly in relation to a collective need to repress this tragic or traumatic past? His brief for abstract painting succeeds in that partial repression, and therefore that painting performs a kind of social function.

HF: There is that connection, but we have to make it more indirectly. In a sense what we see as a process of repression they saw as a process of conservation. On the one hand, abstract painting is one of the great avant-garde ruptures; on the other hand, it is also, as "modernist painting," committed to the centrality of painting and the maintenance of its traditions. It serves to bracket or to suspend other avant-garde breaks, to keep other avant-garde paradigms to one side, at least in the States—I mean ▲ the paradigms that the German critic Peter Bürger,[2] the author of the third narrative that we want to discuss here, underscores: readymades and constructed sculptures, collages and photomontages. Historical memory is displaced and concentrated onto the memory of one medium, advanced painting, which then provides the basis for a historical continuity that cannot be maintained otherwise—not in art and not in history in general. There is also a displacement of political revolution onto formal innovation. That's implicit in the Greenberg remark I cited about looking back on the thirties from the fifties. Fried also states as much in a retrospective passage in "Three American Painters: Noland, Olitski, Stella" in 1965.[3]

YAB: What is also striking is that Greenberg never takes into consideration the political claims of the artists themselves. For ● example, Mondrian saw his work as a blueprint for a future socialist society—hard to believe though this might seem. In a manuscript that appeared only posthumously, *The New Art—The New Life: The Culture of Pure Relationships*, he directly appropriated a passage from a political pamphlet by his friend the anarcho-syndicalist militant Arthur Lehning. Lehning was, among other things, the editor of an extraordinary journal called *1:10* that appeared in 1927–8, which, besides offering the first serious analysis of the Stalinization of the Soviet Union, published texts not only by Mondrian, Kurt Schwitters, and László Moholy-Nagy but also Walter Benjamin, Ernst Bloch, and Alexander Berkman (an old ally of Emma Goldman). It is this type of information, this kind of link, that is obliterated in Greenberg's view of modernism. The ■ same thing happens with his treatment of Newman. Newman recognized the role Greenberg played in his sudden rise to fame in the late fifties, but he still disliked the critic's interpretation of his work because it failed to address its anarchistic implications. I'm not saying that Mondrian and Newman were right about their own painting, only that Greenberg was oblivious to these aspects of it.

HF: At the same time he was far and away the best contemporary critic of their aesthetic ambitions.

BB: Greenberg does address those ambitions, in their continuity with past painting too, but as far as Newman is concerned this continuity also had to be ruptured. For him it's not Newman and Mondrian; it's Newman versus Mondrian. Newman claims a radical break with Mondrian: both his pictorial concepts and his utopian visions are invalidated, no longer possible.

HF: According to Newman.

BB: According to Greenberg too.

YAB: But not for the same reasons. It took Newman a long time to see why he was so different from Mondrian. Until the mid-sixties he repeated all the clichés of the Mondrian literature—that his work was not really abstract but grounded in nature, or that it was ▲ decorative design, etc. His young Minimalist admirers (Donald Judd in particular) provided him with a new critical vocabulary (that's when he begins to speak in terms of the "wholeness" or his paintings as opposed to the "part-to-part" aesthetic of Mondrian), but in the end he coins his criticism of Mondrian in political terms: the Dutch painter was not an anarchist, though he might sometimes have felt he was—he was too Hegelian, too totalistic in his ideas not only about painting but also about the state. Newman, who had always professed anarchistic positions (he prefaced the memoirs of Kropotkin) felt that Mondrian's utopianism was the exact opposite of his stance. Greenberg never addresses that: he never says that Mondrian's and Newman's suggest two totally different world views.

HF: But other artists of the time did not claim such a definitive caesura. Or if they did so, it was out of an Oedipal struggle—especially with Picasso, of course—in which a break at one level is staged in order to forge a connection at another level, a kind of trumping that is both psychological and stylistic. Political differences were usually overwhelmed by such aesthetic positioning.

YAB: Pollock's involved there.

● **HF**: And Gorky, de Kooning, and others. So the story of continuity, troubled or not, opportunistic or not, makes some sense. Again, it also makes great sense institutionally: the postwar period saw enormous growth in museums and universities, and there was a powerful demand for a narrative of recovery and reclamation. The Greenbergian version in particular is also a story, a technique, that could be reproduced, and it was, extensively—it was a great discursive success, curatorially and pedagogically. In a way its success parallels that of the modern discipline of art history when its German founders like Erwin Panofsky flee Hitler for Britain and the States: it, too, gets streamlined and simplified into a technique—primarily that of iconography—which is then circulated and passed down to subsequent generations.

BB: I would twist that, and say again that this narrative of modernism also has the specific *telos* of postwar American liberal democracy. It wants to implement, in response to the catastrophe of the bourgeois nation states of Europe, a different kind of access to education, a different kind of egalitarianism in aesthetic experience. I would not reduce it all to reconstruction ideology; I think there is a more complicated *telos*, with other political implications, in the institutionalization of the discourse of modernism. That, too, is part of avant-garde culture in New York at

▲ Introduction 1, 1960a ● 1913, 1917, 1944a ■ 1951 ▲ 1965 ● 1942a, 1947b, 1959c

the time, and certainly part of Greenberg's project as well. And, as you say, though his omissions are disastrous, he deals with the artists that he selects, American and European, more profoundly and more precisely than anyone else does. He is the one who, in a sense, redeems the modernist legacy for postwar memory.

YAB: It becomes clear now how he was able to do so. Greenberg pretended to a kind of ideological neutrality; this allowed him to make his positivist turn of seeming simply to describe the art. And this turn freed him from the pathos of existentialist critics like Rosenberg. Everything was discarded: an ex-Marxist, Greenberg could present himself as objective—as objective as an engineer or a scientist. So he became the pure empiricist who only describes. And he did it perfectly well …

HF: Let's move on to a third important model of prewar art, the one ▲ proposed by Peter Bürger in *Theory of the Avant-Garde*. Bürger makes two opposed claims: on the one hand, that a modernist autonomy of art was achieved in the late nineteenth century (earlier than in the Greenbergian narrative), and, on the other hand, that this aesthetic autonomy was attacked by "the historical avant-gardes" in the early twentieth century, both in forms of art (for example, the Dadaist assault on painting and sculpture) and in institutions of art (for example, the Futurist assault on the museums). Bürger goes on to construct a story about the tragic failure of this avant-garde and its farcical repetition in the postwar period, a project he dismisses as a "neo-avant-garde," as a recuperation of the historical critique of autonomous art as a new form of art.

roundtable

BB: There are two things to add immediately: Bürger is a German *literary* historian, and he published that book in 1974. Even for this relatively early date it is very schematic; and yet, as you said before, he does realert us to those legacies that American formalists like Greenberg and Fried as well as European writers in their wake had disallowed or disavowed—Dada culture in all of its forms, Surrealism, Russian Constructivism and Soviet Productivism. Bürger was not the only one to do this; he wrote in a post-1968 moment that brought all of those practices back into view. In a sense he sums up this work.

HF: And as you pointed out once, he obscures one of his own conditions of possibility—contemporary artists like Marcel ● Broodthaers and Hans Haacke, who commented not only on the historical avant-garde but also on the neo-avant-garde—on the limits of this neo-avant-garde as well, the very limits that Bürger castigates so strongly.

BB: Yes, he concludes a process that was in the works for ten years or so in both scholarly and artistic practice.

YAB: And in exhibitions too.

BB: Bürger also failed to understand how those historical avant-garde models had differed tremendously from one another; this point was discussed extensively by his critics, at least in Germany when his text was first published. Of course these differences were both theoretical and political. For example, while Freudo-Marxism was constitutive of Surrealism, Dadaism had departed from rather different theoretical positions, ranging from mysticism to the beginnings of structural linguistics to Leninism in Berlin Dada. There was also an anarchistic, even nihilistic quality in Dadaism, which was not at all present in Russian Constructivism, let alone in Soviet Productivism. And while a reorientation toward collectivity was foundational to the Russian and Soviet avant-garde, it was not the kind of collectivity that De Stijl proposed in Holland. And so on. One should challenge Bürger's model on these points, and ask what exact features of the various avant-garde models he was bringing back into view at that time. One aspect that was *not* brought back by Bürger is the way that the bourgeois public sphere was not only contested by the historical avant-garde but also eroded and/or displaced by the rise of mass-cultural spheres—in Weimar Germany, in Italy both prior and during Fascism, and then under the totalitarian regimes of Germany and the Soviet Union.

HF: As important as the Bürger text is, it is schematic not only about the different avant-gardes, but also in its opposition of "the institution of art" and "life practice," of "art" and "reality." To begin with, the institution of art is radically different in different countries, and sometimes in different cities—think of the diverse contexts of Dada alone around World War I: Zurich, a neutral but tempestuous site; Berlin, in political revolt; Cologne, occupied; Hanover, an enclave; Paris, vectored by different political forces, artistic movements, antimodernist sentiments; New York, distant from these troubles, a scene of salon and exhibition scandals more than anything else.

YAB: What is also strange is that Bürger never alludes to the invention of the art market at the time of the historical avant-garde or to its enormous growth at the time of the neo-avant-garde. The ▲ auction consortium "Peau de l'Ours" was the first time that modern art made a profit, and this had an enormous impact. And yet it's as though the market doesn't exist for Bürger. In Germany too the art market was already very developed before WWI, with Herwarth Walden's der Sturm and other galleries …

HF: That's in part what I mean: the opposition of "autonomous art" and "life practice," if it can be posited historically at all, is already breaking down at the time of the historical avant-garde because of economic forces.

YAB: Yes. In a funny way Bürger treats the problem of the avant-garde in a historical vacuum.

BB: This oversight is especially surprising coming from a member of the 1968 generation for whom the problem of art's rapidly increasing commodification had become such a key question.

HF: What about a related question—the "mediation" of the historical avant-garde, the fact that it sometimes emerged in the very space of mass-media forms like the newspaper? One ● example is given in our "1909" entry on Futurism: Marinetti publishes "The First Manifesto of Futurism" in *Le Figaro*. Another

▲ Introduction 2, 1960a ● 1971, 1972a, 1972b ▲ 1914 ● 1909

▲ occurs in 1925 in the context of the "Arts décoratifs" exhibition at the World Fair in Paris ...

YAB: Yes: the transformation of the avant-garde into design, into luxury goods—Cubism turned into Art Deco tables.

HF: It happens fast—in that case in ten years or so—and it happens again and again.

YAB: And it completely saturates the perception of what modernism is. Here it's fascinating to look at Italy under Fascism where you have luxurious villas for Fascist leaders decorated with Cubist paintings, Eileen Gray tables, and so on.

HF: That too is not part of the Bürger account—or any other familiar one, for that matter. Also, on the one side his opposition of institution of art and life practice tends to occlude the various projects to *transform* the institution of art or to construct a new one altogether, as in the Russian Constructivist attempt to found different kinds of schools, different modes of making and exhibiting, production and distribution, to make a proletarian cultural or indeed public sphere. On the other side Bürger seems very romantic about life practice. This is a criticism that Jürgen Habermas makes too: What does it mean to break apart the putative autonomy of art under conditions of mass media and culture?

BB: As of the present day we know: it means the regime of total desublimation.

YAB: A good test case is the "Congress of International Progressive ● Artists" held in Düsseldorf in May 1922—that gives us a range of positions. The one that ends up as the most Leftist, most avant-gardist, is made up of such different figures as Hans Richter, El Lissitzky, and Theo van Doesburg—a German Dadaist, a Russian artist connected to both Suprematism and Constructivism, and the ■ Dutch head of De Stijl. They protest that the others in the Congress don't have a definition of what a new and progressive art is: "All you want to do," they say, "is to federate your movements so as to build up an art market." There's an amazingly clear analysis of the avant-garde, especially from Lissitzky, in its own historical moment: a recognition of its imminent failure and dispersal if the project is not carried beyond what I would call a "guild" mode.

HF: Isn't there, hidden in your example, another side of this failure, another side of the condition of mass media and culture, which is to say the possibility, for the first time, of a real internationalism of the avant-garde? And isn't there also a utopian dimension there, not only in individual projects but in the collective coming-together of such diverse figures at events like the Congress, which was not immediately commodified then and should not be forgotten now? How can we restore those dimensions to that moment of international meetings, exhibitions, manifestos, and so on? There were enormous hopes for modernism. We might see it now as just another ruse of history, but it wasn't all delusion.

BB: It depended on the programmatic theorization of what a real culture of the proletarian public sphere might become at the time, and the Congress addressed the possibilities of its realization. One necessary condition for artistic practice was to live up to the aspirations of post-nation-state identities—identities that are not only defined by proletarian class and collectivity but also understood in terms of a subjectivity that could be constructed outside the parameters of the nation state. That's the reason why internationalism at that moment could be political and proletarian as well as aesthetic and avant-garde.

HF: One might have thought that World War I would have dashed the hope of such internationalism, as even most socialist parties submitted to nationalist imperatives, but it didn't: internationalism revived, and thrived, in the twenties. And in part it did so on account of the war, in reaction against it.

YAB: The case of Berlin in the early twenties is relevant here, especially after the end of the blockade isolating Russia, which was immediately followed by the arrival of many Russian artists and writers of all persuasions (not that many belonged to the old guard linked to the Czarist regime, as these tended to go to Paris). Members of the Hungarian avant-garde also came to Berlin fleeing the military coup that had ended a Soviet-like republic after just a few months in 1919. So in those years Berlin became a kind of platform of internationalism. The German intellectuals (and Berlin Dada in particular) were the most forceful: "We don't want to be caught in that horrible nationalistic butchery again." There was also still the hope, on the part of Russian pro-Soviet artists and writers (such as Lissitzky, who arrived in Germany in 1922), that they could export new means for the production and reception of art and culture. In fact one of the things that Bürger does not discuss is the will, on the part of many avant-garde practitioners in the late teens and twenties, to produce new kinds of distribution for their art—all their journals, for example, are also "art projects" in a way. The proliferation of those little magazines is very different from the immersion in mass media of Futurism, with Marinetti publishing his manifesto in *Le Figaro*. On the other hand, one might argue that, because those journals were not mass-produced, there was already a sort of retrenchment—but that was due to a lack of means as much as anything else.

HF: There's another possibility here, though one very dependent on particular political conditions, and that is the example of John Heartfield, who published some of his most critical photomontages as covers of mass worker magazines like the illustrated weekly ▲ *Arbeiter Illustrierte Zeitung* with circulations in the hundreds of thousands. But you're right: there is a real divide between the micro media of the journal and the mass media of the newspaper; there are some attempts, however, to cut across the gap, and not to be satisfied with either side.

BB: Marinetti simply accepted the given media apparatus as an institution that could not be contested. That is what happens again in a later moment, closer to our own time. But there is an interim moment when other distribution forms are conceived and alternative public spheres, whether proletarian or simply avant-gardist, are claimed. And sometimes they are acted upon, and

▲ 1925a ● 1928 ■ 1915, 1917, 1920, 1921, 1926 ▲ 1920, 1930a

eventually asserted as actually existing—for example, the imaging ▲ of a proletarian public sphere in Heartfield's work—but then the whole space collapses.

YAB: There are also moments of great aberration—like Mayakovsky's books of poems *150,000,000* being printed in editions of five thousand by the Soviet State Publishing House in 1920 (Lenin was furious about that, and severely criticized Lunacharsky, the minister of culture and education, for what he considered a stupid mistake). Or Naum Gabo's "Realist Manifesto"—it was also printed in great numbers because the Soviet authorities thought he was a realist painter!

HF: One thing that Bürger does do is to put into play critical and philosophical texts, mostly from the Frankfurt School, that are roughly of the same period as these modernisms. He has enough historical distance to juxtapose writings about the avant-garde and mass culture by Benjamin and Adorno with actual practices of the artists; in fact one of his important theses is the shared historicity of the concepts at work in such texts and works alike. In this textbook we have attempted similar moves. Frequently these are connections not of causal influence so much as of discursive affinity: epistemological fields that different artists and intellectuals share, often without knowing it.

RK: Like the role of the index in Duchamp or of the uncanny in ● Surrealism. That conceptual clarity allows for a kind of critical archaeology of artistic practice.

YAB: And it also allows for phenomena that fall outside the usual histories of modern art to be discussed.

HF: The question I wanted to ask is different: now that we can look back at what we have written about the prewar period, what are our own occlusions? (Our exclusions might be clear enough.) What other kinds of connections have we failed to see in this historical field?

BB: My first statement in this register of self-critique would be that we too, like everyone else in our field, have not managed to address what has emerged as one of the key questions about the century: the apparatus of mass culture in the totalitarian public sphere (that's a contradiction in terms and meant to be). With its annihilating antimodernisms, that apparatus precipitated the great hiatus in avant-garde culture from 1933 to 1945 in Western Europe (in many countries, some voluntarily, some as the victims of occupation). How might it be understood now as an anticipation of the eventual breakdown of the boundaries of avant-garde culture and the mass-cultural public sphere in the postwar period? The boundaries between those spheres were much more porous, damaged, indeed destroyed in the period 1933 to 1945 than we have long assumed, and we believed, also for far too long, that the reconstruction of those boundaries in postwar neo-avant-garde culture could actually hold up. What we see now is that they didn't hold up, that they haven't for a long time.

RK: Can you give me an example?

HF: Maybe I can. Part of the story of the triumphal renewal of modernist art after the war was its radical separation from unsavory politics: if it was to represent liberal democracy, freedom of expression, and so on, any contamination of this sort had to be corrected. (Obviously this was overdetermined: the presentation of ▲ Abstract Expressionism as the epitome of the liberal spirit, for example, was made in the face of a prior attack from the McCarthyite Right, which associated abstraction with ● Communism.) In any case the connections between Futurism and Fascism, say, had to be obscured; or, to choose a case that strikes closer to home for some of us, the connections between Russian Constructivism and Stalinism. Now obviously these are occlusions that have prompted very reactive counterreadings in our own time, almost antimodernist readings—for example, that Constructivism ■ somehow leads to Stalinism, that the Constructivist paragon of the artist as engineer of a new proletarian cult is actually embodied in Stalin. But those arguments are simply reactions against a reaction, and so are doubly reductive, and they don't get at the ways not only that some modernists lined up on the far Right but also that some modernisms were bound up, paradoxically, with antimodern positions—were "reactionary modernisms" in that sense. This imbrication has become historically available now in a way that it wasn't for people who had to purify modernism of any such political taint or tie, either to Fascism or to Communism.

YAB: There was a separation of modernism from totalitarianism, but there was also a purification of modernism from the avant-garde, so to speak, from the movements we've discussed—Dada, Constructivism, and so on. The avant-garde became a side dish to the great feast of modernism from Picasso and Matisse through Mondrian to Newman.

BB: But those are your artists!

YAB: Yes, but I also see how they were used to push the avant-garde into an ornamental role in the epic of modernism.

HF: At least we have put some of those stories back into play together: the story of modernism with that of the avant-garde, and both with that of antimodernism—not with adequate depth, to be sure, but at least it is sketched.

YAB: Do we want to discuss here the second argument of Bürger, the failure of the historical avant-garde (he never puts any quotation marks around "failure"). What was this failure exactly? The failure to transform the world? As Hal says, that's a little harsh on the part of Mr. Bürger.

BB: Let alone the failure of the postwar neo-avant-garde.

YAB: It's bizarre from a Marxist critic. What did he expect?

HF: That might be a hangover from 1968 too.

BB: That's right, and he's German.

HF: Well, that explains it all.

BB: It's a traditional German task to give grades to history. The

▲ Introduction 2, 1920 ● 1918, 1924, 1930b, 1931, 1935, 1942b

▲ 1947b, 1949 ● 1909 ■ 1921

Constructivist side of the historical avant-garde is one part of the story; another part is the Surrealist side, and I want to return to it for a moment. In Surrealism a post-nation-state identity was put forward on the basis of radically emancipatory psychoanalytic models of subject-formation. These contested national identity as violently as a politically class-bound model of subject-formation did in the context of the Soviet avant-garde. It's not clear that Bürger treated that dimension, in his conception of the Surrealist subject, either, or whether William Rubin did, when, as chief curator at the Museum of Modern Art, he mounted his show of Dada and Surrealism in 1968. How did Surrealism come back then? We said that these exhibitions predate Bürger's text, and the Bürger–Rubin axis is an interesting one to consider in that light. Did the reception of Surrealism at that time recover its full historical scope, or did it come back already as a highly confined and fetishized historical construct in the form of particular images and objects?

HF: And another question: how was its model of the unconscious treated? Was it seen, in keeping with the sixties, in affirmative ▲ terms, à la Herbert Marcuse or Norman O. Brown, as a liberatory unconscious, an Eros-unconscious, an unconscious, moreover, that unlike in Marcuse and Brown was too often thought of in terms of a body that is private and not collective?

RK: In Rubin's hands Surrealism came back as painting and sculpture, not in terms of photography and texts. Twenty years later, when I did my show of Surrealist photography with Jane Livingston, "L'Amour fou: Surrealism and Photography" (1985), it was a historical and theoretical project, and it developed in resistance to the repression of that part of Surrealist history.

YAB: In reexamining the issue you redefined the way we look at Surrealism, because, as Benjamin said, what Rubin attempted to do—which is strange coming from him—was to rescue Surrealism ...

RK: To rescue it as painting and sculpture. Whereas what interested me was how important photography was, and how Surrealism was disseminated through its magazines ...

YAB: If Rubin had been more open to that, he would have had an easier case to make, because he couldn't find a lot of ammunition in Surrealism for the grand narrative of modernist painting. He had Miró, Masson, Matta ...

HF: Yes, Surrealism was still seen in Bretonian terms as a story of a liberatory desire with painting conceived as its primary vehicle of expression. What the "L'Amour fou" show did was to move the • conversation away from Breton toward Georges Bataille, and from painting to photography, and to see Surrealism more as an attack on form, indeed as the disintegration of the very notion of form-giving mediums, which was pursued further in your exhibition "L'Informe" (1996). A very different understanding of psychoanalysis also emerged here: that the Surrealist unconscious had a dark side, not simply in relation to desire, which is not only liberatory but also bound up with lack, but also in relation to the drives, drives that can be destructive, even deadly, as with the death drive. Perhaps the sixties reading was inflected by the Marcusean discourse of Eros; by the eighties, things looked different, and this difference speaks to the different politics of the two moments, one marked by revolts of many sorts, the other by ▲ despair about Reaganite reaction and AIDS deaths.

BB: Perhaps we should also ask what Rubin's approach to Dada was—for Dada was also included in his exhibition and its catalogue, "Dada, Surrealism, and Their Legacies." Not to belabor the point, but he did the same thing to the Dada legacy that he did to Surrealism: it became a constellation of astonishing objects and assemblages. Dada was not the photomontages of John • Heartfield, for example; typically, Heartfield didn't even appear in either the show or the book.

HF: Rubin saw Dada in part through the prism of the objects and assemblages that emerged in the Rauschenberg–Johns moment. There was also the precedent of William Seitz's MoMA show "The Art of Assemblage" (1961), which favored Duchamp, Schwitters, Joseph Cornell, Rauschenberg ...

RK: We have to realize too that Rubin was in constant dialogue with Greenberg, trying to convince him that he, Rubin, was not on the wrong track, and that within Surrealism and even Dada there were worthy modernist practices. He was pleading with Greenberg—

BB: And with Barr too, no?

YAB: I want to add two things to this discussion of Dada and Surrealism. Rubin also made his show in response to a wave of neo-Surrealist work in New York—early Oldenburgs, for example, ■ his soft objects, which Rubin saw in relation to Yves Tanguy, say. That's how Rubin thought—in terms of those kinds of juxtapositions. And he always disagreed with Greenberg on Pop; Rubin supported it. And so if he could justify his interest in this new work by finding historical precedents in Surrealism, well, that was one strategy.

BB: Magritte via Johns, for example.

YAB: Yes. My other point about the rereading of Dada and Surrealism in this period concerns the exhibition mounted by Dawn Ades and David Sylvester in London.

HF: That's ten years later, though—1978.

YAB: Yes, but it was the first time there was a show of material entirely based on journals. It was very intelligently organized in relation to what they thought was the crucial medium of those movements (again, the journals were not mass circulation).

RK: One thing that I discovered as I began to work on "L'Amour fou" is that nobody had read the articles in those magazines, for ◆ example in *Minotaure*. There was all this very interesting material, and it wasn't being taken into account.

BB: In light of that legacy we've just discussed, it's all the more astonishing that the reconstitution of an American avant-garde was

▲ Introduction 2 • 1924, 1930b ▲ 1987 • Introduction 2, 1920 ■ 1961 ◆ 1924, 1930b

so programmatically defined in terms of nation-state identity. Both political internationalism and avant-garde internationalism were totally reversed in the constitution of a New York avant-garde. Its very names are foundational: the New York School, American art, and so on.

YAB: "The Triumph of American Painting."

BB: Yes, the sheer triumphalism of the discourse—I don't blame it on the artists.

HF: Some embraced it.

YAB: But others were not happy with it at all. Newman again was absolutely opposed, for example.

HF: But might some of this triumphalism be compensatory, that is to say, wish-fulfilling? I mean there was an enormous sense of inferiority among American artists around World War II vis-à-vis ▲ European art—in Gorky, in early Pollock ...

BB: I've always disliked that argument because I think American modernism was fairly sophisticated even then.

YAB: And the inferiority complex mostly disappeared when the ● Surrealists arrived in New York and were demystified.

HF: But in an earlier moment it was still active, and Pollock and company didn't have the earlier American modernism—of Stieglitz and his circle—to draw on as a resource.

BB: Why is that edited out or forgotten? By Greenberg and other critics, and by us too, again and again, generation after generation? We all tend to say American modernist art begins with Pollock. I would find the argument of the inferiority complex more generative as an idea if I could understand what it originated in, and why it resorted to a nation-state identity.

RK: But early on there were already international connections. For example, the Museum of Modern Art founded an international council in 1953; early on they decided to make a concerted incursion into European art. When this council revved up, its effect was to promote the idea of an imperial cultural modernism that went with the Marshall Plan.

YAB: But that started even before, and at first outside of MoMA—in the State Department immediately after the war. The first major exhibition of this program was called "Advancing American Art," and it was shown at the Met in October 1946 before splitting into two groups of works, one small exhibit traveling to Cuba and Latin America, the other, larger one going to Paris and other European capitals such as Prague. It contained works by the first generation of American modernists—the Stieglitz group was well represented—but it was on the whole a mixed bag (Thomas Hart Benton, Ben Shahn, etc.). It was a rather successful diplomatic coup in Europe, though its reception in the States was very controversial, with angry congressmen protesting against the use of taxpayers' money. The State Department program continued its activity until 1956, when it was abruptly terminated after protests against "communist-inspired art." It was at this point that MoMA's International Council began to really roll.

BB: That's a nice arc: to go from the dream of a proletarian cultural sphere to avant-garde internationalism, and from there to the State Department and International Council of the Museum of Modern Art!

1 See Serge Guilbaut, *How New York Stole the Idea of Modern Art: Abstract Expressionism, Freedom, and the Cold War* (Chicago and London: University of Chicago Press, 1983) and T. J. Clark, *Farewell to an Idea* (New Haven and London: Yale University Press, date), respectively.

2 Peter Bürger, *Theory of the Avant-Garde* (1974), trans. Michael Shaw (Minneapolis: University of Minnesota Press, 1984).

3 "This would amount to nothing less than the establishment of a perpetual revolution—perpetual because bent on unceasing radical criticism of itself. It is no wonder such an ideal has not been realized in the realm of politics, but it seems to me that the development of modernist painting over the past century has led to a situation that may be described in these terms." (Michael Fried, *Art and Objecthood* [Chicago: University of Chicago Press, 1998], p. 218.)

▲ 1942a ● 1942a, 1942b

1945 – 1949

332 1945 David Smith makes *Pillar of Sunday*: constructed sculpture is caught between the craft basis of traditional art and the industrial basis of modern manufacturing. RK

337 1946 Jean Dubuffet exhibits his "*hautes pâtes*," which confirm the existence of a new, scatological trend in postwar French art, soon to be named "*informel*." YAB
box • *Art brut* HF

343 1947a Josef Albers begins his "Variant" paintings at Black Mountain College in North Carolina a year after László Moholy-Nagy dies in Chicago: imported to the United States, the model of the Bauhaus is transformed by different artistic imperatives and institutional pressures. HF

348 1947b The publication of *Possibilities* in New York marks the coalescence of Abstract Expressionism as a movement. YAB

355 1949 *Life* magazine asks its readers "Is he the greatest living painter in the United States?": the work of Jackson Pollock emerges as the symbol of advanced art. RK

1945

David Smith makes *Pillar of Sunday*: constructed sculpture is caught between the craft basis of traditional art and the industrial basis of modern manufacturing.

Suspended equally between the primitive and the puritanical, David Smith's (1906–65) *Pillar of Sunday* [**1**] perfectly expresses the formal and technical ambivalence of constructed sculpture in the forties. Organized as a totem pole, the work is a vertical agglomeration of mementos to the sculptor's rigid upbringing in the American Midwest (the church choir, for example, or the Sunday family dinner), topped by the image of a liberating, sexualized bird.

Executed in forged and welded steel that was then painted, the object declares a technical allegiance to the sculptural idiom through which Smith entered the field in the mid-thirties, namely the Cubist-identified constructed sculpture that had evolved out of ▲ collage at the hands of Pablo Picasso in the mid-teens and had been brought to a pitch of accomplishment in the late twenties in the work of Julio González (1876–1942). But if welded metal construction had meant the use of warped fins and bent wires in order to achieve the visual openness of what González called "drawing in space" [**2**], it had also implied the opportunistic incorporation of ordinary metal objects into the assembly, as when Picasso pressed a kitchen colander into service as the head of an otherwise schematic figure (*Head of a Woman* [**3**]), a throwback to his having used a real sugar spoon as the crowning element of his Cubist *Absinthe Glass* of 1914. And from this formal exploitation of the found object it was only a short jump to the possibilities of sounding its psychological resonance, which the Surrealists explored in a very different ● development of the idea of sculpture as a collage or an assemblage.

Free-standing collage

At the hands of the Surrealists, two variations were struck on sculpture-as-construction. The first was formal; the second, technical. The formal one had to do with the Surrealists' willingness to abandon the whole idea of drawing in space, which had been Cubism's original way of defying traditional sculpture, with its fetishization of closed volumes, whether in carved stone or cast bronze. If the objects chosen to enter a sculpture become candidates not on formal grounds, however, but on those of psychological association, then they might come in any shape or substance—glass ■ bottles just as well as metal scrap, fur-covered teacups just as easily as

1 • David Smith, *Pillar of Sunday*, 1945
Steel and paint, 77.8 x 41 x 21.5 (31 x $16\frac{5}{8}$ x $8\frac{1}{2}$)

▲ Introduction 3, 1912 ● 1931 ■ Introduction 1

iron grids. Salvador Dalí's *Venus de Milo with the Drawers* (1936)—a copy of the famous statue in the Louvre, with a row of little drawers, that one can slide in or out, stacked along the nude figure's torso—is a perfect example of the way Surrealist sculpture transgressed the modernist, formal credo of openwork construction.

At the technical level there was yet another transgression. The depths the Surrealists wished to plumb being those of the unconscious, they were also understood to be at variance with both the refinements of high culture and the rationalism of modern technology. Primitive in nature, the unconscious had been most forcefully given form, the Surrealists argued, by primitive art, a sculptural example which was both opportunistic—incorporating anything at hand, from trading beads to feathers to tin cans—and agglomerative, things hinged and hung and stuck together. So if the Cubist base for constructed sculpture placed the emphasis on *construction,* thus opening the way for a technological, highly industrialized model to interpret "drawing in space" as steel and ▲ glass forms of building (as in the work of Vladimir Tatlin or Naum Gabo), the Surrealist reception of it reinterpreted construction as *bricolage,* which is to say, a primitive form of making-do, of quasi-irrational, associative thinking.

2 • Julio González, *Woman Combing Her Hair*, 1936
Wrought iron, 132.1 x 34.3 x 62.6 (52 x 13½ x 24⅝)

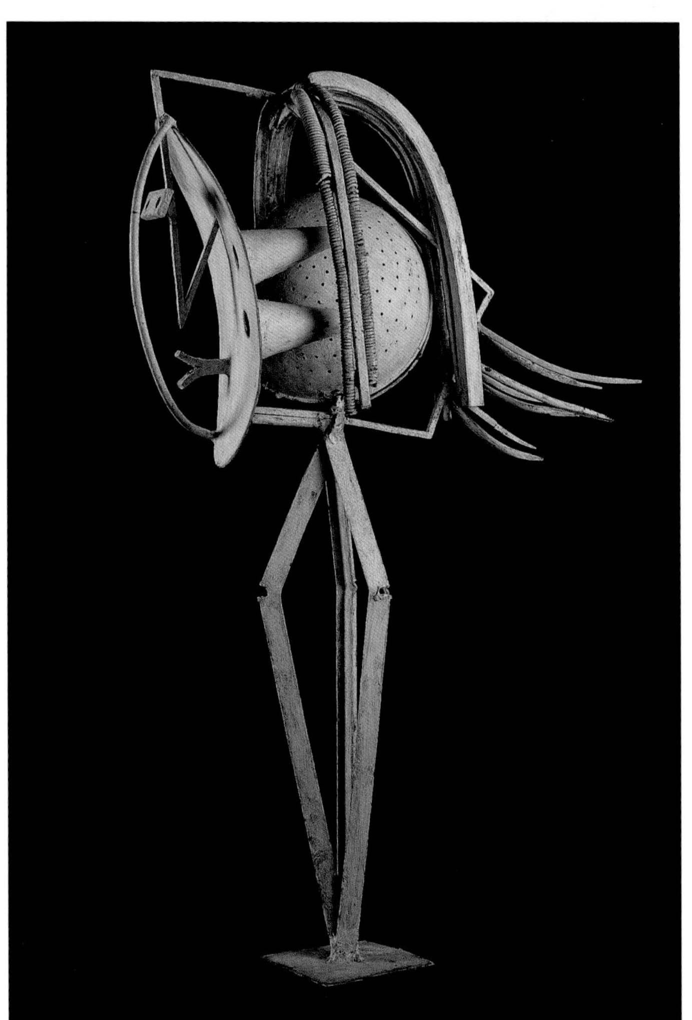

3 • Pablo Picasso, *Head of a Woman*, 1929–30
Iron and mixed media, 100 x 37 x 59 (39⅜ x 14⅝ x 23¼)

This is the significance of the totem's having taken over the structural order of Smith's work in the mid-forties, as well as of his desire to exploit the charged memories of his youth and his willingness to incorporate figurative forms that, like the bird, are classically volumetric in nature. And, given the strength of this claim on his imagination, the artisanal and the figurative would continue to do battle with the industrial and the abstract throughout the rest of his career.

The most obvious place to see this is in the series of *Tanktotems* that Smith made during the fifties and into the sixties [**4**]. The "totem" half of this designation signals the persistence of a certain kind of emotive content, while the "tank" half—which refers to the industrial materials to which Smith was now turning, specifically here the tops of boiler tanks—addresses Smith's modernist ambitions, his desire for abstraction and technology. The struggle between these models is itself the source of the great formal interest of Smith's sculpture, as he managed his own peculiar marriage of abstraction and totemism in his ensuing work.

▲ 1914, 1921, 1937b, 1955b

4 • David Smith, *Tanktotem V*, 1955–6
Varnished steel, 245.7 x 132.1 x 38.1 (96¾ x 52 x 15)

If the totem is basically figurative, a real object or animal invested with great significance for the human subject whose identity depends on it and who must therefore protect it, totemism is inimical to the aims of abstract art. The former can be brought into a relationship with the latter only if the sculptor's move to "protect" the totem-object takes the form of a kind of visual camouflage, the dissolution of the object's intelligible gestalt from any given viewpoint, something in turn made possible only by the feats of engineering—of suspension and near detachment—uniquely available to the industrial techniques of welding, cantilevering, etc.

Totem and taboo

This theme of the "totem-object both proffered and withdrawn" forms the consistent organizational armature of Smith's later sculpture, whether in the series of *Voltri-Boltons* (1962–3), welded of found steel parts, or in the sequence of *Cubis* (1961–5), put together of polished, stainless-steel polyhedrons, the last and most nearly abstract of his work. For in *Voltri-Bolton XXIII* [**5**], for example, the primitive setting of the sacrificial table, which Smith had examined in far more figurative works such as *Head as a Still Life II* (1942), *Sacrifice* (1950), or *The Banquet* (1951), is once more made into the pedestal for a still-life assemblage that implies the presence, as well, of a human, sacrificial figure. This "figure" which consists of three elements tack-welded one above the other—a rectangular plane, an I-beam section set perpendicular to the plane and balanced on it only at one point, an equally precariously poised tank top—is unintelligible as a coherent, figurative form from most angles, reading instead as part of a collection of geometric shapes. Indeed, one of these shapes, a large, open rectangle, seems to be a kind of picture frame through which the artist is giving us a clue as to the correct approach to his work. It is only, however, by moving out of the axis of this frame and thereby eclipsing one's view of it, that the totem-object comes into miragelike focus, only to vanish again as the physicality of the steel forms (the forward thrust of the I-beam, for example) pushes it out of the "picture."

In this resistance to the idea of stereometric rationalism, whereby the intersection at right-angles of identical or similar profiles creates an object of maximum intelligibility, *Voltri-Bolton XXIII* refuses the ▲Constructivist models that Smith's allegiance to modern materials and fabrication practices might otherwise seem to claim. The literal transparency sought by Tatlin, Rodchenko, or Gabo via their use of openwork mesh or clear plastics was only the material vehicle for an even more insistent conceptual transparency, as repetitive forms

5 • David Smith, *Voltri-bolton XXIII*, 1963
Welded steel, 176.5 x 72.7 x 61 (69½ x 28⅝ x 24)

▲ 1914, 1921

exfoliated from a coherent core in an imitation of technology's rationalization of both form and its production. And indeed, if the Russians' concept of stereometry further emphasized the possibility of simultaneous, collective experience of the work, which would be intelligible from any place within a space it thereby declared as truly public, the American's exploitation of unique, shifting points of view places his totems in the realm of the subjective.

Perhaps no one expressed the ambivalence that had settled onto postwar American and European sculpture more eloquently than ▲ the American critic Clement Greenberg, who set the critical terms for constructed sculpture in the late fifties. Arguing that sculpture's "genius" was now the function of a technologically modern concept of volume—"Feats of 'engineering' that aim to provide the greatest possible amount of visibility with the least possible expenditure of tactile surface belong categorically to the free and *total* medium of sculpture. The constructor-sculptor can, literally, draw in the air with a single strand of wire"—Greenberg interpreted the implications of this in a way that turned its back on the objectivity of "engineering" and instead embraced the subjectivism of a kind of visual phenomenon that he himself would call a "mirage." Characterizing the new technology through its release of open forms into "the continuity and neutrality of a space which light alone inflects, without regard to the laws of gravity," Greenberg drew from this fact what some (in particular, the Minimalists) would see as perverse conclusions, insisting on its consequences as a form of opticality that "brings anti-illusionism full circle." Now, he argued, "Instead of the illusion of things, we are offered the illusion of modalities: namely, that matter is incorporeal, weightless, and exists only optically like a mirage" ("Sculpture in Our Time" [1958]).

The radical subjectivity of "opticality" could be associated with the open "frame" through which *Voltri-Bolton XXIII* had registered the importance of point of view for the understanding of the work, even if in this case its particular rectangle did not yield the "correct" aspect. For the frame not only opposes a visual to a tactile field, it also denies simultaneous collective connection to the meaning of the work, since only one person at a time can look through the frame at the precise angle perpendicular to its opening. It is this stress on point of view that the English sculptor Anthony Caro (born 1924), David Smith's most obvious formal heir, then carried forward.

This is perhaps most obvious in a work like Caro's *Carriage* [**6**], in which two large planes stand opposed to one another across eight feet of space through which only a bent steel pipe bridges along the floor between them. Both of these planes are composed

6 • Anthony Caro, *Carriage*, 1966
Steel painted blue, 195.5 x 203.5 x 396.5 (77 x 80 x 156)

▲ 1942a, 1960b

of expanded metal to form a shimmering, optical mesh or screen, each being braced on three sides by steel channel elements which create for one of the planes a closed upper left corner, and for the other a closed lower right one. If the scale of the work appeals to one's tactile experience, since the object's physical expanse invites and allows entry into its midst and inspection of its parts, the filigree of its mesh, painted a sea green, is clearly pointing to the reabsorption of that physical, tactile condition by one that is more specifically immaterial and visual. The sense, furthermore, that this is indeed where the meaning of the work lies comes at the moment at which one's movement around the sculpture produces the coherence of the two sets of braces into the single gestalt of a "frame," one that collapses the physical space within the work and re-creates the sculpture as the function of a singular and purely optical point of view. But in turn, the physical openness of the object allows that "meaning"—which we could read as an abstract statement of coherence, the "praegnanz" of Gestalt psychology—to invade the sculpture from every other point of view so that, to use Michael Fried's terms for this, "at every moment the work itself is wholly manifest." Using language that clearly connects to Greenberg's idea of opticality, in his influential essay "Art and Objecthood" (1967) Fried characterized his experience of Caro in terms of the simultaneity and immediacy of the visual field itself:

> *It is this continuous and entire* presentness, *amounting, as it were, to the perpetual creation of itself, that one experiences as a kind of* instantaneousness, *as though if only one were infinitely more acute, a single infinitely brief instant would be long enough to see everything, to experience the work in all its depth and fullness, to be forever convinced by it.*

The gauntlet Fried threw down in "Art and Objecthood" articulates the divide between the two self-proclaimed heirs of constructed sculpture: the hand-wrought, welded sculpture of Smith and Caro, with its craft associations of applied color and unique assemblage, on the one hand, and the industrially fabri- ▲cated work of the Minimalists, with its commitments to technological coloration—enamels, plastics—and serial production on the other. But it is in the work of John Chamberlain (born •1927) in the United States, and that of Arman or César in Paris, that one sees a third, far more pessimistic option. For whether opticalist or minimalist, the former two positions declare the positive, even utopian, possibilities encoded in modern materials and forms of production. It is the third, however, that marries "construction" with "production" and comes up with the conclusion of planned obsolescence and waste.

Indeed, pushing the found-object component of the medium, present within constructed sculpture from its very inception, way past Surrealist *bricolage* and into the ravages of consumer society, a sculptor like Chamberlain exploited the ready-made surfaces of the automobile body, recovered now from the crash-heap to which it had been consigned, as expendable scrap. Loaded with irony, a work like *Velvet White* **[7]** seems to project a whole history of modernist sculptural debate within its form—the tension between the claims of monolithic volume and openwork construction; the opposition between rationalized structure and Surrealist caprice; the distinction between craft and industrial color, as well as that between the mass-produced and the unique object, the ▲former stripped of "aura," the latter clinging to it—even while, with its switch from production to consumption, from construction to readymade, it seems to announce the obsolescence of •sculpture itself as a category. Perhaps this is why Donald Judd, in a move that seems surprising from a formal point of view, included a work by Chamberlain as one of the illustrations for his essay "Specific Objects," his declaration of the end of sculpture as a specific medium.

7 • John Chamberlain, *Velvet White*, 1962
Painted and chromium-plated steel, 205.1 x 134.6 x 124.9 (80¾ x 53 x 49⅛)

FURTHER READING

Michael Fried, "New Work by Anthony Caro," "Caro's Abstractness," and "Art and Objecthood," *Art and Objecthood* (Chicago: University of Chicago Press, 1998)

Clement Greenberg, "Sculpture in Our Time" and "David Smith's New Sculpture," *The Collected Essays and Criticism, Vol. Four: Modernism with a Vengeance, 1957–1969*, ed. John O'Brian (Chicago and London: University of Chicago Press, 1993)

Rosalind Krauss, *Passages in Modern Sculpture* (New York: Viking Press, 1977)

▲ 1965 • 1960a ▲ 1935 • 1965

1946

Jean Dubuffet exhibits his *"hautes pâtes,"* which confirm the existence of a new, scatological trend in postwar French art, soon to be named *"informel."*

"After Dadaism, here is Cacaism." Those words were penned by the French critic Henri Jeanson in response to "Mirobolus, Macadam & Cie, Hautes Pâtes," the infamous exhibition of Jean Dubuffet (1901–85) held at the Galerie René Drouin in Paris in May 1946. Though published in the satirical weekly *Le Canard enchaîné*, they were perfectly in line with the general response to the show: from everywhere, from left and right, one could hear shrieks of disgust at Dubuffet's "scatology." This was not the first time that the painter had been decried by the press—his first solo exhibition of neoprimitivist, highly colorful scenes of urban life, a year and a half before, in the aftermath of the Liberation of Paris in August 1944, had been mocked as the feat of an infantile dauber—but now the uproar had reached a peak. If one excludes the commotion surrounding Picasso's exhibition at the Salon de la Libération in October 1944—with demonstrations in the streets and iconoclastic attacks on the works—nothing had so shocked the French art world ▲ for decades, perhaps even since the Fauve scandal of 1905.

Jeanson's witticism was less eloquent than the sarcasm of most critics, who took an obvious pleasure in detailing the "filth" they so condemned, but his reference to Dadaism points to a particular nexus of postwar Paris. The collective shame in the city was immense: shame for humanity as a whole at having implemented the Holocaust, but also more specifically shame for France and its collaboration with the Nazi machine. Because it could drape itself in martyrdom—calling itself "*le Parti des 75,000 fusillés*" (the party of the 75,000 gunned down), but also "*le Parti de la renaissance française*" (the party of the French Renaissance)—the Communist Party was seized upon as a moral buoy by a host of artists and intellectuals (Picasso being the most prominent of them). But it had little appeal for those who were appalled by the Communist-backed "*épuration*" following the Liberation—the public humiliation of petty collaborationists, the "popular" justice, and the execution of writers—this reminded them too much of the Stalinist purges of the late thirties), all the more since the Communist Party's demand • for a "socialist realism" was becoming louder every day.

Dubuffet was tempted neither by such self-righteousness nor by a mere return to the prewar status quo, with its perfunctory opposition, within the avant-garde, between the dreamland of Surrealism and the utopia of abstraction (which he saw as the two sides of the same coin). In a climate as politically charged as that of the Liberation, there was little room for maneuvering. The Nazis had treated humanity as if it were sheer disposable or usable matter (photographic reports on the camps—showing piles of corpses but also of human hair—began to pour into Paris during the spring of 1945), and this demotion had been confirmed, at the other end of the world, by the atomic explosions of Hiroshima and Nagasaki. What was expected from art, in the reconstruction period, was a redemptive, sublimatory reaffirmation of humankind's humanity —something akin, in the aesthetic realm, to the political "*épuration*" that was daily publicized in the press (in the sense that, despite the bad faith covering up a mere urge for revenge, the purges and punishments were intended to have the effect of a moral elevation). This is where the Dada provocation seemed a useful model of disobedience—for it, too, had originated in a climate of despair about humanity—even if, in the face of the most recent horrors, unprece- ▲ dented even by the carnage of World War I, it had a sophomoric ring.

The catalogue of the "Mirobolus" exhibition, printed on cheap colored paper and folded in fours, contained a text by Dubuffet entitled "The Author Answers Some Objections." The piece was also reprinted in several journals at the time, and republished just a few months later in the first (and most remarkable) of Dubuffet's many books, *Prospectus aux amateurs de tout genre*, as "Rehabilitation of Mud." Though this final title of the essay became famous as a catchword for Dubuffet's whole enterprise, it blurs its initial polemical stance—the fact that it was addressing the anticipated reaction of an • audience. The text opens on the issue of deskilling. Dubuffet underlines the fact that no special gift had presided over the making of the works in the exhibition, and that he had worked "here with [his] finger, there with a spoon." Even though he rhetorically denies any intention of provocation, Dubuffet appropriates confrontational techniques of earlier modernism, and pushes the envelope in proposing even more radical gestures than those represented by the works on view, dreaming, for example, of paintings solely made of a "monochromatic mud." To those who would question his attraction to "dirty things," he replied in advance: "In the name of what—except perhaps the coefficient of rarity—does man adorn himself with necklaces of shells and not spiders' webs, with fox fur and not fox innards? In the name of what, I want to know? Don't dirt, trash, and filth, which are

▲ 1906 • 1934a ▲ 1916a, 1920 • 1968b

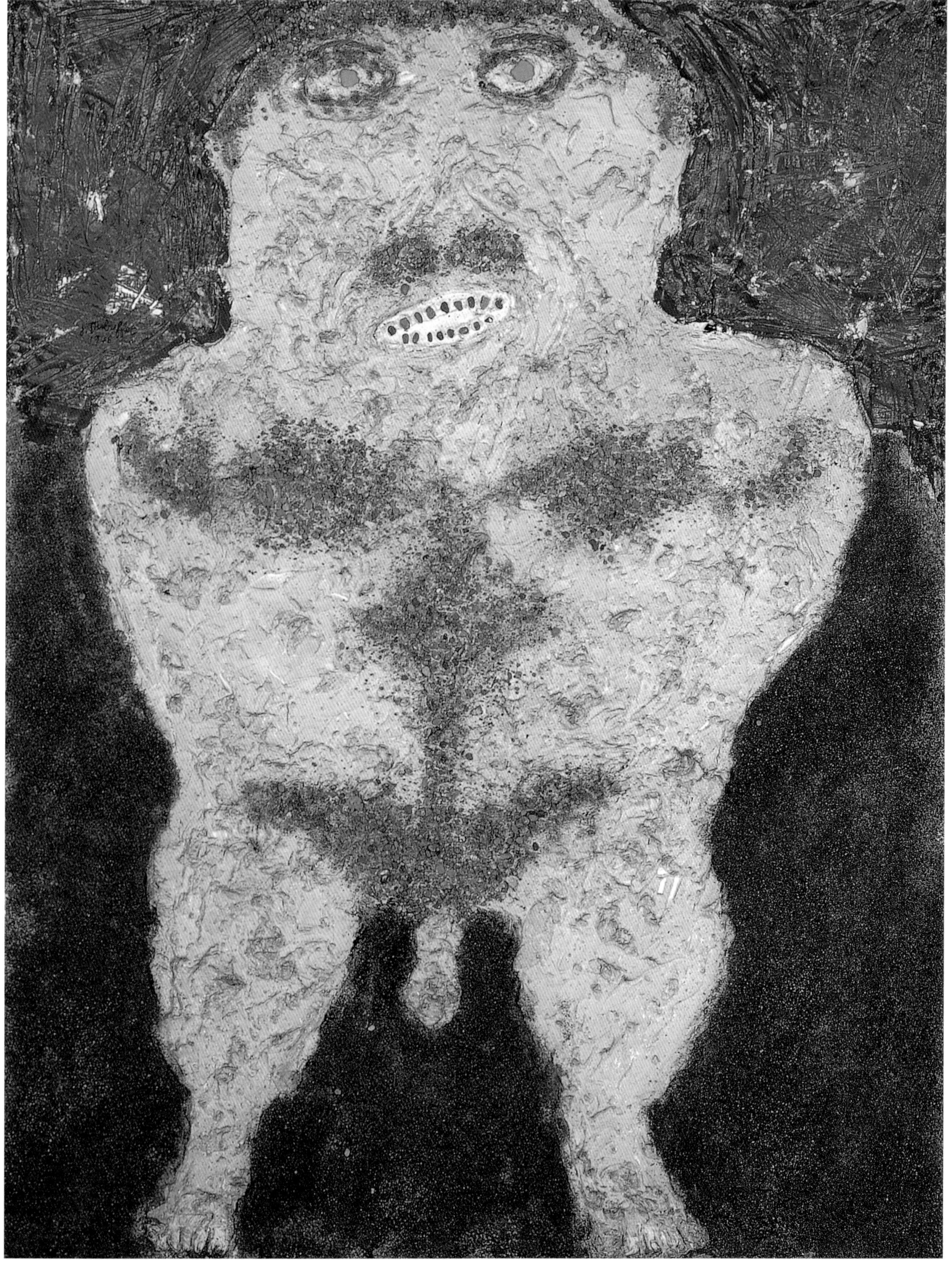

1 • Jean Dubuffet, *Volonté de puissance*, 1946
Oil on canvas, 116 x 89 (45⅝ x 35)

man's companions during his whole lifetime, deserve to be dearer to him, and isn't it serving him well to remind him of their beauty?"

Critics were prompt to read the mention of beauty as a deliberate provocation. They zeroed in on the "monochromatic mud" and gave "the dirt, trash and filth" its predictable excremental name. They were encouraged in that by the paintings themselves, with their brownish/grayish colors and their thick impasto (the *haute pâte*) of various materials, into which figures in full or three-quarter length had been incised [**1**]. Accentuated by the avoidance of any indication of the third dimension (all graffiti-like figures are either frontal or in full profile), the allusion to children's drawing was unmistakable. But if these works recalled kindergarten finger painting, gone were the attendant connotations of playful naivety. Brute matter had replaced color: for most critics it meant to say that the joy of life was no more. Dubuffet had expected to offend the "well read," as he called them, and the ensuing racket gave him confirmation that he had touched a sensitive nerve.

Dubuffet's few partisans, however, noticed that in wanting to rehabilitate mud he was not exactly claiming that "civilization" had ended—for them, on the contrary, he was offering the only redemptive strategy that could be found amid the rubble left after a cataclysm: to rehabilitate mud was to start anew, not exactly with a clean slate but from what was available, from what society *had* and *was* at this point of history. It was, in a dialectical twist whose irony appeared only later, to perfect a certain kind of "*épuration*." For if Dubuffet insisted that the sheer materiality of his work was on a par with the stuff and noise of the real, it meant that in the complex properties of natural objects "there was a certain order to discover." Nothing could better indicate how much Dubuffet's "*matièrisme*" is ▲foreign to Georges Bataille's (1897–1962) notion of "base materialism" or "formless" in which matter is posited as that which cannot be framed by any discursive category, any systematic thought, or poetic displacement—as that which stubbornly resists the sublimatory function of the image and deflates it with a low blow. To discover an order (an image) within the formlessness of matter so that one can rehabilitate that matter is diametrically opposed to the operation of debasement envisioned by Bataille as the task of the formless.

Not only was a whole section of Dubuffet's catalogue essay devoted to the "suggestive power" of the various components of his pastes, but the catalogue itself was doubled by a small book written on the exhibited works by the critic-impresario Michel Tapié. Tapié's turgid prose is not only utterly unreliable but almost unreadable today (except for the amusing anecdote of a picture that Dubuffet had given to the writer Jean Paulhan, and that had melted), but Dubuffet's detailed captions of all the works, duly reproduced, were striking. They parodied entries of museum catalogues in giving succinct information about the material employed, but inevitably they slipped into a metaphoric mode (mostly in the culinary realm). *Monsieur Macadam* was described as "Entirely painted in ceruse [white paint] and real tar mixed with gravel. The kind of white batter thickly buttered upon the figure takes on the color of toasted bread where it meets the tar, like a used meerschaum pipe." *Madame mouche*: "Rough matter, matte at places and shiny at others, or as if it had been cooked and had vitrified. Figure with colors of caramel, eggplant, blackberry jelly, and caviar, adorned with egg-white holes in which a syrupy varnish of a molasses color has accumulated here and there." Each caption thus becomes a small prose poem in which the precedence of vision over

Art brut

Like other modernists, Jean Dubuffet was influenced by the study of the *Artistry of the Mentally Ill* by Hans Prinzhorn. Throughout the thirties Dubuffet corresponded with various doctors, and in the mid-forties he visited institutions in Switzerland, where he first encountered the psychotic art collected by the Geneva psychiatrist Charles Ladame. These experiences prompted Dubuffet to gather art of the mentally ill as well as tribal, naive, and folk art under the rubric *art brut*—*brut* as in "crude" or "raw" as opposed to "refined" or "cultural." Along with André Breton, Jean Paulhan, Charles Ratton, Henri-Pierre Roché, and Michel Tapié, Dubuffet formed the Compagnie de l'Art Brut in 1948, and soon thereafter they presented the first exhibition of its holdings (roughly 2,000 works by 63 artists) at the Galerie René Drouin in Paris. For this show Dubuffet wrote his best-known text on the subject, "Art Brut Preferred to Cultural Art," which casts the *brut* artist as a radical version of the Romantic genius free of all convention:

> *We understand by this term works produced by persons unscathed by artistic culture, where mimicry plays little or no part (contrary to the activities of intellectuals). These artists derive everything—subjects, choice of materials, means of transposition, rhythms, styles of writing, etc.—from their own depths, and not from the conceptions of classical or fashionable art. We are witness here to a completely pure artistic operation, raw, brute, and entirely reinvented in all of its phases solely by means of the artist's own impulses.*

Like other modernists such as Paul Klee, then, Dubuffet idealized the art of the mentally ill as a return to pure "depths." But, unlike Klee, he defined these depths not as an *origin* of art, which one might hope to reclaim redemptively, so much as an *outside* to art, which one might cause to break into its cultural spaces transgressively. However, even as Dubuffet sought to undo the opposition between the normal and the abnormal ("this distinction ... seems quite untenable: who, after all, is normal?"), he reaffirmed the opposition between the *brut* and the cultural—an opposition that affirms rather than transgresses "civilization." And far from "unscathed, "as Dubuffet imagines, the psychotic is scarred by trauma, and this psychic disturbance might be registered in the bodily distortions often evident in *art brut*—for example, eyes and mouths grossly enlarged or disruptively plunged into other parts of the body—disruptions that Dubuffet often reproduced in his own art. Indeed, through such derangements of the body image, he sometimes evokes a schizophrenic sense of literal self-dislocation, which would seem very far indeed from the "completely pure artistic operation" that Dubuffet otherwise wished to see in *art brut.*

▲1930b

other senses, or at least the disembodied separateness of vision, is challenged (it should be noted that Maurice Merleau-Ponty's ▲ *Phenomenology of Perception*, in which this very feature of Western metaphysics was attacked, had appeared in 1945). But in the end, this anti-Cartesianism short-circuits, for Dubuffet's literary translation of the tactile given of the paste into the realm of food imagery remains based on the recentering force of metaphor, and thus on the illusionistic power of the gestalt, the form.

Food was on everyone's mind in postwar Paris (supplies were still very low and, contrary to one's expectations, they remained rationed for quite some time). It is thus not by chance that a high impasto that made paintings look like reliefs would invite culinary associations. Dubuffet encouraged critics to pursue this oral vein, for he began the text accompanying his next exhibition (held in October 1947), which was entirely devoted to portraits of friends and acquaintances in literary Paris, with a long excursus on the advantages of modest bread over the luxury of pastry (once again, Dubuffet's point concerned the beauty of the ordinary). But the first writer to allude to food as a trope for painterly paste was the poet Francis Ponge, whom Dubuffet knew well (Ponge had written the preface to the catalogue of his April 1945 exhibition of lithographs). In his first text on art—a small book on the impastoed paintings of an artist Dubuffet greatly admired, Jean Fautrier (1898–1964)—Ponge had laconically written: "It is part rose petal, part Camembert spread."

A deliberate frustration of vision

Soon both painters would reluctantly be cast as the founding fathers of a movement baptized "*informel*" by Paulhan and "*art autre*" by Tapié. A third "founder" was later spotted in the person of Wols (1913–1951), a German émigré whose real name was Wolfgang Schulze (but he had already died before the concoction of these labels). The exhibition of Wols's miniature watercolors at the Galerie Drouin in December 1945 went almost unnoticed: immediately after Fautrier's brute *Otages* in the same gallery, Wols's abstract landscapes populated by biomorphic forms were too clearly indebted to Paul • Klee's meticulousness to raise even a stir. But things changed almost instantly when Wols began to work in oil on canvas, and his second one-man show in 1947 was a triumph. Though Jean-Paul Sartre (1905–80) would not write his essay on the painter, "Fingers and Non-fingers," until 1963, Wols was unanimously seen as the quintessential ■ "existentialist" artist who undergoes a metaphysical crisis and seeks to demonstrate the contingency of being. The drama of his life as an alcoholic bum, the alleged automatism of his pictorial procedures, the spasmic gesturality of his paintings—all these signs of "sincerity" led Sartre to cast Wols as an "experimentator who understood that he is necessarily part of the experiment." But in the end, for all the grand claims made about Wols's abstract canvases, each similarly composed of a centralized (often vulvalike) vortex out of which energetic rays spout in all directions [**2**], his art remained an invitation to "reading in," to deploy an "imaging" attitude (Sartre's word) that would always save us from having to contemplate the abyss of nothingness.

The sudden success of Wols's cosmic hallucinations was prepared by the scandal of Dubuffet's "*hautes pâtes*," whose scatology now seemed too crude a shock tactic. But the discomfort engendered by Fautrier's October 1945 exhibition of his *Otages* also played a major, if unrecognized, role. The fact that Fautrier belonged to the same intellectual milieu, exhibited in the same gallery, and was defended by the same writers as Dubuffet has clouded for too long what distinguishes them—even if, at least with regard to color, one could not fail to notice that they evolved in opposite directions (Dubuffet from vivid colors to mud, Fautrier, the reverse).

Ponge's inaugural "Notes sur les Otages" (Notes on the Hostages) was written in January 1945 at the request of Jean Paulhan (Paulhan's own "Fautrier l'enragé" had appeared in the catalogue of the painter's show in 1943). It was commissioned as a preface for Fautrier's exhibition of his *Otages* series, which opened at the Drouin gallery in October 1945. In the end, a short essay by André ▲ Malraux (1901–76) was preferred, and Ponge's extraordinary text was published in early 1946 as an independent book. Malraux had long been a supporter of Fautrier's art (he had already written about it in 1933), and, given his phenomenal notoriety at the time as a writer and a hero of the Resistance, it is not surprising that his text

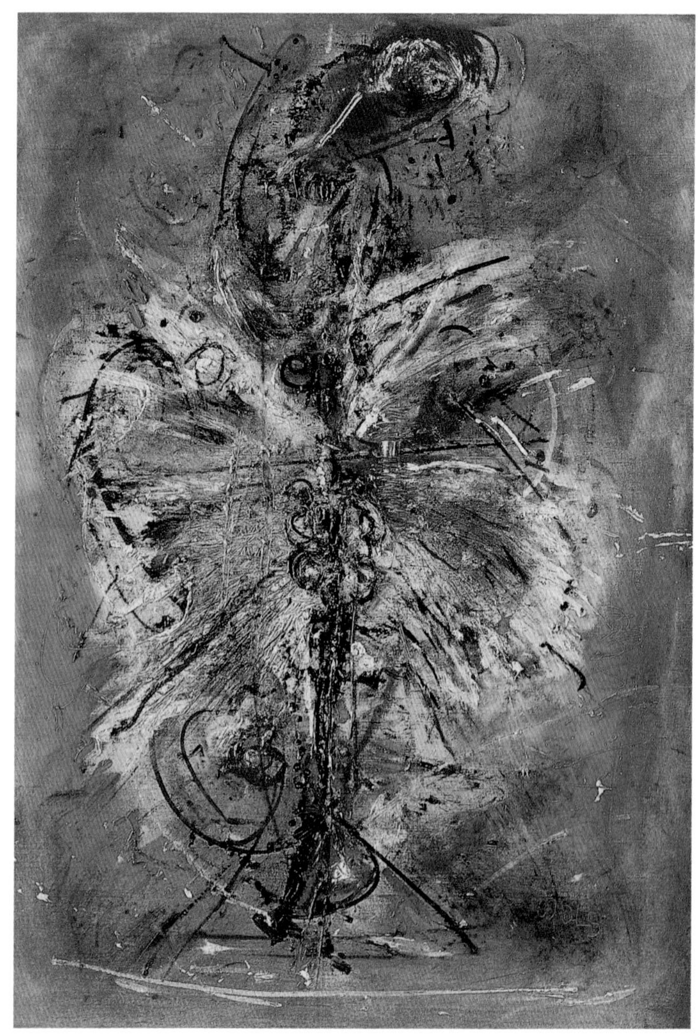

2 • Wols, *Bird*, 1949
Oil on canvas, 92.1 x 65.2 ($36\frac{1}{4}$ x $25\frac{5}{8}$)

▲ 1965 ● 1916a, 1922 ■ 1959c ▲ 1935

3 • Jean Fautrier, *Head of a Hostage no. 22*, 1944
Oil on paper pasted on canvas, 27 x 22 (10⅝ x 8⅝)

should have been given precedence over that of Ponge, who was then far less illustrious. But commercial plotting and public relations might not be the only reasons for the substitution, for Ponge's text was troubling, as Paulhan acknowledged upon its reception—just as troubling as the works themselves.

In his *Otages*, Fautrier was directly addressing the question that was on everyone's mind (even before the full revelation on the camps), though only Ponge dared formulate it as such about his work: how can one, in art, respond to the Nazi reign of terror without spectacularizing it? Fautrier had begun the series in 1943 while hiding from the Gestapo in a psychiatric asylum outside Paris, and after hearing the sounds of the torture and summary execution, in the surrounding woods, of civilians randomly picked by the German authorities. That Fautrier's point of departure was not visual but auditory (gunshots, cries) explains in part his unusual handling of the atrocities. Presented in monotonous rows that accentuated their seriality—and by extension the statistical, assembly-line nature of Nazi atrocity—the forty or so pictures all followed a similar formula in which not much was to be seen of the horror suggested in the generic titles (many works, mostly small, are simply called *Hostage* or *Head of Hostage*, followed by a number [**3**]). This dichotomy between alleged theme and frustration of vision was even more exacerbated with the titles of the somewhat larger works belonging to the same series but withheld from the 1945 exhibition: *Le Fusillé* (The Gunned-Down); *L'Ecorché* (The Flayed); *La Juive* (The Jewess [**4**]); or *Oradour-sur-Glane* (the name of a village where the Nazis burned alive hundreds

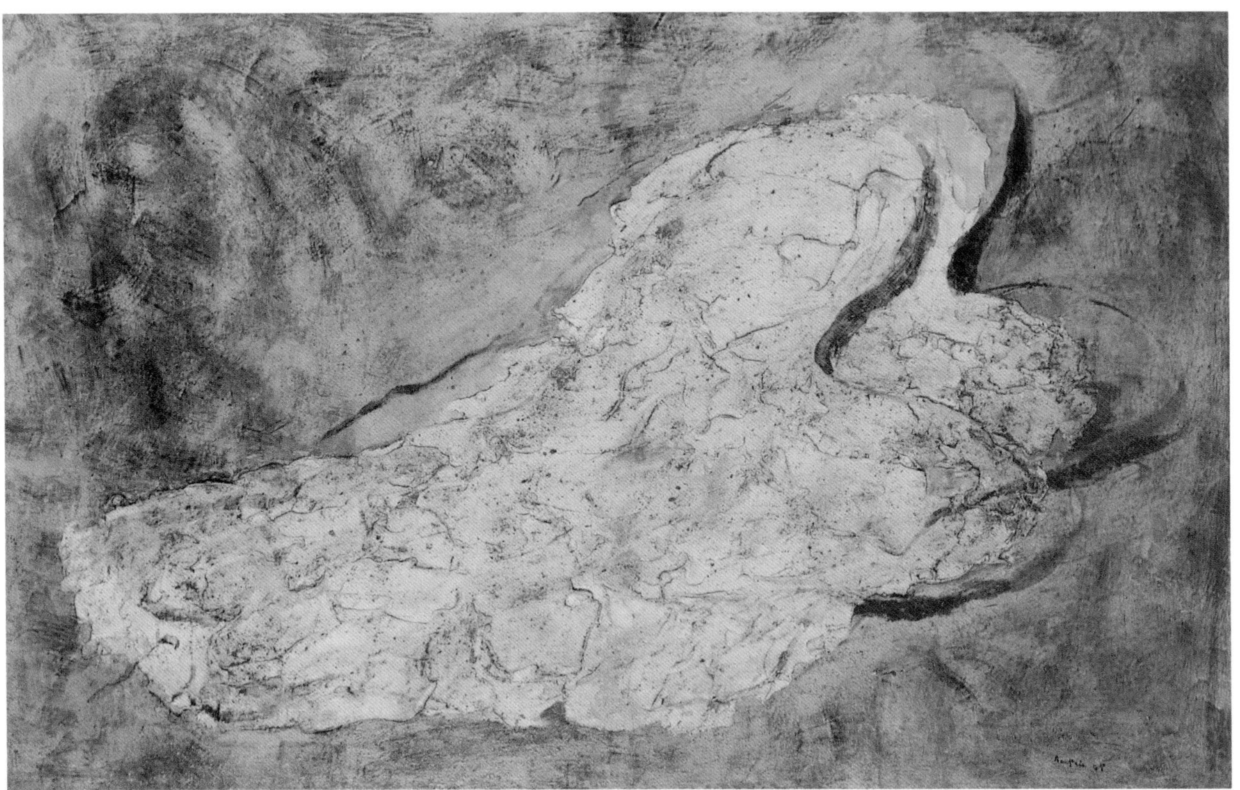

4 • Jean Fautrier, *The Jewess*, 1943
Oil on paper pasted on canvas, 73 x 115.5 (28¾ x 45½)

of women and children who had taken refuge in a church), though the first title of this painting was *The Massacre*.

All these works shared the same characteristics—and what most troubled certain critics was that, formally speaking, very little distinguished them from some of the landscapes and still lifes exhibited by Fautrier during the Occupation: indeed, the formula was set up around 1940, when he abandoned both oil painting and the dark tones he had been using for decades. Working on his canvas (or rather paper premounted on canvas) placed horizontally on a table and previously coated with a thin preparation sprayed with pastel, Fautrier was part plasterer, part pastry-cook. With a spatula he would spread a central blob of stuccolike whitish matter into a vague shape (roughly oval in the case of a *Head of Hostage*), and before this paste had hardened, he would dust it with various pastel powders and adorn it with a few brushed contours. The result would always be that of a highly centralized, and often quite undecipherable, figure silhouetted in relief in the middle of a dirtied atmospheric ground.

Both the choice of colors (pink, purple, turquoise—the whole candy spectrum found in cheap chromos) and the marked dissociation between texture and color send a potent signal of inauthenticity, of kitsch. This odd but deliberate breach of decorum had struck Paulhan as early as 1943—he wrote then of cosmetic creams and makeup—but he felt he had to defend Fautrier's art against accusations of decorative prettiness and of gratuitous virtuosity. Malraux, too, briefly expressed his unease, compounded by his appreciation for the flayed rabbits and other still lifes that Fautrier had painted in brown colors from the late twenties on, works that had often been associated with Goya. Noting that in his *Otages* series Fautrier had gradually abandoned any suggestion of bloody colors and substituted tones "devoid of any rational link with torture," he asked: "Are we always convinced? Are we not disturbed by some of those tender pinks and greens?

For both these writers, the cheesy tongue of seduction spoken by Fautrier's paintings was a problem they did not know how to handle. Of all Fautrier's supporters, Ponge alone understood that the strength of his work resided in the pairing of rapture and horror, and it is not only because Fautrier had illustrated Bataille's erotic fiction *Madame Edwarda* that Ponge alludes in his "Notes" to the latter's conception of scatology. Bataille had imagined the Marquis de Sade as having "the most beautiful roses brought to him only to pluck off their petals and toss them into a ditch filled with liquid manure." Ponge is more in keeping with the current obsession of the time when he speaks of Camembert, but the image is similar: unlike Dubuffet's rehabilitation, Fautrier's kitsch is a pessimistic, nihilist defilement.

True, Dubuffet would occasionally depart from his sublimatory trajectory, either by the sheer ferocity with which his caricatures assault the beholder's expectations, or in swerving from his usual course, in refusing to move from formlessness to figure. To the first strategy belongs his grotesque *Corps de dames* series of the early fifties, where the whole tradition of the nude in Western art is debunked as "metaphysical" bombast and flattened out [**5**]. And the

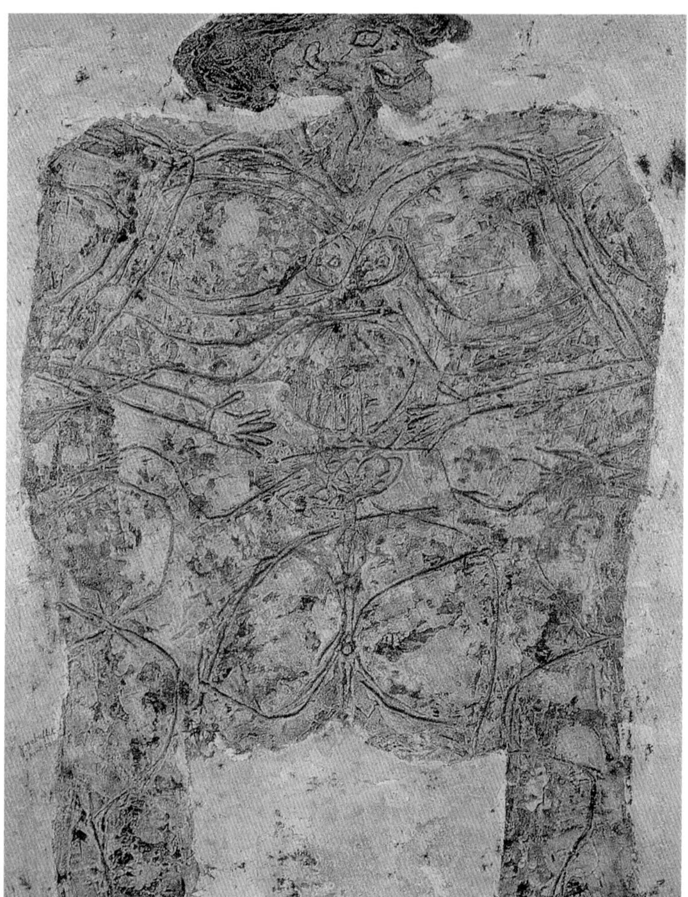

5 • Jean Dubuffet, *La Métafisyx*, 1950
Oil on canvas, 116 x 89 (45¼ x 34¾)

remarkable allover *Matériologies* of the late fifties and early sixties, realized in crumpled tinfoil or papier mâché and looking like maps of lunar terrains, are of the second mode. But even in these rare cases a metaphor would always creep in (the woman as Mother Nature, the canvas as native soil). Immensely prolific as a writer of pamphlets against the "asphyxiating culture," he would end up an official artist of the French Republic. Fautrier, by contrast, steadily put into practice his contempt for high art's pretense—he even embarked on the creation of textured reproductions of modernist art, from van Gogh to Dufy, which he labeled with the oxymoron "multiple originals." Refusing the "pharmaceutic style," as he called it, of those who wanted to read him as an expressionist (or as an *informel*) artist, he would create ever flashier monuments to bad taste until his death. Ponge's text ends with this sentence: "With Fautrier, 'beauty' returns." Beauty, that is, can return only in quotation marks.

FURTHER READING

Curtis L. Carter and Karen L. Butler (eds), *Jean Fautrier* (New Haven and London: Yale University Press, 2002)

Hubert Damisch, "The Real Robinson," *October*, no. 85, Summer 1998

Jean Dubuffet, *Prospectus et tous écrits suivants*, four volumes, ed. Hubert Damisch (Paris: Gallimard, 1967–91) and "Notes for the well read" (1945), translated in Mildred Glimcher, *Jean Dubuffet: Towards an Alternative Reality* (New York: Pace Publications and Abbeville Press, 1987)

Rachel Perry, "Jean Fautrier's *Jolies Juives*," *October*, no. 108, Spring 2004

Francis Ponge, *L'Atelier contemporain* (Paris: Gallimard, 1977)

Jean-Paul Sartre, "Fingers and Non-Fingers," translated in Werner Haftmann (ed.), *Wols* (New York: Harry N. Abrams, 1965)

1947a

Josef Albers begins his "Variant" paintings at Black Mountain College in North Carolina a year after László Moholy-Nagy dies in Chicago: imported to the United States, the model of the Bauhaus is transformed by different artistic imperatives and institutional pressures.

When the Nazis came to power in 1933, they forced the closure of the Bauhaus, the paradigmatic school of ▲ modernist design. Walter Gropius (1883–1969), its first director, had already left in 1928, soon followed by László Moholy-Nagy (1895–1946), who was in charge of its *Vorkurs* or preliminary course (he was replaced in that capacity by Josef Albers [1888–1976]). Relocated in Berlin, Moholy-Nagy continued to ● experiment with new materials, photography, light machines, and various forms of design (mostly books and exhibitions); he also ventured into film, theater, and opera production. In 1934 the spread of Nazism led him to move to Amsterdam and, a year later, to London. Then, in 1937, he left Europe altogether to direct the fledgling New Bauhaus in Chicago launched by a group of patrons and businessman called the Association of Arts and Industries (they had asked Gropius, but he had already accepted the post of Chair of Architecture at Harvard). Due to mismanagement of stocks, the Association had to close the school within a year. However, in 1939, and with only scant resources, Moholy-Nagy was able to reopen it—now renamed the School of Design—with much the same faculty, including the Russian-born American sculptor Aleksandr Archipenko (1887–1964), the Hungarian theorist György Kepes, and the American philosopher Charles Morris. (The Bauhaus veterans Herbert Bayer [1900–85] and Alexander [Xanti] Schawinsky [1904–1979] ■ and the French abstractionist Jean Hélion [1904–87] were listed on the New Bauhaus roster, but they did not teach in the first years.) In 1944 the school was renamed the Institute of Design, and it remains a division of the Illinois Institute of Technology to this day.

Other partial re-creations of the Bauhaus were attempted: Albers brought his version of the *Vorkurs* to Black Mountain College in North Carolina in late 1933, for example, and the Swiss artist and ◆ architect Max Bill (1908–94), who studied at the Bauhaus in 1927–9, launched the Institute of Design in Ulm, West Germany, in 1950. Each version was guided by a different agenda and adapted to a particular setting: Albers integrated his courses in drawing and color into a liberal arts college, while Bill foregrounded technological design for a postwar Germany under reconstruction. A one-time socialist associated with other artists and designers on the Left, Moholy-Nagy was now partnered in Chicago with industrialists such as Walter P. Paepcke, the president of the Container Corporation of America, who chaired the board of the Institute of Design (during his Chicago years Moholy-Nagy also designed for such companies as Parker Pens). How, apart from economic necessity, can we understand this reorientation of the Bauhaus idea?

To open eyes

Moholy-Nagy gives us some clues as early as his signature book *Von Material zu Architektur* (1929), translated into English as *The New Vision: From Material to Architecture* (1932). Throughout the twen- ▲ ties he was steeped in debates about photography, which were most lively in Germany and the Soviet Union. As perspectival painting informed the Renaissance, Moholy-Nagy argued, so photography has informed the modern age, and the arts must be rethought ● according to this "new vision." (In a sentence that Walter Benjamin might have written, he stated that "the illiterates of the future will be ignorant of the use of the camera and the pen alike.") Moholy-Nagy cited "eight varieties of photographic vision," some of which also affected the sciences: abstract (as in cameraless photograms), exact (as in reportage), rapid (as in snapshots), slow (as in prolonged exposures), intensified (as in microphotography), penetrative (as in X-rays), simultaneous (as in photomontage), and distorted (as in various manipulations of the negative and/or the print). Clearly, if seen as a matter of such techniques alone, the idea of a "new vision" could be adapted with relative ease to the different social, economic, and political conditions of corporate America. In *The New Vision* Moholy-Nagy also included a description of his *Vorkurs* and an account of the formal potentials of different materials, as well as a sketch of the evolution of sculpture (blocked out, hollowed or modeled, perforated or constructed, hung or suspended, kinetic). In other words, he offered both a pedagogy of visual fundamentals and a model of history that was almost Hegelian in its faith in the progress of technological vision. These ideas, too, could be embraced by a country committed to the pragmatic instruction and application of new technologies. In short, despite his own utopian aspirations, Moholy-Nagy suggested a way to make modernist design not only teachable but exploitable.

The *Vorkurs* of the New Bauhaus adopted that of the old with slight but significant additions: the training still began with analyses

▲ 1923 ● 1929 ■ 1937b ◆ 1955a, 1957a, 1957b, 1967c ▲ 1929 ● 1935

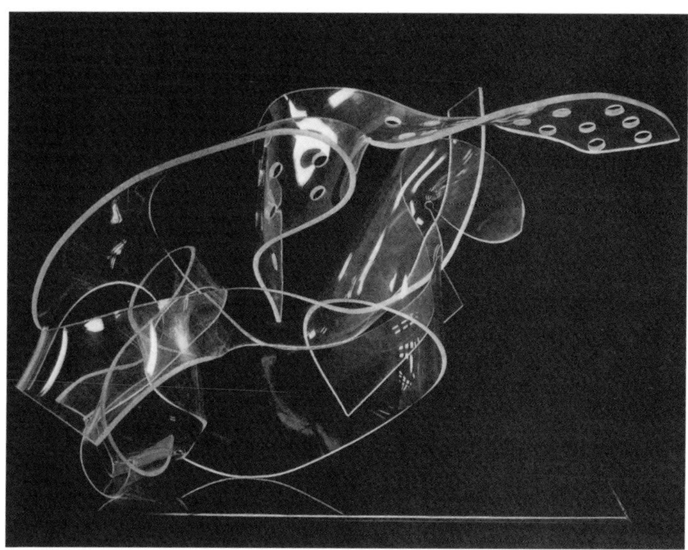

1 • László Moholy-Nagy, *Spiral*, 1945
Plexiglas, 49 x 37.5 x 40 (19¼ x 14¾ x 15¾)

of materials, tools, construction, and representation, but there was new emphasis placed on the sciences, photography, film, display, and publicity. "Our concern," Moholy-Nagy wrote in the program announcement, "is to develop a new type of designer"—note that he does not say "artist," much less "craftsman"—a designer who can integrate "specialized training in science and technique" with "fundamental human needs." This squaring of the circle—of technological science with human biology, of divisions in labor and knowledge with a "universal outlook"—became the American version of his Bauhausian utopia. Some of the subject headings of his next essay "Education and the Bauhaus" (1938), such as "The Future Needs the Whole Man" and "Not Against Technical Progress, but With It" also tell this tale. In an improbable dialectic, Moholy-Nagy sought his utopia of restored unity on the other side of techno-scientific specialization, which, unlike his predecessors in the Arts and Crafts movements, he embraced rather than rejected. For Moholy-Nagy, only through its "new vision" might "the whole man" be remade:

> *We are faced today with nothing less than the reconquest of the biological bases of human life. Only when we go back to these can we reach the maximum utilization of technical progress in the fields of physical culture, nutrition, housing and industry—a thoroughgoing rearrangement of our whole scheme of life.*

This project became ever more urgent due to World War II; in *Vision in Motion*, an updating of *The New Vision* (published in 1947 after his premature death from leukemia at fifty-one), Moholy-Nagy proposed a kind of United Nations of design culture that might "embody all specialized knowledge into an integrated system through cooperative action." A modernist to the end, he never understood how his own utopia might be turned to ideological ends. In modernist fashion his art of his last years, especially his twisting Plexiglas and chrome sculptures [**1**], are true to materials and inventive of forms, but, seen with a skeptical eye, they also look, from one angle, like so much formal "experimentalism" for ▲ its own sake (as Theo van Doesburg once cautioned about the younger Moholy-Nagy) and, from another angle, like so much corporate research-and-development—research into new substances, development of new products.

Shortly after the Bauhaus in Berlin was closed in 1933, Black Mountain College was opened in the hills near Asheville, North Carolina by a small group of professors led by John Andrew Rice (1888–1968)—a coincidence that worked well for Josef and Anni Albers. The new school wanted to make the arts central to the curriculum, even primary for first-year students, and on the recommendation of Philip Johnson, the architecture curator at the Museum of Modern Art who had visited the Bauhaus with Alfred ● Barr in 1927, the Albers were invited to join the faculty. They were the first Bauhausians to teach in the United States, and at first Anni, a gifted weaver who spoke English, received more attention than Josef. "All I knew was Buster Keaton and Henry Ford," Josef recalled later. "I spoke no English." Asked on his arrival what he hoped to accomplish at the school, he stuttered, "To open eyes." Here, too, "vision" was the modernist password.

The college stressed holistic teaching and collective participation. "At Black Mountain," the historian Mary Emma Harris writes, "the principles of democracy were to be applied not just to the classroom, as was usually the case in progressive schools, but to the entire structure of the college. There were to be no legal controls from the outside: no trustees, deans, or regents." This structure was more radical than that of the Bauhaus, new or old. And though Black Mountain College was marginal in the thirties (there were only about 180 students in total), there was no more influential community in American arts from the mid-forties through the mid-fifties. Apart from the Albers, semiregular faculty included poets Charles Olson and Robert Creeley, drama historian Eric Bentley, photography historian Beaumont Newhall, abstract painter Ilya Bolotowsky, and designer Alexander Schawinsky (who was also involved in the New Bauhaus), among others. From 1944 to 1949 Albers arranged summer sessions with diverse artists and writers often foreign to his own tastes and teachings, and the practice continued after he left the school: composer John Cage and dancer-choreographer Merce Cunningham in 1948, 1952, and 1953; photographer Harry Callahan in 1951; painter Willem de Kooning in 1948; poet Robert Duncan in 1955; old Bauhausian Lyonel Feininger in 1945; visionary designer Buckminster Fuller in 1948 and 1949; writer Paul Goodman and critic Clement Greenberg in 1950; Walter Gropius in 1944, 1945, and 1946; painter Franz Kline in 1952; composer Ernst Krenek in 1944; painter Jacob Lawrence in 1946; designer Alvin Lustig in 1945; painter Robert Motherwell in 1945 and 1951; painter-critic Amédée Ozenfant in 1944; cultural theorist Bernard Rudofsky in 1944 and 1945; composer Roger Sessions in 1944; painter Ben Shahn in 1951; photographer Aaron Siskind in 1951; painter Theodore Stamos in 1950; musician David Tudor in 1951, 1952, and 1953; painter Jack Tworkov in 1952; and sculptor Ossip Zadkine in 1945—and

▲ 1917, 1928 ● 1927c

these are only some of the names on the list. The roster of art students was almost as impressive (and not as male-dominated). It included Ruth Asawa, John Chamberlain, Elaine de Kooning, Robert de Niro (father of the actor), Ray Johnson, Kenneth Noland, Pat Passloff, Kenneth Snelson, Robert Rauschenberg, Dorothea Rockburne, Cy Twombly, Stan Vanderbeek, and Susan Weil. The encounters between faculty, guests, and students were often catalytic, as evidenced by the collaborations of Cage, ▲ Cunningham, Tudor, and Rauschenberg alone.

Everything has form

To this experimental community within an egalitarian college, Albers brought the analytical rigor of his own modernist practice: he offered courses in drawing, which stressed techniques of visualization; in design, which focused on proportion, arithmetic and geometric progression, the golden section, and spatial studies; and, most famously, in color, which was analyzed not with paints but with papers received from manufacturers. Albers taught painting only as an advanced color course, and then mostly in watercolor (he painted little at the Bauhaus too; this emphasis came only later). In formulations reminiscent of Moholy-Nagy, Albers proclaimed that "abstracting is the essential function of the Human Spirit" and that it requires the "disciplined education of the eye and the hand." However, his application of this Bauhausian credo was different from that of his old colleague, for, again, it occurred in the context of a liberal arts college, not a professional design school. This setting led Albers to two basic revisions of the Bauhaus idea. Firstly, he gave it a more humanist, almost Goethean inflection: "Every thing has form, every form has meaning," he once wrote, and art concerns "the knowledge and application of the fundamental laws of form." In other words, he complemented the new study of vision (which was not as technologically inflected for Albers as it was for Moholy-Nagy) with an old attention to form, to *Gestaltung*. Second, he reoriented the Bauhausian analysis of materials and structures along the lines of the American pragmatism of such philosophers as John Dewey (who was not unknown at the Bauhaus). For example, at Black Mountain Albers called his preliminary course not *Vorkurs* but *Werklehre*, instruction through work, or learning by doing. Although the goal remained much the same as at the Bauhaus—"*Werklehre* is a forming out of materials (for instance, paper, cardboard, metal sheets, wire), which demonstrates the possibilities and limits of materials"—the focus was less on fixing a meaning or a function to a substance and more on inventing a form out of it. Albers brought to his classes nontraditional materials and found things like autumn leaves and eggshells, and he was interested more in appearance than in essence—in what he called *matière*, which he defined as "how a substance looks" and how this semblance changes with different marking, lighting, and setting **[2]**. This explains his particular obsession with the combination of forms and the interaction of colors, which he juxtaposed "to make obvious how colors influence and change each other." "Nothing can be one thing but a hundred things," Albers once remarked in his odd English; "all art is swindle." Part of educating the eye was fooling the eye, and therein also lay a primary interest of art for Albers—in "the discrepancy between the physical fact and the psychic effect."

Albers was considered severe as a teacher—both at Black Mountain in 1933 to 1949 and at Yale University in 1950 to 1958 as Chair of Painting and Sculpture (then renamed Design)—and his art is still regarded as austere, as a reductive form of abstract painting. But his work allowed for certain openings, and his pedagogy was fecund for many different students. (His influence at both schools continued long after he left; indeed, Yale was as important a training ground for American artists in the sixties as Black Mountain had been in the fifties.) These openings might be understood in two ways. First, Albers was not quite the other extreme to the avant-garde wing of Black Mountain—Olson in poetry, Cage in music, Cunningham in dance, and so on—that he is often seen to be. The rigorous German committed to the disciplining of the eye might appear antipodal to the rumbunctious Americans pledged to the opening of poetry, music, and dance to the breath of the body, to the vagaries of chance, and to nonsymbolic movement, yet Albers and Cage were also aligned in their opposition to other aesthetic models then on the rise—to an art based on expressive *subjectivity* (as represented by some young Abstract Expressionists ▲ who passed through Black Mountain such as de Kooning, Kline, and Motherwell) or on extreme *objectivity* (as in the medium-● specific model of painting later developed by Clement Greenberg). Moreover, both Albers and Cage were involved, each in his own way, in a pragmatic approach to research and experiment, and ■ Black Mountain students like Rauschenberg and Twombly might be seen, in part, as the unlikely offspring of their odd coupling. (Listen to the mix of alienation and affinity that Rauschenberg evokes in this retrospective remark: "Albers was a beautiful teacher and an impossible person ... what he taught had to do with the entire visual world.... I consider Albers the most important teacher

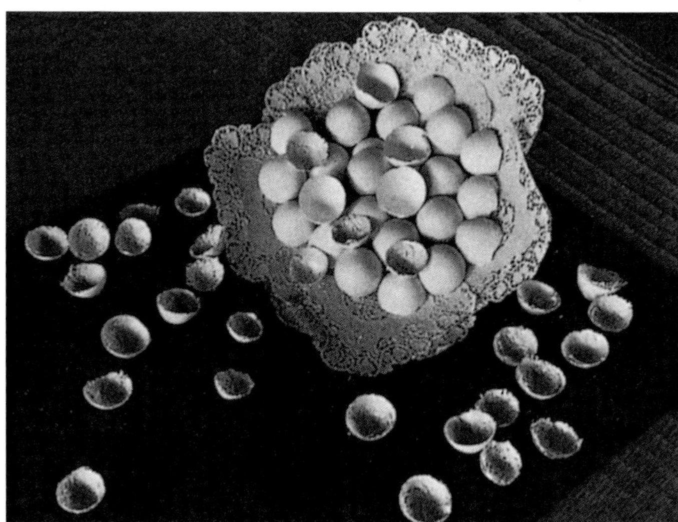

2 • Josef Albers and Jane Slater Marquis, *matière* study using eggshells at Black Mountain College

▲ 1953

▲ 1947b, 1959c ● 1960b ■ 1953

I've ever had, and I'm sure he considered me one of his poorest students.") In short, Albers was a primary element in the chemical reaction that made Black Mountain so important for advanced art in postwar America: after all, it was a crucible where a Constructivist impulse, or a modernism focused on vision, material, form, and structure, was combined with a Dadaist impulse, or an avant-gardism pledged to transgressive play, in a way that triggered many significant artists of the fifties and sixties, directly and indirectly.

Second, Albers helped to mediate not only between different modernist and avant-gardist impulses, but also between various prewar and postwar forms of abstraction, especially those focused ▲ on light and color. His earliest works at the Bauhaus were assemblages of glass shards mounted with chicken wire and placed by windows (they resemble some of the later *matière* studies of his Black Mountain students), and he also produced glass pieces in pure colors for private houses in Germany. "I wanted to work with direct light," he recalled to critic Margit Rowell, "the light which comes from behind the surface and filters through that surface plane." This concern with light as color in volume persisted not only in his early reliefs in glass, both transparent and opaque (whose banded compositions are similar to Anni's contemporaneous weavings), but also in his later paintings, which continued the implicit window format with rectangles of luminescent color. The abstract motif of his "Variant" paintings (1947–55) derived from two adobe houses that the Albers saw on one of many trips to the Southwest. This series presents nested rectangles of various colors in doubled or bilateral compositions, and it leads directly to his most famous series, *Homage to the Square* (1950–76), which consists of many paintings (usually in a four-foot-square format) of exact squares of pure colors that are also nested in one another **[3]**. Applied with a palette knife straight from the tube, the paint is flat and smooth on its support (usually the rough side of masonite panel), but it is also luminescent enough to suggest depth, either projective or recessional; there is much repetition and difference, symmetry and reversal, within each painting and between works. Yet all these experiments with forms depend on the interaction of colors—their relative transparency, intensity, depth, openness, warmth, and so on. "Painting is color acting," Albers liked to say; "character and feeling alter from painting to painting without any additional 'hand writing'": "All this [is] to proclaim color autonomy as a means of plastic organization."

The modernist in the university

These concerns had different ramifications for subsequent artists. For example, his *Homages to the Square* seem to anticipate the spare • geometric canvases of the young Frank Stella; but Albers still allowed for spatial illusion in his paintings, whereas Stella squeezed it out with the white lines of his exposed ground and the extreme depth of his often shaped supports. With Stella "what you see is what you see," as he once famously remarked; with Albers one is never so sure: for all his interest in proper gestalt forms, he was also fascinated, again, with "the discrepancy between the physical fact and the psychic effect." This gap between *known* form and *perceived* form is the space in which Minimalist artists also worked (as, for example, in 1965 when Robert Morris placed three identical L-beams in different positions in a New York gallery and dared ▲ the viewer to see them as the same right angle). Such attention to the complexities of perception might also have influenced not only Op artists such as Bridget Riley but also light artists such as • Robert Irwin and James Turrell, all of whom were also provoked by the phenomenological investigations of Minimalism. Rowell has written of the "lambent incandescence" of a typical Albers painting: "We are as in the presence of real light, not the kind of illusionism through which light is artificially projected from an outside source." So it is with the light installations of Irwin and Turrell, with this obvious difference: Albers worked at the scale of easel painting, careful to retain an intimate relationship with the viewer, not with environmental space that is often manipulated in such a way as to overwhelm the viewer.

Nevertheless, the opening up of "vision" is the most important legacy of both Moholy-Nagy and Albers. Again, Moholy-Nagy studied this vision primarily in terms of light, which he understood in a technologically evolutionary way (one that might have some ■ bearing on the development of Pop and kinetic art in the sixties). Albers understood it primarily in terms of color, which he investigated in a phenomenological way (again, with some ramifications for Minimalist, Op, and light art in the same decade). But more important are the different institutional inflections that the two men gave to these studies, with the Bauhaus program implicitly retooled by Moholy-Nagy for technological design institutes and by Albers for liberal arts schools. As Howard Singerman has argued in *Art Subjects: Making Artists in the American University*: "The discourse of vision and the tropes that go with it are crucial to adapting art to the university campus; it is both professionalizing and democratizing. Vision counters the vocational, the local, and the manual; the visual artist shapes the world, designing its order and progress." Under this dispensation, which was pioneered largely by Moholy-Nagy and Albers, "the fine arts" of the old Beaux-Arts tradition were reworked as "the visual arts" of the modernist period, in which guise they could be relocated in the university in alignment less with the humanities than with the sciences, with the artist-in-the-studio patterned after the scientist-in-the-laboratory, both engaged in research. (This analogy was made explicit by György Kepes of the New Bauhaus, who later founded the Center for Advanced Visual Studies at the Massachusetts Institute of Technology, in his influential *Language of Vision* of 1944: "the task of the contemporary artist is to release and bring into social action the dynamic forces of visual imagery.") This repositioning of the artist involved changes in pedagogy for which the Bauhaus was the best precedent. As Singerman suggests: "Assignments that allow students to discover for themselves the order of vision, the forces and relations of two-dimensional design and three-dimensional space, and the properties of materials—

▲ 1908, 1913, 1915, 1947b, 1949, 1957b, 1960b • 1958 ▲ 1965 • 1998 ■ 1955b, 1960c, 1964b

3 • Josef Albers, *Homage to the Square*, 1970
Oil on masonite, 40.6 x 40.6 (16 x 16)

at least of paint, perhaps of paper and clay—mark the presence and the difference of Bauhaus education in the United States, its difference from the sameness and repetition of the academy and its resemblance to the goals of the modern research university." And: "Over and over again in the teaching of art at the Bauhaus and in its teaching in America, the re-creation of design as vision is represented by the field or, more familiarly, by the picture plane as the gridded, ordered, law-bound rectangle with which, and on which, art fundamentals begin. The rectangle marks the teaching of modernism as the visual arts, displacing and containing the human figure that stood at the center of the academic fine arts."

This is not a question of simple cooption: there is no direct line from the Bauhaus *Vorkurs* to the design and color courses that became tediously standard in many postwar universities. A dialectical view is far better: Moholy-Nagy and Albers also radicalized design and color instruction, just as they both preserved the Bauhaus idea *and* allowed it to be transformed by cross-fertilization with other avant-garde models. Moreover, the very importance of Moholy-Nagy, Albers, and other Europeans to art, design, and education in the postwar period must complicate the old stories of a simple passage in prominence from Paris to New York of the "Triumph of American Painting" sort. For all the differences and disruptions, there was also a continuity from continent to continent, from one postwar period to another—a continuity, despite change and through change, at the level of artistic practice, industrial design, and educational method.

FURTHER READING

Josef Albers, *Homage to the Square* (New York: Museum of Modern Art, 1964)

Mary Emma Harris, *The Arts at Black Mountain College* (Cambridge, Mass.: MIT Press, 1987)

Margret Kentgens-Craig, *The Bauhaus and America: First Contacts 1919–1936*, trans. Lynette Widder (Cambridge, Mass.: MIT Press, 1999)

László Moholy-Nagy, *An Anthology*, ed. Richard Kostelanetz (New York: Da Capo Press, 1970)

Howard Singerman, *Art Subjects: Making Artists in the American University* (Berkeley and Los Angeles: University of California Press, 1999)

1947b

The publication of *Possibilities* in New York marks the coalescence of Abstract Expressionism as a movement.

Every study of Abstract Expressionism begins with a disclaimer about its label, echoing that made by the artists themselves. The coinage itself is quite apt (it came somewhat late into use, around 1952) and is not in question. What is resented is the fact that it groups very diverse talents under the same umbrella, homogenizing and unifying a cast of characters, each of whom strove for singularity. Yet this disclaimer is something of a paradox, for in insisting on the individualism of the Abstract Expressionist artists, and on the idiosyncratic nature of their pictorial marks, it does single out what they had in common: a longing for what could be called the autographic gesture, the inimitable, signature-like dribble of paint that would translate private feelings and emotions directly onto the material field of the canvas—without the mediation of any figurative content.

This is not to say that these artists had little else in common, or that they did not band together—they often did, especially to show collective muscle in the face of a shared enemy. A case in point is their May 1950 boycott of a juried exhibition organized by the Metropolitan Museum in New York in protest against that institution's "hostility to advanced art," a public gesture initiating a six-month-long turmoil and celebrated by a notorious photograph published in *Life* in January 1951 [**1**]. Among the "Irascible Eighteen," as they were nicknamed by the *New York Herald Tribune*, one could count almost all the major Abstract Expressionist painters, including the older Hans Hofmann (1880–1966), a mentor to several of them. The only conspicuous absences, apart from Arshile Gorky, who had died two ▲ years before, were those of Franz Kline (1910–62) and Philip Guston (1913–80). Along with lesser figures and all the sculptors often • (though incorrectly) associated with the movement (David Smith the foremost among them), there were William Baziotes (1912–63), Adolph Gottlieb (1903–74), Willem de Kooning (1904–97), Robert Motherwell (1915–91), Barnett Newman (1905–70), Jackson Pollock ■ (1912–56), Mark Rothko (1903–70), and Clyfford Still (1904–80). They all signed the angry open letter to Roland Redmond, President of the Metropolitan Museum (published on the front page of the *New York Times* on May 22, 1950); and, urged and cooed by Newman, who acted as their chief organizer, most made an effort not to miss the *Life* photo opportunity. Similar protests a few years before (such as the letter to the *New York Times* signed by Rothko and Gottlieb and written with the help of Newman, which was published on June 13, 1943) had led nowhere—but now the time was ripe. Even though commercial success was still a few years away, Abstract Expressionism was suddenly entering the pantheon of high art with the full support of the Museum of Modern Art. It would soon be deemed the quintessential "American-Type Painting" (Clement Greenberg) and enlisted in the Cold War as an efficient cultural battalion against Soviet Communism.

1 • Nina Leen, *The Irascibles*, 1951
Black-and-white photograph published in *Life* magazine, January 1951

Shared experiences

The *Life* photograph vastly exaggerated the bond between the artists it portrayed, as many of them later protested. But for all their posing as proud loners, most indeed had a common background.

▲ 1942a • 1945 ■ 1942a, 1949, 1951, 1959c, 1960b

▲ First, many had worked for the Works Progress Administration (WPA) during the thirties (among them Baziotes, de Kooning, Gorky, Gottlieb, Pollock, and Rothko), and during this period of extreme poverty most had a brush with radical politics (including for some, such as Pollock, membership of the Communist Party). This meant that they had all participated in one way or another, between the Spanish Civil War (1936–7) and the massive disillusionment following the Nazi–Soviet nonaggression pact (1939), in the great debate of the time concerning the relationship between art and politics—some looking toward Picasso and his *Guernica* • (1937) as a model, others toward the Mexican muralists, others yet toward the American Regionalist painter Thomas Hart Benton (the young Pollock being unique among his peers in striving to synthesize those three trends).

Second, with the possible exception of the Dutch-born de Kooning, they all had an enormous feeling of inferiority with regard to the European avant-garde, whose artistic production they knew remarkably well. One could even say that, with the opening in New York of collector A. E. Gallatin's Museum of Living Art in 1926, that of the Museum of Modern Art in 1929, and that of the Solomon R. Guggenheim Museum (then called the Museum of Non-Objective Painting) in 1939—not to forget the multiple touring exhibitions of the collection (selected by Marcel Duchamp) of Katherine Dreier's Société Anonyme in the twenties and thirties, ■ and, last but not least, the militant activity of Peggy Guggenheim at her "Art of This Century" gallery, again in New York, from 1942 on—the Abstract Expressionists had, by the early forties, accumulated a better first-hand knowledge of their immediate European predecessors than any other contemporary artists (and certainly better than anyone in Europe). Their awe for their European seniors was at first paralyzing. A man like Gorky, for example, began to emancipate himself from the Miró-cum-Picasso system of Surrealist automatism only in 1944, but then it was suddenly to raise the stake of the painterly accident higher than ever before in the history of art: admiring the violent bravado of Gorky's 1944 painting *How My Mother's Embroidered Apron Unfolds in My Life* and its conspicuous runoffs of liquid paint, one should not forget that it dates from only four years before his death. But the arrival of many European exiles in New York at the beginning of World War II paradoxically relieved some of the endemic "anxiety of influence": luminaries like ◆ Fernand Léger, André Breton, Max Ernst, and Piet Mondrian were suddenly seen to be not titans after all, but (somewhat aging) human beings. In turn, this discovery fueled a certain nationalistic pride among the American artists: with Europe now almost entirely muzzled by totalitarian regimes, it was up to the US boys to save the flame of culture from its barbaric extinction. Often exhibiting in group shows, and in the same (handful of) galleries and marginal cultural institutions, they slowly began to feel a momentum amid a generally indifferent if not hostile context. Their resentment at the lack of early support from the Museum of Modern Art and that part of the critical establishment that was embracing European modernism helped draw them closer together.

Those difficult early years had a lot to do with the formation of a collective identity. Depending on the swing of the pendulum, these emotional artists felt elated or tortured. Newman captured both the mood and what was at stake: "In 1940, some of us woke up to find ourselves without hope—to find that painting did not really exist.... The awakening had the exaltation of a revolution. It was that awakening that inspired the aspiration ... to start from scratch, to paint as if painting never existed before. It was that naked revolutionary moment that made painters out of painters." Better than his peers (they considered him a kind of benevolent impresario presiding over their own careers), Newman presented what was thought to be the only possible way out: a third path, between pure abstraction (represented by Mondrian) and Surrealism.

An early enthusiasm for, and gradual rejection of, Surrealism was the third trait the Abstract Expressionists held in common, and perhaps more than anything else it determined their ideology. They soon turned their backs on the Surrealists' symbolist imagination and fascination for mythology, but retained a strong primitivist impulse and, at least for the majority of them, a marked interest in psychoanalysis. True, by the mid-forties their *Reader's Digest*-like incursions into anthropological, psychoanalytic, or philosophical literature were hardly a sign of originality. In view of the recent calamities that had plagued humanity (fascism, Stalinism, the Holocaust, the atomic bomb), a new type of theoretical hodgepodge that had emerged in the United States shortly before the war, aptly called the "Modern Man discourse" by art historian Michael Leja, was suddenly becoming enormously popular in the media. Central to this discourse was the idea that "the human mind harbored an unconscious" (Leja)—this seemed the only possible explanation for the unprecedented levels of cruelty and irrationality that man had just displayed. But if the public rise of the concept of the unconscious had a soothing effect on a traumatized population (quickly capitalized on by Hollywood), it also provided the Abstract Expressionists with a potent rhetoric with which they could hide their rapid retreat from the elusive possibility of "pure automatism"—a Grail for which the Surrealism had long searched in vain—to the much more practicable cult of the "autograph."

From the automatic to the autographic

The key years were 1947 and 1948. In the course of just a few ▲ months, Pollock began to work in his allover dripping technique • (in late summer or early fall 1947); Newman painted *Onement I* ■ (in January 1948); de Kooning had a triumphant first solo show (in ◆ April–May 1948); Gorky, who alone among his peers had been welcomed by the Surrealists, committed suicide (in July 1948), marking the definitive end of an old allegiance; and Rothko realized his first mature canvases—the "multiform" paintings that he no longer titled but identified solely by number or color, a sure indication that he had turned a page. Furthermore, 1948 was also the year when The Subjects of the Artist school, founded by Baziotes, Motherwell, Newman, Rothko, Still, and the sculptor

▲ 1936 • 1933, 1937a ■ 1942b ◆ 1942a, 1944a ▲ 1949, 1960b • 1951 ■ 1959c ◆ 1942a

David Hare, opened its doors. This pedagogic experience was short-lived, with the school closing in the spring of 1949, but the very fact that its founders thought, even for a moment, that an academy could function as an outlet for the type of art they were inventing pointed to what was to come.

A particularly significant record of Abstract Expressionism at the very moment of its coalescence as a movement—because it encapsulates the shift from the automatic to the autographic—is provided by the first, and only, issue of *Possibilities*, published at the end of 1947 by Motherwell and the critic Harold Rosenberg (who would ▲ later father the label "action painting"). This "journal" was as ambitious as its title was pregnant. It addressed many media (including music, strongly present with John Cage in command, and literature), and aimed at securing or renewing links with the historical avant-garde (an interview with Miró, a poem and illustrations by • Arp). It is best known today, however, for having published Pollock's and Rothko's statements on their own art. Other texts should not be overlooked, though, such as Baziotes's and, above all, Rosenberg's. Together they form a symptomatic nucleus.

"The source of my paintings is the unconscious," Pollock had written in the draft of his statement, but he deleted this general affirmation, by then already something of a cliché, in favor of a more descriptive note alluding to the drip technique with which he was beginning to experiment (though none of his drippings are reproduced among the six accompanying illustrations, all of which are from works of 1944–6). While for some time he had derived the imagery of his paintings (such as *Birth* [c. 1941], *Bird* [c. 1941], or ■ *Moon Woman Cuts the Circle* [c. 1943]) from his acquaintance with Jungian analysis (he was himself in therapy), he now clearly aligned his new method and its wholly abstract results with unmediated spontaneity: "When I am *in* my painting, I'm not aware of what I'm doing. It is only after a sort of 'get acquainted' period that I see what I have been about.... Painting has a life of its own. I try to let it come through. It is only when I lose contact with the painting that the result is a mess. Otherwise there is pure harmony, an easy give and take, and the painting comes out well." A similar attitude is found in Baziotes ("What happens on the canvas is unpredictable and surprising to me.... Each painting has its own way of evolving") and Rothko ("I think of my pictures as dramas; the shapes in the pictures are the performers.... Neither the action nor the actors can be anticipated, or described in advance.... It is at the moment of completion that in a flash of recognition, they are seen to have the quantity and function which was intended").

But while Pollock clung steadfastly to the notion of automatism, the others did not. Although we can marvel today at Pollock's amazing technical know-how in interweaving numerous meshes of color, and at the remarkable assurance with which he alternated between thread-thin rivulets and thick puddles of wet paint, the fact is that in his drip paintings he relinquished part of his authorship. By avoiding any direct contact with the canvas splayed on the floor, by letting gravity and the viscosity of the paint play a major role in the outcome of his works, and by abandoning the paint-brush, Pollock lost the anatomical connection that had traditionally linked artist's hand, brush, and canvas. He wavered on the issue of control, depending on the critical response ("I *am* nature" versus "No chaos, damn it!"), but even if in the end his marks proved utterly inimitable, his attempt at automatism was deemed by his peers to be too much of a breakdown of authorial mastery. Their taming (repression) of Pollock's radicalism had a defining role in the formation of the Abstract Expressionist canon.

"The aspect of the freely made"

This rapid evolution can be bracketed between two texts, one written at the dawn of the movement—Rosenberg's short essay published in *Possibilities*—and the other when it was already showing definite signs of exhaustion—Meyer Schapiro's "The ▲ Liberating Quality of Avant-Garde Art" of 1957. Rosenberg's "Introduction to Six American Artists," initially the catalogue preface for a spring 1947 exhibition presenting Baziotes, Motherwell, and Gottlieb (among others) to a French audience for the first time, laid the groundwork for a theory of art that would become the pillar of the pictorial practice of Abstract Expressionism. These artists, he wrote, long for "a means, a language, that will formulate as exactly as possible what is emotionally real to them as separate persons ... Art to them is ... the standpoint for a private revolt against the materialist tradition that does surround them.... Attached neither to a community nor to one another, these painters experience a unique loneliness of a depth that is reached perhaps nowhere else in the world." "Emotionally real to them as separate persons," "private revolt," "loneliness": for Rosenberg, the stuff of the Abstract Expressionist painter is his uniqueness; his duty is to let us enter the inner sanctum of his feelings; his art is bound to reveal his very own self as the kernel of his originality. But at the same time, Rosenberg claims that the pangs of suffering registered by the art (a much-dated leitmotiv in his existentialist prose) are universally human and thus universally accessible. In short, the Abstract Expressionist canvas is an affirmation of the ego, a half-romantic, half-petty-bourgeois version of the Cartesian "Cogito ergo sum," which is to say, the seat, as T. J. Clark has argued, of much vulgarity. No wonder that the acompositional monotony of Pollock's allover drips was not long deemed by his peers to fill the brief.

Echoing Rosenberg's notion of a revolt against the "materialist tradition" (meaning here not the tradition of philosophical anti-idealism but the bourgeois mode of life predicated upon the acquisition of goods), Schapiro's text confirms that the myth of "spontaneity" was the locus of a smooth conversion from the unknown and the unpredictable (the unconscious) to a concept of subjective freewill that fitted the ethos of American democracy particularly well: "Paintings and sculptures," he starts, "are the last hand-made, personal objects within our culture. Almost everything else is produced industrially, in mass, and through a high division of labor. Few people are fortunate enough to make something that represents themselves, that issues entirely from their

▲ 1960b • 1913, 1916a, 1918, 1924, 1930b ■ 1949 ▲ Introduction 2, 1942a

hands and minds, and to which they can affix their names.... The painting symbolizes an individual who realizes freedom and deep engagement of the self within his work." This argument is not dissimilar to that given almost a century before by the defenders of Impressionism (a historical antecedent many Abstract Expressionist painters were prompt to celebrate), but it has gained for Schapiro a new poignancy:

> *The consciousness of the personal and spontaneous in the painting and sculpture stimulates the artist to invent devices of handling, processing, surfacing, which confer to the utmost degree the aspect of the freely made. Hence the great importance of the mark, the stroke, the brush, the drip, the quality of the substance of the paint itself, and the surface of the canvas as a texture and field of operation—all signs of the artist's active presence. The work of art is an ordered world of its own kind in which we are aware, at every point, of its becoming.*

Between the "aspect of the freely made" and the work of art as an "ordered world" lies the shift from the automatic to the autographic (but also the risk of fraudulence and of academization). This slippage ran two simultaneous courses, often, but not necessarily, in tandem, and did so almost right from the start (beginning in 1948): the claims of spontaneity were dimmed in favor of principles of good composition; and the autographic unit grew in size from the simple gesture to the immediately recognizable trademark style—almost like the artist's own logo—filling the whole canvas. De Kooning's immediate canonization, in the wake of his first solo show at the Charles Egan Gallery in New York in 1948, tells how much the need of the first move was felt (Greenberg was almost alone in these years in praising Pollock's allover mode, and he had to overcome his own initial resistance). In many ways, the subservience of de Kooning's white-on-black canvases to Pollock's most recent development was a kiss of death [**2**]: gone were the looseness and risk-taking of the drip technique, now replaced by a tight grip on the brush and nervous twists of the wrist. The sigh of relief uttered by sympathetic critics grew even louder in response to de Kooning's second exhibition, in 1951: "There is no destruction but instead constant wiping out and

2 • Willem de Kooning, *Untitled*, 1948–9
Enamel and oil on paper on composition board, 89.7 x 123.8 (35⅜ x 48¾)

3 • Robert Motherwell, *At Five in the Afternoon*, 1949
Casein on board, 38.1 x 50.8 (15 x 20)

starting over," wrote Thomas B. Hess, "and the whole image [is kept] under rigorous control."

Signature style

As for designing a "logo," a trap that Newman called the "diagram" and which he paradoxically avoided by addressing the issue at the outset when he opted for the simplest possible spatial markers (his ▲ immediately recognizable vertical "zips"), one can also date its beginning to 1948. A case in point is Motherwell's lifelong *Elegy to the Spanish Republic* series (more than 140 paintings), based on an ink drawing conceived in 1948 as an illustration for a poem by Rosenberg and destined for the second (never published) issue of *Possibilities*: pulling out the tiny sketch from a drawer one year later, Motherwell scrupulously reproduced it, with all its scumbling contours and paint runoffs, on a somewhat larger canvas now given the title *At Five in the Afternoon*, the famous refrain of an elegy by the Spanish poet and dramatist Federico García Lorca lamenting the death of a bullfighter [**3**]. Such posturing does not necessarily characterize the working method of all the Abstract Expressionists, but the very fact that it was possible at all (and that it would be thoroughly imitated by legions of younger artists once the movement had become widely successful, that is, by the mid-fifties) merits consideration. Gottlieb's clouds hovering above an allusive horizon, Kline's broad and energetic brush-strokes in slicker and slicker black paint [**5**], and Still's dry shards quickly became patented figures of style. Even Rothko's horizontal partitions of his vertical canvases [**4**] fit into this category: were it not for the sustained inventiveness of his color chords, and the ensuing enigmas of figure–ground relations that his works continued to pose till the end, his art may have been exhausted by the artist's manic overproduction.

In short, the seriality of Abstract Expressionism, in the end, had much in common with that of the movement said to have precipi- ▲ tated its demise—Pop art. Jasper Johns and Robert Rauschenberg, whose rise to fame immediately preceded that of Pop and cleared

▲ 1951

▲ 1953, 1958, 1960c, 1964b

4 • Mark Rothko, *Number 3/No. 13 (Magenta, Black, Green on Orange)*, 1949
Oil on canvas, 216.5 x 163.8 (85¼ x 64½)

5 • Franz Kline, *Cardinal*, 1950
Oil on canvas, 197 x 144 (77½ x 56¾)

the way for it, saw through the posturing. Johns mimicked the rapid splashes of the Abstract Expressionist canvases but in encaustic, the slowest possible and most ancient medium, and Rauschenberg painstakingly duplicated the painterly accidents of his *Factum I* onto its pendant *Factum II*, both of 1957. Despite Johns's and Rauschenberg's irony, however, one should not underestimate their concern for mark-making as such, an emphasis on the process of ▲ art that they, and many artists after them, such as Robert Morris, retained from Abstract Expressionism. It is what Robert Rauschenberg had in mind when he declared to Emile de Antonio: "The Abstract Expressionists and myself, what we had in common was touch. I was never interested in their pessimism or editorializing. You have to have time to feel sorry for yourself if you're going to be a good Abstract Expressionist, and I think I always considered that a waste. What they did—and what I did that looks like Abstract Expressionism—is that with their grief and art passion and action painting, they let their brushstrokes show, so there was a sense of material about what they did."

FURTHER READING

T. J. Clark, "In Defense of Abstract Expressionism," *October*, no. 69, Summer 1994

Clement Greenberg, "American-Type Painting" (1955), *The Collected Essays and Criticism, Vol. 3: Affirmation and Refusals, 1950–1956*, ed. John O'Brian (Chicago and London: University of Chicago Press, 1993)

Serge Guilbaut, *How New York Stole the Idea of Modern Art: Abstract Expressionism, Freedom, and the Cold War* (Chicago and London: University of Chicago Press, 1983)

Michael Leja, *Reframing Abstract Expressionism: Subjectivity and Painting in the 1940s* (New Haven and London: Yale University Press, 1993)

Meyer Schapiro, "The Liberating Quality of the Avant-Garde," retitled "Recent Abstract Painting," *Modern Art: 19th and 20th Century, Selected Papers, vol. 2* (New York: George Braziller, 1978)

▲ 1965, 1968b, 1969

1949

Life magazine asks its readers "Is he the greatest living painter in the United States?": the work of Jackson Pollock emerges as the symbol of advanced art.

In the immediate postwar years, one sign of the New York art world's continuing status as a small village is that a mass-circulation magazine like *Life* should have felt the need to introduce its readers to Jackson Pollock in the first place. It happened, however, that one of its researchers was married to the art historian Leo ▲ Steinberg, then just starting out as a critic of contemporary art as well, and through this connection *Life* got wind of what it considered a *succès de scandale*, yet another story of the peculiar excesses of modernism. Ambivalent through and through, *Life*'s presentation of Pollock was part contemptuous (the captions under the "drip paintings" spoke of them as "drools," the text as "doodling") and part serious. The article had to report, after all, the estimation of Pollock's work as great by "a formidably high-brow New York • critic" (Clement Greenberg) as well as its embrace by American and European avant-garde audiences, and, as an illustrated weekly, it had to picture both the artist and his work in generous, large-scale reproductions.

Breaking the ice

In this sense, the *Life* piece reflected what was even then happening in two other domains. In the specialized art press a formerly derisive account of Pollock's drip pictures ("baked macaroni" or "a mass of tangled hair") was turning cautiously positive, so that responses to the November 1949 exhibition at the Betty Parson Gallery now spoke of "tightly woven webs of paint" or "myriad tiny climaxes of paint and color," each one "elegant as a Chinese ▲ character." As Willem de Kooning, observing collectors and museum directors now abandon their more traditional purchases to vie for Pollock's work, put it at the time, "Jackson has finally broken the ice." And in the institutional world of both museum and government cultural policy, Pollock and the other Abstract Expressionists began to be seen as important emissaries of the American experience: wildness now starting to be recoded as freedom—a liberated sensibility increasingly deemed as setting a good example

1 • Jackson Pollock, *One (Number 31, 1950)*, 1950
Oil and enamel on unprimed canvas, 269.5 x 530.8 (106⅛ x 209)

▲ 1960b • 1960b ▲ 1947b, 1959c

for the cause of democracy in Cold War-torn Europe; thus, to accompany the Marshall Plan of financial aid to European countries, which was instituted in 1948, a variety of cultural exports, including museum and gallery exhibitions, was shipped abroad. In the late forties this was officially funded by the USIA (United States Information Agency) but in the fifties (due to Congressional "red-baiting" of the State Department) the Museum of Modern Art's International Council carried the ball for the US government.

For Pollock himself, however, the stardom brought on by this media and institutional success (in 1950, he shared the US pavilion ▲ at the Venice Biennale with de Kooning and Arshile Gorky; the Museum of Modern Art purchased a major drip painting; and he • became the focus of both a sequence of photographs and ultimately a film by Hans Namuth showing him at work actually making the drip pictures) pushed him to a crisis. In the summer of 1950 he rode the crest of his fame long enough to complete four magisterial canvases (*One [Number 31, 1950]* [**1**], *Lavender Mist*, *Autumn Rhythm* [**5**], and *No. 32*); then his will to abstraction failed him. In 1951 he began to make black-and-white paintings [**2**] with, as he put it, "some of my early images coming through," meaning that he returned to the figurative mode of his artistic beginnings in ■ the thirties and early forties: a mixture of Mexican mural painting and the American Regionalist style of his teacher, Thomas Hart Benton [**3**]. This return, accompanied by the resurgence of his alcoholism, meant that by 1953 Pollock was painting with such great difficulty that his 1955 show at the Sidney Janis Gallery had to be conceived as a retrospective, since there was no recent output. Deeply depressed by a work block that appeared to be permanent, he drove his car into a tree in the summer of 1956, killing himself in an act that most people think was intentional.

If there was a war inside Pollock over the competing values of figurative and abstract art, there has been a war ever since about how these options should be understood in the interpretation of Pollock's work. Given the centrality of that work within the history of modernism, not only in the United States but also elsewhere ▲ (both the Gutai group in Japan and Piero Manzoni's *Lines* depend on Pollock), this interpretive battle has unusually high stakes, for it pits various views about the meaning and even the very possibility of abstraction against one another.

The champion of Pollock's work who had no doubt about the artist's commitment to abstraction (the "formidably high-brow critic" whom *Life* had mentioned), and indeed to the necessity of • that abstraction to the success of his art, was Clement Greenberg. A supporter of Pollock's from the early forties, Greenberg initially appreciated his art for the spatial compression of its surfaces, which created what he termed a "fuliginous flatness" that, expanding laterally along the face of the painting, transformed the conditions of the traditional easel picture, with its virtual, illusionistic space, into those of the wall-like mural painting, which Greenberg associated with modern science's commitment to observable, objective fact. This flattening could still be compatible with figuration, however, as Greenberg pointed out in the case of ■ Jean Dubuffet's similarly compressed and scarred, yet representational, surfaces.

But by the late forties, the necessity of abstraction had entered into Greenberg's assessment, since he had reorganized his reading

2 • Jackson Pollock, *Number 14, 1951*, 1951
Enamel on canvas, 146.4 x 271.8 (57⅝ x 107)

▲ 1942a, 1947b, 1959c • 1955a ■ 1933

▲ 1955a, 1959a • 1942a, 1960b ■ 1946, 1959c

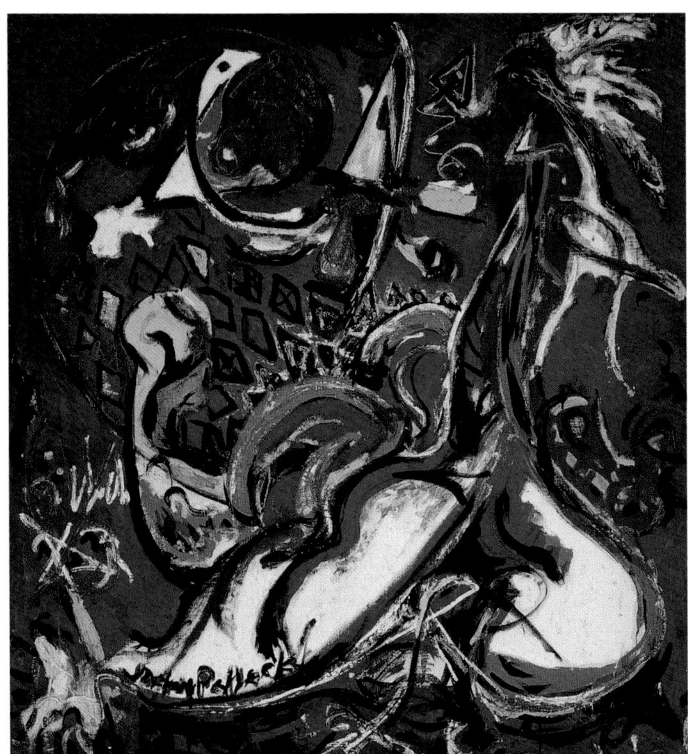

3 • Jackson Pollock, *Moon Woman Cuts the Circle*, c. 1943
Oil on canvas, 106.7 x 101.6 (42 x 40)

of modernism from a scientific model to a reflexive one: the visual arts were not to pattern themselves on the rigor of positivist science but on the modality of their own experiential grounds of possibility, namely the operations of vision itself. Grasped abstractly, these operations were not organized around the object that might be seen but, rather, in the subjective conditions of seeing: the fact that vision is projective; that it grasps its field synchronously rather than sequentially; that it is free from the gravitational field of the body. Modernism's highest ambition would thus be to picture the form of consciousness peculiar to vision: "To render substance entirely optical and form as an integral part of ambient space—this brings anti-illusionism full circle. Instead of the illusion of things, we are now offered the illusion of modalities: namely, that matter is incorporeal, weightless and exists only optically like a mirage."

Eyesight alone

The skeins of Pollock's drip pictures, now recoded as "hallucinated literalness" capable of creating the "counter-illusion of light alone," were thus endowed with a new mission: that of pulverizing or, in Greenberg's terms, "volatilizing" the object, creating this incorporeal weightlessness that could only transmit its effects abstractly. The skeins, constituted of pure line, the very stuff of drawing, managed to undermine the goal of drawing, which is to bound an object by describing its contour. Constantly looping back on themselves, they not only disallowed the formation of anything like a stable contour but they also dispersed any sense of a focal point or compositional center within the optical field. In this sense, line was put to the service of the creation of a kind of luminous atmosphere, formerly the province of color, and in thus canceling or suspending the distinction between line and color, Pollock's skeins further transcended, so Greenberg (along with his colleague Michael Fried) argued, the conditions of reality in order to enter the dialectical terms of abstraction. For, as Fried put it, Pollock's line succeeded in bounding and delimiting "nothing—except, in a sense, eyesight."

But if Pollock's work seemed to have, once and for all, delivered on the promise of a half century of struggle to establish the viability of abstract art, proving that it was not simply a function of mechanism or geometry but could also be sweeping and emotive, its maker's own indecisiveness—his backsliding into figuration in 1951 with the "early images coming through"—opened the door to two alternate readings. Based on a challenge to the very idea of abstraction, one such reading is personal or biographical in nature; the other, more deeply structural. The first type argues that Pollock (who underwent various psychoanalytic treatments for alcoholism throughout his life), was painting out of his unconscious, with memory images (according to the Freudian account) or archetypal images (the Jungian version) shaping the figurative works of the thirties and early forties and then underlying the dripped skeins that covered them over in a kind of denial or refusal in the period 1947–50, only for them to reemerge, triumphant, in the early fifties. According to this argument, the abstract Pollock is a figment of the misguided "formalist" imagination; Pollock's painting is always laden with content, obfuscated or not.

Since the skeins of the dripped pictures are often extremely transparent, it is clear that there are no figures beneath them. This puts one part of the foregoing argument in jeopardy, at least for that aspect of Pollock's work—the dripped pictures—that is taken as central to the history of modernism. Further, it would seem from all available evidence that Pollock's ambition during this period was indeed for nonfigurative, abstract work (although the nature of that abstraction is still a matter of contention, as will become apparent below). It is whether such an ambition (that is, for work that will escape the image altogether) is structurally possible within the domain of painting that concerns the second of these "figurative" readings, the one offered by T. J. Clark.

Arguing that Pollock's drive for abstraction arose from a sense that "likeness" or figuration could only repeat representational clichés, Clark comments on the frequency of Pollock's use of the title *One* or *No. 1* [**4**], even to his renumbering members of a series so as to produce yet another "first" object, another "one." This he sees as symptomatic of Pollock's need to achieve either some kind of absolute wholeness, before the parturition of the field into representational units, or some kind of absolute priorness, before a mark transforms itself for its (primitive) maker from the index of his or her presence—as in a palm-print deposited on the walls of the prehistoric cave—into a representation or image or figure of that presence.

The first type of oneness is, in Clark's account, parallel to the indivisible optical plenum of the Greenberg/Fried (modernist) reading. The difference is that Clark views this cloudlike vortex as an "image"—a metaphor for the idea of order or wholeness rather than a rendition of it in all its abstractness. It is the inescapability of this condition of metaphor that Clark sees Pollock fighting in the second form of oneness, in which a "before figuration" is sought in the stress on the index. That these traces of his process of painting brought with them associations of desecration and violence against the canvas itself—the stains and crusts of thrown paint, the wrinkled scabs of uneven drying—seems to declare not only this condition of firstness, a marking that occurs before metaphor takes over, but also an attack on the other type of oneness and its condition as image.

Yet, Clark argues, even this second option is unable to outrun the metaphorical, since it, too, becomes an image: a picture of accident, of stridency, of chaos. Thus, in Clark's reading, Pollock's art has failure always built into it, and his ability to continue falters when he is no longer able to imagine an outside to the figurative. This occurs in the summer of 1950, when his pictures, ever larger and ever more seemingly authoritative, fully submit to the metaphor of oneness that was lying in wait for them all the time. They become, that is, pictures of nature, massive crypto-landscapes: *Autumn Rhythm*, *Lavender Mist*, *One*.

The total "one"

But is the index or trace of process really fated, as Clark would have it, to coalesce into metaphor? A whole generation of Process ▲ artists thought it was not. As Robert Morris argued in the late sixties, "Of the Abstract Expressionists, only Pollock was able to recover process and hold on to it as part of the end form of the work. Pollock's recovery of process involved a profound rethinking of the role of both material and tools in making." To this reconception Morris gave the name "Anti-form." Noting that Pollock had opened his work to the conditions of gravity, he argued that if all of art has been an effort to maintain the rigidity and thus the verticality of its materials—canvas is stretched, clay is formed on internal armatures, plaster is applied to lath—this is because form itself is a fight against gravity; it is a battle to remain intact, to continue to adhere as a formal gestalt, as a coherently bounded whole, as "one." By famously laying the canvases of his dripped paintings on the floor and flinging liquid paint onto them from sticks dipped into open cans, Pollock had given his work over to gravity and had thus opened them to antiform. Though he did not explicitly draw this conclusion, the implication of Morris's argument was that antiform was structurally incompatible with the creation of the figure—any figure.

4 • Jackson Pollock, *No. 1*, 1948
Oil and enamel on unprimed canvas, 172.7 x 264.2 (68 x 104)

▲ 1969

5 • Jackson Pollock, *Autumn Rhythm*, 1950
Oil on canvas, 266.7 x 525.8 (105 x 207)

Indeed, it would be possible to push Morris's reasoning further and to say that gravity vectors the phenomenological field, separating experience itself into two domains: the optical one and the kinesthetic, bodily one. The Gestalt psychologists, writing in the twenties and thirties, understood the field of sight as fundamentally vertical, and thus freed from the pull of gravity. They described the visual subject's relation to its image-world as "frontoparallel" to it, a function of its standing erect, independent of the ground. This means that the image or gestalt is always experienced as a vertical and that its very coherence as a form (in their terms, its "praegnanz") is based on this uprightness, this rise into verticality which is how the imagination constitutes its images.

In this, the Gestalt psychologists were in accord with the Freudian account of a separation of perceptual fields into vertical and horizontal, a division that in Freud's view occurred at the point when the human species became erect, thereby separating itself from an animality oriented toward the horizontal of the ground and the dominance (for hunting and mating) of the sense of smell. Standing up produces the importance of the vertical and of the visual, of a field that is distanced from the immediate grasp of the perceiver. A function of this distanced viewing would be the sublimation of the carnal instincts and the possibility of a conception, Freud argued in *Civilization and its Discontents* (1930), of beauty.

By returning painting to the field of the horizontal, Pollock attacked all these sublimatory forces: uprightness, the gestalt, form, beauty. At least this was the conviction held by many of the artists convinced by the antiform drive of his work. That the canvases were returned to a formal decorousness by being hung—vertically—on the wall of either Pollock's studio or the museum, did not deter them in their view. For them, the traces of process to which Clark points—the puddling, the scabbing, the lateral ooze of liquid into cloth—are all marks of the horizontal, marks that continue to disrupt the uprightness of the work, its effective coming together as image. All the other Abstract Expressionists worked on easels or with their canvases tacked directly to the wall. This meant that in de Kooning's or Gorky's work liquid paint would form a vertical runoff, the spatters would themselves be oriented toward form. Pollock alone resisted this, and such resistance maintains itself in any view of his work: a horizontal antiform as an abstractness uncolonized by the vertical "one."

FURTHER READING

T. J. Clark, "Jackson Pollock's Abstraction," in Serge Guilbaut (ed.), *Reconstructing Modernism* (Cambridge, Mass.: MIT Press, 1990)

Eva Cockcroft, "Abstract Expressionism, Weapon of the Cold War," *Artforum*, vol. 12, June 1974

Michael Fried, *Three American Painters* (Cambridge, Mass.: Fogg Art Museum, 1965)

Rosalind Krauss, *The Optical Unconscious* (Cambridge, Mass.: MIT Press, 1993)

Steven Naifeh and Gregory White Smith, *Jackson Pollock* (New York: Clarkson Potter, 1989)

William Rubin, "Pollock as Jungian Illustrator: The Limits of Psychological Criticism," *Art in America*, no. 67, November 1979, and no. 68, December 1979

Kirk Varnedoe, *Jackson Pollock* (New York: Museum of Modern Art, 1998)

1950–1959

362 1951 Barnett Newman's second exhibition fails: he is ostracized by his fellow Abstract Expressionists, only later to be hailed as a father figure by the Minimalist artists. YAB

368 1953 Composer John Cage collaborates on Robert Rauschenberg's *Tire Print*: the indexical imprint is developed as a weapon against the expressive mark in a range of work by Rauschenberg, Ellsworth Kelly, and Cy Twombly. RK

373 1955a The first Gutai exhibition in Japan marks the dissemination of modernist art through the media and its reinterpretation by artists outside the United States and Europe, also exemplified by the rise of the Neoconcretist group in Brazil. YAB

379 1955b The "Le mouvement" show at the Galerie Denise René in Paris launches kineticism. YAB

385 1956 The exhibition "This is Tomorrow" in London is the culmination of research into postwar relations between art, science, technology, product design, and popular culture undertaken by the Independent Group, forerunners of British Pop art. HF

391 1957a Two small vanguard groups, the Lettrist International and the Imaginist Bauhaus, merge to form the Situationist International, the most politically engaged of all postwar movements. HF
box • Two theses from *The Society of the Spectacle*

398 1957b Ad Reinhardt writes "Twelve Rules for a New Academy": as avant-garde paradigms in painting are reformulated in Europe, the monochrome and grid are explored in the United States by Reinhardt, Robert Ryman, Agnes Martin, and others. RK

404 1958 Jasper Johns's *Target with Four Faces* appears on the cover of *Artnews* magazine: for some artists like Frank Stella, Johns presents a model of painting in which figure and ground are fused in a single image-object; for others, he opens up the use of everyday signs and conceptual ambiguities alike. HF
box • Ludwig Wittgenstein RK

411 1959a Lucio Fontana has his first retrospective: he uses kitsch associations to question idealist modernism, a critique extended by his protégé Piero Manzoni. YAB

415 1959b At the San Francisco Art Association, Bruce Conner shows *CHILD*, a mutilated figure in a high chair made in protest against capital punishment: a practice of assemblage and environment is developed on the West Coast by Conner, Wallace Berman, Ed Kienholz, and others that is more scabrous than its equivalents in New York, Paris, or elsewhere. YAB

421 1959c The Museum of Modern Art in New York mounts "New Images of Man": existentialist aesthetics extend into a Cold War politics of figuration in the work of Alberto Giacometti, Jean Dubuffet, Francis Bacon, Willem de Kooning, and others. RK
box • Art and the Cold War RK

426 1959d Richard Avedon's *Observations* and Robert Frank's *The Americans* establish the dialectical parameters of New York School photography. BB

1951

Barnett Newman's second exhibition fails: he is ostracized by his fellow Abstract Expressionists, only later to be hailed as a father figure by the Minimalist artists.

Barnett Newman's second one-man show, in April–May 1951, at the Betty Parsons Gallery in New York was even more unsuccessful than the first a year before. At the close of the exhibition (where nothing was sold), Newman took back all his works the gallery had in stock. He would occasionally display a painting or two in group shows during the fifties, but waited until 1958 for his next solo exhibition (at Bennington College), soon followed by his first retrospective in New York (at French & Co. in 1959). It was only after this last event that Newman's status altered: "He changed in about a year's time from an outcast or a crank into the father figure of two generations," wrote art critic Thomas B. Hess, referring to the admiration of artists as diverse as ▲Jasper Johns and Frank Stella, Donald Judd and Dan Flavin.

What must have been particularly distressing to Newman in 1951 was not so much the continuing hostility or silence of the press, but that of the fellow artists he had generously helped over the years—organizing their exhibitions, prefacing their catalogues, editing their statements, acting as their spokesman and impresario. Newman later claimed that at his first show at Betty Parsons' in 1950, where the small New York art world of the time had rushed, Robert Motherwell had told him: "We thought that you were one of us. Instead your show is a critique against all of us." With hindsight this remark is highly perceptive—for Newman's work contrasts indeed with the gestural rhetoric governing the paintings •of Motherwell and other Abstract Expressionists—but at the time it was meant to hurt, and it did. Motherwell's disapproval was widely shared by his colleagues, who stayed away from the opening of Newman's second show a year later, with the notable exception of Jackson Pollock. (Pollock had in fact been instrumental in persuading Newman to hold this second exhibition at all, joining Betty Parsons in her encouragement and helping with the installation.)

The works selected by Newman were extremely diverse—no doubt in part to break down the nascent journalistic cliché that all his canvases were the same (this cliché was particularly offensive to him, given the extreme care he always took to avoid redundancy and repetition, keeping his entire output in all media to fewer than three hundred items). Only one painting, *Onement II* of 1948, directly referred to his pictorial breakthrough of that year: it consists, like the much smaller *Onement I* [**1**], of a red-maroon vertical field symmetrically bisected by a narrow "zip" (to use the odd term Newman

1 • Barnett Newman, *Onement I*, 1948
Oil on canvas and oil on masking tape on canvas, 69.2 x 41.2 (27¼ x 16¼)

adopted later on when speaking of his vertical dividers, preferring it to "band" for it connoted an activity rather than a motionless state of being). Next to *Onement II* he proposed a series of pairings, sometimes with the help of titles, as in the case of *Eve* and *Adam*. (The latter painting, now bearing the date 1951 and 1952, would be subsequently reworked by Newman, like several other canvases:

▲ 1958, 1962c, 1965 • 1947b, 1949

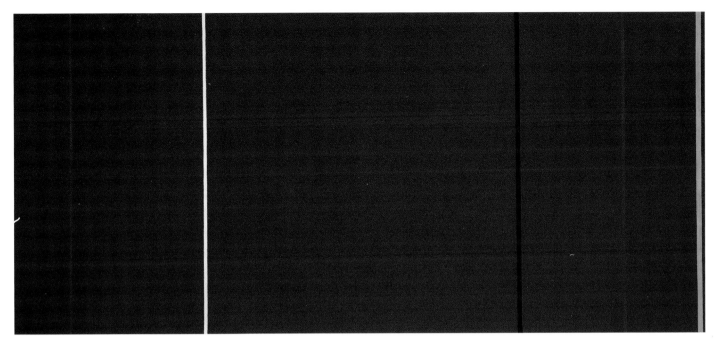

2 • Barnett Newman, *Vir heroicus sublimis*, 1950–1
Oil on canvas, 242.2 x 541.7 (95⅜ x 213¼)

"I think the idea of a 'finished' picture is a fiction," he once said.) The two paintings that most enraged Newman's detractors were *The Voice* and *The Name II*, both consisting of a white field about eight feet square and divided by white zips (one single off-center zip for *The Voice* and four evenly placed in *The Name II*, including zips at the right and left limits of the canvas)—a drastic economy of means that the artist himself had wanted to emphasize by printing the show's invitation elegantly white on white. And then there was the huge *Vir heroicus sublimis* [**2**], an expansive eighteen-foot-wide wall of an evenly vibrant red punctuated by five zips of various colors at irregular intervals, to which *The Wild*, a painting of the same height (eight feet) but only one and a half inches wide, and consisting entirely of a single red zip with a tiny margin of darker red on either side, must have at first seemed the strangest pendant.

The logic of this last correlation, however, is crystal clear. In *Vir heroicus sublimis*, the traditional oppositions of figure and ground, contour and shape, line and plane are dramatically suspended in that the rightmost zip and the tiny band of red "ground" it demarcates at the edge of the canvas are of the same width. With *The Wild* [**3**], painted in its wake, it is as if an extra zip from the large red canvas had migrated onto the wall, taking on an existence ▲of its own as one of the first "shaped" canvases in the history of postwar American art. And to make sure that *The Wild*'s "objecthood" would be neither overlooked nor overstated (as well as that of several smaller vertical paintings in the same vein, for which Pollock had designed simple wooden frames almost three inches deep), Newman exhibited it next to his first sculpture, *Here I* [**3**], where two white "zips," now cutting into real space, had completed their journey toward autonomy. In short, the show was masterfully composed—Newman had always been a brilliant curator. But this seems only to have made the resistance to it all the stronger.

3 • Barnett Newman, (left) *Here I*, 1950; (right) *The Wild*, 1950. Plaster and painted wood, 243.8 x 67.3 x 71.8 (96 x 26½ x 28¼) excluding base; oil on canvas, 243 x 4.1 (95¾ x 1⅝)

▲ 1958

Perhaps he should have foreseen such difficulties. After all, he knew better than anyone else that his art was not easy to grasp—it had taken him eight full months, dedicated to nothing else, to understand what he had achieved in *Onement I.* Hess wrote an account of Newman's revelation: "On his birthday, January 29, 1948, he prepared a small canvas with a surface of cadmium red dark (a deep mineral that looks like an earth pigment—like Indian red or a sienna) and fixed a piece of tape down the center. Then he quickly smeared a coat of cadmium red light over the tape, to test the color. He looked at the picture for a long time. Indeed he studied it for some eight months. He had finished questing."

As countless statements testify, Newman's search had long been for a "proper" subject matter. Yet the by-now standard interpretation of this painting as a pictorial equivalent to the division of light and dark at the beginning of the Book of Genesis fails to account for its radical novelty. For at least three years Newman had been translating his desire "to start from scratch, to paint as if painting never existed before" into a thematics of Origin. His first "automatic" drawings of 1944–5, with their imagery of germination and mythological titles (one of them is called *Gea*, the goddess of the earth, offspring of the original chaos), and his many canvases of 1946–7 (*The Beginning, Genesis—The Break, The Word I, The Command, Moment, Genetic Moment*), with their titles directly alluding to the dawn of the world as it is conveyed in the Old Testament, attest to this central concern—and at some level Newman's art would always evolve around the same issue.

So if the subject matter is not new in *Onement I*, is the form that conveys it? The answer is surprisingly complex. At a formal level, one would be justified in thinking, once again, that there is nothing strikingly original about this modest canvas, for *Moment* [**4**], realized two years before, had already consisted of a vertical rectangular field divided symmetrically by a central vertical element. Conceptually and structurally, however, a gulf separates *Moment* from *Onement I.* One could even say that with *Onement I* and all subsequent works, Newman undermined the philosophical idea that a form merely conveys a preexisting content.

A hint is given by the "ground," which is treated differently in the two paintings. While the field of *Onement I* is painted as evenly as can be (it was initially conceived only as a first layer, as a "prepared ground," according to Hess), in *Moment* we are confronted with a differentiated field that functions as an indeterminate background and is pushed still farther back in space by the "band"—the "band" is not yet a "zip," it still functions as a *repoussoir*, as an element in the foreground pushing back in space the rest of the picture, much like the stenciled letters in an Analytical Cubist ▲ canvas by Braque or Picasso. As Newman would later say of this work and the few other paintings that remain of the period, it gives a "sense of atmospheric background," of something that can be conceived as "natural atmosphere." Or, as he would also say later, he had been "manipulating space," "manipulating color" in order to destroy the void, the chaos that existed before the beginning of all things. As a result, what he had procured with *Moment* was an image, something that was not congruent with but applied to its field and thus could pretend to extend beyond its limits—something that had no adherence to its support (conceived as a neutral receptacle) and could have been worked out previously in a sketch (as indeed it was).

4 • Barnett Newman, *Moment*, 1946
Oil on canvas, 76.2 x 40.6 (30 x 16)

Onement I, Hess reports, was to look something like *Moment*: "Newman was about to texture the background; then he would have removed the tape and painted in the stripe inside the masked edges." But to "texture the background" and to "paint in" the stripe are precisely what Newman renounced in *Onement I.* Nothing existed here that could have been "painted in" or textured, that is, nothing existed beforehand, no "ground" per se, waiting to be filled. While *Gea, Genesis—The Break*, or *The Word*,

▲ 1911

The Command, and even *Moment contained* ideographs, visual symbols of the idea of Creation, *Onement I is*, in itself, an ideograph of Creation. (One has only to recall that *Gea* had figured in the show entitled "The Ideographic Picture," curated by Newman in January 1947, to measure the distance he had traveled since then in his understanding of the concept of ideograph.) The title *Onement*, an Old English word from which "atonement" derives, means "the fact of being made into one": the painting does not *represent* wholeness but *declares* it in uniting the field and the zip into a single entity. Or, to put it differently, the field asserts itself as such through its stark symmetrical division by a zip.

Of course, the zip is still a simple vertical "line," hence a ready-made sign that preexisted in some absent stock of signs that—like all linguistic symbols—could be convoked and used at will. There is no escape, in other words, from the play of absence and deferral inherent to all forms of language; but at least the significance of the zip depends entirely on its coexistence with the field to which it refers and which it measures and declares for the beholder. *Onement I* is indeed an ideograph or, to put it more generally, a sign, but it is a sign of a special kind, one that emphasizes a certain circularity between its signification of the sign and the actual situation of its utterance: it partakes of the category of words that ▲ linguists call "shifters," such as all the personal pronouns but also "now," "here," "not there—here" (which are, not coincidentally, some of the names given by Newman to his later works). Like all previous paintings by Newman, *Onement I* is concerned with the myth of origin (the initial split), but for the first time this myth is told in the present tense. And this present tense is an attempt to address the spectator directly, immediately, as an "I" to a "you."

A sense of place

After the long rumination of 1948, Newman's most productive year (with nineteen canvases, almost one fifth of his entire pictorial oeuvre) was 1949. The largest work of that year, *Be I*, dominated his 1950 show. Not only did it radicalize *Onement I*'s flash of light (the thin central zip dividing the dark red field is razor-sharp and white), but its injunctive title made it clear that the beholder was summoned: "You! Be!" It is as if Newman had intuitively understood that the perception of bilateral symmetry is essential to our status as erect, human beings (as opposed to apes). Bilateral symmetry, to which Newman's work was to have recourse periodically throughout his career, presupposes the vertical axis of our body as the structuring factor of our visual perception, of our situation in front of what we see; it solidifies for us the immediate equivalence between the awareness of our own body and the orientation of our field of vision. Its perception is instantaneous and self-evident. • According to French philosopher Maurice Merleau-Ponty, whose *Phenomenology of Perception* (1945; English translation, 1962) was to become a bible for the Minimalist sculptors in the sixties, it is our verticality since early childhood, more than anything else, that gives us, without our noticing, a sense of our being in the world.

With the large canvases he exhibited in 1951, and particularly with *Vir heroicus sublimis*, Newman turned to the issue of scale, another of his lifelong obsessions, but one closely related to the phenomenology of presence explored in *Onement I*. Of all the postwar American artists, he is the only one prior to the sculptor ▲ Richard Serra for whom scale took on an ethical dimension. Like Matisse, he deemed it morally wrong to figure out a composition in a tiny sketch and then to square it up on canvas. And if he finally got involved in the medium of printmaking, at the end of his life, it was only after he had discovered that he could clearly manifest how a slight modification in the cropping of margins radically transforms the internal scale of a single image (his succinct preface for his 1964 portfolio of lithographs, *18 Cantos*, provides the best analysis of the question of scale, as opposed to size, written in this century).

Vir heroicus sublimis is a very large canvas. So is *Cathedra*, completed shortly after Newman's 1951 show, or *Uriel* (1955), *Shining Forth* (1961), *Who's Afraid of Red, Yellow, and Blue II* (1967–8), and *Anna's Light* (1968), the largest of all (nine by twenty feet). But size itself is not the issue. If these works seem much larger than the equally gigantic canvases produced by Newman's fellow Abstract Expressionists (with the exception of Pollock, in whose webs we easily get lost), it is in great part because they provide us with far less visual incident and require us to take them in at once even while, confronted with the sheer color saturation of their flooding expanse, we realize that we cannot. Attempting to fix one of the several zips that perform a scansion of these vast color fields, we find ourselves tempted to zoom on to the next one. Thus, solicited by the vibrating ocean of violent color, never able to survey the whole and yet forced to acknowledge its existence, we experience it as "here—not there," full in our face.

"There is a tendency to look at large pictures from a distance. The large pictures in this exhibition are intended to be seen from a short distance." This statement, a handout that Newman typed for his second (1951) Betty Parsons show, makes it clear that size was for him a means of exceeding our visual field (and he drove the point home a few years later by having himself photographed staring at *Cathedra* while standing barely three feet away from the canvas). Most commentators have associated this excess, through which we are forced to relinquish our mastery over the visual field, with the theory of the Sublime, which Newman broached in one of his most famous texts, "The Sublime is Now," written in 1948 while he was mulling over *Onement I*. However, given that this short essay was a commission (for which Newman read the classical philosophical treatises by Longinus, Burke, Kant, and Hegel on the issue—all of which he summarily dismissed), and that the concept of the Sublime entirely disappeared from his vocabulary afterward (with one exception), one is tempted to deem it a misnomer. In fact, "sublime" is the name momentarily given by Newman to what he calls everywhere else "tragedy," a term absent from "The Sublime is Now." Which is to say that his understanding of sublimity had little to do with the philosophical texts he had just read. The exception just mentioned is a case in point: referring

▲ Introduction 4, 1918 • 1965
▲ 1969, 1970

to the title of *Vir heroicus sublimis*, Newman told David Sylvester in 1965 that "man can be or is sublime in his relation to his sense of being aware." The Sublime, for Newman, is something that gives one the feeling of being where one is, of *hic et nunc*—of the here and now—courageously confronting the human fate, standing alone in front of chaos, without the props of "memory, association, nostalgia, legend, myth." From 1948 on, he was to insist on the fact that what he wanted to give the beholder was a sense of place, a sense of his or her own scale.

The Sublime of the Enlightenment philosophers and that of Newman were not entirely opposed, however. In August 1949, in front of an Indian mound in Ohio—"a work of art that cannot even be seen, so it is something that must be experienced there on the spot"—Newman had an experience that was not foreign to the eighteenth-century British philosopher Edmund Burke's understanding of the Sublime as a feeling engendered by a vastness one cannot comprehend, nor to the German Immanuel Kant's description, when referring to the perception of the Egyptian pyramids, of the role of temporality in this sudden blank of comprehension. But for them the concept remains a universal category: they define it in terms of a temporary feeling of lack with regard to an idea of totality. Newman wants to speak not of space as concept, but of his own "presence"; not of infinity, but of scale; not of "the sense of time," but of "the physical *sensation* of time." This is what *Onement I* had meant to him and what the Ohio encounter confirmed. In that sense, it also meant farewell to the philosophical concept of the Sublime: soon it would seem too universal to express "the ideal that Man Is Present."

The "universal" (which he often called the "diagram") has always been a bad word for Newman (as early as 1935, in a list that he compiled for *The Answer*, an anarchist journal he was editing, the works of Hegel and Marx are prominent among the books not to read, while Spinoza's and Mikhail Bakunin's are high on the must-read ledger). Thus his unabashed demonization of Piet ▲ Mondrian, whom he already considered his nemesis three years before *Onement I*. (In his first long aesthetic tract, "The Plasmic Image," which he wrote and kept rewriting in 1945, but in the end never published, Newman, like others at the time, interpreted Mondrian's painting both as either mere geometric art or good design and as "abstraction from nature"—despite the fact that Mondrian had spent a considerable energy attacking both these views.) In short, Newman made a straw man of Mondrian by eagerly repeating the clichés of the mediocre literature available to him. But while this imaginary antagonism energized him, his difficulty in overcoming what he called the "neo-plastic mortgage" long remained a sore spot (the triumphalism of such titles as *The Death of Euclid* or *Euclidean Abyss*, two canvases that immediately precede *Onement I*, was premature). It was only in the mid-sixties that Newman understood that the "Mondrian" he had been fighting all along was a fiction, and that his own art and theory had much in common with those of the real Mondrian, notably in the cardinal role ascribed to intuition. But acknowledging at last what he shared with the European veteran of abstraction, Newman was also able to grasp the nature of his twofold feelings of resistance toward him. First, partly thanks to his discussions with his young Minimalist admirers (with whom he did not want to be confused but whose company he obviously enjoyed), he realized that his concept of "wholeness" was utterly contradictory to Mondrian's reliance upon the traditional practice of relational composition— ▲ something derided by Frank Stella as "You do something in one corner and you balance it with something in the other corner." Second, Newman was able to make the connection between this relational aesthetic and Mondrian's social utopia, associating the latter with dogmatism, rationalism and State terror. Rather than condemning Mondrian's "formalism" and the "lack of subject matter" of his art as he had done in the past, he now explained his dislike for the social project inherent in Mondrian's abstraction in terms of his own anarchist politics.

This revaluation led to a series of four paintings entitled *Who's Afraid of Red, Yellow, and Blue* dating from 1966 to 1968, the first and the third being asymmetrical, and the two others, symmetrical. (Symmetry had been a standard feature in Newman's art, but now it was directly aimed, as had been Stella's black paintings several years before, at Mondrian's prohibition of it.) Each pair consists of a small or medium canvas and a very large one. Both of the large paintings from the series have subsequently been vandalized, *Who's Afraid of Red, Yellow, and Blue III* most savagely. This disaster should perhaps not be dismissed as random lunacy (all the more since Newman's paintings have endured an unusual rate of vandalism): one wonders if such a visceral, iconoclastic response was not in part encouraged by the art itself. *Who's Afraid ... III* derives from the first painting of the series [**5**], from which it borrows the two lateral zips, a tiny yellow one on the right edge, and a broader and quasi-translucent blue one on the left, but in laterally expanding the central red plane to a width of nearly eighteen feet, Newman has heightened the color saturation to a point of maximum tension. The engulfing red is overwhelming: one cannot dodge its blow. Presumably, the man who knifed the painting, furiously slashing it three times across, could not bear the heat. In his own, misguided way, he paid homage to Newman's sense of tragedy and his Baudelairean plea for an "impassioned criticism."

FURTHER READING

Yve-Alain Bois, "On Two Paintings by Barnett Newman," *October*, no. 108, Spring 2004

Yve-Alain Bois, "Perceiving Newman," *Painting as Model* (Cambridge, Mass.: MIT Press, 1990)

Mark Godfrey, "Barnett Newman's *Stations* and the Memory of the Holocaust," *October*, no. 108, Spring 2004

Jean-François Lyotard, "Newman: The Instant" (1985), reprinted in *The Inhuman* (Stanford: Stanford University Press, 1991)

Barnett Newman, *Selected Writings and Interviews*, ed. John O'Neill (New York: Alfred Knopf, 1990)

Jeremy Strick, *The Sublime Is Now: The Early Work of Barnett Newman, Paintings and Drawings 1944–1949* (New York: PaceWildenstein, 1994)

Ann Temkin, "Barnett Newman on Exhibition," in Ann Temkin (ed.), *Barnett Newman* (Philadelphia: Philadelphia Museum of Art, 2002)

▲ 1913, 1917, 1944a

▲ 1958

5 • Barnett Newman, *Who's Afraid of Red, Yellow, and Blue I*, 1966
Oil on canvas, 190.5 x 122 (75 x 48)

1953

Composer John Cage collaborates on Robert Rauschenberg's *Tire Print*: the indexical imprint is developed as a weapon against the expressive mark in a range of work by Rauschenberg, Ellsworth Kelly, and Cy Twombly.

Imagine a canvas panel, four feet square, painted flat white. Now imagine a drawing not quite as white, since there are extremely faint residues of ink and crayon streaking the paper, on the archival mat of which is a label that reads "Erased de Kooning Drawing/Robert Rauschenberg/1953." [1] Finally, imagine a twenty-three-foot scroll on which a continuous band of black inscribes the track of an automobile tire that has been driven down the paper's center. What do these three objects have in common?

That was the question surrounding Robert Rauschenberg's art in the wake of his 1953 exhibition at the Stable Gallery in New York, in which several of his *White Paintings*, their matte panels arranged to form diptychs or polyptychs, were shown along with massive all-black works painted on grounds of crumbled newspaper. Critics greeted the young artist's show by dismissing the black pictures as "handmade debris," and the white ones as a "gratuitously destructive act." News of the tire print and the erased de Kooning soon followed, and, given the intensity of ▲admiration for Willem de Kooning in the early fifties, the idea of destroying one of his drawings instantly promoted scandal among those who heard about it, endowing Rauschenberg with a reputation as some kind of nihilist or Dadaist rerun. And indeed, •Rauschenberg did know something about Marcel Duchamp (1887–1968) and his presence in New York at the time, even though he did not meet him until a few years later.

Yet the most obvious thread that ties these three works together is their hostile attitude toward Abstract Expressionism and its dominance over advanced art-world thinking in the late forties and early fifties. Rauschenberg, who had begun art school on the G. I. Bill (a program providing college-level study to all soldiers who had fought for the United States in World War II), first in ■Paris, then at Black Mountain College in North Carolina in 1949, and then in New York in 1950 at the Art Students League, was surrounded by fellow students for whom this had become the universal aesthetic language. From the Abstract Expressionists ◆who were teaching at Black Mountain (such as de Kooning, Robert Motherwell, and Jack Tworkov), to the students at the League who worshiped these artists (such as Alfred Leslie, Joan Mitchell, and Raymond Parker), the idea of the painted mark as a unique trace of the individual who makes it, along with the entire conceptual baggage of authenticity, spontaneity, and risk that accompanied this ideology of the mark, had become a kind of creed.

Dada redux

Nothing could be less spontaneous and redolent of the character of its maker than a line as mechanically produced as that of a tire track [2]. Similarly, nothing could withdraw from the theater of "risk" so totally as a blank canvas that turns the famous arena on which the action painter battled to declare what Harold Rosenberg had called the "metaphysical substance" of his "existence" into a kind of monochromatic readymade. And even more openly avowing that its sights were set on the Abstract Expressionist celebration of the meaning invested in the uniqueness of the artist's touch, the *Erased de Kooning Drawing* makes it clear that nothing could be more contrary to this ethos than the repeated strokes of the eraser, the trace of which does not register the imprint of the worker's identity but is instead a mechanized effacement of both the drawing's marks and its own counterstrokes.

If these three objects united around a critique of action painting it was not, however, in the service of nihilism. The positive aspirations that Rauschenberg invested in the *White Paintings*, made for the most part in the summer of 1951, were allied with the positions then being developed by the American experimental composer John Cage, himself teaching at Black Mountain. Cage's thinking, influenced by Zen Buddhism, celebrated passivity as against the strain and thrust of "action" or, indeed, the activity involved in any conception of composition. Interested in the idea that chance and randomness are universal modalities that structure the universe, Cage thought about music as an aleatory interweaving of silence and ambient sound. That summer at Black Mountain, a brilliant young pianist, David Tudor, performed Cage's newly composed *4′33″* by sitting quietly at the piano and signaling, rather than playing, the piece's movements by silently opening and closing the keyboard cover.

It was in the context of his interaction with Cage that Rauschenberg made his *White Paintings*. Their multiple panels were generated simply by a serial progression—single panel, diptych, triptych, four-, five-, and seven-panel paintings—and their shapes were seen as containing neither narrative nor any other frame of

▲1947b, 1959c ● 1914, 1918, 1935, 1942b, 1966a ■ 1947a ◆ 1947b

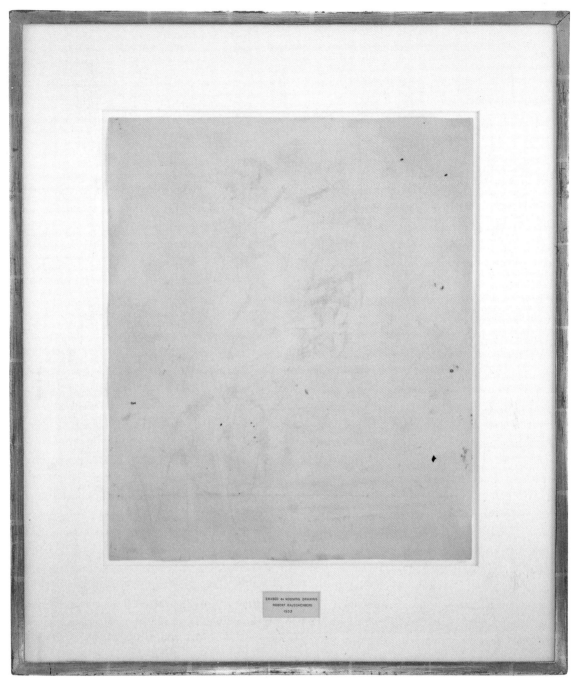

1 • Robert Rauschenberg, *Erased de Kooning Drawing*, 1953
Traces of ink and crayon on paper with mat and hand-lettered label in gold-leaf frame, 64.1 x 55.2 (25¼ x 21¾)

2 • Robert Rauschenberg with John Cage, *Automobile Tire Print*, 1953
Ink on paper mounted on canvas, 41.9 x 671.8 (16½ x 264½) fully extended

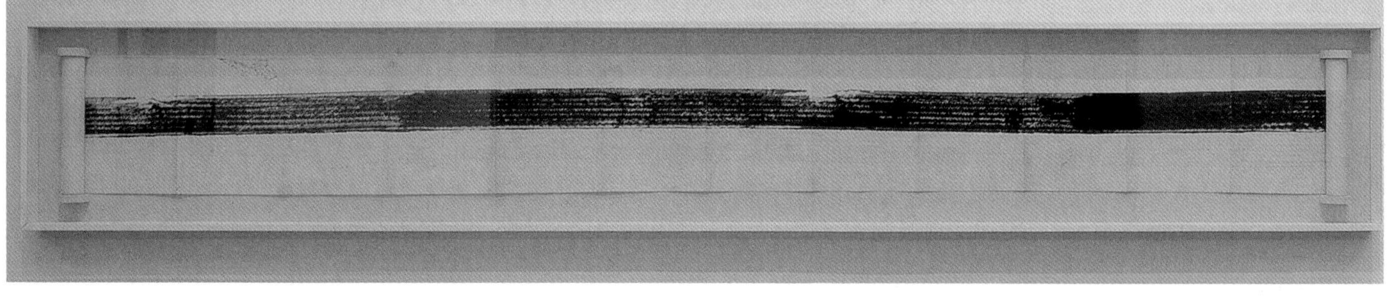

reference. What they were meant to do instead was to attract fleeting, ambient impressions the way that Cage's music opened itself to the noise of its audience's breathing or coughing. Indeed, Cage referred to the *White Paintings* as "landing strips" for dust particles, light, and shadow, and Rauschenberg himself would always speak of them as "the white paintings that would pick up the shadows."

Rauschenberg, who was active as a photographer during these years, would also make a connection between this sense of the painting as a screen onto which the shadows of passersby would be cast and the photo-sensitized surfaces that allow the photograph to register the impressions focused on them by the camera's lens. And even closer in terms of the activity of the cast shadow, there is the parallel between the white paintings and the massive "rayograms" that Rauschenberg had executed on blueprint paper the year before, in which feet, hands, ferns, and the nude female body were fixed as fragile two-dimensional shadows on the cerulean ground. This same connection between photography and cast shadow had been made before, of course, in the elaboration of Duchamp's *Large Glass* (1915–23) and in the parade of the cast shadows of his ▲ own readymades drawn across the surface of *Tu m'* (1918). Just as in Duchamp's case, where the crux of the relationship turned on the nature of the indexical mark—shared not only by shadow and photograph but also by the way the readymade is the "index" of the "rendezvous" or temporal moment of its selection—so in Rauschenberg's practice, the *White Paintings*' relation to photography broadened in the tire print and erased de Kooning drawing to a general consideration of the indexical trace.

That the index could invest three such different objects with the same logic of "noncomposition" testifies to Rauschenberg's grasp of its underlying principles, of the way the mark registers a depthless trace of its physical cause, stenciled, so to speak, off the world outside it but nowhere resonant with a symbolic meaning—as in the "expressive" mark's supposed inner life. Cage's own desire for such noncomposition had been reinforced by his acquaintance • with Duchamp, who had been in New York since the mid-forties; Cage was thus in a position to reinforce Rauschenberg's own interest in traces (as in his blueprint works) by pushing this toward a more general sense of its structural logic. Rauschenberg thus did not need a direct contact with Duchamp—to whom he was finally introduced by Cage only in 1957—to put together the readymade and the imprint, the shadow and the rubbing.

Formulae for noncomposition

Ellsworth Kelly's trajectory was strikingly similar to Rauschenberg's in these same years in that he, too, plumbed the logic of the index to find a way to suppress the autographic mark and to break through to a form of noncomposition. The differences between the two turn on the fact that Kelly had no instruction from Duchamp's example, even indirectly, and that Kelly's battle was not with Abstract Expressionism but with geometric abstraction. Mobilized in 1943, fighting in France the following year, and back in Paris in 1948 on the G. I. Bill, Kelly had no connection to what was happening in New York or to the spread of Piet Mondrian's legacy into academic dogma at the hands of artists like Georges Vantongerloo ▲ and Max Bill. The ideology of the balanced composition of geometrical parts, whose achieved unity would serve as a metaphor for a future utopia of social harmony, had taken hold of European practice. If the geometric delineation of this composition had nothing to do with the individual anguish purportedly folded into the action-painting stroke, it was still seen as expressive: resonating with the chords of "reason," it instituted the artist as Creator.

Kelly's struggle was, then, against this ethos of "composition." And as his disgust with the painting around him mounted he began to sketch the masonry of old buildings and bridges. As he put it, "The found forms in a cathedral vault or in a panel of asphalt on a roadway seemed more valuable and instructive, an experience more sensual than geometrical painting. Rather than making a picture that would be the interpretation of something I saw or the representation of an invented contents, I found an object and I presented it 'as is'."

The most remarkable of these early works presenting a found object "as is" was made in late 1949, when Kelly was struck by the elongated rectangle and mullion patterns of the windows in the Palais de Tokyo, which housed the Museum of Modern Art in Paris. Reproducing this "as is," he fashioned two panels, one for each casement, and projected the mullions of the lower one in wooden relief. Appearing as an abstract painting, *Window, Museum of Modern Art, Paris* **[3]** had the advantage of having used its referent (the object in the world from which it had been traced or stenciled) to relieve its author of any compositional duties, while at the same time dissembling the referent itself. Originally called *Black and White Relief*, the work did not advertise its basis in the principle of the readymade, and indeed, describing the process it now unleashed in his art, Kelly referred to its status as "already made." From this time forth, he said, "painting as I had known it was finished for me. The new works had to be unsigned painting-objects, anonymous. Everywhere I looked, everything I saw became something to be made, as is, without having to add anything whatever.... There was no more need to compose. The subject was there, already made and I could avail myself of it everywhere."

Sometimes these found forms, indexically transferred to the surface of Kelly's work, were objects, such as the paving stones in the garden of the American Hospital in Neuilly-sur-Seine, just outside Paris, reproduced to form a low relief (*Neuilly*, 1950), or the arch of a bridge joined to its reflection (*White Plaque*, 1951–5); sometimes they were cast shadows, falling over stairways (*La Combe I*, 1950) or building facades. Transferring their shapes to the surface of his works with the care that Duchamp had taken for the cast shadows of *Tu m'*, Kelly was able to exploit the same strategy of making an index (the colored transfer) of what was already an index (the cast shadow) but without giving away the source or reference of the mark so produced, even while that mark divided the canvas surface without his having "composed" it.

In the summer of 1949 John Cage, who had come to Paris to see the French composer Pierre Boulez, met Kelly and saw work that was

▲ 1914, 1918 • 1942b

▲ 1913, 1917, 1937b, 1944a, 1955a, 1957b, 1967c

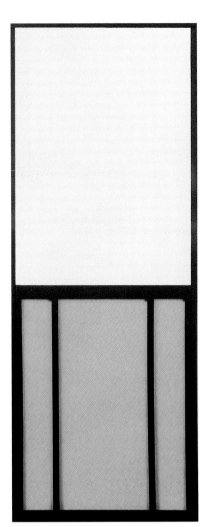

3 • Ellsworth Kelly, *Window, Museum of Modern Art, Paris*, 1949
Oil on wood and canvas, two joined panels, 128.3 x 49.5 x 1.9 (50½ x 19½ x ¾)

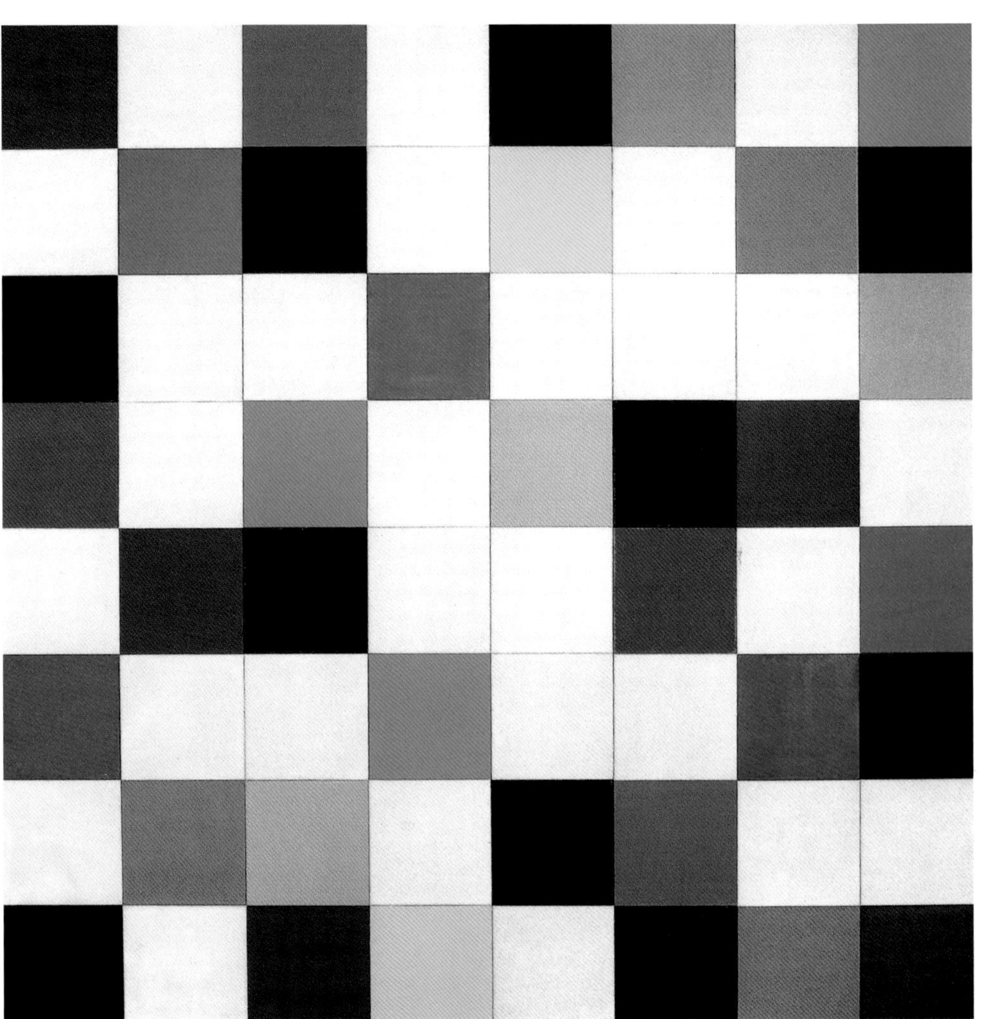

4 • Ellsworth Kelly, *Colors for a Large Wall*, 1951
Oil on canvas, mounted on sixty-four joined panels, 243.8 x 243.8 (96 x 96)

already, though somewhat tentatively, operating on the principle of the indexical transfer of the found object. Refraining from making the comparison to Duchamp lest it discourage the younger man, Cage did speak of the advantages of chance as this operated in his own work, and, indeed, chance is yet another avatar of the index (which is the trace of its occurrence) and, uninterfered with by its witness, is another way to avoid composition. The combination of chance with Kelly's found objects was fully available in the cityscape around him in, for example, the colored oblongs of the awnings of public buildings that would be unequally unfurled from one window to the next to form what seemed to be random patterns. But his own most masterful use of chance was in the modular grids he began in 1951 (as in *Colors for a Large Wall* [**4**]), in which the principle of the "already made" unit of the grid is employed as a way of avoiding internal drawing, hence each module is a separate canvas panel, and the principle of the readymade determines the colors themselves (based on color samples), which are, then, arranged by chance.

That Kelly was exploiting the index as a weapon against geometric abstraction was an unusual case in the early fifties, so much so that it went unnoticed long into Kelly's career, during which he was first mistaken as yet another version of just such abstraction and then seen as a Minimalist before there were any Minimalists. It was, indeed, easier to read the index as resistance to Abstract ▲ Expressionism's expressive stroke, as when Jasper Johns embarked on a series of paintings, beginning with *Device Circle* (1959), that used a paint-mixing stick affixed by one end to the canvas and then rotated so as to smear the colors below it in an imitation—albeit now mechanized—of the dragged paint, wet into wet, of de Kooning's notorious marks.

Return of the index

Cy Twombly, who had been at Black Mountain College in 1951, rejoined Rauschenberg in 1953 at the Stable Gallery, where his work shared the space with Rauschenberg's *White Paintings* and glossy black collages. But rather than setting its sights on de Kooning, Twombly's work in this show, and what he did in the years afterward, fixated on the drawing of Pollock's dripped paintings, turning their looped skeins into the violent furrows dug by the sharp point of his pencils and other instruments into the pigment

▲ 1958

5 • Cy Twombly, *Free Wheeler*, 1955
House paint, crayon, pencil, and pastel on canvas, 174 x 189.2 (68½ x 74½)

covering his canvases. Thus for Twombly the weapon against Abstract Expressionism's autographic mark was not the strategy of transforming the spontaneous stroke into a "device" but of recoding the mark itself as a form of graffiti, which is to say, the anonymous trace of a kind of criminal violation of the unspoiled surface, like so many declarations of the fact that "Kilroy was here."

Less apparent as a form of index than, say, a cast shadow or a tire print, the graffiti mark shares with broken branches in the forest or clues left at the scene of a crime the trace of a foreign presence that has intruded into a previously unviolated space. It exists, that is, as residue. In this sense it breaks with a fundamental premise of the action painter's credo: that the work function as a mirror reflecting the artist's identity, producing a moment to measure one's authenticity in an act of self-recognition. For if the mirror is a model of presence—the self-presence of the subject to his or her own reflection—the graffiti mark is a registration of absence, of the mark that rests in the aftermath of the event and which, as Jacques Derrida, in ▲ his *Of Grammatology*, explains of every graphic trace, has the formal character of wrenching self-presence (the present moment when the marker makes the mark) away from itself by dividing the event into a before and an after; it is a mark that forms itself in the very presence of its maker *as residue*, as remains. In testifying thus to the structural absence of the graffitist to the mark he makes, the graffiti not only does violence to the surface it defaces, but strikes against its author as well, shattering his supposed reflection in the mirror.

Gaining in power and coherence in a work like *Free Wheeler* [**5**], made several years after the *Erased de Kooning Drawing*, Twombly's mark brings the violence inherent in the strokes of Rauschenberg's eraser out into the open. Both are deployments of the index in the face of action painting's drive to authorial self-presence, just as both are engaged in repetition and randomness as a strategy for "not composing."

FURTHER READING

Yve-Alain Bois, "Ellsworth Kelly in France: Anti-Composition in Its Many Guises," in Jack Cowart (ed.), *Ellsworth Kelly: The French Years* (Washington, D.C.: National Gallery of Art, 1992)

Jacques Derrida, *Of Grammatology*, trans. Gayatri Spivak (Baltimore: The Johns Hopkins University Press, 1976)

Walter Hopps, *Robert Rauschenberg: The Early Fifties* (Houston: Menil Foundation, 1991)

Leo Steinberg, "Other Criteria," *Other Criteria: Confrontations with Twentieth-Century Art* (London, Oxford, and New York: Oxford University Press, 1972)

Kirk Varnedoe, *Cy Twombly* (New York: Museum of Modern Art, 1994)

▲ Introduction 4

1955a

The first Gutai exhibition in Japan marks the dissemination of modernist art through the media and its reinterpretation by artists outside the United States and Europe, also exemplified by the rise of the Neoconcretist group in Brazil.

In the fifth issue of the journal *Gutai*, published in October 1956, ▲ this brief statement appeared: "The US artist Jackson Pollock, whom we highly esteemed, has passed away all too early in a road accident, and we are deeply touched. B. H. Friedman who was close to him, and who sent us the news of this death, wrote: 'When recently I looked through Pollock's library, I discovered issues two and three of *Gutai*. I was told that Pollock was an enthusiastic disciple of the Gutai, for in it he had recognized a vision and a reality close to his own.'" This last sentence is subject to doubt, to say the least (was Friedman excessively polite, was his letter tampered with?), and we should not make too much, as far as Pollock's interest in Gutai is concerned, of the oddball presence in his East Hampton studio of the two October 1955 issues of a confidential Japanese journal among those of more familiar magazines about American or European art.

The reference tells a lot, however, about what Pollock represented for the collaborators of the journal (for it was most probably they, despite the feigned surprise of the statement quoted above, who had sent it to the American painter): he was the imaginary audience, the revered master. Just a decade after Hiroshima and Nagasaki, in a schizophrenic Japan endorsing Americanization at the economic level but resisting it at the cultural one (the two most trodden paths were a "return to order" that called for the rehabilitation of age-old Japanese practices on the one hand, or "socialist" realism, on the other), this enthusiastic endorsement of an American artist was deliberately shocking.

A creative misreading of Pollock

Jiro Yoshihara (1905–72), the mentor and financial backer of the Gutai group, had enthusiastically written about Pollock in 1951 when several of his paintings had toured Japan, and he would persist in acknowledging his and his friends' debt. But more than an actual contact with the works themselves, it was no doubt the famous photographs by Hans Namuth (1915–90) [**1**] and Rudy Burckhardt showing Pollock dripping and pouring paint that galvanized the young artists gathered around Yoshihara. By December 1954 (that is, at the time of the group's foundation), Yoshihara had already acquired a national reputation as a painter—his works then were competent yet rather provincial versions of European postwar abstraction. It is not so much his own art as his independence of mind, his defiance of bureaucracy, his willingness to seize the opportunity of a clean slate afforded by the historical situation of postwar Japan, and his encouragements to be as radical as possible that explain the attraction he exerted on artists who were a generation younger. His interest in performance and in the theater—the only domain where he was as innovative as the other members of Gutai—also played a major role in defining the group's activity.

It is this performative angle from which Gutai looked at Pollock that resulted in one of the most interesting, albeit short-lived, "creative misreadings" of twentieth-century art. Because they knew

1 • Hans Namuth, *Jackson Pollock painting Autumn Rhythm*, 1950

▲ 1949, 1960b

next to nothing about the context that had presided over the invention of Pollock's drip technique, because they read it through cultural codes that were utterly foreign to the American artistic ambience, the Gutai artists were able to zero in on aspects of Pollock's art that would become available to Western artists (notably the post- ▲ Minimalist proponents of "antiform") only fifteen years later.

But Gutai's eccentric reading of Pollock did have a American origin. Even before the group was formed, the Gutai artists had ● endeavored to literalize Harold Rosenberg's (antiformalist) notion that the Abstract Expressionist canvas is an "arena for action" and that the pictures themselves are far less significant than the gestures that produced them. In fact, it is the new technique adopted in 1954 by Kazuo Shiraga (born 1924), who was to become the most brilliant member of the group, that functioned as a catalyst: abandoning his brush, Shiraga began to paint with his feet [**2**], con- ■ ceiving of this bodily method as a radicalization of Pollock's horizontality. Upon seeing Shiraga's pictures, other artists such as Shozo Shimamoto (born 1928), who had been puncturing holes in thick screens of painted paper, or Saburo Murakami (born 1925), who had been throwing balls dipped in ink, realized that they had a double interest in common: in order to prevent a protectionist return to the traditional artistic practices of Japanese art (the extremely codified calligraphy, for example), one had not only to invent radically new modes of engendering a mark, but also to take advantage of the highly ritualistic nature of Japanese culture in order to transform the artistic act into a transgressive and ludic performance. It is this dual investigation that characterizes the most interesting productions of Gutai. The word itself is formed of two characters: "gu," signifying tool or means, and "tai," which means body or substance; it is translated as "concreteness."

The inventiveness of Gutai artists in their choice of material and working method for their paintings—most often realized during their exhibitions (several of them outdoors)—is staggering. The spectacularization of the production, especially during the two first years of the group's existence, almost inevitably called for an emphasis on chance and contingency (like Pollock, they insisted on severing the link that—via the brush—had always tied hand, gesture, and inscription). To apply paint or ink, Akira Kanayama

2 • Kazuo Shiraga, *Work II*, 1958
Oil on paper, 183 x 243 (72 x 95⅝)

▲ 1969 ● 1960b ■ 1949

3 • Kazuo Shiraga, *Challenge to the Mud*, October 1955
Performance

(born 1924) used an electric toy car, Yasuo Sumi (born 1925), a vibrator, Toshio Yoshida (born 1928), a sprinkling can held ten feet above his waiting surface; Shimamoto smashed jars of pigment on a rock placed on his canvas, or he used a rifle, while Shiraga favored arrows to pierce pouches of paint.

Not surprisingly, the resulting pictures were of no great interest (Shiraga's numerous "foot paintings" are among the very few pictorial traces of those events that do not look drab—undoubtedly because the indexical footprints clearly register the temporality of the act). But the Gutai artists knew as much and, initially at least, they did not particularly value these remnants, considering them as mere props for their performances or multimedia installations.

The performances proper, later somewhat mistakenly celebrated ▲ by Allan Kaprow as anticipating his happenings, also pay a direct tribute to Rosenberg's trope of the "arena." For the opening of the first indoor Gutai exhibition, held in Tokyo in October 1955, Shiraga threw himself into a pile of wet mud, where he thrashed around half naked while the audience gathered round him [**3**]. The same evening, Murakami thunderingly crashed through a row of six large paper screens, the gaping holes he left deliberately assaulting that icon of traditional Japanese interior architecture, the paper partition [**4**]. But soon the very theatricality of these actions developed to the stage where, from 1957 on, Gutai mounted grandiose audiovisual shows whose main characteristic was, in a manner that ▲ recalled Dadaist theater, a predilection for the grotesque and an aggressive stance toward the audience (just as in 1924 Francis Picabia had blinded the Parisian public of the ballet *Relâche* by pointing at it 370 automobile lights, Sadamasa Motonaga [born 1922] chased his spectators away with his "smoke cannon").

It is, however, in its conception of exhibitions as vast amusement parks containing pockets of meditative spaces and delicate sculptural objects that the Gutai group excelled. In its second outdoor show (July 1956), for example, held like the first in a pine forest, Motonaga hung between the trees long sheets of plastic filled with colored water that filtered the sun's light; Michio Yoshihara (born 1933) dug a hole in the sand where he almost buried an electric light; Shimamoto constructed a catwalk of planks, supported by uneven springs, on which people were invited to walk; Kanayama zipped through the entire ground with a 300-foot-long strip of white vinyl, adorned with black footprints that made it looked like a runway and ending up in a tree. A sense of play was pervasive (many works exhibited in Gutai shows were directly inviting the spectators to participate), but also a genuine interest in new materials (with a definitive fascination for plastic, which marked worldwide the period of reconstruction after World War II), both often combining in an appeal to the uncanny. A case in point is the *Electric Dress* of Atsuko Tanaka (born 1932), a costume made of several dozen incandescent bulbs and colored neon tubes with which she wrapped herself, risking electrocution, for the opening of an exhibition in Tokyo in 1956.

By the time Gutai was presented at the Martha Jackson Gallery in New York in October 1958, however, it had grown stale. The main cause of this debacle was a shift of emphasis: in great part as a result of French critic Michel Tapié's visit to Japan, during which this ● champion of *art informel* in Paris had managed to persuade them that this was to be their forte, the Gutai artists now concentrated their energy on painting. Tapié's cynical marketing strategy had a devastating effect: no longer considered mere props, the material products of Gutai's theatrics were exhibited as autonomous, idealized abstractions. Understandably the Martha Jackson show, curated by Tapié at the very juncture when the notion of action painting had become utterly academic in America, was very badly received. The group never recovered from the fiasco and slowly degenerated into a caricature of itself. Gutai disbanded only in 1972 (at the death of Jiro Yoshihara), but it had long lost its flame.

Geometry turned against itself

It is interesting to compare this fate with that of the Neoconcretist movement which emerged in Brazil at the end of the fifties—just as Gutai was slackening—for it was similarly born out of the

▲ 1961 ▲ 1916a ● 1946

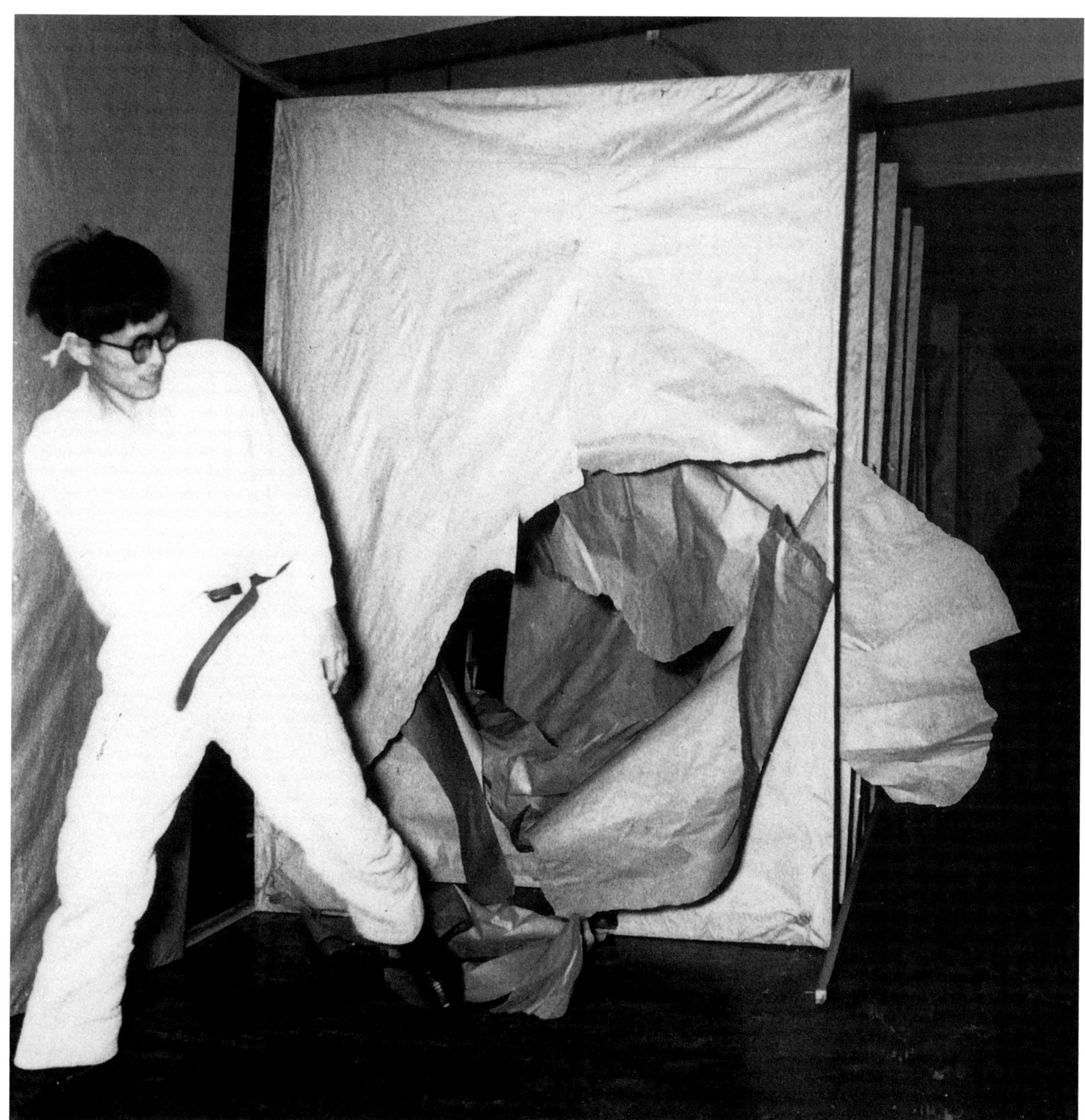

4 • Saburo Murakami, *Passage*, October 1956
Performance

reinterpretation, from a peripheral outpost, of a canonical trend of Western modernism, this time the geometric abstract art that had ▲ been institutionalized in the thirties. It all started with the retrospective of the work of Swiss painter, sculptor, and architect Max • Bill at the Museu de Arte Moderna in São Paulo in 1950, followed by his reception of the Grand Prize at the first Biennale of Rio de Janeiro in 1951: enthusiasts of Bill's "Concrete Art" (in which everything had to be planned by arithmetic calculations) suddenly flooded the tiny Brazilian art world, which had been, until then, recalcitrant toward modern art.

Returning to her native Brazil in 1952, after a year in Paris (where she had studied with Fernand Léger), Lygia Clark (1920–88) quickly assimilated Bill's rationalist catechism and soon began to sap it from within. Noting that Bill often borrowed his forms from topology, she resolved to go beyond his purely iconographic appeal to this scientific field. Her first mature paintings (1954) were modular jigsaw

▲ 1937b • 1937b, 1947a, 1967c

puzzles in wood in which she endeavored to give a positive role to the black interstices (empty joints) between the color blocks, and to transform the frame into a pictorial element: as she insisted at the time, her goal was to undo the empty/full, inside/outside oppositions upon which planar geometry and rationalism are based.

Her next step, following her discovery of the ambiguous spaces ▲ of Josef Albers's *Structural Constellations*, was a series of pictures (or rather wood reliefs) in which a square mechanically painted in a matte black is bordered on one or several of its sides (and sometimes divided) by a recessed white line which functions more like a hinge than like a frame. In these, she had managed to illusionistically torque the plane, an accomplishment she verified in a tondo called *Linear Egg* (1958), a black disk bordered by an interrupted white line. Because the white line laterally dissolves into the surrounding white wall, we refrain from the gestaltist habit of closing the circle, and the black area tends to shift visually in depth with the line, one area receding while the other seeming to protrude toward us. It is this perceptual to and fro, conceived as a "suppression of the plane," that propelled Clark to secede publicly from Bill's school and to found "Neoconcretismo," with several younger artists, in March 1959.

The only major figure besides Clark to emerge from this movement, Hélio Oiticica (1937–80), rallied to the cause only after the publication of the group's manifesto penned by the poet and critic Ferreira Gullar (this text was entirely based on Clark's reinterpretation of the tradition of geometric abstraction through the lenses of the phenomenology of perception, often quoting Maurice Merleau- • Ponty's philosophical work, which she had recently discovered and which would remain a lifelong interest). The publication of the Neoconcretist manifesto coincided with Clark's elaboration of a series of reliefs called *Cocoon* **[6]** and *Contra-reliefs*, in homage to Vladimir ▲ Tatlin, all dating from 1959, in which she translated the perceptual instability of her preceding works into the real, phenomenal space of our senses (Oiticica soon proposed his own version, which he called *Spatial Relief*). Each *Cocoon* is made of a single rectangular sheet of metal partially cut and folded (but not cut out—nothing is deleted nor added) so that its frontal proportion, whatever its projection in space, is always a square (hiding, so to speak, an interior space that the beholder discovers when stepping aside). The fold engenders the fantasy of unfolding and of the plane as a compression of volume, an idea developed further in the *Contra-reliefs*, where void is sandwiched between layers of black or white boards.

That plane has a volume, and that this volume can be opened up (as a cocoon) is at the core of Clark's most celebrated works, the *Animals* of 1960–4 **[5, 7]**, free-standing structures made of hinged plates of metals that one can manipulate to give the sculpture various shapes (when stored, an *Animal* is perfectly flat—just • like the suspended sculptures of Aleksandr Rodchenko). The articulation and disposition of the metal plates determine a set of possibilities that are often unforeseeable. In these first participatory works, Clark transposed her topological investigations (concerning the possible abolition of the reverse side of a plane) into the mode of relations between subject and object: neither is passive nor entirely free. The *Animal* is conceived as an organism that reacts, with its own laws and limitations, to the movements of whoever manipulates it to modify its configuration. Often it requires certain gestures or unexpectedly turns itself inside out: the dialogue between *Animal* and "beholder" is at times exhilarating, at times frustrating, but it always undermines the notion that one could ever be in control of the other.

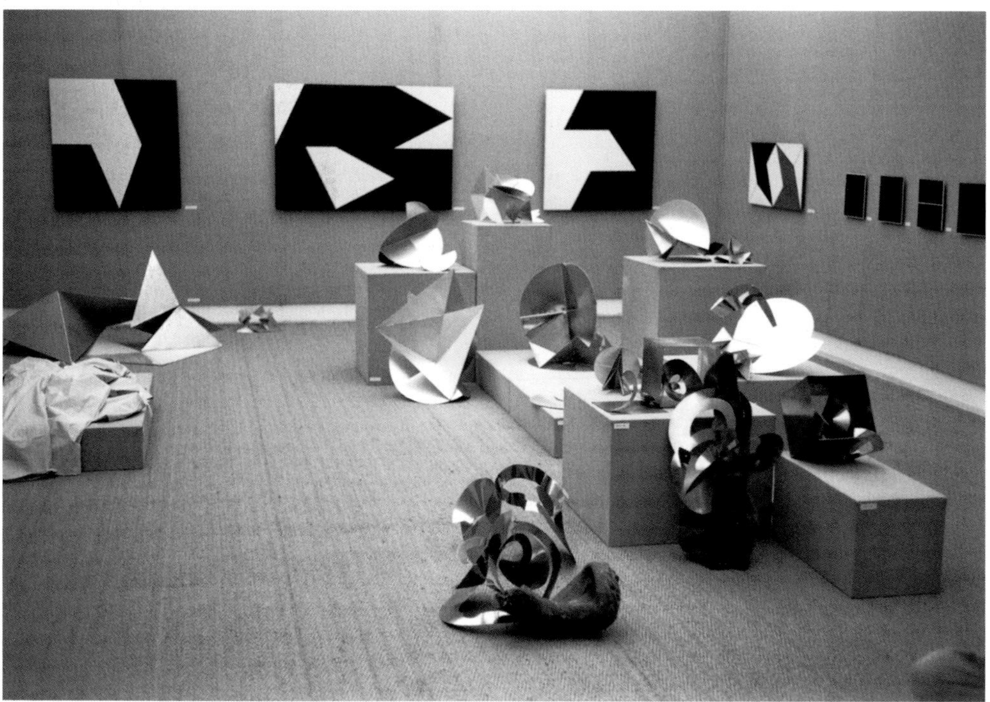

5 • Lygia Clark, installation in the Brazilian Pavilion at the Venice Biennale, 1968
Clark's *Animals* can be seen on the plinths and on the floor under the black-and-white painting in the upper left corner.

▲ 1947a • 1965 ▲ 1914, 1921 • 1921

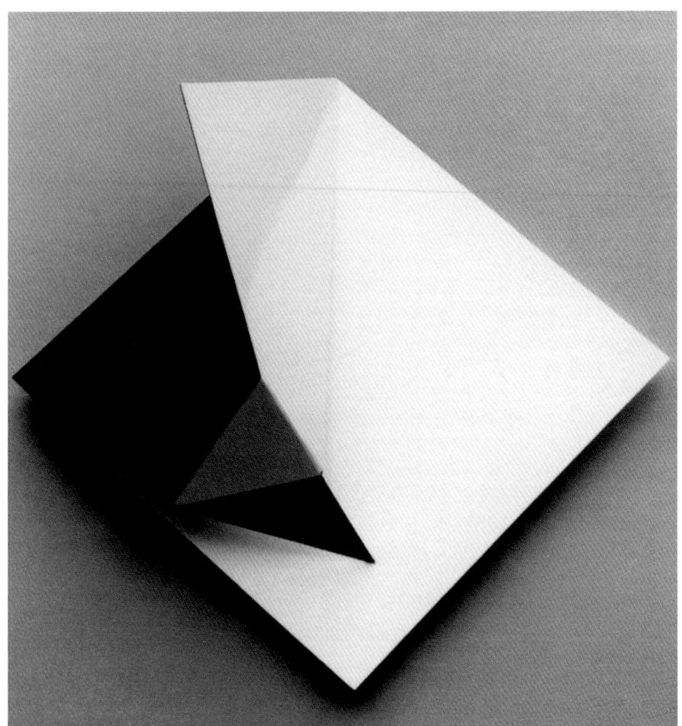

6 • Lygia Clark, *Cocoon*, 1959
Nitrocellulose paint on tin, 30 x 30 x 30 (11¾ x 11¾ x 11¾)

7 • Lygia Clark, *Animal*, 1960
Steel, 45 x 50 (17¾ x 19⅝)

From painting and sculpture to the absence of objects

It is at this juncture that Clark invented the *Caminhando* (poorly translatable as "Trailing," "Walking along"), which in 1964 marks both her definitive farewell to geometric art and the beginning of a trend in her work and in that of Oiticica that one could characterize as the progressive disappearance of the art object as such. (In other words, perhaps because of their total disregard for the strictures of the art market, the logical development of the Neoconcretists followed a path rigorously inverse to that of Gutai: they began with pictures and ended with props that were nothing if not manipulated.) The *Caminhando* returned one more time to Bill's infatuation with the morphological wonders of topology, but rather than being an object it is conceived as an existential experience that has to be lived through: the basic material is a paper Moebius strip, a shape that Bill had many times carved in granite. Here are Clark's do-it-yourself instructions: "Take a pair of scissors, stick one point into the surface and cut continuously along the length of the strip. Take care not to converge with the preexisting cut—which would cause the band to separate into two pieces. When you have gone the circuit of the strip, it's up to you whether to cut to the left or to the right of the cut you've already made. The idea of choice is capital. The unique meaning of this experience is in the act of doing it. The work is your act alone. To the extent that you cut the strip, it refines and redoubles itself into interlacings. At the end the path is so narrow that you can't open it further. It's the end of the trail."

What's left, a pile of paper spaghetti on the floor, is ready for the wastebasket: "There is only one type of duration: the act. The act is that which produces the *Caminhando*. Nothing exists before and nothing afterwards," writes Clark, adding that it is essential "not to know—while you are cutting—what you are going to cut and what you have already cut." And then: "Even if this proposition is not considered as a work of art, and even if one remains skeptical in relation to what it implies, it is necessary to do it."

From the *Caminhando*, Clark and Oiticica developed, throughout the sixties and beyond, a complex interactive practice that steered away not only from any consideration of the object per se, but also from any notion of theatricality (no performance, not even in the "propositions" that involved multiple "participants"—to use the words that now respectively replaced "object" and "beholder" in their numerous texts). More important yet, the very concept of the artist gradually became irrelevant (as "art" became a kind of therapy or social work): the Neoconcretists' propositions might very well be "arenas for action," to refer again to Rosenberg's coinage, but not as vehicles for the expression of an authorial subject. If a cathartic liberation is indeed the goal, it is that of the participant.

FURTHER READING

Barbara von Bertozzi and Klaus Wolbert (eds), *Gutai: Japanese Avant-Garde 1954–1965* (Darmstadt: Mathildenhöhe, 1991)

Manuel J. Borja-Villel (ed.), *Lygia Clark* (Barcelona: Fundacio Antoni Tapies, 1997)

Guy Brett et al., *Hélio Oiticica* (Minneapolis: Walker Art Center, 1994)

Lygia Clark, "Nostalgia of the Body," *October*, no. 69, Summer 1994

Rosalind Krauss and Yve-Alain Bois, *Formless: A User's Guide* (New York: Zone Books, 1997)

Alexandra Monroe, "To Challenge The Mid-Summer Sun: The Gutai Group," *Japanese Art After 1945: Scream Against The Sky* (New York: Harry N. Abrams, 1994)

Harold Rosenberg, "The American Action Painters," *Artnews*, December 1952

1955b

The "Le mouvement" show at the Galerie Denise René in Paris launches kineticism.

On April 6, 1955, when she went for a drink with four artists participating in the exhibition "Le mouvement" which had opened earlier that evening at her Paris gallery [**1**], Denise René did not expect a beating (smug gratitude was more what she had in mind: after all, it was the first time the artists had been hand-picked to show their works in her respectable space). But the Venezuelan Jesús-Rafael Soto (born 1923), the Israeli Yaacov Agam (born 1928), the Belgian Pol Bury (born 1922), and ▲ the Swiss Jean Tinguely (1925–91) all ganged up on her to express their frustration. The "four musketeers," as René called them, were furious that Victor Vasarély (1908–97) had been the only artist invited to publish a text in the foldout printed on yellow paper on the occasion of the show (the whole leaflet was subsequently nicknamed "The Yellow Manifesto"), and thus appeared to be their leader. Defending herself, René argued that Vasarély was no better represented than anybody else in the exhibition, which had been

1 • The Galerie Denise René in April 1955 at the time of the "Le mouvement" exhibition

▲ 1960a

his idea in the first place. Furthermore, she said, everything had been done very quickly in order to forestall competition from a forthcoming show in Lausanne (which would indeed be completely overshadowed), adding that there were other artists she would have liked to include as well, such as Vassilakis Takis (born 1925), but had failed to do so for lack of time.

Abstraction in motion

This tempest in a teapot is quite telling, not only with regard to the Parisian atmosphere in the mid-fifties but also as an omen for the rise and fall of the *ism*, soon dubbed "kinetic art" or "kineticism," that was being launched. Inaugurated in 1944 with an exhibition of Vasarély's early "optical" designs for advertisements or the fashion industry (all figurative), the Galerie Denise René had progressively become the main French outlet for what was then called *art construit*, that is, a form of geometric abstraction that was trying to reconnect with the prewar production of groups such as *Cercle et Carré* or ▲ *Abstraction-Création*. Without counting the still formidable (and paralyzing) presence of grand Old Masters of modernism such as ● Pablo Picasso or Georges Braque (1882–1963), the French art world was then entirely dominated by late and mediocre by-products of Cubism and Surrealism, by a sentimental form of figuration that was oddly associated with existentialist philosophy (Bernard Buffet was the star of that genre), and by *tachisme* (or "lyrical abstraction"). Placing the works of young artists under the tutelage of pioneers of geometric abstraction who had been forgotten in France (such as Mondrian, whose first one-man show in Paris would be held in René's gallery as late as 1957; or the Polish Constructivists Wladys- ■ law Strzeminski (1893–1952) and Katarzyna Kobro (1898–1951), whom she introduced to the French public, together with Kazimir ◆ Malevich, in the same year), Denise René was on a mission: she was the midwife of an art of "clarity, stability and order" that, in her view, perfectly fitted with the post-traumatic needs of the reconstruction period. Such a neoclassicist interpretation of abstraction as a kind of "return to order" would have repelled Mondrian or Malevich, but it was the only critical discourse through which their work was seized in postwar Europe. (In France its main proponent was Mondrian's friend and would-be biographer Michel Seuphor, who organized the landmark exhibition "Premiers maîtres de l'art abstrait" ["First Masters of Abstract Art"] at Paris's Galerie Maeght in 1949.)

The first abstract works exhibited by Vasarély in 1947, at his second Denise René show, had nothing to do with his early graphic designs based on the flickering of competing positive/negative, black-and-white patterns, a kind of optical violence that he had learned to master during his apprenticeship in the Bauhaus-type school directed by Sandor Bortnik in Budapest. His compositions of the late forties—elegant exercises in precariously balancing a few large unmodulated geometrical planes on a neutral background—fully belonged to the new tradition of *art construit* of which he was fast becoming the spokesman. But dissent was already in the air and in 1950 this very tradition was lambasted in the pamphlet "*L'art abstrait est-il un académisme?*" ("Is abstract art academic?") published by Charles Estienne, a critic who had been until then a staunch supporter of the Denise René pool. It is at this juncture that Vasarély introduced into his pictures the optical illusionism he had so far relegated to his commercial production and began to articulate an artistic program centered around the idea of virtual movement. The large *Photographismes* which he exhibited in 1951 set the tone: as in Bridget Riley's works ten years later, an illusion of movement (and of volume) is engendered by the destabilization of a regular pattern and the continually confusing inversion of figure and ground.

Destabilization is the key word. Vasarély's retinal titillations had the immediate effect of casting the quieter production of all his geometric abstract colleagues as old-fashioned: taking stock of his ascendancy, a good half of René's artists left the gallery. By 1955, Vasarély had streamlined his compositions and developed new techniques (such as sandblasting thick slabs of glass with a different pattern on both sides, which produced shifting moiré effects at the slightest move of the spectator), and he was now ready for a public takeover.

The "Le mouvement" exhibition of 1955 was a brilliant coup: at once it baptized a new movement (with Vasarély as its self-appointed head) and replenished the gallery with new recruits. In order to legitimize this latest trend historically, René secured the loans of several works by Alexander Calder (whose first mobiles date from 1932) and, even more savvy, of Marcel Duchamp's ▲ *Rotary Demisphere* (*Precision Optics*) of 1925 (unlike Calder, who had benefited from the critical support of the then immensely famous philosopher/writer Jean-Paul Sartre for his spectacular show at the Galerie Louis Carré in 1946, Duchamp, who had long ago emigrated to the United States, was only just beginning to be remembered in postwar France). Furthermore, a short chronology of the role of movement in twentieth-century art was published in "The Yellow Manifesto": beginning with Italian Futurism, it mentioned Duchamp more than any other artist—from his first ● readymade of 1913 (*Bicycle Wheel*) to his first optical machine (*Rotary Glass Plates*) of 1920, his abstract film *Anemic Cinema* (1926), and his *Optical Disks* of 1935. Also noted were Naum ■ Gabo's (1890–1977) astonishing *Kinetic Construction*, in which a tiny electric motor functioning as a base triggers an oscillating movement in a thin vertical metallic rod and thus engenders a virtual volume [**2**], Viking Eggeling's abstract film *Diagonal Sym-* ◆ *phony* of 1921, and László Moholy-Nagy's high-tech automaton, the *Light Modulator* of 1935. (Other historical precedents that could cast some doubt on Vasarély's claim to originality—such as Henrik Berlewi's *Mecano-faktura* of 1922 or Josef Albers's compositions on glass realized at the Bauhaus in the late twenties, and many of his subsequent drawings—were conspicuously absent.)

The protective guardianship of two prewar pioneers could not have been more welcomed by the "four musketeers." Just like Calder after his visit to Mondrian's studio (which prompted him to invent his mobiles [**3**]), all had succumbed to the same desire of setting painting into motion; and all were eager to pursue

▲ 1937b ● 1944b ■ 1913, 1917, 1928, 1944a ◆ 1913, 1915 ▲ 1918, 1993a ● 1914 ■ 1937b ◆ 1923, 1929, 1947a

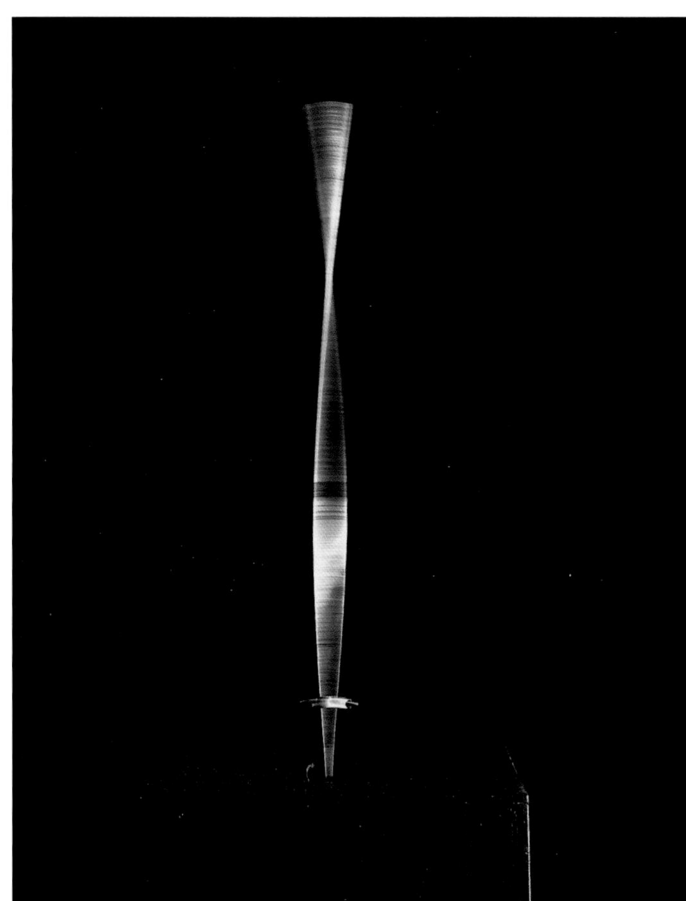

2 • Naum Gabo, *Kinetic Construction*, 1919–20 (1985 replica)
Metal, painted wood, and electrical mechanism, 61.6 x 24.1 x 19 (24¼ x 9½ x 7½)

Duchamp's critique of the subjective authority of the artist as God-like Creator. Both Bury and Agam exhibited transformable reliefs whose elements could be displaced and rearranged on a peg-board, the spectator being invited to become the de facto coauthor of the work (the Argentinian group Madi had exhibited works based on the same principle in the Salon des Realités Nouvelles in Paris as early as 1948, but these had been almost unanimously condemned by French critics for their lack of seriousness). Tinguely's neo-Dadaist bent was the most radical: in his *Meta-Malevich* reliefs, he submitted Suprematist compositions to the test of contingency by having their geometric shapes animated by a motor that rotated them on a black ground, undermining the very notion of the work as a definitive unity; in his *Metamechanical Sculpture*, an elementary linear combination of wheels and gears activated by the simplest electric motor, he was ridiculing all the self-congratulatory discourses concerning the technological advance of the West, plethoric at the time. Not least, it was at this exhibition that he exhibited the first of his *Metamatics* (*Drawing Machines*), robots furnished with markers or chalks and designed to produce an abstract (albeit gestural) work on paper. As for Soto, at first he seemed much closer to Vasarély in that he too was making ample use of superimpositions and their attendant moiré effects (though his model had rather been Moholy-Nagy's painted Plexiglas reliefs of the mid-thirties in which the geometric figures painted on a transparent sheet of Plexiglas cast their shadow on another composition set a few inches behind). But on closer inspection, Soto's works constituted a radical critique of Vasarély's program of mere destabilization of traditional abstract compositions: like François Morellet at the same moment, and following the example of ▲ Ellsworth Kelly's production during his stay in France, he was explicitly exploring noncompositional systems (modular allover grids, serial progressions) in order to prevent the final hierarchical *stasis* of any formal arrangement.

Kinetic art gathers momentum—and loses it

Although the press was reticent at first, the exhibition had an enormous impact. In its aftermath a myriad of groups that gathered kinetic artists together was constituted in various European countries (including the Eastern bloc—in Zagreb and Moscow, for example), and by 1960 the "new tendency," as it was often called at the time, had conquered the market while museums worldwide were devoting major exhibitions to this trend. In 1965, capitalizing on the public success of kineticism, René organized a recapitulative exhibition celebrating the tenth anniversary of "Le mouvement." The fold-out catalogue of "Mouvement 2," with an eye-popping orange and green cover, reproduced the works of sixty artists living in ten countries (the great majority based in Paris, however, and many of those being South American expatriates). Intended as a victorious celebration—and indeed it was enormously popular (this time around the press was won over)—the show effectively marked the beginning of the end for kinetic art. Just a few months later, the exhibition "The Responsive Eye" at the Museum of Modern Art in New York, would be another kiss of death, only topped in 1966 by the attribution of the Grand Prize for Painting of the Venice Biennale to the Argentinian artist Julio le Parc, and by that for Sculpture in 1968 to the Hungarian Nicolas Schöffer, both prolific protégés of Denise René. The bubble burst, much more quickly than it had inflated, and it took only a few years for kinetic art to utterly vanish from the scene: René's staggering commercial expansion followed the classic scenario of ending in bankruptcy, both financial and aesthetic, and with this fiasco the baby was thrown away with the bath water.

There are many factors to this spectacular fall, but none more important than the gradual domination of the "Op" branch of kineticism over all the others: it was Vasarély's ascendancy, in a sense, that killed kineticism (his tendency reigns in both "Mouvement 2" and "The Responsive Eye," even if it was not he but Bridget Riley who carried "Op" into the New York limelight). The "four musketeers" were right to complain after all: things could have been different if Vasarély had not stolen the show in 1955.

Indeed, the initial "Le mouvement" had nothing of the homogeneity of its offspring of a decade later. Several types of instability were competing in 1955: illusory movement, by simple optical activation of a surface (Vasarély would stick to this); abruptly changing aspects of the work according to the movement of the

▲ 1953

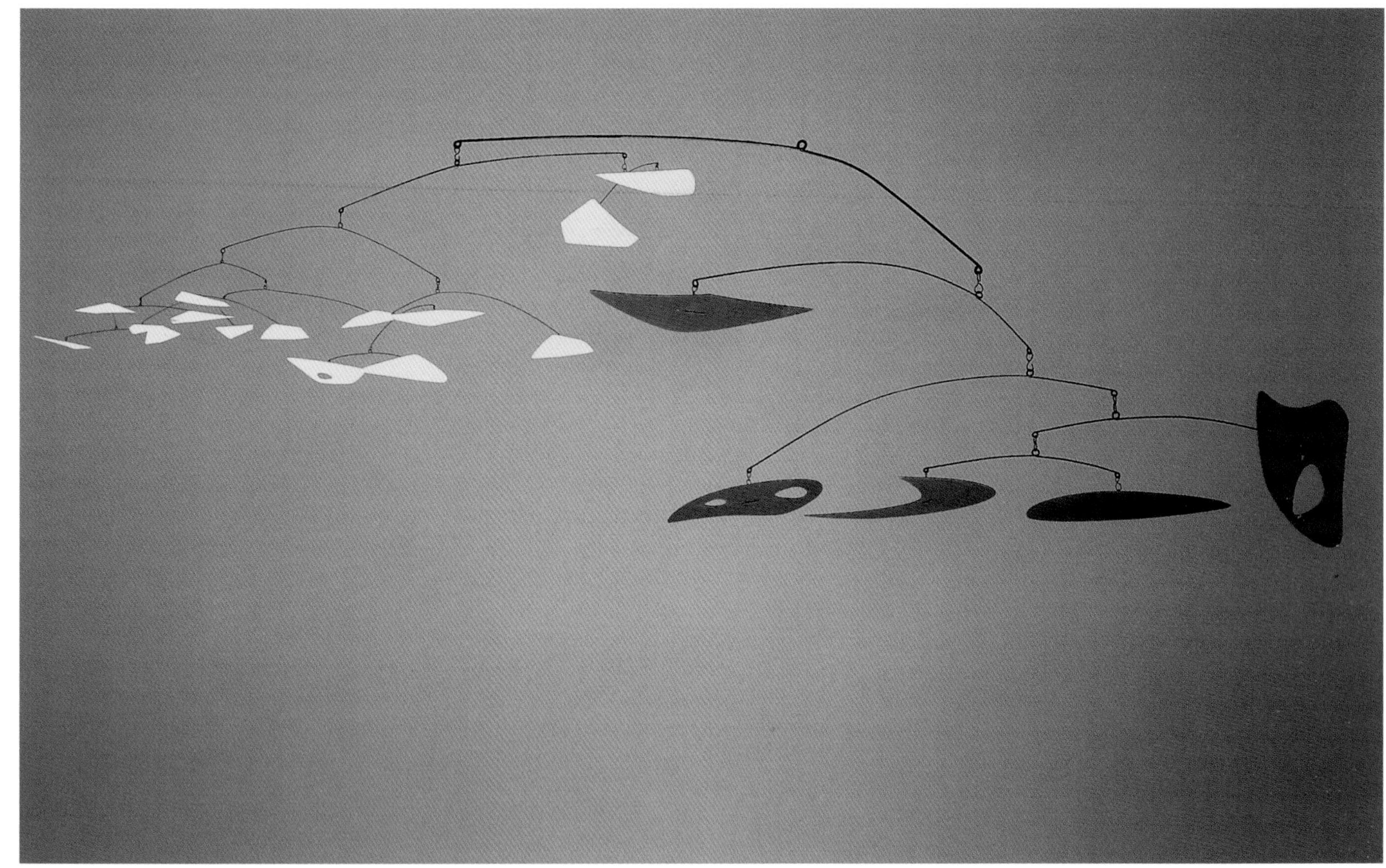

3 • Alexander Calder, *1 Red, 4 Black plus X White*, 1947
Sheet metal, wire, and paint, 91.4 x 304.8 x 121.9 (36 x 120 x 48)

spectator (Vasarély and Soto, who would soon be joined by Agam); manipulation of the object by the spectator (Bury and Agam, who would both soon abandon this ludic vein); movement of the object itself either through a natural form of energy (Calder: wind, gravity) or a mechanical one (Tinguely). Furthermore, contradictory attitudes with regard to the role of art and its relationship to reason and above all to science (which, after all, was easily conceived as *the* most pregnant discourse, in this atomic age, to be dealing with movement and energy) almost immediately undermined the unity of the new "ism." Vasarély's utopic stance (a humanist hodge-podge of old tropes about the universal language of abstract art bridging the class divides and solving all social ills, and the democratization of art by the infinite multiplication of its objects—the production of "multiples" that contributed to a nauseating saturation of the market) was based on a rationalist philosophy that Tinguely's archaic automata were parodying, as were Soto's attack on compositionality in its evacuation of the self.

Agam rejoined Vasarély's cohort (Op destabilization of *art construit*). ▲ Adapting a device invented by El Lissitzky in his *Abstract Cabinet* (parallel wood slats set perpendicular to the picture plane, painted a different color on each side), Agam spent most of his artistic career creating ever larger geometric compositions that provided three different aspects according to the beholder's position. (In 1967 he strayed away from this limited gimmick in a spartan environment consisting of a dark room lit by a single electric bulb responding to sound, its wattage proportional to the volume of noises produced by the visitors—but this was as much a fluke as Gabo's 1920 work to which it was paying tribute.)

Tinguely was to run out of the Galerie Denise René, which was fast becoming Vasarély's turf. Lured by his friend Yves Klein ▲ (1928–62), he joined the ranks of the Nouveaux Réalistes and continued to produce ironic motorized machines assembled from material gathered at junk yards. The climax of his career was • undoubtedly his gigantic *Homage to New York* of 1960. Built in three weeks in the sculpture garden of the Museum of Modern Art, it was made to self-destruct, a feat that it accomplished in a flurry of fire and sounds in less than half an hour.

Bury, too, escaped from Vasarély's bastion—paradoxically at the very moment when, after the 1955 show, he realized his first motorized reliefs. Among the works that stand out from this extremely inventive period are his *Elastic Punctuations* from 1960, his *Erectiles* series begun in 1962, or his *White Points* series of 1964 to 1967. In the first, a sheet of latex, stretched across a frame, is pressed from behind in different spots, after which these peaks recede, the slow rhythm of this alternative movement inevitably lending organic connotations—sex, breathing—to the piece. In *White Points* the very brief, spasmodic motion of the myriad points extending at the tips of black nylon threads projecting from a wooden bollard (all potential targets of our focus), but only one or two at a time, insures that we can never ascertain that we have

▲ 1926

▲ 1960a, 1967c • 1960a

actually seen something moving, or that we have seen everything that has moved. The effect is at once comical (because it is humbling) and disquieting, as always with any confusion between the organic and the inorganic (which Freud characterized as one of the features of the uncanny).

Kinetic deskilling

Soto's evolution is perhaps the most informative in that it fluctuated between the Op/geometric pole and the organic or bodily one. Often reflected in his institutional allegiances (as when he left the Denise René team for a while to join the gallery of Yves Klein, Jean Tinguely, and Vassilakis Takis, or participated, along with his friend Lucio Fontana in the exhibitions of the Düsseldorf-based Group Zero formed by Heinz Mack, Gunter Ucker, and Otto Piene), the oscillations of Soto's stance further indicate that things were initially less cast in stone than one might retrospectively imagine. Immediately after the "Le mouvement" show, Soto stumbled upon an elementary means to achieve the vibratory suspension of form he had been trying to achieve with his superimpositions on Plexiglas: a regularly striated background is enough to optically dematerialize the contour of any form that projects in front of it, as long as the spectator moves laterally. In 1957, Soto almost entirely abandoned the geometric vocabulary he had been using until then, and he set into his signature vibratory motions wire drawings that clearly imitate gestural abstraction—even combined with the thick blobs of matter one finds in Dubuffet's or ▲ Fautrier's paintings. But even after his definitive return to geometric elements in 1965, in reliefs that steadily grew in scale and projected ever more into the space of the spectator, to the point that they became environments, he kept underlining the discrepancy between the simplicity of his material means and the strength of the dissolution effect in his pieces. The most striking (and last) work of this period is perhaps the four-hundred-square-meter *Pénétrable* he realized outdoors for his 1969 retrospective at the Musée National d'Art Moderne in Paris, which consisted of many thousands of thin plastic tubes hung from a grid canopy: the atmosphere became entirely vibratile, as if gaseous, and spectators entering and roaming the vast space could perceive their peers only as fleeting, deformed, and ever-changing silhouettes.

One particular episode of Soto's career casts some light on the ambivalence of his position (taking stock of geometry in order to produce inchoate bodily sensations) and on the history of kineticism at large: his 1965 exhibition at the Signals Gallery in London. For though Signals did not deliberately attempt to be uncommercial (it was, and closed after just eighteen months), its *eminence grise*, the young Filipino artist David Medalla, saw it as a melting pot, a kind of "alternative space" inviting artists from around the world to collaborate in total freedom, and at times funding their creation of then wholly unsaleable "environments."

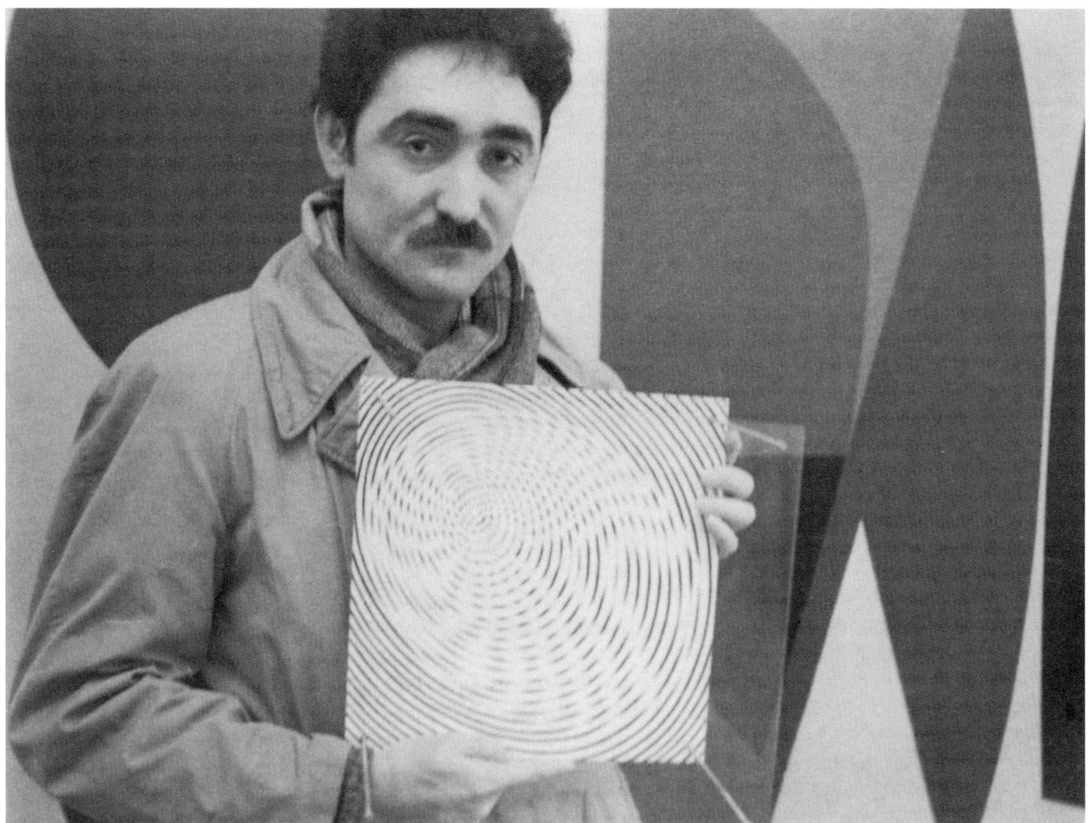

3 • Jesús-Rafael Soto holding his *Spirale* at Galerie Denise René in 1955
In the background is a painting by Richard Mortensen.

▲ 1946, 1959c

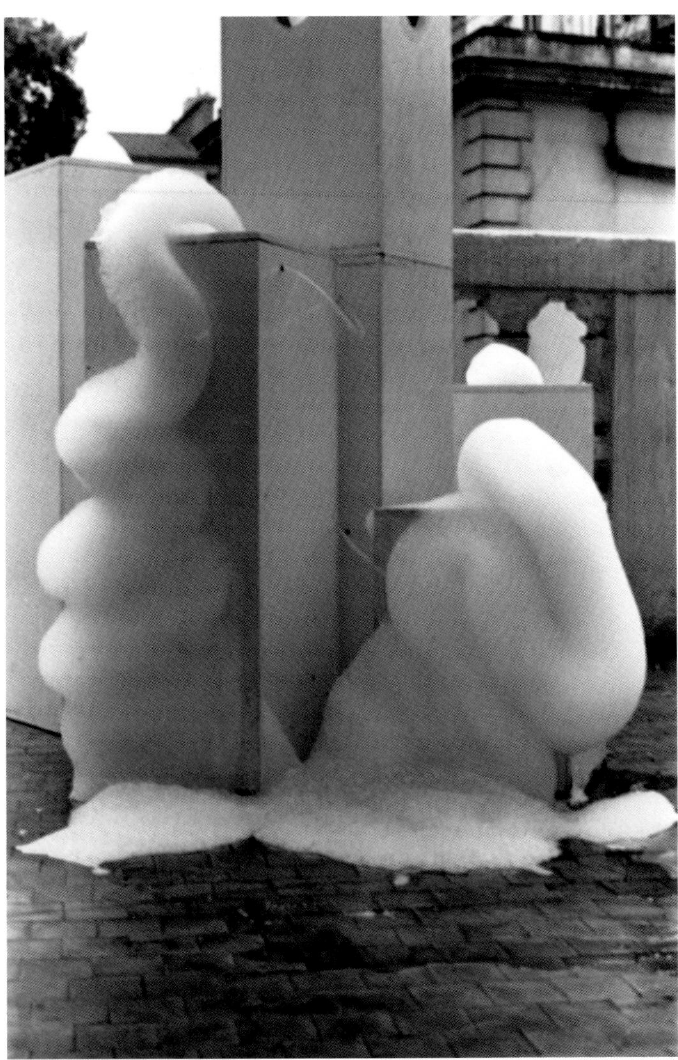

5 • David Medalla, *Cloud Canyons no. 2*, 1964 (detail)
Bubble-machines = auto-creative sculptures

(Among the founding members of this cooperative—whose original name was the Centre for Advanced Creative Study—one counts Gustav Metzger, the apostle of "auto-destructive art.") Its bulletin, more often than not coinciding with a one-man show, reflected this rare openness. It contained many texts by and about the artist being celebrated, but also about others—companions-in-arms, so to speak—and poems, scientific material, songs, political protests, and a host of documentary items pertaining to the activity of the gallery. (The issue on Soto includes among other things the translations of a 1877 text by German physicist Hermann von Helmholtz [1821–94] on the composition of vibrations, and of several "dreams" by Argentine author Jorge Luis Borges [1899–1986].) With its large format and deskilled typography (both borrowed from daily newspapers), the *Signals* bulletin had all the characteristics of an underground "zine" of the period (according to Medalla, the gallery folded when its backer withdrew his financial support after the publication of the historian Lewis Mumford's and the poet Robert Lowell's respective addresses against the Vietnam War).

For all Medalla's playful anarchism, the Signals Gallery had a serious program, by which it proposed a version of kineticism that had little to do with that offered at "Mouvement 2" or "The Responsive Eye." Its first exhibition, in 1964, was devoted to the electromagnetic sculptures of Takis—called, precisely, *Signals* (arrows and balls suspended in space, intermittent lights and simultaneously pulsating dials on disconnected switchboards, a whole histrionic, and in many ways antiquated, hardware mobilized in praise of an "invisible force" and celebrated in the gallery's bulletin by William Burroughs). This was immediately followed by a show of Medalla's *Cloud Canyons* [**5**], primitive machines made of rectangular wooden boxes filled with a mix of liquid soap and water that a pump transformed into a stream of foam that slowly oozed from the top and adopted the sensual curves of Hans Arp's late marble sculptures while mocking their claim to perennity. Among the exhibitions organized by Signals, many of them of kinetic artists *not* represented by René, one of the most memorable remains the retrospective of Lygia Clark in 1965, which was to be followed by an "environment" ▲ of Hélio Oiticica. (The gallery closed before the realization of this project, but it became the famous installation called *Tropicalia*, which the artist mounted at the Whitechapel Gallery in 1969.)

Such is the context in which Soto was greeted in London: the ease with which he meshed with the Signals group explains better than anything else why he vigorously refused to participate in "The Responsive Eye" exhibition (going against the urging of René). Sadly, this resistance did not last long enough: his work gradually edged towards gadgetry and the cheap "Op" effects dear to Vasarély. By the time he definitely joined in (after his 1969 *Penetrable)* his art was no longer alive. This particular fate is by no means atypical. Another example would be that of the Groupe de Recherche d'Art Visuel (GRAV), officially founded in 1960, soon after Piero Manzoni had invited several of its future members to show their work at the Azimuth Gallery in Milan (where the Italian artist would hold his famous exhibition of edible art). Such a link might seem strange for a group best known for its emulation of Vasarély's program, but at the beginning of GRAV's activity, there was much greater interest in the active participation of the spectator than in optical illusions. This ludic impetus climaxed on April 19, 1966, with *Une journée dans la rue* (A day in the street), during which passersby in various areas of Paris were invited to walk on moving tiles, construct a kinetic sculpture, enter into several others, prick balloons, adorn special glasses that segmented vision, etc. But this marked the end of both the collective nature and the experimental attitude of GRAV. Two months later, when GRAV member le Parc won his Venice prize (and started lambasting Manzoni's anti-aesthetic stance), Op became the orthodoxy—and the group almost immediately collapsed.

FURTHER READING

Jean-Paul Ameline et al., *Denise René, l'intrépide* (Paris: Centre Georges Pompidou, 2001)

Yves Aupetitallot (ed.), *Strategies of Participation: GRAV 1960–68* (Grenoble: Le Magazin, 1998)

Guy Brett, *Exploding Galaxies: The Art of David Medalla* (London: Kala Press, 1995)

Guy Brett, *Force Fields: Phases of the Kinetic* (Barcelona: Museu d'Art Contemporani; and London: Hayward Gallery, 2000)

Pamela Lee, *Chronophobia: On Time in the Art of the 1960s* (Cambridge, Mass.: MIT Press, 2004)

▲ 1955a

1956

The exhibition "This is Tomorrow" in London marks the culmination of research into postwar relations between art, science, technology, product design, and popular culture undertaken by the Independent Group, forerunners of British Pop art.

The Independent Group was less a tight artistic movement than a multifarious study group. Its leading members were artists: Richard Hamilton (born 1922), Nigel Henderson (1917–85), John McHale (1922–78), Eduardo Paolozzi (born 1924), and William Turnbull (born 1922). But its prime movers were critics: architectural critic Reyner Banham (1922–88), art critic Lawrence Alloway (1926–90), and cultural critic Toni del Renzio (born 1915). And its signal achievements—its ambitious series of lectures and extraordinary run of exhibitions, the latter abetted by innovative designers in the group like the Brutalist architects Alison Smithson (1928–93) and Peter Smithson (1923–2003)—were discursive and curatorial. The principal legacy of the Independent Group might well be its "art" of discussion, design, and display.

The fine art–popular art continuum

The history of the Independent Group proper (1952–5) is bound up with that of the Institute of Contemporary Arts (ICA) in London, which it served as an unruly research-and-development arm. This testy relation is suggested by the successive appellations of the Independent Group: first *Young* Group, then Young *Independent* Group, and finally Independent *Group*. The ICA was set up in 1946 in emulation of the Museum of Modern Art (MoMA) in New York by established writers like Roland Penrose (1900–84) and Herbert Read (1893–1968), its first president, in order to champion modernism. But the ICA version of modernism, a ▲ watered-down mix of Surrealism (represented by Penrose) and • Constructivism (represented by Read), was seen by a new guard of artists, architects, and critics as an academic holdover from the prewar period (Banham dubbed it an "Abstract-Left-Freudian aesthetic"). And when a new director, Dorothy Morland, took office in 1951, these young rebels began to militate for a forum of their own.

Like MoMA, the ICA also wanted to probe connections between modernist art, architecture, and design. But because of economic austerities it was not yet established enough to do so; its leadership was thus relatively open to suggestions from the Independent Group for experimental discussions and displays: if Paris had its cafés and New York its art bars, London might have its art forum. The Independent Group turned this position between the two art capitals of New York and Paris to its advantage, as it engaged new North American art and popular culture in part to revise the academic modernisms of continental Europe. At the same time, it fought on local fronts too, not only *against* the ICA in a generational dispute about modernism and mass culture, but also *with* the ICA against the British art establishment (specifically in the person of art historian and curator Kenneth Clark and company), whose

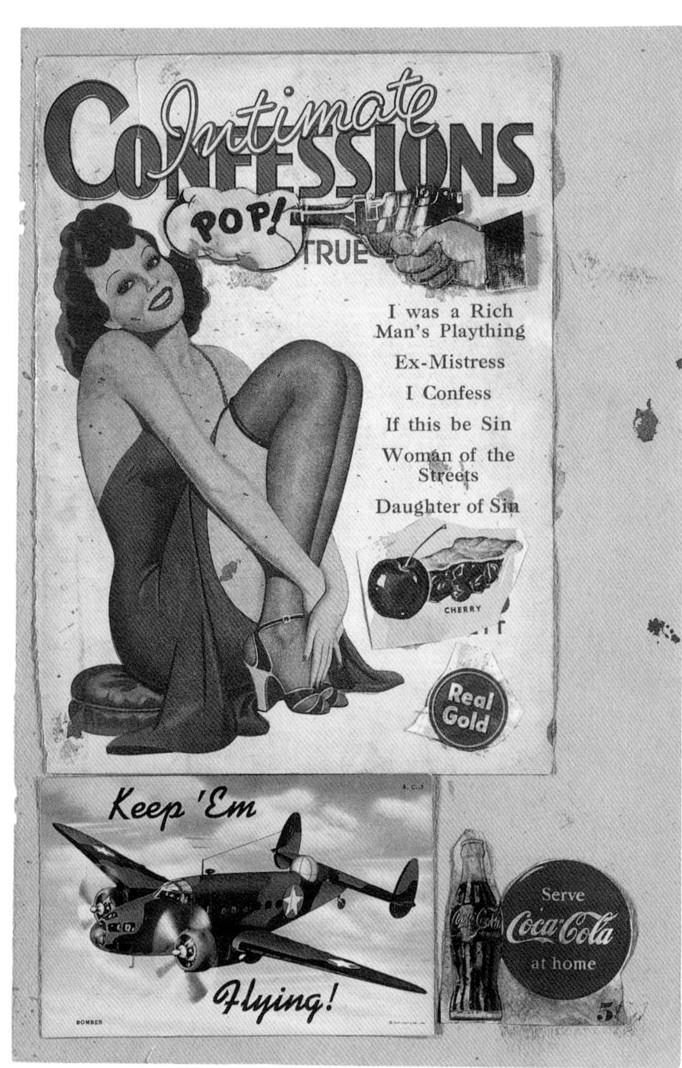

1 • Eduardo Paolozzi, *I Was a Rich Man's Plaything*, c. 1947
Collage mounted on card, 36 x 23 (14⅛ x 9)

▲ 1924, 1930b, 1931 • 1921, 1928

head-in-the-sand elitism regarded anything American as the height of vulgarity, perhaps even the end of civilization. This, then, was the ideological situation in which the Independent Group emerged: the slow death of the British Empire and the continued austerity after World War II (rationing would not cease until 1954), the abrupt advent of the Cold War (with its threat of an atomic end of the world) and a new age of technological advance (with its contrary promise of a new utopia, or at least of a new beginning). This situation was complicated, again, by the old age of European modernism on the one hand and the sex appeal of American mass culture on the other—its promise of plenty on the horizon in contrast to the actuality of scarcity at home.

As a forum, the Independent Group passed quickly through three formations oriented around display and design, science and technology, and art and popular art respectively. In April 1952 a young ICA assistant named Richard Lannoy arranged three events for invited guests. The first was a now-legendary show of images projected by Paolozzi from his collection of magazine tearsheets, ads, postcards, and diagrams, which he labeled "Bunk" and presented with scant order or commentary [**1**]. The second was a light show by an American discovered by Lannoy called Edward Hoppe; and the third was a talk by a de Havilland aircraft designer. Such odd presentations would prove characteristic of the Independent Group, as would the interest in collage, display, and design, even though the status of these formats was as yet obscure—were any of these presentations "art"? After Lannoy left in July 1952, Reyner Banham emerged as master of ceremonies. A doctoral student at the Courtauld Institute of Art under the architectural historian Nikolaus Pevsner, Banham would soon develop an account of modernist architecture that stressed its techno-futurist aspect over its formal-functionalist aspect, which was privileged by Read and others (Banham's revised thesis, published in 1960 as *Theory and Design in the First Machine Age*, transformed this field of study). His interest in science and technology surfaced in his first year of Independent Group meetings, which included talks on the machine aesthetic (by Banham), as well as on helicopter design, proteins, and the principle of verification (by the philosopher A. J. Ayer). But this interest dominated the nine-seminar course convened by Banham in 1953–4, "Aesthetic Problems of Contemporary Art," which included Banham on "the impact of technology" (on environment and art), Hamilton on "new sources of form" ("under the impact of microphotography, long-range astronomy, etc."), Colin St. John Wilson on "proportion and symmetry," and Alloway on "the human image" in art (as transformed by "new factors—cinema, anthropology, archaeology"). After the course Banham returned to his dissertation, and a lull ensued until Alloway and McHale were asked to reconvene the Independent Group. They turned the program for 1955 away from science and technology toward "the fine art–popular art continuum" (Alloway), with sessions led by Hamilton on "popular serial imagery in a fine art context," by Banham on the "sexual iconography" of automobile styling (important to such paintings by Hamilton as *Hommage à Chrysler Corp.* [**2**]), by E. W. Meyer on information theory, by Alloway and del Renzio on the "social symbolism" of advertising, movies, music, and fashion, and by Banham and Gillo Dorfles on Italian industrial design.

2 • Richard Hamilton, *Hommage à Chrysler Corp.*, 1957
Oil, metal, foil, and collage on panel, 121.9 x 81 (48 x 31⅞)

Perhaps the shift from science and technology was not so great: as Hamilton remarked in retrospect, the Independent Group had always addressed popular representations. But the art–pop continuum seemed to suit the ICA directorship, for formal meetings of the Independent Group ended in 1955 when its program was assimilated into that of the ICA proper (Alloway became assistant, then deputy, director). In the early sixties, important members emigrated—first Alloway to the United States (where he soon became a curator at the Guggenheim Museum), followed by McHale and Banham. The site of the British avant-garde also shifted to the Royal College of Art, first with Richard Smith (born 1931) and Peter Blake (born 1932), then with Derek Boshier (born 1937), David Hockney (born 1937), Allen Jones (born 1937), and Ronald B. Kitaj (born 1932). However different, most could be packaged under the new label "Pop art" made current by Alloway. Indeed, most became active agents rather than ambivalent students of the pop-culture industry of art, music, and fashion of the sixties.

A tackboard aesthetic

Parallel to the Independent Group lectures were its exhibitions, in which members served as curators of culture more than artists on display. Four shows stand out. The first, "Growth and Form," arranged by Hamilton in summer 1951, before the official founding of the Independent Group, used multiple projectors and screens to produce a photographic environment of different structures found in nature. It introduced key elements of Independent Group shows to come: nonart imagery, multiple media, and exhibition design as art form. It also adapted the device of collage and offered a principle of its own—transformation. For the exhibition drew on the 1917 classic of mathematical biology *On Growth and Form*, in which the Scottish zoologist D'Arcy Thompson put forth his theory of morphological transformation. Both the device of collage and the principle of transformation governed the three other Independent Group shows that followed. "Parallel of Life and Art," arranged by Henderson, Paolozzi, and the Smithsons in the fall of 1953, presented transformations across culture in a spatial collage of roughly one hundred enlarged images of modernist paintings (Kandinsky, Picasso, Dubuffet), tribal art, children's drawings, and hieroglyphs, as well as anthropological, medical, and scientific photographs, hung without commentary at various angles and heights throughout the ICA gallery [**3**]. Its use of photographic reproduction and viewer disruption recalled both ▲ Constructivist and Surrealist installations, and it also drew on such textual image-repertoires as *Foundations of Modern Art* (1931) by • Amedée Ozenfant, *The New Vision* (1932) by László Moholy-Nagy, and *Mechanization Takes Command* (1948) by Sigfried Giedion. Like Independent Group lectures, both "Growth" and "Parallel" implied that science and technology had impacted society, culture, and indeed art far more than art had. The same is true of the third show, "Man, Machine, and Motion"; presented by Hamilton at the ICA in summer 1955, it focused on transformations of the human

3 • Installation view of "Parallel of Life and Art," 1953
The exhibition was held in the grand Regency rooms of London's Institute of Contemporary Arts.

▲ 1921, 1926, 1931, 1942b • 1923, 1925a, 1929

image. Here again were enlarged photographs, now of bodies and machines in motion, under the sea, on the earth, in the sky, and in space: a futuristic sublime of technological man. Yet most of these visions were already archaic or simply phantasmatic, and this points to a delight, characteristic of the Independent Group, in the obsolescence of "the future," perhaps its own included. Set on Plexiglas panels, the images hung on steel frames in a maze that activated the viewer as an ambulatory collagist of past and present techno-tomorrows.

This rigor of exhibition design and motivation of spectatorship climaxed in "This is Tomorrow." Arranged by Theo Crosby in the summer of 1956 at the Whitechapel Gallery in east London (it was too vast for the ICA and, with one thousand visitors a day, too crowded), "This is Tomorrow" consisted of twelve exhibits. "Split up like market stalls in a fair" (St. John Wilson), they were designed by twelve different teams, each made up of a painter, a sculptor, and an architect. As befit the ICA milieu, some exhibits were Constructivist or Surrealist in spirit, while others explored the interface of art with technology and popular culture. No one aesthetic paradigm or disciplinary agenda governed the exhibits; once again the show as a whole was the primary work. The two most celebrated displays presented extreme versions of the British "tomorrow" of 1956. "Patio and Pavilion," designed by "Group Six" (the Smithsons, Paolozzi, and Henderson), consisted of a pavilion of old wood, corrugated plastic, and reflective aluminum on a patio covered with sand [**4**]. In terms of human needs, the Smithsons presented a zero degree of architecture as shelter, while inside Paolozzi and Henderson suggested a bare minimum of human activities—a wheel, a sculpture, various crude objects. The effect was at once primitive, modern, and post-apocalyptic: barred by barbed wire, the interior resembled a ramshackle reliquary of debris after a nuclear blast, especially as it was dominated by *Head of a Man* by Henderson, a modern Frankenstein similar to the busts of broken machine-men for which Paolozzi was known at the time.

4 • The Whitechapel Art Gallery at the time of the "This is Tomorrow" exhibition, with detail of the "Patio and Pavilion" exhibit designed by "Group Six," 1956

5 • The Whitechapel Art Gallery at the time of the "This is Tomorrow" exhibition, with detail of three-dimensional collage installation designed by "Group Two," 1956

The other display, designed by "Group Two" (architect John Voelcker, Hamilton, and McHale), posed an alternative "tomorrow"—not a dystopia of the military-industrial complex but a utopia of capitalist spectacle [**5**]. Here, rather than peer into a spare shack, the visitor passed through a cacophonous funhouse given over to popular images and perceptual tests. These included a movie poster of Robby the Robot with a starlet from *Forbidden Planet* (1956) juxtaposed with a famous shot of Marilyn Monroe from *Seven-Year Itch* (1955), a Cinemascope collage with stars like ▲ Marlon Brando, rotoreliefs and other optical diagrams à la Marcel Duchamp (with whom Hamilton was deeply engaged), and various information postings. Rather than a post-atomic Frankenstein mangled in his senses, the guardian spirit of this place was a contemporary man who seemed to advertise, through word balloons ("look," "listen," "feel"), the new sensorium of capitalist spectacle. (Lest we miss the point, a huge image of spaghetti and a gigantic bottle of Guinness Stout were placed nearby, along with a jukebox, live microphones, and air freshener.) All senses and most arts were engaged here, but engaged as entertainment to the point of distraction, indeed of enervation (the man looked both aggravated and fatigued). Thus the figureheads of the two exhibits, a horrific mutant and an overwhelmed consumer, were not opposites so

▲ 1918, 1993a

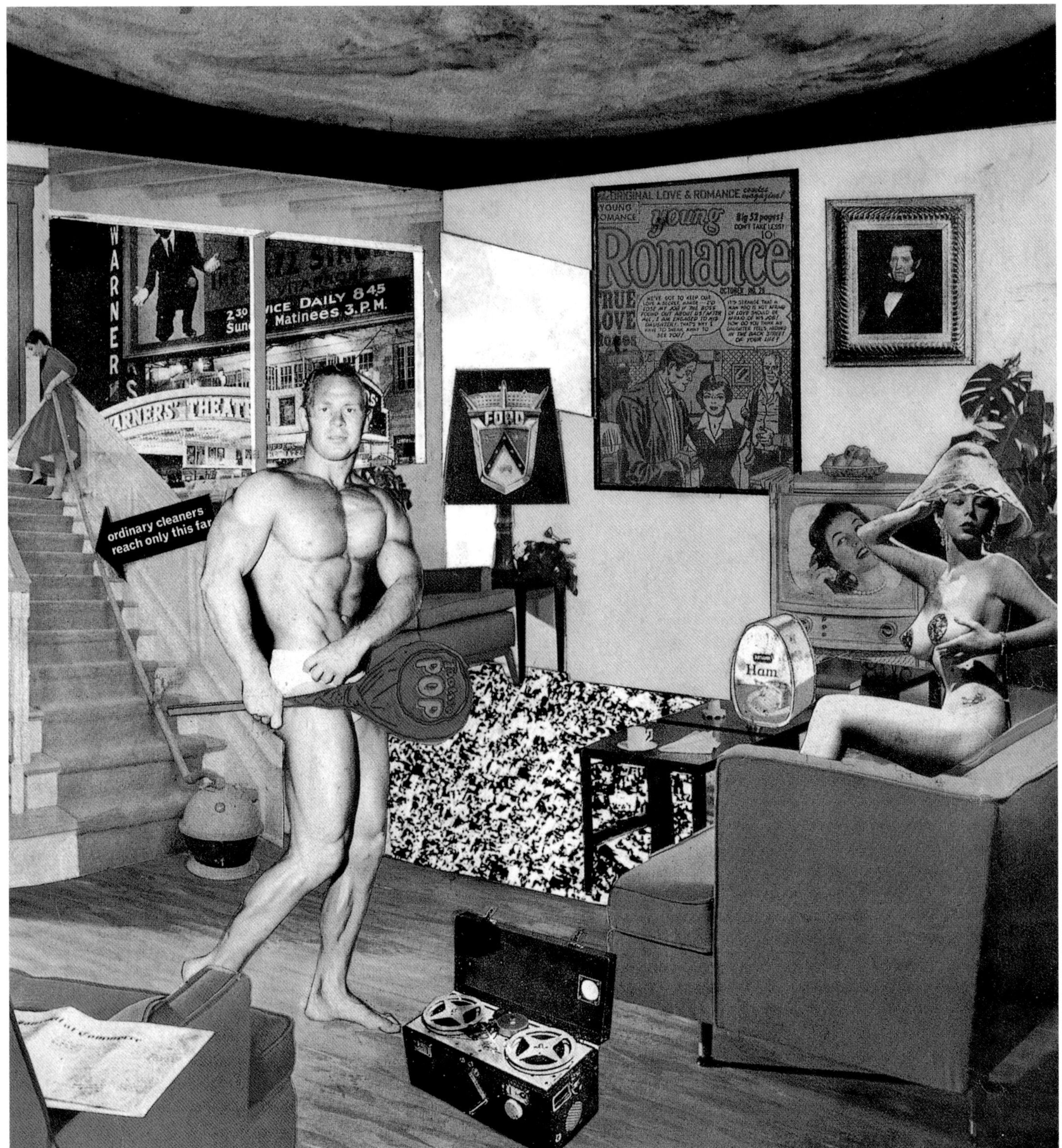

6 • Richard Hamilton, *Just what is it that makes today's homes so different, so appealing?*, 1956
Collage on paper, 26 x 25 ($10\frac{1}{4}$ x $9\frac{7}{8}$)

much as complements. As in "Man, Machine, and Motion," so here in "This is Tomorrow:" Hamilton and company seemed to question the very spectacle that they celebrated.

This is also the case with the emblematic image of the show, *Just what is it that makes today's homes so different, so appealing?* [**6**], a small collage designed by Hamilton not as an art object but for reproduction as a poster and in the catalogue. Like prior collages by Paolozzi, such as *I Was a Rich Man's Plaything* [**1**], it is a pop-psychological parody of postwar consumer culture made with its own ad-slogans and image-bits, and it too reads like a scripted Freudian dream. In this domestic interior, two contemporary Noble Savages pose, a body-builder with a Tootsie Pop for a penis and a well-endowed woman with a lampshade hat and sequined breasts. These two narcissists are connected only by the pop-penis and primped breasts that point at each other and by the surrogates and commodities that surround them (like the can of ham set on the coffee table). On the right a woman speaking on the telephone appears on TV, while on the left her double, an ad-come-alive, vacuums the staircase with an extra-long hose that repeats the theme of the commodity-appliance-as-phallus.

Woman seems to rule this interior, but she too is a commodity; and even as she may fantasize about the body-builder, she is overseen by the portrait of a patriarch on the wall and the absent lord of the house evoked by the armchair with newspaper. Moreover, the interior is thoroughly penetrated by the outside world: distinctions like private and public are effaced by commodities and media (a television and a tape deck, forerunners of video recorders and camcorders, and a *Young Romance* comic on the wall, forerunner of soap operas). There is even a Ford hood ornament emblazoned on a lampshade as the heraldic emblem of this household. Here it is as if Hamilton foresaw the relay of car, television, and commodity that would soon become the very nexus of consumer capitalism. Finally, modernism is also taken in, commodified and domesticated, as the Bauhaus returns here as Danish furniture, and a Pollock drip painting reappears as a mod rug. The only threat from the outside comes from the movie-marquee image of Al Jolson in black face, which cannot quite contain the specter of race, and the face of Mars that hovers above the interior as an ambiguous signifier of all that is alien (in the fifties, sci-fi aliens were often Communists in disguise).

▲ This delirious crossing of fetishisms—sexual, commodity, and technological—was a persistent topic for the Independent Group. Broached by Paolozzi, who soon after the war played with juxtapositions of female bodies and military weapons, it was developed by Hamilton, who rehearsed the sublimations of female bodies in product designs of the fifties (as in *Hommage à Chrysler Corp.*). It • was then passed on to American Pop artists like James Rosenquist (born 1933) and Tom Wesselmann (born 1931) in the sixties, for whom such inorganic eroticism was not exotic at all. How are we to evaluate such Independent Group enthusiasms? Obviously they pose a drastic alternative to the different denunciations of mass culture made by Anglo-American formalists like Clement Greenberg and Frankfurt School critics such as Theodor Adorno. But the Independent Group was neither celebratory nor campy in the manner of much Pop art.

The Paolozzi term "bunk" suggests the equivocal relation of the Independent Group to mass culture. Recall that the first presentation of his collage material, though catalytic, was also tentative, somewhere between an obsessive hobby and an art project, in any case not a stern exercise in ideology-critique. Paolozzi found the word "bunk" in a Charles Atlas advertisement. It is tough-guy American slang, short for "bunkum," which is defined as "nonsense" or "ostentatious talking" (appropriately it was first used to describe the speeches of a Congressman). But what exactly is "bunk" here—the popular source materials or the collages? Perhaps it is both, and the implication is not to take either mass culture or its artistic elaboration too seriously—to *de*bunk both, in fact. Yet "bunk" has another association with which Paolozzi was likely familiar, the famous saying of Henry Ford that "history is bunk." In his caustic collages of *Time* magazine covers, Paolozzi seems to agree. But perhaps he also suggests a reversal: not only that official history is bunk but that bunk has a history too; or, more precisely, that it provides another way into history—bunk as a form of "nonsense" used to debunk history as a form of "ostentatious talking."

As we have seen, a "tackboard aesthetic" was "fundamental to Independent Group notions" (del Renzio), to its splicing of art with science and technology, its exploring of the art–pop continuum, its cracking of commodified bodies. But collage had also become a device of the culture industry. "Magazines were an incredible way of randomizing one's thinking," Turnbull remarked later, "food on one page, pyramids in the desert on the next, a good-looking girl on the next; they were like collages." This suggests that surreal juxtapositions were already the stuff of ads, that collage was in need of a critical reinvention that the Independent Group did not quite provide (this task was left to the ▲ Situationists). Indeed, when Hamilton decided "to produce work" out of "the investigations of the previous years," he returned to painting, and soon traffic on the art–pop continuum became one-way, toward art, as in most Pop art.

In retrospect, the very need of the Independent Group to splice art with science and technology points to the divide between them; it demonstrates more than disproves the famous thesis of the gulf between the "two cultures" of the arts and the sciences presented by English novelist and physicist C. P. Snow in 1959. Much the same may be said of the insistence on an art–pop continuum. In "The Long Front of Culture," an essay also of 1959, Alloway opposed this new horizontal, egalitarian "continuum" of culture to the old hierarchical, elitist "pyramid" of art, fully aware of the class war at stake in this culture war. But, like much recent cultural studies, the Independent Group tended to oscillate between an absorption in this continuum as fans and a looking down on this continuum from on high, that is, from the dandyish perspective of a consumer-connoisseur. (Alloway also wrote of a new culture of different "channels," a term that anticipates the consumerist "choice" of the distracted media-subject of today.) And yet even as its critique of art tilted toward an advocacy of capitalist technology and spectacle, the Independent Group did point to a historic shift from an economy centered on production to one based on consumption, a shift that entailed a repositioning of the postwar avant-garde as well.

FURTHER READING

Julian Myers, "The Future as Fetish: the Capitalist Surrealism of the Independent Group," *October*, no. 94, Fall 2000

David Robbins (ed.), *The Independent Group* (Cambridge, Mass.: MIT Press, 1990)

Brian Wallis (ed.), *"This is Tomorrow" Today* (New York: Institute for Art and Urban Resources, 1987)

Victoria Walsh, *Nigel Henderson: Parallel of Life and Art* (London: Thames & Hudson, 2001)

▲ 1931 ● 1960c ▲ 1957a

1957a

Two small vanguard groups, the Lettrist International and the Imaginist Bauhaus, merge to form the Situationist International, the most politically engaged of all postwar movements.

The Situationist International (SI, 1957–72) has a complicated history. It developed out of two movements: the Lettrist International (1952–7) led by the Frenchman Guy Debord (1931–94), the central theorist of the SI, and the International Movement for an Imaginist Bauhaus (1954–7) led by the Dane Asger Jorn (1914–73), the central artist of the SI. The Lettrist International grew out of the Lettrist Group (founded in 1946, it lives on to this day), and the Imaginist Bauhaus out of yet another group, Cobra (1948–51), an acronym of *Co*penhagen, *Br*ussels, and *A*msterdam, the home bases of its various members. The sheer number and short lives of these movements point to the volatility of cultural politics in postwar Europe. But they all shared a critical involvement in Surrealism and Marxism; or, more precisely, they all sought to supersede the aesthetic strategies of Surrealism and to defy the political strictures of the Communist Party. The first was ▲ deemed conservative in its reconsolidation under André Breton after the war, and the second was considered abhorrent in its ● Stalinism and reactionary in its Socialist Realism. To these two critical engagements a third must be added: like the Independent ■ Group in Britain, the SI confronted the rise of consumer society. But whereas the Independent Group saw open "channels" for desire in this new mass culture, the SI saw that a closed "spectacle" had transformed our very alienation into so many commodities to consume. Moreover, whereas avant-gardes like the Independent Group embraced one side of the cultural dialectic of twentieth-century capitalism in order to contest the other—mass culture against modernist art, or vice versa—the SI were able to comprehend both sides critically, strategically, at least for a time.

Besides Jorn, Cobra had included the Belgian poet-critic Christian Dotrement (1922–79), painters Karel Appel (born 1921), Pierre Alechinsky (born 1927), and Corneille (born 1922), and the Dutch painter-turned-urbanist Constant (born 1920); the last would figure in the SI too. Although Marxists, they were contemptuous of Socialist Realism in the East; and although Expressionists, they were suspicious of Abstract Expressionism in the West. Thus neither figurative nor abstract, Cobra practiced forms of coloristic "disfiguration" suggestive of the fierce scrawling of children, if not of the insane. This brought Cobra close to Surre- ◆ alism, and closer still to the *art brut* of Jean Dubuffet; but as the SI would do later, it rejected the Surrealist unconscious as too individualistic or "subjectivist." Cobra sought a collective basis of art and society, and to this end it stressed totemic figures, mythic subjects, and collaborative projects like journals, exhibitions, and murals. However, the Paris art world of the time, governed by an academic coalition of Surrealists and abstractionists, did not fall before this onslaught, and Cobra broke apart in 1951.

Critique of everyday life

▲ Jorn had studied with Fernand Léger and assisted Le Corbusier briefly before the war. Perhaps it was this training that led the Swiss abstract painter Max Bill, a former Bauhaus student, to contact ● Jorn in 1953 about the founding of a "new Bauhaus." Yet Jorn was too marked by his Cobra experience to accept the functionalist pedagogy outlined by Bill. "Experimental artists must get hold of industrial means," Jorn agreed, but they must "subject them to their own nonutilitarian ends." His idea of a new Bauhaus was experimental, not technocratic, and in this polemical spirit he founded the Imaginist Bauhaus in November 1954 with his old Cobra comrade Constant and a new Italian associate, Giuseppe Pinot Gallizio (1902–64). In 1955 they started an "experimental laboratory" in Albisola, Italy, in order to experiment with new materials in painting and ceramics (Pinot Gallizio was trained as a chemist). Yet, even as the Imaginist Bauhaus suggested a working-through of the unfinished projects of Surrealism and Constructivism, it was little more than a way-station between Cobra and the SI. In 1956 representatives of the Imaginist Bauhaus and the Lettrist International met to discuss a coalition, and the SI was founded a year later.

To an extent the original Lettrist Group was an early postwar ■ reprise of Dada. Apart from actions designed as scandals to shock the bourgeoisie, the Lettrists, clustered around the charismatic Romanian Isidore Isou (born 1925), pushed the Dadaist decomposition of word and image further, both in poems that broke language down to the letter and in collages that mixed verbal and visual fragments. Not content with such experiments, Debord split from this group with a few other Lettrists to form the Lettrist International in 1952. Over the next several years they adapted some

▲ 1924, 1942a, 1942b ● 1934a, 1937a ■ 1956 ◆ 1946, 1959c ▲ 1925a ● 1923, 1947a ■ 1916a, 1920

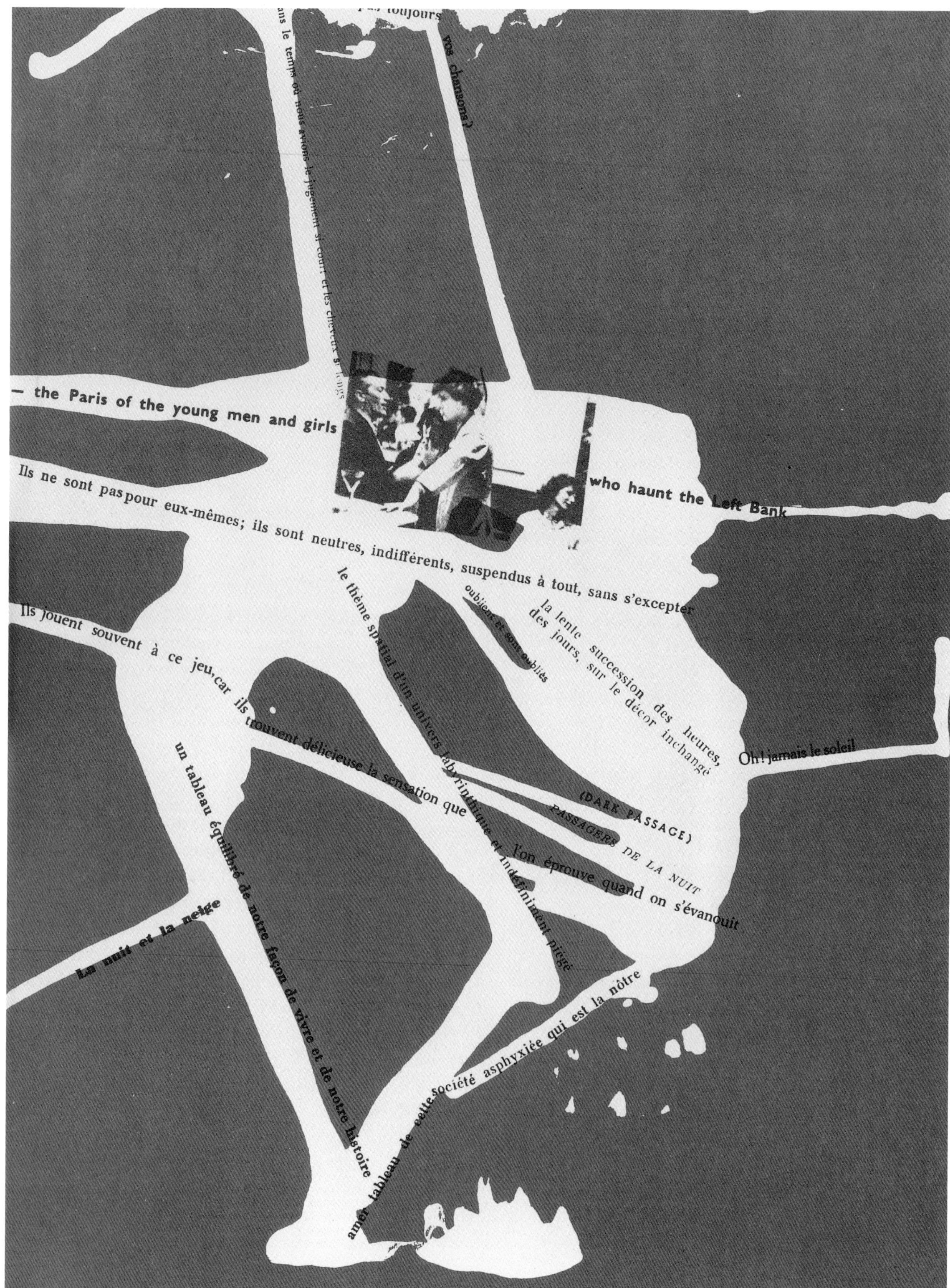

1 • Guy Debord and Asger Jorn, page from *Mémoires*, 1959
Oil, ink, and collage on paper, 27.5 x 21.6 (10½ x 8½)

Lettrist notions, invented others, and recast the whole project according to a newfangled Marxism pledged to a "critique of everyday life" (developed from the Marxist sociologist Henri Lefebvre [1901–91]) through the construction of subversive "situations" ▲ (derived from the existentialist philosopher Jean-Paul Sartre). They sought, in short, to advance the "class struggle" through the "battle of leisure." Debord and Jorn documented the brief life of the Lettrist International in *Mémoires* (1959), a collage that literally intercuts the subjective and the social, the artistic and the political [**1**]. It is a labyrinth of quotations snipped by Debord from poems and novels, histories and political economies, newspapers and film scripts, ads and cartoons, etchings and woodcuts, all scored by Jorn in streaks and splotches of paint that trace passionate connections between people, places, and events.

It is often said that the SI developed as an artistic avant-garde until 1962, when a schism divided the activists from the artists, and that it continued as a political avant-garde until its dissolution in 1972. Yet the SI sought to transform art and politics together at every stage of its development, and its signal contribution was to devise a cultural politics able to critique consumer capitalism. It did so even as it also insisted on some old political principles (like the idea of workers' councils) and challenged some new ones (such as the fiery Maoisms of the time). However, the schism within the SI in 1962 was real. Preceded by several departures—Pinot Gallizio was expelled in 1960, charged with art-world opportunism; Constant resigned the same year; and Jorn withdrew to the margins a year later—the division occurred when the Paris section led by Debord stipulated that Situationist art and politics could *not* be separated. Some artists from the Scandinavian, German, and Dutch sections disagreed, and, led by Jorgen Nash (younger brother of Jorn), they formed a rival Situationist group, only to be expelled by the SI in turn. At this point, fueled by new members not formed by the art movements of the fifties and driven by the political crises of the early to mid-sixties, the SI sought to realize its critical strategies in political interventions. In 1966 it was involved in the first student revolt in France, at the University of Strasbourg, which was guided by the Situationist pamphlet *On the Misery of Student Life* by Mustapha Khayati. And in 1967 the SI published its two greatest critiques of capitalist culture, *The Revolution of Everyday Life* by Raoul Vaneigem (born 1934) and *The Society of the Spectacle* by Debord. These texts were crucial to the student uprisings of May 1968, in which the SI was also active (its advocacy of workers' councils was especially important at this time). However, in the meltdown of the left after 1968, the SI also began to fall apart. Its last conference occurred in 1969, its last journal appeared in the same year, and in 1972 it dissolved altogether.

Dérive and *détournement*

The SI has had an afterlife, however, through texts like *The Society of the Spectacle*, in which Debord focused insights into capitalist culture developed since the founding of the Lettrist International in 1952. Many of its theses elaborate or quote central texts of Hegelian Marxism: the young Marx on "alienation," the young György Lukács on "reification" from *History and Class Consciousness* (1923), as well as Sartre and Lefebvre (in this respect Debord liked to cite the nineteenth-century poet and Surrealist favorite Lautréamont: "plagiarism is necessary; progress implies it"). But this caustic text is also highly original, for it updates both Marx on the fetishistic effects of the commodity and Lukács on the fragmentary effects of mass production in order to expose the workings of a new stage of capitalism centered on the image and driven by mass consumption. Debord analyzed this society of marketing, media, and mass culture in terms of "spectacle," defined most succinctly as "capital accumulated to such a degree that it becomes an image." Although written out of a specific conjuncture, *The Society of the Spectacle* allows one to grasp the trajectory of modern culture vis-à-vis capitalist development. And today, as two former SI members, T. J. Clark and Donald Nicholson-Smith, have argued, its greatest strengths might well be what critics on the Left have long deemed its greatest weaknesses: its emphasis on political organization (at a time of dispersal on the Left) and its will to totalize (in the face of a capitalism that becomes ever more total in its own right).

Two theses from *The Society of the Spectacle*

#190:
Art in the period of its dissolution, as a movement of negation in pursuit of its own transcendence in a historical society where history is not yet directly lived, is at once an art of change and a pure expression of the impossibility of change. The more grandiose its demands, the further from its grasp is true self-realization. This is an art that is necessarily *avant-garde*; and it is an art that *is not*. Its vanguard is its own disappearance.

#191:
The two currents that marked the end of modern art were Dadaism and Surrealism. Though they were only partially conscious of it, they paralleled the proletarian revolutionary movement's last great offense; and the halting of that movement, which left them trapped within the very artistic sphere that they had declared dead and buried, was the fundamental cause of their own immobilization. Historically, Dadaism and Surrealism are at once bound up with one another and at odds with one another. This antagonism, involvement in which constituted for each of these movements the most consistent and radical aspect of its contribution, also attested to the internal deficiency in each's critique—namely, in both cases, a fatal one-sidedness. For Dadaism sought *to abolish art without realizing it*, and Surrealism sought *to realize art without abolishing it*. The critical position since worked out by the Situationists demonstrates that the abolition and the realization of art are inseparable aspects of a single transcendence of art.

▲ 1946, 1959c

The SI cannot be reduced to its practice of art, but neither can this be dismissed as superfluous. "Culture reflects," Debord wrote in 1957, "but also prefigures, the possibilities of organization of life in a given society." And it is to this end that the SI elaborated its cultural strategies, four of which stand out: *dérive*, "psychogeography," "unitary urbanism," and *détournement*. A *dérive* is defined as "a technique of transient passage through varied ambiances." Literally "a drifting," a *dérive* is undertaken in the interest less of a chance encounter that might trigger the unconscious, as with Surrealist wandering, than of a subversive relation to everyday life in the capitalist city. Here the Baudelairean connoisseur of leisure—the *flâneur*—becomes the Situationist critic of leisure, defined simply as the other side of alienated work. A "psychogeography" might follow from a *dérive*; it is "a study of the specific effects of the geographical environment, consciously organized or not, on the emotions and behavior of individuals." Debord provided a good example in *The Naked City* (1957), which consists of nineteen sections of a Paris map reordered according to one such hypothetical itinerary **[2]**. Together the *dérive* and the psychogeography point toward "unitary urbanism," or "the combined use of arts and techniques for the integral construction of a milieu in dynamic relation with experiments in behavior." Constant

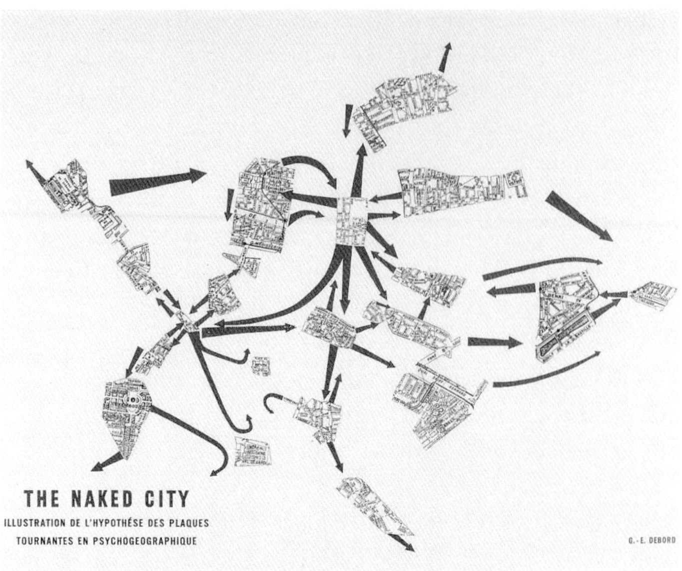

2 • Guy Debord, *The Naked City*, 1957
Color psychogeographical map on paper, 33 x 48 (13 x 18⅞)

3 • Constant, *New Babylon/Amsterdam*, 1958
Ink on map, 200 x 300 (78¾ x 118⅛). Installation at Amsterdams Historisch Museum.

prefigured such constructions in his project "New Babylon" [**3**]. Devoted to a notion of urban design as a set for nomadic movement and mass play, he proposed a series of high-tech megastructures across various European cities that could be reformed by residents at will like giant pieces of Lego. (At least this was the idea; even some Situationists were not persuaded by his drawings and models, in which utopian lines of escape and dystopian forms of surveillance become difficult to distinguish.)

More than a wandering, a *dérive* is a recoding of urban spaces and symbols. This recoding is part of the central strategy of Situationist practice: *détournement*, defined as "the integration of present or past artistic production into a superior construction of a milieu." *Détourner* is to divert—in this case, to divert purloined images, texts, and events toward subversive viewings, readings, and ▲ situations. Derived from Dadaist and Surrealist collage, *détournement* ● was opposed to the quotations of media in Pop art and the ■ accumulations of products in Nouveau Réalisme. Rather than a univocal appropriation, the Situationists sought a "dialectical devaluing/revaluing" of the diverted artistic element. Moreover, the result was not intended as art or antiart at all: "There can be no Situationist painting or music," the first issue of *Situationniste Internationale* declared in June 1958, "but only a Situationist use of these means." In this way *détournement* is a double performance: it simultaneously exposes the ideological nature of a mass-cultural image or the dysfunctional status of a high-art art form *and* refunctions it for a critical political use. With its use of extracted texts and images, *Mémoires* is an early example of *détournement*, but the exemplary instance is the six films made by Debord from 1952 to 1978, mostly from appropriated ads and news photos, media clips and film footage, texts and soundtracks.

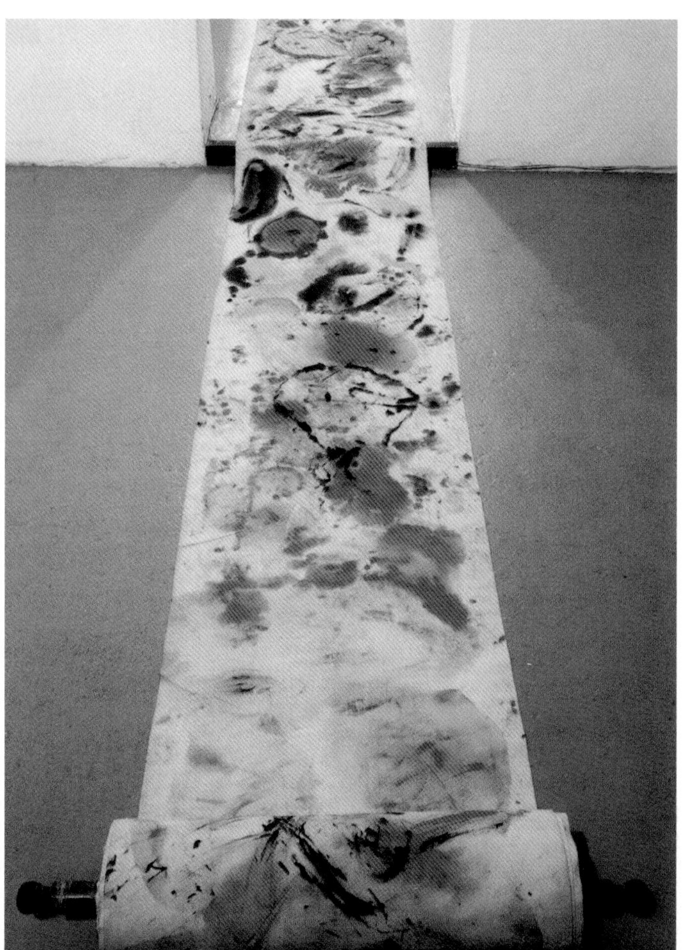

4 • Giuseppe Pinot Gallizio, *Rotolo di pittura industriale* (Industrial Painting), 1958
Mixed media, 74.5 x 7,400 (29³⁄₈ x 2,913³⁄₈)

Production and consumption

As the critic Peter Wollen has indicated, the Situationist *détournement* of art came to a head in 1959 when Pinot Gallizio displayed his "industrial paintings" and Jorn exhibited his "modifications," both in Paris. In his show Pinot Gallizio covered the entire Galerie René Drouin with rolls of canvas painted as if automatically in lurid colors; he added lights, mirrors, sounds, and smells to create a total environment. Yet, rather than another extension of action painting into Installation art, this "grotto of anti-matter" was meant to prefigure a future world of play that automation, once diverted from its capitalist logic, might afford (this was true of "New Babylon" as well). It was also intended to parody the present world of capitalist production and consumption, for not only were the canvases made on a mock assembly line with paint-machines and spray guns, but they could also be cut up for sale by the meter [**4, 5**]. The "modifications" bear the marks of capitalism in another way. They are kitsch pictures, mostly anodyne landscapes and city views produced for *petit-bourgeois* decoration, that Jorn had scavenged in flea markets and painted over with primitivist figures and abstract gestures à la Cobra.

5 • Giuseppe Pinot Gallizio and his son Giors Melanotte working on the Industrial Painting in Alba, Italy, c. 1956

▲ 1920 ● 1960c, 1964b ■ 1960a

5 • Asger Jorn, *Paris by Night*, 1959
Oil on reused painting, 53 x 37 ($20\frac{3}{4}$ x $14\frac{1}{2}$)

Lately the "modifications" have prompted divergent readings. For some critics they "crack open" traditional genres that have become academic kitsch in order to make them live again as contemporary signs. In doing so, they overcome, symbolically at least, the split between avant-garde and kitsch that long deformed modern culture. For other critics, however, the "modifications" suggest the reverse. They rehearse avant-garde styles (for instance, primitivist, Expressionist, abstract) as so many dead letters; thus, rather than a resolution of avant-garde and kitsch, they show the former reduced to the latter. Yet neither account seems adequate to a modification like *Paris by Night* **[5]**. In the original painting a lone bourgeois man leans on a balcony and gazes over the nocturnal city. It is a prewar scene, perhaps turn of the century, that is designed to seduce us, to allow us to identify our contemplation of the figure in the painting with his contemplation of the spectacle of Paris. The gestural overpainting does not shatter this absorption; rather, it injects a different moment of interiority and spectacle—▲ the moment of Abstract Expressionism and postwar culture. In this way, the kitsch original is not enlivened any more than the avant-garde overpainting is deadened. Instead the two bracket one another as historical, and so carve out a critical distance for the viewer with which to evaluate both moments, both formations. "Painting is over," Jorn wrote in a statement that accompanied his show of "modifications" in 1959. "You might as well finish it off. Detourn. Long live painting." Like the old king, Jorn suggests, painting may be dead; but like the new king it may live on—not as an idealist category that never dies but as a materialist corpse that rots subversively. "Our past is becoming," Jorn concludes, "one needs only to crack open the shells."

For Debord the prewar precedents of the SI were complementary failures: "Dadaism sought to abolish art without realizing it," he wrote in *The Society of the Spectacle*, "and Surrealism sought to realize art without abolishing it." The SI should not make this same mistake: it needed to "surpass" both the prewar avant-gardes and the revolutionary politics that emerged with them (from the Russian Revolution in 1917 onward). It could not be just another postwar repetition. But the SI possessed a possibility other than • Debordian refusal or neo-avant-garde rehearsal of the historic avant-garde. In 1962, around the time of the SI schism, Jorn produced another set of modifications called "new disfigurations," which are mostly portraits of proper subjects disfigured by childish doodles or deranged doubles. In one kitsch original, a girl who appears to be dressed for confirmation—that is, for social-religious initiation as an adult—gazes out at us; but she still holds the jump rope of a child **[6]**. In the overpainting Jorn puts a mustache and goatee on her as Marcel Duchamp had done with the *Mona Lisa* in 1919, perhaps with this warning of Debord in mind: "Since the negation of the bourgeois conception of art and artistic genius has become pretty much old hat, the drawing of a mustache on the *Mona Lisa* is no more interesting than the original version of that painting." One can read this disfiguration as an admission of the pathetic status of the belated artist—the avant-garde should just give up, or, as Debord would say, its negation of art, now taken *as* art, should be negated in turn. But around this girl, amidst other assorted grotesqueries, Jorn has scrawled "l'avangarde se rend pas" (*sic*)—the avant-garde *doesn't* give up. How are we to read this defiance, and to whom is it addressed? Is it serious or silly? Does Jorn imply that the avant-garde should give up (as many, both pro-Situationist and con, insisted) but doesn't, and that ridiculous recalcitrance is the greatest mockery of all, a nose-thumbing to the Left as well as to the Right? In any case, just as Duchamp was able to jazz up old Mona Lisa (he renamed her "L.H.O.O.Q.", which in French sounds like "she has a hot ass"), so Jorn has turned this girl into a tough little customer: her jump rope begins to look like a whip, maybe even a garotte.

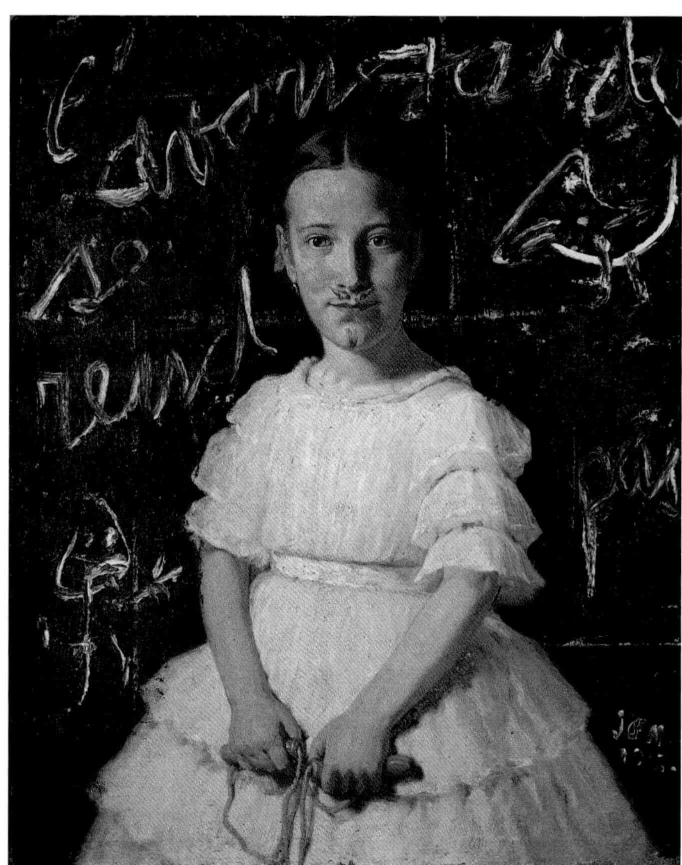

6 • Asger Jorn, *l'avangarde se rend pas* (the avant-garde doesn't give up), 1962
Oil on reused painting, 73 x 60 (28¾ x 23⅝)

FURTHER READING

Iwona Blazwick (ed.), *An Endless Adventure—An Endless Passion—An Endless Banquet: A Situationist Scrapbook* (London: Verso, 1989)

Guy Debord, *The Society of the Spectacle* (1967), trans. Donald Nicholson-Smith (Cambridge, Mass.: MIT Press, 2002)

Ken Knabb (ed.), *Situationist International Anthology* (Berkeley: Bureau of Public Secrets, 1981)

Thomas F. McDonough (ed.), *Guy Debord and the Situationist International* (Cambridge, Mass.: MIT Press, 2002)

Elisabeth Sussman (ed.), *On the Passage of a Few People Through a Rather Brief Moment in Time: The Situationist International 1957–1972* (Cambridge, Mass.: MIT Press, 1989)

▲ 1947a, 1949, 1960b • 1960a

1957b

Ad Reinhardt writes "Twelve Rules for a New Academy": as avant-garde paradigms in painting are reformulated in Europe, the monochrome and grid are explored in the United States by Reinhardt, Robert Ryman, Agnes Martin, and others.

In the midst of working on his first set of black paintings—a series of tall oblongs each articulated by a stately grid, three modules wide by seven high, the difference between the units almost impossible to discern in certain of the pictures, so close in tone is one "black" to its neighbor—Ad Reinhardt (1913–67) submitted "Twelve Rules for a New Academy" to the May 1957 issue of *Artnews*. Often doubling as a mordant critic of the art world, Reinhardt, one might think, wrote this essay with his tongue in his cheek, for, one might say, "academic" art, particularly in its abstract guises, was everywhere at that time.

From the late thirties and into the forties and early fifties, the American Abstract Artists' Association had established and then consolidated a local version of the international language of abstraction, which was then being practiced in France under the ▲ banner of *Abstraction-Création*, and being taught in European schools like the Ulm Institute of Design, under the tutelage of Max Bill, and at the postwar continuations of the Bauhaus in the United ● States, under the guidance of László Moholy-Nagy, Josef Albers, and György Kepes. In an essay written in 1959—"Is There a New Academy?"—Reinhardt acknowledged this presence of a type of abstraction-become-academic, which is to say, formulaic and routine, corrupted by the need to place abstraction in the service of design, advertising, or architecture. But he castigated this as "extract art," having nothing to do with real abstraction, which, he said, "cannot be 'used' in education, communication, perception, foreign relations, etc."

It was for this reason that Reinhardt truly wanted a "new academy," which would function like those of the seventeenth century: protecting a notion of aesthetic purity and maintaining the difference between high art and its applied derivatives. Such an academy would make clear, he said, that art is essentially "'out of time,' art made fine, art emptied and purified of all other-than-art meanings."

A black marriage

Reinhardt's own efforts at such purification took the form of marrying the two major paradigms of abstraction that had been brought to their pitch of perfection early in the century: ▲ the grid and the monochrome. For by all but suppressing the demarcations of the grid, Reinhardt's black paintings [1] produce something that approaches the unbroken surface of monochrome painting, thereby doubly ruling out the possibility of distinguishing anything like a "figure" as distinct from a "ground" and, with the same stroke, rejecting any sense that the work could summon an "elsewhere," whether through the association to a window or to a mirror. The resultant self-reference is the supposed guarantee of both grid and monochrome: beginning and ending with themselves (if the grid "describes" anything, this is merely the very surface it serves to map and thereby to redouble), there are no "other-than-art meanings" involved.

But Reinhardt's blithe insistence that this art, and these paradigms, are "out of time" is where the seeming obviousness of his argument breaks down. For, on the contrary, temporality haunts abstract art, even though, in its rage to purge all forms of narrative from its domain, abstraction strives to establish the pure simultaneity characteristic of a spatial art as distinct from a temporal one. Abstract art's involvement with time consists of the historical dimension that supports abstraction as a specific project, making every pure painting the "ultimate" or last work of its kind, the final, culminating member of a progressive series, or alternatively, as a peculiar extension of this logic, the first in a completely new type of art whose history is yet to be written. This had been the logic behind Aleksandr Rodchenko's triptych of monochrome panels ● *Pure Red Color, Pure Yellow Color, Pure Blue Color* (1921), which the Russian critic Nikolai Tarabukin saw as the "last picture," but which Rodchenko himself considered the emergence of the ■ work-as-object. This was also the logic that drove Piet Mondrian "forward" toward an ever purer sublation of the oppositions within painting so that eventually painting itself could be transcended—both preserved and *overcome* by passing beyond itself and into the social field as a whole. Reinhardt participated in this aim when he stated of his black paintings: "I'm merely making the last paintings which anyone can make."

This sense of a historical tide that buoys these projects contains other temporal aspects as well. Undertaken as a form of resistance against the historical forces threatening to penetrate the domain of the work—either from the "left," by contaminating its purity with

▲ 1937b ● 1947a, 1955a, 1967c

▲ 1911, 1913, 1915, 1917, 1921 ● 1921 ■ Introduction 3, 1917, 1944a

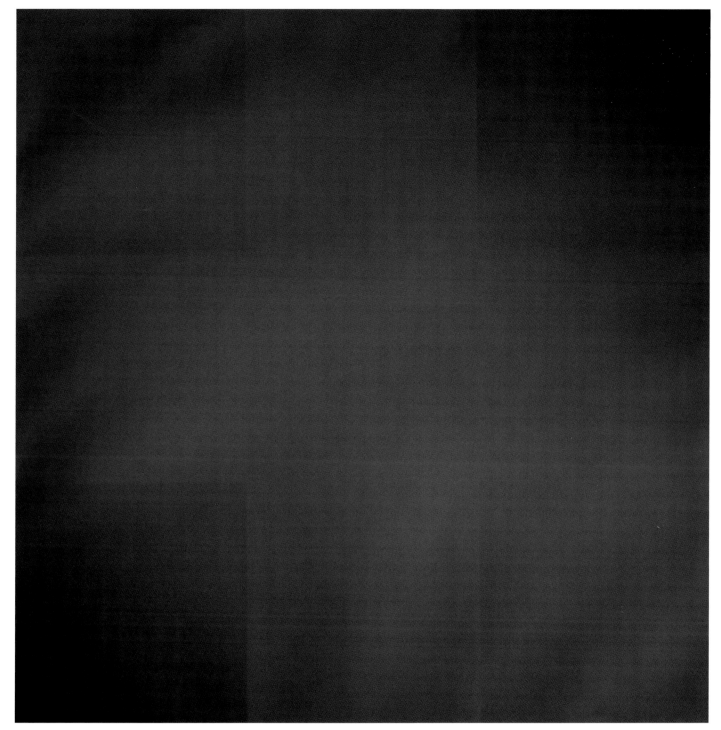

1 • Ad Reinhardt, *Abstract Painting, No. 5*, 1962
Oil on canvas, 152.4 x 152.4 (60 x 60)

elements of social ideology and utility, or from the "right," by corrupting its materiality with the signs of privilege, specialized skill, etc.—an artist's withdrawal into the grid or the monochrome is, if only implicitly, an acknowledgment of those very forces. Each instance of abstraction is historically specific, the circumstances surrounding the onset of Rodchenko's primary color panels in the thirties (Soviet revolutionary production), for instance, differing ▲ widely from those conditioning Lucio Fontana's or Yves Klein's own practices of monochromy in the forties and fifties (the advertising and "spectacle" culture of the aftermath of World War II).

By referring to this phenomenon of reinvention or repetition so characteristic of abstract art—in which we experience wave after wave of the modular grid or absolute monochrome—we encounter another dimension of abstraction's inherent temporality. This aspect has less to do with the idea of each purified painting as the last of its kind than with the notion that each is a total break from anything that could have come before it; and that being thus an origin, each instance of this paradigm is an original. The self-deception necessary to maintain the fiction of one's "originality" when manifesting a form that is as old as cave painting (as is the

▲ 1959a, 1960a, 1967c

case with the modular grid) calls, however, for an explanation. For, while certain parts of the early twentieth-century avant-garde turned to these forms precisely as a badge of anonymity to be worn against the decadence of individualism in art, the postwar avant-garde increasingly asserted its repetitions of these identical paradigms as acts of original invention.

It is possible to suggest that the very ambivalence built into these paradigms of abstract art—suspended as they are between the polar ▲ oppositions of pure idea versus absolute matter—means that however simple such a paradigm might be it is characterized by an unresolvable internal conflict. Further, one could argue, it is just this conflict that drives the need to "reinvent" the form at the same time that it fuels the denial that such occurrences are in fact repetitions. The French structural anthropologist Claude Lévi-Strauss was struck by the phenomenon of this type of repetition as it manifests itself in myths, in which the same story is layered with repeated "mythemes," or kernels of identical meaning-structure, that are restaged by different characters and within seemingly different episodes of the narrative. Lévi-Strauss's structuralist explanation for this repetition turns on the very question of ambivalence that characterizes the phenomenon of visual abstraction. The myth itself, he claimed, is a response to a deep cultural contradiction that cannot be resolved but only returned to over and over, like the loose tooth one continually probes with one's tongue. Myth is the form of these returns; it is a type of narrative in which an unresolvable problem in the real is temporarily relieved by being repeatedly suspended in the realm of fantasy.

This analogy with the myth's compulsion to repeat permits two aspects of the painterly situation to come into focus at once. First, it illuminates the way the abstract paradigm will be the vehicle of serialization within a given artist's practice: the repetition of the *same* format spun out in a long chain of minutely varied replicates. And second, it underscores the fact that the utterly simple form will nonetheless generate a sense of internal contradiction: the anonymous character of the unadorned monochrome taking on, in Yves Klein's case, the insistent individualism of the "signature" object (as he slightly rounds the corners of his rectangular panels or applies his patented [!] pigment "International Klein • Blue"); or in the case of the nine-square grid of Reinhardt's last black paintings, the reduction of the work to its purest logical statement—the "idea"—paradoxically promoting an experience of the most indefinably and irrationally optical shimmer—"matter"—that constantly eludes the viewer's grasp.

Pure paradox

Two careers that developed at about the same time as Reinhardt's last series of black paintings (executed 1960–4) adopted the same fusion of grid and monochrome and demonstrated the same contradictory conditions of the form. One of these careers was Agnes Martin's (born 1912), the other was Robert Ryman's (born 1930).

Coming to New York in the early fifties from the open planes of Northern Saskatchewan, where she grew up, and of New Mexico, where she studied, Agnes Martin gravitated toward that part of the New York School that had avoided gestural painting, adopting instead fields of unbroken color and vastly simplified, geometricizing compositional strategies: Mark Rothko, Ad Reinhardt (his grid pictures of the early fifties having for the most part been either all ▲ red or all blue), and Barnett Newman. Wanting to express subjective thoughts and emotions that have no objective counterpart in nature, Martin turned to abstraction as a way to achieve "not what is seen," as she put it, but "what is known for ever in the mind."

The method she had developed by 1963—and which she never changed thereafter—consisted of penciling a fine linear, edge-to-edge grid onto six-foot-square canvases treated with a thin layer of gesso. In the first of these grids she used colored pencils, but by 1964 Martin had switched to simple graphite so that monochromy took over these pictures, which, nonetheless—to the astonishment of their observers—were able to achieve an extraordinary visual variety **[2]**. Because she endowed that variety with titles evocative of the natural world—*Falling Blue*, *Leaf in the Wind*, *Milk River*, *Orange Grove*—and because of the strong impression of effulgence generated by the gridded fields as they appear to give off an indefinable light, Martin's paintings were soon seen as analogues of nature. They came to be read along the lines that had begun to be applied to Newman, Rothko, and Reinhardt in the seventies, when a rage to thematize abstract art insisted on interpreting even the starkest grid or the most ascetic monochrome phenomenologically • in iconographic terms associated with the idea of the "Sublime." As we have seen, this possibility is something that appears endemic to the grid itself: its even spread of potentially limitless, identical units always capable of generating metaphysical, transcendentalist associations, no matter how seemingly "mechanical" or "automatist" such a schema might be.

The strength of Martin's art, however, is that it mobilizes the very spiritual/material ambivalence built into the grid to effect another order of meaning altogether, one we could characterize as "structuralist." For the luminous, atmospheric haze exhaled by Martin's surfaces occurs only as a middle term between two other experiences of the paintings. The first, when one views the works close to, is of overwhelming material specificity: the unevenness of the penciled lines as they skim the top of the canvas weave but fail to enter its crevices; the ghost of a set of lines visible under the coat of gesso, echoed by their double on top of it, etc. It is only when one backs away from the surface far enough for the mesh of the grid to dissolve, visually, that the sensation of luminous atmosphere replaces the one of particular matter. But then, as one backs up even further, this visual mist opacifies into a densely flattened wall, becoming thus another, more general, form of the material itself. In other words, the canvases become "luminous atmosphere" only in relation to—that is, by *differing* from—the other experiences of the works as material objects, and vice versa.

In this sense we could say that Martin's art is not involved in "picturing" anything specific, whether that be clouds or sky or light or sublime immensity. Instead, working as a structuralist might,

▲ 1908, 1913 • 1967c

▲ 1951 • 1913, 1951

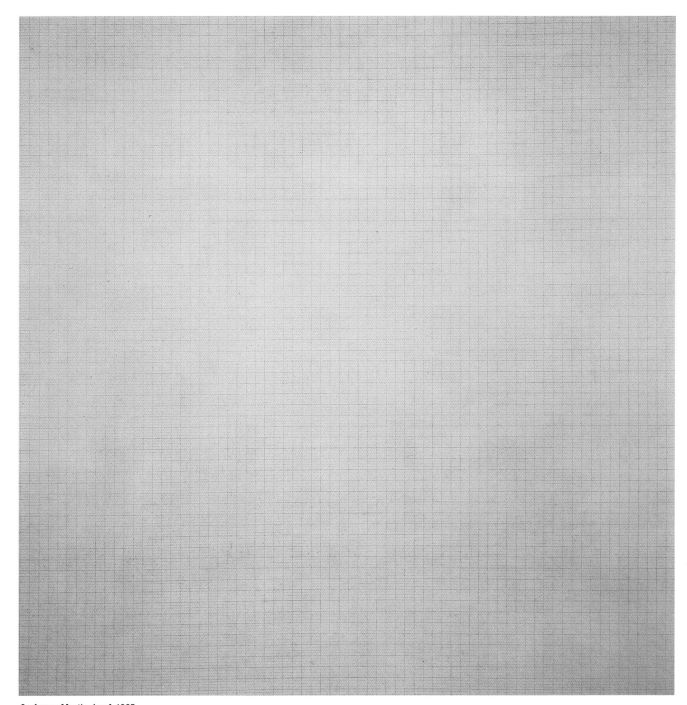

2 • Agnes Martin, *Leaf*, 1965
Acrylic and graphite on canvas, 183 x 183 (72 x 72)

▲ she has generated a structural paradigm in which atmosphere becomes less a question of intuition and more a unit in a system, one that converts it from a signified (the content of an image) to a signifier—"atmosphere"—the open member of a differential series: "wall" as opposed to "mist"; "canvas weave" as opposed to "unlocatable luminosity"; "form" as opposed to "formlessness."

The operation of the structural paradigm means, then, that something is experienced not in terms of a phenomenological plenitude ("this luminous mist I *see* before *me*") but in constant relation to what it is not ("luminosity" = "not opacity")—a presence always shadowed by its own absence. It is this that makes a reductive reading of Martin's work as "pure spatial immensity" or "pure spirit" impossible.

Painting the paint

In the case of Robert Ryman the drive toward a phenomenological interpretation has been equally common, except that here it moves not in the direction of "spirit" but in that of "matter." Emerging in the late sixties (his first solo exhibition was in 1967; in 1969 he ▲ participated in "When Attitudes Become Form" in Berne and London and in "Anti-Illusion: Procedure/Materials" at the Whitney

▲ Introduction 3, 1912

▲ 1969

3 • Robert Ryman, *Winsor 34*, 1966
Oil on linen canvas, 160 x 160 (63 x 63)

Museum in New York), Ryman was seen as a Process artist, his gridded all-white surfaces the sum total of a series of manipulations of the brute materials of painting itself. In the group of works called *Winsor* [**3**], for example, it is self-evident that the two-inch-wide brush has been charged with white oil paint and dragged across the canvas in parallel rows, with each swipe of the brush covering from eight to ten inches before running out of pigment and having to be reloaded. The slight breaks in facture between the tailing off of the stroke and the ridge of material where the stroke starts again create a series of verticals in counterpoint to the horizontal gaps between the rows through which the warm brown of the canvas is visible. Describing this process as his attempt to "paint the paint," Ryman restricted his materials to types of white pigment—casein, gouache, oil, Enamelac, gesso, acrylic, etc.—which he laid onto a wide range of supports—newsprint, gauze, tracing paper, corrugated cardboard, linen, jute, fiberglass mesh, aluminum, steel, copper, etc.—and manipulated with a variety of applicators—brushes of varying widths (up to twelve inches), knives, ballpoint pen, silverpoint, etc. This has cast a spell of pure positivism over his work; it is seen as the sum of a set of past operations that can be reconstructed in the present from the evidence before one. It is thus understood as both pure matter and the states of its evolution as that unfolded in time.

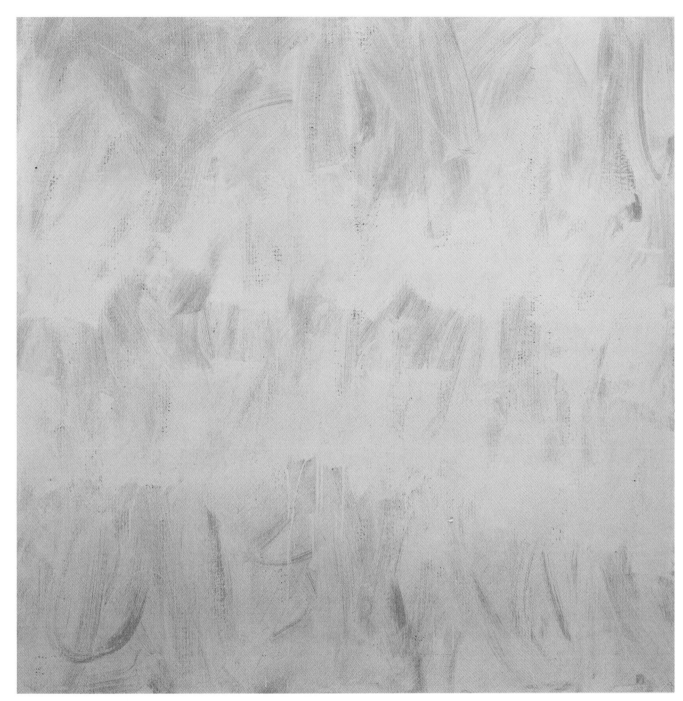

4 • Robert Ryman, *VII*, 1969
Enamelac on corrugated paper (seven units), each 152.4 x 152.4 (60 x 60)

But Ryman defies this temporal continuum, just as Martin defies the notion of an unbroken spatial immensity. He is also operating in relation to the structural paradigm when, for example, in the series *III*, *IV*, *V*, and *VII* [**4**], he applies three obliquely scumbled rows of Enamelac (a flat-white-pigmented shellac primer) to thirteen five-foot-square panels of corrugated paper, carrying out this continuous gesture over only three units of the series at a time. The result is that in *VII*, say, there are discontinuities in the stroke that make the "process" of the gestures impossible to reconstruct, thereby opening up the continuity of process to its opposite: the discontinuity of the unique, implosive object. Ryman's "matter," as fungible in the binary operations of the system as is Martin's "spirit," unpacks and is unpacked by the internal contradictions of the grid.

FURTHER READING

Yve-Alain Bois, "Ryman's Tact," *Painting as Model* (Cambridge, Mass.: MIT Press, 1990) and "The Limit of Almost," *Ad Reinhardt* (New York: Museum of Modern Art, 1991)

Benjamin H. D. Buchloh, "The Primary Colors for the Second Time," *October*, no. 37, Summer 1986

Rosalind Krauss, "Grids," *The Originality of the Avant-Garde and Other Modernist Myths* (Cambridge, Mass.: MIT Press, 1985) and "The/Cloud/," *Bachelors* (Cambridge, Mass.: MIT Press, 1999)

Robert Storr, *Robert Ryman* (New York: Harry N. Abrams, 1993)

1958

Jasper Johns's *Target with Four Faces* appears on the cover of *Artnews* magazine: for some artists like Frank Stella, Johns presents a model of painting in which figure and ground are fused in a single image-object; for others, he opens up the use of everyday signs and conceptual ambiguities alike.

On January 20, 1958, only two weeks after the *Artnews* cover appeared, Jasper Johns (born 1930) opened his first solo show at the Leo Castelli Gallery in New York. It consisted of six paintings of concentric targets, including *Target with Four Faces* [**1**]; four paintings of the American flag, including the first *Flag* [**2**], five paintings of stenciled numbers, both single and serial; as well as a few paintings with literal objects attached like *Drawer* and *Book* (both 1957). The show sold out, with four paintings ▲ bought by the legendary curator Alfred H. Barr, Jr. for the Museum of Modern Art alone. Such a debut was unprecedented, and it seemed to signal changes in the culture of the art world. There was a new premium on youth (Johns was only twenty-seven at the time) and promotion (how else could an unknown artist appear on the *Artnews* cover?). The turnover of styles was also accelerated, for the banal references and impersonal brush-strokes of the paintings were immediately seen as a trumping of the lofty subjects and charged gestures of Abstract Expressionism, which was still very much on the scene. Yet Johns was no wild child. The show represented three years of sustained production (in the fall of 1954 he had destroyed most prior work as derivative). And he ● was already active in a circle that included Robert Rauschenberg, with whom he was intimate, artistically and romantically, from 1954 to 1961, the composer John Cage and the choreographer Merce Cunningham, for whom he designed sets and costumes, and others such as the performance artist Rachel Rosenthal.

A constant negation of impulses

In part, the association with Cage and company led early critics such as Thomas B. Hess, director of *Artnews*, and Robert Rosenblum to affix the new label "neo-Dada" to Johns. But Johns was involved less with the anarchic attacks on art made by Dada than with the ironic investigations of its significance undertaken by ■ Marcel Duchamp, whose work he encountered in 1958 at the Philadelphia Art Museum (they met a year later). Duchamp would remain a crucial point of reference for Johns. The same is true of the philosopher Ludwig Wittgenstein, whose critiques of language appealed to his sense of "physical and metaphysical obstinacy," as Johns wrote in a sketchbook note (he began to read Wittgenstein around 1961, an interest soon picked up by other artists of his ▲ generation, especially Conceptual artists).

The influence of both men, especially Duchamp, can be seen in the signature strategies of his early work. Johns used "pre-formed, conventional, depersonalized, factual, exterior elements" (as he described his "Flags" and "Targets" to his best critic, Leo Steinberg). He played with different orders of signs—visual and verbal, ● public and private, symbolic and indexical (that is, signs made by physical contact, like handprints or plaster casts). He also liked to render literal things ambiguous, even allegorical; for instance, the "Flags" are at once advanced paintings, obdurate objects, and everyday emblems. So, too, he tended to evoke a self that was divided by its own language, by its different signs, in opposition to the Abstract Expressionist self said to be made whole in the very act of painting. Again, much of this provocation resonates with Duchamp, whom Johns also inflected for other artists, just as Cage had inflected Duchamp for Johns. At issue here, then, is less influence than transformation. As Johns commented after Duchamp died in 1968, one of his lessons—again in opposition to Abstract Expressionist belief—was that no artist determines his work finally. Not only does the viewer have a share, but subsequent artists also interpret a body of work, reposition it retroactively, and so carry it forward as well.

Duchamp, Johns wrote, "moved his work through the retinal boundaries which had been established with Impressionism into a field where language, thought and vision act upon one another." Johns inaugurated a similar shift in relation to Abstract Expressionism. Yet, in order to break with it effectively, he first had to be connected with it. And his "Flags" and "Targets" exceed Abstract Expressionism on its own criteria—that is, they are flatter as surfaces, more "allover" as images, more fused as picture and support, than any Abstract Expressionist precedent. In this way, Johns raised the ante of advanced American painting in the late fifties, only to change the game, for he scored these formal points through means forbidden to Abstract Expressionism—by recourse to everyday cultural signs like flags and targets. This was a twist with a knife attached, for Johns responded to Abstract Expressionism with terms that seemed opposed to it: here was painting that was abstract but also representational in mode, gestural but also

▲ 1927c ● 1953 ■ 1914, 1918, 1935, 1966a, 1993a ▲ 1968b ● 1953

1 • Jasper Johns, *Target with Four Faces*, 1955
Assemblage, encaustic on newspaper and cloth over canvas surmounted by four tinted plaster faces in wood box with hinged front, 85.3 x 66 x 7.6 (33⅝ x 26 x 3)

2 • Jasper Johns, *Flag*, 1954–5
Encaustic, oil, and collage on fabric mounted on plywood (three panels), 107.3 x 154 (42¼ x 60⅝)

impersonal in facture (his brush-strokes often appear repetitive), self-referential but also allusive in image (abstract stripes and circles that are also flags and targets), pictorial but also literal in association (in the otherwise nonobjective *Canvas* [1956], a little stretcher is simply attached to the canvas), and so on.

For this suspension of opposites Johns found a perfect medium in encaustic, a wax base that preserves each gesture of the brush—but preserves it dead, as it were, like a fly in flypaper. Encaustic also allowed Johns to bind the picture to its support in such a way as to render the painting as much an object as an image. Finally, it permitted the suspension of other materials as well, such as the collage of newspaper and fabric that Johns often used in his early work, in a dense palimpsest of surfaces. This layering injects a sense of time into the space of the painting—not only the actual time of the complicated making of the work, but also an allegorical time of different meanings and/or suggested memories. For example, over the bedsheet that provides the base of *Flag* [**2**], near the center amid other bits of newspaper that make up its ground, appear the ghostly words "pipe dream." This phrase might allude to the story that the flag first appeared to Johns in a dream (which characteristically renders this public sign a private talisman as well). At the same time, it also points to the conundrum of a painting of a flag that is not a flag (in 1954, at the Sidney Janis Gallery in New ▲ York, Johns had seen a version of *The Treachery of Images* (1929) by René Magritte, the famous Surrealist puzzle-picture of a pipe captioned with its own verbal disclaimer "Ceci n'est pas une pipe"—"This is not a pipe"—beneath it). Already at work in his debut painting, then, is this distinctively Johnsian play with contradiction and paradox, irony and allegory. Again and again Johns states one thing, only to imply another (this is one definition of irony), or he collides different levels of meaning or different kinds of signs (this is one definition of allegory). As he wrote in a sketchbook note circa 1963–4, "One thing working one way/Another thing working another way/One thing working different ways at different times." The trick here is that this ambiguity is effected by means of the literalism of his flags, targets, numbers, maps, and the like, not in opposition to it—by means of "things the mind already knows," Johns added in an early statement. "That gave me room to work on other levels."

"My work became a constant negation of impulses," Johns remarked in retrospect. This negation is not just a display of sophistication, as it first appeared to Steinberg, for whom "the

▲ 1927a

moral" of the early work was that "nothing in art is so true that its opposite cannot be made even truer." Nor did the collision of the visual and the verbal, the pictorial and the literal, simply cancel the ▲ aesthetic of Abstract Expressionism. Rather, it preserved the model of painting as represented by Jackson Pollock in a tense suspension with its avant-gardist opposite as represented by Duchamp. The "impulses" negated here are thus aesthetic imperatives as much as personal inclinations. Indeed, one reason why Johns became central so quickly is that he was able to suspend the contradiction between the basic imperatives at work in the postwar avant-garde—the legacy of Pollock (after his death in 1956) *and* the provocation of Duchamp (whose work became current again around the same time). More precisely, he was able to develop these opposed paradigms into a distinctive art of ambiguity.

The watchman and the spy

And yet, despite all the European wit drawn from Duchamp, Magritte, and Wittgenstein, Johns also possessed the homespun wisdom of an American pragmatist (early on, the critic Hilton Kramer disparaged his art as "a kind of Grandma Moses version of Dada"). This aspect led Steinberg, in his brilliant essay on Johns, to rehearse the making of the early work as if it were a recipe found in an almanac: a recipe of "man-made things" that are "commonplaces of our environment," of "whole entities or complete systems" with "conventional shapes" that underscore the flatness of the painting and prescribe its dimension. These procedures suggest how Johns could be adapted by both Pop artists (who also would use "commonplaces of our environment") and Minimalist • artists (who also would use "whole entities or complete systems"). Yet the implications of his method were both less matter-of-fact and more far-reaching.

First, Johns advanced a novel paradigm of the picture. Especially in paintings after 1958 he used stencils, often of words of colors at odds with the actual painted colors on the canvas (as in *Periscope [Hart Crane]* **[3]**, where we read primary colors but see mostly grays and blacks). In front of such works, Steinberg intuited "a new role of the picture plane: not a window, not an uprighted tray, nor yet an object with active projections into actual space, but a surface observed during impregnation, observed as its receives a message or imprint from real space." Several years later, in a celebrated essay on Rauschenberg, Steinberg saw in this reorientation of the picture—as a site for the reception of signs rather than as a screen for the projection of views—a "postmodernist" shift from "nature" to "culture" as the primary frame of reference of art. For Steinberg this shift required "other criteria"—other, that is, to the ■ formalist criticism of Clement Greenberg that was dominant at the time—and its first suggestion was here with Johns. Second, Johns intimated a novel persona of the artist. "Everything has its use and its user, and no need of him," Steinberg remarked of the pragmatic objectivity of materials and methods in Johns, and this withdrawn subject suggested a posture of "sufferance rather than action"—again in opposition to Abstract Expressionism. This is the beginning of another "postmodernist" shift to a sometimes affectless or antisubjective stance—an "aesthetics of indifference" (as the critic Moira Roth later termed it) that became radical with some Pop and Minimalist artists (think of Andy Warhol).

Johns may "insinuate absence" with his given signs, as Steinberg remarked, but a personal subject is nonetheless residual in his everyday emblems, suspended brush-strokes, and fragmentary casts. It is a subject that seems split in both its "memory imprints" (as Johns wrote in 1959) and its "changing focus" (no phrase is more recurrent in his early sketchbooks) as it moves across different kinds of motivations and meanings. It is also a subject that seems split in relation to the viewer. In an extraordinary elliptical note from 1964 that is again evocative of Duchamp, Johns allegorized this split subjectivity in terms of two personae, "the watchman" and "the spy," and there is little doubt with whom he identifies: "The watchman falls 'into' the 'trap' of looking.... That is, there is a continuity of some sort among the watchman, the space, the objects. The spy must be ready to 'move,' must be aware of his entrances and exits.... The spy stations himself to observe the watchman." It might be this spying on our watching that often lends to his work, even in its most literal aspect, its uncanny effect of gazing back on us as we gaze on it.

Ludwig Wittgenstein (1889–1951)

Defiantly anti-idealist, the Viennese-born philosopher Ludwig Wittgenstein labored to purge our conceptions of language of their persistent Platonism. His *Philosophical Investigations* (1953) performed a radical critique of the very idea of "expression," a concept essential to various forms of abstract art, especially Abstract Expressionism. Expression depends on the idea of an intention to express a meaning; intention is thus understood as a will to meaning that precedes its verbal or visual articulation. In this light, Wittgenstein argued, intention involves a picture of mental life that is private, unknowable to others but immediately available to ourselves.

Instead of this idea of private meanings to which each of us has unique access, Wittgenstein maintained that "the meaning of a word is its use." In particular he advanced the idea of "language games" based on "forms of life." Language games are patterns of verbal behavior that are social in nature and are learned interpersonally. Private expression makes no sense in such a universe: "If a lion could talk," Wittgenstein wrote, "we could not understand him."

One of the first artists to mediate on the implications of this critique for art was Jasper Johns. His use of rulers as "devices," for example, questioned the autographic stroke as the expression of a private meaning; indeed, much of his work can be seen as the performance of "language games." Minimalist, Conceptual, and Process artists then developed the Wittgensteinian skepticism regarding private language in various ways.

▲ 1949, 1960b • 1960c, 1964, 1965 ■ 1960b

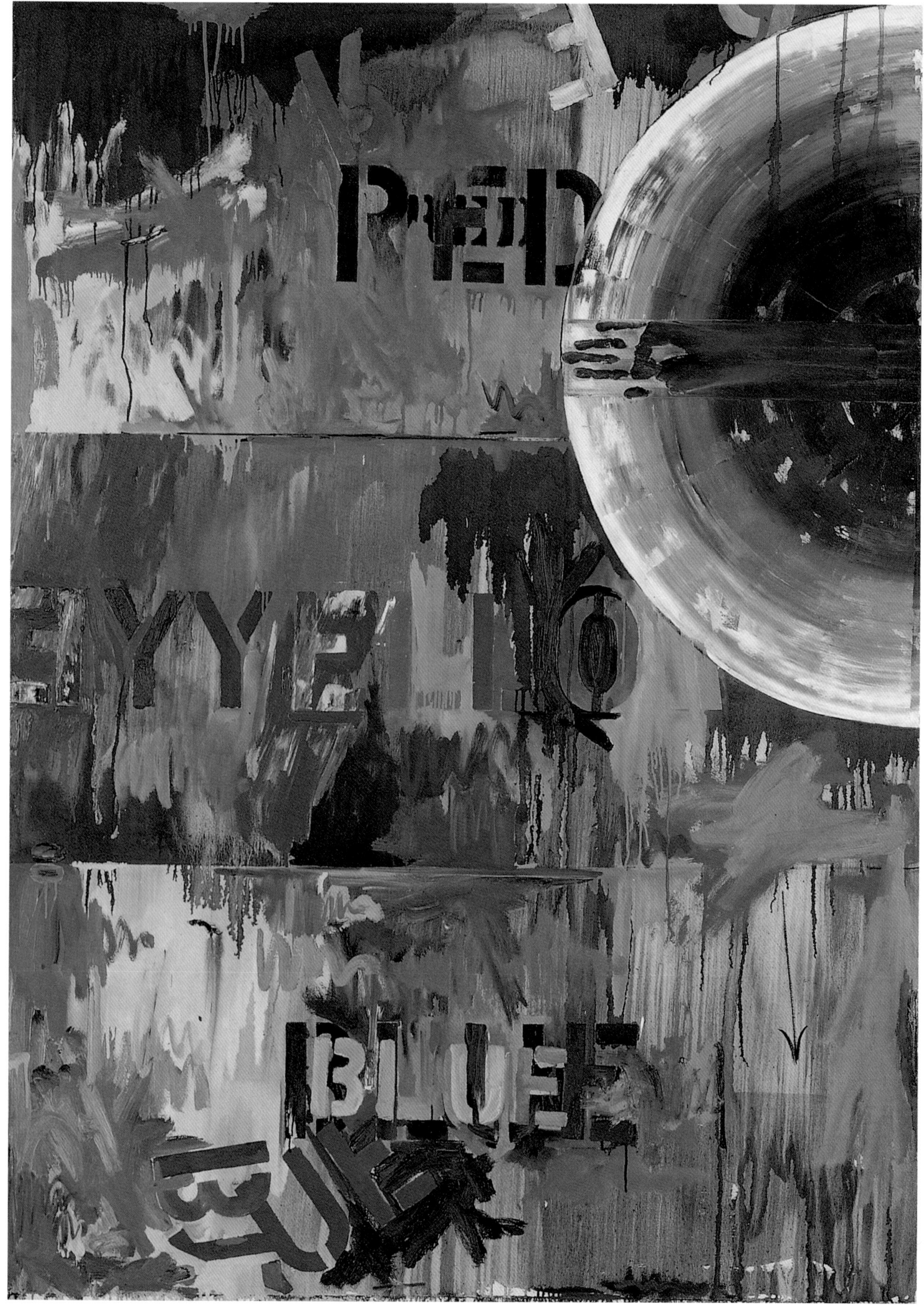

3 • Jasper Johns, *Periscope (Hart Crane)*, 1963
Oil on canvas, 170.2 x 121.9 (67 x 48)

In 1964 Johns had an exhibition at the Jewish Museum in New York, which disclosed how provocative his early work was to various artists. Its philosophical puzzles were crucial to Conceptual ▲ artists like Sol LeWitt (born 1928) and Mel Bochner (born 1940), whose slogan "Language is Not Transparent" could stand as a Johnsian motto as well. Its indexical markings (for example, the handprint in *Periscope* or the piece of wood spun on its axis so as to smear circles of paint in *Device* [1961–2]) were suggestive to • Process artists, even though the actual making of most works by Johns is difficult to reconstruct. And, of course, its use of cultural signs supported Pop art just as its insistence on painting as an object abetted Minimalism (some works, such as *Flag on Orange Field* [1957] where a "Pop" image floats on a "Minimalist" monochrome, combine both tendencies). The connection to Pop is obvious enough; the relation to Minimalism was explained suc- ■ cinctly by Robert Morris (born 1931) in 1969, in the fourth installment of his "Notes on Sculpture": "Johns took the background out of painting and isolated the thing. The background became the wall. What was previously neutral became actual, while what was previously an image became a thing."

What you see is what you see

In this passage from the Johnsian image-thing to the Minimalist object a crucial mediation was provided by Frank Stella (born 1936), whose debut in the important "Sixteen Americans" show curated by Dorothy Miller at MoMA in 1959 was even more precocious (he was twenty-three) than that of Johns in 1958. Stella did not delight in Johnsian ambiguities; he seemed to see them as "dilemmas" to resolve rather than paradoxes to indulge (one painting is titled *Jasper's Dilemma*). His early work kept the stripes of the "Flags" but dropped the symbol. *Coney Island* (1958), for example, is an abstract banner, an island of black on a sea of orange and yellow stripes. But Stella wanted to expunge even this residue of a figure–ground relation, which his "Black Paintings" (1959) did without mercy. *Die Fahne Hoch!* **[4]** is the best-known work in this series, in part because its notorious title ("Flags on High!") cites the official marching song of the Nazis. Yet this reference is more formal than thematic: the painting is sized like a banner, cruciform like a swastika, even black like a fascist uniform. It is also huge (ten feet by six), with a stretcher almost three inches in depth; and this depth suggested the width of the stripes, which Stella graphed in enamel on the canvas in a way that reiterates the cruciform of the stretcher. The cross at the center repeats the most basic form of a vertical figure against a horizontal ground, but this figure–ground relation is underscored here, only to be undone. This occurs not only through the excessive elaboration of the black stripes, but also because the whitish lines between them, lines that appear to be "the figure" on top, are in fact "the ground" underneath—they are the unpainted ground of the canvas showing through the black paint. Where Johns might be playful about this fact, Stella is positivistic; where all is "changing focus" in Johns,

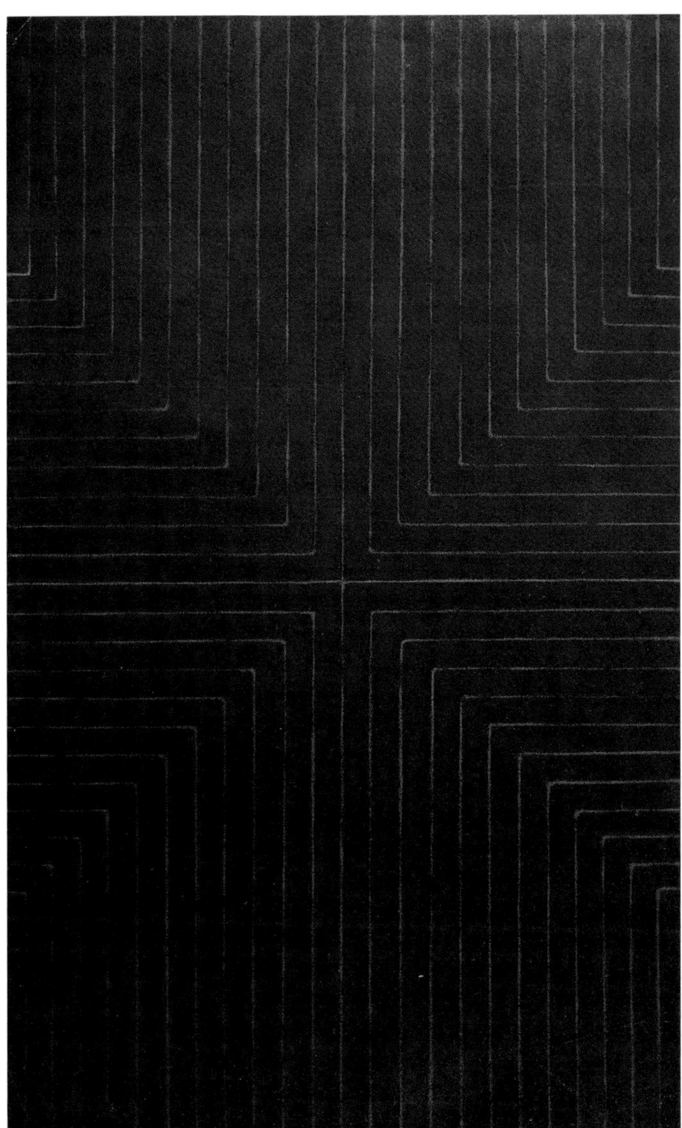

4 • Frank Stella, *Die Fahne Hoch!*, 1959
Black enamel on canvas, 308.6 x 185.4 (121½ x 73)

"what you see is what you see" in Stella (this deadpan line is his best-known comment on his early work).

"There are two problems in painting," Stella remarked in this same manner in 1960. "One is to find out what painting is and the other is to find out how to make a painting." In effect his solution was to combine the two problems—to show what painting is through a demonstration of its making. For his college friend, the critic Michael Fried, who wanted to enlist Stella in his narrative of ▲ modernist abstraction, this logic stemmed from Cubism by way of • Mondrian. For his schoolboy friend, the Minimalist Carl Andre, who was at work on a different genealogy of modernism, this logic was Constructivist in its materialism (Stella applied "identical, discrete units," Andre once commented, "[that] are not stripes, but brushstrokes"). "Carl Andre and I were fighting for his soul," Fried remarked in retrospect, and the debate continued through the mid-sixties at least. In 1960 Stella began to use metallic (aluminum and copper) and house paints; he also began to shape his canvases, first with small notches that redirected the stripes, then with large planar

▲ 1968b • 1969 ■ 1965

▲ 1911, 1913, 1917, 1944a • 1962c

5 • Frank Stella, *Takht-i-Sulayman*, 1967
Polymer and fluorescent polymer paint on canvas, 304.8 x 609.6 (120 x 240)

additions. For Fried these new paints effected a sheer opticality; for Andre they signified a banal materiality. For Fried the new shapes structured the images "deductively," internally, without the need of a found image like a flag to do so; this shaping rendered the paintings even more autonomous. For Andre the shapes called out for three-dimensional objects in actual space; they suggested a site-specific practice, not an autonomous one. In short, just as Johns answered both expectations raised by Pollock and Duchamp with an enigma of his own, so Stella could be claimed by some artists and critics as the epitome of late-modernist painting and by others as the origin of Minimalist objects.

Both camps saw a strict logic in Stella, a declarative logic of the stretcher mapped onto the canvas in the "Black Paintings," of the image made coincident with the support in the notched paintings, of the painting grounded in known shapes and simple signs, and so on. Yet as the shapes became more eccentric, this logic became more arbitrary. Image and support were still coterminous in the "Protractor" series [**5**], but they began to be conflicted as well, and the structures did not appear so necessary or persuasive. By the middle of the seventies the works became hybrids, neither painting ▲ nor sculpture, that first quoted Cubist collage and Constructivist construction, and then mixed different codes of historical and modernist art. This assemblage was pushed to the point in the eighties where fragments of semi-Baroque forms, skewed grids, pop-geometric forms, and exorbitant colors and gestures might collide in the same aluminum construction. Stella seemed to pass from a modernist analysis of painting to a posthistorical pastiche of styles. If one moral of Johns is that "nothing in art is so true that its opposite cannot be made even truer," one moral of Stella is that no pictorial logic is so guaranteed that it cannot be repudiated.

But this crisis in pictorial logic is not his alone. It points to a greater crisis in histories of modernism in the seventies and eighties—histories in which one great artist is seen to father the next master in a strict line of influence, and in which the importance of this heir depends on his furthering of the grand succession of artists. Like his guardian angels Fried and Andre, Stella is of a generation that possesses a heightened consciousness of modernism and an ambitious sense of place in its unfolding (or undoing). In the debates about this unfolding, there is a fine line between historicist narratives of influence and succession and other accounts of historical connection and disconnection. Historicist accounts can be very enabling, indeed ennobling, but they can also be constraining. "Stella wants to paint like Velázquez," Fried is reported to have commented once, "and so he paints stripes." The very rigor of the implicit narrative of painting here—a rigor that offers lofty connection to the past but at the price of severe reduction in the present—suggests why Stella might have wanted to break out of this late-modernist history, perhaps to repudiate it histrionically, even though he is deemed one of its principal protagonists.

FURTHER READING

Michael Fried, *Art and Objecthood* (Chicago: University of Chicago Press, 1998)
Jasper Johns, *Writings, Sketchbook Notes, Interviews* (New York: Museum of Modern Art, 1996)
Fred Orton, *Figuring Jasper Johns* (Cambridge, Mass.: Harvard University Press, 1994)
William Rubin, *Frank Stella* (New York: Museum of Modern Art, 1970)
Leo Steinberg, *Other Criteria: Confrontations with Twentieth-Century Art* (London, Oxford, and New York: Oxford University Press, 1972)
Kirk Varnedoe, *Jasper Johns* (New York: Museum of Modern Art, 1996)

▲ 1912, 1921, 1928

1959a

Lucio Fontana has his first retrospective: he uses kitsch associations to question idealist modernism, a critique extended by his protégé Piero Manzoni.

At the time of the first fully fledged retrospective of his work in the fall of 1959 (in galleries in Rome and Turin), Lucio Fontana (1899–1968) had just begun the series of *Tagli* (or cuts) that would dominate the last decade of his production and become his trademark (he had exhibited his first attempts in this vein, pastel-colored canvases punctuated by many short slices that dated from the previous year, in February in Milan and March in Paris). This near coincidence was a mixed blessing. Dramatized by Ugo Mulas's cannily staged photographic sequence showing the process of creation, from the artist's meditative hesitation in front of his blank canvas to his satisfied contemplation after the act, Fontana's iconographic gesture—the razor-sharp slashing of a monochrome stretched canvas—would overshadow the rest of his enormously diversified production. The scores of *Tagli* that would invade the market in the sixties and the Janus-like rhetoric they would generate—quasi-mystical paeans to a so-called "search for the absolute" on the one hand, and hyperbolic glorifications of the theatrics of violence on the other, a couplet quite similar to that ▲ consciously exploited by Yves Klein—would cast a long shadow over the seriousness of Fontana's enterprise.

The dialectic of avant-garde and kitsch, undone

Though a *catalogue raisonné* of his work had appeared as early as 1974, it was only in the late eighties, after the large exhibition at the Centre Georges Pompidou in Paris, that Fontana's critical fortune changed and he began to be seen, at last, as one of the most important postwar European artists. Such a belated recognition is not a rare phenomenon in itself, but it is particularly striking in the case of Fontana—an artist who unashamedly dallied with the culture industry of the Reconstruction period (with a particular attraction for the glitz of glamour) and who never recoiled at any commission for a decorative piece (from the ceiling of a movie theater or a shop to the monumental door of a cathedral). It is, in fact, Fontana's immersion in the universe of kitsch that paradoxically accounts for the slow emergence of his centrality, as this recognition could happen only at the moment when the dialectical opposition between kitsch and the avant-garde that had dominated cultural criticism ever since the origins of modernism had begun to lose its edge.

Simultaneously (and independently) theorized by both Clement ▲ Greenberg and Theodor Adorno in response to the totalitarian threats of fascism and Stalinism, this dialectical account posits that the experimental work of the avant-garde is the only possible safeguard against the inevitable devolution of any cultural practice and form of production into the condition of the commodity under the rule of capitalist economy. Inadvertently, Fontana threw a monkey wrench into the mechanism of this well-established explanatory model. Unlike the Nouveaux Réalistes in the sixties (who hailed • him as a forerunner) or the Pop artists, he did not consciously rebel against the suffocating effects described by the Greenberg/Adorno argument by elevating the debased commodity to the status of a cultural artifact—an oppositional stance that would only confirm the grip of the dialectical model. Fontana did not *appropriate* kitsch, which would have presupposed a critical, highbrow point of view (for, in order to exploit kitsch, to enjoy kitschiness, one must stand at some remove from it, protected by ironic distance and by a smug confidence in one's own good taste). He did not have to appropriate kitsch (nor could he have done so), for he was mired in it ever since the very beginning of his career: with him, the tight wall separating commercial kitsch from avant-garde art had become utterly porous—a deconstructive endeavor that becomes apparent only if one examines the work that has been eclipsed by the *Tagli*. This means, for the most part, paying attention to his vastly underrated sculpture, keeping in mind that he did not begin to paint until 1949, at the age of fifty.

As the son of an Italian commercial sculptor who emigrated to Argentina (and specialized in funerary monuments), Fontana was exposed to the epitome of kitsch: nineteenth-century *pompier* sculpture. Entering the Milan School of Fine Arts (academic kitsch) at the end of World War I, he returned to Argentina in 1922 (where he ■ emulated Art Deco, Maillol, and Archipenko—modern kitsch). Back in Italy six years later, he was tempted for a while by the antimodernist revisionism of Novecento (revisionist kitsch), a movement soon to receive a stamp of approval from Mussolini's regime.

If up to 1930 Fontana had only been following the well-trodden path of what could be called an "officially sanctioned bad taste," in that year his endorsement of kitsch suddenly became *outré*, extravagant—in direct contradiction to the request for decorum made by

▲ 1960a, 1967c

▲ 1960b • 1960a, 1960c, 1964b ■ 1900b, 1925a

1 • Lucio Fontana, *Butterfly*, 1938
Polychrome ceramic, 16 x 30 x 20 (6¼ x 11¾ x 7⅞)

2 • Lucio Fontana, *Ceramica spaziale*, 1949
Polychrome ceramic, 60 x 60 x 60 (23⅝ x 23⅝ x 23⅝)

the Italian state, whose bureaucrats were prompt to criticize this new direction in his work. The "primitivist" polychrome marble sculpture *L'Uomo nero* (Black Man) that Fontana made in that year was followed in 1931 by sculptures of enameled terracotta, polychrome bronze, gilded plaster, and ceramic, as well as engraved slabs of polychrome cement. Despite the great variety of styles employed in these works (most of the cement slabs are abstract, the terracottas are "expressionist-primitivist," the bronze and gilded plasters are academic), their common denominator is polychromy, an attribute of sculpture that had so offended the sensibilities of the German art theorist Johann Joachim Winckelmann in the eighteenth century, and which had subsequently been an anathema to modernist artists. True, there had previously been notable transgressions of the taboo against sculptural polychromy—by Gauguin, Picasso, and, closer to Fontana, the Polish Constructivist ▲ sculptor Katarzyna Kobro and the American inventor of mobiles, • Alexander Calder. But these artists were mostly interested in testing the respective limits of painting and sculpture in relation to each other, an analytical inquiry that, as Fontana himself discovered after a brief modernist interlude of geometric abstraction in the mid-thirties, had little to do with his enterprise.

Rather than attempting to "paint in space," Fontana plunged back into a premodernist tradition—specifically that of the statuary and decorative objects produced in France during the Second Empire (1852–71), where the simultaneous use of many materials surreptitiously reintroduced polychromy—in order to reverse the very terms of this tradition. For whereas academic kitsch venerated finish and used color to conceal the materiality of the sculptural medium, Fontana made of color the very emblem of a radical materiality, its intrusion into the realm of sculpture becoming a rude noise disturbing the homogeneous harmony advocated by aesthetic discourse. The numerous polychrome ceramic pieces he realized in the late thirties exacerbated the obscene basis of bad taste with a vengeance. For example, his *Lions* (1938), two enameled animals lying side by side, one pink, the other black (the colors of genitalia), and his pearly *Butterfly* of the same year **[1]** are reminiscent of Émile Gallé's Art Nouveau vases (which Le Corbusier detested and whose floral sexuality excited the Surrealists).

Fontana's base materialism

Returned to Argentina in World War II, Fontana once again followed his father's footsteps and became an official sculptor: back to square one—the hyperacademic style. But this was just a step back that allowed Fontana to jump forward, for in 1946, he and his students launched the *Manifesto bianco* (White Manifesto), in which he broke with both abstraction and figuration, attacked aesthetics, rationalism, and formalism, and announced his own concept of art called Spatialism (*Spazialismo*). A call for an atavistic regression, this text is an invocation to create an art of the instinct and of the undifferentiated, an art "in which our idea of art cannot intervene," an art, so to speak, liberated from ideas. As soon as he returned to Italy, in 1947, Fontana began to carry out this program in his work.

He took stock of his "base materialism," to use the term that ▲ Georges Bataille had elaborated in his journal *Documents*, that is, a materialism not grounded in concepts, in which matter is not subject to any ontology but is the agent of debasement of everything that is "high." Here again Fontana concerned himself with polychromy (in neo-Baroque, semiabstract reliefs in terracotta), but then he quite rapidly arrived at sculptures that look like shape-

▲ 1928 • 1955b ▲ 1930b

less piles of mud, that seem to advocate the possibility of formlessness—of the material manifestation of what Bataille called the *informe*. From that point on, sculptural polychromy was no longer the essential medium through which Fontana issued his scatological cry, but just one among many as his base materialism got further and further down to earth.

A comparison between two of his sculptures allows one to locate rather precisely the moment at which his work definitively tipped toward the low. The first, dating from 1947 and currently entitled *Scultura nera* (Black Sculpture), since it is now in bronze, while originally a colored plaster, is a kind of ring made of balls of matter, positioned vertically like those flaming hoops through which circus animals are forced to jump. At the center a vaguely anthropomorphic, vertical excrescence emerges. The crown of balls still bounds an arena, like a stage on which something is about to happen. This last vestige of narrative is entirely swept away in Fontana's *Ceramica spaziale* of 1949 [**2**]: a cubic mass of blackish matter, with glossy and iridescent reflections on an extremely agitated surface, it seems to have fallen on the ground like an enormous turd. Geometry (form, the Platonic "idea") is not suppressed here but *debased*, brought down to the level of matter, which until then, in the history of Western culture, it had had the task of "suppressing by overcoming" (to use the classical term of Hegelian dialectics). Reason is being dealt a "low blow": there is no antithesis, merely a single obscenity lodged in the aesthetic house of cards, and one that threatens to topple it.

Now that he had identified his impulse as scatological, Fontana could at last begin to work in painting without having to fear the optical idealization that seemed to plague the medium (an idealization that had prompted Aleksandr Rodchenko before him and ▲ Donald Judd after him to leave painting altogether for the realm of objects). Indeed, in Fontana's hands, oil paint—the noblest material of pictorial art—often becomes a repugnant paste, and the myriad holes that puncture his very first canvases (the *Buchi* series that runs from 1949 to 1953) ostensibly highlight the materiality of the support. Furthermore, Fontana's courting of "infantile regression" gave a new, playful twist to his infinite appetite for kitsch: from the fake gems added to the punctured canvases (often painted in the sugar-sweet tones of a wedding cake's frosting) of the *Pietre* (Stones) series of 1951–8, to the diamond dust sparkles or acidic colors (candy pink or apple green) of the oval-shaped *La Fine di Dio* (End of God) series from 1963–4 [**3**]—not to speak of gold paint—Fontana never ceased to declare (*contra* Greenberg and Adorno, but also *contra* the aestheticism and Zen-like simplicity of his "cut" paintings) that in the midst of late capitalism the only morally tenable position is that of the irresponsibility of the toddler discovering the scintillating riches of a bazaar. And this "innocent" marveling extended to all the favorite domains of the postwar spectacle: television (for which Fontana wrote a manifesto and hoped to work); fashion (he designed jewels and was delighted when asked to provide props for photo shoots); commercial fairs and discothèque decors, where he often introduced what would become the vernacular use of new hardware equipment such as loopy neon tubes or black light.

The fundamentally nihilist undertone of Fontana's art did not escape his much younger compatriot Piero Manzoni (1933–63), whom he took under his wing in 1957. This date marks the abrupt beginning of Manzoni's meteoric career (until then his production was not-so-promising student work). What triggered this take-off ▲ was the exhibition of Yves Klein's blue monochromes in January of that year in Milan, which Manzoni assiduously studied. His first response was indebted to the pauperist aesthetic of yet another mentor, Alberto Burri (1915–95), whose assemblages of burlap bags, soon followed by pieces of burnt plastic, had also fascinated • Robert Rauschenberg during his sojourn in Italy in 1952–3. Resisting the monochrome, Manzoni realized "compositions" in which layers of melted tar crack open to reveal, in variously disseminated streaks or craters, blobs of fiery reds or yellows. But by 1958, with his first *Achromes* (literally, "without color") Manzoni imported this *matiériste* and resolutely anti-idealist stance within the modernist trope of the monochrome, recently reactivated by Klein. The *Achromes*, which are all white, would constitute an ongoing series until Manzoni's untimely death at the age of thirty, but they evolved dramatically during such a short span.

At first, with pieces made of squares of cotton sewn into a grid, or of cleated sheets, both types whitewashed with the earthy yet milky substance of kaolin (a superfine clay used for porcelain),

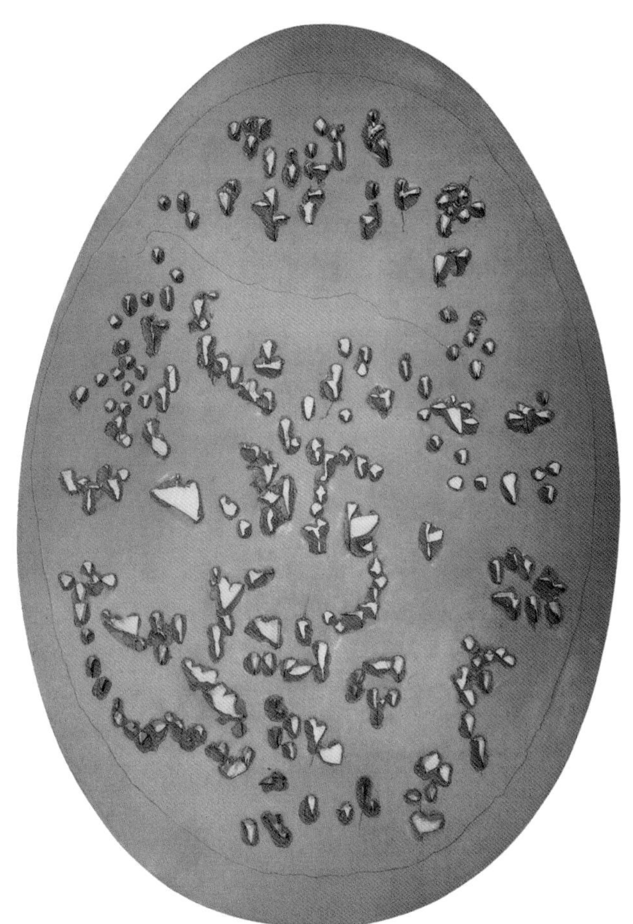

3 • Lucio Fontana, *Concetto spaziale/La Fine di Dio*, 1963
Oil on canvas, 178 x 123 ($70\frac{1}{8}$ x $48\frac{3}{8}$)

▲ 1921, 1965

▲ 1960a, 1967c • 1953

Manzoni's *Achromes* seem only to conjure a genuine admiration for Klein (though the definitive censure of color could already be interpreted as a poke at Klein's grandiloquent aesthetics, largely based on the spectacular effects of chromatic saturation). Soon, however, Manzoni's vast array of white works would point in the ▲ direction of Klein's ultimate nemesis, that is, Marcel Duchamp, and thence return to Fontana in order to sharpen his negative lesson. This is because unlike the first *Achromes*, whose textile material highlighted their belonging to the pictorial tradition, the next batch, still bathed in kaolin, leaned toward the status of the object. These collages of rows of bread rolls stacked in grid fashion, or of pebbles, produce a strange combination, half macabre, half silly, of abstraction (monochrome) and readymade. The definitive step is when Manzoni decides to limit his intervention to a minimum (no collage, no whitewashing) and uses fragments of white materials untouched. This time the materials in question, such as Styrofoam or fiberglass, have nothing to do with the realm of painting but smack, on the contrary, of the toxicity of industrial production and the dangers of construction sites (an omnipresent reality in the immediate postwar Italy). Thus Manzoni's fiberglass *Clouds* [**4**], sometimes set in a red velvet box in order to strike the fetishist chord that connects disgust with erotic (once again, infantile) affect, spell out the nature of Fontana's attraction to kitsch: it is the culture of trash.

Furthermore, and directly mocking Klein's rhetoric of authorial grandeur and pseudomysticism, Manzoni leaned once again on Duchamp in order to single out the bodily impulses that had been at the core of Fontana's production. Against Klein's posturing and his appeal to immateriality, Manzoni conceived of the artist not as an ideal superhero but as an excremental machine: his edition of

4 • Piero Manzoni, *Achrome*, 1962
Fiberglass on board, 31 x 34 (12¼ x 13⅜)

5 • Piero Manzoni, *Socle du monde* (Base of the World), 1961
Iron, 82 x 100 x 100 (32¼ x 39⅜ x 39⅜)

Merda d'artista (Artist's Shit), identical cans, all numbered, supposedly containing the said matter, is the best-known example of this particular vein in his work, but the red balloons that he inflated (*Fiato d'artista* [Artist's Breath]) and left to their eventual fate of deflation are perhaps more telling. And it is not by chance that such an ironical attack against the very notion of the artistic, expressive, subject should have gone hand in hand with an investigation of the nature of the mark. In 1959–61, Manzoni mechanically generated a single line symmetrically bifurcating the length of rolls of paper (varying from less than a meter to more than seven kilometers). Each of these *Lines* was boxed individually in a tube, which means that, contrary to other gestures similarly steeped in a Duchampian ▲ tradition, such as Rauschenberg's *Tire Print* of 1953, the "lines" themselves are not visible: all you see is their tube, most often in cardboard but twice in chromed metal—a derision of Brancusi?—while the cylinder containing the longest *Line* is made of lead.

This deliberate frustration of our visual sense as a strategy of resistance against the spectacularization of culture, a strategy that makes of Manzoni one of the most important father figures of ● Conceptual art, climaxed in *Socle du monde* [**5**], a hollow parallelepiped of iron inscribed with its title (and the subtitle *Hommage à Galileo*) written upside down—a "base of the world" that rhymes with Fontana's regressive fantasies in signaling that, confronted with the entropic indifferentiation that is the future promised to us by late capitalism, there is no other solution than an utopian wish that everything be upturned.

FURTHER READING

Yve-Alain Bois, "Fontana's Base Materialism," *Art in America*, vol. 77, no. 4, April 1989

Germano Celant (ed.), *Piero Manzoni* (London: Serpentine Gallery, 1998)

Jaleh Mansoor, "Piero Manzoni: 'We Want to Organicize Disintegration'," *October*, no. 95, Winter 2001

Anthony White, "Lucio Fontana: Between Utopia and Kitsch," *Grey Room*, no. 5, Fall 2001

Sarah Whitfield, *Lucio Fontana* (London: Hayward Gallery, 1999)

▲ 1914, 1918, 1935, 1966a, 1993a

▲ 1953

● 1968b

1959b

At the San Francisco Art Association, Bruce Conner shows *CHILD*, a mutilated figure in a high chair made in protest against capital punishment: a practice of assemblage and environment is developed on the West Coast by Conner, Wallace Berman, Ed Kienholz, and others that is more scabrous than its equivalents in New York, Paris, or elsewhere.

In June 1957, officers from the vice squad of the Los Angeles Police Department entered the Ferus Gallery that the future curator and museum director Walter Hopps and the artist Edward Kienholz had opened just three months earlier. Following up on two anonymous complaints regarding the first (and last) exhibition of Wallace Berman's work, the squad officers were looking for pornographic material. Amazingly, they failed to notice the main offender, a lean assemblage entitled *Cross* [**1**], consisting solely of a battered wood cross planted on a wooden crate, from which hung, suspended by an iron chain at the end of its left arm, a small shadow-box framing the photographic close-up of an act of heterosexual intercourse inscribed with the Latin words "Factum Fidei" (fact of faith). In their blind zeal to find incriminating evidence, they leafed through the first issue of Berman's journal *Semina*, scattered among other printed matter on the floor of a telephone-booth-sized reliquary entitled *Temple*. They felt vindicated, at last, when zeroing in on the reproduction, within the pages of the journal, of a mediocre surrealizing and cartoonish drawing of a woman's rape by a phallus-headed monster. Confiscating the publication, they arrested the artist on the spot.

The event is a twofold historical marker: the policemen's myopia reveals how much visual literacy has evolved in half a century (after decades of coopting of avant-garde practices by the advertising industry, nothing could be more explicit now than the then illegible zoom-in on four thighs, two pelvises, a penis, and a vagina); the obsessive search and the arrest signal how much the legal definition of public decency has changed during the same period. The raid on Ferus was not isolated—the United States were still not over the McCarthy years, even though the right-wing senator had been censured by Congress in December 1954. Just a few weeks before Berman's show was closed, the City Lights Bookstore in San Francisco, mecca of the beat culture, was stormed by two plainclothes officers who arrested the shop's owner Lawrence Ferlinghetti for publishing—and (then illegally) selling—Allen Ginsberg's banned poetry book *Howl* celebrating (among many other things) gay sex and drug use. A lawsuit of immense consequence ensued: on October 3, 1957, Ferlinghetti was declared not

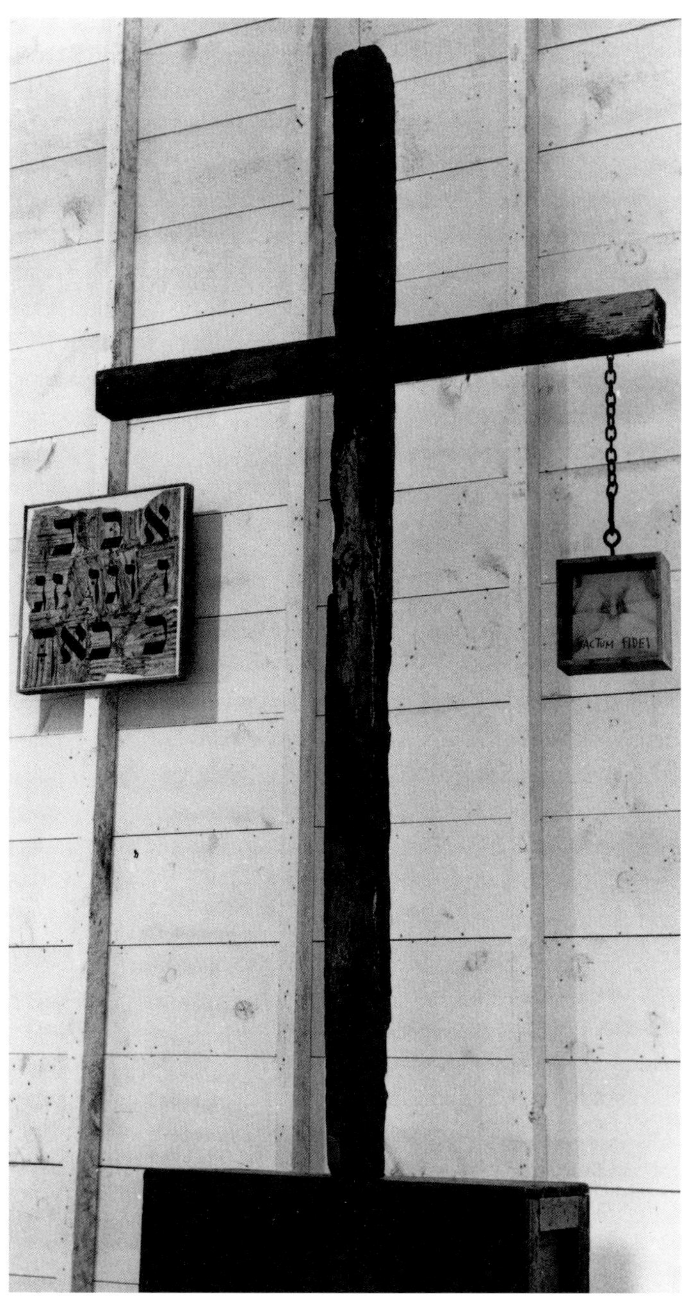

1 • Wallace Berman, *Cross*, 1956–7
Wood, metal, chain, and photograph, c. 274.3 x 152.4 (108 x 60)

guilty by a judge (surprisingly, a conservative one) who argued that the book, whatever its merit, deserved constitutional protection. Berman was not that lucky and he would have served time in prison if an actor friend had not come up with bail money. Fuming at the trial, he shouted "There is no justice, there is only revenge." Shattered, he moved to San Francisco and vowed never to show in a commercial art gallery again, instead devoting most of his energy to the editing of *Semina*, a beacon of counterculture until its publication ceased in 1964.

Berman's aesthetic critiques mass culture

Around that time, Berman moved back to Los Angeles (in the hippie community of Topanga Canyon), living in a shack where he remained a semi-recluse till his death in a car crash at the age of fifty, occasionally organizing home exhibitions of his works. Little known but cherished by his friends, for whom he was a model of integrity, his production was essentially limited to two categories: the rocks that he covered with Hebrew letters, and the so-called *Verifax* collages. The pebbles pursued a trend initiated in the drawings on torn and wood-stained parchment paper that he had shown in his ill-fated Ferus exhibition: mounted on canvas, these fragments imitated the display of archaeological finds, particularly those of the Dead Sea Scrolls—but with the major difference that Berman's groups of letters did not coalesce in any words. Although the *Verifax* collages—for which he used, as their nickname indicates, an ancestor of the photocopy machine—did not refer to such an antique past, their sepia tone and fading imagery conveyed a nostalgic sense of the ▲ vestigial. Responding to Andy Warhol's entropic strategy of repetition, to which Berman was exposed at Warhol's famous 1962 "Campbell's Soup" show in the Ferus Gallery, these works are a paean to the subjectivity of memory as a weapon against "mass culture." An invariable element is multiplied (most often in a grid formation) in each of the *Verifax* collages: a hand holds up a small AM-FM transistor radio, whose face is parallel to the picture plane (the smallest grid holds four of these units, the largest fifty-six). The variable elements are the images inserted where the radio speaker would be (generally, photos of an isolated item: a nude torso, the moon, Earth, a snake, a native American warrior, a jaguar, the US Capitol, a tree, a church, a rose, a pope, a gun, etc.), blips of information salvaged from the outside world, messages tossed at sea—the sum of which constitutes indecipherable rebuses but still asserts the possibility of escaping the Orwellian universe. Such a naive hope—the ground for much of the hippie counterculture of the sixties—would become the easy target of Warhol's cynical contempt.

Conner's assemblages oppose "society"

One of Berman's closest friends during his San Francisco stay, Bruce Conner, was just as adamant in his rejection of the rules of the establishment game, particularly those that govern an artist's career: as soon as a particular kind of work secured him some recognition, he would stop producing, only to reemerge a few years later with works belonging to a whole different genre or medium. The assemblages he began to create in 1957 were put on the map by the deliberately repulsive *CHILD*, exhibited in 1959 in San Francisco [**2**]. Based on the famous case of Caryl Chessman, a death row inmate condemned for sexual molestation and gassed in San Quentin after twelve years amidst an immensely vociferous international campaign to save his life, it consists of the mutilated figure of a child-sized man (at least, clad with adult male genitalia) modeled in brown wax, tied to a highchair by shreds of nylon stocking, its mouth agape, its limbs partially cut off, its flesh like bulbous magma.

Although *CHILD* might be Conner's best-known sculpture, it departs from his other assemblages. Like those, it harbors the nylon stockings that soon became a signature item. But unlike *CHILD*, whose simple message is patent (the death penalty is barbarous),

2 • Bruce Conner, *CHILD*, 1959
Wax figure with nylon, cloth, metal, and twine in high chair, 87.9 x 43.2 x 41.9 (34⅝ x 17 x 16½)

▲ 1964b

most of Conner's works from the late fifties and early sixties are not only remarkably polysemic—with their array of objects and photographs gathered from various sectors of life and affixed on various supports—but often hard to perceive, as the nylons that cover their discrete elements and help maintain them in place slowly gather dust and end up functioning as veils [**3**]. Like Berman's early pieces, Conner's assemblages abound in religious and erotic imagery (crosses, rosary beads, the face of Christ, nude women, etc.), but embedded within the obsolete bric-à-brac one finds in a junk store (laces, sequins, fake jewels, plastic flowers, toupées, camp cosmetic items of a forlorn drag queen, etc.). The sense of "pastness" they distill is not based on the illusion that one could retrieve and make sense of memory, but on the accumulation of pathetic dross.

The first identity Conner claimed for himself as an artist came in 1958 when, with the poet Michael McClure, he founded the Rat Bastard Protective Association (RBP), and was that of the quintessential ragpicker (the Association's name was derived from that of a garbage-collection company in San Francisco: The Scavengers' Protective Association). The professional scavengers "went around the city with big trucks, gathering the trash by emptying trash cans onto big flat burlap sheets," declared Conner to Peter Boswell. "They would gather it up on their backs and dump it into the truck. Or, when the truck was full, they would hang them on the sides like big lumpy testicles. So they were using all the remnants, refuse, and outcast of our society. The people themselves who were doing this were considered the lowest people employed by society." Likewise, RBP was for "people who were making things with the detritus of society, who themselves were ostracized or alienated from full involvement with the society." It is not only his glorification of the outcast that most differentiated Conner's stance from that of a Robert Rauschenberg and even more from that of then emerging ▲ Pop artists, but also the fact that the content of the bins he rummaged was decidedly retro (the initials of RBP, Boswell notes, were intended to evoke "PRB," those of the Pre-Raphaelite Brotherhood). The stuff he gathered for his assemblages was pre-Holocaust, pre-Hiroshima, pre-Cold War—not the contemporary waste of the postwar industrial boom, not the surplus of empty images produced by the mass media. For several years, and like his friends of the beat generation, Conner identified with the nine- • teenth-century Bohemia that Walter Benjamin, in his essay on the French poet Baudelaire (1821–67), "Charles Baudelaire: A Lyric Poet in the Era of High Capitalism," closely linked to the figure of ■ the ragpicker. But like Theodor Adorno in a scathing letter criticizing Benjamin's romanticization of Baudelaire's *chiffonnier* (ragpicker), he might have come to the conclusion that merely recycling antiquated trash did not offer a sustainable means to escape the all-pervasive condition of the commodity. The commercial success of his assemblages disturbed him and when it reached the point at which he was dubbed the "nylon master," he sought ways to change course. He moved to Mexico in 1961 and gradually abandoned his production of objects (for one thing, there was no

3 • Bruce Conner, *THE TEMPTATION OF ST. BARNEY GOOGLE*, 1959
Assemblage, wood, stocking, rubbish, 140 x 60 x 22 (55⅛ x 23⅔ x 8⅔)

▲ 1953, 1960c, 1964b • 1935 ■ Introduction 2

trash around, the poor local population being far more adept than he was in making use of refuse). His last assemblage proper dates from 1964, after his return to the United States.

In parallel to his assemblages, Conner had begun to make films out of found footage. His first, entitled *A Movie* and dating from 1958, sets the tone of all his subsequent ones—a tone that differs sharply from the nostalgia of his objects in that it consists of an aggressive deconstruction of the medium itself. *A Movie* conventionally starts with its title and its maker's name (which would be suppressed in later works), but this is followed by the countdown leader (this normally unseen bit of white noise would appear in most of Conner's films and become the exclusive material of *Leader*, in 1964). The "first" image (a woman undressing) is swiftly introduced during the countdown which resumes to end up in a blackout screen followed by the familiar title card: "The end." And that is only the very beginning! The rapid succession of miniclips that make up most of the twelve-minute movie amounts to a montage overdose. Very few sequences stand out (the most memorable is perhaps that of a submarine commander looking through a periscope, cut to a pinup girl in basic suit, back to the commander who lowers the periscope, cut to the launching of a torpedo and to an atomic mushroom—all this in a manner of seconds). Speed is numbing—this is part of *A Movie*'s lesson. Conner's overload of images was intended as a critique of the mass media's increasingly efficient means of psychological manipulation in the fast-developing TV age. To his surprise, this underground, homemade collage, together with his second film in the same mold, the 1961 homage to Ray Charles entitled *Cosmic Ray*, would soon acquire a cult status—which led him, true to form, to abandon the cinematic medium. But in this case his defection was momentary: when he returned to film several years later (he made twenty-five movies from 1964 to 2002), speed was no longer of the essence; in its stead were repetition and slow motion. In *Report* (1963–7), several televised sequences of Kennedy's assassination are rehearsed many times with different soundtracks; in *Marilyn Times Five* (1968–73) it is a song by Monroe that is repeated while the found footage of a starlet posing half-nude as the actress is spliced into irregular beats, the sequence never beginning at the same point in each of the five "takes," and revealing only little by little her various "sex acts" (simulating a blow job on a Coke bottle, or rubbing her abdomen with an apple).

Flickering his identity had been one of Conner's favored strategies right from the start. The invitation to his first solo show, in 1959, announced, with black borders: "Works by the Late Bruce Conner." In 1964, he planned a Bruce Conner national convention in a Holiday Inn, to which all his namesakes would be invited ("All the guests would register at the hotel as Bruce Conner. Major Speeches and elections of officers. The minutes of the meeting: 'Bruce Conner elected President. Bruce Conner elected Vice-President. Bruce Conner, Treasurer. Bruce Conner disagreed with Bruce Conner on this point.'"). Though the idea was never realized, it generated various paraphernalia such as the columns of fake ads he placed in *Joglars*, a small literary journal published by Harvard students, using the name, occupation and address of several of his "twins." Another by-product of his conceptual convention was a set of two buttons (the red one reads "I AM BRUCE CONNER" and the green, "I AM NOT BRUCE CONNER") which he reused a few years later when campaigning for the public office of Supervisor in the city of San Francisco. Having to specify his occupation in an official questionnaire for his candidacy, Conner answered "My business or occupation is Nothing," which landed him the votes of 5,228 citizens on November 7, 1967.

Few of his voters knew that two months earlier he was the subject of a fully illustrated article in *Artforum*, signed Thomas Garver and entitled "Bruce Conner Makes a Sandwich." Based on the famous series published in *Artnews* from the late forties on (the most memorable being "Pollock Paints a Picture" by Robert Goodnough in March 1951), even imitating its layout with the artist's signature included in the title, the article delivered exactly what it promised, the excruciatingly detailed account of a "making": food too needs to be prepared, and it is just as consumable as art, but it declares their common fate more honestly, ending in excrement while art winds up in gilded frames or a gallery's white cube.

Parody was Conner's preferred way of absenting himself, self-immolation his most devastatingly antisublimatory weapon. But his *Artforum* spoof was not only targeting his own (past) practice; it was the whole ethos of junk art—by then just as academicized ▲ a movement as Abstract Expressionism had become ten years earlier—that Conner was lambasting. In view of the last image reproduced in the article (the completed "artwork"—that is, the sandwich—full page), one could easily conclude that his prime • objects of ridicule were Daniel Spoerri's *tableaux pièges* (one of them was included in the 1961–2 Museum of Modern Art show "The Art of Assemblage," to which Conner contributed and whose last venue was San Francisco). But it is more likely that his pique was aimed closer to home, at the only California assemblagist to attain early on—and maintain—international fame: Ed Kienholz (1927–94).

Kienholz tries too hard

At first sight, Kienholz's sculptural production—from isolated objects to large-scale installations such as *The Portable War Memorial* of 1968, which he called *tableaux*, presumably after the old aristocratic pastime of the *tableau vivant*—seems to partake of the same aesthetic as Conner's and Berman's work. But a gap separates Kienholz's conception of art from theirs (even though he considered Berman his mentor ever since having hosted the latter's show at Ferus). Contrary to the decidedly ambiguous and often obscure assemblages created by his peers, each of Kienholz's works combines elements whose semantic information goes in one single direction, the sum total force-feeding the beholder with a heavy, unmistakable, unidimensional message. While *CHILD* represents an exception in Conner's oeuvre—it is his least equivocal assemblage—*The Psycho-Vendetta Case* of 1960, based on the same Caryl Chessman story, is typical of Kienholz's maniacal redundancy **[4]**.

▲ 1947b, 1949 • 1960a

4 • Ed Kienholz, *The Psycho-Vendetta Case*, 1960
Painted wood, canvas, tin cans, and handcuffs, 58.4 x 55.9 x 40.6 (23 x 22 x 16)

5 • Ed Kienholz, *Portable War Memorial*, 1968
Environmental construction with operating Coke machine, 289 x 243.8 x 975.4 (114 x 96 x 384)

In order to make sure you'll get the point, Kienholz alludes in the title to the famously butchered trial and execution of Sacco and Vanzetti in the twenties (framed testimony, planted evidence, biased prosecution), and to the immense international scandal accompanying this spectacular breakdown of the American justice system. On the outside of the wooden suitcase, to quote Walter Hopps, "the 'California Seal of Approval' features Mickey Mouse astride the California bear symbol. Inside, the viewer is presented with the backside of a shackled Chessman. Looking through the periscope glass at the top of the torso, the viewer's mouth is aligned with the figure's anus. The message visible inside reads, 'If you believe in an eye for an eye and a tooth for a tooth, stick your tongue out. Limit three times.'" The description is somewhat inaccurate (unless the sum of a bottom, a pair of testicles and thighs can be termed a torso) and, moreover, it is incomplete—it does not mention, for example, that the figure is modeled out of striped cloth (read: prisoner); that it is stained dirty pink (read: blood); nor that two grotesque arms jot out from the back of the box to hold the periscope (read: strangling); nor that the opened lid is adorned by the US and California flags (read: criminal government). But it scarcely matters: Kienholz never understood that piling up multiple symbols of the same idea, no matter how noble this idea, was giving in to the worst tactics of the mass media that Berman and Conner had struggled so hard to keep at bay. No matter what topic he picked—abortion, the dismal treatment of prisoners or of patients in psychiatric wards, rape, prostitution, car crash, drunkenness, war, boredom, etc.—Kienholz never had faith in his public (nor in his advocates, for whom he always provided long captions painstakingly deciphering the elements of his yet all-too-clear allegories). Like any advertisement, his works are one-liners pounded into the beholder's head with a skull-crashing baseball bat. No abdication to the law of commodity could be more total. With Kienholz's spectacular tableaux, replete with the sensational violence to which Hollywood and TV news have made us addicted, junk art, once conceived as a strategy of resistance, had completed a full circle [**5**].

FURTHER READING

Theodor Adorno and Walter Benjamin, *The Complete Correspondence, 1928–1940*, ed. Henri Lonitz, trans. Nicholas Walker (Cambridge, Mass.: Harvard University Press, 1999)

Walter Benjamin, "The Paris of the Second Empire in Baudelaire," first section on the Bohème, *Charles Baudelaire: A Lyric Poet in the Era of High Capitalism,* trans. Harry Zohn (London: New Left Books, 1973)

Peter Boswell et al., *2000 BC: The Bruce Conner Story Part II* (Minneapolis: Walker Art Center, 2000)

Walter Hopps (ed.), *Kienholz: A Retrospective* (New York: Whitney Museum of American Art, 1996)

Christopher Knight, "Instant Artifacts" and "Bohemia and Counterculture," *Wallace Berman* (Amsterdam: Institute of Contemporary Art, 1992)

Lisa Phillips (ed.), *Beat Culture and the New America 1950–1965* (New York: Whitney Museum of American Art, 1996)

1959c

The Museum of Modern Art in New York mounts "New Images of Man": existentialist aesthetics extend into a Cold War politics of figuration in the work of Alberto Giacometti, Jean Dubuffet, Francis Bacon, Willem de Kooning, and others.

In the twentieth and twenty-first centuries, historians have become increasingly preoccupied with the phenomenon of repetition, not as Hegel described it by saying that everything in world history happens twice, but rather as Marx expanded this when he corrected what Hegel "forgot to add: the first time as tragedy, the second as farce" (*The Eighteenth Brumaire of Louis Napoleon* [1852]). Such a historical two-step would seem inapplicable to the entirely continuous battle between representation and abstraction that dogged the history of early modernism and came to represent the attempts of the academy to hold on to classical forms of figuration as the utopian drives of advanced art tried to break through to an unknown vision.

The rise of fascism, however, caused a remapping of this terrain, especially in France, as the Popular Front government united liberal and Communist forces in an anti-Nazi campaign that used "humanism" as its watchword and set up an appeal to artists to become politically engaged: which would mean abandoning their elitist, avant-garde forms and making their art accessible to the working classes. Figurative representation as applied to art had thus been wrenched from the protected privilege of the academy to become a matter of world-historical import. Further, not only did this version of realism come to be connected with a historical moment that stretched from the late thirties into the war years, and was thus seen as a product of the politics of the Resistance and the Liberation, but also its uniqueness was established by the existentialist terms of one of its major theorists, the philosopher Jean-Paul Sartre.

Man in a situation

As their perfect demonstration, the aesthetics of existentialism focused on the transformation that Alberto Giacometti's (1901–66) sculpture had undergone during these years. Up to 1935 it was ▲ grounded in a Surrealist-derived imagery of dream, couched in forms that moved toward abstraction; during the war it was reborn in terms that were resolutely figurative, based on working from the model and engaged with what Sartre was always calling for: man in a situation.

But if the tragedy of the war had produced this realism of the human subject thrown into the full uncertainty of "existence"—an existence unballasted by the comforting absolutes of an "essence" (a set of universal laws, truths, or conditions) that had preceded it and could thus prescribe to it—the years that followed were to turn existentialist aesthetics (about which more below) into farce. As the postwar forties became the Cold War fifties, replete with Marshall Plan and Pax Americana, existentialism became a product of the culture industry and found itself wearing toreador pants and singing along with Juliette Greco in jazz joints. "Man in a situation" became a slogan along with "Existence precedes essence," and both, in relation to aesthetics, could be used to promote almost any kind of realism, as was the case with the exhibition "New Images of Man," which the Museum of Modern Art mounted in 1959.

In this context, all breaks with the code of abstraction were seen to resemble one another. Thus Willem de Kooning's "Woman" series, departing as it did from the wholly nonfigurative cast of his Abstract ▲ Expressionist production, or Jackson Pollock's black-and-white pictures of 1951, similarly allowing recognizable imagery to reenter the abstract skeins of his earlier dripped pictures, were held up as comparable to Giacometti's renunciation of Surrealism. It did not matter that de Kooning's women were less in a "situation" of existential dread than of spritely American advertising, inspired as they were by the voracious smiles of the beer-advertising Miss Rheingolds and movie starlets to be found in glossy magazines. Nor did it matter that Pollock's figurative moment lasted just one year before he returned to a desperate attempt to reconnect with abstraction in the few years remaining before his death. With its attempt to use an ● earlier generation of "realists"—Giacometti, Jean Dubuffet—as a vehicle to justify an intermediary generation—de Kooning, Pollock, Francis Bacon (1909–92)—"New Images of Man" was involved in promoting a third generation of neo-Expressionists—Karel Appel, César (born 1921), Richard Diebenkorn (1922–93), Leon Golub ■ (1922–2004), Eduardo Paolozzi—as a "new" movement at just the moment when Pop art was to enter the picture and throw all these ideas about the link between the figurative and the expressive onto the junkheap of history.

To understand the distance that separated the aesthetics of 1948, the year when Sartre wrote "The Search for the Absolute," his catalogue essay for Giacometti's first exhibition since abandoning Surrealism, and 1959, when "New Images of Man" appeared, it is necessary to know a little more about existentialism and how it meshed with Giacometti's postwar project. Ironically, Sartre's

▲ 1930b, 1931

▲ 1947b, 1949 ● 1946 ■ 1956, 1957a, 1960a, 1987

philosophical writing opened in the very domain of Giacometti's Surrealist practice, which is to say with an investigation of the realm of mental images: dreams, fantasies, memories, hallucinations. But with this book, *L'Imaginaire* (1940; translated as *The Psychology of the Imagination*), Sartre's interest was definitely not to celebrate the imaginary world as the product of an unconscious welling up within the subject, as Surrealism had done. Indeed, Sartre's entire philosophical position was that there is no "unconscious," since there are no contents of consciousness lying inside it of which it could be either aware or, as in the case of the unconscious, unaware.

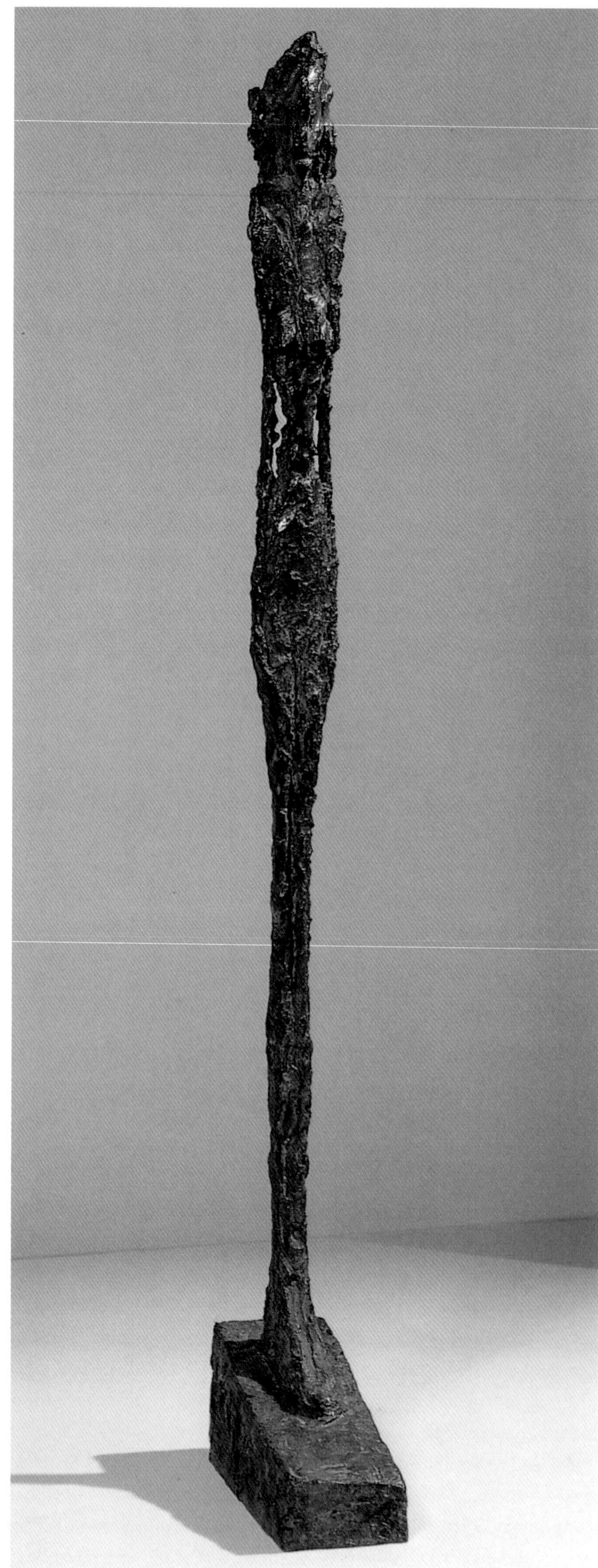

1 • Alberto Giacometti, *Femme debout (Leoni)* (Standing Woman [Leoni]), 1947
Bronze, 135 x 14.5 x 35.5 (53⅛ x 5¾ x 14)

Sartre begins with the perception, adopted from Edmund Husserl's ▲ phenomenology, that consciousness is always consciousness of something other than itself. It is what Husserl had called "intentional consciousness," which means that it comes into being only in the act of perceiving, grasping, directing itself toward an object. It is thus always a movement beyond itself, a projection that empties itself out, leaving no "contents" behind. Consciousness is "nonreflexive": I do not hear myself speaking any more than I see myself seeing. Empty and transparent, consciousness traverses itself without ever finding anything in its path on the way to its object. And that object is marked by its own transcendence, its outsideness to consciousness itself.

The result of this exteriorization is that man becomes one with his projects, with the world that both motivates him and is the site for the exercise of his freedom. This act of synthesis, this unity with the world, stands opposed in Sartre's thinking to the philosophy of immanence, in which consciousness is always attempting to capture itself in its own mirror: seeing itself seeing, touching itself touching. This attempt at analysis, Sartre argues, merely doubles the subject. As Denis Hollier explains in his study of Sartre, "From that impossibility for the subject to catch up with himself comes his necessity to double up every time he approaches himself.... So that a subject who touches himself, divides himself by touching himself, becomes contiguous to himself, finds (and loses) himself alongside himself, being his own neighbor, having taken his own place."

Reflexive consciousness, analytic thinking, the attempt to grasp myself in the act of being myself, is thus always serial, repetitive, productive only of a sum of contiguous parts. Instead, the synthesis of which Sartre speaks strips man of his very properties: making him only what he does, only his deeds, only what unites him to his situation in the world.

Sartre's two models of this totalizing synthesis were the unity of the work of art and, as a result of both the Resistance and the heady days of the Liberation, what he would call the "group in fusion," a real, even if ephemeral collectivity. And in Giacometti's postwar sculpture he was able to celebrate both at once. On the one hand Giacometti had fashioned his sculptures as figures always seen at a distance, as being twenty or thirty or however many feet away from their viewer no matter how close he or she came to them [**1**]. "Giacometti," Sartre wrote, "has restored an imaginary and indivisible space to statues. He was the first to take it into his head to sculpt man as he appears, that is to say, from a distance." And because this is man as he is perceived, it is fitting that these sculptures should all

▲ 1965

be vertical, since Sartre equates perception with walking, traversing space, doing things, just as he links imagining with the body's repose. If one dreams lying down—as in the sculptor's earlier, Surrealist, sleeping women—one perceives standing up.

And man so sculpted, so imbricated with the perceptual field in which he is caught is never anything but a synthesis in which the body is one with its projects. Like the cave paintings in which the silhouettes "outlined an airy future; to understand these motions, it was necessary to start from their goals—this berry to be picked, that thorn to be removed—and not from their causes," Giacometti's sculpture, Sartre writes, "has suppressed multiplicity. It is the plaster or the bronze which can be divided: but this woman who moves within the indivisibility of an idea or of a sentiment, has no parts, she appears totally and at once."

Further, to this effect of perceptual unity there is added, in Giacometti's work, the affect of the "group in fusion" **[2]**. For the triumph of this sculpture is that each figure reveals man "as he appears in an intersubjective world ... [and] at a proper human distance; each shows us," Sartre insists, "that man is not there first and to be seen afterwards, but that he is the being whose essence is to exist for others." There were other writers, however, for whom the isolation and immobility of Giacometti's figures, some of them even presented in cagelike structures, defined "intersubjectivity" itself as a condition of unbreachable separation, loneliness, and dread. Accordingly, Francis Ponge offered his own interpretation in 1951: "Man—and man alone—reduced to a thread—in the ruinous condition, the misery of the world—who looks for himself—starting from nothing. Thin, naked, emaciated, all skin and bone. Coming and going with no reason in the crowd."

Indeed, this idea of scarring and caging would be the hallmark of an existentialist position less optimistic than Sartre's, less focused on commitment's projects geared toward a future and more on dread, on what Friedrich Nietzsche had called the "wounds of existence" or on what Martin Heidegger would speak of as anxiety, namely a fear of "the nothing" or the nonbeing that lies behind existence. In the early thirties, when Heidegger's "What is Metaphysics?" appeared in France, the French literary avant-garde found the idea of nonbeing liberating, exciting. Raymond Queneau, a former Surrealist, had a character in his first novel, *The Bark Tree* (1933), speak in "Heideggerian" even though he was a concierge. Musing on a piece of butter, he says: "The lump of butter isn't everything it is, it hasn't always been and won't always be, ekcetera, ekcetera [*sic*]. So that we can say that this lump of butter is up to its eyes in an infinity of nonbeing.... It's as simple as Hello. What is, is what isn't; but it's what is that isn't. The point is that nonbeing isn't on one side and being on the other. There's nonbeing, and that's all, seeing that being isn't."

Giacometti's figures might have projected nonbeing for Sartre as a function of the mottled, pitted surfaces that could emit the flash of an expression or the lift of a breast as seen from a distance but that would never yield any more-solidly wrought details of surface or shape when seen up close, thus making nonbeing function as the motivation of perception. But this same work could signal nonbeing for Ponge as "the ruinous condition" of "starting from nothing." For Ponge, the cage pinned man as "at once executioner and victim," or the flayed surface produced him as "at once the hunter and the game."

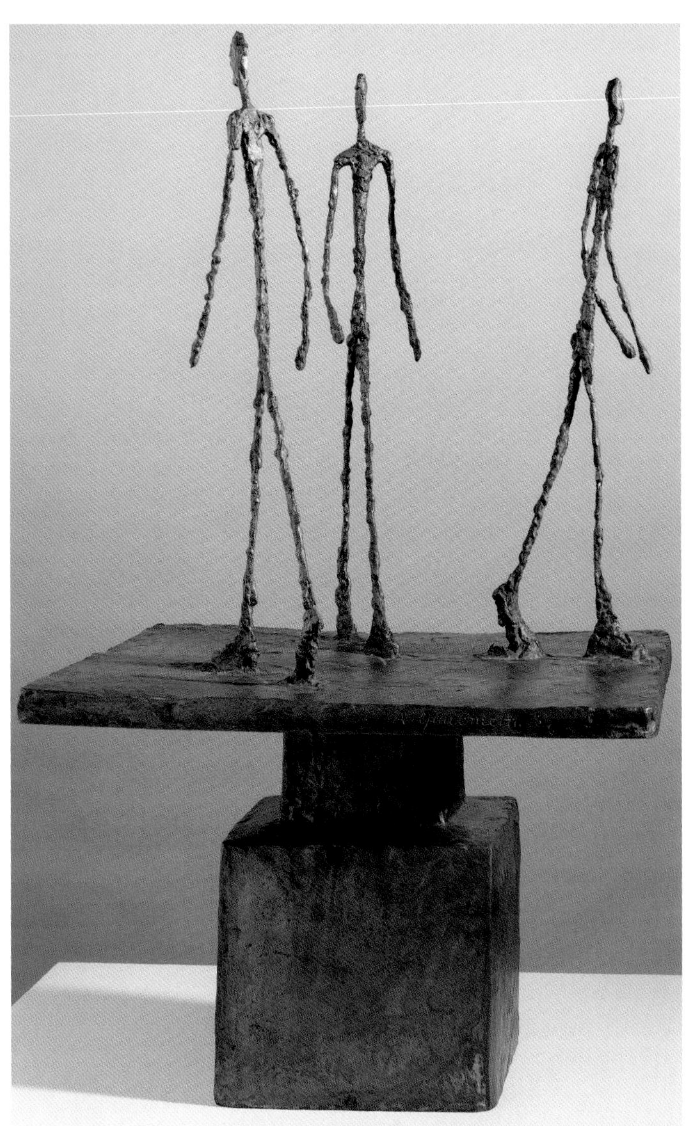

2 • Alberto Giacometti, *Trois hommes qui marchent* (Three Walking Men), 1948
Bronze, 72 x 43 x 41.5 (28⅜ x 16⅞ x 16⅜)

If they were united with their physical surrounds, the scarred and ravaged surfaces of Dubuffet's postwar portraits and women's bodies had less to do with the unity of an instance of perception than with a sense of the human subject as nothing but an oilspot or a stain fused with the corrugated surface of an urban ruin. Calling one of these ▲ bodies *La Métafisyx*, Dubuffet's version of the Heideggerian question ("What is Metaphysics?") was to deflate the metaphysical, producing it instead as something "grotesquely trivial" and, far from conceding to man a formal essence or a stable being, embodying the aim of attacking form. "My intention," he wrote, "was that the drawing should deny the figure any particular shape; that on the contrary, it should prevent the figure from assuming this or that particular form." The gauging, stabbing lines with which Dubuffet executes these figures, in their push toward the defiling character of graffiti,

▲ 1946

Art and the Cold War

When Clement Greenberg broadcast "Modernist Painting" for "The Voice of America" in 1960, avant-garde art joined cause with American Cold War politics, which was then focused on the rebuilding of a devastated postwar Europe, itself part of the cause of anticommunism in the United States. By the late sixties, the US government deemed the propaganda value of art important enough to support the Congress for Cultural Freedom as a way to promote the idea of individual liberty and autonomy as a defense against the menace of totalitarianism. Members of the Congress included Greenberg, Jackson Pollock, Robert Motherwell, and Alexander Calder. But it was not simply the government that promoted modernism in Europe. The Museum of Modern Art was also active through its program of traveling exhibitions, which sent American art abroad. *Life* magazine joined with a spread titled "Arms for Europe." That these "arms" would be cultural as well as military incited the Communist Party's reaction against American abstraction as "decadent" and "reactionary." With Germany the battlefield for a capitalist–communist confrontation, the desire to flaunt the rewards of West German postwar reconstruction in the face of East Germany led to the establishment of an international exhibition, Documenta, in Kassel, an industrial city in the northeast corner of the FDR, just a few miles away from an installation of international ballistic missiles pointed at the Soviet Union. The first Documenta was held in 1945 and every four or five years thereafter. The American entries in the early years stressed the importance of Pollock and the other Abstract Expressionists as well as the commercial splendor of Pop art.

thus invoke both the attack on the whole body's "good form" so common to graffiti's obsession with genitalia (and thus with the body reduced to merely a "part-object") and the semiautomatic character of the graffiti mark, the seeming lack of intellection behind it.

Emerging slightly later than Dubuffet, but contemporaneously with the postwar Giacometti, Francis Bacon's early work is marked by both the cagelike isolation of his figures and the blur of their features that projects them at a perpetually unbridgeable distance. But they are far more expressive than Giacometti's impassive figures. Characteristically, their mouths are wide open in a scream but their eyes are veiled and the sides of their faces corroded. Even without the isolation booths in which Bacon stranded his various figures based on Velázquez's portrait of Pope Innocent X **[3]**, the figures always seem overwhelmed by the space in which they find themselves.

Although they were conceived at the same time as Dubuffet's *corps de dame* pictures, de Kooning's "women" seem to inhabit a different moral universe, and this despite the fact that Harold ▲ Rosenberg had espoused existentialist ideas to justify the group of artists he identified as "The American Action Painters," of which de Kooning was a major, perhaps *the* major, figure. But Rosenberg's thesis, following Sartre, involved the absolute uniqueness of the event in which the painter discovers himself in the process of taking the risk of a leap into the unknown. A wholly synthetic moment, this act of projection and perception was thus to be as unrepeatable as it was ephemeral. The act itself was what was important; the end results—reified in the finished product—were of little interest.

Though such rhetoric might be applicable, in part, to the improvisatory look of the abstract painting de Kooning pursued during the forties, it seemed increasingly out of place in relation to the "women." Indeed, de Kooning stressed that he fell back on this image precisely because it was pregiven, repeatable, a fixed convention. "It eliminated composition, arrangement, relationships, light," he explained. "So I thought I might as well stick to the idea that it's got two eyes, a nose and mouth and neck." His women, singly or in groups, give off the sense of a seriality at the heart of their conception, perhaps because de Kooning used a furtive collage technique that meant that forms he had taken from media sources—toothy smiles, mascara-laden eyes—are doubled over the surfaces of the bodies, as so many repeated mouths, breasts, vulvas **[4]**. It is the ▲ proto-Pop, serial quality of these images, then, their lack of individuality, that makes their relation to existential aesthetics problematic.

FURTHER READING:

Jean-Paul Sartre, "Fingers and Non-Fingers," translated in Werner Haftmann (ed.), *Wols* (New York: Harry N. Abrams, 1965)

Denis Hollier, *The Politics of Prose* (Minneapolis: University of Minnesota Press, 1986)

Peter Selz, *New Images of Man* (New York: Museum of Modern Art, 1959)

Eva Cockcroft, "Abstract Expressionism, Weapon of the Cold War," *Artforum*, vol. 12, June 1974

3 • Francis Bacon, *Study after Velázquez's Portrait of Pope Innocent X*, 1953
Oil on canvas, 152.7 x 118.1 (60⅛ x 46½)

▲ 1960a

▲ 1960c, 1964b

4 • Willem de Kooning, *Woman*, 1953
Oil and charcoal on paper mounted on canvas, 65.1 x 49.8 (25⅝ x 19⅝)

1959d

Richard Avedon's *Observations* and Robert Frank's *The Americans* establish the dialectical parameters of New York School photography.

In the twentieth century, photography's emergence as a major force in cultural representation usually marked a shift in power relations between the avant-garde and everyday industrial mass culture. This ▲ is well known in relation to Soviet and Weimar avant-garde photography around 1928, but less known and understood in relation to photography in New York after World War II, a cultural context • considered mostly in terms of the "Triumph of American Painting."

Two families of photography

Edward Steichen's (1879–1973) blockbuster exhibition of postwar photographic ideology, "The Family of Man," at the Museum of Modern Art in 1955, included a large number of both American social documentary photographers, such as Dorothea Lange (1895–1965), Russell Lee (1903–86), Ben Shahn (1898–1969), and Margaret Bourke White (1904–71), and photographers who would subsequently emerge as the key figures of New York School photography, such as Lisette Model (1901–83), Helen Levitt (born 1913), Sid Grossman (1913–55), Roy DeCarava (born 1919), Richard Avedon (1923–2004), Diane Arbus (1923–71), Robert Frank (born 1924), and Louis Faurer (1916–2001). The exhibition signaled in many ways the intensity with which the relations between photographic avant-gardes and the mass public, and between two generations of American photographers, had to be reorganized.

The first group of New York School photographers emerged from the Film and Photo League (founded in 1928), and its offshoot from 1936, the Photo League, initially hoping to forge a union between progressive sociopolitical forces and photographic practice. Most postwar photography in New York served capitalist consumer culture, almost entirely subject to fashion and advertising. Throughout the thirties, books and magazines had disseminated American social documentary via the Works Progress Administration (WPA) ■ and Farm Security Administration (FSA), for example Margaret Bourke White and writer Erskine Caldwell's (born 1903) *You Have Seen Their Faces* (1937); Berenice Abbott's (1898–1991) *Changing New York* (1939); Dorothea Lange and economist Paul Schuster Taylor's *An American Exodus* (1939) and Walker Evans (1903–75) and James Agee's (1909–55) *Let Us Now Praise Famous Men* (1941). In contrast, postwar photographic books and illustrated magazines such as *Vogue, Harper's Bazaar,* and *Life* magazine, in the paradox of their simultaneous climax and irreversible decline, struggled to survive the growing dominance of the cinema and television.

Alexey Brodovitch (1898–1971) became a key figure in the formation of New York School photography after his appointment as art director at *Harper's Bazaar* in 1934. A White Russian officer who had left the Soviet Union for Paris when the Bolsheviks came to power, Brodovitch came to the United States in 1930, bringing nostalgia for the lost culture of the Czarist empire, and a desire to preserve the *haut goût* of its last cultural flowerings, such as Sergei Diaghilev's ▲ Ballets Russes. He used this almost pathological longing for a revival of aristocratic elegance and style to mask the vulgarity of American consumer culture with the seductive foils of distinction, particularly the deception that fashion could perforate class boundaries: incurable social envy would release the new middle classes' purchasing power. Brodovitch's second resource was his snobbish embrace of the avant-gardes that he had encountered during the twenties in Paris, recruiting their radicality to service the emerging apparatus of mass-cultural domination. Thus, he wrote as early as 1930:

> *The publicity artist of today must be not only a fine craftsman with the faculty of finding new means of presentation ... he must be able to perceive and preconceive the tastes, aspirations and habits of the consumer-spectator and the mob. The modern publicity artist must be a pioneer and a leader, he must fight against routine and the bad taste of the mob.*

Brodovitch's first (and only) photographic book, *Ballet* [**1**], published in New York in 1945, with an accompanying essay by the dance critic Edwin Denby, appears to pay a grand and mournful homage to the beautiful remains of the Ballets Russes. His one-time appearance as a photographer, as Christopher Phillips has lucidly stated, "is equally exhilarating and at the same time haunting ... Indeed, what these fugitive shapes and unexpected transformations ultimately suggest is the phantasmagoria of memory itself."

Ballet is the first New York School book where photography's promise to serve as sociopolitical documentary in the twentieth century is perverted into a melancholic invocation of the vanishing elitist bourgeois culture of the nineteenth. Brodovitch knew that this homage was as futile as the images were fugitive: the price that

▲ 1929, 1930a, 1935 • 1947a, 1949b, 1960b ■ 1936 ▲ 1919

1 • Alexey Brodovitch, page from *Ballet*, 1945

photography had to pay to deliver the reminiscences of elitist culture was to succumb to the demands of an ever-intensifying culture of spectacle (evident in the book's cinematic layout as much as in its shift in focus, from the dancers' bodies to the effects of photographic technologies). Thereafter, Brodovitch refrained from taking photographs, but he became the teacher and art director for a generation of photographers, masterminding the medium's transformation from social documentary into product propaganda.

From *USSR* to *Harper's Bazaar*

When in 1949 Brodovitch conceived what would soon be called "the archetypal graphic design magazine of the twentieth century," he reconfigured many avant-garde strategies (from Picasso to Pollock) to acquire a sophisticated industrial arsenal of advertising. His characteristic layouts for *Portfolio Magazine* and *Harper's Bazaar,* with their extreme variations of image size and cinematic shifts from close-up to long shot, were montaged on double-page spreads that expanded even the panoramic vision of *Ballet.* Ironically, Brodovitch (just like his fellow Russian émigré, Alexander Liberman, art director of *Vogue*) derived his most successful graphic and photographic strategies from work that Russian artists including El Lissitzky and ▲ Aleksandr Rodchenko had produced for Stalin's Ministry of Propaganda in publications such as *USSR in Construction.* Thus Brodovitch accomplished for American magazine design what Edward Steichen had achieved slightly earlier for the new genre of exhibition design. In his famous exhibition "The Road to Victory in 1942" (in collab- • oration with Herbert Bayer), Steichen had resuscitated Soviet photographic (exhibition) design from the late twenties, bringing the new genre to a final American climax in "The Family of Man" (in collaboration with the architect Paul Rudolph).

Brodovitch's legacy is best embodied by his students Richard Avedon and Irving Penn (born 1917), who were enrolled at the legendary Design Laboratory he taught from 1933 at the Philadelphia Museum School of Industrial Arts and from 1941 at New York's New School for Social Research (the home of the Film and Photo League from 1928 until its abolition under McCarthyism in the fifties). Other Design Laboratory students included Arbus, Eve Arnold (born 1913), Ted Croner (born 1922), Saul Leiter (born 1923), Model, Hans Namuth, Ben Rose (born 1916), and Garry Winogrand (1928–84). Penn and Avedon received their first commissions from Brodovitch at *Harper's Bazaar,* Penn later becoming associated with Brodovitch's archrival, Alexander Liberman at *Vogue,* who defined the parameters of New York School photography:

> *There was a thirst for new visual sensations to feed those growing modern monsters, magazines.... Penn and the key editors at* Vogue *were conscious of the very special and historic time in which they were living.... The early forties was a period of violent change, with war and the Holocaust as staggering tragedies. During the war, there was a sense of a new beginning in cultural New York, a tabula rasa of the past and even the dreadful present.... At the same time, there was a curious convergence between Penn's new vision and the great American ready to wear revolution. With war in Europe and the Pacific and USA Fashion on its own,* Vogue *proclaimed a new era.*

More than any of their peers in the New York School (especially those emerging from the Film and Photo League) who remained involved with the sociopolitical legacies of the American documentary tradition, Avedon and Penn embodied the photographic ▲ agenda of the postwar generation. Walker Evans, although revered and supportive of the younger photographers, became the target of generational animus. For example, in an astonishingly erroneous description and historical combination of two utterly unrelated photographers, Richard Avedon stated:

> *I didn't like Walker Evans, that is until now. I thought his work was boring, precious, empty, without emotion, a system. I used to do sort of jokes about Walker Evans and his camera and Ansel Adams and his. I didn't see the sort of social part of it, spending the day in front of a picket fence or a redwood tree waiting for the light to be right.*

Avedon's closest friend, and in many ways his photographic opponent, Diane Arbus, seems to have echoed that attitude on the occasion of the Walker Evans retrospective at MoMA in 1971:

> *First I was totally whammied by it. Like there is a photographer, it was so endless and pristine. Then by the third time I saw it, I realized how it really bores me. Can't bear most of what he photographs.*

From weapon to style

Richard Avedon's first book, *Observations* (1959), a collection of portraits seemingly selected according to the proto-Warholian principle of their subjects' media fame, with "comments" by writer Truman Capote (1924–84), was designed by Brodovitch using his idiomatic, stylized neoclassical Bodoni typeface, the oversized slipcase decorated in the red, white, and blue of a newly affirmed American identity. *Observations* gives a better sense of the new tasks of photography than most publications of that time, firstly by

▲ 1921, 1926, 1935 ● 1923

▲ 1936

announcing, just as all concerns for the social collective had disappeared from the political agenda, that photography would have to completely detach itself from mass culture and the sociopolitical subjects of the thirties and forties. Secondly, rather than representing the mass subject's everyday life within industrial capitalism, American photography would now depict the spectacularized star subject of the culture industries. Functioning as a conduit between the mirage of the subject and the commodity object, photography would compel the mass subject to acquire the substitutions that compensate for the loss of subjective experience. One of Avedon's most celebrated devices is to stage his figures in front of white surfaces, and to print the images with the frame and numbers of the contact sheet, which—in spite of its modernist semblance of self-referentiality—foregrounds the branded identity of the photographer and the production of photography as the actual *subjects* of all photographs. More importantly, it physically dislocates the subject from the actual spaces of social relations and production (urban or rural, work or leisure, public or private) in order to invest it with the scopic magnitude necessary for the idolatry of the star subject.

Irving Penn published his first photographic book, *Moments Preserved*, in 1960. He designed it in Brodovitch style and, just like Avedon, made the portrait his primary "artistic" genre outside of his fashion work, following similar principles of spectacularization. However, Penn's resuscitation of still-life photography for advertising was his lasting hallmark, coaxing even fruits and flowers into the service of the commodity aesthetic. Taking his cues from the magic ▲ realism of thirties photography (a fusion of Neue Sachlichkeit and • Surrealism), Penn mobilized the austerity and sobriety of latent neoclassicism to ennoble something as banal as a cosmetics pot with the radiance of a spiritual object.

Another strand of New York School photography draws more emphatically on those earlier practices where photography was intertwined with social and political realities. Two important figures attempted to maintain this engagement after World War II: Helen Levitt and Lisette Model, who had emigrated from Paris in 1938 to escape Nazi prosecution. Both women had been active in cultural politics, Levitt joining the Film and Photo League, which—following the Soviet models of the late twenties—attempted to conceive of film and photography as publicly accessible, politicized cultural practices. Nevertheless, Levitt's photographs at first seemed suspended between the anecdotal surrealism of Henri Cartier-Bresson (1908–2004) and the documentary realism of Walker Evans. While Cartier-Bresson's theory of the "decisive moment" implied that chance encounters and surreal constellations were compelling evidence of the subject's access to unique forms of independence and self-affirmation, Walker Evans's documentary realism took its confidence from a deep-seated belief that the bonds of social communication and political responsibility would not be abandoned. However, once it had become clear that neither position could be sustained, Levitt's photographs started to expose the disappearance of photography's documentary abilities. She retreated into the theatrical world of children [2], seeing in them the last dimension of authentic subjectivity, acting in spaces of exemption and enacting their utopian versions of a future community in the face of a manifest disappearance of social relations.

Roy DeCarava's work is indebted to Levitt, and similarly emerges from the dual influences of Cartier-Bresson and Walker Evans. It shifts social documentary from universal principles of political and social change to the representation of a particular social group, notably in his extraordinary collaboration with Langston Hughes, *The Sweet Flypaper of Life* (1955), which focuses on the life of an African-American family in Harlem, presented as an autobiographical report from the perspective of its oldest member, the grandmother. The first-person narrative emphasizes not only the singular specificity of the speaker's culture, but also the differences of race and class that the subject represents, both as imposed by the regulations and regimes of its racist oppressors and as voluntarily embraced in a gesture of counteridentification. The introduction of the various family members and the sequencing of the images, alternating between close-ups, medium shots and long shots, simulate the cinematic flow of a documentary film, while the oppositional photographic traditions of narrative and document are equally pronounced.

It sometimes seems that DeCarava's in-depth account of the family narrative with its emphasis on the "normalcy" of social life in Harlem set out to distinguish itself from the anonymous, random documentation of the black population in James Agee and Walker Evans's accounts of the rural South. DeCarava's anchoring of the photographs in a first-person narrative account and his focusing the documentary images on one family invest the subjects and their community with spatial and social groundedness and a sense of agency, redefining the abstract universalizing of earlier documentary photographers. *The Sweet Flypaper of Life* can, therefore, be read either backward—in terms of its differences from the political universality of thirties and forties social documentary photography—or forward—as open opposition to the anomic universality that came to govern books such as *Observations* four years later. The sense of social groundedness, in a space exempt from universal anomy, is conveyed not only through DeCarava's careful depictions of his

2 • Helen Levitt, *New York*, c. 1940
Silver-gelatin print

▲ 1925b, 1929, 1930a, 1935 ● 1924, 1930b

subjects, but also in the photographs' very tonality. Hardly anyone else in twentieth-century photography succeeded in investing the extreme tonality of black-and-white photography with the metaphoric intensity of a refuge of identity, in which the color of racial segregation is turned into the ground of social solidarity.

From caricatures to counterportraits

Lisette Model published her first images in 1932 in *Regards,* the magazine of the French Communist Party (comparable to Willi ▲ Münzenberg's *AIZ* in Weimar Germany). She framed and captioned her images of bourgeois idlers at the Promenade des Anglais with a venomous irony to match the most aggressive caricatures of • Honoré Daumier in the nineteenth century or George Grosz in the twentieth. It would be plausible to situate photography within the tradition of satirical illustration and caricature, reassigning social critique and revelatory travesty to the photograph, especially since progressive artists and writers in Europe during the twenties and thirties had explored communicative aspects of popular culture that had been increasingly obscured by modernism. Before them, caricaturists such as Daumier, Paul Gavarni, and Jean-Jacques Grandville had already addressed the problems of the distribution form as well as the need to engage with a different mass public.

Model did not seek her sitters from glamorous media representation, but in the street. The grotesque authenticity of her images of Manhattan's lumpenproletariat contrasts sharply with Avedon's and Penn's spectacularized subjectivity, and her counterportraits of social deviancy, transvestites, beggars, or inebriated eccentrics [**3**] identify with the marginalized and the social outcasts not in order to romanticize their abject lot and elevate it into a photographic picturesque, but by insisting on the subject's innate incommensurability in the face of its increasing assimilation to spectacle and consumption.

Thus the counterportrait as a photographic genre had already emerged by the thirties, and governed the work of the second generation of photographers, such as Robert Frank and Garry Winogrand but particularly Diane Arbus, whose teacher Model became in 1956. However, the subject of the counterportrait is no longer an emerging proletarian class or the bourgeois subject in the process of ■ disintegration (as in August Sander's [1876–1964] *Antlitz der Zeit* of 1929). Rather, the photograph as caricature now produces images of the grotesque disfigurations of subjectivity under the social policies of neglect and abandonment resulting from increasing class inequality in postwar American history.

Model made some of her most remarkable photographs immediately after her arrival in New York in 1938. Resuscitating Atget's topos of the spatial play of reflections in shop windows, she selected fragments of the body and sutured them into the windows' reflecting surfaces. Like a found montage, these images mapped the bodily fragment and the fetish in a highly compressed photographic representation, seemingly the subject's only accessible space.

Usher Fellig (1899–1968) came to the US aged ten from Zloczew (now in Poland) and took the name Weegee. In many ways Model's

3 • Lisette Model, *Sammy's Bar, New York*, 1940
Silver-gelatin print

counterpart and rival, he apparently introduced himself to Brodovitch at *Harper's Bazaar,* stating that the magazine had published enough of Model's work and urging him to fire her and publish him. The émigré's blatant competitiveness took its cues from his understanding of the behavioral structures of everyday life in his adopted homeland. *Naked City* (1945), Weegee's first book, programmatically identified the new social relations and spaces of his photographs just as Walter Benjamin had diagnosed the sites of Atget's photographs in 1934: as the scenes of crimes. *Naked City* enforced the insight that from now on the photograph could justify its existence only if its iconography, temporality, and locations operated in the spectacular manner of film (ironically, a 1948 film called *Naked City* was inspired by Weegee's book). From Lewis Hine to the ▲ Farm Security Administration, photography had functioned, in part, as social documentary, if not as activist protest and intervention. Now, it recorded crimes and accidents as the primary tropes of the anomic conditions of social life. Weegee's photographs marked the point when documentarian compassion and political responsibility had degenerated to cold voyeurism and a sadistic desire to stare at others' suffering, whether victims of accidents or the defeated enemies of the social order (criminals). Weegee also became the first in a line of early sixties artists—such as Jim Dine, Claes Oldenburg, • and Andy Warhol—who recognized that the forces of random order and breakdown would have to converge in an aesthetic where social relations figure merely as accident or outright catastrophe.

▲ 1920, 1930a • 1920 ■ 1935 ▲ 1936 • 1960c, 1961, 1964b

4 • Weegee, *Coney Island Beach*, New York, 1940
Silver print

5 • Diane Arbus, *Identical Twins, Rozel, New Jersey*, 1967
Silver-gelatin print

One of the most striking images in *Naked City* is Weegee's double-page spread of Coney Island bathers [**4**]: collectively remembered images of the politically activated masses of the thirties appear as the first acephalic mass of leisure culture. (These images clearly inspired Steichen's double-page endpapers in his 1955 *The Family of Man*, where Pat English's *Life* magazine photographs of an even more disciplined mass of English spectators emasculate the once radical concepts of the mass public sphere even more convincingly.)

After his move to New York from Paris in 1947, the Swiss Robert Frank contributed a distinctly different project to postwar New York photography. Initially on a similar trajectory to that of his colleagues (with magazine work for Brodovitch's *Harper's Bazaar*, fashion photography for *McCall's*, and early interest from Steichen, who included six of his images in "The Family of Man"), Frank came to situate his work mainly in an explicit dialogue with Walker Evans (who along with Brodovitch supported Frank's successful application for a Guggenheim fellowship in 1954). His contemplation of the methods and subjects of the American documentary legacy during road trips across the United States led to his book *The Americans*, even in its title paying tribute to Walker Evans's famous *American Photographs*. (Frank's book was first published as *Les Américains* in Paris in 1958, and subsequently in New York in 1959).

The American road trip became a European compulsion, just as the Grand Tour to Italy had been in the eighteenth century. In Frank's case, it led to an account of social and political tendencies in his new country, of roads not taken, and of roads ahead. In many ways comparable to Theodor Adorno's *Minima Moralia* in 1946 (which also looked at the culture of the United States as a panorama of the future), the book's eighty-three images not only articulate a vision defined by Frank's recent departure from the Europe of the Holocaust and totalitarianism's destruction of subjectivity, but they also probe the future of social relations and subjectivity in the most powerful nation state to emerge in the postwar period. The American edition had an introduction by Jack Kerouac, the beat poet of *On the Road*, and its images, such as the barber shop and the interiors, often pay tribute to Walker Evans, simultaneously recognizing that social relations and their political organization—which documentary photography might, erroneously, have considered as accessible, if not transparent—had been lost for ever, shrouded in the sign systems of automobile locomotion and media consumption. Nevertheless, at least four images are still devoted to the recognition of labor, and while Frank's photographs of workers at the conveyor belt are as blurry as Brodovitch's frames of the Ballets Russes fifteen years before, in Frank's case the haze indicates doubt over photography's access to social relations rather than hallucinatory evocations of the past.

Frank's acute observations of the rigid racial segregation that he came to know in fifties America are probably more important. While contemplative, *The Americans* is still marked by the documentary impulse to make photography a tool of political enlightenment and social change and Frank's leitmotivs signal his diagnostic clarity: the repetition and central placement of images of the American flag [**6**], the car, and the technologies of media culture (movie theaters, television sets and juke boxes) identify the forces shaping the growing dominance of American consumer culture and anomic society. At every turn of the road, Frank seems to gaze upon the New World not just with the wide-eyed amazement of the European newcomer, but also with shock that this is the model of things to come.

The career of Diane Arbus embodies all the contradictions of the New York School, and, as its most significant photographer, she concludes its history. After brief training with Berenice Abbott and Alexey Brodovitch, she worked as a fashion photographer with her husband Allan Arbus during the early fifties. In 1956, after abandoning fashion, she took classes with Lisette Model, finding "the courage to be herself." As Allan Arbus noted: "That was Lisette. Three sessions and Diane was a photographer." When it comes to the dialectics between the mass subject and the star subject, one could argue that Arbus is the counterpart to both Avedon and Warhol (her junior by five years), the first "*photographe maudit*" of the twentieth century. Typically, Arbus stated her position early on, saying that she would "much rather be a fan of freaks than of movie stars, because movie stars get bored with their fans, and freaks really love for someone to pay them honest attention." Arbus maps Model's photographic realism onto the archival typology of subjectivity that ▲ August Sander had famously developed in his systematic portrayal

6 • Robert Frank, *Fourth of July—Jay, New York*, no. 43 from *The Americans*, 1955–6

of Weimar society in his *Antlitz der Zeit* , a work to which she was introduced in the late fifties. By constructing a photographic universe of outsiders [**5**], she simultaneously inverts Sander's positivist sociological optimism and Avedon's techniques of isolating and spectacularizing the subject. Her universe is ordered not by class or profession, nor by the sitters' seduction as substitutional image, but by the degree to which their abject social isolation gives evidence that universal assimilation to the principles of the consumerist mass subject had not yet taken hold. Her solidarity with her sitters originates not in compassion, but in her more complex understanding of the fragility of the processes of subject formation, and the tragic consequences of their continuing destruction.

FURTHER READING

Max Kozloff, *New York: Capital of Photography* (New York: Jewish Museum; and New Haven and London: Yale University Press, 2002)

Jane Livingston, *The New York School: Photographs 1936–1963* (New York: Stewart, Tabori, and Chang, 1992)

Janet Malcolm, *Diana and Nikon: Essays on Photography* (New York: Aperture, 1997)

Elisabeth Sussman, *Diane Arbus: Revelations* (San Francisco: San Francisco Museum of Modern Art; and New York: Metropolitan Museum of Art, 2003)

▲ 1935

1960–1969

464 1962b In Vienna, a group of artists including Günter Brus, Otto Mühl, and Hermann Nitsch come together to form Viennese Actionism. BB

470 1962c Spurred by the publication of *The Great Experiment: Russian Art 1863–1922* by Camilla Gray, Western interest revives in the Constructivist principles of Vladimir Tatlin and Aleksandr Rodchenko, which are elaborated in different ways by younger artists such as Dan Flavin, Carl Andre, Sol LeWitt, and others. HF
box • *Artforum* RK

475 1963 After publishing two manifestos with the painter Eugen Schönebeck, Georg Baselitz exhibits *Die Grosse Nacht im Eimer* (Great Night Down the Drain) in Berlin. BB

480 1964a On July 20, the twentieth anniversary of the failed Stauffenberg coup against Hitler, Joseph Beuys publishes his fictitious autobiography and generates an outbreak of public violence at the "Festival of New Art" in Aachen, West Germany. BB

486 1964b *Thirteen Most Wanted Men* by Andy Warhol is installed, momentarily, on the facade of the State Pavilion at the World's Fair in New York. HF

492 1965 Donald Judd publishes "Specific Objects": Minimalism receives its theorization at the hands of its major practitioners, Judd and Robert Morris. RK
box • Maurice Merleau-Ponty RK

496 1966a Marcel Duchamp completes his installation *Etant Donnés* in the Philadelphia Museum of Art: his mounting influence on younger artists climaxes with the posthumous revelation of this new work. RK

500 1966b The exhibition "Eccentric Abstraction" opens in New York: the work of Louise Bourgeois, Eva Hesse, Yayoi Kusama, and others points to an expressive alternative to the sculptural language of Minimalism. HF

505 1967a Publishing "A Tour of the Monuments of Passaic, New Jersey," Robert Smithson marks "entropy" as a generative concept of artistic practice in the late sixties. YAB

509 1967b The Italian critic Germano Celant mounts the first Arte Povera exhibition. BB

515 1967c For their first manifestation, the four artists of the French group BMPT paint in public, each artist repeating exactly from canvas to canvas a simple configuration of his choice: their form of Conceptualist painting is the latest in a line of attacks against "official" abstraction in postwar France. YAB

521 1968a Two major museums committed to the most advanced European and American art of the sixties—the Stedelijk Van Abbemuseum in Eindhoven and the Städtisches Museum Abteiberg in Mönchengladbach—exhibit the work of Bernd and Hilla Becher, placing them at the forefront of an interest in Conceptual art and photography. BB

527 1968b Conceptual art manifests itself in publications by Sol LeWitt, Dan Graham, and Lawrence Weiner, while Seth Siegelaub organizes its first exhibitions. BB
box • Artists' journals RK
box • Deskilling BB

534 1969 The exhibition "When Attitudes Become Form" in Bern and London surveys Postminimalist developments, while "Anti-Illusion: Procedures/Materials" in New York focuses on Process art, the three principal aspects of which are elaborated by Richard Serra, Robert Morris, and Eva Hesse. HF

1960a

Critic Pierre Restany organizes a group of diverse artists in Paris to form Nouveau Réalisme, redefining the paradigms of collage, the readymade, and the monochrome.

Recognizing the public-relations value to be gained from organizing artists into a group operating under the banner of a single name, the French critic Pierre Restany (1930–2003) convinced a group of artists gathered in Yves Klein's Paris apartment on October 27, 1960, to form an avant-garde movement. Such a project naturally warranted a manifesto. This was dutifully designed by Klein in an edition of approximately 150 copies (white crayon on International Klein Blue or pink or gold cardboard) and signed by Restany and the eight artists present for the occasion (Arman [born 1928], François Dufrêne [1930–82], Raymond Hains [born 1926], Yves Klein, Martial Raysse [born 1936], Daniel Spoerri [born 1930], Jean Tinguely, and Jacques de la Villeglé [born 1926]). The manifesto consisted of a single sentence, the one anodyne statement about which all the artists could agree: "The New Realists have become conscious of their collective identity; New Realism = new perceptions of the real."

Twenty minutes after the signing, a fist-fight broke out between Klein and Hains, leading most of the members to consider the movement no longer extant, even though from now on they would frequently exhibit together (and they would be joined a little later by César, Christo [born 1935], Gérard Deschamps [born 1937], Mimmo Rotella [born 1918], and Niki de Saint Phalle [1930–2002]). It was not until 1970, however, that the movement's death would be officially celebrated—with a banquet and the unveiling of Tinguely's sculpture *La Vittoria*, a giant phallic structure spouting fireworks in front of Milan Cathedral.

Neo-avant-garde and spectacle

If all this seems uncannily like a replay of typical avant-garde rituals, that is because this, in fact, is *one aspect* through which the group declared its relationship to the historical avant-garde. Yet if it also shows signs of posturing and ostentatious adherence to the forms of spectacle culture, that is because contemporary spectacle is actually the *other* major historical context within which the group was constituted. And it is this very ambivalence that marks Nouveau Réalisme, along with the Independent Group in London, Cobra, ▲ and the Situationist International, as one of the major instances of a neo-avant-garde formation in Europe in the postwar period.

The Situationist Guy Debord might have referred to the prewar avant-garde for his own formulation of a postwar aspiration "to constitute a new movement which most of all should reestablish a fusion between the cultural creation of the avant-garde and the revolutionary critique of society." But, as is typical of all these groups, the Nouveaux Réalistes were confronting a situation in which, for the first time in the twentieth century, the avant-garde's project had manifestly become problematic. Instead, as critic Peter Bürger has argued, the avant-garde itself had become a highly institutionalized set of themes, practices, and spaces. But perhaps Nouveau Réalisme is the movement that recognized one particular condition of the neo-avant-garde most programmatically: its precarious but unchangeable situation at the intersection between a spurious posture of critical negativity and the affirmative agenda of the culture industry.

In generating its forms, Nouveau Réalisme seems to have taken the ineluctable condition of the neo-avant-garde more literally than the other groups that were developing parallel to it, mentioned above. In an almost systematic fashion, its participants rediscovered, recycled, and redistributed among themselves the modernist paradigms of the 1916–36 period, anticipating the manner in which advertising ▲ agencies would later pilfer avant-garde culture: the readymade ● (Arman), the monochrome (Klein), constructed kinetic sculpture ■ (Tinguely), and the collage (Dufrêne, Hains, Rotella, Villeglé). Yet in almost all instances, these paradigms now appeared as though they had been tuned to articulate the fundamentally different experience of objects and public spaces under a newly formed society of spectacle, control, and consumption. Not surprisingly, the most avid critics of that society at the time, the Lettrists and later the Situationists, would vehemently denounce Nouveau Réalisme as an art of affirmative collusion, a culture of right-wing politics and corrupt complicity.

However, articulating the profound ambiguities of cultural production by inhabiting its contradictions is different from mere complicitous affirmation. What made their practices the most authentic articulation of postwar visual production in France is first of all the fact that these artists made clear the inescapable way that all of postwar culture was caught up in a dialectic of historical repression and memory on the one hand, and an aggressive mode of enforced consumption and submission to the conditions of spectacle, on the other.

▲ 1956, 1957a

▲ 1914, 1918 ● 1913, 1915, 1921, 1928 ■ 1912

It is not surprising then that some of the most important contributions by the Nouveaux Réalistes shifted the status and sites of the work of art from the relative intimacy of the pictorial and sculptural object onto the level of public space. They repositioned the work from the frame of the picture, or the space of sculpture, to architecture, which is to say to institutional and commercial frameworks and to the spaces of the street that had always been presumed to be public.

Beginning with Klein's first installation of *Le Vide* (The Void)—in which the artist presented a completely empty gallery—in 1957 (to be followed by a more famous one in 1958) and culminating with Arman's corresponding *Le Plein* (The Full) in 1960—in which the window of Iris Clert's gallery was filled with a huge accumulation of garbage—the architectural dimension and interaction with public space would become central to the development of a Nouveau Réaliste aesthetic. This would be equally evident in Tinguely's large-scale, self-destructing installation *Homage to New York* [**1**], called by its author a "simulacrum of catastrophe," or in César's shift into Nouveau Réalisme in 1960, when he abandoned his successful career ▲ in welded sculpture, in the tradition of Picasso and González, to exhibit *Three Tons*: three cars that had been compacted by a hydraulic press into sculptural rectangular masses; or, in a shift that was equally emphatic, Spoerri was to declare the totality of a "found" grocery store in Copenhagen as an exhibition in 1961 (almost year ▲ before Claes Oldenburg's *The Store*). Entering public space with equal drama in 1962, Christo and Jeanne-Claude (born 1935) would make *Wall of Barrels, Iron Curtain* [**2**], a blockade of 240 oil barrels in the rue Visconti in Paris, corresponding to the recently constructed Berlin Wall and initiating their lifelong project of expanding sculpture to the scale and the temporariness of spectacle culture and reducing its simultaneous material presence to a mere media image.

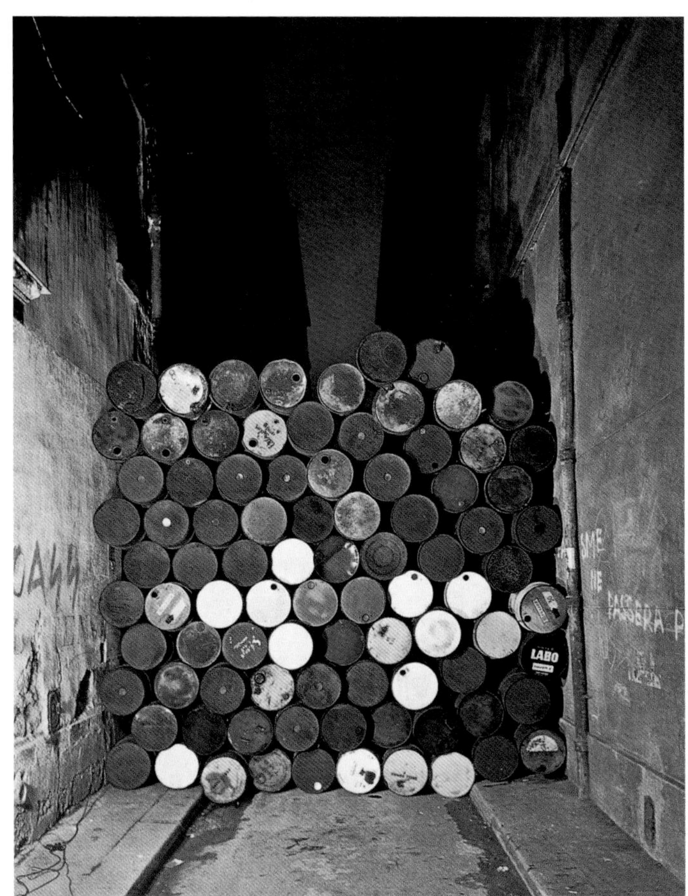

2 • Christo and Jeanne-Claude, *Wall of Barrels, Iron Curtain*, 1961–2
240 oil barrels, 430 x 380 x 170 (168 x 156 x 66)

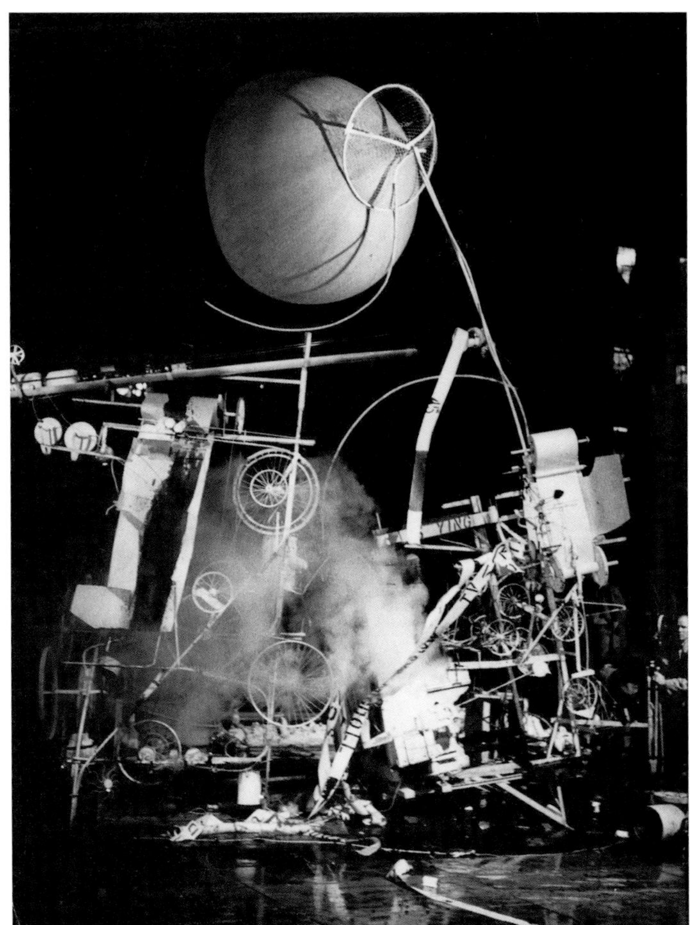

1 • Jean Tinguely, *Homage to New York*, 1960
Self-destructing installation

The same desire to situate the work within public space and position it within the discursive apparatus of consumer culture is evident in the transformation of collage by the *décollage* artists. From ● an object of intimate reading and viewing (for example, Kurt Schwitters), collage was reconceived as a large-scale fragment detached from advertising billboards. In an act of piracy, posters were ripped by the artists from public walls, not only in order to collect aleatory linguistic and graphic configurations but equally to make permanent the acts of vandalism in which anonymous collaborators (named by Villeglé's *Le Lacéré anonyme*) had protested against the domination of public space by advertising's product propaganda. In the first ■ Paris Biennial, inaugurated by André Malraux in 1959, the French *décollage* artists—Hains, Villeglé, and Dufrêne [**3**]—presented their work for the first time in a public institution, culminating in Hains's first "*palissade*," which consisted of the entirety of a large construction-site fence covered with an open field of anonymous acts of *décollage* intervention in a sequence of ravaging gestures.

▲ 1945 ▲ 1961 ● 1926 ■ 1935

Social spaces and frames

Repositioning their practices explicitly in these different social spaces and frames, the Nouveaux Réalistes created works that had an aesthetic of industrial production and collaboration. The sheer quantity of objects produced, their relative interchangeability and equivalence no longer foregrounded the originality of one author's vision or the unique features of an individually crafted work. Instead, we now not only encounter the intrinsically collaborative principle of *décollage* but also the actual collaborations between the artists, beginning with Villeglé and Hains's astonishingly early *décollage, Ach Alma Manétro* in 1949 **[4]** and moving to the subsequent collaborations between Klein and Tinguely, Tinguely and Niki de Saint Phalle, and many others.

More important, however, is the fact that the collaborative principle itself now became a central paradigm, as when Spoerri proposed a patent in 1961 to have his *tableaux pièges* **[5]** produced by other artists or by anyone else. This principle culminated in Klein's ultimate performances, a few months before his death in June 1962, in which the artist sold "Zones of Immaterial Pictorial Sensibility" to collectors who, in exchange for certain quantities of gold, received a certificate of ownership as the only legal proof of the work's existence. This protoconceptual critique of objecthood and authorship would gain considerable importance in the discussions of Minimalist and Conceptual art only a few years later.

Adopting advertising strategies for the dissemination of their ideas, the Nouveaux Réalistes often operated in an apparent parallel to their politically more radical and theoretically more consequential opponents of the Lettrist International and the later Situationist International (among the *décollagists*, Dufrêne had in fact been a member of the former). The Situationists' key strategies, *dérive* ▲ (drifting) and *détournement* (diversion or misapplication), certainly share aspects of the *décollagist* principle of *ravir* (ravishment), that is, the transformation of reality in an act of violent abduction and seduction. Other spectacular examples, such as Tinguely's decision in 1959 to drop 150,000 copies of a manifesto on Düsseldorf and its suburbs, could certainly be recognized as a form of counterpropaganda strangely reminiscent of the Allies' attempts to enlighten the population of National Socialist Germany by dropping leaflets from airplanes behind enemy lines. By contrast, the publication in 1960 of Klein's *Journal d'un seul jour*, feigning the features of a newspaper that celebrates the universally victorious presence of Yves le Monochrome (including the notoriously fake photographic "proof" of Klein's levitation in space), deployed, rather than "*détourned*" (or subverted from within), all the emerging media and advertising strategies of disinformation and massive manipulation of the public.

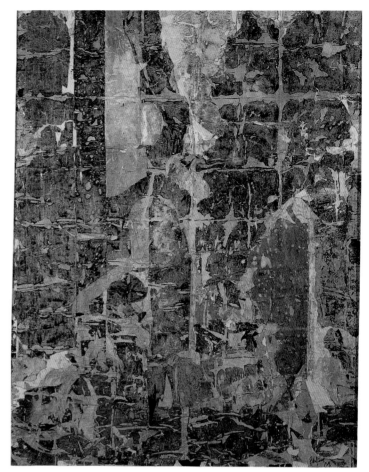

3 • François Dufrêne, *⅛ of the ceiling of the first biennial of Paris*, 1959
Lacerated posters on canvas, 146 x 114 (57½ x 4 ⅞)

With the 1954 publication of Klein's books *Yves: Peintures* and *Hagenault: Peintures*, modernist abstraction had appeared for the first time transformed into a conceptual metalanguage. Pretending to give an account of Klein's extensive production of monochrome

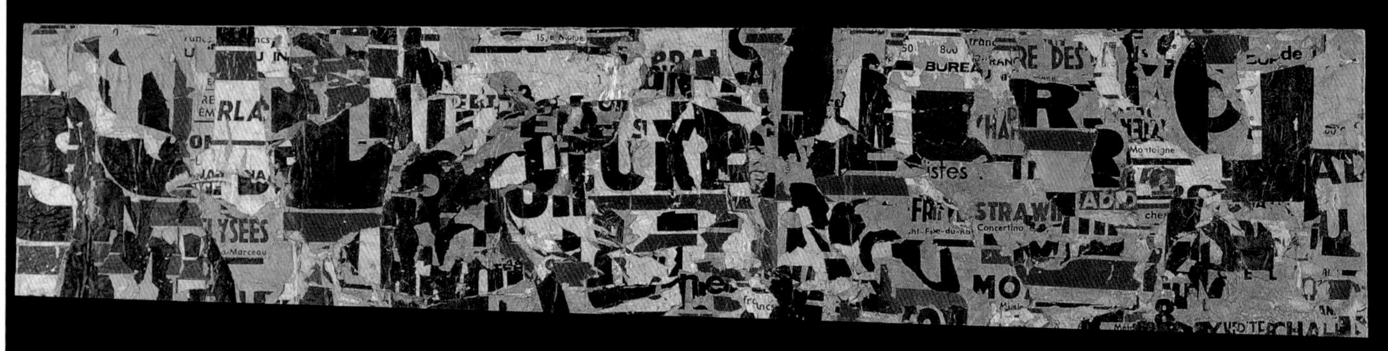

4 • Jacques de la Villeglé and Raymond Hains, *Ach Alma Manétro*, 1949
Lacerated posters on canvas, 58 x 256 (22⅞ x 100¾)

▲ 1957a

5 • Daniel Spoerri, *Kishka's Breakfast, no. 1*, 1960
Wood chair hung on wall with board across seat, coffee pot, tumbler, china, egg cups, eggshells, cigarette butts, spoons, tin cans, etc., 36.6 x 69.5 x 65.4 (14⅜ x 27⅜ x 25⅘)

paintings (their sizes and dates, their sites of production, sometimes even the location of their collections), the two books were entirely fictitious. Thus, at the very moment of Klein's (fraudulent) claim to have invented monochromy, he presents it already as absent, accessible only through fiction and technical reproduction. Insofar as these "paintings" constitute the first instance in which the central modernist paradigm of the monochrome (with all of its claims for presence and purity, optical and empiricist self-evidence) has been shifted to the registers of linguistic, discursive, and institutional conventions—presence displaced, that is, by a textual apparatus—they ▲ open onto what could be called an "aesthetic of the supplement."

Klein's notorious 1957 exhibition in Milan of eleven identical, differently priced monochrome blue paintings (subtle variations being discernible only in the surface texture of the works) could be seen as the first climax of this new aesthetic. The artist's decision to mount the seemingly identical paintings on stanchions made these panels appear as contingent hybrids between autonomy and function, in need of a prosthesis for public display. Suspended between pictorial convention as *tableaux* and their newly gained assignment as *objects/signs*, these paintings articulated a strange new dialectic of pure visuality and pure contingency. Thus, Klein initiated his painterly project as a paradox in which the spiritual transcendence of the aesthetic object is both energetically reclaimed and simultaneously displaced by an aesthetic of the spectacularized supplement. The latter aspect culminates in Klein's decision to subject the serialized paintings to a willful hierarchical order that articulated the opposition between "immaterial pictorial sensibility" and randomly • assigned price, anticipating Jean Baudrillard's semiotic formulation of the phenomenon of "sign exchange value". It is not just the exhibition's emphasis on painting as *production* that distances it from all previous forms of abstraction but, instead, the fact that it does not consider the order of the "exhibition" as a mere accumulation of individual works first made and then put on display but, rather, conceives of painting itself as always being on the order of an "exhi- ▲ bition" (a strategy to be deployed by Andy Warhol in 1962 in his first solo exhibition of "Campbell's Soup" paintings).

Expanding on these concepts in his first installation of *Le Vide* in 1957, Klein declared the empty gallery space itself a zone of heightened pictorial, protomystical sensibility. *Le Vide* was not, then, a reflection on the critical implications of reductivism; it refused to connect with the historical specificity of modernist conventions of vision, their discursive and institutional constructions of spectators and the order of architectural and museological systems of display. But, to the very degree that Klein recognized that a

The neo-avant-garde

Peter Bürger's *The Theory of the Avant-Garde* (1974) divides the last hundred and fifty years of art practice into three distinct phases: the period of modernism, with its claim to the autonomy of the aesthetic field (and its institutions); the intervention of the pre-World War II avant-garde whose practices turned precisely on the critique of that autonomy; and the moment of what he calls the neo-avant-garde, a third phase during which European and American postwar culture produced a rerun of those critiques, albeit leveling them to a set of empty gestures. All three phases are interrelated, but Bürger grants only the second the status of avant-garde radicality since it is within the project of this "historical avant-garde" (the period 1915–25, roughly from Cubism through Russian Constructivism and Dada to Surrealism) that the traditional assumptions about modernism's claim to an autonomous status are rejected in favor of what Bürger calls an attempt to reposition artistic practices within the life practice itself. Examples of this would be, on the one hand, Surrealism's use of chance operations as a way of abolishing the separation between high art and mass culture as well as that between art and everyday experience and, on the other, Russian Constructivism's and German Dada's deployment of collage and photomontage as ways of breaking down the separateness of the bourgeois public sphere in favor of the conception of a newly emerging proletarian public sphere. In opposition to those, Bürger claims that all postwar avant-garde practices are mere farces of repetition of the original interventions, but ones that work neither to dismantle the founding modernist claim to autonomy nor to achieve a displacement of art practice into everyday life; rather they simply provide an existing and expanding apparatus of the culture industry with marketable goods and objects. As typical examples Bürger points to postwar Pop, either in its American or Nouveau Réaliste guise, in which he sees the mere replay of collage and photomontage operations, but now addressing neither the questions raised by the original avant-garde with regard to the institutions of aesthetic autonomy nor of art's necessary interrelationship with new mass audiences and new forms of distribution.

▲ Introduction 4 • 1980 ▲ 1960c, 1964

modernist aesthetic of spiritual or empirico-critical autonomy had failed, he made the persistence of abstraction's spiritual afterlife evident and questioned the fate of these aspirations once spectacle culture had taken over the spaces of the avant-garde.

Klein's merit is precisely to have constructed this couplet—spirit/consumption—in open public view, making clear that the attempt to redeem spirituality with artistic means at the very moment of the rise of a universal control of consumer culture would inevitably cloak the spiritual in a sordid guise of travesty. A typical acknowledgment of this is a remark by him like: "We are not artists in revolt, we are on vacation." By making his work manifestly dependent on all of the previously hidden *dispositifs* (for instance, the spaces of leisure and consumption, and the devices of advertisement), he would become the first postwar European artist to initiate not only an aesthetic of total institutional and discursive contingency, but also one of a seemingly inescapable affirmative assimilation.

When Arman, Klein's closest ally, decided to abandon his stamp paintings in 1953 in favor of the direct presentation of the object ▲ itself, the ramifications of Duchamp's readymades had hardly been recognized in France. Yet Arman's formal strategies not only derive from the readymade, they transfigure two other central ▲ paradigms of modernism as well: the grid and chance. If the post-Cubist grid still governs Arman's *accumulations* and works such as the slightly later *poubelles* and *portraits-robots* (as in the *Premier Portrait-robot d'Yves Klein* [**6**]) follow the organization of matter either according to the physical laws of gravity or the principle of chance encounter, Arman's object aesthetic neither shares the utopian promise of the techno-scientific avant-gardes, nor does it • generate the unconscious resonance of the Surrealist object that had been liberated—if by no other force than the passage of time—from its everyday functions. With Arman, all objects seem to emerge from a limitless expansion and a blind repetition of production, appearing as so many specimens of an unclassifiable world of arbitrary variations, merely arranged according to the universal administration of sameness. If Duchamp's readymade had still suggested a radical equivalence between the constitution of selfhood through the subject's acts of speech and the formation of subjectivity in a relation to the objects of material production, Arman's objects firmly opposed such a parallel. Linguistic repetition, the principle according to which subjectivity is constituted in the production of speech, finds its objective correlative here in the repetition of the act of choosing an object of consumption.

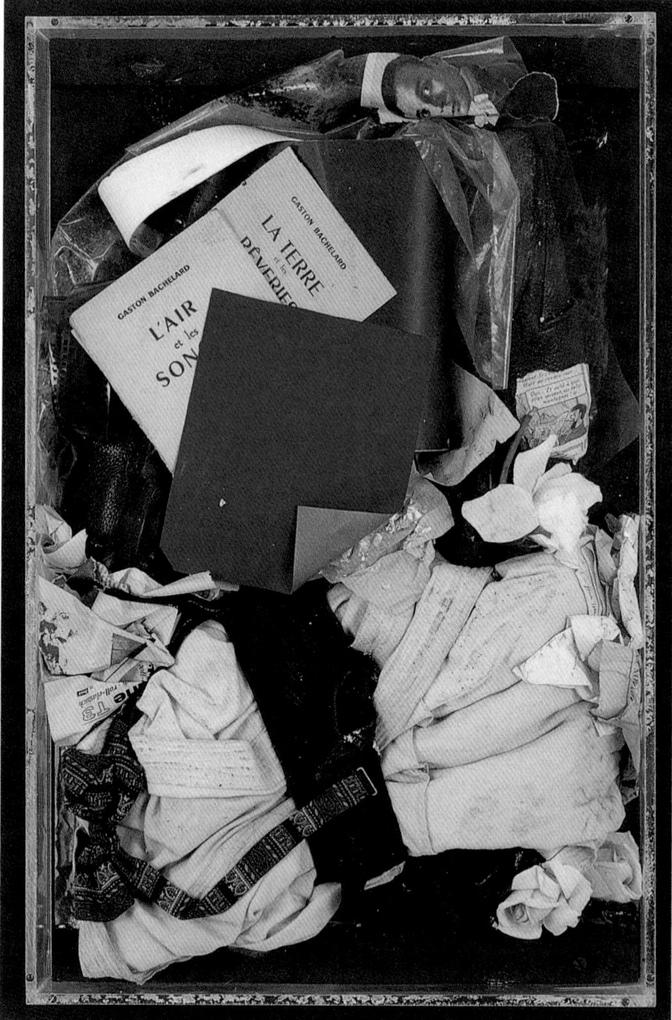

6 • Arman, *Premier Portrait-robot d'Yves Klein*, 1960
Accumulation of Klein's personal belongings, 76 x 50 x 12 (29⅞ x 19⅝ x 4¾)

Arman had understood that sculpture from now on would have to be situated within the display devices of the commodity, and that conventions of museum presentation would merge increasingly with those of the department store (the showcase and the shop window). As in the climactic moment of Klein's *Le Vide*, Arman recognized that the changes in how the subject is constituted and how objects are experienced, as well as the dialectic between memory and spectacle, would become most apparent in the object's situation in public space. His window installation of garbage, *Le Plein* of 1960, would demarcate one of the single most important changes in the paradigm of sculpture in the postwar period.

In their extreme forms, Arman's *accumulations* and *poubelles* cross the threshold to become memory images of the first historical instances of industrialized death. Some objects in his warehouse seem to echo the accumulations of clothing, hair, and private belongings that filmmaker Alain Resnais had recorded in *Night and Fog* (1955), the first documentary of the Nazi concentration camps, which Arman saw at the time of its release. Yet these accumulations set up a temporal dialectic that holds past and future in tension; for at the very moment when they seem to contemplate the catastrophic destructions of the recent past they open up a glimpse toward the imminent future. Anticipating another form of the industrialization of death, Arman's immobile arrangements evoke an emerging ecological catastrophe resulting from an accelerating and expanding consumer culture and its increasingly unmanageable production of waste.

FURTHER READING

Jean-Paul Ameline, *Les Nouveaux Réalistes* (Paris: Centre Georges Pompidou, 1992)

Benjamin H. D. Buchloh, "From Detail to Fragment: Décollage/Affichiste," *Décollage: Les Affichistes* (New York and Paris: Virginia Zabriske Gallery, 1990)

Bernadette Contensou (ed.), *1960: Les Nouveaux Réalistes* (Paris: Musée d'Art Moderne de la Ville de Paris, 1986)

Catherine Francblin, *Les Nouveaux Réalistes* (Paris: Editions du Regard, 1997)

▲ 1914

▲ 1913, 1915, 1917, 1918, 1944a, 1953, 1957b

• Introduction 1, 1931

1960b

Clement Greenberg publishes "Modernist Painting": his criticism reorients itself and in its new guise shapes the debates of the sixties.

From the late forties through the early sixties, the American critic Clement Greenberg worked to forge a descriptive vocabulary, a set of terms that would address with great precision and muscularity those features that counted as new in the postwar art he admired. One of these was the term "allover," which he used to describe the uniformity of surface of certain Abstract Expressionist ▲ painting, most conspicuously Jackson Pollock's, in its condition as a tight mesh of repetitions [1]. To make this term count, Greenberg contrasted it with the idea of the "easel picture" in which the illusion of a boxlike cavity is cut into the wall behind it to create the stage for some kind of dramatic, and thus focused, event; the allover surface, by contrast, organizes its contents in terms of flatness, frontality, and lack of incident ("The Crisis of the Easel Picture" [1948]).

Another term was "homeless representation," which Greenberg invented to account for the paradox of abstract painting that nonetheless seemed to describe the kinds of shallow hills and valleys generally used to model the illusion of a three-dimensional object; it was as if the tonal modulations of de Kooning's smeared paint (and later, Jasper Johns's encaustic "touches") were waiting for a representational object to return to them. In opposition to this, Greenberg pitted the idea of "color-space," as in the work of • Barnett Newman ("After Abstract Expressionism" [1962]), a luminous openness he was also to qualify as "optical," here following the lead of early art-historical writing where "haptic" or tactile qualities were opposed to "optic" ones—the art historian in question ▲ was the nineteenth-century Austrian Alois Riegl.

Given this effort at accurate, formal characterization, it is not surprising that Greenberg should have exploded into the exasperation of an essay such as "How Art Writing Earns Its Bad Name" (1962). It is already the mark of the simplicity and directness of Greenberg's prose that he should have avoided the term "criticism" and adopted the workmanlike connotations of "art writing" instead. But his target was not verbal archness or preciosity. Rather, it was the position, first enunciated by Harold Rosenberg's "The American Action Painters" (1952) but taken up in England a few years later by critics such as Lawrence Alloway, that the avant-garde is no longer concerned with making art but rather in performing a kind of self-revealing gesture, or "event," the by-product of which (the painting) is of no real concern to either artist or onlooker. As Rosenberg had put it: "The new painting has broken down every distinction between art and life." For Greenberg, however, the scandal of such a remark's claim to being criticism is that it has no way of explaining why the "painted leftovers of 'action' should be looked at and even acquired by others."

It was Greenberg's sense that in its jettisoning of art, the avant-garde had come to stand for a position he characterized, negatively,

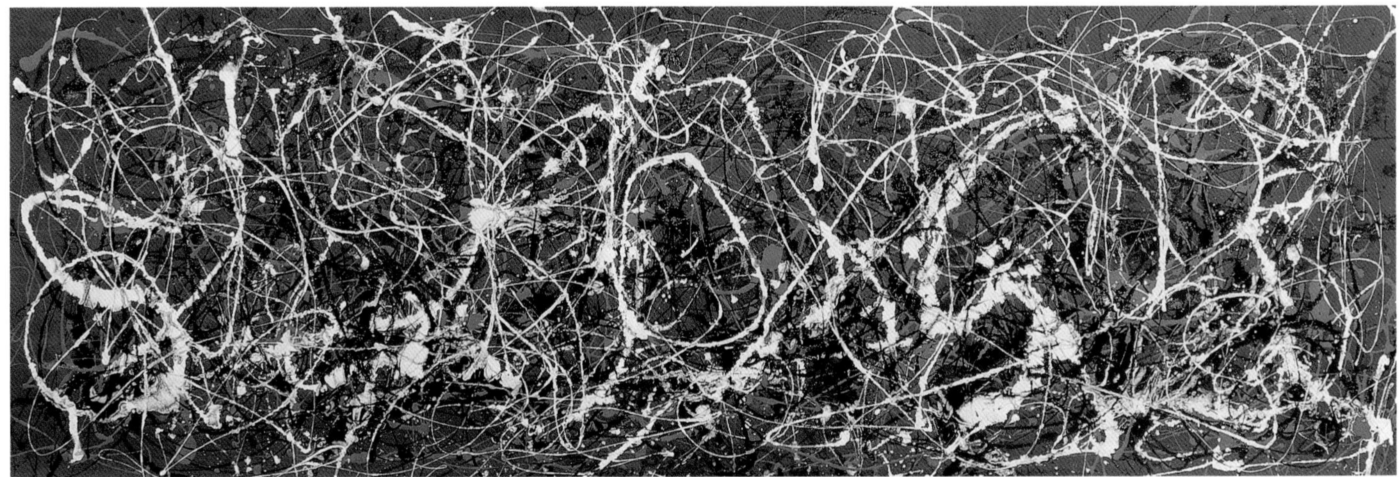

1 • Jackson Pollock, *Number 13A, 1948: Arabesque*, 1948
Oil and enamel on canvas, 94.6 x 295.9 (37¼ x 116½)

▲ 1947b, 1949 • 1951 ▲ Introduction 3

2 • Morris Louis, *Saraband*, 1959
Magna on canvas, 256.9 x 378.5 (101⅛ x 149)

as merely "subversive and futuristic" and that, on the contrary, art was necessarily the renewal (no matter how seemingly violent) of a continuous pictorial tradition. Such is the view that seems to ballast his most famous essay, "Modernist Painting" (1960).

Areas of competence

By characterizing the eighteenth-century German philosopher Immanuel Kant as "the first real Modernist," Greenberg's essay announces from its very outset that the phenomenon he is addressing, no matter how much of "a historical novelty" it might be, sinks its roots at least as far back as the eighteenth century and the Enlightenment. Drawing a parallel between the way "Kant used logic to establish the limits of logic" and what Greenberg calls the self-critical procedures of the modernist arts, he sees these as using "the characteristic methods of a discipline to criticize the discipline itself," not he adds, "in order to subvert it, but to entrench it more firmly in its area of competence."

For the arts, he argued, this area of competence, this domain that is specific to every separate aesthetic discipline, was historically to be found in what was unique in the nature of the medium of each. And in order to arrive at this, each art had begun to divest itself of those conventions that could be shown to be dispensable, mainly because such conventions had been borrowed from another art: the narrative in history painting, for example, having been borrowed from literature; or the stagelike depth in illusionist painting, having been taken over from the theater. Beginning with Édouard Manet's painting in the early 1860s, this logic began to reveal the extent to which the one characteristic absolutely unique to painting was the flatness of the picture plane itself. "Because flatness was the only condition painting shared with no other art, Modernist painting oriented itself to flatness as it did to nothing else."

It may sound as though "Modernist Painting" is simply a reprise of the arguments Greenberg had developed two decades earlier, at the outset of his career as an "art writer" when in 1939 and 1940 he published "Avant-Garde and Kitsch" and "Towards a Newer Laocoon." In the latter, he had also set the history of modernism within the context of the Enlightenment, calling upon Gotthold Ephraim Lessing's 1766 tract *Laocoön: An Essay upon the Limits of Poetry and Painting* for the theorization of the necessary separation of the various artistic mediums. The difference, however, lies in the history he projects of art's development thereafter. In "Modernist Painting" this history is purely internal, each art striving to achieve its own "purity." The only (veiled) reference to anything outside

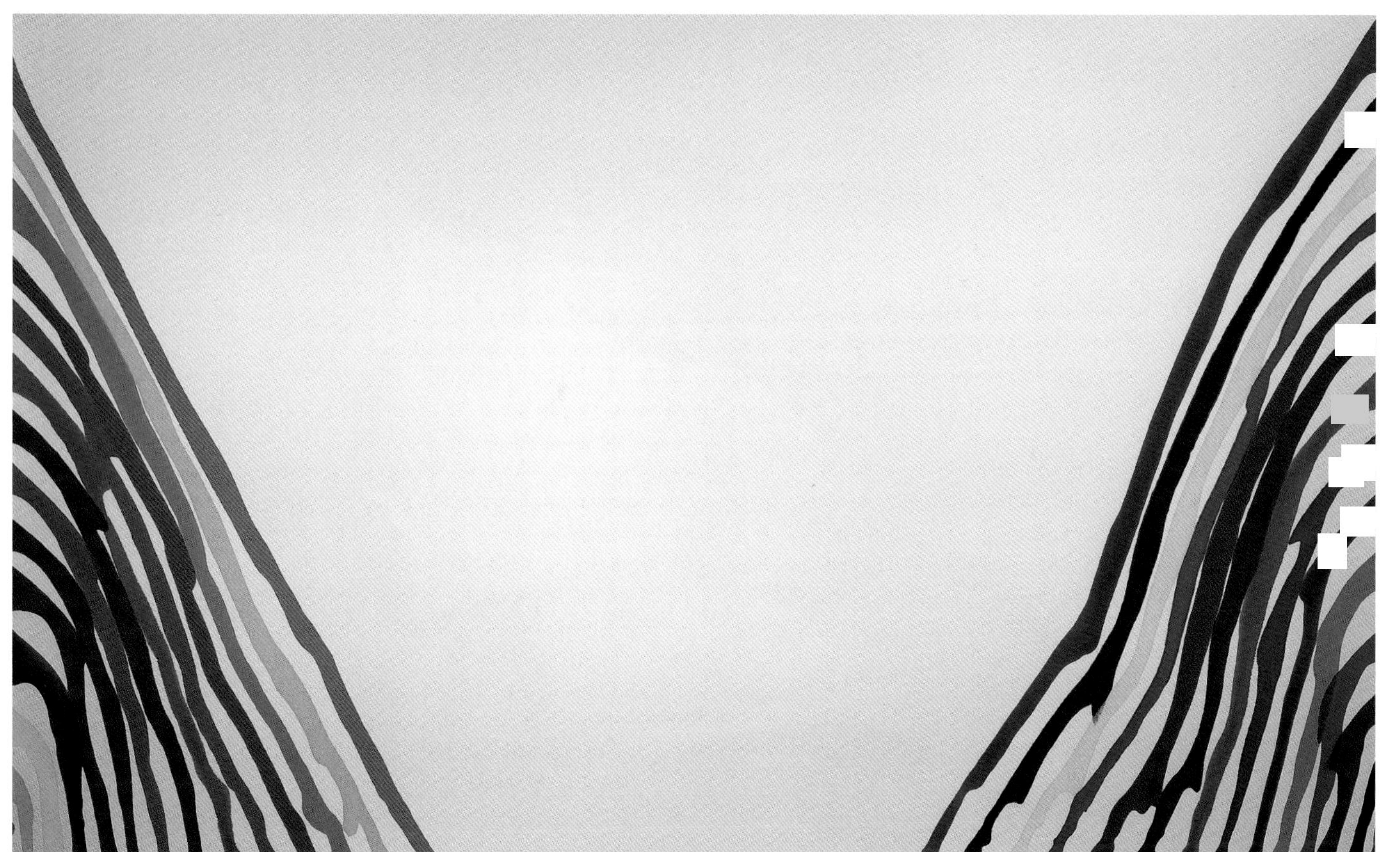

3 • Morris Louis, *Beta Kappa*, 1961
Acrylic resin on canvas, 262.3 x 429.4 (103¼ x 173)

the aesthetic domain is a sentence acknowledging that it seemed as if the arts were to be assimilated to entertainment, and as an escape from this they set themselves to "demonstrating that the experience they provided was valuable in its own right."

But in the "Newer Laocoon" the history, far more detailed, relates to the social conditions under which modernism evolved as first an authentic conveyor of bourgeois values and then, as capitalism advanced, an ever more vehement denial of and flight from an increasingly materialist and philistine society into the domain known as Bohemia. Thus in the forties Greenberg was projecting this history specifically in the name of the avant-garde as a project "to perform in opposition to bourgeois society the function of finding new and adequate cultural forms for the expression of that same society," without, he adds, "at the same time succumbing to its ideological divisions and its refusal to permit the arts to be their own justification." This notion of the arts as self-justifying, however, is itself qualified in terms that bring the aesthetic and the social domains together, since Greenberg saw modernism's acknowledgment of its medium as a form of materialist objectivity that this kind of painting shared with contemporary science. Indeed, he viewed modernism's focus on method and its striving for detachment as further instances of the relation to science, and when he came to summarize the findings of the visual arts in their search for their medium, he wrote that this "is discovered to be physical."

This emphasis carries into the terms of Greenberg's criticism during the forties in, for example, his ideas about the easel picture's replacement by mural painting. For the latter is a form that can declare the wall's impermeable surface in all the "positivity" of its observable fact, a continuous planar object that will function as an analogue for positivist science's continuous space of fact.

The orientation to science in this account connects back to the idea of the avant-garde's relation to the Enlightenment project; for it was to physics that philosophers such as Kant had looked for a model of critical thinking and merciless refinement of method. An orientation to science as a vanguard project could, then, be seen to be natural to an avant-garde that was bent on keeping alive what was valid in cultural experience. And indeed the social and materialist dimension of Greenberg's account of this history of the modernist arts becomes most obvious when he charts its course specifically in terms of the avant-garde. For it is to the avant-garde, he argues, that the task has fallen to preserve culture, in any form we could call genuine, from its ersatz, fake, dissembling version produced by modern consumer societies, a version to which Greenberg attached the word *kitsch* ("Avant-Garde and Kitsch").

If these early arguments were made in the name of socialism ("Today we look to socialism *simply* for the preservation of whatever living culture we have") and of the avant-garde, twenty years later "Modernist Painting" not only drops the social dimension of the account but now sees the avant-garde (along with the positivist science it avowed) as the enemy of art. Turning on science by saying that its "kind of consistency promises nothing in the way of aesthetic quality," Greenberg now qualifies the materialist,

Leo Steinberg (born 1920): the flatbed picture plane

In 1968, at a lecture at the Museum of Modern Art, art historian Leo Steinberg first raised his voice against Clement Greenberg's dogmatic account of the power of modernist painting. Himself a historian of Renaissance art, Steinberg bristled at the idea that modernism's canny revelation of painting's own medium (the flatness of its support) contrasted with the supposed naivety of Old Master painting. For while "Modernism used art to call attention to art," Greenberg deplored that "Realistic, illusionist art had dissembled the medium, using art to conceal art." Arguing that great art never masks its own process, covering it over with illusionism, Steinberg pointed to the absurdity of maintaining that Rembrandt was not formally self-conscious.

He wrote in his essay "Other Criteria," "The notion that Old Master paintings in contrast to modern dissemble the medium, conceal the art, deny the surface, deceive the eye, etc., is only true for a viewer who looks at the art like those ex-subscribers to *Life* magazine." Summarizing the modernist idea of a progressive mainstream in terms of Greenberg's notion of the "allover" composition (generated in relation to Abstract Expressionism) he wrote: "In formalist criticism, the criterion for significant progress remains a kind of design technology subject to one compulsive direction: the treatment of the whole surface as a single undifferentiated field of interest. Arguing that modernism's cherished idea of flatness needed considerable complication since the imaginative experience of Dubuffet's graffiti-like effects or Jasper Johns's *Flags* and *Targets* which "relegated the whole maintenance problem of flatness to 'subject matter'," Steinberg went on to develop a conception of imaginative experience, which is to say the orientation a given picture assumes toward a viewer standing in front of it.

Most painting, no matter how radical, he wrote, operates with "the conception of the picture as representing a world, some sort of worldspace which reads on the picture plane in correspondence with the erect human posture." Further, "A picture that harks back to the natural world evokes sense data which are experienced in the normal erect posture. Therefore the Renaissance picture plane affirms verticality as its essential condition." But beginning in 1950, in the work of Dubuffet and Rauschenberg, he went on, something happened to challenge this verticality, since their pictures "no longer simulate vertical fields, but opaque flatbed horizontals." Steinberg drew his term "flatbed" from the print-shop, since typographers must arrange their separate lines of type into forms that hold the fragile pieces of metal together. This new kind of picture, he added, "no more depends on a head-to-toe correspondence with human posture than a newspaper does. The flatbed picture plane makes its symbolic allusion to tabletops, studio floors, charts, bulletin boards—any receptor surface on which objects are scattered, on which data is entered, on which information may be received, printed, impressed—whether coherently or in confusion."

Steinberg's next move was decisive, hooking as it did into one of the central binaries of structuralist anthropology: "To repeat: it is not the actual physical placement of the image that counts. There is no law against hanging a rug on a wall, or reproducing a narrative picture as a mosaic floor. What I have in mind is the psychic address of the image, its special mode of imaginative confrontation, and I tend to regard the tilt of the picture plane from vertical to horizontal as expressive of the most radical shift in the subject matter of art, the shift from nature to culture."

Although this cataclysmic shift may have been prepared by a work like Duchamp's *Tu m'* (1918), it was currently being exploited by Rauschenberg's silkscreen paintings in which a variety of printed material—from color reproductions to newspaper photos, to maps or calendars—gathered. "To hold all this together, Rauschenberg's picture plane had to become a surface to which anything reachable-thinkable would adhere. It had to be whatever a billboard or dashboard is, and everything a projection screen is, with further affinities for anything that is flat and worked over—palimpsest, canceled plate, printer's proof, trial blank, chart, map, aerial view. Any flat documentary surface that tabulates information is a relevant analogue of his picture plane—radically different from the transparent projection plane with its optical correspondence to man's visual field." And it seemed at times that Rauschenberg's work surface stood for the mind itself—dump, reservoir, switching center, abundant with concrete references freely associated as in an internal monologue—the outward symbol of the mind as a running transformer of the external world, constantly ingesting incoming unprocessed data to be mapped in an overcharged field. If the vertical, optical picture addressed a viewing subject imagined as a Romantic, seeking to immerse him or herself into a turbulent landscape, the horizontal flatbed picture imagined an entirely different subject since the pictorial surface was now "as hard and tolerant as a workbench.... The 'integrity of the picture plane'—once the accomplishment of good design—was to become that which is given. The picture's 'flatness' was to be no more of a problem than the flatness of a disordered desk or an unswept floor." The subject this new type of picture addressed was no longer the Romantic but the denizen of urban spaces, both receiving and programmed by the fragmented messages processed by the media—radio, TV, advertising—or slipped into his or her domestic spaces through the mail slot.

physical implications of pictorial *flatness* in a way that will have great resonance for the critical debates of the sixties, as it both reorients his own writing and spawns that of a younger generation.

For here, suddenly lodging his idea of the medium of painting not on the physical properties of its support but on the specific nature of its perceptual experience as it is encountered by a viewer, Greenberg exchanges the physical for the phenomenological. Eyesight itself, he reasons, is projective. Thus "the first mark made on a canvas destroys its literal and utter flatness," meaning that absolute flatness is never possible for a field that opens itself to *vision*. What *is* possible, Greenberg maintains, is a special kind of spatiality which, like flatness, denies the viewer imagined physical entry, as though he or she were able to walk through the depicted space. What it substitutes for this is a sense of space that is unique

4 • Kenneth Noland, *Whirl*, 1960
Magna on canvas, 178.4 x 176.5 (70¾ x 69½)

to visuality—what Greenberg calls a specifically "optical illusion" —something that "can be traveled through, literally or figuratively, only with the eye."

The date of "Modernist Painting," initially broadcast in 1960 by "The Voice of America," coincided with an essay Greenberg devoted to two emerging artists—Morris Louis (1912–62) **[2, 3]** and Kenneth Noland (born 1924) **[4]**—in whom he saw the notion of "optical space" take on both a new dimension and the beginnings of something he could identify as a new school of American art. Throughout the fifties Greenberg had been changing the terms ▲ of his own appreciation of Pollock's drip paintings to correspond to the character of a space available to eyesight alone. It was in the work of these younger painters, and in that of their contemporary Helen Frankenthaler (born 1928) **[5]**, that he saw the luminosity produced by Pollock's linear (and relatively monochrome) web translated into ranges of intense color, color now identified as the most nontactile aspect of the visual field. In Louis's hands, Pollock's use of liquid paint spilled onto unsized canvas had been adopted into a far more general form of staining, so that the color is both identified with the woven canvas of its support but also manages to dematerialize that support into a series of shimmeringly "optical" veils that "open and expand the picture plane" ("Louis and Noland").

The power broker

It must be said that during the fifties Greenberg had identified himself with two aspects of the social field that his writing of the early forties might have seen as inimical to the avant-garde's cultural (and political) mission. One of these was the US State Department, which sponsored various speaking tours by Greenberg to both Europe and Asia in a promotion of American culture that many have identified with a concerted policy of Cold War propaganda. Another was the art market: buoyed by the prescience of ▲ his early support for Jackson Pollock and David Smith, Greenberg's reputation as a critic had attracted the attention of those, from museum directors to magazine editors, who wished to trade in emerging talent. Beginning in 1959, Greenberg organized exhibitions for the gallery French & Co. in New York just as he was, around the same time, advising other dealers. In all of this he could be seen to have a stake in a kind of American jingoism that took a delight in the demise of European painting and the "triumph" of a specifically American art. For Greenberg this meant "post-Cubist • painting," Cubism being a category into which he not only put everything produced in Europe in the twentieth century but also all ■ of Abstract Expressionism, even including Pollock, whose work, he had said in "How Art Writing Earns Its Bad Name" has "an almost completely Cubist basis." Thus the "exclusively visual" terms of what he would now call "post-painterly abstraction" and also "color-field painting" were both new and American. Further, in their opening and expanding of the picture plane they could also, self-evidently, be connected with the tradition that Greenberg saw modernist painting as continually renewing. In this they were clearly opposed to the avant-garde.

That the avant-garde had transformed itself in Greenberg's eyes from the upholder of cultural value to its enemy was a function of the emergence of "neo-Dada," which in his view cheapened and confused the modernist project in an embrace of the very commercial sphere from which the avant-garde, so he argued, had earlier ◆ fled. Dismissing that aspect of Jasper Johns's work that trafficked with the readymade, he spoke of, for example, "the literary irony that results from *representing* flat and artificial configurations which in actuality can only be *reproduced*" as having a merely journalistic, not formal or plastic, interest ("After Abstract Expressionism"). In the same context he spoke of the threat to modernism of a generalized infection of painting by the logic of the readymade: if flatness and the delimitation of flatness are the two constitutive norms that form the essence of painting, then "a stretched or tacked-up canvas already exists as a picture"—readymade—"though not necessarily as a successful one."

Greenberg's closest ally among a young generation of critics deeply affected by him deepened this observation. "It is not quite enough to say that a bare canvas tacked to a wall is not 'necessarily' a successful picture," Michael Fried wrote in 1967, "it would, I think, be more accurate to say that it is not *conceivably* one" ("Art and Objecthood"). For Fried, any future circumstances that might lead one to believe that it *could* be successful would so radically change the enterprise of painting "that nothing more than the name would remain." Carrying on Greenberg's attack on the avant-garde's obliteration of the distinction between art and life, "Art and Objecthood" staked the coherence of art on the possibilities and conventions generated by and within the limits of the

▲ 1949 ▲ 1945, 1949 • 1911 ■ 1947b, 1949 ◆ 1958

5 • Helen Frankenthaler, *Mountains and Sea*, 1952
Oil on canvas, 220.6 x 297.8 (86⅞ x 117¼)

individual medium. What exists *between* these, Fried said, is theater and "theater is now the negation of art." In fact, he insisted: "The success, even the survival, of the arts has come increasingly to depend on their ability to defeat theater." In this argument, Fried's "theatre" parallels Alloway's "event."

From Greenberg's notion, in 1940, that the survival of culture depended on the avant-garde's ability to defeat the bourgeoisie's stripping art of value, to his idea that it depended on modernist logic's securing the project of art as self-validating, one arrives in 1967 at Fried's notion that that survival now depends on defeating the avant-garde itself. Fried's aim now generalized the avant-garde's "neo-Dada" manifestation to those aspects of the ▲ readymade to be found in Minimalism, such as the use of found, industrial materials and parts or the deskilling of the work's fabrication by having it made in series, in a factory.

The result of his and Greenberg's position was that by the late sixties color-field painting and "opticality" stood on one side of a divide, lined up with what Greenberg had found missing in scientific methodicalness, namely "aesthetic quality"; while on the other side ranged all those practices for which the logic of modernism had led either to a reduction to the literal or physical nature of the support—Minimalism—or to a tautological notion of art as self- ▲ definition—as in some forms of Conceptual art.

FURTHER READING

T. J. Clark, "More on the Differences between Comrade Greenberg and Ourselves," in Serge Guilbaut, Benjamin H. D. Buchloh, and David Solkin (eds), *Modernism and Modernity* (Halifax: The Press of the Nova Scotia College of Art and Design, 1983)

Thierry de Duve, "The Monochrome and the Blank Canvas," *Kant after Duchamp* (Cambridge, Mass.: MIT Press, 1996)

Michael Fried, "Three American Painters," *Art and Objecthood* (Chicago: University of Chicago Press, 1998)

Clement Greenberg, *The Collected Essays and Criticism*, vols 1 and 4, ed. John O'Brian (Chicago: University of Chicago Press, 1986 and 1993)

Serge Guilbaut, *How New York Stole the Idea of Modern Art: Abstract Expressionism, Freedom, and the Cold War* (Chicago and London: University of Chicago Press, 1983)

▲ 1962c, 1965

▲ 1968b

1960c

Roy Lichtenstein and Andy Warhol start to use cartoons and advertisements as sources for paintings, followed by James Rosenquist, Ed Ruscha, and others: American Pop art is born.

In 1960, independently of each other, Roy Lichtenstein (1923–97) ▲ and Andy Warhol (1928–87) began to make paintings based on tabloid cartoons and advertisements. They were drawn to familiar characters like Popeye [1] and Mickey and generic products like tennis shoes and golf balls; a year later, Lichtenstein added comic strips of romance and war to this image repertoire [2]. Quickly dubbed "Pop"—a term first associated with the Independent • Group in England—this kind of art was roundly condemned: with its cold surfaces it seemed to mock the emotive depths of Abstract Expressionist painting, and mainstream critics, who had only just come around to Jackson Pollock and company, were not happy about this new turn of events. In 1949 *Life* had showcased Pollock ■ under the banner "Is he the greatest living painter in the United States?" In 1964 the same magazine profiled Lichtenstein under the heading "Is he the worst artist in America?"

1 • Roy Lichtenstein, *Popeye*, 1961
Oil on canvas, 106.7 x 142.2 (42 x 56)

The charge of banality

Critics charged the work with banality, which in the first instance had to do with content: Pop threatened to open the floodgates of commercial design and to drown out fine art. Of course, modern artists had long poached the brash forms of mass culture (popular prints, posters, newspapers, and so on), but they did so mostly to reinvigorate staid high forms with feisty low contents; with Pop, on the other hand, the low appeared to overrun the high. The accusation of banality also involved procedure: since Lichtenstein seemed to reproduce the cartoons, advertisements, and comics directly (in fact he modified them more than Warhol), he was branded with a lack of originality and, in one case at least, menaced with a charge of outright copying. In 1962 Lichtenstein had adapted a couple of didactic diagrams of portraits by Cézanne made by an art historian named Erle Loran in 1943; Loran surfaced to protest loudly. Not coincidentally, when ◆ Duchamp presented his readymade urinal as art forty-five years before, he was charged with similar crimes, only then the terms were a little more severe—"obscenity" and "plagiarism."

Lichtenstein did copy, but he did so in complicated fashion; even his use of the comic strips was not as automatic as it might appear. He would select one or more panels from a strip, sketch one or more motifs from these panels, then project his drawing (never the comic) with an opaque projector, trace the image on the canvas, adjust it to the picture plane, and finally fill it in with stenciled dots, primary colors, and thick contours—the light ground of the dots first, the heavy black of the outlines last. Thus, while a Lichtenstein might look industrially readymade, it is actually a layering of mechanical reproduction (the comic), handwork (the drawing), mechanical reproduction again (the projector), and handwork again (the tracing and the painting), to the point where distinctions between hand and machine are difficult to recover. In different ways, Warhol, Richard Hamilton, James Rosenquist (born 1933), Ed Ruscha (born ▲ 1937), Gerhard Richter, and Sigmar Polke produced a related conundrum of the painterly and the photographic; it is a prime characteristic of Pop art at its best.

Lichtenstein abounds in manually made signs of mechanically reproduced images, but his signature dots crystallize this paradox of "the handmade readymade," for they are a painted depiction of a printed code, the so-called Ben Day dots devised by Benjamin Day in 1879 as a technique to produce a printed image by means of gradations of shading translated into a system of dots. More importantly, the Lichtenstein dots convey the sense, still fairly novel at the time, that appearance had undergone a sea change of mechanical reproduction, that life was somehow "mediated" and

▲ 1964b • 1956 ■ 1949 ◆ 1914

▲ 1956, 1964b, 1967a, 1968b, 1972b, 1988

2 • Roy Lichtenstein, *In the Car*, 1963
Oil and magna on canvas, 172.7 x 203.2 (68 x 80)

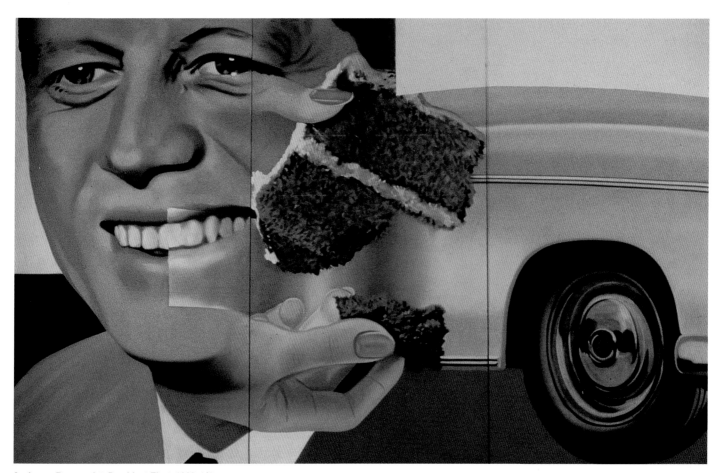

3 • James Rosenquist, *President Elect*, 1960–1/4
Oil on masonite, three panels, 213.4 x 365.8 (84 x 144)

all images somehow "screened"—that is, printed, broadcast, or otherwise viewed beforehand. This is another strong theme of Pop, again with significant variations wrung by Warhol, Hamilton, Rosenquist, Ruscha, Richter, and Polke.

Where did Lichtenstein stand in this brave new image-world? Did he "cling" to notions of originality and creativity, as art historian Michael Lobel has argued? True enough, when Lichtenstein appropriated images of products, he did efface the brand names (Warhol retained "Campbell's," "Brillo," and all the rest); as Lobel remarks, he "Lichtensteinized" his objects, and worked "to make the comics look like *his* images." This tension between traces of distinctive authorship and signs of its evident eclipse is pronounced in Lichtenstein, but apparently it did not trouble him much. "I am not against industrialization, but it must leave me something to do," Lichtenstein commented, modestly enough, in 1967: "I don't draw a picture in order to reproduce it—I do it in order to recompose it. Nor am I trying to change it as much as possible. I try to make the minimum amount of change." This is the ambiguous line that Lichtenstein hewed: to copy print images, but to adapt them to painterly parameters; to "recompose" them in the interest of pictorial form and unity, in the name of distinctive style and subjectivity, but only enough to register these values (perhaps to register them as threatened) and no more.

Rosenquist also recomposed his images, which were most often drawn from magazines, but his paintings retain the disjunctive quality of his preparatory collages of source illustrations, which he cropped and otherwise manipulated. For the most part Rosenquist used bland images of everyday objects, "common enough to pass without notice [and] old enough to be forgotten," which he then painted, with his skills as both an abstract artist and a billboard painter, in spectacular passages of lush illusionism that often traverse several panels and sometimes evoke the wide-screen cinema of the time. In some works, however, his subjects are charged, and his version of Pop approaches social commentary. For example, with the twelve-foot expanse of *President Elect* (1960–1/4) **[3]**, we move, as along a highway of billboards or through the pages of a magazine, from a beaming John F. Kennedy to manicured female fingers breaking apart a slice of cake, to the rounded surfaces of the right side of a '49 Chevrolet: the juxtaposition is almost Surrealist, but, ▲ as with Richard Hamilton, the mood is mostly upbeat, suggestive of a new age of products and promises. However, a short time later, in *F 111* (1965), an eighty-six-foot extravaganza that connects a jet fighter and an atomic blast with, among other disparate images, a little girl under a hairdryer and a mess of spaghetti, the mood is far less sanguine: the smiling president is dead, the Vietnam War is in full swing, and "the military-industrial complex" is exposed as the dark support of American consumer affluence.

The charge of banal content that greeted Pop is more difficult to refute than the accusation of dumb procedure, but here too appearances are not so simple. The lowly subjects often favored by Lichtenstein, Rosenquist, and others did offend aesthetic taste attuned to the lofty themes of Abstract Expressionism, but Lichtenstein in particular was not so contrarian. In fact, he showed that tacky advertisements and melodramatic comics could serve some of the same goals set not only for traditional art (such as pictorial unity and dramatic focus) but also for modernist art (such as the "significant form" prized by Roger Fry and Clive Bell and the ▲ vaunted "flatness" demanded by Clement Greenberg). Jasper Johns had played a similar trick with his paintings of flags, targets, and numbers of the fifties; as Leo Steinberg pointed out, these works met the Greenbergian criteria for modernist painting—that it be flat, self-contained, objective, immediate—by means that Greenberg found utterly alien to such painting—the kitschy images and found things of mass culture. Lichtenstein and company forced together the poles of fine art and commercial design with more sparks than did Johns, for their advertisements and comics were as flat as any flag or target, and more vulgar to boot.

Ed Ruscha also followed this Johnsian lead into Pop. He moved to Los Angeles from Oklahoma in 1956, and there, a year later, while still an art student at Chouinard Art Institute (now CalArts), he saw a • magazine reproduction of a Johns work, *Target with Four Faces* (1955), which combined a simple sign with four molds. The painting struck Ruscha as both matter-of-fact and mysterious, and he responded to the provocation with an even blunter move: a simple word painted in one color on a flat ground painted in another color. His first such works were monosyllabic exclamations—"guttural utterances like *Smash*, *Boss*, and *Eat*"—that were nonetheless ambiguous **[5]**. "These words have these abstract shapes," Ruscha later remarked, "they live in a world of no size." He went on to explore "the idea of visual noise" in a variety of word-image combinations, and the result was a kind of deadpan Duchampian aesthetic of his own, redolent of both Midwestern straight-talk and LA sophistication. If every major Pop artist complicates the high art of painting through cross-pollination with other mediums—Lichtenstein with comics, Warhol with newswire photographs, Rosenquist with billboards, and so on—Ruscha has introduced a cinematic quality into pictorial practice: often his colors have a celluloid gloss, and his paintings oscillate between deep, airy spaces and flat, word-inscribed screens—as though they were projected as much as painted **[4]**. ■ In this respect, too, his version of Pop exploits its Los Angeles locale.

Screening and scanning

In various ways, then, Lichtenstein, Rosenquist, Ruscha, and others seemed to challenge the oppositions on which pure painting of the twentieth century was founded: high versus low, fine versus commercial, even abstract versus representational. In *Golf Ball* **[6]** Lichtenstein presents an iconic representation of a dimpled sphere in black and white on a light gray ground. It is as banal as possible, but it is also not too distant from the pure plus-and-minus abstrac- ◆ tions of Mondrian also painted in black and white. On the one hand, the near abstraction of *Golf Ball* tests our sense of realism, which here as elsewhere Lichtenstein shows to be a conventional code, a matter of signs that do not always resemble things in the

▲ 1924, 1930b, 1931, 1956

▲ 1906, 1960b • 1958 ■ 1967a, 1968b ◆ 1913, 1917, 1944a

4 • Ed Ruscha, *Large Trademark with Eight Spotlights*, 1962
Oil on canvas, 169.5 x 338.5 (66¾ x 133¼)

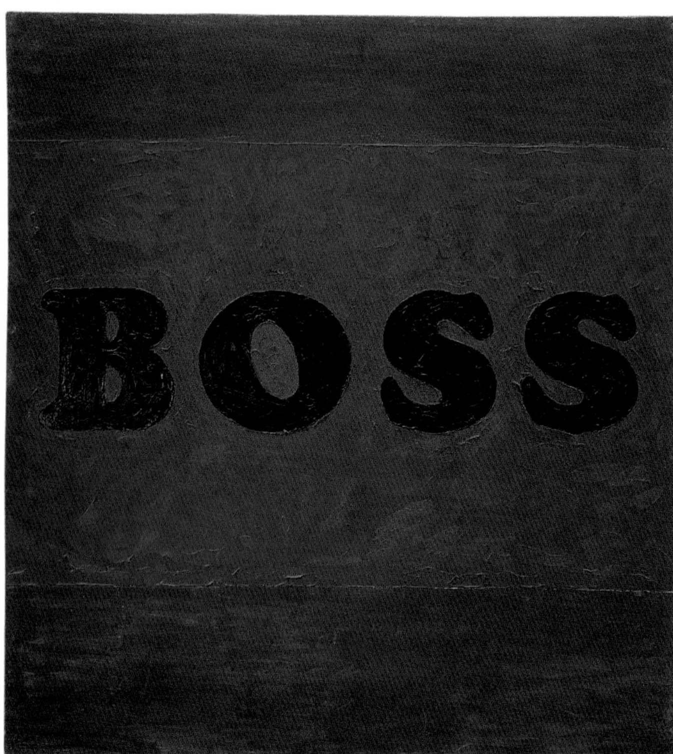

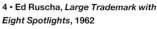

5 • Ed Ruscha, *Boss*, 1961
Oil on canvas, 182.9 x 170.2 (72 x 67)

world (around this time he read *Art and Illusion* [1960] by Ernst Gombrich, who defined realism in this "conventionalist" manner). On the other hand, when a Mondrian begins to look like a golf ball, then the category of abstraction is in trouble too. Modernist painting often worked to resolve figure into ground, to collapse spatial depth into material flatness (Mondrian is again the great example). Like his Pop peers, Lichtenstein gives us both—the illusion of space *and* the fact of surface—and if there is a radical edge in Pop it lies here: less in its thematic opposition of low content and high form, and more in its structural identity of simple sign and exalted painting. One can see why, when cartoons and commodities appeared in the metaphysical space once reserved for the numinous rectangles of Mark Rothko and the epiphanic stripes of ▲ Barnett Newman, some people got upset.

Lichtenstein in particular performs a kind of visual short circuit: he delivers both the immediate effect of a modernist painting and the mediated look of a print image. Consider an early Pop work like *Popeye* [**1**], which shows the spinach-enriched sailor knocking out his rival Bluto with a roundhouse left. It might be an allegory of the new Pop hero taking the tough Abstract Expressionist to the canvas with a single blow. Yet the important thing is the blow: *Popeye* is arguably as instantaneous in its impact as a Pollock; it smacks the viewer in the head as well. (Lichtenstein likes to underscore the force of this blow with the onomatopoeic terms of the comics: his punches go "Pow," his guns fire "Brattata.") Thus at the level of effect too, Lichtenstein suggests that Pop is not so different from a modernist painting like a Pollock: they project a similar sort of viewer, one that is all eye, that takes in the image in a flash, in a "Pop" of immediacy.

But to what end is this demonstration made? With Warhol, the appearance, in the exalted space of painting, of a newswire photo- ● graph of a gruesome car crash or a poisoned housewife is difficult to take even today. For the most part Lichtenstein puts high and low together with less subversive effects; he was proud of his formal sense, his tasteful ability to make good paintings out of banal pictures or mawkish stuff. Yet his reconciliation of high and low is not only a matter of his formal skill; it also registers a historical convergence of these old binaries. Lichtenstein was well prepared for this convergence. In the late forties as a G. I. Bill student at Ohio State University and in the fifties as a teacher in Ohio and upstate New York, he worked through his own catechism in modernist art: he painted along Expressionist lines first, then in a faux folk style (to which he adapted Americana themes, such as *Washington Crossing the Delaware* [1951], that anticipate his Pop art), and briefly in an abstract mode. He became adept in a repertoire of modernist styles and avant-garde devices, such as the gestural stroke, the Cubist play ■ with signs (a few strokes to signify a shadow, a white patch to signify ◆ a reflection, and so on), the abstract forms of grid and monochrome

▲ 1947b, 1951 ● 1964b ■ 1911, 1912 ◆ 1913, 1915, 1917, 1921, 1947a, 1957b

▲ painting, as well as the readymade object and the found image, all of which he received secondhand. These devices appear in his work as mediated, as if in review, held together by the iconic shapes supplied by the advert or the comic strip—held together, that is, by the very representational mode that avant-garde art had worked to overthrow. This is one aspect of his Pop art that does have an edge.

Edgy too is his demonstration of how much the codes of advertisements and comics have in common with the devices of the avant-garde (throughout the century the influence in this high–low relationship ran both ways). Of his own pictorial language Lichtenstein once remarked: "Mine is linked to Cubism to the extent that cartooning is. There is a relationship between • cartooning and people like Miró and Picasso which may not be understood by the cartoonist, but it definitely is related even in the ■ early Disney." He might have added Matisse, Mondrian, and Léger, among others; they are all there, read through the comics, in his paintings: the ambiguous signs of light and shadow in Picasso, the bold but suave contours in Matisse, the strict primary colors in Mondrian, the semicartoonish figures in Léger, all put to different purposes, of course (for example, if the primaries signify pure painting in Mondrian, in Lichtenstein yellow is also likely to signal a beautiful blonde, red a dress, blue the sky). Lichtenstein recomposed his advertisements and comics to fit them to the picture plane, but also to expose these modernist connections and to exploit them rhetorically. (Soon these connections became patent when he began to "Lichtensteinize" some of these masters directly, with paintings done after Picasso, Matisse, Mondrian, and others.) One can draw a dire conclusion from this commingling of modernist art and comic strip: that by the early sixties most devices of the avant-garde had become little more than gadgets of commercial design. And certainly this is one dilemma of the postwar or neo-avant-garde: that some of the antiart measures of the prewar or "historical" avant-garde had become the stuff not only of art museums but of spectacle industries. Or one can take the benign view that both fine art and commercial design benefited from this exchange of forms and contributed to values that, again, are rather traditional—unity of image, immediacy of effect, and so on. This is how Lichtenstein saw the matter.

6 • Roy Lichtenstein, *Golf Ball*, 1962
Oil on canvas, 81.3 x 81.3 (32 x 32)

Lichtenstein was adept not only in modernist styles but also in different modes of seeing and picturing, some of which date to the Renaissance, if not to antiquity: specific genres of painting like portraiture, landscape, and still life, all of which he Lichtensteinized, as well as general paradigms of painting—of painting as stage, as ▲ window, as mirror, and as abstract surface. Leo Steinberg detected yet another paradigm in the collage-paintings of Rauschenberg and • Johns, which he termed "the flatbed picture plane": the picture no longer as a vertical frame to look at or through as if onto a natural scene (like a window, a mirror, or indeed an abstract surface), but as a horizontal site where very different images can be brought together textually, a "flat documentary surface that tabulates information." For Steinberg this paradigm signaled a "postmodernist" break with modernist models of picturing, and certainly it influenced Lichtenstein. Yet Lichtenstein also suggests a variant of this model, which is crystallized in his Ben Day dots: a model of the picture as a screened image—and, as such, a sign of a postwar world in which everything seems subject to processing through mechanical reproduction and electronic simulation. This screening bears not merely on the actual making of his art (its commingling of handmade and readymade); it also addresses the mediated look of the contemporary world at large, and affects seeing and picturing as such. As Lobel notes, Lichtenstein often chose comic-strip figures placed in front of viewing screens—gun sights and televisual monitors as well as windshields and dashboards—as if to "compare or correlate the surface of the canvas" with such surfaces [**2**]. In effect, we too are thus positioned: our looking is also correlated with such viewing. Emergent here is a mode of seeing that has become dominant only in our own age of the computer screen: not only do all images appear screened, but our reading and looking alike have become a kind of "scanning." That is how today we are trained to sweep through information, visual or other : we scan it (and often it scans us, tracking keystrokes, counting website hits, and so forth). Early on Lichtenstein seems to have sensed this shift, both in appearance and in seeing, latent in the comic strip.

FURTHER READING

Russell Ferguson (ed.), *Hand-Painted Pop: American Art in Transition, 1955–92* (Los Angeles: Museum of Contemporary Art, 1992)

Walter Hopps and Sarah Bancroft (ed.), *James Rosenquist* (New York: Guggenheim Museum, 2003)

Michael Lobel, *Image Duplicator: Roy Lichtenstein and the Emergence of Pop Art* (New Haven and London: Yale University Press, 2002)

Steven Henry Madoff (ed.), *Pop Art: A Critical History* (Berkeley and Los Angeles: University of California Press, 1997)

Ed Ruscha, *Leave Any Information at the Signal* (Cambridge, Mass.: MIT Press, 2002)

▲ 1914, 1918 • 1907, 1911, 1912, 1924 ■ 1903, 1906, 1910, 1913, 1917, 1925a, 1944a, 1944b ▲ 1960b • 1958

1961

In December, Claes Oldenburg opens *The Store* in New York's East Village, an "environment" that mimicked the setting of surrounding cheap shops and from which all the items were for sale: throughout the winter and the following spring, ten different "happenings" would be performed by Oldenburg's Ray Gun Theater in *The Store* locale.

Allan Kaprow's (born 1927) essay "The Legacy of Jackson Pollock" was published in the October 1958 issue of *Artnews*, ▲ only two years after the painter's tragic death. By that time, the fact that Abstract Expressionism had become academicized had finally dawned on the editor of the journal, which for a decade had been the main promoter of the "10th Street touch," to use Clement • Greenberg's disparaging characterization of the art produced by "second-generation" Abstract Expressionists. In January of that year, ■ Jasper Johns's *Target with Four Faces* had appeared on the cover of *Artnews*, in preview of the painter's first solo exhibition which turned out to be a spectacular success. A year later, Frank Stella's black paintings would mesmerize the New York art world. Pop art and Minimalism would soon follow: the inevitable demise of an already exhausted Abstract Expressionism was well under way. Kaprow's text, however, was the first to address head-on the issue of its legacy, or rather that of its main protagonist. Perhaps because he had been trained as an art historian (Kaprow studied with Meyer Schapiro at Columbia University, where he wrote a master's thesis on Mondrian), and was teaching the discipline (at Rutgers), he felt it was not enough, or too easy, to repudiate—rather, one had to sublate.

Kaprow's utopia

It is true, Kaprow starts, that Pollock's innovations are "becoming part of textbooks": "The act of painting, the new space, the personal mark that builds its own form and meaning, the endless tangle, the great scale, the new materials are by now clichés of college art departments." But taking something for granted and replicating it is not understanding it, and there is more to Pollock's enterprise than what this stereotypical take suggests. Indeed, "some of the implications inherent in these new values are not as futile as we all began to believe," adds Kaprow, before commenting upon each feature he had just listed in order to demonstrate that, if Pollock "created some magnificent paintings ... he also destroyed painting." The immediacy of the act, the loss of self and identity in the potentially infinite, allover space of painting, the new scale that undermines the autonomy of the canvas as an art object and transforms it into an environment: all of that, and more, points to Pollock's art as one "that tends to lose itself out of bounds, tends to fill our world with itself." Then, "What do we do now?" asks Kaprow. "There are two alternatives," he answers. "One is to continue in this vein. Probably many good 'near-paintings' can be done varying this esthetics of Pollock's without departing from it or going further. The other is to give up the making of painting entirely—I mean the single flat rectangle or oval as we know it. It has been seen how Pollock came pretty close to doing so himself." There is, on the one hand, the taming of Pollock's work (and there is little doubt that Kaprow's target, at this juncture, was the school of artists presented by Greenberg as Pollock's true heirs: Helen Frankenthaler, ▲ Morris Louis, etc.); on the other, the dissolution of painting as we know it, and more precisely, its "dissolution into the environment," • to speak like Mondrian from the mid-twenties on.

Kaprow knew very well that his call had a precedent in Mondrian's utopia, but rather than dwelling on this—which would have forced him to take into account the wedge separating the context of ■ the historical avant-gardes and that of the postwar neo-avant-garde, and perhaps to temper his optimism—he concluded his essay with a blueprint for the immediate future, worth quoting in full:

> *Pollock ... left us at the point where we must become preoccupied with and even dazzled by the space and objects of our everyday life, either our bodies, clothes, rooms, or, if need be, the vastness of Forty-second Street. Not satisfied with the suggestion through paint of our other senses, we shall utilize the specific substances of sight, sound, movements, people, odors, touch. Objects of every sort are materials for the new art: paint, chairs, food, electric and neon lights, smoke, water, old socks, a dog, movies, a thousand other things that will be discovered by the present generation of artists. Not only will these bold creators show us, as if for the first time, the world we have always had about us but ignored, but they will disclose entirely unheard-of happenings and events, found in garbage cans, police files, hotel lobbies; seen in store windows and on the streets; and sensed in dreams and horrible accidents. An odor of crushed strawberries, a letter from a friend, or a billboard selling Drano; three taps on the front door, a scratch, a sigh, or a voice lecturing endlessly, a blinding staccato flash, a bowler hat—all will become materials for this new concrete art.*
>
> *Young artists of today need no longer say, "I am a painter" or "a poet" or "a dancer." They are simply "artists." All of life will be*

▲ 1949 • 1960b ■ 1958 ▲ 1960b • 1917, 1944a ■ 1960a

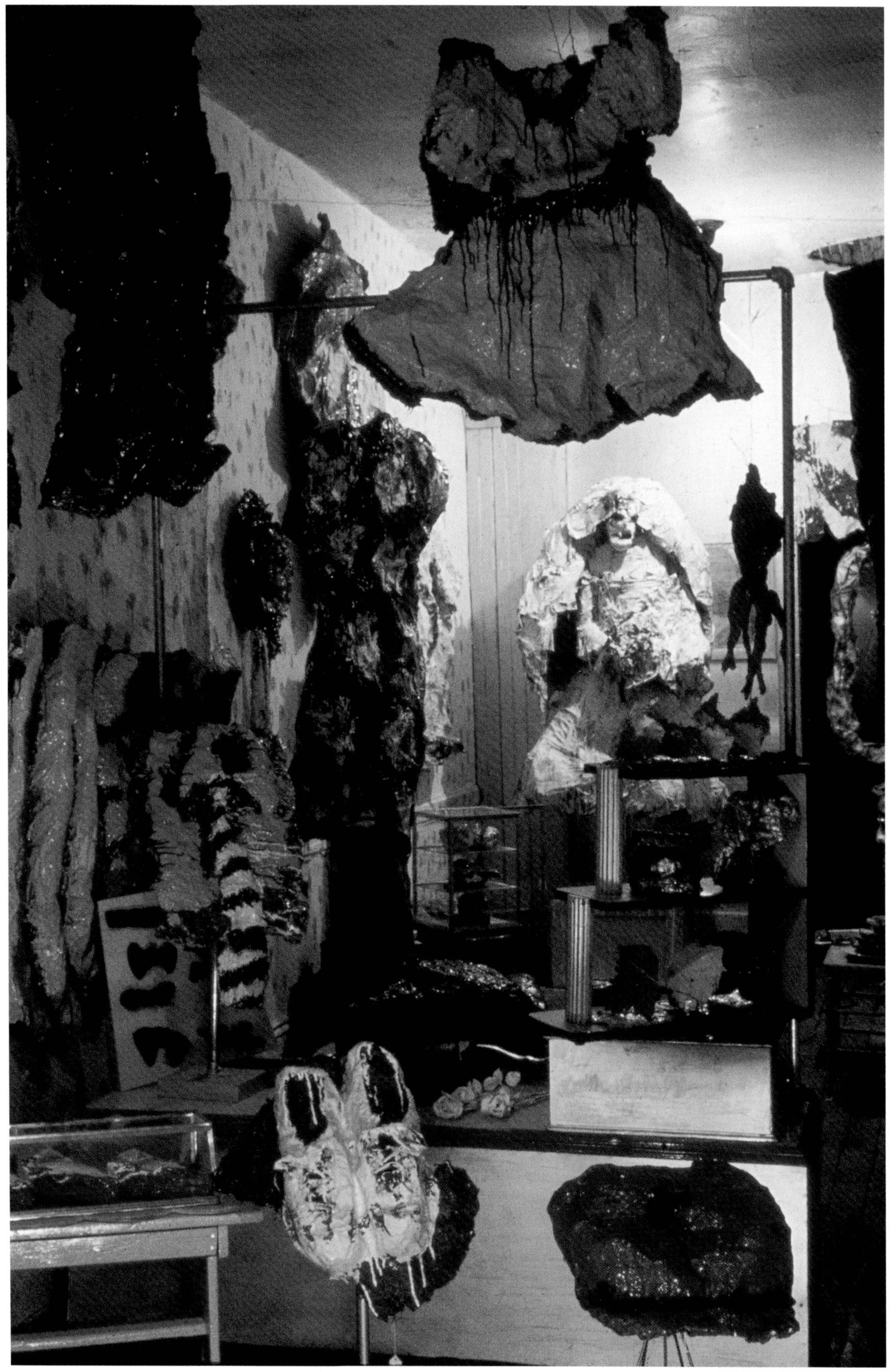

1 • Claes Oldenburg, interior of *The Store*, 107 East 2nd Street, New York, December 1961

open to them. They will discover out of ordinary things the meaning of ordinariness. They will not try to make them extraordinary but will only state their real meaning. But out of nothing they will devise the extraordinary and then maybe nothingness as well. People will be delighted or horrified, critics will be confused or amused, but these, I am certain, will be the alchemies of the 1960s.

One cannot but admire Kaprow's foresight here. Much avant-garde art produced in the sixties does fulfill his prophecy, or at least fits this or that aspect of his prospective description. Three interconnected elements need to be singled out, because they directly concern Kaprow's own art and in particular the form that he was inventing at the time, dubbed the "happening": the availability of the world at large—not only the manifold of its objects, particularly its refuse, but also events unfolding in time—as the new, all-encompassing material of art; the dissolution of all hierarchies and value-systems; the suppression of medium-specificity and the simultaneous inclusion of all realms of perception into the aesthetic sphere.

Kaprow had been exhibiting paintings for several years, but toward the end of 1957 he began to create spatial "environments," which he dubbed "action collages," and which he conceived as direct extensions of Pollock's art—in his *Assemblage, Environments & Happenings* of 1966, he reproduced an aerial view of *Yard,* dating from 1961, for which he famously filled a courtyard with an accumulation of used tires [**2**], next to a photograph by Hans Namuth of Pollock at work (quietly smoking his pipe and trailed by a child, Kaprow looks less heroic than Pollock, but he was definitively more "in" his work). It was while he was was trying to introduce sound in his environments—to open them further to the world, according to his logic of infinite extension—that Kaprow stumbled upon the happening. Dissatisfied with the paucity of effects he could muster, he sought ▲ advice from John Cage, who was then giving a course on composition at the New School for Social Research in New York. Fascinated by what he saw of the class on this first visit, he decided to join the ranks of several nonmusicians who were also in attendance, such as ● George Brecht and Dick Higgins, later to become pillars of Fluxus. It was there, in the spring of 1958, and with the encouragement of Cage, from whom he learned about chance as a compositional, or rather anticompositional, device, that he developed his idea of the happening. Randomness had long been a foundational principle of Cage's musical practice, fostering a genuine interest in the issue of notation. Kaprow's responses to Cage's class assignments were all performed whilst following a score listing objects to be used in noisy actions as well as the duration of each of these actions (which could be simultaneous). The model was obviously musical, but in adding the dimension of space—of the movement and placement of the participants (often hidden from view)—Kaprow emphasized both the theatrical dimension of these events, and their reliance upon a ■ collage tradition derived from Dada.

Between this embryonic stage and the first fully fledged public happening, *18 Happenings in 6 Parts,* nothing fundamentally changed but the structure got more complex. For this event, which

2 • Allan Kaprow, *Yard*, 1961
Environment in the backyard of the Martha Jackson Gallery, New York

marked the inauguration of the Reuben Gallery—a space that would function for the next two years as the Mecca of the new art form (with happenings by Red Grooms, Robert Whitman, Claes Oldenburg, George Brecht, Jim Dine)—Kaprow had divided the space into three rooms by temporary partitions made of wood, sheets of plastic and canvas, either covered with assemblages of various objects to be used as props by the participants, or, if still blank at the beginning of the performance, destined to be painted over during its unrolling. Sounds—electronic, mechanical, and live—as well as lighting (including slide projections) were constantly altering this multipart environment into which six participants (three women and three men) evolved and executed a whole range of disconnected actions and uttered disconnected sentences while keeping as expressionless as possible. The "happenings" were carried out simultaneously in the three rooms (six in each of them) and the spectators were required to change room twice, during the overall one-hour performance (the seats were numbered and the changes of their occupiers were timed in the score). This modest audience participation (it grew in importance in Kaprow's later happenings and in those of others), as well as the absence of plot and character and the simultaneity of the "three-ring circus" insured that no one among the public could claim to have anything more than a fragmentary grasp of the whole event. Even returning the following days—*18 Happenings in 6 Parts* was performed during six evenings, starting on October 4, 1959—would not have much augmented one's mastery of the performance's overall structure, since the likelihood of obtaining a radically different seating arrangement each time was statistically very small.

The breakdown of the barrier separating performers and audience is what most struck commentators on the first happenings (there

▲ 1953 ● 1962a ■ 1916a, 1918, 1920

was no stage, no ideal setting: in fact, as they grew more complex and involved more participants, happenings tended to occur outdoors, as would Kaprow's *Household* in 1964 [**3**]). This breakdown, particularly when it was marked by aggressivity, was what distinguished happenings from pure theater (Oldenburg's happenings would perhaps be the most violent or rather discomfiting of all, but Kaprow did not hesitate to abuse his public—for example in *A Spring Happening*, in March 1961, when the audience was chased out by someone operating a power landmower at the end of the performance.) Critics also noted that this collapse of the performer/audience boundary was in keeping with happening's deliberate disregard of any cause-and-effect relations as well as of any principle of constancy. Likening it to the "alogic of dreams" that have "no sense of time," no past, are without "climax or consummation," often repetitive, and "always at the present tense," Susan Sontag remarked that its lack of storyline (particularly, as often, when the sequence of actions had been determined by chance) was at odds with the basic modernist concept of the work of art as an autonomous totality, and troubling even for the small, "loyal, appreciative, and for the most part experienced audience" of happenings who "frequently does not know when they are over, and has to be signalled to leave." Another dissolution of categories noticed by Sontag concerns the materials used in the happenings: "one cannot distinguish among set, props, and costumes in a Happening, as one can in the theater." One cannot even distinguish among people and objects (all the more since people were "often made to look like objects, by enclosing them in burlap sacks, elaborate paper wrappings, shrouds, and masks," or stay as immobile as the props around them). There is only a global environment, often deliberately messy, in which mostly fragile materials are used and often destroyed in the course of a series of non-sequential acts. "One cannot hold on to a Happening, and one can only cherish it as one cherishes a firecracker going off dangerously close to one's face," concludes Sontag.

Such impermanence became a key element of Kaprow's concept (after the initial experience of *18 Happenings in 6 Parts*, he often stated that happenings should never be repeated in order to preserve what he deemed their most important quality, their immediacy, their "suchness," as he called it). This has little to do with any interest in spontaneity (happenings were scripted and rehearsed, no matter how aleatory their structure), but with a somewhat naive belief, derived from Cage's Zen-like philosophy, that uniqueness as such was a guarantee of "presence," and that "presence" as such, when thought of as a natural process, was a guarantee against the blatant commodification of all things that characterized the postwar consumerist society.

3 • Allan Kaprow, *Household*, 1964
Happening

(Kaprow's disdain for the art market and the "white walls, tasteful aluminum frames, lovely lighting, fawn—gray rugs, cocktails and polite conversation" pertaining to the modernist gallery had been one of the motivations for his environments.) While he misunderstood Cage, for whom repetition was properly impossible (since no two performances could ever be alike), which made its proscription senseless, Kaprow perhaps inadvertently touched a nerve whose sensitivity among his audience at this time of history might explain more than any other factor the shock value of the happening. This nerve was the economic one, which he irritated, as art historian Robert Haywood pointed out, by enacting the corporate strategy of "planned obsolescence" destined to quicken commodity production and consumption (Haywood's prime example is the 1967 multipart happening *Fluids*, which consisted of erecting and then letting melt fifteen large geometric ice formations spread throughout diverse locations in Pasadena and Los Angeles). Yet though it was intended as a critique of instrumental labor—a critique that his mentor Meyer Schapiro had deemed to be at the core, if not the purpose, of modern art since Impressionism—Kaprow's superlatively gratuitous recourse to a capitalist trick did not really hold as strategy and slowly devolved into an inoffensive spectacle that, as such, only extended further the alienation it pretended to reveal.

Asked by arts critic Richard Kostelanetz "Are not most of us opposed to planned obsolescence? I would prefer more permanent cars. Is it bad for me to want things that would last longer?", Kaprow offered a reply that could have been undersigned by any corporate mogul: "I suggest that this is a myth of the wrong kind—that you really don't want a permanent car; for if you and the public did, you wouldn't buy cars that are made impermanently. Planned obsolescence may have its bad sides.... It also is a very clear indication of America's springtime philosophy—make it new is *renew*; and that's why we have a cult of youth in this country." Those words, uttered in 1968, could not have clashed more dramatically with what the rebelling youth demonstrating in the streets was thinking at the time. In the end, it might have been Kaprow's incapacity to reflect and seize upon the politico-economical meaning of the art form that he had invented that led to its oblivion: in light of the 1968 "real-life" events, far more violent than his own and often as festive, the happening suddenly looked irrelevant and rapidly faded away.

Art for dime stores

But while Kaprow might have been too indirect in his wish to underscore the hold of market forces on our lives and on our consumption of art in particular, Oldenburg addressed this issue head on. Though ▲ his starting-point was not Pollock but rather Jean Dubuffet's "rehabilitation of mud," Oldenburg's early take was quite similar to that of Kaprow, particularly in his glorification of refuse as the prime material of art. But things began to shift right from Oldenburg's first mature manifestation, the "Ray Gun Show" at the Judson Gallery between January and March 1960 (the gallery was administered by the Judson Memorial Church, soon to host the Judson Dance Theater, including performances by Yvonne Rainer, Carolee ▲ Schneemann, and the Minimalist sculptor Robert Morris). For this show, Oldenburg constructed his first environment, *The Street*, which became the disheveled setting of his first happening, *Snapshot from the City* [**4**]. It consisted of an accumulation of silhouettes made from torn or torched rubbish collected in the streets (lots of corrugated cardboard, of burlap, of old newspapers), and of more garbage spread on the floor. Foremost and recurrent among these silhouettes was that of the "Ray Gun," a parodic sci-fi toy (between a hair-dryer and a gun) devised by Oldenburg as the emblem of all commodities. To enhance the market metaphor, Oldenburg offered the audience of *Snapshot from the City* large sums of "money" in Ray Gun currency (bills ranged from 1,000 figures to 7,000) with which to buy stuff from *The Street* and other junk that he and his fellow artist Jim Dine had been adding to it for the occasion.

What was left over from this fake yardsale was installed as a much sparser version of *The Street* in the Reuben Gallery in May 1960, after which Oldenburg retreated to the country for the summer. It is there, while reflecting upon his dissatisfaction with the second, clean, version of *The Street* in a typical modernist "white cube," that he fully elaborated his concept of the Ray Gun, particularly its ubiquity: any object shaped in a right angle, even a blunt one, can be a Ray Gun, which, in a humorous appropriation of Mondrian's phrase, Oldenburg crowned with the title of "universal angle." "Examples: Legs, Sevens, Pistols, Arms, Phalli—simple Ray Guns. Double Ray Guns: Cross, Airplanes. Absurd Ray Guns: Ice Cream Sodas. Complex Ray Guns: Chairs, Beds." In short, just as gold had for long functioned as the standard of monetary circulation, the Ray Gun was a "general equivalent," the empty sign through which all kinds of things could be compared and exchanged. Although it

4 • Claes Oldenburg, *Snapshots from the City*, 1960
Performance at Judson Gallery, Judson Memorial Church, New York

▲ 1946

▲ 1965, 1968b, 1969

would be far-fetched to imagine that Oldenburg spent his summer musing about political economy, his next project, *The Store* [**1**], indicates that his ruminations led him to discount his earlier, Kaprowesque aestheticization of refuse as irrelevant. In what seems in retrospect like a direct allusion to his Reuben show, he wrote: "These things [art objects] are displayed in galleries, but that is not the place for them. A store would be better (Store—place full of objects). Museum in b[ourgeois] concept equals store in mine."

Though a partial realization of *The Store* took place in the group show "Environments, Situations, Spaces" at the Martha Jackson Gallery in May–June 1961, it was only in December of that year that Oldenburg opened the outlet of his "Ray Gun Manufacturing Company" on 107 East Second Street, in an area of Manhattan replete with "dime stores" selling cheap or secondhand goods. In this new location *The Store* was conceived as a duplicate of the neighboring shops, where ill-assorted items endlessly succeeded each other on the shelves—with this difference: Oldenburg's shelves were filled with obvious replicas of perishable foodstuffs or tiny objects of mass consumption. Often oversized, made of cloth soaked in plaster and clumsily painted in garish colors applied with broad brush-strokes ▲ (in overt parody of Abstract Expressionism), these baked potatoes, sausages, ice-cream cones or blue shirts were never intended to pass for the real thing (though their price was a far cry from those commanded by art works in even the least prestigious gallery—they ran from twenty-five dollars to over eight hundred). Rather, their purpose was to demonstrate that since there was no fundamental difference between the rarefied commerce of art and the trade of a thrift-store, as both art works and bibelots were nothing but commodities, one might as well skip the pretense and drop the fig-leaf.

If Oldenburg's assault on the institutions of art as sheer marketplace went much further than that of his predecessor, it is because, through the symbol of the Ray Gun (and he displayed countless "Ray Guns" for sale in *The Store*), he had understood that the status of the work of art as commodity rested on its exchangeability. To his delight, a visitor trying to identify one of these poorly shaped objects exclaimed: "It's a lady's handbag.... No, it's an iron. No, a typewriter. No, a toaster. No, it's a piece of pie." But once this metaphoric structure of the art work as exchangeable good had been identified, there was no stopping it from looming everywhere, making of any object the equivalent of at least another one. *Store Days*, a book in which Oldenburg has assembled all the notes pertaining to this ongoing installation and the events that took place in it, abounds in lists of comparisons: "cock and balls equals tie and collar/equals leg and bra/equals stars and stripes/flag equals cigarette package and cigarettes/heart equals balls and triangle/equals (upside down) girdle and stockings/equals (sidewise) cigarette package equals flag."

This potentially infinite chain of associations would hardly pass for economic analysis (foremost because it rests on the deliberate disregard of any opposition between use- and exchange-value). In the end, Oldenburg knew full well that his replicas would end up marketed as art and be given the special care that luxury goods enjoy. But combining with his longstanding interest in psychoanalysis, the parody propelled him into the next stage of his production, with which he has been engaged ever since. It was in his subsequent solo exhibition at the Green Gallery, in September–October 1963, that he presented for the first time his large-scale "soft" objects sprawled on the floor (*Floor-Burger*, *Floor-Cone*, *Floor-Cake*, etc.): with the unescapable eroticism of these mock edible items (as well as that of the more scatological objects that would follow, such as his *Soft Toilet* [**5**]), Oldenburg was further aiming his pan-metaphoricity at American mass culture and declaring that if its fixation on consumption was an open secret, its covert obsession was with the body.

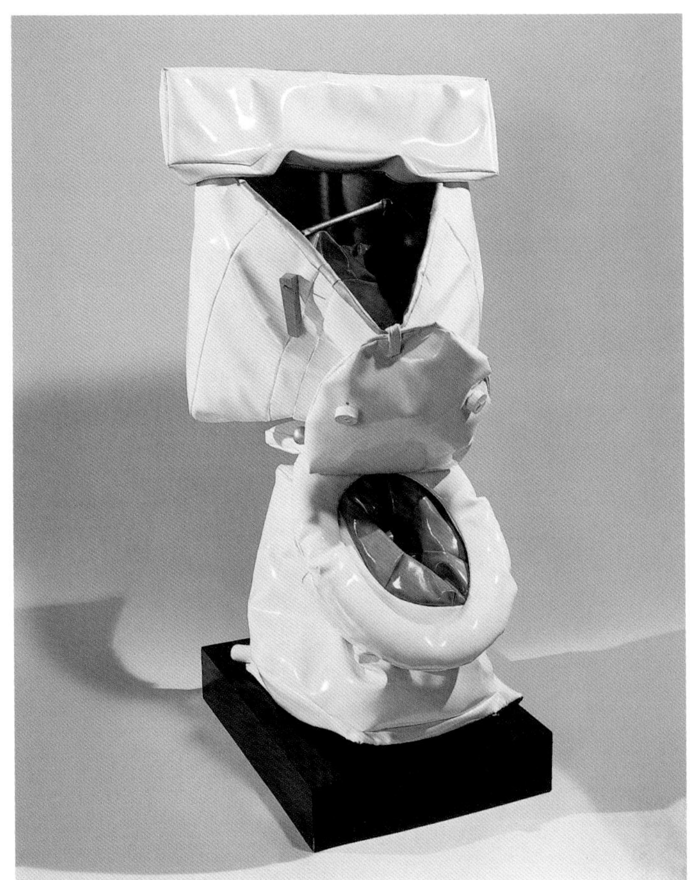

5 • Claes Oldenburg, *Soft Toilet*, 1966
Wood, vinyl, kapok, wire, Plexiglas on metal stand and painted wood base, 144.9 x 70.2 x 71.3 (57⅛ x 27⅝ x 28⅛)

FURTHER READING

Robert Haywood, "Critique of Instrumental Labor: Meyer Schapiro's and Allan Kaprow's Theory of Avant-Garde Art," in Benjamin H. D. Buchloh and Judith Rodenbeck, *Experiments in the Everyday: Allan Kaprow and Robert Watts* (New York: Columbia University, 1999)

Allan Kaprow, *Essays on the Blurring of Art and Life* (Berkeley and Los Angeles: University of California Press, 1993)

Michael Kirby, *Happenings* (New York: Dutton & Co, 1966)

Barbara Rose, *Claes Oldenburg* (New York: Museum of Modern Art, 1969)

Susan Sontag, "Happenings: An Art of Radical Juxtaposition," *Against Interpretation* (New York: Dell, 1966)

▲ 1947b

1962a

In Wiesbaden, West Germany, George Maciunas organizes the first of a series of international events that mark the formation of the Fluxus movement.

1 • George Brecht, *Solo for Violin, Viola, Cello, or Contrabass*, 1962
Performance

Fluxus remains the most complex—and therefore widely underestimated—artistic movement (or "nonmovement," as it called itself) of the early to mid-sixties, developing in parallel with, and often in opposition to, Pop art and Minimalism in the ▲ United States and Nouveau Réalisme in Europe. More open and international in scope (and counting more female artists among its participants) than any other avant-garde or neo-avant-garde since • Dadaism and Russian Constructivism, Fluxus saw no distinction between art and life, and believed that routine, banal, and everyday actions should be regarded as artistic events, declaring that "everything is art and everyone can do it." With its diverse activities, which included "Flux" concerts and festivals, musical [**1**, **2**] and theatrical performances, innovatively designed publications and pronouncements, mail art, and other ephemeral events, gestures, and actions [**3**], ■ it initiated many key aspects of Conceptual art, such as the insistence on viewer participation, the turn toward the linguistic performative, ◆ and the beginnings of institutional critique.

The force fields of Fluxus

Fluxus was named (if not "founded") in 1961 by George Maciunas (1931–78), a postwar émigré from Lithuania who—after spending a few years at high school in West Germany—came to the United States in 1948. Maciunas claimed to have found the name—derived from the Latin *fluere*, to flow—by sticking a knife or finger into a ▲ dictionary, the very method by which the Dadaists claimed to have found theirs. The term "fluxus" already had a certain resonance. The fifth-century BC philosopher Heraclitus of Epheseus is reputed to have said that "everything is in flux … everything flows" and that "you cannot step into the same river twice." Hegel took up the idea in the eighteenth century when he formed his concept of the dialectic, saying that everything in nature is in continuous flux and that "struggle is the father of everything." And in the early twentieth century, the French philosopher Henri Bergson saw natural evolution as a process of constant change and development—as a "fluxion." Bergson also argued that we do not experience the world moment by moment but continuously in one flow, as we hear music. Beyond these philosophical connotations, Maciunas also explicitly associated the word "fluxus" with the medical processes of cathartic

2 • Alison Knowles, *Newspaper Music*, 1967
Concert in the Lund Kunsthalle, Sweden

▲ 1960a, 1960c, 1964b, 1965 • 1916a, 1920, 1921 ■ 1968b ◆ 1971 ▲ 1916a

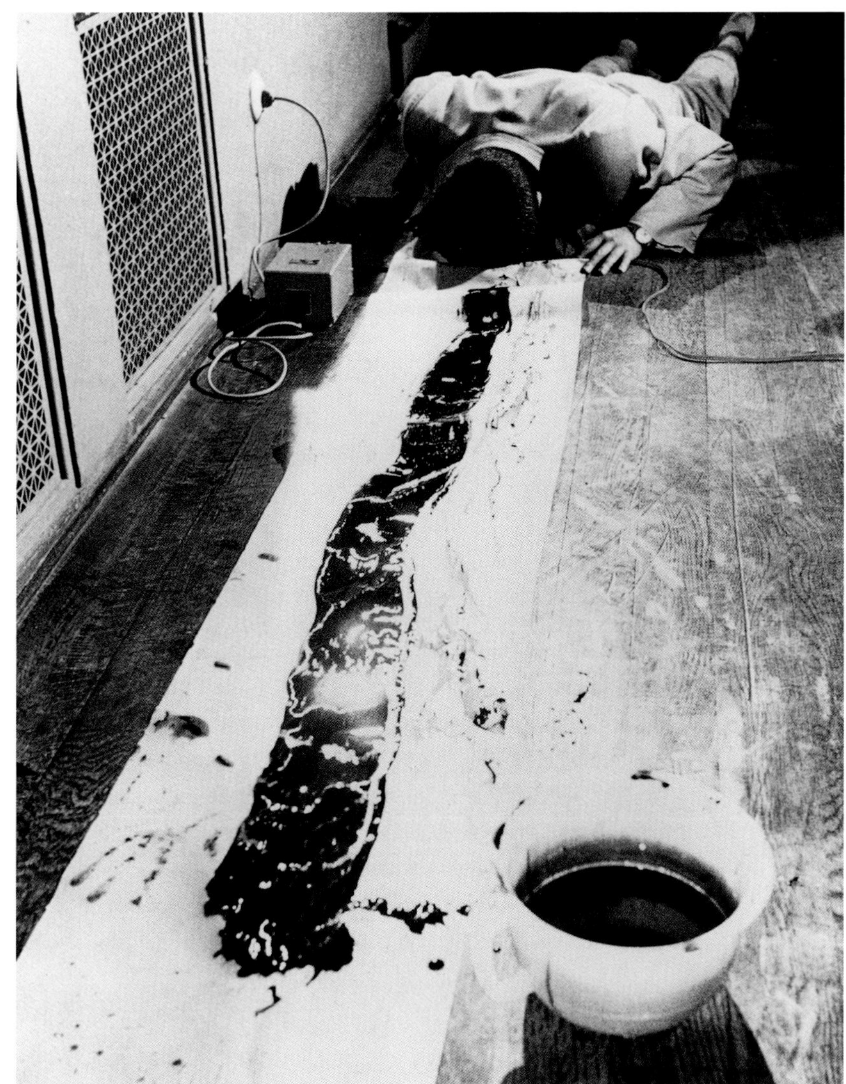

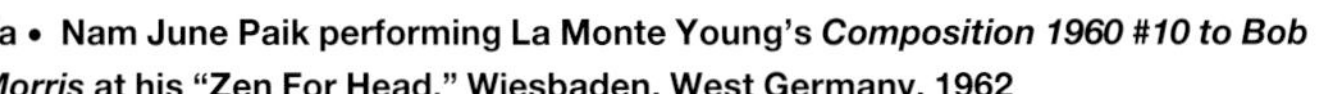
3a • Nam June Paik performing La Monte Young's ***Composition 1960 #10 to Bob Morris*** **at his "Zen For Head," Wiesbaden, West Germany, 1962**

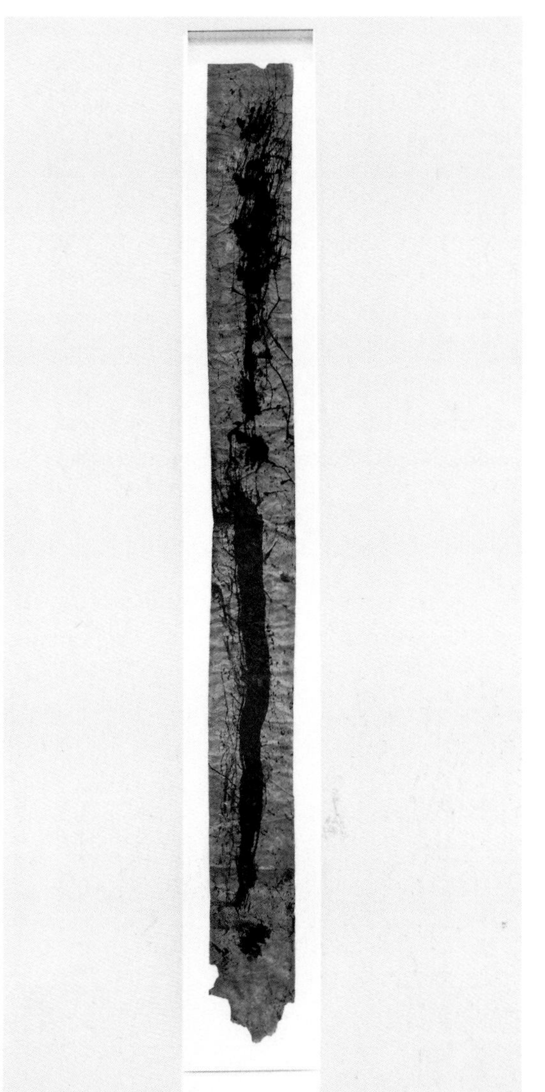
3b • Nam June Paik, *Zen for Head*, 1962
Ink and tomato on paper, 404 x 36 (159 x 14¹⁵⁄₁₆)

bodily and excremental discharge and the scientific processes of molecular transformation and chemical fusion.

The Fluxus movement emerged at the crucial moment when postwar artists were beginning to turn away from the hegemonic ▲ dominance of American Abstract Expressionism. This shift was prompted to a considerable degree by the publication of Robert Motherwell's anthology *The Dada Painters and Poets* in 1951, and more specifically by the teachings of the composer John Cage (an • early and avowed follower of Marcel Duchamp) at the New School for Social Research in New York between 1957 and 1959. A whole generation was now directed away from the overpowering pres- ■ ence of Jackson Pollock toward Dadaism in general and the work of Duchamp in particular, and was guided in this by the pervasive influences of Cage's models of chance operations, an aesthetic of ◆ the everyday, and a new type of (artistic) subjectivity.

Perhaps more surprising, however, than the programmatic recovery of Dada and Duchamp's readymade was Maciunas's early and explicit association of the Fluxus project with the most radical legacies of the Soviet avant-garde, those of the LEF (Left Front of ▲ the Arts) group and the Productivists, then barely known to anyone in either Europe or the United States. But this attempt to fuse the crucial features of Dada/Duchamp and Productivism, the most radical avant-garde models of the twentieth century, while being fully aware of the impossibility of achieving any of their historic aims in the present, may have generated the unique and paradoxical mix of the melancholic and the grotesque-comical that came to characterize Fluxus.

Another of the Fluxus group's many remarkable characteristics was its internationalism, since most other avant-gardes in the postwar period had either reasserted nationalist ideologies (for instance, American Abstract Expressionism) or had engaged with • discourses of traditional identity (such as Joseph Beuys). In manifest distinction, however, from Dada's hopeful aspirations for a post-nation state, or the proletarian internationalism of the Soviets, the internationalism of Fluxus might be described as *cataclysmic* rather than *utopian*, since it originated primarily in the artists' experiences of exile, of involuntary displacement from their ravaged homelands during and after World War II. This was clearly the case with

▲ 1947b • 1914, 1918, 1935, 1966a ■ 1949, 1960b ◆ 1953 ▲ 1921 • 1964a

▲ refugees like Maciunas and Daniel Spoerri, but it also held true, though in a very different way, for artists from Korea and Japan, such as Nam June Paik (born 1932), Yoko Ono (born 1933), Ay-O (born 1931), Shigeko Kubota (born 1937), Mieko Shiomi (born 1938), and others who joined Fluxus in subsequent years. The opposite form of *voluntary* displacement also contributed to the movement's internationalism: Emmett Williams (born 1925), Benjamin Patterson (born 1934), and Maciunas all lived and worked in postwar West Germany under the auspices of the US Army, while Robert Filliou (1926–87) first came into contact with Asian culture (as crucial for his own personal development as it was for Fluxus as a whole) when he was stationed in Korea on behalf of the United Nations Korean Reconstruction Agency in the early fifties.

Fluxus, use and amuse

Beyond its complex internationalism and its insistence on group practices, Fluxus also engaged from the beginning with a radical critique of conventional concepts of identity and (artistic) authorship. This took an antimasculinist, if not yet an explicitly feminist, stance. An outstanding example of this attitude was Shigeko Kubota's *Vagina Painting* [**4**], in which the artist brushed red paint onto a sheet of paper on the floor with a brush hanging from her crotch, thereby dismantling the seemingly never-ending • mythology of Pollock's virile painting performances with a single scandalous gesture.

4 • Shigeko Kubota, *Vagina Painting*, 1965
Performed during the "Perpetual Fluxus Festival," New York

Kubota first publicly executed this work at the Perpetual Fluxus Festival, held in 1965 at the New York Cinemathèque. In the same year, Maciunas announced the Fluxus project in the following "official" statement:

FLUXUS ART-AMUSEMENT

To establish artist's nonprofessional status in society,
he must demonstrate artist's dispensability and inclusiveness,
he must demonstrate the selfsufficiency of the audience,
he must demonstrate that anything can be art and that anybody can do it.

Therefore, art-amusement must be simple, amusing, unpretentious,
concerned with insignificances, require no skill or countless rehearsals, have no commodity or institutional value.
The value of art-amusement must be lowered by making it unlimited, massproduced, obtainable by all and eventually produced by all.

Fluxus art-amusement is the rear-guard without any pretention [sic]
or urge to participate in the competition of "one-upmanship" with the avant-garde. It strives for the monostructural and nontheatrical qualities of a simple natural event, a game or gag.
It is the fusion of Spike Jones, Vaudeville, gag, children's games and Duchamp.

If Productivism had insisted on the necessity of responding to the needs of the postrevolutionary proletarian masses by replacing aesthetic self-reflexivity with utilitarian production, and by changing the elitist distribution form of cultural texts and objects, ▲ Dadaism, by contrast, had attempted to posit popular and mass-cultural forms of exhibition and entertainment polemically against the institutionalization of high art and its separation from the sphere of everyday life. Accordingly, Fluxus set out to erase the traditional boundaries between linguistic and visual production, between text and object. Typically, it was one of Duchamp's late • works, his *Boîte-en-valise* (1935–41)—which, in the early sixties, was taken seriously by hardly anyone—that became a crucial point of departure for Fluxus reflections on the dialectics of object status, institutional frame, and distribution form.

But, exceeding Duchamp, Fluxus aimed to efface the last remaining divisions between the readymade (that is, the suspended utilitarian or commodity object) and the very means of its suspension (that is, the devices of framing and presentation); and one of the ways it did so was by collapsing the differences between the linguistic and discursive formations of the "work" and those of its containers—which is to say, the differences between the cultural discourses that declare "This is the art" and "This is the ■ frame." For Fluxus considered both framing and presentational devices, with their typography and graphic design, as *languages* in their own right, not just as separate and lesser *carriers* of a language

▲ 1960a • 1949, 1960b ▲ 1916a, 1920 • 1935 ■ Introduction 4, 1971

that takes the higher form of "art." It thereby equated work and frame, object and container. Yet at the same time, it dismantled the "magic" of the "art" object that has been made so *by* its presentational frames (such as the Surrealist vitrine or Joseph Cornell's ▲ boxes), and replaced these with an aesthetic of archival accumulation, one in which the textual, visual, or audio recording of a work's production and subsequent display or performance were as much part of the finished "art work" as the object or event itself (this aesthetic would receive its fullest articulation with Robert • Morris's *Card File* of 1962.

From *Store* to box

Positioning its production wholly within the sphere of consumer culture, Fluxus defined the commodity as the exclusive object-type and distribution form within which art could be produced and perceived. On several occasions, this took the form of simulating "institutional" and "commercial" frames of presentation and ■ distribution (Claes Oldenburg's *The Store* from 1961 was an important predecessor to these concerns): the Fluxshop, founded by Maciunas at 359 Canal Street in New York in 1965, Robert Watts's (1923–88) *Implosions*, the *Cédille qui sourit*, initiated by Robert Filliou and George Brecht (born 1926) in 1965 in Villefranche-sur-Mer in France—all of these "enterprises" posed as artistic schemes to produce and distribute a variety of radically democratized gadgets and objects.

Filliou's *Galerie légitime* **[5]** was another early example of Fluxus institutional critique. "Founded" in 1966, the "gallery" was in fact the artist's bowler hat (or sometimes his Japanese cap or his beret), which contained a variety of handmade objects, notations, and photographic records of his own works or those by other artists who had chosen, or whom he had chosen, to "exhibit" in one of its touring "exhibitions." Filliou himself described one of these "shows":

> *In July 1962, the Galerie légitime—a hat in this case—organized an exhibition of works by the American artist Benjamin Patterson. We walked round Paris from 4 o'clock in the morning until 9 at night, starting from Les Halles, finishing up at La Coupole.*

Both the gallery's perpetual mobility and its reduction of the work of art to a pure notation or documentary record are reminiscent of Duchamp's *Boîte-en-valise.* But the proximity of the institutional space and its "artistic objects" to the sphere of the artist's body (his head), and the fusion of the utilitarian object (the hat) with the frame of the institution (the "gallery"), imbued the *Galerie légitime* with a grotesque urgency: it not only insisted on the work's egalitarian intimacy with both the body and the utilitarian object, but also, at the same time, withdrew all perceptual presence from the alienating institutional, discursive, and economic frames beyond the quasi-umbilical container of the hat.

The self-deprecatory humor of Fluxus that regarded these radical activities as those of a "rear-guard" is evident in Maciunas's pronouncement that during the entire year of its operation the Fluxshop did not sell a single object from its vast array of low-priced boxes, books, gadgets, and multiples. It is equally present in Emmett Williams's proudly stated confession that there were often more performers than audience members at the early Fluxus festivals. One of Williams's most startling works from the early sixties, the *Counting Songs*, in which he counted aloud the members of the audience, was first performed at the "Six Pro- and Contragrammer Festival" at the Nikolai Kerke in Copenhagen in 1962. Appearing as though he were counting the audience in a modernist self-referential manner, Williams was actually doing so because he thought the organizers had cheated him out of his full share of the minimal admission charge.

5 • Robert Filliou, *Galerie légitime*, c. 1962–3
Assemblage, 4 x 26.5 x 26.5 ($1\frac{5}{8}$ x $10\frac{3}{8}$ x $10\frac{3}{8}$)

One could argue that Fluxus was the first cultural project in the postwar period to recognize that collective constructions of identity and social relations were now primarily and universally mediated through reified objects of consumption, and that this systematic annihilation of conventional forms of subjectivity necessitated an equally reified and internationally disseminated aesthetic articulation. In order to implement this, Fluxus had to dismantle *all* of the traditional conventions that had offered a cultural guarantee for the continuity of the bourgeois subject. First, it would have to rupture the foundationalist certainty that language itself had provided to literature and bourgeois subjectivity. This premise had remained ▲ more or less valid until the arrival of Dadaism and Gertrude Stein, both "rediscovered" by Fluxus. Their "rediscovery" was largely the result of the editorial interests of the poet and performer Dick Higgins (1938–98), one of Cage's students at the New School for Social Research in 1957, who from 1964 republished many important works such as Richard Huelsenbeck's *Dada Almanach* and Gertrude Stein's *The Making of Americans* through his exceptional Something Else Press publishing house.

But Fluxus also systematically eroded the securities of the literary genres, by scrambling all the codes and conventions that had categorized literary writing (such as poetry, drama, and the narrative

▲ 1931 • 1968b ■ 1961 ▲ 1907, 1916a

novel) and had confined "other" linguistic enunciations to the realm of the "nonliterary" (for instance, the journalistic documentary or factual narrative, private letters, the performative, or chance-derived texts): all of these became the bases of Fluxus activities.

The removal of the boundaries between these literary genres was not the result of a revolutionary aspiration toward a *Gesamtkunstwerk*, in which all of the arts of the past could be reunited within a structure that adequately responded to the actually existing social conditions of collective participation in the formation of wealth. Rather, the disintegration of boundaries in Fluxus acknowledged the rapid decline of options, the diminishing returns of the traditional genres and conventions, which have all, one by one, lost their license and historical credibility under the conditions of extreme separation and reification. It was in recognition of the impact of massive dedifferentiation—the process under advanced consumer capitalism whereby experience becomes homogenized, where everything in the world is made the same, without difference—that Fluxus articulated these diminishing options and discursive opportunities by collapsing all traditional genres and artistic conventions.

Shifting registers

Within each contested category of Fluxus activity, however, particular confrontations were systematically enforced. In fact, the highly diverse projects of the group's members helped bring about the most crucial change by shifting artistic production from the register of the object to registers operating somewhere between theatricality and musicality: if Duchamp had predicted in the mid-sixties that at some point in the near future the entire galaxy of objects would have to be considered as an inexhaustible resource of ▲ readymades, Fluxus had already responded by displacing this paradigm with an aesthetic of the universal "event" [**6**]. Indeed, when Robert Watts retrospectively defined the "Yam Festival"—a year-long festival planned for 1962–3, during which one performance or event was to be delivered each day—his description echoed Duchamp's statement almost exactly: "a loose format that would make it possible to combine or include an ever expanding universe of events." (Organized according to the principles of chance and play, the "Festival" culminated with a finale in May [that is, "Yam" spelled backward] 1963.)

This paradigm shift implied that the systematic destabilization of the visual object enacted by the readymade would find its equivalents in the theatrical register. Fluxus achieved this by fusing the most elementary forms of the linguistic performative with a virtual infinity of chance operations to forge a new dramaturgy of "event performances," recorded in "event scores." Actually formulated by Cage (that is, prior to Fluxus itself), the idea of the "event" became central to the aesthetics of his students, in particular George Brecht, Dick Higgins, and Jackson MacLow (born 1922). Higgins recalled how Cage's teachings first defined "events" as a new paradigm:

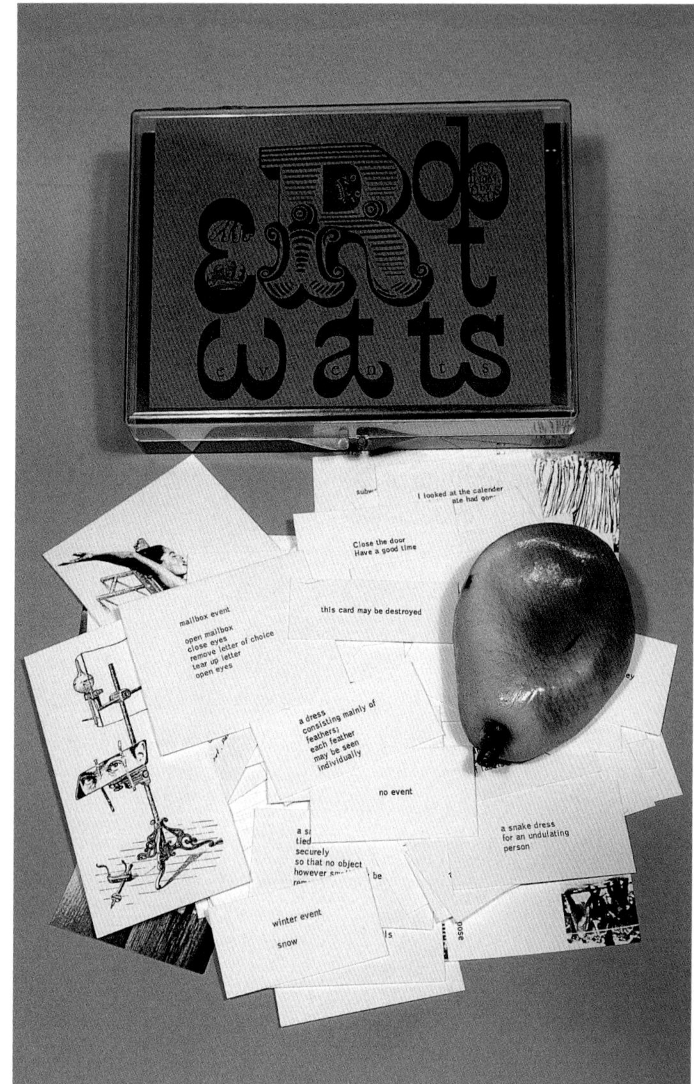

6 • Robert Watts, ***Robert Watts Events (Fluxus Edition)***, **1963**
Plastic box, offset labels, 97 offset cards, rubber pear, 13 x 28.6 x 17.9 (5⅛ x 11¼ x 7 1/16)

> *Cage used to talk about a lot of things going on at once and having nothing to do with each other. He called it "autonomous behaviour of simultaneous events."*

Brecht first identified the "event" as a new paradigm in his essay "Chance Imagery" (written in 1957 and published in 1966), defining it later as "very private, like little enlightenments I wanted to communicate to my friends, who would know what to do with them." One, by now classic example of Brecht's events was his *Drip Music (Drip Event)*, which he first proposed in 1959 and was "published" by Maciunas in 1963 in *Water Yam*, a collection of Brecht's "event score" cards and one of the earliest Fluxus boxes to be produced:

> *For single or multiple performance. A source of dripping water and an empty vessel are arranged so that the water falls into the vessel. Second Version: Dripping.*

This "event" marks precisely the transition from a chance aesthetic that—at the moment of "Chance Imagery"—was still defined ▲ primarily by the encounter with Pollock's painting toward a Cage-

▲ 1914

▲ 1949, 1960b

inspired aesthetic of chance operations that critiqued the idea of painting as a heroic site and an exceptional practice of virile authority and authorial identity. Brecht snatched the crucial dimensions of the ludic, the aleatory, and the performative away from the painterly spectacle that Pollock (or rather the reception of his work) had recently triggered and embedded them in the most intimate forms of the subject's experience of everyday reification.

Another example of such early "event scores," partially readable against the background of Abstract Expressionism's masculinist athletics, and testifying to Cage's impact on the artists of that generation, is the work of Alison Knowles (born 1933), who studied painting with Adolph Gottlieb at the Pratt Institute. Her *Proposition No. 2 (October 1962)*, also entitled *Make a Salad*, was first performed at the Institute of Contemporary Arts in London in 1962 and consisted "quite simply" of the public execution of the proposition by the artist. A year later, in *Proposition No. 6*, Knowles suggested another event, entitled *Shoes of Your Choice*:

> *A member of the audience is invited to come forward to a microphone if one is available and describe a pair of shoes, the ones he is wearing or another pair. He is encouraged to tell where he got them, the size, color, why he likes them, etc.*

In a later project, *Identical Lunch* (1968), Knowles demonstrated that anyone wanting to be an artist/performer need only to record the circumstances of an event or action to have produced a work:

> *The Identical Lunch: a tunafish sandwich on wheat toast with lettuce and butter, no mayo and a large glass of buttermilk or a cup of soup was and is eaten many days of each week at the same place and at about the same time.*

▲ At first glance one might associate these "event scores" with Pop art's early sixties rediscovery of the iconography of everyday life (such as Claes Oldenburg's persistent focus on American food as an iconic object). But it is precisely at this juncture where the profound differences between Fluxus and Pop become all the more transparent. While the Pop artists ultimately insisted that the spheres of painting and sculpture were essentially different from that of the readymade object, let alone from that of everyday objects, the Fluxus artists emphasized the exact opposite: that it was only on the level of the object itself that the experience of reification could be combated in the radical transformation of artistic objects (and genres) into events.

Thus Fluxus not only acknowledged the "poverty of reality" that the Surrealists had already bemoaned in the twenties, or the ● "poverty of experience" that Walter Benjamin had analyzed critically in the thirties, it also attempted to overcome these. Fluxus "events," in their quasi-religious devotion to the everyday, and in their emphasis on the repetitive and mechanistic forms of daily consumption and on the instrumentalized "simplicity" within which subjectivity is constituted and contained, resuscitated and articulated the individual subject's limited capacity to recognize the collectively prevailing conditions of "experience."

▲ 1960c, 1964b ● 1935

Sublimation and desublimation

Fluxus artists gave a dialectical answer to Pop art's inherent traditionalism and its implicit aestheticization of reification by dissolving both the artistic genres and the readymade object's centrality. In public acts that reintegrated the "object" within the flow of consciously "performed" everyday activities, Fluxus provided an artistic analogue to psychoanalysis' recovery of object relations or capacities of experience that have been split off from the subject through trauma or repression, or that have been simply "lost" in the general processes of socialization.

These dialectics of sublimation and desublimation are at the core of the difficulties with which Fluxus confronted its audiences ever since its first performances, and they are doubly overdetermined. On the one hand, Fluxus acknowledged that collective subjectivity has no access to space and time within which it can constitute itself other than in the leftover spaces and temporal structures that have remained mysteriously outside an ever-increasing process of commodification, and also that it is only in extremely decentered gestures that an *artistic* instantiation of a self-determining subject can be conceived and articulated.

On the other hand, it recognized this condition of being condemned to utter ephemerality, to extreme forms of linguistic, visual, and theatrical-musical fragmentation, and associated itself explicitly with counterforms of cultural experience, with the "low" arts of popular entertainment, of the gag, the joke, and vaudeville theater, at a moment when these antiquated forms appeared diverse and subversive in comparison with the massive homogeneity of postwar spectacle culture.

It is not surprising, therefore, that we find new and often hybrid models of (artistic) subjectivity and its critique in Fluxus: from Cage's infatuation with Zen Buddhism and the discovery of non-Western and nonbourgeois philosophical or religious conceptions to the political claims expressed by Maciunas (he was widely perceived throughout the sixties and seventies as a Marxist-Leninist), who attempted to collectivize artistic production, abolish the class character of culture, alter the work's distribution form, and deprofessionalize the artist in order to transform the social division of labour that had positioned the artist in the role of the exceptional specialist of cognitive and perceptual competence.

Such hybridity was a particularly notable feature of Fluxus typography and graphic design. These had been two of the areas in ▲ which the Dadaists and the Soviet Productivists had enacted their own radical aesthetic, semiotic, and political aspirations. For them, typeface and layout functioned as the forms and grounds on which the first steps of a collective perceptual and linguistic revolution were to be taken. In this respect, once again, these two early avant-gardes provided a model for Fluxus. But its typography and design also engaged in a dialogue with yet another avant-garde, Surrealism, as mediated through the work of the collage novels of Max Ernst and through Duchamp's collaborator on the *Boîte*, Joseph ● Cornell, who was of considerable importance in the formation of

▲ 1920, 1921, 1926, 1928 ● 1931, 1935

the early work of Brecht and Watts. Surrealism's use of *obsolescence* as an oppositional practice against contemporaneity as mere fashion and compulsory consumption came to characterize the objects and presentational devices of Fluxus as well. One example of this was Maciunas's paradoxical insertion of late-nineteenth-century steel engravings from popular advertisements and illustrations into his otherwise rigorous designs for Fluxus publications, publicity, and pronouncements, which he produced on the then newly developed IBM Composer typewriter. This machine imbued all of Maciunas's typographic designs, from La Monte Young's *An Anthology* in 1962 onward, with an administrative rationalization and immediacy that would become compulsory under the reign of Conceptualism.

The name cards designed by Maciunas for his colleagues around 1966 **[7]** illuminate both Fluxus' distance from its radical predecessors and the paradoxes of its wider project. Maciunas might have envisaged the movement as a collective, aiming at anonymity in order to dissolve the cult of artistic subjectivity, but the actual group of original Fluxus participants consisted of a very loose-knit association of extremely independent and autonomous figures, and each of them was given a separate and unique identity through the typography and design of Maciunas's cards. The spectrum of typefaces used ranged from nineteenth-century ornamental type (as in one of two cards designed for Robert Watts) to the more bureaucratic, rationalized, and serialized sans-serif type of Maciunas's IBM machine. He used the latter to spell out Robert Filliou's name ten times, each one followed by a question mark, and an eleventh time, only now followed by an exclamation mark. In the typographical design of these name cards, individual subjectivity hovers somewhere between allegorical ornament and corporate trademark, between Fluxus' utopian abolition of the exceptional artist and the existing rule of corporate culture, which dismantles any form of subjective

7 • George Maciunas, *Name Cards of Fluxus Artists*, c. 1966

experience. To have brought out the precariousness of this historical dialectic is one of the movement's many achievements.

Another example of early Fluxus typography, one that shows the extent to which design constituted an integral element of the group's project, was the *Yam Festival Newspaper*, coproduced by Brecht and Watts in 1963, which served primarily to publicize the activities and products of the "Yam Festival." Simulating the format of an antiquated small-town broadsheet, the *Newspaper* ▲ performed a Situationist-like *détournement* of the traditional daily newspaper's framework of text and image with its fusion of information and ideology, advertisements and cartoons. Constructing in typography and design a parallel to the playful and chance-derived "Festival," the *Yam Newspaper* restructured the way a traditional newspaper is normally read (the way a reader is deliberately led through its pages in a particular direction) by adopting a scroll format, constant reversals of the reading axis, and repeated fragmentation. It thus enacted on the level of reading the very same principles of chance and play that governed the "Festival" itself as a collective liberation from the regulation and control of experience in everyday life.

The dialectics of radicality

Contradictions of theory and practice characterized the Fluxus project. Vehemently opposed to the object-ness and commodity status of the work of art, Fluxus nonetheless produced endless commodities of the lowest and cheapest sort. Insisting on the universal accessibility of artistic objects across geopolitical and class boundaries, Fluxus nonetheless became one of the most inaccessible and esoteric cultural formations of the twentieth century. Demanding collectivist group identity and the demolition of the artist as cult figure, Maciunas nonetheless maintained a petulant control over the group that matched earlier examples of avant-garde authoritarianism in the context of Dada and Surrealism (for example, the orthodox • fanaticism of Tristan Tzara and André Breton) and corresponded to Guy Debord's autocratic control over the Situationist International.

But one of the most difficult aspects of Fluxus to assess is the ■ vandalism of its (quasi-Futurist) desire to annihilate European high-art (and avant-garde) traditions. When Maciunas formulated his *Fluxus Manifesto* in 1963 [**8**], he revealed both the radicality of his ideas and—involuntarily—their "avant-gardiste" deficiencies:

> *Purge: the world of bourgeois sickness, "intellectual," professional & commercialized culture, PURGE the world of dead art, imitation, artificial art, abstract art, illusionistic art, mathematical art, — PURGE THE WORLD OF "EUROPANISM"!*

Though Fluxus claimed to have successfully eliminated all the experiential differences between aesthetic and everyday objects, it did so without fully reflecting on the radically altered conditions of production and experience that emerge in an advanced culture industry. In making its own coincidental events and ephemeral objects an aesthetic standard, Fluxus risked becoming an unknowing part of a larger social project of enforced dedifferentiation and desublimation. The group could be misperceived, therefore, as having implicitly endorsed the prominent social tendency that relegates the artistic object to the realm of the ephemeral, dischargeable and disposable along with all other objects among the infinity of commodities.

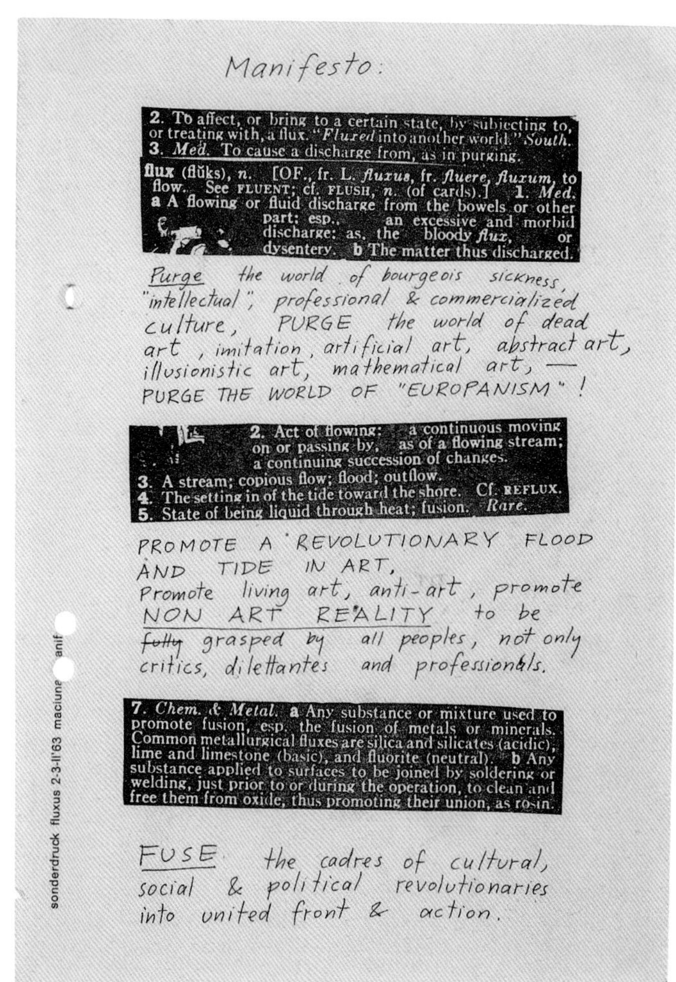

Manifesto:

2. To affect, or bring to a certain state, by subjecting to, or treating with, a flux. "*Fluxed* into another world." *South.*
3. *Med.* To cause a discharge from, as in purging.

flux (flŭks), *n.* [OF., fr. L. *fluxus*, fr. *fluere, fluxum*, to flow. See FLUENT; cf. FLUSH, *n.* (of cards).] **1.** *Med.* **a** A flowing or fluid discharge from the bowels or other part; esp., an excessive and morbid discharge: as, the bloody *flux*, or dysentery. **b** The matter thus discharged.

Purge the world of bourgeois sickness, "intellectual", professional & commercialized culture, PURGE the world of dead art, imitation, artificial art, abstract art, illusionistic art, mathematical art, — PURGE THE WORLD OF "EUROPANISM"!

2. Act of flowing: a continuous moving on or passing by, as of a flowing stream; a continuing succession of changes.
3. A stream; copious flow; flood; outflow.
4. The setting in of the tide toward the shore. Cf. REFLUX.
5. State of being liquid through heat; fusion. *Rare.*

PROMOTE A REVOLUTIONARY FLOOD AND TIDE IN ART, Promote living art, anti-art, promote NON ART REALITY to be ~~fully~~ grasped by all peoples, not only critics, dilettantes and professionals.

7. *Chem. & Metal.* **a** Any substance or mixture used to promote fusion, esp. the fusion of metals or minerals. Common metallurgical fluxes are silica and silicates (acidic), lime and limestone (basic), and fluorite (neutral). **b** Any substance applied to surfaces to be joined by soldering or welding, just prior to or during the operation, to clean and free them from oxide, thus promoting their union, as rosin.

FUSE the cadres of cultural, social & political revolutionaries into united front & action.

sonderdruck fluxus 2-3-II'63 maciun anif

8 • George Maciunas, *Fluxus Manifesto*, February 1963
Offset on paper

FURTHER READING

Elizabeth Armstrong and Joan Rothfuss (eds), *In the Spirit of Fluxus* (Minneapolis: Walker Art Center, 1993)

Jon Hendricks (ed.), *Fluxus Codex: The Gilbert and Lila Silverman Collection* (New York: Harry N. Abrams, 1988)

Thomas Kellein, *Fluxus* (London: Thames & Hudson, 1995)

Thomas Kellein (ed.), *Fröhliche Wissenschaft: Das Archiv Sohm* (Stuttgart: Staatsgalerie Stuttgart, 1987)

Emmett Williams and Ann Noël (eds), *Mister Fluxus: A Collective Portrait of George Maciunas* (London: Thames & Hudson, 1995)

▲ 1957a ● 1916a, 1924 ■ 1909

1962b

In Vienna, a group of artists including Günter Brus, Otto Mühl, and Hermann Nitsch come together to form Viennese Actionism.

The formation of the Wiener Aktionsgruppe (Viennese Actionists group) follows what seems to have been the inexorable course of all postwar artistic activities, facing, on the one hand, the ruined conditions of the European avant-garde, either obliterated or destroyed by fascism and totalitarianism, and on the other hand the overwhelming promises of the American neo-avant-garde, in its emergence during the period of European reconstruction. In Vienna—as elsewhere—the seemingly universal impact of, in Allan Kaprow's words, "The Legacy of Jackson Pollock" became central (either by the direct encounter with his work, or via its highly misread mediations in the paintings of Georges Mathieu [born 1931] and Yves Klein, who exhibited in Vienna to great acclaim in the late fifties). Other European artists such as Manolo Millares (1926–72) and Alberto Burri (1915–95) (strangely enough Lucio Fontana was never mentioned) were equally cited by the Viennese Actionists as providing license for the destruction of the canvas and the spatialization of the painterly process.

The desecration of painting as ritual

The first steps for the evacuation, if not outright destruction, of easel painting, its traditional formats, materials, and processes, were taken by the Viennese artists Günter Brus (born 1938), Otto Mühl (born 1925), and Hermann Nitsch (born 1938) around 1960. From then on, painting would be forced to regress to infantile smearing (Brus), to aleatory processes of application (as in the staining and pouring of the *Schüttbilder* [Pouring Paintings] by Nitsch), or to the actual defacement of the surface in the tearing and cutting of painting's support, the shift from relief to object (Mühl), making it evident that the canvas itself had become *one* surface among other surfaces, merely an object littered with other objects.

As a second step, the Viennese recognized the necessity of noncompositionality to the decentering of perspectival order. They deployed the principles of permutations as well as (predominantly violent) chance operations. The third, and possibly most important, step was their push for painting's inevitable expansion into public space, theatrical if not social. Yet the perceptual parameters of that spatial expansion initially seem to have remained opaque to the artists, since they either ignored or disregarded all earlier historical transformations of the interrelationships between painterly space and social space (for example, the work of El Lissitzky and that of the Soviet avant-garde in general).

Paradoxically, in spite of the Viennese histrionics about the absolute originality of their inventions, the actual works produced in the period prior to the development of the Viennese Actionist movement are in many instances similar to slightly earlier work by American artists: the paintings by Brus and Adolf Frohner (born 1934) exacerbate the desublimatory effects of the somatic graphemes of Cy Twombly in the late fifties, and Mühl's and Nitsch's *Materialbilder* (Material Pictures) uncannily resemble (if not repeat) the funk and neo-Dada assemblages by artists such as Jasper Johns, Robert Rauschenberg, Bruce Conner, or Allan Kaprow. Clearly, the Viennese Actionists misread Pollock's latent, yet inexorable spectacularization of painting as a celebratory legitimation of art's return to ritual (which Pollock's own rhetoric had fueled). The Viennese writer and theoretician Oswald Wiener (born 1935)—a founding member of the Wiener Gruppe who subsequently became to some extent the aesthetic and theoretical mastermind of the Viennese Actionists—had already declared in his *Cool Manifesto* in 1954 that artistic production would have to move away from *objects*, to focus on the work of art as an *event structure*. Thus, Wiener anticipates the prophecy of Kaprow's essay "The Legacy of Jackson Pollock" (written in 1956, published in 1958), stating that "not only will these bold creators show us, as if for the first time, the world we have always had about us but ignored, but they will disclose entirely unheard of *happenings and events*."

With the example of Pollock established, American artists began to engage painting's performance structure—with its implications of action and duration—as early as 1952 (for example when John Cage enacted his protohappening *Theatre Piece No.1* with Robert Rauschenberg, Mary Caroline Richards, Merce Cunningham, and others at Black Mountain College). This was followed in 1959 by the first such work to use the term "happening" (coined by its maker): Allan Kaprow's *18 Happenings in 6 Parts* at the Reuben Gallery in New York. It is important to acknowledge immediately the specific differences between the early "happenings" of Kaprow, Dine, and Oldenburg and the performances of the Viennese

▲ 1961 ● 1960a ■ 1959a ▲ 1921, 1926 ● 1953 ■ 1958, 1959b ◆ 1947a

1 • Otto Mühl, *Materialaktion*, 1965
Photographic documents

Actionists, beginning in 1962. While the Americans' "happenings" focus on the clash between the body and technology, the mechanical and the mass-cultural environment (for instance, Jim Dine's *Car Crash*, Claes Oldenburg's *Photo Death* and his installation ▲ *The Street*) the artists of Viennese Actionism emphasize the return to ritual and theatricality right from the beginning. Furthermore, even in their very first performances, the Viennese Actionists single out the body itself and treat it as an analytic object, as the libidinal site where the intersection between psychosomatic subjectivity and social subjection can be dramatically enacted.

There are several reasons for these differences. The first is that the Actionists linked action painting and *tachisme* with the specifically local and regional Austrian Expressionist tradition. One of Vienna's foundational cultural characteristics had been the fusion of Catholicism and patriarchy with a powerful and hierarchical imperial order, a fusion that had been internalized and perpetuated most within its bourgeois class. From the beginning of the twentieth century, Viennese Expressionism had opposed these power structures and constituted itself within a poignant and lasting dialectic: on the one hand was a hypertrophic cult of the sexual body, touting its compulsions as subversive of the bourgeois regimes of sublimation and repression; on the other hand was a simultaneous loathing of the body and of sexuality as the very structures where social order and repression were most deeply anchored and acted out in compulsive behavior and neurotic suffering. This Expressionist tradition—beginning with Oskar Kokoschka's 1909 play and poster, revealingly titled *Murderer, the* • *Hope of Woman*, and with the extraordinary drawings of Egon Schiele and Alfred Kubin—served as *one* crucial horizon and point of departure for Viennese Actionism.

Psychoanalysis and polymorphous perversity

The second reason for the cultural divide between the American and Viennese artists is the fact that the Viennese Actionists emerged from a culture of psychoanalysis. The rediscovery of the prewar theories of Sigmund Freud and the rearticulation of psychoanalysis in its various strands and deviations from Wilhelm Reich (who would become crucial for Mühl) to Carl G. Jung (whose theory of unconscious archetypes was of particular importance to Nitsch), are certainly another defining element in Viennese Actionism. Yet the conception of the body in Viennese Actionism is distinctly post-Freudian, since it foregrounds the polymorph perverse origins of the libidinal structure rather than, as Freud had required, conceiving of sexuality as a teleological trajectory in which the subject's earlier and "primitive" stages of instinctual development are surpassed, culminating in a presumably hegemonic and heterosexual genitality. The new postlinguistic theatricality of the Viennese Actionists originates precisely in a recourse to these partial drives, in an almost programmatic and ostentatious regression to, not to say propagandistic staging of, the primitive phases of sexual development. This particular

▲ 1961 ● 1900a

confrontation reminds us of course of a similar conflict between André Breton's Surrealist psychoanalytic theories and Georges ▲ Bataille's and Antonin Artaud's derisive critique of Surrealism and of Freudian orthodoxy. Yet the Actionists were equally influenced by Breton's Surrealism (ignoring Bataille) and of Artaud's "Theatre of Cruelty." They seem to have worked through both positions in the process of formulating the project of Actionism.

Lastly, and perhaps most importantly, the Viennese Actionists positioned themselves and their work quite explicitly within the sociohistorical framework of postfascist Austria. Thus Otto Mühl, the oldest member of the group, spent two years in the German Army during the war and later stated that his Actionism was his personal response to the experience of fascism. After 1945, Austria, like Germany, had been occupied by the four Allies. From the fifties onwards it was systematically restructured according to the laws of a liberal democracy.

Adopting the principles of the so-called free market society, the conduct of everyday life in Austria was rapidly forced into the American mold of compulsive consumption. As was the case in post-Nazi Germany, Austrians seem to have been convinced that this transition could be achieved most efficiently by embracing the principles of solid repression and via a massive amnesia about their own recent fascist past, both in its self-generated variety of Austro-Fascism and in its externally imposed version of the 1938 German Nazi *Anschluss* (Annexation), and the catastrophic consequences of both.

The extraordinary violence with which the work of the Actionists confronts its spectators thus seems to originate in a dialectic that is particular to the postfascist cultures of Europe: on the one hand, the Viennese Actionists seem to have recognized that experience could be resuscitated only by breaking through the armor of collectively enforced repression. Therefore, the ritualistic reenactment of brutal and excessive forms of human defilement and the theatrical debasement of the human body would become mandatory, since all cultural representation from that point onward would have to be measured against the destruction of the subject, which had now been historically established on a massive scale. On the other hand, Viennese Actionism voluntarily seems to have enforced the total reritualization of artistic practices under the newly emerging aegis of spectacle culture. While the grotesque performances of Georges Mathieu and Yves Klein seemed to indicate at least an ironic glimpse of understanding their condition, there is little evidence that the Viennese Actionists actually grasped this external determination.

Gesamtkunstwerk and travesty

As early as 1960, Nitsch had begun to produce his variations on the legacies of *tachisme* and action painting by pouring (mostly blood-red) paint directly onto (or rather *into*) his canvases. The blood-stained appearance of these *Schüttbilder*—as Nitsch would call them—attempted to simulate sacrifice using modernist monochromy. These paintings declared that a flat canvas was not just an object of neopositivist self-reflexivity but that it should become, once again, a vessel of ritualistic and transcendental experience. Accordingly, Nitsch's titles, such as *Stations of the Cross*, *Wall of Flagellation*, and *Triptych of the Blood of the Cross*, situate each work programmatically outside of modernist painting and reclaim its putative access to the spheres of the sacred, of myth, and of liturgical performance. Nitsch would later state in his "Blood Organ Manifesto" in 1962:

> *Through my art production (a form of devotion to life) I take upon myself that which appears to be a negative, perverse and obscene lust and the sacrificial hysteria resulting from it, so as to spare you the defilement and shame of a descent into the extreme.*

By contrast, Mühl's first *Materialbilder* (begun in the summer of 1961) owe more to his encounter with the idiom of junk sculpture, ▲ by then universally practiced in the work of Jean Tinguely in Paris ● and David Smith, Richard Stankiewicz, and John Chamberlain in New York, all of whom had introduced contemporary industrial refuse to form countermachinic sculptures by that time. Rather than continuing as a painter/sculptor in the assemblage tradition of ■ Kurt Schwitters, whom the Viennese venerated as one of their greatest predecessors, Mühl subsequently identified himself only as a "poet and director" beginning in 1963. Already pointing in the direction of his subsequent *Materialaktionen* (Material Action Performances), he describes his assemblage work in the following terms: "a sensual expansion and movement in space, ground up, mixed up, broken up, piled up, scratched, hacked up and blown up." Mühl declares his artistic project to be one of *destructivism* ◆ (presumably in opposition to *Constructivism*) and he announces its anarchist and nihilist dogma to be one of "absolute revolt, total disobedience, and systematic sabotage.... All art will be destroyed, annihilated, terminated and something new will begin."

Deriving directly from the Futurist proclamation that *industrial* materials are equally valid for artistic production, Mühl now celebrates the incorporation of the most banal substances of everyday consumer culture. Thus, in Mühl's theatrical performances (which he called "Happenings" after 1963, when Kiki Kogelnik [1935–77], an Austrian artist living in New York, told him about Kaprow's term), it is no longer the forces of industrialization, but the universal regime of commodification that sets the terms for the individual's subjection. At the moment of the breakthrough from action painting to *Materialaktion*, Mühl states that "meals and meat, vegetables and sauces, jam and breadcrumbs, liquid paint and powdered pigment, paper, rags, dust, wood, stones, whipped cream, milk, oil, smoke, fire, tools, machines, airplanes etc., etc." are all equally valid for the production of a *Materialaktion*. And we find a very similar position in the writings of Nitsch at that time when he states that "all the normal substances of everyday life, like oil and vinegar, wine and honey, egg yolks and blood, meat as matter, intestines, and talcum powder were discovered for Actionism because of their substance and material sensuality." Both statements inevitably recall once again Allan Kaprow's essay

▲ 1924, 1930b

▲ 1960a ● 1945 ■ 1926 ◆ 1921

"The Legacy of Jackson Pollock" and *its* lists of newly discovered materials from everyday life:

> *We shall utilize the specific substances of sight, sound, movements, people, odors, touch. Objects of every sort are materials for the new art: paint, chairs, food, electric and neon lights, smoke, water, old socks, a dog, movies, a thousand other things that will be discovered by the present generation of artists.*

Mühl's *Materialaktionen* from 1963 onward deploy two crucial strategies, that of *Entzweckung* (disfunctionalization) and that of *Entwirklichung* (derealization). Both detach objects and materials from their common functions and achieve the estrangement effect for performances of everyday activities within the context of the *Materialaktion*, aiming quite explicitly at a newly experienced immediacy of sensation and cognition comparable to ▲ the tradition of the Soviet Formalist model of *ostranenie*. Despite their explicit antitheatrical claims, and beyond the tremendous impact on the Viennese Actionists at large of the theories and writings of Artaud, the *Materialaktionen* seem to fuse the endless despair of Samuel Beckett's *Endgame* (1958) or *Happy Days* (1961) with a Viennese variation of Buster Keaton's and Charlie Chaplin's slapstick comedies (such as "Modern Times" of 1936) about the subject's hapless and helpless submission to the forces of advanced industrialization [**1**].

Viennese Actionism thus operates across a spectrum ranging from the sacred to the grotesque. Nitsch's *Orgien Mysterien Theater* (Orgies Mysteries Theater), sincerely attempting to reconstitute the intensity of experience once offered by catharsis in the classical tragedies, the redeeming rituals of Christianity, opera, and Baroque theater, occupies one extreme of that spectrum. The simultaneous totality of objects, materials, and actions, and the ensuing conditions of synesthesia, inevitably lead to a new conception of the *Gesamtkunstwerk* (and Nitsch of course considered Richard Wagner a heroic precursor worthy of following). In Nitsch's modern mystery shows, acoustic and optical, haptic and olfactory perceptions are fused with a range of activities on the stage that shift from ritual to provocation, from mere object performance to hieratic celebration. As Nitsch states: "Everything comes together in the reality of our actions. Poetry becomes painting, or painting becomes poetry, music becomes action, action painting becomes theater, informal theater becomes primarily an optical event." [**2**]

By contrast, Mühl's cornucopia of negated objects, and his proliferation of matters of consumption, often engulfing, if not actually physically burying the performers, of course demarcates the opposite extreme of the spectrum. Even the titles of the *Materialaktionen* manifestly separate them from the project of Nitsch's *Orgien Mysterien Theater: The Swamping of a Nude, OMO* (named after what was then the most "prominent" laundry detergent), *Mama and Papa*, or *Leda and the Swan*. All of these stagings of scandal, public defilement, and the denigration of the subjects' bodies perform grotesque exorcisms of consumption more in the manner of a travesty or a satyr-play than that of ritualistic redemption and tragedy.

2 • Hermann Nitsch, *4. Aktion*, 1963
Performance

Positivism and pathology

The joint performance of Nitsch, Mühl, and Frohner, called *Die Blutorgel* (The Blood Organ) in 1962 is clearly the founding event of Viennese Actionism. Nitsch describes the work as a collective festival, deploying scientific models derived from depth- and mass-psychology, to reignite that experience that cults from antiquity through Christianity had presumably offered. In opposition to what Nitsch perceives as the "collective inability to experience and the collective fear of existence," his *Orgien Mysterien Theater* sought to induce its public "through the ritualistic organization of elementary sensuous forms to attain a breakthrough to life as a continuous celebratory festivity."

By 1966, Mühl had initiated—in collaboration with Oswald Wiener—a project of countercultural activism, called *ZOCK* (an acronym that Peter Weibel (born 1944) took to mean "destruction of order, Christianity and culture," but also a verb, "*zocken*," that means to hit, beat, or play cards in German slang). *ZOCK* takes its ▲ cues explicitly from Dada's antiartistic stances, yet in its pronunciations it reminds us once again of the grandiloquent anticultural • prophecies of Futurism. Thus, Wiener and Mühl announce in their manifesto that "all opera houses, theaters, museums, and libraries should be razed," and they continue their polemic by listing the ■ artists from Pop art and Minimalist art to Land art and Conceptual art as the worst enemies of their own anticultural venture.

▲ Introduction 3, 1915

▲ 1916a, 1920 • 1909 ■ 1960c, 1964b, 1965, 1967a, 1968b, 1970

The centrality of Oswald Wiener as a theoretician of both the Wiener Gruppe and of the Viennese Actionists (a role continued slightly later by Weibel who was to become the most complex critic and historian of both groups, at the same time developing an artistic practice that attempts to overcome the Actionists' historical and geopolitical limitations) points to yet another condition that is very specific to the Vienna avant-garde. At first glance one might assume that the neopositivist approach to poetic language practiced in the Wiener Gruppe and the Viennese Actionists' celebration of the prelinguistic world of polymorph perverse sexuality would be mutually exclusive. In fact, they form the halves not just of the general dialectics of enlightenment, but more specifically of the epistemological duality that has marked Viennese culture since the late nineteenth century, best embodied in the simultaneous emergence of the psychoanalytical project of Freud and the epistemological project of Ernst Mach, whose empirico-criticism had insisted on a theory of intelligibility that was defined solely by material evidence, rather than by metaphysical or historical concepts.

The third—and possibly the most complex—figure of the group, Günter Brus, seems to have been initiated into Actionism under the tutelage of the older Mühl, who in 1964 insisted that Brus abandon his late *Informel Labyrinth Paintings* in favor of direct performance-based actions. From the beginning, Brus explicitly aligned painting with sexuality, stating that painting is a form of masturbation, since both take place in utter privacy. His first performance, *Ana* in 1964, marks his initial step into Actionism.

Brus shifted the painterly process directly onto the performing body (most often the artist's own), exhibiting himself, painted white, in rooms covered with the same paint. Performing in front of his paintings at the Galerie Junge Generation in Vienna in 1965, he paid tribute to the work of Arnulf Rainer (born 1929) (whose *Übermalungen* [overpaintings] were held in great esteem by all of the Actionists). Gradually expanding the sites of his performance activities, Brus positioned himself and his work in direct confrontation with public social space. In his work *Spaziergang* (Promenade; 1965), the artist, painted white, with a black line inscribing a vertical split and dividing his body in half, walked through the streets of Vienna, where he was promptly arrested by the police. What distinguished Brus's work from that of his peers in the movement is that from the very beginning he situated his activities outside of any theatrical enactment, and beyond any promises of a healing redemption by ritual [**3**].

Brus began his project of *Total Aktion* in 1966, once again in collaboration with Mühl. Their first joint performance, staged at the Adolf Loos Villa on June 2, 1966, is significantly titled *Ornament is a Crime*, adding the verb and indefinite article to Loos's famous title ▲ ("Ornament and Crime") to imbue it with a renewed urgency and concreteness. *Total Aktion* combines elements of Nitsch's *Orgien Mysterien Theater* with Mühl's *Materialaktion.* Language is here reduced to its most elementary prelinguistic sounds of stuttering, hissing, heavy breathing, screaming, bordering on a public enactment of psychologist Dr. Arthur Janov's "primal therapy," from *The Primal Scream* (1970).

3 • Günter Brus, *Untitled*, 1965
Photographic documentation of various performance works

4 • Günter Brus, cover of *Der Irrwisch*, Kohlkunst Verlag, Frankfurt, 1971

▲ 1900a

Brus's most important contribution to the culture of postwar Vienna is undoubtedly his prolific output of extraordinary drawings (such as his book *Der Irrwisch* [1971]), in which the martyrium of contemporaneity is recorded in the lapidary manner of a draughtsman for the courtroom in which photography is prohibited **[4]**. Or equally adequate (since the cult of mental alterity in children and deranged adults is yet another central cultural topos among the Actionists), the drawings appear to be made in the manner of those of mental patients, for whom compulsively executed detail promises the highest realization of a vision or the closest proximity to the object of desire.

If there is any oeuvre of drawing in the twentieth century with which Brus's drawings could be compared, it would be the compulsively detailed erotic drawings of Pierre Klossowski (1905–2001), even though they were certainly unknown to Brus (since they were mostly inaccessible during the sixties). Brus's conception of sexuality and bodily experience opens up all the registers of the repressed histories of individual and collective libidinal development. When the body in Brus's drawings is subjected to an infinity of acts of torture and abject degradation, the inflictions suffered by the subject appear, almost always, as highly mechanical not to say neuro-motoric. As a result it becomes apparent that Brus's imaginary torture machines correlate to the actually existing social orders that regulate, dominate, and control the subject's libidinal apparatus. His extreme formulations articulate, in a dialectical manner, the repressions at the root of unquestioned normalcy within the conditions regulating everyday life in late capitalist society.

Reminiscent in that regard of Bertolt Brecht's famous question, "What is the murder of a man by comparison to his lifelong employment?", the semblance of horror in Brus's drawings and Mühl's *Materialaktionen*, the depth of their revulsion and their apparently appalling regressions into the deepest recesses of a polymorph perverse history of the subject, at the same time articulate a manifest opposition to the subject's scandalous reduction, in the process of assimilation, to enforced heterosexuality, to the rules of the monogamous family, to the seeming supremacy of genitality and patriarchal order, and worst of all, to the subjection and extreme reduction of the libidinal complexity of the subject to socially "acceptable" and "desirable" roles and activities (for example, enforced consumption and the total passivity of experience under the regime of spectacle culture).

A turning-point in Viennese Actionism, undoubtedly prepared by the radical contemporaneity and analytical precision of Brus's work, would emerge in the late sixties with the arrival of a younger generation of artists, such as Valie Export (born 1940) and Peter Weibel. It appears that for Export and Weibel, Actionism's perpetual entanglement with reritualization by that time had become as insufferable as the latent, if not manifest, patriarchal sexism that had gone on unquestioned in all of their activities. As had been the case with Surrealism, latent sexism had driven even the Actionists' most radical attempts to trace the formation of a subject's sexuality in patriarchal capitalist society. In this trajectory, Export's extraordinary *Tapp und Tastkino* (Pat and Paw Cinema) **[5]** appears as a paradigmatic reversal of almost all the principles of Viennese Actionism. In her public self-exposure (in a street performance her breasts are being offered to anyone who wants to touch them through the openings of a box entitled the "pat and paw cinema"), the radicality of Brus's self-sacrificial auto-analysis, and the specificity of its transfer into the public social spaces where the self is constituted, are both exceeded and displaced. This happens, first of all, via Export's brilliant shift from ritualistic self-exposure to the real registers where social control and oppression are most powerfully inscribed within sexual behavior. Moreover, the performance makes it blatantly obvious that the engagement with rituals of redemption or cathartic healing no longer have any purchase in a world of advanced technological and industrialized spectacle culture. And lastly, Export, more than anybody among the Actionists, manifestly recodes the radical dimension of self-sacrifice that had been exemplarily performed by Brus. She exchanges ritual for emancipatory shock, by bringing about in her spectators/participants a sudden insight into those registers of socialization where the socialized forms of sexual repression and the eternal infantilization of the subject are anchored with industrial means.

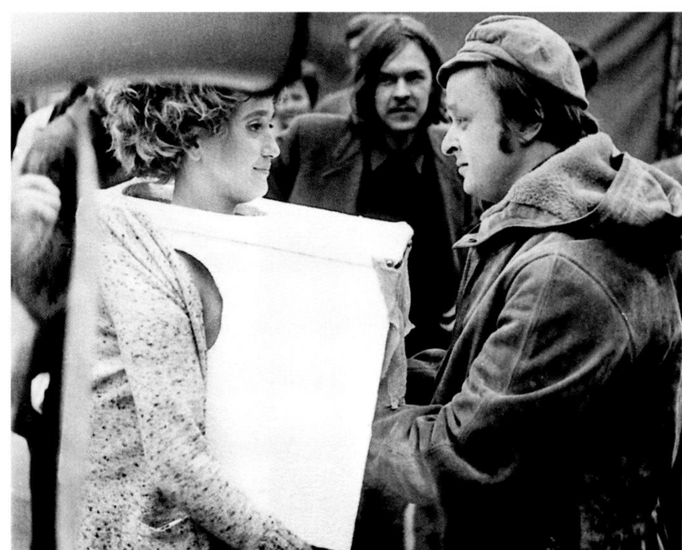

5 • Valie Export, *Tapp und Tastkino*, 1968
Body action

FURTHER READING

Kerstin Braun, *Der Wiener Aktionismus* (Vienna: Böhlau Verlag, 1999)
Malcolm Green, (ed.), *Brus Mühl Nitsch Schwarzkogler: Writings of the Vienna Actionists* (London: Atlas Press, 1999)
Dieter Schwarz et al., *Wiener Aktionismus/Vienna Actionism* (Winterthur: Kunstmuseum; Edinburgh: Scottish National Gallery of Modern Art; and Klagenfurt: Ritter Verlag, 1988)
Peter Weibel and Valie Export (eds), *wien: bildkompendium wiener aktionismus und film* (Frankfurt: Kohlkunst Verlag, 1970)

1962c

Spurred by the publication of *The Great Experiment: Russian Art 1863–1922* by Camilla Gray, Western interest revives in the Constructivist principles of Vladimir Tatlin and Aleksandr Rodchenko, which are elaborated in different ways by younger artists such as Dan Flavin, Carl Andre, Sol LeWitt, and others.

▲ ● Outlawed in the Soviet Union in 1934 when Socialist Realism was declared the official state art, the Constructivism of Vladimir Tatlin and Aleksandr Rodchenko fared better in the West. Yet there it was known primarily through the narrow version promulgated by the émigré brothers Naum ■ Gabo and Antoine Pevsner (1886–1962), both sculptors who saw Constructivism in idealist terms of pure art rather than in materialist terms of applied construction. Grounded in Cubism, Gabo and Pevsner used planar forms to present the abstract idea of a motif (which was often as traditional as a bust or a figure), and technological materials (such as clear Plexiglas) to render this idea conceptually transparent and aesthetically pure. At the same time, they tended to treat these forms and materials as techno-scientific values in their own right. This somewhat fetishistic treatment of formal art is far from the "culture of materials" that original Constructivists like Tatlin and Rodchenko attempted to elaborate into a new order of utilitarian objects for Communist society. Already condemned as bourgeois by these Constructivists in the East, the "Constructive Idea" of Gabo and Pevsner was embraced in the West precisely because its mixture of aesthetic idealism and technological fetishism suited the predispositions of Western institutions—art patrons, museums, and schools alike.

Two instances of the American occlusion of Russian Constructivism are especially telling. In the winter of 1927–8, prior to the opening of the Museum of Modern Art in New York, its young ◆ director-to-be Alfred H. Barr, Jr. toured the not-yet-Stalinist Soviet Union. There he saw "an appalling variety of things," and even though he was initially sympathetic to this diversity, Barr noted in his diary, "I must find some painters if possible." With his museum in mind, he then focused on painting that looked back to Cubist painting rather than forged ahead to the Constructivist overcoming of traditional mediums. The second occlusion, here regarding sculpture, occurred twenty years later when the influential critic Clement Greenberg first sketched a Cold War history of "The New Sculpture" that effectively ignored Russian Constructivism. According to Greenberg, "the new construction-sculpture" evolved from Cubism through Picasso, implicitly via Gabo and Pevsner, to Jacques Lipchitz and Julio González, all of whom aspired to "anti-illusionism." Yet, rather than a Constructivist exposure of material construction, this anti-illusionism produced the opposite effect, mostly through its metallic surfaces—"namely, that matter is incorporeal, weightless and exists only optically like a mirage." Here, in the name of construction, the materialist Constructivism of Tatlin and Rodchenko was inverted, stood on its head, in an idealist genealogy of sculpture engendered by Picasso, Gabo, and Pevsner—an amnesiac history reiterated in many shows, catalogues, books, and reviews.

Incomplete projects

▲ In the fifties the welded constructions of David Smith and Anthony Caro, as well as the massive assemblages of Mark di Suvero, appeared to restore some materialist principles to sculpture. ● But ambitious young artists such as Donald Judd (1928–94), Dan Flavin (1933–96), Carl Andre (born 1935), and Sol LeWitt were soon critical of all three predecessors. However abstract, Smith was still too figurative; however disjunctive, Caro was still too compositional; and the gestural beams of di Suvero combined both vices. Indeed, the work of all three was considered too pictorial, too much like Abstract Expressionist painting turned into sculpture. As Andre remarked, he and his peers sought a "great alternative to the semi-Surrealist work of the fifties such as Giacometti's and the late Cubism of David Smith," and they found it in the Constructivism of Tatlin and Rodchenko. This recovery had two further advantages: it not only reversed the idealist inversion of Constructivism performed by Gabo and Pevsner, but also trumped the model of a medium-specific modernism advanced by ■ Greenberg in his book of essays *Art and Culture* in 1961.

The recovery of Constructivism was abetted by the publication in 1962 of *The Great Experiment: Russian Art 1863–1922* by the English art historian Camilla Gray. Although not focused on Constructivism, this survey did document such formal experiments as the Tatlin reliefs, the Rodchenko constructions, and the "laboratory" work of the Obmokhu group, as well as such utopian and utilitarian projects as Tatlin's *Monument to the Third International* ◆ (1920) and Rodchenko's Workers' Club (1925). "Our tastes [are] dictated by our needs," Andre commented in 1962; and if Flavin was drawn to Tatlin for his demonstration of industrial material, exposed production, and architectural siting, Andre and LeWitt

▲ 1934a ● 1914, 1921, 1925a ■ 1937b, 1955b ◆ 1927c ▲ 1945 ● 1965 ■ 1960b ◆ 1921, 1925a

favored Rodchenko for his transparency of construction and his near-serial generation of structures.

The specific influence of *The Great Experiment* alone is difficult to trace, but a general shift in the meaning of "Constructivism" is clear in this dialogue between Andre and the photographer and filmmaker Hollis Frampton in November 1962:

> HF: *But why "Constructivist"? You flood me with the yellowed celluloid of Gabo and Pevsner.*
> CA: *Let me indicate some shadow of what I mean by a Constructivist aesthetic. Frank Stella is a Constructivist. He makes paintings by combining identical, discrete units. Those units are not stripes, but brush strokes. We have both watched Frank Stella paint a picture. He fills in a pattern with uniform elements. His stripe designs are the result of the shape and limitation of his primary unit.... My Constructivism is the generation of overall designs by the multiplication of the qualities of the individual constituent elements.*

▲ The nomination of Frank Stella as "a Constructivist" suggests how concerned Andre and others were to redirect the Greenbergian trajectory of modernist painting. And the stress on "identical units" suggests that another precedent was also in play, which both assisted in the challenge to Greenberg and complicated the recov-
● ery of Constructivism: the readymades of Duchamp. Although far from unknown, Duchamp had recently returned with a special force: the great Arensberg Collection of his work had opened in Philadelphia in 1954, and his first retrospective would be held in Pasadena in 1963. His model of the readymade also returned in a new light, for Andre and others felt that too much was made of the readymade as a rhetorical gesture (of either antiart sentiments or pop-cultural sympathies or both) and not enough as a structural device. "The results of the Dada experiments have not been fully evaluated to date," he remarked to Frampton in the same dialogue. "I do not think that the true product of Duchamp's experiments is the rising market in Rauschenberg."

By 1963, then, these artists had combined the two radical alternatives to traditional sculpture first proposed, almost as com-
■ plements, fifty years before in 1913: the Tatlin construction and the Duchamp readymade. This was not a historical accident; just as "our tastes [are] dictated by our needs," as Andre remarked, these needs were specific. For Andre the combination of construction
◆ and readymade was mediated by the sculpture of Constantin Brancusi. Unlike Judd, say, Andre had begun as a sculptor, and wanted to redirect the medium rather than depart from it. And Brancusi provided a model of sculpture that, though often idealist in form, was often just as materialist in its articulation of substance and site—a tension that appealed to Flavin as well. In any case, these were the precedents in play at this volatile moment, and the young Flavin, Andre, and LeWitt worked through them in different ways.

Flavin was explicit about his relation to Constructivism—"my joy is to try to build from that 'incomplete' experience as I see fit"—but this relation was not simple. Flavin, who had attended Catholic schools, once studied for the priesthood, and in 1961–2 he made several monochrome paintings with lights attached that he titled "icons" [**1**]. In part, Flavin was inspired by Byzantine icons (his notebooks mention a particular Russian painting at the Metropolitan Museum) whose "physical feeling" and "magical presiding presence" impressed him. As with Tatlin, who once worked as an icon restorer, the icon provided Flavin with an alternative model of the picture, one which was assertively material but also spectrally spiritual; "blank magic" is how he defined his art in 1962. Perhaps he had seen the juxtaposition, posed by Gray in *The Great Experiment*, of a Tatlin relief and a Russian icon. In any case, Flavin paid homage to the Constructivist in 1964 with several light pieces titled *Monument for V. Tatlin* [**2**], whose pyramid of fluorescent lights recalls the proposed spiral of metalwork of
▲ *Monument to the Third International.*

A year before, Flavin had altered his practice slightly but significantly: he began to use the diffuse light of fluorescent tubes—alone, as readymade units, without painting. His first such piece was a common eight-foot gold light set on the wall at a forty-five-degree angle, *the diagonal of May 25, 1963.* Not only was the light unit given, but for Flavin "the diagonal declared itself" as well: "It seemed to sustain itself directly, dynamically, dramatically in my workroom wall." Thus the readymade was also in play here, but it was used in a Constructivist manner to undo traditional composition: "There was literally no need to compose this system definitively," Flavin remarked. At the same time, his historical distance from both paradigms, the construction and the readymade, was made apparent. Unlike in Constructivism, the industrial material here was not futuristic but found, precisely readymade. And, unlike in Duchamp, the readymade was not only pledged to demystify or to defetishize art; Flavin also regarded his light as "a modern technological fetish," "a common lamp become a common industrial fetish, as utterly reproducible as ever but somehow strikingly unfamiliar now."

1 • Dan Flavin, *Icon I (to the light of Sean McGovern which blesses everyone)*, 1961–2
Oil on gesso, masonite and pine, red fluorescent light, 63.8 x 63.8 x 11.7 (25⅛ x 25⅛ x 4⅝)

(right) Dan Flavin, *Icon II (the mystery) (to John Reeves)*, 1961
Oil and acrylic masonite and pine, porcelain receptacle, pull chain, amber-colored fire logs, vacuum incandescent bulb, 63.8 x 63.8 x 11.7 (25⅛ x 25⅛ x 4⅝)

▲ 1958 ● 1914, 1918 ■ 1914 ◆ 1927b ▲ 1921

Artforum

By the opening of the sixties, American art magazines were firmly focused on the past: *Artnews* inherited its commitment to Abstract Expressionism from its eminent editor, Thomas B. Hess, and *Art in America*, as its name suggests, was limited in scope to American production, both fine and folk. The upsurge in productive energy at the end of the fifties created the opportunity for a magazine less narrow than its fellows. In 1962 this occasion was grasped by Philip Leider and John Coplans in San Francisco; soon they moved their fledgling project—*Artforum*—to Los Angeles, where it would find its publisher, Charles Cowles, and its signature square format, designed by Ed Ruscha. However, their eyes were fixed on New York, the actual center of aesthetic production, and the editors were determined to build an editorial board that could report on the activities of the East Coast art world: Michael Fried, Max Kozloff, Annette Michelson, James Monte, Robert Pincus-Witten, Barbara Rose, and Sidney Tillim, soon joined by Rosalind Krauss.

The work of Ellsworth Kelly, emerging in the late fifties as abstract and minimal, signaled the new direction of the artistic production *Artforum* would champion. Although Leider was committed to new and more muscular writing than the vaporous, belle-lettristic style of the other magazines, he was also eager to publish texts by the artists themselves. Donald Judd, who had been an active reviewer for *Artnews* throughout the sixties, established critical discourse as a legitimate vehicle for artists. Robert Morris soon followed his lead, and "Notes on Sculpture," his four essays laying down the conditions for Minimalism, were published in *Artforum* between 1966 and 1969.

Robert Smithson was complicating the conceptual field of sculpture at this time and his "Entropy and the New Monuments" (June 1966) moved beyond the industrial optimism of Minimalist practice. The magazine's enthusiasm for Earthworks such as Smithson's was consolidated in a special issue (Summer 1967). This opening away from Minimalism also made room for Conceptual art, and writings by Sol LeWitt such as "Paragraphs on Conceptual Art" (June 1967) soon appeared.

Leider's insistence on lucid analytical prose forged a close relationship between him and Michael Fried, opening the magazine's pages as well to Clement Greenberg and its covers to artists such as Jules Olitski, Kenneth Noland, and Morris Louis. By 1971 Leider felt his leadership of the magazine to have reached a plateau such that to continue as editor could only mean a repetitive treading water. He therefore resigned, turning the editorship over to John Coplans, who left California to move to New York and to face a badly divided editorial board that he had difficulty holding together. Two of the most productive writers, Max Kozloff and Lawrence Alloway, were hostile to what they characterized as the "formalist" drift of the magazine, insisting that it become more openly political and supportive of the socially relevant mediums like photography. On the other side of this struggle were Fried, Michelson, and Krauss. The latter two resigned from the board in 1975 to start their own magazine, *October*, named for the Sergei Eisenstein film that suffered from the Soviet assault against "formalism."

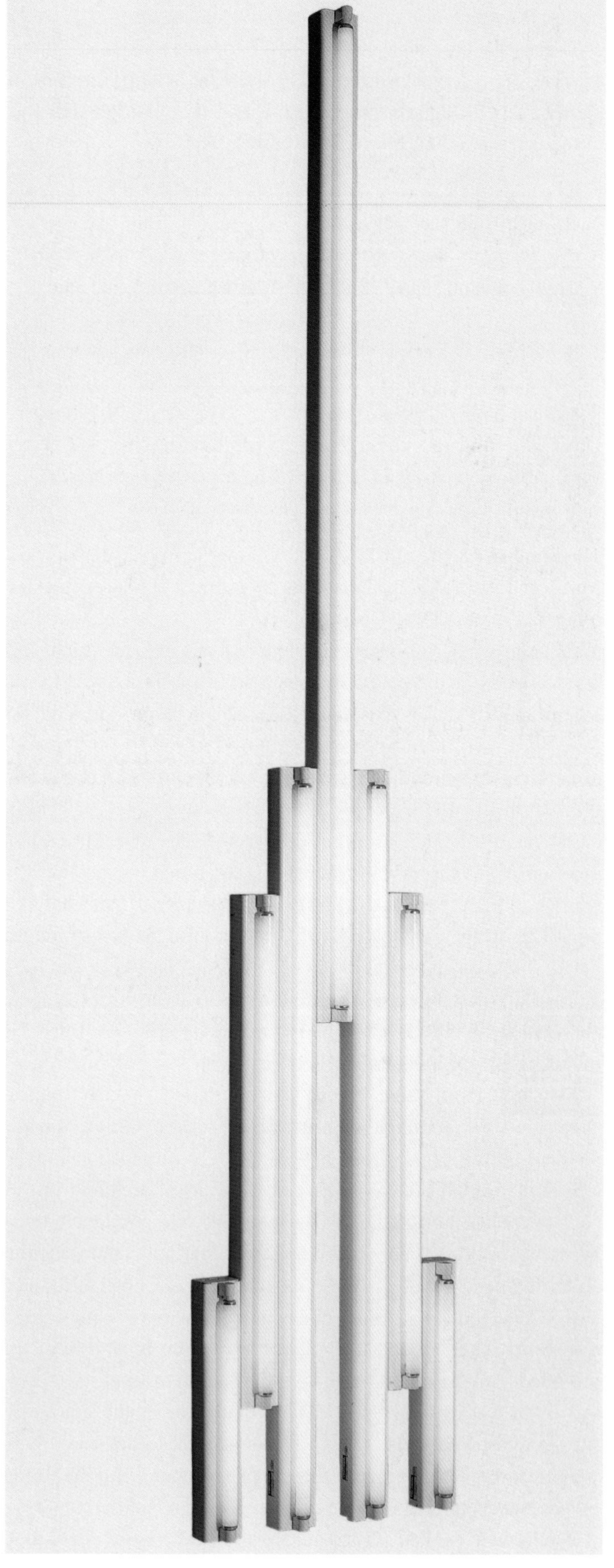

2 • Dan Flavin, *Monument for V. Tatlin*, 1966
Seven fluorescent light fixtures of various lengths, 365.8 x 71 x 11 (144 x 28 x 4⅜)

3 • Carl Andre, (right) unfinished Pyramid; and (left) *Pyramid (Square Plan)*, c. 1959
Wood, 175 x 78.7 (68⅞ x 31) (destroyed)

In this way he held together two contradictory imperatives of modernist art: on the one hand, the imperative to materialize the work of art, here to declare light as light and to expose its physical support (the fluorescent fixture); on the other hand, the imperative to *de*materialize the work of art, here to irradiate it with light, to wash space with color. Perhaps this is why, even as *the diagonal of* ▲ *May 25, 1963* draws on Tatlin and Duchamp, it is dedicated to Brancusi, who also held the two imperatives—the material and the ideal, the worldly and the transcendental—in tense suspension.

Similar precedents are at work in the early pieces of Carl Andre, which alternate between "assisted" readymades à la Duchamp and wooden sculptures first carved, then cut, à la Brancusi (for example, *First Ladder* [1958] seems to stem from *Endless Column* [1937–8] by the Romanian). However, already by 1959—well before *The Great Experiment*—Andre had begun to stack wood units in pyramidal structures in a manner reminiscent of the constructions of Rodchenko [**3**], and in 1961 he ordered "found steel objects" in related ways. Both series declared a Constructivist transparency of construction. Although more literal than Flavin in his use of materials, Andre was not merely positivistic, for he soon elaborated this Constructivist method into "a kind of plastic poetry" in which given elements like bricks, wood blocks, or metal plates are "combined to produce space" [**4**]. This redefinition of sculpture as *place* led him to several series of rectangular units set flat on the floor. Here sculpture was structured by the logic of the unit with little composition, in a way that produced space without a trace of the figure. In effect, Andre turned the readymade into a

4 • Carl Andre, *Equivalent (VIII)*, 1966
Fire bricks, 12.7 x 68.6 x 229.2 (5 x 27 x 90¼)

▲ 1914, 1927b

Constructivist form; that is, he took given elements, and made them speak reflexively about material, structure, and site alike.

Like his peers, Sol LeWitt looked at Constructivism through past models and present needs. *Hanging Structure with Stripes* [**5**], in which different wood blocks are assembled axially, set on a platform, and suspended from the ceiling, seems to cite Rodchenko's ▲ "spatial constructions" (1920–1), some of which were also hung. But it does not articulate substance, structure, and space in a truly Constructivist manner, for the blocks are painted, most in various stripes of black and white, and this obscures more than reveals both material and construction (in this respect, the work is closer • to the Dutch movement De Stijl than to Russian Constructivism). Like the Rodchenko constructions, however, *Hanging Structure* occupies a space between mediums, a "negative" condition that is neither painting nor sculpture, which LeWitt explored further in his "Floor Structures" and "Wall Structures" of 1964–5, in which different angles of wood planes are set on the floor or the wall. These structures are also neither architecture nor furniture. "Architecture and three-dimensional art are of completely opposite nature," LeWitt insisted in 1967, at a time when this distinction ■ seemed blurred by Minimalist objects. "Art is not utilitarian." Here LeWitt declared his distance from this aspect of Constructivism, but this distance was already apparent in his sequences of frames from 1965–6, also set on the floor or the wall, in which sculpture and painting were again negated, literally emptied out. It is in these modular works that one sees the beginning of the serial grids for ▲ which he is best known, and which advance his version of Conceptual art more than look back to Constructivist precedent [**6**]. Although not as idealist in form as much Conceptual art, these structures are not materialist either: "What the work of art looks like isn't too important," LeWitt wrote in his laconic "Paragraphs on Conceptual Art" (1967). Nevertheless, he arrived at this way of working through his own combination of the construction and the readymade, as is suggested in his well-known formula: "The idea becomes a machine that makes the art."

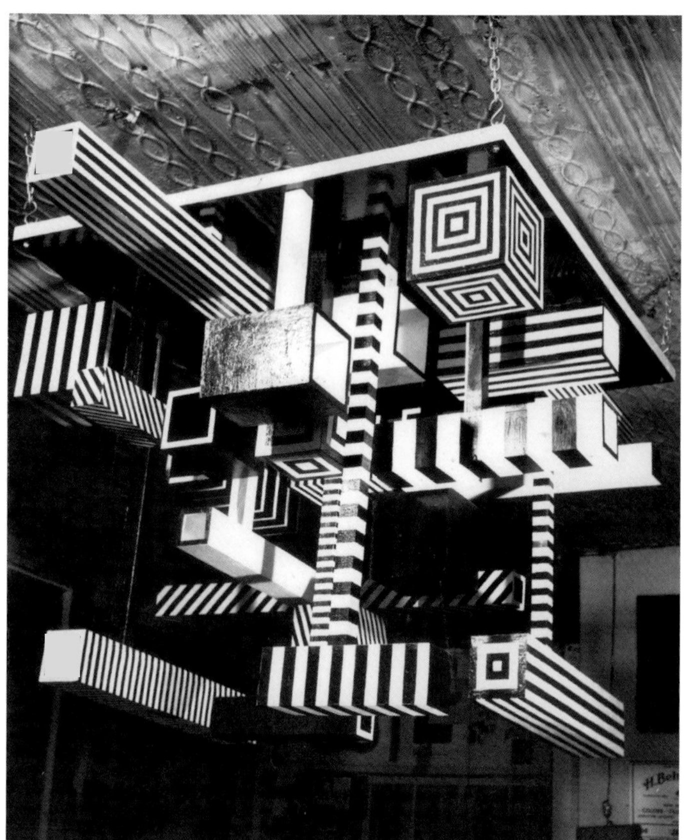

5 • Sol LeWitt, *Hanging Structure with Stripes*, 1963
Painted wood, 139.7 x 139.7 x 56.2 (55 x 55 x 30) (destroyed)

6 • Sol LeWitt, *Modular Structure*, 1966
White painted wood, 62.2 x 359.4 x 359.4 (24½ x 141½ x 141½)

With this formula, however, there is little of Constructivism left. Perhaps the historical distance from its revolutionary moment was such that it could be recovered only as a ruin—that is, an emblematic relic of a modernist practice that sought to articulate and to advance art and politics together. So it is, for example, that in his piece from 1964 Flavin paid homage to the artist Tatlin, not, as Tatlin had done, to a new social order. Indeed, Flavin cites the Tatlin who had withdrawn into his project for a glider, *Letatlin* (1932), and it is a commemoration soaked with the pathos of failure: "*Monument 7* in cool white fluorescent light memorializes Vladimir Tatlin, the great revolutionary, who dreamt of art as science. It stands, a vibrantly aspiring order, in lieu of his last glider, which never left the ground." Nevertheless, if the revolutionary project of Russian Constructivism could not be recovered, some of its artistic proposals could be reinscribed, and this recovery helped to redirect art in the sixties radically.

FURTHER READING

Carl Andre and Hollis Frampton, *12 Dialogues 1962–1963* (Halifax: The Press of the Nova Scotia College of Art and Design, 1980)

Benjamin H. D. Buchloh, "Cold War Constructivism," in Serge Guilbaut (ed.), *Reconstructing Modernism* (Cambridge, Mass.: MIT Press, 1990)

Hal Foster, "Uses and Abuses of Russian Constructivism," in Richard Andrews (ed.), *Art into Life: Russian Constructivism 1914–1932* (New York: Rizzoli, 1990)

Camilla Gray, *The Great Experiment: Russian Art 1863–1922* (1962), republished as *The Russian Experiment in Art 1863–1922* (London: Thames & Hudson, 1986)

Jeffrey Weibs et al., *Dan Flavin* (Washington, D.C.: National Gallery of Art, 2004)

▲ 1921 • 1917 ■ 1965 ▲ 1968b

1963

After publishing two manifestos with the painter Eugen Schönebeck, Georg Baselitz exhibits *Die Grosse Nacht im Eimer* (Great Night Down the Drain) in Berlin.

The exhibition of a group of paintings by Georg Baselitz—including those of a single large-scale masturbating figure, *Die Grosse Nacht im Eimer* [**1**], and a large male nude with an erection—that opened in the Werner & Katz Gallery in West Berlin on October 1, 1963, and their immediate confiscation by the State Attorney, led to one of the first major art scandals in the still young West Germany. It set the stage for the enactment of some of the most crucial contradictions of postwar reconstruction culture.

Baselitz (born Georg Kern in Deutschbaselitz, Saxony, in 1938) had moved from East to West Berlin in 1957 to study at the highly renowned Academy of Fine Arts. His move from the Communist half of postwar Germany to its Western capitalist counterpart was repeated a few months later by Eugen Schönebeck (born 1936), with whom Baselitz would become friends, and who until 1957 had been studying Socialist Realism at the East Berlin Academy; again ▲ four years later by Gerhard Richter (born 1932), who had been ● studying Socialist Realism in Dresden, the younger Sigmar Polke (born 1941), and Blinky Palermo (1943–77); and again, much later still, by A. R. Penck (born 1939).

From Socialist Realism to *tachisme*

From the start, this very movement from a Communist state to a capitalist country that was in the process of being restructured in accordance with advanced American consumer capitalism situated Baselitz and his peers within a complex triangulation. In the first place, these artists had to distance themselves from all residues of Socialist Realism, which was enforced in East German academies as the only valid model of visual culture, and which was represented in particular by the work of German artists such as Bernhard Heisig, Werner Tübke, and Wolfgang Mattheuer, and that of their ■ Soviet precursors (Aleksandr Gerasimov, for instance) and their French and Italian variations (André Fougeron and Renato Guttuso)—all of whom were heroes in the East German art world.

Second, upon their arrival in the West, these young artists all ◆ studied with German *tachistes* and *informel* painters, either in Berlin (Baselitz with Hann Trier, Schönebeck with Hans Jaenisch) or in Düsseldorf (Polke and Richter with Karl Otto Götz and Gerhard Hoehme, respectively). By that time, this older generation of painters was comfortably positioned producing a West German type of "international abstraction," whose Parisian and New York origins were concealed as much as the delayed processes of avant-garde and neo-avant-garde reception in West Germany would allow. This was a form of abstraction, as Klaus Herding has argued when speaking of Willy Baumeister, that had placed itself exactly at the right intersection between primitivism and classicism to fulfill the neutralizing demands of West German political and cultural repression. Its primary function seems to have been to produce a sort of "*Anschluss-Aesthetik*," a link to a noncontaminated culture and a public assimilation to the legacies of European and American modernism, even if only in their already dilapidated state.

Thus, around 1962, Baselitz, Schönebeck, and the others would challenge these governing forms of abstraction with the same fervor with which they had distanced themselves slightly earlier from Socialist Realism. But this oppositionality achieved more than just Oedipal distinction from what had gone before: it assaulted and actually broke down the repressive armor of the painterly practices that the first generation of West German artists had hastily assembled immediately after the war.

A third and related strategy becomes evident in Baselitz's work of 1962: the rebuttal of the presumed inevitability of "internationalism" (oriented primarily at Paris and New York) as an intrinsically necessary condition for the reconstruction of an avant-garde culture (or rather, the foundation of a neo-avant-garde) on the territory of the former Nazi state. This third maneuver of distancing would lead to an ever-increasing opposition, culminating in a profound generational chasm between the two models of artistic production that were to govern the subsequent decades of West German art.

On the one hand, Baselitz now laid the foundations of a new conservative aesthetic by reclaiming a more or less unbroken conventional artistic and historical identity. His work invoked, in particular, that tradition of German modernist painting that had ▲ been destroyed by the Nazi government after the "Degenerate 'Art'" exhibition in 1937 (of specific importance for Baselitz were ● the German Expressionists of the Die Brücke group in Dresden, as well as the work of Ludwig Meidner [1884–1966] and Oskar ■ Kokoschka). But Baselitz's model of continuity even attempted to

▲ 1988 ● 1934a, 1972b ■ 1934a ◆ 1946 ▲ 1937a ● 1908 ■ 1900a

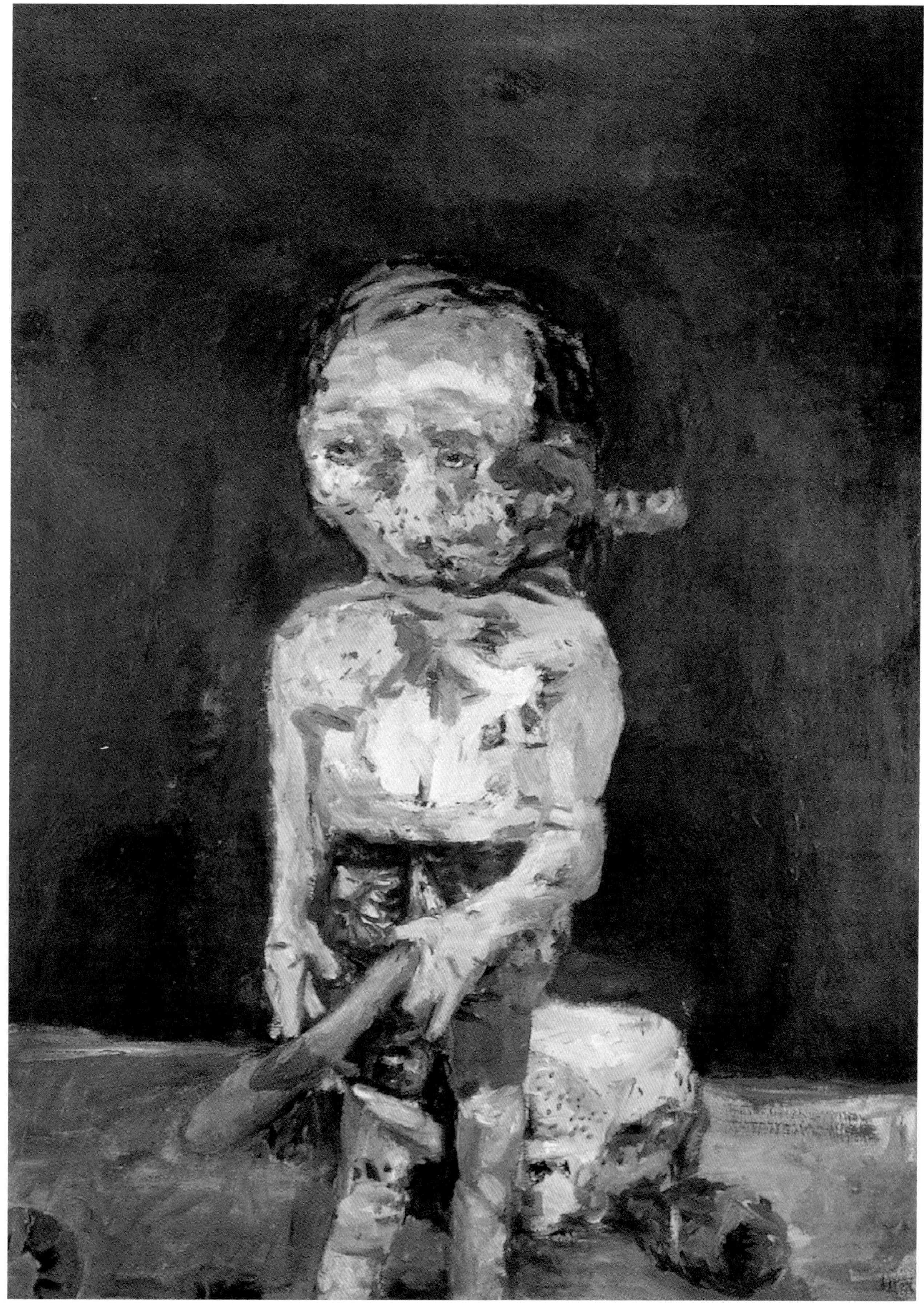

1 • Georg Baselitz, *Die Grosse Nacht im Eimer* (Great Night Down the Drain), 1962–3
Oil on canvas, 250 x 180 (98⅜ x 70⅞)

return to practices developed prior to the formation of Expressionism: the legacies of provincial German modernism in the painterly work of Lovis Corinth (1858–1925) and Max Slevogt (1868–1932).

On the other hand, the model enacted in the work of Richter, Polke, and Palermo in Düsseldorf precisely refused the desirability, if not outright denied the possibility, of traditional identity formations in the painterly practices of the postwar period. Accordingly, these artists situated their work within a more complex set of relations with predecessors by grafting it onto the radical aesthetics of both Parisian and American neo-avant-garde artists. These ranged from Yves Klein and Piero Manzoni to the enormously influential Abstract Expressionist painters of the New York School and the ▲ more recently emerging American Pop and Fluxus artists.

The origins of these two models of aesthetic opposition could be theorized in different ways, and their ramifications for subsequent German art could be interpreted accordingly. But they are perhaps most productively explained in those terms with which German • philosopher Jürgen Habermas has theorized sociopolitical subjects and institutions in postwar Germany as being suspended in the conflict between conventional and postconventional identity formations. Thus, the work of Baselitz in 1962 could be said to have created a "new" painterly aesthetic that not only privileged the continuity of the artisanal production of representations as the primordial definition of art, but also argued for the persistence of a local, regional, and national grounding of artistic practice. In doing so, it established a hierarchy of cultural values and insisted on the continuing, if not exclusive, validity of a conventional national identity as the foundation of German postwar reconstruction culture.

By contrast, the work of Richter and Polke at this time developed a pictorial aesthetic in which the supremacy of the artisanal was continuously challenged by the fact that painterly representation appears as inconceivable outside the parameters of mass-media image production and the apparatus of the culture industry. Thereby painting itself was dislodged from its status as a guarantor of conventional identity and cultural continuity. It was repositioned as a hybrid at the intersection of various conventions and technologies of representation that were not tainted by the cultural ideologies of the nation state, and it acknowledged concepts of post-traditional identity formation as an inevitable necessity for postwar cultural practices in Germany.

These conflicts were initially played out on the level of the concepts and techniques underlying pictorial representation: to the extent that painters like Baselitz and Schönebeck declared the uninterrupted conventionality of painting, they reclaimed the (photographically) unmediated availability of the anthropomorphic figure and insisted on painting's capacity to access the body in mimetic representation. Paradoxically, however, as their work amply demonstrates, it appears that an enforced attachment to the figure at this point in history could be achieved only by subjecting figurative painting to a simultaneous regime of disfiguration, fragmentation, or grotesque hypertrophic distortions.

The problematic insistence on figuration, a reenactment of ■ Picasso's post-1915 dilemma in the specific context of postwar European art (and for the first time in postwar West German culture), now acquired an altogether different layer. The examples upon which Baselitz and Schönebeck **[2]** drew at that time, the international precursors and contemporaries that would seem to legitimize the otherwise all too provincial retrieval of the purely German Expressionist models, were the British painters Francis ▲ Bacon and Lucian Freud and the American Philip Guston, whose then recent conversion from Abstract Expressionism to figuration had also been achieved at the price of depicting the human body in pieces or in grotesque cartoonish disfigurations. But most importantly, it was the discovery of the fragmented bodies and • anthropomorphic forms in the work of Frenchman Jean Fautrier that would become one of the key references for Baselitz. It was in Fautrier's work that the epistemological and perceptual problem of painterly figuration was historically fused for the first time with an anthropological, or rather, an ethical question: namely, whether human subjects after the Holocaust and World War II could at all be represented as "figures," whether, indeed, they could still carry their name and image as human subjects at all.

Disfiguring figuration

This dialectic of a fixation on the representation of the human figure that at the same time has to be distorted and depleted of all its mimetic conventions finds its analogue in the dialectic

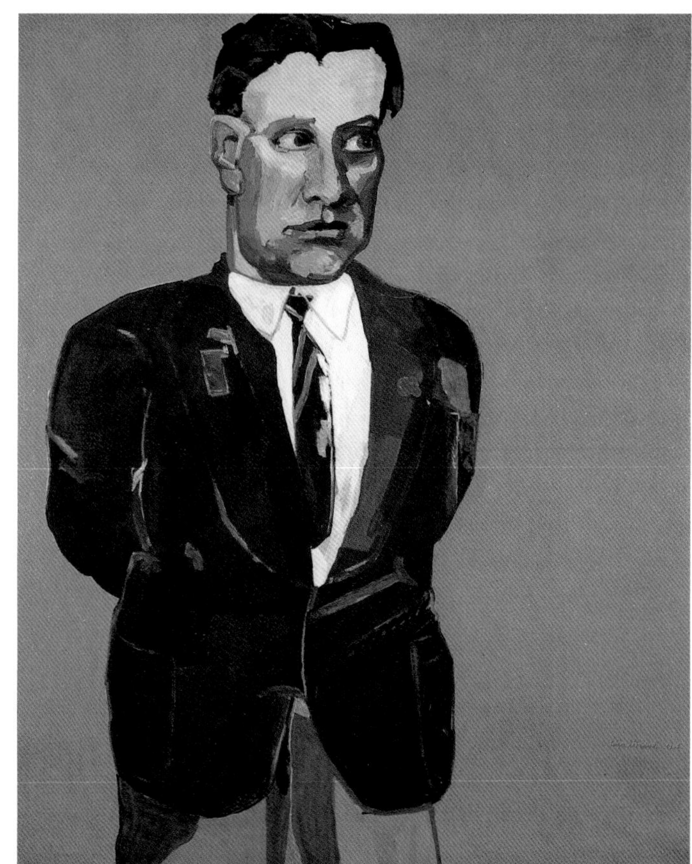

2 • Eugen Schönebeck, *Mayakovsky*, 1965
Oil on canvas, 220 x 180 (85 x 61)

▲ 1947b, 1959a, 1960a, 1960c, 1962a, 1964b • 1988 ■ 1919 ▲ 1959d • 1946 approach to the artisanal practice of painting. While drawing and painterly gesture remain the foundational register of delineation and expression in Baselitz's work, they have to be perpetually debased by inscribing into the act of painting itself the counter-practices of primal pictorial procedures: the fecal smear, the infantile gestural scratch. This antipainterly impulse probably originates in the irrepressible suspicion that the matter of painting cannot ultimately live up to the promise of a fundamental psycho-sexual experience of identity, one that would be grounded in the somatic register of the unconscious alone. In blatant contrast, for a painter like Richter, painting and its processes, conventions, and materials appear as mere tools of the trade, or as technical, physical, and chemical matters. They do not have to be lined with vigorous antipainterly acts, since they have not been invested with psycho-sexual aspirations for a deeper experience, nor do they carry any foundational hopes for an ultimate authenticity.

Baselitz's iconography requires careful description, for it maneuvers constantly between enforcing prohibitions (such as the one against abstraction or the one against photographic mediation) and enacting transgressions (for instance, the desire to return to a presumed ground of a deeper and more authentic German [painterly] history, or the desire to rupture the pretense of a culture of repressive amnesia mediated by the photographic image of consumer culture). Thus Baselitz's series of "*Helden*" ("heroes"), "partisans," and "*ein neuer Typ*" ("a new type") reveals all the markers of the historical fallacies, if not the subjective pathology, of that ambition: from the hypertrophic and disproportionate sizes of the figures and their internal inconsistencies (from thwarted limbs to gigantic growths) to the perpetual laceration of the contour line, where the figure itself is suddenly opened up or discontinued to merge with its pictorial surroundings, the patches of viscous pigment or the suddenly self-conscious planes of flattened modernist painterly space.

This ambiguity between the figure's epiphanic returns and its persistent disappearances within the formal challenges of representation, which Baselitz recognizes as ultimately insurmountable and as pictorial problems of modernism that exist beyond the scope of his subjective ambitions, are a hallmark of his unique contribution to a postwar German aesthetic. On the level of unconscious or conscious conceptions of the artist's public identity and social role, analogous contradictions are at work. Thus, it is the legacy of the Romantic outsider that Baselitz and Schönebeck rediscover in their two *Pandämonium* manifestos, in which they reposition the artist (and themselves) within a framework that—while historically fully predetermined—appeared in 1962 as a radical departure toward the formation of a conservative postwar German aesthetic.

While heavily relying on the aesthetic theories of Gottfried Benn, Germany's supposedly extraordinary prewar Expressionist poet and temporary Nazi sympathizer, who became an eminent cult figure as a postwar nihilist, the antisocial and anticultural impulse of the *Pandämonium* manifestos also brought other elements—with a considerable delay—into the context of German visual culture for the first time. Borrowing from the writings of the Frenchmen Antonin Artaud and Lautréamont, it declared war against all aesthetic practices that define themselves as consciously operative within discursive or social conventions, and that aspire toward culture as a project of communication. By contrast, Baselitz and Schönebeck's manifestos claimed access to a space of radical incommensurability and pure otherness, in which communication is refuted and sealed in aesthetic opacity. The hero of this Nietzschean definition of the artist's role as radical outcast and outsider is invoked in both manifestos as "G." (presumably Vincent van Gogh, to whom Artaud had dedicated one of his most programmatic texts). In terms of art-historical reception, Baselitz and Schönebeck's repositioning of the artist as outsider associated itself with the recovery of multiple legacies, most of them having been deleted from German history by the Nazi destruction of Weimar modernity. This is most explicit in a formulation in which they refer to themselves as partaking in the condition of the "*Entarteten*" ("degenerate artists"), an explicit reference to the ▲ infamous exhibition of that name in Munich in 1937. That recovery ● ranged from the extraordinary centrality of the Prinzhorn ■ Collection, to the dialectics of deskilling and primary expressivity in non-European "primitivism" to the cult of lesser-known, untrained artists such as Frederick Hill, Louis Soutter, and Gaston Chaissac, a position that itself had been recently elaborated more ◆ publicly in Jean Dubuffet's celebration and collection of *art brut*.

Subjects in tatters

The internal contradictions of Baselitz's approach to painting are, then, fairly evident, inasmuch as they are the historically overdetermined attempts to resolve conflicts operating within late-twentieth-century culture at large, and within postwar German painting in particular. First of all is the renewal of the Nietzschean claim of the artist as outsider, even as criminal outcast, in which Baselitz situates himself in manifest opposition to what he would consider a specious and largely compensatory construction of German postwar democracy. But this resuscitation of a right-wing reactionary elitism as an aesthetic counterposition to democratic hypocrisy only prolonged the protofascist disgust with the fallacies of democratic everyday life of the Weimar period (and then of postwar West Germany). As is well known, at that time the majority of the populace's attachment to the prewar ideologies of Nazi fascism was generally stronger than the newly (and largely enforced) commitment to a new democratic culture and consciousness. The claim for the exceptional grandeur of the artist as transcendental being outside of the fetters of socialization and the constraints of cultural and linguistic conventionality only attempted to redeem aesthetically that type of ideology whose political realities had recently proven to be the most devastating experience in human memory.

Baselitz's figures [**3**]—the "new types," the "heroes," the "partisans" (for which cause, one wonders)—are all dressed in tatters: a garb that oscillates between the German Romantic painter stalk-

▲ 1937a ● 1922 ■ 1968b ◆ 1903, 1946

3 • Georg Baselitz, *Die grossen Freunde* (The Great Friends), 1965
Oil on canvas, 250 x 300 (98⅜ x 118⅛)

ing off to the outdoor subject and youthful male figures (somewhere between Boy Scouts and Hitler Youths), half clad in camouflage, half revealing oversized genitals, carrying palettes or canes, often marked by the peculiar homoerotic cult of youthful uniformed males with weapons and war. These prodigal German sons all appear as though they have just returned "home," or as though they are about to depart or begin anew (from where, for where, for what remains unclear).

Repositioning the artist as "hero," but as a hero in patches and tatters, therefore, is not only an attempt to work through the difficulties of a renewed figuration in the evidence of its historic impossibility. It is also an attempt—perhaps a consciously futile one—to construct a new subject, one that has been patched together by its ambition to reconfigure German subjectivity under the circumstances of its self-imposed and willful destruction of its former self, and the destruction it had recently inflicted on millions of others.

FURTHER READING

Georg Baselitz and Eugen Schönebeck, *Pandämonium Manifestoes*, excerpts in English translation in Andreas Papadakis (ed.), *German Art Now*, vol. 5, no. 9–10, 1989

Stefan Germer, "Die Wiederkehr des Verdrängten. Zum Umgang mit deutscher Geschichte bei Baselitz, Kiefer, Immendorf und Richter," in Julia Bernard (ed.), *Germeriana: Unveröffentlichte oder übersetzte Schriften von Stefan Germer* (Cologne: Oktagon Verlag, 1999)

Siegfried Gohr, "In the Absence of Heroes: The Early Work of Georg Baselitz," *Artforum*, vol. 20, no. 10, Summer 1982

Tom Holert, "Bei Sich, über allem: Der symptomatische Baselitz," *Texte zur Kunst*, vol. 3, no. 9, March 1993

Kevin Power, "Existential Ornament," in Maria Corral (ed.), *Georg Baselitz* (Madrid: Fundacion Caja de Pensiones, 1990)

1964a

On July 20, the twentieth anniversary of the failed Stauffenberg coup against Hitler, Joseph Beuys publishes his fictitious autobiography and generates an outbreak of public violence at the "Festival of New Art" in Aachen, West Germany.

When, in the summer of 1964, Joseph Beuys (1921–86) exhibited a small selection of his drawings and sculptures made between 1951 and 1956 at "Documenta 3," Kassel, Germany, a larger public was confronted with his work for the first time. On at least three subsequent occasions that year, Beuys's early notoriety would grow to the condition of scandalous fame, eventually establishing him as the first major, if not the most important, artist of postwar West German reconstruction culture.

The first event occurred when Beuys was attacked by right-wing students during his performance at the "Festival of New Art" at the Technical University of Aachen on July 20, 1964 [**1**, **2**]. While he was melting two large cubes of fat on a hot plate, a soundtrack—apparently not an intentional part of Beuys's performance—played Joseph Goebbels's infamous Berlin *Sportpalast* speech soliciting the unequivocal assent of the masses to "total war." This experience of confrontation triggered, as Beuys put it, "processes of becoming increasingly conscious of the necessity to politicize my attitudes."

The second event, which occurred on the same occasion, was Beuys's publication of his fictitious autobiography *Lebenslauf/Werklauf* (Curriculum vitae/Curriculum opere). In it he constructed

1 • Joseph Beuys, *Aktion Kukei, akoopee – Nein! Braunkreuz, Fettecken, Modellfettecken* (Brown cross, Fat corners, Model fat corners), 1964
Performance at the "Festival of New Art," Technical University of Aachen

a "myth of origin" in which he gave an enigmatic account of his development as an artist. Thus he explained, for example, that his use of fat and felt, the most conspicuous materials of his sculptural oeuvre, had originated in his encounter with tribal people in the Tartar region of the Soviet Union, who had saved his life by wrapping him in fat and felt after his Luftwaffe plane had been shot down during World War II. Only a year before, Beuys had used fat for the first time when he "exhibited" a box of warm fat during a lecture on ▲ happenings given by Allan Kaprow at the Rudolf Zwirner Gallery in Cologne, thus positioning himself—in a maneuver typical of Beuys's subsequent career—in association with artistic practices not necessarily as close to his own as he claimed them to be.

Beuys concluded his autobiographical account with a proposal to raise the Berlin Wall by five centimeters to improve its architectural proportions. This passage set off a public inquisition by his employer, the Minister of Culture of North-Rhine Westphalia, who—several years later and for altogether different reasons—would dismiss Beuys for disobedience from his post at the venerable State Academy of Fine Arts in Düsseldorf, where he had studied from 1947 to 1951 and had been appointed as Professor of Monumental Sculpture in 1961. All these incidents already point to Beuys's future commitment to a model of "*Soziale Plastik*" (social sculpture), which conceived of sculpture as an activist aesthetic practice.

How German is it?

The year 1964 was also the time when Beuys appeared more • frequently as a strange fellow traveler with the international Fluxus movement. After having met the group's chief coordinator and theorist, the Lithuanian-American George Maciunas, in 1962, Beuys had invited fifteen international Fluxus artists and musicians to the "Festum Fluxorum Fluxus" at the Academy of Fine Arts in Düsseldorf in 1963. Yet Beuys would never be fully accepted by his Fluxus colleagues, since they saw his work as a specifically German contribution to a movement whose programmatic internationalism had emphasized a post-nation-state conception of culture.

What made Beuys's work particularly German was first of all a strange eclecticism that resulted from the absence of an avant-garde tradition after Nazi fascism had destroyed (Weimar) avant-garde culture in all its forms: from psychoanalysis to photomontage, from Messianic eschatological thought to orthodox Communism. Rather than recovering German modernism and establishing a cultural continuity with the amazingly complex range of personalities and projects from the Weimar spectrum, West German postwar reconstruction culture embraced, almost ■ fanatically, at first *tachisme* and *art informel* from Paris and then, from the mid-fifties onward, New York School post-Surrealist abstraction in order to internationalize itself. Furthermore, the seemingly mandatory abstraction and the internationalism of reconstruction culture deflected from the necessity to confront the recent German past, and it concealed the collective inability to mourn the victims of fascism.

▲ 1961 • 1962a ■ 1946

2 • Joseph Beuys's Fluxus action in the large auditorium of the Technical University of Aachen, July 20, 1964

It is first of all against this type of an established aesthetic of disavowal that Beuys developed an aesthetic of the mnemonic. The historical avant-garde's radicality of the Dada readymade and of ▲ Constructivism would return in Beuys's hands as mere ruins and as utopian debris, as the irretrievable traces of an avant-garde of the past—a past that was as inaccessible for Beuys as the accumulations of an apparently celebratory commodity culture (in French Nouveau • Réalisme and even more so in American Pop art) would appear unacceptable. Beuys articulated this with the clarity of hindsight in 1980:

> *Actually this shock after the end of the war is my primary experience, my fundamental experience which is in fact what led me to begin to really go into art, that is, to reorient myself in the sense of a radically new beginning.*

Thus, Joseph Beuys can be situated, along with two other artists of the early sixties—that is, Yves Klein and Andy Warhol—at the multiple intersections and within the historically crucial transformations that distinguish the practices of the prewar avant-garde artists from those of the postwar neo-avant-garde artists.

▲ 1914, 1918, 1921 • 1960a, 1960c, 1964b

While not necessarily ensuring his art-historical importance, to have inhabited these intersections has made Beuys a figure upon whom ceaseless readings have been projected since the early sixties. And while these incessant interpretive efforts do not necessarily attest to an oeuvre's inexhaustible complexity, but rather to the inexhaustible desire for "meaningful" cultural production among audiences in general and among specialists of interpretation (art historians and critics) in particular, it is important to reflect upon the wide array of references and combinatory effects that Beuys's work has generated over the thirty years of his prolific production.

The first of these intersections, and perhaps the most striking, is the degree to which Beuys's work (and especially his performances) is inextricably bound up with an emerging culture of spectacle, which had been of secondary importance to the historical avant-garde. When artists in the twenties generated scandal and shock among their audiences, their activities were universally perceived as social or political provocations. We can argue, for example, that in almost all cases ▲ (such as the performances at the Cabaret Voltaire in Zurich in 1916, ● or Kurt Schwitters's public readings of his *Merz* sound poems) the avant-garde not only situated itself in manifest opposition to the ruling conventions of meaning production but also attempted to confront bourgeois society with models of culture as alternate, if not utopian, political and social practice. When artists of the neo-avant-garde engaged in scandal and shock, on the other hand, the most evident effect of their actions would be—in accordance with the rituals of the culture industry—the spectacularization of the artist as "star" and the social role ensuing from that. Beuys (and Klein and Warhol for that matter), in manifest contradistinction to his predecessors, and even to most of his contemporaries, programmatically incorporated for the first time these principles of spectacle culture and strategies of cultic visibility into his persona as much as into his work. ■ Although precursors such as Jackson Pollock may have transposed painting into the register of the spectacle they did not submit fully to its principles. But once cultural practice had been severed from all utopian and political aspirations, perhaps even from its ambitions for ◆ a semiotic revolution, the neo-avant-garde inevitably consummated the shift into an exclusive register of spectacular visuality.

This register had been instituted socially in postwar consumer culture so that its subjects could be extracted from their material and productive participation in the world in favor of a passive specular consumption of its representations. The neo-avant-garde's ineluctable mimetical inscription within this historical process traces the extrapolation of all lived experience into a simulacral mirage. Within representation, so it seems, no function or capacity can be mobilized any longer except that of the specular and totalitarian dislodging of all traditional concepts of subjectivity.

Beuys and the readymade cults

The second set of intersections between the work of Beuys and that of the historical avant-garde on the one hand and that of his international peers on the other (specifically the Nouveaux Réalistes in France and the international Fluxus artists) concerns his relationships to the world of objects at large and to the legacies of ▲ Marcel Duchamp's readymade paradigm in particular. While it still might have appeared possible for the historical avant-garde ● (for instance, in the context of the Bauhaus aesthetic or of *l'esprit nouveau* to contemplate the social functions of objects in terms of their utopian potential, artistic production in the postwar period, by contrast, represented the object as being at the core of disaster, control, and domination (Arman and Warhol, for ■ example). What distinguished Pop and Fluxus artists of the early sixties from the avant-garde artists of the 1919–25 period was the sudden insight that the incessant invasion of all spheres of everyday life by the totality of object production would now border on the totalitarian. Clearly then, these were no longer the times for Duchamp's careful contemplation of the industrial object's emancipatory opposition to the obsolescence of artisanal works of art. This fact alone might already explain why Beuys, again in 1964, in a televised interview/performance, explicitly rejected Duchamp's legacy by painting the notorious placard "The Silence of Marcel Duchamp is Overrated" [**3**].

Beuys—situated between West Germany's avid internalization of American consumer culture and its repression of its fascist history—was qualified to engage in a perpetual project of dual reflection: that of the recent (German) totalitarian past and its entanglement with authoritarian forms of myth, leadership, and the fascist state on the one hand, and that of the emerging totalizing forms of the corporate state in the present, where the domination by commodity objects would increasingly eliminate conventional concepts of subject formation and experience on the other. Since Beuys—at least initially—sought an almost desperate association with the Fluxus artists, one might want to consider their attitudes to object production in general, and to the readymade in particular, and recognize how these differ dramatically from Beuys's own. And furthermore, and perhaps more importantly, one would have to recognize that the concept of performativity developed by Fluxus artists and the actual performances by Beuys are equally, if not fundamentally, different.

Fluxus artists had responded to the totalizing claims of object production under consumer culture with a mimetically totalizing subjection of artistic production to the object's regime. But it is precisely this decision to situate aesthetic practice exclusively in the register of the object (as opposed to the traditional registers of the iconic, the painterly, the sculptural, the photographic) that generates the essential element of the Fluxus aesthetic: a perpetual dialectical flux between object production and performativity. (The name "Fluxus," the Latin for "flowing," suggests a state of continuous movement.) Inducing the object's simultaneous reinvention and defetishization, this aesthetic demands a radically egalitarian mobilization of the artist/performer and the spectator in all registers: the dramatic, the linguistic, the poetical, and the musical.

Beuys, by contrast, conceived of "performance" as a relapse into myth, a return to ritual, as an almost cultic form of psychic healing

▲ 1916a ● 1926 ■ 1949, 1960b ◆ 1912, 1915 ▲ 1914 ● 1923, 1925a ■ 1960c, 1962a, 1964b

3 • Joseph Beuys, *Das Schweigen von Marcel Duchamp wird überbewertet* (The Silence of Marcel Duchamp is Overrated), 1964
Paper, oil color, ink, felt, chocolate, and photograph, 157.8 x 178 x 2 (62⅛ x 70⅛ x ¾)

and of exorcism. His performances attempted to reconnect unconscious conditions of past experiences (even if they have only recently passed as political) with sudden dramatic or grotesque representations in the present. These interventions, in their symbolic/substitutional character and their renewed hierarchical relations of performer and spectator, relapse into a pre-Aristotelian identificatory catharsis, and annihilate every aspect of Enlightenment dramaturgy. Most obviously they eliminate Bertolt ▲ Brecht's model of spectatorial agency and dialectical self-determination, the most crucial of Weimar Germany's theatrical positions.

The epistemological problem with Beuys's definition of the performative as therapeutic and exorcistic, as opposed to the Fluxus definition of the performative as linguistic self-constitution, as participatory and resistant to the condition of reification, is that it led to the cult of Beuys as the "shaman-artist." But "shamanism" • under the conditions of the society of the spectacle and under the conditions of postwar West Germany might not have been the cure to either the aesthetic or the sociopathological problems of that country's population. It remains unclear whether West Germany's "inability to mourn" could in fact have been culturally transfigured by this "homeopathic" structure of a single artist's ritualistic (and substitutional) interventions; or whether it was rather the promise to raise that nation state's devastated culture from the ashes and enact a new cultural model of conventional (German) identity that made the "shaman" particularly attractive to the Germans of the *Wirtschaftswunder* ("wonder of economics"), the name given to the German economy and industrial base's phenomenal recovery after World War II.

Thus, one of the central theoretical questions posed by Beuys's approach to artistic production—to phrase the problem in Walter ▲ Benjamin's terms—is whether "the avant-garde's emancipation of art from its parasitical dependency on ritual" could and should be reversed under the conditions of postwar culture at large and those of Germany in particular. After all, one argument in favor of this reversal, and thereby supporting the position of Beuys, would be to recognize that in order to perform the labor of mourning more profoundly, the actual sites and structures in which repression is enforced have to be first invested with the desire for memory. That investment requires, however, from both the producer and the spectator, a capacity to inhabit those structures of repression explicitly, in a form of homeopathic identification with those threatening historical phenomena that the socially and psychically ordered processes of forgetting had attempted to eradicate in the first place.

▲ Introduction 3 • 1957a ▲ 1935

One could argue, then, that the third of the complexes that distinguish Beuys from his peers is the work's structural and iconic relationship to historical memory. While all art, as Charles Baudelaire had said at the beginning of modernism, is engaged in the construction of the mnemonic, this prognosis had not held true. Avant-garde practices throughout the twentieth century had been for the most part relentless, if not in their orientation toward the future, then in their rabid affirmation of the present. The conditions of a universal "memory crisis," confronted by Baudelaire in the face of urban modernization, were, however, exacerbated beyond imagination in postwar Germany: here, the memory crisis originated in a politically and psychologically motivated repression of the recent past as much as from the rapidly advancing enforced consumption and its inherent erasure of the subject's individual and social history.

The last event in 1964 that defined Beuys's future oeuvre and practices was his decision to assemble his first vitrine. This constituted a new type of assemblage sculpture, a hybrid between the post-Surrealist object accumulation (prominent at that time in the ▲ work of Joseph Cornell and the *accumulations* of Arman that influ- • enced Fluxus artists and the spatialization of the readymade aesthetic that would soon culminate in all types of installation practices. The 1964 vitrine—the first of many to follow—would remain the only one to receive its title directly from Beuys, who named it *Auschwitz-Demonstration* [**5**]. Positioned somewhere between the memorial shrine and the showcase, it assembled various elements from Beuys's preparation for his entry to the competition for the creation of a *Monument for Auschwitz* [**4**], organized by the International Auschwitz Committee in 1958 (its artistic jury consisted ▲ of Hans Arp, Henry Moore, and Ossip Zadkine). Most importantly, it displayed a photographic leporello of the architecture of the camp itself and a drawing of a young woman on a piece of letterhead paper from the Committee. But for the most part, the vitrine combined earlier and more recent objects that were not explicitly related to the subject at hand (most notably the hot plate from the notorious Aachen performance, now carrying two blocks of fat, a printing stone with incisions from the mid-fifties with Christian symbols, the remains of a dead rat, and various hooflike elements made of cut-up sausage and two sausage rings).

Thus ranging from the abject to the uncanny presence of death, from the pomposity of its Christian symbolism to apparent

4 • Joseph Beuys, *Monument for Auschwitz*, 1958
Pencil, watercolor, opaque color, mordant, 17.6 x 24.5 (6⅞ x 9⅝)

▲ 1931, 1960a • 1962a ▲ 1913, 1916a, 1918, 1934b

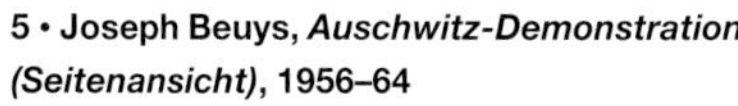

5 • Joseph Beuys, *Auschwitz-Demonstration (Seitenansicht)*, 1956–64
Mixed-media installation

mockery (for instance a cookie lying like a eucharist next to a Christ figure on a dinner plate), the *Auschwitz-Demonstration* (functioning in the manner of a "toy" as Beuys would state later) seems to be a work—if not the first work of visual culture in postwar German art—in which both the necessity to remember and the impossibility to represent adequately are fully articulated. Beuys attempts to synthesize two mutually exclusive epistemes aesthetically: to emphasize the object's investment, if not with cathartic ritual, then at least with a mnemonic dimension, and simultaneously to foreground the object's condition as pure matter and process according to his obsession with proto- and pseudoscientific positivism.

Beuys would later comment on the work, saying "*Similia similibus curantur*: heal like with like, that is the homeopathic healing process. The human condition is Auschwitz, and the principle of Auschwitz finds its perpetuation in our understanding of science and political systems, in the delegation of responsibility to groups of specialists, and in the silence of intellectuals and artists. I have found myself in permanent struggle with this condition and its roots. I find for instance that we are now experiencing Auschwitz in its contemporary character." Thus Beuys delivers his own variation on the *Dialectic of Enlightenment*, the philosophical study by the Germans Theodor Adorno and Max Horkheimer, written in 1947 and most likely unknown to Beuys in 1964, which had summed up and theorized for the first time the conditions of experience and the possibilities and necessities of cultural production after the Holocaust and World War II.

FURTHER READING

Götz Adriani, Winfried Konnertz, and Karin Thomas, *Joseph Beuys: Life and Works* (New York: Barrons Books, 1979)

Mario Kramer, "Joseph Beuys: Auschwitz Demonstration 1956–1964," in Eckhart Gillen (ed.), *German Art from Beckmann to Richter* (New Haven and London: Yale University Press; and Cologne: Dumont, 1997)

Gene Ray (ed.), *Joseph Beuys: The Critical Legacies* (New York: DAP, 2000)

David Thistlewood (ed.), *Joseph Beuys: Diverging Critiques* (Liverpool: Liverpool University Press and Tate Gallery, 1995)

Caroline Tisdall (ed.), *Joseph Beuys* (New York: Guggenheim Museum, 1979)

1964b

Thirteen Most Wanted Men by Andy Warhol is installed, momentarily, on the facade of the State Pavilion at the World's Fair in New York.

Andy Warhol is one of the few postwar artists whose name resonates well beyond the art world. From his public rise in the early sixties to his premature death in 1987, he was a central relay between art and advertising, fashion, underground music, independent filmmaking, experimental writing, gay culture, celebrity culture, and mass culture. Apart from art work that ranged from extraordinary to bathetic, Warhol invented entirely new genres of movies, produced the first album of The Velvet Underground, founded a magazine (*Interview*), and endorsed products with his own logo-persona, among a myriad other ventures (his studio was appropriately named The Factory). He exposed and exploited a new way of being in a world of commodity-images where fame is often subsumed by celebrity, newsworthiness by notoriety, aura by glamor, and charisma by hype: a native informant who always kept his Polaroid, tape recorder, film and video cameras switched on, Warhol had a look of blank indifference, but an eye for killer images.

Critical or complacent?

Born in 1928 to Slovak immigrants in Pittsburgh (his father worked in coal mines, then in construction), Warhol studied design at the Carnegie Institute of Technology, then moved to New York in 1949, where he achieved early success with magazine ads, window displays, stationery, book jackets, album covers, and the like for a range of classy clients from *Vogue* to Bonwit Teller. By the late fifties and early sixties, he was wealthy enough to buy work by ▲ Jasper Johns, Frank Stella, even Marcel Duchamp, before he could sell his own art; and he went on to collect objects and images of many sorts—every day was a time capsule for Warhol. He did his first paintings of comic-strip characters (Batman, Nancy, Dick Tracy, Popeye) in 1960, the year before he saw, at his own future • gallery (Leo Castelli), canvases by Roy Lichtenstein with similar subjects rendered in different styles. Whereas Lichtenstein was clean and hard in his comic-and-ad copies, Warhol played with manual mistakes and media-image blurrings. The year 1962–3 was his *annus mirabilis*: he produced his first paintings of Campbell's soup cans; his first "Disaster," "Do It Yourself," "Elvis," and "Marilyn" paintings; his first silkscreens on canvas; and his first films (*Sleep*, *Kiss*, and so on—the titles declare all the action that we see). In 1963 he moved his studio to East 47th Street (soon to be dubbed The Factory), which became a post-bohemian hangout for scene-makers and "superstars" (another Warhol invention); in the same year, he used a Polaroid for the first time as well.

His greatest period spans the time between his first silkscreens in 1962 and his near-fatal shooting in 1968 (on June 3, two days before Bobby Kennedy was assassinated). Most significant readings of Warhol focus on this body of work, especially on the "Death in America" images (based on newspaper photographs, often too gruesome for publication, of car wrecks and suicides, electric chairs and civil-rights confrontations [**1**]). These accounts tend either to connect such images to real events in the world or, conversely, to propose that the world of Warhol is nothing but image, that Pop images in general represent only other images. Most readings, not only of Warhol but of most postwar art based in photography, divide somewhere along this line: the image as referential *or* as simulacral (a simulacrum is a copy without an apparent original, and in his image repetitions the original often does appear to dissolve).

The *simulacral* reading of Pop is advanced by critics informed by ▲ poststructuralism, for whom the theory of the simulacrum, crucial to the poststructuralist critique of referential representation, sometimes seems to depend on the example of Warhol as Pop. "What Pop art wants," Roland Barthes writes in "That Old Thing, Art" (1980), "is to desymbolize the object," that is, to release the image from deep meaning into simulacral surface. In the process the artist is also released: "The Pop artist does not stand *behind* his work," Barthes continues, "and he himself has no depth: he is merely the surface of his pictures, no signified, no intention, anywhere." With variations this reading is repeated by such French philosopher-critics as Michel Foucault, Gilles Deleuze, and Jean Baudrillard, for whom referential depth and subjective interiority are also victims of the sheer superficiality of Warhol Pop.

The *referential* view is advanced by critics based in social history who tie the work to thematic issues (fashion, gay culture, political struggles). In "Saturday Disasters: Trace and Reference in Early Warhol" (1987), the art historian Thomas Crow disputes the simulacral account of Warhol as impassive and the images as

▲ 1914, 1918, 1935, 1942b, 1958, 1966a • 1960c ▲ Introduction 4, 1980

1 • Andy Warhol, *White Burning Car III*, 1963
Silkscreen on canvas, 255.3 x 200 (100½ x 78¾)

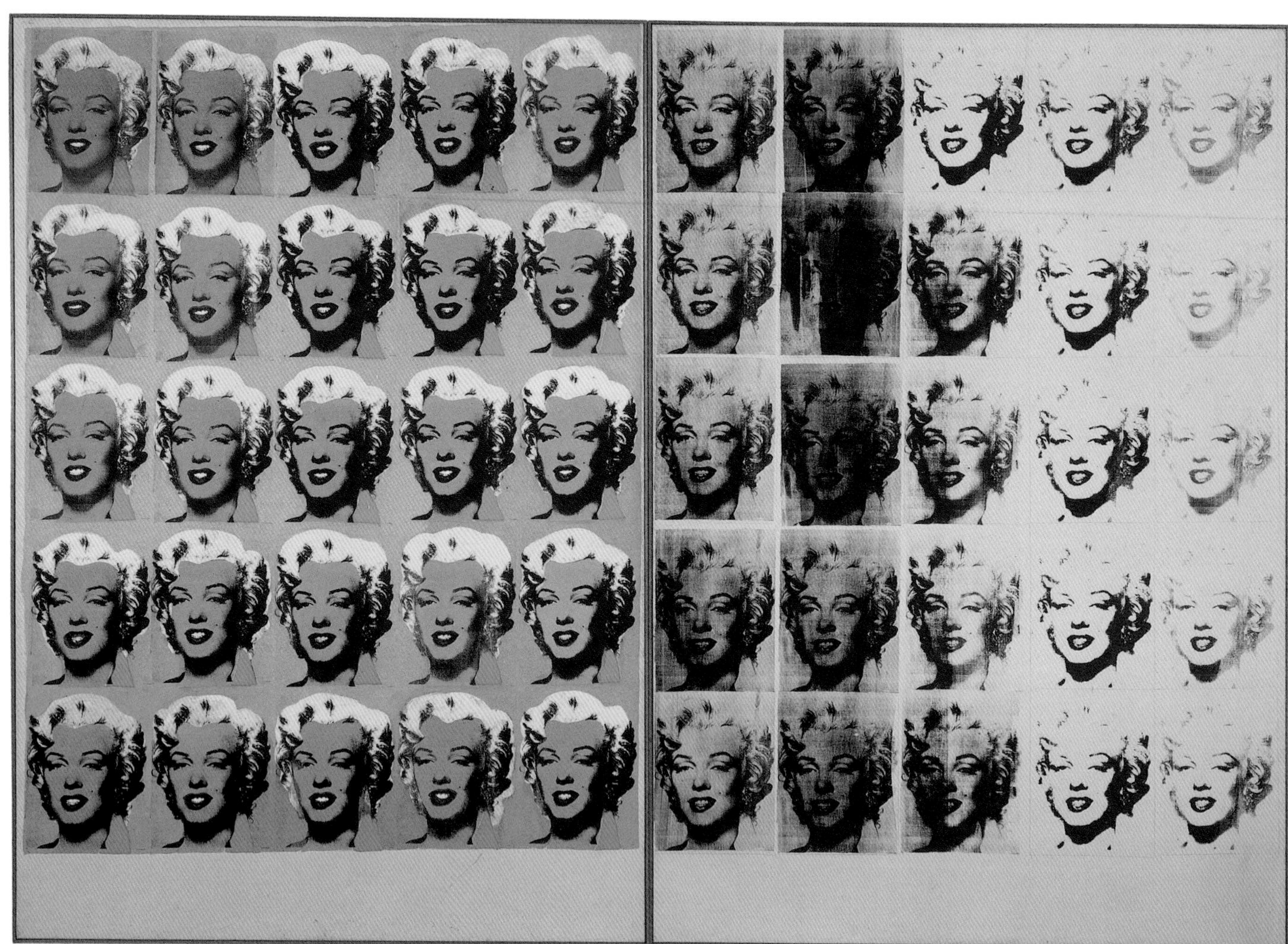

2 • Andy Warhol, *Marilyn Diptych*, 1962
Silkscreen ink and synthetic polymer paint on canvas, two panels, each 208.3 x 144.8 (82 x 57)

indiscriminate. Underneath the glamorous surface of commodity fetishes and media stars, Crow finds "the reality of suffering and death"; the tragedies of Marilyn, Liz, and Jackie in particular prompt "straightforward expressions of feeling" from Warhol [**2**]. Here Crow finds not only a referential object *for* Warhol but an empathic subject *in* Warhol, and here he locates the criticality *of* Warhol—not in an attack on "that old thing art" (as Barthes would have it) through an embrace of the simulacral commodity-image (as Baudrillard would have it), but rather in an exposé of "complacent consumption" through "the brutal fact" of accident and mortality. In this way Crow pushes Warhol beyond humanist sentiment to political engagement. "He was attracted to the open sores in American political life," Crow writes in a reading of the electric-chair images [**3**] as agitprop against the death penalty and of the race-riot images as a testimonial for civil rights. "Far from a pure play of the signifier liberated from reference," Warhol belongs to the popular American tradition of "truth-telling."

In part this reading of Warhol as empathic, even *engagé*, is a projection, but so is the superficial, impassive Warhol—even though this latter projection was his own: "If you want to know all about Andy Warhol, just look at the surface of my paintings and films and me, and there I am. There's nothing behind it." Both camps make the Warhol they need; no doubt we all do (projection is one of his great subjects). In any case neither argument is wrong; but they cannot both be right—or can they? Can we read these early images of disaster and death as referential *and* simulacral, connected *and* disconnected, effective *and* effectless, critical *and* complacent?

Traumatic realism

The most famous Warhol motto is "I want to be a machine," which is usually taken to confirm the blankness of artist and art alike. But it may point less to a blank subject than to a shocked one, who takes on what shocks him as a mimetic defense against this very shock: I am a machine too, I make (or consume) serial commodity-images too, I give as good (or as bad) as I get. "Someone said my life has dominated me," Warhol told the art critic Gene Swenson in an important interview of 1963, "I liked that idea." Warhol had just sworn to having the same lunch for the past twenty years (what else but Campbell's soup?). Together, then, the two statements read as a preemptive embrace of the compulsion to repeat put into play by a society of serial production and consumption. If you can't beat it,

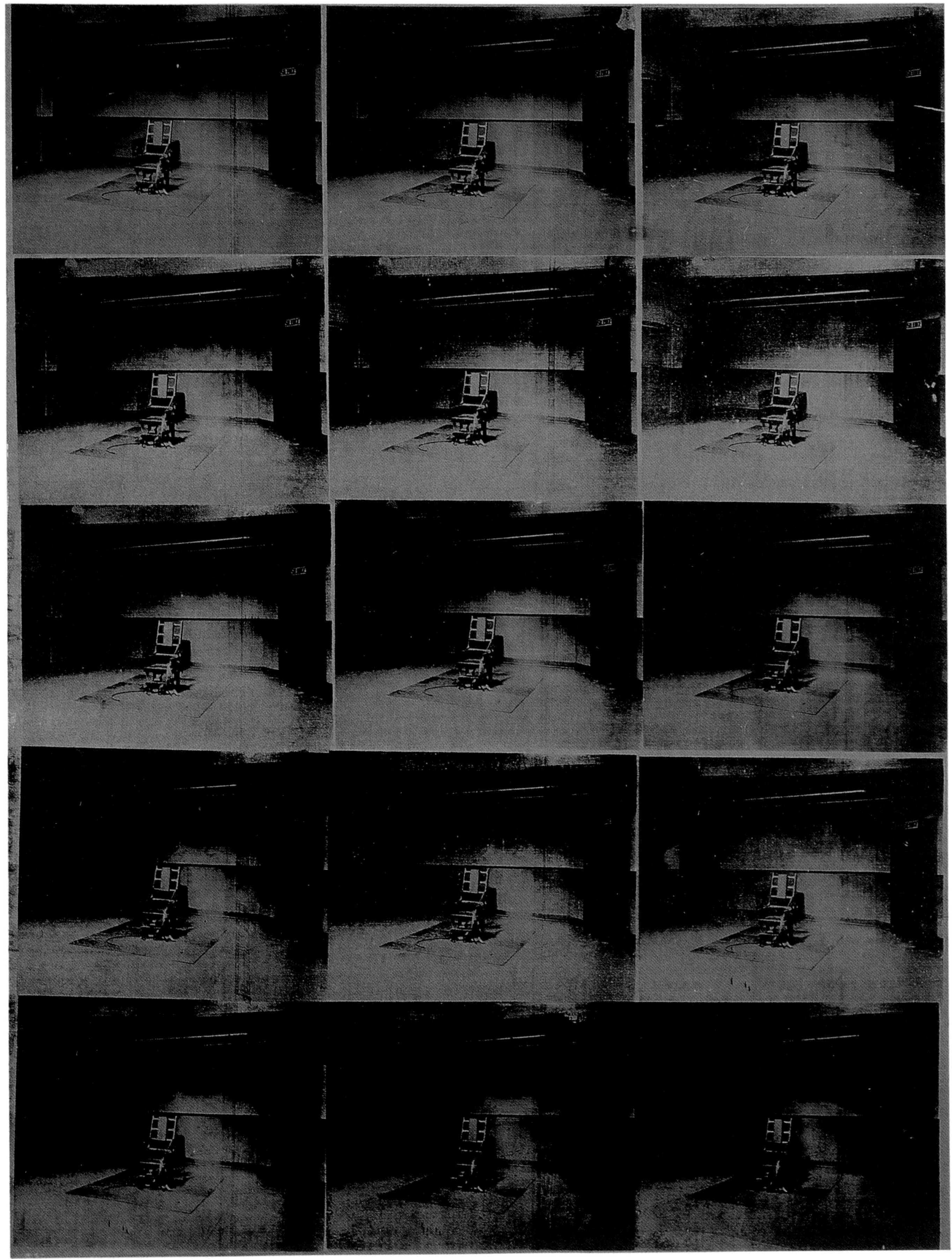

3 • Andy Warhol, *Lavender Disaster*, 1963
Silkscreen ink and synthetic polymer paint on canvas, 269.2 x 208 (106 x 81⅞)

Warhol suggests, join it. More, if you enter it totally, you might expose it; you might reveal its automatism, even its autism, through your own excessive example. Deployed first by Dada, this strategic nihilism was performed ambiguously by Warhol, and ▲ artists such as Jeff Koons have played it out since.

These remarks reposition the role of *repetition* in Warhol. "I like boring things" is another famous motto of his quasi-autistic persona. "I like things to be exactly the same over and over again." In *POPism* (1980) Warhol glossed this embrace of boredom, repetition, domination: "I don't want it to be essentially the same—I want it to be *exactly* the same. Because the more you look at the same exact thing, the more the meaning goes away, and the better and emptier you feel." Here repetition is both a draining of significance and a defending against affect, and this strategy guided Warhol as early as the 1963 interview with Swenson: "When you see a gruesome picture over and over again, it doesn't really have any effect." Clearly this is one function of repetition in our psychic lives: we repeat traumatic events in order to integrate them into a psychic economy, a symbolic order. But the Warhol repetitions are not restorative in this way; they are not about a mastery of trauma. More than a patient release from a lost object in mourning, they suggest an obsessive fixation on a lost object in melancholy. Think of all the *Marilyn* images cropped, colored, and crimped: the "hallucinatory wish-psychosis" of a melancholic (Freud) seems to be in play here. But this analysis is not quite right either, for the repetitions not only *re*produce traumatic effects, but also can *produce* them. Several contradictory operations occur at the same time: a warding away of traumatic significance *and* an opening out to it, a defending against traumatic affect *and* a producing of it.

Repetition in Warhol, then, is neither a representation of a worldly referent nor a simulation of a pure image or a detached signifier. Rather, repetition serves to screen a reality understood as traumatic, but in a way that points to this traumatic reality nonetheless through a rupture in the image—or, more precisely, in the viewer *touched* by the image. In *Camera Lucida* (1980) Barthes called this traumatic point the *punctum*. "It is this element which rises from the scene, shoots out of it like an arrow, and pierces me," he writes. "It is what I add to the photograph and what is nonetheless already there.... It is acute yet muffled, it cries out in silence. Odd contradiction: a floating flash." Barthes is concerned here with straight (unmanipulated) photographs, so he relates the *punctum* to details of content. This is rarely the case in Warhol, yet a *punctum* exists for me (Barthes stipulates that it is a personal effect) in the indifference of the passerby in *White Burning Car III* [**1**]. This indifference to the crash victim impaled on the telephone pole is bad enough, but its repetition is galling, and this points to the operation of the *punctum* in Warhol. It works less through content than through technique, especially in the "floating flashes" of the silkscreen process, in the repetitive "popping" of the images. Here Pop does not register the death of affect (as is sometimes said) so much as the affect of death.

Such disaster and death images evoke the public nightmares of the early age of television, for Warhol selects moments when this ▲ society of spectacle cracks—Jackie Kennedy in mourning after the assassination in Dallas, Marilyn Monroe remembered after her suicide, racist attacks, car wrecks—but cracks only to expand. Content in Warhol is thus not trivial: a white man impaled on a telephone pole, or a black man attacked by a police dog, is shocking. But, again, this first order of shock is screened by the repetition of the image, even as this repetition produces a second order of trauma, here at the level of technique, where the *punctum* breaks through the screen and allows the real to poke through. In this way different kinds of repetition are put into play by Warhol: repetitions that fix on the traumatic real, that screen it, that produce it. And this multiplicity makes for the paradox not only of images that are both affective and affectless, but also of viewers that are neither integrated (which is the ideal of most modern aesthetics: the subject composed in contemplation) nor dissolved (which is the effect of much popular culture: the subject given over to the intensities of the commodity-image). "I never fall apart," Warhol remarks in *The Philosophy of Andy Warhol* (1975), "because I never fall together." Such is the paradoxical subject-effect of his work too, and it resonates in some art after Pop as well ● (for instance, some appropriation art and some abject art).

Mass subjectivity

Barthes was wrong to suggest that the *punctum* is only a private affair; it can have a public dimension as well. The breakdown of the distinction between private and public is traumatic too; seen as a breakdown of inside and outside, it is one way to understand trauma as such. No one points to this traumatic breakdown of private and public as incisively as Warhol. "It's just like taking the outside and putting it on the inside," he once said of Pop in general, "or taking the inside and putting it on the outside." However cryptic, this remark suggests a historically new relay between private fantasy and public reality as a primary topic of Pop.

Warhol was fascinated by the subjectivity produced in mass society. "I want everybody to think alike," he said in 1963. "Russia is doing it under government. It's happening here all by itself." "I don't think art should be only for the select few," he added in 1967. "I think it should be for the mass of American people." But how does one represent "the mass of American people"? One way to evoke this mass subject is through its proxies, that is, through its objects of consumption (thus the serial presentation from 1962 on of the Campbell's soup cans, Coke bottles, Brillo boxes) and/or through its objects of taste (thus the kitschy flower paintings of 1964 and the folksy cow wallpaper of 1966). But can one *figure* this mass subject? Does it have a body to figure? "The mass subject cannot have a body," the critic Michael Warner asserts, "except the body it witnesses." This principle suggests why Warhol evokes the mass subject through its figural projections—from celebrities and politicians such as Marilyn and Mao to all the lurid cover-people of

▲ 1916a, 1920, 1986

▲ 1957a ● 1977, 1980, 1994a

Interview magazine. At the same time he was also concerned to specify this subject in subcultural ways: The Factory was a virtual workshop of campy reinventions of mass icons such as Troy Donahue, and portraits like *Thirteen Most Wanted Men* **[4]** are obvious *double entendres* for gay viewers.

However, Warhol did more than evoke the mass subject through its kitsch, commodities, and celebrities. He also represented it in its very unrepresentability, that is, in its absence and anonymity, its disaster and death, the democratic levelers of famous mass object and anonymous mass subject alike. Here are two more statements from interviews, the first from 1963, the second from 1972:

> *I guess it was the big crash picture, the front page of a newspaper: 129 DIE. I was also painting the Marilyns. I realized that everything I was doing must have been Death. It was Christmas or Labor Day—a holiday—and every time you turned on the radio they said something like, "4 million are going to die." That started it.*

> *Actually you know it wasn't the idea of accidents and things like that ... I thought of all the people who worked on the pyramids and ... I just always sort of wondered what happened to them ... well, it would be easier to do a painting of people who died in car crashes because sometimes you know, you never know who they are.*

These remarks imply that his primary concern was not disaster and death but the mass subject, here in the guise of the anonymous victims of history, from the drones of the pyramids to the statistical DOAs at the hospitals. Yet disaster and death were necessary to ▲ evoke this subject, for in the society of the spectacle the mass subject often appears only as an effect of the mass media (the newspaper, the radio), or of a catastrophic failure of technology (the plane crash), or, more precisely, of both (the news of such a catastrophic failure). Along with icons of celebrity such as Marilyn and Mao, reports of disastrous death are a primary way that mass subjecthood is produced.

For the most part, then, Warhol evoked the mass subject in two opposite ways: through iconic celebrity and abstract anonymity. But he might have come closest to this subject through a compromise representation somewhere between celebrity and anonymity, that is, through the figure of *notoriety*, the fame of fifteen minutes. Consider his implicit double portrait of the mass subject: the most-wanted men and the empty electric chairs, the first a kind of American icon, the second a kind of American crucifix. What more exact representation of our pathological public sphere than this twinning of iconic mass murderer and abstract state execution? That is, what more difficult image? When Warhol made his *Thirteen Most Wanted Men* for the 1964 World's Fair in New York, power—men such as Governor Nelson Rockefeller, Commissioner Robert Moses, and court architect Philip Johnson, men who not only designed the society of the spectacle but also represented it as the fulfillment of the American dream of success and self-rule—could not tolerate it. Warhol was ordered to cover up the image, literally to repress it (which he did, in gay mockery, with his signature silver paint), and the powers that be were not amused when Warhol offered to substitute a portrait of Robert Moses instead.

4 • Andy Warhol, *Thirteen Most Wanted Men*, 1964
Silkscreen on canvas, twenty-five panels, 610 x 610 (240 x 240), on the New York State Pavilion, 1964 World's Fair, New York (no longer exists as one work)

FURTHER READING

Roland Barthes, *Camera Lucida*, trans. Richard Howard (New York: Hill and Wang, 1981)
Thomas Crow, "Saturday Disasters: Trace and Reference in Early Warhol," in Serge Guilbaut (ed.), *Reconstructing Modernism* (Cambridge, Mass.: MIT Press, 1990)
Kynaston McShine (ed.), *Andy Warhol: A Retrospective* (New York: Museum of Modern Art, 1989)
Richard Meyer, "Warhol's Clones," *The Yale Journal of Criticism*, vol. 7, no. 1, 1994
John Russell (ed.), *Pop Art Redefined* (New York: Praeger, 1969)
Paul Taylor (ed.), *Post-Pop* (Cambridge, Mass.: MIT Press, 1989)
Andy Warhol, *The Philosophy of Andy Warhol* (New York: Harcourt Brace Jovanovich, 1975) and *POPism: The Warhol '60s* (New York: Harcourt Brace Jovanovich, 1980)

▲ 1957a

1965

Donald Judd publishes "Specific Objects": Minimalism receives its theorization at the hands of its major practitioners, Judd and Robert Morris.

Looking back from a distance of nearly three decades at his first years as a sculptor, Robert Morris wrote in 1989 of that period in the early sixties: "At thirty I had my alienation, my Skilsaw, and my plywood. I was out to rip out the metaphors, especially those that had to do with 'up,' as well as every other whiff of transcendence." This mood of resistance he recalls as specifically pitted against the values of Abstract Expressionism, a defiance that energized his whole generation: "When I sliced into the plywood with my Skilsaw, I could hear, beneath the ear-damaging whine, a stark and refreshing "no" reverberate off the four walls: no to transcendence and spiritual values, heroic scale, anguished decisions, historicizing narrative, valuable artifact, intelligent structure, interesting visual experience."

The plywood polygons—giant slabs, beams, portals—that Morris was to begin exhibiting in the fall of 1963 coincided with the peculiar transformation that Donald Judd had effected in his own work during the same year. It was then that Judd's paintings had begun to mutate into large, simplified, three-dimensional objects, such as two slabs abutted at right angles, their juncture acknowledged by an elbow of metal pipe or a big, bright-red, wooden box with a shallow trough cut out of its upper face [**1**].

"No" to transcendence

By 1966, with the "Primary Structures" show mounted at the Jewish Museum in New York, these separate acts of defiance could be decreed a movement, since the exhibition's curator, Kynaston McShine, was now able to join forty more British and American sculptors to Judd's and Morris's examples, these including Carl ▲Andre, Anthony Caro, Walter De Maria, Dan Flavin, Robert

1 • Donald Judd, *Untitled (box with trough)*, 1963
Light cadmium-red oil on wood, 49.5 x 114.3 x 77.5 (19½ x 45 x 30½)

▲ 1945, 1962a

Grosvenor, Ellsworth Kelly, Sol LeWitt, Tim Scott, Tony Smith, ▲ Robert Smithson, Anne Truitt, and William Tucker. One among a number of attempts to give this movement a name, the title "Primary Structures" focused on the radical simplification of shapes involved, while in 1968 the Museum of Modern Art employed "The Art of the Real" as a rubric that would highlight the brutally unframed character of the work in its abandonment of any sculptural pedestal in order to share the real space of its viewer. By 1968, however, "Minimalism" had come into widespread usage, edging out all other titles, such as "Systemic Painting," which the Guggenheim Museum had used to emphasize the impersonal quality involved in generating this work—its industrialized, serialized character—only now applied to the movement's production in the two dimensions of painting.

That Minimalist art bridges between painting and sculpture, indeed, that it necessarily erases the distinction between painting and sculpture, was the message of Judd's article in the 1965 *Arts Yearbook*, "Specific Objects," the first extended attempt to theorize what was taking place (the second being Morris's "Notes on Sculpture" of 1966). Turning to the shaped, concentrically striped • canvases that Frank Stella had been making since 1961, Judd saw these as moving past painting—with its inevitable illusion of space (no matter how shallow)—to become slabs that begin to exist as three-dimensional objects. "Three dimensions are real space," Judd explains. "That gets rid of the problem of illusionism and of literal space, space in and around marks and colors." This, he adds, "is riddance to one of the salient and most objectionable relics of European art," a relic he would in another context characterize as linked to rationalistic philosophy "based on systems built beforehand, *a priori* systems."

Having become "three dimensions," Stella's slabs are now "specific objects," which would tend to suggest that Judd thought they would best be called sculptures. Judd, however, had the same objection to sculpture that he did to painting, seeing it as additive and composed. What Stella's rectangular or donut or V-shaped "slabs" achieved was a striking quality of unitariness, of simply being *that* object, *that* shape. He compared this with Duchamp's ■ readymades which, he said "are seen at once and not part by part."

This insistence on a single shape that takes over the experience of a work, eclipsing any sense of its component parts, is thus seen as a correlative of the rejection of "a priori systems." For Judd, such systems inevitably establish a hierarchy among the constituent elements, as they work to achieve balance, to produce compositional relationships. By radically reducing the elements in a work to such a degree that all would connect self-evidently to the unitary shape, Judd hoped not only to cancel composition but also to eliminate the other aspect of the a priori, namely the sense of an idea or intention that exists prior to the making of the work in such a way so that it seems to lie inside the object like its motivating kernel or core. Eradicating illusionism is thus part and parcel of ridding the work of this motivating idea, this sense of a *raison d'être* that the resulting object clothes or expresses. This is what Morris had

2 • Robert Morris, (from left to right) *Untitled (Table)*, *Untitled (Corner Beam)*, *Untitled (Floor Beam)*, *Untitled (Corner Piece)*, and *Untitled (Cloud)*
Installation at the Green Gallery, December 1964–January 1965

meant when he remembered saying "no to transcendence and spiritual values, heroic scale, anguished decisions," in a rejection that covered Judd's "rationalism" and the Abstract Expressionist ▲ "sublime" in one and the same rebuff. When Morris decreed this same anti-illusionism in his own "Notes on Sculpture," he used the term "gestalt" to evoke Judd's idea of unitariness. That nothing, no previous idea, lies *behind* the external shape or gestalt, Morris expressed as: "One does not seek the gestalt of a gestalt." **[2]**

If the spectator was not supposed to plumb the object's depths to discover the rationale for its appearance, this was because such an object "takes relationships out of the work and," Morris explained, "makes them a function of space, light, and the viewer's field of vision." Which is to say that a new model of meaning was being put in place by this sense that everything in the work existed only on its surface, a surface itself constantly vulnerable to the play of light and of the viewer's perspective. "Even [the work's] most patently unalterable property, shape, does not remain constant," Morris maintained, "for it is the viewer who changes the shape constantly by his change in position relative to the work."

The death of the author

Into the art world of the early and mid-sixties there had surfaced two models of meaning that seemed utterly to alter the parameters of aesthetic experience. One of these, linked to the late phase of • Ludwig Wittgenstein's philosophical writings, had already been invoked by Jasper Johns in the late fifties and early sixties when he announced that the *meaning* of any word was its "use." Two conclusions followed from such a statement: first, that the meanings of words are not a function of an absolute definition held inviolate in some kind of Platonic heaven but instead blur and fuzz within the context of their applications; and second, that the meanings of the words we speak are not secured by the intentions we have in our heads prior to having uttered them ("*this* is what I meant") but

▲ 1953, 1962c, 1967a, 1968b, 1970 • 1958 ■ 1914 ▲ 1947a, 1949, 1951 • 1958

instead take on significance in the public space of our exchange with others. Discussing Minimalism in "A.B.C. Art" (1965), one of the first interpretive essays not written by an artist, Barbara Rose emphasized the importance of Wittgenstein's notions of language for the way Morris's and Judd's works stake everything on the context in which they surface into the experience of their viewers.

To reinforce this sense of meaning-as-context Morris resorted to several strategies. One was to make the gestalts of his works out of detachable segments and, over the course of the installation of a group of these ensembles, to "permute" the segments into different arrangements of forms, in such a way that no single work could ever be seen to have a stable, pregiven shape: an inner "idea" that would function as its immutable core. Another strategy was to take the same shape and repeat it several times, only each in a different position, as in his three *L-Beams* **[3]** where, as we confront one of these massive Ls lying on its side, the other "sitting up," and the third arched on its two ends, we cannot see all three of their shapes as the "same." This is because the effect of real space means that each shape takes on a different meaning according to the way a sense of gravitational pull or luminous release affects our experience of the actual thickness and weight of the different "arms."

It was Maurice Merleau-Ponty's *Phenomenology of Perception* (1945; English translation, 1962) that produced the second important model for meaning-as-context, or rather meaning as a function of the body's immersion in its world, which resonates in Morris's *L-Beams* or in the plywood boxes Judd began to make in the early seventies that seem to internalize, and therefore all the more nakedly depend on, the moving spectator's visual trajectory.

Insofar as both these models—meaning as "use" or meaning as a function of the body's connection to its spatial horizon—join in rejecting an idea of either innerness or priorness as securing signification, both of them have sweeping implications for the traditional notion of the author of either a sentence or a work. For nothing inside the author—his or her intentions or feelings—is now believed to serve as a guarantee of the work's meaning; rather, that meaning is dependent on the interchange that occurs in the public space of the work's connection to its viewers. That Judd with his refusal of the a priori, and Morris with his "no" to anguishing decisions, should have embraced these models is not, then, surprising, nor is it an accident that by 1968 the second-generation Minimalist and critic Brian O'Doherty (born 1934) should have brought into the American context an essay by Roland Barthes that carried the significant title: "The Death of the Author."

3 • Robert Morris, *Untitled (Three L-Beams)*, 1965–6
Installation at Leo Castelli Gallery

Various practices by the Minimalists were to reinforce this sense of the eviction of the "author," one of which was to depersonalize the fabrication of the work. Just as Morris and Judd had initially resorted to the use of standardized materials—such as plywood or Plexiglas sheets—so they had also taken the plans for objects too difficult for them to forge themselves to metal shops to have them executed. By the late sixties this recourse to production by others had become far more programmatic in that it had entered their ▲ thinking as a way of exorcising the last remnants of "aura" from the object, whether in the form of the artist's touch or in the uniqueness of the resultant work. Industrial fabrication ensured the utmost depersonalization of the making of the work at the same time as it guaranteed that the object could be produced as a multiple, with no member of the resulting series having any more claim to being the "original" than any other.

The second of these antiauthorial practices was to push the use of standardized materials toward the limit of the readymade and to ● make the object from freestanding store-bought units. Dan Flavin pursued this in the form of fluorescent tubes that he would pair, treble, or quintuple to form what he began to call "Monuments" (e.g., *Monument 7 for V. Tatlin*, thereby acknowledging not so much the ■ Dada aspect of the readymade but the Russian Constructivist and Productivist commitment to industrialized art. For his part Carl ◆ Andre began to employ fire bricks, as in the four-hundred-foot row of them he installed in the "Primary Structures" show and called *Lever*. Given the absolutely aggregate character of the floorbound assemblies that he pursued in both brick and metal plates (often referred to as "rugs"), his work flaunted the idea of "composition" to the utmost and declared itself to be a case of what Judd had said should replace it: an organization that was nothing but "just one thing after another."

"Presentness is grace"

If by 1966 "Primary Structures" had established the breadth of Minimalist practice, *Artforum* magazine would, the following summer, demonstrate its conceptual ambitions by devoting a special issue to this work, an issue in which artists such as Robert Smithson (1938–73) and Sol LeWitt joined Robert Morris in setting forth the logic of their practice. Yet their "joining" was at the same time a subtle form of secession, since Smithson's "Towards the

▲ 1935 ● 1962c ■ 1914, 1921 ◆ 1962c

Development of an Air Terminal Site" was already to announce the coming of a new phase in art that was to be called Earthworks, and ▲ LeWitt's "Paragraphs on Conceptual Art," while they were meant to stress the permutational and serial nature of this practice, were already geared to a relation with language and dematerialized "conception" that was to challenge Minimalism with increasing ferocity. But even more aggressively, Michael Fried's "Art and Objecthood" used the special issue of *Artforum* to launch an attack on Minimalism's rear, ratifying even through his most negative arguments its practitioners' own sense of the degree to which Minimalism constituted a watershed within modernism, changing the most basic terms for the practice of art.

Rebaptizing Judd's "specific" object with the term "literalist," Fried agreed with Judd that such a work constituted itself in the real space of its viewer's engagement neither as painting nor as sculpture but in some kind of category that is between the two. He also agreed that the crucial effect of this work was to engage with its surrounds, including the real time within which its existence unfolds—a "just one thing after another" that is temporal as well as spatial. But where Fried diverged from his adversaries was in his argument that the presence that such an object sets up within its newly real space was analogous to *stage presence*, like an actor who is constantly producing effects on his audience, and hence that the experience of Minimalism was profoundly theatrical. Further he argued, if this theatricality is a result of the insistence on engaging the work with its surrounds, it is also logically continuous with the desire to collapse the distinctions between the specific mediums of art on which the modernist logic had previously depended. For, from Richard Wagner in the late nineteenth century to Erwin Piscator in the twentieth, theater was continually seen as the consummate mixed medium, the melting pot of all the separate arts, or what Wagner had called the *Gesamtkunstwerk* (the total work of art).

Yet this collapse of distinction *between* the arts is nothing, Fried maintained, but the eradication of any distinction between art and the literal, or art and the everyday. For art is not simply a function of something's being in my presence—as though it were in my way—but rather an instant of aesthetic experience which occurs in no real space or time at all, being instead a moment of illumination that suffuses a work with its meaning the way comprehension of a mathematical equation suffuses a bunch of numbers and a group of instances with a kind of timeless truth. To this effect Fried gave the name "presentness" to contrast it with the literalist object's "presence," and by ending his essay with a refusal of dailiness in the startling declaration "presentness is grace," he courted that very possibility of transcendence to which Morris's Skilsaw had screamed its earlier "no."

Between the covers of this 1967 issue of *Artforum* there were collected, then, four voices equally clear about the threshold that Minimalism had crossed. One of them was dismayed at its bringing the specific medium of sculpture to an end; and indeed Fried pre- • sented the work of Anthony Caro as the true, sculptural alternative to Judd's and Morris's literalist work. The other three—Morris, LeWitt, Smithson—greeted the newly mapped field for aesthetic practice as the advent of the greatest possible freedom, entering ▲ thereby into what could be called an "expanded field."

Maurice Merleau-Ponty (1908–61)

Having founded the important postwar journal *Les Temps modernes* with Jean-Paul Sartre and Simone de Beauvoir, Maurice Merleau-Ponty filled the chair of philosophy at the Collège de France, beginning in 1952. Reacting against Descartes, Merleau-Ponty's criticism of his, or any, form of idealism stemmed from his objection to a model of experience based on the knowing mind's harmonious connection to the world, a model which failed to account for the fundamental discontinuities not only between consciousness and the world but between one consciousness and another. Human subjectivity could not be grasped, he felt, without an account of these gaps.

Indebted to the Gestalt psychology of Wilhelm Köhler, Merleau-Ponty focused on what he called the "perceptual milieu" in an effort to describe the uniquely human form of "being-in-the-world," which was grounded, he argued, in the partial nature of visual experience due to the "perspectival" limits of human perception. In *The Phenomenology of Perception* (1945), his chapters on "the Body" opened onto forms of perception that he characterized as "preobjectile," thereby grounding a form of seeing and knowing that would have to be called "abstract." Merleau-Ponty's work entered the active discourse on modernist art through the essays that Michael Fried wrote on the English sculptor Anthony Caro. There, wanting to characterize the disjunctive "syntax" of Caro's work, Fried acknowledged Merleau-Ponty's essay "On the Phenomenology of Language" (1952) among others.

Since Merleau-Ponty's phenomenology places the subject's body—its bilateral symmetry, its vertical axis, its having a front and a back, the latter invisible to the subject him- or herself—at the center of the subject's intention toward meaning—those artistic projects dependent on bodily vectors for their aesthetic experience are particularly open to phenomenological analysis. In addition to the above-mentioned case of Caro, important examples would be Barnett Newman and Richard Serra.

FURTHER READING

Gregory Battcock (ed.), *Minimal Art: A Critical Anthology* (New York: Dutton, 1968; and Berkeley and Los Angeles: University of California Press, 1995)

Francis Colpitt, *Minimal Art: The Critical Perspective* (Seattle: University of Washington Press, 1990)

Michael Fried, "Art and Objecthood" (1967), *Art and Objecthood* (Chicago: University of Chicago Press, 1998)

Donald Judd, *Complete Writings: 1959–1975* (New York: New York University Press, 1975)

Rosalind Krauss, *Robert Morris: The Mind/Body Problem* (New York: Guggenheim Museum, 1994)

Robert Morris, *Continuous Project Altered Daily* (Cambridge, Mass.: MIT Press, 1993)

▲ 1968b, 1970 • 1945 ▲ 1970

1966a

Marcel Duchamp completes his installation *Etant Donnés* in the Philadelphia Museum of Art: his mounting influence on younger artists climaxes with the posthumous revelation of this new work.

One way—and by no means the least telling—of characterizing the aesthetic climate of the sixties is to notice the degree to which Picasso's reputation had become eclipsed by Duchamp's. If Picasso had been the wizard of modernism, the ▲ great inventor of Cubism and of the principle of collage, he had also been the ceaselessly protean producer, keeping alive the tradition of painting in an endless parade of pictorial styles, fanning the dying embers of the printmaking process, pushing the boundaries of traditional sculpture. Duchamp, by contrast, had "stopped painting" in 1920 to take up chess, as he claimed, and to issue a series of ready- • mades under the pseudonym Rrose Sélavy. Compared with the avalanche of publicity, exhibitions, and critical literature that surrounded Picasso, the "serene obscurity" into which Duchamp had settled in New York by the forties was broken only by a special issue ■ of the Surrealist-influenced magazine *View* devoted to him in 1945 (a first monograph on Duchamp would not be published until 1959). Living in a spartanly simple apartment, his only contact with the art world was through a few displaced Surrealists and the avant-garde composer John Cage. But this, it turns out, was enough.

By the fifties Cage, fascinated with Duchamp's ideas about chance, had spread the news of Duchamp's example to his friend, the painter Robert Rauschenberg. Through Rauschenberg some- ◆ thing of Duchamp's procedures was transmitted to Jasper Johns, although Johns claims that the works for his amazing premier exhibition in 1957 (his *Targets* with cast body parts, and his *Flags*) were made before he learned about Duchamp and that it was only after critics labeled his work "neo-Dada" and spoke of their identity as readymades that he and Rauschenberg began to find out about the phenomenon in earnest. By 1959 they had met Duchamp, seen the extraordinary constellation of his work in the Arensberg Collection at the Philadelphia Museum of Art (including *The Large Glass)* and by 1960 they had read the newly published, English version of *The Green Box* (1934), Duchamp's elaborate notes for the *Glass*, and—in the case of Johns—had begun to collect work by Duchamp, particularly the cast pieces Duchamp made in the fifties and had issued in limited editions **[2]**.

Although Johns's work clearly manifested two of the "paradigms" for making art to which the name Duchamp is firmly attached—the readymade and the "index" (the latter indicated by Johns's use of cast body parts as well as various "devices," such as the medium of encaustic, or the use of squeegees for smearing paint, that emphasize the pictorial mark as a form of trace)—he himself signaled the importance of a third. "With Duchamp," Johns wrote in 1960, "language has primacy.... Duchamp's *Large Glass* shows his conception of work as a mental, not a visual or sensual, experience."

Peep show

It was these three "paradigms," or models for how to make a work, that had firmly established themselves in the American context of the early sixties. The readymade was everywhere, thoroughly perme- ▲ ating Fluxus production as well as forming the conceptual armature • of Pop art. The index not only manifested itself in the body casts Johns continued to make, as well as those fashioned by Robert Morris and Bruce Nauman (born 1941) **[1]**, but also spread to a whole network of "traces," such as Morris's registration of his own brain waves in *Self-Portrait (EEG)* (1963), and was additionally to be found in the Fluxus obsession with chance. The language model, which began by staying close to Duchamp's example in *The Green Box*—for instance, Morris's *Card File*, in which the object is nothing but the typed and alphabetized record of its own conception and execution—would develop by the late sixties into Conceptual art, ■ in which the reflections on language by Duchamp and Ludwig Wittgenstein would combine to form what Johns had called a "conception of work as a mental, not a visual or sensual, experience."

The new ascendancy of these three paradigms left that of Cubist collage seeming more and more compromised—nothing but the cynically corrupted language of advertising and other forms of mass media into which it had been incorporated even before World War II. The only way collage could be practiced by the avant-garde in the postwar period was through a dialectical reversal that would use it negatively, in the register of trash: the commodity exposed as planned obsolescence, as in the practice of *décollage* or in ◆ Rauschenberg's assemblages or Arman's "*poubelles.*"

But Duchamp treated his own "dominance" in a typically Duchampian way. He disowned it through the kind of overthrow manifested in the work he had secretly been making throughout the previous two decades and had brought to completion in 1966:

▲ 1907, 1911, 1912, 1937a, 1944b • 1918 ■ 1968b ◆ 1953, 1958

▲ 1914, 1960c, 1962a, 1964b • 1918, 1953 ■ 1958, 1968b ◆ 1960a

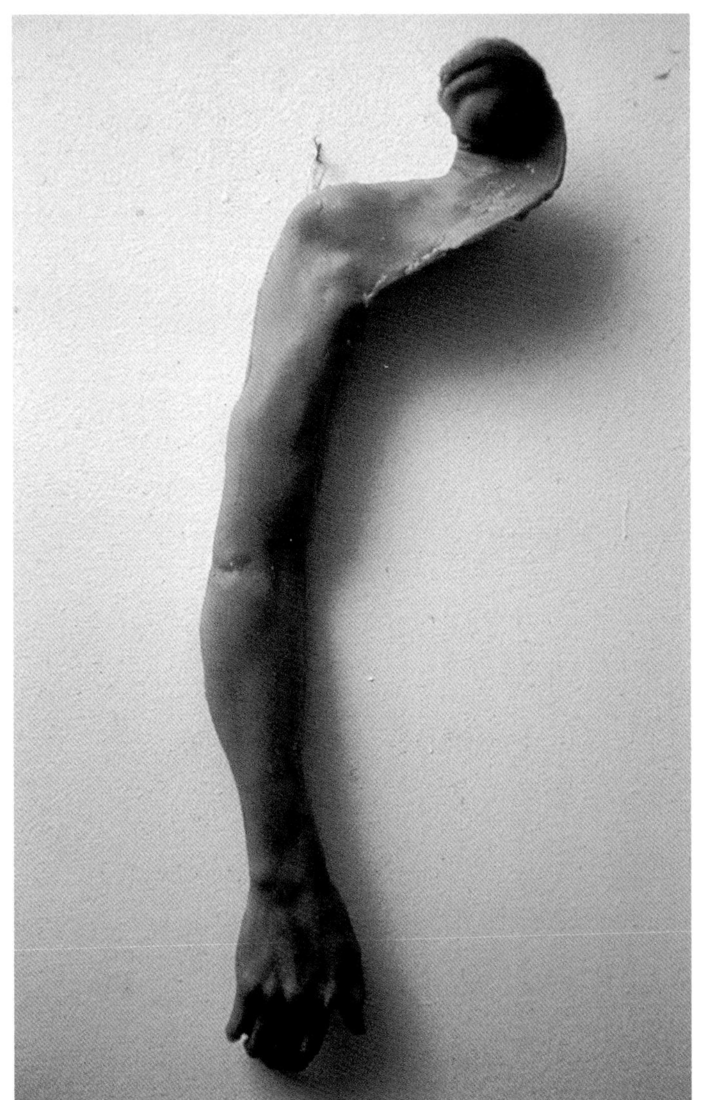

1 • Bruce Nauman, *From Hand to Mouth*, 1967
Wax over cloth, 71.1 x 26.4 x 11.1 (28 x 10⅜ x 4⅜)

2 • Marcel Duchamp, *Feuille de vigne femelle* (Female Fig Leaf), 1950
Galvanized plaster, 9 x 14 x 12.5 (3⁹⁄₁₆ x 5½ x 4¹⁵⁄₁₆)

his *Etant Donnés: 1. La Chute d'eau 2. Le Gaz d'éclairage* (Given: 1. The Waterfall 2. The Illuminating Gas) **[3, 4]**. Arranging for its installation in the Philadelphia Museum just next to the Arensberg Collection's monument to his early production, he intended this new piece to be made available to the public in 1969, the year following his death.

If Duchamp's art had until then been understood as "conceptual," here was a diorama that was startlingly realistic, an erotic display leaving nothing to the imagination. If his art had been seen as transferring all the emphasis in the making of a work from traditional technique to the "deskilled" automatism of the readymade, here was a painstaking labor of handcrafted artifice. And if his art had used photography as a structural, procedural element through which to reveal the operations of the index, here "the photographic" seemed to manifest itself in its crassest incarnation, merely as a drive toward the brutally simulacral: the substitution of the mimetic copy for reality itself.

There were Duchamp scholars who looked aghast at this work as they saw the imaginary, allegorical intricacy of *The Bride Stripped Bare by her Bachelors, Even* (1915–23) turned into a kind of dirty joke, a peep show viewed through holes pierced in a barn door revealing a nude arranged on a heap of twigs, her legs spread wide before the spectator's gaze, while in the landscape behind her could be seen wholly kitsch versions of the mysterious protagonists of *The Large Glass*'s "Preface": the waterfall and the illuminating gas. Despite these scholars' dismay, however, and contrary to the position being promulgated by the late sixties that all the paradigms of avant-garde practice had been invented in the first half of the century, leaving nothing for postwar artists to do but recycle them in a series of repetitions to which the tag "neo-" would be persistently affixed (this is what Peter Bürger would say in his *Theory of the Avant-Garde*), the *Etant Donnés* itself constituted a newly wrought paradigm, one that would profoundly affect work from 1968 onward. For having determined to set itself up in a museum, it would settle into its permanent, institutional context to form the most total and devastating critique of how the aesthetic itself operates and is legitimized.

A function of the Enlightenment, the very idea of aesthetic experience was grounded on the principle of a judgment about something's beauty (its worthiness to be called "art") that would be totally disinterested, which is to say unballasted by either the object's usefulness or its truth content, as for example its correspondence to scientific facts or concepts, a judgment that would nonetheless be pronounced as if for everyone and thus spoken in a "universal voice." If such an experience could be theorized by Immanuel Kant in his *Critique of Judgment* (1790), it would be institutionalized in the great museums that arose in the nineteenth century. Setting their contents apart from the space of everyday life, the palatial containers of the great art collections declared both the autonomy of the aesthetic sphere—hence its withdrawal from "interest," whether at the level of utility or of knowledge—and its public aspect: a place of collective experience where the "universal voice" could be visualized in the community of beholders gathered before the works, each judging as though for all.

▲ 1914, 1968b • 1918 ▲ 1960a

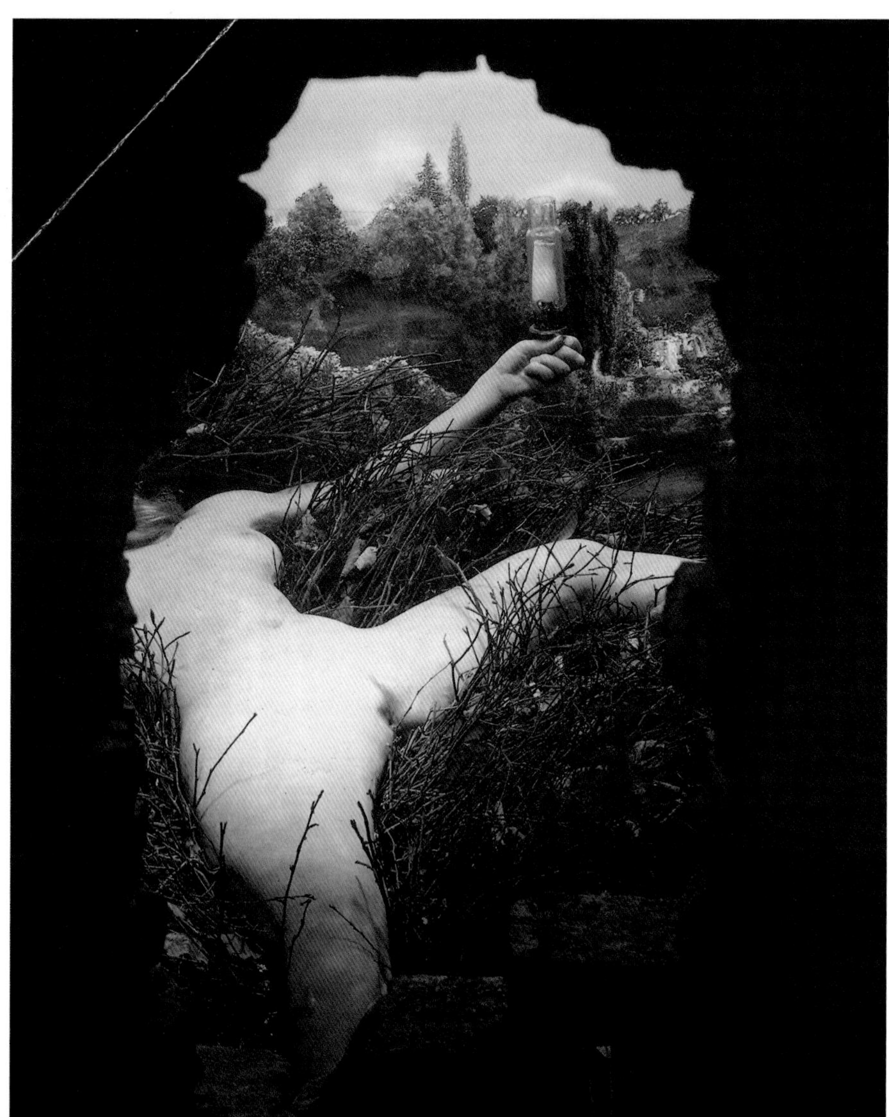

3 • Marcel Duchamp, *Etant Donnés: 1. La Chute d'eau 2. Le Gaz d'éclairage*, 1946–66
Mixed-media assemblage, 242.5 x 117.8 x 124.5 (95½ x 46⅜ x 49)

Duchamp's *Etant Donnés* is placed in just such a building. But against the grain of the public nature of this space of shared experience, the work is perversely hidden. Seen through the peepholes drilled into the oaken door that is its sole visible aspect within its setting at large, the diorama reveals itself to only one viewer at a time. And that viewer, far from assuming the detached posture of aesthetic "disinterest," is forced into an acute awareness that, while glued to the peephole so as to peer into the space of the erotic spectacle, he or she is exposed to being seen from behind by someone else, a guard perhaps, or a third person entering the gallery. Always potentially "caught in the act," this visual experience is never able to transcend the body that supports it in order to connect to the object of its judgment; rather, that body thickens into an object for itself, rendered carnal by its opening to feelings of shame.

The spectacle behind the door is, meanwhile, fashioned to articulate this carnalization of the viewer. Exactly replicating the model of Renaissance perspective, the mise-en-scène presents its nude behind the jagged opening of a brick wall in a parody of Alberti's notion that the plane through which we look in a perspective construction is like that of a window. Further, orchestrating perspective's geometries through which the cone of vision (coming to a point in the viewer's eye—the viewing point) is the exact mirror of the pyramid of projection (coming to a point in "infinity"—the vanishing point), Duchamp's peepholes set the viewing point as mirrored twin to the hole directly opposite them, namely the point between the nude's legs, spread-eagled on her bed of twigs. Writing about Duchamp's transformational systems, the French philosopher ▲ Jean-François Lyotard captured this bipolar collapse of viewing and vanishing point into twinned bodily orifices in the pun "*Con celui qui voit*" (roughly, "He who sees is a cunt").

Caught in the act

The "Modernist Painting" position—itself an outgrowth of Enlightenment pressures to understand the specificity of the visual arts in terms of the separateness of vision from the other senses

▲ 1984b

(vision being spatial, for instance, while hearing is temporal)—had tied the idea of art's autonomy (and its "disinterest") to the ▲ possibility of a purified sense of the visual. This disembodied "opticality" through which painting would acknowledge its distinctness from the other arts—by avoiding any sense of the kinesthetic or the sculptural and instead addressing eyesight alone—staked the aesthetic, then, on the illusion that the viewing point was, as in the Renaissance diagram, truly reduced to a pure speck of light and thus detached from any bodily experience.

If "opticality" was the gauge of "disinterest," and the monumental scale of the color-field painting through which it was manifested the guarantor of the collective space of its viewing, the *Etant Donnés* revokes this warrant of disinterest by carnalizing the viewer twice over. As the theoretical vantage point of the diagram thickens into the eroticized gaze of the voyeur, the space of the museum becomes a labyrinth of separate interests some of whom will have the power to alienate others from themselves by catching them in the act of looking now defined as far from "pure."

• As Roland Barthes never tired of explaining, the Enlightenment theorized its notion of the "universal" as a way of consolidating the bourgeoisie's power by making this power disappear as a historical fact only to reappear, instead, as the order of nature. "Classical art," Barthes says in *Writing Degree Zero*, "could have no sense of being a language, for it *was* language, in other words it was transparent, it flowed and left no deposit, it brought ideally together a universal Spirit and a decorative sign without substance or responsibility."

The act of unmasking this "universality" and exposing it as historically contingent operates in many ways throughout the history of modernism, from collage's denaturalizing of the medium of oil paint, say, to the readymade's insistence on the conventional, social character of art's condition. But the *Etant Donnés* goes beyond the ▲ way *Fountain*, the urinal Duchamp had submitted to the Society of Independent Artists exhibition in 1917, had exposed the social frame around the work—its official place of exhibition, its culture of legitimation in the process of judging and accepting it—as what in fact "constitutes" the work *as* art. For by lodging itself at the heart of the museum—public protector of the values of disincarnated disinterest—the *Etant Donnés* was able to pour its logic along the very fault lines of the aesthetic system, making its framing conditions appear in startling clarity only to make them "strange."

The "institutional critique" that will now focus on the museum • as its site will range from Marcel Broodthaers's work in Belgium to ■ Daniel Buren's in Paris to Michael Asher's and Hans Haacke's in the United States. This focus on the institutional frame of the aesthetic system was energized by many sources, from the Situationist contribution to the events of May 1968 in Paris to the poststructuralist theorization of the conditions of "discourse" in ◆ the work of writers such as Michel Foucault and Jacques Derrida. But the *Etant Donnés*, lying within the very citadel of the museum itself, went to the heart of the aesthetic paradigm, critiquing it, demystifying it, deconstructing it.

4 • Marcel Duchamp, *Etant Donnés: 1. La Chute d'eau 2. Le Gaz d'éclairage*, 1946–66
Mixed-media assemblage, 242.5 x 117.8 x 124.5 (95½ x 46⅜ x 49)

FURTHER READING

Marcel Duchamp, *Manual of Instruction for Etant Donnés: (1) La Chute d'eau (2) Le Gaz d'éclairage* (Philadelphia: Philadelphia Museum of Art, 1987)

Rosalind Krauss, *The Optical Unconscious* (Cambridge, Mass.: MIT Press, 1993)

Jean-François Lyotard, *Duchamp's TRANS/formers* (Venice, California: Lapis Press, 1990)

▲ 1960b • Introduction 3 ▲ 1914 • 1972a ■ 1970, 1971, 1972b ◆ Introduction 4

1966b

The exhibition "Eccentric Abstraction" opens in New York: the work of Louise Bourgeois, Eva Hesse, Yayoi Kusama, and others points to an expressive alternative to the sculptural language of Minimalism.

1960–1969

Born into a middle-class home in Paris, Louise Bourgeois (born 1911) assisted in the family business of tapestry restoration from an early age. Perhaps this repairing of damaged figures was formative for the young Bourgeois, for her future art would oscillate between suggestions of damage and reparation. In her own account this ambivalence was focused on her philanderer father, who installed a mistress in his household and disrupted his family. Years later, Bourgeois would take her revenge in a work bluntly titled *The Destruction of the Father* (1974). First, however, she simply escaped—initially to art school, ▲ then to the studio of Fernand Léger. In 1938 she married the American art historian Robert Goldwater (1907–73), whose *Primitivism in Modern Art*, long the standard book on the subject, might have influenced her as well, and together they moved to New York.

Patricidal aggression

• Her early work includes drawings influenced by Surrealism, such as the *Femmes-Maisons* (House-Women) (1945–7), in which Bourgeois represents the female nude as an exposed, often violated shelter. By the late forties she had begun to make sculpture as well; semiabstract poles in wood or bronze, these "totems" were also in ■ keeping with the late Surrealism still current in New York. Her style became distinctive only in the early sixties when she began to shape plaster, latex, and fabric in ways that evoked abstract body parts. Often formed as if by violent fantasies or aggressive drives, these body parts suggest what psychoanalysts call "part-objects"—that is, parts of the body such as the breast carved out by the drives as their special objects. An early example is *Portrait* (1963), a brownish, viscous mass in latex that slumps down from the wall like an exposed stomach with its tubes cut, a phantasmatic portrait of a self as a body turned inside out. The critic Lucy Lippard, who included this piece in her "Eccentric Abstraction" exhibition at the Fischbach Gallery in 1966, saw it as an ambivalent "body ego" that produces both "appeal" and "repulsion." In the same year Bourgeois made *Le Regard* (The Gaze) at a moment when, with the exception of Marcel Duchamp in his last work *Etant Donnés*, few artists were explicitly concerned with this subject which would ◆ become so central to feminist art. A roundish, labial object in latex over burlap, *Le Regard* is what the Surrealists called *l'oeil-sexe*, a combination of an eye and a genital, in this case an ambiguously vaginal one. Slit open to reveal a bumpy interior, this genital-eye evokes both a wound and a maw as well—like the eye of an infant who "sees" the world through its mouth alone. In this respect *Le Regard* suggests vulnerability and aggressivity at once, an ambivalence typical of most Bourgeois objects. As the art historian Mignon Nixon has suggested, it "reworks the motif of the *oeil-sexe*

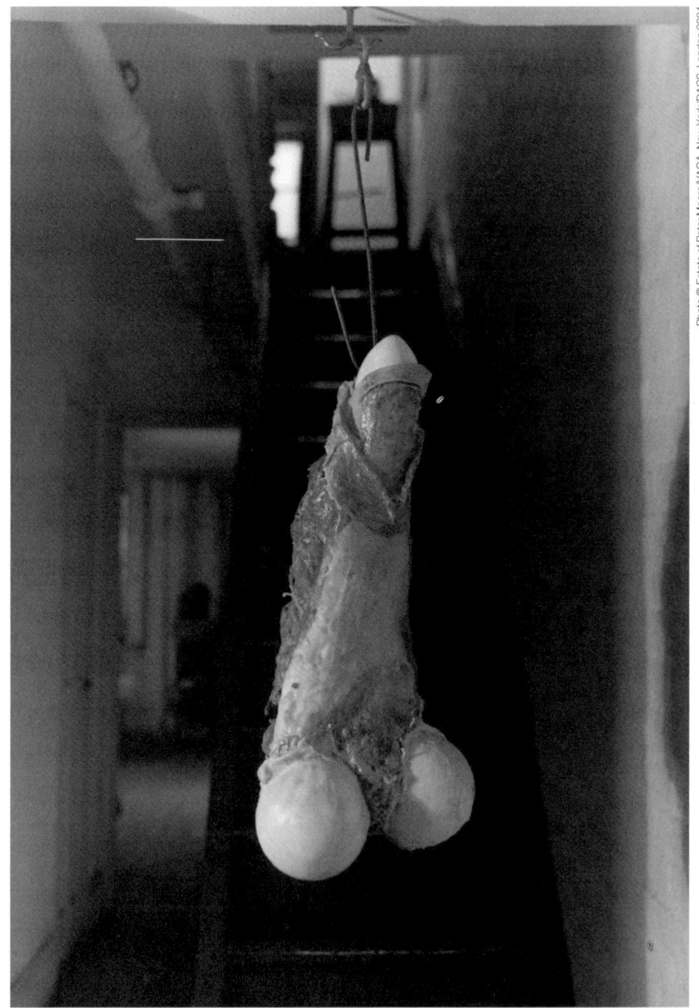

1 • Louise Bourgeois, *La Fillette*, 1968
Latex over plaster, 59.7 x 26.7 x 19.7 (23½ x 10½ x 7¾)

▲ 1913, 1925a ● 1924, 1930b, 1931 ■ 1942b, 1945 ◆ 1966a, 1975

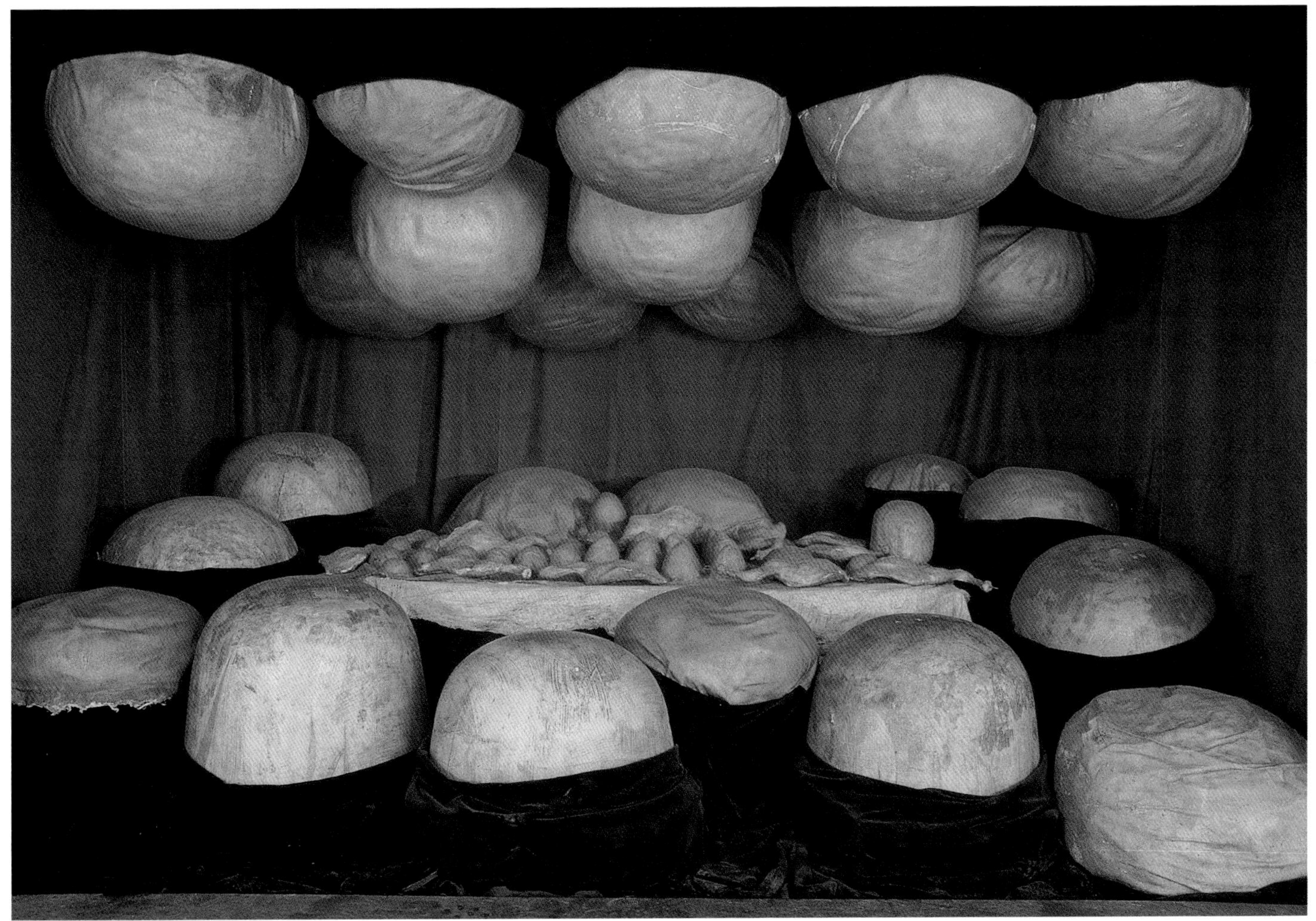

2 • Louise Bourgeois, *The Destruction of the Father*, 1974
Plaster, latex, wood, fabric, and red light, 237.8 x 362.3 x 248.6 (93⅝ x 142⅝ x 97⅞)

from a female subject-position," in a way that troubles "the phallic gaze" of the Surrealists.

Bourgeois gave another twist to the Surrealist object, in this case the sexual fetish, in *La Fillette* (Little Girl) [**1**]. A dirty, penile thing in latex over plaster, *La Fillette* is another "disagreeable object," to borrow the term of the great Surrealist object-maker, Alberto ▲ Giacometti; and like his objects it is fraught with ambivalence. When hung by wire (as it is often displayed), it seems an object of hate, a castrated piece of meat. But when cradled (as it is by Bourgeois in a well-known photograph by Robert Mapplethorpe), it seems an object of love, a baby held by its mother (one can project eyes and mouth onto its "head"). According to Freud, women might • associate penis and baby in order to compensate the lack of the first with the gain of the second. But this "little girl" is no mere fetish or penis-substitute; she is a personage in her own right. In this way *La Fillette* is a bold gesture: if *Le Regard* is a feminist parody of the male gaze, *La Fillette* is a feminist appropriation of the symbolic phallus.

By the late sixties, then, Bourgeois was involved in feminism, and after her husband died in 1973 she began to confront her traumatic past from a feminist perspective; one result was *The Destruction of the Father* [**2**]. By the sixties Bourgeois had already developed her old image of the *Femme-Maison* into a new environment called a "lair," "a protected place you can enter to take refuge." Although "the lair is not a trap," she remarks, "the fear of being trapped has become the desire to trap others." In this regard *The Destruction of the Father* may be her ultimate lair, for here protection turns into aggression, and the hunted becomes the hunter. A large cave made of plaster, latex, wood, and fabric, it consists of forms suggestive of breasts, penises, and teeth that protrude from a ceiling, a floor, and a table. At once cave, body and room, *The Destruction of the Father* is a phantasmatic interior of the sort that, according to the psychoanalyst Melanie Klein, young children sometimes imagine. For Bourgeois it is a lair where the "evening meal" (the alternative title of the piece) has somehow turned into a ritual meal, where the "totem" to be devoured has suddenly become the father. This is how she narrates this fantasy of patricidal aggression:

> *It is basically a table, the awful, terrifying family dinner headed by the father who sits and gloats. And the others, the wife, the children, what can they do? They sit there, in silence. The mother of course tries to satisfy the tyrant, her husband. The children are full of exasperation. We were three children: my brother, my sister, and myself. There were also two extra children my parents*

▲ 1931 • Introduction 1, 1975

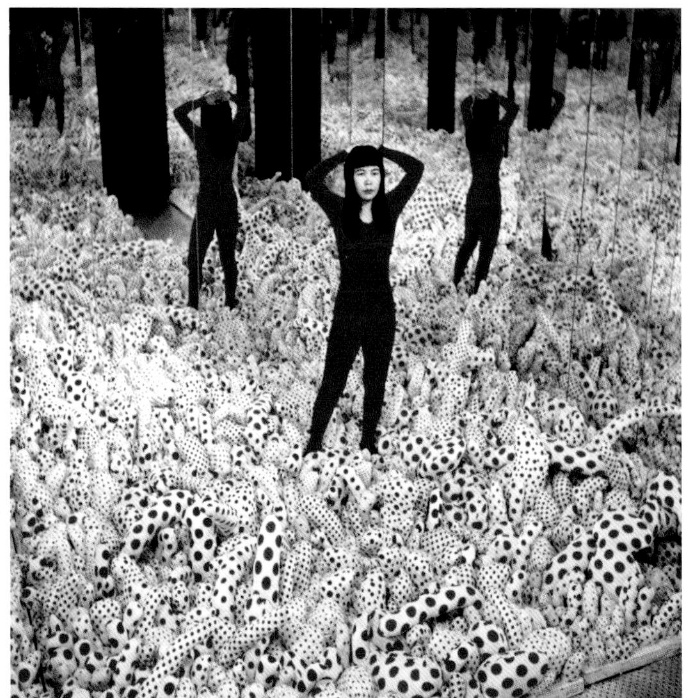

3 • Yayoi Kusama, *Infinity Mirror Room—Phalli's Field*, 1965
Sewn stuffed fabric, plywood mirrors, dimensions variable

adopted because their father had been killed in the war. So we were five. My father would get nervous looking at us, and he would explain to all of us what a great man he was. So, in exasperation, we grabbed the man, threw him on the table, dismembered him, and proceeded to devour him.

Obsessive repetition

Yayoi Kusama (born 1929) approached the lair of patriarchy from another direction: rather than seize the phallus in the manner of Bourgeois, Kusama multiplied it in a way that mocks it, inflated it in a way that "pops" it. A native of Japan, she moved to New York in 1957, and by 1959 had already exhibited five of her "Infinity Nets." Large white canvases (one is thirty feet wide) covered with a light web pattern, they respond not only to the drip paintings of Jackson Pollock but also to the renewed interest in monochrome ▲ works. Two years later her motifs became more material and more ● distinctive. Perhaps inspired by the exhibition of assemblages at the Museum of Modern Art, Kusama began to make her "Accumulations" in fall 1961—household things often found on the street (an armchair, a coat, a stepladder, a baby carriage), covered with small sacks stuffed with cotton batting, and painted white. "The point," Donald Judd remarked laconically in a 1964 review of such work, "is obsessive repetition," but repetition here produced thick fields of phallic growths, not regular Minimalist units or serial Pop images but a strange hybrid of the two. Soon Kusama used this procedure to create entire environments of stuffed phalli, as in *Aggregation: One Thousand Boats* (December 1964), whose centerpiece was a rowboat with oars covered by penile protuberances, like so much alien vegetation. Large photographs of the boat also papered the walls with phallic silhouettes, against which Kusama posed for the camera (as became her wont), in this case nude.

This repetition of the phallic form not only parodied it, but also dispersed it as a vertical figure into a horizontal ground of other phalli. This interest in a camouflage that collapses figure and ground led Kusama to employ red polka dots as well, sometimes with the phalli, sometimes alone, again in an apparent drive both to dedifferentiate her objects and to totalize her environments. This undoing of distinctions was furthered by her use of mirrors, in the first instance in *Infinity Mirror Room—Phalli's Field* [**3**], in which her phalli, polka dots and, in some photographs, her own body (usually clothed in a red leotard) are replicated potentially ad infinitum. "We must forget ourselves with polka dots," she once remarked, as if her own subjecthood might also be at stake in this drive toward indistinction. Thereafter her environments became more deliriously Pop, and often included barrages of light and sound; Kusama experimented with psychedelic culture too. At this point critics routinely accused her of exhibitionism; yet paradoxically, for all her self-exposure, her work can also be seen as a theater of self-immolation as well. Perhaps her apparent schizophrenia came into play here: Kusama had attested to periodic hallucinations since her teens, and in 1972 she returned to Japan to enter a mental institution (where she has continued to produce art nonetheless).

Eccentric abstraction

The sculpture of Eva Hesse (1936–70) is neither as assertive as that of Bourgeois nor as dispersive as that of Kusama, but it is also more innovative formally, and, despite her premature death from a brain tumor at thirty-four, more influential historically. In part this is because it is less referential in its imagining of the body—indeed of the entire world of material objects with which the body is in contact—than it is potentially disturbed by fantasies, desires, and drives. Yet, perhaps to compensate for its relative abstraction, her work is often referred to the vicissitudes of her own life (her Jewish family fled the Nazis, her mother committed suicide) and/or of womanhood as such—"its repugnant and piteous inheritance of pain," in the words of Anne C. Chave. In this way some critics (like Chave) see her evocations of the body as specifically female, as part of an early feminist reclamation of an essential female embodiment, whether understood in terms of womb or wound, while other critics (like Anne Wagner) reject this account of the work as "a symptom of the pathology of the female condition," and read these figures as disruptive of such markers of sexual difference, as less a stable female "body-ego" than a quasi-infantile combination of conflicted drives and part-objects. In either light, her constructions in latex, fiberglass, and cheesecloth evoke the body in extreme ways—as though flayed in a condition of horror, as in *Connection* (1969), or veiled in a contingent of grace, as in *Contingent* [**4**].

One of the sculptures included in "Eccentric Abstraction" is *Ingeminate* [**5**]: two large tubular forms, each wrapped with dark

▲ 1949, 1957b ● 1959b

4 • Eva Hesse, *Contingent*, 1969
Fiberglass and polyester resin, latex on cheesecloth, eight units, each 289.6 to 426.7 x 91.4 to 121.9 (114 to 168 x 36 to 48)

5 • Eva Hesse, *Ingeminate*, 1965
Enamel paint, cord, and papier-mâché over two balloons connected with surgical hose. Each balloon 55.9 x 11.4 (22 x 4½); length of hose 365.8 (144)

rough cord, which also links the two. At the time Lippard pointed to the procedural implications of the title—to double, to emphasize through repetition. More recently Mignon Nixon has stressed its biosexual associations—to inseminate, germinate, disseminate—terms that underscore the ambiguous relation of this object to conventional images of gender, indeed of the body whether part or whole. For what exactly is doubled and tied up here? "To twin and bind the phallus is to make a joke at its expense," Nixon writes, "but also to muddle it up with the breasts, and the breasts with the testicles, and so to set off a spiral of identifications in which the body is both drawn close and lost track of—become ever more profoundly phantasmatic." Hesse delights in this formal muddling, in its pointed provocation of ambivalent interest in the viewer; this is also suggested by her mirthful posing for the camera with her objects (this is true of Bourgeois and Kusama, and points to a performative strategy that the three artists share as well). Hesse also delights in her disruption of the aesthetic field of Minimalism, ▲ with her objects that resemble part-objects, as well as of Postminimalism, with her procedures that insist on the carnal, even the • visceral. As Lippard saw early on, her art stages "a forthright confrontation of incongruous physical and formal attributes: hardness/softness, roughness/smoothness, precision/chance, geometry/free form, toughness/vulnerability, 'natural' surface/industrial construction." *Contingent* plays with all these oppositions, and others as well (falling and floating, gravity and transcendence, etc.), in a way that renders them unstable, insistently material and metaphorical at once.

Crucial to this body of work, then, is "its utter inwardness with artistic languages of the day" (Wagner), with Minimalist forms like the grid and the cube as well as Postminimalist strategies of binding, hanging, dispersing, and so on. This inwardness allowed Hesse to transform these languages effectively—again, to introduce messy carnal associations into their clean conceptual assumptions. At the same time these languages distance the work "from a purely personal range of meanings." "The sculpture is literal about the body," Wagner has argued, "at the same time as it explodes the whole notion of literalness. It insists on its languagelike character—its structures of repetition and transformation—at the same time as it maps those properties onto evocations of a carnal world. The body is there somewhere, at the intersection of structure and reference." This is "eccentric abstraction" indeed, and it continues to touch us today in a way that some art of her time does not.

FURTHER READING:

Louise Bourgeois, *The Destruction of the Father, The Reconstruction of the Father: Writings and Interviews, 1923–1997* (Cambridge, Mass.: MIT Press, 1998)

Lucy R. Lippard, *Changing: Essays in Art Criticism* (New York: Dutton, 1971)

Mignon Nixon, "Posing the Phallus," *October*, no. 92, Spring 2000

Elisabeth Sussman (ed.), *Eva Hesse* (San Francisco: San Francisco Museum of Modern Art, 2002)

Anne M. Wagner, *Three Artists (Three Women): Georgia O'Keeffe, Lee Krasner, Eva Hesse* (Berkeley and Los Angeles: University of California Press, 1997)

Catherine de Zegher (ed.), *Inside the Visible* (Cambridge, Mass.: MIT Press, 1996)

Lynne Zelevansky et al., *Love Forever—Yayoi Kusama, 1958–68* (Los Angeles: Los Angeles County Museum of Art, 1998)

▲ 1965 • 1969

1967a

Publishing "A Tour of the Monuments of Passaic, New Jersey," Robert Smithson marks "entropy" as a generative concept of artistic practice in the late sixties.

In one of his first published essays, "Entropy and the New Monuments" (1966), Robert Smithson singles out a passage from a ▲ review of an exhibition of Roy Lichtenstein's painting, written by • Donald Judd. Judd, notes Smithson, "speaks of 'a lot of visible things' that are 'bland and empty'," such as "most commercial buildings, new Colonial stores, lobbies, most houses, most clothing, sheet aluminium, and plastic with leather texture, the formica-like wood, the cute and modern patterns inside jets and drugstores." "Near the super highway surrounding the city," Smithson adds:

> *We find the discount centers and cut-rate stores with their sterile façades. On the inside of such places are maze-like counters with piles of neatly stacked merchandise; rank on rank it goes into a consumer oblivion. The lugubrious complexity of these interiors has brought to art a new consciousness of the vapid and the dull. But this very vapidity and dullness is what inspires many of the more gifted artists.*

Smithson then proceeds to the analysis of what he calls "hyper- ■ prosaism" in the work of Robert Morris, Dan Flavin, and Judd himself, among others, providing one of the earliest and still among the best, assessments of Minimalism.

That Judd should have been among the early supporters of Lichtenstein's art may come as a surprise—his short articles on the artist ◆ offer perhaps the first bout of a "simulacral" reading of Pop art, such as the one that develops later about Warhol—but only because Minimalist art is often mistakenly read, against the intent of all its practitioners, as a mere continuation of early geometrical abstract art. And if Smithson, still in his twenties, was able to grasp the continuity between Pop and Minimalist art, it is because, informed by structuralist anthropology and literary criticism, of which he was an ardent reader, he had stumbled upon an explanatory model that reached far beyond questions of stylistic discrepancies.

Ruins in reverse

As the title of his essay indicates, this model was the law of entropy, a concept that governs Smithson's entire artistic production, and to which he would return in all his writings (his last interview, conducted a few months before his death, was entitled "Entropy Made Visible"). Formulated in the nineteenth century in the field of thermodynamics (it is the second foundational principle of that science), the law of entropy predicts the inevitable extinction of energy in any given system, the dissolution of any organization into a state of disorder and indifferentiation. It asserts the inexorable and irreversible implosion of any kind of hierarchical order into a terminal sameness. Smithson's example for entropy is very close to the first one given by scientists, which had to do with the temperature of water: "Picture in your mind's eye the sandbox divided in half with black sand on one side and white sand on the other. We take a child and have him run hundreds of times clockwise in the box until the sand gets mixed and begins to turn gray; after that we have him run anticlockwise, but the result will not be a restoration of the original division but a greater degree of grayness and an increase of entropy."

The concept of entropy had fascinated many people since its inception, especially because the example chosen by Sadi Carnot (1796–1832), one of its creators, was the fact that the solar system would inevitably cool down (this understandably fed the millenarian and cosmic pessimism of many books written at the end of the nineteenth century). Very early on—and Smithson directly borrowed from this tradition—the law of entropy was applied both to language (the way words empty out when they become clichés) and to the displacement of use-value by exchange-value in an economy of mass production. The final book of the nineteenth-century French novelist Gustave Flaubert, *Bouvard et Pécuchet*, one of Smithson's favorites, already merged these two lines of enquiry in recounting the growth of the entropic shadow being cast on our lives and our thought under the condition of capitalism. Repetition (of goods on the marketplace, of words and images in the media) is profoundly entropic; it is from this discovery that the theory of information would emerge in the late forties, a mathematical model of communication according to which the content of any fact is in inverse proportion to its probability—Kennedy's assassination was a world event, but if the rule were for every American president to be killed in order to end his term, it would have had no more content than dusk or dawn and would have barely made the headlines.

But while for Flaubert and his peers our entropic fate—a defining characteristic of modernity—was sheer doom, Smithson

▲ 1960c • 1965 ■ 1962c, 1965 ◆ 1964b, 1980

reread the very inexorability of this process as the promise of a definitive critique of man and his pretenses. It was not only the pathos of Abstract Expressionism (long become suspect) that was rendered irrelevant once the entropic logic was followed to the end, but also the modernist struggle against arbitrariness in art (the purported elimination, in each art, of any convention that was not "essential" to it), a notion that had turned increasingly dogmatic in ▲ the writings of Clement Greenberg. Entropy is for Smithson the ultimate in what the structuralists term "motivated," or nonarbitrary. Since it is the only universal condition of all things and beings, there is nothing arbitrary about entropy. It was in order to manifest just this pervasive nature of entropy that soon after the ● 1969 exhibition "When Attitudes Become Form," and perhaps as a rebuttal of the emphasis on *form* in its title, Smithson conceived of ■ *Asphalt Rundown* [**1**] as a reading of Pollock's drip process and its gravitational pull as profoundly entropic.

Writing in "Entropy and the New Monuments" that Minimalist art had eliminated "time as decay," Smithson indicated his disenchantment with the movement as failing to push into the domain of entropy: "Instead of causing us to remember the past like the old monuments, the new monuments seem to cause us to forget the future," he wrote. But what if one were to connect the future with the distant past—what if posthistory (time after the demise of man) were nothing but the mirror image of prehistory? Smithson's childlike fascination with dinosaurs and fossils stemmed from his essentially antihumanist conception of history as a cumulative succession of disasters. Time as decay thus became one of his strongest concerns and with it the necessity of creating not merely "new" monuments, but "antimonuments," monuments to the wane of all monuments.

In fact, one did not even need to create such artifacts, the world was already full of them. This is what Smithson discovered when, in September 1967, with his Instamatic camera hung from his shoulder just like a tourist in Rome ("Has Passaic replaced Rome as the Eternal City?" he asked), he revisited his small, industrial home town. The result, "A Tour of the Monuments of Passaic, New Jersey," is a mock travelogue documenting various "monuments" to decay (the last of them being the sandbox mentioned above), particularly construction sites that Smithson saw as factories of "ruins in reverse": "this is the opposite of the 'romantic ruin' because the buildings don't *fall* into ruin *after* they are built but rather *rise* into ruin before they are built." Everything, whatever its past, even before it has any past, is geared in the end toward the same equal state—which also means that there is no justifiable center, no possible hierarchy. In short, what might at first seem a dire prospect—the fact that man, though he often chooses to ignore it, has created for himself a universe without quality—can also be liberating, for a world without center (which is also a world where the self has no boundaries, no propriety) is a labyrinth open to infinite exploration.

Smithson was alone in making entropy the most important generative concept of art practice at the end of the sixties: his

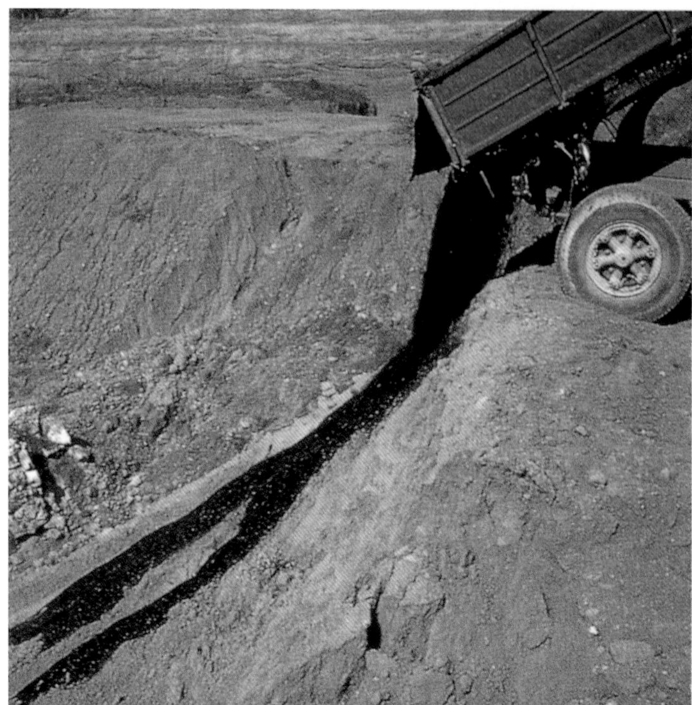

1 • Robert Smithson, *Asphalt Rundown*, Rome, October 1969
Dump truck, asphalt, quarry cliff (destroyed)

▲ *Spiral Jetty*—an Earthwork that was covered by the water of Utah's Great Salt Lake shortly after its "completion" in 1970, and which has now temporarily reemerged, whitened by salt crystals, as the water receded—remains the quintessential "monument" to this decade of radical expansion of the sculptural field. But many other artists—often before him, yet without theorizing it—also adopted an "entropic" mode in their work.

Deadpan transience

● One such artist was Bruce Nauman. Working in California, and thus in relative isolation from the New York art world, Nauman produced his first casts of interstitial spaces in the mid-sixties (for example *A Cast of the Space under My Chair* [**2**], or *Platform Made Up of the Space between Two Rectangular Boxes on the Floor* [1966]). Thus even before *Upturned Tree* (1969), in which Smithson had shown that in an entropic universe, because it is shorn of any other meaning than the irreversibility of time, everything is reversible but time, and everything is equally devoid of signification, Nauman explored this same depletion of meaning: were it not for their titles, we would never have guessed what Nauman's concrete pieces were cast from.

Both Smithson and Nauman, in fact, were fascinated by the disseminating role of mirror reflections once the very notion of center (of identity, of self) is suspended: in Nauman's *Finger Touch No. 1* (1966), for example, it is not only impossible for us to fathom which is the "real" pair of hands and which is its mirror image, but further we have no way of reassembling into a bodily synthesis the sensory fields that are signified. Trying to imagine a tactile sensation corresponding to what we see—the twirling of hands pressed

▲ 1960b ● 1969 ■ 1949 ▲ 1970 ● 1966a, 1973

2 • Bruce Nauman, *A Cast of the Space under My Chair*, 1965–8
Concrete, 44.5 x 39.1 x 37.1 (17½ x 15⅝ x 14⅝)

against the cold surface of a mirror—we soon find ourselves at the brink of a vertigo from which we recoil. Similarly, in Smithson's ephemeral *Mirror Displacements* (1969)—in which a loose grid of square mirrors was disposed and photographed at various sites during a trip that Smithson took in the Yucatan—the very notion of beholding is called into question, as the mirrors become potentially invisible within the landscape they reflect. What these images record can only paradoxically be called "incidents," for they are, in a strict sense, nonevents. They convey no information other than the sheer fact of their transience. Finally—another mark of affinity between Nauman's and Smithson's way of thinking—in 1968, shortly after the latter had rejoiced, in "Entropy and the New Monuments," at Sol LeWitt's project of putting "a piece of Cellini's jewelry into a block of cement," Nauman produced a work whose first (descriptive) title was *Tape Recorder with a Tape Loop of a Scream Wrapped in a Plastic Bag and Cast into the Center* (the center in question being that of a block of concrete).

Another Californian artist whose work is overdetermined by entropy is Ed Ruscha, especially in the many large canvases, from ▲ the mid-sixties on, that "depict" words—that is, in which a single word ("Automatic," "Vaseline") or a nonsensical group of words ("Another Hollywood Dream Bubble Popped," "Those Golden Spasms") is stenciled on an illusionistic sky against which words seem to hover and then dissipate, like clouds. But it is Ruscha's little photographic books, which Smithson mentioned several times, and whose deadpan tone is matched only by the early films of Andy Warhol, that provided one of the earliest critiques of aesthetic judgment under the banner of the "vernacular"—that is, of • the visual cliché. In *Twenty-Six Gasoline Stations*, Ruscha records exactly what the title announces: every gas station he encountered in a trip from Oklahoma City to Los Angeles, one for each letter of the alphabet, is dryly photographed from the other side of the road. The same tautological and exhaustive impulse is to be found in *Every Building on Sunset Strip* [**3**], a foldout panorama that provides an inventory of every building, but also every crossroad and every empty lot, along a famous section of Sunset Boulevard (same reversibility as in Smithson's *Upturned Tree*: the book can be "read" in both directions, since the two sides of the boulevard symmetrically oppose one another on each page, one right side up, the other upside down). Photographed at noon in order to accentuate its quality of desolation, the Sunset Strip appears as a simulacrum, the set of a Hollywood movie. "It's like a Western town in a way," Ruscha would note. "A store-front plane of a Western town is just paper, and everything behind is just nothing." Endlessly reporting the same anonymous nothingness, Ruscha's dozen or so books do

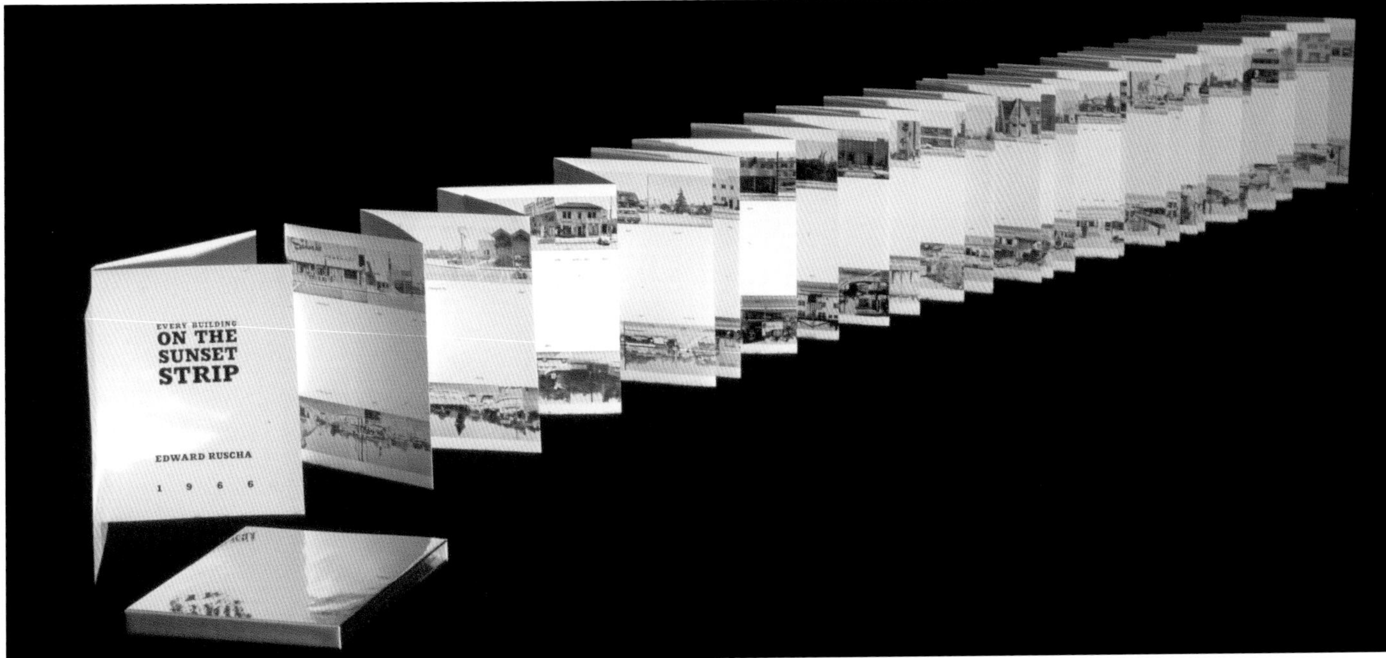

3 • Ed Ruscha, *Every Building on the Sunset Strip*, 1966
Offset lithograph on paper in silver-mylar-covered box, closed, 18.1 x 14.3 x 1 (7⅛ x 5⅝ x ⅜)

▲ 1960c ● 1968b

not constitute a damning commentary on the vacuity of life at the end of the twentieth century—there is not an inch of nostalgia in them. They are practical guides to entropy, showing a possible ▲ way of relishing, with no small dose of what André Breton called *humour noir* (dark humor), a world depleted of difference and thus of meaning.

Matta-Clark's anarchitecture

If Nauman and Ruscha preceded Smithson, Gordon Matta-Clark (1943–78) proceeded from him. The starting-point of his short career was indeed his encounter with Smithson, during an "Earth Art" show at Cornell University in 1969, just a few months before the latter realized his *Partially Buried Woodshed* on the campus of Kent State University. Conceiving this as a "nonmonument" to the process he called "de-architecturization," Smithson had a dump truck unload earth onto the roof of an old woodshed to the point where its ridge beam cracked. Matta-Clark was at the time an unhappy architecture student and this attack on an existing building must have had an immense appeal for him (he soon dropped out of Cornell). At the same time, however, as is often the case in the relation of a younger artist to his mentor, Matta-Clark began to think that Smithson had not carried out his program fully: he had frozen the de-architecturization of *Partially Buried Woodshed*, entrusting Kent State University, to whom he had bequeathed the work, with its "maintenance" in its original condition.

While Smithson was suspicious of architecture (and never tired of deriding architects for their naivety in believing that they had any control over their work), Matta-Clark was hostile to it. He had started by considering waste as architectural material, building a wall out of garbage in 1970, but this gesture had a redemptive ring that utterly contradicted his entropic bent: he soon turned around, now considering built architecture as trash. His first "anarchitectural" piece, to use one of his favorite expressions, was called *Threshole* (1973). Under this generic term Matta-Clark cut out the thresholds of apartments in abandoned buildings in the Bronx, often on several floors, opening the gloomy spaces to light. With this work Matta-Clark had found the medium in which he would operate in increasingly complex fashion for the five remaining years of his life: a building that has been marked out for imminent destruction, and which he would pierce here and there, hollowing out negative spaces in its mass conceived as inert matter, without much consideration for its constructive structure (his provisional spaces were dangerous to enter) and none whatsoever for the original distribution of functions. An essential aspect of his work was that it was itself destined to waste, that it should have only a fleeting existence, for it partook of the war against architectural meaning (built for eternity) waged by Matta-Clark. Not only do a door, a floor, a window, a lintel, a threshold, a wall lose all their prerogatives as such—every architectural element being equally unprotected against the cuts made through the building as a whole—the cuts themselves are never long enough in place to solidify as figures, as fetishes. From the simplicity of *Splitting* in 1974, a suburban house split vertically in two **[5]**, up to the last Piranesi-like cutouts in an office building in Anvers **[4]** or in neighboring townhouses of Chicago (*Circus Caribbean Orange* [1978]), Matta-Clark's spaces became increasingly vertiginous as the differentiation between the vertical section and the horizontal plan, essential to our perception and habitation of architecture, was made almost wholly illegible.

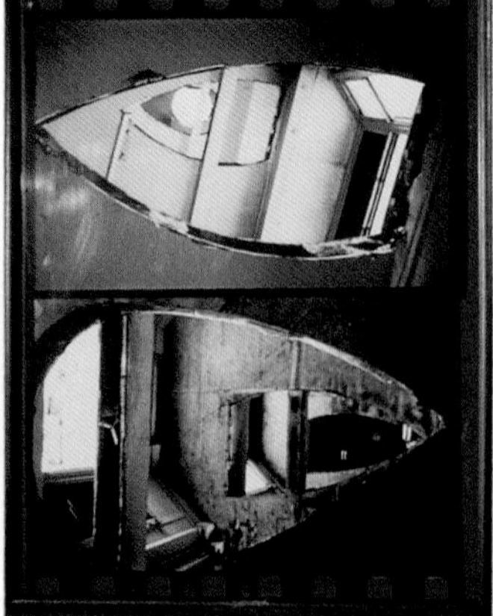

4 • Gordon Matta-Clark, *Office Baroque*, 1977
Cibachrome photograph, 61 x 81.3 (24 x 32)

5 • Gordon Matta-Clark, *Splitting*, 1974
Cibachrome photograph, 76.2 x 101.6 (30 x 40)

FURTHER READING

Yve-Alain Bois, *Edward Ruscha: Romance with Liquids* (New York: Gagosian Gallery and Rizzoli, 1993)
Yve-Alain Bois and Rosalind Krauss, *Formless: A User's Guide* (New York: Zone Books, 1997)
Tom Crow et al., *Gordon Matta-Clark* (London: Phaidon Press, 2003)
Robert Hobbs, *Robert Smithson: Sculpture* (Ithaca, N.Y.: Cornell University Press, 1981)
Jennifer Roberts, *Mirror-Travels: Robert Smithson and History* (New Haven and London: Yale University Press, 2004)
Joan Simon (ed.), *Bruce Nauman: Catalogue Raisonné* (Minneapolis: Walker Art Center, 1994)
Robert Smithson, *The Collected Writings*, ed. Jack Flam (Berkeley and Los Angeles: University of California Press, 1996)
Maria Casanova (ed.), *Gordon Matta-Clark* (Valencia: IVAM; Marseilles: Musée Cantini; and London: Serpentine Gallery, 1993)

▲ 1924

1967b

The Italian critic Germano Celant mounts the first Arte Povera exhibition.

No other European avant-garde was as riddled with profound contradictions as that in Italy during the period 1909–15. Just as it was within the Italian framework that the first explicit and programmatic link between avant-garde artistic production and advanced forms of technology was forged by the Futurists, so it was within this same context that the first countermove against modernity and modernism was undertaken by Giorgio de Chirico. ▲ In de Chirico's *pittura metafisica*, artisanal forms of work were reintroduced as the sole foundation of artistic practice, thereby assuming an antitechnological, antirational, antimodernist posture.

Those were the parameters within which postwar Italian artistic production reestablished itself, as it issued into Arte Povera (poor or impoverished art) with the first exhibition organized by the critic Germano Celant, who coined the term in 1967. It was this group of twelve artists that produced the most authentic and independent series of European artistic interventions of the late sixties. Pitted in certain ways against the hegemony of American art, specifically • Minimalist sculpture, it also recuperated the legacy of the prewar Italian avant-garde—with all its internal contradictions—but now in a postwar context. Between those early decades and the emergence of Arte Povera, however, three neo-avant-garde figures—Alberto ■ Burri, Lucio Fontana, and Piero Manzoni—served as mediators to relay the early contradictions, with their specifically Italian cast, to the next generation.

The first pivot around which these contradictions turned was technology. To the extent that the Italians' misreading of American Minimalist sculpture emphasized technology as the primary orientation or mode of production in Minimalism, Arte Povera took up an explicitly antitechnological stance. Secondly, while photography and the wide variety of artistic modes of production associated with it had been almost totally excluded from the prewar Italian avant-garde, photography was excised from Arte Povera as well. Indeed there was what one could call a programmatic elision of photographic practices as they had emerged in West Germany, France, and the United States in the context of Pop and Conceptual art.

The third distinguishing feature was Arte Povera's peculiar relationship to materials and processes of production, one that both recuperated and denied certain conventions as they had been established in other parts of avant-garde activity. Specifically, the absence ▲ of Surrealism, with its fallen-commodity-object culture, along with the absence of an avant-garde photographic culture such as had • operated in prewar French, Soviet, and American contexts, negatively demarcated a point of departure for Arte Povera. For if these absences can be felt in Arte Povera's renewed emphasis on the artisanal, something that defines the specifically Italian condition of the movement in 1967, this same artisanal condition is nonetheless set in perpetual juxtaposition with those advanced forms of technology that characterize post-Pop consumer culture. And in this very juxtaposition Arte Povera reinvented for itself an experience of what one could call the "retrieval of obsolescence." Thus, in a manner parallel to the way Surrealism had exploited the very condition of obsolescence that haunts commodity culture in order to reinvest the fallen object of fashion with the power of memory, Arte Povera sought to retrieve the mode of obsolescence from its own historical project for much the same ends.

The design of the archaic

Arte Povera is most clearly defined by a group of works made in the mid-sixties by Mario Merz (1925–2003) **[1]**, Jannis Kounellis (born 1936), and Pino Pascali (1935–68), who even prior to the official coining of the term produced a peculiar type of assemblage that was dependent neither upon technology nor upon the paradigm of the readymade or the *objet trouvé*. Rather, their structures were able to interrelate those strategies continuously, thereby corrupting the technological element with obsolescence and investing the artisanal aspect with a renewed sense of purification.

Kounellis's 1968 installation at the Galleria L'Attico, *12 Cavalli* (12 Horses) **[2]** was one such instance. Insofar as it staged the natural within an institutional framework, it pronounced the aesthetic of Arte Povera by producing the shock of the reappearance of nature within the spaces of acculturation. Consisting of twelve workhorses displayed in the gallery over the duration of the exhibition, *12 Cavalli* emphatically countered any assumption about the sculptural object as either a discrete form, or a technologically wrought thing, or a discursive structure. Instead it insisted on the model of prelinguistic experience, as well as on nondiscursive structures, and nontechnological, nonscientific, nonphenomenological artistic conventions.

▲ 1909 • 1965 ■ 1959a ▲ 1931 • 1916b, 1930b, 1935

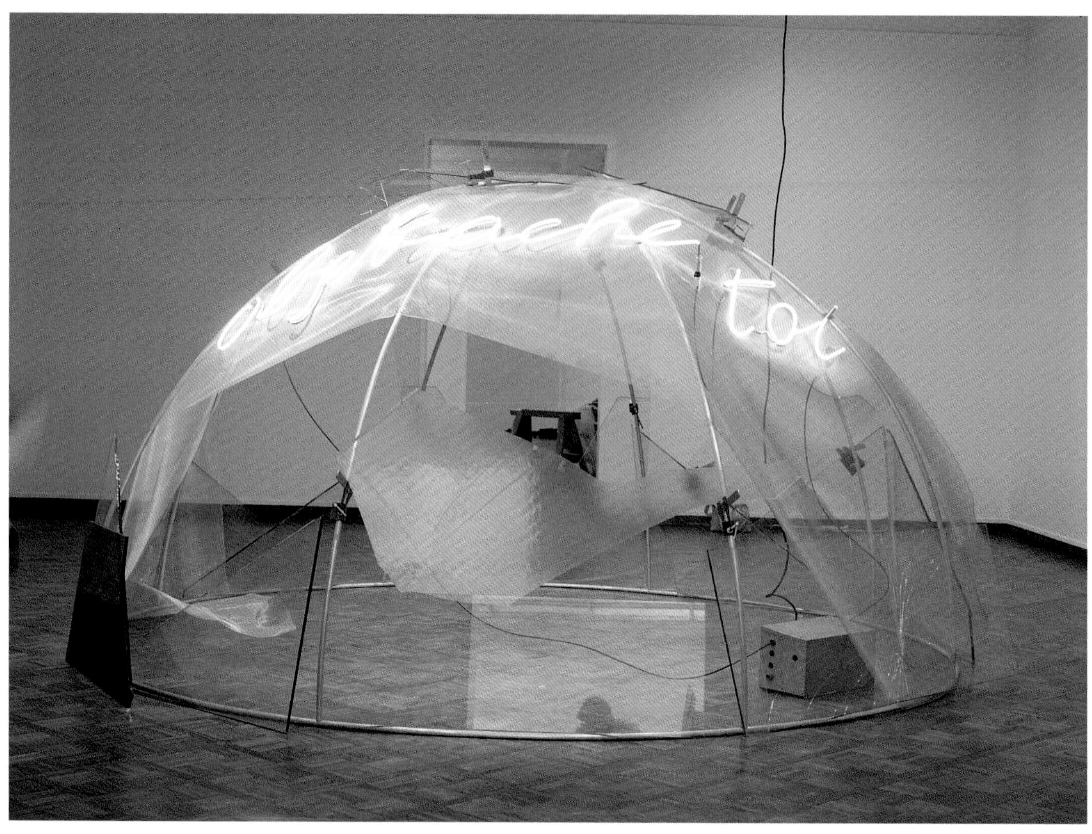

1 • Mario Merz, *Objet Cache Toi*, 1968–77
Metal tubes, glass, clamps, wire mesh, neon, height 185 x 365 (72⅞ x 143¾)

2 • Jannis Kounellis, *12 Cavalli* (12 Horses), 1969
Installation at Galleria L'Attico, Rome

12 Cavalli's emphasis on a mythology of local specificity—namely, Italy's continuing connection to a preindustrial, rural economy—its foregrounding of the natural, the unformed, the nondiscursive, even the prelinguistic, could be compared with work by Pino Pascali of the mid-sixties, where conventions of theatricality, narrative, and representation are also reinserted into the making of painting and sculpture. Once again this clearly contradicts those concepts of a ▲ phenomenological or modernist approach to the making of sculpture that had governed American production throughout the decade. The pertinent example would be *Teatrino* [**3**], a composite work from 1964, in which a painting is dismantled or a sculpture is transformed into the hybrid condition of a theater set. In this form, Pascali was able to pose the question of the degree to which late-modernist art had to prohibit narrative and excise language and performance from its project of self-definition. Yet as Kounellis's and Pascali's works suggest, the supposed purity of the artistic medium or the aesthetic category or genre is already irredeemably hybrid; and this demonstration of the hybrid is one of the fundamental principles of the Arte Povera aesthetic.

Of the figures behind the formulation of this aesthetic, a central example is Pier Paolo Pasolini, who in 1962 had declared that the key references for his own writing and films were the subproletariat of southern Italy and the Third World and Greek mythology, with its recourse to ritual. Both these references were thought to mobilize experience that countered the discursive registers of science and rationalism; specifically, in Pasolini's connection to antique tragedy and its participation in ancient ritual, he wished to counter the discursive through recourse to the prelinguistic experience figured through myth. Pasolini thus provided a framework of countermodernist practice within which Arte Povera could situate itself, as it drew on its internal Italian tradition of countermodernity, specifically the work of de Chirico, but with different parameters, ones that were now recoded within a political program of the Left. For Arte Povera's • refusal to enter into Pop art and Minimalism signaled a refusal to participate in a practice of advanced consumer culture. Further, the resistance to an aesthetic of modernist and late-modernist notions of autonomy assumed a political implication as Arte Povera emphasized the need to reposition the work of art within the socially shared spaces of political activism and a new mode of address to its audience. Arte Povera thus mobilized the antimodernist legacy of de Chirico in order to reinvest artistic practice with the dimension of the mythical, the theatrical, and the corporeal, not only to oppose the instrumental logic and rationality of Minimalist sculpture but also to oppose the homogeneity of advanced forms of spectacle culture in which the global suppresses an experience of the local, and instant communication obliterates the functions of memory and history.

If Pasolini functioned as a precursor for Arte Povera in the field of cinema, Burri, Fontana, and Manzoni played this role in the domain of the visual arts. As early as 1949 Burri began to reinsert materials such as burlap and wood into the pictorial surface in nonnarrative but also nonconstructivist and nonmodernist manners. In his work from the late fifties and early sixties he exploited a variety of decaying industrial materials such as rusted metal and burnt plastic for their quality of obsolescence (without the precedent for doing this in Italy that Surrealism had provided in France). So materials in Burri's work—always presented as wrecked, faded, torn, or burnt—are thus devoid of function, of the utopian promise encoded in the avant-garde's embrace of technological forms of production.

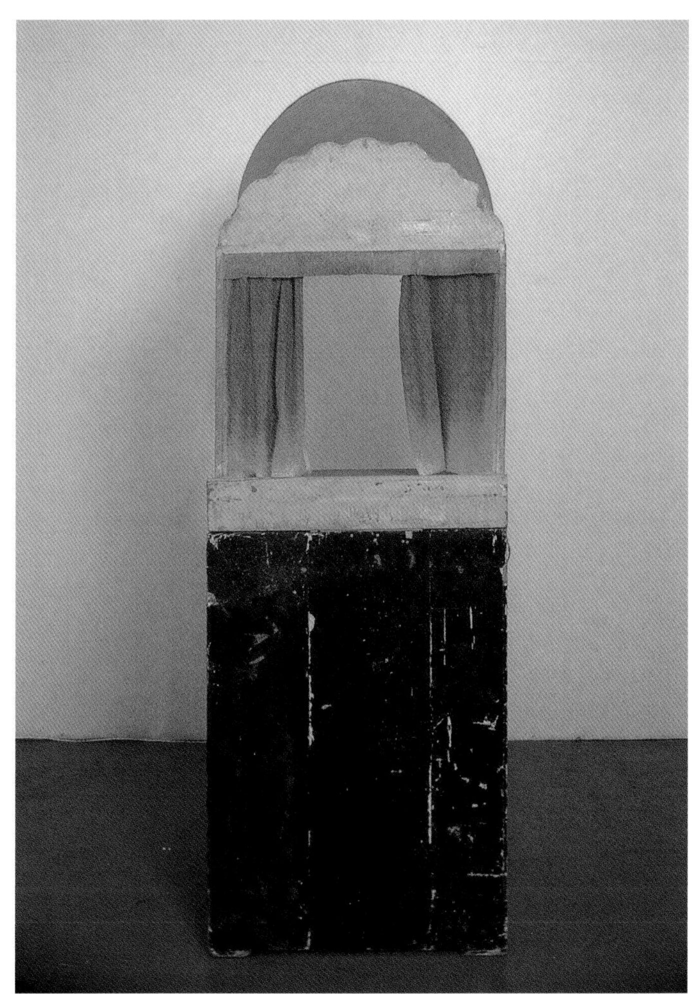

3 • Pino Pascali, *Teatrino* (Little Theatre), 1964
Painted wood and fabric, 217 x 74 x 72 (85½ x 29 x 28¼)

▲ Fontana's example was also crucial for the formation of some of Arte Povera's major figures, but in a different way from Burri, since in accepting the legacy of monochrome painting, Fontana had participated in the neo-avant-garde's attempts to reposition itself in a discourse of self-reflection, purification, and extreme reduction. Yet his operations of slashing and puncturing the monochrome's surface simultaneously emphasized process and performance. And this pointed toward the intricate contradictions of neo-avant-garde production, since the theatrical dimension of his work very quickly entered—via the decors he made for design exhibitions—the very register of public spectacle that Arte Povera would both struggle against and be entangled with throughout the sixties and seventies.

Probably the most important among the three predecessors was Piero Manzoni, who could be described from the perspective of Arte Povera as the artist who had pushed that initial dilemma between modernism and its opposite, between a scientific-technological

▲ 1965 ● 1960c, 1964b ▲ 1959a

4 • Luciano Fabro, *Piedi da seta* (Silken Feet), 1968–71
Pink marble, marble, glass, pure silk, natural silk, brushed bronze, iron, and suede. Installation of twelve *Piedi* at Centre Georges Pompidou, Paris, 1972

modernity and an artisanal connection to the primitive—with its hope for a return to foundational forms of somatic and prelinguistic experience—to the threshold of the absurd. This is obvious in his emphasis on the bodily foundations of perception in the *Fiato* ▲ *d'artista* (Artist's Breath), the *Merda d'artista* (Artist's Shit), or in the pieces including the artist's blood, which were meant to be quasi-ritualistic returns to the origins of the aesthetic experience. These provided crucial points of departure for artists such as Kounellis and Pascali in the late sixties to take that legacy into the next register.

The language of the mnemonic

One of the paradoxes of Arte Povera, perhaps intentional, is its attempt to mobilize the revolutionary potential of outdated and thus antimodernist objects, structures, materials, processes of production. For inasmuch as it involved the artisanal forms of sculptural production, as for example in Luciano Fabro's (born 1936) *Piedi da seta* (Silken Feet) **[4]**, in which the crafting of marble signaled a return to a specifically Italian art-historical legacy, and inasmuch as Arte Povera emphasized the separateness of artistic production, it also came into a precarious proximity—in various instances and to varying degrees—with what could be called the advanced forms of design and fashion culture. So the ambivalence, which is peculiar to Italy, of an industrial production that, since it does not show its technological underside, still carries the banner of artisanal values, or of a commodity production that, by sublimating itself in extreme forms of refinement, disguises itself as the unique and differentiated object, is the dilemma of Arte Povera itself. For the movement could be accused of sharing precisely those conditions of advanced forms of Italian design in its own ranks and within its own perimeters. Michelangelo Pistoletto's (born 1933) *Venere degli stracci* **[5]** also combines references to outdated forms (the classical statue) with artisanal modes of production (the statue is made from concrete). Furthermore, it juxtaposes "high" art with everyday detritus (the rags of discarded clothes).

Minimalism was not the only reference in the dialogue between Arte Povera and American art of the sixties. In fact, Celant seems to have perceived a continuity, if not direct correspondence, between some American Postminimalists (e.g., Bruce Nauman, Eva Hesse, Richard Serra) and the Arte Povera artists, when he presented them side by side in his first comprehensive account of the movement in 1969. Furthermore, he also recognized a third dialogue emerging: ▲ that with American Conceptual art (Robert Barry, Joseph Kosuth, and Lawrence Weiner are included in his first Arte Povera monograph). From the beginning of their activities, the Italian artists responded to or shared an increasing focus on the linguistic elements within artistic production as well.

In Giovanni Anselmo's (born 1934) *Torsione* **[6]** we can recognize the Italian sculptor's preoccupation with the innate forces of gravity, material resistance, and tension, as factors that determine the morphology of a sculpture suspended between material and process. But the suspension of weight and time here (comparable in this regard to contemporaneous work by Nauman and Serra) also seems to barely control an element of physical threat to the spectator, and the seemingly passive and presumably neutral and protected process of looking. The weighty steel bar is kept from falling or from swirling in a violent rotation against the wall and the spectator only by the extreme tension of the relatively light fabric that suspends the bar in its precarious position. What distinguishes Anselmo's work from

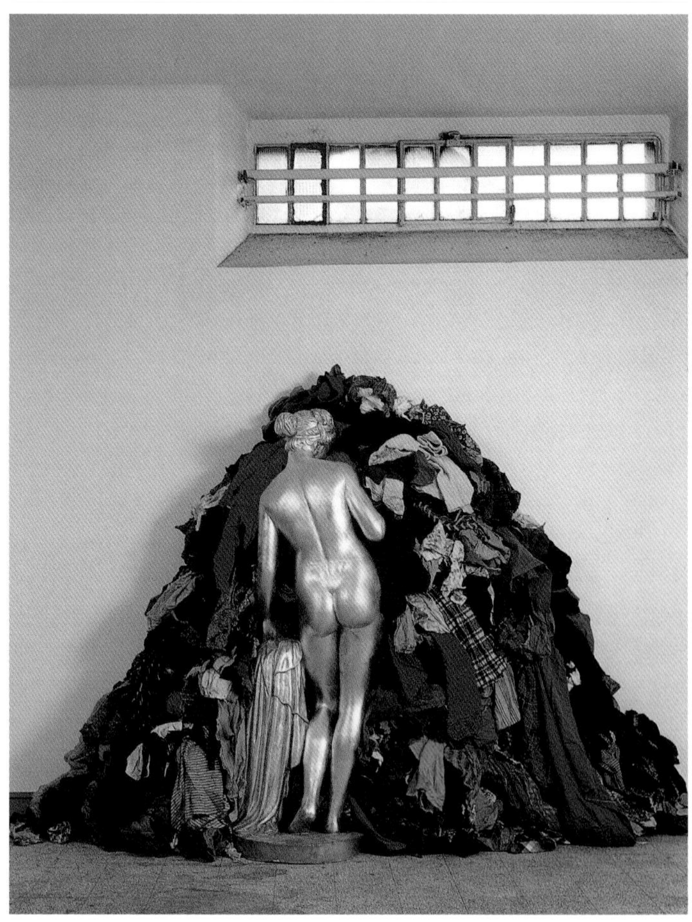

5 • Michelangelo Pistoletto, *Venere degli stracci* (Venus of Rags), 1967
Concrete with mica and rags, 180 x 130 x 100 (70⅞ x 51⅛ x 39⅜)

▲ 1959a

▲ 1968b

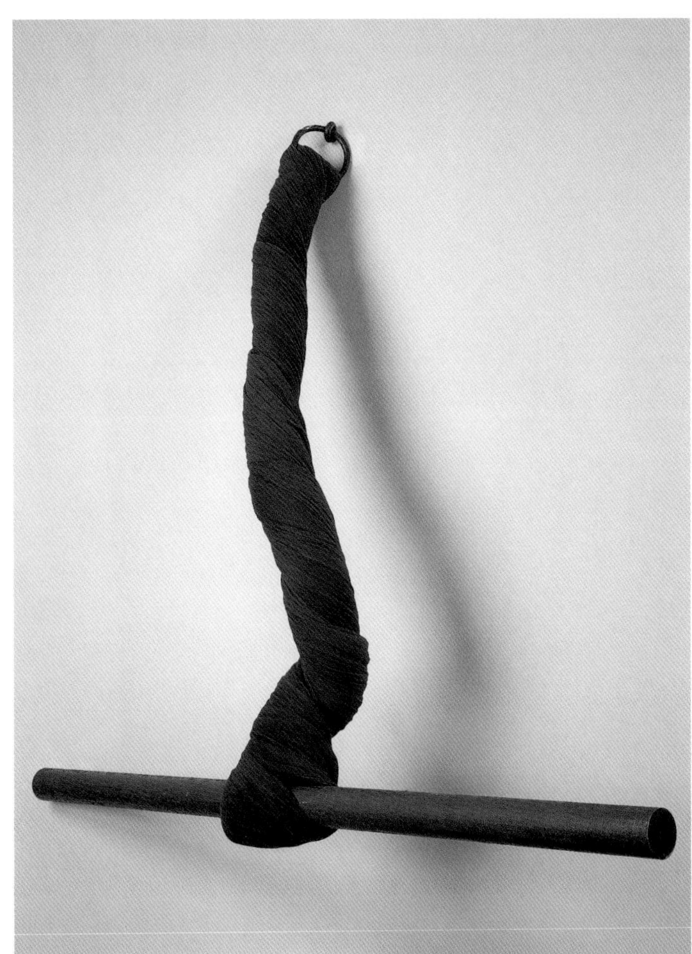

6 • Giovanni Anselmo, *Torsione* (Torsion), 1968
Iron bar and fabric, 160 x 160 (63 x 63)

7 • Giuseppe Penone, *Alberro di 8 metri* (Eight Meter Tree), 1969
Wood, 80 x 15 x 27 (31½ x 5⅞ x 10⅝)

that of his American peers, however, is first of all the choice of materials that articulate an extreme opposition of texture and tactility (i.e., fabric and steel). But it is also an opposition of temporalities, since the display of the fabric's intense torsion inevitably reminds the viewer of the history of Italian Baroque sculpture. At the same time the foregrounding of these forces makes the viewer recognize the conditions and materials that actually govern sculptural production in an age of industrial technology and scientific knowledge.

This almost structuralist preoccupation with oppositional couples evidently determines also the conception and execution of Giuseppe Penone's (born 1947) work, such as *Alberro di 8 metri* [**7**]. In distinction from the American focus on an empiricist model of process and temporality, here the processes of industrial production are reversed and shown in slow motion, a playback from culture to nature that would be unthinkable in any American work of the Postminimalist moment. Penone literally *undoes* the manufacturing process of the industrial object, in this case a construction beam, by removing layer after layer from the beam to reveal its interior core. Thus, in a dialectical countermove, and in an extremely careful process, that is both anti-industrial and—paradoxically—anti-artisanal—the artist retrieves the natural origins of the industrial product, revealing a tree and its branches and stems to be the kernel of the geometricized form of the beam.

It is this complexity of gestures and operations that avoids a mere "return" to craft or artisanal modes that salvages the work of the Arte Povera artists from lapsing into either the reactionary attitudes of *pittura metafisica* or into an attitude of fashion and design culture that would merely fetishize a return to the materials and procedures of a preindustrial age. Nevertheless, it has been tempting to a number of commentators to point out either their latent desire for historical regression (for example, when Daniel Buren referred to the work of Kounellis as "de Chirico in three dimensions"), or to celebrate their work's intrinsically "poetical" dimensions, a numinous quality that would of course be programmatically eliminated from the work of the American artists of that generation. But what makes the work of the Italians often appear as "poetical" is their unique capacity to fuse sudden epiphanies of historical memory with a simultaneous radicality to critique the present.

This duality of approach determines also the sculpture of Mario Merz, in particular in works that deploy the thirteenth-century Fibonacci series of numbers as a mode of spatial progression. Here, in a deliberate counterargument to Donald Judd's Minimalist insistence on the positivist verifiability of composition by deploying purely quantificatory principles, Merz engages an ancient mathematical principle of spatio-temporal expansion that exceeds and complicates the simplistic logic of Judd's progressions. The fact that

8 • Alighiero Boetti, *Mappa* (World Map), 1971–3
Embroidery, 230 x 380 (90½ x 149⅝)

this invocation of mathematical and compositional differences has political implications is foregrounded by Merz in his construction of sculptural volumes whose spiraling growth follows the Fibonacci principle, resembling the architecture of igloos made by the Inuit population. These sculptures in the guise of nomadic shelters are constructed out of glass shards and a variety of other materials (leather, branches, sandbags, tree bark), and often carry an electric neon inscription. One of the igloos carries the ominous inscription "Objet cache toi" **[1]**, clearly articulating not only the desire of the artists of that generation to criticize the social obsession with the production and possession of objects of consumer culture, but also—precisely because of that universal obsession—to negate the object's viability and withhold that very same object status from the sculptural work.

Like his European or American Conceptualist peers (such as ▲ Douglas Huebler), Alighiero Boetti (1940–94) **[8]** engaged with the quantification of seemingly unquantifiable phenomena bordering on infinity. Typical in this Conceptualist approach to quantify the transcendental is his work *Classifying the Thousand Longest Rivers in the World*, a book project he realized in 1970. Or, we recognize a similar desire for the simultaneous transcendence of traditional boundaries (of genres, of techniques, of identities, of nation states, of political borders) in an even more astonishing project, the series of world maps entitled *Mappe del Mundo*. Begun in 1971, they articulate Boetti's recognition that the artist's traditional language elements—colors and signs—are only credible in the present when they are anchored within a preexisting functional social system of communication (rather than in a putatively creative or mythical artistic subjectivity). Yet, paradoxically, Boetti counteracts this Conceptualist withdrawal of all traditional forms of artistic production and the emphasis on artistic anonymity with a dialectical gesture, by assigning the task of executing the *Mappe del Mundo* to the hands of anonymous weavers, who fabricated the large-scale woven maps and their political symbols in Afghanistan (then Boetti's second home after Rome). This counterconceptualist gesture, in its ostentatious return to the preindustrial modes of production, seems at first to be motivated by a peculiar form of primitivism. Yet in retrospect it is transparent that Arte Povera artists understood the dialectics of enlightenment better than their American colleagues. Unlike the latter, the Italians did not suffer from the delusions of unilateral technological process; more importantly, they continuously engaged in the definition of artistic practices that engendered the subject's sense of place and identity at a contradictory crossroad of returns and progressions, of remembrances and prospects.

FURTHER READING

Germano Celant, *Arte Povera* (Milan: Gabriele Mazzotta; New York: Praeger; London: Studio Vista, 1969)

Germano Celant, *The Knot: Arte Povera* (New York: P.S.1; Turin: Umberto Allemandi, 1985)

Carolyn Christov-Bakargiev (ed.), *Arte Povera* (London: Phaidon Press, 1999)

Richard Flood and Frances Morris (eds), *Zero to Infinity: Arte Povera 1962–1972* (Minneapolis: Walker Art Gallery; London: Tate Gallery, 2002)

Jon Thompson (ed.), *Gravity and Grace: Arte povera/Post Minimalism* (London: Hayward Art Gallery, 1993)

▲ 1984a

1967c

For their first manifestation, the four artists of the French group BMPT paint in public, each artist repeating exactly from canvas to canvas a simple configuration of his choice: their form of Conceptualist painting is the latest in a line of attacks against "official" abstraction in postwar France.

▲ One of the most chauvinistic statements ever made by an American artist is this comment by Donald Judd: "I'm totally uninterested in European art and I think it's over with." It was uttered during a famous interview with the • sculptor and his fellow artist Frank Stella, conducted by Bruce Glaser and broadcast on the radio in March 1964. The spiteful remark was not made by chance and Judd made no attempt to tone it down when an edited transcript of the broadcast was printed in *Artnews* (September 1966); it has been anthologized several times since then. In fact, throughout the interview, which contains perhaps the earliest and most detailed articulation of the Minimalist program, both Stella and Judd were eager to explain their anti-European stance.

Alluding to those European geometric painters to whom he has been compared, Stella declared: "they really strive for what I call relational painting. The basis of their whole idea is balance. You do something in one corner and you balance it with something in the other corner.... In the newer American painting ... the balance factor isn't important. We're not trying to jockey everything around." Asked to comment on why he would want to avoid such compositional effect, Judd added, "those effects tend to carry with them all the structures, values, feelings of the whole European tradition.... The qualities of European art so far ... are linked up with a philosophy—rationalism, rationalistic philosophy."

A false transatlantic divide

Judd's important point about the deliberately antirationalist stance of his attempt, as well as the attempts of all his Minimalist friends, to eschew part-to-part relations and to conceive of "logical" systems that would eliminate subjective decisions, was lost on critics and public alike, and he spent his life trying to get it across. But despite the fact that Judd and Stella had every right to protest against the assimilation of their art into that of the European tradition of geometric abstraction initiated by Kazimir ■ Malevich and Piet Mondrian, their view that the dichotomy was geographic (American/European) was ill-founded, based on sheer ignorance. For in pre-World War II Europe there had already been what could be called an antitradition of nonrelational art—a tradi▲tion for which certain of Malevich's own works (the *Black Square* of 1915 and related canvases of the same period), as well as Mondrian's nine modular grid paintings from 1918 to 1919, constituted essential benchmarks. (Other early contenders included Giacomo Balla's *Compenetrazione iridescente* of 1912, Hans and Sophie Taeuber-Arp's *Duo-collages* of 1916 to 1918, Rodchenko's • modular sculptures and his monochrome triptych of 1921, or ■ Wladyslaw Strzeminski's Unist paintings [either those based on a deductive structure in 1928 to 1929 or his monochromes of 1931 to 1932]—and this list is by no means exhaustive). Stella and Judd were not aware that this tradition, just as old as that of compositional abstraction, was being revived by a host of artists in postwar Europe. Furthermore, the reasons for this European revival were not so different from those behind the rise of noncompositionality in American art at the same time.

On both sides of the Atlantic, what was at stake was the nature of agency, of authorship, in art. The Holocaust and Hiroshima were still very much on everyone's mind in the late fifties and early sixties; the Cold War combined with the spread of colonial conflicts kept reminding every Western citizen that a return of barbarity on one's doorstep was always possible. In this charged atmosphere, it is not surprising that young painters asked "What does it mean to be an artistic subject, an author?", given that the humanity of *any* individual subject had just been cast in doubt by the massive demonstration of the inhumanity of the species.

That the geographic divide was a red herring is nowhere more apparent than when examining the context of Stella's criticism of "relational art," which directly followed his other attacks against ◆ not only Victor Vasarély's Op art but also the Groupe de Recherche d'Art Visuel (or GRAV), which he viewed as essentially composed of Vasarély's minions:

> *The Groupe de Recherche d'Art Visuel actually painted all the patterns before I did—all the basic designs that are in my paintings.... I didn't even know about it, and in spite of the fact that they used those ideas, those basic schemes, it still doesn't have anything to do with my paintings. I find all that European geometric painting—sort of post-Max Bill school—a kind of curiosity—very dreary.*

▲ 1965 • 1958 ■ 1913, 1915, 1917a, 1944a ▲ 1915 • 1913, 1921 ■ 1928 ◆ 1955b

It is not completely untrue that the GRAV was gathering followers of the "Pope of Op," as Vasarély was nicknamed at the time (one of its members, Yvaral, was Vasarély's own son), but another of the group's participants stands out—he had joined it partly by mistake, as he himself recognized later—and he is probably the one artist that Stella had in mind: the French painter François Morellet (born 1926).

In the rarefied context of the French art world of the early fifties, dominated by *tachisme* and post-Cubist abstraction, the two favorite styles of the Jeune École de Paris (or JEP), it is not all that ▲ surprising that Morellet knocked at the door of the Galerie Denise René with his portfolio—it was the only possible outlet for any kind of art that smacked of geometry. Neither is it surprising that he should have been turned down, eventually joining the gallery—as a member of GRAV—only after the group's formation in 1961. For, despite the fact that his work appeared fully indebted to that of Max Bill, it actually represented one of its most salient critiques, as would the work of Stella a few years later.

Chance *contra* Max Bill's systematic art

Morellet discovered Swiss artist Bill's work in Brazil in 1950, meeting a swarming school of his devotees there in the aftermath of his major retrospective. By 1952, he had perfectly grasped Bill's • notion of systematic art, borrowed from Theo van Doesburg)—that of an art entirely programmed by a set of a priori rules, an art that in principle leaves no room for the artist's subjectivity and the arbitrariness of composition—in fact he had gone further than Bill in this direction. Contrary to what Bill's various manifestos stated at the time, his art always remained the prisoner of good taste, always strove for compositional balance, for equilibrium. He "programmed," but edited out anything that did not pass the test of his subjective judgment. (It is not by chance that Bill later ■ became the heir of Georges Vantongerloo, the veteran of De Stijl.) Just like the algebraic equations on which Vantongerloo's paintings were supposedly based, the arithmetic computations that Bill presented as the justification for the formal arrangement of his works were often mere smokescreens (especially since the beholder could very rarely perceive the system in use, and since color, an important feature of Bill's canvases, was always conceived as a surplus, as a supplement ungoverned by the system).

Very early on, Morellet set out to eradicate any element of personal taste, using only generative systems of flagrant simplicity and programmatically refusing to meddle with them. As many other artists before him, Morellet wanted to find out what was the minimum required to produce an abstract painting. Although by no means the first artist to be obsessed by the Holy Grail of a "zero degree," he was perhaps the most articulate in his conclusion that this was an unattainable goal. His search began with a work flatly entitled *Painting*, from 1952, where a pattern of green stripes (horizontal-vertical zigzags) fills, in allover fashion, a white background. As in Stella's aluminum canvases ten years later, the whole structure is deducted from an arbitrary generative element: in Stella's works it is the shape of the canvas; in Morellet's, the position of one broken line—the only one to be partly aligned to both the right and left limits of the support—onto which all the other stripes align.

The fact that an initial arbitrary choice was at the core of the configuration of this work led Morellet to one of his most radical experiments, *16 Squares* of 1953. Although this modular, allover grid (a white square divided into sixteen equal parts) is not much more than a readymade, Morellet calculated that no fewer than eleven decisions had determined its elaboration (two for the format: the square and the length of its sides; five for the elements: the lines, their two directions—horizontal and vertical—their number and their width; one for the interval that uniformly separates them; two for the colors: white and black; and finally, one for the lack of texture). Those eleven decisions were, in the logic of the "zero degree," ten too many. This outcome signaled to Morellet that one could never entirely suppress choice, arbitrary decisions, invention, and thus composition. As long as he kept total control of his canvas, even if the system he devised was entirely impersonal, he could not avoid subscribing to a romantic dream according to which, through the example of his art, through the rational and relational ordering of his canvas, he would be helping to shape the universe, or at least proclaiming such a mastery to be possible [**1**].

A major change in approach, at this point, was Morellet's use of chance, something that Bill would never have accepted in his own arsenal. In order to counteract the arbitrariness of subjective choice that even the most determinist system could not entirely suppress, Morellet came to adopt chance (the absolute lack of system, the absolute arbitrariness) as the principal means of organizing his work. This change did not happen in a vacuum: it was ▲ very clearly indebted to Ellsworth Kelly, an artist who shared his noncompositional drive and to whom Morellet was so close in the early fifties that his works often seem like systematic versions of the American painter's aleatory noncompositions.

Though he began using chance in the mid-fifties, Morellet's most eloquent works in this vein are probably the canvases and silkscreens called *Random distribution of 40,000 squares using the odd and even numbers of a telephone directory*, dating from 1960, in which a square field is divided into a regular grid that is colored in a binary (positive/negative) fashion according to the series of digits picked up from a telephone directory. Constituting a programmatic farewell to the tradition of geometric abstraction—for the assault was unmistakable, plainly stated in the title itself which functioned as an explanatory caption—these works also confirm a turning-point in Morellet's career. Their optical flickering seemed a logical offspring of the moiré effects engendered by the chance superimposition of grids in a series of canvases begun in 1956, and it persuaded him (wrongly, as he soon realized) that he was speaking the same language as the artists of the newly constituted GRAV. But if Morellet was momentarily deluded about his own development, others were not: it was precisely his superimposed grids that

▲ 1955b • 1917, 1928, 1937b, 1947a, 1955a ■ 1917, 1937b ▲ 1953

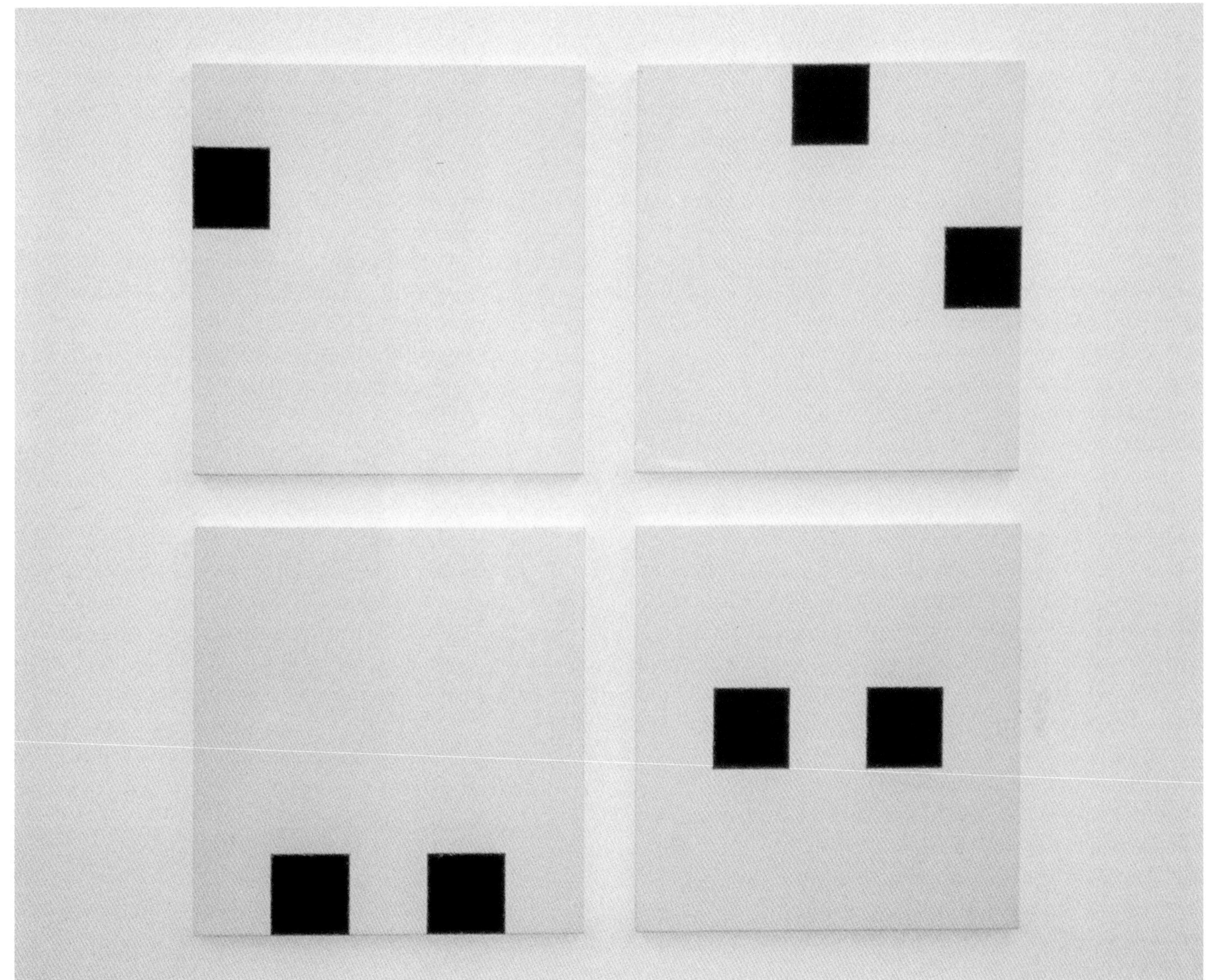

1 • François Morellet, *4 random distributions of 2 squares using the numbers 31-41-59-26-53-58-97-93*, 1958
Oil on wood, four squares 60 x 60 (23⅝ x 23⅝)

prompted Piero Manzoni to invite him to a group show he was organizing in 1959 in Milan, where the third work he had ever sold ▲ was purchased by Lucio Fontana.

Yves Klein as litmus test

The evocation of these last two names introduces a different paradigm in the Parisian postwar context, that represented by the French • alter ego of the two Italian artists, Yves Klein. Just as Morellet had needed the encouragement of a Kelly to break up his allegiance to Bill, Klein's works, and in particular his monochromes, perceived by many artists of the Jeune École de Paris as a direct affront, became the dividing line. A case in point was the letter that the painter Martin Barré (1924–93), then a rising star of JEP, sent to critic Michel Ragon upon reading the draft of the little monograph he was devoting to him: "In speaking of Yves Klein," Barré notes, "you say 'such a contested artist.' I want you to state that for me he is uncontestable." Ragon complied, quoting the sentence verbatim in the published version of the book that appeared in 1960, but failing to grasp its consequences, framing Barré's statement with this caveat: Barré's fascination for Klein, Ragon explained, can be ▲ understood only via their common interest in Malevich.

Ragon's tone and that of other sympathetic critics would very soon change radically: in the reviews of the one-man show that coincided with the publication of Ragon's book, Barré was accused of having succumbed to Klein and having betrayed the cause of JEP. The only positive review of this 1960 exhibition was written by • Pierre Restany, Klein's lifelong hagiographer: "In one scoop Barré, with true intellectual courage, got rid all of the outmoded apparatus, a whole vocabulary of anachronistic forms he had been till now trying to revive. And please do not tell me there is almost nothing left—I'd say there is still too much." In particular, Restany thought that Barré was unnecessarily beguiled by color and that he should concentrate on line, which he saw as his forte. For Restany, *color*

▲ 1959a • 1960a ▲ 1913, 1915 • 1960a

was Klein's domain—which he approached as a "monist," eschewing any dualism, any concept of balance—and Barré had the potential to be the "monist" poet of *line*.

In order to understand the nature of Barré's "betrayal" or conversion, as well as that of many others of his contemporaries, a brief summary of what the JEP was about is required. The "Jeune École de Paris" is an umbrella term repeatedly used in the fifties to designate the type of abstraction (either gestural or post-Cubist or rather post-Klee) initiated by the likes of Pierre Soulages, Jean Bazaine, Alfred Manessier, Viera da Silva, Serge Poliakoff, Jean Esteve, Bram van Velde, and Hans Hartung in the immediate postwar period and then emulated by an army of academic imitators. (This phenomenon is comparable to the mass production of watered-down Abstract Expressionist works in the New York of the early fifties, a production Clement Greenberg disparagingly labeled "10th Street" art in reference to the proliferation of art galleries on that very locale.) JEP theory and practice were modeled on those of early ▲ Kandinsky, who ponderously made detailed, elaborate sketches of so-called "improvisations" that the spectator was to view as faithful portraits of the painter's "inner being." Poseur and composer, the JEP artist was a Cartesian subject who felt secure as the master of his (or, more rarely, her) pictorial universe. Even when endorsing an Expressionist cloak, the JEP painter remained the pure product of an artistic education that has been largely governed by late, classicizing, highly compositional Cubism.

It is unfair to group the first and the second JEP wave together, but by the late fifties the distinction was blurred by their common saturation of the market and the support both were receiving from the State and from the belle-lettristic intelligentsia as a whole. It was to celebrate the JEP, with great pomp, that the first Paris Biennale was set up in 1959. Instead, its organizers were confronted head-on by the entries, all unusually large, of several artists soon to • be grouped by Restany under the label "Nouveaux Réalistes," not to mention the three *Combine Paintings* sent by Robert Rauschenberg (in the American section): a *Meta-Matic* machine by ■ Jean Tinguely, producing gestural abstract drawings at will, a blue monochrome by Yves Klein [**2**], and numerous *décollages* by ◆ Jacques de la Villeglé, François Dufrêne, and Raymond Hains (the latter's *Palissade des emplacements réservés*, a row of planks from a billboard covered with remnants of posters, directly imported from the streets, led to a full-blown scandal).

Although Klein was neither the first nor the only artist to rebel against the JEP, he was the most talented at directly borrowing its histrionics, notably the exhibitionist tactic of a Georges Mathieu painting a large canvas on stage in a matter of minutes. Klein continued using paint and canvases, the traditional tools of a painter: this explains in great part the impact of his work upon artists who were wary of the JEP but unwilling to leave painting altogether—which does not necessarily mean that they approved of his grand mystique. In fact, to come back to Barré, in the works that follow his discovery of Klein's monochromes one perceives a matter-of-fact critique of the return to the Romantic position of the aesthetic Sublime that Klein was advocating. The paintings that Barré exhibited in 1960, all harboring simple inscriptions (a corkscrew curve, a ball of scribbles) made by directly pressing out the paint from a tube onto the white canvas, are clearly parodic and akin to the ▲ more famous "brush-strokes" canvases realized by Roy Lichtenstein from 1965 on, which are rightly celebrated for their gentle mockery of Abstract Expressionism.

The process of production in these works was laid bare, exposed, without any frills. The line was both the indexical sign of a spatial journey (it started there, finished here) and of a temporal unfolding (for example, the thicker section indicating where the hand slowed down). But it was only in the following year, when Barré began to use the spray-can—a device that was then unmistakably of its time, with the walls of Paris covered with graffiti alluding to the war in Algeria—that he understood, as Kelly and Rauschenberg had done ten years earlier, that his assault against the JEP's conception of authorship and agency had to proceed from an analysis of the pictorial sign as index [**3**]. The reasons why Barré was seduced by the rudimentary technique of the spray-can are obvious: its user's only difficulty is the control of speed, especially since he did not want any run-offs that would be interpreted as *tachisme* (as expressive); and the marks are produced without any contact between the body of the artist and his support. There is next to no material or psychological mediation between the canvas and the gesture that is transcribed in the mark, and there is no texture, no painterly "cuisine" (this might account for the fact that the first,

2 • Yves Klein, *Monochrome Blue IKB 48*, 1956
Oil on wood, 150 x 125 (59 x 49)

▲ 1908 ● 1960a ■ 1955b ◆ 1960a ▲ 1960c

3 • Martin Barré, *63-Z*, 1963
Spray paint on canvas, 81 x 54 (31⅞ x 21¼)

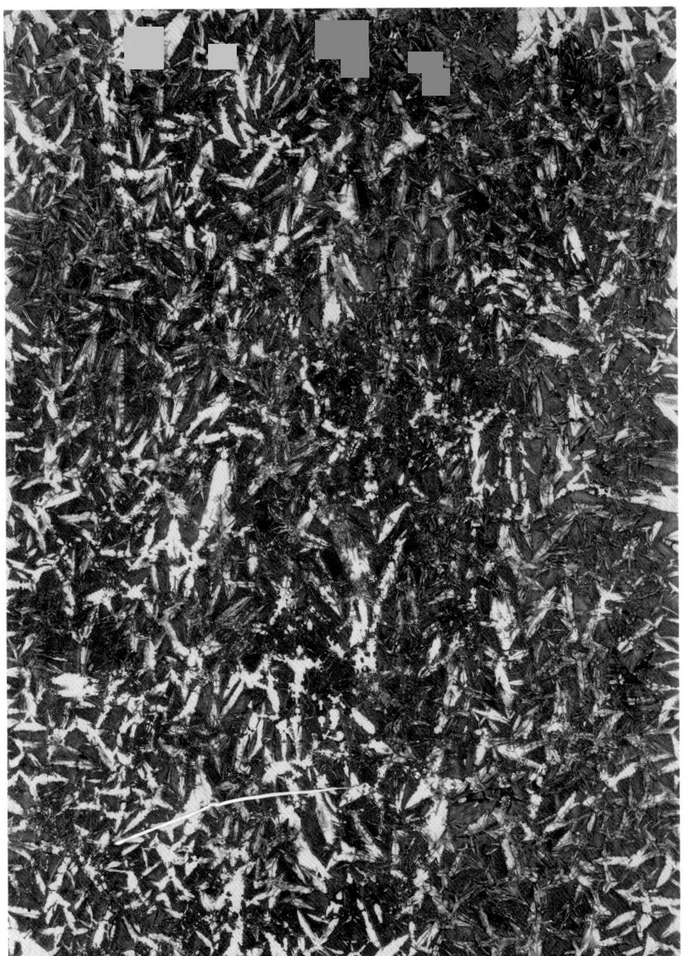

4 • Simon Hantaï, *Mariale 3*, 1960
Oil on canvas, dimensions unknown

mostly hostile, commentators on these works thought they were photographs). The most spectacular of these first spray-can pictures is a 1963 canvas that is striped with parallel oblique lines from edge to edge, all over [**3**].

Hantaï and the allover mode

That the allover goes hand-in-hand with an investigation of indexicality is a conclusion that was also reached, at around the same time, by Simon Hantaï (born 1922). While Morellet had stumbled upon this structure when battling against Bill's legacy, and Barré when discarding the old recipes of the JEP, Hantaï's nemesis was Surrealism. Though it is clear today, with hindsight, that Surrealism was utterly moribund in postwar France, it still occupied a major position of power at the time. André Breton remained very active until his death in 1966, and both the French art market and public institutions were inundated with works by his protégés, basically third-generation imitators of the artists the poet had regrouped under his banner in the mid-twenties. Hantaï had begun as a Surrealist in the early fifties, then gradually moved into gestural abstraction, swiftly scraping a few strokes off the dark wet paint of the ground of his large canvases with a broad palette knife or spatula. By 1959, his large allover paintings—oddly resembling, but with more luscious effects, Dubuffet's strictly contemporary *Matériologies*—mark a turning-point in his oeuvre [**4**]. While the allover mode of that year represents an exception in Dubuffet's whole output, it became a springboard for Hantaï, who never parted with it thereafter: through Pollock, whom he had recently discovered, Hantaï understood that he had to invent a new method for marking his canvases and dividing their surfaces. This method, which was set in place the following year, is *pliage* (literally "folding," though it has more the effect of crumpling). From then on, Hantaï folded his canvases before coating them with color, the variously sized tongue/flame/leaf-shaped creases that the paint did not reach being revealed as white at the moment of unfolding. At first he would paint in those creases with another color, or with another shade of the same color, giving the surface of his canvases the reticular and hardened feel of a reptile's skin, but soon, using a more fluid paint and working on a larger scale, he would let the reserved spaces remain untouched and their whiteness luminously contrast with the monochrome, decorative, and aleatory pattern of the painted areas. Whatever the variations, his pictorial practice always toyed with the issue of automatism and with the possibility of uncontrol, and Hantaï's most successful works convey what one imagines to be the sheer pleasure of his surprise at the moment of unfolding.

▲ 1924, 1930b, 1931

▲ 1946, 1959c

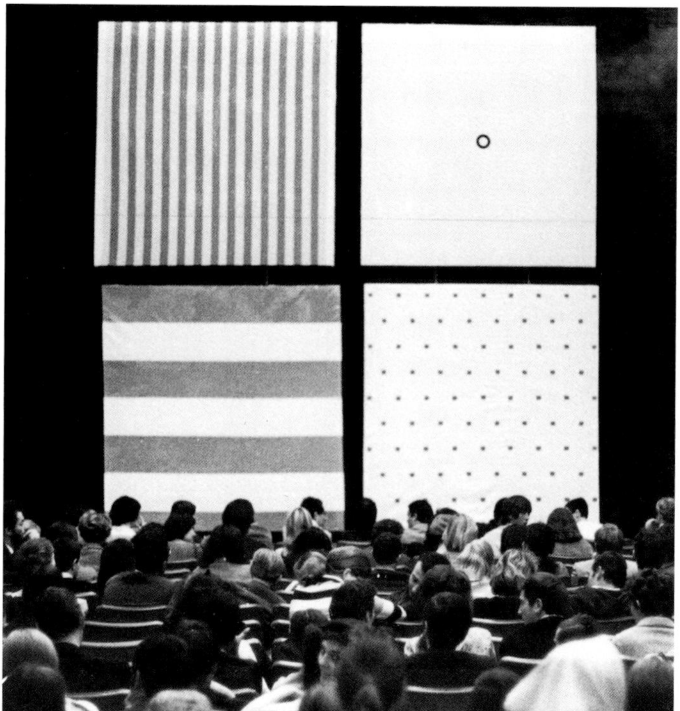

5 • Daniel Buren, Photo-souvenir: *"Manifestation no. 3: Buren, Mosset, Parmentier, Toroni,"* Musée des Arts Décoratifs, Paris, 1967 (detail)

Morellet, Barré, and Hantaï all renounced the considerable skills they owed to their traditional backgrounds in order to develop procedures that would flaunt composition and the myth of interiority that this pictorial equivalent of the *cogito ergo sum* entails (the Cartesian "I think, therefore I am" being translated into "I am able to 'do something in one corner and to balance it with something in the other corner' [Stella], therefore I am"). They would, however, be outrun on this score by a younger artist who was to become one of the most important players in the international ▲ field of Conceptual art: Daniel Buren. It took Buren less than two years to digest the lesson of his elders (Hantaï was particularly • important to him, but so were Ellsworth Kelly and Frank Stella for, unlike his peers, he was keenly aware of the American situation). By mid-1965 his expansive canvases, almost all contrasting a regular pattern of colored stripes (usually the ground) and flat areas of color (usually biomorphic figures) were forcefully pleading ■ for a revival of Matisse's notion of the decorative.

It was at this point that Buren underwent the same deskilling sacrifice as his predecessors in deciding to use ready-made pieces of striped canvas, bought at fabric stores, for the background of his compositions. At first he tinkered with the colorful printed pattern, "correcting" it, to use Duchamp's phrase, but soon he left it as such, contenting himself to paint his biomorphs over it. His next step was to multiply the biomorphs so that they also would become an allover pattern (in competition with the "first," striped one and thus calling into question the traditional opposition between figure and ground). By early 1966, he had adopted the standard binary pattern he would use ever after—alternating bands of white and of a single color per work, each band being of the same width (8.5 centimeters). By the end of the summer of that same year, he had dispensed with any "figuration," with any silhouetting—his only intervention consisted of stretching the striped fabric (bought by the yard) and highlighting one of the white bands in white acrylic paint.

He also decided to team up with three other artists engaged in a similar reductive course: Olivier Mosset, Daniel Parmentier, and Niele Toroni, with whom he founded the group BMPT [**5**]. Rebelling against the myth of inspiration and other art world follies, each artist chose a configuration that they would invariably repeat in all their works: to Buren's standard vertical stripes, Parmentier responded with large horizontal bands, Toroni with a regular distribution of isolated brush-strokes of equal dimensions, Mosset with a black circle in the middle of the canvas. Their first exhibition together, during the "Salon de la Jeune Peinture" on January 3, 1967, was a parody of Klein parodying Mathieu: during a whole day, from 11 a.m. to 8 p.m., each artist executed as many of his trademark works as time allowed, while this slogan was broadcast through a loudspeaker: "Buren, Mosset, Parmentier, Toroni advise you to become intelligent." At the end of the day, they left the Salon for good, taking their work with them and leaving only this banner on the walls: "Buren, Mosset, Parmentier, Toroni are not exhibiting." The "Jeune Peinture" was dead and buried, paving the way for institutional critique. A little over a year later, the political upheavals of May 1968 would further radicalize the guerrilla ▲ tactics of BMPT.

FURTHER READING

Yve-Alain Bois, "François Morellet/Sol Lewitt: A Case Study," in Thomas Gaehtgens, *Artistic Exchange, Acts of the 28th International Congress of Art History, Berlin, July 15–20* (Berlin: Akademie Verlag, 1993)

Yve-Alain Bois, *Martin Barré* (Paris: Flammarion, 1993)

Benjamin H. D. Buchloh, "Hantaï/Villeglé and the Dialectics of Painting's Dispersal," *Neo-Avantgarde and Culture Industry* (Cambridge, Mass.: MIT Press, 2000)

Daniel Buren, *Entrevue: Conversations with Anne Baldessari* (Paris: Musée des Arts Décoratifs, 1987)

Bruce Glaser, "Questions to Stella and Judd," in Gregory Battcock (ed.), *Minimal Art: A Critical Anthology* (New York: Dutton, 1968; and Berkeley and Los Angeles: University of California Press, 1995)

Serge Lemoine, *François Morellet* (Zurich: Waser Verlag, 1986)

▲ Introduction 4, 1971 • 1953, 1958 ■ 1910 ▲ 1971

1968a

Two major museums committed to the most advanced European and American art of the sixties—the Stedelijk Van Abbemuseum in Eindhoven and the Städtisches Museum Abteiberg in Mönchengladbach—exhibit the work of Bernd and Hilla Becher, placing them at the forefront of an interest in Conceptual art and photography.

In 1957, Bernd (born 1931) and Hilla Becher (born 1934) initiated a photographic project that has continued to preoccupy them until the present day: the systematic recording of European industrial architecture, which at that time was under threat of imminent disappearance through neglect and decay. Like many photographic archives before them, from Charles Marville's nine-▲teenth-century topography of Parisian streets to Eugène Atget's magisterial attempts slightly later to record the disappearance of Paris under the impact of modernization, the Bechers' project has been marked from the very beginning by a particular dialectic: a struggle between, on the one hand, an almost obsessive will for an exhaustive record, a desire to make permanent, and, on the other, an equally deep sense of loss, the melancholic insight that the spatial and temporal disappearance of the object can never be arrested.

Two photographic turns: 1928–1968

Two other photographic projects—one central to the very history and culture from which the Bechers emerged (that is, the photo-●graphy of German Neue Sachlichkeit [New Objectivity]); the other from the context of reception within which their work became internationally known—should be mentioned at once. ■ The first is the work of the German photographer August Sander, to whom the Bechers have referred on many occasions as a key influence. Sander's best-known project *Antlitz der Zeit* (Face of Our Time), conceived in the first decade of the twentieth century and partially published in 1929, was an attempt to provide an exact and complete record of the social subjects of the Weimar Republic, a physiognomy of all its social strata, genders and ages, professions and types.

The second "archive" was constituted by the use of photography by American artists such as Ed Ruscha, Dan Graham, and Douglas ◆ Huebler who, starting in the early to mid-sixties, resituated the photograph at the center of artistic production. In the Bechers' initial reception, from the late sixties onward, the couple were frequently associated with these artists (and with some of them they have maintained lifelong friendships). Typically, one of the first—and possibly still the most important—essays on their work and their first book *Anonyme Skulpturen: Eine Typologie technischer Bauten* (Anonymous Sculptures: A Typology of Technical Constructions) ▲ was written by Carl Andre, the central sculptor of Minimalism.

Some of the earliest photographs the Bechers produced were composite images of mining architecture, a strangely antiquated type of montage that resurrects the original photographic promise to supply the greatest quantity of empirically verifiable detail in the formation of a positivist record of the visible world. But these images were problematic for the couple, for they were disturbingly reminiscent of photomontage—the menacing political "other" to the latent conservatism of Neue Sachlichkeit photography that served as the Bechers' primary historical resource. Furthermore, the tradition of photomontage had recently resurfaced in the postwar period in an American reincarnation, namely in the work ● of Robert Rauschenberg, a reference that the Bechers would have wanted to avoid altogether at that time.

This might explain why they soon replaced the composite photograph with a unique combination of two modernist photographic orders: the traditionally crafted, single-image print and the principle of the sequential or the serial image. From now on their photographs were displayed in two different formal arrangements: either in what the Bechers call a "typology" (generally a series of nine, twelve, or fifteen images of the same type of architectural structure, such as nine different lime kilns or fifteen different cooling towers [**1**]), or in what they identify as a "development," (*Abwicklung*), that is, a series of single images in which one particular individual structure (for instance, a mining tower or a house) is presented in a sequence of rotating views [**2**].

The actual development of the Bechers' work over this period is infinitely more complex, however, than this brief summary suggests, inasmuch as it could be identified as one of the few artistic projects in postwar Germany to establish a historical continuity with the Weimar avant-garde. This is in contradistinction to the majority of ■ the postwar West German artists, such as Gerhard Richter, who explicitly situated themselves outside the orbit of the Weimar legacy, establishing a link instead with the American neo-avant-garde phenomena of the fifties and sixties. In opposition, the Bechers worked to resuscitate the legacy of Weimar Neue Sachlichkeit photography by openly emulating the ideals and achievements of its canonical figures: August Sander, Albert Renger-Patzsch, and Werner Manz.

▲ 1935 ● 1925b, 1929 ■ 1935 ◆ 1967a, 1968b, 1984a ▲ 1962c ● 1953 ■ 1988

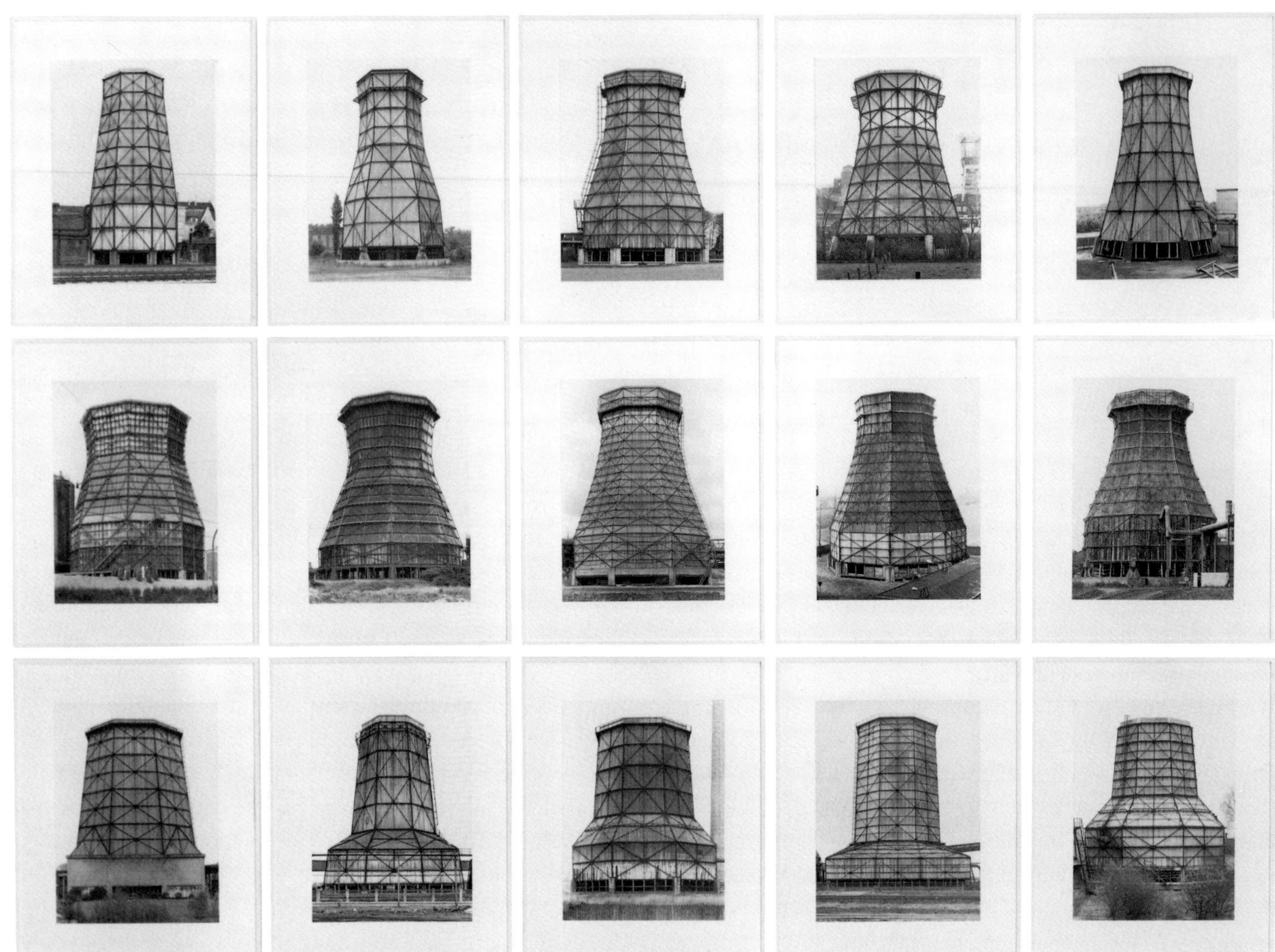

1 • Bernd and Hilla Becher, *Cooling Towers*, 1993
Fifteen black-and-white photographs, 173 x 239 (68¼ x 94¼)

Beyond this claim of continuity with Weimar, the Bechers also asserted a new credibility for photography itself, which under the impact of Abstract Expressionism and the rise of American and French painting of the fifties had been completely overshadowed in the reconstruction period in Germany. Quite clearly, then, they were working to establish a double continuity: first with an alternate Weimar culture; second with an alternate system of imaging practices as they had been fully developed within the context of the "historical avant-garde."

Further, it is important to recognize that in its focus on industrial buildings, such as coal tipples, water towers, mine-entrance structures, the Bechers' project also entered into an explicit dialogue with the rise of welded sculpture and its reception in Germany in the late fifties and early sixties. This work, by sculp-▲tors ranging from David Smith to Jean Tinguely and based on machine parts taken as industrial debris, had become central to the postwar redefinition of sculpture. By their own account, the key figure against which the Bechers defined themselves in the early sixties was the Swiss Nouveau Réaliste Tinguely with his junk sculpture aesthetic to which they opposed their own work both in its photographic dimension and in its use of an actual, historical foundation as industrial archaeology to combat the aestheticizing of industrial ruins. In opposition to the romanticization of industrial waste and to what they perceived to be a reductive understanding of the intersection between artistic and industrial practices, the Bechers explicitly wanted to put themselves in a relation to this type of architecture that would recognize its historical importance, its structural and functional probity, and its aesthetic status. A conservationist impulse therefore motivated their work to the same extent as did an artistic one. While these structures do not quite yet appear as ruins, they are certainly structures on the wane. Thus it is perhaps no surprise that the relatively new discipline of "industrial archaeology," in which conservationists rescue selected examples of industrial architecture from their definitive disappearance, received some of its initial impulses from the work of the Bechers. And it is not surprising either that industrial archaeologists commissioned the pair on various occasions to assist in the scientific exploration and photographic documentation of industrial sites to ensure their archaeological preservation.

▲ 1945, 1960a

From seriality to site-specificity

Clearly, the intersections in the work of the Bechers become yet more complex as one reads them against the various historical strands on which they depended, from Sander and Renger-▲ Patzsch, to Le Corbusier, who in 1928, in his journal *L'Esprit Nouveau*, had published a manifesto to launch an aesthetic based on industrial structures (such as grain silos) as examples of the formal strength of anonymous engineering design. This aesthetic not only argued that form should be nothing more than the pure articulation of function, but also it implied an early (psychological) critique of authorship, as well as an early (sociopolitical) emphasis on the collective participation in social production. Le Corbusier was opposed to the *auteur* aesthetic of the modernist architect on the same grounds as were the Bechers, when in *Anonymous Sculptures* they argued that the anonymity of industrial design deserves to be taken as seriously as authorial claims for individuality. Thus at the moment of 1968, a lineage within modernism could be traced from Le Corbusier through Neue Sachlichkeit to the Bechers, for which collectivity, anonymity, and functionalism are seen as key artistic values.

▲ In his enthusiastic response to *Anonymous Sculptures*, Andre read their work as though it were primarily defined by its compulsive attention to serial repetition. This reading, which immediately brought the Bechers into the context of Minimalist and Postminimalist aesthetics, was made possible by the way the Bechers arrange their images as pristine, gridlike taxonomies by which to present the minute structural differences between each of their examples. This emphasis on repetition, seriality, minute inspection, and structural differentiation is obviously what attracted Andre's attention, engendering his Minimalist reception of the work and its canonization within the context of Minimalist and Postminimalist sculpture. But there were other aspects that helped to locate the Bechers within the dialogue on sculpture that was developing in the late sixties. One was their work's stress on anonymity, the other was its obvious foregrounding of the issues of site. Andre in particular had developed an internal logic for sculpture in which it would cease to be defined as constructed object and would instead be understood as place, as a node at the intersection of architecture and environment.

Another quality that placed the Bechers within the context not only of Minimalism but also of emerging Conceptualism was the

2 • Bernd and Hilla Becher, *Eight Views of a House*, 1962–71
Eight black-and-white photographs

▲ 1925a, 1929, 1935

▲ 1962c

replacement of material structures by the photographic document, particularly as it was accumulated in their work in serial ▲ alignments. From Ed Ruscha and Dan Graham onward, serial, systematic photography figured crucially within the rise of Conceptual art. What distinguishes the Bechers' work, however, from all of Conceptual art is their emphasis on skill. If Conceptual • photography is defined by deskilling, the Bechers' work is focused on reskilling: they emphatically resuscitate the ambition to produce the highest quality black-and-white photography they can possibly achieve, in the same way that photographers of the ■ Neue Sachlichkeit context, such as Sander and Renger-Patzsch, insisted on the highest artisanal accomplishment of the photographic project. The Bechers go to great lengths to produce the right photograph, framed at the right height and taken, without shadows, on the right day in order to get the right light and thereby to obtain the most minute gradations of tonal values; further, they insist on the most immaculate presentation of the object. Insofar as it then appears to be unmediated by any authorial perception, this is in line with the legacy of Neue Sachlichkeit that the Bechers push to a new threshold of ambition.

This insistence on continuity with the Weimar culture of Neue Sachlichkeit, in its refusal to allow German neo-avant-garde production to be mediated in its entirety through postwar American ▲ art, parallels Georg Baselitz's exactly contemporaneous attempt • to resuscitate German Expressionism. Such claims for continuity are problematic, however, on two fronts at once. Insofar as artistic practices and strategies are in and of themselves historically circumscribed and thus perpetually surpassed and devalorized, the idea of a valid model of "new objectivity" photography that could be transplanted from the twenties to the sixties is questionable. Further, in a situation such as the German one, the political and historical caesura of World War II blocks access to an unproblematic relation to the idea of the nation state as the basis for the subject's identity, and thus the project of trying to construct artistic identity on such conventional models becomes ever more difficult. The other side of the effort to create an artistic practice that transcends the chasm of the historical rupture opened by World War II and the Holocaust is, then, an attempt to blind oneself to the degree to which all cultural practices after 1946 were deeply affected by that caesura and would have had to

3 • Thomas Struth, *Clinton Road, London*, 1977
Black-and-white photograph, 66 x 84 (26 x 33)

▲ 1967a, 1968b • 1968b ■ 1929, 1935 ▲ 1963 • 1908

take it into account. This is the additional dimension of the Bechers' problematic claim for historical continuity which needs to be contrasted with other practices in Germany of the ▲ same period, such as Gerhard Richter's, where no such assertion is being made.

Precisely in its attempt to bypass the questions of historical mourning, the work displays the symptoms of a repressive apparatus; it is not accidental in that sense that the melancholia hovering over the Bechers' work is generated by the almost phobic prohibition of the subject within the photographs' exclusive focus on industrial ruins (that applies even to the category of mid-nineteenth-century rural housing, a series that is also presented solely for the type's structural beauty, rather than for any sociological dimension). For the melancholic contemplation of the past to be effective, then, the social and historical context has to be excised from their work in order to make the architectural the undisturbed object of • attention. With the major exception of August Sander, this move to dehistoricize had, of course, been a defining charac- ■ teristic of the original Neue Sachlichkeit photography as well, given its perpetual endeavor to aestheticize the object.

From concepts to color

The second generation of artists to emerge from the Bechers' "school"—Bernd Becher taught at the Düsseldorf Academy from the mid-sixties onward—was a group of photographer-artists that included Thomas Struth (born 1954) **[3]**, Thomas Ruff (born 1958) **[4]**, Candida Höfer (born 1944) **[5]**, and ◆ Andreas Gursky (born 1955) **[6]**. All of them picked up from the Bechers' point of departure and extended it, also extending some of the predicaments inherent to their approach. For example, in the photographs of Struth and Ruff, the emphasis on the absence of human agency is as compulsively enacted as it is in the Bechers' own work.

Beginning by photographing empty streets in Düsseldorf in 1976, Struth replaced the pure industrial object with the pure urban, structural fabric. Yet, as had been the case with the Bechers, the capacity to skirt actual historical questions operates in the way Struth systematically found urban sites where the absence of human activity allowed for a melancholic reading of the city. But with the transformation from architectural to urban archaeology that took him on incessant travels through urban centers—ranging from small towns in Belgium, Germany, England, and the United States to large cities such as Tokyo—Struth recorded a peculiar type of public urban space. And in retrospect this appears as a systematic accounting of the actual experience of the disappearance of public urban space in a parallel with the vanishing landscape preserved only in the photographic archive the Bechers have produced.

In Struth's and Ruff's early work, the insistence on black-and-white photography—doubly obsolete in its dimension

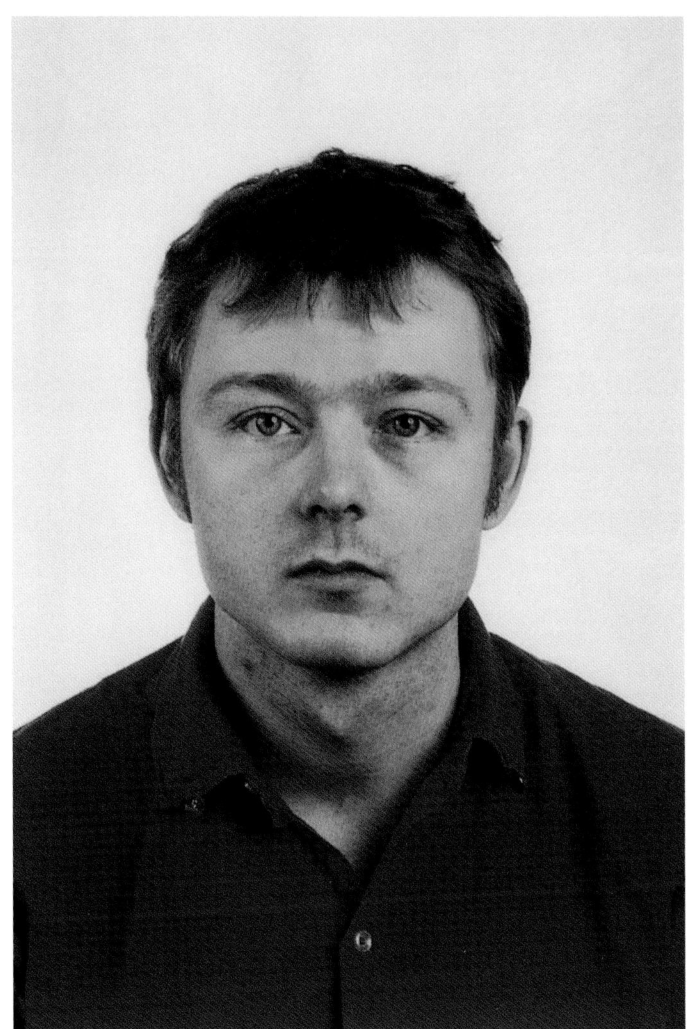

4 • Thomas Ruff, *Portrait*, 1989
Chromogenic color print, 119.6 x 57.5 (47 1/16 x 22 5/8)

as material support and as vehicle of artisanal skills—brings to the foreground the question of whether and to what extent an antimodernist impulse is operative here, one that could best ▲ be compared to the lineage of Giorgio de Chirico in painting. It is an antimodernism that greets the present through the lens of melancholia, that is manifestly disconnected from the model of an avant-garde and its necessary link with advancing scientific and technological means of production, and that positions itself with regard to the question of the reconstruction of memory under the conditions of loss, a question that is important in the postwar period.

There is a later phase of this development when color suddenly makes its appearance in the work of Ruff, Struth, Gursky, and Höfer as though it has been released from a prohibition. Yet this introduction of color, and along with it the admission of human agency and social context in great quantities and detail, does not resolve the historical limitations of Struth's or Ruff's photographic practice. Quite the opposite would be true, in fact, for the large and continuing series of photographic portraits that Ruff produced from the late eighties onward, which resuscitates the traditional model of the portrait as it had been practiced in

▲ 1988 • 1935 ■ 1929 ◆ 2001 ▲ 1909, 1924

5 • Candida Höfer, *BNF Paris VII*, 1998
Chromogenic color print, 85 x 85 (33½ x 33½)

6 • Andreas Gursky, *Salerno*, 1990
Chromogenic color print, 188 x 226 (74 x 89)

Weimar Neue Sachlichkeit. This places Ruff at the center of a counterconceptual approach—the portrait having been the object of explicit deconstruction by the Conceptualists who regarded it as a historically obsolete model through which false claims for an accessible physiognomic depiction of subjectivity and identity were made. With Ruff's reconstitution of the genre of photographic portraiture, one such countermodernist impulse thus reaches its apogee and points toward the radicality of photo-▲ conceptual practices.

FURTHER READING

Alex Alberro, "The Big Picture: The Art of Andreas Gursky," *Artforum*, vol. 39, no.5, January 2001
Carl Andre, "A Note on Bernhard and Hilla Becher," *Artforum*, vol. 11, no. 5, December 1972
Douglas Eklund (ed.), *Thomas Struth: 1977–2002* (New York: Metropolitan Museum of Art, 2002)
Peter Galassi (ed.), *Andreas Gursky* (New York: Museum of Modern Art, 2001)
Susanne Lange (ed.), *Bernd und Hilla Becher: Festschrift. Erasmuspreis 2002* (Munich: Schirmer/Mosel, 2002)
Armin Zweite (ed.), *Bernd and Hilla Becher: Typologies of Industrial Buildings* (Düsseldorf, Kunstsammlung Nordrhein-Westfalen; and Munich: Schirmer/Mosel, 2004)

▲ 1984a

1968b

Conceptual art manifests itself in publications by Sol LeWitt, Dan Graham, and Lawrence Weiner, while Seth Siegelaub organizes its first exhibitions.

Conceptual art emerged from the confluence of two major legacies of modernism, one embodied in the readymade, the other in geometric abstraction. Through the practices ▲ of Fluxus and the Pop artists, the first legacy was transmitted to ● younger postwar artists; through the works of Frank Stella and the ■ Minimalists, a similar bridge was formed between prewar abstraction and conceptual approaches at the end of the sixties.

At the beginning of the decade, prior to the organized onset of Conceptual art in 1968, the fusion of Fluxus and Pop had led to works such as Robert Morris's *Card File* (1962) and Ed Ruscha's *Twenty-Six Gasoline Stations* [**1**], in which certain positions that would subsequently determine Conceptual art were firmly established: in Ruscha's work this meant an emphasis on photography and the form of distribution of the printed book; in Morris's, it entailed a focus on a revised, linguistic definition of modernist self-reflexiveness—or art asserting its own autonomy through strategies of self-reference—which Morris pushed to the point of undermining the very possibility of aesthetic autonomy.

Both Morris and Ruscha are, in turn, indebted to the way ▲ Duchamp's readymade had yielded a more complex model of ● practice in the hands of Jasper Johns and Andy Warhol. These two were also central to the subsequent unfolding of photographic and textual strategies as they were being put in place in the mid-sixties by the first "official" generation of Conceptual artists, namely Lawrence Weiner (born 1940), Joseph Kosuth (born 1945), Robert Barry (born 1936), and Douglas Huebler (1924–77). These artists formed the group that was shown in 1968 in New York by the art dealer Seth Siegelaub (born 1941).

The second element that contributed significantly to the formation of a Conceptual aesthetic was Minimalist abstraction as embodied in the work of Frank Stella, Ad Reinhardt, and Donald ■ Judd. In his manifesto-like essay "Art After Philosophy" (1969), Joseph Kosuth acknowledged all of these as predecessors in the development of the Conceptual aesthetic. What is at stake in this aesthetic is a critique of the modernist notion of visuality (or "opticality"), here defined as a separate, autonomous sphere

1 • Ed Ruscha, from *Twenty-Six Gasoline Stations*, 1962
Artist's photobook

▲ 1960c, 1962a, 1964b ● 1958 ■ 1965 ▲ 1914 ● 1958, 1964b ■ 1957b, 1958, 1965

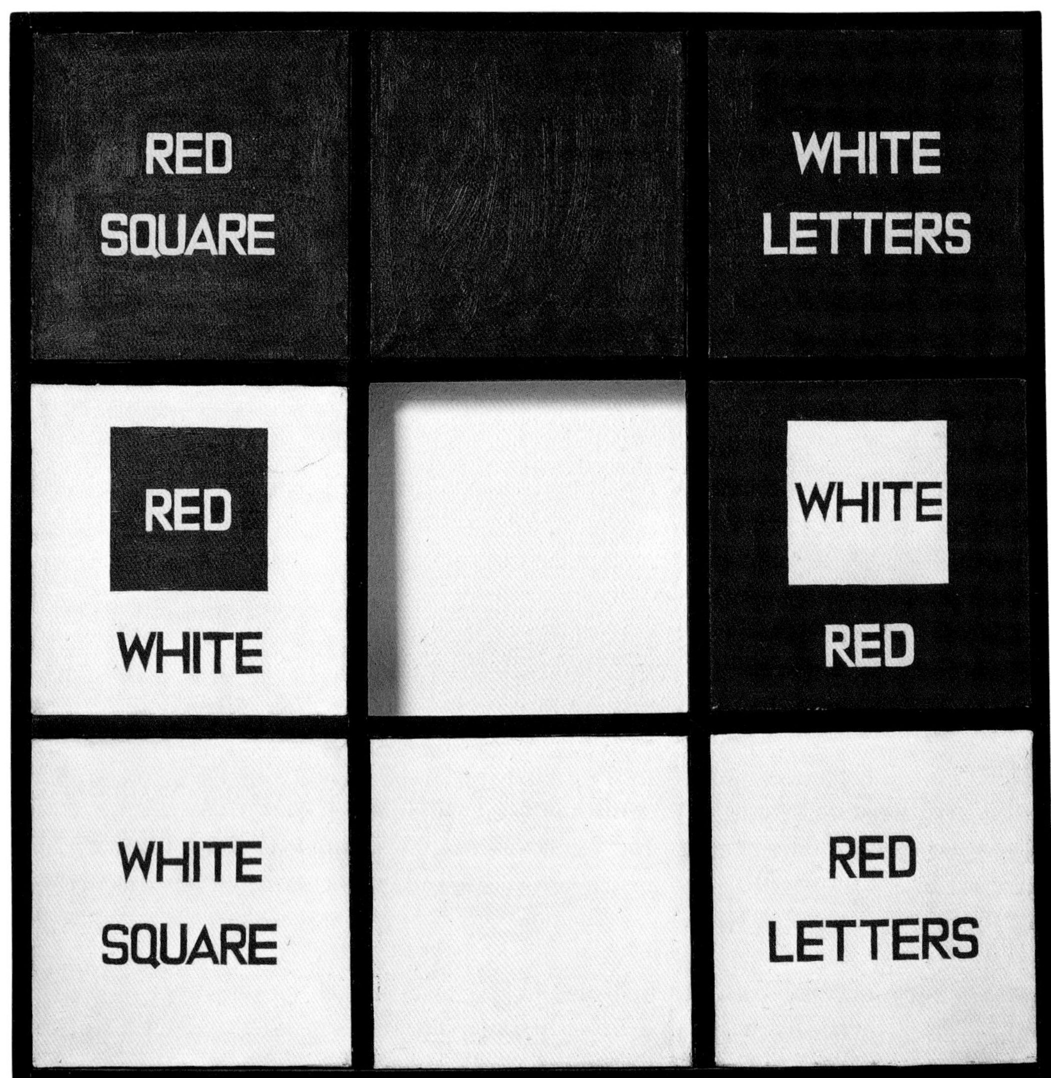

2 • Sol LeWitt, *Red Square, White Letters*, 1963
Oil on canvas, 91.4 x 91.4 (36 x 36)

▲ of aesthetic experience. What is further at issue is the question of the problematic uniqueness of the art object as well as the new mode of distribution (the book, the poster, the journal) and the "spatiality" of that object—namely, the pictorial rectangle or the sculptural solid (despite Minimalism's embrace of industrial pro- • duction and technological reproduction, Minimalist work had ultimately remained wedded to the singular object).

Developing the critique

If visuality, physical concreteness, and aesthetic autonomy are some of the modernist aspects that Conceptual art began to critique from within, this critique had already manifested itself as early as 1963 in work such as Sol LeWitt's *Red Square, White Letters* [**2**]. As a result of the extreme reductivism of late-modernist painting and sculpture in its drive to secure its autonomy through self-definition, it became a relatively plausible step to challenge visual and formal self-reflexiveness through a strategy of producing literal, which is to say linguistic, "definitions." And if the idea of definition as a basis for art practice started to enter the work of future Conceptual artists by 1965, the model of definition transmitted to them by the example of Sol LeWitt was clearly what one would call a *performative model.* This is because, in replacing the visual structure of the work by the color- and shape-names of its visual units ("White Square" printed on a white square; "Red Letters" printed in red on a white square, and so on), LeWitt transforms the work's spectator into a reader: in the act of pronouncing the information inscribed on the canvas, the viewing relationship becomes a performative reader relationship. This in turn parallels the transformation of the visual object—as autonomous—into an understanding of that object as highly contingent, depending as it does on the context of its particular engagement with its receiver.

With Morris's early work it also became evident that one aspect ▲ of the readymade that had been overlooked in the history of Duchamp's reception in the postwar period was that it already contained a performative, linguistic dimension—a work of art can be "created" merely by naming it so—which could open in turn onto what one could call the administrative or legalistic definition

▲ 1960b, 1993a • 1965 ▲ 1914

of the work. Specifically, Morris's *Statement of Aesthetic Withdrawal* [**3**] canceled the artistic value of his slightly earlier work *Litanies* (also 1963)—because, as the notarized document contained in *Statement* attests, the collector of *Litanies* did not pay for it—thereby, in effect, voiding its "name." This legalistic or administrative system of conventions within which meaning is (temporarily) fixed is one strategy that was then adopted by Conceptual art to displace the ontological or "intrinsic" definition of the work of art.

In the way such conventions are obviously external to the idea of the work as self-contained and autonomous, they participate in ▲ what could be called an "aesthetic of the supplement." And it is this notion of supplement that operates in other ways in those works, such as Morris's *Card File* or his *Box with the Sound of Its Own Making* (1961), that forms the immediate prehistory of Conceptual art. There, Morris's strategy is to point toward those features that so exceed the containment and the relative autonomy demanded by the modernist paradigm that it begins to break down in the face of this experience of excess. Thus in *Box with the Sound of Its Own Making* the traditional sculptural cube (the classic correspondent to the traditional pictorial square) is presented, but—with the taped sounds of the process of its own production emanating from within it—this seemingly "pure" form is shown to be a hybrid of supplements of history, memory, texture, sound, and technology of fabrication that led to this supposedly self-contained object.

In *Card File* [**4**], which consists entirely of a box of cards carrying notations of the production of the object itself (hence the self-referential stance), the supplement system appears through the written record of all the chance encounters that entered the process of production and opened it up to an economic, social, biographical, historical system that, in all its randomness and even in its • triviality—related to Fluxus and Pop aesthetics—is not extrinsic to the aesthetic object but indeed *necessary* to it. In this, the resultant work is unimportant compared with the complexity with which its process of making intertwines with a variety of "external" structures. And it is the emphasis on these structures that one would call an aesthetic of the supplement. (A wonderful instance in *Card File* is the reference to Morris's chance meeting—on the ■ way to purchase the file itself—with Ad Reinhardt who, as a key representative of the type of self-referential, late-modernist aesthetic to which Morris is saying farewell, is folded into the work as an "insider" who enters the object from outside to distance the "inside" from itself.)

With the first exhibitions organized in 1968 by Seth Siegelaub, who acted as both critic and manager of the Conceptual aesthetic, several additional aspects became evident that were to have a great impact on the definition of Conceptual art. One of these was the way Siegelaub's strategies made the supplement yield a shock value that produced the strange paradox of a simultaneous withdrawal from the field of the visual *and* a staging of that withdrawal as a form of spectacle. Saying "We show in an office space; we don't need a gallery. We show printed matter. We show work that is

Artists' journals

The success of the Dada and Surrealist journals in forging an international audience and a far-flung network for artistic practice was not lost on New York artists who had also seen the prestige and publicity generated by Alfred Stieglitz's magazines *291* and *Camera Work*. In 1947, the year Peggy Guggenheim closed her "Art of This Century Gallery," artists emerging with New York exhibitions at Samuel Kootz Gallery, Charles Egan Gallery and Betty Parsons Gallery felt the need to consolidate a movement using journals as its platform. Accordingly, *The Tiger's Eye* and *Possibilities* were founded as the support for the group practice of Abstract Expressionism. *Possibilities* had only one issue (Winter 1947–8) with statements in it by Robert Motherwell, Jackson Pollock, and Mark Rothko. *The Tiger's Eye* was somewhat longer-lived, with Barnett Newman writing and editing for it.

With the Surrealists Tanguy, Matta, Ernst, and Man Ray in New York in the early forties, it was not surprising that two journals devoted to the movement would be founded: *View* and *VVV*. In April and May 1942, *VVV* published special issues devoted to Ernst and Tanguy, while the first issue of *View* in 1945 was devoted to Marcel Duchamp, who designed its cover; extracts of André Breton's essay "Lighthouse of the Bride," were included. *VVV* and *View* were vehicles for the Abstract Expressionists to voice their concern with subject matter and to wonder whether it would be possible to forge new structures of myth based on American Indian narratives. In 1944, Pollock wrote: "I have always been very impressed with the plastic qualities of American Indian art." Barnett Newman joined him and organized an exhibition of Northwest Coast Indian painting at the Betty Parsons Gallery.

By the late sixties the evolving practice of Conceptual art was focusing on print as the support for its work, with books and magazines as mass-circulation, inexpensive supports for the publication of material centered on photography's own logic of the multiple. Not only were Ed Ruscha's books (*34 Parking Lots*; *Twenty-Six Gasoline Stations*; *Every Building on the Sunset Strip*; *Various Small Fires*) the reasonable outcome of this new conviction, but the publication of manifesto-like essays in established art journals formed part of the Conceptualists' activities. Joseph Kosuth's "Art After Philosophy" was a three-part statement of the way art was being refocused by a new set of issues, published in *Studio International* (1969). It was thus a next step for Kosuth to found the movement's own journal, *The Fox* in 1975, as well as becoming the American editor of *Art-Language* (1969).

The centrality of photographic documentation as evidence of the existence of geographically remote Earthworks led to the frequent publication of artist statements and essays in magazines such as *Artforum*. Robert Smithson, Michael Heizer, Walter De Maria were all published there, as were the Minimalists Robert Morris, Carl Andre, and Donald Judd. This in turn encouraged the development of a journal devoted to Earthwork art, *Avalanche*, edited by Willoughby Sharp and Lisa Bear from 1970. In addition to its interviews with Earthwork artists, *Avalanche* also introduced Joseph Beuys to Anglophone readers.

▲ Introduction 4 • 1960c, 1962a, 1964b ■ 1957b

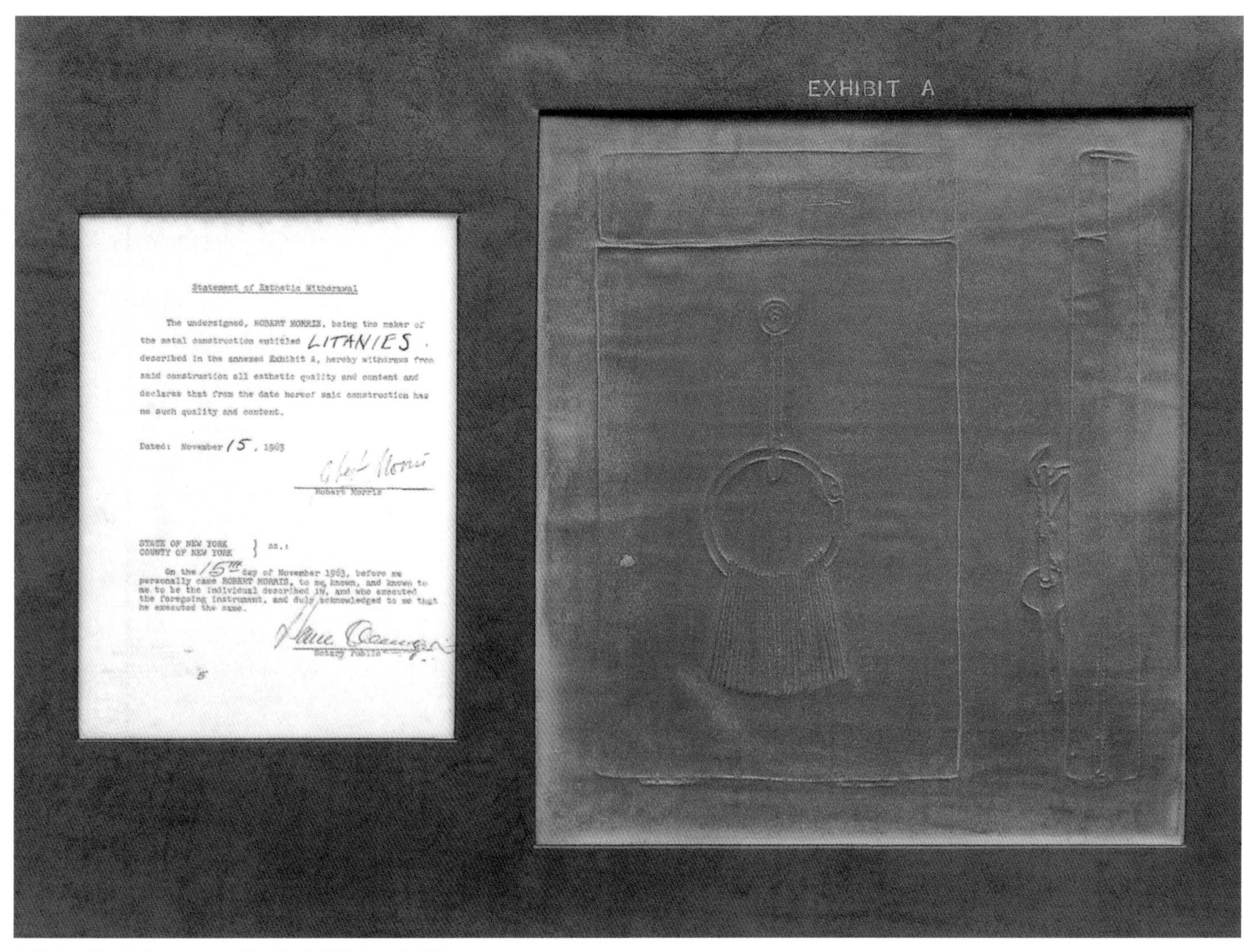

3 • Robert Morris, *Statement of Aesthetic Withdrawal*, 1963
Typed and notarized statement on paper, sheet of lead over wood, mounted in imitation leather mat, 45 x 60.5 (18 x 24)

ephemeral, that is only temporally defined, that is textually based and does not need an actual material institution," Siegelaub underscored the historical obsolescence of the visual work in favor of a mass-cultural, reproduced object; but in doing so, he produced the kind of impact on art audiences that one associates with the most effective kind of advertising. Thus the first few exhibitions of the Siegelaub Gallery repeated what had already appeared in the mid- ▲ to late fifties in the work of Robert Rauschenberg and Yves Klein, in which the gesture toward the supplement also came across, paradoxically, as a "spectacular" withdrawal from visuality and from traditional concepts of artistic production.

Strategies and *Statements*

When Siegelaub published Lawrence Weiner's *Statements* in 1968, a broad spectrum of strategies had thus been put into play. And clearly one of these strategies was the focus on the distribution form as it had been laid out by Ruscha. For in resisting a merely painterly engagement with technical reproduction, such as Warhol's, where the outcome turned out to be no different from previous forms of art, Ruscha was demanding that the product itself partake in the technologies of reproduction. He thereby shifted from Warhol's "Campbell's Soup" paintings to his own photographic books in which the photograph defines the distribution form rather than merely redefining the pictorial structure (as in Warhol) to resuscitate it, paradoxically, from within.

Weiner's book *Statements* carries the idea of distribution even further. Broken down into two halves—the first including works that are in "the public freehold domain" (that is, never able to become private property), which Weiner called "General Works," and the second including those he called "Specific Works"—everything in *Statements* is guided by a tripartite formula in which Weiner pronounces: (a) the artist may construct the piece; (b) the piece may be fabricated; (c) the piece may not be produced at all. In doing so, he indicates that it is the condition of receivership that controls and ultimately determines the material status of the work of art, thereby completely reversing the traditional hierarchy of artistic production. For Weiner, "the owner [receiver] of the work contributes to what the material status of the work will be to the very same extent as its producer."

▲ 1953, 1960a

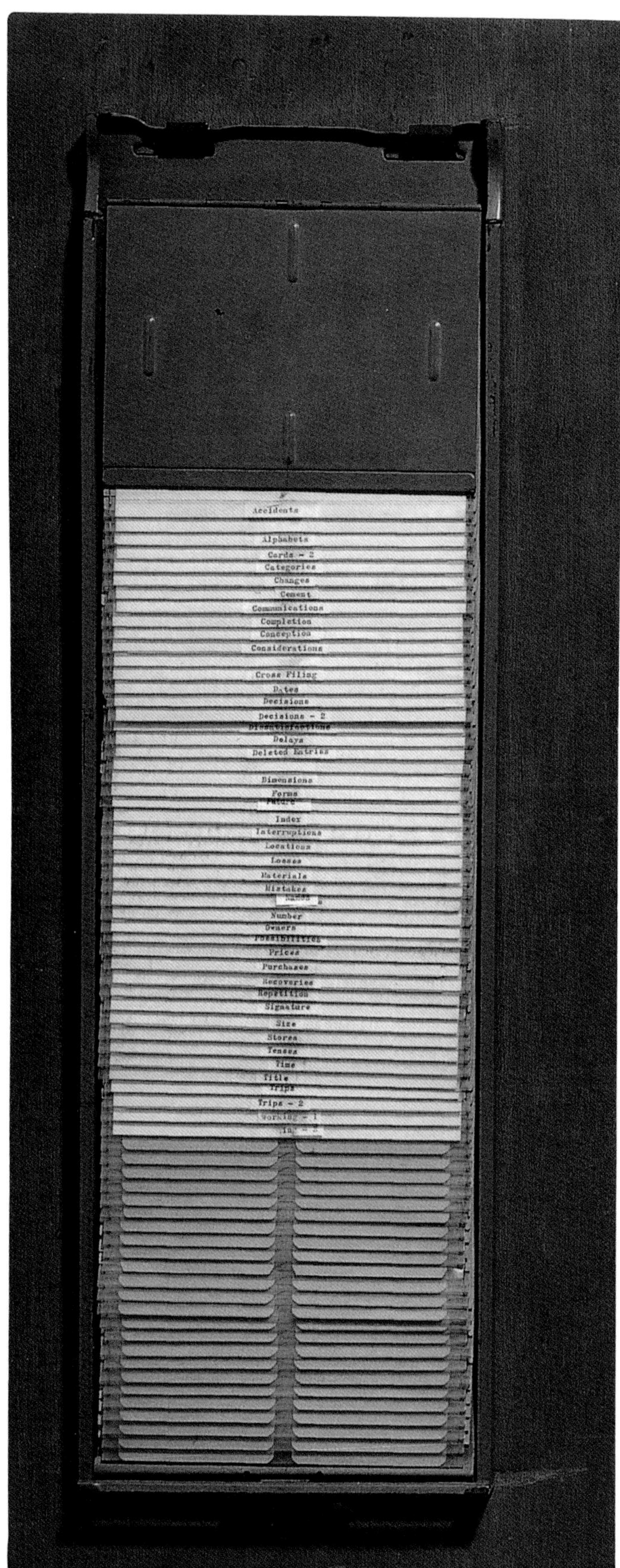

4 • Robert Morris, *Card File*, 1962
Metal and plastic wall file mounted on wood, containing forty-four index cards, 68.5 x 26.5 x 5 (27 x 10⅜ x 2)

Deskilling

The term deskilling was first used in Ian Burn's essay, "The Sixties: Crisis and Aftermath (Or the Memoirs of an Ex-Conceptual Artist)" in *Art & Text* in 1981. It is a concept of considerable importance in describing numerous artistic endeavors throughout the twentieth century with relative precision. All of these are linked by their persistent effort to eliminate artisanal competence and other forms of manual virtuosity from the horizon of both artistic production and aesthetic evaluation. Deskilling appears for the first time in the late nineteenth century in the work of the Impressionists and of Georges Seurat, when the traditional emphasis on virtuoso draftsmanship and painterly finish was displaced by a breakdown of the application of pigment into visibly separate brush-strokes, displacing the smooth surfaces of academic painting with the marks of manual labor in an almost mechanically executed and serially deployed arrangement of pigment. Deskilling first climaxed in the context of Cubist collage, as found cut-paper elements displaced both painterly execution and the function of drawing altogether, substituting the "merely" found tonalities and found graphic schemes that the cut papers took on. The second major moment—perhaps the high point of such a critique of virtuosity and manual skill—came in the immediate wake of Cubist collage with the assumption of the readymade. With this declaration of the found, industrial object from which all artisanal (manual) process has been banished as the work of art, the collective production of the serialized, mechanical object took the place of the exceptional work crafted by the gifted virtuoso.

Here, then, is a logical expansion of the initial collaborative or contingency model that had been introduced in the postwar reception of Duchamp that began with Johns and extended through Morris to LeWitt. For *Statements* emphasizes that neither collaboration, nor industrial production, nor the elimination of authorial originality alone are sufficient to define the condition of contextuality within which the work of art functions. The fact that from *Statements* onward Weiner's work became exclusively language-based corresponds, precisely, to that complex definition inasmuch as the reading of the work, its presentation on the printed page, and its distribution in book form all point to the multiplicity of performative options that the work can assume. All of the work in *Statements* maintains the possibility of a material, sculptural definition [**5**]; all of it could in fact be executed by anyone who cared to: yet all of it retains its full definition as "art" even if it does not acquire a material form. A typical example is a piece such as "A 36 inch × 36 inch square removal from a wall," which was in fact installed in the exhibition ▲"When Attitudes Become Form." In this work the transition in Weiner's own history—he had started out as a painter/sculptor—is rewritten as the move from Minimalist and modernist self-reflexive and highly reductive visual practices to the linguistic transcription of such practices. For the square as the quintessential topos of

▲ 1969

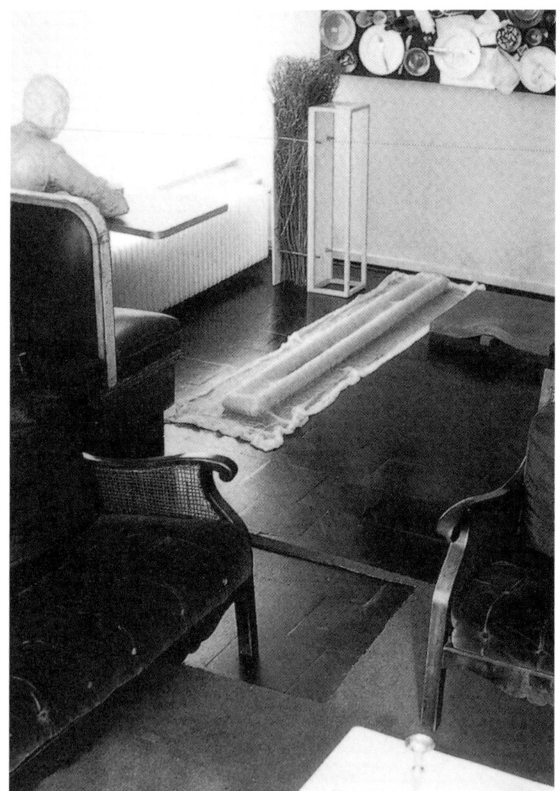

5 • Lawrence Weiner, *a square removal from a rug in use*, 1969
Installation in Cologne, West Germany, dimensions unknown

modernist self-reflection is still in play but now it is literally "inscribed," or written. It is thus linked with the quintessentially antimodernist strategy of visual withdrawal. Inasmuch as the "statement" ties the form to the wall that constitutes its frame, it denies the possibility of a separate visual entity by integrating it into the display surface as much as into the institutional support structure. That paradox, in which the quintessence of visual self-reflexivity is embedded within the contingency and the contextuality of these supports, is a classic conceptual strategy in Weiner's *Statements.*

Another major strand in Conceptual art was photoconceptualism, ▲ developed by figures such as Douglas Huebler, also a member of the Siegelaub group, Dan Graham (born 1942), and John Baldessari (born 1931). These artists introduced models of photographic practice that once again performed a peculiar fusion of Minimalist, late-modernist, and Pop art strategies manifestly derived from a more complex understanding of the implications for photography of Duchamp's readymade. Insofar as Graham's photographs, starting in 1965, focused on the peculiar echoes of modernity in its most debased forms of vernacular architecture—suburban housing developments—the readymade can be seen to be operative. In a work such as *Homes for America* [**6**], produced in several parts in 1966–7, Graham recognized the coding system of Minimalist sculpture—simple geometries arranged through serial repetition—in the found structures of vernacular architecture in New Jersey and elsewhere. That was the first subject of his photographic inquiry, but at the same time he also introduced an approach to photography that was then to be dominant in both Huebler's and Baldessari's use of the medium. This is what one could call the extreme forms of "deskilling" photography that supplanted both the tradition of American documentary and that of American and European fine arts photography. Photography in the hands of these artists—post-Warhol and post-Ruscha—becomes a mere randomly accumulated set of indexical traces of images, objects, contexts, behaviors, or interactions in an attempt to make the complexity of both the architectural dimensions of public space and the social dimensions of individual interaction the subject matter of conceptual approaches. The third figure to be mentioned in this context, in dialogue with those figures mentioned above as photoconceptualists (although clearly positioning himself ▲ outside of their immediate circle), is Hans Haacke, who also deployed systems of photographic records in a deskilled production as an integral element for a "documentary" approach. In the work of these artists, documentation certainly claims no continuity with the ● documentary traditions of, say, FSA photography.

Joseph Kosuth deducted his own theory of Conceptual art from a dogmatic synthesis of the various, and contradictory, strands of modernism, ranging from Duchamp to Reinhardt (for Kosuth, Duchamp's readymades were the "beginning of 'modern' art" because they changed the nature of art "from 'appearance' to 'con-

6 • Dan Graham, *Homes for America, "Split Level" and "Ground Level," "Two Home Homes,"* 1966
Two photographs, 25.5 x 17.5 (10 x 17)

▲ 1984a

▲ 1971, 1972b ● 1936

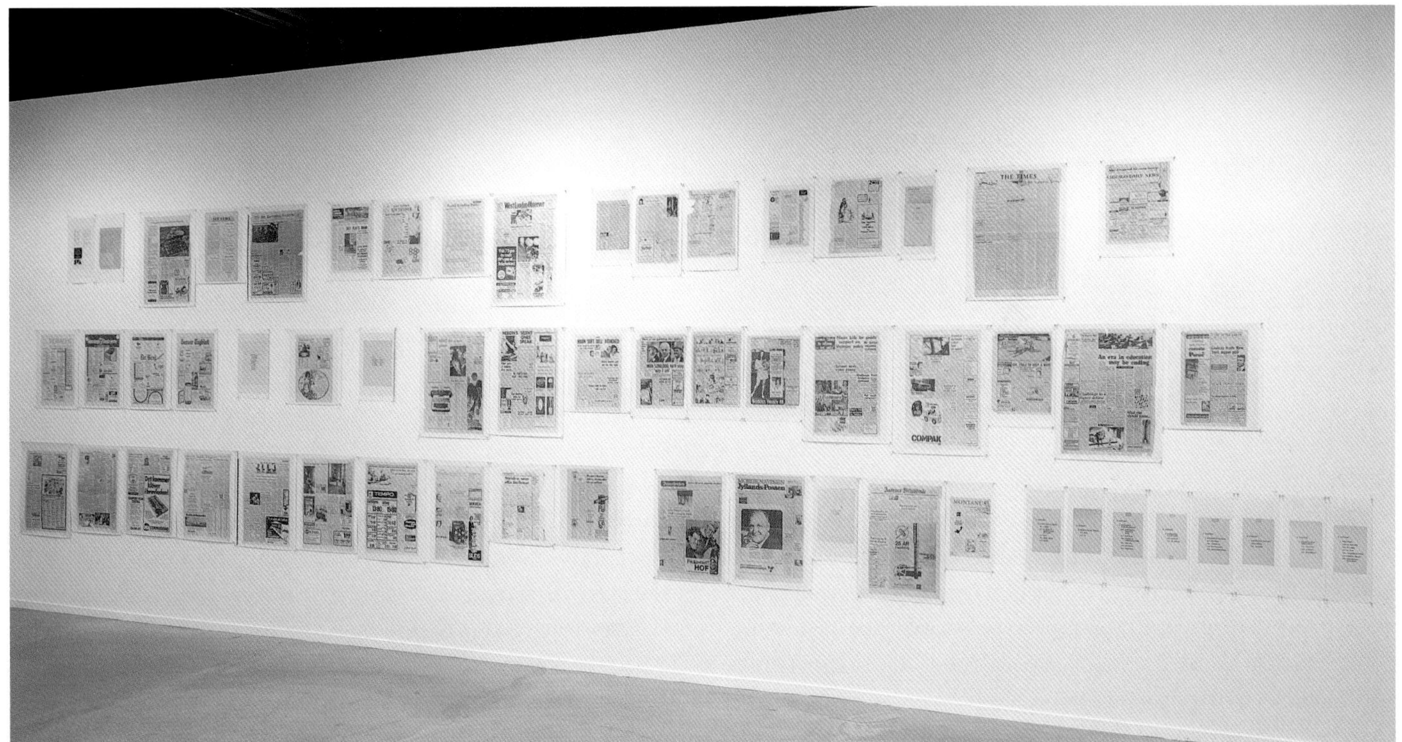

7 • Joseph Kosuth, *The Second Investigation*, 1969–74
Installation view

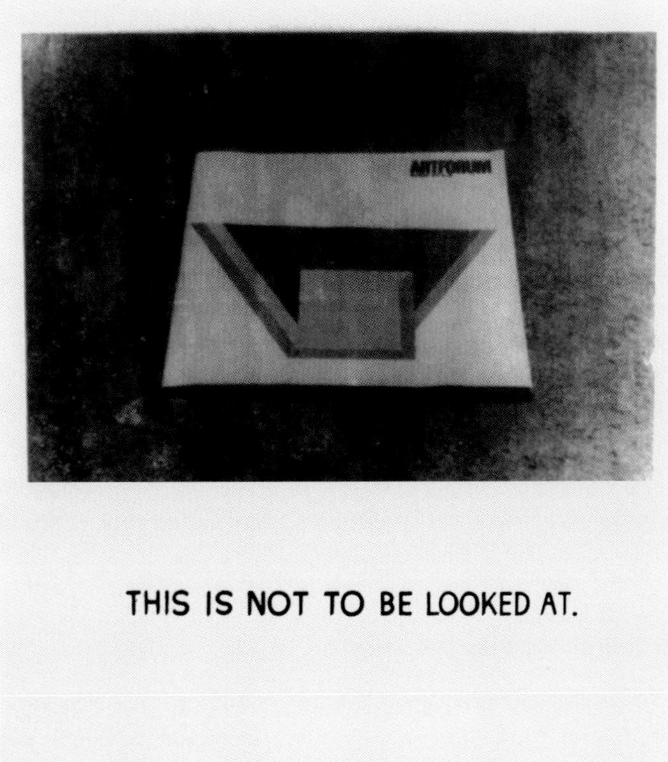

ARTFORUM
THIS IS NOT TO BE LOOKED AT.

8 • John Baldessari, *This Is Not To Be Looked At*, 1968
Acrylic and photoemulsion on canvas, 149.9 x 114.3 (59 x 45)

ception'"). In *One and Three Chairs* (1965), he extended the readymade by breaking it into a tripartite set of relations—object, linguistic sign, and photographic reproduction—and in works such as *The Second Investigation* [**7**] he put into practice his assertion, as expressed in "Art After Philosophy," that the work of art is a "*proposition* presented within the context of art as a comment on art." Influenced by linguistic models, the laws of mathematics, and the principles of logical positivism, Kosuth defined his project—"and, by extension, other artists'"—as an "inquiry into the foundations of the concept 'art,' as it has come to mean." And yet, while valid for his own investigations, such a rigorously analytical approach was hardly applicable to any of the other practices emerging at that time. One artist who was explicitly excommunicated from Kosuth's late-modernist doxa was John Baldessari. Instead of turning Duchamp into doctrine, as Kosuth had done, Baldessari took his subversive legacies and applied them to the false orthodoxies with which Conceptualism was about to install itself as the new authoritative movement. Baldessari's work anticipated these new art-world pieties early on: he annihilated them with an antiartistic humor in both his paintings and his books [**8**].

FURTHER READING

Alexander Alberro, *Conceptual Art and the Politics of Publicity* (Cambridge, Mass.: MIT Press, 2001)
Alexander Alberro and Patricia Norvell (eds), *Recording Conceptual Art* (Cambridge, Mass.: MIT Press, 2000)
Benjamin H. D. Buchloh, "From the Aesthetics of Administration to the Critique of Institutions," *October*, no. 55, Summer 1995, reprinted in *Neo-Avantgarde and Culture Industry* (Cambridge, Mass.: MIT Press, 2001)
Michael Newman and Jon Bird (eds), *Rewriting Conceptual Art* (London: Reaktion Books, 2001)
Peter Osborne (ed.), *Conceptual Art* (London: Phaidon Press, 2002)
Blake Stimson and Alexander Alberro (eds), *Conceptual Art: An Anthology of Critical Writings and Documents* (Cambridge, Mass.: MIT Press, 2000)

▲ 1971 ● 1936

1969

The exhibition "When Attitudes Become Form" in Bern and London surveys Postminimalist developments, while "Anti-Illusion: Procedures/Materials" in New York focuses on Process art, the three principal aspects of which are elaborated by Richard Serra, Robert Morris, and Eva Hesse.

▲ With its move into "specific objects" Minimalism signaled a definitive crisis in notions of the medium. The old standard of *quality*, assessed in relation to traditional painting and sculpture, was challenged by the new criterion of *interest*, which was not medium-specific: "a work of art needs only to be interesting," Donald Judd declared. If so, it followed for Judd, "any material can be used," and with new materials came new procedures, as explored in • Process art, Arte Povera, Performance, Body art, Installation, and site-specific art. Often called "Postminimalist," these practices do follow Minimalism, some to extend its principles, most to react against them, but the term "Postminimalist" is no more coherent than the term "Postimpressionist." It did not help comprehension that these reactions came fast and furious. For example, 1966 was the year not only of "Primary Structures," the first museum survey of Minimalism in New York (held at the Jewish Museum), but also of ■ "Eccentric Abstraction," the initial gallery show (again in New York) of art deemed eccentric to Minimalism both formally and psychologically. For its curator, the critic Lucy Lippard, the odd substances wrought in strange shapes by Louise Bourgeois, Eva Hesse, Bruce Nauman, Keith Sonnier, and others posed an "emotive or erotic alternative" to Minimalism, which was thus seen as normative as early as 1966. And if 1968 saw another museum review of Minimalism, "The Art of the Real" at the Museum of Modern Art, 1969 witnessed early institutional assessments of Postminimalism: as the titles suggest, "Anti-Illusion: Procedures/Materials" at the Whitney Museum focused on Process art, whereas "When Attitudes Become Form," first at the Kunsthalle in Bern, then at the Institute of Contemporary Arts in London, surveyed an international panoply of Postminimalist modes (its subtitle read "Works—Concepts—Processes—Situations—Information").

How are we to understand this heady round of position and counterposition, show and countershow, which is accelerated even by avant-garde standards? Does Postminimalism signal a new moment of artistic freedom and critical debate, or of aesthetic confusion and discursive anxiety? Is it a breakthrough into new materials and methods, or a breakdown in convention, a collapse in medium? Or is it both at once, an innovation born of crisis when, after the apparent supercession of painting and sculpture in Minimalism, the manipulating of substances and systems in ▲ Process and Conceptual art, and the marking of bodies and sites in Performance and Installation art, emerged both as creative possibilities and as default positions—medium-substitutes, as it were?

However different, all these practices responded to this crisis in medium, which forced two questions with special urgency: Is there a limit to the materiality of the art work, a zero degree of its visuality? And can the intentionality of the artist also be reduced, or at least transformed in its effects? The responses to these two questions were often divided, sometimes internally so. If some Conceptual artists "dematerialized" art (the famous term of Lippard), most Process artists rematerialized it with a vengeance: one thinks of the latex • creatures of Eva Hesse or the polyurethane growths of Lynda Benglis (born 1941); "eccentric abstraction" is a mild term for such works. As for intentionality, some Process artists saw new materials as mere vehicles for expressive intent (e.g., Benglis, who indeed turned "attitudes" into "form"), while others saw intrinsic properties that the work might disclose automatically, as if without authorial intervention: Morris let his felt strips hang limply **[1]** and his threadwaste sit humped, while Serra allowed the ambient architecture to shape his lead splashings **[2]**. As in Conceptual art, which was divided between the concept as pure intention (e.g., Joseph Kosuth) and the concept as quasi-automatic "machine" (Sol LeWitt), this split over intentionality stemmed in part from different readings of ■ Duchamp—of the readymade seen as an act of declarative choice ("I nominate this urinal to be a work of art") or as an attempt to annul choice altogether ("a reaction of visual indifference ... a complete anesthesia," as Duchamp once claimed).

A search for the motivated

Two aspects of this "postmedium" condition are relevant to Process art. First, however restrictive, traditional mediums offer practical rules for making and meaning: art may seem free without such constraint, but it may also become *arbitrary*. This was a primary point of anxiety not only for critical foes of Minimalism ◆ and Postminimalism, such as Clement Greenberg and Michael Fried, but also for artist proponents like Morris, for whom Process art was driven by a "search for the motivated" now that the protocols of medium-specificity seemed to be voided—a search, that is,

▲ 1965 • 1967b, 1970, 1974 ■ 1966b ▲ 1968b • Introduction 1 ■ 1914 ◆ 1960b

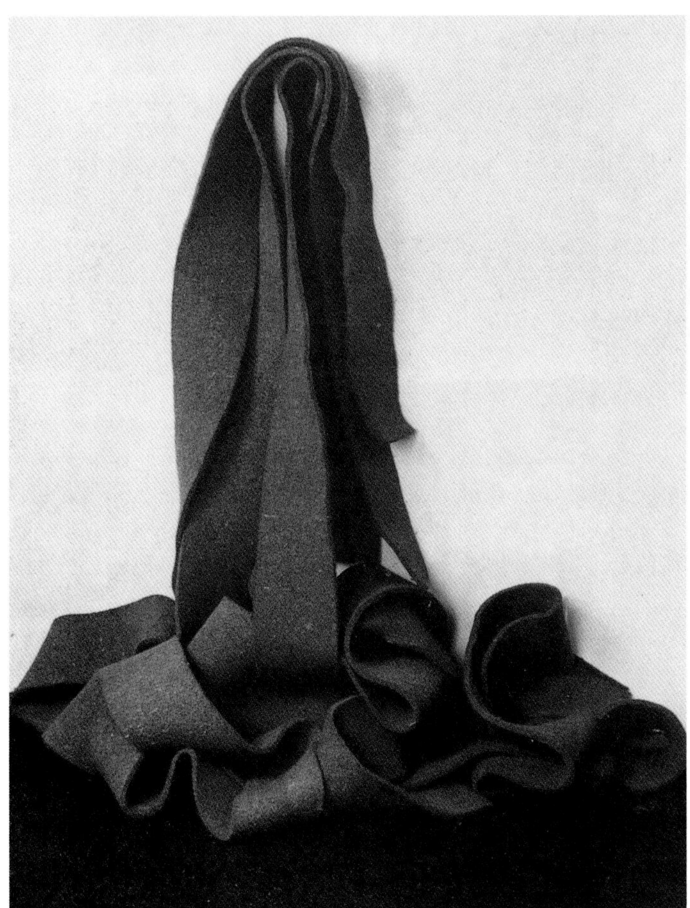

1 • Robert Morris, *Untitled (Tan Felt)*, 1968
Nine strips, each 304.8 x 20.3 (120 x 8). Installation, 172.7 x 182.8 x 66 (68 x 72 x 26)

for other ways to ground art, as in the "logic of materials" proposed by Serra, or in the "order of making behavior" (triangulated by "the nature of materials, the restraints of gravity, the limited mobility of the body interacting with both") proposed by Morris. This is the first point to stress about Process art. The second is that it also *continued* a critical engagement with traditional mediums; in particular it continued the Minimalist critique of the illusionist space and relational composition thought to be residual in abstract painting and sculpture. This is why the first imperative of most Process art was to overcome the traditional oppositions of form and content (stressed by Lippard) and of means and ends (stressed by Serra and Morris)—to reveal the process of the work in the product, indeed *as* the product. This is also why the second imperative of some Process art was to overcome the no-less-traditional opposition of figure and ground, of a vertical image read against a horizontal field (whether this field be illusionist, as in painting, or actual, as in sculpture). It is this second imperative that led artists such as Morris, Serra, Alan Saret (born 1944), and Barry Le Va (born 1941) to scatter different materials (e.g., threadwaste, felt, wire, shattered glass) in gallery spaces in such a way that "the figure is literally the ground" (Morris). Already in "Eccentric Abstraction," Lippard described this field effect as "an alogical visual compound, or obstreperous Sight," an elliptical account that points to a third imperative of some Process art. For with the object often disturbed, if not dissolved, and the gaze of the viewer often diffused, if not deranged (made "obstreperous"), a new nonfigurative intimation of the body became possible. Early on, Lippard called this corporeal evocation (it was most apparent in Hesse) a "body-ego"; more recently, critics such as Rosalind Krauss and Anne Wagner have discussed it instead as a nonrepresentational registering of psychic fantasies and bodily drives. It is these three dimensions that are distinctive to Process art—a logic of materials, a field effect, and a phantasmatic corporeality—and they are probed most effectively by Serra, Morris, and Hesse respectively.

In his protean way, Robert Morris followed his essays on Mini-▲ malism with a suite of texts equally important to Postminimalism: "Anti-Form" (1968), "Notes on Sculpture, Part 4: Beyond Objects" (1969), and "Some Notes on the Phenomenology of Making: The Search for the Motivated" (1970). Just as Minimalism had questioned the relational composition of abstract painting and sculpture, so Morris now questioned the arbitrary ordering of Minimalist objects: "What remains problematic about these schemes," he writes in "Anti-Form," is "that any order for multiple units is an imposed one," with "no inherent relation to the physicality of the units." Here Morris extended the Minimalist criterion of unity beyond the object to its making, which effectively returned Pollock as the exemplary artist who was most able to retain his process "as part of the end form" of his work through a "profound rethinking" of his tools and materials—in particular, his use of sticks in the drip paintings to disclose the essential fluidity of the • paint. This account of Pollock differs dramatically from the pure painter of opticality presented by Greenberg, but also from the existential actor of painting as performance and the great predecessor of happenings, as proposed by Harold Rosenberg and Allan ■ Kaprow respectively. With Morris the ideal derived from Pollock became a work united less in its image than in its process, self-evident in its making.

Perhaps paradoxically, this theory of procedural unity often inspired a practice of antiformal dispersal. Yet for Morris, Serra, Saret, and Le Va such dispersive gestures were not intended to continue Abstract Expressionism by other means: they were meant to reveal not the subjectivity of the artist, but the materiality of the work ◆ as resistant to ordering, as bound to entropy. To this end gravity was deployed as a force of (de)composition, "chance [was] allowed and indeterminacy [was] implied," as "random piling, loose stacking, hanging, [gave] passing form to the material" (Morris). Morris was most programmatic in his demonstrations. In *Continuous Project Altered Daily* (1969)—the title delivers the procedure as well as the point of the work—he manipulated such materials as earth, clay, asbestos, cotton, water, grease, felt, and threadwaste for three weeks, with no final form. In *Threadwaste*, a tangle of threadwaste, felt, copper tubing, and mirrors, and in *Dirt* (1968), a mound of earth, grease, peat moss, bricks, felt, and assorted metals, he refused to aestheticize his materials at all. Here the attack on the verticality of painting and sculpture resulted in a debasement that was both literal and symbolic: the art work, scattered on the floor almost as refuse

▲ 1965 • 1949, 1960b ■ 1961 ◆ 1967a

with minimal manipulation, was disincorporated to the point where "scatter" began to evoke "scatological."

A "dedifferentiating" of vision

Richard Serra (born 1939) also turned to process to attack figure–ground conventions in painting and sculpture. His performance of tasks, resistant to imagery and detached from subjectivity, was similar to Minimalist dance and serial music of the ▲ time, and indeed he was intimate with dancers such as Joan Jonas and Yvonne Rainer and composers like Philip Glass and Steve Reich. In 1967–8 Serra generated a list of verbs ("to roll, to crease, to fold ...") that generated in turn a set of works. One instance, *Casting* [**2**], is paradigmatic of Process art, for here the process became the product without remainder. Yet this convergence of material, action, and site (of lead, casting, and wall) also anticipated his site-specific sculpture. As with Morris, then, process led Serra to • field effects, with "the discrete object dissolved into the sculptural field which is experienced in time." But Serra differed from Morris in two respects. First, he held that many antiformal scatterings were not as subversive of figure–ground conventions as they purported to be. "A recent problem," he wrote in 1970, "with the lateral spread of materials, elements on the floor in the visual field, is the inability of this landscape mode to avoid arrangement qua figure-ground: the pictorial convention." Second, Serra retained the category of sculpture, even though he redefined it as a relation between "the sculptural field" and the viewer set in temporal motion within this field. Thus he saw Process art, as he would its site-specific successor, as a way not to exceed sculpture but to render it appropriate to the industrial conditions of modern society (Serra worked in steel mills as a young man, while Carl Andre, who ■ shared his Constructivist concerns, worked on railroads). Thus he foregrounded particular processes of engineering, fabricating, and rigging, especially in his "prop" pieces [**3**], as a means not only to disclose the inherent properties of materials such as lead (weight, density, rigidity) but also to demonstrate "the axiomatic principles" of sculpture as *building*.

For Morris, on the other hand, process was a way less to continue sculpture than to move "beyond objects" altogether. This "beyond" was not, however, a conceptual reduction of art to an essential idea but an enquiry into its fundamental visuality: "to take the conditions of the visual field" as its "structural basis." To this end Morris would present an array of materials such as threadwaste or dirt that could not be grasped, in profile or in plan, as an image at all—less to set the viewer in motion (as with Serra) than to shift from a focal gaze on a specific object to a "vacant stare" on a visual field. Here the Minimalist undoing of spatial illusionism became a Postminimalist "dedifferentiating" of vision that was rendered "a structural feature of the work" as such ("dedifferentiating" was derived from art theorist Anton Ehrenzweig, whose *The Hidden Order of Art* [1967] was suggestive for Morris, Robert ▲ Smithson, and others). Oddly, then, process here concerns visuality more than materiality. Or, more precisely, it concerns a visuality that is at once materialized in stuff and scattered in space, decentered from any subject—as if to register that vision is somehow in the world too, that the world gazes back at us as well. Interestingly, these implications are in keeping with "the phenomenology of perception" of Maurice Merleau-Ponty (translated into English in 1962), as well as "the psychoanalysis of the gaze" of Jacques Lacan (delivered as seminars in Paris in 1964).

In this liminal moment between modernism and postmod- • ernism, Eva Hesse was especially inventive, and she has remained influential because, as with Louise Bourgeois, her twisting of figure–ground conventions allowed her to implicate the body in new ways—the body as disturbed by the psyche, as the material of fantasy and obsession, desires and drives. A year before Serra

2 • Richard Serra, *Casting*, 1969
Lead casting, c. 10.2 x 762 x 762 (4 x 300 x 300) (destroyed)

3 • Richard Serra, *One Ton Prop (House of Cards)*, 1969
Lead antimony, four plates, each 122 x 122 (48 x 48)

▲ 1973 • 1970 ■ 1962c ▲ 1965 • 1966b

4 • Eva Hesse, *Hang Up*, 1966
Acrylic paint on cloth over wood; acrylic paint on cord over steel tube, 182.9 x 213.4 x 198.1 (72 x 84 x 78)

constructed his work-order verb list, the Conceptual artist Mel Bochner made a *Portrait of Eva Hesse* (1966) that consisted of very different verbs ("secrete, bury, cloak ...") written in circles with "wrap" in the center. These verbs are erotically charged activities intimate with the body understood as a psychic site, not rationally detached procedures of the body seen as a taskmaster. Her work thus evokes a particular erotic body, not an anonymous, neutral one of much Minimalist art. Some critics have seen this body as specifically female—as part of an early feminist reclamation of an essential female embodiment, whether understood in terms of a womb or a wound. Other critics have read it as a body that upsets such markers of sexual difference—less a stable female "body-ego" (Lippard again) than a quasi-infantile congeries of conflicted drives and part-objects.

Early on, Hesse set up a space between painting and sculpture where such phantasmatic figurations might arise. With a frame that, though meticulously painted in different shades of gray, is left empty save for a loop that extends absurdly into our space, *Hang Up* **[4]** both declares the conventions of painting (as bound, painted, and hung up) and empties them out. In this way painting seems to mutate here into a thing possessed of obsessions of its own (as bound, painted, and hung up in another sense). This witty play, sometimes light, sometimes dark, is characteristic of Hesse, whose constructions in latex, fiberglass, and cheesecloth can evoke the body in extreme ways. Serra and Morris often force our bodies into a phenomenological confrontation with an object or a field that undoes any purity or stability of form. With Hesse, this undoing is also psychological: it is as if, charged in a strange empathy with her objects, our bodies are disrupted *from within*. Rather than painting or sculpture that reflects a proper figure, an ideal body-ego, back to us as in a mirror, Hesse evokes a body "deterritorialized" by desires and drives that just might be our own.

FURTHER READING

Rosalind Krauss, "Sense and Sensibility: Reflections on Post-'60s Sculpture," *Artforum*, vol. 12, no. 3, November 1973, and *The Optical Unconscious* (Cambridge, Mass.: MIT Press, 1993)

Lucy R. Lippard, *Changing: Essays in Art Criticism* (New York: Dutton, 1971) and *Six Years: The Dematerialization of Art* (New York: Praeger, 1973)

Robert Morris, *Continuous Project Altered Daily* (Cambridge, Mass.: MIT Press, 1993)

Richard Serra, *Writings Interviews* (Chicago: University of Chicago Press, 1994)

Anne M. Wagner, *Three Artists (Three Women): Georgia O'Keeffe, Lee Krasner, Eva Hesse* (Berkeley and Los Angeles: University of California Press, 1997)

1970–1979

540 1970 Michael Asher installs his Pomona College Project: the rise of site-specific work opens up a logical field between modernist sculpture and Conceptual art. RK

545 1971 The Guggenheim Museum in New York cancels Hans Haacke's show and suppresses Daniel Buren's contribution to the Sixth Guggenheim International Exhibition: practices of institutional critique encounter the resistance of the Minimalist generation. BB
box • Michel Foucault RK

549 1972a Marcel Broodthaers installs his "Musée d'Art Moderne, Département des Aigles, Section des Figures," in Düsseldorf, West Germany. BB

554 1972b The international exhibition "Documenta 5," held in Kassel, West Germany, marks the institutional acceptance of Conceptual art in Europe. BB

560 1973 The Kitchen Center for Video, Music, and Dance opens its own space in New York: video art claims an institutional space between visual and Performance art, television and film. HF

565 1974 With *Trans-fixed*, in which Chris Burden is nailed to a Volkswagen Beetle, American Performance art reaches an extreme limit of physical presence, and many of its adherents abandon, moderate, or otherwise transform its practice. HF

570 1975 As filmmaker Laura Mulvey publishes her landmark essay "Visual Pleasure and Narrative Cinema," feminist artists like Judy Chicago and Mary Kelly develop different positions on the representation of women. HF
box • Theory journals HF

576 1976 In New York, the founding of P.S.1 coincides with the Metropolitan Museum's "King Tut" exhibition: important shifts in the institutional structure of the art world are registered by both alternative spaces and the blockbuster show. RK

580 1977 The "Pictures" exhibition identifies a group of young artists whose strategies of appropriation and critiques of originality advance the notion of "postmodernism" in art. RK

1970

Michael Asher installs his Pomona College Project: the rise of site-specific work opens up a logical field between modernist sculpture and Conceptual art.

▲ In his 1966 "Notes on Sculpture: Part II," Robert Morris had described the Minimalist object as taking "relationships out of the work" by making them "a function of space, light, and the viewer's field of vision," adding that "one is more aware than before that he himself is establishing relationships as he apprehends the object from various positions and under varying conditions of light and spatial context." By the end of the decade this aesthetic of "varying conditions of light and spatial context" had dispensed with the object altogether to create instead an altered site: a space, sometimes public (a city street), more often private (a gallery or museum interior), into which the artist had minimally intervened.

One could say, then, that site-specificity—the name attached to such interventions—was a kind of Minimalism by other means. And while in fact it constituted a critique of Minimalism, which it saw as still dependent on the work of art as actual, consumable object, it nonetheless extended the feel of the earlier movement. For in its stripping away of all surface incident, in its proclivity for industrial building materials (steel in the case of Richard Serra, sheet rock in the case of Michael Asher, plywood in the case of ● Bruce Nauman), and in its love of simple, geometric shapes, even if these were now the shapes of spaces rather than objects, site-specific work was clearly extending some of Minimalism's principles.

Walk-in Minimalism

This relationship is clear in Richard Serra's twenty-six-foot-wide ring embedded into a derelict street in the Bronx (*To Encircle Base Plate Hexagram, Right Angles Inverted* [**1**]). Though its title derives from the list of transitive verbs that Serra had drawn up as a basis ■ for the process pieces he made, such as *Splashing* (1968) or *Casting* (1969), its drive is away from the figure–ground ambiguity that such process work courted and instead toward an extreme simplicity of shape, so that this "minimal" gesture intervenes in the urban setting as a kind of liminally perceived signal of order.

Michael Asher's (born 1943) project at the Pomona College Art Gallery in Claremont, California, which lasted barely a month (February 13–March 8, 1970), was another such intervention, this time organized within a private setting. Based on the architectural givens of the gallery itself, the project focused on the institution's

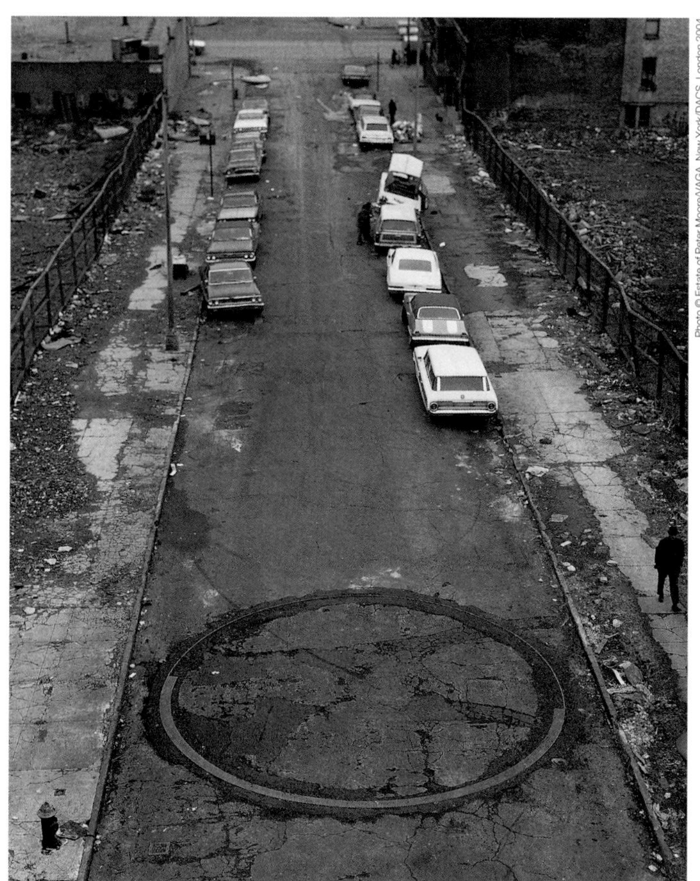

1 • Richard Serra, *To Encircle Base Plate Hexagram, Right Angles Inverted*, 1970
Steel, diameter 792.5 (312)

main exhibition space and its lobby, including the entry doors facing the street. Into these rooms Asher inserted a series of new walls that altered the shapes of the two spaces, turning them into opposing isosceles triangles—one relatively small, the other quite large—fused at their tips to leave a two-foot-wide passage from one to the other [**2**]. As well, a false ceiling lowered the space from its height of approximately twelve feet to a clearance exactly flush with the entry doors (6 feet 10 inches), which had been removed to leave a square, unimpeded opening onto the street. The experience was, then, like walking into the inside of a hugely inflated Minimalist sculpture in which visual incident had been pared down to changes of light over the surfaces of the walls and

▲ 1965 ● 1966a, 1967a, 1969, 1973 ■ 1969

shifting perspectives caused by one's own movement. This, however, is too aestheticized a consideration of the "experience," since the wrenching open of the private confines of the museum to make them entirely porous to public entry, twenty-four hours a day, moved the work beyond the aesthetic domain and into something that is more properly called the sociopolitical.

In one way it could be said that the work was wholly about "entry" (forced or not), since the angled walls seemed to have converted the exhibition space into nothing but continuous corridor. But the way the onset of this passageway was articulated from each of the two sides of its threshold was significant about what Asher was doing in the work. For from inside the gallery, the perfectly square opening framed the street beyond as a "picture," an aestheticized object submitted to the controlling conditions of the museum, with its presumption about the specialness, or autonomy, of the experience it provides; while from the street side, the yawning orifice expressed the way the museum's privilege had been breached, rendered continuous with the conditions of its surrounds. The work was thus able to comment on the museum's assumptions of autonomy even while refusing to allow those same assumptions to continue to operate. In this sense, Asher's critique was directed simultaneously against the (Minimalist) production of objects open to commodification and consumption and against the institutional apparatus of the museum as the space constituted to endow such activity with cultural legitimacy.

Insofar as the *Pomona College Project* was tailor-made to its physical confines, it could be called site-specific. But insofar as it was cut to the measure and geared to expose the logic of its sociocultural container, it joined a type of work that identified itself as a ▲ critique of institutions. Involving both a dematerialization of the art object and a focus on the conventions, or social pact, that invisibly underwrite the supposedly "universal" conditions of aesthetic judgment, the *Pomona College Project* could also be connected to • the aims of Conceptual art. But there is another sense in which the phenomenological richness of the work, its invitation to its audience to move through it bodily and thus to participate in the constitution of its meaning, identifies it with other, more materialized types of interventions, such as the work of Serra, or Nauman, ■ or Robert Smithson, work that would indeed have trouble sailing under the flag of Conceptualism.

A case in point is Richard Serra's *Strike: To Roberta and Rudy* [**3**], a massive steel plate whose dimensions, 8 feet high by 24 feet long by 1 inch thick, leave the viewer in no doubt about how much it weighs, but whose simplicity both of shape and of construction—it is maintained as a vertical simply by being butted into the corner of the gallery in which it is installed—could be said to be Minimalist, except that the experience goes beyond this into something else. For the work exists in the contradiction between the threat of its

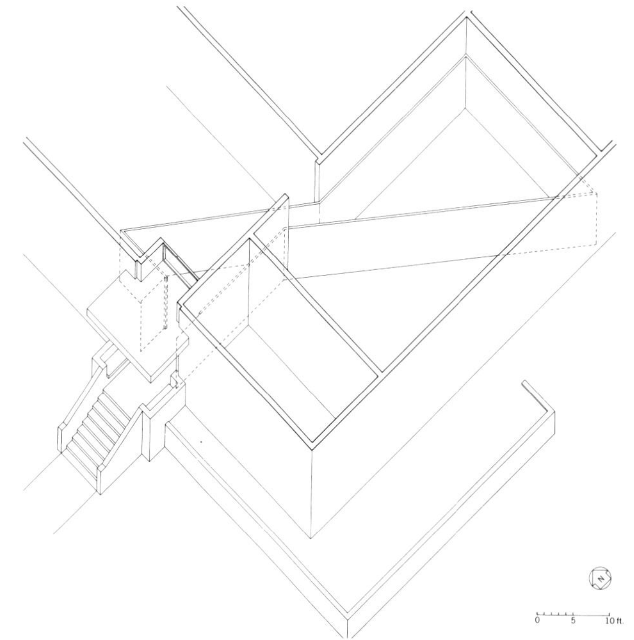

2 • Michael Asher, *Pomona College Project*, 1970
(top) Axonometric drawing of the installation for the Gladys K. Montgomery Art Center Gallery; (middle) view out of gallery toward street from small triangular area; (bottom) entry/exit and view into constructed triangular area

▲ Introduction 4, 1971 • 1968b ■ 1967a

tonnage bearing down on one's body and the sense of its dematerialization into the mere condition of a "cut"—a line that both separates and connects, like the splice between two pieces of film across which our imaginations leap to connect one shot to another in the creation of the illusion of a whole, continuous spatio-temporal field. For, projecting out from its corner, *Strike*'s bafflelike plane slices the space's volume in half, leaving only a few open feet to circulate around one of its edges. As the viewer moves around the work, its plane is perceived as contracting to a line (or edge) and then expanding back into a plane. Reciprocally, the space is blocked off and then opened out and subsequently reblocked. In this movement, closed–open–closed, the space itself is experienced as the matter on which the cut, or slice, of *Strike* operates, a cut that knits together the raveled sleeve of experience, uniting it beyond the split into the splice. Moreover, because it is the viewer, traversing the space, who is him- or herself the operator of this cut, its activity becomes a function of the viewer's perceptual work as well; the viewer is working with it to reconvene the continuity of his or her own lived world.

3 • Richard Serra, *Strike: To Roberta and Rudy*, 1969–71
Hot rolled steel, 243.8 x 731.5 x 2.5 (96 x 288 x 1)

Not everything is possible

If Serra and Asher were making insertions, both material and conceptual, into architectural spaces, other artists at this same moment had moved beyond the locatable, sculptural object by operating directly on the landscape. Famously, Smithson projected his *Spiral Jetty* fifteen hundred feet out into the Great Salt Lake at Rozel Point, Utah **[4]**; while Michael Heizer (born 1944) cut two enormous (1,100 × 42 × 30 feet) notches out of opposing mesas in Mohave Desert, Nevada, to form his *Double Negative* (1969). Although these installations were built to last, the idea of such "Earthwork" did not necessitate permanence and, indeed, the British artists Richard Long (born 1945) and Hamish Fulton (born 1946) operated in the landscape more conceptually, taking walks or making temporary mounds or rings of stones that they documented photographically.

In the early seventies, then, it appeared as though a wide range of entirely diverse practices had canceled what had been the strict ▲ formal logic of Minimalism in both the sculpture and painting that had seemed to rule the previous decade. All kinds of materials could be used, from wheat crops cut into giant patterns by harvesters (Dennis Oppenheim) to acoustical soundproofing tiles into the holes of which tiny rolls of paper were inserted (Sol LeWitt); all kinds of operations could be conducted, from the crushing and burying of a cabin (Smithson) to the stringing of hundreds of miles of parachute material across the countryside (Christo); all kinds of "engagement" could be encompassed, from the political commitment of institutional critique (Michael Asher) to the aestheticization of an organized lightning field (Walter De Maria). It thus seemed, as the song had put it, "Anything goes."

It is, however, always worth looking beyond claims of "pluralism"—the kind of explanation that was being offered by critics in the seventies—for an underlying logic that unites what would appear as mere randomness or the diversity of individual choice. For pluralism presupposes that everything is available to every artist at every moment in history, that there are no overriding historical factors that limit the available options and organize behavior no matter how independent it might appear. Against this ▲ notion the early art historian Heinrich Wölfflin had cautioned, however: "Every artist finds certain visual possibilities before him, to which he is bound. Not everything is possible at all times."

We began by noticing how Asher's Pomona project, like other site-specific work, was both a critique and a continuation of Minimalism. In its foregrounding of the phenomenology of bodily experience, Serra's *Strike* also accepts certain aspects of the earlier movement while rejecting others; and both *Spiral Jetty* and *Double Negative* can be added to this list. The issue, then, is to try to map the logic of the way this diversity exfoliates from Minimalism itself, while never forgetting Minimalism's own dialectical relation to modernist sculpture, which it both refined and terminated.

Expanded fields

To do this we might back up a bit and permit ourselves to make a series of generalizations about traditional sculpture as a whole, modernist sculpture in general, and Minimalism in particular. We might start by observing that through the ages sculpture had functioned in relation to what could be called the logic of the monument, itself an earlier form of "site-specificity." Sculpture, that is, had operated to mark a real site—grave, battleground, ceremonial axis—with a representation of its meaning: funerary figure, *pietà*, equestrian statue. By lifting the field of such a representation off the ground of real space, the pedestal of this statuary had a liminal function: it established the virtual, symbolic nature of the representation even while physically linking that to the actual site—either landscape or architecture—that it marked.

▲ 1957b, 1965, 1967c

▲ Introduction 3

4 • Robert Smithson, *Spiral Jetty*, 1970
Rock, salt, crystals, earth, and water, 45,720 x 460 (18,000 x 181), Great Salt Lake, Utah

It is in the late nineteenth century that we experience the waning of this logic of the monument, perhaps because of the split between the aims of artists and the tastes of their patrons—as when the ▲ group that had commissioned Auguste Rodin to make a monument to the writer Honoré Balzac rejected his work —or perhaps because the enormity of historical events outstripped the possibility of "representing" them (we think of the World War I dead). Just as the failure of Rodin's commission occasioned the multiplication of his Balzac statue so that it now appears in many different sites, to none of which it is logically connected, so modernist sculpture in general can be seen to establish the "autonomy" of the representational field of the work, its absolute withdrawal from its physical context into a wholly self-contained formal organization. There were, of course, certain attempts to break from this • autonomy—as in Vladimir Tatlin's Monument to the Third ▲ International or in the readymade's refusal of the condition of sculpture altogether—but the main thrust of modernist sculptural production sought to reinforce the privileged space of the autonomous • object as much as possible. In Brancusi's case this drive led to the extension of the representational field downward to include the pedestal itself in a declaration that no part of the work, not even its formerly mundane, physical support, would escape the reign of the formal and the virtual.

Given this resolute removal of the object's symbolic concerns from what were its earlier conditions of possibility, namely architecture and landscape, modernist sculpture might, then, be projected in terms of this rejection, defining its condition as a kind of pure negativity, the combination of exclusions. In this sense it is the exact inverse of the basis for traditional sculpture, the positivity of the logic of the monument.

▲ 1900b • 1921 ▲ 1914 • 1927b

▲ Structuralism provides us with a model that helps to conceive of social forms in terms of logically related inclusions and exclusions. Based on a logical structure, sometimes referred to as a Klein group, this model shows how a set of two opposing terms, a binary opposition, can be opened up into a quaternary (or fourfold) field without changing the character of the opposition itself.

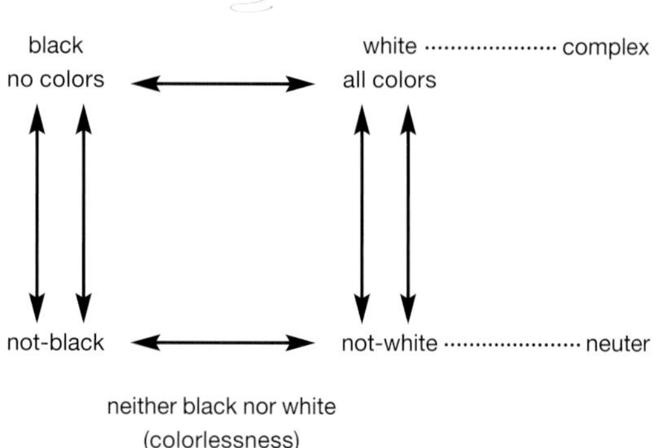

Projecting the "strong" form of the opposition on what it calls the "complex axis"—black vs. white, say—the Klein group demonstrates that the same binary can be expressed in a less vehement way—as not-black vs. not-white—thus converting the strong statement (both/and) to a "neutralized" one (neither/nor).

Applying this model to what we have observed in the field of sculptural practice we could say that in ceasing to be the positivity that • marked its site, modernist sculpture was now the category resulting from the addition of the not-landscape to the not-architecture.

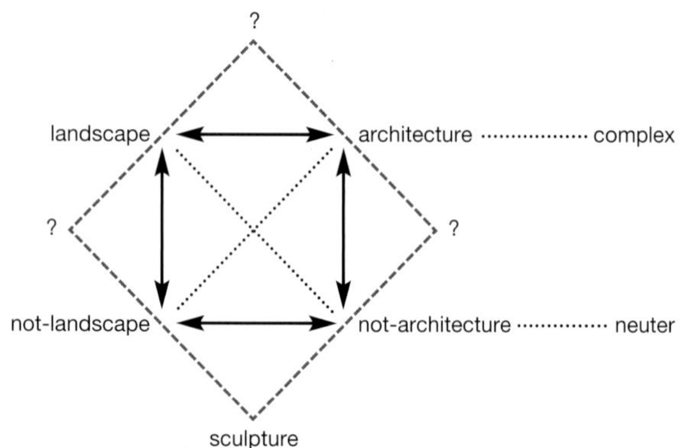

■ And further, with the onset of Minimalism, this withdrawal drew fire from the sculptors who wanted their work to engage its context, becoming as we have seen "a function of space, light, and the viewer's field of vision." If Minimalism still generated the sculptural object, however, site-specific works and Earthworks, in their abandonment of that object, extended the Minimalist engagement with the site—which modernist sculpture had voided—and began to work instead with the positive terms architecture and landscape.

This was not merely a return to traditional sculpture's acknowledgment of its site, however, since that had always before occurred symbolically—in a "virtual" field of representation. Instead, this new work engaged it directly. It now imagined the possibility of an exact inverse of modernism in the "both/and" in a way that had been seen before only in structures such as labyrinths, Japanese gardens, or the ritual playing fields and processionals of ancient civilizations, which, occupying the complex axis, were both landscape and architecture. An example of this assumption of the complex term might be Smithson's *Partially Buried Woodshed* (1970). But such new work also took advantage of the other possibilities of the quaternary field, namely a combination of landscape and not-landscape, which we could call the "marked sites" of Earthworks such as Smithson's *Spiral Jetty* or his *Mirror Displacements in the Yucatan* (1969); and a combination of architecture and not-architecture, which could be called "axiomatic structures," and in which we would include Asher's *Pomona College Project*.

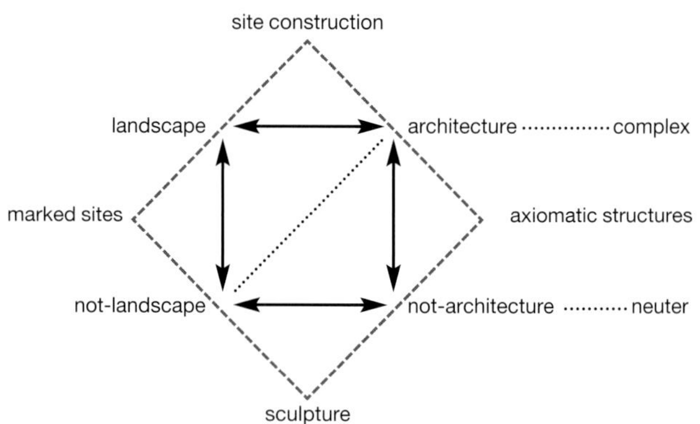

The structuralist diagram of this quaternary "expansion" of the simple binary allows two aspects of the new practices of the seventies to come to light. The first is a sense of the logical connection between the practices, and the possibilities of moving from one position to another within a given artist's practice. The second is the clarity with which it shows how focus has moved from a concentration on the rules internal to a given medium—sculpture as a physically bounded, three-dimensional object—to the cultural conditions, far larger than the medium, that are now seen as ballasting it. The practices identified with site-specificity wanted to operate directly on those cultural conditions; directly, we could say, on the frame of the world of art. The term "expanded field" is one way of mapping that frame.

FURTHER READING

Michael Asher, *Writings 1973–1983 on Works 1969–1979* (Halifax: The Press of the Nova Scotia College of Art and Design, undated)

Benjamin H. D. Buchloh, *Neo-Avantgarde and Culture Industry* (Cambridge, Mass.: MIT Press, 2000)

Hal Foster, "The Crux of Minimalism," *Individuals* (Los Angeles: Museum of Contemporary Art, 1986)

Fredric Jameson, *The Political Unconscious: Narrative as a Socially Symbolic Act* (Ithaca, N.Y.: Cornell University Press, 1981)

Rosalind Krauss, "Sculpture in the Expanded Field," *The Originality of the Avant-Garde and Other Modernist Myths* (Cambridge, Mass.: MIT Press, 1986)

▲ Introduction 3 • 1900b, 1914, 1921, 1927b, 1931, 1934b, 1945 ■ 1965

1971

The Guggenheim Museum in New York cancels Hans Haacke's show and suppresses Daniel Buren's contribution to the Sixth Guggenheim International Exhibition: practices of institutional critique encounter the resistance of the Minimalist generation.

▲ Two major incidents of censorship at the Guggenheim Museum in 1971 involved artists of the Postminimalist generation. Perhaps more accidentally, both placed European artists in opposition to American art institutions and, in the second case, in dialogue with certain American artists. The first scandal emerged on the occasion of the retrospective exhibition scheduled for Hans Haacke (born 1936), which was canceled at the last minute because of the request by the Museum's Director Thomas Messer to eliminate two pieces from the exhibition, a request with which both the artist and the curator, Edward Fry, refused to comply. This led to the cancellation of the exhibition in its entirety and to the firing of the curator.

It is particularly important to take into account the multiple causes and ramifications of this confrontation in order to understand its historical complexity. First of all, it concerns work that points, at a relatively early moment, to the deneutralization and ● repoliticizing of photoconceptualist practices. It is not the first but one of the earliest major projects by Haacke in which the assumed neutrality of photographic imagery is explicitly repositioned with regard to social, political, and economic fact-finding, in the manner of muck-raking journalism.

As almost always in Haacke's case, the two works, *Shapolski et al. Manhattan Real Estate Holdings* [**1**] and *Sol Goldman and Alex DiLorenzo Manhattan Real Estate Holdings* (both 1971), consisted quite simply of cumulative recorded facts available in the New York Public Library and collected and presented by the artist. These concerned the extensive real-estate dealings of two or three families who, under the various guises of holding companies and corporate entities, had assembled vast empires of slum housing in different parts of New York. By tracing the interrelationships and connections between, and the often hidden titles of, these various owners, Haacke revealed the structure of these slum empires. Simple, matter-of-fact trackings of tenement holdings, the pieces are without any accusation or polemical tone.

1 • Hans Haacke, *Shapolski et al. Manhattan Real Estate Holdings, a Real-Time Social System, as of May 1, 1971*, 1971
142 photos with data sheets, 2 maps, 6 charts, slide excerpt

▲ 1969 ● 1968b, 1984a

In Messer's argument against the inclusion of the two pieces in the exhibition, he called them "work that violates the supreme neutrality of the work of art and therefore no longer merits the protection of the museum." This confrontation operated, then, on the level of what defines the neutrality of the work of art and of what defines artistic, aesthetic practices as opposed to political, journalistic ones. It was around this threshold that the actual conflict and the ensuing polemics would then develop.

The exclusion of Haacke's work points to another dimension that was becoming problematic within the discourse of the art world, for it coincided with the very moment when works incorporating photography and text had become a crucial format for ▲ Conceptual art as a whole and when the status of such strategies as artistic production was increasingly being contested by a variety of critics and historians. Rosalyn Deutsche has convincingly argued that there was an additional dimension of the real-estate works that led to their suppression, namely the fact that through them Haacke brought two types of architectural space, two sociopolitical models of urban condition, into stark confrontation: the slum housing of New York's massive underclass and the luxurious "neutrality" of the uptown, exclusionary, high-art institutions with their total obliviousness to the situation of the large majority of people who share the same urban space. Deutsche's reading of Haacke's work—as an effort to juxtapose social spaces as defined by architectural structures—is an important additional interpretation of his practice.

The limits of Minimalism

The second scandal occurred a few months later, on the occasion of the Sixth Guggenheim International Exhibition, in which the French artist Daniel Buren attempted to install a huge bannerlike work slicing through the cylindrical space of the building's central atrium [**2**], matching that banner with a smaller external element to be installed across the street at 89th Street and 5th Avenue. Having been approved by the show's curator, Diane Waldman, the work's troubles arose only at the point of its being put in place, when several artists participating in the International opposed the installation and insisted on its removal, threatening to withdraw from the exhibition otherwise. The argument of these artists— • Donald Judd, Dan Flavin, Joseph Kosuth, and Richard Long—was that the size and placement of the huge banner obscured the view of their own installations throughout the Guggenheim.

The absurdity of the argument becomes evident when one realizes that Buren's work was a piece of cloth that, as the viewer descended the spiraling ramp, continuously expanded and contracted—from the width of a frontal view to the linear profile of a side view within which the work was almost imperceptible. Thus, as Buren anticipated, for at least half the time all of the museum and the works in its galleries were fully visible from across the ramps. In the end, this conflict was resolved by Waldman's giving in to the demands of the other artists. Buren's banner was removed.

2 • Daniel Buren, Photo-souvenir: *"Peinture-Sculpture,"* work in situ, at the Sixth Guggenheim International Exhibition, Guggenheim Museum, New York, 1971 (detail)

But beyond the smokescreen of the artists' explanation of their objection is the more important question of a clash between two generations: the Minimalists on the one hand and Buren, as representative of an emerging Conceptualist position with a clear focus on institutional critique, on the other. As Minimalists, Judd and ▲ Flavin, who were the most outspoken in their aggression against Buren, clearly sensed that Buren's work revealed several fallacies in their own positions. The first of these was the assumption of the neutrality of the phenomenological space within which the viewer interacts with the work. This assumption was counteracted by Buren's programmatic formulation of the theory of institutional space, within which a purely visual or a purely phenomenological experience can not be conceived. This is because institutional interests, which are always mediated by economic and ideological interests, inevitably reframe and redefine the production, the reading, and the visual experience of the artistic object.

The second fallacy was revealed through the way that Buren's piece set up a confrontation between museum architecture and sculptural work, specifically in the Guggenheim Museum, where Buren provocatively countered Frank Lloyd Wright's extraordinary building—in its control, its containment, its utterly unmanageable

▲ 1968b • Introduction 4, 1962c, 1965, 1968b, 1970 ▲ 1962c, 1965

imposition on any traditional pictorial or sculptural work installed within its confines—by manifestly piercing the space, the spiraling funnel of the museum, with his own work. In contrast to this, the other objects were fully but naively confident in their assumption about the availability of a neutral, architectural space.

This dialogue, which then escalated into confrontation, in the course of which Judd called Buren a "paperhanger" and other such insults were thrown around, in fact points to one of the crucial intersections of the late sixties and early seventies. For the beginnings of an artistic practice related to Conceptualism but not defined by it—▲ one of the key figures of American Conceptual art, Joseph Kosuth, had after all joined with Judd and Flavin in excluding Buren—were being forged at that time in the European variation on Conceptual art that would come to be called institutional critique.

Testing repressive tolerance

As it is formulated by both Haacke and Buren in these years, institutional critique is a project that could be associated with the development of poststructuralist and critical theory in their impact on visual practices. We could say that for Haacke this effect is evidently the legacy of Frankfurt School thought and Jürgen • Habermas, while for Buren it is evidently the structuralist and ■ poststructuralist legacy of Roland Barthes, Michel Foucault, and Louis Althusser that led to artistic practices taking into account the inescapable subjection of art to ideological interests. In Buren's case, this also led to the recognition of the extent to which the discourse on art (its criticism, its history) is defined by and subjected to institutional networks, an issue articulated by him as early as 1970 in his essay "Limites Critiques."

If institutional critique in Haacke's hands is different from that in Buren's, this might be a function of their respective theoretical backgrounds. For Haacke, institutional critique is an attempt to recontextualize the sphere of the aesthetic, with its socioeconomic and ideological underpinnings, in a somewhat mechanistic manner. This is fully embodied in *Solomon R. Guggenheim Museum Board of Trustees* [**3**], a work people have, not erroneously, seen as a belated response to the initial censorship and cancellation of his 1971 show. At the time, journalists mistakenly connected the owners of the slum properties to the Guggenheim Board, although they actually had no connection whatever to the Museum's Trustees.

The timing of the work, however, indicates that it is motivated by a much more urgent reflection than personal revenge, since it is sited at the point of the crisis in Chile, the democratically elected President Ferdinand Allende having been overthrown and murdered in a CIA-sponsored coup by the Chilean military. It is at that moment that Haacke reveals the profound connection between a large number of the Trustees of the Guggenheim and the Kennecott Copper Corporation in Chile. One of the driving forces behind the intervention of the CIA in Chile at that time was the massive threat to the Corporation's (and the American military's) interests posed by the nationalization of the copper mines by its newly elected president.

The second piece that would point to Haacke's persistent attempts to recontextualize the art object within cultural practices at large is a work installed in 1974 in his home town of Cologne when, on the occasion of the 150th anniversary of the Wallraf-Richartz Museum, Haacke was invited to participate in an exhibition called "Projekt '74." For this he provided a series of ten panels tracing the provenance of Manet's *Bunch of Asparagus* (1880), a painting that had been donated to the Museum in 1968 by the Friends of the Wallraf-Richartz Museum, under the leadership of its chairman, Hermann Josef Abs, in memory of Konrad Adenauer, the Federal Republic of Germany's first chancellor. As was the case for all the other panels, the final panel—the conclusion of this history—presents an analysis of Abs's background, since he functioned as the head of the entity that donated the work to the Museum. In this instance what it reveals is that Abs, who had been the most prominent banker and financial adviser of Hitler's Reich from 1933 to 1945, had been reinstated after the war in positions of similar influence from the time the Adenauer government took office in 1949, and had remained in a place of extraordinary power throughout the sixties up to the moment of his gift of the still life to the Museum.

That final panel is one of ten that trace the history of the painting from its first owner, Charles Ephrussi (a French Jewish art historian and collector who was reputed to be one of the models for Proust's character Charles Swann), to figures such as the German publisher

SOLOMON R. GUGGENHEIM MUSEUM

CORPORATE AFFILIATION OF TRUSTEES

Kennecott Copper Corporation

FRANK R. MILLIKEN, President, Chief Exec. Officer & Member Board of Directors

PETER O. LAWSON-JOHNSTON, Member Board of Directors

ALBERT E. THIELE, past Member Board of Directors

Multinational company mining, smelting, refining copper, molybdenum, gold, zinc and coal. Copper based mill products.

Operates in the U.S., Australia, Brazil, Canada, Colombia, Costa Rica, England, Indonesia, Italy, Netherlands Antilles, Nigeria, Peru, South Africa.

El Teniente, Kennecott's Chilean copper mine, was nationalized July, 1971 through Constitutional Reform Law, passed unanimously by Chilean Congress. Chilean Comptroller General ruled profits over 12% a year since 1955 to be considered excess and deducted from compensation. His figures, disputed by Kennecott, in effect, eliminated any payments.

Kennecott tried to have Chilean copper shipments confiscated or customers' payments attached. Although without ultimate success in European courts, legal harassment threatened Chilean economy (copper 70% of export).

President Salvador Allende addressed United Nations December 4, 1972. The New York Times reported:

The Chilean President had still harsher words for two U.S. companies, the International Telephone & Telegraph Corp. and the Kennecott Corp., which he said, had "dug their claws into my country" and which proposed "to manage our political life."

Dr. Allende said that from 1955 to 1970 the Kennecott Copper Corp. had made an average profit of 52.8% on its investments.

He said that huge "transnational" corporations were waging war against sovereign states and that they were "not accountable to or representing the collective interest."

In a statement issued in reply to Dr. Allende's charges, Frank R. Milliken, president of Kennecott, referred to legal actions now being taken by his company in courts overseas to prevent the Chilean Government from selling copper from the nationalized mines:

"No amount of rhetoric can alter the fact that Kennecott has been a responsible corporate citizen of Chile for more than 50 years and has made substantial contributions to both the economic and social well-being of the Chilean people."

"Chile's expropriation of Kennecott's property without compensation violates established principles of international law. We will continue to pursue any legal remedies that may protect our shareholders' equity."

President Allende died in a military coup Sept. 11, 1973. The Junta committed itself to compensate Kennecott for nationalized property.

1973 Net sales: $1,425,613,531 Net after taxes: $159,363,059 Earn. per com. share: $4.81

29,100 employees

Office: 161 E. 42 St., New York, N.Y.

3 • Hans Haacke, *Solomon R. Guggenheim Museum Board of Trustees*, 1974 (detail)
Seven panels, each 50 x 61 (19⅝ x 24), brass frames (central panel shown here)

▲ 1968b • 1988 ■ Introduction 3, Introduction 4

and art dealer Paul Cassirer and the German-Jewish painter Max ▲ Liebermann (whose work was outlawed by the Nazis), finally to be bought from Liebermann's American granddaughter (his own daughter having emigrated) by the Friends of the Museum led by Abs. But it was the panel focusing on Abs's own political background, revealing him as an ex-Nazi and showing how easily the posture of cultural benefactor allows an individual to "launder" their more-than-problematic past, that was seen as scandalous. Haacke's proposal for the work, although approved by the exhibition's curator, was "democratically" voted down by the Museum's administration (in a curiously tied decision) in obvious deference to the Friends' Chairman.

With the second major scandal of Haacke's career, it becomes evident that his project of connecting social and ideological interests with cultural practice in the broad variety of repressive disguises, making those disguises to which culture lends itself part of the site-specific and institutional-critical focus of the work, is hard for the institutions themselves to reincorporate and reneutralize. It is in this context that Haacke defines his major work of the seventies.

In a manifest act of solidarity—as had been the case for Buren in 1971, when several other artists such as Sol LeWitt, Mario Merz, and Carl Andre, opposed to the removal of Buren's piece from the Guggenheim, had withdrawn their own pieces from the exhibition —Buren now responded to the censorship of Haacke's work by inviting him to photocopy his panels and to glue these onto Buren's own work, consisting of green and white stripes covering large areas of wall within the Museum. Buren's stripes were to have functioned • in "Projekt '74" as they had done in "Documenta 5" two years earlier, for example, where white-on-white stripes were distributed throughout the exhibition, sometimes as sculptural bases, sometimes as backgrounds for the installation of paintings. (The way these recontextualized the works of art, with their claims to autonomy and to security within their own frames, so to speak, is most evident in the example of the clash between Buren's stripes and ■ those of a Jasper Johns *Flag*, where the internal logic of the painting was suddenly leached out into the larger context of the architectural framework as well as that of the politics of the exhibition.) To the distress of the organizers, the piece was therefore fully legible on the day of the opening of the exhibition, since Haacke's work was now being presented as a work by Buren. This led to further reprisals by the authorities of the Museum who, that night, tore off the Haacke photocopies, thereby defacing Buren's installation in an act of triple censorship: the double exclusion of Haacke and the vandalizing cancellation of Buren.

Michel Foucault (1926–84)

Michel Foucault's work was utterly transformed by his experience of antiwar and other political demonstrations in 1968, during which students occupied the administrative offices of the Sorbonne in Paris. In response, the officials called in the police, who had not entered the precincts of the university since the middle ages. It was this violation of the university's independence that allowed Foucault to see the normally transparent frame of the institution, a frame that is supposed to guarantee the "objectivity" and "neutrality" of academic knowledge—to see this frame and suddenly to recognize its ideological cooption by forces of power. Foucault's strategic acknowledgment of the unacknowledged frame of the university, his unmasking of its political imbrication, was soon adopted by artists who wished to unmask the interests at work in the institutional frames of the art world. Called "institutional critique," this revelatory strategy informed the work of Daniel Buren, Marcel Broodthaers, Hans Haacke, and many others.

Perhaps Foucault's most profound effect on scholarly discourse was his transformation of historical narrative, exhorting that, instead of the seamless evolution of forms of knowledge, it was necessary to understand that knowledge undergoes abrupt changes that totally shift the conditions of understanding, each new set of conditions producing an entirely new organization of facts—which he termed *epistemes*. Foucault was identified with structuralism because of the importance his argument gave to the linguistic sign as the organizational trope (or figure of speech) that orders knowledge, creating the links between relevant facts. For example, Renaissance thought proceeded metaphorically, explaining phenomena by resemblances: since the brain looks like a walnut, walnuts must be good medicine for mental maladies. Foucault argued that Renaissance resemblance was abruptly displaced by Enlightenment thought (which he called "classical"), which orders phenomena by means of grids that can relate similarities and differences; this in turn was displaced by modern (or nineteenth-century) forms, which Foucault called synechdochic, marked by "analogy and succession," where gradual and continuous genesis replaces the separation of species. The classical organization was spatial, but this new episteme was temporal, historical. Thus the naturalists' table is pushed aside by biology or evolution, comparative analyses of wealth by economics (Marx's histories of production), and the study of the logic of the sign by linguistics. The shift from the visual to the temporal (and invisible) was given a special emphasis in Foucault's study of prisons *Discipline and Punish* (1977). He called his new methods of excavating the epistemic orders "archaeology," to distinguish it from "history," whose commitment to gradual genesis consigned it to the episteme of the nineteenth century and thus to obsolete forms of understanding.

Foucault died in the midst of writing and publishing a sweeping study of the *History of Sexuality*, which was organized around the epistemic shift from a decorous silence on the subject and practice of the sexual, to the exhortation to talk about it (as in psychoanalysis), thus transforming its very practice.

FURTHER READING

Alexander Alberro, "The Turn of the Screw: Daniel Buren, Dan Flavin, and the Sixth Guggenheim International Exhibition," *October*, vol. 80, Spring 1997

Daniel Buren, Hans Haacke, Thomas Messer, Barbara Reise, Diane Waldman, "Gurgles around the Guggenheim," *Studio International*, vol. 181, no. 934, 1971

Rosalyn Deutsche, "Property Values: Hans Haacke, Real Estate, and the Museum," in Brian Wallis (ed.), *Hans Haacke—Unfinished Business* (New York: New Museum of Contemporary Art, 1986)

Guy Lelong (ed.), *Daniel Buren* (Paris: Centre Georges Pompidou/Flammarion, 2002)

Gilda Williams (ed.), *Hans Haacke* (London: Phaidon Press, 2004)

▲ 1937a • 1972b ■ 1958

1972a

Marcel Broodthaers installs his "Musée d'Art Moderne, Département des Aigles, Section des Figures," in Düsseldorf, West Germany.

The career of Belgian artist Marcel Broodthaers was marked by several publicly announced reinventions, the first of which took place in 1963 when he decided to complement his previous work as a poet by working as a visual artist, with an exhibition at a Brussels gallery [**1**]. The second major shift of roles was his transformation from artist to museum director on the occasion of the founding of the "Musée d'Art Moderne, Département des Aigles, Section XIXième siècle," in 1968, also in Brussels. Several theoretical models could be applied in any analysis of the transformations that were taking place in Broodthaers's work in this period, as well as those that were occurring in the art-historical and theoretical climate of the mid- to late sixties.

From poetry to production

First, Broodthaers's relation to the work of art was defined, from its inception, by a profound skepticism concerning the contemporary condition of the object-status of the work of art as opposed to its historical function and context. Broodthaers's puns on the work of art as the inevitable object of commodity exchange began as early as 1963 when he deposited the last fifty copies of a recent volume of his poetry into a mass of plaster and declared the result to be a sculpture [**2**]. Given that once the books had been transformed into a visual object and could no longer be read, Broodthaers's action implicitly asks the spectator why he or she refused to be a reader and wished to become a viewer instead. Henceforth, all of Broodthaers's work would take as one of its key questions the status of the work of art as commodity.

The second key question concerns the impact of the institution of the museum on the discourses (teaching, theorizing, historicizing) surrounding artistic practices, as well as on their reception (their criticism, collection, market). Within this framework, Broodthaers's interventions can be viewed first of all as defining the museum as a normalizing, disciplinary institution. Yet at the same time the museum for him was also an integral element of the enlightenment culture of the bourgeois public sphere that has to be defended against the onrush of the forces of the culture industry. If one reads his attempts to situate the museum within this dichotomy, one will come closer to an understanding of the actual oppositions and dialectical tensions that Broodthaers's work tries to generate.

On the one hand, from 1968 on, he continually emphasized the operations of the museum as institution in the discursive formation of the work of art; this underscores the fact that aesthetic claims for the separateness and relative autonomy of the sphere of modernist visual art no longer have any validity; they must be replaced by a

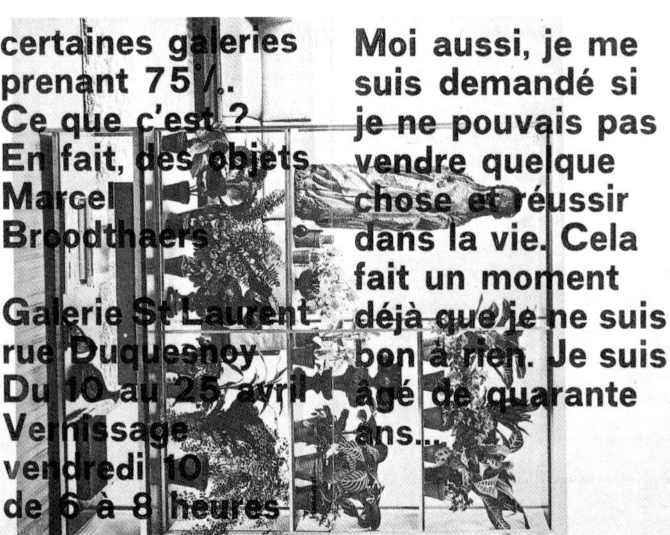

1 • Marcel Broodthaers, *Moi aussi, je me suis demandé*, invitation card for exhibition at Galerie St. Laurent, Brussels, April 10–25, 1964 (front and back)
Magazine tearsheet, 25 x 33 (9⅞ x 13)

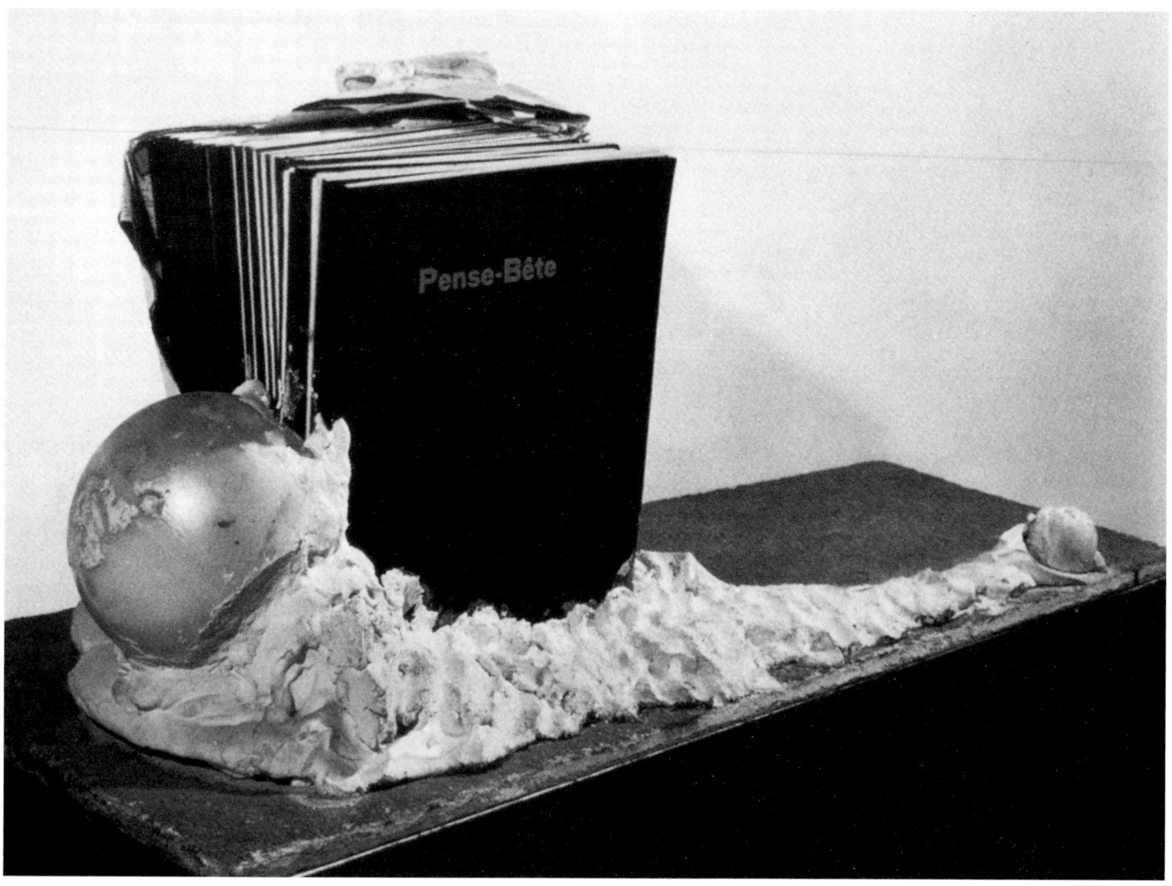

2 • Marcel Broodthaers, *Pense-Bête*, 1963
Books, paper, plaster, plastic spheres, and wood, 98 x 84 x 43 (38⅝ x 33⅛ x 16⅞)

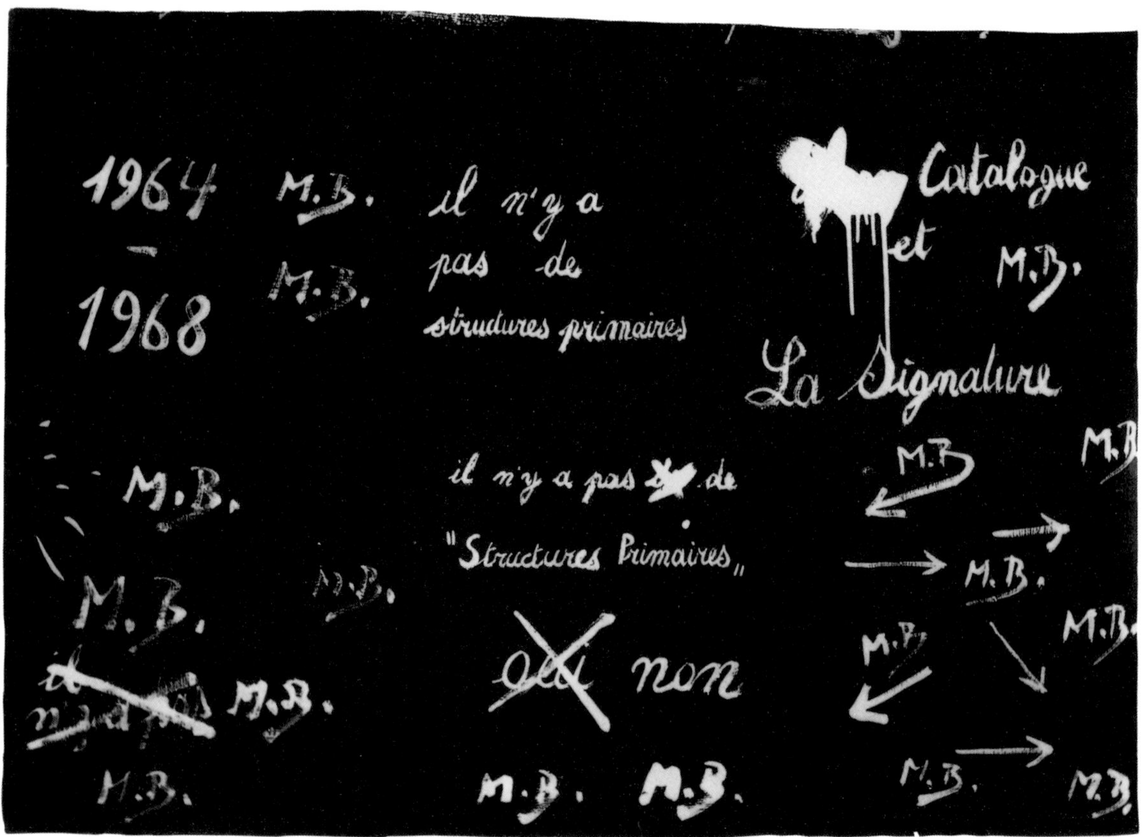

3 • Marcel Broodthaers, *Il n'y a pas de Structures Primaires*, 1968
Oil on canvas, 77.5 x 115 (30½ x 45¼)

4 • Marcel Broodthaers, "Musée d'Art Moderne, Département des Aigles, Section XIXème siècle," opening ceremony, September 28, 1968

recognition of the contextuality and contiguity within which all discursive formations—including aesthetic ones—are located. It is this increasing relativization of aesthetic practices that Broodthaers—in the moment of 1968 and in the context of Conceptualism—uses to counteract all the delusions and deceptions surrounding the emancipatory experience of the work of art [**3**].

On the other hand, and in direct contrast to this, it is important to recognize that Broodthaers's criticism of the museum institution per se also consistently entails a sometimes even more intense criticism and skepticism toward the development of artistic practices once they have left the traditional museum behind and have made the museum into the institution of the production of contemporary art instead. It is in the context of just such a contradictory approach that Broodthaers's work must be situated. Its skepticism about the museum as a site of production emerges directly out of the insight that once it is so transformed it will also inevitably become part-and-parcel of those larger formations of the culture industry—such as entertainment, spectacle, marketing, advertising, public relations—from which it had previously been exempted. And it is precisely that transformation that Broodthaers insistently tried to clarify by pointing to the "historical" museum as having been an institution of the bourgeois public sphere that was relatively free from commercial interests and thus relatively determined by the necessity to contribute to self-differentiation in the historical development of bourgeois subjectivity. One should recognize that Broodthaers's series of museum sections are suspended in a dialectic between, on the one hand, historical mourning over the destruction of this institutional site and, on the other, critical analysis of the museum as an institution of power, ideological interest, and external determinacy.

"Musée d'Art Moderne"

In September 1968, having participated in the May student riots in Brussels, Broodthaers publicly opened his newly founded museum by introducing himself as its director [**4**]. It is in this reversal, grotesque and comical, that his historical insight was first articulated: that the artist no longer functions or defines himself as a producer but rather as an administrator, occupying the site of institutional control and determination, voluntarily inhabiting the source of the institutional codification normally imposed upon the work of art. Thus, by making his work itself the very center of administrative and ideological power, Broodthaers positioned himself within those frameworks that had been previously excluded from the conception and reception of the work of art, and was simultaneously able to articulate a critique.

The elements Broodthaers assembled within his first section—"Section XIXème siècle"—consisted of items used in museum and gallery exhibitions: crates used for shipping, lamps used for illumination, ladders used for installation, postcard reproductions used for identification, signs used to give information about the gallery's entrance policy [**5**] and to direct visitors, and a truck used for transport (visible outside the window of his former studio on the rue de la Pépinière) [**4**]. Not only do all these objects evoke the museum as their source, but with their resounding emptiness, they strip that source of its meaning, substance, and historical significance, thereby constituting it as an "allegorical structure."

Contrary to the symbol's positing of the work of art as a form of plenitude, of organic wholeness and self-containment, of direct relationship to substantial meaning, and thus of epiphanic power, ▲ Walter Benjamin stresses allegory's character as "inorganic"—dependent on ancillary interpretive systems that are merely added on to the allegorical emblem like so many captions in an endlessly open series—and, therefore, as subjected to external forces exiting beyond its "own" frame: imbricated within powers of domination and institutional order. Insofar as allegory mimetically inscribes itself within all that is "external" to the traditional work of art, it opens onto the strategy Broodthaers used to develop his museum "fiction" into a project of critical negativity and opposition. Further, it questions the confidence with which Conceptual art, emerging at the same time, assumed that it had itself been able to transcend the frames within which modernism is institutionalized.

5 • Marcel Broodthaers, *Museum: Enfants non admis*, 1968–9
Plastic, two parts (black, white), 83 x 120 (32⅝ x 47¼)

▲ 1968b

▲ 1935

Secondly, and of equal importance for Broodthaers's work, is the association of allegory with the melancholy of mourning and decay, thereby opening the allegorical structure onto the mnemonic inscription of reflections on history, on the legacies that have been displaced or obscured by recent activities, thus allowing them to be reinscribed within contemporary practice. Broodthaers's perpetual foregrounding of the legacy of modernist poetry, beginning with Charles Baudelaire and Stéphane Mallarmé, the two writers with whose work his own continually engaged, opened the field to two questions central to his work. One is clearly the question of the exclusion, not to say the repression, of the literary and mnemonic dimension of visual modernist practices, with their utter denial of the credibility or accessibility within contemporary visual art of any of the legacies of literary modernism. The other, in another dialectical reversal, involves an immediate historicization of the claims of Conceptualism as a critical means of transcending modernism in its foregrounding of the analytical proposition and the linguistic signifier as models that have successfully displaced the legacy of modernist autonomy. In that act of a constant relativization effected by Broodthaers's pointing back to and identifying with Mallarmé, the dialectical connection to language is achieved.

Broodthaers's museum culminated in 1972 with its presentation within the institution of the Kunsthalle in Düsseldorf [**6, 7**]. For this occasion he organized an exhibition of hundreds of objects all unified by the iconographic marker of the eagle and presented as the "Section des Figures" of his "museum" under the title "The Eagle from the Oligocene to the Present." Many of these objects, borrowed from European museums, were of historical and aesthetic value, including Assyrian sculptures and Roman *fibulae*; others were items of utter banality such as postage stamps, product labels, and champagne bottle corks. Seeming to trace the universality and omnipresence of this icon of power and domination throughout all European and non-Western cultures, Broodthaers here undermines the very idea of coherence upon which such domination depends by creating in this wild, parodic collection something that French philosopher Michel Foucault would have called a heterotopia—the ▲ wholly illogical system of classifications he derives from Jorge Luis Borges's short story about a fantasized "Chinese Encyclopedia" in the preface to his *The Order of Things: An Archaeology of the Human Sciences* (1966, English translation 1970).

Broodthaers's absurdist taxonomy should be situated within his own specific context as well. Among its many reverberations, his choice of the eagle as symbol also pointed to a continuing ambivalence regarding postwar German culture, with which he was critically involved throughout in his writings and his statements, and which the presence of the exhibition in Düsseldorf highlighted.

At another level, Broodthaers's invented iconography, to include all media, all genres, high and low, including commissions • to living artists—such as Gerhard Richter—to produce paintings of eagles for the exhibition, once again emphasizes the complex dialogue with the continuing foreclosure of the realm of the visual

6 • Marcel Broodthaers, "Musée d'Art Moderne, Département des Aigles, Section des Figures," 1972 (installation view)

that was dominating all advanced artistic practices of the late sixties and early seventies. One could argue that at precisely the ▲ moment when Conceptual artists emphasized the disappearance of the iconographic, the elimination of the visual, and the transcendence of all historical strictures imposed by the classificatory systems of the museum (with its emphasis on the development of historical styles), Broodthaers reintroduced with a vengeance all the traditional taxonomic features and discursive formations that the museum represented. In doing so his intention was to expose as empty Conceptualism's claim to having established a truly democratic, egalitarian art form that had transcended the object, its forms of distribution, and its institutional frame, instead denouncing all such claims as typical avant-garde myth and self-mystification, and opposing them by making persistent reference back to the continuing (if not increased) validity of all those methods Conceptualism claimed to have left behind.

In this respect Broodthaers's "museum" work can be seen as being a conservative *blague* as a reactionary response to Conceptualism's claims. It is important to recognize how Broodthaers's critique inscribes itself in other, previously established, models of antimodernism as an attempt both to recognize the artistic affinity of earlier art with narrative and poetic practices and to emphasize the previously available—but now repressed and thus no longer accessible—relationship between artistic practices and the construction of historical memory.

The dialectics of fables

The last of Broodthaers's museum "sections" took place five months after the Düsseldorf show, on the occasion of "Docu- • menta 5" in Kassel in 1972. Founding another wing to his own museum named "Section Publicité" (Public Relations Section), in the context of this international exhibition, Broodthaers displaced his own collection of original objects gathered for the "Section des Figures" exhibition by photographing all the objects that had been

▲ 1971 • 1972b, 1988 ▲ 1968b • 1972b

on display in Düsseldorf and mounting these in large photopanels on the wall in Kassel. Consistently questioning how meaning is produced within given institutional structures, whether museum galleries or the pages of catalogues, Broodthaers mobilizes his "Public Relations Section" toward the reiteration of his often used strategy of displacement—here from real object to its photographic reproduction, as in earlier instances it had moved from the actual object to the supporting elements and various framing devices (packing cases, lighting, etc.) that make up the institutional and discursive order. In an anticipatory deflection of the reception of his own work, then, he now presented the Düsseldorf installation of the eagle exhibition as having already been through the channels of its own publicity. He thereby anticipated the transformation of the work of art under all circumstances from object to photographic reproduction and its dissemination in forms of critical writing and marketing.

This displacement from the object to the apparatus of its display ▲ and dissemination could be called "the aesthetic of the supple- • ment." Sharing such a strategy with artists of the same generation, such as Daniel Buren and Michael Asher, Broodthaers identifies his work with those structures of dissemination and distribution that are generally considered mere subproducts—the banal accoutrements to the centrality of the work of art as a substantial object—as an act of critical resistance. It is precisely by inhabiting those structures that would have to be called supplements—the page of the catalogue, the site of the poster, the framing devices of the institution—and by going as far as the banality of the tools of installation and shipping—that Broodthaers denies the continuing validity of an aesthetic of centrality, of substantiality, and by so doing also denies the commodity status of the work of art, for the supplement can never itself acquire commodity-value.

The "Section Publicité" plays critically on yet another dimension as well. As Broodthaers saw his own rise to fame in 1972, he anticipated the transformation of his own work in accord with the very mechanisms of the culture industry that the art world was even then in the process of adopting. He mimetically repositioned himself by founding his own advertising and promotion agency and thus making his own work disappear within the public-relations campaign launched for his own project, thereby denying once again the substantiality and historical specificity of his own initial practice.

It is in respect of this denial that one can look back at the peculiar difference, not to say opposition, between Broodthaers's relation- ▲ ship to the museum and Peter Bürger's model of the "historical avant-garde"—understood as involved in a rupture of the enclosure of an autonomous realm for the work of art as institutionalized by the museum, this rupture being defined by Bürger as the true function of a radical, avant-garde practice. In almost exact opposition to such a theoretical model, however, Broodthaers insists that it is not the function of artistic practice to dissolve the institution of art, but rather to recognize the extent to which the dismantling of the autonomous sphere of aesthetic practice is part of a historical tendency of the rise into domination of the culture industry, which will no longer tolerate any heterogeneity at all within the differentiation process of the various cultural spheres.

7 • Marcel Broodthaers, "Musée d'Art Moderne, Département des Aigles, Section des Figures," installation at the Städtische Kunsthalle, Düsseldorf, 16 May–9 July, 1972

FURTHER READING

Manuel Borja-Villel (ed.), *Marcel Broodthaers: Cinéma* (Barcelona: Fundacio Antoni Tapies, 1997)
Benjamin H. D. Buchloh (ed.), "Marcel Broodthaers: Writings, Interviews, Photographs," special issue, *October*, vol. 42, Fall 1987
Catherine David (ed.), *Marcel Broodthaers* (Paris: Galerie Nationale du Jeu de Paume, 1991)
Marge Goldwater (ed.), *Marcel Broodthaers* (Minneapolis: Walker Art Center; and New York: Rizzoli, 1989)
Rachel Haidu, *Marcel Broodthaers: The Absence of Work*, dissertation (New York: Columbia University, 2003)

▲ Introduction 4 • 1970, 1971 ▲ 1960a

1972b

The international exhibition "Documenta 5," held in Kassel, West Germany, marks the institutional acceptance of Conceptual art in Europe.

Two foundational exhibitions, both organized by the Swiss curator Harald Szeemann, demarcate the origins and the zenith of the production and the institutional reception of Conceptual art in Europe. The first was the (by now famous) exhi- ▲ bition "When Attitudes Become Form" that took place at the Berne Kunsthalle and elsewhere in 1969, and the second was "Documenta 5", the fifth installment of what had become the most important international group show of contemporary art, organized in Kassel, Germany, every four or five years since 1955.

These two exhibitions demarcate—in their initial omissions as much as in their eventual inclusions—the changing orientations that occurred in the late sixties and early seventies in different centers of artistic production (New York, Paris, London, Düsseldorf). Artists like the group Art & Language, Bernd and Hilla ● Becher, Marcel Broodthaers, Daniel Buren, and Blinky Palermo were still excluded from "When Attitudes Become Form." (Buren was prosecuted by the Swiss police for illicitly pasting his color-white-striped paper signs throughout Berne—his contribution to an exhibition in which he thought he should have been represented.) However, three years later all these artists were given a central role in "Documenta 5," where they installed works that would subsequently be seen as the foundational models of European Conceptual art and its strategies of institutional critique.

"Documenta 5" used its institutional resources on the level of the exhibition as much as that of the catalogue to enact the legalistic-administrative dimensions of Conceptual art and to transform these into operative realities. The catalogue (designed by Ed ■ Ruscha to look like an administrative loose-leaf binder or a technical training manual with a thumb index) carried one of the first systematically philosophical and critical essays on the commodity status of the work of art (written by the philosopher Hans Heinz Holz). More importantly perhaps, it reproduced "The Artists Reserved Rights Agreement," a contract developed by New York art dealer Seth Siegelaub and New York lawyer Robert Projansky. Originally published in *Studio International* in 1971, this contract would allow artists to participate in decisions concerning their work after it had been sold (exhibition participation and reproductions in catalogues and books) and would also oblige collectors to offer the artist a reasonable, if minimal, share in the increasing resale value of their work. This was obviously an arrangement that would be loathed by most collectors; so much so that they refrained from buying works by any artists who had signed the contract, thereby deterring other artists from engaging in the project altogether.

Conceptualism's encounters

Several factors came together to transform 1972 into the *annus mirabilis* of European Conceptual art, culminating in the emergence and institutional reception of the work of the Bechers, Broodthaers, Buren, Hanne Darboven (born 1941), Hans Haacke, ▲ Palermo, and Gerhard Richter [**1**]. The first factor was that the politically radical student movement of 1968 and the cultural radicality of Conceptual art entered into a dialogue in 1972, rather than—as had been the case with "Documenta 4" in 1968—remaining entangled in a polemical confrontation. Thus, the work of Broodthaers and of Buren at "Documenta 5" turned some of the critical tools of 1968 (that is, the Frankfurt School tradition of a Marxist critique of ideology and the poststructuralist practices of semiological and institutional critiques) back onto the actual institutional frameworks of the museum, the exhibition, and the market.

The changing relations of that generation of postwar artists to the legacies of European avant-garde culture undoubtedly constituted the second factor. A particular tension emerged from the simultaneous reception not only of the recently rediscovered practices of the most advanced forms of European abstraction (Constructivism, Suprematism, and De Stijl) but also American ● Minimalism: both practices were evidently fused and operative in the work of Buren, Darboven, Haacke [**2**], and Palermo.

Thirdly, all of these artists contested the dominant positions of ■ Joseph Beuys in Germany and Yves Klein and the Nouveaux Réalistes in Paris (and in Düsseldorf). Throughout the early sixties, Beuys, Klein, and the Nouveaux Réalistes had developed an aesthetic in which memory and mourning had unknowingly confronted the effects of their instant spectacularization. The new generation of artists recognized the fallacies of these earlier positions, displacing them with self-critical acuity that focused on the

▲ 1969 ● 1968a, 1968b, 1971, 1972a ■ 1960c, 1967a, 1968b ▲ 1988 ● 1915, 1917, 1921, 1928, 1965 ■ 1960a, 1964a

1 • **Gerhard Richter, *48 Portraits*, 1971–2**
Oil on canvas, forty-eight paintings, each 70 x 55 (27½ x 21⅝)

social and political power structures governing the production and reception of culture in their own time. Furthermore, since the younger artists had already engaged in an explicit dialogue with ▲ American art of the early to mid-sixties, in particular with Pop art (in the cases of Broodthaers and Richter, for example) and Minimalism (Buren, Darboven, Haacke, and Palermo were especially • concerned with the work of Sol LeWitt, Carl Andre, and Robert ■ Ryman), they were fully prepared to confront the recent formulations of a Conceptualist aesthetic that was first articulated by the artists around Seth Siegelaub in New York in 1968 (Robert Barry, ◆ Douglas Huebler, Joseph Kosuth, and Lawrence Weiner). Yet in all of the European responses to Conceptualism, even in their most esoteric and hermetic variations (such as the work of Darboven) one of the principal differences from Anglo-American Conceptual art was a dimension of historical reflexivity that now appeared as inextricably intertwined with Conceptualism's neopositivist self-reflexivity on the epistemological and semiotic conditions of its own languages.

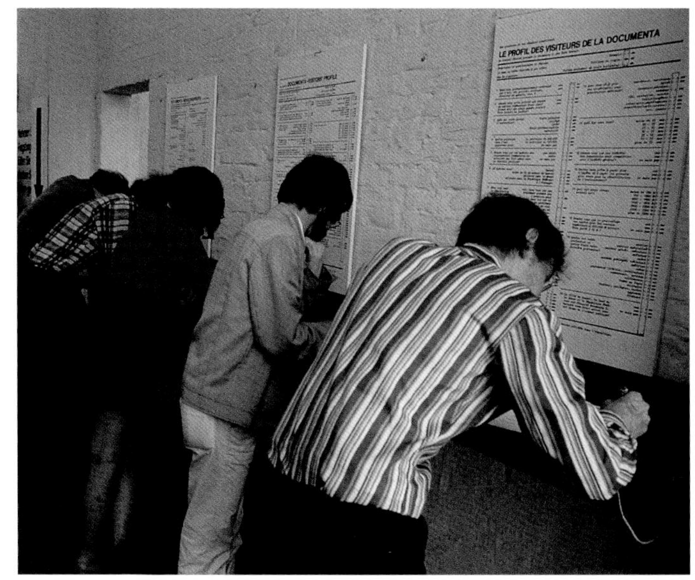

2 • **Hans Haacke, *Documenta Besucher Profil* (Documenta Visitors' Profile), 1972**
Audience participatory installation

▲ 1960c, 1964b • 1962c, 1994b ■ 1957b ◆ 1968b, 1984a

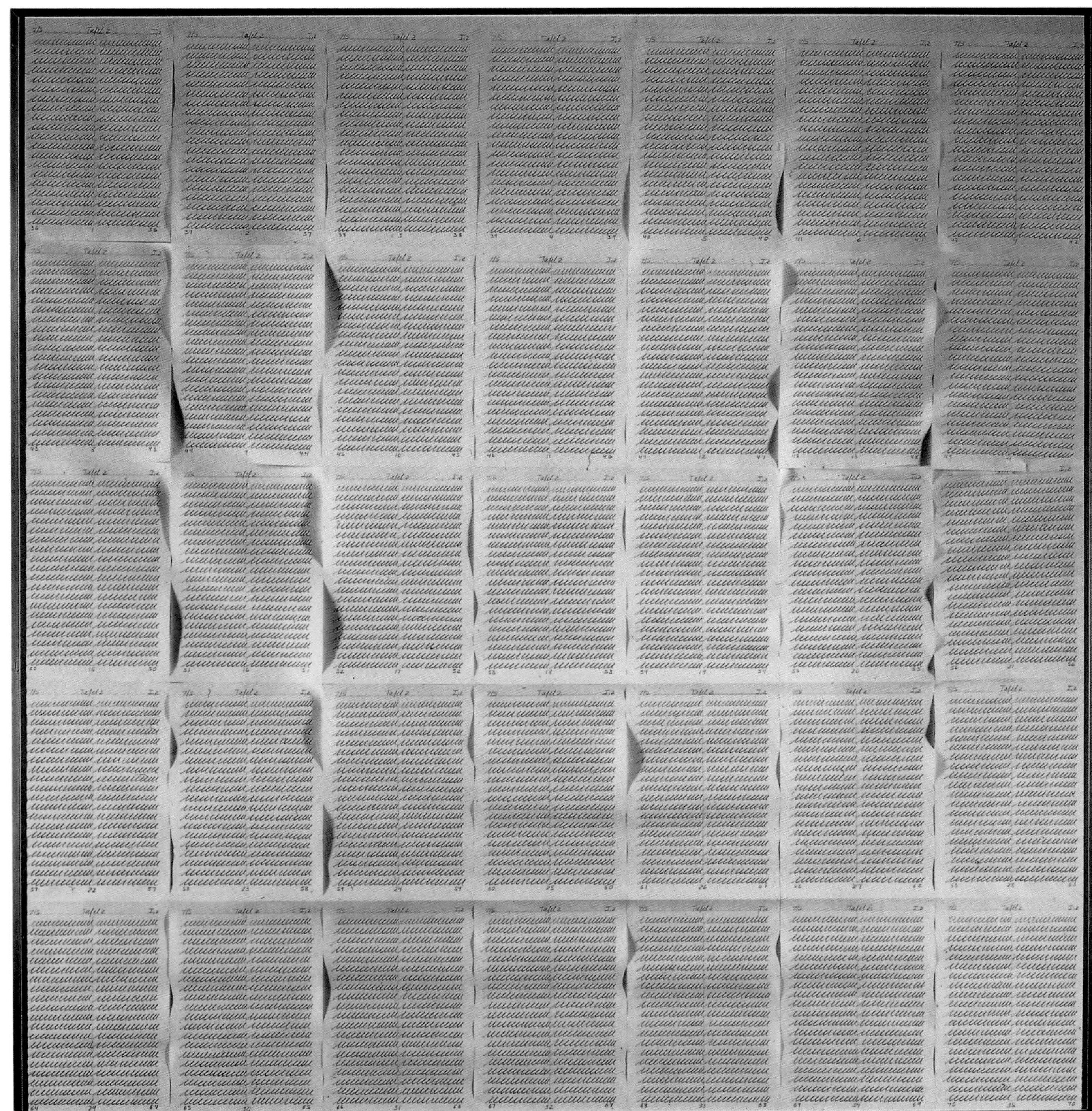

3 • Hanne Darboven, *Seven Panels and an Index*, 1973 (detail)
Graphite on white wove paper, panels 177.8 x 177.8 (70 x 70), index 106 x 176 (41¾ x 69¼)

One could argue that Darboven's work [**3**] originated to some ▲ extent in her earlier encounter with kineticism (as represented in the work of Almir Mavignier [born 1925], her teacher at the Hochschule für Bildende Kunst [Academy of Fine Arts] in Hamburg, and his attempt to innovate postwar abstraction by mechanizing and digitalizing its permutations and chance operations). The second formative encounter for Darboven was her friendship with Sol LeWitt during the three years she spent in New York from 1966 to 1968. Darboven's trajectory synthesized the oppositions between an infinity of spatio-temporal proliferation and processes of digitalized quantification, the dialectics of mathematically determined operations with a new type of drawing bordering on the iterative order of writing. Furthermore, she fused the order of the scriptural with the public performance of compulsive repetition, investing the concept of automatism with significations that were radically different from its initial definition in Surrealism or its postwar resuscitation in ▲ Abstract Expressionism.

● Jasper Johns and Cy Twombly had of course initiated the process of denaturing drawing in favor of drawing that repeated a more-or-less fixed and contained grapheme or that approached

▲ 1955a

▲ 1924, 1947b ● 1953, 1958

the condition of writing (initiated in the postwar period as a dialectic structure of somatic and libidinal loss and emancipation from myth). Once the features of iconic representation (e.g., figurative line, volume, chiaroscuro) had been completely stripped from the body of drawing's mimetic relationship to nature, the order of ▲ language and iterative enumeration (in Johns) appeared as a perforation of the body of drawing itself, as the surfacing of its social skeleton of inexorable constraints.

Yet Darboven's work traces this process in even more minute detail, and exacerbates the quantification of the temporality of its proper production. Thereby she inscribes drawing mimetically within an advanced social organization where experience is increasingly governed by an infinite proliferation of administrative rules and operations that prevent drawing from appearing any longer as an exemplary enactment of the subject's immediate access to psychosomatic or spiritual experience. Darboven registers these ruling patterns of the collective forms of spatio-temporal experience, and she identifies the automatic repetition of an infinity of eternally identical acts as the microscopic matrix of drawing itself.

This infinity of possibilities (an infinity of permutations, of processes, of quantities) is very much at the center of Conceptual- • ism. The extent to which this model would inform European practices of Conceptual art became poignant in Hans Haacke's contribution to "Documenta 5" when he installed the third version of his series of "Visitors' Polls" **[2, 4]**. This work made the historical dialectics of Conceptual art painfully obvious. On the one hand it offered (or subjected) the spectator to the most complex form of viewer participation that neo-avant-garde parameters had ever allowed for (by asking them for the full statistical accounts of their social and geopolitical identities). At the same time, however, the work articulated the extreme poverty of spatio-temporal, psychological and perceptual/phenomenological experiences available both to the conceptions of the artist and to a realistic estimation of spectatorial capacities and dispositions.

Haacke's synthesis of a seemingly infinite number of random participations (the size and scale of the work are totally open and dependent on the number of visitors who choose to participate in the statistical accounts) and a very limited number of factors of total overdetermination (since only a very limited series of questions could be asked in the ready-made statistical questionnaire) makes up the constitutive opposition of the work. In that reductivist instantiation of each participant as explicitly unique and different, yet at the same time a merely quantifiable statistical unit, Haacke's work acquires the same intensity of having mimetically internalized the order of the administrative world that we had encountered in the work of Darboven.

A similar dialectic can be discerned in the development of the work of Blinky Palermo (Peter Schwarze/Heisterkamp) who—like his friends and fellow artists, Sigmar Polke and Gerhard Richter— ■ had arrived in West Germany from Communist East Germany, where he had spent his childhood. The definition of Palermo's abstraction lies in the triangulation between the ruins of the heroic

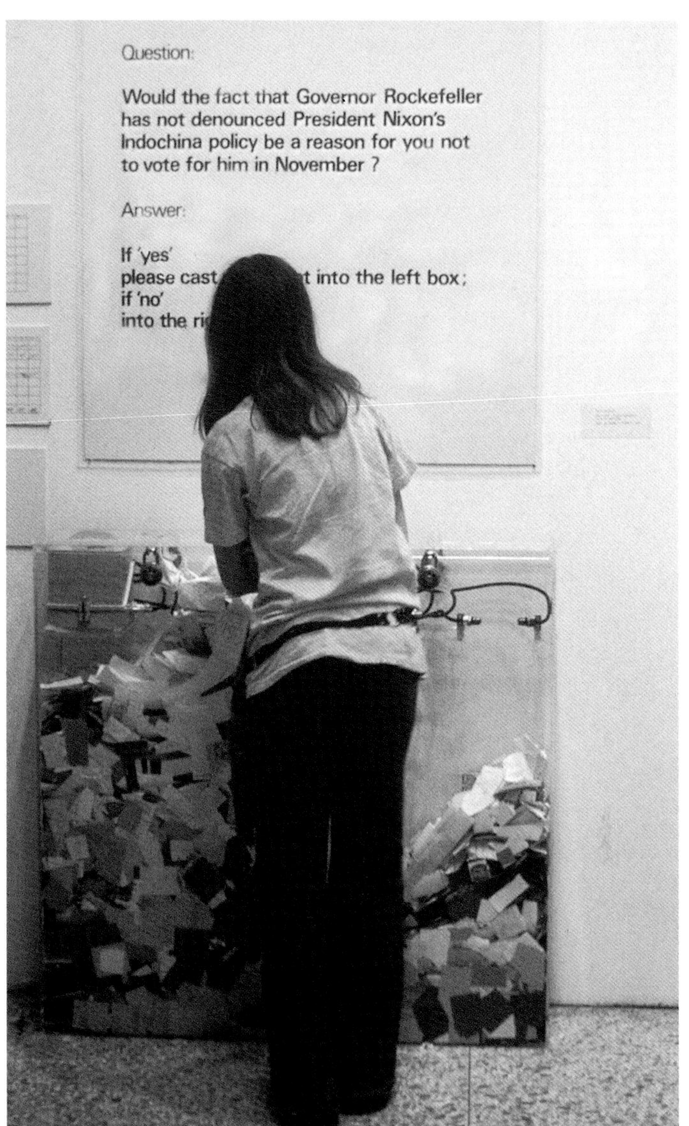

4 • Hans Haacke, *MOMA-Poll*, 1970
Audience participatory installation, two transparent acrylic ballot boxes, each 40 x 20 x 10 (15¾ x 7⅞ x 3⅞), equipped with photoelectic counter, text

abstractionists of the prewar avant-garde (Mondrian and Malevich ▲ in particular), the radical revisions of these legacies of abstraction in the postwar period in Europe (in particular in the work of • his teacher Joseph Beuys and in the presence of Yves Klein in Düsseldorf at the moment of Palermo's emergence), and thirdly, the dialogue with American postwar abstraction in its most reductivist models, ranging from Ellsworth Kelly and Barnett Newman ■ to Sol LeWitt.

While Palermo clearly recognized that the spiritual and utopian ◆ aspirations of the Bauhaus and De Stijl, of Suprematism and Constructivism lay in historical ruins, he also realized that all attempts to resuscitate them would inevitably turn out to be travesties. As with the radical departures in the work of Darboven, Palermo equally emancipated abstraction from its entanglement with myth and utopia (as it had still appeared in the hands of Beuys) and at the same time he severed abstraction from its entanglement in spectacle culture (as it had been inadvertently or cynically proffered by

▲ 1958 • 1968b ■ 1988

▲ 1913, 1915, 1917, 1944a • 1960a, 1964a ■ 1951, 1953, 1962c ◆ 1915, 1917, 1921, 1923, 1928

1970–1979

5 • Blinky Palermo, *Wall Painting*, 1972
Red lead on card, 22.7 x 16.5 (8⅞ x 6½)

Klein). Thus the neopositivist and empiricist formalism of the American Minimalists provided Palermo with a counterforce that allowed him to articulate the contradictory predicaments of abstraction in postwar Germany all the more.

Palermo's work consists of three principal types: the reliefs and wall objects, the fabric paintings, and the wall paintings. All three rehearse, and some of them repeat, the fundamental problems facing postwar abstraction. The first group (which is also chronologically the earliest) departs from the most advanced forms of postwar reflections on the transition from easel painting to the relief as they had been embodied in Barnett Newman's ▲ works such as *Here I* (1950).

Palermo's wall objects, however, rapidly move to a more explicit reflection on their simultaneous status as both reliefs and architectural elements, comparable in many ways to the Postminimalist work of Richard Tuttle. As in Tuttle's reliefs, Palermo's *Wand-Objekte* (1965) oscillate between organic and geometric form as though they literally wanted to reembody abstraction, against its rationalist and technological tendencies. The *Wand-Objekte* seem to be reflecting on the contradictions between autonomous pictorial presence and public architectural space. Yet the intensity of their intimacy and phenomenological presence appears first of all to compensate for the absence of that horizon of collectivity toward which the heroic abstraction of the twenties had been able to define itself. All these oppositions are as much articulated in the reliefs' formal definition as they are generated by the tensions between natural and industrial qualities in the chromatic definition of the objects, and it is far from accidental that in these wall reliefs Palermo frequently quotes Yves Klein's supposedly patented "International Klein Blue," modifying it ever so slightly, yet remaining within its spectrum, publicly exposing the absurdity of Klein's attempt to brand a color and to own the copyright in a particular tint.

In Palermo's fabric paintings, store-bought lengths of commercial decorator's fabric are sewn together in bipartite or tripartite horizontal divisions to compose a painting. Reiterating a model that ▲ had been developed in the first and only Ellsworth Kelly painting that was made with the colors of industrially produced fabrics, entitled *Twenty-Five Panels: Red Yellow Blue and White* in 1952, Palermo's fabric paintings withdraw two crucial elements from conventional abstraction: first of all they eliminate even the last traces of drawing and facture, where the process of paint application—even ● in its most reduced form of staining, as in Mark Rothko's work for example—had itself become an integral element in the production of painterly meaning. Secondly, the fabric paintings perform a denaturing of color in exact analogy to the denaturing of drawing in the work of Darboven. Choice of color and color itself now appear as suspended between their innate relation to the realm of the natural and their new conception as a commercially produced readymade. But the cheapness of the materials and their ready-made character are constantly counteracted by Palermo's determination to conceive the most differentiated chromatic constellations and chords from the extreme poverty of his own means.

The third group in Palermo's oeuvre is that of the wall drawings and wall paintings that he first executed in 1968 in a work for the Heiner Friedrich Gallery in Munich. Undoubtedly resulting in part from Palermo's attention to the development of painterly and sculptural practices in the context of Minimalism (in this case, the ■ wall drawings of Sol LeWitt in particular), Palermo's wall drawings/paintings address the dialectics between painting's internal order (its figure–ground hierarchies, its morphologies, its relations of color) and its external "situatedness" within public social space.

Palermo was among the first to recognize that painting's transition into architectural space would no longer carry any of the ◆ promises that this shift had entailed in the work of El Lissitzky, for example. Typically, in his installation at "Documenta 5," Palermo positioned his bright-orange wall painting [**5**] (executed with industrial rust-proofing paint) in a mere leftover space (in terms of the public display functions of exhibition architecture) and he also placed it in what was structurally the most functional space (a staircase that—while not intended for exhibition usage—connected two floors of the exhibition spaces). Palermo's wall paintings, in their explicit referral to outside spaces, to overlooked spaces, to the functional and utilitarian dimensions of architecture and painting (even more evident in his deployment of lead primer from the shipyards in Hamburg in his installation for the Hamburg Kunstverein

▲ 1951 ▲ 1953 ● 1947a ■ 1994b ◆ 1926

in 1974) insist on their dislocation and their industrial materiality principally to contest notions of autonomous plasticity. Yet if they open up to architectural space, they do so only as a mnemonic image of the lost promises of radical abstraction that had once engaged in the production of a new industrial culture of the collective.

If Palermo's work still bracketed industrial use-value and painterly surplus value, and remained suspended within an ambiguous space between an architectural surface as a carrier of painterly plasticity and an exhibition wall as an institutional space, Daniel Buren's installation for "Documenta 5" foregrounded an almost systematically analytical approach. In his work *Documenta* the exhibition walls were treated as mere carriers of information, as discursive sites. The work consisted of inserting white-on-white striped paper underneath an array of extremely different objects (such as Jasper ▲ Johns's painting *Flag* [1954], the base of an architectural model by Will Insley, or posters as examples of contemporary advertising) throughout the various segments of the vast and complex exhibition. Thus, the elements of Buren's installation functioned primarily as markers of the discursive condition of the institution, the exhibition, and its architecture.

Inevitably, the white stripes on white paper called forth a comparison with the long history of instances in which reductivism attenuated painting to the highest level of perceptual and phenomenological differentiation. Yet it became instantly clear that Buren's white-on-white work probably shared as much with • Kazimir Malevich's famous climax of Suprematist reductivism and ▲ Robert Ryman's most advanced forms of extremely differentiated reductivist painting of the early-to-mid-sixties, as it engaged with a conception of spatiality and visuality from which pure plasticity had withered away. This conceptual evacuation made room for a discursive analysis and institutional critique of the usages of space in a society driven by administration, where the difference between two whites was more likely to be derived from two types of paper or two coats of wallpaint than from the anticipation of two highly differentiated spiritualities.

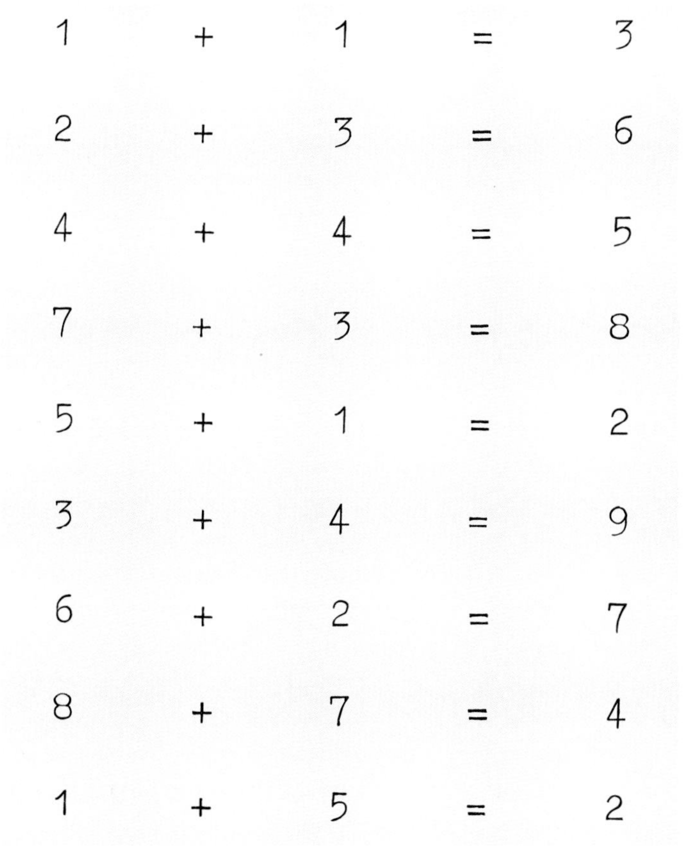

If the work of these artists seems to mourn the lost utopian potential of avant-garde practices, and of abstraction's aspirations toward progressive and emancipatory functions, the work of Sigmar Polke by contrast assumes a position of Romantic irony. Yet it is not any less aware of the tragic losses that postwar culture had to confront. Polke's travesties of abstract painting would eventually even incorporate the Conceptualist impulse to a linguistic reductivism, as in his series of *Lösungen* (Solutions) [**6**]. Thereby both abstraction's historical failure and the preposterousness of its radical promises in the present day become the target of Polke's sardonic and allegorical humour.

What the work of this generation of artists acknowledged—and responded to accordingly—was the fact that the spaces and the walls of the "white cube" had in fact been permeated by a network of institutional powers and economic interests and that they had been irreversibly removed from the neutrality of a phenomenological space within which the subject would constitute itself freely in its acts of pure perception. It might have appeared difficult at the time to recognize that the work's emphatic radicality was enforced by an almost ethereal withdrawal of what one might traditionally have regarded as the tasks of the aesthetic. Thus one could argue that Buren, Darboven, Haacke, Palermo, and Polke operate from within a highly contradictory, not to say aporetic form of melancholic modernism, attempting to redeem the radical utopianism of avant-garde abstraction, yet mourning at the site of its irreversible devastation. But to the very extent that their work yields its structural and formal organization in its entirety to the ruling principles of social administration, in the very semblance of an affirmation of the totality of these principles as the solely valid forms that actually structure experience, the aesthetic, within its radical negation, attains an unforeseen transcendence.

6 • Sigmar Polke, *Lösungen V*, 1967
Lacquer on burlap, each 150 x 125 (59 x 49¼)

FURTHER READING

Vivian Bobka, *Hanne Darboven* (New York: Dia Center for the Arts, 1996)
Brigid Doherty and Peter Nisbet (eds), *Hanne Darboven's Explorations of Time, History and Contemporary Society* (Cambridge, Mass.: Busch Reisinger Museum, Harvard University Art Museums, 1999)
Gloria Moure (ed.), *Blinky Palermo* (Barcelona: Museu d'Art Contemporani; and London: Serpentine Gallery, 2003)
Harald Szeemann (ed.), *Documenta V: Befragung der Realität—Bildwelten Heute*, (Kassel: Bertelsmann Verlag/Documenta, 1972)
David Thistlewood (ed.), *Joseph Beuys: Diverging Critiques* (Liverpool: Liverpool University Press/Tate Gallery, 1995)
David Thistlewood, (ed.), *Sigmar Polke: Back to Postmodernity* (Liverpool: Liverpool University Press/Tate Gallery, 1996)

▲ 1958 ● 1915 ▲ 1957b

1973

The Kitchen Center for Video, Music, and Dance opens its own space in New York: video art claims an institutional place between visual and Performance art, television and film.

By 1960 ninety percent of American households owned a television; it had become the dominant, even definitive medium of mass culture. By this time some artists had already taken it up, not only as a source of images, as in some projects of the Independent Group, but also as an object to ▲ manipulate, as in some happenings, performances, and installations. Fluxus artists in particular, such as the German Wolf Vostell (born 1932) and the Korean Nam June Paik, subjected television to different kinds of deformation, even destruction, in a way that Vostell modeled after the *décollage* of billboard posters by • Nouveau Réaliste artists Jacques de la Villeglé and Raymond Hains. From 1958 on Vostell produced several events generically titled *TV Dé-collage*. In one such event in 1963, at the New Jersey farm of sculptor George Segal (1924–2002), the site of several happenings, he put a television set in a picture frame, wrapped it with barbed wire, and then buried it "in a mock ceremonial interment" (in the words of curator and critic John Hanhardt). Yet this example points to the limits of such "critique": it rarely got beyond mockery, and it was often spectacular in its very attack on the spectacle of television culture.

This contradiction reappears in Paik, who complemented the histrionic rage against the television in Vostell with his own whimsical assemblage of electronic devices. In 1963 he too began to alter ■ televisions along the lines of the "altered pianos" of composer John Cage, whom Paik first met as a student in West Germany. In fact, after his move to New York in 1964, Paik popularized the Cagean mix of Duchamp and Zen in his own persona as a mystical madcap inventor of electronic contraptions. At first he manipulated the sync pulse of the television, then simply distorted its image with a magnet. He dislocated the actual sets as well, placing them randomly around rooms, on ceilings, on beds, in shapes such as a cross, amid plants on the floor, and so on. With his *Participation TVs* (1969), which viewers could modify through microphone hookups, Paik combined video with performance. One of the first artists to use video, he explored this combination most intensively in his collaborations with musician Charlotte Moorman (1933–91). He invented such devices as *TV Bra for Living Sculpture* (1968–9), *TV Glasses* (1971), and *Concerto for TV, Cello, and Videotapes* [**1**], all of which Moorman wore and/or performed. In *Concerto for TV, Cello, and Videotapes* she "played" three monitors stacked in the rough shape of a cello, on which appeared videotaped performances by Moorman and others as well as live images of the actual space. Already evident here is the tension between bodily presence and technological mediation fundamental to much video art, a tension that Paik sought to resolve—in his own words, to humanize, even to eroticize, technology. But his very attempt to reconcile the difference between man and machine often only exacerbated it, sometimes at the expense of Moorman (who was arrested during a topless performance in 1967). Certainly, *TV Bra for Living Sculpture*, in which two cameras, focused on her face, were reflected in two circular mirrors worn on her breasts, can be seen as an objectification of woman more than as an eroticization of technology.

Haunted by television

Another tension, no less important to much video art, soon became evident in Paik. Even as he was led to attack television, he also wanted to realize it—that is, to transform it from an apparatus of passive spectatorship into a medium of creative interaction, in which receivers of video might become transmitters as well. A similar ambivalence runs through communications theory of the time, especially the influential writings of the Canadian media guru Marshall McLuhan (1911–80). Like many other artists and critics of the time, Paik participated in McLuhanite mood swings between paranoid and mystical attitudes about media and between defeatist visions of technological control and grandiose fantasies of a "global village" of electronic interconnection (the internet has given new life to both attitudes). After other video artists like Douglas Davis (born 1933) produced live satellite performances, Paik created his own electronic happenings across distant sites (such as his *Good Morning, Mr. Orwell* performed between Paris and New York on January 1, 1984). Yet just as Fluxus attacks on television spectacle were sometimes spectacular in their own ways, so these attempts at interactivity often merely combined the passive spectatorship of most media events with the private conception of most art works.

As with radio, there was nothing technical about television that prevented its adaptation as a reciprocal medium between

▲ 1956, 1961, 1962a • 1960a ■ 1953

1 • Nam June Paik and Charlotte Moorman, *Concerto for TV, Cello, and Videotapes*, 1971
Performance with video monitors

transmitter and receiver—nothing, that is, except its corporate capitalist deployment. For this reason "television haunt[ed] all exhibitions of video art," as poet and critic David Antin wrote in 1975, in its potential for communication as much as in its failure to approach that ideal. This critique of television took many different forms over the years. In the seventies it ranged from *Television Delivers People* (1973), a didactic video-essay by Richard Serra of scrolled texts that condemned television as corporate propaganda, to the notorious *Media Burn* video performance (1975) staged by Ant Farm (Doug Hall, Chip Lord, Doug Michels, and Judy Procter) in San Francisco, a spectacular attack on spectacle culture in which a stack of televisions was set on fire and run through by a souped-up 1959 Cadillac at high speed. In the eighties this critique extended from the "guerrilla television" of Paper Tiger Television, a collective based in New York that produced alternative accounts of news events as well as incisive analyses of corporate media for cable television (such as *Born to be Sold: Martha Rosler Reads the Strange Case of Baby S/M* [1985], a textual video-performance by ▲ Martha Rosler on the politics of surrogate motherhood), to multimonitor video installations such as *PM Magazine* (1982–9) by Dara Birnbaum (born 1948), which manipulated footage from the television show of the same name in such a way as to foreground new techniques of viewer fascination like hyperkinetic image and sound editing.

As might be expected, video art has also had a technophiliac side. Its own early technological developments include the coming to market of videotape in 1956, of the Sony Portapak in 1965 (as the first portable video camera, it was the single most important material precondition of video art), of the half-inch reel-to-reel CV Portapak in 1968 (with its thirty-minute tapes, it provided the basic structure of much early work), and of the three-quarter-inch color cassette in 1972. In these years some artists actually assisted in video research and development; for example, in 1970 Paik designed a synthesizer for image manipulation with Japanese electronics engineer Shuya Abe. More recently, some artists have also assisted, consciously or not, in video marketing and promotion, ▲ especially where technically sophisticated artists like Bill Viola and Gary Hill (both born 1951) have exploited elaborate computer programs and special digital effects in their multimonitor, multichannel video-sound installations. Also to be expected, then, is a tilt toward technological determinism, on which score this early pronouncement of Paik remains typical: "As the collage technique replaced oil-paint, the cathode ray tube will replace the canvas." Yet with video, as with photography and film before it, the deep question was not "Is video art?" but rather "In what ways might video transform art—or at least participate in the transformation of the aesthetic field undertaken in the sixties and seventies?" In search of provisional answers, some video artists looked to nonart audiences and sites (first public television, then cable channels), while others brought video to bear on advanced art issues in given art settings. By the time The Kitchen Center for Video, Music, and Dance opened its new quarters in 1973, video art ranged vitally across this wide spectrum of activity.

Dislocations and decenterings

In the early days, artists could both explore the new technology of video and respond to the old modernist imperative that each art • form seek out its ontological "specificity"—in this case, that they investigate video not as a device to record (much less as an object to attack) but as a medium whose intrinsic properties might be foregrounded as the very substance of the work. Since the late sixties Woody and Steina Vasulka (born 1937 and 1940), the founders of The Kitchen Center, have pursued this double inquiry. They did so first through direct manipulations of the video signal, of its electronic waveform, as in *Matrix* [**2**]. This was a bank of nine monitors in which abstract forms and sounds generated by such manipulations drifted fluidly across the three rows of screens. Such video might recall the cameraless photography of the twenties and ■ thirties, such as the "photograms" of László Moholy-Nagy and others, but it is closer in spirit to the structural cinema of ◆ Canadian Michael Snow (born 1929), Hollis Frampton (1936–84),

▲ Introduction 2, 1984a
▲ 1998 ● 1960b ■ 1929 ◆ 1962c

Paul Sharits (1923–91), and others, who foregrounded the material and formal characteristics of film in the sixties and seventies. ▲ "The content was the medium," Viola remarked of video art of this time (when he too was initiated into the form), "like structural film in a way." But the materiality of video seemed more difficult to specify than film stocks and flicker effects, and its formal language more difficult to articulate than film montage. Unlike film, video can also be an instantaneous medium, a closed circuit of camera and monitor in which the production of the image is simultaneous with its transmission. To adapt a title of a video work by Gary Hill, video seemed stuck, ontologically speaking, "between cinema and a hard place"—the hard place of television. Moreover, as Rosalind Krauss wrote in her classic essay "Video: The Aesthetics of Narcissism" (1976), "The mirror-reflection of absolute feedback is a process of bracketing out the object. This is why it seems inappropriate to speak of a physical medium in relation to video."

Yet this apparent immediacy of video also made it attractive, ● especially to artists involved in Process and Performance art. Discontent with medium-specific definitions, these artists wanted to invent new supports and spaces for art that were ever more direct and present. After Minimalism, video became an important player in this "expanded field" of art where it served in part as a continuation of Process and Performance art by other means. Thus prominent practitioners of these forms—like Serra, Bruce Nauman, Lynda Benglis, Joan Jonas (born 1936), Vito Acconci (born 1940), and others—also experimented with video at this time. As extensions of sculpture, Process and Performance art implicated the body both as material and in movement, and video seemed well suited to record bodily manipulations and motions alike; in some instances, it seemed almost to prompt these things. More than just another object to manipulate, then, video became a performance space in its own right, where the viewer was sometimes invited (or impelled) to participate too, whether in the actual space of a video installation or in the virtual space of a closed-circuit transmission. Yet the desire for immediacy that drove so much Process and Performance art ran up against the reality of mediation in video—the fact that video remains a time-based, technology-laden medium that is never quite as instantaneous or immediate as it seems, and in which artist and viewer are never quite as present or transparent to each other as they might think.

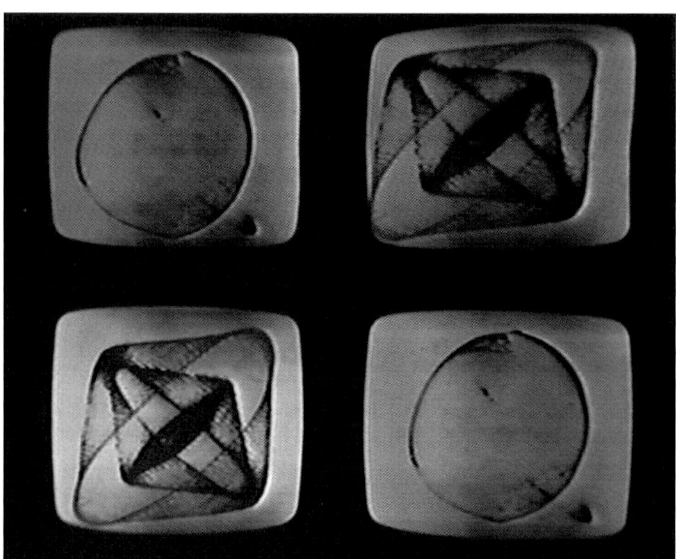

2 • Steina and Woody Vasulka, *Matrix*, 1978 (detail)
Videotape, 28 minutes 50 seconds

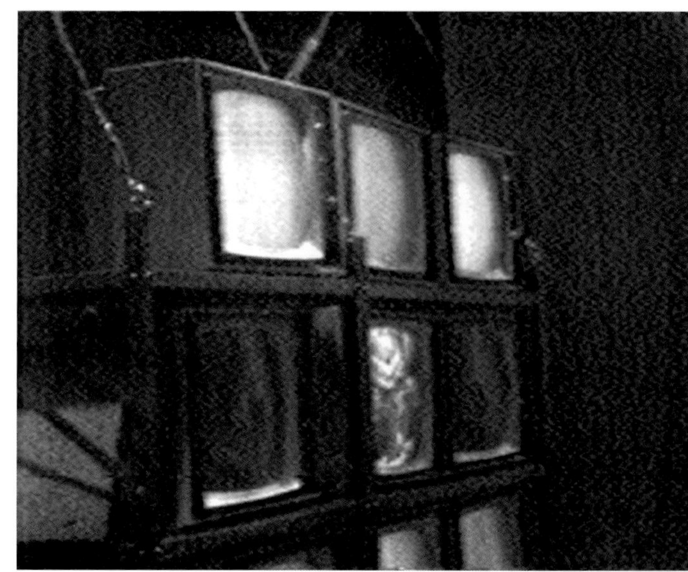

3 • Frank Gillette and Ira Schneider, *Wipe Cycle*, 1969 (detail)
Nine-screen interactive video installation

Very quickly, however, some artists made a virtue of this mediation, as they took up, as a central subject of video work, this very gap between the self and its images—and often between the artist and the audience as well. This was done in ways that were theatri- ▲ cally aggressive, as in the videotaped performances of Acconci, as well as formally simple, as in the use of transmission-delays in image and/or sound. For example, in *Wipe Cycle* [**3**] by Frank Gillette (born 1941) and Ira Schneider (born 1939), which was first presented at the landmark exhibition "TV as a Creative Medium" in New York, a bank of nine monitors played an array of broadcast television, prerecorded material, and closed-circuit images of the gallery entrance—both live and on delays of eight and sixteen seconds. Each viewer had to negotiate the different space-times of these images, including those of the immediate past—a process of dis/orientation that was further complicated by the rotation of the images from monitor to monitor. Such spatial decentering could also be effected without the use of transmission delays, as it was by Nauman in his various "Corridors" of the late sixties and early seventies [**4**]. Typically, one entered a long and narrow corridor; set behind and above the viewer was a video camera that looked down the corridor; on the floor at the end to which one walked sat a monitor that relayed what the camera viewed. As the viewer looked at the monitor, then, he or she saw an image of his or her own back. More disruptively, as the viewer approached the monitor, he or she saw this image recede, so that even though one came nearer the monitor and so felt bigger, as it were, one looked smaller. A double dislocation was produced between action and image and between perceiving body and perceived body—a dislocation that, again,

▲ 1998 ● 1969, 1974 ▲ 1974

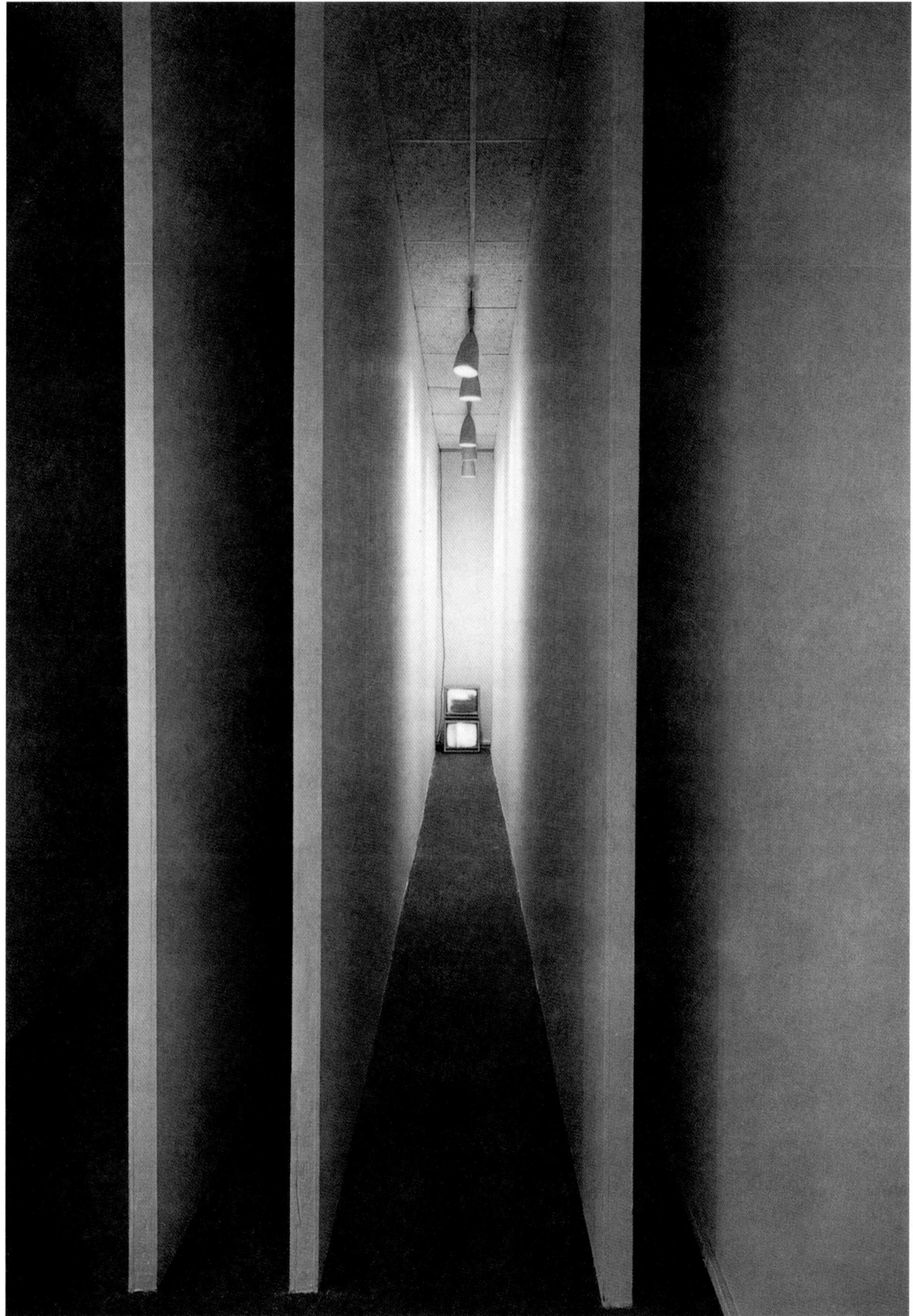

4 • Bruce Nauman, *Corridor Installation (Nick Wilder Installation)*, 1970 (detail). Wallboard, three video cameras, scanner and mount, five video monitors, videotape player, videotape (b/w, silent), dimensions variable, 335.3 x 1219.2 x 914.4 (132 x 480 x 360) overall as installed at the Nick Wilder Gallery, Los Angeles

was in keeping with other experiments in the expanded field of art at the time.

The impossibility of a pure present

By the early seventies many artists had assumed these spatial dislocations and subjective decenterings as almost givens of video art; some worked to overcome them while others sought to exacerbate them. For example, in his "video fields" of disjunctively positioned cameras and screens, Peter Campus (born 1937) challenged his viewers to attempt "the coordination of direct and derived perception." Meanwhile, in his video designs, which often included reflective and/or transparent panes set up in front of the audience, Dan Graham sought to heighten the discoordination between such perceptions, discoordinations that were always temporal as well as spatial. In his retrospective essay "Video into Architecture" he remarked:

> *A premise of sixties modernist art was to present the present as immediacy—as pure phenomenological consciousness without the contamination of historical or other a priori meaning.... My video time-delay, installations, and performance designs use this modernist notion of phenomenological immediacy, foregrounding an awareness of the presence of the viewer's own perceptual process; at the same time they critique this immediacy by showing the impossibility of locating pure present tense.*

This ambivalent relation to modernist immediacy suggests that early video art was on the threshold of some other, perhaps post- ▲ modernist, kind of practice. So was early feminist art, and artists like Joan Jonas and Lynda Benglis used video to explore perception in ways that also went beyond the strictly phenomenological. In such work the spatial-temporal dislocations of video were treated almost as analogues of subjective decenterings. For example, in *Left Side, Right Side* [**5**] Jonas performed before the camera with hand-held mirrors that bifurcated her face. As the viewer of the video saw a reverse image in any case, it became all but impossible to tell which side was which, all the more so as Jonas constantly repeated, "This is my left side, this is my right side." Another version of this subjective decentering, which stressed the temporal dimension, was performed by Benglis in *Now* (1973), in which the artist attempted to conform physically, in the present time of the video, to prerecorded images of her own face in close-up. The "now" of this meeting was never quite achieved, as her insistent whisperings of this word only underscored.

Because the medium of video was difficult to specify in its physicality, and because its artists seemed more interested in images of the self than in objects in the world, Krauss had argued that its "real medium" might be "a psychological situation"—that of narcissism. But, as we have seen with Jonas and Benglis, this narcissistic situation was never a perfect mirroring. In a sense it was closer to narcissism as understood by the French psychoanalyst Jacques Lacan in his celebrated "Mirror Stage" essay—a kind of mirroring

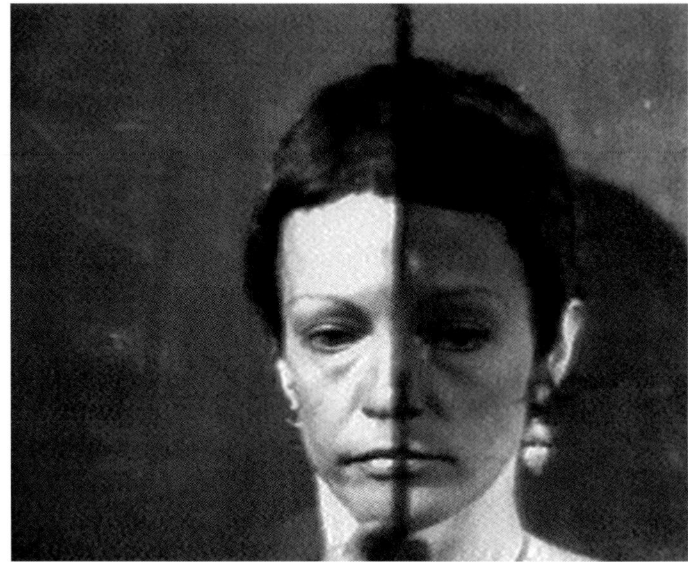

5 • Joan Jonas, *Left Side, Right Side*, 1972 (detail)
Videotape, 2 minutes 39 seconds

that is always disturbed by a slight mediation, an identification with the image of the self that is always undercut by an alienation from this same image as a little alien. Sometimes, especially with ▲ Acconci, this alienation seemed to provoke an aggression against the self or its images that was difficult to distinguish from an aggression against the viewer or the audience. But it may be that this aggression was also born out of another kind of anxiety as well—an anxiety about the interest, perhaps even the existence, of the viewer, of the audience, of any public. In this regard, this aggression might be read allegorically as a probing for a viewer, a search for an audience, a provocation of a public—at a time when, with traditional media and spaces of art transgressed, it was not clear who might show up where, and to what ends or effects. In this light, "the aesthetics of narcissism" explored by Acconci and others represent the other side of the aesthetics of interaction espoused by Paik and others: on the one hand, there is the reality of the autobiographical performer who is often left alone with his or her own body as both a kind of medium-substitute and a kind of audience-surrogate; on the other hand, there is the dream of the video wizard who calls into being a global village of interconnected transmitter-receivers.

FURTHER READING

Doug Hall and Sally Jo Fifer, *Illuminating Video: An Essential Guide to Video Art* (New York: Aperture, 1990)

John G. Hanhardt (ed.), *Video Culture: An Investigation* (Layton, U.T.: G. M. Smith Books, 1986)

Rosalind Krauss, "Video: The Aesthetics of Narcissism," *October*, no. 1, Spring 1976

Ira Schneider and Beryl Korot (eds), *Video Art: An Anthology* (New York: Harcourt Brace Jovanovich, 1976)

Anne M. Wagner, "Performance, Video, and the Rhetoric of Presence," *October*, no. 91, Winter 2000

▲ 1975, 1977, 1980, 1984b

▲ 1974

1974

With *Trans-fixed*, in which Chris Burden is nailed to a Volkswagen Beetle, American Performance art reaches an extreme limit of physical presence, and many of its adherents abandon, moderate, or otherwise transform its practice.

Performance art extends, internationally, across the century; in the postwar period alone it is central to Gutai, happenings, Nouveau Réalisme, Fluxus, Viennese Actionism, and the Judson Dance Theater, to name a few disparate contexts ▲; and there is a performative dimension in many other practices as well. Thus it may be impossible to define Performance art strictly; it may also be thankless, for many practitioners refused the label once it became current in the early seventies. Here performance will be limited to art where the body is "the subject and object of the work" (as the critic Willoughby Sharp defined "body art" in 1970 in *Avalanche*, the most important review of such work), where the body of the artist in particular is marked or otherwise manipulated in a public setting or in a private event that is then documented, most often in photographs, films, or videotapes. As this description suggests, Body art was involved in the same "postmedium" predicament as its Postminimalist complement, • Process art; and so we might ask of it a question similar to the one asked of Process: does Body art represent a liberatory extension of materials and markings, or does it signal an anxious default of representation onto the body, a literal collapse of the "figure" of art into the "ground" of the body, which might indeed be taken as the primal ground of art?

Three models of Body art

In retrospect much Body art can be seen to elaborate three models of performance of the late fifties and early sixties. First, there is performance as *action*, as developed out of Abstract Expressionist painting in the interart activities of happenings, Fluxus, and related groups. Frequently called "neo-Dada," such actions attacked the conventional decorum of the arts, but they affirmed the heroic, often spectacular gesture of the artist (assumed to be male). Second, there is performance as *task*, a model elaborated in the Judson Dance Theater in which antispectacular bodily routines (such as nonmetaphorical movements like walking and running) were substituted for symbolic dance steps. Set in protofeminist opposition to action performance, task performance was advanced primarily by women dancers like Simone Forti, Yvonne Rainer, and Trisha Brown in a spirit of radical egalitarianism that was sexual as well as social. And, third, there is performance as *ritual*, ▲ different versions of which were proposed by Joseph Beuys, the • Viennese Actionists Hermann Nitsch, Otto Mühl, Günter Brus, and Rudolf Schwarzkogler, and practitioners of "destruction art" such as Gustav Metzger and Raphael Montanez Ortiz, among others. Whereas most task performance worked to demystify art, most ritualistic performance sought to remythify it, indeed to resacralize it—which might point, from another direction, at the same crisis in artistic convention. At times these models of performance overlapped, but important differences remained, and they guided the three directions in which Body art developed from the mid-sixties to the mid-seventies, to be represented here with the

1 • Carolee Schneemann, *Eye Body: 36 Transformative Actions for Camera*, 1963
Silver-gelatin print, 27.9 x 35.6 (11 x 14)

▲ 1955a, 1960a, 1961, 1962a, 1962b • 1969

▲ 1964a • 1962b

signal work of Carolee Schneemann (born 1939), Vito Acconci (born 1940), and Chris Burden (born 1946), respectively.

Schneemann was the first American to extend the action model of performance into Body art in the early to mid-sixties; her use of "flesh as material" moved from the perceptual interests of the time, first to erotic expressions, then to feminist commitments in a way that was soon shared by an entire generation of women artists in the United States and abroad. For his part, in the late sixties Acconci turned the task model of performance into a testing of body and self, first in quasi-scientific isolation, then in intersubjective situations; in doing so, he opened up task performance to a Body art that was a social theater of the psyche as well. Finally, in the early seventies Burden combined task and ritual models of performance to produce a sacrificial form of Performance art; ▲ though less literal than, say, the Orgies Mysteries Theater of Nitsch, which was explicitly posed as "an 'aesthetic' substitute for a sacrificial act" (replete with the tearing up of dead lambs and the like), the violations of Burden were nonetheless literal enough to test the ethical limits of the artistic use of the body.

In her early "Notebooks" (1962–3), Schneemann drew on the • phenomenological notions of bodily perception that had begun to circulate in her milieu; thus when she introduced her nude body into her painting-constructions, she did so less for sexual titillation than for "empathetic-kinesthetic vitality." *Eye Body* **[1]** was her first piece of Body art: it consisted of private actions, documented in photographs, that were performed in an environment of painted panels, mirrors, and umbrellas: "Covered in paint, grease, chalk, ropes, plastic, I establish my body as visual territory. Not only am I an image maker, but I explore the image value of flesh as material." The title of the piece was programmatic: Schneemann wanted her "visual dramas" to "provide for an intensification of all faculties simultaneously," and *Eye Body* did indeed extend the "eye" of painting into the "body" of performance. Within six months, however, her focus shifted to sexual embodiment, perhaps under the influence of Simone de Beauvoir's feminist classic, *The Second Sex* (1949), as well as the psychoanalytical theories of Wilhelm Reich that condemned sexual repression as the greatest of all evils. Her next piece, *Meat Joy* (1964), performed first in Paris, then in London and New York, presented the body as fully "erotic, sexual, desired, desiring." Here a group of near-naked men and women cavorted (along with any onlookers who would participate) on a set of wet paint, plastic, and rope spiced with pieces of raw meat, fish, and chicken. The title signals the move from *Eye Body*: beyond a phenomenological extension of painting to performance, *Meat Joy* proposed an ecstatic reconfiguration of the solitary "meat" of the body in the communal "joy" of sex.

Schneemann continued to work in Body, Performance, and Installation art, as well as in photography, film, and video, but already by 1964 she had suggested these possibilities: that action models of art called out for literal embodiment; that this embodiment allowed an erotic affirmation of the female body; that this affirmation in turn effected a protofeminist appropriation of action models, heretofore dominated by men, for women as "image makers"; and that this appropriation might support further explorations of feminine sexuality and subjectivity. Of course, Schneemann was not alone in these early feminist developments. ▲ For example, in *Vagina Painting* (1962) Shigeko Kubota had brushed red paint onto a sheet of paper on the floor with a brush suspended from her crotch in a performance that symbolically shifted the locus of action models away from the phallic sticks of Pollock and company. Meanwhile, as artists like Schneemann and Kubota assumed new active positions in art, others like Yoko Ono underscored the old passive positions in society to which patriarchy has long submitted women. Thus in *Cut Piece* **[2]**, performed first in Tokyo, then in New York, Ono invited her audience to cut away her clothing; in a manner resonant with some antiwar protests of the time, vulnerability was here transformed into resistance, as her audience was forced to confront its own capacity for violence, both actual and phantasmatic. Such troublings of cultural associations of active and passive modes with masculine and feminine positions (and, here at least, Western and Eastern ones as well) proved to be a fertile topos of Body art, feminist and • otherwise, both for single performers (such as Valie Export) and for collaborative pairs (Marina Abramovic and Ulay, for example); it became a central arena for Vito Acconci as well.

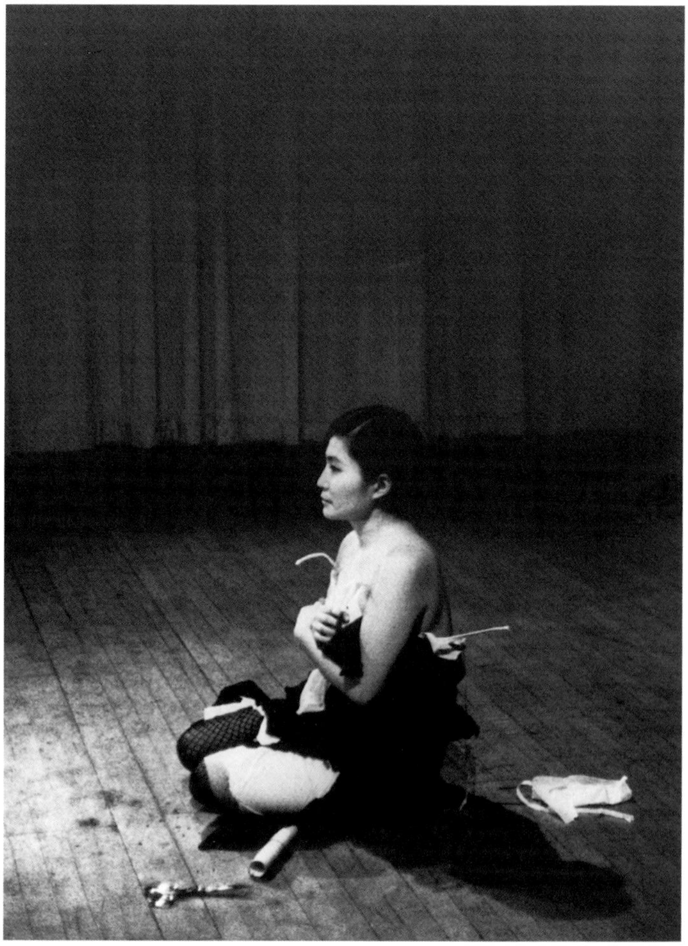

2 • Yoko Ono, *Cut Piece*, March 21, 1965
Performance at Carnegie Recital Hall, New York

▲ 1962b • 1965 ▲ 1962a • 1962b

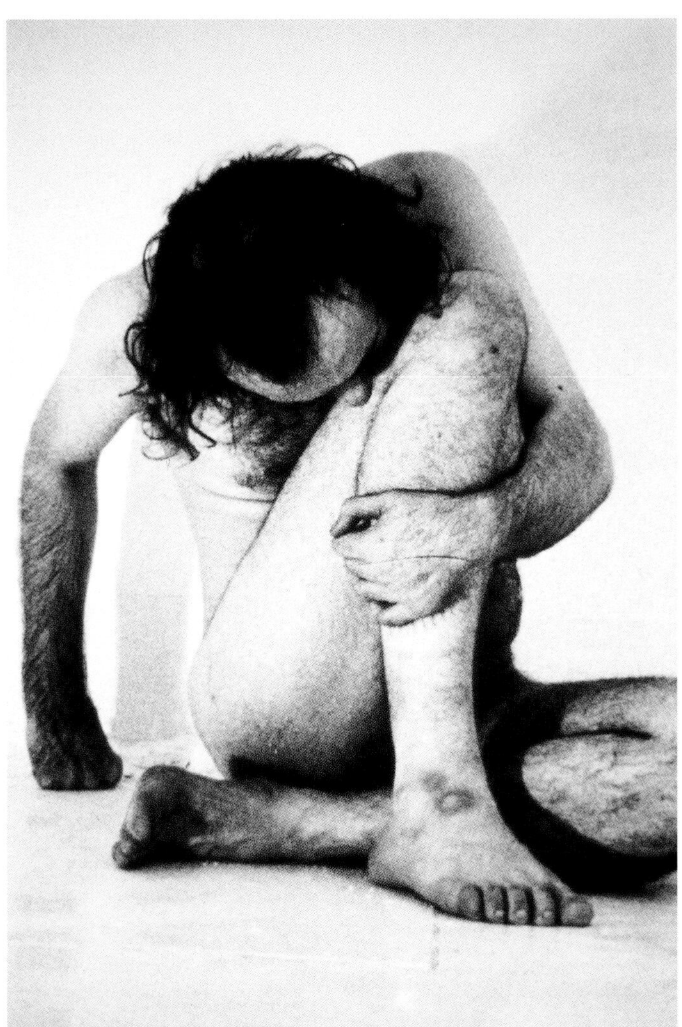

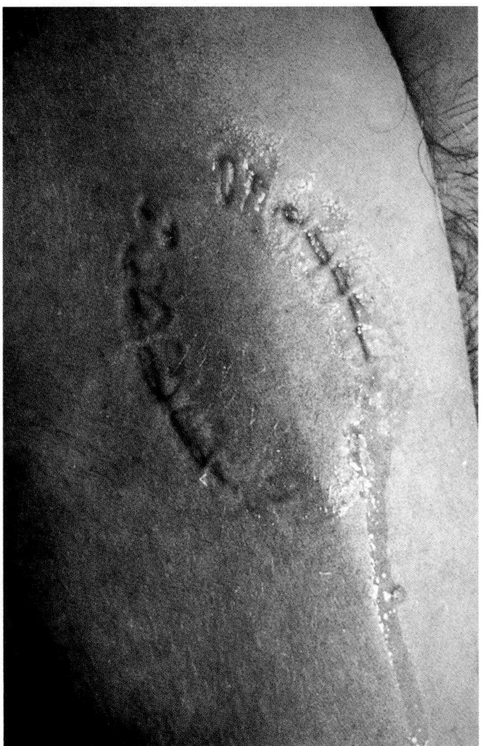

3 • Vito Acconci, *Trademarks*, 1970 (details)
Photographed activity

Trust and violation

Acconci first experimented with concrete poetry, a mode of writing that foregrounds the materiality of language. By 1969 he had shifted to a task model of performance, which he adapted into "performance tests" documented for an art public, first through reports and photographs, later through films and videos. Like the ▲ related performances of Bruce Nauman, Acconci subjected the body to apparently rational regimes for apparently irrational purposes (Acconci seemed to suffer the indignities impassively; Nauman seemed to delight in them secretly). For example, in *Step Piece* (1970) Acconci mounted an eighteen-inch stool in his apartment each morning at a rate of thirty steps a minute until he was exhausted. His stamina increased over the duration of the performance, but so did the absurdity of the task. His *Adaptation Studies* (1970) tilted these tests further toward failure. In one piece a blindfolded Acconci was thrown a rubber ball again and again—a recipe for errors. In another piece he plunged his hand into his mouth, also in repeated fashion, until he choked. These performances did test the reflexes of his body, but, more, they exposed its mundane incompetencies to the point where a strange aggressivity against the self predominated in his work.

About this time Acconci began to mark his body directly. In *Trademarks* **[3]** he bit into his flesh, turning it into a graphic medium of indentations, which were then inked and impressed on paper. This is a *reductio ad absurdum* of the autographic mark in art: at first it seems an act of absolute self-possession ("to claim what's mine," as he said), but this marking split Acconci into an active subject and a passive object—a self-alienation deepened by the suggestion of a sadistic–masochistic polarity in play, as well as by the implication of the body (and perhaps of Body art) as a commodity "trademark." No doubt prompted by feminist developments, Acconci explored this self-othering in gender terms too: in a set of filmed performances titled *Conversions* (1971), he attempted, hopelessly, to alter bodily signs of sexual difference, burning away "male" hair, shaping "female" breasts, tucking his penis between his legs. At the same time he also turned his theater of aggression round on others—to test the boundaries between bodies, selves, and spaces. At first the violations were minimal: in *Following Piece* (1969) he followed randomly chosen people on the street until they entered a private space, while in *Proximity Piece* (1970) he crowded randomly chosen people in art museums until they moved away. But the violations became more insistent with subsequent performances. In *Claim* **[4]** a blindfolded Acconci crouched in a Soho basement, armed with lead pipes and a crowbar, and threatened any intruders into his space, intruders who were also nominal invitees to the performance; this relation between trust and violation is an important aspect of his work. And in the infamous *Seedbed* (1972) he inhabited, twice a week, the space beneath a raised floor of the Sonnabend Gallery in New York, where he would often implicate visitors in his sexual fantasies, relayed over a microphone, to which he would also sometimes masturbate.

▲ 1966a, 1967a, 1973

4 • Vito Acconci, *Claim*, 1971
Performance with closed-circuit video monitor and camera, three hours

As Acconci explored such imbrications of self and other, privacy and publicity, trust and violation, he tested different kinds of limits—physical and psychological, subjective and social, sexual and ethical. But when these lines seemed broken—for example, in a 1973 performance involving a story of seduction, a young woman from the audience embraced him on the stage—Acconci backed away from such practice. For Chris Burden, on the other hand, the crossing of such lines *constituted* his practice. His first body piece, performed in 1971 when he was still a graduate student at the University of California at Irvine, made him notorious: for his master's thesis he squeezed into a school locker for five days and nights, attached only to two five-gallon water bottles, a full one above, an empty one below. Here task performance was taken to an ascetic extreme—Body art as a spiritual exercise without the religion, except perhaps for the faith demanded of performer and onlookers alike. This attenuation of ritualistic performance into an ascetic regime would later be pursued by teamed performers like Abramovic and Ulay and Linda Montano and Tehching Hsieh.

Like Acconci, Burden alternated such quasi-masochistic performances with quasi-sadistic events, but he concentrated on acts that placed his own body at primary risk, even as his studied irresponsibilities also tested the spontaneous responsibilities of others. There are several examples from the early seventies, but two stand out. In *Shoot* (1971) Burden had a marksman shoot him in the arm (his left bicep was grazed), while in *Trans-fixed* **[5]** he was nailed, with his arms extended à la Christ, onto the hood of a Volkswagen Beetle: the garage door was then opened, the car with the crucified Burden rolled out, the engine raced for two minutes (to signify his screams), then the car was rolled back in, and the door dropped. However inflected by Pop parody (regarding, perhaps, the sacramental value of the car in American culture), the ritualistic basis of Body art is blatant here. Transfixed, Burden also transfixed his viewers (the performance continues to have this mesmeric effect through photographs), and indeed the remnants of his actions, such as the nails, are often called "relics." To the ambivalent positions of narcissism and aggressivity, voyeurism and exhibitionism, sadism and masochism already evoked by Acconci, Burden added another ambiguous dimension, a sacrificial theater that, as with its other celebrants like Nitsch, Schwarzkogler, or Gina Pane, touched on the extremes of art—its ritualistic origins as well as its ethical limits (ethical limits in two senses: what can an artist do to self and to other, and when does the viewer intervene?).

Between the real and the symbolic

Our initial definition of Body art—in which the body is "both subject and object of the work"—seems innocent by comparison. But this innocence, this "immediacy" of Body art, should not be lost: it is what attracted its first practitioners and impressed its first viewers. It is also what aligned Body art with the modernist mandate to expose the materiality of art, to pursue an idea of sheer presence. But, as we have seen, Body art did not render "subject and object" one; on the contrary, this polarity was exacerbated, and it set up other binarisms as well—the body as active or passive, Body art as expressive, even liberatory (as in Schneemann), or withdrawn, even debilitated (as in Acconci, Nauman, and sometimes Burden), and so on. But the definitive ambiguity of Body art might be this: even though it was regarded as an art of presence—positively as an avant-gardist reuniting of art and life, negatively as a nihilistic obliterating of aesthetic distance—it was also a marking

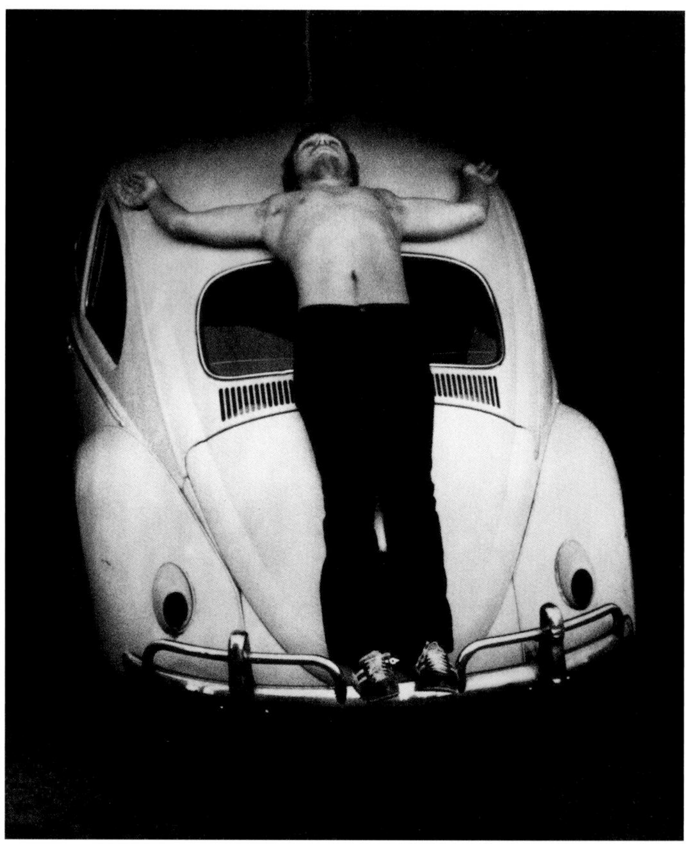

5 • Chris Burden, *Trans-fixed*, 1974
Performance, Venice, California

▲ 1960c, 1964b

▲ 1962b

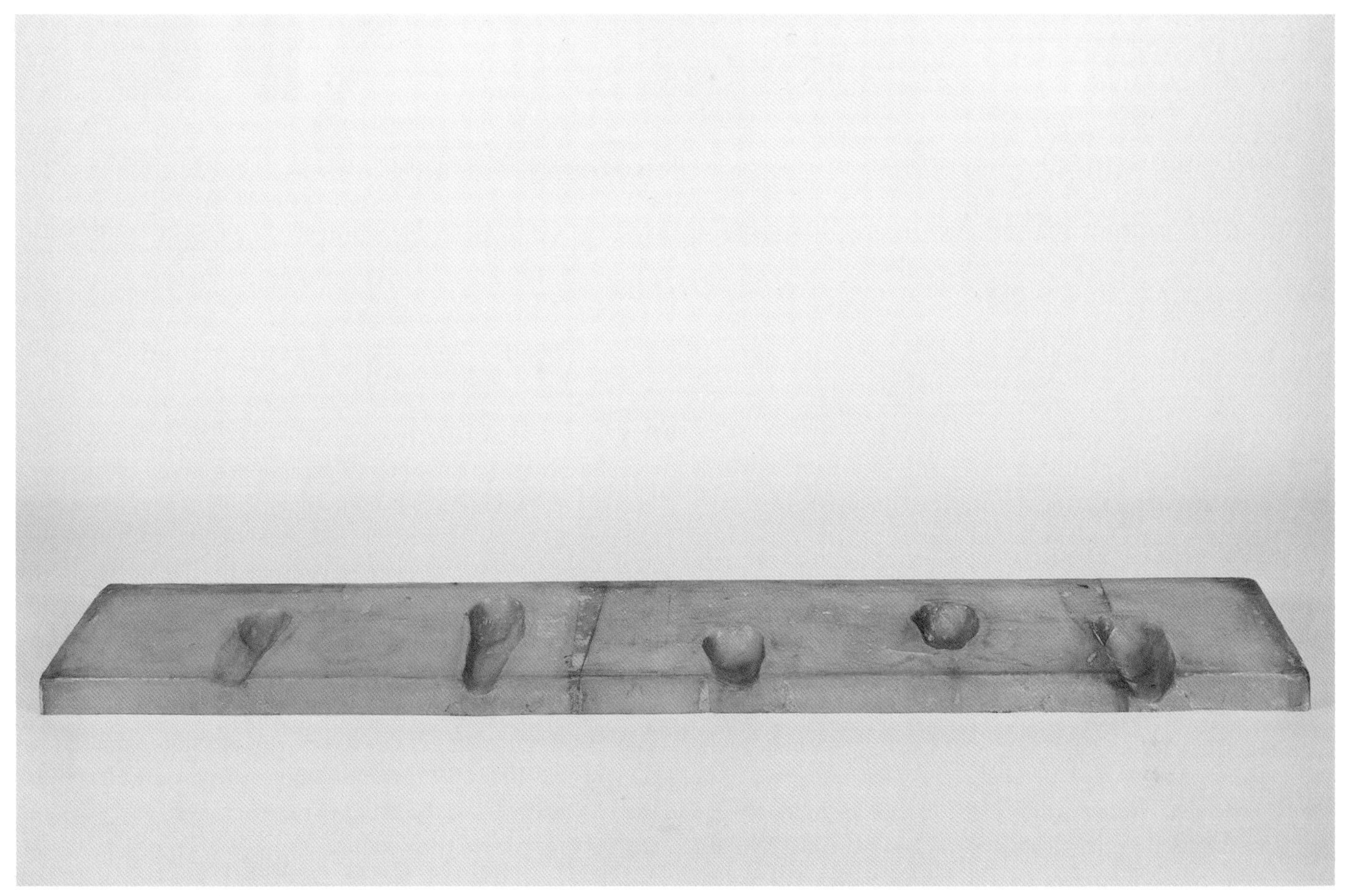

6 • Bruce Nauman, *Wax Impressions of the Knees of Five Famous Artists*, 1966
Fiberglass, polyester resin, 39.7 x 216.5 x 7 (15⅝ x 85¼ x 2¾)

of the body as a representation, as a sign, indeed as a semiotic field. Perhaps the essence of Body art is this difficult shuttling between presence and representation, or, more exactly, between indexical markings of the real (this arm bitten or shot, right now, before your eyes) and grandiose invocations of the symbolic (especially evident in ritualistic performance). For some practitioners like Acconci, this vacillation—of representation collapsed into the body, of the body raised into representation—seemed almost traumatic. For others like Nauman, the great ironist of Postminimalist art, it was an occasion for subversive play. For example, his *Wax Impressions of the Knees of Five Famous Artists* **[6]** mocked both the indexical markings and the ritualistic pretensions of Body art almost before they were proposed: all five sacred impressions here are faked—they are his alone (indeed this relic is not even wax).

Perhaps the ambiguity of the body as both natural flesh and cultural artifact is irreducible, and Body art only confronts us with the ambivalence of this condition. But Body art also complicates this ambiguity with another, for it not only presents the body as a marked thing but also invokes it as a psychic site. For the most part Body art preceded the psychoanalytic engagements in art ▲ first prompted by feminism in the mid-seventies; when its models of the subject were not phenomenological, they tended to be behavioral, even sociological. Nonetheless, its involvement in subject–object relations led it toward an abstract theater of psychosexual positions: as we have seen, Body art often seems to stage the Freudian couplets of narcissism and aggressivity, voyeurism and exhibitionism, sadism and masochism, indeed to play out the Freudian "vicissitudes of the instincts"—the constant "reversals" of active and passive positions, the perpetual "turnings round" from subject to object and back again. In this way, Body art anticipates rather than illustrates the psychoanalytic theories of ▲ subjectivity and the political critiques of power that became prominent from the late seventies onward.

FURTHER READING

Amelia Jones, *Body Art: Performing the Subject* (Minneapolis: University of Minnesota Press, 1998)
Kate Linker, *Vito Acconci* (New York: Rizzoli, 1994)
Carolee Schneemann, *More Than Meat Joy: Complete Performance Works and Selected Writings* (New Paltz, N.Y.: Documentext, 1979)
Kristine Stiles, "Uncorrupted Joy: International Art Actions," in Paul Schimmel and Russell Ferguson (eds), *Out of Actions: Between Performance and the Object 1949–1979* (London: Thames & Hudson, 1998)
Fraser Ward, "Gray Zone: Watching 'Shoot'," *October*, no. 95, Winter 2001

▲ 1975

▲ 1975, 1987, 1993a

1975

As filmmaker Laura Mulvey publishes her landmark essay "Visual Pleasure and Narrative Cinema," feminist artists like Judy Chicago and Mary Kelly develop different positions on the representation of women.

Feminism is a complicated topic in its own right, and as it provoked women to transform art in the late sixties and early seventies, it became more complicated. There is no single feminist art; indeed, most significant art of the last three decades has shown some influence of feminist concerns, such as the social construction of gender identity (including that of the artist) and the semiotic import of sexual difference (especially regarding the image). There is also, then, no separate history of feminist art.

Nonetheless, feminist art can be narrated in relation to the women's movement, which developed along the lines of the civil-rights movement. Thus in a first phase (underway in the sixties) women struggled for equal rights, and feminist artists struggled for equal access to modernist forms such as abstraction. The second phase (underway by the late sixties) was more radical than this first egalitarian stage. Here the movement tended to insist on the fundamental difference of woman from man, and to claim a special intimacy with nature, a unique culture of histories and myths, indeed an essential womanhood to express. And feminist artists moved away from modernist forms associated with men, like abstraction, reclaimed devalued forms of craft and decoration associated with women, contested oppressive stereotypes, and advanced positive images of women. A third phase (underway by the mid-seventies) was skeptical both of the equality pursued in the first phase and the separation proclaimed in the second. The movement still critiqued the positioning of women within patriarchal society, but it did so aware that this order could not be simply transcended. Meanwhile, feminist artists passed from a utopian imaging of women apart from men to a critique of given images ▲ within high art and mass culture alike. In a shift from a "representation of politics" to a "politics of representation," images of women—from nudes in museums to models in magazines—were treated as signs, even as symptoms, of male desire and dread, and the category of woman was seen to be "constructed" in social history, not grounded in natural biology or in "essential" being.

These phases are not strictly consecutive; they can coexist, conflict, and recur. And although some artists may view woman as "essential," and others as "constructed," this opposition is rarely absolute. Finally, even as feminist art is distinctive, it is not produced in a vacuum. It is in constant dialogue with other art—with marginal forms developed by obscure women as well as with privileged forms dominated by famous men. Thus even as feminist art elaborated the shift toward the perceptual conditions of the viewer ▲ inaugurated by Minimalism, it also questioned the Minimalist assumption that all viewers, all bodies, are the same perceptually and psychologically. So too, even as feminist art elaborated the ● critique of visuality begun in Conceptual art, it also questioned the Conceptualist assumption that language is essentially neutral, transparent, and rational. The same is true of feminist transforma- ■ tions of early Body, Performance, and Installation art, all of which were particularized and politicized, often according to the feminist slogan "the personal is the political."

Challenging the canon

The first order of business for feminist artists was to secure spaces for working and exhibiting, "raising consciousness" and teaching. This was a collective project involving the founding of such artist-run galleries as AIR (Artist in Residence) in New York in 1972. Yet the signal achievements in this regard occurred away from the male-controlled Manhattan art world. In 1971 Miriam Schapiro (born 1923) and Judy Chicago (born Judy Cohen in 1939) began the Feminist Art Program at the California Institute of the Arts in Valencia. In 1972 this group created Womanhouse, a temporary exhibition space in Los Angeles, which was soon followed by the Woman's Building in the old Chouinard art school (it closed only in 1991). According to Chicago, Womanhouse "fused collaboration, individual artmaking, and feminist education to create a monumental work with openly female subject matter." One must imagine a ribald theater where the domestic roles of women were caustically critiqued in a series of rooms. It opened with "Bridal Staircase," a mannikin in a wedding gown atop a flight of stairs. In "Sheet Closet" this bride became a housewife, a mannikin with shelves lined with sheets literally cut into her. "Nursery" implied her next role as mother, but its adult-scale crib and hobbyhorse suggested that the domestic structure of the nuclear family infantilizes all its members, especially the mother. Finally, in "Nurturer's Kitchen" and "Menstruation Bathroom" the body of this mother-and-wife became unruly. In the kitchen, a feminist

▲ 1977 ▲ 1965 ● 1968a, 1993a ■ 1974

revision of a Surrealist fantasy, eggs mutated into breasts and covered the wall and ceiling, while in the bathroom tampons soaked in fake blood spilled out of a wastebasket.

At Womanhouse, performance was also turned into a feminist form of critical expression. Along with the installations were "duration" pieces by Faith Wilding (born 1943) and others, who acted out domestic work usually left to women—scrubbing floors, ironing shirts, simply waiting—in pained silence. Other performances treated traumatic events. In *Ablutions* **[1]**, performed by Chicago, Suzanne Lacy, Sandra Orgel, and Aviva Ramani a few months after Womanhouse was dismantled, some of the women were immersed in tubs full of different fluids, then wrapped in bandages by the others, all in a space surrounded by kidneys tacked to the walls and filled with a taped testimony of a rape. Here ▲ task performance and ritual performance were combined to work through extreme experiences of "binding, brutalization, rape, immersion, body anxiety, and entrapment" (Chicago).

Just as early feminism sought to reclaim bodies of women (for instance, in abortion rights), so early feminist art sought to reclaim images of women—and by women as well. This involved the revaluation of such devalued forms as decorative arts and utilitarian crafts historically gendered female. For example, Schapiro adapted different sewing techniques in her feminist transformation of collage, which she dubbed "femmage," while Faith Ringgold (born 1930) also transformed collage in her "story quilts" of African-American life **[2]**. For her part Chicago used both ceramics and needlework in *The Dinner Party* (1974–9), her monumental "femmage" to women historical and legendary. This "personal search for a historical context for my art" began with a series of paintings called "Great Ladies," in which abstract forms mutate into floral and vulvar images, and it culminated in *The Dinner Party* **[3]**. Conceived "as a reinterpretation of the Last Supper from the point of view of women, who, throughout history, have prepared the meals and set the table," this Last Supper positioned women as "the honored guests." Three

1 • Judy Chicago, Suzanne Lacy, Sandra Orgel, Aviva Ramani, *Ablutions*, 1972
Collaborative performance, Venice, California

Theory journals

The seventies witnessed an unprecedented flourishing of journals of criticism. During this time, critical theory became a dynamic part of cultural practice: if an avant-garde existed anywhere, it might be argued, it existed there—in such publications as *Interfunktionen* in Germany, *Macula* in France, *Screen* in Britain, and *October* in the United States. More politically committed than traditional philosophy, but also more intellectually rigorous than conventional criticism, such theory was interdisciplinary in its very nature: some versions attempted to reconcile different modes of analysis (e.g., Marxism and Freudianism, or feminist inquiry and film studies), while others applied one model to a wide range of practices (e.g., the structure of language adapted to the study of art, architecture, or cinema). The master thinkers who had emerged in France in the fifties and sixties, such as the structuralist Marxist Louis Althusser, the structuralist psychoanalyst Jacques Lacan, and the poststructuralist philosophers and critics Michel Foucault, Jacques Derrida, Roland Barthes, and Jean-François Lyotard, were already influenced by modernist poets, filmmakers, writers, and artists, so that the application of such "French theory" to visual art seemed logical.

Among the preconditions of the boom in theory was a growing discontent with both formalist and belle-lettristic modes of criticism, especially as they failed to grapple with new developments in Conceptual art, Performance, and institution-critical art, which were sometimes influenced by "theory" in their own ways. Second, there was an embrace, in both art and academia, of the French thinkers mentioned above, as well as a developing interest in the critical elaboration of such figures, especially by feminists involved in psychoanalysis (such as Julia Kristeva, Luce Irigaray, Michèle Montrelay). Third, there was a delayed reception of interwar German critics associated with the "Frankfurt School" of critical theory such as Walter Benjamin and Theodor Adorno. And, fourth, there was an intensive refinement of feminist theory, especially concerning the question of spectatorship and the structure of sexuality. All four of these developments were mediated by the new critical journals.

Interfunktionen was perhaps the most engaged in radical art practice, while *October* and *Macula* responded selectively to both new art and French theory. *New German Critique* was the principal interpreter of German criticism in the States, while *m/f* in the UK and then *Camera Obscura* and *Differences* in the US elaborated on feminist theory (journals such as *Heresies* focused on feminist art). Other reviews such as *Block*, *Wedge*, *Word and Image*, and *Art History* addressed both the new art and "the new social art history" that was emerging. And still other journals, such as *Critical Inquiry* and *Representations*, were developed to consider the academic ramifications of these different phenomena. But in the early days of these journals perhaps the most dynamic was *Screen*, for it was in this British review that the Marxist orientation of the New Left, a strong commitment to cultural studies, early translations of such various thinkers as Brecht, Benjamin, Barthes, Althusser, and Lacan, and feminist readings of film, mass culture, and psychoanalysis, all came into critical conversation.

▲ 1962b, 1974

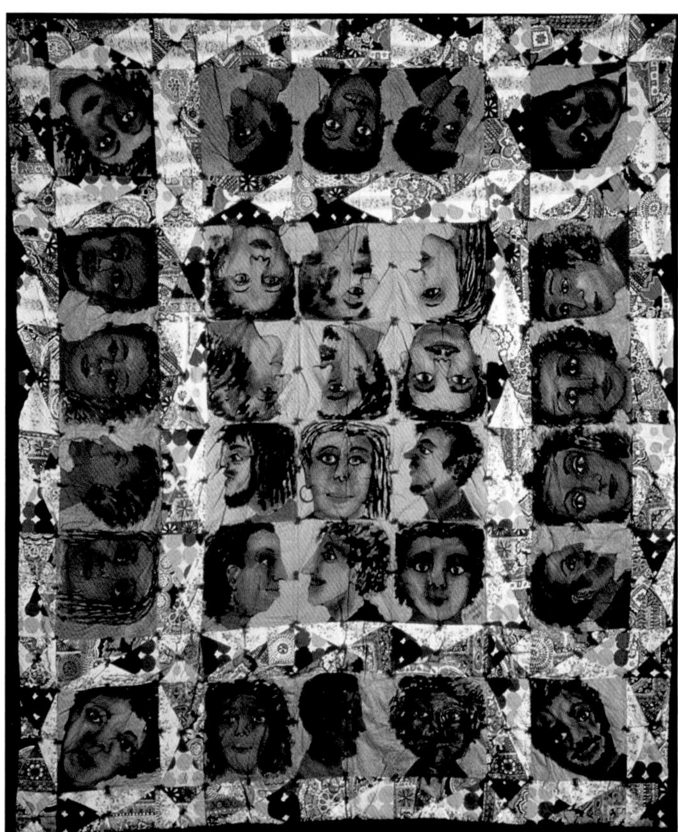

2 • Faith Ringgold, *Echoes of Harlem*, 1980
Acrylic on canvas, dyed, painted, and pieced fabric, 243.8 x 213.4 (96 x 84)

long tables are set in an equilateral triangle on a "Heritage Floor" made up of over 2,300 porcelain tiles inscribed with the names of 999 women. These obscure women "support" the illustrious women honored, with distinctive painted plates, on the tables, which are also set with linen tablecloths, goblets, flatware, and napkins. The first table celebrates women from matriarchal prehistory through antiquity; the second, from the beginnings of Christianity through the Reformation; and the third, from the seventeenth to the twentieth centuries. *The Dinner Party* thus "takes us on a tour of Western civilization, a tour that bypasses what we have been taught to think of as the main road" (Chicago). This challenge to the canon was also raised by feminist art historians, from the first essay on the systematic exclusion of women, "Why Have There Been No Great Women Artists?" (1971) by Linda Nochlin, to the first book on the subject, *Old Mistresses: Women, Art, and Ideology* (1981) by Roszika Parker and Griselda Pollock. Feminist criticism of different orientations was also supported by new journals, such as *Feminist Art Journal* and *Heresies* in North America and *Spare Rib* and *m/f* in Britain.

A new language of desire

The Dinner Party is emblematic of the second phase of American feminist art in several respects. Although Chicago assumed authorship, it was a collaborative project; it sought to revalue arts and crafts associated with women; and it worked to recover lost figures for a feminist history. But what made it exemplary of this second phase was its celebratory association of woman and body as well as its gynocentric view of cultural history. Other feminist artists advanced more anguished versions of womanly embodiment during this time. In the long scrolls of her *Codex Artaud* **[4]**, Nancy Spero (born 1926) mixed violent statements from Antonin Artaud (1896–1948), the French writer and founder of "the theater of cruelty," with "images I had painted—disembodied heads, defiant phallic tongues on tense male, female, and androgynous figures, victims in strait-jackets, mythological or alchemical references, etc." And in her *Siluetas* series of the seventies **[5]**, Ana Mendieta (1948–85) inscribed her own profile into various landscapes, an association of female body and maternal nature that reads ambiguously as joyous reunion or deathly embrace or both. This second phase of feminist art was thus governed by an identification of woman and body, of woman and nature, that was at times triumphant and at times depressive.

Perhaps in the face of patriarchy this identification was necessary to feminist solidarity. But it was soon seen as a reduction of women to nature, as an "essentialist" impediment to feminist repositioning of women in society. Also confronted with sexist stereotypes in mass culture, some feminists advocated a moratorium on representations of women in art, while others explored other ways to register the desires of women and the disruptions of sexual difference. This investigation was more advanced in Britain than in North America. There, too, feminists first focused on economic inequities (as in the informational project "Women and Work: A Document on the Division of Labour in Industry," mounted by Kay Hunt, Margaret Harrison, and Mary Kelly in London in 1975); and artists first sought out autonomous spaces (as in A Woman's Place, a site somewhat similar to Womanhouse, also staged in London in 1975). But British feminisms were closer both to socialist politics and to psychoanalytic theory than their North American counterparts. Indeed, Freud, Jacques Lacan, and French feminist analysts like Luce Irigaray and Michèle Montrelay guided feminist debates in Britain. Of course, feminist relations to psychoanalysis could only be ambivalent, given that in Freud femininity is associated with passivity, and that in Lacan woman is made to signify "castration" or "lack." But psychoanalysis also provided feminists, first in Britain and then elsewhere, with critical insight into the positioning of woman—in the unconscious and in the symbolic order, in high art and in everyday life.

The text that pioneered this feminist use of psychoanalysis for cultural critique was "Visual Pleasure and Narrative Cinema" (1975) by the filmmaker and critic Laura Mulvey (born 1941), who, with her partner Peter Wollen (born 1938), also made such feminist films as *Riddles of the Sphinx* (1976). In her essay Mulvey articulated two primary concerns of the third phase of feminist art: the construction of woman both in mass culture (in her case, classic Hollywood film) and in psychoanalysis. In Britain artists like Mary Kelly (born 1941) were already at work on the second topic, while in the States artists like Barbara Kruger, Cindy ▲ Sherman, and Silvia Kolbowski (born 1953) would soon turn to the first. According to Mulvey, the visual pleasure of mass culture

▲ Introduction 1, 1977, 1993a

3 • Judy Chicago, *The Dinner Party*, 1974–9
Mixed-media installation,
121.9 x 106.7 x 7.6 (48 x 42 x 3)

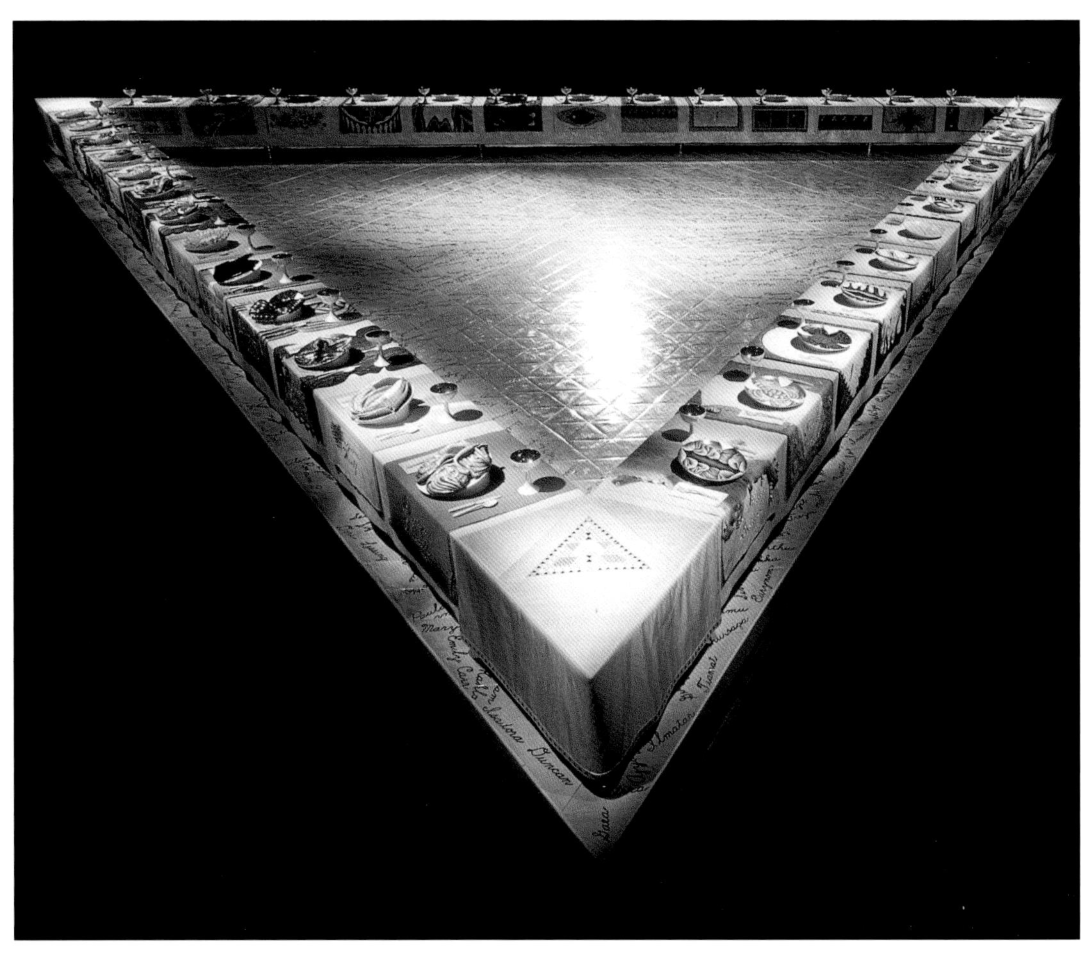

1970–1979

4 • Nancy Spero, *Codex Artaud VI*, 1971 (detail)
Typewriter and painted collage on paper, 52.1 x 316.2 (20½ x 124½)

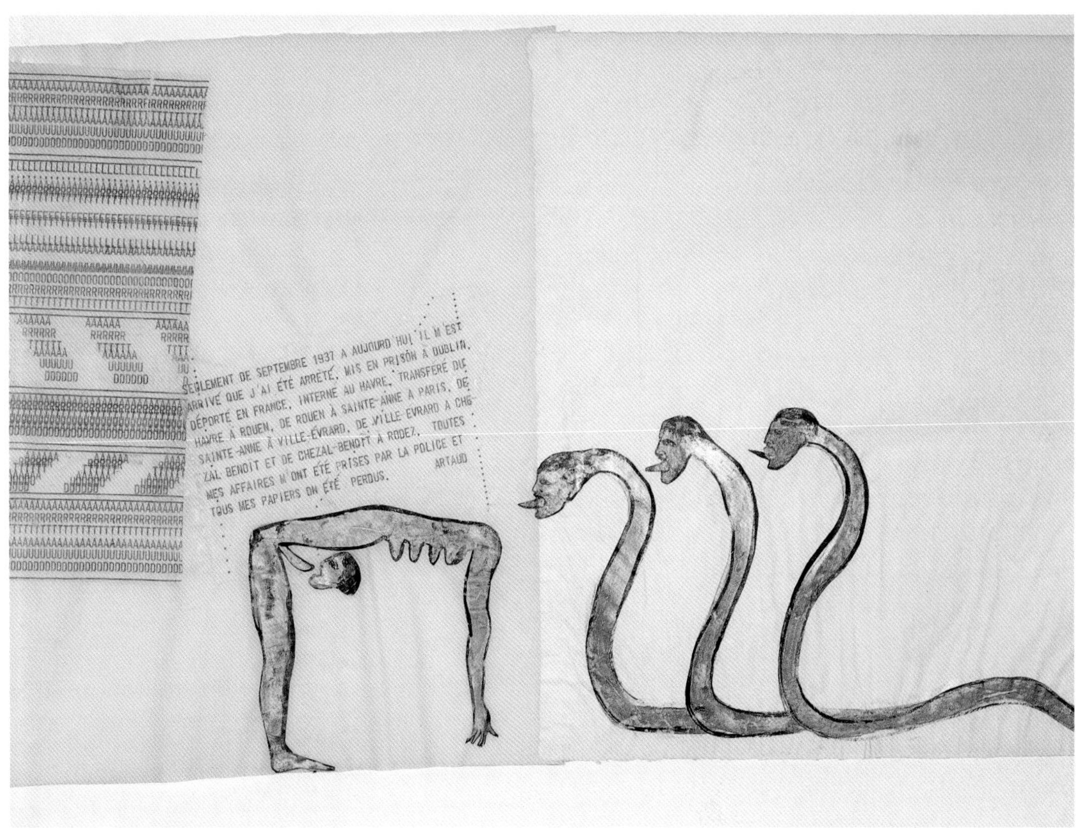

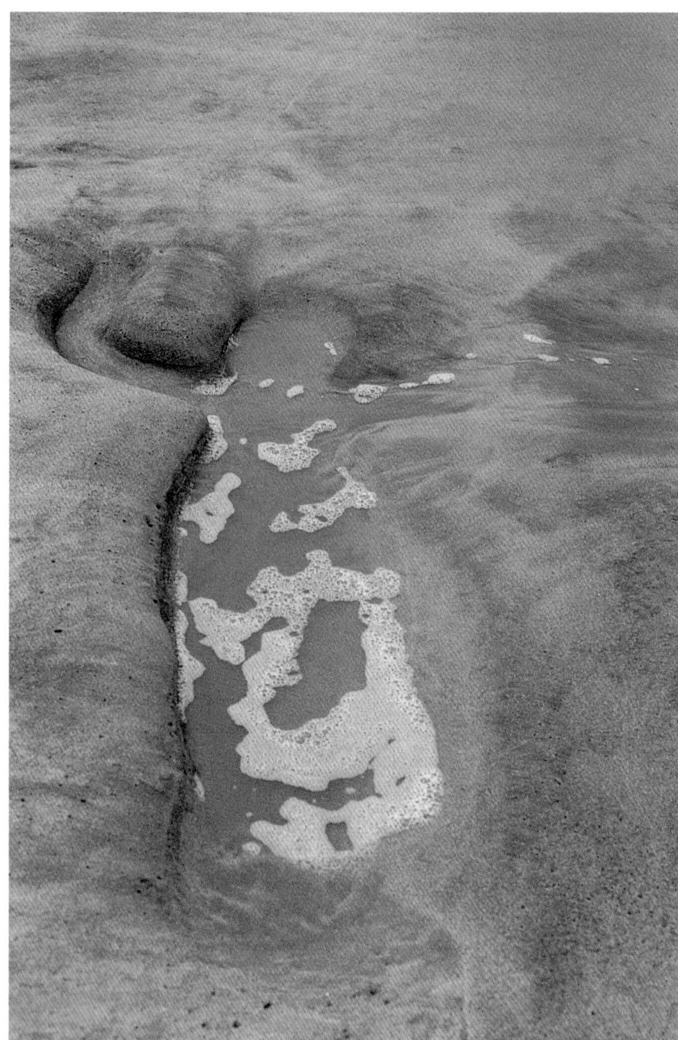

5 • Ana Mendieta, *Untitled*, from the *Silueta* series, 1976
Red pigment *silueta* on the beach, Mexico

is not "mass" at all; it is designed primarily to suit the psychic structure of the heterosexual male, to allow his enjoyment of the female image as an erotic object. Thus, in the famous formula of her text, patriarchal culture positions "woman as image" and "man as bearer of the look." The politics of the essay follow from this account: Mulvey calls for the destruction of this masculinist pleasure in favor of a "new language of desire." This recognition—that patriarchal culture, high and low, is structured around "the male ▲ gaze"—was fundamental: it empowered many feminist practices in art and criticism alike. But it also had a few blind spots of its own, as Mulvey came to see. Are gazes strictly male, female, • straight, gay, white, black, and so on? Such claims can fix identity more than free it up. Nonetheless, like the claim of an essential womanhood, the notion of a male gaze was a strategic necessity. And its own essentialism was soon complicated by male artists like ■ Victor Burgin, who was also prompted to investigate the construction of this gaze, indeed of masculinity in general.

When Mulvey published "Visual Pleasure and Narrative Cinema," Mary Kelly had almost completed the first part of her *Post-Partum Document* of 1973–9 [**6**]. Although the two works are nearly contemporaneous, *Post-Partum Document* is as emblematic of the third phase of feminist art as *The Dinner Party* is of the second. Here Kelly developed her model of an art project that exists somewhere between a psychoanalytic case-study and an ▲ ethnographic field-report. Made up of six sections with a total of 135 units, *Post-Partum Document* mixes different kinds of images and texts in a double narrative. On the one hand, it recounts the entry of her son into family, language, school, and social life. On the other hand, it recounts her response to the "loss" of her child to such institutions. In doing so, Kelly explores "the possibility of • female fetishism," in particular that of the mother. For Freud the fetish is a substitute for an erotic object that appears lost—as the maternal breast might sometimes appear lost to the infant, the penis of the mother to the child, or indeed the grown child to the mother. Kelly focuses on this last loss as she presents the residues of her child—his diapers, baby clothes, first scribbles, initial letters, and so on—as fetishes of the mother, as "emblems of [her] desire." At the same time she juxtaposes these traces with notes, some anecdotal, others theoretical, which confirm as well as contest psychoanalytic accounts of both childhood and motherhood. The result is an "archaeology of everyday life"—of weaning, speaking, schooling, writing, and so on—that is also a narrative of "the difficulty of the symbolic order for women."

Kelly has completed further projects that are particularly important in this context. *Interim* (1985–9) considers the middle age of women as an interim period, putatively after erotic and maternal services, a dark age lost to cultural representation. And *Gloria Patriae* (1992) tackles the pathologies of military masculinity, especially as displayed in the Gulf War of 1991. Both projects attempt to connect theoretical inquiries into psychic life with political demands for social change, and they did so in a reactionary period ruled by Ronald Reagan and Margaret Thatcher and their immediate heirs. It may be little consolation to feminist art, given the great backlash against feminism in general, that it has so transformed contemporary art. But it has done so, as Kelly suggests, "by transforming the phenomenological presence of the body into an image of sexual difference, extending the interrogation of the object to include the subjective conditions of its existence, turning political intent into personal accountability, and translating institutional critique into the question of authority."

FURTHER READING

Judy Chicago, *Beyond the Flower: The Autobiography of a Feminist Artist* (New York: Viking, 1996)

Joanna Frueh, Cassandra L. Langer, and Arlene Raven (eds), *New Feminist Art Criticism: Art, Identity, Action* (New York: HarperCollins, 1994)

Mary Kelly, *Imaging Desire* (Cambridge, Mass.: MIT Press, 1997)

Lucy R. Lippard, *The Pink Glass Swan: Selected Essays in Feminist Art* (New York: New Press, 1995)

Linda Nochlin, *Women, Art and Power: And Other Essays* (New York: Harper & Row, 1988; and London: Thames & Hudson, 1989)

Roszika Parker and Griselda Pollock, *Framing Feminism: Art and the Women's Movement 1970–85* (London: Pandora, 1987)

Griselda Pollock, *Vision and Difference: Femininity, Feminism, and Histories of Art* (New York: Routledge, 1988)

Catherine de Zegher (ed.), *Inside the Visible: An Elliptical Traverse of 20th-Century Art* (Cambridge, Mass.: MIT Press, 1994)

▲ 1977, 1993a • 1987, 1993c ■ 1984a ▲ 1992 • 1931

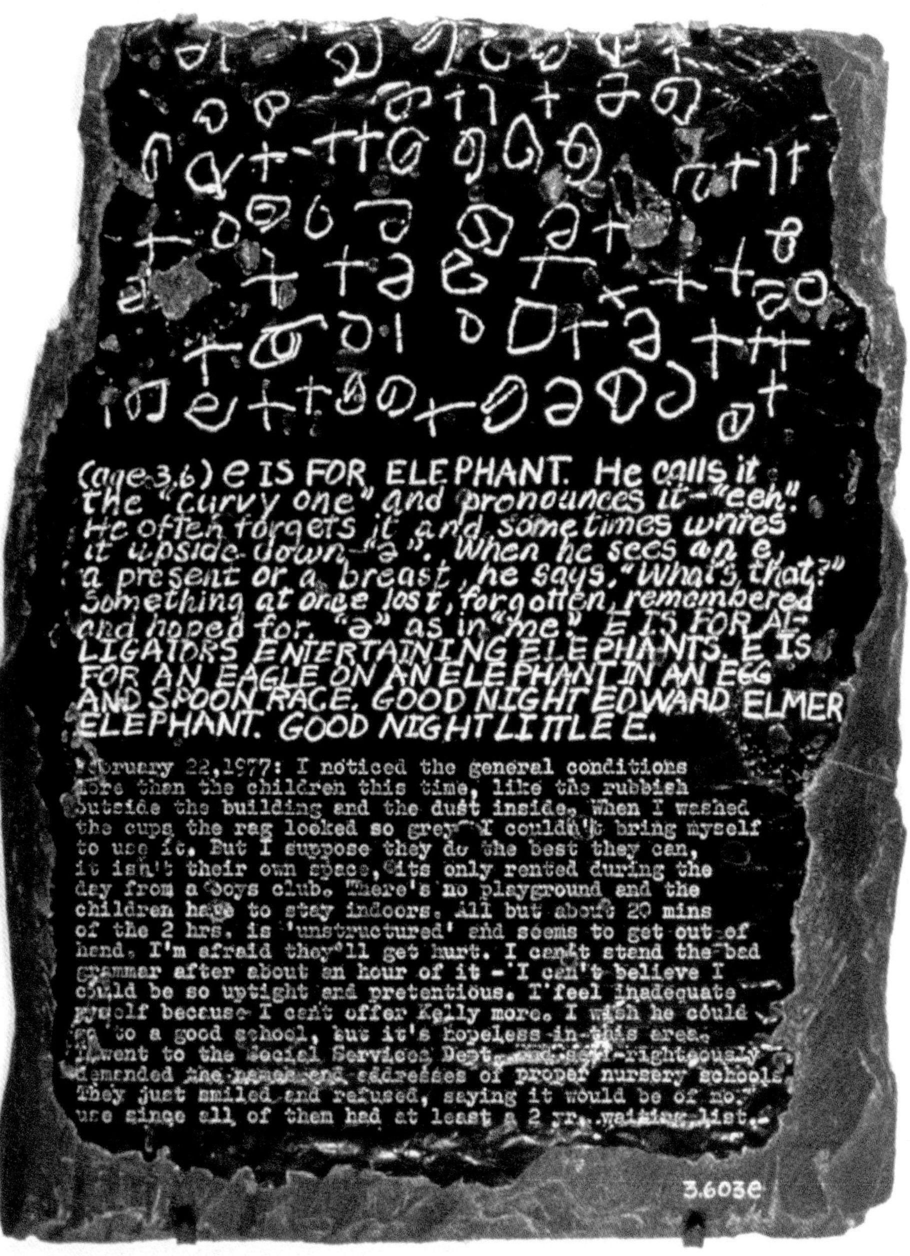

6 • Mary Kelly, *Post-Partum Document: Documentation VI, Pre-Writing Alphabet, Exergue and Diary*, 1978 (detail)
Perspex units, white card, resin, and slate, one of fifteen units in this section, 20 x 25.5 (7⅞ x 10)

1976

In New York, the founding of P.S.1 coincides with the Metropolitan Museum's "King Tut" exhibition: important shifts in the institutional structure of the art world are registered by both alternative spaces and the blockbuster show.

In the summer of 1966, as *Time* magazine announced that the art market was "expected to hit $7 billion a year by 1970," this overheated situation was having a double effect. On the one hand it was skewing museum finances, making purchases and temporary exhibitions exorbitantly expensive. On the other, it was encouraging more and more aspiring artists to try for success and embark on a serious artistic career. It also coincided with the first US ▲ government program to finance the arts since the WPA and the days of the Depression.

President Lyndon Johnson had signed the Arts and Humanities Bill on September 29, 1965, and in 1966 he pushed Congress to authorize a grant of $63 million, of which the newly founded • National Endowment for the Arts would have $10 million to allocate in its first year (roughly equivalent to the $11 million [£4 million] the British government gave in the same year to the Arts Council of Great Britain). Such public funding for the arts began to address the double pressure of money on the art world. First, it made grants available to museums for the type of exhibition they would increasingly see as the only solution to their problems, namely big "box office" shows that would enormously increase the money they could make on admissions. Second, it began to open a channel of funding outside the system of the commercial gallery by helping the kind of service-oriented organizations that operated what came to be called alternative spaces.

But addressing financial pressure is also a way of feeding it. As would soon become apparent, the house that the NEA had built was also constructing a new cultural "subject" to inhabit it; and, as Guy Debord had already predicted at the end of the fifties, it would be impossible to address the nature of that subject without speaking ■ at the same time of "spectacle."

A decade after the NEA was established the effects were beginning to show. In 1976 the Metropolitan Museum in New York opened the "Treasures of Tutankhamen," a lavish display popularly known as the "King Tut" exhibition that brought record numbers to the museum, consolidating the new form of spectacular exhibition, now routinely referred to as "blockbuster," that had been introduced in 1969 with the Met's crowd-pleasing "Harlem on My Mind" show. A few years later, in 1980, the Museum of Modern Art took Picasso's recent death as the opportunity to put its entire painting and sculpture collection in storage so that it could house a complete retrospective of the Spanish master. Crowds lined up around the block, and tickets were reserved months in advance. The museum, formerly so assiduous in accompanying its exhibitions with carefully researched catalogues, chose this time to offer a lavishly produced picture book, without texts and nearly without scholarly apparatus. The "complete" Picasso unfolded in floor after floor of galleries in an atmosphere of crowd-driven excitement. It was an atmosphere—feeding off itself, so to speak—that grew increasingly familiar as the blockbuster exhibition became a staple, often structured around the theme of gold ("King Tut's Treasures," "The Search for Alexander" [Mycenean precious objects]) but always geared to the broadest taste (van Gogh, Impressionism, Matisse, Impressionism, Cézanne, Impressionism ...).

The gold shows

It was not the broadest taste, however, that shaped the programs of the alternative spaces but, rather, an escape from the very commercialism that the museum's contemporary courting of that taste represented. Partly in reaction to the sixties boom in the art market, many artists took flight from a practice rooted either in the creation of marketable objects or in the "user-friendliness" of traditional mediums. The alternative space became a theater of the experimental and the ephemeral: video, performance, music, mammoth-scale mixed-media installations, site-specific works that were quasi-architectural.

In 1971, 112 Greene Street opened its doors to welcome the work ▲ of Gordon Matta-Clark, Richard Nonas, Gene Highstein, George Trakis, and Charles Simonds. In 1971, The Kitchen Center, a • response to excited speculations about the coming impact of video, began life in the kitchen of the Broadway Central Hotel and then moved in 1973 to Broome Street [**1**]. As a performance and video space, it hosted Vito Acconci, William Wegman (born 1942), and ■ Lawrence Weiner; in the domain of music, it sponsored John Cage, Steve Reich, and Philip Glass.

Perhaps the most symptomatic organization of this type was the Institute for Urban Resources, founded by Alanna Heiss. Impressed by her experience of the freely available studio and

▲ 1936 • 1987 ■ 1957a

▲ 1967a • 1973 ■ 1968b, 1974

1 • Vito Acconci, *VD Lives/TV Must Die*, 1978
Rubber, cable, bowling balls, and video with sound. Installation at The Kitchen Center, May–November 1978

exhibition facilities she had seen in London, particularly at St. Catherine's Dock where Bridget Riley and Peter Sedgely ran a warehouse called simply "The Space," Heiss set up an organization to provide these same services in New York; by 1973, the Institute had moved into the Clocktower in Lower Manhattan—the upper floors of an office block designed in 1912 by McKim, Mead, and White. In 1976 the Institute acquired P.S.1, a derelict public school building in Queens, which it rented from New York City for twenty years at the cost of $1 per year. Rebaptized Project Studios 1, P.S.1 now had studio space to offer on a vast scale along with acres of exactly the "alternative" space required by the kind of art that had in part been bred by such arenas in the first place. In June 1976, P.S.1 opened "Rooms," its first exhibition of such work.

The third term in this symbiosis between kinds of space and kinds of work was, of course, money. By 1976 The Kitchen Center was operating on a $200,000 budget, nearly half of which was being supplied by the federal government. Brian O'Doherty, who had succeeded Henry Geldzahler as director of the NEA's Visual Arts Program, was particularly enthusiastic about alternative spaces and was increasingly willing to fund them. Support for these service-organizations thus followed the establishment of the government's Art in Public Places program, which had already begun to institutionalize, and thus deradicalize, Earthwork art.

Founded on a shoestring and without much thought of real survival, these projects were suddenly becoming administrative operations of their own. Artists Space, an exhibition venue and slide register for artists unaffiliated with commercial galleries, was begun to take advantage of the public money now available. In 1976, it moved into the Fine Arts Building, a piece of Soho real estate temporarily donated by its owner, which housed the offices of other organizations such as Richard Foreman's Ontological-Hysteric Theater and the New Museum.

By the late eighties, more than a decade after this initial institutionalization of alternative spaces, a peculiar fusion began to appear between the two consequences of the money pressures of the sixties. The museum, its blockbuster mentality still intact, now began to see the alternative space itself as a kind of commercial opportunity, in the form of something like an art theme park.

Nowhere was this more spectacularly evident than in the restructuring of the self-image of the Solomon R. Guggenheim Museum in New York, wrought through the activities of its new director, Thomas Krens. Having sold the Massachusetts legislature the idea of converting a massive (750,000 square feet) derelict factory site in the western part of the state into a huge art-exhibition space and hotel-and-shopping complex, so that a $35 million bond issue was voted in 1989 to begin the project (called MassMoCA), Krens was catapulted from a small college museum position into leadership of the Guggenheim in the same year. Instantly, he began to reconceive the institution as a global operation and started to explore opening Guggenheim "branches" in Europe (Salzburg, Venice, and Moscow were all discussed), in Asia (Tokyo), and, of course, in Massachusetts (the Guggenheim/MassMoCA). One such branch was realized, in Bilbao, Spain, with a spectacular structure designed by the American architect Frank Gehry (born 1929) **[2]** and organized according to Krens's master plan, in which the local government pays for the building and its operating costs in addition to supplying a massive annual fee to the Guggenheim in exchange for the museum's programming services (the delivery of temporary

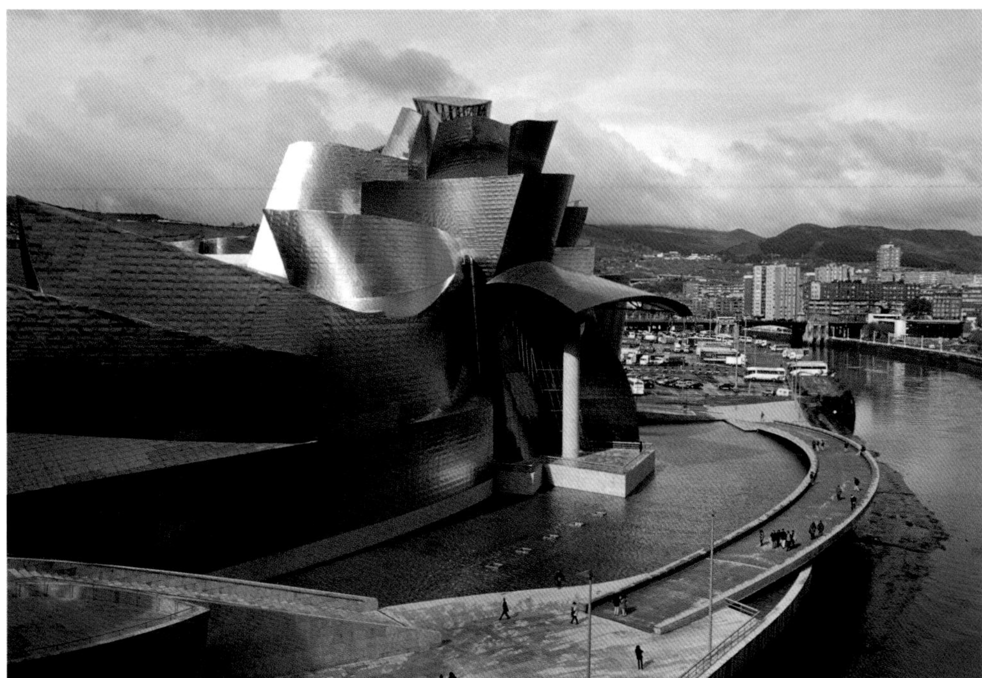

2 • Frank O. Gehry, Guggenheim Museum, Bilbao, Spain

exhibitions as well as the temporary circulation into the site of the Guggenheim's own permanent collections).

Leveraging the collection

Participating in the very logic of globalization that was reshaping the economic sphere at large, Krens's plan exploits the capitalist idea of centralizing and consolidating the operations through which a "product" is conceived (and sometimes made) and then of reaping the economic benefits of multiple markets in which to deliver this "product." If the "product" here is in part curatorial (the planning of exhibitions, the writing of catalogues, etc.), it is also made up of something that had never before been thought of under such a rubric, namely, works of art. And, further, the idea of propelling the works in one's collection into circulation in order to fulfill obligations to one's foreign outlets partakes of the attitude toward capital accumulation that had become epidemic within the free-market spirit of the eighties: leveraging, in which outsized amounts of money are borrowed on the basis of current assets. By shifting the collection from an earlier condition as untouchable cultural patrimony to a new state in which it inhabits the credit sector, this move participates in what is characteristic of "late" capitalism's falling rate of profit: the forced unlocking of noninvested surplus capital and the propulsion of it into motion. This is the way late capitalism has industrialized sectors of social life—such as leisure, sport, and art—hitherto thought impenetrable by industry's hallmarks: mechanization, standardization, overspecialization, and division of labor. As the Belgian economist Ernest Mandel (1923–95) described it: "Far from representing a 'post industrial society' late capitalism thus constitutes generalized universal industrialization for the first time in history."

If the foregoing provides more than just an interesting example of socioeconomic historical shifts during the final decades of the twentieth century but goes on to address developments deep within the production and experience of art itself, this is because the model of the globalized museum, being spatial rather than temporal, represents—as Krens has been the first to insist—a shift in discourse. The modern museum was resolutely historical, endlessly rehearsing the unfolding of modernism's discoveries in the field of formal research, of social analysis, of psychological rebellion. In order to mount this narrative, such a museum had to be encyclopedic. The new museum, Krens argued, would need to forgo this array, replacing it with just a few artists shown in great quantity over vast amounts of space. History would thus be jettisoned in favor of a kind of intensity of experience, an aesthetic charge that is not so much temporal (historical) as it is now radically spatial.

Specifically lodging his own conversion from the old type of museum "discourse" to the new one within his experience of Minimalism and within the effect of the mammoth exhibition sites recently set up for its display (such as warehouses in Schafhausen, ▲ Germany, or Donald Judd's airplane hangars in Marfa, Texas), Krens set out to acquire Minimalist work *en masse*, purchasing the extensive Panza collection for $30 million (and selling three of the Guggenheim's modern masterworks, including a major Kandinsky, in order to do so). For it was Minimalism, seen in long rows of glistening, inter-reflecting cubes or elusive aureoles of fluorescent light or gleaming pavements of steel plates, that provided Krens with the model for this idea of art as pure intensity [**3**].

Now if Krens's hallucinatory version of Minimalism—Minimalism as pure spectacle—could be the basis for a vision of the museum as scintillating funfair, occupying multiple sites around the world, like Disneyland, this is because something had happened in the perception of Minimalism itself, something that had reprogrammed the movement from the meanings and experiences it had supported in the sixties to this new condition in the late eighties and

▲ 1965

▲ nineties, a condition that critic Fredric Jameson would call "the hysterical sublime." Nothing could be farther from the hallucinatory than the experience Minimalism originally sought. Denying that the work of art is an encounter between two previously fixed and complete entities—on the one hand, the work as a repository of known forms: the cube or prism as a kind of geometric given; and on the other, the viewer as an integral, biographically elaborated subject who cognitively grasps these forms because he or she knows them in advance—Minimalism tried to make the work "happen" on a perceptual knife-edge, at the interface between the work and its beholder. Further, it understood this experience as going beyond the visual to connect with the full bodily sensorium. Its model of perception was one that would break with what it saw as the decorporealized and therefore bloodless, algebraicized condition of abstract painting, in which a visuality cut loose from the rest of the body and now remade in the model of modernism's drive toward autonomy had become the very picture of an entirely rationalized, instrumentalized, serialized subject. Its insistence on the immediacy of the experience, understood as a bodily immediacy—feeling • the gravitational pull of Richard Serra's *House of Cards* in one's stomach, for example —was intended as a release from the drive of modernist painting toward an increasingly positivist abstraction.

But the contradiction lodged within this ambition was that if the desire was to invoke bodily plenitude as a resistance against and compensation for the serialized, stereotyped, banalized character of modern life, the means the Minimalists used were double-edged. For Plexiglas and aluminum, chosen to destroy the interiority signaled by traditional sculpture's wood or stone, were also materials of commodity production; simple polygons, invoked as vehicles of perceptual immediacy, were also forms of rationalized mass production; and repetitive, aggregate arrangements, used as a resistance to traditional composition, deeply partakes of just that serialization that structures consumer capitalism. Thus, even while it wished to attack commodification and technologization, Minimalism paradoxically always carried the codes of those very conditions. It is this potential that is then released by the museum newly organized as funfair exploitation of a simulacral Minimalism.

Houses of cards

Such cultural reprogramming has been characterized by Fredric Jameson as the inner logic of modern art's own relation to advanced capital, a relation in which, in their very resistance to a particular manifestation of capital—to technology, say, or commodification, or the reification of the subject of mass production—artists produce an alternative to that phenomenon which can also be read as a function of it, another version of the very thing against which they were reacting. Thus while the artist might be creating a utopian alternative to, or a compensation for, a certain nightmare induced by industrialization, he is at the very same time projecting an imaginary space that, if it is shaped by the structural features of that same nightmare, works to produce the possibility for its receiver to fictively occupy the territory of what will be a next, more advanced level of capital. The globalized museum, its contents a display of derealized, simulacral spectacle, becomes another example of the working out of this logic.

FURTHER READING

Hal Foster, "The Crux of Minimalism," *The Return of the Real* (Cambridge, Mass.: MIT Press, 1996)
Fredric Jameson, *Postmodernism, or The Cultural Logic of Late Capitalism* (Durham, N.C.: Duke University Press, 1991)
Rosalind Krauss, "The Cultural Logic of the Late Capitalist Museum," *October*, no. 54, Fall 1990
Brian O'Doherty, "Public Art and the Government: A Progress Report," *Art in America*, vol. 62, no. 3, May 1974, and *Inside the White Cube: The Ideology of the Gallery Space* (Berkeley and Los Angeles: University of California Press, 1999)
Phil Patton, "Other Voices, Other Rooms: The Rise of the Alternative Space," *Art in America*, vol. 65, no. 4, July 1977

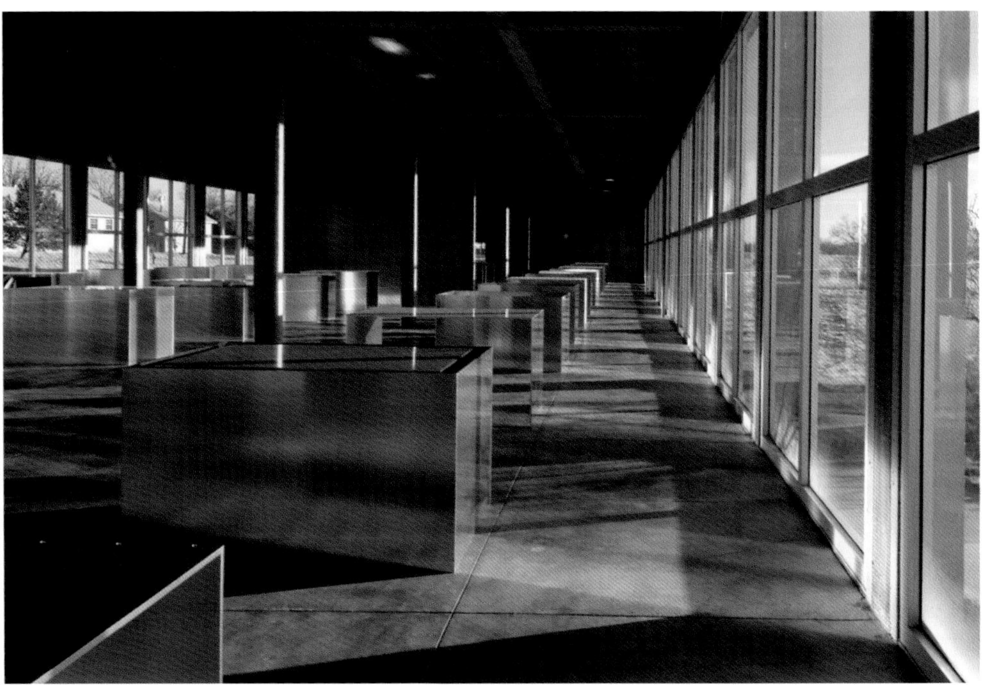

3 • Donald Judd, *100 Untitled works in mill aluminum*, 1982–6 (detail)
Permanent collection at the Chinati Foundation, Marfa, Texas

▲ 1984b • 1969

1977

The "Pictures" exhibition identifies a group of young artists whose strategies of appropriation and critiques of originality advance the notion of "postmodernism" in art.

1970–1979

In early 1977 the critic Douglas Crimp was invited by Helene ▲ Winer, the director of Artists Space, to mount a show of artists relatively new to New York: Troy Brauntuch, Jack Goldstein, Sherrie Levine (born 1947), Robert Longo, and Philip Smith. • Winer, who would later open the gallery Metro Pictures, steered Crimp toward young artists who, like others in their milieu—Cindy Sherman (born 1954), Barbara Kruger (born 1945), Louise Lawler (born 1947), and so on—were linked not by any one medium (they used photography, film, and performance, as well as traditional modes such as drawing) but by a new sense of the image as "picture"—that is, as a palimpsest of representations, often found or "appropriated," rarely original or unique, that complicated, even contradicted, the claims of authorship and authenticity so important to most modern aesthetics. "We are not in search of sources of origins," Crimp wrote, "but of structures of signification: underneath each picture there is always another picture." "Picture" was meant to transcend any given medium, delivering its message equally from the pages of magazines, books, billboards, and all other forms of mass culture. Further, it mocked the idea that a specific medium might serve as a resistant fact, a kind of bedrock of truth that might itself serve as an aesthetic origin in the modernist sense, whether by "truth to materials" or as revealed ■ essence. "Pictures" have no specific medium, they are as transparent as beams of light, as flimsy as decals meant to dissolve in water.

The postmodernist "picture"

As this collective work developed over the next few years, it became clear that the challenge to authorship was most radical in Levine's practice. In 1980, with her series *Untitled, After Edward Weston*, she blatantly pirated a group of images from those Weston had taken in 1925 of his young son Neil posed nude and cropped to include no more than the boy's torso [**1**]. Absolutely fusing her own status as author with that of Weston's, Levine was seen as going beyond merely challenging his legal status as the creator, and therefore the holder of the copyright to his own work. Instead, her appropriation was taken as extending to Weston's very claim to originality, in the sense of being the origin of his images. For in framing his son's body in such a way as to yield a series of graceful nude torsos,

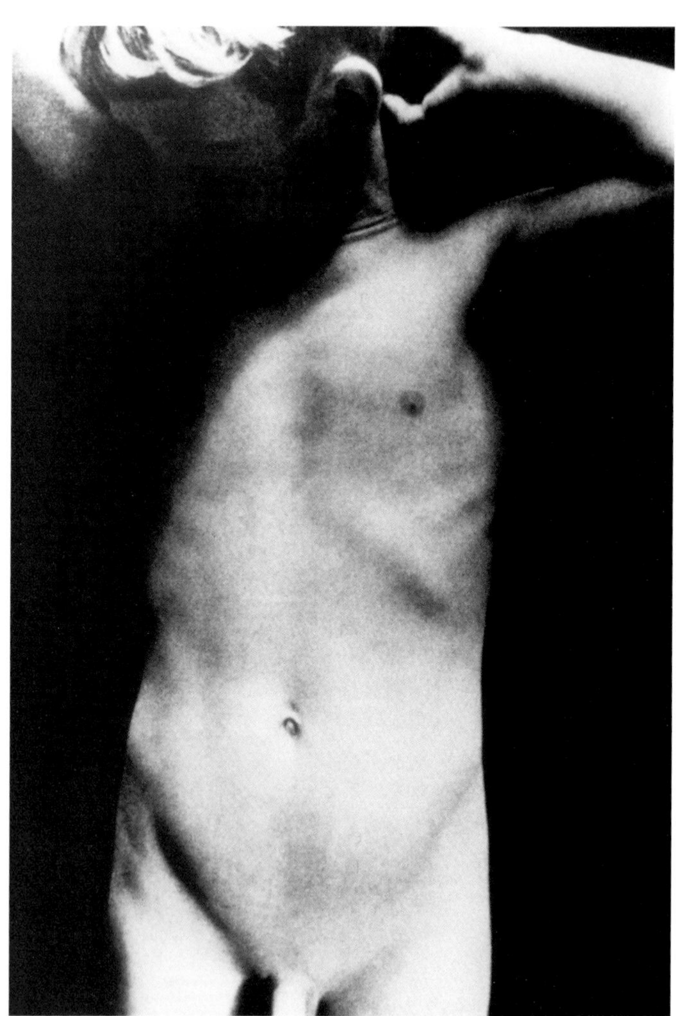

1 • Sherrie Levine, *Untitled, After Edward Weston I*, 1980
Photograph, 25.4 x 20.3 (10 x 8)

it could be argued that Weston was in fact helping himself to one of the most culturally disseminated visual tropes in Western culture: going back certainly to the male nude of Greek high classicism, itself the model for endless Roman copies, but filtered through the form in which these antiquities were received in the post-Renaissance world, namely as decapitated, armless fragments, the cut-off torso had come to symbolize the body's rhythmic wholeness. The "author" of this image is, therefore, dazzlingly multiple: from the nameless antique sculptors who trafficked in copies, to the teams of

▲ 1976 • 1980 ■ 1914, 1921, 1960b, 1962c

archaeologists who excavated ruins, to the museum curators who put these bodies on display, to the modern advertisers who use versions of such images to promote their products. It is this perspective that Levine's violation of Weston's "authorship" opens onto his work, setting up a long line of claimants to this privilege and making a mockery of the very idea of Weston himself as the image's origin.

That Levine would have dramatized this appropriation with a photograph of another photograph was intended, moreover, to address the special role that photography itself had had in dispelling the mystique of "origin" that had settled onto the work of art. Belonging to a generation of artists for whom the lessons ▲ of Walter Benjamin's seminal 1936 essay "The Work of Art in the Age of Mechanical Reproduction" were now second nature, Levine thoroughly understood the condition of the photograph as a "multiple without an original." Thus the cult-value of the unique object, the artistic original whose aesthetic magic or "aura" would be voided by the invalidity of a copy or a fake, was held up to question by the very nature of photography. Benjamin: "From a photographic negative ... one can make any number of prints; to ask for the 'authentic' print makes no sense." Indeed, one of the motives of the "Pictures" artists was to counter the growing market for fine photography, with its canceled negatives and vintage prints, with the lowly, derisive term "picture."

Building on this demystification of one type of origin (the aesthetic original), it was easy for Levine to transfer it to another (the author's originality). Photography, she implied, only made it technically easier and more transparent to do the kind of stealing—politely called "appropriation"—that has always been endemic to the "fine arts" whose fundamentally decorative status photography now reveals. As Benjamin's essay had already predicted: "Earlier much futile thought had been devoted to the question of whether photography is an art. The primary question—of whether the very invention of photography had not transformed the entire nature of art—was not raised." Levine and other appropriation artists were now raising it. One of the terms under which their critique sailed was "postmodernism."

Although not represented in the "Pictures" show, Louise Lawler most consistently took up this term to refer to her own production, as in show after show—"How Many Pictures," "It Could Be Elvis, and Other Pictures," "Paint, Walls, Pictures"—she integrated her work into the serialized world of mass production, injecting her photographs into the little domes of glass paperweights, projecting her images in the ephemeral form of slides, presenting her output as a kind of cultural detritus: matchbook covers, souvenir glasses, phonograph records. And in the grip of the same logic that had operated for Levine, Lawler extended the structure of multiplicity from the technical fact of copies generated from a matrix to the aesthetic domain of authorship, thereby dissolving herself as her work's point of origin into the bath of a diverse social continuum.

Many of her photographs bear titles like *Arranged by Barbara and Eugene Schwartz* **[2]**; *Desk Light by Ernesto Gismondi*, to signal

2 • Louise Lawler, *Arranged by Barbara and Eugene Schwartz*, 1982
Black-and-white photograph, 40.6 x 59.7 (16 x 23½)

the mutations in authorship they are documenting. The submission of works of art to the forces of the market has meant that they are not just integrated into the world of commodities, thereby taking on the personality of their owners, like the artfully ▲ arranged wall of August Sander portraits hanging in Mr. and Mrs. Schwartz's study. It has also meant that the form of commodity to which they are assimilated is one in which their exchange-value exists at the disembodied level of the sign, making them the equivalent of so many fashion logos worth far more than the incidental handbag or leather moccasin to which they might be attached. This • status of art as nothing but "sign exchange value" is implied again and again by Lawler's images in which, in a work like *Pollock and Tureen* (1984), a dining room sideboard neatly splits our attention between a piece of eighteenth-century porcelain and the segment of the Jackson Pollock painting we can see on the wall above it; or in *Who Are You Close To?* (1990), where Andy Warhol's *S&H Green Stamps* hang on a magenta wall between symmetrically placed green Chinese horses, all of it a study in color coordination (magenta and green) worthy of *House and Gardens* magazine. By ceding her compositional privileges to the collectors of the works, by relinquishing her stylistic prerogatives to a whole range of mass-media vehicles—the photographic styles of fashion magazines, of high-end advertising, of brute documentation—and by sustaining the implied logical reciprocity through which "sign exchange value" will overtake not only Pollock's work but her own as well, Lawler suspends her own claims as author.

Readymade selves

All of these "pictures" issues generated by photography and affecting the fine-arts triumvirate—originality, original, origin—by leaching the autonomous world of the art object into the explosive domain of mass culture, found their way into the work of Cindy Sherman, a contemporary and colleague of Levine's and Lawler's. Elaborating the series she called *Untitled Film Stills* between 1977 and 1980 **[3, 4]**, Sherman rang extraordinary changes on the idea of self-portraiture as she disappeared behind the guises of the

▲ 1935

▲ 1929, 1935 • 1980

movie stars she impersonated (Monica Vitti, Barbara Bel Geddes, Sophia Loren), the characters she implied (gun moll, battered wife, heiress), the directors whose styles she pastiched (Douglas Sirk, John Sturges, Alfred Hitchcock), and the film genres she dissimulated (film noir, suspense, melodrama).

Beyond jettisoning her selfhood as author and individual, however, the implication of these works is that the very condition of selfhood is built on representation: on the stories children are told or the books adolescents read; on the pictures the media provide through which social types are generated and internalized; on the resonance between filmic narratives and fantasy projections. Hence the transparency of the persona to the roles and situations that form in the public image-world, the one cannily projected first by film and then by television. If Sherman's work could be authored by so many Hollywood gambits, her pictures seem to be saying, this is because Sherman herself, standing in for all of us, is constructed by those same gambits. And in this form of the argument, not only does every author appropriate his or her images, but every author appropriates his or her "self."

By the mid-eighties and in the aftermath of feminist arguments ▲ such as Laura Mulvey's "Visual Pleasure and Narrative Cinema," however, it was no longer possible to see Sherman as standing in "for all of us," or to take the manipulations operated by Hollywood film as gender neutral. Not only was it obvious that the roles in

3 • Cindy Sherman, *Untitled Film Still #7*, 1978
Black-and-white photograph, 25.4 x 20.3 (10 x 8)

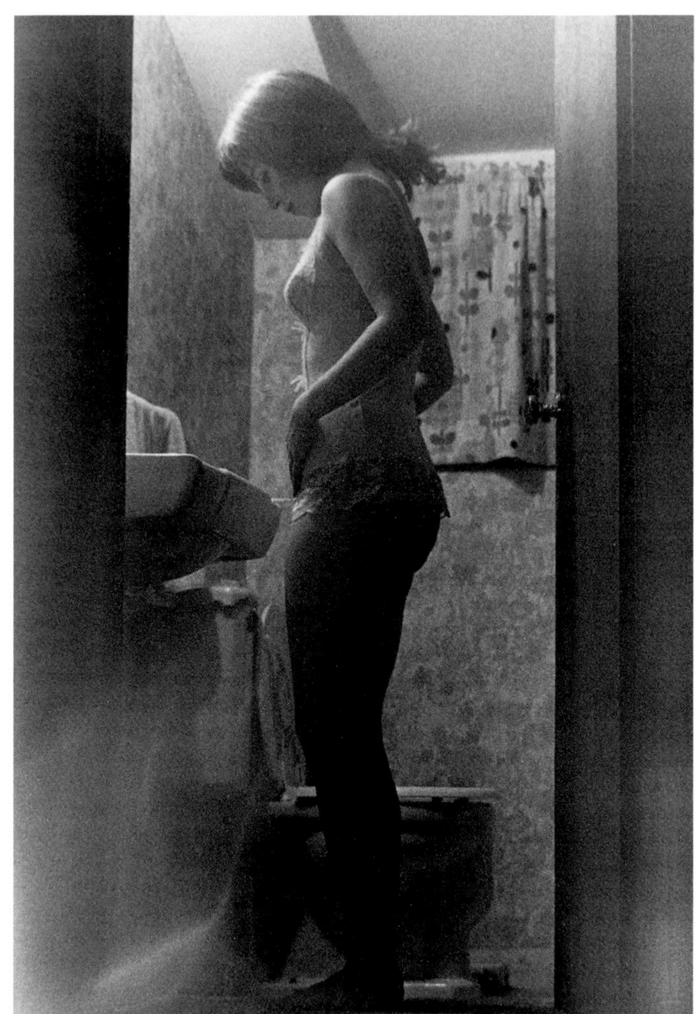

4 • Cindy Sherman, *Untitled Film Still #39*, 1979
Black-and-white photograph, 25.4 x 20.3 (10 x 8)

question in Sherman's *Film Stills* were feminine, but the feminist argument according to which those roles should be understood had shifted. Mulvey was no longer exhorting a kind of consciousness-raising by which women were asked to put aside the roles into which they had been cast, like a set of disguises they could change if only they would. She was making a far more structural argument according to which the division of labor under patriarchy could not be shifted: men were the actors in a world in which women were the passive objects; men were the speakers, the makers of meaning, while women—the spoken for—were the bearers of meaning. If Hollywood followed this pattern, producing female stars as somnolent visual fetishes and male ones as vigorous agents, this was because these assignments were hard-wired into the social psyche, unavoidable. Accordingly, Sherman's settings came to be analyzed less for their mass-cultural associations and more for their visual vectors: the traces of a male gaze trained on a waiting ▲ and defenseless female; the ways the female reacts to this gaze, entreating it, ignoring it, placating it.

As Mulvey's essay had also argued, the division of roles in terms of action and vision also apply to—or are structurally imbricated with—language. If she says that the woman is the bearer of

▲ 1975

▲ 1975, 1993a

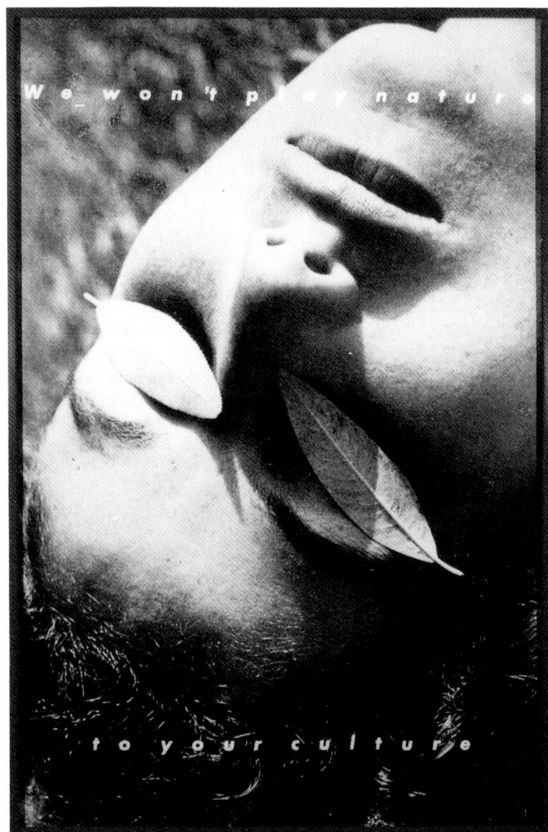

5 • Barbara Kruger, *We Won't Play Nature to Your Culture*, 1983

meaning she is referring to the sense in which the woman's body is organized by what the French psychoanalyst Jacques Lacan called the signifier of difference, namely the phallus that she does not have but that—marked by castration and its threat—she is. Another way of describing this would be to say that her body—complete in its beauty but damaged in its phallic absence—is the ▲ fetish that marks the site of a lack. It is on this site and according to this lack that the difference that founds the very possibility of meaning, or language, is built.

The work of Barbara Kruger, another contemporary and colleague of the "Pictures" group, is constructed on acknowledging this linguistic division of labor only to suspend it. Like Sherman's, Lawler's, and Levine's, the basis of Kruger's work is appropriated mass-cultural imagery, here in the form of found photographs taken from magazines and other mass-circulation sources. But onto this visual foundation she collages trenchant verbal statements. In *We Won't Play Nature to Your Culture* [**5**], for example, these words ride atop the photograph of a young woman sunbathing with her eyes masked by leaves. Referring to the binaries that structure not only language but all cultural forms of meaning—the nature/cultural opposition being almost as fundamental as the male/female one—Kruger's young woman is indeed "playing" nature. As she lies prone on a barely visible field of grass, not only do the leaves covering her eyes encourage a sense of her as yielding to the natural conditions of her surroundings, ● like Roger Caillois's mimetic animals, but also this mask confirms the sexual dynamics of vision as described by Mulvey: the young woman is the object, not the agent of vision.

Our bodies, ourselves

But working at cross purposes to this confirmation of the gender stereotypes is the text that mobilizes another aspect of the linguistic ▲ analysis proposed by the structuralists. This is the argument about the nature of pronouns put forward by the French linguist Émile ● Benveniste. Dividing language into two forms, narrative and discourse, the first the form of historical or objective accounts, the second the form of interactive dialogue (conversation), he pointed to another type of division of labor, that between the third person pronouns—he, they—joined to the (historical) past tense, and the first and second person pronouns—I, you, we—connected with the present tense. The former, he says, is the matrix through which purportedly objective, scientific fact is related and it is thus the medium of knowledge. The latter is the medium of active, lived experience, through which speakers assume their subjecthood, taking on the responsibility of entering the position "I." This is the dimension of language that the linguists would also call the "performative" and what it lacks in supposed truth-value it makes up in its assumption of power and agency. The two messages of Kruger's image are, then, decidedly "mixed," one playing to the narrative system in which the woman is the object of knowledge, her passivity constituting its very "truth," the other taking up the discursive system and, saying "I" (or in this case "we"), assuming a performative position. In doing so, the woman's voice aggressively returns the male gaze.

The work of these four women constituted an important part of what was identified as "critical postmodernism," a term that associated their critique with that of the theorists of mass culture who, ■ from Adorno to Habermas, had denounced the "consciousness industry." This qualifier was necessary to differentiate the work from another form of postmodernism that was eagerly promoted by the very media the "Pictures" group was exposing. For an antimodernist postmodernism had declared war on "formalism" by returning to ◆ the classicist modes of painting in oil and sculpting in bronze (for example, the Italian Sandro Chia), as it waved goodbye to a progressive notion of history by eclectically assuming odd assortments of past pictorial styles, as though none of these had any historically fixed, internal meaning (for example, the American David Salle). The "Pictures" group, insofar as it declared that artistic mediums were no longer value neutral but had now, infected by the (communications) media, become part of the battle zone of modern culture, was itself an emblem of postmodernism understood as critique.

FURTHER READING

Douglas Crimp, *On the Museum's Ruins* (Cambridge, Mass.: MIT Press, 1993)

Hal Foster, "Postmodernism," *The Anti-Aesthetic* (Seattle: Bay Press, 1983) and "The Crux of Minimalism," *The Return of the Real* (Cambridge, Mass.: MIT Press, 1998)

Craig Owens, *Beyond Recognition: Representation, Power, and Culture* (Berkeley and Los Angeles: University of California Press, 1992)

▲ Introduction 1, 1931 ● 1930b ▲ Introduction 3 ● Introduction 4 ■ Introduction 2, 1988 ◆ 1984b

1980–1989

586 1980 Metro Pictures opens in New York: a new group of galleries emerges in order to exhibit young artists involved in a questioning of the photographic image and its uses in news, advertising and fashion. HF

box • Jean Baudrillard RK

590 1984a Victor Burgin delivers his lecture "The Absence of Presence: Conceptualism and Post-Modernisms": the publication of this and other lectures by Allan Sekula and Martha Rosler signals a new approach to the legacies of Anglo-American photoconceptualism and to the writing of photographic history and theory. BB

596 1984b Fredric Jameson publishes "Postmodernism, or the Cultural Logic of Late Capitalism," as the debate over postmodernism extends beyond art and architecture into cultural politics, and divides into two contrary positions. HF

box • Cultural studies RK

600 1986 "Endgame: Reference and Simulation in Recent Painting and Sculpture" opens in Boston: as some artists play on the collapse of sculpture into commodities, others underscore the prominence of design and display. HF

605 1987 The first ACT-UP action is staged: activism in art is reignited by the AIDS crisis, as collaborative groups and political interventions come to the fore, and a new kind of queer aesthetics is developed. HF

box • The US Art Wars HF

612 1988 Gerhard Richter paints *October 18, 1977*: German artists contemplate the possibility of the renewal of history painting. BB

box • Jürgen Habermas BB

617 1989 "Les Magiciens de la terre," a selection of art from several continents, opens in Paris: postcolonial discourse and multicultural debates affect the production as well as the presentation of contemporary art. HF

box • Aboriginal art HF

1980

Metro Pictures opens in New York: a new group of galleries emerges in order to exhibit young artists involved in a questioning of the photographic image and its uses in news, advertising, and fashion.

"I don't think of myself as a photographer. I've engaged questions regarding photography's role in culture ... but it is an engagement with a problem rather than a medium." With this statement Sarah Charlesworth (born 1947) spoke for an entire group of young artists who, along with Cindy Sherman, Barbara ▲ Kruger, Sherrie Levine, and Louise Lawler, came to sudden prominence in the late seventies and early eighties—artists such as Richard Prince (born 1949), James Welling (born 1951), James Casebere (born 1953), and Laurie Simmons (born 1949), among others. Some were recent graduates of vanguard schools like the California Institute of the Arts (CalArts), where teachers like John Baldesarri, Douglas Huebler, and Michael Asher had initiated them • into the strategies of Conceptual art and institutional critique. But they were all marked by new developments of the time, such as an increased sophistication in feminist theory, which foregrounded the question of sexual difference in visual representation, and a qualitative transformation in the mass media, which changed the entire context of image production, distribution, and reception. If some of their predecessors contended with the divided "legacy of Jackson Pollock," some of these baby-boomers struggled with the ■ ambiguous model of Andy Warhol, who appeared to collude with the spectacular image-world that he also exposed.

The serial and the simulacral

Most of these artists used photography along the lines described by Charlesworth: rather than reground the medium "in its area of competence" in a modernist manner as understood by formalist critics, they worked to problematize its usual claims to expressive ◆ abstraction or documentary referentiality in a postmodernist fashion. This problematizing operated on several fronts: on one side they were opposed to art photography that assumed the values of the unique image associated with painting; on another side they were suspicious of media photography that worked to produce effects of consensus in the news and of persuasion in advertising. Often made of purloined images, this photobased art was also positioned against neo-Expressionist painting and its forced reclamation of the auratic artist-genius. These postmodernists treated the photograph not only as a "serial" image, a multiple without an original print, but also as a "simulacral" image, a representation without a guaranteed referent in the world. That is, they tended to regard the photograph less as a physical trace or indexical imprint of reality than a coded construction that produces "effects of the real," and with different accents they worked to investigate these effects. In this exploration of the rhetoric of the photograph Roland Barthes was a crucial guide, as were Jean Baudrillard, Michel Foucault, and Gilles Deleuze for their accounts of the simulacrum, a notion that Baudrillard used to understand recent transformations in the commodity, and Foucault and Deleuze used to challenge old Platonic conceptions of representation.

As an editor of the short-lived journal *The Fox*, Sarah Charlesworth was involved with the Conceptual art of Joseph ▲ Kosuth and Art & Language in the mid-seventies. Feminism prompted her to make her own art, and her first pieces adapted Pop as well as Conceptual idioms in an emergent critique of media representations of women (here she was aligned with Kruger, Silvia Kolbowski, and many others). In 1977 Charlesworth initiated a series that drew on the alterations of newspaper formats in early Warhol as well as in early Dan Graham. For the month of September she photocopied the front pages of the *International Herald Tribune* and whited out everything except the masthead and the photographs. At first glance this subtraction produced arbitrary montages, but the patriarchal structuring of the news soon became apparent, especially through the dominant representation of male heads of state. Charlesworth also applied this strategy to an array of North American newspapers, with similar effects of manifest randomness and latent patterning. For example, in all the papers surveyed on April 21, 1978, one figure appears: the Italian minister Aldo Moro kidnapped and killed by the Red Brigade [**1**]. Here, with the simple device of "the assisted readymade," Charlesworth exposed the first priority of dominant media: the maintenance of state authority. In part this post-Watergate "hermeneutics of suspicion" concerning the news was also a critical reaction to the conservative turn in politics of the late seventies and early eighties.

Like some of her peers, Charlesworth proceeded to the patterning of images in advertising and fashion. In a series titled *Objects of Desire* she appropriated images from magazines, edited them further, then rephotographed them on saturated fields of single

▲ 1977, 1993a • 1968b, 1970, 1971, 1984a ■ 1949, 1960b, 1960c, 1964b ◆ 1977, 1984b ▲ 1968b

colors. These fragments—of posed models and displayed accessories—pointed to a language of desire that is highly fetishistic, an effect that Charlesworth underscored with the fetishistic gloss of her own Cibachrome prints. Some of these works presented solitary traces of the female body such as a chic scarf, while others juxtaposed two images for critical comparison. In *Figures* (1983) a female torso wrapped in a dinner dress on a red ground is set next to a female body bound in fabric on a black ground; here, as the critic Abigail Solomon-Godeau wrote, "the (desirable) female body is bound not only by the gown, but by the cultural conventions of desirability, and the delimiting and defining convention of representation itself." Again like some of her peers, Charlesworth applied the strategy of a doubling of the stereotype in such a way as to expose its ideological or "mythical" operations (in the sense of ▲ Roland Barthes)—operations that work to naturalize the particular interests of one group, gender, or class.

Richard Prince also focused on the conventions of advertising and fashion images for what they reveal about subjective modeling. At stake in this patterning of images, Prince implies, is the patterning of identities, of identities *as* images, which are now shaped by media representation far more than was any older cultural form. In the mid-seventies he worked as a cataloguer in the periodical library of Time-Life Incorporated, where he collected images of models and products. He then arranged these images by type and rephotographed them, first in black and white, then in color, but always at the same scale in order to reveal the generic repetitions of poses and gestures, displays and effects **[2]**. Rather than the celebrity figures favored by Pop, Prince reframed anonymous subjects, and he did so less in a register of celebration or critique than in a mode of testing—a testing of our own ambivalent fascination with such models.

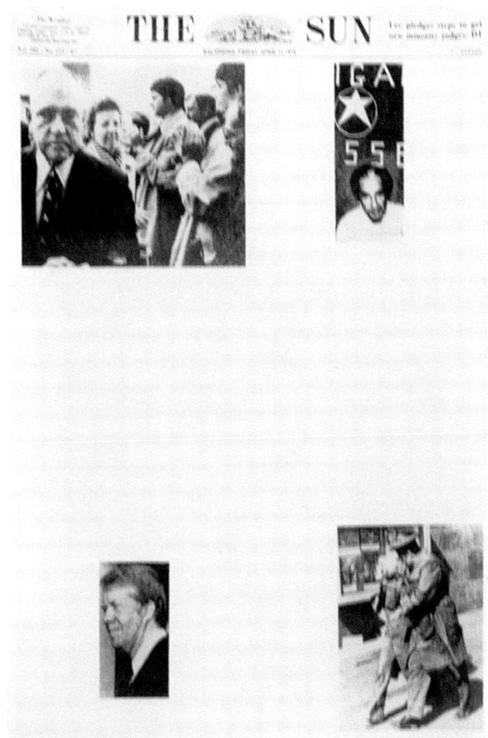

1 • Sarah Charlesworth, *April 21, 1978*, 1978
One of forty-five black-and-white prints composing one work, varying sizes, each c. 55.9 x 40.6 (22 x 16)

Jean Baudrillard (born 1929)

In the late sixties, French sociologist Jean Baudrillard led Marxian analysis into the structural-linguistic domain of the sign, arguing that it is signification that controls ideology. Beginning with *The System of Objects* (1968) and *The Society of Consumption* (1970), this project was developed in *For a Critique of the Political Economy of the Sign* (1972) and *The Mirror of Production* (1973). His most provocative formulation of this shift is the term "sign exchange value," which points to the displacement of exchange-value from commodities to their representatives, such as the logos of companies.

In order to think this displacement, Baudrillard focused on simulacra, in which reality is replaced by its representation. Disneyland is one of his favorite examples: "Disneyland is there to conceal the fact that it is the 'real' country, all of 'real' America, which *is* Disneyland (just as prisons are there to conceal the fact that it is the social in its entirety which is carceral)," he writes in "The Precession of Simulacra."

It is Baudrillard's conviction that the commodity and the sign have become one, facilitated by the operations of a "code" through which meanings are exchanged in discourse. Baudrillard was not happy with the idea of "commodity fetishism," which imagines objects endowed with magical value; instead, he argued, objects are abstracted into signifiers in order to enter into the exchange of meaning governed by the "code."

The effacement of objects by signifiers that turn them into meaning and prepare them for "exchange" occurs everywhere, Baudrillard argued, even on the body, where signifiers proliferate and replace physiological substance. "Rewriting the cultural order on the body," tattooes, bound feet, eye shadow, mascara, bracelets, and jewelry, all show that "the erotic is the reinscription of the erogenous in a homogeneous system of signs."

Like other postmodernist artists who use photography, Prince works in series, for only a serial structure can deliver the play of repetition and difference that interests him. In 1981 he began to rephotograph two genres of ads that traffic in semimythic lifestyles. The first involved the famous Malboro campaign with the Western cowboy, often on horseback, that associates cigarette smoking with macho masculinity. Prince developed a hyperbolic catalogue of this Western frontiersman in a manner that appeared equally suspicious of the legend and seduced by it. The second series concerned vacation ads of the beach, that utopia where sexual pleasure and family life are somehow made to coexist. In his version, however, the seaside vacationers, shot in grainy black-and-white against sunburst backgrounds, experience a holiday that looks like an atomic holocaust. Prince then turned to social subjects below the usual purview of the middle class. In *Entertainers*

▲ Introduction 3

2 • Richard Prince, *Untitled (four women looking in the same direction) #1–#4*, 1977–9
Set of four Ektacolor prints, 50.8 x 61 (20 x 24)

he rephotographed the murky photographs of nightclub performers used in newspaper ads, and floated them in black Plexiglas panels; frozen in lurid display, these blurry faces are offered up for our own obscure voyeurism. Later Prince grouped such images in formats that he called "gangs"—essentially slide sheets blown up to big grids that also capture a play of repetition and difference. Often the subjects are indeed gangs—motorcycle gangs and biker chicks, drag racers and surfers, and so on—"subcultures that operate outside the hegemony of high literacy," as the critic Jeffrey Rian has put it. Once again, as these figures "filter through the media and mutate in our minds," Prince offers up our own voyeurism for our inspection. Not as critical as the Barthesian analyses of Kruger or Charlesworth, his work is not as removed either; he admits to his own partial identification and ambivalent participation in the image-world on display.

Reality effects

The work of James Welling and James Casebere is more internal to photography, more committed to its traditions and techniques, but also more deconstructive of it as a result. Rather than challenge the referential dimension of the photograph, they insist on it, as the critic Walter Benn Michaels has argued, but in a nonrealist way that exploits the slight ambiguity of the photographic signifier. They are also less interested in simulation and seduction than in the differences between how we see and how the camera sees; in their photographs the "effects of the real" are all produced by staging and lighting, camera position, and image scale.

Welling opened this line of inquiry as early as 1974, while still a student at CalArts, with a videotape of scatterings of ash that resemble entire landscapes. In 1980, in New York, he photographed crinkled surfaces of aluminum foil in extreme close-up again with ambiguous effects—they could pass for semiabstract studies of rock formations by Minor White or of weathered doors by Aaron Siskind. A year later his photographs of pastry dough scattered on lush drapery also appeared equally representational and abstract, at once full of spatial depth and nothing but surface. With titles like *Wreckage*, *Island*, and *The Waterfall*, they evoke Romantic landscapes only enough to make us reflect on our own projections about photographic reality (here, as Barthes argued, "connotation" precedes "denotation," not vice versa as is usually thought). The very simplicity of means opens up these images to different readings: *In Search Of…* **[3]** suggests an alpine ridge or a glacial floe as well as flakes of dough caught in rifts of cloth. With Welling, the "search" for Romantic experience becomes a quest for elusive reference.

James Casebere has also played with the ambiguity of the photograph since the late seventies, but here the uncertainty is effected through quasi-architectural models, made of white mat board, plaster, and Styrofoam, which Casebere stages and lights like miniature movie sets. At once specific and generic, these tableaux only evoke their subjects, which, in his early work, tend to vernacular scenes of the American West, the Civil War, the ante-Bellum South, and so on. Sometimes these scenes are entirely fictional, as in *Sutpen's Cave* [**4**], which alludes to a neoclassical mansion built out of the wilderness by a diabolical character in William Faulkner's novel *Absalom! Absalom!* (1936). Like Welling, Casebere creates his reality effects through his medium and titles alone. But again these effects are only partial or part-way: all his images are suspended in a no man's land between model and referent, fiction and document. His places have the uncanny consistency of dreams or myths; they are akin to phantasms in which representation rises up to replace reality.

In all this photobased work the hierarchies of reality and representation and original and copy become somewhat unstable, and in this slight unfounding of the image is a subtle subverting of the viewer: the mastery that the photographs usually afford the subject—an empowered point of view and precision of vision—is partially withdrawn. Sometimes the viewer feels almost engulfed by these simulacra; as Deleuze writes, "the spectator is made part of the simulacrum, which is transformed and distorted according to his point of view." In this phantasmal disturbance the reality effects of the photograph are put into question, as are its conventional status as a "message without a code" (Barthes), as a document that renders things obvious and events natural. Twenty years ago this was still a critical insight, and challenges to the truth claims of photographic representation—in the news and elsewhere—were urgent. But more and more in our contemporary image-world the simulacral triumphs over the referential; perhaps what we need today is less a critique of representation than a critique of simulation.

4 • James Casebere, *Sutpen's Cave*, 1982
Silver-gelatin print, 40.6 x 50.8 (16 x 20)

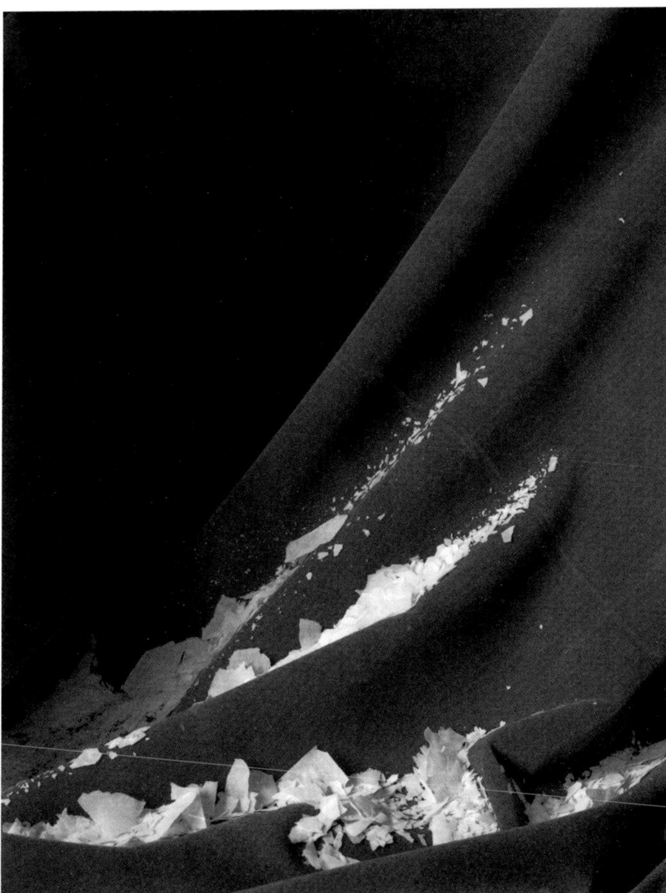

3 • James Welling, *In Search Of ...*, 1981
Silver-gelatin print, 22.9 x 17.8 (9 x 7)

FURTHER READING

Roland Barthes, *Image-Music-Text*, trans. Stephen Heath (New York: Hill and Wang, 1977)
Jean Baudrillard, *Selected Writings*, ed. Mark Poster (Stanford: Stanford University Press, 1988)
Gilles Deleuze, *The Logic of Sense*, trans. Mark Lester (New York: Columbia University Press, 1990)
Louis Grachoes (ed.), *Sarah Charlesworth: A Retrospective* (Santa Fe: SITE Santa Fe, 1997)
Jacques Guillot (ed.), *Richard Prince* (Grenoble: Centre National d'Art Contemporaine, 1988)
Sarah Rogers (ed.), *James Welling: Photographs 1974–1999* (Columbus: Wexner Center for the Arts, 2000)
Abigail Solomon-Godeau, *Photography at the Dock: Essays on Photographic History, Institutions and Practices* (Minneapolis: University of Minnesota Press, 1991)

1984a

Victor Burgin delivers his lecture "The Absence of Presence: Conceptualism and Post-Modernisms": the publication of this and other essays by Allan Sekula and Martha Rosler signals a new approach to the legacies of Anglo-American photoconceptualism and to the writing of photographic history and theory.

It is important to realize that the founding concerns of Conceptual art—the focus on analytical propositions and on linguistic ▲ definitions—had a visual correlative in an increasingly analytical • approach to the photographic image. If Postminimalist art had shifted the perception of language and of the body into the registers of performativity, photography's elementary indexicality had supplied the exacting medium with which these temporal and spatial dimensions could be recorded. Thus the photographic medium extended the Postminimalist concerns with the processes of production, specific locations, and the minute tracing of contingency and contextuality. Not surprisingly, photography's unique qualification to record the smallest spatio-temporal displacement and incremental or sequential performative changes made it also the ideal tool for Conceptualism's increasingly intense focus on the processes and the production of *signification* itself. British artist Victor Burgin's (born 1941) *Photopath* [1] demarcates that transition from contextual aesthetics to an analysis of photographic meaning at the very moment (1969) when Burgin was initiating the theorization of site-specificity in his crucial theoretical text "Situational Aesthetics," in the British journal *Studio International.*

Burgin's first book, *Work and Commentary: 1969–1973* from 1973, still adhered in its overall theoretical and artistic projects to the orthodoxies of late-sixties Anglo-American Conceptualism, in particular to the challenges posed by the late-modernist self-criticality of the Art & Language group and its journal *Art-Language.* But Burgin eventually became the first to systematically criticize that position in the pages of that very journal, arguing that "The optimum function of art is to modify institutionalized patterns of orientation towards the world and thus to serve as an agency of socialization. No art activity therefore is to be understood apart from the codes and practices of the society which contains it; art in use is bracketed ineluctably within ideology.... We must accept the responsibility of producing an art which has more than just Art as its content."

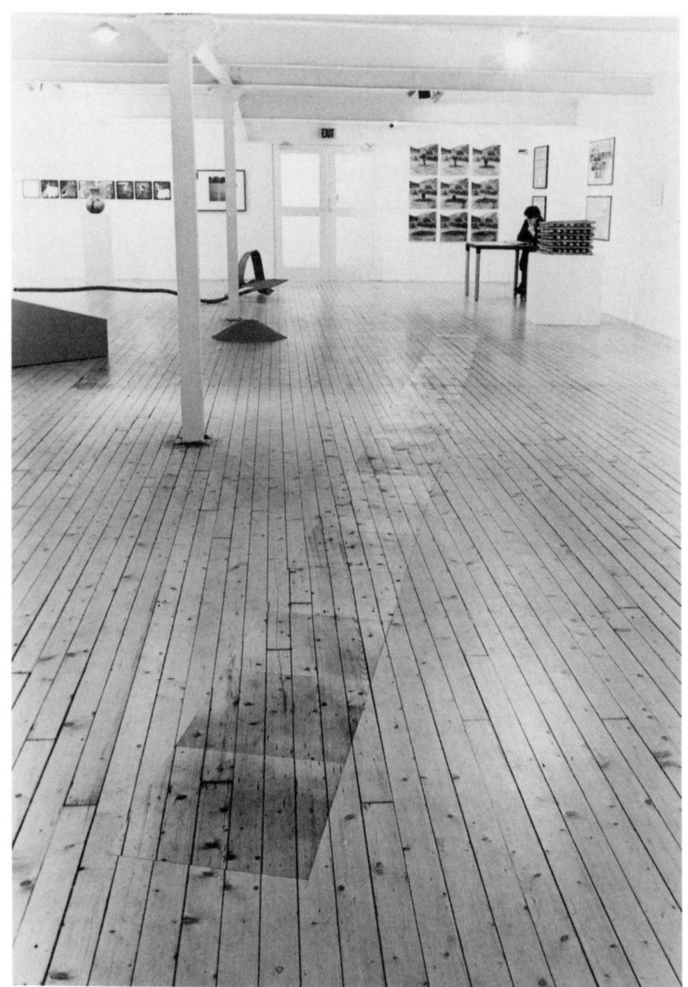

1 • Victor Burgin, *Photopath*, July 1969
Twenty-one photographs of twenty-one continuous sections of floor boards

■ Clement Greenberg's American-type formalism had kept English artists (up to and including the members of the Art & Language group) in its spell for an astonishingly long time. It was the discovery of two theoretical legacies, introduced initially to an Anglophone audience of filmmakers, artists, and writers by the editors of *Screen* magazine, that accelerated the disintegration of formalist modernism. The first one would be the rediscovery of ▲ Russian and Soviet Formalist thought; and the second one, the • encounter with French structuralist semiology and psychoanalytic theory from Freud to Lacan. Both discoveries provided a new ■ theoretical foundation for artists such as Burgin and Mary Kelly in England and would motivate Burgin to finally sever his ties with modernism and Conceptualism, as manifested in his 1984 essay "The Absence of Presence." If Burgin's work was largely based on

▲ 1968b • 1969 ■ 1960b ▲ 1915 • Introduction 1, Introduction 3 ■ 1975

semiology and the theories of the photographic image as they had been developed in several essays by Roland Barthes, the work of ▲ Michel Foucault would become Allan Sekula's (born 1951) central theoretical focus, eventually leading to his groundbreaking essay "The Body and the Archive" (1986). And Mary Kelly's Lacanian feminism would find its counterpart in Martha Rosler's (born 1943) highly politicized critique of photographic representation as much as in an activist definition of feminist and artistic practices.

The photographic turn

The legacy of photography entered American art of the sixties in several contradictory ways. First of all there was the incorporation of "found" photography in the work of Robert Rauschenberg and subsequently in that of Andy Warhol through which a peculiar • transformation of the photomontage aesthetics of Europe of the twenties took place. Secondly, but in a much more complicated and at first unrecognizable way, there were the multiple references back to the specifically American traditions of photography from the twenties on: the great tradition of American straight photography from Paul Strand to Walker Evans; and that of the Farm ■ Security Administration (FSA) photographers and the documentary tradition as it had been programmatically formulated in the thirties. It was thus in a variety of ways that artists of the early sixties, after Warhol, contributed to the reemergence of the photographic image in the context of neo-avant-garde production.

One of the first figures in the rise of what could be seen as a specifically photographic aesthetic was Ed Ruscha, whose books from ◆ the early sixties onward, starting with *Twenty-six Gasoline Stations* (1962) and *Every Building on the Sunset Strip* (1966), introduced a peculiar type of photography. Inasmuch that one could characterize this as amateurish and popularist, it was involved in the principle of deskilling the photographic image; and indeed it is in the context of Pop art (with its own methods of deskilling the work of art) that Ruscha's books were first received. In the dialogue between Ruscha and Warhol, the latter's use of "found" photographs was translated into a principle of treating parts of the urban landscape as "found" material, to be recorded by Ruscha in the most banal way possible.

By the mid-sixties a different type of photographic production emerged in what could be called the protoconceptual photography of Dan Graham. While largely still dependent upon the work of Ruscha, Graham placed his work in a more manifest dialogue with the traditions of American documentary photographers, and specifically with the work of Walker Evans. Graham's deadpan photographic images of vernacular architecture in New Jersey—such as the suburban housing developments of his *Homes for America* (1966–7)—hark back directly to Evans's deadpan photographs of industrial architecture in Pittsburgh. But as much as it establishes a continuity with vernacular architectural imagery, Graham's work operates a kind of distancing from the high, ambitious quality of thirties and forties photography. Adding the idea of vernacular, popular, photographic practice to that of vernacular architecture as image, Graham exacerbated Ruscha's original ▲ project of deskilling the making of the photograph. His use of a cheap hand-held camera, of cheap color film, and of cheap commercial printing creates results that look as if they had been taken on the run by a tourist lost in New Jersey.

In the context of Conceptual art, photography assumed numerous functions beyond those established by Graham. First of all it addressed the problem of the form of distribution for the work of art. Starting with Ruscha, photography was embraced as a device for insisting on the mediatization, or mass distribution, of the work of art, a device that therefore contributes to the dismantling of the conception of the work of art as unique object. Although Warhol had already teased painting's condition as a unique original, he had ultimately returned to this very condition in all instances of his production. The result was that while his paintings were determined by the photographic image and by the silkscreen process, the end product of this process was inevitably a unique original object. With Ruscha, the end product was in fact the multiple object, the cheaply produced book, open to mass distribution, which therefore positioned itself in manifest contradiction to the • Pop art painting with its "aura" paradoxically intact.

Secondly, photography entered the protoconceptual and conceptual context by introducing a whole range of previously unthinkable and invisible subject matter. It is with Ruscha that we can say that urbanism—questions of architecture, questions of vernacular urban space, questions of traffic circulation—reentered artistic practice by means of subjects that had not figured in anyone's work, either in Europe or the United States, for a good thirty years. Up to the moment of high modernism in the thirties it was, of course, fully understood that architecture and urbanism were subjects for avant-garde consideration. In the postwar period, however, all subjects concerning the conditions of collective, urban, public space had dramatically disappeared from artistic production. Only with Ruscha's work and with the subsequent practices of Graham and the Conceptual artists did the issues of public urban space, of architecture, of "publicness"—and how to conceive of it in the first place—reenter the field of avant-garde reflection.

From index to information

One of the American artists in whose Conceptual work these concerns became central was Douglas Huebler, who specifically linked the temporality and the spatiality of his activities to the photographic image and detached his practice of the medium from high-art iconography. In 1971 he initiated a project—*Variable Piece #70 (in process) Global*—to produce a universal collective portrait of everyone living on Earth, which in and of itself functions both as a critique of the genre of portraiture and as an attempt—in its vast spatial, temporal, and quantitative expansion—to radicalize the traditionally limited focus on representation and representational conventions [**2**].

▲ 1971 • 1920, 1953, 1960c, 1964b ■ 1916b, 1936 ◆ 1967a, 1968b ▲ 1968b • 1960c, 1964b

2 • Douglas Huebler, *Variable Piece #70 (in process) Global*, 1971–97 (details)
Documentation photographs, text, dimensions variable

By the late sixties, however, in specific confrontation with the photographic practices of the Conceptualists, numerous artists repositioned themselves through a critique of Conceptualism on the one hand and, as is so often the case in the formation of a new artistic position, with a rediscovery and rereading of earlier legacies on the other: in this case that of the American documentary tradition. Beginning in California in the context of the group ▲ that studied with Allan Kaprow, John Baldessari, and the poet David Antin, these artists—primarily Sekula, Rosler, and Fred Lonidier—defined their work in opposition to the seeming neutrality of Conceptualism. One of the most important examples through which this historical turnabout can be recognized is Fred Lonidier's *29 Arrests* [**3**], which recapitulates the exact structure • of Ruscha's books and the deadpan, almost campy neutrality with which seemingly random accumulations of found objects are made into their subjects. In his own project, Lonidier took photographs of people being arrested during an antiwar protest in San Diego harbor while military ships depart for Vietnam with new weaponry and new supplies of Army contingents. Thus Ruscha's seemingly neutral practice is critiqued by a sudden infusion of just those contingencies—political, contextual, historical—that Conceptualism had rejected.

One reason for this generation to oppose the Pop and Conceptualist mentality of artists such as Huebler, Baldessari, and Ruscha is precisely that at that time, belated as it might be, they rediscovered the legacies of the New York Film and Photo League of the twenties with its emphasis on Russian film. Thus, feeding into their work in the late sixties were not only the films of Sergei Eisenstein and Vsevolod Pudovkin but also the social documentary practices of the Film and Photo League, taken together with a ▲ serious reconsideration of figures such as John Heartfield. In some instances this occurred through the explicit mediation of the work of Hans Haacke. The latter's photographic work in 1970–1 • (such as the real-estate piece *Shapolski et al.*, which in its focus on architecture and its serializing format also parallels Ruscha's and Graham's practice) is another such turning-point where the Pop neutrality of an approach without either comment or contextualization is transformed into a model of activist intervention.

From Pop to photomontage

Artists such as Rosler and Sekula take the models of both photomontage and political documentary as historical points of departure. This first approach is visible in Rosler's late sixties work

3 • Fred Lonidier, *29 Arrests*, (top) *#10: Headquarters of the 11th Naval District*; (bottom) *#18: Headquarters of the 11th Naval District*, May 4, 1972, San Diego
Thirty black-and-white photographs, 12.7 x 17.8 (5 x 7)

▲ 1961, 1968b • 1967a, 1968b
▲ 1920 • 1971, 1972b

Bringing the War Home: House Beautiful [**4**], which is a series of photomontages almost literally taken from the Heartfield model (although Rosler claims not to have known Heartfield at that time), in which images of the devastation in Vietnam are inserted into the slick imagery of advertising and fashion and home decoration magazines. Rosler attempted to produce this series of colored photomontages for mass distribution; although she failed to realize that goal, it was one of the first instances in which the politicization of the photomontage aesthetic reached its apogee in the American context.

The second approach, other than the rediscovery of photomontage, involved a complicated reconsideration of the legacy of American documentary traditions. In this group's orientation, there was a distinct desire to Americanize its practice, looking at local vernacular historical contexts and traditions rather than European ones alone. This interest in regional culture, which Pop art had already introduced to some degree by its persistent emphasis on the Americanness of its own project, is the background for the dialogue that Rosler and Sekula opened with the ▲ Film and Photo League as well as with the legacies of FSA photography in their effort to draw on existing traditions and cultures within American history.

The last element that is crucial to their work is the internal debate over the status of photography itself. Not only are both these artists prolific critics, theorists, and historians of photography, but it was largely as a result of their writings that the whole relationship between modernism and photography became increasingly problematized. It is important to recognize to what degree documentary photography entered the public awareness of American cultural history at that moment largely as a result of their contribution in their various essays, such as Rosler's "In, Around, and Afterthoughts on Documentary Photography" (1981) and Sekula's "Dismantling Modernism, Reinventing Documentary" (1984). Neither suggests a blind continuation of the documentary project. In fact the opposite is true; both are extremely critical and careful to point out the historical inadequacies of the legacy of FSA photography, for example.

First of all, what is clearly understood by these writer-artists is that, in the face of the political deployment of their work, the political neutrality of photographers like ▲ Walker Evans or Dorothea Lange was a severe shortcoming; for both of them were unaware of or disinterested in the actual political framework within which their work was going to be used under the auspices of Roy Stryker's FSA project. The conflict that both Rosler and Sekula continuously

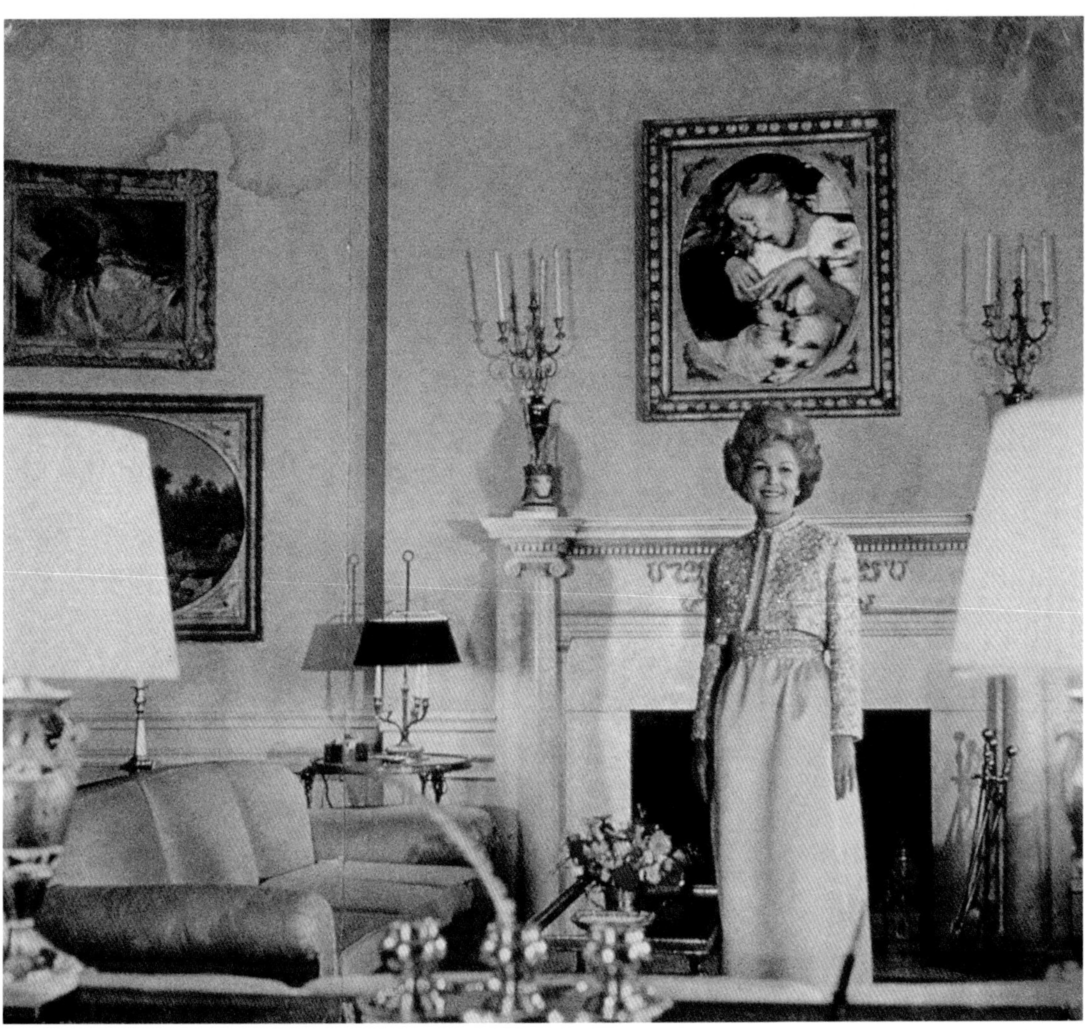

4 • Martha Rosler, *First Lady (Pat Nixon)* from the series *Bringing the War Home: House Beautiful*, 1967–72
Photomontage printed as color photograph, 61 x 50.8 (24 x 20)

▲ 1936

▲ 1936

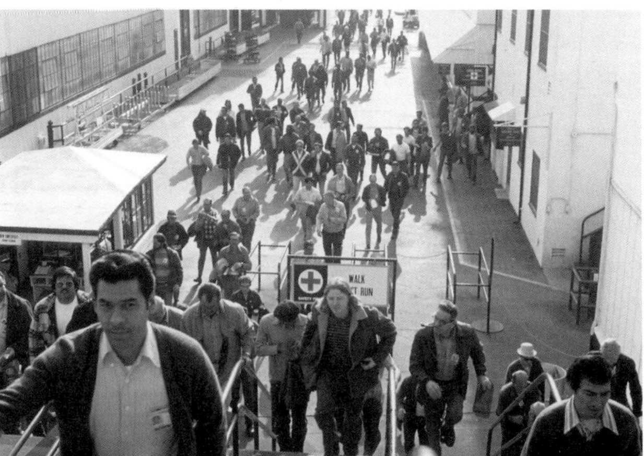

5 • Allan Sekula, *Untitled Slide Sequence*, 1972

explore is the question of the degree to which photographic practices can take on an activist, interventionist, agitprop approach, or to what degree, as photographs, they are contained within the discursive conventions and institutional frameworks that prevent them from ultimately attaining political efficacy.

Between seriality and agency

This is one of the dilemmas that face photographers both in their writings and their practices. It is in projects such as Sekula's *Untitled Slide Sequence* **[5]** or Rosler's *The Bowery in Two Inadequate Descriptive Systems* **[6]** that one can see their efforts to go beyond the limitations of traditional documentary practice. Sekula's work, projected as slides in a continuously repeating cycle, is a series of eighty images of workers at the end of the day shift leaving the General Dynamics Convair Division aerospace factory in San Diego. It clearly responds to the California transformation ▲ of Conceptualism at the hands of someone like Huebler, as it also responds to images of the working-class movement in both the Weimar and American documentary traditions. The fact of its transformation from the static black-and-white photograph to a continuously running slide sequence, and its random shots of workers that point to the difficulty of identifying working-class subjects (as opposed to middle-class or white-collar workers) therefore gives us a much more accurate and complex image of the subject of the documentary photograph. On the one hand, then, the semiotic reflection on what the photograph is (its status as "indexical sign"), how it produces meaning, and how it is institutionally and discursively placed and disseminated, is crucial to this practice, which distances itself from a naive return to a political claim for photographic documentary. Yet at the same time, and in an opposite gesture, it goes beyond this purely semiotic critique by emphasizing the necessity and possibility for contextualization or historical specificity in the reflection of the subject matter. We could say, then, that the critique of a naive assumption about the political efficacy of American documentary joins the critique of the pure neutrality of Conceptualist photography.

Rosler's *The Bowery in Two Inadequate Descriptive Systems* is an exemplary project in this respect. It addresses documentary photography in its more debased forms—what Rosler calls "the find-a-bum school of photography"—in its gritty black-and-white imagery and the internal historical meaning that this type of work had acquired by the seventies. It also performs a critique of a certain type of New York street photography celebrated by MoMA's John Szarkowski at the time, especially in the work of Garry Winogrand, where, with a detached cynicism, the decrepitude and misery of everyday life are made the spectacular subject • matter. In going back to the tradition of Walker Evans—many of the photographs function like quotations of Evans's work—Rosler positions herself in what she calls "the inadequacy of the photographic representation." Simultaneously, she constructs the manifest inadequacy of the linguistic system as a representation for

▲ 1968b • 1936

sot

tippler

winebibber

elbow bender

overindulger

toper

lushington

6 • Martha Rosler, *The Bowery in Two Inadequate Descriptive Systems*, 1974–5
Forty-five black-and-white photos and three black panels, each 20.3 x 25.4 (8 x 10), edition of five

drunkenness. Juxtaposed with the photographic images, the facing pages carry lists of terms for being inebriated—ranging from the most debased slang and the most archaic expressions to literary language. In their serial accumulation, these lists mimic the seriality of Pop repetitions even while they oppose, both by their subject matter and by their linguistic status, the claims of Conceptual art to have acquired a pure linguistic self-reflexivity. By linking language back into the sphere of the somatic—as into the sphere of the deranged, the digressive, the socially disqualified—a dimension of counterrationality is introduced into the rational project of Conceptual art that is typical for this moment of dialogue between these two generations.

FURTHER READING

Richard Bolton (ed.), *The Contest of Meaning* (Cambridge, Mass.: MIT Press, 1989)
Victor Burgin, *The End of Art Theory: Criticism and Postmodernity* (Atlantic Highlands, N.J.: Humanities Press International, 1986)
David Campany (ed.), *Art and Photography* (London: Phaidon Press, 2003)
Martha Rosler, *Decoys and Disruptions: Selected Writings 1975–2001* (Cambridge, Mass.: MIT Press, 2004)
Allan Sekula, *Photography Against the Grain: Essays and Photoworks 1973–1983* (Halifax: The Press of the Nova Scotia College of Art and Design, 1984)
Abigail Solomon-Godeau, *Photography at the Dock: Essays on Photographic History, Institutions and Practices* (Minneapolis: University of Minnesota Press, 1991)

copy it, to subject us to stereotypes more than to reveal the truth about us. And yet, as we will see, these two contrary positions might now be seen to share a historical identity, one that neither could have foreseen.

In art and architecture neoconservative postmodernism favored an eclectic mix of archaic styles and contemporary structures. In architecture, as represented by Philip Johnson (born 1906), Charles W. Moore (1925–93), Robert Venturi (born 1925), Michael Graves (born 1934), Robert Stern (born 1939), and others, this practice tended to use neoclassical elements like columns as so many popular symbols to dress up the usual modern building, rationalized in structure and space for efficiency and profit. And in art, as represented by Francesco Clemente (born 1952), Anselm ▲ Kiefer (born 1945), David Salle (born 1952), and Julian Schnabel (born 1951), it tended to use art-historical references as so many clichéd quotations to decorate the usual modern painting (the references differed with the national cultures of the artists—here Italian, German, and American, respectively [**1**]). So in what way was such work postmodernist? It did not argue with modernism seriously or exceed it formally. Rather it sought a reconciliation with the public (which is also to say with the marketplace) that was said to be alienated by the overly conceptual art and architecture of the sixties and seventies. Far from democratic (as was sometimes proclaimed), this reconciliation tended to be both elitist in its historical allusions and manipulative in its consumerist clichés. "Americans feel uncomfortable sitting in a square," Venturi once remarked, "they should be home with the family looking at television."

In this regard, neoconservative postmodernism was less postmodernist than antimodernist; and like the antimodernisms of the ▲ interwar period, this one sought stability, even authority, through reference to official history. More than a stylistic program, then, this postmodernism was a cultural politics, the strategy of which was twofold: first to foreclose modernism, especially in its critical aspects (in the neoconservative scheme of things culture was to be only affirmative of the status quo), and then to impose old cultural traditions on a complex social present that was far beyond such stylistic solutions.

It was here that the great contradiction of this postmodernism began to surface, for even as it cited historical styles, its mix of quo- • tations, often called "pastiche," tended to deprive these styles not only of context but also of sense. Ironically, then, rather than a return to tradition, this postmodernism pointed to its fragmentation, even its disintegration, at least as a coherent canon of styles. Indeed, "style," understood as the singular expression of a distinctive individual or period, and "history," understood as the basic ability to place cultural references at all, were undermined more than reinforced by this postmodernism. In this way, neoconservative postmodernism was exposed by the very cultural moment that it wanted to flee. For, as Jameson in particular has stressed, the eighties were marked not by a return of style but by its breakdown in pastiche, not by a recovery of historical consciousness but by its erosion in consumerist amnesia, and not by a rebirth of the artist as genius but by "the death of the author" (in the famous phrase of the French poststructuralist Roland Barthes), understood as the unique origin of all meaning.

1 • Julian Schnabel, *Exile*, 1980
Oil and antlers on wood,
228.6 x 304.8 (90 x 120)

▲ 1988

▲ 1919, 1934a, 1937a • 1919

Cultural studies

Insofar as semiology scanned the whole of the cultural horizon for examples of covert political speech, its field extended to advertising as well as television, packaging, and fashion. This semiological opening to the wider field of mass-cultural activity was contemporary with the attack mounted by Michel Foucault on the internal coherence of the various disciplines that make up the field of humanities: literature, history, art, etc. In England, at the University of Birmingham, scholars began to object to the idea that mass culture was simply a matter of manipulating passive consumers. Instead, argued cultural critics such as Stuart Hall (born 1932) there are strategies of consumption that slip over into forms of resistance. Rap would be one example of a reprogramming of music that turns it into a vehicle of aggression against middle-class values of decorum and obedience. It was even argued that the most degraded forms of popular storytelling, so-called "romance novels," could be a form of resistance that enabled lower-class women to carve out a space of privacy and fantasy.

That the divide between high art and mass entertainment would mirror class warfare was articulated by the French sociologist Pierre Bourdieu (1931–2002), who, in *Distinction* (1979), argued that skill in the consumption of high art was tantamount to having "cultural capital," and thus translates in Western, industrialized societies into monetary advantage and power.

▲ The other postmodernism, "poststructuralist postmodernism," differed in most respects. It differed, first of all, in its opposition to modernism. From the neoconservative point of view, modernism had to be overcome because it was too critical. From the poststructuralist point of view, it had to be overcome because it was no longer critical enough—it had become the official art of the museums, the favored architecture of the corporations, and so on. But it was on the question of representation that these two postmodernisms differed most clearly. As noted above, neoconservative postmodernism advocated a return to representation, and it took the truth of its representations for granted. Poststructuralist postmodernism, on the other hand, was driven by a critique of representation that questioned this truth, and it is this critique that aligned such postmodernist art most closely with poststructuralist theory.

Indeed, this art borrowed the poststructuralist notion of the fragmented "text" as a counter to the modernist model of the unitary "work." According to this argument, the modernist "work" suggested a work of art that was a symbolic whole, unique in its making and perfect in its form. The postmodernist "text" suggested a very different kind of entity: in the influential definition of Barthes, "a multidimensional space in which a variety of writings, none of them original, blend and clash." This notion of "textuality" seemed well suited to the strategy of appropriated images and/or anonymous writings, as used in the early phototexts of Barbara Kruger • and poster-statements of Jenny Holzer (born 1950) [**2**], as well as ▲ in the early copied works of Sherrie Levine and photographic arrangements of Louise Lawler. In these practices postmodernist textuality was first brought to bear on the modernist ideas of "master" works and "master" artists, which were viewed as ideological "myths" to expose—to "demystify" or to "deconstruct." As these myths were seen to be gendered male, it was no accident that • this critique was led by feminist artists.

Pastiche and textuality

As models of artmaking, then, the modernist "work" and the postmodernist "text" are distinct enough. But what about neoconservative "pastiche" and poststructuralist "textuality"—how different, finally, are they in effect? Consider, as an example of each practice, the work of two artists who were lionized circa 1984: the neo-Expressionist paintings of Julian Schnabel on the one hand and the multimedia performances of Laurie Anderson (born 1947) on the other [**3**]. Schnabel mixed high-art allusions (such as to Caravaggio in *Exile*) with low-culture materials (such as velvet and deer antlers), but not in order to question either set of terms. On the contrary, along with many other artists of the time, he turned the modernist techniques of collage and assemblage into contemporary devices dedicated to bolster the very medium that they once were used to break open: painting. Certainly some of his pictorial elements are fragmented (such as broken plates), but all are held together by the conventions of modern painting—such as expressive gestures, excessive frames, and heroic Abstract Expressionist posturings—that Schnabel attempted to resuscitate. Anderson, on the other hand, did play with art history and pop culture as clichés. In her performances, which tended to be allegories of disorientation in contemporary American life, she orchestrated a profusion of artistic media and cultural signs—projected images, taped narratives, electronically altered music and voice, and so on. This

2 • Jenny Holzer, *Truisms*, 1977–9
Poster, 91.4 x 61 (36 x 24)

▲ Introduction 4 • Introduction 1, 1977 ▲ 1977 • 1975

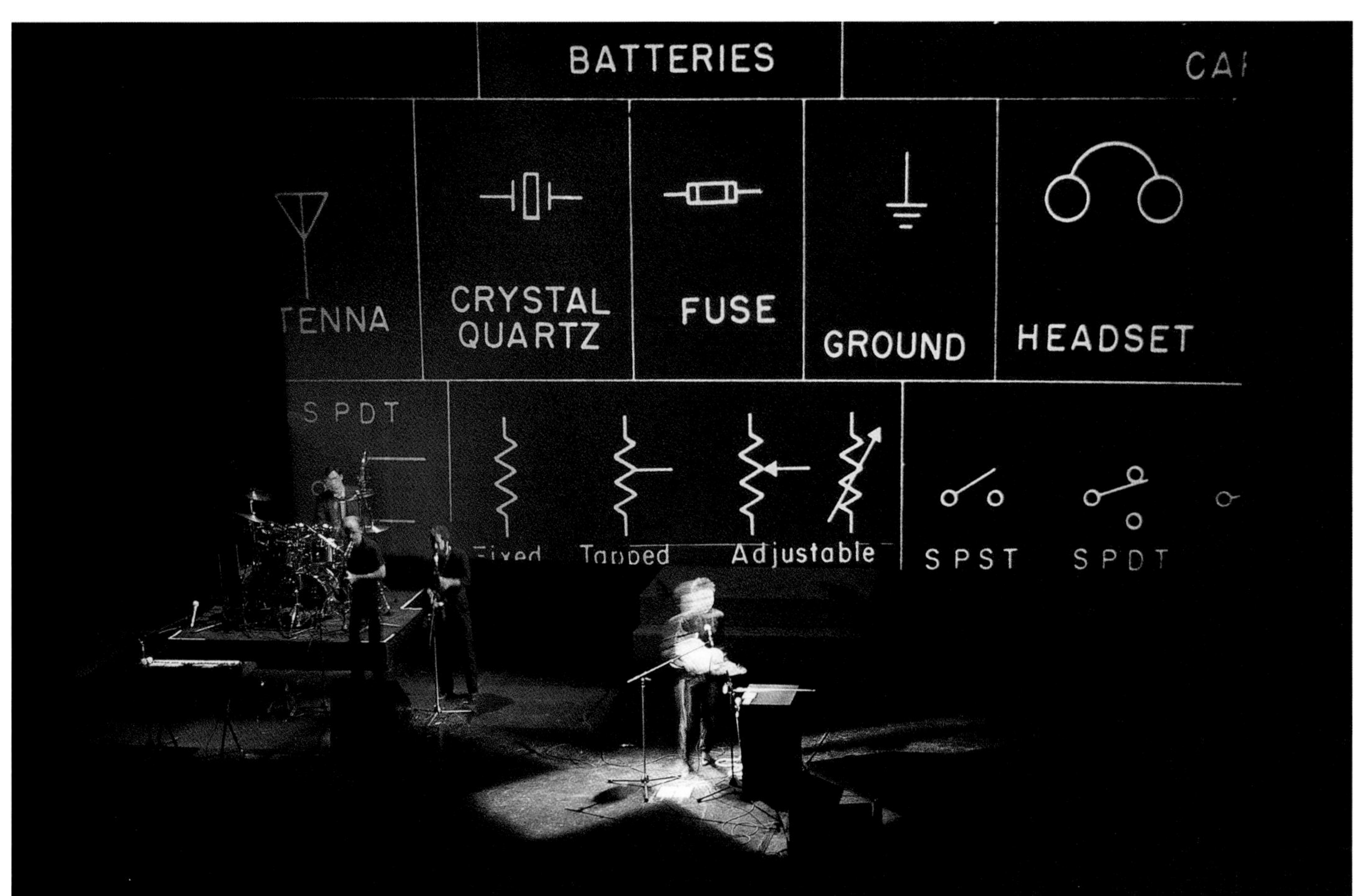

3 • Laurie Anderson, detail of the performance *United States*, 1978–82

mélange rendered ambiguous the personal position as well as the social reference of her representations, and it did so outside of any one medium that might recontain them as high art.

Granted these great stylistic and political differences, did these respective practices of pastiche and textuality differ in any structural sense? Both tended to disrupt the idea of stable subjectivity and to shatter the notion of traditional representation—Anderson intentionally so, Schnabel inadvertently so. If this is the case, then the neoconservative "return" to individual style and historical tradition (as exemplified here by Schnabel) might be revealed, twenty years after its peak moment, to be similar in effect to the poststructuralist "critique" of these things (as exemplified here by Anderson). In short, pastiche and textuality might now be seen as complementary symptoms of the same crisis of subjectivity and narrative that comprised "the postmodern condition" for Lyotard, of the same process of fragmentation and disorientation that informed "the cultural logic of late capitalism" for Jameson.

But then what exactly were this subjectivity and that narrative that were supposed to be in crisis in the first place? They were presumed to be general, even universal; critics of "the postmodern condition" soon came to see them as more particular—as mostly white, middle-class, male, Western European and North American. For some, any threat to this subjectivity and that narrative, to the great modern tradition, was indeed grave, and it provoked both laments and disavowals concerning the end of art, history, the canon, the West. But for others, especially for people marked as ▲"other," whether sexually, racially, and/or culturally, postmodernism did not signal an actual loss so much as a potential opening to other kinds of subjectivities and narratives altogether.

FURTHER READING

Roland Barthes, *Image-Music-Text*, trans. Stephen Heath (New York: Hill and Wang, 1977)
Hal Foster (ed.), *The Anti-Aesthetic: Essays on Postmodern Culture* (Seattle: Bay Press, 1983)
Fredric Jameson, *Postmodernism, or The Cultural Logic of Late Capitalism* (Durham, N.C.: Duke University Press, 1991)
Rosalind Krauss, *The Originality of the Avant-Garde and Other Modernist Myths* (Cambridge, Mass.: MIT Press, 1986)
Jean-François Lyotard, *The Postmodern Condition: A Report on Knowledge*, trans. Geoff Bennington and Brian Massumi (Minneapolis: University of Minnesota Press, 1984)
Craig Owens, *Beyond Recognition: Representation, Power, and Culture* (Berkeley and Los Angeles: University of California Press, 1992)
Brian Wallis (ed.), *Art after Modernism: Rethinking Representation* (Boston: David R. Godine, 1984)

▲ 1975, 1987, 1989, 1993c

1986

"Endgame: Reference and Simulation in Recent Painting and Sculpture" opens in Boston: as some artists play on the collapse of sculpture into commodities, others underscore the prominence of design and display.

Like other movements in the sixties, Pop and Minimalism worked against traditional notions of artistic composition, and they did so partly through a serial mode of production: one image after another, as often in the silkscreened paintings of Andy Warhol; "one thing after another," as often in the sculptural units of ▲ Donald Judd. This serial ordering also oriented Pop and Minimalism to the everyday world of serial commodities more systematically than any previous art. In our world of consumer capitalism, the primary term of consumption is not necessarily the use of a given product so much as its difference as a sign from other such signs. According to ● the French sociologist Jean Baudrillard, it is often this "factitious, differential, encoded, systematized aspect of the object" that we consume more than the object as such; it is the brand name that ■ triggers our desire, the commodity-as-sign that becomes our fetish.

Codes of consumption

Once serial production and differential consumption penetrated art in this manner, distinctions between high and low forms became blurred in a way that exceeded any thematic borrowing of imagery or sharing of subject matter. Evident in Pop and Minimalism, this blurring became explicit in the early eighties when artists like Jeff Koons (born 1955) and Haim Steinbach (born 1944) equated art works with commodities directly; this work first came to broad attention in a 1986 show titled "Endgame" at the Institute of Contemporary Art in Boston. With his early basketballs half-submerged in aquarium tanks, Koons produced an almost Surrealist affect of ambivalence [**1**], yet his glossy ad campaigns and luxury objects thereafter seemed bent on little more than self-promotion, as Koons appeared to delight, nihilistically, in the commodity fetish and the media celebrity as the historical replacements of the auratic art work and the inspired artist. ◆ In effect he acted out what Walter Benjamin had predicted long ago for capitalist society: the cultural need to compensate for the lost aura of art and artist with "the phony spell" of the commodity and the star. Here his most famous precedent among artists was Andy Warhol. "Some company recently was interested in buying my 'aura'," he wrote in *The Philosophy of Andy Warhol* (1975). "They didn't want my product." It was left to Koons to make this redefinition of aura as "phony spell" not only the subject but the operation of an art career.

1 • Jeff Koons, *Two Ball 50/50 Tank (Spalding Dr. J Silver Series, Wilson Supershot)*, 1985
Glass, steel, distilled water, and two basketballs, 159.4 x 93.3 x 33.7 (62¾ x 36¾ x 13¼)

And if Koons, a stockbroker-turned-artist, presented commercial hype as the contemporary substitute for artistic aura, then no-less-savvy artists like Damien Hirst (born 1965), the most notorious of the "Young British Artists" who emerged in the late eighties and early nineties and gained notoriety with the 1997 "Sensation" show at the Royal Academy in London, did much the same thing with media sensationalism. Koons had only placed kitschy products in his cases; Hirst went the whole hog and presented sectioned animals in his containers [**2**]. In this regard the outraged opponents of these artists played right into their hands, for together they produced a packaged simulacrum of artistic provocation.

Whereas Koons focused on the fetishistic aspect of the commodity-sign, Steinbach concentrated on its differential aspect.

▲ 1964b, 1965 ● 1980 ■ 1931 ◆ 1935

2 • Damien Hirst, *This Little Piggy Went to Market, This Little Piggy Stayed at Home*, 1996
Steel, glass, pig, formaldehyde solution, and two tanks, each 120 x 210 x 60 (47 x 82 x 23½)

A 1985 piece titled *related and different* displays a pair of Nike basketball shoes alongside five plastic goblets, as if to suggest that Air Jordans were a contemporary version of the Holy Grail. This is typical of his work: to set selected products on simple shelves or pedestals in clever juxtapositions of shape and color in a way that shows them to be "related and different"—related as commodities, different as signs. Steinbach frames art objects in these terms too: they are presented as signs to be appreciated—that is, consumed—as such. Like Koons he positions the viewer as shopper, the art connoisseur as commodity-sign fetishist, and celebrates the idea that our "passion for the consumerist code" (Baudrillard) seems to subsume all other values—use-value, aesthetic value, and so on. With Steinbach this code of consumption is first and foremost a matter of design and display, and its logic appears total, able to absorb any object, however bizarre, into any arrangement, however surreal. In his work such oppositions as functional and dysfunctional, rational and irrational, which structured the definition of the modern object since the ▲ Bauhaus and Surrealism, appear to be collapsed, which is indeed one "endgame" played out by this kind of "commodity sculpture."

These artists "pretend to engage in a critical annihilation of mass-cultural fetishization," Benjamin Buchloh has argued, but in doing so "they reinforce the fetishization of the high-cultural object even more: not a single discursive frame is undone, not a single aspect of the support systems is reflected, not one institutional device is touched upon." In this account they do not confront the contemporary status of the institution of art; rather, they perform (as one practitioner, Ashley Bickerton [born 1959], once boasted) a "strategic inversion of the deconstructive techniques" developed to critique this institution by such artists as Marcel Broodthaers, Michael Asher, ▲ and Hans Haacke in the sixties and seventies. If those older artists • had expanded the presentational device of the readymade object in order to reflect on conditions of exhibition, these younger artists returned the readymade to its status as a product—indeed, they often transformed it into a luxury commodity on display.

Yet not all artists concerned with the commodification of art in the eighties succumbed to this cynical inversion of the old avant-garde device of the readymade. Allan McCollum (born 1944) demonstrated the same positioning of art—as object of desire and as vehicle of prestige—as did Koons and Steinbach, but he withheld the goods, so to speak, and so invited us to consider conventions of display as triggers of consumption. His *Surrogate Paintings* **[3]**, which consist solely of minimal frame, mat, and rectangle in lieu of the usual image, are so many blank signs for easel painting (first painted in acrylic on wood, they were later cast in plaster); while his *Perfect Vehicles* (1985), urns cast in solid Hydrocal and painted in enamel bands of different colors, are equally generic tokens of sculptural objects. As with several subsequent series, both "the Surrogates" and "the Vehicles" come in various sizes and in extreme

▲ 1923, 1931

▲ 1970, 1971, 1972a, 1972b • 1914

3 • Allan McCollum, *Surrogate Paintings*, 1978–80
Acrylics and enamels on wood and museum board, sizes vary

numbers: McCollum oversees a studio that functions, like a cottage industry, somewhere between a workshop and a factory, and he uses it to produce a superabundance of unique multiples that frustrates rather than satisfies our desire. In this way he calls up differences in production at the same time that he provokes reflections on consumption, and so carves out a place of critical distance on various kinds of making, showing, viewing, and owning from within an economy that works to foreclose awareness of alternative modes of production and distribution altogether.

John Knight (born 1945) has also worked to develop the deconstructive techniques of institution-critical art, with an eye not only to the increased commodification of art but also to its literal incorpora-▲tion into big business, indeed *as* big business. This led him to mimic the forms of design and display in advertising and architecture that became pervasive during the Reagan-Thatcher years when corporate merging and culture marketing expanded exponentially. Thus for "Documenta 7" (1982), the international exhibition in Kassel, • Germany, Knight made eight logotypes from his own initials abstracted in italicized Helvetica font (which he deemed "the ultimate mainstream corporate font"), mounted them in wood relief, and covered them with color reproductions of travel posters (in one piece he substituted an advertisement for a California bank). In this way he pointed to the historical recuperation of modernist forms of abstraction, relief, and collage "for the dissemination of the ideology and the products of corporate postwar culture" (Buchloh). At the same time, positioned in the two main staircases in the principal hall of "Documenta," his logotypes equivocated between art work and commercial logo, between private, individual signature and public, anonymous sign. In a sense Knight incorporated his own initials here, a rhetorical move that underscored the double condition that critical artists faced at this moment: not only the corporate domination of art-world institutions (along with the financial manipulation of art collectors like Charles Saatchi in England, whose first line of business is indeed advertising), but also the forced revival of Expressionist ▲ painting. His *Mirror* series [4] reflected on both developments, and suggested that the apparent subjectivity of the painting served as small compensation (and no little mystification) for the actual sovereignty of the corporation. According to Buchloh, Knight shaped his pseudocorporate logos in different geometric forms faced with mirrors so as to "remind us of the ultimate corporate reality that controls and determines the most secluded interior reflection. In the same manner, the trivial domesticity of the mirrors leaves no doubt that the aesthetic withdrawal from its public social function has no other place than that of the private framed reflex."

Other artists at the time also underscored the corporate designing of our identities. For example, Ken Lum (born 1956) has arranged standard modern furniture in bizarre positions—sofas standing, leaning, sometimes combining and coupling—as if they

▲ 1976 • 1972b ▲ 1984b

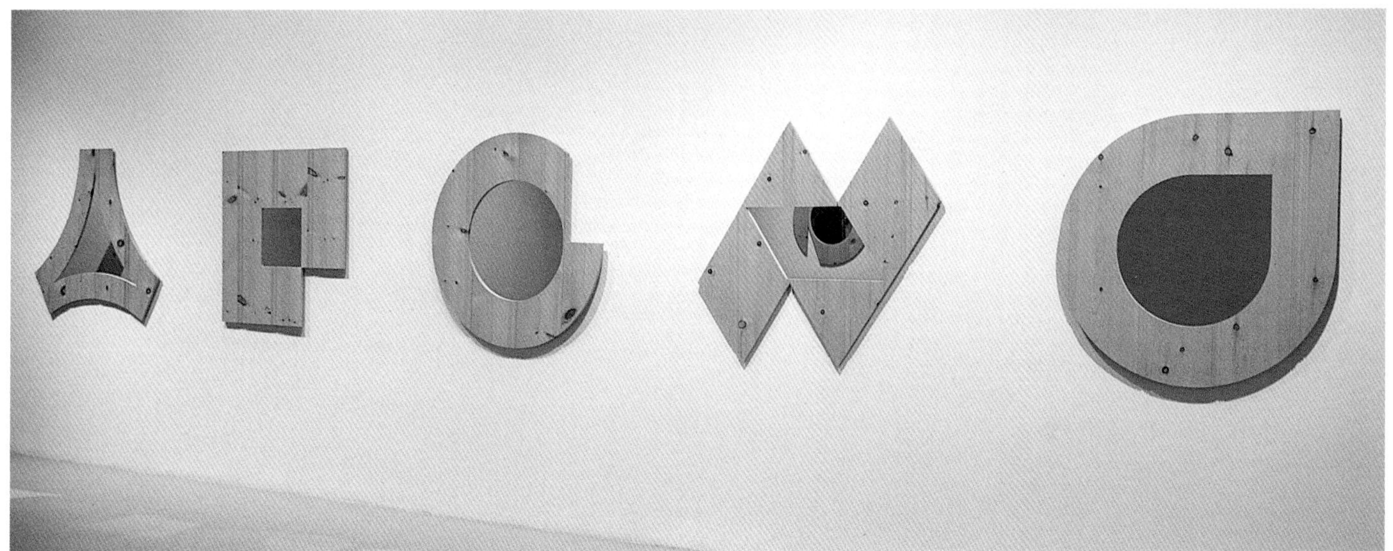

4 • John Knight, *Mirror* series, 1986
Installation view

had taken on a life of their own and displaced their human owners. And Andrea Zittel (born 1965) has explored the modularization of our contemporary habitats in a series of mock models of streamlined offices and homes. Still other artists have sought to reclaim a subjective dimension in this new order of everyday life under mega-corporations. Like Knight, Lum, and Zittel, Barbara Bloom (born 1951) has also mimicked cultural forms that shape social identity. Among other things, she has produced posters and advertisements, book jackets and film trailers, in a sly sort of deconstructive ▲ mimesis of these genres of the culture industry. "In all my work 'seeming' and 'appearing as if' play a large role," Bloom explains, "but this looking 'like,' this chameleonic means of achieving my purpose is, on the surface, a first impression. The images, often through irony, offer commentary upon the medium in which they are placed and cultural images (clichés) in general."

● Bloom developed her early work out of feminist concerns of the late seventies and early eighties, which focused on questions of fetishism and spectatorship; in a 1985 installation titled *The Gaze*, which took the form of a showroom, she worked to catch our fascination with designer shoes in the act. However, her later work is not so distanced; especially in her exhibitions staged as private collections Bloom has introduced fragments of stories, both fictional and (auto)biographical, through photographs and books, personal items and household objects, often redolent of the past [**5**]. Here rather than adopt the guise of the public curator, as many contemporary artists have done, she performs the role of the private collector. Other artists had taken up this part before her, or combined it with that of ■ the curator (Broodthaers, for example), but Bloom is concerned less to critique the gallery–museum nexus than to transform it into an alternative theater to explore the secret lives of words and things. ◆ Like Walter Benjamin before her, Bloom sees the collector as a figure who resists the reduction of the object to either use-value or exchange-value, and who mobilizes a personal kind of fetishism—what she calls "the potency of detail"—against the abstract fetishism of the commodity-sign. "Collectors are the physiognomists of the world of objects," Benjamin wrote in "Unpacking My Library" (1931); they elevate the commodity "to the status of allegory," finding hidden stories therein. Bloom performs a similar narrativization with her objects: "I seem to spend an inordinate amount of time contemplating whether an object can be imbued with enough meaning to become a stand-in for a person or event."

In the eighties, artists responded to the market pressures and corporate interests in the art world (and beyond) in dialectically ▲ different ways. Some acted out these financial arrangements in their work, as if to exacerbate them might be to damage them somehow; while others attempted to reflect on these new forces critically, and to develop rather than to collapse the framing effects of the readymade device in order to do so. Although economic conditions shifted, temporarily, after the minicrash of the stock market in 1987, the mid-nineties saw another round of capitalist expansion, and some artists began to focus less on the commodification of art, which they considered a given by this time, than on the ubiquity of *design*, or the manner in which objects or practices are so often recoded, subsumed into a greater ensemble, turned into an element of decor or lifestyle. This shadowing, even doubling, of avant-garde art by "good design" is not a new story; it has haunted abstract art through much of its development. In this ● regard consider the trajectory of the Bauhaus, the most celebrated of modernist schools: if the Bauhaus did indeed transform the arts and crafts as they were traditionally taught, it also facilitated, as Baudrillard has argued, "the practical extension of the system of exchange-value to the whole domain of signs, forms and objects." This is one version of "the bad dream" of modernism—that its utopian transformations of art forms might be recouped as market ■ advances in fashion and other commodity lines.

Some contemporary artists, such as Jorge Pardo (born 1963) and Karim Rashid (born 1960), appear to take this recuperation as a given, and to work within the parameters of a design logic. In this

▲ 1977, 1980 ● 1975 ■ 1972a ◆ 1935 ▲ 1992 ● 1923, 1947a ■ 1925a

1984b

Fredric Jameson publishes "Postmodernism, or the Cultural Logic of Late Capitalism," as the debate over postmodernism extends beyond art and architecture into cultural politics, and divides into two contrary positions.

No word in postwar criticism is more disputed than the term "postmodernism." This is so largely because it can be understood only in relation to other broad terms that are equally difficult to grasp, such as "modernism," "modernity," and "modernization." "Postmodernism" is also paradoxical in its own right. On the one hand, it suggests that "modernism"—whether understood as the refinement of each art form to its separate essence or, on the contrary, as the critique of all aesthetic separation—is somehow finished, and its death was indeed announced by many theorists. On the other hand, in the work of some artists and critics also associated with the term, postmodernism has provided new insights into modernism, especially into historical avant-gardes long scanted by dominant accounts (as Dada and ▲ Surrealism had been, for example, by Clement Greenberg and his followers). In this way, postmodernism has served as a way to revisit modernism as much as to declare it dead.

Like modernism, postmodernism does not designate any one style of art. Rather, its most ambitious theorists have used the term to mark a new cultural epoch in the West. For the American critic Fredric Jameson, whose "Postmodernism, or the Cultural Logic of Late Capitalism" is a classic Marxist analysis, the postmodern is less a clean break with the modern than an uneven development of old (or "residual") and new (or "emergent") elements. Nevertheless, it is distinct enough to "periodize" as a new moment in culture in relation to a new stage in capitalism, often called "consumer capitalism," which emerged after World War I. Thus • for Jameson the spectacular images associated with postmodern culture—seductive simulations in magazines and movies, on TV and the internet, that rarely represent anything real at all—reflect "the cultural logic" of an economy driven by consumerist desire. However, for the French philosopher Jean-François Lyotard, whose *The Postmodern Condition* (1979) inaugurated the philosophical debate over the term, the postmodern marked the end of any such Marxist narrative, indeed of all "grand narratives" of "modernity," whether told as a story of progress (such as the spread of enlightenment) or as a tale of decline (the enslavement of the proletariat). And yet, even as these two opponents in the debate about postmodernism disagree on its ramifications, they concur that its motive force remains "modernization," or the ceaseless transformation of modes of production and consumption, transportation and communication, in the interest of profit. On this score there may be an end to the artistic formation that is called "modernism," perhaps even an end to the cultural epoch called "modernity," but no end to the socioeconomic process called "modernization" is in sight. On the contrary, the postmodern may only signal the near-global extent of this process.

Rival postmodernisms

But what did the term "postmodernism" signify in art and architecture at the height of this debate—that is, circa 1984, the year that Ronald Reagan was reelected president? (I include architecture because the debate first became public there.) In the United States this was the peak moment of neoconservativism in politics, which called for a return to original values of family, religion, and country—in short, of cultural tradition. But it was also, at least in the art and academic worlds, the peak moment of poststructuralism in theory, which put into question all such origins and returns. Hardly matched as antagonists—the first was a political force, the second an intellectual orientation—these two philosophies nonetheless governed the two basic positions on postmodernism at the time, and for convenience I will label them accordingly.

Then as now "neoconservative postmodernism" was the more familiar of the two. Defined mostly in terms of style, it reacted against modernism, which it reduced to abstract appearance alone—to the glass-and-steel International Style in architecture, to abstract painting in art, and to linguistic experimentation in fiction. It then countered this modernism with a return to ornament in architecture, to figuration in art, and to narrative in fiction. Neoconservative postmodernism justified these returns in terms of a heroic recovery not only of artistic individuality in opposition to the supposed anonymity of mass culture, but also of historical memory in opposition to the supposed amnesia of modernist culture. "Poststructuralist postmodernism," on the other hand, questioned both the originality of the artist and the authority of the tradition. Moreover, rather than a return to representation, ▲ this postmodernism advanced a critique of representation, in which representation was held to construct reality more than to

▲ 1916a, 1920, 1924, 1930b, 1931, 1942a, 1942b, 1960b • 1956, 1957a ▲ 1977, 1980

5 • Barbara Bloom, *The Reign of Narcissism*, 1989
Mixed media, dimensions variable

space of design, categories and terms that a generation ago were held in productive contradiction—for example, "sculpture" versus ▲ "architecture" in site-specific art—appear as compounds without much generative tension, as in the many combinations of pictures, objects, and spaces in Installation art. In this state of reversion, site-specific art becomes a kind of ambient art, and the situational aesthetics developed by institution-critical artists like Michael • Asher transmutes into a sort of design aesthetics. Indeed, artists like Pardo and Rashid use elements of decor—color-coded tile and wallpaper, super-sleek fixtures and furniture—to subsume the space of art into a total environment. In this sense, if some artists once pushed sculpture out into the realm of architecture, others now submit sculpture to the dictates of design.

Yet here too, as with the heightened commodification of art in the eighties, there are dialectically different responses to this pervasive design logic. The artist-architect Judith Barry (born 1949) has long appropriated aspects of this logic for critical purposes in her installations and exhibitions. And rather than exacerbate the implosive effects of this logic, some artists, such as Glenn Seator (1956–2002) and Sam Durant (born 1961), have sought to recover the "expanded field of sculpture" in the sixties, and to resist the totality of design through an explicit remotivation of site-specific practices. In the case of Durant, this has meant a recovery of the site/non-site dialec- ▲ tics of Robert Smithson, but now read through funky references to both subcultures and mass culture. In the case of Seator, it meant a • recovery of the architectural cuts of Gordon Matta-Clark, but now performed in a manner in which the exposed architectural history becomes a systematic index of an exposed social history.

FURTHER READING

Brooks Adams et al., *Sensation: Young British Artists from the Saatchi Collection* (London and New York: Thames & Hudson, 1998)

Benjamin H. D. Buchloh, *Neo-Avantgarde and Culture Industry* (Cambridge, Mass.: MIT Press, 2000)

David Joselit (ed.), *Endgame: Reference and Simulation in Recent American Painting and Sculpture* (Boston: Institute of Contemporary Art, 1986)

Lars Nittve (ed.), *Allan McCollum* (Malmo: Rooseum, 1990)

Peter Noever (ed.), *Barbara Bloom* (Vienna: Austrian Museum of Applied Arts, 1995)

▲ 1967a, 1970 • 1970

▲ 1967a, 1970 • 1967a

1987

The first ACT-UP action is staged: activism in art is reignited by the AIDS crisis, as collaborative groups and political interventions come to the fore, and a new kind of queer aesthetics is developed.

In response to conservative governments in the United States, the United Kingdom, and (then) West Germany, the early eighties ▲ witnessed a resurgence of art devoted to progressive politics, the most important since the height of the Vietnam War. Different events overlapped to provoke this resurgence: military interventions in Central America, corporate takeovers on Wall Street, the continued threat of nuclear holocaust, the phobic attacks of the religious Right, backlashes against civil rights and feminist gains, slashes in welfare and other social programs, and—most tragic of all for the art world—the AIDS epidemic, the indifference of most governments to it, and the brutal scapegoating of gay men in particular on account of it. As the decade wore on, political art in the United States was also galvanized by a number of beatings and other violent events that were racially and/or sexually motivated, as well as by ideological conflicts that pitted the art world against the very governmental agencies founded in part to support it—above all the National Endowment for the Arts.

These responses were framed in two basic ways. The first tended to a "representation of politics," in which social identities and political positions were treated as given contents, to be communicated as

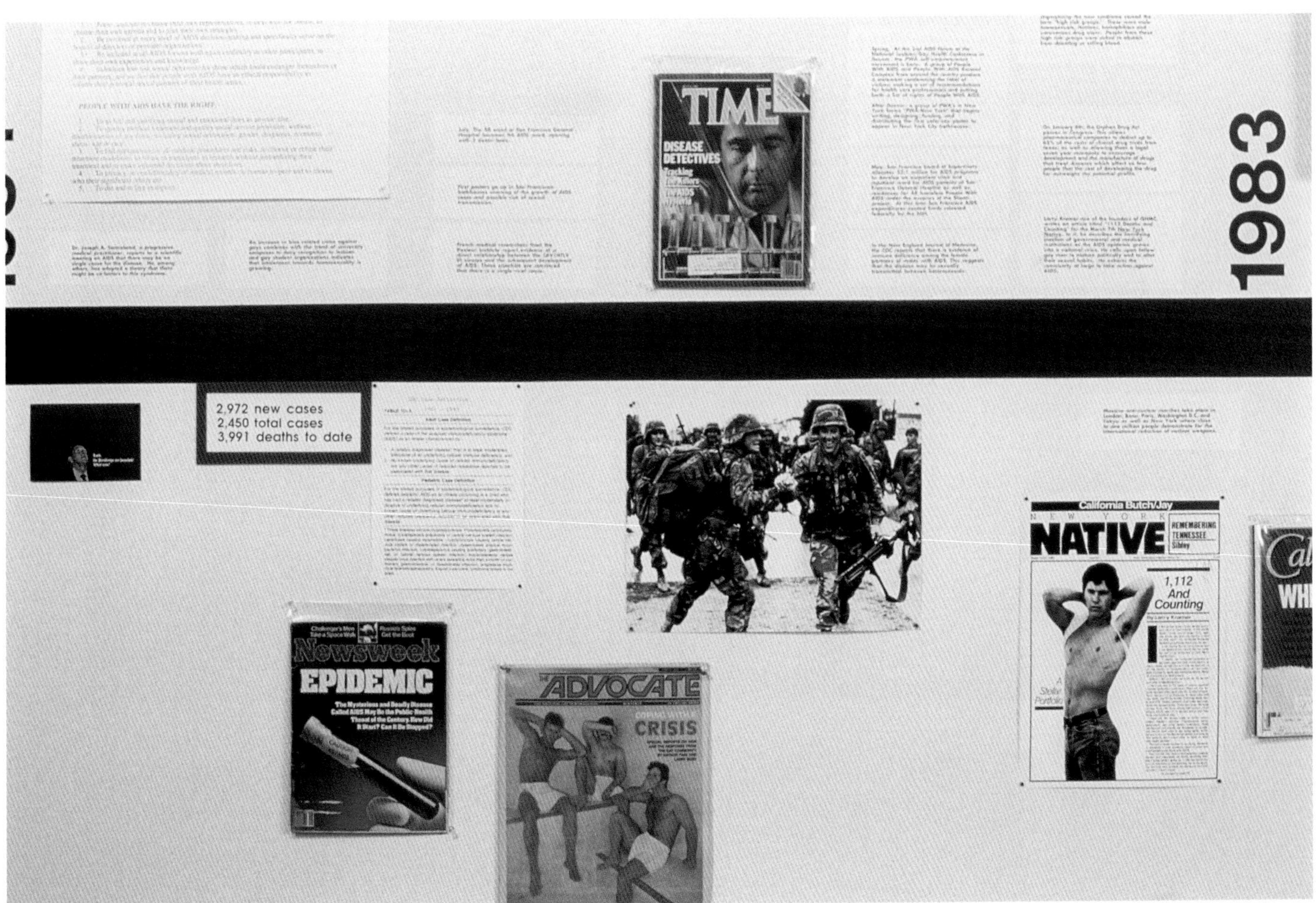

1 • Group Material, *AIDS Timeline*, 1989
Mixed-media installation

▲ Introduction 2, 1984a

immediately as possible. The second tended to "a politics of representation," in which these identities and positions were treated as constructed representations, to be interrogated on formal as well as ▲ ideological levels. Thus, while some artists worked to present political problems in direct ways, others brought poststructuralist • critiques of representation to bear on them. One danger of the first approach was that it sometimes confirmed the stereotypes that it sought to challenge; and one danger of the second was that its very sophistication sometimes obscured its own critique.

The reactionary turn in politics was accompanied by one in aesthetics, as was manifest in the resurrection of old forms like oil painting and bronze sculpture; the common enemy here was the radical transformations in the sixties of politics and art alike. And yet, even as humanist myths of master art and artists were revived, the art world was given over to market forces like never before, especially to the financial manipulations of collector-investors (like the British advertising executive Charles Saatchi) who extended the rampant privatization of the public sphere under Reagan and ■ Thatcher to the institutions of art. Among other changes for the worse, this meant the trumping of curators and critics by collectors and dealers as arbiters of artistic importance and value.

In resistance to the ideological regression in art as well as the overt manipulation of its market, some artists pursued "collaborative, collective, cooperative, communal projects," as one New York group called COLAB put it. Often these collectives set up alternative spaces, sometimes for temporary exhibitions in abandoned storefronts, sometimes to engage communities not served by the art world and removed from its centers. One example of guerrilla exhibitions in New York was "The Real Estate Show" (1980), which combined ad hoc objects and installations by local artists with wall drawings and graffiti by neighborhood children in a derelict storefront in the East Village owned by the city. Almost immediately the show was closed by the authorities, who thereby only underscored the real-estate problems that the event sought to dramatize. One example of community spaces in New York was Fashion Moda, a storefront gallery in the South Bronx set up by Stefan Eins and Joe Lewis to connect various artists with local residents (some of whom were portrayed, in painted plaster busts, by John Ahearn and Rigoberto Torres). The activities of such collectives as Group Material in New York and Border Art Ensemble in San Diego also ranged from message shows and guerrilla interventions (such as illegal postering) to community projects [**1**].

2 • Leon Golub, *Mercenaries (IV)*, 1980
Acrylic on canvas, 304.8 x 585.5 (120 x 230½)

▲ 1975, 1977 • 1977, 1980, 1984b ■ 1976

The mission statement of Group Material—"to maintain control over our work, directing our energies to the demands of the social conditions as opposed to the demands of the art market"—captures the spirit of this movement of politically motivated artists who sought to be socially site-specific as well, a spirit that has lived on in other groups like RePo History.

The resurgence of political art associations in the eighties revived interest in such precursors as the Art Workers' Coalition, which was formed at the height of the Vietnam War in order to advance the cause of an artist union and to protest the absence of woman and minority artists in exhibitions and collections. The spotlight also fell again on engaged artists like Leon Golub, who updated his graphic paintings of the atrocities of American soldiers in Vietnam with the new subjects at hand, such as the mercenaries of the undeclared "dirty wars" of the eighties [**2**]. Intercut with this representation of politics, however, was a politics of representation, which led some artists to mimic Situationist strategies of ▲ *détournement* in particular—that is, the reworking of public symbols and media images with subversive kinds of social meanings and historical memories. Thus, from 1980 onward the Polish-born Krzysztof Wodiczko (born 1943) projected specific images at night, at first in guerrilla fashion, onto different monuments and buildings redolent of political and financial power: nuclear missiles on war memorials, presidential pledges of allegiance on corporate buildings, homeless people on heroic statues, and so on [**3**]. His goal was to counter the official languages and to expose the suppressed histories of these architectures, with the result that under his projections they often seemed to erupt, symptomatically, with repressed contents and connections. Others like Dennis Adams (born 1948) and Alfredo Jaar (born 1956) used similar strategies. In his site-specific bus shelters, Adams confronted passersby with photographs of political demons who still haunt the present, such as the anti-Communist demagogue Joseph McCarthy and the Nazi executioner Klaus Barbie. In a related set of substitutions, Jaar displaced the slick subway ads that glorify businesses and banks at home with graphic phototexts that detailed their real work of exploitation abroad.

Agitprop appropriations

The most effective of these neo-Situationist interventions were made by the numerous artist groups associated with ACT-UP, the acronym of AIDS Coalition To Unleash Power, founded in March 1987 "to undertake direct action to end the AIDS crisis." As sophisticated in poststructuralist critiques of representation as the aforementioned artists, these groups (among them Gran Fury, Little Elvis, Testing the Limits, DIVA TV, Gang, Fierce Pussy) deployed different mediums and techniques depending on the occasion: bold posters of appropriated images and invented texts for specific demonstrations, subversive reworkings of corporate ads and newspaper pages for general circulation, video cameras to counter police abuse and media misrepresentations of ACT-UP

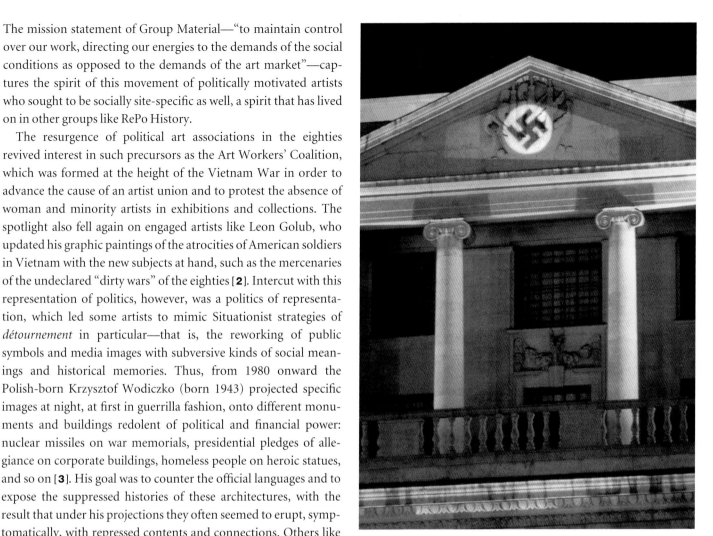

3 • Krzysztof Wodiczko, *Projection on South Africa House*, 1985
Trafalgar Square, London, dimensions variable

activities, and so on. In doing so, they drew on a wide range of art practices—the photomontages of John Heartfield, the graphics of Pop art, the outrageousness of Performance art, the reflexivity of institutional critique, the image-savvy of appropriation art, and the ▲ caustic wit of feminist artists like Barbara Kruger. "The aesthetic values of the traditional art world are of little consequence to AIDS activists," critic Douglas Crimp commented in 1990. "What counts in activist art is its propaganda effect; stealing the procedures of other artists is part of the plan—if it works, we use it." Or, as a 1988 poster by Gran Fury put it succinctly, "With 42,000 Dead Art Is Not Enough: Take Collective Direct Action To End The AIDS Crisis."

Some of these strategies were already at work in an anonymous poster that surfaced in downtown New York before the founding of ACT-UP: the mordant and mournful "Silence = Death" (1986). These two words were set in white type on a black ground with a pink triangle, the Nazi emblem for gays in the concentration camps. With the simple strength of its conviction, this sign indicted governmental inaction and public indifference regarding the AIDS epidemic (spelled out in a series of questions and exhortations in fine print at the bottom); indeed it equated this passivity with murder. At the same time, this sign turned the stigma of the

▲ 1957a

▲ 1920, 1956, 1960c, 1964b, 1971, 1975, 1977, 1980, 1992

pink triangle into an emblem of proud identity—a characteristic transvaluation, in the political development of an oppressed group, of an abusive stereotype (a similar reversal was performed on the word "queer" during this time). Scores of signs followed. Many, like "Silence = Death," were made in various forms (posters, placards, T-shirts, buttons, and stickers), and all were used as tools for organizing and reporting, raising consciousness and support, surviving and fighting back.

ACT-UP groups knew that the ideological war over AIDS was fought through the media as well as in the streets, and with a membership of many artists, film- and videomakers, architects, and designers, they devised signs and events that not only critiqued and corrected the media but also played on its procedures and propensities. Some used graphic horror, such as a 1988 poster by Gran Fury that showed only a handprint in blood red, the sign of a murderer, with the texts "The Government Has Blood On Its Hands" above and "One AIDS Death Every Half Hour" below [**4**]. Others used campy humor, such as a 1989 poster, also by Gran Fury, that substituted the word RIOT for the old Pop icon of LOVE painted by Robert Indiana in 1966 (the poster also responded to a prior substitution, by the Canadian group General Idea, of AIDS for LOVE). Designed to commemorate the twentieth anniversary of the Stonewall Rebellion, the uprising after an abusive raid at a Greenwich Village gay bar that is often taken to mark the beginning of the gay-rights movement, this sign was at once a call to memory and a call to arms, with the captions "Stonewall '69" above and "AIDS Crisis '89" below. ACT-UP groups also targeted bureaucratic officials and reactionary politicians (from commissioners of health to presidents), as well as drug-company profiteers. The infamous 1988 election pledge of George Bush against new taxes—"Read My Lips"—became a different kind of promise altogether in announcements of gay and lesbian "kiss-ins." (When the group Gang substituted a beaver shot for the kissing couples, and added the words "Before They are Sealed," "Read My Lips" took on yet another meaning—an indictment of the Bush gag-order against the discussion of abortion at medical clinics.) Such edgy appropriations were practiced by other artist collectives too, feminist groups like the Guerrilla Girls and antiracist groups like Pest, both of which posted statistically terse condemnations of sexual and racial discrimination in the art world and beyond.

A queering of art

Empowered by ACT-UP, many gay and lesbian artists began to explore homosexuality as a subject of art in different ways—Robert ▲ Gober (born 1954), Donald Moffet (born 1955), Jack Pierson (born 1960), David Wojnarowicz (1954–92), Felix Gonzalez-Torres (1957–96), and Zoe Leonard (born 1961) prominent among them. (The death from AIDS of two of the six here is a small indication of the ghastly toll suffered by the gay and art communities.) In a sense these artists telescoped the different claims made by feminist artists • of the first two generations, and "queered" them. That is, they

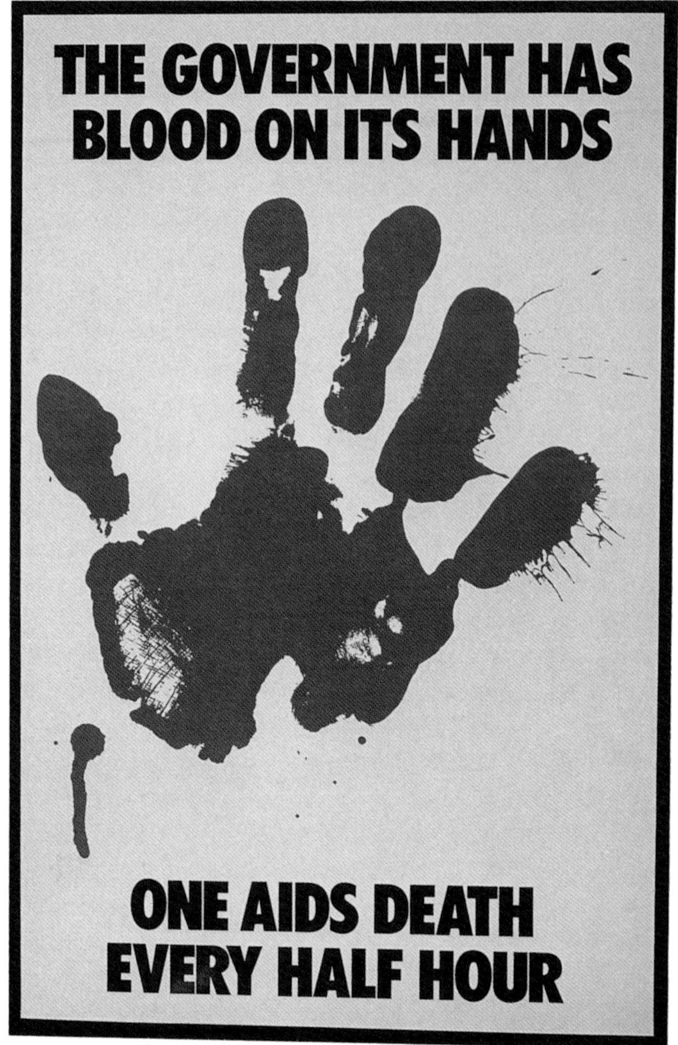

4 • Gran Fury, *The Government has Blood on its Hands*, 1988
Poster, offset lithography, 80.6 x 54.3 (31¾ x 21⅜)

explored homosexuality not only as a subjective experience that was essential in its nature (precisely what its enemies denied), but also as a social construction subject to cultural and historical variation.

More gentle than many of the ACT-UP appropriators urged on by Crimp, Felix Gonzalez-Torres, who was also a member of Group Material, performed a queering of other artistic forms of the sixties and seventies. "In our case," he once remarked, "we should not be afraid of using such formal references, since they represent authority and history. Why not take them?" And so Gonzalez-Torres did, with particular twists. He would arrange thousands of paper sheets, often lithographed with colors or images that bordered on kitsch (such as birds in the sky), in perfect ▲ stacks that recalled Minimalist volumes. Or he would spill thousands of gaily wrapped candies in the form (or antiform) of • Postminimalist scatter pieces. Or he would paint an elliptical list of historical events in homosexual rights on public billboards in the ■ laconic manner of Conceptual art.

One such billboard appeared in 1989 at Sheridan Square in New York near the site of the Stonewall Rebellion. It consisted simply of a black ground captioned in white italics as follows: "People with

▲ 1994a • 1975

▲ 1965 • 1969 ■ 1968b

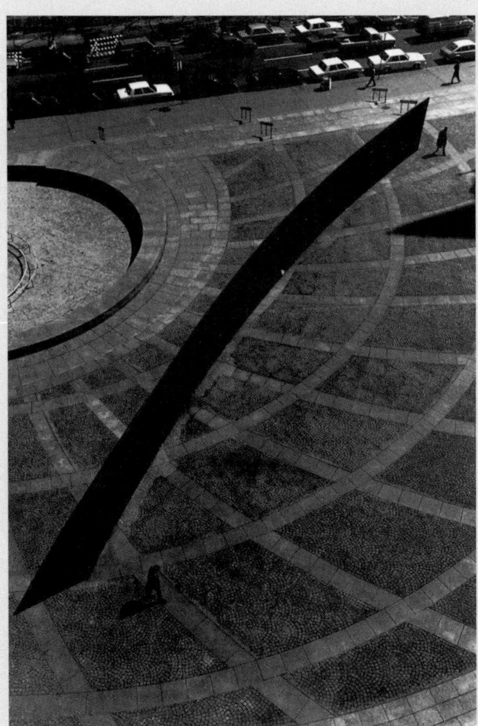

The US Art Wars

In 1987 a US District Judge dismissed a lawsuit filed by Richard Serra to prevent the General Services Administration, a federal agency, from removing his sculpture *Tilted Arc* (above), which the same GSA had commissioned in 1981 for the Federal Plaza in downtown Manhattan. "To move it," Serra argued persuasively of his site-specific work, "is to destroy it." Nevertheless, two years later *Tilted Arc* was moved under the cover of night. This was hardly the first case of the seizure or outright destruction of an art work, nor would it be the last, but it did open a new era of marked intolerance toward the work of advanced artists.

Also in 1987 the artist Andres Serrano (born 1950) was awarded a $15,000 grant from the Southeastern Center for Contemporary Art (SECCA) in Winston-Salem, North Carolina, which was funded indirectly by the National Endowment for the Arts (NEA). During his grant period, Serrano produced a Cibachrome photograph that showed a small plastic crucifix submerged in a bubbly amber liquid. Mostly on the basis of its title, *Piss Christ*, Serrano was accused of "religious bigotry" by the Reverend Donald Wildmon, director of the American Family Association. Again in 1987 the Philadelphia Institute of Contemporary Arts received $35,000 from the NEA to assist in a retrospective of the photographer Robert Mapplethorpe (1947–89), which contained five images of homosexual acts. Fearful of controversy, the Corcoran Gallery canceled the Washington version of the show. The exhibition then moved on to Cincinnati where Dennis Barrie, the director of the Cincinnati Museum of Contemporary Art, was charged with peddling obscenity. Led by Senator Jesse Helms, conservatives in Congress exploited the Serrano and Mapplethorpe controversies to call for the outright abolition of the NEA, an attack to which its supporters responded but meekly.

The greatest struggle concerning art since the Vietnam era was in full roar; and at least three lessons could be drawn from these events: public support for contemporary art had eroded drastically; the religious Right had exploited this failure for its own purposes; and a cultural politics of homophobia had gripped the United States. The work of other artists singled out by Congress also foregrounded homosexuality (for example, the performance artists Holly Hughes and Tim Miller). All such art was deemed antifamily, antireligion, and anti-American.

A literalism dominated these battles from the start. Many thought of *Piss Christ* as an actual desecration of Jesus by urine. "The pictures are the state's case," the prosecutor declared of the Mapplethorpe images as if their crime was self-evident. For its part *Tilted Arc* was once likened to a terrorist device.

The immediate upshot of these cases was that *Tilted Arc* was destroyed, an antiobscenity clause was inserted into NEA contracts (unconstitutionally, it was argued), and the case against Dennis Barrie was dismissed. But there were other ramifications. Contemporary art became political fodder for the Right; when not associated with obscenity or scandal, it was ridiculed as hype, and so a waste of taxpayers' money in this respect too, with the result that many liberal supporters also turned away from art. An enormous pall was cast over public art in particular, with the NEA (and other institutions such as Public Broadcasting Stations and National Public Radio) under almost constant assault. And tolerance toward non-normative sexualities was met with murderous reaction at a time when AIDS therapies cried out for massive financing.

AIDS Coalition 1985 Police Harassment 1969 Oscar Wilde 1895 Supreme Court 1986 Harvey Milk 1977 March on Washington 1987 Stonewall Rebellion 1969." Sooner or later one realized that all of the dates were landmark events—associations and demonstrations, trials and rulings, killings and uprisings—in the last century of gay life, but they were not in any order or sequence. The narrative was left to the viewer to construct, and the need to do so was underscored by the vacancy of the image, as if this history were always threatened by invisibility or illegibility.

The candy spills are ambiguous in another way. *Untitled (USA Today)* **[5]** consists of three hundred pounds of candies in gaudy red, blue, and silver wrappers heaped in a corner. The piece flies in the face of taboos in art against touching, let alone eating. It also brings together stylistic cues usually kept apart: a Postminimalist- ▲ like arrangement (Robert Morris and Richard Serra, among others, did corner pieces) with Pop-like materials (the glitziness ● reminds one of Andy Warhol in particular). It even seems to undo, if only for a moment, the old opposition between the avant-garde

▲ 1965, 1969, 1970 ● 1960c, 1964b

and kitsch. But these artistic allusions are complicated by more worldly ones. The subtitle points to the sugary news that the national paper *USA Today* delivers for our daily consumption, and consumption is literally foregrounded here, as a telling portrait of "USA Today" in another sense too. At the same time, the excess of the piece also conveys a sense of generosity, a spirit of offering so different from the cool cynicism of other uses of the readymade ▲ device by Jeff Koons, Damien Hirst, and others. Gonzalez-Torres solicits our participation in the register not only of consumption but of gift-exchange. Like his paper stacks, his candy spills are listed as "endless supply," which reminds us, in a utopian sense, that mass production once had democratic possibilities latent within it.

For all its spirit of offering, however, this art is also imbued with the pathos of loss. In *Untitled (March 5th) #2* (1991), for example, two light bulbs are suspended, supported by their own intertwined cords—a simple testament to love threatened by loss, as one light must burn out before the other. (March 5 was the birthday of his partner, who died of AIDS in 1991, five years before Gonzalez-Torres himself.) And in a 1992 billboard we see only a black-and-white photograph of an empty double bed, ruffled where two bodies recently lay—an elegy to absent lovers that also condemns antigay legislation criminalizing the bedroom [**6**].

Gender trouble

Like many of his generation, Gonzalez-Torres was influenced by poststructuralist critiques of the subject. Yet his art is concerned more with the making of a gay subjectivity than with its unmaking, for the simple reason that such a deconstruction would assume that gay identity is secure and central in a way that cannot be assumed in our heterosexist society. In his art, then, Gonzalez-Torres attempted to carve out of heterosexual space a lyrical-elegiac place for gay subjectivity and history. In her art Zoe Leonard finds such places in moments of "gender trouble" within straight society. In a 1992 poster made with the ACT-UP group Fierce Pussy, Leonard simply reframed a 1969 photograph of her second-grade class in Manhattan with the typewritten question "Are you a boy or a girl?" This is typical of her twofold tactic: to trouble gender, to expose what she calls the "the bizarreness" of its categories, and to construct a gay identity out of this trouble, to invent a lesbian history in the "place where expectations fall apart."

Leonard plays with this "bizarreness of gender" in her photographs of a *Preserved Head of a Bearded Woman* (1992) found in storage at the Musée Orfila in Paris. (She often searches the backrooms of medical and natural history museums for such "specimens.") Yet the true bizarreness here is not the woman's; for Leonard "it is her decapitation, the pedestal and the bell jar. What is disturbing is that someone or some group of people thought that was acceptable." And so Leonard photographs the "specimen" in such way that she seems to gaze back at her spectators, to put them on exhibit. A similar reversal occurs in the photograph *Male Fashion Doll #2* (1995), a toy that Leonard found in a flea market in Ohio. She describes him as "a little drag queen," with the face and body of a girl, as "usually rendered in plastic, completely sexless and pink," but with a little mustache drawn on him—a figure of gender trouble that Leonard reframes as a question for us.

"I wasn't interested in re-examining the male gaze," Leonard has remarked; "I wanted to understand my own gaze." But the objects of desire and/or identification of this gaze are not readily found in heterosexual culture—a vacancy that she seems to figure in her

5 • Felix Gonzalez-Torres, *Untitled (USA Today)*, 1990
Red, silver, and blue wrapped sweets, dimensions variable

6 • Felix Gonzalez-Torres, *Billboard of Bed*, 1992
Installed at a New York location

▲ 1986

7 • Zoe Leonard, *Strange Fruit*, 1992–7 (detail)
295 banana, orange, grapefruit, and lemon peels, thread, zips, buttons, needles, wax, plastic, wire, and fabric, dimensions variable

photographs of mirrors that reflect an empty glare more often than any image. As with Gonzalez-Torres, then, Leonard responds to the need not only to critique what is given as identity or history but also to imagine other kinds of constructions. This mandate may lead to archival work, to historical invention, or to both. For example, in her *Fae Richards Photo Archive* (1996), made in conjunction with the 1996 film *The Watermelon Woman* by Cheryl Dunye, Leonard helped to construct, through different genres of photographs artificially aged in the darkroom, the documentary life history of an imaginary woman, a black lesbian of the early 1900s who performed in Hollywood "race films." "She is not real," Leonard attests of Fae Richards, "but she is true."

Along with her gender troublings and historical imaginings, Leonard has also worked toward an art of AIDS mourning, and in ▲ this project she is joined by such artists as Robert Gober and Gonzalez-Torres. Her *Strange Fruit* is a poignant instance of this coming to terms with loss: a community of hundreds of fruits whose peels she sewed back together once the fruit was extracted [**7**]. Inspired in part by her friend David Wojnarowicz, who once cut a loaf of bread in half, then stitched it back together with blood-red embroidery thread, *Strange Fruit* alludes not only to the old slang for homosexual but also to a Billie Holliday song about lynching—about hatred and violence, death and loss. "It was sort of a way to sew myself back up," Leonard has commented; but the stitched peels attest more to holes than to healing, more to "the inevitability of a scarred life" than to the possibility of a redeemed one. In this regard they are pathetic in a profound sense, "repositories for our grief." This mnemonic model of art, this nonredemptive idea of beauty that allows for aesthetic sublimation but also works toward social change, is an important offering of artists like Gober, Gonzalez-Torres, and Leonard.

FURTHER READING

Anna Blume, *Zoe Leonard* (Vienna: Secession, 1997)
Judith Butler, *Gender Trouble: Feminism and the Subversion of Identity* (New York: Routledge, 1989)
Douglas Crimp (ed.), *AIDS: Cultural Analysis/Cultural Activism* (Cambridge, Mass.: MIT Press, 1988)
Douglas Crimp and Adam Rolston (eds), *AIDS DEMOgraphics* (Seattle: Bay Press, 1990)
Lucy R. Lippard, *Get the Message? A Decade of Social Change* (New York: Dutton, 1984)
Nancy Spector, *Felix Gonzalez-Torres* (New York: Guggenheim Museum, 1995)

▲ 1994a

1988

Gerhard Richter paints *October 18, 1977*: German artists contemplate the possibility of the renewal of history painting.

In depicting the impact of the Baader-Meinhof Group's violent attempts to overthrow capitalism, Gerhard Richter's 1988 cycle of paintings titled *October 18, 1977* [**1, 2**] concluded a long, complex succession of German artists' attempts to reposition painting as a critical reflection on German history. While most postwar visual art, certainly in Europe and the United States, had avoided references to the immediate past, whether the prewar years or the war experience itself, it was German painting from the sixties onward that specifically tried to oppose the elision of historical references that the artistic neo-avant-garde in general mandated.

Within the context of German postwar art there were attempts to relocate painting in relation to history from as early as 1963, with ▲ the exhibition of Georg Baselitz's *Die Grosse Nacht im Eimer* (and the subsequent scandal and censorship of the painting). First of all, with almost manifesto-like fervor, this type of work tried to reconstruct the site of a specifically German cultural tradition and to create some continuity for it by opposing all the standards that had been adopted in the first seven years of postwar visual culture—primarily the standards of *informel* painting and those imposed • by the rise of American Pop art. Instead, Baselitz's work clamors to be seen as the result of a direct lineage linking it to pre-Weimar German painterly traditions, specifically to the legacies of Lovis ■ Corinth and of German Expressionism. It thereby set out not only to skirt all postwar international avant-garde movements, but, typically and importantly, to avoid all photographically based ◆ practices that were specific to Weimar Dada, and to do so by reestablishing painting as the center of visual culture.

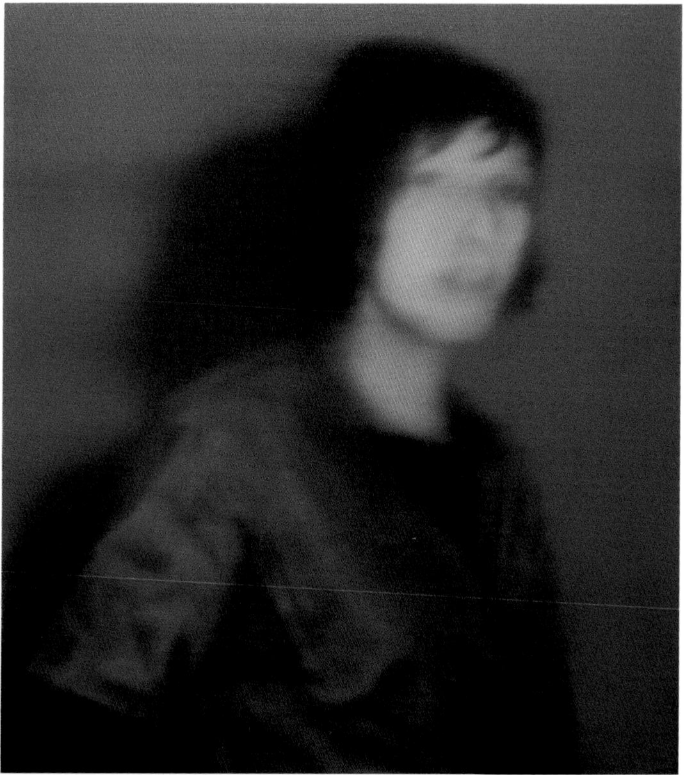

1 • Gerhard Richter, *October 18, 1977: Confrontation 1 (Gegenüberstellung 1)*, 1988
Oil on canvas, 111.8 x 102.2 (44 x 40¼)

The problem of history

Like Baselitz, Gerhard Richter had arrived in West Germany from the East German Democratic Republic, and, also like him, Richter had confronted the question of whether and how recent German history could be made the subject of visual culture. This was also in direct opposition to the *informel* abstractionists such as Winter, Trier, Götz, Hoehme—who were the teachers of Richter, Baselitz, and their peers—and their attempt to internationalize postwar German art. As early as 1962, Richter explicitly addressed the repressed legacy of Germany from 1933 to 1945 by painting a portrait of Adolf Hitler (which he later destroyed). At the same time he began to collect the photographs that would form his huge *Atlas* project [**3**], in which images of private family narrative were increasingly juxtaposed with images of public German history. Over the years this resulted in the panels in which Richter collected photographs from Buchenwald and Bergen-Belsen.

It can therefore be argued that the project to make German painting assume the function of dismantling postwar historical repression could be credited to both Richter and Baselitz. However, the means with which those strategies were implemented were in fact very different; the difference culminated in the late sixties in the opposition between the work of Richter and Anselm Kiefer.

▲ On the one hand, by continuously looking at Nouveau Réalisme and the work of Andy Warhol—the French and American examples who served as the two poles of reference for his early

▲ 1963 • 1946, 1960c, 1964b ■ 1908 ◆ 1920, 1929 ▲ 1960a, 1960c, 1964b

2 • Gerhard Richter, *October 18, 1977: Funeral (Beerdigung)*, 1988
Oil on canvas, 200 x 320 (78¾ x 126)

work—Richter upheld the need to situate German painting in relation to all the other artistic practices that emerged in the early sixties. On the other, Baselitz almost programmatically denounced and denied both mass culture and photography, seeing them as conditions that painting had to counteract. Accordingly, the underlying argument (operative in work from Baselitz to the younger Kiefer)—that it was possible to establish an unbroken model of national identity and regional specificity right through ▲ from Corinth to Expressionism, to antimodernism, to Baselitz and Kiefer themselves—was refused by Richter, who insisted that all visual practices are determined both by their susceptibility to mass culture and by their entanglement in the postnational identity model of global cultural production.

Soon after 1962, Baselitz's work was seconded by numerous followers, among them Markus Lüpertz, all of whom tried to establish a specifically West German form of painting, to serve as the regional idiom of contemporary culture. At that time, links were already being made within painting between such a project and the problematic attempt to set up the foundations of a broader German cultural identity. Even so, Baselitz and his fellow neo-Expressionists avoided confronting the question of whether either of these two claims—for the continuity of national identity on the one hand or for the model of identity in cultural production on the other—were credible after fascism's destruction of any model of national identity in cultural production (in particular the German one). Yet the establishment of this continuity—one that obscured the actual breakdown, the ruptures, the actual historical destruction that German fascism had brought about—was inherent in the project to renationalize and reregionalize cultural production. Thus, while painterly practices are not inherently reactionary, any attempt to project a continuity of experience outside the hiatus of fascism is necessarily both in and of itself a reactionary fiction.

It is along this axis of an opposition between the claim for a return to historical authenticity embedded in painting and the claim for a recognition of the various moments where that claim had been dismantled—by media culture, by political transformations, by the critique of the very idea that a model of national identity could be articulated by cultural production—that Richter and Kiefer can be situated. This opposition, as it reemerged in the eighties, when an international surge of interest in the fiction of a return to regional and national cultures made itself felt (specifically in the American reception of German neo-Expressionism) could be described as a question of mediation. First, since Kiefer's work explicitly addresses the legacy of German Nazi fascism, whereas Richter's focuses on events of German political life in the recent past (as in the *October 18, 1977* series), the issue of mediation occurs around the actual historical events the works address.

▲ 1908, 1925b, 1937a

3 • Gerhard Richter, *Atlas: Panel 9*, 1962–8
Black-and-white clippings and photograph, 51.7 x 66.7 (20⅜ x 26¼)

On that level, the question of the possibility of the representation of German history is already infinitely more complicated in Richter's work than in Kiefer's since, unlike Kiefer, Richter questions even painting's access to and capacity for representing historical experience. Secondly, mediation occurs at the level of painterly execution, since Kiefer's work claims access to German ▲ Expressionist painting as the means of executing his own project of historical representation. Richter, on the other hand, emphasizes both the degree to which history, if it is accessible at all, is mediated by photographic images, and also how not just the construction of historical memory but its very conception are dependent on photographic representation.

Richter's *October 18, 1977* cycle embodies a doubt, then, about the possibility of unmediated access to historical experience through the means of painting just as it asserts the possibility that painting could actually intervene in the process of critical, historical self-reflection. At the same time, the focus on the Baader-Meinhof Group as the subject of recent German history leads in a much more complicated way to a prolonged reflection on the questions of postwar Germany. Writers on the post-1968 student movement and the events leading to the formation of the Baader-Meinhof Group had made it clear that this rebellion against the neocapitalist German state was triggered largely by an underlying horror at both the complicity of the postwar generation's participation in the history of Nazi Germany and its insistent refusal to acknowledge this complicity. Richter's reflection on the fate of the Baader-Meinhof Group is thus part of a larger project of understanding the formation of postwar German identity by addressing the second and third generations of that historical trajectory rather than by returning to the actual events of the Nazi past as they were staged in Kiefer's work.

The staging of such events emerged in Kiefer's first work, his 1969 *Occupations* series [**4**], in which he placed himself in various majestic landscapes (reminiscent of German Romantic pictorial settings) or in monumental architectural complexes and, from a relatively great distance, had himself photographed making the "Heil Hitler!" salute. The fact that this series was accomplished

▲ 1908

photographically complicates the contradictions between Richter's and Kiefer's positions tremendously. First, Kiefer's work situates itself in an explicit dialogue with the photoconceptualist and ▲ performance practices of the sixties, but reorienting both of these within a tainted context of specific German historicity. That was the shock and the aesthetic interest of the project when it was first seen, primarily because it *attempted* to relocate European artistic • practices—under the spell of either American Minimalism or Conceptualism in the late sixties—within the focus of addressing history in a specifically German context; and secondly, because the work tried to criticize the blind spots of the perpetual renovation of West German cultural practices in their approach to history. However, what is crucial in Kiefer's use of the photograph in this series is that unlike Conceptual art's approach to documentary photography at that time, Kiefer consistently treats the photograph as a hybrid, as a residue, as the one tool of representation that is just as discredited as painting. Thus there is a deeply antiphotographic impulse in Kiefer's collection of photographic remnants, as there is an antipainterly impulse in his use of nonpainterly materials such as straw, earth, and other matter in the construction of his paintings. Nonetheless, unlike Richter and artists of the Pop art generation, Kiefer never questions the authenticity or auratic ■ originality of the painting as a singular object, or that of painting as a craft that generates a unique aesthetic experience. Indeed, as far as the continuous visual trope of the *Occupations* series is a reference to Caspar David Friedrich's German Romantic imagery (such as his *Wanderer above the Mist* [c. 1818]), photography is asked to participate in the sublimity of experience to which painting presumably had access in the early nineteenth century and to which neo-Expressionism assumed it could once more connect.

Jürgen Habermas (born 1929)

The last of the major German philosophers to emerge from the so-called Frankfurt School of Critical Theory, Jürgen Habermas, was born in the year the Frankfurt Institute for Social Research was founded. At age the age of twenty-four, when still a doctoral candidate, he published a forceful critique of Martin Heidegger's infamous "Introduction to Metaphysics" (1935), which had announced that philosopher's conversion to Nazism, and which Heidegger had republished in 1953 without a single word of self-criticism, let alone an apology. In 1956 Theodor W. Adorno invited Habermas to join the recently reopened Institute for Social Research in Frankfurt. Under the tutelage of his mentor and the tradition of the Institute, Habermas would develop a synthesis of empirical social research and critical theory, addressing the particular conditions of postwar societies.

In his first groundbreaking work, *The Structural Transformation of the Public Sphere* (1962), Habermas developed a concept that would have important ramifications for an art-historical understanding of the museum and the functions of the avant-garde: the bourgeois public sphere, tracing it from its emancipatory beginnings in the eighteenth century to its imminent dissolution under the impact of late corporate capitalism. In *Knowledge and Human Interest* (1968), his second major work, and one that would bring him international recognition, he formulated the concepts of communicative reason and communicative action as normative models for the subjective and sociopolitical realization of a present-day enlightenment project founded in language itself.

In analyzing Kiefer, the cultural historian Eric Santner proposes that Kiefer's strategies should be seen as a "homeopathic" approach to the conditions of repression. He hails Kiefer's project of confronting the legacy of thirties and forties German history as a necessary attempt to dismantle the repressive apparatus, the almost phobic inhibition, that was established in postwar Germany. In addition to blanking out the Nazi past, this repression also blocked any attempt by the German people actually to articulate their historical experience, by barring their access to the culture of the late nineteenth and early twentieth centuries as well, since the principal figures who made up German culture in this period had been considerably tainted by their abrogation in Nazi ideology. In his portraits Kiefer provocatively mingled figures ranging from Heidegger to Hölderlin, from Moltke to Bismarck, paintings that are seen by Santner not as a project of resuscitating the heroicization of a tainted history but as necessary attempts to open up the repressive apparatus that German culture had internalized and imposed upon itself in the postwar period. Santner thereby follows a similar logic to the one that had been developed by Hans Jürgen Syberberg in his seventies film *Hitler: A Film from Germany*, which was a similar project to open up the question of how German cultural history could be reestablished across the historical hiatus.

Whether or not one finds the model of the "homeopathic" approach to repression an acceptable one, Richter's work, in contrast, seems to take the inextricability of postwar German culture and its repression as its point of departure rather than claiming that it can be remedied. It also seems to take the various layers of postwar German cultural involvement with certain forms of internationalization, and of Americanized consumer culture (e.g., an Americanized model of Pop art production) as a historical condition that cannot be undone. With this act of specifically disclaiming any possibility of access to German cultural history, Richter's project both criticizes and also perhaps—as some artists and critics would say—perpetuates false internationalization and its intrinsic intertwinement with the act of historical repression.

Richter's paintings of the Baader-Meinhof Group members, the various scenes, the arrest, and the members' funerals, are necessarily from the very recent past. They represent what one could call the conclusion of the utopian aspirations of the "moment of 1968," in its calamitous ending with the supposed suicides of Andreas Baader and Ulrike Meinhof in the Stammheim Prison in 1977. As a result of their iconography, the paintings have been widely recognized as an elegiac expression of German doubt and skepticism about the possibilities of utopian political transformation.

▲ 1962a, 1962b, 1968b • 1965 ■ 1935, 1956, 1960c, 1964b

4 • Anselm Kiefer, *Besetzungen (Montpellier)* (Occupations [Montpellier]), 1969
Eight photographs on cardboard

They have also been recognized as an allegory of the life and the history of the postwar German generation in its dual attempt to dissociate itself from and reassociate itself with German history, to overcome the repression of its fathers' generation and at the same time to develop countermodels and alternative political possibilities in the sixties radicalization and mobilization of leftist German thought. Richter himself has denied any aspect of these readings, refusing to be associated with any political interpretation of the paintings and claiming that if there is any connection between them and political thought, his aim was to articulate the problematic nature of *all* utopian projects.

FURTHER READING

Benjamin H. D. Buchloh, "A Note on Gerhard Richter's 18.October 1977," in Gerhard Storck (ed.), *Gerhard Richter: 18. Oktober 1977* (Cologne: Walther König; Krefeld: Kunstmuseum Krefeld; and London: Institute of Contemporary Arts, 1989)

Stefan Germer, "Unbidden Memories," in Gerhard Storck (ed.), *Gerhard Richter: 18. Oktober 1977* (Cologne: Walther König; Krefeld: Kunstmuseum Krefeld; and London: Institute of Contemporary Arts, 1989)

Andreas Huyssen, "Anselm Kiefer: The Terror of the History, the Temptation of Myth," in Andreas Huyssen, *Twilight Memories: Marking Time in a Culture of Amnesia* (Routledge, London, 1995)

Lisa Saltzman, *Anselm Kiefer and Art After Auschwitz* (Cambridge: Cambridge University Press, 1999)

Robert Storr, *Gerhard Richter: October 18, 1977* (New York: Museum of Modern Art; and London: Thames & Hudson, 2000)

1989

"Les Magiciens de la terre," a selection of art from several continents, opens in Paris: postcolonial discourse and multicultural debates affect the production as well as the presentation of contemporary art.

In the eighties two exhibitions at major museums in New York and Paris served as lightning rods for postcolonial debates about art, and also focused new attention on the old problem of the Western collection and exhibition of art from other cultures. The first show, "'Primitivism' in 20th Century Art: Affinities of the Modern and the Tribal" directed by William Rubin and Kirk Varnedoe at the Museum of Modern Art in 1984, consisted of brilliant juxtapositions of modern and tribal works that resembled one another in formal ways. For critics of the show, however, these juxtapositions only rehearsed the mostly abstract understanding of tribal art by ▲ European and American modernists, a noncontextual appropriation which the curators did not adequately question. To an extent the second exhibition, "Les Magiciens de la terre" (Magicians of the Earth), directed by Jean-Hubert Martin at the Centre Georges Pompidou in 1989, took such critiques into consideration. It included only contemporary practitioners, fifty from the West, fifty from elsewhere, many of whom made work specifically for the show. In this way "Magiciens" struggled against some of the formalist appropriations and museological abstractions of non-Western art that were replayed in "Primitivism." Yet for *its* critics "Magiciens" went too far in the opposite direction in its implicit claim of a special authenticity for non-Western art, a special aura of ritual or magic. ● "Who are the magicians of the earth?" Barbara Kruger countered in her skeptical contribution to the show. "Doctors? Politicians? Plumbers? Writers? Arms Merchants? Farmers? Movie Stars?"

The nomadic and the hybrid

The year 1989 was a time for reappraisal of rhetoric on several fronts. Not only had the opposition between the First and Third Worlds already fallen apart, along with the dichotomy between metropolitan centers and colonial peripheries that had structured the relation between modern and tribal art. But so, too, had the opposition between the First and Second Worlds broken down, as signaled by the fall of the Berlin Wall in November. A "new world order," as George Bush would dub it triumphally after the Gulf War in 1991, was emerging—a mostly American order of released multinational flows of capital, culture, and information for privileged people, but of reinforced local borders for many more others.

This mixed development affected many artists profoundly. "Hybridity" became a catchword for some, as postmodernist cri- ▲ tiques of modernist values of artistic originality were extended by postcolonial critiques of Western notions of cultural purity. These postcolonial artists sought a third way between what the critic Peter Wollen has called "archaism and assimilation," or what the artist Rasheed Araeen has termed "academicism and modernism." Content to be neither illustrators of folklorish pasts nor imitators of international styles, they attempted to work out a reflexive dialogue between global trends and local traditions. Sometimes this postcolonial dialogue demanded an additional negotiation between the often nomadic life of the artist and the often site-specific positioning of the project that he or she was asked to produce. Indeed, in this new time of cosmopolitanism, artists were on the move as much as artifacts were in earlier moments of primitivism.

The search for a third way had precedents in art of the eighties. Some artists involved in political groups had already rejected institu- ● tions of art, while others involved, say, in graffiti art like Jean-Michel Basquiat (1960–88) had already played with signs of hybridity. This search was also supported by developments in theory, the most important of which were the critiques of Western self-fashioning and discipline-building in postcolonial discourse, which, after the Palestinian-American critic Edward Said (1935–2003) published his epochal study *Orientalism* in 1978, flourished in the work of theorists Gayatri Spivak, Homi Bhabha, and many others. Of course, postcolonial art and theory has assumed diverse forms depending on context and agenda; between the United States and the United Kingdom alone, for example, there is a difference of focus on the subject of racism, inflected historically by slavery in the States, and by colonialism in Britain. There are also conflictual demands on artists and critics alike, who are often torn between the call for positive images of given identities long subjected to negative stereotypes on the one hand, and the need for critical representations of what the critic Stuart Hall has called "new ethnicities" complicated by sexual and social differences on the other. Sometimes this very conflict between notions of identity—as given naturally or as constructed culturally—is foregrounded, as in some work by black British artists such as the filmmaker Isaac Julien (born 1960), the photographers ■ Keith Piper (born 1960) and Yinka Shonibare (born 1962), and the

▲ 1903, 1907 ● Introduction 1, 1977
▲ 1977, 1980, 1984b ● 1987 ■ 1993c

Aboriginal art

The most renowned form of Aboriginal art in Australia are the "Dreamtime" paintings produced in the northern and central regions (six Dreamtime artists from the Yuendumu community near Alice Springs were represented in "Les Magiciens de la terre"). In Aboriginal belief, Dreamtime was the period of Creation when ancestral beings shaped the land and its inhabitants, and Dreamtime paintings evoke these activities; the imaging of the creator-figures, which assume different forms (human, animal, and plant), tends to be more representational in the northern country, and more abstract, structured around vivid dots and lines, in the central area.

Dreamtime art is a good example of the third way between "archaism" and "assimilation" in contemporary global culture. On the one hand, its designs derive from motifs and patterns used in sacred ceremonies from archaic times (some paintings in rock shelters date back as far 20,000 years). On the other hand, the efflorescence of Dreamtime paintings on canvas is little more than three decades old, spurred technically by the assimilation of acrylic paints in the early seventies and commercially by the market for exotic images among Western collectors whose own culture appears ever more homogeneous. (The market for Maori art also boomed in the eighties, as did the demand for the arts of Africa, the Arctic, Bali, and so on.) Thus, even as Aboriginal art is still based in the ceremonial practices of specific communities—each painting is in part a reenactment of a cosmology passed on from generation to generation—it is also shot through with global forces of touristic taste, cultural commerce, and identity politics.

However, like similar forms of hybrid art in Africa and elsewhere, Dreamtime painting has seemed to thrive on its contradictions. Although it is often dismissed as a pidgin language, its mixing of indigenous idioms and foreign materials is part of its creativity. While its abstraction is attractive to elite tastes schooled in modern art, it also remains true to its own old traditions; and while it borrows such modern techniques as acrylic on canvas, it continues to elaborate ancient motifs otherwise applied to human bodies, tree bark, or the earth. In short, Dreamtime painting is an art that has remained authentic in its own terms even as it plays on the desire for "the authentic" on the part of outsiders. This use of forms is also not one-way: modern Australian artists have drawn on Aboriginal motifs too, and Qantas Airlines once painted one of its fleet in Aboriginal style. At work here then is a kind of exchange that, though hardly equal, must still be distinguished from prior episodes of exoticism in modern art, such as the use of African sculpture in the primitivist work of Picasso, Matisse, and others in the first decades of the century, as well as the projection of Native American art as primordial by some Abstract Expressionists, and the positing of an absolute *art brut*, or uncivilized "outsider art," by Jean Dubuffet and others, both at mid-century. In the case of Dreamtime painting and other forms like it, there is a borrowing from the West by "the other" as well.

"There is a very strong connection between the use of symmetry in Aboriginal art and the powerful commitment to the balance of reciprocity, exchange and equality in Aboriginal art," Peter Sutton, curator of the South Australian Museum, has remarked. At the same time we do well to remember that Aboriginal peoples of Australia, like other indigenous peoples on other continents, were long subject to forced resettlement and worse. To quote Frantz Fanon again: "The zone where the natives live is not complementary to the zone inhabited by the settlers."

painter Chris Ofili (born 1968). More often this conflict has led to divergent conceptions of the role of postcolonial art—to express and reinforce identity, or to complicate and critique its construction.

For Homi Bhabha the search for a third way in postcolonial art suggests a repositioning of the avant-garde—away from the pursuit of a utopian "beyond," a vision of a unitary social future, and toward an articulation of a hybrid "in-between," a negotiation between diverse cultural space-times. This theoretical notion has found its parallel development in the art of such diverse figures as Jimmie Durham (born 1940), David Hammons (born 1943), ▲Gabriel Orozco (born 1962), and Rirkrit Tiravanija (born 1961).

Although different in generation and background, these artists have several things in common. All work with objects and in sites that are somehow hybrid and interstitial, not readily placed within the given discourses of sculpture or the commodity, or in the given spaces of museums or the street, but usually located somewhere in transit between these categories. To an extent photographs figure in this art, but like the other objects they are often residues of performative activities, or what Orozco calls "leftovers of specific situations." This work thus extends across performance and installation too, without resting easily in either. To be sure, such an idiom of found objects, reclaimed debris, and documentary leftovers has precedents, especially in the sixties: one is reminded of the performance props of such artists as ▲Piero Manzoni and Claes Oldenburg, •the "social sculpture" of Joseph Beuys, the assemblages of archaic and technological materials in Arte Povera, and so on. (Importantly, Durham and Hammons, who were active by the early seventies, witnessed some of these practices, while Orozco and Tiravanija encountered them later in museum shows.) Nevertheless, all four contemporary artists are suspicious of the aestheticizing tendencies of such precursors. Although often lyrical as well, their aesthetic is even more provisional and ephemeral, in opposition not only to the old idea of timeless art but also to the new fixities of identity politics.

Subversive play

To different degrees all four artists work with what the critic Kobena Mercer has called "the stereotypical grotesque," and here they are joined by such African-American artists as Adrian Piper, ■Carrie Mae Weems, Lorna Simpson, Renée Green, and Kara

▲ 2003

▲ 1959, 1961 • 1964a, 1967b ■ 1993c

Walker. Essentially this means that they play with ethnic clichés, sometimes with light, acerbic wit, sometimes with exaggerated, explosive absurdity. Thus Durham has fabricated "fake Indian artifacts," and Orozco, stereotypically Mexican skulls; Hammons has used loaded black symbols, and Tiravanija, stereotypically Thai cuisine. They have also engaged different models of the primitive ▲ object, such as the fetish and the gift, which they often juxtapose with "modern" products or debris. In some sense these subversively hybrid things are symbolic portraits of a similarly disruptive kind of complex identity.

Like the Performance artist James Luna (born 1950), who has acted out such stereotypes of the Indian as the warrior, the shaman, and the drunk, Jimmie Durham pressures primitivist clichés to the point of critical ridicule. This is most evident in *Self-Portrait* (1988), in which he summons up the smokeshop chief of American lore, only to tag this wooden figure with absurdist responses to racist projections about Native-American men. Durham first produced his fake Indian artifacts from old car parts and animal skulls; then he mixed in other kinds of commodity debris to produce "artifacts from the future" whose "physical histories ... didn't want to go together." One such artifact juxtaposes, on a craggy board, a portable phone and an animal pelt, on top of which is inscribed this quotation from the anticolonial revolutionary and theorist Frantz Fanon: "The zone where the natives live is not complementary to the zone inhabited by the settlers" [**1**]. Such hybrid art, which reworks the Surrealist object to postcolonial ends, is wryly anticategorical in a way that resists any further "settlement" into separate "zones."

David Hammons also puts ethnic associations into subversive play. In the early seventies he did a series of images and objects with spades, at once a tool of manual labor and a slang word for African-American. One such object, *Spade with Chains* (1973), is especially provocative in its simultaneous suggestion of slavery and strength, bondage and resistance [**2**]. Hammons has since made many sculptures out of discarded or abject things that are culturally fraught, such as barbecue bones in bags, African-American hair wound into balls on wires and woven onto screens, chicken parts, elephant dung, and found bottles of cheap wine stuck on stripped branches or hung from trees. For some viewers these objects and installations evoke the desperation of the black urban underclass. Hammons, however, sees a sacred aspect in these profane things, a ritualistic power. "Outrageously magical things happen when you mess around with a symbol," he has remarked. "You've got tons of people's spirits in your hands when you work with that stuff." His contradictory contemporary fetishes return art to the street, and at once demystify and reritualize it there.

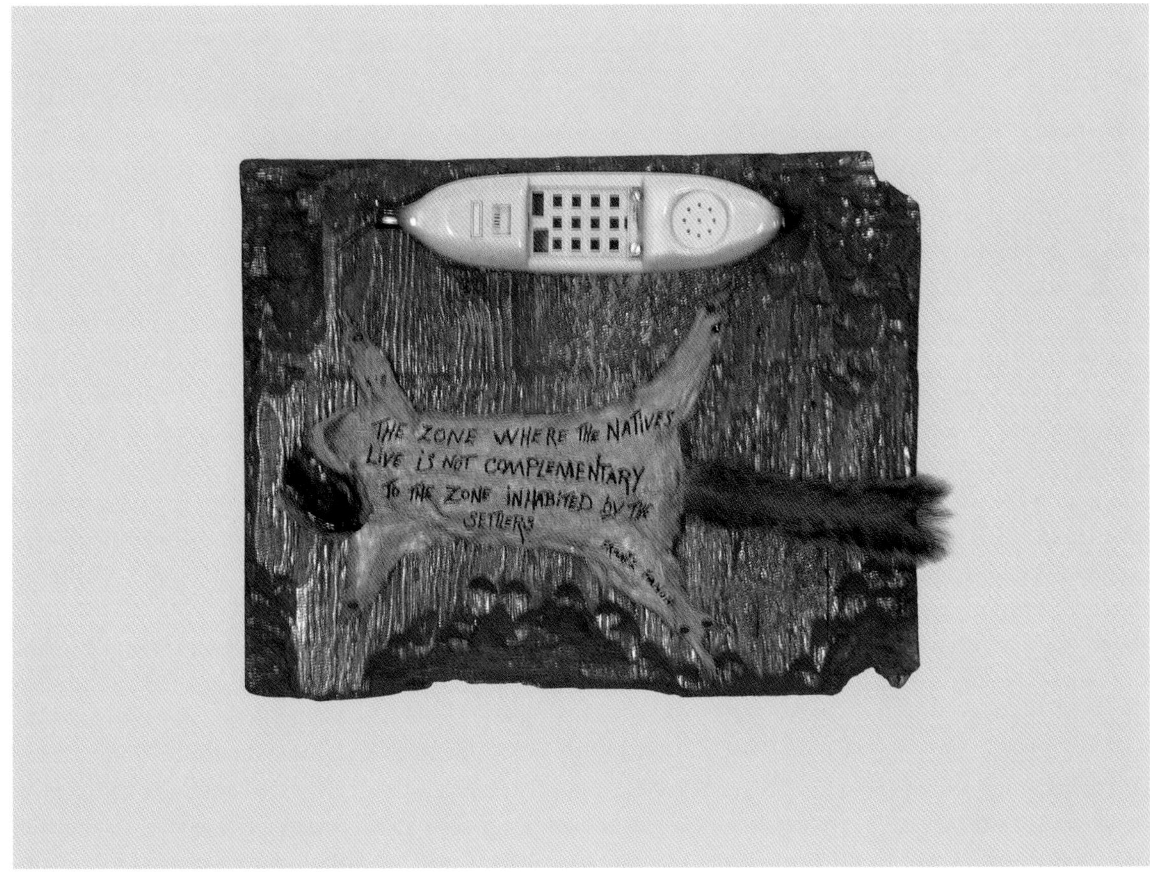

1 • Jimmie Durham, *Often Durham Employs ...*, 1988
Mixed media, wood, squirrel skin, paint, and plastic, 30.5 x 40.6 x 12.7 (12 x 16 x 5)

▲ 1931

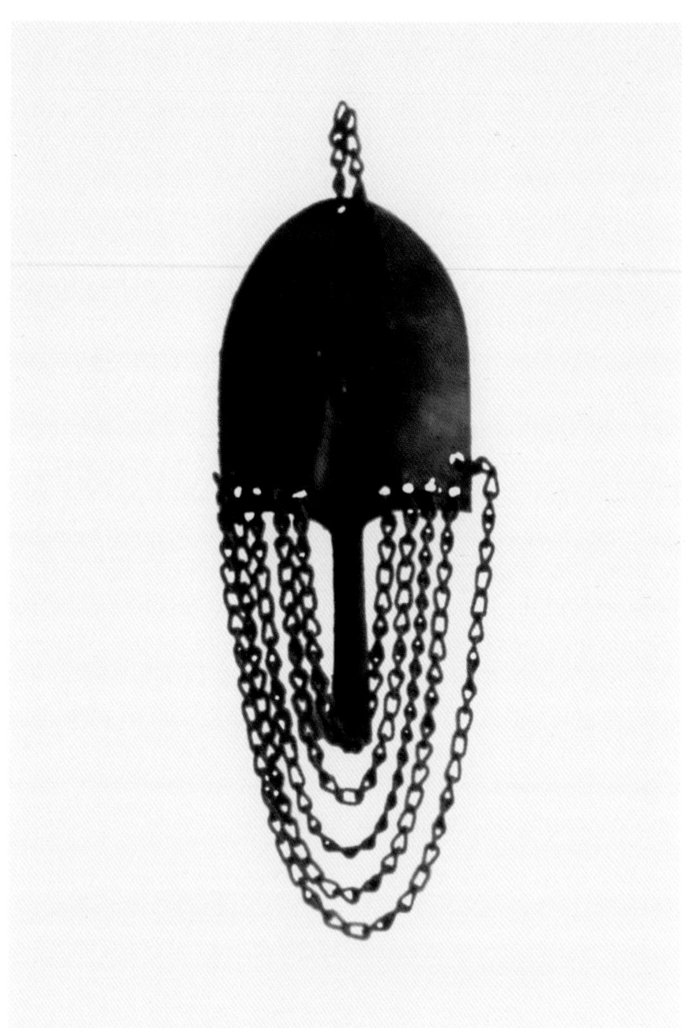

2 • David Hammons, *Spade with Chains*, 1973
Spade, chains, 61 x 25.4 x 12.7 (24 x 10 x 5)

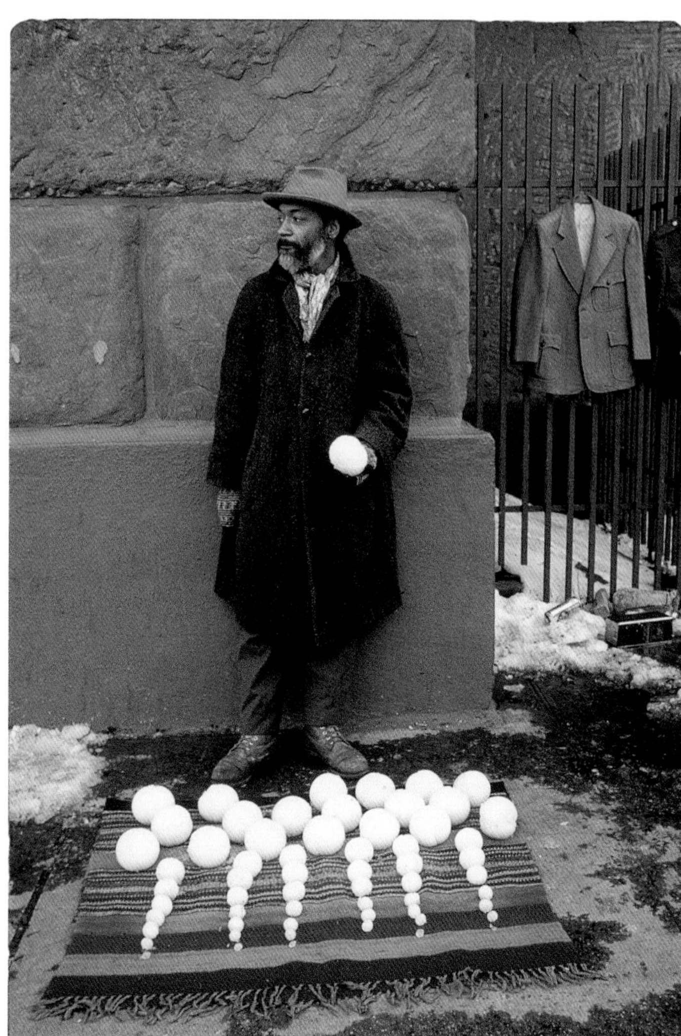

3 • David Hammons, *Bliz-aard Ball Sale*, 1983
Installation in Cooper Square, New York

Often indirect, the work of Hammons and Durham nonetheless possesses the edge of political commitment—Hammon's to the civil rights and Black Power movements, Durham's to the American Indian movement, in which he was an activist. Born of less confrontational times, the work of Orozco and Tiravanija is more lyrical. A 1983 performance piece by Hammons can help us track the directions that they take. In *Bliz-aard Ball Sale* Hammons presented several rows of different-sized snowballs for sale, next to other vendors of disused things on the street, in front of Cooper Union in downtown Manhattan [**3**]. This piece cut across private and public spaces, and confounded valued and valueless things, in a way that suggested that these distinctions are often artificial and only afforded by the privileged—a demonstration made by Orozco as well. At the same time, the snowballs, like the rubber-doll shoes that Hammons has also offered on the street, exist in a pathetic and parodic relation to commodity exchange, and point to a system of resale, barter, and gifts that Tiravanija has also explored as a critical alternative to the capitalist network of art.

One instance of each practice must suffice here. In a 1993 project for the Museum of Modern Art, Orozco invited neighbors in the apartment building north of MoMA to place an orange in each window sill that fronted the museum [**4**]. Here was a sculpture, wittily titled *Home Run*, that exceeded the physical space of the museum ball park. At the same time it brought into ambiguous contact different kinds of objects (perishable fruit on the window sills, bronze sculpture in the museum garden), agents (semiprivate residents and semipublic curators), and spaces (homes and ▲ museums). This is institutional critique with a lyrical touch, which, as with Tiravanija, does not mean that it is inconsequential.

In a signal piece of 1992, Tiravanija also used the dislocating of space and the offering of food as a means to confuse the normal positions and conventional roles of art, artist, viewer, and intermediary (in this case the art dealer). At 303 Gallery in New York he moved the private unseen rooms of the gallery, which contained the business office, the packing, and shipping areas, and all the other materials of its daily functioning, into its public viewing spaces [**5**]. The director and assistants at desks were on display in the central gallery, while Tiravanija worked over a stove in the back gallery where he cooked and served Thai curry vegetables over jasmine rice to interested gallery visitors, often with conversation added. In subsequent works he has often played on such reversals of physical space, substitutions of expected function, and displacements of

▲ Introduction 4, 1971, 1992

4 • Gabriel Orozco, *Home Run*, 1993
Installation in apartment building, view from the Museum of Modern Art, New York

5 • Rirkrit Tiravanija, *Untitled (Free)*, 1992
Tables, stool, food, crockery, and cooking utensils, dimensions variable

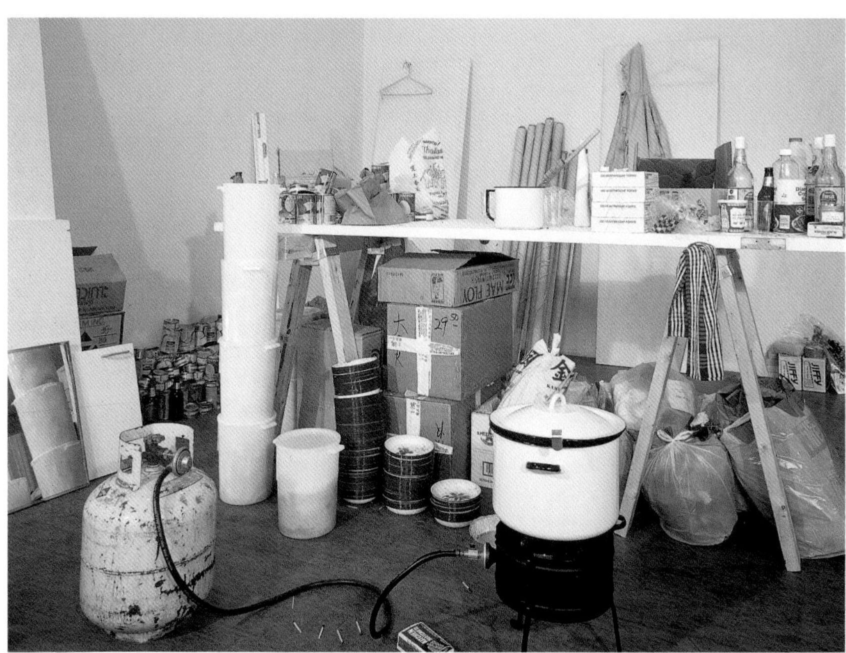

object exchange that invite one to reflect on the enforced conventionality of all of these categories in the art world and beyond.

"Not the monument," Durham has remarked of his work in a way that relates to the other artists as well, "not the painting, not the picture." Rather, he seeks an "eccentric discourse of art" that might pose "investigatory questions about what sort of things it might be, but always within a political situation of the time." In this way the work of these artists constitutes the equivalent of the "minor literature" defined by the French critics Gilles Deleuze (1925–95) and Felix Guattari (1930–92) in their 1975 study of Franz Kafka: "The three characteristics of minor literature are the deterritorialization of language, the connection of the individual and the political, the collective arrangement of utterance. Which amounts to this: that 'minor' no longer characterizes certain literatures, but describes the revolutionary conditions of any literature within what we call the great (or established)."

FURTHER READING

Homi Bhabha, *The Location of Culture* (London: Routledge, 1994)
Tom Finkelpearl et al., *David Hammons* (Cambridge, Mass.: MIT Press, 1991)
Jean-Hubert Martin et al., *Les Magiciens de la terre* (Paris: Centre Georges Pompidou, 1989)
Laura Mulvey et al., *Jimmie Durham* (London: Phaidon Press, 1995)
Molly Nesbit et al., *Gabriel Orozco* (Los Angeles: Museum of Contemporary Art, 2000)
Peter Wollen, *Raiding the Icebox: Reflections on 20th Century Culture* (Bloomington: Indiana University Press, 1993)

1990–2003

624 1992 Fred Wilson presents *Mining the Museum* in Baltimore: institutional critique extends beyond the museum, and an anthropological model of project art based on fieldwork is adapted by a wide range of artists. HF
box • Interdisciplinarity HF

630 1993a Martin Jay publishes *Downcast Eyes*, a survey of the denigration of vision in modern philosophy: the critique of visuality is explored by a number of contemporary artists. RK

635 1993b As Rachel Whiteread's *House*, a casting of a terrace house in east London, is demolished, an innovative group of women artists comes to the fore in Britain. HF

639 1993c In New York, the Whitney Biennial foregrounds work focused on identity amid the emergence of a new form of politicized art by African-American artists. HF

645 1994a A mid-career exhibition of Mike Kelley highlights a pervasive concern with states of regression and abjection, while Robert Gober, Kiki Smith, and others use figures of the broken body to address problems of sexuality and mortality. HF

650 1994b William Kentridge completes *Felix in Exile*, joining Raymond Pettibon and others in demonstrating the renewed importance of drawing. RK

654 1998 An exhibition of large video projections by Bill Viola tours several museums: the projected image becomes a pervasive format in contemporary art. RK/HF
box • The spectacularization of art HF

659 2001 A mid-career exhibition of Andreas Gursky at the Museum of Modern Art in New York signals the new dominance of a pictorial photography, which is often effected through digital means. HF

664 2003 With exhibits such as "Utopia Station" and "Zone of Urgency," the Venice Biennale exemplifies the informal and discursive nature of much recent artmaking and curating. HF

1992

Fred Wilson presents *Mining the Museum* in Baltimore: institutional critique extends beyond the museum, and an anthropological model of project art based on fieldwork is adapted by a wide range of artists.

One way to understand some of the shifts in materials and methods over the last forty years of advanced art is to see them as a sequence of investigations: first into the constituent elements of a traditional medium like painting, as in the ▲ self-critical modernist painting advocated by Clement Greenberg; then into the perceptual conditions of an art object defined in • terms less of a given medium than of a given space, as in Minimalist art; then into the material basis of such artmaking and perceiving, ■ as explored variously by Arte Povera, Process art, and Body art. Along the way, Conceptual art also shifted attention away from the specific conventions of painting and sculpture to the general questions of "art as art" and "art as an institution."

At first the institution of art was understood mostly in physical terms, as the actual spaces of art studio, gallery, and museum, and artists worked to underscore these parameters and/or to expand them. One thinks of the systematic exposés of these art spaces by Michael Asher, Dan Graham, Marcel Broodthaers, and Daniel Buren, who also wrote an important set of critical texts on such ◆ subjects. Such "institutional critique" revealed that the institution of art was not only a physical space but also a network of discourses (including criticism, journalism, and publicity) that intersected with other discourses, indeed with other institutions (including the media and the corporation). It also suggested that the viewer of art could not be defined strictly in perceptual terms, for he or she was also a social subject marked by multiple differences of class, race, and gender—a point stressed by feminist artists above all others. Of course, this expansion of the definitions of art and institution, artist and viewer, was also driven by social developments (especially the civil rights and feminist movements early on, and postcolonial and queer politics later), as well as by theoretical critiques of the oppositions of high and low culture and modernist and mass art. Together these forces, both internal and external to art, prompted a wider engagement of the culture at large. Thus was the field of art and criticism expanded to "cultural studies," with culture understood in an almost anthropological sense.

This sequence of investigations can also be understood as a set of transformations involving the site of art: from the surface of painting and the armature of sculpture to the structure of the studio, gallery or museum, as well as to the alternative spaces of site-specific installations and the distant locations of Earthworks. Here, too, a gradual shift occurred from a literal, physical understanding of site to a more abstract, discursive understanding—to the point where, in the late eighties and early nineties, artists and ▲ critics could treat desire or death, AIDS or homelessness, as so many sites for art projects. Along with this expanded notion of site came an expanded operation of "mapping," which also ranged from the literal to the discursive—for example, from the cartographic markings of (semi)natural sites by Robert Smithson and • others to the sociological mappings of (sub)urban sites by Dan Graham and others (such as his *Homes for America* [1966–7], a magazine report of the "Minimalist" structures to be found in a tract-housing development in New Jersey).

An ethnographic turn

Sociological mapping became more programmatic in institutional critique during the seventies, especially in the work of Hans ■ Haacke. Haacke moved from profile polls of gallery and museum visitors and archival exposés of real-estate moguls in New York (1969–73), to detailed reports of the successive owners of particular paintings by Manet and Seurat (1974–5), to continued investigations of the financial and ideological arrangements made by museums, corporations, and governments. Such work questioned these social authorities incisively, but it did not often reflect on its own sociological authority, its own voice of truth. This reflexivity was more pronounced with artists, such as Martha Rosler, who were involved in a critique of documentary modes ◆ of representation as somehow transparent to the world. In her phototext work *The Bowery in Two Inadequate Descriptive Systems* (1974–5), Rosler mimicked documentary photographs as well as sociological descriptions of alcoholic destitution in order to show the "inadequacy" of both "descriptive systems" in the face of this recalcitrant social problem.

In feminist art the suspicion of documentary representation converged with an elaboration of institutional critique in the work of such artists as Louise Lawler and Silvia Kolbowski. This convergence was complicated by an interest in quasi-ethnographic modes of fieldwork, as some artists assumed the roles of both

▲ 1960b • 1965 ■ 1967b, 1969, 1974 ◆ 1968b, 1970, 1971, 1972a ▲ 1984a, 1987 • Introduction 2, 1968b, 1970 ■ 1971, 1972b ◆ Introduction 2, 1984a

ethnographer and native-informant in everyday life under patriarchy. (A few of these artists, like Susan Hiller [born 1942], were trained in anthropology.) It was in this manner that Mary Kelly reported on patriarchal conventions of language, schooling, artmaking, and aging in such projects as *Post-Partum Document* ▲ (1973–9) and *Interim* (1985–9). By the early nineties art based on personal reportage, fieldwork and/or archival research had become pervasive, as more and more artists were invited to do site-specific projects at museums and related institutions around • the world. The combination of the nomadic condition of the artist and the project basis of the art made installation the preferred mode of this work.

There were several reasons for this ethnographic turn in some art of the nineties, such as an involvement in nonart forms of cultural representation that was also encouraged by the growth of cultural studies in the academy. Yet anthropology also possessed its own attractions for artists and critics alike. First, anthropology is the discipline that takes *culture* as its object, and this expanded ■ field of operations was desired by many postmodernist artists. Second, anthropology is *contextual* in nature, another attribute much valued in recent art and criticism. Third, it is seen as intrinsically *interdisciplinary*, a further characteristic prized in such practice. Fourth, it is a discipline that studies *otherness*, which has made anthropology, along with psychoanalysis, the common language of much recent art and criticism. And, finally, the *critique* of "ethnographic authority" launched in the eighties also rendered anthropology attractive, for it suggests a special self-awareness on the part of the ethnographic artist.

Such self-awareness was essential for artists who took up the model of fieldwork. Lothar Baumgarten (born 1944) was one of the first to do so in his mappings of indigenous cultures of North and South America, which were often based on his extensive travels. In several projects over the last two decades, Baumgarten has inscribed the names of native societies of both continents—names often imposed by explorers and ethnographers alike—onto various settings. These sites have ranged from Northern museums (such as the neoclassical dome of the Museum Fridericianum in Kassel, Germany, in 1982 [**1**] and the modernist spiral of the Guggenheim Museum in New York in 1993) to Southern settings (such as in Caracas, Venezuela) that Baumgarten has sometimes marked with the names of threatened local species and extracted raw materials as well. The names of the various native societies often appeared somewhat distorted in these installations, with letters placed upside down or reversed, as if to underscore the historical misrepresentation of these groups, but also to challenge this misrepresentation in the present. Thus in Kassel the mute Indian names seemed to suggest that the other side of Old World Enlightenment (as evoked by the neoclassical dome of the museum) was New World Conquest. Meanwhile in New York these names seemed to suggest that some other mapping of the globe (as evoked by the spiral of the Frank Lloyd Wright building) was required, one without hierarchies of North and South or modern and primitive.

The last examples point to a potential problem with these quasi-ethnographic projects: they are often commissioned by the museums, and it can appear as if these institutions import this kind of critique as a substitute for an analysis that they might have undertaken internally. This complication has led some critics to declare institutional critique recuperated by the museums, and the flurry of international shows of commissioned site-specific projects in the mid-to-late nineties did not contradict this view (this trend culminated in the 1999 survey at the Museum of Modern Art with the telling title "The Museum as Muse"). On the other hand, this location within the museum is necessary if these

1 • Lothar Baumgarten, *Documenta installation project*, rotunda of the Museum Fridericianum, Kassel, 1982

▲ 1975 • 2003 ■ 1977, 1980, 1984b

projects are to remap its space or to reconfigure its audience in any way; indeed, this internal position is a premise of all work that purports to be deconstructive. And this argument held for the most incisive of these projects, such as *Mining the Museum* by Fred Wilson (born 1954).

The artist as curator

In *Mining the Museum*, sponsored by the Museum of Contemporary Art in Baltimore, Wilson took an ethnographic approach to the Maryland Historical Society. First he explored its collection of historical artifacts, especially ones deemed marginal and placed in storage; this excavating was a first meaning of the "mining" in the title. Then he reclaimed certain objects in the collection, most evocative of African-American experiences, which were not part of the official history on display; this repossessing was a second kind of "mining." Finally he reframed still other objects that were already part of the official history. For example, in an existing exhibit of exquisite goblets and pitchers captioned "Metalwork 1793–1880" [**2**], Wilson placed a rough pair of slave manacles found in storage; this third kind of "mining" wrenched the objects on view into a different context of meaning, from one kind of ownership to another. In this way Wilson served as an anthropologist not only of the Maryland Historical Society but also of the African-American communities not adequately represented there—a situation that the Society at least began to ameliorate through this very exhibition. Wilson had previously worked as a curator; as an artist he has continued this work, critically, by other means.

Andrea Fraser (born 1965) is best known for her barbed performances of various art-world types, including the curator, but she has also made several ethnographic probes into museum culture. In *Aren't They Lovely* (1992), for example, she reopened a private bequest to the art museum of the University of California at Berkeley in order to investigate how the heterogeneous domestic objects of a specific collector (from everyday eyeglasses to Renoir paintings) are transformed into the homogeneous public culture of a general art museum. Whereas Wilson has focused on the problem of institutional repression, here Fraser addressed the process of institutional sublimation; in both cases the artists play with museology in order first to expose and then to reframe the institutional codings of art and artifacts—how specific objects are translated into historical evidence and/or cultural exemplars by museums, invested as such with meaning and value, and for what constituencies this is done (or not done).

Renée Green (born 1959) has also adopted an ethnographic approach, in a way that often extends beyond the art museum. In her site-specific projects she has focused on the residues of ▲ racism, sexism, and colonialism that remain inscribed in various kinds of representations: popular movies and travel literature, domestic decor and institutional architecture, as well as private collections and museum displays. A few of her installations have sketched a critical genealogy of the principal figure of primitivist • fantasy, the exotic and erotic female, from the "Hottentot Venus," a nineteenth-century European stereotype of an excessive African sexuality, to the American jazz dancer Josephine Baker, who ■ enthralled young modernists like Le Corbusier in the Paris of the

2 • Fred Wilson, *Mining the Museum*, 1992 (detail)
Slave manacles placed in metalwork display

▲ 1993c • 1903, 1907 ■ 1925a

Interdisciplinarity

Many positions in postwar art are articulated between or across the mediums and the disciplines: one thinks of the experiments at Black Mountain College, the aesthetics of John Cage and Robert Rauschenberg, the investigations of the Independent Group and the Situationists, the various practices of assemblage, happenings, and environments, as well as such disparate movements as Fluxus, Neoconcretism, Nouveau Réalisme, Minimalism, Process art, Performance art, video, and so on. Some of these practices recovered precedents from the prewar period that either attacked traditional art forms, like Dada and Surrealism, or sought to transform them utterly, like Constructivism. But they also reacted against a strong reading of modernist art that understood its mission to be the perceptual refinement of the specific mediums (e.g., the "opticality" of painting). "The concepts of quality and value—and to the extent that these are central to art, the concept of art itself—are meaningful, or wholly meaningful, only *within* the individual arts," Michael Fried insisted, famously, in his 1967 essay "Art and Objecthood." "What lies *between* the arts is theater." Clearly he had in mind some of the aforementioned practices, whose interdisciplinary methods and temporal involvements ("theatrical" in his lexicon) he deemed improper to visual art.

Yet this opposition overlooks several forces even more important to the general tendency toward interdisciplinary art over the last four decades. First, there was the inspiration of both the critique of political institutions and the expansion of cultural spaces in the social movements of the sixties and seventies—student, civil rights, antiwar, and feminist movements above all. Second, along with a crossing of mediums there was an erosion in hierarchies at this time—of high and low forms, elite and popular audiences, fine and media arts (we tend to forget, in the midst of our own technological retoolings, that the sixties and seventies experienced great transformations in this respect too). Third, there were, especially in the eighties, the interdisciplinary provocations of poststructuralist theory—a loose term that gathered together such disparate thinkers as Roland Barthes, Jacques Derrida, and Michel Foucault. However different their interests, all these figures practiced a critical suspicion of whatever appeared to be originary and authoritative, purely proper and simply present—a suspicion that was extended to artistic forms and institutional frames, and without which postmodernism could not have been theorized. Finally, there was, in the nineties, the effect of postcolonial discourse, which elaborated the poststructuralist deconstruction of conceptual oppositions in the political context of decolonialization—a deconstruction of such binaries as First World and Third World, center and periphery, and Occident and Orient. In related art, critiques of identity and notions of hybridity came to the fore.

The latter two developments are sometimes described, respectively, as a semiotic turn, in which the linguistic sign is the privileged term of analysis, and an ethnographic turn, in which cultural practice becomes the primary object of study. In the first instance, some artists, architects, filmmakers, and critics adapted semiotic models in order to rethink their work in textual terms. And in the second instance they did much the same thing with anthropological notions of culture. Sometimes, it must be admitted, these exchanges followed a used-car principle whereby, as one practice or discipline wore out a paradigm, it passed it on to another; but such exchanges also greatly expanded the fields of art and criticism alike. In the present, however, both fields show signs of a stalled relativism in which no one paradigm is strong enough to orient practice, or to make for relevant debate with any real purchase on the culture at large. Moreover, the inflation of design and spectacle in contemporary art and architecture sometimes appears as part of a greater revenge of advanced capitalism on the expanded fields of postmodernist culture—a recouping of its crossings of arts and disciplines, a routinization of its transgressions. Not long ago, when late modernism seemed to petrify into medium-specificity, postmodernism promised an interdisciplinary opening. What might renew postmodernism in turn?

twenties. In *Seen* **[3]** Green had the viewer stand on a special platform in order to see her images of these women, which in effect aligned the contemporary spectator with the historical voyeur of such figures—one could not assume a moral superiority with temporal distance. Green has also focused our gaze on aspects of primitivism closer to the present: in *Import/Export Funk Office* (1992), for example, she explored our urban legends concerning hip-hop culture music and black masculinity.

Mark Dion (born 1961) has taken the ethnographic approach even further afield: the "culture" that he studies is that of nature—how it is studied in science, represented in fiction, and staged in natural history museums. For Dion nature is "one of the most sophisticated arenas for the production of ideology," and his projects attempt to expose aspects of this production with techniques inspired by various artists and intellectuals—the wry fictional ▲ museums of Broodthaers, the site/non-site strategies of Smithson, the historical investigations of scientific discourses of Michel ● Foucault, and so on. For all its criticism of the ecological disasters precipitated by colonial history and postcolonial economics, his art is hardly one of disdainful critique: Dion is also an avid amateur, with his own collections of insects and other curiosities often on display; his work has drawn, too, on his many trips to the tropics and elsewhere. In this manner Dion plays the naturalist and the environmentalist in ways that are both straight and sardonic. Most often his installations have taken the form of works in progress, and they exist somewhere between a site in the field, the home office of a bizarre naturalist, and a finished museum display **[4]**. "I take raw materials out of the world and then act upon them in the space of the gallery," Dion has remarked. "When the collection is complete, when I've run out of space or raw material or time, the work is finished."

▲ Introduction 4, 1970, 1972a ● 1971

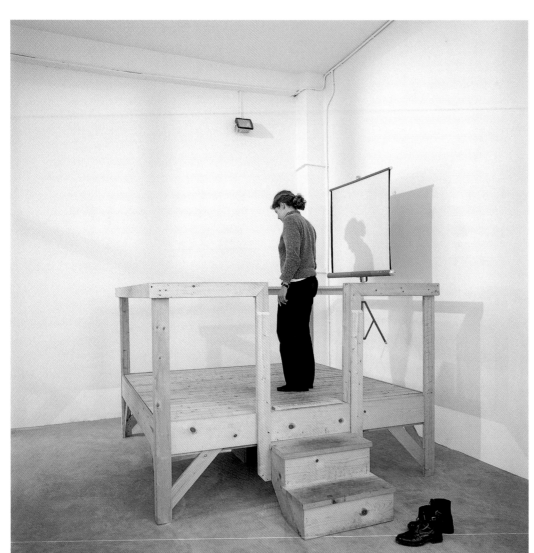

3 • Renée Green, *Seen*, 1990
Wood structure, height 207 x 207 x 136 (81½ x 81½ x 53½), lens, hologram, screen, light, and audio system

4 • Renée Green, *Seen*, 1990 (detail)
Wood structure, height 207 x 207 x 136 (81½ x 81½ x 53½), lens, hologram, screen, light, and audio system

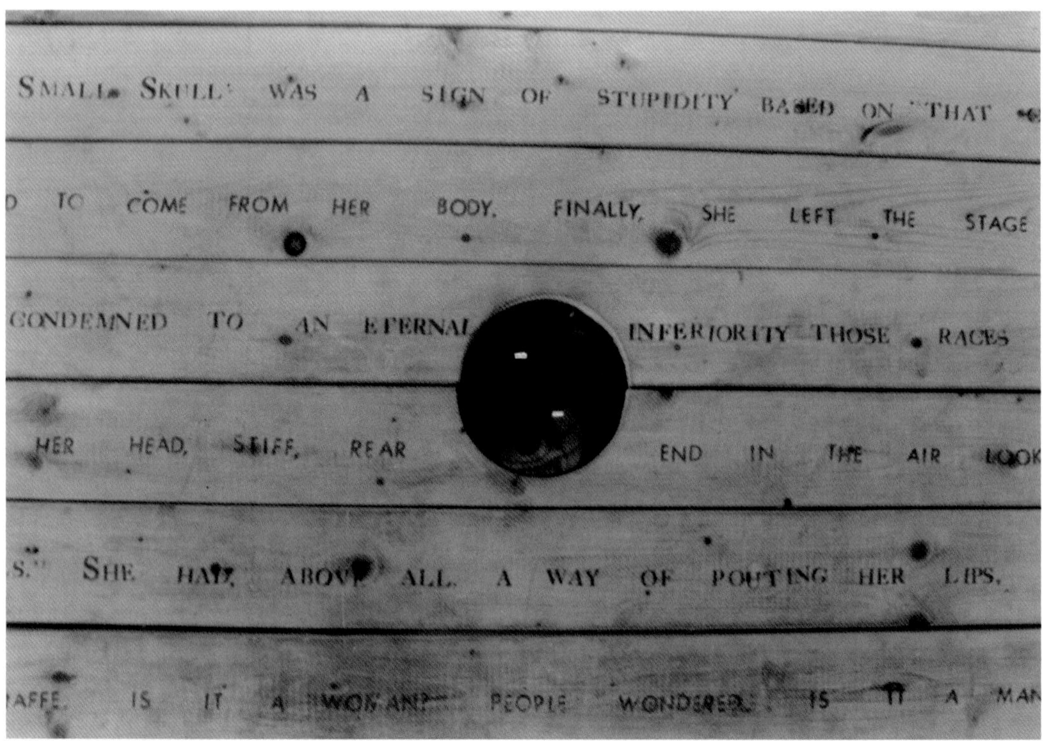

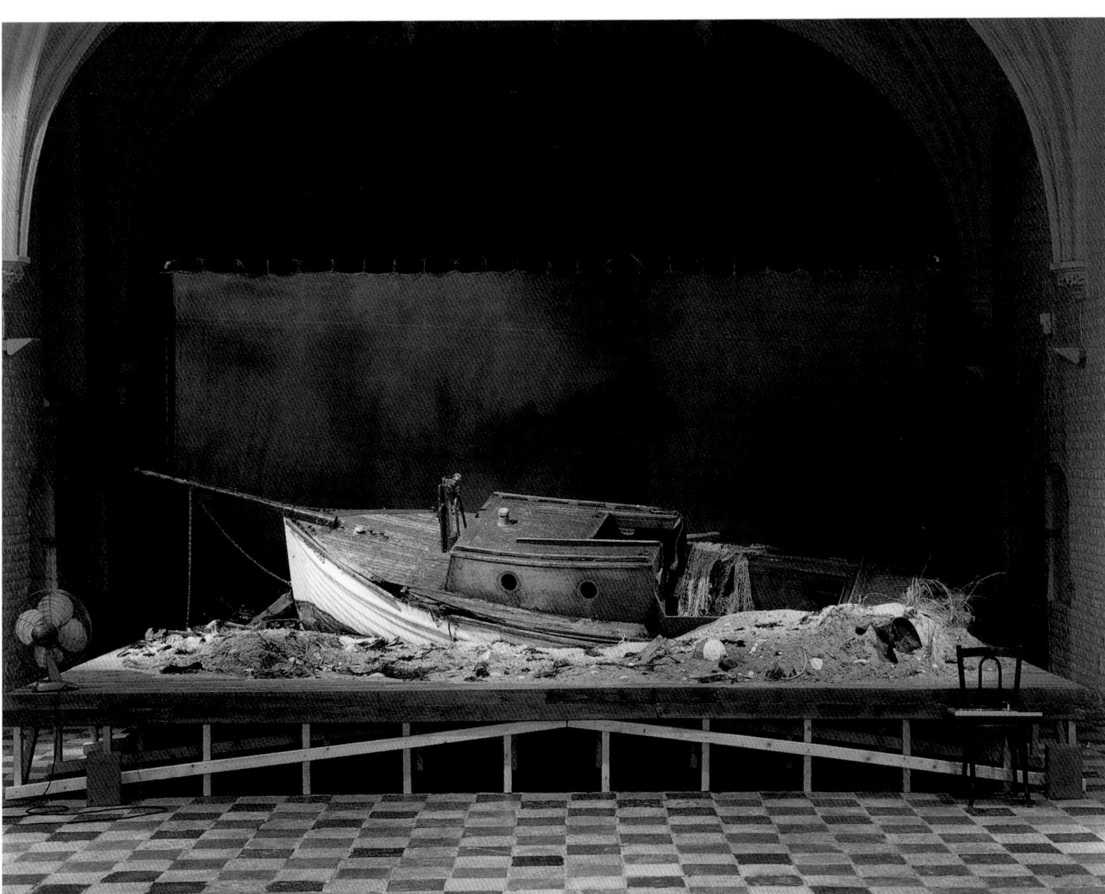

4 • Mark Dion, *Flotsam and Jetsam (The End of the Game)*, 1994
Mixed-media installation

Each of these artists complicates the ethnographic approach with ▲ other models: Fraser is interested in the sociology of art pioneered by the French sociologist Pierre Bourdieu; Green, in the postcolonial discourse of critics like Homi Bhabha; Dion, in the study of disciplines developed by Foucault; and so on. But the ethnographic turn in recent art has also raised certain questions. The quasi-anthropological role set up for the artist can promote a presuming of ethnographic authority as much as a questioning of it. In some instances the artist might be asked to represent a neglected community, only to stand in for this community at the museum, and so confirm as much as contest its absence there. The curatorial role might also prompt an evading of institutional critique as much as an extending of it. In some instances the artist might become a curator • for hire, an adviser in an educational program, or even a consultant in a public-relations campaign. Indeed, the nineties witnessed the rise not only of the artist-as-curator but of the complementary figure of the curator-as-artist, whose orchestration of a show or a set of site-specific projects often appeared to be the primary creative act. This development of curating as a pervasive "medium" of contemporary art suggests an uncertainty about the domains of artmaking and curating alike, just as the development of socially site-specific projects bespeaks an anxiety about the status of the public not only for art museums but for contemporary art in general.

There is a final question about this ethnographic turn that bears consideration. Such art is impressively inventive and smartly contingent: "We hold dear the belief," Dion has commented, "that our production can have many different forms of expression—making a film, teaching, writing, producing a public project, doing something for a newspaper, curating or presenting a discrete work in a gallery." But sometimes its very multiplicity might confuse its audience, or invite the charge that it is dilettantish. Moreover, with art conceived in terms of projects, and projects conceived in terms of discursive sites, these artists might be led to work horizontally, in a lateral movement from social issue to issue, or from political debate to debate, more than vertically, in a diachronic engagement with the historical forms of a genre, medium, or art. Granted, a strict focus on its own intrinsic problems can lead to an art that is involuted and detached, but a strict focus on extrinsic debates can lead art to forget its own repertoire of forms, its own memory of meanings—to relinquish the critical possibilities of its own semi-autonomous sites.

FURTHER READING

James Clifford, *The Predicament of Culture* (Cambridge, Mass.: Harvard University Press, 1988)
Lisa Corrin et al., *Mark Dion* (London: Phaidon Press, 1997)
Hal Foster, *The Return of the Real* (Cambridge, Mass.: MIT Press, 1996)
Andrea Fraser, "What's Intangible..."?, *October*, no. 80, Summer 1997
Miwon Kwon, *One Place After Another: Site-Specific Art and Locational Identity* (Cambridge, Mass.: MIT Press, 2002)

▲ 1989 • 2003

1993a

Martin Jay publishes *Downcast Eyes*, a survey of the denigration of vision in modern philosophy: this critique of visuality is explored by a number of contemporary artists.

With a subtitle announcing his book as treating "The Denigration of Vision," the American historian Martin Jay's *Downcast Eyes* could easily have appeared as yet another theorization of postmodernism, joining the rising chorus of voices either producing or analyzing that challenge to vision ▲ familiar to the art world since the sixties. From Conceptual art's use of language to chase any experience of lush visuality from the visual arts, to the strategies of hiding, wrapping, or secreting that had been • developed by certain kinds of Performance and Body art, the idea that aesthetic production should be geared to either optical display or ocular pleasure was opened to the severest attack.

And if this was happening in the domain of practice, at the level of criticism the break between modernism and postmodernism was being understood in terms of a transformation of the senses—here, the sense of sight—which were themselves no longer taken to be biological givens and thus transhistorical, but were seen to be specifically shaped by history. Thus, in order to analyze the onset of ■ postmodernism, Fredric Jameson first describes the modernist experience of the visual, achieved by the time of Impressionism, as the constitution of a semiautonomous mode of perception. If Realism's drive was to express the experience of the world as a totality that therefore engages the sensory field of the whole body—touch, hearing, smell, balance, motion, as well as seeing—Impressionism breaks off this one perceptual channel from the whole and makes it instead into a quasi-abstract source of pleasure that could attain new heights of fullness and purity. In the postwar period, however, within the conditions of advanced capitalism, Jameson argues, this abstract but full visuality is transformed into a new and disorienting form of unreality, a generalized kind of seeing that Jameson names "the hysterical sublime." Still others would interpret this sense of an image-world divested of anything real behind it and thus become "simulacral" as a function of an ◆ ever-deepening effect of "spectacle."

But *Downcast Eyes* projects the attack on vision as more than a postwar or postmodern phenomenon; the book's full subtitle reads: "The Denigration of Vision in Twentieth-Century French Thought." Once regarded as the culture of En*light*enment thinking, in which vision's capacity to survey and order, to abstract and model the elements within a given field, had made it into the privileged vehicle of reason itself, France was now seen as covering vision with the utmost suspicion throughout the whole of the twentieth century. In Jay's account, this opens with Henri Bergson's repudiation of space as the dominant model of experience to which other orders, such as the temporal, are submitted. Contrasting the homogeneity of space—a matrix of repeatable equivalent units, each outside the other—to the heterogeneity of time, in which memory and projection are inextricably telescoped into the present, Bergson formulated the idea of duration—the *durée*—as radically unassimilable to space and thus also to vision. From Bergson, this opposition continues, in different terms, to the ▲ Surrealists and Georges Bataille, and thence to Jean-Paul Sartre's near paranoia, in his *Being and Nothingness*, about the other's "gaze," which, by trapping the subject in its beam like a deer caught in headlights, objectifies that subject and limits his or her freedom. As the roll call of French theorists suspicious of vision lengthens to include the psychoanalyst Jacques Lacan (with his idea of misrecognition), the Marxist Louis Althusser (with his concept of interpellation), the philosopher Jacques Derrida (with his formulation of "phallogocentrism"), the feminist Luce Irigaray (with her notion of the speculum), and the intellectual historian Michel Fou- • cault (with his ideas of surveillance), Jay argues that "although the reasons are still uncertain, it is legitimate to talk of a discursive or paradigm shift in twentieth-century French thought in which the denigration of vision supplanted its previous celebration."

Precision optics

In the case of twentieth-century art, it may seem counterintuitive to characterize the period of high modernism as "antiocular." Wave after wave of modernist artists had followed Impressionism's move to establish a "purified" optical stratum as a semiautonomous field of experience. From Robert Delaunay's extrapolation of the optical blur of an airplane propeller into an abstract set of circular bands, to Giacomo Balla's Futurist search for the laws of pure iridescence, to Wassily Kandinsky's attempt to render the whole field of human emotion through symphonic surges of color, to the Bauhaus desire for a systematic exploration of color married to geometric form, ■ conducted by Johannes Itten, Paul Klee, and Josef Albers, and in the

▲ 1968b • 1974 ■ 1977, 1980, 1984b ◆ 1957a, 1980 ▲ 1924, 1930b, 1946, 1959c • 1971 ■ 1908, 1909, 1913, 1923, 1947a

postwar period, to the phenomenon of "color-field painting" and ▲ Clement Greenberg's campaign for the idea of "opticality," which he also extended to sculpture, we feel the pressures of a strictly visual thinking.

Working counter to this opticalist euphoria, however, was quite another tradition, one given theoretical articulation in Bataille's • concept of "formlessness." A generation of Surrealist artists embraced this attack on *form* and on the privilege it gave to the visual domination of experience—from Joan Miró's "antipainting" to Salvador Dalí and Luis Buñuel's *Un Chien d'Andalou* (with its razored eyeball). But they were not alone in this. The Dada artist ■ Hans Arp was also attacking the stability of form through the collages he was making of torn and crumpled paper, arranged by chance. Speaking of the way these works promoted a withering away of form through the devastating effects of entropy, Arp asked:

> *Why strive for accuracy and purity if they can never be attained? I now welcomed the decomposition that always sets in once a work is ended. A dirty man puts his dirty finger on a subtle detail in a painting to point it out. That place is now marked with sweat and grease. He bursts into enthusiasm and the painting is sprayed with saliva.... Moisture creates mildew. The work decomposes and dies. Now, the death of a painting no longer devastated me. I had come to terms with its ephemeralness and its death, and included them in the painting.*

For his part Marcel Duchamp had by now entered into the phase of his work he mockingly called "precision oculism," signaling its antiartistic nature by the fact that the oculist "machines" he was producing, from the sculpturelike *Rotary Demisphere* (1925) to the film *Anemic Cinema* (1925–6) to his visual phonograph records, the *Rotoreliefs* [**1**], was now the scientifico-commercial exploration ◆ conducted by his alter ego "Rrose Sélavy," who invariably defied the idea of art's inherent defense against reduplication by submitting such inventions either to copyright or patent. The ironic turn on opticality wrought by these oculist machines was the havoc they were able to wreak with form. For as the turning spirals of the "oculist charts" opened onto a pulsatile movement from concavity to convexity and back again, the throb of this motion dizzied and destabilized the field of vision, eroticizing and carnalizing it instead, by filling it with a suggestive play of "part-objects": now a breast, now an eye, now a uterus.

This idea of an attack on visuality itself continued and even intensified in the postwar period. On the one hand, as noted above, it involved the kind of inoculation of the work against the optical that occurred at the hands of Conceptual art, either by filling the field with the nonvisual substance of language as in the case of Lawrence Weiner or by so banalizing the image as to render it unexploitable by the mass-cultural forces of spectacle. On the other hand, it went beyond the negative strategy of an avoidance of the visual to the more positive one of an active aggression against the very prerogatives of vision.

1 • Marcel Duchamp, *Rotorelief No. 6: Escargot*, 1935
One of set of six cardboard discs printed on both sides, diameter 20 (7⅞)

One dimension of this strategy organized itself around a reprise of the pulsatile force of Duchamp's *Rotoreliefs*. Adopting both the medium of film and that of video in the late sixties, artists like ▲ Richard Serra and Bruce Nauman made works employing a repetitive rhythmic beat, in Serra's case the opening and closing of a fist in his film *Hand Catching Lead* [**2**], in Nauman's, the truncated image of an upside-down lower face and neck with the mouth saying "lip sync" over and over (although out of synchronization) in *Lip Sync* (1969). In both cases the body part performing the gesture becomes organlike (as in Duchamp's spirals), and the visual field, unstable. With Serra in particular, the example of contemporary cinematic practices in the field of avant-garde film was important, especially the phenomenon of the "flicker film," in which alternations of colored frames with more or less equal amounts of black leader produce rapid-fire flashing lights. While it might seem that the visual dazzle set up by the "flicker" is just another instance of "opticality," in fact the phenomenon sets off a strange bodily, or tactile, experience due to the way the light stimulates the viewer's production of an afterimage, which is then projected onto the empty field of the momentary stretch of blackness. So what we "see" in those interstitial spaces is not the material surface of the "frame" nor the abstract condition of the cinematic "field," but the bodily production of our own nervous systems, the rhythmic beat of the neural network's feedback, of its "retention" and "protention," as the nerve tissue retains and releases its impressions.

This kind of beat is what James Coleman's (born 1914) *Box (ahhareturnabout)* [**3**] takes as its subject. Here, a filmed boxing match, cut into short bursts of between three and ten frames, interrupted by equally short spurts of black, is turned into a pulsing

▲ 1960b • 1930b ■ 1913, 1916a, 1918 ◆ 1918

▲ 1966a, 1967a, 1969, 1970, 1973

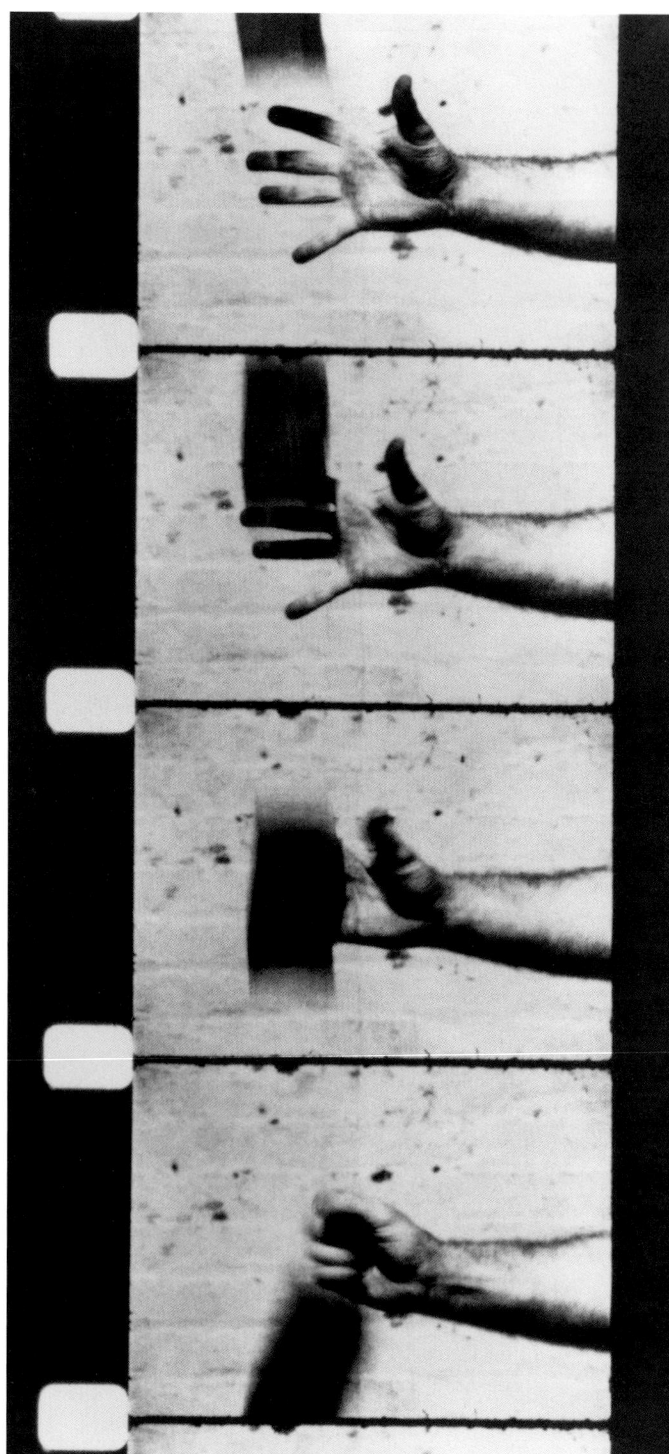

2 • Richard Serra, *Hand Catching Lead*, 1968
Black-and-white 16mm film, silent, 210 minutes

movement that both breaks apart and flows together over those breaks, which is to say, emphasizes movement itself as a form of repetition, of beats that are separated by intervals of absolute extinction, even while the urgency of the rhythm promises the return of another beat and another. The gestures of the boxers, and thus of the representational field of the work—which is spun out of a few minutes of found footage documenting the historic Gene Tunney vs. Jack Dempsey fight of 1927—would seem to embody this rhythm, with their repeated jabs and feints, and their always threatened dive into oblivion. Further, this field of visual representation is doubled aurally by a voiceover that emphasizes both the drive of repetition—"go on/go on," "again/again," "return/return"—and the ever-waiting possibility of the onset of nothingness—"break it/break it," "stop/s-t-o-p i-t," "regressive/to win/or to die."

The fact, however, that the viewer's own body, in the guise of its perceptual system and the projected afterimages it is automatically "contributing" to the film, is also being woven into the work, means that *Box*'s subject matter is somehow displaced away from the representational plane of the sporting event, and into the rhythmic field of two sets of beats or pulses: the viewer's and the boxers'. And it also means that the frequent projections of the sound of breathing—expressed in the track as "ah/ah," "aha/ah," "p-a-m/p-u-m"—is giving voice not just to the boxers' bodily rhythms but to those of the viewer as well.

In all these cases, then, the attack on modernism's notion of visual autonomy is thus staged in relation to the invasion of the body and its rhythms into the optical field now robbed of both its purity and its formal stability. But another strategy also developed in the following decade to assault the prerogatives of vision, one that could be called the "uncanny gaze," by which it was meant to return *against* the controlling system of the "gaze" itself by using its own power to overthrow it.

The theory of the controlling gaze emerged from various analyses of the operations of state power and the way modes of surveillance, for example, cause individual subjects to internalize systems of prohibition and thereby reproduce themselves as subjects of disciplinary force (the shopper who fears the closed-circuit television camera, for instance, and thus restrains him- or herself from stealing). Imported into the field of artistic practice as ▲ a theory of the "male gaze," visual control—now gendered as a function of patriarchy and therefore as masculine—froze women into the position of fetish-objects, rendered immobilized and mute by the force of male desire. Reorganized as the helpless body made intact in the unity of her own beauty, the object of this gaze is now coerced into functioning as a kind of "proof" that the male body is itself unthreatened, that there is no castrating power that can touch him. And if the theory of the male gaze was developed in relation to the mass-cultural construction of women—within advertising, films, pornography, etc.—it could easily be seen as applying to modernist painting, too, with its reciprocity between the visual object as autonomous unity and the individual viewer as independent subject.

• Cindy Sherman's early work *Untitled Film Stills* (1977–80) had taken on the mass-cultural construction of the woman's image, as the artist photographed herself convincingly posed in a variety of cinematic types (gun moll, dumb blonde), genres (film noir, melodrama), and styles (Douglas Sirk, Michelangelo Antonioni, Alfred Hitchcock). But as her work developed into the eighties the idea of a perspective that might fix the identity of the woman as a focal point controlled by the viewing point of the (male) spectator mutated into a kind of shattered visual field. Sometimes this is the

▲ Introduction 1, 1975 • 1977

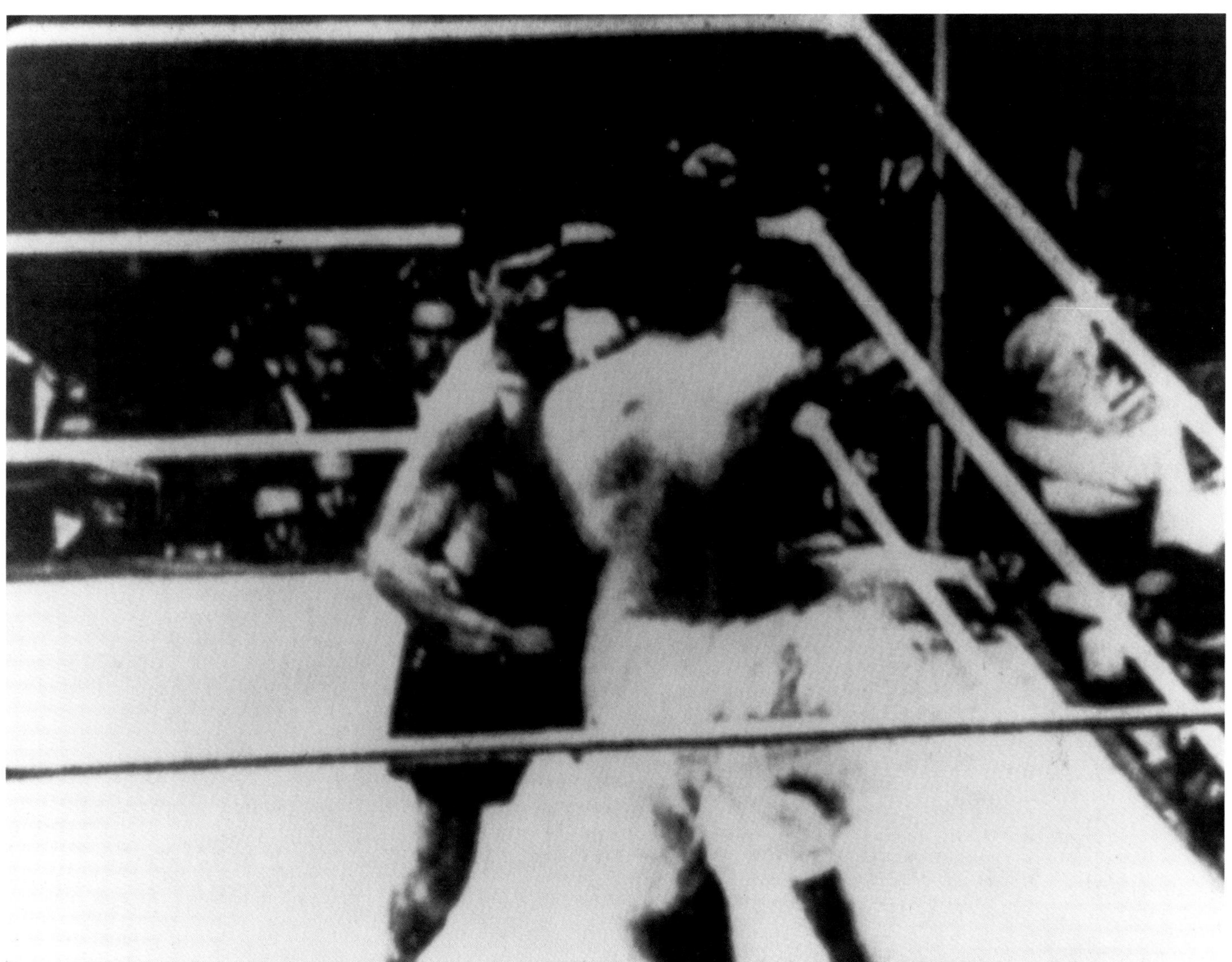

3 • James Coleman, *Box (ahhareturnabout)*, 1977
Black-and-white 16mm film, continuous projection with synchronized audio

effect of a kind of backlighting that forces a glow to emerge from the ground of the image to advance outward at the viewer and thus to disrupt conditions of viewing, producing the figure herself as a kind of blindspot. In others this corrosive visual dispersal is the result of a kind of "wild light," the scattering of gleams around the otherwise darkened image as though refracting it through the facets of an elaborate jewel. This is the case in *Untitled #110* [**4**], where Sherman has concentrated on creating a sense of the completely aleatory quality of the illumination. For while the lighting plunges three quarters of the field in total blackness, it picks out the arm and draped edge of the figure's garment to create a glowing, knotted complex of near unintelligibility.

In opposition to the stability of traditional perspective in which the subject is fixed, its gaze taking in, capturing, controlling everything in its sight from a given point, this recourse to ricocheting light opens onto a very different idea of the "gaze," one that destabilizes its subject, making it the victim rather than the master of vision. This new gaze, theorized by Lacan as the gaze-as-*objet-a*, or the uncanny gaze, is modeled on the idea of the light that surrounds each of us. Such an irradiation beaming at us from everywhere in space cannot be assimilated to the single focus of perspective. Instead, to describe this luminous gaze, Lacan turned ▲ to the model of animal camouflage, which Roger Caillois had described in the thirties as the effect of space at large on an organism that, yielding to the force of this space's generalized gaze, loses its own organic boundaries and merges with its surroundings in an almost psychotic act of imitation. Making itself into a kind of shapeless camouflage, this mimetic subject now becomes a formless part of the "picture" of space in general. "It becomes a stain," Lacan wrote, "it becomes a picture, it is inscribed in the picture."

Insofar as our body is the target of this luminous, uncanny gaze, its relation to the world establishes our perception not in the transparency of a conceptual grasp of space, but in the thickness and density of a being that simply intercepts the light. It is in this sense that to be "in the picture" is to feel dispersed, subject to a picture organized not by form but by formlessness. None of Sherman's works so captures this idea of entering the field as "stain," perhaps, as does *Untitled #167* [**5**], where the camouflage-effect of mimicry

▲ 1975

▲ 1930b

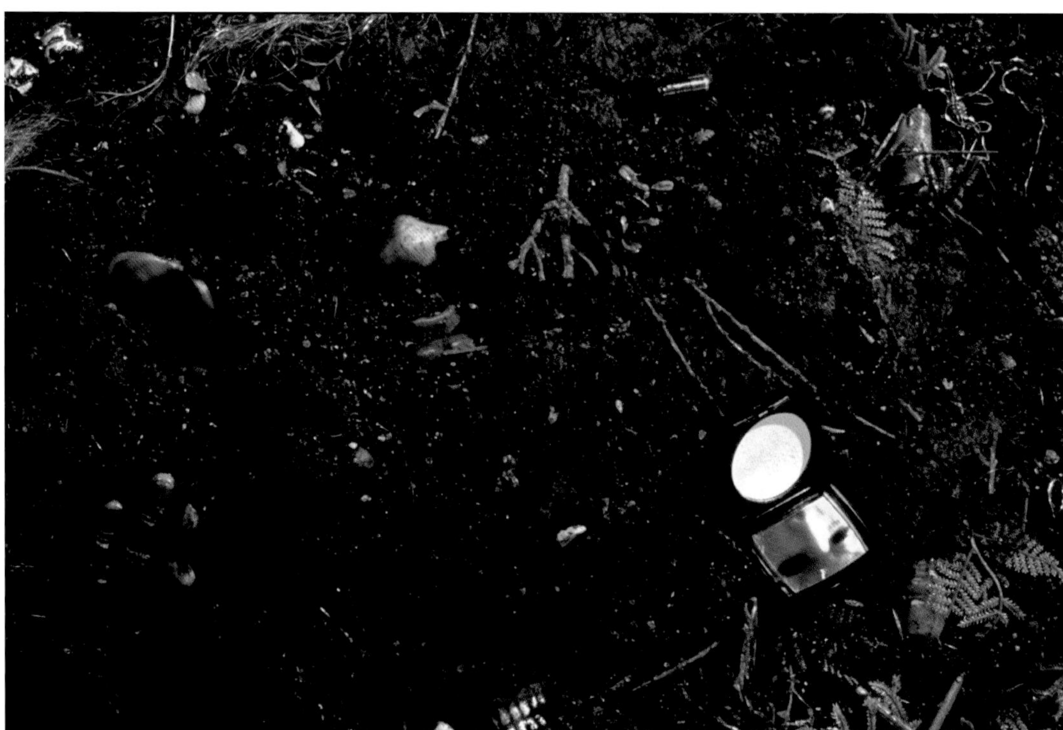

5 • Cindy Sherman, *Untitled #167*, 1986
Color photograph, 152.4 x 228.6 (60 x 90)

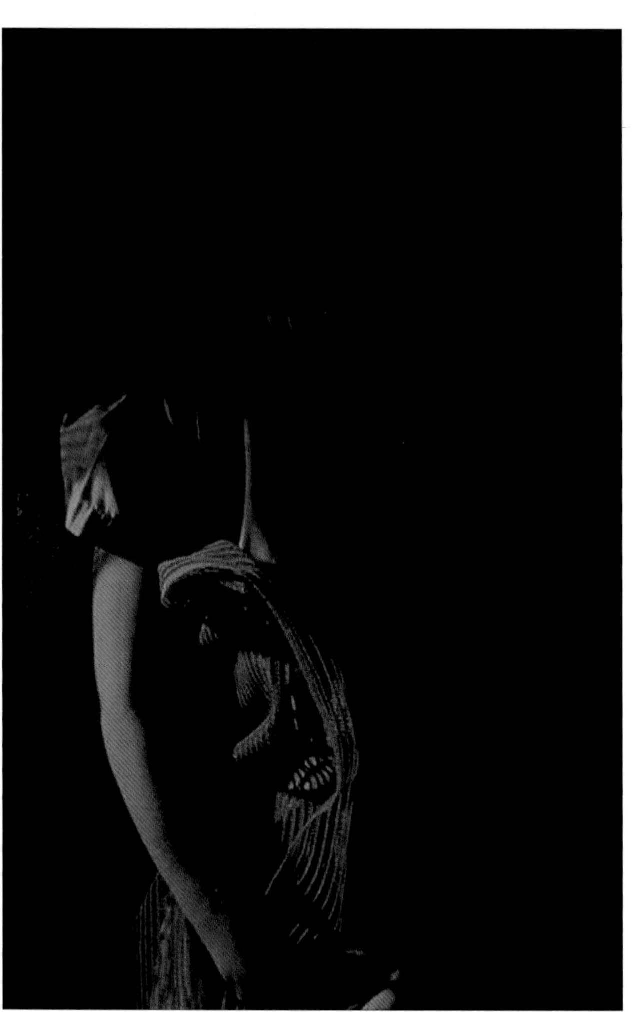

4 • Cindy Sherman, *Untitled #110*, 1982
Color photograph, 114.9 x 99.1 (45¼ x 39)

is in full flower. The figure, now absorbed and dispersed within the background, can be picked out only by a few remnants still visible, though only barely, in the mottled surface of the darkened detritus that fills the image. We make out the tip of a nose, the emergence of a finger with painted nail, the detached grimace of a set of teeth. Classical perspective sets two unities opposite one another: the viewing point and the vanishing point. Each reinforces the other's sense of focus and singularity. The unfocused, dispersed gaze gives the subject no support, nothing to identify with, unless it is dispersal itself. The fragmentation of the "point" of view here prevents the invisible, unlocatable gaze from being the site of coherence, meaning, unity. Desire is thus not mapped here as the desire for form, and thus for sublimation; desire is modeled in terms of a transgression against form.

FURTHER READING

George Baker (ed.), *James Coleman* (Cambridge, Mass.: MIT Press, 2003)

Douglas Crimp, *On the Museum's Ruins* (Cambridge, Mass.: MIT Press, 1993)

Hal Foster, "The Return of the Real," *The Return of the Real* (Cambridge, Mass.: MIT Press, 1996)

Martin Jay, *Downcast Eyes: The Denigration of Vision in Twentieth-Century French Thought* (Berkeley and Los Angeles: University of California Press, 1993)

Rosalind Krauss, "Cindy Sherman," *Bachelors* (Cambridge, Mass.: MIT Press, 1999)

1993b

As Rachel Whiteread's *House*, a casting of a terrace house in east London, is demolished, an innovative group of women artists comes to the fore in Britain.

In the nineties many artists began to look back to the sixties and seventies for new points of departure—to Minimalist and Conceptual art, Performance and video art, Installation and site-▲specific art. The most provocative of these reconnections were made by young women in Britain such as Mona Hatoum (born 1952), Sarah Lucas (born 1962), Cornelia Parker (born 1956), Gillian Wearing (born 1963), and Rachel Whiteread (born 1963). The motives of these returns were various, but one factor in some was a discontent with a sensationalist art world that by the late eighties seemed dominated by marketing strategies and hyped •scandals. More important, however, was the changed status of movements like Minimalism and Conceptualism by the nineties. On the one hand, the trajectories of such work seemed cut short in the eighties, pushed prematurely into the past. On the other hand, now that they were historical objects, these movements constituted a new archive of forms and devices for different kinds of appropriation in the present. This liminal, almost paradoxical status—as both a vital beginning of postmodernist practice and an enshrined moment in art history—attracted young artists, critics, curators, and historians alike.

Minimalism was especially ambiguous in this regard. Some artists, like Whiteread and Hatoum, reworked its language of simple forms and serial orderings to new psychological and political ends. However, other artists, like the American Janine Antoni (born 1964), reacted against its apparent austerity, which they saw, reductively, as macho authority, and reintroduced what Minimalism had worked so hard to expunge—namely, a conception of art as a matter of images, and a model of meaning dictated by iconographic referents and/or themes. Of course, Minimalism was hardly ignored in its own time. Already in the late sixties and early seventies it was developed in ways that artists like Whiteread and Hatoum would elaborate in the nineties. Thus, for example, its modular forms were repositioned in a social context by artists such ■as Dan Graham, whose *Homes for America* (1966–7) discovered Minimalist objects ready-made in the repetitive tract-houses of a ◆New Jersey development. Other artists like Eva Hesse detected an irrational, even absurdist dimension in Minimalism, which they turned against its official position of extreme objectivity. Rather than a phobic reaction, however, this was an ambivalent critique, as suggested by the strange compliment paid by Hesse to Carl Andre in 1970: "I feel, let's say, emotionally connected to his work. It does something to my insides. His metal plates were the concentration camp to me."

Minimalism with a twist

Artists like Hesse, Ree Morton (1936–77), Dorothea Rockburne (born 1921), Jackie Ferrara (born 1929), and Jackie Winsor (born 1941) were fluent with such Minimalist devices as the mono-▲chrome, the grid, and the cube. But they also twisted these devices in order to evoke structures of feeling more or less alien to Minimalism. For example, Ferrara constructed Minimalist forms like pyramids out of non-Minimalist materials like cardboard, rags, rope, fur, and flax. Her constructions were also just irregular enough to further undo the ideality of geometric forms. This is true, too, of Winsor, who gouged, burned, or otherwise marked her wood cubes in ways that registered the body through these fraught acts [1]. Like the irregularity of form in Ferrara, the intensity of process in Winsor intimated a psychology, even an irrationality,

1 • Jackie Winsor, *Burnt Piece*, 1977–8
Concrete, burnt wood, and wire, 36 x 36 x 36 (14⅛ x 14 x⅛ x 14⅛)

▲ 1965, 1967a, 1968b, 1970, 1973, 1974 • 1976, 1987 ■ Introduction 2, 1968b ◆ 1969 ▲ 1957b, 1962c, 1965

that Minimalism had seemed to expunge. These artists thus opened up Minimalist forms, only to turn them inward, as it were, to make of marked cubes and open boxes so many metaphors of the interi- ▲ ority not only of the body but of the psyche. At the same time, this Postminimalist art remained abstract or structured enough not to become reductively referential or personal. In this regard it did not reverse the most radical achievement of Minimalism—the opening • of art onto the phenomenological field of the body—as is the case with recent treatments of Minimalism that tend to picture, pastiche, or otherwise package its forms as so many theatrical images. (This spectacularization is extended to Process and Performance art in the baroque installations and films of the American Matthew Barney [born 1967].)

Often fragile and ephemeral, much of this Postminimalist work is now neglected, when it is not lost altogether. Some practitioners such as Hesse and Morton died young, while others have fallen between the cracks of institutional categories of Minimalist, ▲ Process, and feminist art. However, in the late eighties and early nineties this line of working was picked up again by artists like Whiteread and Hatoum, who may have inadvertently benefited from the somewhat delayed reception of Minimalism in Britain. Although pledged to other purposes, their art also exists, enigmatically, between abstraction and figuration, structure and reference, the literal and the metaphorical.

Born in Beirut to Palestinian parents, Hatoum was stranded in London in 1975 when war broke out in Lebanon. This condition of displacement became a subtext of her art, as in a 1985 performance in which she walked barefoot through Brixton, a London community torn by racial strife, with Dr. Marten boots laced to her ankles like a ball and chain. Somewhat reminiscent of • Vito Acconci, her early performances also tested taboos of the body (what is considered clean and unclean, fit and unfit), while her early videos focused on structures of surveillance. Hatoum continues to elaborate both of these interests in her installations,

2 • Mona Hatoum, *The Light at the End*, 1989
Angle iron frame, six electric heating elements, 166 x 162.4 x 5 (65⅜ x 63⅞ x 2)

▲ 1969 • 1965 ▲ 1975 • 1974

which sometimes include abject residues of the human body like nails, skin, and hair. Indeed, her 1994 video *Corps étranger*, which explores the interior of her own body through a microscopic camera, takes surveillance of the body to an extreme. This tracing of boundaries (both corporeal and social) complements her tracking of displacements (both personal and political), and together they structure her art.

One installation in 1989, *The Light at the End* **[2]**, signaled "a whole new way of working" for Hatoum. In a dark apex of a triangular gallery in London, she set six electrical rods in a vertical steel frame in a way that resembled an abstract cage. The viewer was attracted by the sheer beauty of the red-hot rods, only, on approach, to be repelled by the extreme heat: here the threat often projected onto Minimalist objects became actual. *Contra* the cliché, "the light at the end" of this particular tunnel brooked no escape or reprieve; as Hatoum commented, only "imprisonment, torture, and pain" were evoked. Positioned on the open side of the space, one might identify with the implied jailer. And yet, as one saw that there was just enough space under the rods to slip through, one might also identify with the implied prisoner. In this way Hatoum used a Minimalist aesthetic—the modular repetition ▲ of a Donald Judd, the spatial luminosity of a Dan Flavin—to produce a situation that was psychological as well as phenomenological, a theater of ambivalence in which spatial positions became phantasmatic positions of power as well. In effect Hatoum reread • Minimalism through the French philosopher Michel Foucault, in particular through his analysis of architectural surveillance in *Discipline and Punish* (1975). And she continued to explore these effects in such installations as *Light Sentence* (1992), a maze of wire-mesh lockers made fantastically carceral by the shadows cast by a single lightbulb slowly moving up and down at its center.

The social body

Bodies that are both fragile and porous, boundaries that are at once intractable and reversible, subjects that are both displaced and disciplined—these are experiences that Hatoum evokes through materials, structures, and spaces, more than themes that she illustrates in images. (When she does picture her concerns in this way, it must be said, her work is less effective.) This is true too of Rachel Whiteread, who is also concerned with experiences of exposure, displacement, and homelessness. By the late eighties Whiteread began to cast objects associated with homes—bathtubs and mattresses, closets and rooms—in materials like rubber and resin, plaster and concrete. Often, as the objects are used as molds, the ■ castings are of the negative spaces of these things, the voids that they form. In this way they are at once obvious in production and ambiguous in reference. For example, although her sculptures are based on utilitarian objects and everyday sites, they negate function and harden space into mass. At the same time, although they appear whole and solid, they also seem fragmentary and spectral. More ambiguously still, these literal traces suggest symbolic traces as well, especially memories of childhood and family. As the critic Jon Bird has argued, they conjure up "the cultural space of the home" as a place of beginnings and endings, departures and returns, as a place haunted by the actuality of loss and the presence of absence. The effect of these works is thus often associated with ▲ "the uncanny"—that is, with the return of familiar things made strange by repression. And indeed, as "death masks" of familial objects and maternal spaces cast in hard rubber and cold plaster, they do render the homey somewhat *unheimlich* (German for uncanny, literally "unhomelike"). But precisely as death masks they can also appear more melancholic than uncanny, suggestive less of the return of the repressed than of the persistence of the lost. Some of the objects, especially the tubs and the mattresses, evoke the body as emptied of desire, even as dead and calcified, and in fact Whiteread has also cast mortuary slabs.

The effects of these castings are not only psychological; they also "carry the marks of history written on the social body" (Bird). On the one hand, the hard pitted mattress of *Untitled (Amber Double Bed)* **[3]** suggests archetypal events of the bed—loving, birthing, and dying. On the other hand, it has a specific social resonance: slumped against the wall as if on the street, it recalls the stained bedding of a homeless person. And it is homelessness, as much as *Unheimlichkeit*, that Whiteread treats. This is especially true of her most-celebrated work to date, *House* **[4]**, a concrete

3 • Rachel Whiteread, *Untitled (Amber Double Bed)*, 1991
Rubber and high-density foam, 106 x 136 x 121.5 (47 x 54 x 41)

▲ 1962c, 1965 • 1971 ■ 1967a, 1974

▲ 1924, 1931

4 • Rachel Whiteread, *House*, 1993
Internal casting of 193 Grove Road, Bow, east London (destroyed)

internal casting of a house (minus its roof) in an old working-class neighborhood of east London. In collaboration with the art foundation Artangel, Whiteread negotiated with the local council to cast a terrace house scheduled for demolition. This negative imprint of now-vanished rooms, inscribed not only with the faint outlines of window sills, door frames, and utility lines but also with the slight traces of past inhabitants, stood in a small park for a few months like the unrequited ghost of some social past. On the same evening that Whiteread won the Turner Prize, the most prestigious award for contemporary art in Britain, a vote to demolish *House* was passed by the local council, and a firestorm of controversy ensued. As Bird has suggested, the great provocation of *House* was to link the psychic and the social, "the lost spaces of childhood" and the lost working-class culture of east London, both threatened by rampant capitalist development. (The new business area Canary Wharf, the most egregious example of this development in London, was on a sight-line with *House*.) Perhaps its opponents grasped this connection subconsciously, or perhaps they simply refused a public sculpture that did not idealize social life or monumentalize historical memory. For *House* was indeed a public sculpture that, however abstract, was both specific and obdurate. It stood like an involuntary memorial, in a contemporary Pompeii, of catastrophic socioeconomic forces.

Through different inversions of interiors and exteriors, Hatoum and Whiteread point to a social world in which private space often appears obscenely exposed and public space nearly collapsed; they also point to a melancholic culture fixed on traumatic events. And they make these comments count through a pertinent elaboration of postwar art. The particular antecedents differ in each case—besides various Minimalists, Hatoum draws on Piero Manzoni and Arte Povera with her charged materials, while Whiteread recalls ▲ Gordon Matta-Clark and Bruce Nauman with her architectural molds. But they adapt these different antecedents to similar ends—as psychological and mnemonic instruments. Again, Hatoum and Whiteread represent only two instances of a pervasive redeploy-● ment of art of the recent past. Just as the "neo-avant-garde" of the fifties and sixties returned to the various devices of the "historical avant-garde" of the teens and twenties, so, too, it might be argued, have many artists in the nineties returned to the different paradigms of the sixties and seventies. And, as with the neo-avant-garde, some recoveries were opportunistic and reductive, and so spectacularized the past, while others were innovative and expansive, and so elaborated it critically and pertinently. It is crucial to distinguish between these returns, for at stake is the alternative, in a time of pervasive amnesia, between an artistic culture given over to a static consumerist recycling and an artistic culture that still seeks to reclaim different pasts to open up different futures.

FURTHER READING

Guy Brett et al., *Mona Hatoum* (London: Phaidon Press, 1997)

James Lingwood (ed.), *Rachel Whiteread: House* (London: Phaidon Press, 1993)

Susan L. Stoops (ed.), *More Than Minimal: Feminism and Abstraction in the '70s* (Walthram, Mass.: Rose Art Museum, 1996)

Chris Townsend (ed.), *The Art of Rachel Whiteread* (London: Thames & Hudson, 2004)

Catherine de Zegher (ed.), *Inside the Visible* (Cambridge, Mass.: MIT Press, 1996)

Lynne Zelevansky, *Sense and Sensibility: Woman Artists and Minimalism in the Nineties* (New York: Museum of Modern Art, 1994)

▲ 1959a, 1967a, 1967b, 1970, 1974 ● 1960a

1993c

In New York, the Whitney Biennial foregrounds work focused on identity amid the emergence of a new form of politicized art by African-American artists.

▲ In recent decades the different politics of identity—racial, multicultural, feminist, and queer—have sometimes followed similar trajectories, at least as they are taken up in art. In a first phase, an essential nature—of blackness, ethnicity, femininity, or homosexuality—is often claimed in the face of negative stereotypes, and positive images of this nature are put forward (that is, once minority artists have won access to art institutions at all). Then, in a second phase, this critique of stereotypes is pushed to the point where such identity is seen as a social construction more than an essential nature, and the assumption of simple categories is complicated by the fact of multiple differences (e.g., that one might be black, female, and/or gay at the same time). The undoing of stereotypes is an especially urgent task for artists concerned with the imaging of race, and they have developed a number of strategies to this end, including critiques of documentary forms of representation, testimonials of personal experience, and turns to alternative traditions of art.

Turning the tables

One of the most prominent artists involved in this project is Adrian Piper (born 1948). Already active in avant-garde circles in the late sixties and the early seventies, Piper adapted several devices of Per● formance and Conceptual art in her own investigation of the "visual pathology" of racism. In her "Mythic Being" series (1973–5), for example, she staged performances in public spaces that underscored the ideological construction or "mythic being" of the macho image of the African-American male, whom she impersonated. Later, in *My Calling (Card) #1* (1986), she used the Conceptualist technique of the written declaration, here in the guise of a business card that informed the recipient of the card, after he or she had made a racist remark, that its bearer (Piper) was black. Piper also turned techniques of Installation and video art to her own critical purposes. For instance, *Four Intruders Plus Alarm Systems* (1980) confronts its audience with four large photographs of "angry young black men"; as viewers process their own reactions to these images, they also hear a taped recitation of hypothetical reactions from (other) white viewers. *Cornered* [**1**] confronts its audience as well, here with an overturned table set in a corner that in turn "corners" viewers with a videotape in which Piper considers the likelihood

1 • Adrian Piper, *Cornered*, 1988
Video installation consisting of videotape, monitor, table, chairs, birth certificate, dimensions variable, 17 minutes

that the white people among them also have black ancestors: once again the myth of a simple or pure identity is challenged.

In the seventies Piper trained in Kantian philosophy, which she teaches to this day. Her dissertation adviser at Harvard was John Rawls, whose *A Theory of Justice* (1971) is a landmark in the field of political philosophy, and in her art Piper has consistently posed her specific arguments regarding racial inequity within the general framework of human rights issues. Other artists involved in the questioning of racial representations have tended in the opposite direction, toward a postmodernist suspicion about universal claims. Yet Piper is skeptical of any position that forgoes "the potent tools of rationality and objectivity," which she regards as necessary to the critique of the "pseudorationality" of racism, "the defenses we use to rationalize away the uniqueness of 'the other'." "All you have to do," Piper argues, "is to echo or depict those defensive categorizations as they are, without too much aesthetic or literary embellishment, in order to generate a certain degree of self-awareness of how inadequate and simplistic they are." Piper sometimes renders this "echoing" concrete through photographic and documentary testimony of her own experience and history.

Carrie Mae Weems (born 1953) often employs personal images and stories as well. However, trained at the California Institute of the Arts and the University of California at San Diego—two

▲ 1975, 1977, 1987, 1989 ● 1968b, 1974

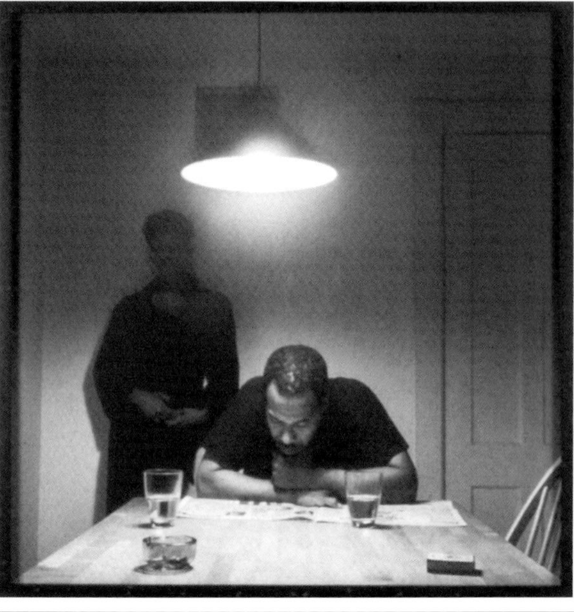

hotbeds of postmodernist art and theory—Weems is more inclined than Piper to question objective claims of truth-value. On the other hand, she draws less on avant-garde models of the sixties and seventies than on African-American precedents of the Harlem Renaissance in the forties, especially the writer Zora Neale Hurston and the photographer Roy DeCarava (his 1955 portrait of his Harlem neighborhood, *The Sweet Flypaper of Life*, is a particular ▲ touchstone for her). In her phototext work, Weems is content neither with strictly positive representations of African-American identity nor with merely negative demystifications.

Weems developed her signature combination of intimate photographs and narratives in *Family Pictures and Stories* (1978–84). Here, accompanied by texts and tapes, 35-millimeter snapshots tell the tale of four generations of her extended family in their various migrations from Mississippi. Even as the work reports on harsh conditions of racism, poverty, and violence, it also resists automatic assumptions about black victimization. As the critic Andrea Kirsh has argued, "*Family Pictures* takes two practices as points to resist: first, the imaging of black people as 'other' in the photo-documen- ● tary tradition (a tradition that is almost the exclusive property of white photographers); second, the official sociological studies commissioned by the US government in the 1960s" (such as the famous Moynihan Report on "the black family"). Weems questions the objectifying often produced in the sociological tradition, with a nuanced account of black families drawn from her own stock of memories and experiences; and she questions the othering often produced in the documentary tradition through an alternative vision of black communities as developed in the work of DeCarava and others. (Informed in folklore—Weems also did graduate work in anthropology at UC Berkeley—she has since extended her gaze to black societies in the Sea Islands, Cuba, and elsewhere.)

In the "Kitchen Table" series [**2**], Weems refined her complex approach. This work consists of views of one or two black subjects (a man and a woman, two female friends, and so on) seated at a kitchen table under a stark light; beneath the images run narrative texts in a third-person voice (usually that of a woman, sometimes of a man) that mulls over the different demands of personal longings, romantic relationships, domestic arrangements, and workaday obligations. It is rare in American art, not to mention American culture at large, that such subjectivities are given such evocative expression.

Like Piper and Weems, Lorna Simpson (born 1960) also frames racial images for our critical reflection, yet her phototext works are neither as confrontational as those of Piper nor as intimate as those of Weems (her classmate at UCSD). Although also concerned with the alienation produced by stereotypes, Simpson concentrates on the use of photography as evidence, especially in the construction of pseudo-objective typologies of black identities. The manipulation of photos and texts for purposes of identification and surveillance was developed in the nineteenth century by the French criminolo-

2 • Carrie Mae Weems, *Untitled (Man Reading Newspaper)*, from the *Kitchen Table* series, 1990
Three silver-gelatin prints, each 71.8 x 71.8 (28¼ x 28¼)

▲ 1943, 1959d ● 1936, 1959d, 1984a

gist Alphonse Bertillon and the English statistician Francis Galton, but clearly the deployment of "the body as archive" for reasons of discipline and punishment continues in the present, for instance in the "profiling" used (programmatically or not) by police, employers, and everyday people on the street. In her early work, Simpson was concerned to mirror this typological gaze—to catch it in the act, as it were—and to trouble its prejudicial classifications.

This work features simple photographs of black figures, most of them female, often with hairstyles and clothes that suggest a particular group or class identity (chignons or Afros, a white cotton servant shift or a black business suit). Rarely does Simpson show entire faces, and often her models are turned away from us: such partial or obscure views solicit our curiosity, but they also frustrate any desire to master the figures through either fetishistic details or holistic images. The short texts that accompany the photographs, often single words or simple phrases, further challenge any habit of reading that is either voyeuristic or sociological or both: although often elliptical, the texts can be cautionary, even accusatory. For example, *Guarded Conditions* (1989) consists of eighteen Polaroid prints of a black woman of unknown age in servant clothes, seen from behind with her arms crossed behind her back. Below the photos run two texts in block letters that alternate throughout the sequence: "SKIN ATTACKS ... SEX ATTACKS ... ". Here, with great economy and force, Simpson conveys the condition of many black women as double targets of racism and sexism. At the same time, like Weems, she does not indulge in victimology: the poses can be read as defensive or defiant or both, and the markings of "skin" and "sex" are underscored in a way that seems to strengthen rather than to debilitate the woman pictured.

Again like Weems, Simpson combines critique and beauty in her work, as if to refute advocates of either principle who deem the combination somehow impossible. For example, her exquisite early work *The Waterbearer* [**3**] presents a black girl, once again in a white cotton shift and with her back turned to us. In her right hand, the girl holds a plastic bottle by its neck and in her left a silver pitcher, and almost nonchalantly she lets water pour out of both. Underneath the image is this text in simple capitals: "She saw him disappear by the river. / They asked her to tell what happened. / Only to discount her memory." *The Waterbearer* "declares the existence of subjugated knowledge," as the critic bell hooks has argued, but it is a knowledge that appears resistant even when it is ignored, for the action of the girl indicates a small refusal, a slight subversion: spilling the water, releasing her burden, forgoing her task, she nonchalantly spites her implied deniers (she seems oblivious to her observers as well). Her pose is also subtly transformative: her unbalanced arms suggest a tilted scale of justice, and her *contrapposto* stance recalls any number of canonical figures in Western art—from ancient muses, through the maids of Vermeer, to paintings by Ingres, Seurat, and a host of others—only to redirect them toward a subject matter rarely represented in Western art at all. *The Waterbearer* thus recalls a classical tradition of beauty and grace in order to refashion it almost insouciantly. In her recent films and videos, Simpson has developed this aesthetic of subversive beauty further still.

The stereotypical grotesque

If Piper, Weems, and Simpson resist and redraw racial stereotypes, other artists exaggerate them to the point of critical explosion—a complementary strategy that the critic Kobena Mercer has termed "the stereotypical grotesque." Pioneered in the early seventies by ▲ artists in the States such as Betye Saar (born 1929), Faith Ringgold • and David Hammons, this kind of parody was developed in the eighties and nineties by artists in Britain such as Rotimi Fani-Kayode (1955–89), Yinka Shonibare, and Chris Ofili, among others, in photography, painting, and other media. Influenced by the homoerotic portraits of Robert Mapplethorpe, the Nigerian-born Fani-Kayode (who delighted in his own outsider status as a gay African man in London) exaggerates the primitivist clichés of

3 • Lorna Simpson, *The Waterbearer*, 1986
Silver-gelatin print with vinyl lettering,
114 x 194 x 4 (45 x 77 x 1½)

▲ 1975 • 1989

African sexuality in his portraits of near-naked black men, who are shown painted, feathered, or otherwise costumed in exotic "tribal" garb **[4]**. Meanwhile, his compatriot Shonibare caricatures the other side of the primitivist fantasy: for example, in the three photos of his "Effnick" series **[5]** he assumes the sumptuous costume and haughty pose of a bewigged English gentleman of the late eighteenth century, a leisured man of letters (or perhaps a Victorian dandy who adopts this artificial style anachronistically). This fictional aristocrat, whose holdings might include colonial plantations worked by slaves, could well be the subject of a painting by Sir Joshua Reynolds—except for the fact that he is black. The imposture thus becomes a kind of travesty that renders the cultivation of the aristocrat more than suspect.

In Britain, of course, racist ideology is keyed to a complex history of colonialism more than to a traumatic legacy of slavery. One result is that "black" is a broader category in the Britain than in the United States, and its investigation involves many different subjects, cultures, and traditions. Indeed, British black art and film has explored a wide range of issues of the African diaspora and "the Black Atlantic." And in the eighties and nineties this great multiculturalism of multiple differences and hybrid states provoked an extraordinary efflorescence of painting, photography, and filmmaking by such different artists as Isaac Julien, Sonia Boyce, Steve McQueen, Keith Piper, and Ingrid Pollard, to name only several.

Of special relevance here is the work of Julien, which has spanned feature films, television documentaries, and film installations. From *Who Killed Colin Roach?*, a 1983 documentary about the suspicious death of a young black man while in police custody, through *Looking for Langston*, a luscious short film of 1988 evoking the gay life and aesthetics of the great poet Langston Hughes, ▲ a leader of the Harlem Renaissance, to his film installations with double and triple projections of the 1990s, such as *The Attendant* and *The Long Road to Mazatlán*, Julien has explored different representations of race, class, art, and homosexuality in British and American culture at large. Again and again he has used the force of desire to disrupt any rigidity in the definition of these categories, and he has doubled his thematic blurring of the edges between genders and sexualities with a formal blurring of the lines that divide genres and disciplines: fiction and nonfiction; imagistic and narrative; art and documentary; film and video. A cofounder of Sankofa Film and Video, a collective of young black British filmmakers, in the early 1980s, Julien has long collaborated on projects in which politics and aesthetics are never pitted against each other; at the same time he has developed a cinematic style, rooted in gay black sensibility but not confined to any restrictive identity, that is distinctly his own.

Legibilities of race

The strategy of "the stereotypical grotesque" is also developed by young American artists such as Kara Walker (born 1969), whose tableaux and installations consist of postings and projections, on the

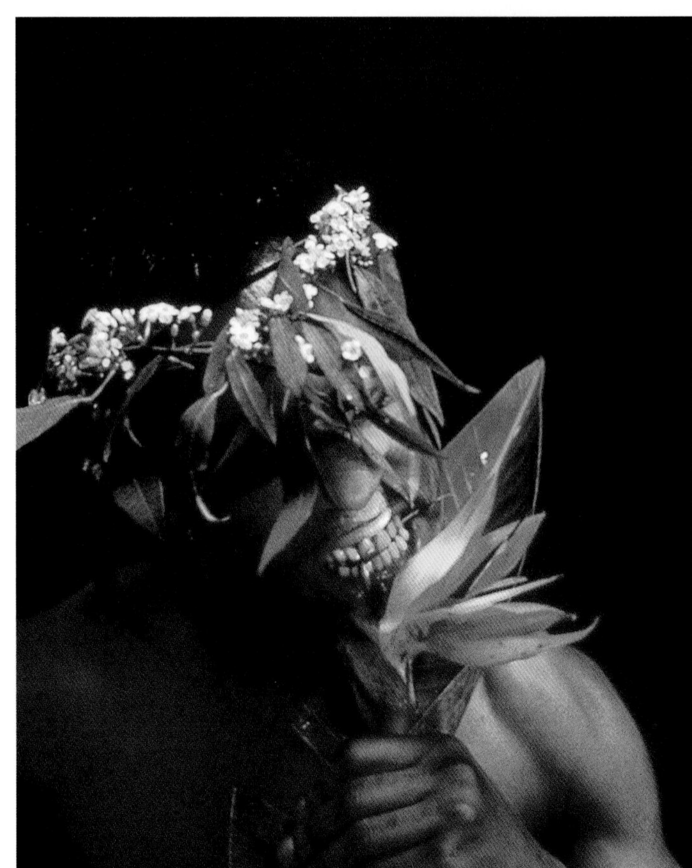

4 • Rotimi Fani-Kayode, *Nothing to Lose IV (Bodies of Experience)*, 1989

white walls of galleries and museums, of black-paper cutouts **[6]**. Walker cites the genres of the cameo and the silhouette, but where one might expect the safe profiles of loved ones that are typical of these discreet forms, Walker restages ante-Bellum caricatures of Deep South slaves and slave-owners involved in wild scenes of sex and violence. In effect, she restages the myths of racist lore, but in a ribald fashion that undermines them at the same time. These fantasies persist outrageously in the American unconscious, Walker suggests; at the same time she subjects them to subversively excessive reimaginings.

The Walker silhouettes are both very visible and quite anonymous in a way that points to the ambiguous legibility of race in social relations today. This ambiguity is treated by some artists in the medium of painting, often through analogies of canvas with skin and paint with skin color. Ellen Gallagher (born 1965) has developed a language of tiny pictographs set on large fields of paper and canvas **[7]**. Often built up in shallow relief, her symbols look from a distance to be abstract forms; their combination of repetition and variation is sometimes associated with the rigorously nonobjective ▲ paintings of Agnes Martin. Only on closer examination are these forms revealed to be eyes, mouths, faces, hair styles, and the like—that is, physical attributes that are singled out for special significance in racist physiognomies. Even as Gallagher mimes this typological process, however, she breaks down its constituent parts, its loaded details, nearly to the point of their utter deconstruction.

▲ 1943

▲ 1957b

5 • Yinka Shonibare, *Untitled*, from the "Effnick"series, 1997
C-print, reproduction Baroque frame, edition two of five, 122 x 91.5 (48 x 36)

6 • Kara Walker, *Camptown Ladies*, 1998 (detail)
Cut paper and adhesive on wall, dimensions variable

7 • Ellen Gallagher, *Preserve (Yellow)*, 2001
Oil, pencil, and paper on magazine page, 33.7 x 25.4 (13¼ x 10)

Glenn Ligon (born 1960) also plays with the legibility of race, here through the trope of paintings in black on white and white on black [**8**]. He has borrowed texts and images involving race, often drawn from writers like James Baldwin and critics like Frantz Fanon, setting them on canvas with various degrees of contrast between figure and ground, surface and depth. In effect, Ligon turns the formal issues of modernist painting into perceptual tests of racial readings, and vice versa. Here the structural questioning of abstraction and signification—from the early canvases of Jasper Johns through the continued investigations of Robert Ryman—takes on new social meaning and political valence.

FURTHER READING

Coco Fusco, *The Bodies That Were Not Ours* (New York: Routledge, 2001)
Thelma Golden, *Black Male: Representations of Masculinity in Contemporary Art* (New York: Whitney Museum of American Art, 1994)
Stuart Hall and Mark Sealy, *Different: Contemporary Photography and Black Identity* (London: Phaidon Press, 2001)
Kellie Jones et al., *Lorna Simpson* (London: Phaidon Press, 2002)
Kobena Mercer, *Welcome to the Jungle: New Positions in Cultural Studies* (Routledge, 1994)

8 • Glenn Ligon, *Untitled (I Feel Most Colored ...)*, 1990
Oil on wood, 203.2 x 76.2 (80 x 30)

1994a

A mid-career exhibition of Mike Kelley highlights a pervasive concern with states of regression and abjection, while Robert Gober, Kiki Smith, and others use figures of the broken body to address questions of sexuality and mortality.

▲ Although well known in the sixties and seventies, Louise Bourgeois and Eva Hesse became truly influential only in the eighties and nineties, as they had to await a context once again sympathetic to an exploration of body and space shaped psychologically by drives and fantasies. This reception was prepared by feminist artists such as Kiki Smith (born 1954), Rona Pondick (born 1952), and Jana Sterbak (born 1955), who wanted to return to the female image after its partial taboo in feminist art of the late seventies, but not necessarily in the "positive" manner of ● feminist art in the early seventies. It was also assisted by gay artists ■ like Robert Gober, who, in response to the AIDS crisis, worked to transform Surrealist fetishes of heterosexual desire into enigmatic tokens of homosexual mourning and melancholy. Like Bourgeois, these artists have developed a model of art as "the re-experiencing of a trauma," which they understand sometimes as a symptomatic acting-out of a traumatic event, in which the art work becomes a site where memory or fantasy can be attempted, as it were, and sometimes as a symbolic working-through of such an event, in which the work becomes a place where "treatment" or "exorcism" can be attempted (Bourgeois).

Fantasies objectified

As the critic Mignon Nixon has argued, some of these artists appear to objectify the fantasies of a child. For example, in her installations Rona Pondick has set up a quasi-infantile theater of oral-sadistic drives, not only in *Mouth* [**1**], an array of dirty mouths with nasty teeth, but also in *Milk Milk* (1993), a landscape of mammarian mounds with multiple nipples. Meanwhile other artists have focused on the imagined effects of such fantasies, especially the effects on mother and child. Like Bourgeois, Kiki Smith evokes both subjects, but in a way that is more literal than Bourgeois. Smith has often cast organs and bones like hearts, wombs, pelvises, and ribs in various materials like wax, plaster, porcelain, and bronze. In *Intestine* (1992) we see a clotted line in bronze, as long as an actual intestine (thirty feet), that stretches out, inert, on the floor. "Materials are also sexy things," Smith has remarked, "that have either life in them or death in them." Here it is mostly death, and if there is a primary drive evoked in her work, it is the death drive. Smith imagines the insides of the body not as animated by aggression, as they are in Bourgeois, so much as evacuated by it; all that remains are the hardened scraps of viscera, bare bones, and flayed skin.

1 • Rona Pondick, *Mouth*, 1993 (detail)
Rubber, plastic, and flax, six hundred parts, dimensions variable

Smith has spoken of this loss of "insides" as a loss of self, as intimated in *Intestine*. But more often this anxiety about loss seems to center on the maternal body, as suggested by *Tale* (1992), a naked female figure on her hands and knees who trails a long straight tail of spilled entrails. This figure recalls the maternal body as conceived, according to the psychoanalyst Melanie Klein, as the medium of the ambivalent child who imagines it damaged and

▲ 1966b, 1969 ● 1975 ■ 1987

2 • Kiki Smith, *Blood Pool*, 1992
Painted bronze 35.6 x 99.1 x 55.9 (14 x 39 x 22). Cast two of an edition of two

restored in turn. In the plaster *Trough* (1990) this body lies cut in half, an empty vessel long dead and hollowed out, while in the bronze *Womb* (1986) it appears intact, even impervious. Smith echoes this ambivalent imagining of the mother in her representation of the child. In one untitled figure in wax with white pigment (1992), a girl crouches low, her submissive head tucked down, her elongated arms extended with palms upward in a gesture of extreme supplication. Smith also presents the child in a manner as abused as the mother: in the grisly *Blood Pool* [**2**], a malformed female child, painted a viscous red, is posed in a fetal position, her spine a double row of extruded bones like teeth. It is as if the oral sadism of the child evoked by Pondick in *Mouth* had returned, now to attack the child. As often with Bourgeois, Smith suggests an assault on patriarchy, but whereas Bourgeois imagines the man destroyed, Smith focuses on the woman violated and/or mourned.

Mourning of another kind is evoked by Robert Gober, who also casts body parts like male legs and buttocks in wax and other materials, set alone on the floor or in spare settings with strange decor. Often these parts, nearly all male, appear truncated by the wall, and they are clad, with boots, trousers or underpants, only enough to seem all the more exposed. Even more oddly, they are sometimes tattooed with bars of music or planted with candles or drains [**3**]. Like Bourgeois, Smith, and Pondick, Gober presents these body parts in order to query the intricate relations among aesthetic experience, sexual desire, and death. His art is also involved with memory and trauma: "Most of my sculptures," he has remarked, "have been memories remade, recombined, and filtered through my current experiences." Often his tableaux do not evoke actual events so much as enigmatic fantasies, and in this respect Gober is both more realistic and less literal than Smith. Indeed, he has called his installations "natural history dioramas about contemporary human beings," and sometimes they do possess the hyperreal, almost hallucinatory dimension of such displays. They place us in an ambiguous space—as in a dream we seem to be both inside and outside the scenes—that is also an ambiguous time—"memories filtered through my current experiences." In this way we are like ▲ sudden voyeurs of forgotten events, as if from our own lives. The result is an uncanny experience that seems both past and present, imagined and real.

But unlike Bourgeois, Smith, and Pondick, Gober stages adult desires more than infantile drives. Thus with his enigmatic female breast (1990) presented in relief as a part-object, Gober seems to ask: "What is a sexual object, and for whom?" And with his strange hermaphrodite torso (1990), one side coded male, the other female, he seems to wonder: "What is a sexual subject, and how do we know which kind we are?" Even as he questions the origins of desire, Gober also considers the nature of loss. In effect he reworks the Surrealist aesthetic of desire, tilted strongly to the heterosexual, into an art of melancholy and mourning, here tinged gay—an art ● of loss and survival in the age of AIDS. "For me," Gober remarked in 1991, "death has temporarily overtaken life in New York City."

Abject states

When we look back on such art of the early nineties, and wonder at its many figures of damaged psyches and wounded bodies, we must remember that this was a time of great anger and despair about a persistent AIDS crisis and a routed welfare state, about invasive disease and pervasive poverty. In this grim period many artists staged regression as an expression of protest and defiance, often in the form of performances, videos, and installations. This regression was especially aggressive in the work of Paul McCarthy (born 1945) and Mike Kelley (born 1954), both based in Los Angeles with continuous ties to Performance art there, whether focused on the pathos of failure, as with Bruce Nauman, or on the pathologies of ■ transgression, as with Chris Burden. McCarthy and Kelley combined both modes of Performance and took them to new extremes.

◆ In the mid-sixties, unaware of the precedent of Yves Klein, Paul McCarthy torched his canvases, and called the charred remains "black paintings." In the early seventies he developed these antiaesthetic actions into outright performances in which his own body became the brush, with food products like ketchup as paint: a portrait of the artist as infant or madman or both. In his performances thereafter, many of which were filmed or videotaped, McCarthy attacked conventional figures of male authority, with the aid of grotesque masks and bizarre costumes sometimes based on deranged pop-cultural icons. Some of these characters performed roles or functions entirely alien to them—in *My Doctor* (1978) the male protagonist gave bloody birth to a doll out of his head like some horror-movie Zeus—while others (fathers and grandfathers, a sea captain, *Mad* magazine's Alfred E. Newman) are pushed beyond stereotype to grotesquerie. McCarthy reserved his nastiest ridicule for the figure of the artist, especially the expressionistic painter, whom he presented as a monster of regression.

▲ 1966b ● 1924, 1931, 1987 ■ 1974 ◆ 1960a, 1967c

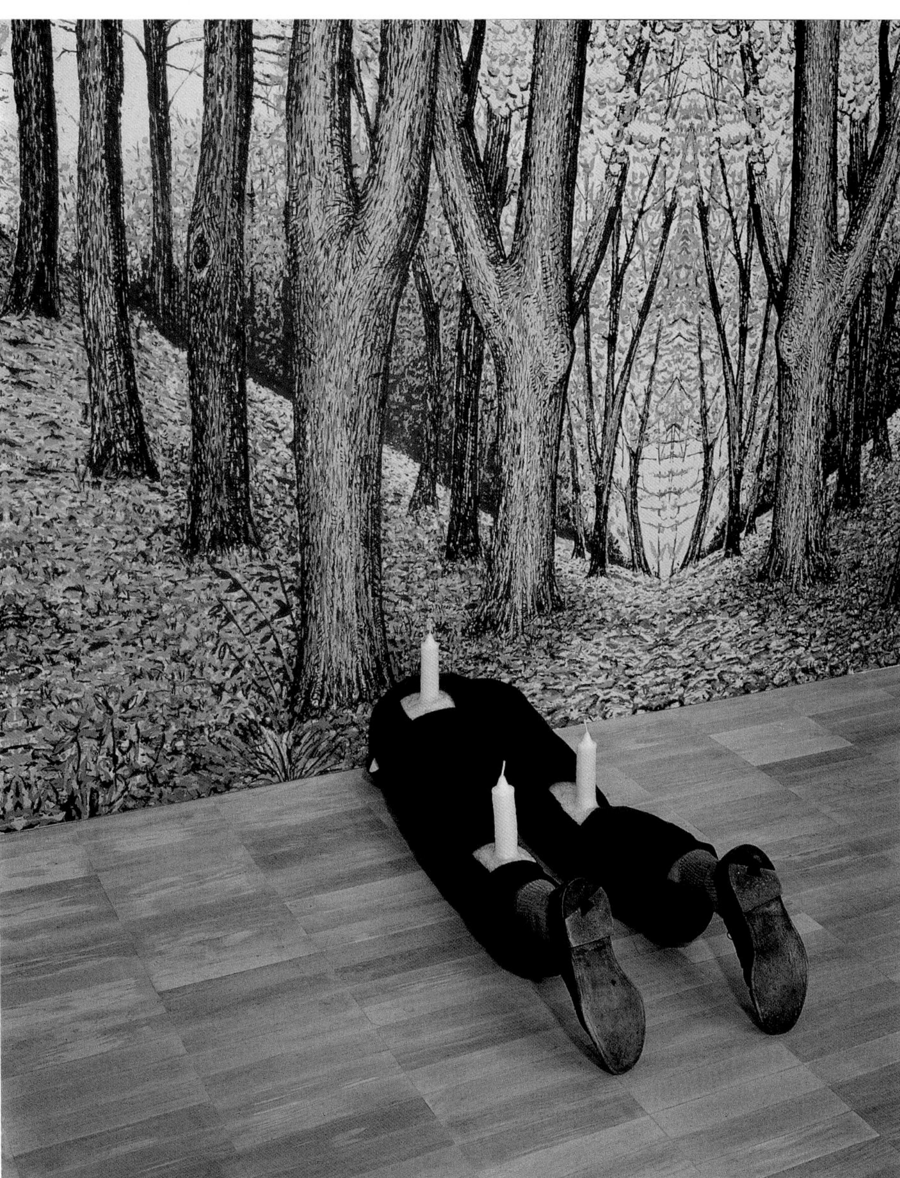

3 • Robert Gober, *Untitled*, 1991
Wood, beeswax, leather, and fabric
38.7 x 42 x 114.3 (15¼ x 16½ x 45)
(shown with *Forest*, silkscreen on paper)

In the eighties and nineties McCarthy often displayed the props of his performances as installations—such things as stuffed animals, dolls, and artificial body parts found on the street or in junk shops. Some of these installations turned into contraptions that staged outrageous actions, such as couplings of figures that defy all lines of difference—young and old, human and animal, person and thing [**4**]. In his own account McCarthy uses his props "as a child might use them, to manipulate a world through toys, to create a fantasy." Yet, even when comic, these fantasies are usually obscene, darker than any precedent in American Gothic art or fiction, for again and again McCarthy shows the orders of both natural and cultural worlds in disarray, and all structures of identity—especially the family—in dissolution.

On several points Mike Kelley is close to McCarthy, with whom he has collaborated on several performances and videos (their *Heidi* [1992] recasts the Swiss family tear-jerker as an American horror home-movie). Kelley also deploys carnivalesque reversals of character and inversions of role, but in a way that is more specific in its social references and cultural targets. Often he draws on aspects of his Roman Catholic, working-class childhood as well as his rock-and-roll, subcultural adolescence; and like his long-time associates John Miller (born 1954) and Jim Shaw (born 1952), he is very alert to connections between social oppression and artistic sublimation, between hierarchies in class and values in culture (Shaw, for example, has curated shows of found amateur paintings, placing marginal works in central galleries). If McCarthy assaults the symbolic order with performances of infantile regression, Kelley reveals this order to be already cracked in installations that often track the deviant interests of the adolescent male. Kelley uses this persona, whom he calls "the dysfunctional adult," to dramatize failures (or refusals) of accepted socialization, and in this respect he is drawn more to "the abject" than to the grotesque. Indeed, his work favors found things that, even if reclaimed, cannot be quite redeemed—things like worn stuffed animals and

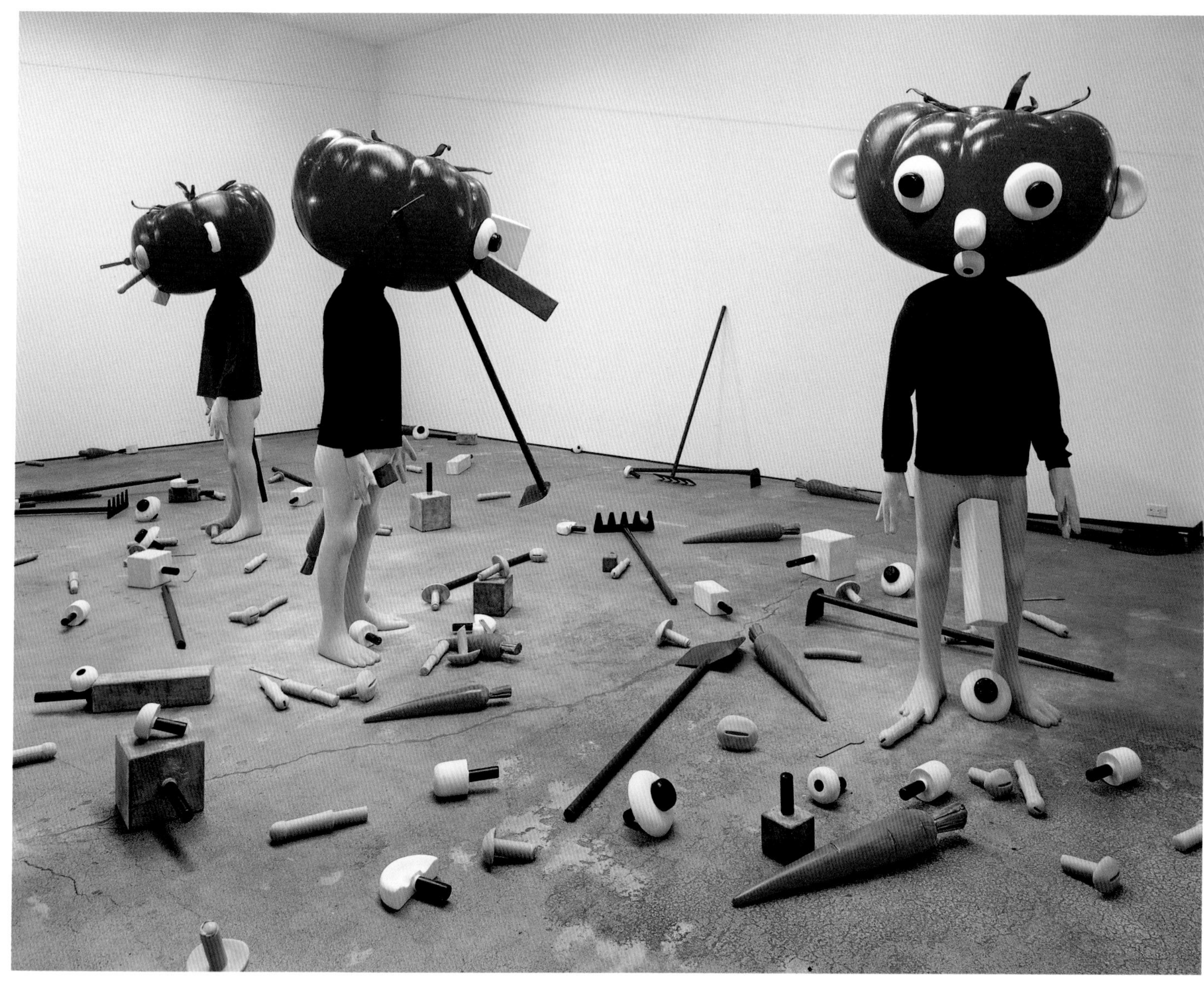

4 • Paul McCarthy, *Tomato Heads*, 1994
Sixty-two objects, fiberglass, urethane, rubber, and metal clothing, 213.3 x 139.7 x 111.7 (84 x 55 x 44)

dirty throw rugs from the Salvation Army, things that have dropped out of use, let alone exchange, things that Kelley renders even more pathetic through juxtaposition and combination.

The notion of the abject took on great currency in art and criticism of the early nineties. According to the canonical definition of the psychoanalytical theorist Julia Kristeva, the abject is a psychically charged substance, often imagined, which exists somewhere between a subject (or person) and an object (or thing). At once alien to us and intimate with us, it exposes the fragility of our boundaries, of the distinctions between what is inside and what is outside. Abjection is thus a condition in which subjecthood is troubled, "where meaning collapses" (Kristeva)—hence its attraction for artists like Kelley, McCarthy, and Miller, who often figure it through social detritus and bodily remains (which are sometimes equated). Indeed, art of the early nineties often seems pervaded by the dejected and the rejected, mess and scatter, dirt and shit (or shit-substitute). Of course, these are states and substances resistant to social order; in fact, in *Civilization and its Discontents* (1930) Freud argues that civilization was founded on the repressing of the lowly body, of the anal region and the olfactory sense, and the privileging of the erect body, of the genital region and the visual sense. In this light it is as if abject art sought to reverse this first step into civilization, to undo repression and sublimation, especially through a flaunting of the anal and the fecal. Such defiance is a strong subcurrent in twentieth-century art, from the coffee ▲ grinders of Duchamp, through the cans of shit of Piero Manzoni, to the messy practices of Kelley, McCarthy, and Miller, with whom it is often self-conscious, even self-parodic. "Let's Talk About Disobeying" reads one home-made banner by Kelley that is emblazoned with an image of a big cookie jar. "Pants-shitter and Proud of It" reads another.

However pathetic, this defiance can also be perverse, a twisting of laws of sexual difference, a staging of regression to an anal universe where difference as such is obscured. This is the fictive space that artists like Kelley, McCarthy, and Miller set up for transgressive play. For example, in *Dick/Jane* (1991) Miller stained a blonde,

▲ 1959a

5 • Mike Kelley, *Dialogue #1 (An Excerpt from "Theory, Garbage, Stuffed Animals, Christ")*, 1991
Blanket, stuffed animals, and cassette player, 30 x 118 x 108 (11¾ x 46½ x 42½)

blue-eyed doll brown and buried her neck-deep in shit-substitute. Familiar characters in old school primers, "Dick" and "Jane" taught several generations of North American children how to read—and how to read sexual difference. In the Miller version, however, Jane is turned into a phallic composite and plunged into a fecal mound. Like the stroke between the names in the title, the difference between male and female here is both erased and underscored, as is the difference between white and black. In this way Miller creates an anal world that tests the conventional terms of difference—sexual and racial, symbolic and social.

Kelley also often places his creatures in an anal universe. "We interconnect everything, set up a field," Kelley has the bunny say to the teddy bear in *Theory, Garbage, Stuffed Animals, Christ* [**5**], "so there is no longer any differentiation." Like McCarthy and Miller, Kelley explores this space where symbols mix, where "the concepts *faeces* (money, gift), *baby* and *penis* are ill-distinguished from one another," as Freud wrote of the anal stage. Like the others, Kelley does so less to celebrate material indistinction than to trouble symbolic difference. *Lumpen*, the German word for "rag" that gives us *Lumpenproletariat* ("the scum, the leavings, the refuse of all classes" that so interested Karl Marx), is a crucial term in the Kelley lexicon, a kind of cognate of the abject. And his art is indeed one of lumpen forms (dingy toy animals stitched together in ugly masses, dirty throw rugs laid over nasty shapes), lumpen themes (pictures of dirt and trash), and lumpen personae (dysfunctional men who build weird devices ordered from obscure catalogues in basements and backyards)—an art of degraded things that resist formal shaping, let alone cultural sublimating or social redeeming.

FURTHER READING

Russell Ferguson (ed.), *Robert Gober* (Los Angeles: Museum of Contemporary Art, 1997)

John Miller, *The Price Club* (Geneva/Dijon: JRP Editions, 2000)

Mignon Nixon, "Bad Enough Mother," *October*, no. 71, Winter 1995

Helaine Posner (ed.), *Corporal Politics* (Cambridge, Mass.: MIT List Visual Arts Center, 1992)

Ralph Rugoff et al., *Paul McCarthy* (London: Phaidon Press, 1996)

Linda Shearer (ed.), *Kiki Smith* (Columbus: Wexner Center for the Arts, 1992)

Elisabeth Sussman et al., *Mike Kelley: Catholic Tastes* (New York: Whitney Museum of American Art, 1993)

1994b

William Kentridge completes *Felix in Exile*, joining Raymond Pettibon and others in demonstrating the renewed importance of drawing.

In the Renaissance, artistic self-consciousness split the pictorial arts in two, associating each half of the enterprise with the city that seemed to stand for the workshop of its most intense practice. These were Rome and Venice, the former the center of drawing (*disegno*), the latter the headquarters of color (*colore*). Raphael and Michelangelo were the great exemplars of *disegno*, demonstrating the conceptual powers of this art of contour and composition. In Venice, the leading practitioners of *colore* were Bellini, Giorgione, Titian, Tintoretto, and Veronese, whose great altarpieces and multipanel installations showed how painting could dissolve away the solidity of plaster and stone to fill interior spaces with a disembodied radiance.

In France, the Académie des Beaux-Arts institutionalized the Renaissance division of painting in the competition for the prestigious Prix de Rome, the prize being to work at a State-sponsored studio at the Medici Palace in Rome. The prize required mastery of figure drawing in the production of an "academy," or study of the male nude, and of multifigure composition in the execution of a complex history painting. Jacques-Louis David (1748–1825) won the Prix in the late eighteenth century, followed soon by J.-A.-D. Ingres (1780–1867). The privileging of *disegno* was not challenged until Eugène Delacroix (1798–1863) emerged not only as a great colorist but as an ardent "Orientalist," his imagination fired by the patterns and palette of the Middle East: its mosques, its harems, its opiates. Encouraged by Delacroix's success, the landscape painters who emerged in the 1870s and became known as Impressionists hunted down the effects of color through *plein air* (out-of-doors) painting in which they discovered how the actual color of shadows cast by the golden sun is violet. Stroking such complementary colors onto the surfaces of their figures in short, fragile traces, the brushwork they practiced dissolved drawing into a shimmer of colored light. By the 1880s, Claude Monet and Auguste Renoir, the leading Impressionists, worried about the dissolution of line and thus of form that was a consequence of their attention to color. The emergence of neo-Impressionism, in the work of Georges Seurat and Paul Signac, was the acknowledgment of this resurgence of the rights of drawing.

The split between color and drawing seemed to continue, ▲ unabated, into the twentieth century as Cubism came to dominate avant-garde practice with an art of monochrome shading ▲ (chiaroscuro); only Matisse mounted a serious challenge in the name of color. Yet, as Yve-Alain Bois has shown, Matisse himself spoke of "color by design," or "color by drawing," a formulation that collapses the centuries-old distinction that had formed the logic of the pictorial arts. When Mondrian began to draw in colored line, weaving the florid masking tapes he discovered in ● New York into the late canvases for *New York* and *Victory Boogie-Woogie*, he joined Matisse in imploding the difference between line and color and discovered a form of abstraction that synthesized the oppositions that occur within the visual experience of reality: color vs. contour; figure vs. ground; light vs. shadow, etc.

Perhaps the most spectacular such synthesis was achieved by the ■ major "drip pictures" Jackson Pollock executed in 1950 and 1951, immense canvases filled with nothing but huge skeins of dripped and thrown liquid paint, weaving colored lines into one another in such a way as never to permit the bounding of an individual shape and thus the formation of a contour. The effect, as the critic Michael Fried expressed it, was to bound or delimit "nothing except, in a sense, eyesight." Once again, then, line emerged as the master-resource, a component of painting that was capable of generating the experience of light and color without surrendering its own abstractness.

This paradoxical deployment of line (the ultimate resource of representation) in the service of abstraction reflects the development of the two major aspects of drawing within the twentieth century. As Benjamin Buchloh has argued, drawing was essentialized as either a form of matrix or a form of grapheme. The first was the flattened and abstracted representation of the spatial ambience, as when the Cubists' grid simplified the geometricized lattice of Renaissance perspective, generalizing it into the description of the infrastructure of the woven canvas; the second was the expressive mark, as when some ◆ Abstract Expressionists exploited the bodily trace, or Cy Twombly used a graffiti-like scrawl, in order to effect the indexical registration of neuromotor and psychosexual impulses. According to Buchloh, if the matrix model of drawing delivers an abstract form of the object, the grapheme model performs an abstract version of the subject.

In the sixties Sol LeWitt developed a species of wall drawing that repeated Pollock's act of synthesis as it similarly dissolved recognizable form within a luminous matrix of line, one capable of generating the experience of color and light as well. But LeWitt's

▲ 1911

▲ 1903, 1906, 1910, 1944a ● 1944a ■ 1949, 1960b ◆ 1947b, 1949, 1953, 1957b work, executed by assistants following formulaic instructions (for example, *Ten thousand one-inch long lines evenly spaced on each of six walls* [**1**]), acknowledges the incursion into handicraft of industrialized and technologized forms of drawing such as commercial rendering and computer graphics. This demonstration of the obsolescence of drawing continued in the practice of ▲ Pop artists Andy Warhol and Roy Lichtenstein, in whose hands drawing was once again placed in the service of representation rather than abstraction. Indeed, the industrialization of representation by mass-cultural forces, which have exploited drawing for magazine advertisements and comic-book narrative, has withdrawn graphic expression from the sphere of the private and the expressive, from which it had always seemed to have issued, and forced it into the domain of the commercial and the public.

The Californian artist Raymond Pettibon (born 1957) takes up drawing exactly at that intersection between public and private by situating it within the culture of the comic books and "zines" that developed on the ruins of the West Coast counterculture of the late

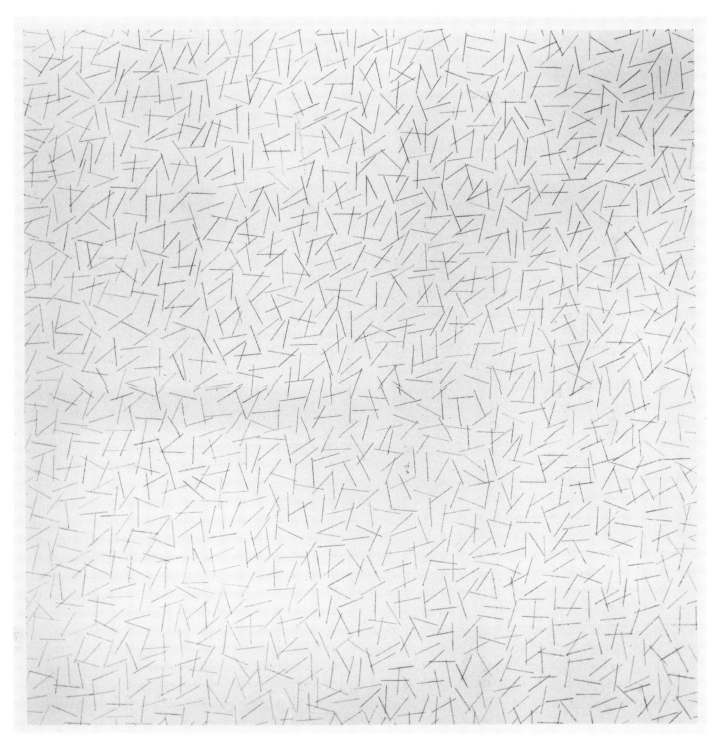

1 • Sol LeWitt, *Wall Drawing #150, Ten thousand one-inch (2.5cm) lines evenly spaced on each of six walls*, 1972 (detail)
Black pencil, dimensions variable

▲ 1960c, 1964b

sixties. Basing his style on the linear simplifications that Francisco Goya and Honoré Daumier adopted in order to make their work available to replication techniques such as lithography, Pettibon sets his art within a domain from which individual subjective life has been removed, having been replaced by the most impersonal, stereotypified, caricatures of individuality. Batman becomes the man-at-large in a series of "zines" set in Gotham City. The grip of mass-cultural practice at work on Pettibon's graphic expression not only displays the flattened character of subjective life within the world of what the Frankfurt School calls the "consciousness industry," but it also manifests the opacity of the forms of social communication within the sphere of developed consumer culture. But Pettibon works as well to pay homage to his modernist predecessors: from the great draftsmen such as Henri Matisse to the ▲ commercial stylists such as Roy Lichtenstein. His drawing *No Title (I think the pencil)* [**2**], recalls Lichtenstein's imitation of comic-book auditory bursts such as "BLAM, BRATATATATA! TAKA TAKA"; it also restricts the contours of the figure to the uninflected lines of a deskilled illustrator. This mechanical quality, given the human body part, reflects ironically on the promise of expressive gesture bodied forth by the pencil in the hand, as well as by the effusive "SNAP."

The South African artist William Kentridge (born 1955) takes a different tack with regard to drawing, making pictures in charcoal whose minute erasures and corrections are individually filmed in a stop-shoot technique that causes the finished drawing to appear "animated" once the run-on film is projected. The world of animated films (cartoons) is not far from that of "zines"; thus Kentridge's art inhabits a sphere, somewhere between the subcultural and the mass-cultural, which abuts that of Pettibon. Kentridge's cartoon world takes the form of a serialized "story" about the lives of a restricted set of characters: the mine-owner Soho Ekstein and his wife; and the artist Felix Teitelbaum, erotically involved with Mrs. Ekstein. But Kentridge's "story" is also about the form he practices, and it dares to focus on the resources and possibilities of drawing. That these resources are now threatened by a technological fluency that will soon render them obsolete is communicated by the mechanical metamorphoses that animation effects. But it is that very fluency that allows Kentridge to depict his own process, as when the motion of windshield wipers mimics the action of his own erasures, necessary to his work's production.

In *Felix in Exile*, Felix Teitelbaum is in a hotel in Paris looking through a suitcase of drawings, all of which represent slaughtered bodies of black protesters as they lie, fallen in the fields around Johannesburg. The author of these drawings is Nandi, a black woman surveyor whose activity seems to be forensic since she not only makes representations of the bodies but also draws lines around their contours as an index of where they have fallen in the fields. This is a • regression back along the history of drawing toward a "deskilled" graphic mark that is nothing but the mechanical trace of an object. Nandi's drawings also record the rivulets of blood that ooze from the ■ wounds on the bodies, drippings which inevitably recall Pollock's development of line and are an ironic manifestation of the tradition

2 • Raymond Pettibon, *No Title (I think the pencil)*, 1995
Pen and ink on paper, 61 x 34.3 (24 x 13½)

of the grapheme. Nandi's optical instrument (the theodolite) allows her, as a surveyor, to objectify her view of the mutilated human flesh she must record. It is the theodolite that then forms a bridge between Felix, standing at his hotel-room mirror to shave [**3**] and Nandi, looking back at him from faraway Africa, and allows Felix to observe the murder of Nandi, shot down as she draws [**4**]. Kentridge is thus determined that subjectivity and, indeed, extreme forms of emotion, can enter and develop within the field of mass-cultural entertainment that his medium occupies.

Kentridge's approach to drawing is neither matrix nor grapheme but a form of erasure, in which the traces of erased lines remain on the page, forming a faint charcoal mist. This type of linear overlay has the technical name "palimpsest" and attaches to the oldest forms of human graphic activity. In the paleolithic renderings of the caves, such as those at Ruffignac, we find animals layered one over

▲ 1903, 1906, 1910, 1944b, 1960c • 1968b ■ 1949, 1960b

3 • William Kentridge, *Felix in Exile*, 1994 (detail)
Charcoal on paper, 120 x 160 (47¼ x 63)

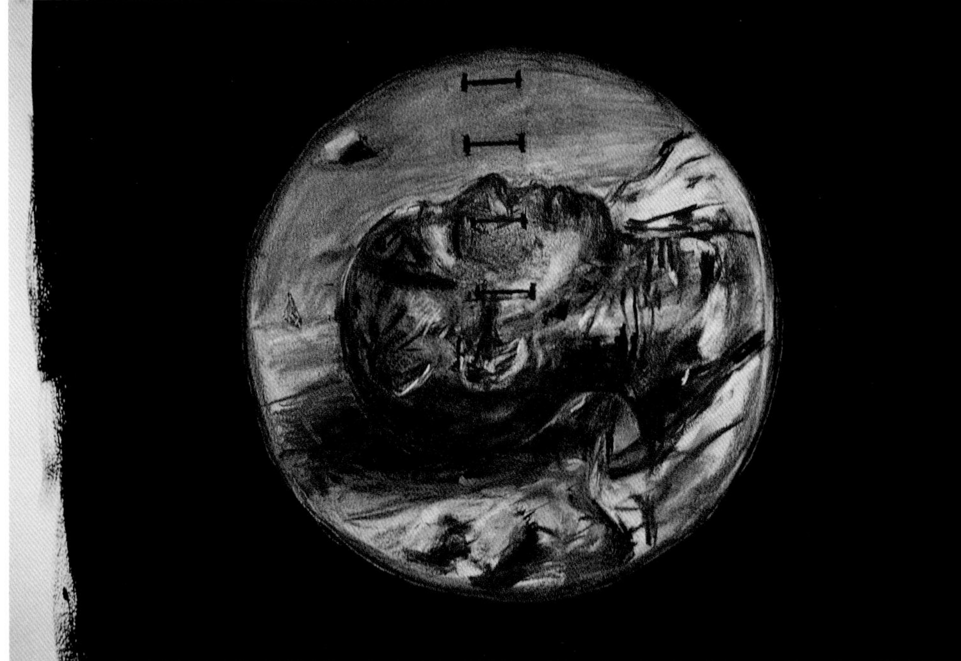

4 • William Kentridge, *Felix in Exile*, 1994 (detail)
Charcoal on paper 45 x 54 (17¾ x 21¼)

the other, bison covering up and canceling groups of mammoths. Palimpsest does for time what matrix had done for the object and grapheme for the subject: it renders it abstract. Rather than a narrative or history composition, we are given erasure and layering.

If the indexical outlines of the bodies is a way of acknowledging the outmoding of drawing, as hand work is made obsolescent by mechanized graphic forms, Kentridge's practice of animation is a meditation on the fate of the arts under the pressures of advanced ▲ technologies. Walter Benjamin has written that various artistic media have sometimes faced their superannuation at the hands of technology by summoning up the earliest history of the medium, a history within which is inscribed the utopian promise of the medium itself. In the case of Kentridge, this is to recall the earliest forms of film in which the little drawings pasted onto the drum of the zootrope or the phanokistoscope made possible a collective experience, thereby transforming the private consumer into the collective ensemble of the audience.

FURTHER READING

Benjamin H. D. Buchloh, "Raymond Pettibon: Return to Disorder and Disfiguration," *October*, no. 92, Spring 2000

Carolyn Christov-Bakargiev, *William Kentridge* (Brussels: Palais des Beaux Arts, 1998)

Rosalind Krauss, "The Rock: William Kentridge's Drawings for Projection," *October*, no. 92, Spring 2000

Raymond Pettibon, *Plots Laid Thick* (Barcelona: Museu d'Art Contemporani, 2002)

▲ 1935

1998

An exhibition of large video projections by Bill Viola tours several museums: the projected image becomes a pervasive format in contemporary art.

▲ Perception in all its complexity is the principal concern of the philosophy of phenomenology, and, as such, it was of special interest to Minimalist artists like Robert Morris who moved to "take relationships out of the work and make them a function of space, light, and the viewer's field of vision." Phenomenology cast particular doubt on ideal geometries such as cubes, spheres, and regular polyhedrons, arguing that the body of the viewer interrupts the field of vision and so complicates any reading of such forms. "Even the most unalterable property, shape, does not remain constant," Morris claimed, "for with each shift in position the viewer also constantly changes the apparent shape of the work." Foregrounding the seeming variability of simple forms in their installations, the Minimalists made explicit Marcel Duchamp's notion that it is the viewer who completes the work.

The art of suture

If Minimalist art acknowledged the conditions of both the ambient space and the viewing subject, it did so strictly in physical and perceptual terms. For this reason its phenomenological basis was called into question in the seventies and eighties by some artists and critics who claimed that the space of art is never so neutral and that the viewer considered in an abstractly phenomenological way is likely to be male, white, and heterosexual. Practitioners informed by ● feminist, postcolonial, and queer theories moved to undercut these assumptions and to set up other kinds of spectatorship; this work on representation vis-à-vis identity often took the form of a critical ■ manipulation of given images, usually in photographs. Yet other ◆ practices—Performance, video, and Installation art in particular—continued the opening to the body and its spaces inaugurated by Minimalism, thus elaborating on its phenomenological concerns. Performance and video engaged the viewer directly, but restrictions of staging in the former and dependence on monitors in the latter often kept the spectator at a distance. It was Installation that threw everything onto the experience of the viewer, and nowhere more clearly than in the work of James Turrell (born 1943), who sets up enormous fields of colored light [**1**]. Often these fields are produced through a slight opening in a gallery wall backed by an oblique plane that is brilliantly illuminated but whose exact location is almost impossible to determine for that very reason. A Turrell installation seems to exist as a spatial afterimage, appearing as a phantom shape projected by our own retinal activity and nervous system rather than as a fixed object in its own right. Instead of the reflexive viewers and delineated spaces of Minimalism, such art tends to effect a kind of sublime experience in which the spectator is overwhelmed by an apparition that he or she seems to project into being. For many viewers this free-floating aestheticism is exhilarating; for some,

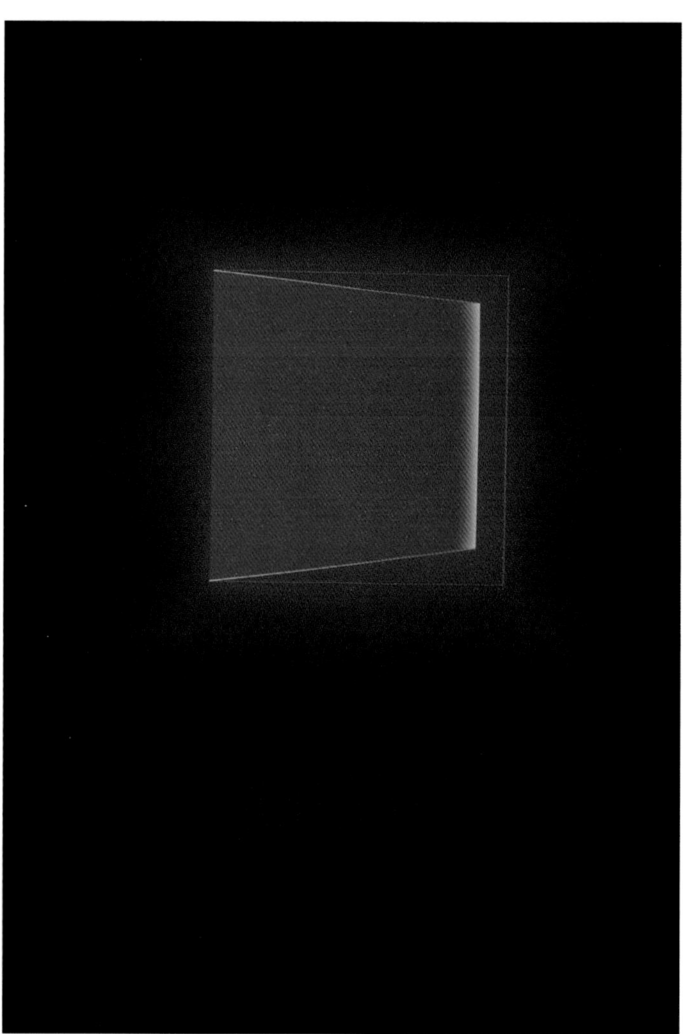

1 • James Turrell, *Milk Run III*, 2002
Light into space

▲ 1965, 1969 ● 1975, 1987, 1989, 1994a ■ 1977, 1980 ◆ 1973, 1974 however, it bears a disturbing relation to dazzling forms of technological spectacle.

▲ Installation artists such as Turrell complemented video artists such Peter Campus and Bruce Nauman who used the video camera to draw the viewer directly into the field of the work, often folding the time of perception onto the time of the video through its capacity for immediate transmission and rapid replay. It was left to subsequent video artists like Bill Viola and Gary Hill to combine the different effects of such Installation and video art, with viewers drawn into darkened spaces punctuated by luminous projections. Prompted by advances in projection devices in the eighties, Viola and Hill transcended the limited scale of the video monitor, sometimes making the field of display the size of a museum wall, and so creating an image-space that was immense yet mysterious, thoroughly mediated yet seemingly immediate. In some respects these video projections, which often include color and sound as well, partake equally of the fixity of grand painting and the temporality of narrative cinema. This reformatting of video transforms the terms of its space and its viewer alike: the former is literally obscure, and the latter is positioned somewhere between the contemplative and the awestruck. Yet the phenomenological effects of Minimalist installations do not disappear altogether; in some respects they are heightened, but in a manner that often confounds bodily perception and technological mediation.

Of course, seductive luminosity and immense projection were already combined in Hollywood cinema, which also activates another kind of projection, a psychically charged identification of the audience with the figures presented to it as visual models or ego ideals. Film theory has analyzed the experience of such cinema as a matter of projective identification through "suture," the process by which the audience is woven into the matrix of the filmic event through its alignment with the point of view of the camera; as the camera turns to a figure within its visual field, the audience imagines itself entering the field of the narrative, thereby joining the actors and their shifting points of view as well. In this way cinema doubles psychological projection with imagistic projection. For the most part this doubling is adapted rather than rejected in large video installations by Viola, Hill, and others, for though they are far less narrative than movies, less suturing of the viewer through camera and story, they are sometimes even more enveloping, more immersive of the viewer in a total image-sound space. Even when the video screens are arrayed in different configurations, sometimes confronting the viewer and sometimes surrounding them, the space often seems even more virtualized, the medium even more derealized, than in cinema. To what ends are these effects produced?

In his video installations Viola has consistently sought to represent, indeed to reproduce, different bodily experiences. Tranquil and agitated states often collide in the same work: in *The Sleep of Reason* (1988) a video monitor shows a close-up of a sleeping person; randomly, as if in a dreaming fit, the room darkens and violent images appear on the walls as roaring sounds fill the room; then the space returns to normal. Further, these bodily states frequently evoke extreme mental conditions: in *Reasons for Knocking at an Empty House* (1982) a monitor shows a man periodically struck from behind (again to the accompaniment of sound bursts), while the viewer sits in a wood chair listening via headphones to chattering voices telling of a horrible head injury. Moreover, these mental conditions are often analogues of spiritual experiences: in *Room for St. John of the Cross* (1982) images of mountain peaks are accompanied by sounds of a violent storm while turbulent poems by the sixteenth-century Spanish mystic are recited. Again and again, Viola foregrounds ritual passages and visionary states: from the baptismal *Reflecting Pool* (1977–9), in which a man leaps above a pool only to vanish, to *Nantes Triptych* (1992), which juxtaposes a young woman giving birth, a clothed man suspended under water, and an old woman dying, to *The Crossing* [**2**], which shows a figure consumed by fire on one side of the screen and a figure inundated with water on the other. In his most elaborate work to date, *Going Forth by Day* (the title is derived from the Egyptian *Book of the Dead*), the viewer is surrounded by five vast videos projected in slow motion. Inspired in part by the Giotto frescoes at the Scrovegni Chapel in Padua (c. 1303–5), the different parts of this "cinematic fresco" are titled *Fire Birth*—another baptism, here in waters of fire and blood; *The Path*—a parade of people along a forest path; *The Deluge*—the flooding of an apartment house; *The Voyage*—the dying of an old man by a riverside; and *First Light*—the witnessing of a saved person

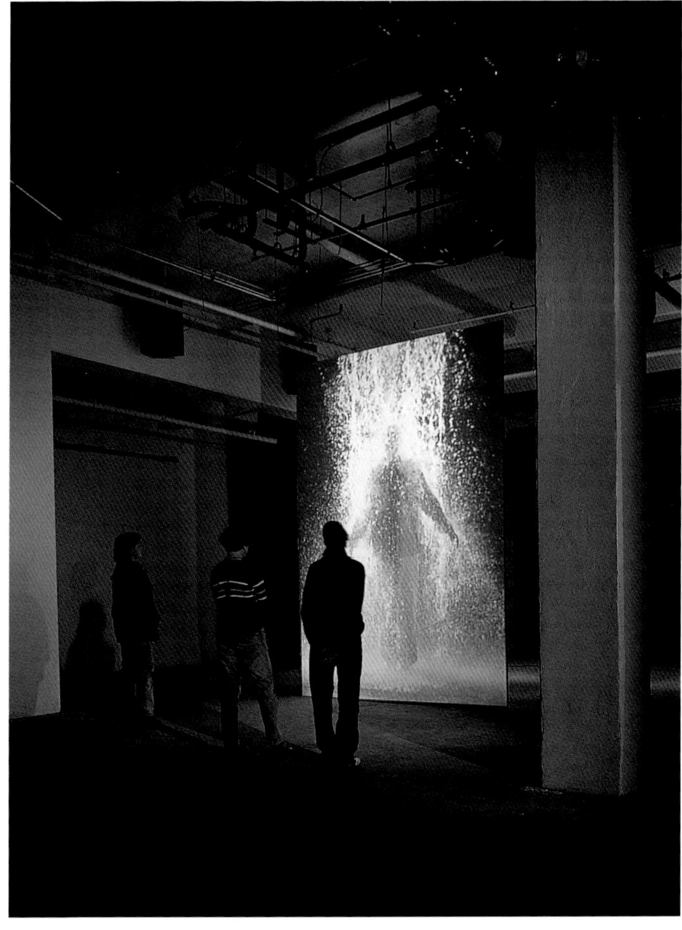

2 • Bill Viola, *The Crossing*, 1996
Video and sound installation at the Grand Central Market, Los Angeles

▲ 1973

The spectacularization of art

In the nineties architecture and design acquired a new importance in culture at large. Although this prominence stemmed from the initial debates about postmodernism, which centered on architecture, it was confirmed by the inflation of design and display in many aspects of consumerist life—in fashion and retail, in corporate branding and urban redevelopment, and so on. This economic emphasis on design and display has affected both curatorial practice and museum architecture as well: every large exhibition seems to be conceived as an installation piece in itself, and every new museum as a spectacular *Gesamtkunstwerk* or "total work of art." To take two prominent examples, the Guggenheim Museum (1991–7) designed by Frank Gehry in the Basque city of Bilbao, and Tate Modern (1995–2000) renovated by Herzog and de Meuron along the Thames in London, are now tourist attractions themselves. Like other mega-museums, they were designed to accommodate the expanded field of postwar art, but in some ways they also trump this art: they use its great scale, which was first posed as a challenge to the modern museum, as a pretext to inflate the contemporary museum into a gigantic space-event that can swallow any art, let alone any viewer, whole. In part the new significance granted architecture has a compensatory dimension: in some respects the celebrity architect is the latest figure of the artist-genius of old, a mythic creator endowed with magisterial vision and worldly agency that the rest of us in a mass society cannot possess.

In *The Society of the Spectacle* (1967) Guy Debord defined spectacle as "capital accumulated to such a degree that it becomes an image." This process has become more intensive in the last four decades, to the point where media-communications-and-entertainment conglomerates are the dominant ideological institutions in Western society. In this way the corollary of the Debordian definition has become true as well: spectacle is "an image accumulated to such a degree that it becomes capital." Such is the logic of many museums and cultural centers, as they are designed, alongside theme parks and sports complexes, to assist in the postindustrial refashioning of the old industrial city—that is, in its being made safe for shopping and spectating, which often involves the displacing of working and unemployed classes and the furthering of "brand equity" for global corporations (including museums like the Guggenheim).

by a group of exhausted rescue workers. The *New York Times* described the piece as "an ambitious meditation on the epic themes of human existence—individuality, society, death and rebirth." This ambition suggests why Viola works to virtualize his space and to derealize his medium: so that his ahistorical vision of spiritual transcendence can be effected—that is, it can come across as an effect. ▲ From the start, video art was prone to a technological kind of mysticism (with Nam June Paik it is more Zen Buddhist in flavor; here it is more Christian). Of course, cinema has long been similarly inclined, and it continues to strive for ever more intense effects of immediacy through ever more elaborate forms of mediation. (As Walter Ben- ▲ jamin remarked long ago of film in "The Work of Art in the Age of Mechanical Reproduction" (1936): "the equipment-free aspect of reality here has become the height of artifice; the sight of immediate reality has become a blue flower in the land of technology.") As with Turrell, how one feels about such illusion will guide how one feels about such work: for many, this mystical experience is a genuine effect of much great art; for some, it is just that—mystification.

The traumatic sublime

Much contemporary art of the projected image recalls the two-part movement of the Sublime, as discussed by German philosopher Immanuel Kant, with a first moment in which the viewer is almost overwhelmed, even shattered, by an awesome sight and/or sound, followed by a second moment in which he or she comprehends the experience and so recoups it intellectually, and feels a rush of power, not of loss, for doing so. Viola privileges the second, redemptive moment. A partial list of other artists involved with video and film projections who favor the first, traumatic moment might include Matthew Buckingham (born 1963), Janet Cardiff (born 1957), Stan Douglas (born 1960), Douglas Gordon (born 1966), Pierre Huyghe (born 1962), Steve McQueen (born 1969), Tony Oursler (born 1957), Paul Pfeiffer (born 1966), Pipilotti Rist • (born 1962), Rosemarie Troeckel (born 1952), and Gillian Wearing. Sometimes these artists (who are of many different nationalities, interests, and commitments) project images of both beauty and violence. For example, in her video diptych *Ever is Over All* (1997), Pipilotti Rist shows a luscious field of red and yellow flowers on one screen, and a young woman in a blue dress strolling down a city street on the other, gaily smashing car windows as she does so. For his part Douglas Gordon focuses more strictly on the traumatic; indeed, he seems obsessed with splittings of many sorts—imagistic, formal, thematic, and psychological. Often Gordon uses split screens to project his appropriated films (he has favored Hollywood *auteurs* from Alfred Hitchcock to Martin Scorsese), sometimes mirroring the extracted scenes on the two halves; usually he deploys these devices to highlight a divided subjectivity. One video projection, *Confessions of a Justified Sinner* (1996), contains all these elements: extracts of *Dr. Jekyll and Mr. Hyde* are projected on two screens, the one image in positive, the other in negative, as if the split personality of the protagonist had penetrated everything, including its re-representation here. Gordon appears to identify with this division: *Monster* (1996–7) includes a double self-portrait with one photograph of his face expressionless and the other of his face Scotch-taped into a grotesque mask. (Perhaps there is a religious dimension here as well: he grew up in Glasgow in a Calvinist family with a Manichean view of good and evil in the world.) His most famous work appropriates the most famous movie about schizophrenia, *Psycho*; however, Gordon slows the Hitchcock film to a hypnotic, almost catatonic pace—hence his title, *24 Hour Psycho* **[3]**.

Sometimes Gordon interrupts his appropriated films in a manner that produces a hysterical effect of fitful starts and stops. Hysteria is a

▲ 1973 ▲ 1935 • 1993b

common interest of several of these artists, especially Martin Arnold and Paul Pfeiffer, both of whom also use found footage (Arnold tends to old Hollywood films, Pfeiffer to recent commercial spectacles), which they subject to compulsive repetitions. These concerns suggest particular precedents: if one model (for Gordon in particular) is the cinema of Andy Warhol, with its often fixed camera, prolonged shots, and split screens, another model is the "flicker" films pioneered by Peter Kubelka in Vienna and developed by Hollis ▲ Frampton, Paul Sharits, and others in New York in the sixties and seventies. The flicker effect is produced through a rapid-fire alternation between clear frames of film and opaque ones; this visual stutter allows the viewer actually to see the separate integers that make up the cinematic medium in the very course of its projection. On the one hand, this visual attack interrupts any identification based on suture; on the other, it stimulates the nervous system in specific ways. As the clear light triggers the retina to project its shapes onto the visual field as afterimages in the complementary color, purple rectangles begin to dance on the field of black, as projections of the clear frames join the experience of the opaque ones; the body thus seems propelled into the field of the screen. Inspired by modernist investigations of the medium (for example, those of Sergei Eisenstein and Dziga Vertov), the flicker-filmmakers were interested in revealing not only the reflexes of the body but also the materiality of the celluloid, the apparatus of the camera and the projector, the space of screening, and so on. Some contemporary artists develop these materialist interests; most, however, do not. Unlike their modernist predecessors, they use flicker and related effects in order to induce an experience of bodily shock, of traumatized subjectivity. And unlike their postmodernist predecessors as well, they seem concerned to produce image-spaces of psychological intensity more than critical reflections on given representations.

Film as archive

Along with recent advances in image technologies has come an increased appreciation of outmoded devices; renewed interest in flicker films is only one instance of this concern. Not long ago film was considered the medium of the future; now it appears as a privileged index of the recent past (perhaps it will enter the art museums as it becomes outmoded elsewhere). Early cinema in particular has emerged as an archive of historical experience, a repository of old sensations, private fantasies, and collective hopes, and it is often ▲ treated in these terms by Buckingham, Cardiff, Tacita Dean (born 1965), Douglas, Huyghe, McQueen, and others. "Both in terms of presentation and the subject matter of my work," Stan Douglas has remarked (in a comment that might represent the others as well), "I have been preoccupied with failed utopias and obsolete technologies. To a large degree, my concern is not to redeem these past events but to reconsider them: to understand why these utopian moments did not fulfill themselves, what larger forces kept a local

3 • Douglas Gordon, *24 Hour Psycho*, 1993
Video projection installation

▲ 1973, 1993a

▲ 2003

4 • Stan Douglas, *Overture*, 1986
Black-and-white 16mm film with looping device and mono optical soundtrack, each rotation seven minutes

moment a minor moment: and what was valuable there—what might still be useful today." To cite only one instance of this collective concern, *Overture* [**4**] is a film installation by Douglas that combines archival footage from the Edison Company from 1899 and 1901 with audio text from Marcel Proust's *Remembrance of Things Past* (1913–22). The old film was shot from a camera mounted on a train engine as it passed along cliffs and through tunnels in British Columbia; the Proust is a meditation on the state of semiconsciousness that exists between sleeping and waking. There are six extracts from Proust and three sections of film (with tunnel passages extended by leader film), so that when the footage recurs it is matched with a different text, in a way that tests our sense of repetition and difference, memory and displacement. *Overture* is concerned not only with the transition from sleeping to waking, with the rebirth of consciousness that is also a return to mortality, but also with the shift in dominance from one kind of narrative medium (the novel) to another kind (the film). It juxtaposes moments of rift—in subjective experience as well as in cultural history—when other versions of self and society are glimpsed, lost, and glimpsed again. "Obsolete forms of communication," Douglas has commented, "become an index of an understanding of the world lost to us." To recover these forms is to "address moments when history could have gone one way or another. We live in the residue of such moments, and for better or worse their potential is not yet spent."

In this way recent projections of video and film suggest a dia-▲lectic of advanced and outmoded techniques, of future and past possibilities in media. On the one hand, more and more contemporary art seems to be reworked in cinematic terms, a development aided by the ready availability of digital cameras and editing programs since the mid-nineties (the trajectory of a prominent artist like Matthew Barney—from elaborate installation-performances to a mammoth film cycle titled *Cremaster*—is telling in this regard). On the other hand, there is a counterimpulse to complicate media history as never before, to find new avenues of expression in surpassed modes. Why this turn to the cinematic in art? No doubt one reason is the sheer legibility of movies: "I try to use film as a common denominator," Douglas Gordon has remarked. "They [movies] are the icons of a common currency." Perhaps, too, these artists see the medium as best suited to treat fundamental transformations in experience and subjectivity in contemporary society—that is, experience that is so often routed through imaging devices, and subjectivity that has learned not only to survive but even to thrive on technological shocks.

FURTHER READING

Russell Ferguson et al., *Douglas Gordon* (Los Angeles: Museum of Contemporary Art, 2001)
Lynne M. Herbert et al., *James Turrell: Space and Light* (Houston: Contemporary Arts Museum, 1990)
Chrissie Iles et al., *Into the Light: The Projected Image in American Art, 1964–1977* (New York: Whitney Museum of American Art, 2001)
David Ross et al., *Bill Viola* (New York: Whitney Museum of American Art, 1998)
Chris Townsend (ed.), *The Art of Bill Viola* (London: Thames & Hudson, 2004)
Scott Watson et al., *Stan Douglas* (London: Phaidon Press, 1998)

▲ 2003

2001

A mid-career exhibition of Andreas Gursky at the Museum of Modern Art in New York signals the new dominance of a pictorial photography, which is often effected through digital means.

The photograph appears distant from the digital image. With its chemical registration of continuous gradients of ambient light on chemically treated paper, the photograph might be taken to exemplify the analogical image: the photograph as a direct imprint of things in the world in opposition to the digital image as a manipulated screen of information scanned with a computer. Slowly but surely, however, digital techniques have penetrated photographic image-production in various forms of media—and, in some instances, displaced it altogether. Many artists have explored the uneasy commingling of the photographic and the digital—Jeff Wall (born 1946) and Andreas Gursky most prominent among them—and sometimes they have done so in ways that exploit our uncertainty about the physical status, even the ontological nature, of the resultant image. At least for the time being, the traits long associated with photography—monocular perspective, realistic detail, and, above all, documentary referentiality—remain natural enough to us so that any digital alteration of these terms still appears disruptive, but perhaps this will soon change. (Of course, there are other kinds of digital art too, as well as different experiments in web or internet art, but the practical terms of such work, let alone the critical terms of its evaluation, are not yet in place; this too might soon change.)

Ersatz unities

The last decade has witnessed a transformation in image technologies as dramatic as those changes registered by the photography debates in the late twenties and early thirties and by the various ▲ Pop manifestations in the late fifties and early sixties. As Wall observed as early as 1989, "The historical consciousness of the medium [of photography] is altered": rather than a direct "message without a code" (as Roland Barthes defined it in "The Photographic Message" [1961]), the photograph might now be shot through with complicated codes of various sorts (including the computer sense of "code"). This new status of the photograph not only qualifies its presumed referentiality but also revises its possible • applications in art. Consider photocollage and photomontage: the uses of these devices in modernism were diverse, but they all depended on the explicit juxtaposition of referential photographs for their effects, whether these were aesthetically subversive as in Dada, psychically charged as in Surrealism, or politically agitational as in Constructivism (and indeed in much Dada also). However, with digital manipulation—that is, of images taken with a digital camera or of photographic negatives scanned into digital files that can then be revised or changed utterly, with entirely new negatives printed as a result—the old logic not only of documentary photographs but also of montaged ones is transformed. Proportions can be adjusted, perspectives corrected, color changed (Gursky, for example, makes all these alterations routinely); and, for that matter, novel images can be synthesized. In the process montage becomes not only hidden but also internal to the single image, almost intrinsic to it: more a seamless join than a physical cut, more a morphing than a montaging, the digital composite exists somewhere between a photographic document and an electronic puzzle.

At the same time that digital photography signals technological advance, in the hands of practitioners like Wall and Gursky it often evokes historical art (a related dialectic is active in art involving ▲ projected images). Quite apart from its frequently grand scale and sometimes explicit references, this work tends to pictorial composition, even to narrative themes, in ways that often align it with figurative painting or classical cinema more closely than with unmanipulated or straight photography. If the pictorial image was under assault in advanced art after Minimalism (especially in • Process, Body, and Installation art)—in large part because it seemed to promise a virtual space that a private consciousness or a unitary subject might enter and inhabit—the pictorial image now returns triumphant in digital photography (and much other art besides). Moreover, if "pictorialism" dominated painting and photography ■ *before* modernist art, it now seems to reign supreme *after* it as well. This has led some critics to decry artists like Wall and Gursky as conservative, but they might also be understood to recover a semiotically hybrid and temporally heterogeneous type of image that was pervasive before abstract painting and straight photography became dominant—to recover (as the curator Peter Galassi has put it vis-à-vis Gursky) a "long tradition of fluid mendacity."

Wall is explicit about the restorative dimension of his practice. In his view the avant-garde aesthetic of the fragment—of collage and montage—has become almost rote, as has the privilege given

▲ 1929, 1930a, 1930b, 1935, 1959d, 1964b, 1968a, 1968b • 1920, 1924, 1930b ▲ 1998 • 1969, 1974 ■ 1916b

1 • Jeff Wall, *The Storyteller*, 1986
Color transparency in lightbox, 229 x 437 (90⅛ x 172)

any rupture with art history; for Wall this is a misbegotten celebration of discontinuity that overlooks the greater continuity "which is that of capitalism itself." "The rhetorics of critique have had to make an 'other' out of the pictorial," he has charged; "this truth has been totalized, and transformed into what [Theodor] Adorno called 'identity'. I am struggling with that identity." According to this argument, the fragmentation of both the art work and the viewing subject is now normative, "our orthodox form of cultural lucidity," in a way that renders a return to the unified picture and the centered viewer a critical move, a "transgression against the institution of transgression" (Wall).

For some critics of Wall this argument is sophistry, yet it is not all, or not precisely, that Wall performs with his large color transparencies set in luminous light boxes. Even as his format mimics advertisement display, his images often suggest historical painting, and sometimes they are composed in a manner that specifically recalls the neoclassical tableau—that is, a staged ensemble of painted figures captured in a significant action or pregnant moment. *Diatribe* (1985), which shows two welfare mothers, one with a child on her hip, in the vague terrain of a working-class backlot, is calculated to resonate—in difference as much as in similarity—with such Old Master paintings as *Landscape with Diogenes* (1648) by Nicolas Poussin. And *The Destroyed Room* (1978), which stages the violent trashing of the apparent apartment of a prostitute, with clothes strewn and mattress slashed, is meant to evoke *The Death of Sardanapalus* (1827) by Eugène Delacroix, his Romantic (indeed Orientalist) vision of an entire harem put to the sword. Yet Wall focuses his art-historical gaze not only on traditional painting but also on modernist painting at its very birth. As the critic Thierry de Duve has written, "It is as though Wall had gone back to the fork in the roadway of history, to that very moment when, around Manet, painting was registering the shock of photography; and as though he had then followed the route that had not been taken by modern painting, and had incarnated the painter of modern life as a photographer." In this way, even as Wall seeks to reinscribe "the painting of modern life" in contemporary photography, he also wants to redeploy its social critique—to expose new myths of capitalist society, as Manet often did with old myths, at the same time that he stages them. Wall has cited Manet a number of times. *Woman and Her Doctor* (1980–1), which shows these two affluent figures seated together at a cocktail party, updates the ambiguous rendezvous of a bourgeois couple depicted by Manet in *In the Conservatory* (1879); and *The Storyteller* **[1]** resituates his famous *Le Déjeuner sur l'herbe* (1863) in a wasteland under a highway bridge, where Wall replaces the leisurely Parisian bohemians of Manet with the homeless native Canadians of his home town Vancouver.

For some critics the unities of this art are forced; for others it is its very lack of consistency, its pastiche of references, that is problematic. For his part Wall seems to intend both effects: to produce a pictorial order that reflects (on) a social order, and to suggest that both are in decay, with the former a symptom of the latter. This is the principal lesson that he takes from Manet, who, according to Wall, inherited a traditional painting (again, the tableau) that was in crisis, a crisis that the spread of photography only exacerbated.

What once seemed organic and composed in traditional painting had become mechanistic and fragmented in Manet, who opposed the "ersatz unity" of contemporary Salon pictures with what Wall terms a "negative, almost memorializing unification of the image around a ruined, or even a dead concept of the picture." Wall seeks to recover and to advance this dialectic of "unity and fragmentation" ("I feel that my work is in fact both classical and grotesque"), and to make it the instrument of "profane illuminations" of his own social world.

Delirious spaces

Sam Taylor-Wood (born 1967) also cites historical paintings in some of her work, which includes video and sound installations as well as large photographs; her *Wrecked* (1996), for example, is a contemporary version of *The Last Supper* of Leonardo. "These allusions and quotations are a self-discipline that I impose on my history," Taylor-Wood has remarked; but as with Wall there are contemporary social insights to be gleaned here as well. Her series *Five Revolutionary Seconds* (1995–8), for instance, presents a panoramic frieze of mostly bored subjects in mostly affluent homes, connected only by intermittent acts or gestures of violence. Like many of her peers who use projected images, Taylor-Wood is concerned with extreme states (this is evident from her titles alone): "I have an interest, both personal and social, in ungluing the setting." In her *Soliloquy* series [**2**], she presents large portraits of a figure above with smaller panoramas of various scenes below, on the model of the Renaissance altarpiece with its underlying "predella" pictures. Here an Old Master format, developed to convey different orders of existence (heavenly and earthly) in the scenes of a saintly life, is updated to evoke different orders of experience, objective and subjective, public and private, perhaps conscious and unconscious.

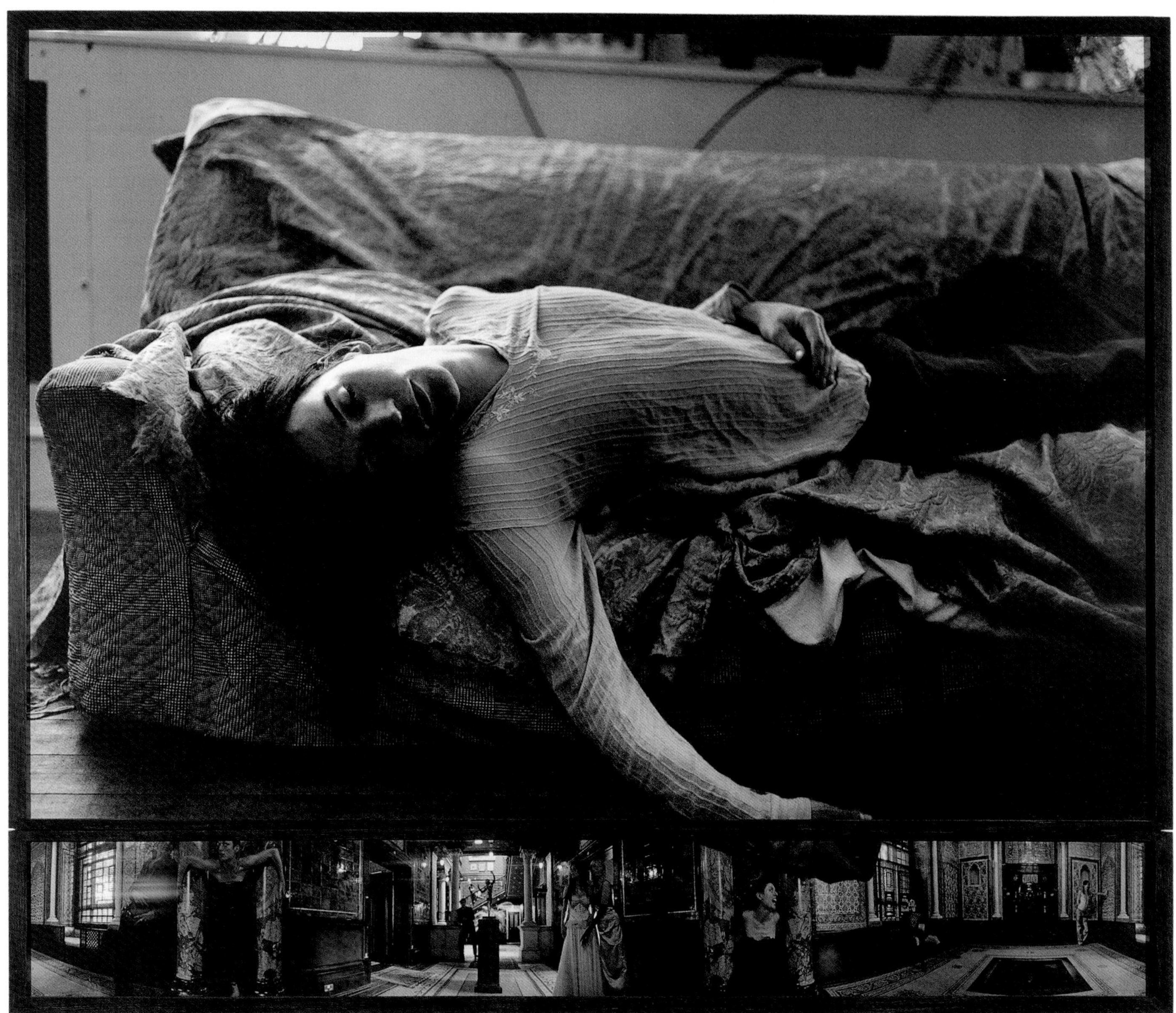

2 • Sam Taylor-Wood, *Soliloquy I*, 1998
C-type color print (framed), 211 x 257 (83⅛ x 101⅛)

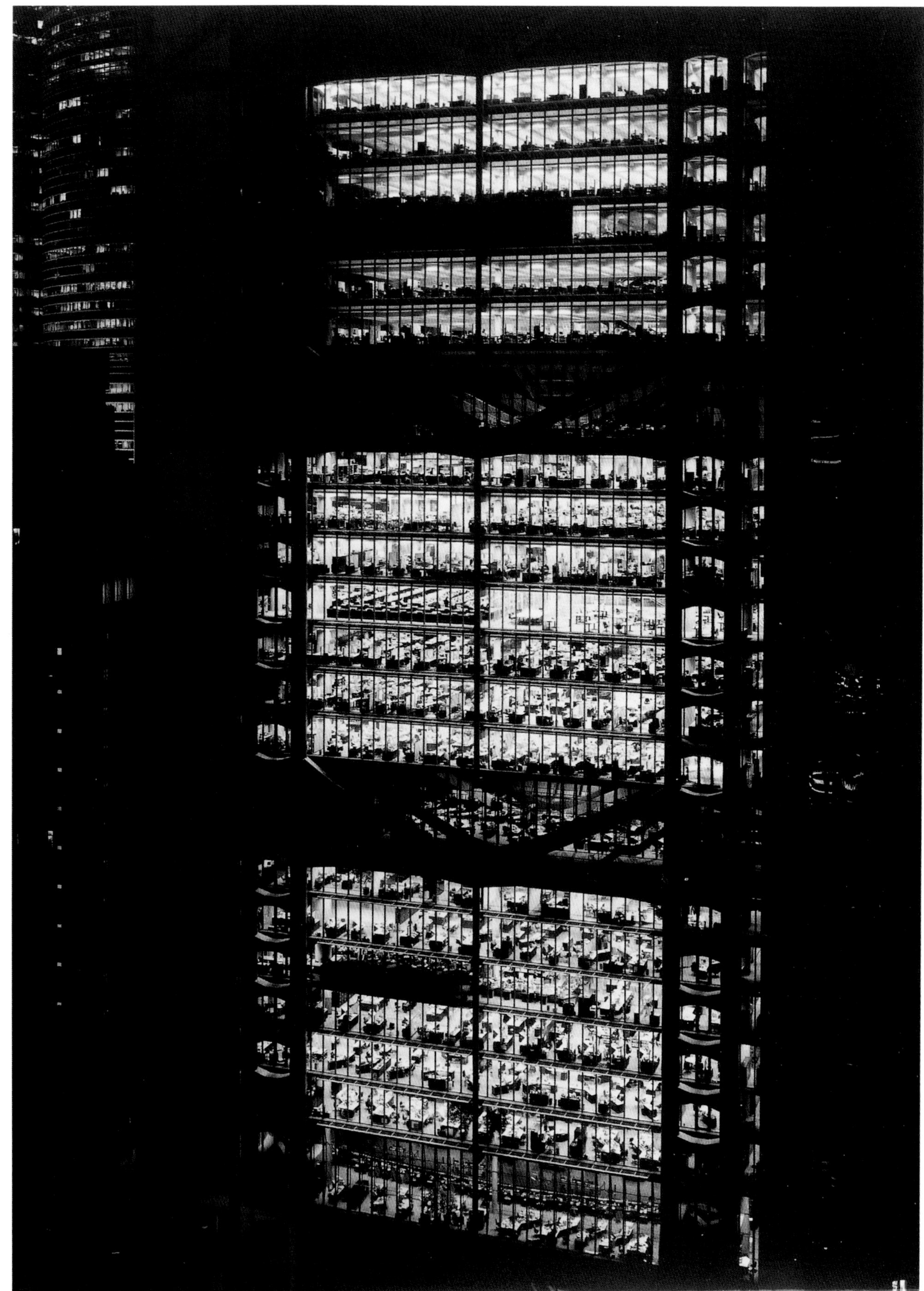

3 • Andreas Gursky, *Hong Kong and Shanghai Bank*, 1994
Chromogenic color print, 226 x 176 (89 x 69¼)

▲ Influenced by James Coleman, Taylor-Wood draws on precedents in cinema, theatre, and the *tableau vivant* as much as in ● painting and photography, and like her peers (such as Tacita Dean) she moves back and forth between mediums in an attempt "to offer a 'provocation' of meanings." Andreas Gursky is far more focused on traditions of photography; but he too produces a kind of pictorial tension, here produced in part through digital montage. In the early eighties, along with Thomas Struth, Thomas Ruff, and Candida ■ Höfer, Gursky studied with Hilla and Bernd Becher at the Düsseldorf Art Academy, where he was schooled in the distinctive Becher approach: photograph a single subject as uniformly and objectively as possible, usually in black and white; then display the results typologically, usually in grids or series. His early photographs of security guards and Sunday activities adapted these principles. However, unlike the Bechers, Gursky worked in color (his is the first generation of German photographers to use it extensively), and soon he experimented with digital splicing as well (at first to create sleek urban panoramas). By the nineties most of his prints had become large and pictorial, though he was never as concerned with art-historical allusions as Wall (whom Gursky nonetheless acknowledges as an important influence at this time). Gursky does produce the occasional "Romantic" landscape (e.g., *Aletsch Glacier* [1993]), but his primary interest lies in a different sort of contemporary "sublime"—in the intense spaces of detailed commodity production (*Siemens* [1991]), furious financial exchange (*Tokyo Stock Exchange* [1990]), spectacular professional sports (*EM, Arena, Amsterdam I* [2000]), rave youth culture (*May Day IV* [2000]), excessive product display (*99 Cent* [1999]), and other such "hyperspaces" characteristic of global capitalism both at work and at play **[3]**.

Many of these spaces are already spectacular, with people and products alike arranged in total designs or as "mass ornaments" (to use the term of the critic Siegfried Kracauer, who first pointed to this phenomenon in industrial culture); yet Gursky also manipulates his panoramic images to further heighten photogenic patterns of repeated forms and colors. Sometimes his digital stretching of the photograph—spliced images with two or three perspectives and the like—seems driven by a desire to image spaces that might not otherwise be given to sight or to representation, that test our "cognitive map" of the postmodern world (to borrow a ◆ term from the critic Fredric Jameson). For example, *Salerno* (1990) is a vast panorama of color-coded vehicles, containers, cranes, and freighters, a "second nature" of commercial distribution that has overwhelmed the ancient landscape of this Mediterranean port, and still it is the merest fragment of the contemporary network of maritime transport. Other spaces pictured by Gursky appear almost abstract (the tarmac in *Schilpol* [1994], the warehouses in *Toys "R" Us* [1999], the river banks in *Rhine II* [1999], and so on); they attest to a deterritorializing of space that is also characteristic of advanced capitalism, a stripping-down that Gursky underscores with further digital edits.

For Jameson delirious spaces are a distinctive attribute of postmodern culture, and his prime example are the vast atriums of John Portmann hotels, which Gursky has attempted to image, again through digital edits, more than once. In *Times Square* (1997), for example, he montaged two views of one such atrium, seen in opposite directions along a single line of sight, to convey its vertiginous extent. Again, one stake of his photography is the very representability of a post-Fordist order where capital seems in ceaseless flux, and architecture and urban space seem overwhelmed by images—indeed where the "photographic face" of the modern world described by Kracauer in 1928 seems outdone by "the communicational signifier" of a postmodern world in which media and environment are often difficult to distinguish. Perhaps this world cannot be imaged by the old means of painting and photography, which still tend to locate viewers punctually, in one place. Perhaps this can be done only by the kind of "computer vision" that Gursky and others affect—precisely because this vision seems to exceed any human perspective, any physical placement. But the danger is that such vision might also render this world natural, even beautiful or again sublime, all in a fetishistic manner that fully delivers on the appearances of the image but otherwise obscures the reality of labor. (I echo here the famous ▲ critique that Walter Benjamin made of Neue Sachlichkeit photographers like Albert Renger-Patzsch in 1931—that they beautified the industrial world.) In other words, these beautiful images might help to reconcile us to a world without qualities where the human subject has little place. In this regard Gursky might take away too finally what Wall seems to restore too quickly—the authority of a unified subjectivity.

FURTHER READING

Hubertus von Amelunxen (ed.), *Photography After Photography* (Amsterdam: G&B Arts, 1996)

Michael Bracewell et al., *Sam Taylor-Wood* (London: Hayward Gallery; and Göttingen: Steidl, 2002)

Thierry de Duve et al., *Jeff Wall* (London: Phaidon Press, 1996)

Peter Galassi, *Andreas Gursky* (New York: Museum of Modern Art, 2001)

▲ 1993a ● 1998, 2003 ■ 1968a ◆ 1968a, 1984b ▲ 1929, 1935

2003

With exhibits such as "Utopia Station" and "Zone of Urgency," the Venice Biennale exemplifies the informal and discursive nature of much recent artmaking and curating.

In a gallery over the last decade you might have happened on one of the following: a room empty except for a mound of identical ▲ candies wrapped in brilliant foils, the candies free for the taking. Or, space where the office contents are dumped into the exhibition • area, and a couple of pots of Thai food are on offer to visitors, who might be puzzled enough to linger, eat, and talk. Or an array of abstract bulletin boards, drawing tables, and discussion platforms, some concerning a role player of the near past (such as Robert McNamara, Secretary of Defense under Presidents Kennedy and Johnson), as though a documentary script were in the making or a history seminar had just let out [**1**]. Or, finally, a makeshift altar, monument, or kiosk, cobbled together out of plastic, cardboard, and tape, and filled, like a homemade study-shrine, with images and texts devoted to a particular artist, writer, or philosopher (e.g., ▲ Piet Mondrian, Raymond Carver, or Georges Bataille) [**2**]. Such works, which exist somewhere between a public installation, an

1990–2003

1 • Liam Gillick, *McNamara*, 1994
Brionvega Algol TVC 11R, 35mm film transferred onto appropriate format, Florence Knoll table (optional), copies of various drafts of the film *McNamara*, dimensions variable

▲ 1987 • 1989 ▲ 1913, 1917, 1930b, 1944a

2 • Thomas Hirschhorn, *Raymond Carver Altar*, 1998–9
Mixed-media installation at The Galleries at Moore, Philadelphia

obscure performance, and a private archive, can also be found in nonart spaces, which might render them even more difficult to decipher in aesthetic terms; nonetheless, they can be taken to indicate a distinctive turn in recent art. In play in the first two examples—works by the Cuban-American Felix Gonzalez-Torres ▲ and the Thai Rirkrit Tiravanija respectively—is a notion of art as an ephemeral offering, a precarious gift; and in the second two instances—works by the English Liam Gillick (born 1964) and the Swiss Thomas Hirschhorn (born 1957) respectively—a notion of art as an informal probing into a specific figure or event in history or politics, fiction or philosophy. There is also a utopian dimension in the first approach and an archival impulse in the second.

This way of working includes other prominent practitioners • such as the Mexican Gabriel Orozco, the Scot Douglas Gordon, the French Pierre Huyghe, Philippe Parreno (born 1964), and Dominique Gonzalez-Foerster (born 1965), the Americans Renée ■ Green, Mark Dion, and Sam Durant, and the English Tacita Dean. They draw on a wide range of artistic precedents such as the performative objects of Fluxus, the humble materials of Arte Povera, and the site-specific strategies of institution-critical artists like Marcel ◆ Broodthaers, Michael Asher, and Hans Haacke. Yet the current generation has also transformed the familiar devices of the readymade, collaboration, and installation. For example, some of these artists treat television shows and Hollywood films as found images: in *The Third Memory* (2000) Huyghe reshot parts of the 1975 Al Pacino movie *Dog Day Afternoon* with the real-life protagonist (a reluctant bank robber) returned to the lead role **[3]**, and Gordon ▲ has adapted a couple of Hitchcock films in drastic ways. For Gordon such pieces are "time readymades," given narratives to be sampled in large image-projections (a pervasive medium in contemporary art), while the French critic Nicolas Bourriaud has championed such work under the rubric of "post-production." This term underscores the secondary manipulations (editing, special effects, and the like) that are almost as pronounced in this art as in film; it also suggests a changed status of "the work" of art in an age of information. However one regards this age (if it exists as a distinct epoch at all), "information" does often appear as a kind of ultimate readymade, as data to be reprocessed and sent on, and some of these artists work accordingly "to inventory and select, to use and download" (Bourriaud), to revise not only found images and texts but also given forms of exhibition and distribution.

One upshot of this way of working is a "promiscuity of collaborations" (Gordon) in which the postmodernist complications of • artistic originality and authorship are pushed to the limit. Consider

▲ 1987, 1989 • 1989, 1998 ■ 1992, 1993c, 1998 ◆ 1962a, 1967b, 1970, 1971, 1972a ▲ 1998 • 1977, 1980, 1984b

3 • Pierre Huyghe, *The Third Memory*, 1999
Double projection, Beta digital, 4 minutes 46 seconds

a collaborative work like *No Ghost Just a Shell* (1999–2002) led by Huyghe and Parreno. After they learned that a Japanese animation company wanted to sell some of its minor characters, they bought one such person-sign, a girl named "AnnLee," and invited other artists to deploy her in their own work. Here the art piece becomes a "chain" of pieces: for Huyghe and Parreno *No Ghost Just a Shell* is "a dynamic structure that produces forms that are part of it"; it is also "the story of a community that finds itself in an image." Or consider another group project that also adapts a ready-made product to unusual ends. Here Gonzalez-Foerster, Gillick, Tiravanija, and others detail how to customize a coffin out of cheap furniture from IKEA; the work is titled *How to Kill Yourself Anywhere in the World for Under $399.*

The tradition of ready-made objects, from Marcel Duchamp ▲ to Damien Hirst, often mocks high art or mass culture or both; in these examples it is mordant about global capitalism as well. Nevertheless, the prevalent sensibility of the new work tends to be expansive, even ludic—again an offering to other people and/or an opening to other discourses. At times a benign image of globalization is also advanced (this international group of artists finds one of its preconditions there), and again there are utopian moments as ▲ well: for example, Tiravanija has spearheaded a "massive-scale artist-run space" called "The Land" in rural Thailand that is designed as a collective "for social engagement." More modestly, these artists aim to fashion passive viewers into temporary communities of active discussants. In this regard Hirschhorn, who once worked in a communist collective of graphic designers, sees his makeshift structures dedicated to artists, writers, and philosophers as a species of passionate pedagogy, and they do partake a little of the agitprop kiosks of the Constructivist Gustav Klutsis as well • as of the obsessive constructions of the Dadaist Kurt Schwitters. With these works Hirschhorn seeks to "distribute ideas," "radiate energy," and "liberate activity" all at once: he wants not only to familiarize his audience with an alternative public culture but also to charge this relationship with affect. Other figures, some of whom were trained as scientists or architects (such as the Belgian Carsten Höller [born 1961] and the Italian Stefano Boeri [born 1956] ■ respectively), adapt a model of collaborative research and experi-

▲ 1914, 1986

▲ 1989 • 1920, 1926 ■ 1992

ment closer to the science laboratory or the design firm than the traditional artist studio. "I take the word 'studio' literally," Orozco remarks, "not as a space of production but as a time of knowledge."

"A promiscuity of collaborations" has also meant a promiscuity of installations: installation is the default format, and exhibition the common medium, of much contemporary art. (In some measure this tendency is driven by the increased importance of huge shows in the art world: there are now biennials and triennials in Venice, Saõ Paulo, Istanbul, Johannesburg, Gwangju, Seoul, Yokohama). Often entire exhibitions are given over to messy juxtapositions of projects—photos and texts, images and objects, videos and screens—and occasionally the effects are more chaotic than communicative: in these instances legibility as art is sacrificed without great gains in other kinds of literacy. Nonetheless, discursivity and sociability are central concerns of the new work, both in its making and in its viewing. "Discussion has become an important moment in the constitution of a project," Huyghe comments, while Tiravanija aligns his art, as "a place of socialization," with a village market or a dance floor.

Interactive aesthetics

In this time of mega-exhibitions the artist often doubles as a curator. "I am the head of a team, a coach, a producer, an organizer, a representative, a cheerleader, a host of the party, a captain of the boat," Orozco comments, "in short, an activist, an activator, an incubator." This rise of the artist-as-curator is complemented by the rise of the curator-as-artist; maestros of large shows have become very prominent over the last decade. Often the two groups share models of working as well as terms of description. For example, several years ago Tiravanija, Orozco, and other artists began to speak of projects as "platforms" and "stations," as "places that gather and then disperse," in order to underscore the casual communities that they sought to create. In 2002 "Documenta 11," curated by an international team led by the Nigerian Okwui Enwezor (born 1963), was also conceived in terms of "platforms" of discussion, scattered around the world, on such topics as "Democracy Unrealized," "Processes of Truth and Reconciliation," "Creolité and Creolization," and "Four African Cities"; the actual exhibition in Kassel, Germany, was only the final such "platform." And in 2003 the Venice Biennale, curated by another international group headed by the Italian Francesco Bonami (born 1955), featured sections titled "Utopia Station" and "Zone of Urgency," both of which exemplified the informal discursivity of much recent artmaking and curating. Like "kiosk," the terms "platform" and "station" call up the old modernist ambition to modernize culture in accordance with industrial society (El Lissitzky ▲ spoke of his *Proun* designs as "way-stations between art and architecture"). Yet, these terms also evoke the electronic network, and many artists and curators do use the internet rhetoric of "interactivity," though the means applied to this end are usually far funkier and more face-to-face than any chat room on the web.

Along with the emphasis on discursivity and sociability, a concern with the ethical and the everyday is often voiced: art is "a way to explore other possibilities of exchange" (Huyghe), a model of "living well" (Tiravanija), a means of being "together in the everyday" (Orozco). "Henceforth," Bourriaud declares, "the group is pitted against the mass, neighborliness against propaganda, low tech against high tech, and the tactile against the visual. And above all, the everyday now turns out to be a much more fertile terrain than pop culture." The possibilities of such interactive aesthetics seem clear enough, but there are problems here as well. Sometimes radical politics are ascribed to the art by a shaky analogy between an open work and an inclusive society, as if a desultory form might evoke a democratic community, or a nonhierarchical installation predict an egalitarian world. Hirschhorn sees his projects as "never-ending construction sites," while Tiravanija rejects "the need to fix a moment where everything is complete." But one service that art can still render is to make a stop, take a stand, in a concrete register that constellates the aesthetic, the cognitive, and the critical. Moreover, formlessness in society might be a condition to contest rather than to celebrate in art—a condition to make over into form for purposes of reflection and resistance (as some modernist painters attempted to do). ▲ The artists in question frequently cite the Situationists as a model of critique, but the Situationists valued precise intervention and rigorous organization above all other things.

"The question," Huyghe argues, "is less 'what?' than 'to whom?' It becomes a question of address." Bourriaud also sees art as "an ensemble of units to be reactivated by the beholder–manipulator." In many ways this approach is another legacy of the Duchampian provocation, but when is such "reactivation" too great a burden to place on the viewer? As with previous attempts to • involve the audience directly (as in some Conceptual art), there is a risk of illegibility, which might return the artist as the principal figure and the primary interpreter of the work. At times, it must be admitted, "the death of the author" has meant not "the birth of the reader," as Roland Barthes speculated in his 1968 essay of that title, so much as the befuddlement of the viewer. Moreover, when has art *not* involved discursivity and sociability, at least since the Renaissance? Such an emphasis might risk a strange situation of discussion and interaction pursued for their own sakes. Collaboration, too, is often regarded as a good in itself: "Collaboration is the answer," the peripatetic curator Hans Ulrich Obrist has remarked wryly, "but what is the question?"

Perhaps discursivity and sociability are foregrounded in art today because they appear scarce in other spheres (at least in the United States), and the same might hold true for the ethical and the everyday: it is as if the very idea of community has taken on a utopian inflection. Even art audiences cannot be taken for granted but must be conjured up every time, which might be one reason why contemporary exhibitions sometimes feel like remedial work in socialization ("come play, talk, learn with us"). Yet if participation appears threatened in other areas of life, its privileging in art

▲ 1926

▲ 1957a • 1968b, 1971, 1972b, 1984a

must function in part as a compensatory substitute. At one point Bourriaud almost suggests as much: "Through little services rendered, the artists fill in the cracks in the social bond." And only when he is most grim is he most revealing: "The society of spectacle is thus followed by the society of extras, where everyone finds the illusion of an interactive democracy in more or less truncated channels of communication." The situation in the global art world would seem to be no different.

An archival impulse

Yet there are hopeful signs here as well, not only in the utopian aspiration of this art, but also in its archival impulse, which might be taken as a tacit paradigm in contemporary practice. This impulse, which has many precedents in postwar art, is manifest in a will to make historical information, often lost, marginal, or suppressed, physical and spatial, indeed interactive, usually through found images, objects, and texts arranged in installations. Like any archive, the materials of this art are found but also constructed, public but also private, factual but also fictive, and often they are put together simply for the occasion. Frequently this work also manifests a kind of archival architecture, a physical complex of information (as in the kiosks of Hirschhorn or the platforms of Gillick), as well as a kind of archival logic, a conceptual matrix of citation and juxtaposition. Hirschhorn speaks of his process as one of "ramification," and much of this art does branch out like a tree or, rather, like a weed or a "rhizome" (a term drawn from the philosopher Gilles Deleuze that others like Gillick and Durant also use). Perhaps the life of any archive is a matter of mutative growth of this sort, through connection and disconnection, which this art also reveals. "Laboratory, storage, studio space, yes," Hirschhorn has remarked, "I want to use these forms in my work to make spaces for the movement and endlessness of thinking...."

The archival impulse is strong in Tacita Dean, who works in a variety of mediums in photography, drawing, and sound, but ▲ primarily in short films and videos accompanied by texts that she calls "asides." Dean is drawn to people, things, and places that have become lost somehow, sidelined or stranded. Typically she begins with one such event and traces it as it ramifies into an archive as if of its own accord. Consider *Girl Stowaway* (1994) an 8-minute, 16-millimeter film in color and black and white with a narrative aside. Here Dean happened on a photograph of a young stowaway named Jean Jeinnie who, in 1928, sneaked onto a ship named *Herzogin Cecilie,* bound from Australia to England. Several years later the ship was towed to Starehole Bay on the South Devon Coast, where it eventually broke up.

The archive of *Girl Stowaway* forms as a tissue of coincidences. First Dean loses the photograph in a bag mishandled at Heathrow, another "stowaway" that turns up later in Dublin. Then, as she researches Jean Jeinnie, she hears echoes of her name everywhere—from the author Jean Genet to David Bowie's song *Jean Genie.* When Dean travels to Starehole Bay to inquire about the ship, a girl is murdered on the cliffs above the harbor on the very night that Dean also spends there. *Girl Stowaway* is thus an archive that includes the artist-as-archivist within it. "Her voyage was from Port Lincoln to Falmouth," Dean writes. "It had a beginning and an end, and exists as a recorded passage of time. My own journey follows no such linear narrative. It started at the moment I found the photograph but has meandered ever since, through uncharted research and to no obvious destination. It has become a passage into history along the line that divides fact from fiction, and is more like a journey through an underworld of chance intervention and epic encounter than any place I recognize. My story is about coincidence, and about what is invited and what is not." In this way archival work is also an allegory of archival work.

In another film-and-text piece Dean tells the story of another lost-and-found figure. In 1968 one Donald Crowhurst, a failed businessman from Teignmouth, a coastal town in England hungry for tourist recognition, was driven to enter the Golden Globe Race to be the first to sail solo nonstop around the world. Yet neither sailor not boat, a trimaran christened *Teignmouth Electron,* was prepared, and Crowhurst soon faltered: he faked his logs, then broke off all radio contact. He began to suffer from time-madness, with incoherent log entries that amounted to a private discourse on God and the Universe. Eventually Crowhurst jumped overboard with his chronometer, just a few hundred miles from the coast of Britain.

Dean treats this event obliquely in three short films. The first two, *Disappearance at Sea I* and *II* (1996, 1997) were shot at different lighthouses: in the first, filmed near Berwick, images of the lighthouse bulbs alternate with blank views out to the horizon as darkness slowly descends; in the second, filmed in Northumberland the camera mounted on the lighthouse apparatus provides a continuous panorama of a sea bereft of human life. In the third film, *Teignmouth Electron* (2000) Dean travels to Cayman Brac in the Caribbean to document the remains of the trimaran. It has "the look of a tank or the carcass of an animal or an exoskeleton left by an arrant creature now extinct," she writes. "Whichever way, it is at odds with its function, forgotten by its generation and abandoned by its time." In this extended work, then, "Crowhurst" is a term that implicates others in an archive that reveals an ambitious town, a misbegotten race, a metaphysical seasickness, and an enigmatic remnant.

And Dean lets this archive ramify further. While on Cayman Brac she happens on another derelict structure dubbed "the Bubble House" by locals [**4**], and documents this "perfect companion" to the *Teignmouth Electron* in another short film and text (1999). Designed by a Frenchman jailed for embezzlement, the Bubble House was "a vision for perfect hurricane housing, egg-shaped and resistant to wind, extravagant and daring, with its Cinemascope-proportioned windows that look out onto the sea." Never completed and long deserted, it now sits in ruin "like a statement from another age." "I like these strange monoliths that sit in this no place," Dean remarks of another "failed futuristic vision" that she has reclaimed as an archival object, fully aware that a

▲ 1989

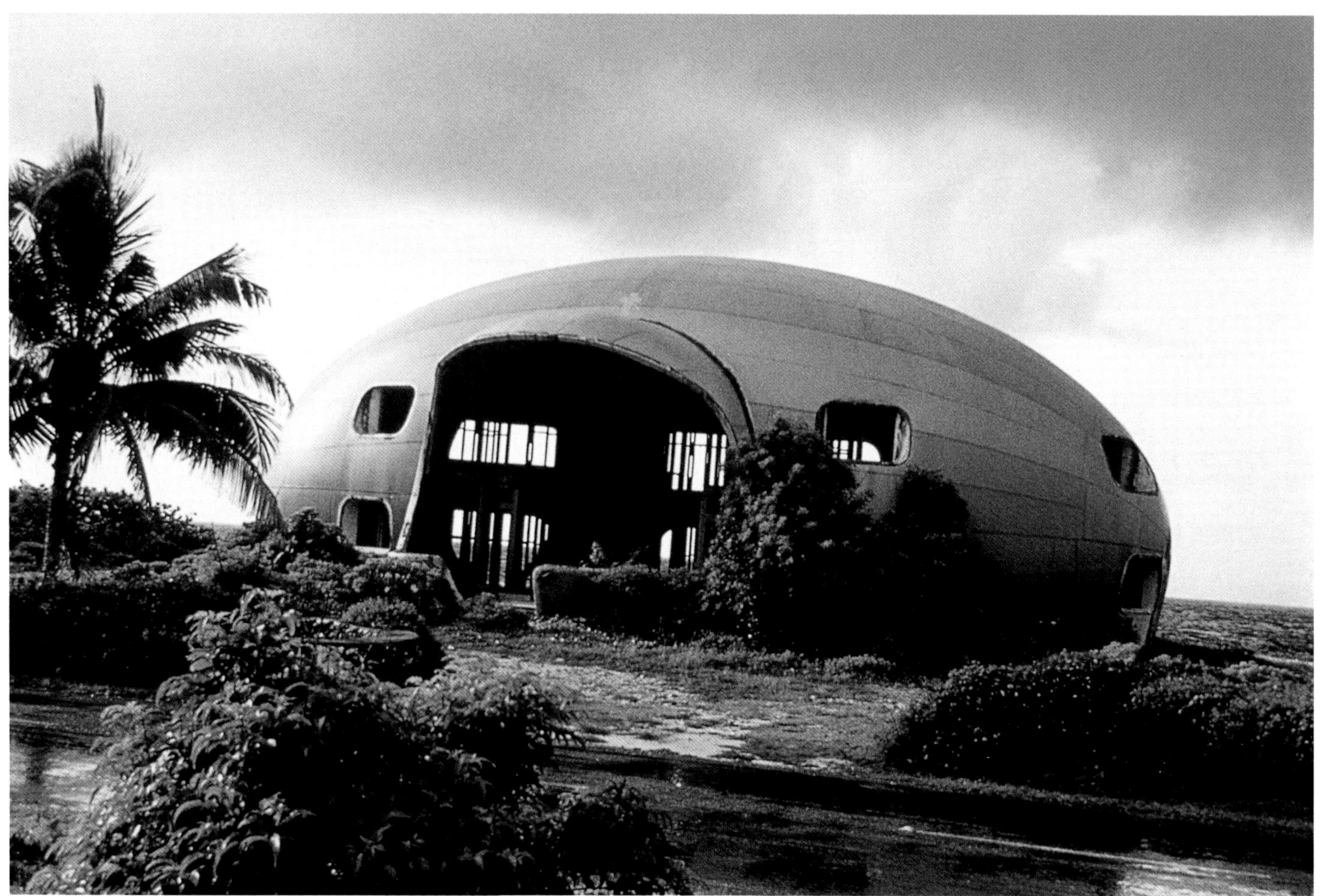

4 • Tacita Dean, *Bubble House*, 1999
R-type photograph, 99 x 147 (39 x 57⅞)

"no place" is the literal meaning of "utopia" and that it conjures up a "no time" as well. In a sense all her objects serve as arks of uncertain temporalities, in which the here-and-now of the work functions as a crux between an unfinished past and a reopened future. And herein lies the most extraordinary aspect of such archival art: its ability to turn failed visions of the past into scenarios of alternative futures—in short, to turn the no-place of archival remains into the no-place of utopian possibility.

FURTHER READING

Claire Bishop, "Antagonism and Relational Aesthetics," *October*, no. 110, Fall 2004

Laurence Bossé et al., *Tacita Dean: 7 Books* (Paris: Musée d'Art Moderne de la Ville de Paris, 2003)

Nicolas Bourriaud, *Postproduction* (New York: Lukas & Sternberg, 2002) and *Relational Aesthetics* (Dijon: Les Presses du Réel, 1998)

Okwui Enwezor (ed.), *Documenta 11_Platform 5* (Ostfildern-Ruit: Hatje Cantz Verlag, 2002)

Tom McDonough, "No Ghost," *October*, no. 110, Fall 2004

Hans Ulrich Obrist, *Interviews, Volume I* (Milan: Edizioni Charta, 2003)

roundtable

The predicament of contemporary art

RK: We've structured our entries on twentieth-century art through the analytical perspectives that each one of us tends to favor: Hal's is a psychoanalytic view; Benjamin's, a social-historical view; Yve-Alain's, a formalist and structuralist view; and mine, a poststructuralist view. One way to look back on the development of postwar art is to consider what happened to those methodological tools—how their relevance grew or diminished.

YAB: None of us is married to a particular method.

HF: Right: my commitment to psychoanalysis is not as strong as you suggest; frequently the art led me somewhere else, methodologically, altogether. But your question is really about the *fate* of these different methods in postwar art and criticism. On that score, as far as psychoanalysis is concerned, the Surrealist concern with the unconscious continues after World War II, but in a register more private than political. Many artists from Abstract ▲ Expressionism to Cobra attempt to open up this private unconscious to a more collective dimension; there's a turn, for example, from a Freudian focus on desire to a Jungian interest in archetypes. Yet that move is soon stunted, at least in the United States, by the rise of ego psychology, and another reaction sets in. An aversion to the private ego as the source of artmaking is palpable in milieux from John Cage, Robert Rauschenberg, and ● Jasper Johns to the Minimalists: to different degrees they all try to de-psychologize art, and, in the face of much pathos-laden work in the fifties, one can understand why.

One irony of Minimalism is that, despite its making art more public in its meaning, more objective in its situation, it also puts the subject back into play in a phenomenological form, embodied in ■ space. And as Postminimalists like Eva Hesse moved to complicate this general subject, and to reveal it to be marked differently by fantasy, desire, and death, psychoanalysis returns. This is explicit in the seventies when feminist artists and theorists question how the subject is riven by sexual difference, and how such difference informs both the making and the viewing of art. Psychoanalysis is extremely productive for many feminists, even as they also critique its presuppositions, and the same holds for some queer artists and theorists thereafter, as well as some postcolonial critics.

On a more abstract level, psychoanalysis has provided insights into artistic forms that other models don't grasp well—for example, the persistent evocation of the "part-object" from Duchamp, through Johns, Louise Bourgeois, Hesse, and Yayoi Kusama, to many artists today. However, psychoanalysis is not consistently important in the postwar period: its presence waxes and wanes as questions of subjectivity and sexuality advance and recede.

YAB: The postwar fate of the methodological tools of formalism and structuralism is partly discussed in my introduction. There I trace the transformation of a morphological conception of formalism (à la Roger Fry in the prewar period, but revived by ▲ Clement Greenberg in the postwar era) into a structuralist one, and then the transformation of the structuralist position into the "poststructuralist" one, which Rosalind in turn explains in her introduction. She discusses how many artists in the middle seventies and early eighties found in "poststructuralism" a powerful theoretical ally that helped them sort out issues in their own production. (By the way, if, as I do with "postmodernism," I put "poststructuralism" in quotation marks, it is because, as far as I know, it was never used by the authors designated by that label.) Here I want to stress that structuralism also left a mark on the artistic production of the sixties. We know that a number of artists in New York were reading Roland Barthes and Claude Lévi-Strauss ● (for example, their books were in Robert Smithson's library) and, perhaps more importantly, the novels of the French Nouveau Roman (such as Alain Robbe-Grillet's), which were written in a structuralist context (Barthes was the biggest champion of Robbe-Grillet's early novels). In many ways the antisubjectivism that is an essential element of structuralism was parallel to the de-psychologizing tendency, just mentioned by Hal, of many artists opposing the pathos of Abstract Expressionism in the ■ US or *art informel* in Europe. The anticompositional impulse that characterizes so much of the art produced from the mid-fifties through Minimalism—the serial attitude, the interest

▲ 1947b, 1949, 1957a, 1960b ● 1953, 1958, 1965 ■ 1966b, 1969

▲ 1906, 1960b ● 1967a, 1970 ■ 1946

▲ in indexical procedures, the monochrome, the grid, chance, etc.—goes hand in hand with the rebellion of structuralism against existentialism.

This brings me to the other methodology alluded to by Hal, which does not appear in our official quartet: phenomenology. It's very interesting that Maurice Merleau-Ponty's *Phenomenology of Perception* became a bedside book for many American artists ● (e.g., Robert Morris) as well as critics (e.g., Michael Fried) soon after it was published in English in 1962. Merleau-Ponty's theoretical formation was identical to that of Sartre and his existentialism (the founding text for both was the philosophical work of Edmund Husserl), but Sartre had a limited appeal to artists (mainly in Europe, and just for a short while). I wonder if it's not because, unlike Merleau-Ponty, who wrote beautifully about Ferdinand de Saussure, Sartre remained hostile to the structuralist position (not to mention his awkward position with regard to psychoanalysis). In other words, Sartre continued to presuppose a "free subject," and so in part remained a prisoner of the classical philosophy of consciousness inherited from Descartes. As such he was out of touch with what many artists were dealing with after ■ Abstract Expressionism (his champion in the US art world was Harold Rosenberg, himself identified with a "pathos" formulation of the Abstract Expressionist aesthetic). By contrast, Merleau-Ponty, even though he had little knowledge of the artistic avant-garde of his time (his best pages on art concern Cézanne), was touching on points that resonated with the concerns of artists of the sixties.

RK: Hal, when Yve-Alain and I curated the exhibition "L'Informe: Mode d'Emploi" at the Centre Pompidou in 1996, we foregrounded the operation of "the formless" in a great range of artistic production from Duchamp to Mike Kelley; in order to understand this formlessness it was important for us to think through the problem of "desublimation," and psychoanalysis was still fresh, still urgent, for that investigation.

YAB: It's a question of different uses of the same model. This is something we also learned from Georges Bataille, from whom we borrowed the anticoncept of the *informe* or "formless." Bataille ◆ opposed the literary way in which André Breton had applied psychoanalysis in his Surrealism, reducing Freud's dynamic discourse to a treasure trove of myths and symbols. For Bataille symbols and myths were to be contested; they were illusions, on the side of the dominant ideology of representation, and psychoanalysis was a means of dissecting and dissipating them. His work forced us to rethink what aspects of psychoanalysis might speak to the art practices that interested us, how it might be used to configure a different constellation of objects and concepts that were not addressed in other sorts of readings—in part because they were involved in an operation of desublimation. Maybe that is the project of each of us in this book: to suggest different kinds of reconfigurations.

For Bataille the same model could be used in a conservative way and in a revolutionary way (I guess we wouldn't use that term today); that's a constant in all his writings concerning not only psychoanalysis but also Marxism, Nietzsche, de Sade, and almost every other philosophical system or mode of interpretation he discussed. And I think this is linked to our mode of approach here. For example, Hal wrote an essay in the early eighties ▲ stressing that there were two kinds of "postmodernism" in art, an authoritarian one and a progressive one, and he also wrote in a similar way about the divergent legacies of Russian Constructivism and Minimalism. This goes hand in hand with what I mentioned about the two kinds of formalisms, a morphological one and a structural one.

HF: Perhaps "desublimation" is a way to raise the question of social art history in the postwar period. The attack on reified forms and codified meanings à la Bataille is one version of the process, but there is also the spectre of "repressive desublimation" in the Marxist sense of Herbert Marcuse. What are the social effects when artistic forms and cultural institutions are desublimated—i.e., when they are cracked open by libidinal energies? It's not always a liberatory event: it can also open up those spheres to a depoliticized rechanneling of desire by "the culture industry."

BB: As I develop in my introduction, the dialectic of sublimation and desublimation plays an enormously important role in the history of postwar art. Perhaps it is even one of the central dynamics of the period, certainly more so than in the history of the prewar avant-gardes. It is defined differently by different theoreticians, both as an avant-garde strategy of subversion and as a strategy of the cultural industry to achieve incorporation and subjection. One axis on which this dialectic is played out more programmatically in the postwar period than ever before is the relationship of the neo-avant-garde to the ever-expanding apparatus of cultural industrial domination: as of the fifties, in the ● context of the Independent Group in England, for example, or in ■ early Pop art activities in the United States, appropriating imagery and structures of industrial production became one of the methods with which artists tried to reposition themselves between a bankrupt humanist model of avant-garde aspirations and a emerging apparatus whose totalitarian potential might not have been visible at first. Desublimation in England served as a radical strategy simultaneously to popularize cultural practice and to recognize the conditions of collective mass-cultural experience as governing. Desublimation in Andy Warhol, by contrast, operated more within the project of a final annihilation of whatever political and cultural aspirations the artists of the immediate postwar period might still have harbored.

As schematic as this might sound, my own work is situated, methodologically, between two texts: one from 1947, *The Dialectic of Enlightenment* by Theodor Adorno and Max Horkheimer, the

▲ 1957b ● 1965 ■ 1947b, 1949, 1960b ◆ 1924, 1930b, 1931 ▲ 1984b ● 1956 ■ 1960c, 1964b

chapter on "The Culture Industry" in particular, and the other ▲ from 1967, *The Society of the Spectacle* by Guy Debord. The more I think about those texts the more they seem to historicize the last fifty years of artistic production, for they demonstrate how the autonomous spaces of cultural representation—spaces of subversion, resistance, critique, utopian aspiration—are gradually eroded, assimilated, or simply annihilated. This is what occurred in the postwar period with the transformation of liberal democracies in the United States and in Europe: from my perspective not only has the prognosis of Adorno and Horkheimer in 1947 been bitterly fulfilled, but so too has the even more nihilistic prognosis of Debord in 1967—exceeded even. The postwar situation can be described as a negative teleology: a steady dismantling of the autonomous practices, spaces, and spheres of culture, and a perpetual intensification of assimilation and homogenization, to the point today where we witness what Debord called "the integrated spectacle." Where does that leave artistic practices in the present, and how can we, as art historians and critics, address them? Are there still spaces situated outside that homogenizing apparatus? Or do we have to recognize that many artists themselves don't want to be situated outside it?

HF: Are you content with the finality of that narrative?

YAB: It's a dire diagnostic (after all, Debord committed suicide), but one I think we all share to some extent.

HF: Yes, but if you agree entirely with Adorno and/or Debord, little more can be said.

BB: I take the last statement I made seriously: I'm not concluding that every artist in the present defines her or his work as inextricably integrated and affirmative. The artistic capacity still might exist not only to reflect on the position that the art work assumes within the wider system of infinitely differentiated representations (fashion, advertisement, entertainment, etc.), but also to recognize its susceptibility to becoming integrated into those subsets of ideological control. And yet, if there are artistic practices that still stand apart from this process of homogenization, I'm less convinced than ever that they can survive, and that we as critics and historians are able to support and sustain them in a substantial and efficient manner, to prevent their total marginalization.

HF: Let's look back over the last few decades to instances where critical alternatives were proposed. Indicating some "incomplete projects" might help us look ahead as well.

BB: Yes: what place does neo-avant-garde practice have in the present compared to the one it held in the moment of 1968, for example? Or even in seventies, when the relative autonomy of such practice had a role in the liberal bourgeois public sphere as a site of differentiating experience and subjectivity? It was supported then, or at least taken seriously, by the state, the museums, and the universities. As of the eighties, artistic production was subsumed into the larger practice of the culture industry, where it now functions as commodity production, investment portfolio, and entertainment. Consider Matthew Barney in this regard: even more than Jeff Koons, he has articulated, that is to say exploited, those tendencies. In that sense he is a proto-totalitarian artist for me, a small-time American Richard Wagner who mythifies the catastrophic conditions of existence under late capitalism.

HF: Again, can't we complicate the Adornian position that the totalitarian cultural sphere is simply continued in the American culture industry, and that that industry has entirely subsumed art?

YAB: There were energetic expressions of artistic freedom in the aftermath of 1968—and before as well ...

BB: Of course there's an important artistic culture in the postwar United States—from Abstract Expressionism, through Pop and Minimalism, to Conceptualism at least. That has to be taken into account. Why was it possible? Because the United States was a liberal democracy at its highest level of differentiation. But no more.

HF: Other possibilities also opened up in other parts of the globe, especially in various encounters with different modernisms. For example, Yve-Alain discusses the elaboration of Constructivism ▲ among the Neoconcretists in Brazil, as well as of performance after Pollock with the Gutai artists in Japan. Those practices alone complicate the old story of a simple shift from Europe to North America or, even more reductively, from Paris to New York. It's an alternative narrative of cultural *différance*—of avant-garde practices in other place-times.

YAB: At first, though, the usual paradigm isn't changed much: for at least two decades those avant-garde activities on various continents still define themselves in relation to the old centers. For example, the Brazilians still look to Paris, and for Gutai it's all New York, Pollock especially, whom they read through the photographs of Hans Namuth. It's only later, once they have had some history in their own way of working, that they give up the competitive relation to the old centers. On this level 1968 marks a very important date: there's an extraordinary internationalization not only of political rebellion but of its its artistic offspring, with social unrest all over Europe, the States, and elsewhere (the Prague Spring and its crushing by the Soviet Union; the Chicago Democratic convention followed by violent riots, and so on), all in the context of the Vietnam War. That was a strong political unifier for progressive minds around the world, let us not forget; and certain aspects of the present situation are reminiscent of that period—notably the fact that the Bush administration has unified much of the world against American imperialism. It remains to be seen, of course, if this "negative internationalism" will have any direct consequences in the cultural sphere.

▲ 1957a

▲ 1921, 1928, 1955a

HF: Much before 1968, too, the postwar period witnessed an international resurrection of some movements—like Dada, ▲ Surrealism, and Constructivism—that were international in ambition in the first instance. The Bauhaus alone had several afterlives in different sites after World War II. This is further complicated by a centrifugal move outward from Paris and • New York. Cobra, for instance, initiates a partial shift away from Paris to other European cities; and later, to take another example, Arte Povera emerges in Italy. So there's a remapping of Europe, a relativizing of Paris as art capital, which is slight but significant. There's also a remapping of the United States, with a similar relativizing of New York, especially by artists in California—beat performance and assemblage artists in San ■ Francisco and in Los Angeles, and later California Pop and abstract artists as well.

BB: Yes, but then if we turn back to the present, what do we see? Look at Michael Asher, in many ways the most radical of the figures involved in institutional critique from the late sixties onward, and long based in Los Angeles: his work is now mostly neglected; the very radicality of its contestation appears forgotten. Clearly the complexity of Asher's work seems to pose, now more than ever, insurmountable obstacles to its reception within the present parameters of the art world. So, as with social repression at large, the way to respond to the work is simply to eradicate it from historical memory and to isolate its producer as an outsider. And ◆ Daniel Buren, another radical artist of institutional critique, is the pendant on the European side, only Buren has now transformed himself, willingly, into an affirmative state artist in order to avoid the fate that has befallen Asher.

HF: Once again, can't your narrative be complicated? It carries a teleology of its own that is reductive, indeed defeatist.

RK: Perhaps a different narrative will help, though it might be no less dire. In my view postmodernism, understood through the prism of poststructuralism, constituted a great critique of essentialist thinking—of what is proper to a given category or activity. It annihilated the very idea of the self-same, and launched an especially strong attack on the idea of the medium (this is explicit in Jacques Derrida's essay "The Law of Genre"). So the medium came under a concerted assault from the most sophisticated thinkers of the sixties and seventies, and that critique joined a similar attack in Conceptual art on medium-specificity in art (that painting be only about the forms of painting, etc.); this was supported in turn by the reception of Duchamp at the time, which only underscored the Conceptualist contempt for the medium. And then video entered the field of aesthetic practice, which also disturbed the idea of the medium (it's very hard to find the specificity of video). So poststructuralism, Conceptual art, Duchamp reception, video art: together they effectively dismembered the concept of the medium. The problem is that this dismemberment then became a kind of official position (the pervasiveness of installation art is one sign of t his state of affairs), and now it's a commonplace among artists and critics alike: it's understood as given. And if I as a critic have any responsibility now, it is to dissociate myself from this attack on the medium, and to speak for its importance, which is to say for the continuance of modernism. I don't know if poststructuralism will help me do this, and thus I don't know if I can maintain my earlier commitment to this methodological option.

HF: That's a strange position for the author of "Sculpture in the Expanded Field"—among other essays that theorized the intermedial and interdisciplinary dimensions of postmodernism—to take. What do you intend by "medium" now? Surely not medium-specificity in a Greenbergian sense.

RK: No: I mean the technical support for the work. It needn't be a traditional support—like canvas, which is the support of oil painting, or metal armature, which is the support of modeled sculpture. A medium grounds an artistic production, and provides a set of rules for that production. It can be complicated even when it appears simple; a good example is Ed Ruscha's use of the automobile as a kind of medium—it's a consistent support of his ▲ work. His early book of photographs, *Twenty-Six Gasoline Stations* (1962), documents a number of gas stops on his drives from Oklahoma City to Los Angeles and back; that idea gave him a rule for making his book. Again, a medium is a source of rules that prompts production but also limits it, and returns the work to a consideration of the rules themselves.

HF: This notion of medium still seems a little arbitrary to me, almost free of historical motivation, let alone of social convention. In that respect it's not clear how much of a corrective it could be to the relativistic condition of contemporary art. Surely a medium is a social contract with an audience as well as a private protocol for form-making.

RK: Sometimes it only appears arbitrary. At one point in his work Ruscha could use almost anything as a support for color—like blueberry extract, chocolate sauce, axel grease, and caviar. What he did with this comestible mess was to do a portfolio of prints (actually they're dirtied sheets of paper) titled "Stains", and those works hooked back into the history of stained painting—from • Pollock through Helen Frankenthaler and color-field painting. It got him away from the arbitrary back into the history of recent art.

YAB: If I understand you, it's a question not of the materiality of the medium so much as of the concept of the medium. The medium can fluctuate from one series of work to another, but the artist has to have a set of rules to work.

RK: The idea of a coherent set of rules means that the structure of the work will be recursive, that it will generate analogues for the medium itself.

▲ 1916a, 1920, 1921, 1924, 1928, 1930b, 1931 • 1957a ■ 1959b, 1960c ◆ 1971 ▲ 1968b • 1949, 1960b

HF: Now your definition of medium sounds formalistic as well as arbitrary.

RK: Without the logic of a medium art is in danger of descending into kitsch. Attention to medium is one way modernism tried to defend against itself against kitsch.

HF: Now that really is Greenberg come again.

YAB: As a concept kitsch seems very dated—it has been replaced by spectacle.

RK: I don't think it's dated at all. Kitsch is the meretricious, and we see that everywhere. On the other hand, Greenberg's was a blanket condemnation of kitsch, and, as Yve-Alain has argued elsewhere, some kitsch practices, such as Lucio Fontana's use of ▲ ceramics or Jean Fautrier's use of color, take on the presumption that "advanced" art, such as Cubist-compositions or elegant monochromes, is the epitome of good taste. The late paintings of Francis Picabia are another case of the mobilization of kitsch. And ● how can we speak of an artist like Jeff Koons without recourse to the concept of kitsch?

BB: I disagree with many of the statements you've made. I'd like to support your demand for a continuation of modernism—rather than look back at its demise with a melancholic attitude—but whether one can preserve its practices is not a matter of voluntaristic decisions within the cultural sphere. What is aesthetically achievable is not in the control of critics or historians or even artists, unless artistic practice is to become a mere preserve, a space of self-protection. And there are problems even there. One might argue ■ that Brice Marden, for example, or Gerhard Richter retains a space of exemption for painting in a relatively credible way, as does ◆ Richard Serra in sculpture. But the moment they formalize that position they border on a conservative position that contradicts their initial project. And the question becomes whether preserving modernism is desirable, even if it were possible.

HF: I'm also not happy with this story of a modernism of medium-specificity, followed by a postmedium condition, which is then recouped somehow by a renewal of the medium, even if in an extended sense. There are multiple ruptures in the postwar period that can't be sutured so easily. One transformation has to do with the eclipse of the very tension between avant-garde and kitsch that Rosalind still insists upon. Many artists—perhaps most under fifty—assume that that dialectic is now overwhelmed, that they have to work within a condition of spectacle. That's not to say they capitulate to it, although we see extravagant examples of that embrace too. (Spectacle is the very logic of a Matthew Barney, his "medium" if you like, and for many people he turns it to his advantage.) Some artists also find productive cracks within this condition; it's not as seamless as Benjamin makes it out to be.

BB: Give us an example.

▲ **YAB**: There was Warhol earlier. That's one reason why he became so important to subsequent artists: they understood how he worked with spectacle.

BB: Yes, he was the oracle of things to come.

HF: I hope you don't mean that Warhol was *only* an agent of spectacle. To take but one instance from his work, is there a more critical exposé of the dark side of spectacle than his 1963 images of consumerist "death in America"—of car wrecks and botulism victims? Or another instance already mentioned, the photobooks of Ruscha from the sixties: I don't see them as affirmative of the car-commodity landscape (as is so often claimed); they show its null aspect, or document its space as so much gridded real estate, or both. Another example is Dan Graham, who has also become ● important to younger artists: his *Homes for America* (1966–7), for instance, indicates how the serial logic in play in Minimalism and Pop was already at work in capitalist society at large, specifically in the development of suburban tract-homes. There, in the very similarity in production-logic between avant-garde art and capitalist development, Graham was able to point to the possibility of both critical insight and artistic innovation. And many other examples ■ could be cited here—in Fluxus, for instance, and work closer to the present too. Cindy Sherman has generated her art out of an ambivalent play with the restrictive types of women offered up by spectacle. Mike Kelley has produced his out of a fascinated exploration of the wayward subcultures of "dysfunctional adults" that spectacle cannot always conceal. And, with his tacky installations of kitsch items, fan photos, and tin foil, Thomas ◆ Hirschhorn does all he can (in that great old line of Marx's) to make "life's reified conditions dance once again" by "playing them their own tune." And so on. So we can't say that artists haven't diagnosed the problem and produced work that addresses it.

YAB: Yet perhaps conditions have changed again now, and, instead of a polar opposition à la Adorno between resistant high art and mass-cultural trash, both have become, in the context of global media, so many bits in the planetary web. The paradigm isn't resistance versus dissolution any more: resistance is immediately dissolved in the new situation. Young artists are not necessarily suicidal about it (there I agree); they want to do something with it.

BB: Certainly, artists as diverse as Allan Sekula, Mark Lombardi, and Hirschhorn address the condition of artistic production under the rule of an intensely expansionist form of late-capitalist and corporate imperialism, now generally identified with the anodyne and meaningless term "globalization." All of them have succeeded to articulate the fact that nation-state ideology and traditional models of conventional identity-construction are no longer available to relevant cultural production, since the internationalization of corporate culture would desire nothing more than a cultural retreat into mythical models of compensatory

▲ 1946, 1959a ● 1986 ■ 1972b, 1988 ◆ 1969, 1970

▲ 1964b ● Introduction 2, 1968b ■ 1962a ◆ 2003

identity-formations. At the same time such artists have made it one of their priorities to *work through* the intensely complicated networks of political, ideological, and economic intersections that make up the supposedly liberating forms of globalization. Thereby they achieve a critical analysis of phenomena that are generally presented by the media, but also by cultural organizers and functionaries, as an emancipatory and almost utopian achievement.

But globalization is only one of the driving factors. There are at least two others. One is technological development, which confronts artists, historians, and critics today with problems that none of us really foresaw in the sixties or seventies. The second factor is more complicated, and it's difficult not to sound conspiratorial about it: the very construct of an oppositional sphere of artists and intellectuals appears to have been eliminated; certainly this is true in the realm of cultural production. That production is now homogenized as an economic field of investment and speculation in its own right. The antinomy between artists and intellectuals on the one hand and capitalist production on the other has been annihilated or has disappeared by attrition. Today we are in a political and ideological situation that, while it is not quite yet totalitarian, points toward the elimination of contradiction and conflict, and this necessitates a rethinking of what cultural practice can be under the totalizing conditions of fully advanced capitalist organization.

HF: The postwar acceleration of new technologies was already evident in the early sixties, and it was addressed not only by media gurus like Marshall McLuhan but also by artists involved in Minimalism, Pop, and other movements. These artists treated new and/or nonartistic materials and techniques (e.g., Plexiglas in ▲ Donald Judd, fluorescent lights in Dan Flavin, silkscreen seriality in Warhol) within the formats of sculpture and painting the better to register their effects there. These examples (to say nothing of video) suggest that "new media" already has a complicated history within postwar art—indeed all history is littered with "new media." So are the consequences of "new media" really so total today? For example, isn't there a dialectic here, however feeble it might appear, whereby "new media" also produce outmoded forms as a by-product—outmoded forms that then stand as ciphers of surpassed or suppressed aesthetic and social experiences that contemporary artists can recover critically? Alongside the embrace of "new media" there is a recovery of displaced modes, which can ● be mined as an archive of past subjectivities and socialities.

I grant that these attempts to open up cultural history through old media are humble, and certainly they appear overwhelmed by the institutional attention given to "new media." Here I have in mind such technophiliac extravaganzas as the recent video installations of Bill Viola, who seems to want to deliver what Walter Benjamin once called, in the thirties in relation to film, "the blue flower in the land of technology"—that is, the effect of spiritual immediacy through the means of intensive mediation. This effect is a kind of techno-sublime that overwhelms body and space alike, but which today goes well beyond simple distraction (Benjamin's concern in the thirties) to outright immersion. An immersive, even mesmeric experience seems to be the desired effect of much art today (you see it in much digital photography too), and it's very popular, in part because it aestheticizes, or "artifies," an already-familiar experience—the mind-blowing intensities produced by media culture at large. In this art we get the rush of special effects along with the surplus-value of the aesthetic. Nevertheless, there are also artists who sketch a different project, again a sort of archaeology of outmoded forms, and, interestingly, they do so often in film, now that film is no longer the medium of the future or even the present but is already touched with archaism ...

BB: Artists such as?

▲ **HF**: Stan Douglas, Tacita Dean, Matthew Buckingham, to name just a few.

● **RK**: Another artist engaged with the outmoded is William Kentridge.

■ **HF**: Right. And one reason why James Coleman is so interesting to younger artists is that he has consistently explored the social spaces of outmoded media. One might argue that the separateness of these spaces is illusory, that the culture industry is always there to recolonize them, but we shouldn't say they never existed in the first place.

BB: We've seen that recuperation already with Surrealism and advertising.

HF: Absolutely, but we shouldn't declare the dialectic foreclosed for ever.

YAB: The outmoded is resistant only to a certain point and only for a certain time. I was struck to hear that the radical filmmakers Jean-Marie Straub and Danièle Huillet refuse video and DVD: they only want their films to be projected on the screen. How long can they sustain that position, and not be forgotten? In this regard they're the equivalent of Asher in the universe of film.

RK: Yet the way the outmoded works is that new technologies—maybe even DVD—will fail, or at least be surpassed, rendered outmoded, too. What will Coleman do, for example, when Kodak no longer makes slide projectors? They're being outmoded by digital projection and PowerPoint.

YAB: The digitization of images is going to be the Esperanto of globalization. There's a becoming-uniform of format at the level of production and distribution alike. Young artists want to address that frame.

BB: To return for a moment to the opposition of Bill Viola and James Coleman: they reveal two tendencies that are very

▲ 1962c, 1964b, 1965 ● 1998

▲ 1998 ● 1994b ■ 1993a

complicated in their interrelationship. One is the intensification for the desire of myth—that's the secret of Viola's success. He succeeds in reinvesting technological representation with mythological imagery, even religious experience …

HF: One sees that kind of cultic reenchantment through new media everywhere. Benjamin saw a fascistic dimension to this manipulated immediacy, and maybe that's still accurate.

RK: Viola produces the video monitor as a black box meant as an analogue of the viewer's own head: the psychic space externalized as the physical surround. Once physical space is converted to psychological space in this way (notice I'm not saying phenomenological space), all connection to the reality of his artistic means is dissolved.

HF: Right: it's a "faux-phenomenological" experience: experience reworked, keyed up, given back to us in a very mediated fashion—as immediate, spiritual, absolute.

RK: In that respect the concept of kitsch is relevant again.

BB: That's the treacherous tendency. In opposition to it Coleman succeeds in bringing together two things that seem mutually exclusive—namely, the mnemonic dimension of art and a technological format of representation. That's extraordinarily important in the present; and yet, as we've just remarked, the potential of tapping the mnemonic through the outmoded is extremely fragile. There's no more innate resistance in the mnemonic than there is in the outmoded: both are very precarious. We know that the mnemonic dimension in art (intrinsic to modernism since Baudelaire) is the most susceptible to fetishization and spectacularization, as such work as Anselm ▲ Kiefer's has amply proven. On the one hand, the effort to retain or to reconstruct the capacity to remember, to think historically, is one of the few acts that can oppose the almost totalitarian implementation of the universal laws of consumption. On the other hand, as artists such as Viola and Barney demonstrate, to deliver the aesthetic capacity to construct memory images to the voracious demands of an apparatus that entirely lacks the ability to remember and to reflect historically, and to do so in the form of resuscitated myth, is an almost guaranteed route to success in the present art world, especially with its newly added wing of "the memory industry."

HF: There's a further danger there. As you suggest, the mnemonic easily tips into the memorializing, that is to say, into a demand that the historical be monumentalized, and often today what is monumentalized is the traumatic. The chief example here, among countless others, is the new World Trade Center design by Daniel Libeskind, with its vast memorial preserve and immense glass spire: historical trauma is here made not only monumental but spectacular and triumphal as well. Paradoxically enough, then, there might be no contradiction between a blinding fixation on historical trauma and a culture industry that produces historical amnesia as a precondition of ever-renewed consumption (next to the memorial there'll be the usual Gap, Starbucks, etc.). This condition is in stark contrast to the utopian dimension of so much modernist art and architecture of the early twentieth century that also experienced great trauma: we seem to live in a culture fixed on horrific pasts, not in a culture desirous of transfigured futures. From my perspective its political effects are disastrous: we live under the repressive dread of antidemocratic blackmails ("9/11," "the war on terrorism," etc.).

RK: By the nineties the question of trauma becomes a kind of intellectual fashion. Essentially it is a way of reinserting the subject into the discourses of history and culture. Trauma discourse effectively reconstitutes the subject—even if it is a subject absented somehow, by definition not alert to the traumatic event. This way of privileging the subject again slips into a reconstitution of the biographical subject, and that project is very suspect from a poststructuralist perspective.

HF: Yet in one sense the poststructuralist critique of the biographical subject is continued in the psychoanalytic understanding of the traumatized subject, even as, from another angle, it is also recouped there. I don't think the two discourses are as opposed as you suggest: both fix on slippages and breakdowns—on aporias—in a way that sometimes suggests another contemporary version of the sublime.

BB: But why hold out for a poststructuralist critique of the subject now, or even then? Hasn't it become evident that such a critique prevents not only a reflection on the historical foundations of postwar culture but also an understanding of their traumatic conditions?

▲ **YAB**: Why do you say that? How would Michel Foucault, for example, prevent such an understanding?

BB: As far as I know, Foucault did not reflect on those conditions of postwar culture in the way that Adorno, for example, did from the forties onward. Adorno's critique is always directed at both cultural practice and the subject in post-Holocaust European and American society.

YAB: Foucault's critique of subjectivity doesn't imply any disjunction from historical struggles. He was very politically engaged, as you know, especially at the time he was writing *Discipline and Punish* and reflecting on the nature of power. And through his political engagement, notably at the side of prisoners struggling for their rights, he became very attentive to the way in which collective memory—especially what he called "popular memory"—is violently erased by the state and by the media. This is probably why, unlike Adorno, he was reluctant to single out the Holocaust as a kind of absolute limit of evil. And that is probably what prevented him, contrary to Adorno, from being deaf to the student uprising in 1968.

▲ 1988

▲ 1971

HF: I agree, but the poststructuralist critique of the subject was questioned in other ways as well. It was seen to concern a particular kind of subject only: this was a critique initiated by feminist theory and advanced in postcolonial discourse. Both argued that many groups had not yet acceded to the very privileges that the poststructuralist critique wanted to throw into doubt or to dispense with altogether. Why critique a subjecthood, these groups argued, that was denied one in the first place?

BB: That was a very important argument.

HF: Yes, and another problem with the poststructuralist critique of the subject was that it was sometimes turned into a cliché about the construction of the subject—that we are all fashioned, top to bottom, socially—and this reductive version of the poststructuralist critique was not resistant enough to the consumerist modeling of the subject: that we can be made and remade continually in terms of new clothes, cars, and cuisines too—and art as well. For many people "postmodernism" is not much more than hip, knowing consumerism.

▲ **BB**: The reception of Cindy Sherman, for example, supports that account.

HF: As I see it, the interest in the nineties in a traumatic subject—a subject fixed by trauma, stuck in abjection—was in part a reaction to that consumerist version of the constructed subject. It called into question the idea that we just float along as so many combinations of signs and commodities. So, however reductive it might seem now, and however grim then, trauma discourse did have a certain point, even perhaps a certain politics, and Cindy Sherman was important there as well (it's not as though she was blind to how her work was being taken up).

BB: Your first argument concerning the postcolonial caution about the poststructuralist critique provides a way to return to the question of globalization. There was a move to open up the focus of practices and institutions in Western Europe and the United States—to recognize that cultural representation can also be a form of political representation. With an almost missionary zeal the art world responded to the aspiration that all cultures, all countries, at whatever stage, might have access to contemporary artistic practices. That is politically progressive, even radical, but it is also naive, and sometimes problematic, because one problem in the globalization of culture is a failure to recognize the dialectics of dissemination—that inherent in this dissemination is the possibility of new forms of commodification and blockage as well as of new forms of self-constitution and self-representation. That contradiction is not well understood in the avid globalizing of current curatorial enterprises.

HF: To make this point more specific, we might consider what ● occurred between the moment of the "Les Magiciens de la Terre" show at the Centre Pompidou in 1989 and the present flourishing of international biennials, where the formats of work seem both fairly restricted and generally available (prominent models include installation art, the projected image or video, the vast pictorial photograph or photographic sequence, the chat-room filled with all sorts of texts, documents, images ...). "Magiciens" was an emphatic attempt to open up the center to the peripheries, even if it came at a time when the two couldn't be opposed in that manner any more. There was a great diversity of work and a concerted attention to local traditions. That was as recent as 1989, and yet today international exhibitions—Documenta, the biennials in Venice, Johannesburg, Gwangju, Istanbul, and so on—feel very different.

YAB: The model of "Les Magiciens de la Terre" was not so dissimilar to any colonial show. Things are different now in part because the market is two-way. Work flows in from South Africa, for example, but part of the art world also goes there, and its net can pick up anything. It's not exoticism any more; it's feeding the network of markets.

BB: A curator like Okwui Enwezor might say that we're looking at this phenomenon only from a hegemonic Western perspective, and that we don't see that the development of cultural activities within these countries has tremendous consequences for producers and receivers alike. They develop forms of representation, communication, and interrelation that might not have been so readily established without the globalization of cultural practices.

YAB: In South Africa there has been a great surge in artistic practice since the end of apartheid, and alternative spaces of art have mushroomed. So has the number of artists.

BB: But we don't know yet at this moment whether a quantitative expansion is a desirable effect in and of itself. From the perspective of an art world that is more crowded than ever before, marked by extraordinary overproduction, the simple multiplication of artistic practices and alternative spaces might not be desirable if it's not linked to an actual agenda of new forms of political articulation through cultural means.

YAB: It's too early to say. But we can say now that there's an unbelievably sharp acceleration in artistic production and reception in many countries as a result of globalization.

RK: One possible positive of globalization is the internationalism of the art world today. This was very important in the early aspirations of the avant-garde—to turn away from nationalist culture and to move into a set of international connections.

HF: But, as we discussed in the first roundtable, that aspiration was often driven by faith in socialist revolution. What social projects guide the present internationalism?

BB: Corporate culture.

▲ 1977, 1993a ● 1989

HF: OK, what *other* social project? There are counters to corporate culture, to American Empire, even if at this point those counters often seem rather romantic (as those are articulated, for example, by Toni Negri and Michael Hardt). But then none of us is in a position to comment on what projects might be emerging in other parts of the globe. There is much interest, for instance, in contemporary art in China: what role might it assume internationally? Or art produced in the Indian subcontinent, which has its own modern history of national forms and international responses? Or in contemporary Islam? And so on. Postcolonial discourse gave us some conceptual tools with which to address these formations—to do with hybrid spaces and complicated temporalities—but how are those practices to be articulated with ones more familiar to us, in a manner that is neither restrictively particular nor glibly synthetic?

This opens up a question we haven't confronted, but it goes to the heart not only of our own double status as modernist art historians and contemporary art critics, but also of the latter part of this book. Are there plausible ways to narrate the now myriad practices of contemporary art over the last twenty years at least? I don't point to this period of time arbitrarily: in the last several years the two primary models we've used to articulate different aspects of postwar art have become dysfunctional. I mean, on the one hand, the model of a medium-specific modernism challenged by an interdisciplinary postmodernism, and, on the other, the model of a historical avant-garde (i.e., ones critical of the old bourgeois ▲ institution of art such as Dada and Constructivism) and a neo-avant-garde that elaborates on this critique (we discussed both models in the first roundtable). Today the recursive strategy of the "neo" appears as attenuated as the oppositional logic of the "post" seems tired: neither suffices as a strong paradigm for artistic or cultural practice, and no other model stands in their stead; or, put differently, many local models compete, but none can hope to be paradigmatic. And we should note too that the methods discussed again here—psychoanalysis, Marxian social history, structuralism, and poststructuralism—are hardly thriving. For many this condition is a good thing: it permits artistic freedom and critical diversity. But our paradigm of no-paradigm has also abetted a flat indifference, a stagnant incommensurability, a consumerist-touristic culture of art sampling—and in the end is this posthistorical default in contemporary art any great improvement on the old historicist determinism of modernist art à la Greenberg and company? And then we have to compound this problem with the question of the narrativity of art in a global context.

The problem is not abstract: it's there in the museum galleries (but not, interestingly, in the auction halls). It's evident in the proliferation of single-artist and single-period museums—the • Dia:Beacon shrine to Minimalism and Postminimalism is just one instance. It's also apparent in the mix-and-match thematics of the Tate Modern, for example, with works from across the century clustered under iconographic headings like "Nude/Action/Body" or "Still Life/Object/Real Life." And this sense of *post-histoire* is, paradoxically enough, a common institutional effect today: we wander through museum spaces as if after the end of time.

BB: For the most part participants in the contemporary art world (and that includes ourselves) have not yet developed a systematic understanding of how that once integral element of the bourgeois public sphere (represented by the institution of the avant-garde as much as by the institution of the museum) has irretrievably disappeared. It has been replaced by social and institutional formations for which we not only do not have any concepts and terms yet, but whose modus operandi remains profoundly opaque and incomprehensible to most of us. For example, we have more artists, galleries and exhibition organizers than ever before in the postwar period, yet none of these operate in any way comparable to the way they functioned from the 1940s to the 1990s. We have ever larger and evermore imposing museum buildings and institutions emerging all around us, but their social function, once comparable to the sphere of public education or the university, for example, has become completely diffuse. These new functions range from those of a bank—which holds, if not the gold standard, at least the quality and value warranties for investors and speculators in the art market—to those of a congregational space, semi-public at that, in which rites are enacted that promise to compensate for, if not to obliterate, the actual loss of our sense of a once given desire and demand for political and social self-determination.

YAB: But couldn't we say that such a current amnesia is in great part what motivated us to write this book? I don't think we should delude ourselves into thinking that we are going to change the global colonization of the cultural sphere by spectacle, but I don't think we should whine either. After all, we've been united in our desire to reshuffle the cards, not only to revisit canonical moments of modernism and "postmodernism," but also to retrieve from oblivion many aspects of the cultural production of these past hundred-plus years that had been ignored or deliberately repressed. In doing so, I think, we have presented a much more complex tableau than the one served to us when we were students. Who knows, it might have some liberatory effect.

▲ 1916, 1920, 1921, 1926, 1928 • 1965, 1966b, 1969

glossary

CAPITALS indicate other glossary terms

affirmative culture

The concept of an affirmative culture was initially coined by the philosopher Herbert Marcuse in his essay "On the Affirmative Character of Culture," where he argued that cultural production inherently supported existing political, economical, and ideological power structures by the very fact of its innately legitimizing character. This means that cultural production not only provides presumably compelling evidence of social and subjective autonomy to any given political system, but also prohibits contestation and change since it corroborates the *status quo* as valid and productive by its very existence; or as T. W. Adorno once said, "culture by the mere fact of its existence prohibits the sociopolitical change that it promises." Artists since the sixties in particular have attempted to overcome Marcuse's pessimistic totalization (represented best by Andy Warhol's universal affirmation), and have responded by developing a variety of specific critiques and contestations. And in fact it could be argued that the momentary successes of artistic practices such as institutional critique of the seventies, feminist interventions of the eighties, and gay activism of the nineties have proven that forms of cultural opposition can raise public and political consciousness successfully. This does not imply, however, that the continuously expanding arsenal of instant recuperation that transforms cultural opposition into mere market—and museum—goods does not pose a permanent challenge to artists and requires a perpetual change of strategies.

Alexandrianism

The avant-garde assumed different positions in its lifetime: opposed to academic art, engaged in political critique, turned inward toward its given materials, or outward toward mass culture, and so on. Yet common to all these positions was the imperative of *advance*—"to keep culture *moving*," as Clement Greenberg put it in "Avant-Garde and KITSCH" (1939), "in the midst of ideological confusion and violence" (note the date of the essay, on the brink of World War II). Paradoxically, in a society in transformation or turmoil when the "verities" of tradition are thrown into question, "a motionless *Alexandrianism*" can take over cultural practice: "an academicism in which the really important issues are left untouched because they involve controversy, and in which creative activity dwindles to virtuosity in the small details of form, all larger questions being decided by the precedents of the old masters." According to Greenberg, the avant-garde first emerged in the middle of the nineteenth century to challenge this stalled state of affairs; but such Alexandrianism is hardly a one-time event. The illusion of great movement that conceals the reality of oppressive stasis might well be the rule more than the exception in capitalist society; and if this is the case—if the problem of Alexandrianism has not disappeared—then perhaps the need for an avant-garde has not either.

alogism

This term, coined by Kazimir Malevich around 1913–14, refers to a body of works that he realized at the same time as he was transforming the idiom of Synthetic Cubism into his own particular brand of abstraction, Suprematism, which came to light in 1915. By superposing onto his alogic canvases unrelated figures, represented as they would be in an illustrated dictionary and sharply contrasting in terms of scale, that could not possibly belong to the same scene, Malevich sought to create the pictorial equivalent of the "transrational" (or *ZAUM*) poetry of his friends Aleksei Kruchenikh and Velemir Khlebnikov.

alterity

Etymologically, "alterity" is the condition of "otherness," which was a longtime goal of many modernists (note the famous statement of the young French poet Arthur Rimbaud in 1871: "Je est un autre"). Often this otherness was projected onto faraway cultures; the most famous instance here is Paul Gauguin, who traveled to Tahiti in search of a new way not only to make art but to live life. But it could also be sought in places closer to home—in native traditions, folk art, peasant culture, and so on. Sometimes, too, this alterity was seen to exist even more intimately, if no less strangely, in the unconscious—the otherness of obscure dreams and vague desires explored by Surrealists like Max Ernst above all. In short, many modernists pursued alterity for its disruptive potential, but it never had a fixed location. In the wake of feminist theory and postcolonial discourse, the term has taken on a renewed valence, wherein alterity is privileged as a position of radical critique of the dominant culture—of what it cannot think or address or permit at all—more than as a place of romantic escape from it.

anomie/anomic

This term, first defined by Émile Durkheim in 1894, has been generally deployed in social history and theory in order to describe particular historical formations of social deregulation, periods in which the fundamental contracts of social ethics that had traditionally regulated the interaction among subjects, and between subjects and the state, have been canceled. In the present time, typical examples of the expansion of social anomie could be found in the overall attitudes of capitalist neo-liberalism that has systematically dismantled fundamental social institutions such as education, healthcare, and the elementary political processes of participation and representation (e.g., unionization). Transferred into aesthetic and art-historical debates, the term anomic identifies the working conditions of cultural producers for whom utopian avant-garde aspirations, or even the desire for a minimum of sociopolitical relevance, have become extinct. The absence of a sociopolitical dimension within artistic production inevitably leads to anomic conditions in culture at large (e.g., Jeff Koons, Matthew Barney) where the neo-liberal principles of speculation and investment opportunities driven by the promise of profit maximization govern the politics of artists, collectors, and institutions alike. Culture under the conditions of anomie acquires at best the features of a SIMULACRUM of legitimation and prestige, and at worst those of a closed-circuit system of specialized investment expertise.

aporia/aporetic

Originating in philosophy and rhetorics, the terms aporia and aporetic describe what seems to be an almost inextricably necessary condition of the work of art: that it generates intrinsically unresolvable structures of paradoxical contradiction. For example, to be at once representational yet self-referential; to claim autonomy status while being totally subjected to ideological interests; or to claim freedom from instrumentalization, yet be determined by mass-cultural frameworks and massive economic interests—these are just some of the more obvious cases of artistic aporias in the present. More subtle aporetic structures would be the claims of the aesthetic to be universally legible, yet to be always confined to privileged situations of reading and reception. Aporetic is also the work's desire to expand its audiences to disseminate critical reflection, only to end up in the mass-cultural formations of a voraciously recuperative spectacle culture. Thus one could argue that the aporetic has become in fact *one* of the fundamental rhetorical TROPES of the aesthetic at this moment. It remains unclear whether it is reactive, in the sense that that every work of art has to face unresolvable contradictions, or whether it is proactive in the sense that it is precisely the function of the work of art to subvert and implode fixities and certainties in the behavioral and perceptual structures of everyday life by confronting them with an incessant barrage of unresolvable contradictions.

art autre

Meaning "a different art," or, more literally, "an art that is other," this expression was launched in 1952 by the French critic Michel Tapié to group together the art of Jean Dubuffet, Jean Fautrier, and Wols (who had died in 1951), as well as that of their imitators and of an eclectic compendium of Abstract Expressionist and neo-Surrealist artists, under a single banner. Tapié soon replaced it, and with more lasting success, with the phrase *art informel* (although Dubuffet and Fautrier reviled that just as much as *art autre*). SEE *ART INFORMEL*

art informel

When in 1962 French writer Jean Paulhan published his book *L'Art informel*, the phrase, coined by Michel Tapié a decade earlier, had not gained much in clarity. By then it designated a post-Cubist pictorial (or eventually sculptural) mode in which the figures, abstract or not, were not readily legible but would gradually emerge from a tangle of gestures or accumulation of matter before the consciousness of the spectator. Most of the painters satisfied with this label were also to be called *TACHISTES*.

atavism

From the Latin for "great-grandparent," "atavism" signifies the tendency to resemble, in a given trait, an ancestor more than a parent. In the nineteenth century, largely under the influence of racialist biology, "atavism" took on a pathological shading, whereby such resemblance was taken to suggest a reversion to a diseased state that had passed into remission for a generation or two. Used in this way, the term connoted a regression to a primitive or degenerate condition, ambiguously physical, psychological, or both, and this negative connotation still echoes in its use in art criticism and cultural discourse today.

biographism

With the eclipse of modernism in the seventies, the formal logic of abstract art began to fade, making way for a new conviction that the meaning of avant-garde works was to be found in the artist's life, for which the art objects could be seen to serve as an emblem. This was the same period during which biographism came under fierce attack, as in Roland Barthes's essay "The Death of the Author" (1968) and Michel Foucault's truculent "What matter who's speaking?" ("What is an author?"[1969]). Following Freud's *Leonardo da Vinci and a Memory of his Childhood* (1910), art historians and critics searched within the biographical information for a symptomatic detail that would "unlock" the work. Picasso's habit of signing his paintings and drawings not only with his name but with the precise dates and even hours of their execution lent credibility to this belief. Jaume Sabartés, Picasso's secretary, predicted that once this trail of clues was followed, "We would discover in his works his spiritual vicissitudes, the blows of fate, the satisfactions and annoyances, his joys and delight, the pain suffered on a certain day or at a certain time of a given year."

calligramme/calligram/calligrammatic

In 1918, Guillaume Apollinaire published a volume of his *calligrammes*, composed while he was sequestered in the trenches during World War I. *Calligrammes* are poems fashioned so that the words take the shape of the object named by the poem. One example is "Il pleut" (It is raining), with the letters descending in vertical channels to imitate rain; another is "The necktie and the pocket watch," with both objects represented by the words of the poem. The similar combination of language and image, as in Cubist collages or the paintings of Jasper Johns and Edward Ruscha, are therefore designated "calligrammatic."

Concrete poetry

As a historical term, Concrete poetry identifies the postwar resurrection and academicization of the linguistic and poetical experiments of the radical avant-gardes of the teens and twenties that had been conducted in the context of Russian Futurism, and the practices of international Dadaism in Berlin, Zurich, Hanover, and Paris. If the Dada painters and poets (such as Hugo Ball and Raoul Hausmann) were engaged in a radical opposition to traditional painterly and poetical languages (e.g., Berlin sound poetry as a travesty of the German cult of the poet Rainer Maria Rilke or of German Expressionism), the Russian and Soviet sound poets (e.g., the *ZAUM* poetry of Velemir Khlebnikov) developed a theoretical understanding of poetical processes and functions that would correspond to the new theoretical analysis of linguistic functions in Russian and Soviet Formalism. The Concrete poets of the postwar period typically emerged in areas that had been both remote and protected from the cataclysms of World War II, both privileged and disadvantaged with regard to the naivety of their early rediscovery of these avant-garde projects. Thus we find early resuscitations named Concrete poetry in the context of Latin American countries and in Switzerland in the forties, often working in tandem with the academicization of abstraction (for example, Eugen Gomringer and Max Bill). Here the celebration of a newfound ludic irrelevance and of typographical gamesmanship displaced both the political, the graphic, and the semiological radicality of the originary figures.

condensation

Sigmund Freud developed this term in his interpretation of dreams, but it also signified a basic process of the unconscious in general, whereby a single idea—image and/or word—comes to represent multiple meanings through association. This idea attracts different lines of associated meanings, "condenses" them, and so takes on a special intensity (as well as a particular obscurity) through them. In this light one can understand its function in dreams, the "manifest content" of which (the narrative that we seem to see) is more concentrated and confused than its "latent meaning" (the sense that we might decode); yet condensation is also in play in the formation of symptoms, which can also combine different desires into one trait or action. To the limited extent that images are analogous to dreams or symptoms, "condensation" has some use-value in art criticism as well. Its complement in psychoanalysis, as a fundamental process of the unconscious, is DISPLACEMENT, and its parallel in linguistics, as a layering of associated meanings, is metaphor (*see* METONYMY).

décollage

Décollage was initially envisioned by the late Surrealist writer Léo Malet, who in 1936 predicted that in the future the process of collage would be transferred from the small scale and intimate collections of found and glued remnants of the everyday (e.g., Kurt Schwitters) via an aggressive expansion to the large-scale frameworks of advertisement billboards, then increasingly taking control of what were once public urban spaces. It is only in the immediate postwar period in Paris that Malet's prognosis would be fulfilled by a group of young artists who were equally disenchanted with Surrealism as with *art brut* or *ART AUTRE*. Jacques de la Villeglé and Raymond Hains initiated *décollage* in 1946 by collecting lacerated billboards and transferring the remnants into pictorial formats, identifying their work as deliberate acts of collaboration with anonymous vandals who oppose the power of product propaganda. This collaborative dimension, as much as the totally aleatory nature of the found lacerations, was an important aspect of the process. *Décollage* positioned itself in a complex dialogic relationship with the cult of Pollock's *painterly allover* by replacing it with an *allover structure of textuality*. It was also the first postwar activity to resituate artistic production at the intersection of urban architectural space, advertisement, and the conditions of textuality and reading under the newly emerging regimes of advanced forms of consumer culture.

deductive structure

The Cubist grid is, perhaps, the first instance of the kind of pictorial composition that would later in the twentieth century come to comprise the whole of Frank Stella's paintings. Derived from the shape of the canvas and repeating its vertical and horizontal edges in a series of parallel lines, the grid is an instance of drawing that does not seem to delimit a representational object, but, mirroring the surface on which it is drawn, "represents" nothing but that surface itself. Stella would make this "mirroring" much more emphatic by casting his paintings into eccentric shapes, such as Vs or Us. With his drawing paralleling these edges, to create a series of concentric stripes, there was not only no question that anything but the shape itself was being represented, but also no possibility of reading "depth" or illusionistic space into the surface, which was stretched as tight as a drum-head by the constant representation of itself. Writing about Stella's work, the critic Michael Fried called this procedure "deductive structure."

desublimation

The concept of desublimation figures in contradictory ways within criticism and psychoanalytically informed writing on art history. In its obvious response to Freud's model of SUBLIMATION as the presumed precondition for any type of cultural production, the countermodel describes first of all the social conditions that foil the subject's capacities to sublimate libidinal demands and to differentiate experience within increasingly complex forms of social relations, knowledge, and production. Adorno's critique of the "desublimation" of musical listening, arising with the technologies of musical reproduction such the radio and the gramophone, would be a case in point. Here desublimation is identified as a socially and historically determining factor of cultural decline caused by mass-cultural formations. But in its opposite definition, desublimation has taken on the meaning of a strategy to foreground the conflicting impulses within the aesthetic object itself. The social enforcement of sublimation is counteracted in antiaesthetic gestures, processes, or materials that discredit the sublimatory triumphalism made by the work of high art. Desublimation is played out in the dialectics of high art versus mass culture, performed throughout the twentieth century as a counteridentification with the iconographies and the technologies of mass culture in order to debase the false autonomy claims with which modernism had propped up its myths. At the same time, these antiaesthetic gestures underline that all acts of sublimation are always also acts of libidinal repression, and that the work of art is the sole site to make these contradictions manifest by its emphatic invocation of the somatic origins of artistic production.

diachronic

Although this term, derived from the Greek language, existed before the Swiss linguist Ferdinand de Saussure, its modern acceptation was forged in his *Course of General Linguistics*, posthumously published in 1916, where it is used in direct opposition to SYNCHRONIC. Meaning "lasting through time," diachronic designates any process observed from the point of view of its historical development. The diachronic study of a language deals exclusively with its evolution (for example, from Old English to present-day English).

dialogism/dialogical

The writings of Mikhail Bakhtin entered the world of structuralism in the sixties, when a group of Eastern Europeans—Tzvetan Todorov and Julia Kristeva among them—emigrated to France, bringing with them knowledge of Russian linguistic work that had previously been unknown in the West. *Discourse in the Novel* (1934) and *Problems of Dostoevsky's Poetics* (1929) were important sources of Bakhtin's notion of dialogism, or the dialogical principle. Dostoevsky's novels, Bakhtin observed, are polyphonic, which means that "a plurality of independent and unmerged voices and consciousnesses" takes up existence there. "What unfolds in his work," Bakhtin writes, "is not a multitude of characters and fates in a single objective world, illuminated by a single authorial consciousness; rather a plurality of consciousnesses, with equal rights and each with its own world, combine but are not merged in the unity of the event." The conventional novel, to which this technique is opposed, attempts to synthesize these voices within the vision of a single consciousness—that of the author—creating, thus, a monological universe. The dialogical principle carries over to Bakhtin's understanding of the linguistic utterance, which structuralism pictured as a coded message sent between a sender and a receiver. Instead, Bakhtin's dialogism assumed that any such message would already take the receiver's position into account and thus be conditioned by that position: supplicating it, refuting it, placating it, seducing it.

displacement

The complement of CONDENSATION in psychoanalysis, "displacement" is the other essential process at work in dreams, or the DREAM-WORK, according to Freud. Rather than a layering of meanings in a vertical (or metaphorical) association as in condensation, displacement signifies a slippage of meanings in a horizontal (or METONYMIC) connection. In the case of displacement, then, one idea—a word and/or an image "cathected" or invested with special energy or significance—passes on some of this charge to an adjacent idea, which, as in condensation, gains in intensity as well as obscurity. As in condensation, too, displacement is often at work in the formation of symptoms and other unconscious productions, and it might also be applied, with caution, to a reading of art—in terms of the unconscious processes involved in both making and viewing a work.

dream-work

In psychoanalysis this term encompasses all the operations of the dream as it transforms its various materials (bodily stimuli while asleep, traces of the events of the day, old memories, and so on) into visual narratives. The two essential operations are CONDENSATION and DISPLACEMENT; yet two other mechanisms are important as well: "considerations of representability" and "secondary revision." The first mechanism selects the dream-thoughts that can be represented by images and reformats them (as it were) accordingly. The second mechanism then arranges these dream-images so that they might form a scenario fluid enough to stage the dream in the first instance. In some sense both operations—"representability" and "revision"—already suggest activities of picture-making, and so they might appear to be of rather direct use in matters of art. But this proximity is also a danger: a painting that takes the dream as its model—as Paul Gauguin, say, or the young Jackson Pollock sometimes did implicitly, or as some Surrealists did explicitly—risks a reductive circularity whereby the painting illustrates the dream, which in turn delivers the key to its meaning.

durée

The French philosopher Henri Bergson, whose work was highly valued by the Italian Futurists, opposed "objective time" and "subjective time," which he called *durée* (duration). While "objective time" is space in disguise, argued Bergson (thus the spatial means used to measure or represent it: the clock, the arrow), the subjective time of experience flows indivisibly, and its intuitive apprehension is one of the means by which human consciousness accedes to its central unity. Bergson's views, enormously successful in the teens and twenties (he was awarded the Nobel Prize for literature in 1927) were eclipsed by psychoanalysis, for which the human psyche is a field divided by conflicting forces, but they have been regaining some currency from the sixties on, in a large measure thanks to the work of the French philosopher Gilles Deleuze.

entropy

The law of entropy, which is the second law of thermodynamics, a branch of physics founded in the nineteenth century, predicts the inevitability of the deperdition of energy in any given system, thus the future and irreversible dissolution of any organization and return to a state of indifferentiation. The concept of entropy had an immediate and enormous effect on the popular imagination, especially because the example chosen by Sadi Carnot, one of its creators, was the fact that the solar system would inevitably cool down. It was soon imported into many fields of knowledge, not only in hard sciences but also in the humanities, drawing the interest of authors as different as Sigmund Freud in psychology, Claude Lévi-Strauss in anthropology, and Umberto Eco in aesthetics. While the way in which words become clichés and gradually lose their meaning—a topic of immense concern for modernist writers, starting with Stéphane Mallarmé—can be characterized as an entropic process, it is only with the adoption of the concept of entropy by the theoreticians of information Claude Shannon and Norbert Wiener in the late forties that it was directly applied to the field of communication. In their definition, the less informational content a message carries the more entropic it is: were all American presidents assassinated, for example, the announcement of their death would be highly entropic; conversely, since American presidents are very rarely assassinated, the murder of John F. Kennedy was of exceptional informational value for the media. Until Robert Smithson's choice of entropy for his main motto in the sixties, however, it had always been understood as a kind of dark inevitable doom. Fascinated by the strength and inevitability of entropy in any process, Smithson viewed it, positively, as performing in itself a kind of critique of humankind and its pretenses that it is the only universal condition of all things and beings.

epistemology

Derived from the Greek words *episteme* (science, knowledge) and *logos* (study, discourse), this term first meant the theory of knowledge or of science. At the beginning of the twentieth century, however, a major crisis in the foundations of mathematics and physics led epistemological inquiries—that is, critical analyses of the general principles and methods of sciences—into the realm of pure logic, a current that still dominates in Anglo-Saxon epistemology. Another trend, particularly active in France in the immediate postwar period (with Gaston Bachelard, Alexandre Koyre, and Georges Canguilhem) and represented in the United States by Thomas Kuhn, focuses on the formation of scientific disciplines and the internal evolution of scientific theories. It from this branch of epistemology that derives Michel Foucault's use of the concept of episteme, in *The Order of Things*, as the specific way knowledge is articulated in various sciences, or rather discursive practices, during any specific period, determining what is thinkable at any given time. While the historical shift from one episteme to another is always marked by a rupture, each episteme is characterized by a specific grouping of several dominant discursive practices that all conform to the same cohesive model. In *The Order of Things*, Foucault identified and discussed three successive epistemes in Western thought, that of the Renaissance, obsessed by resemblance, that of the Classical Age, for whom representation was crucial, and that of modernity, which presided over the advent of human sciences.

estrangement

This term, often mistranslated from the German or Russian as "alienation," originated in Russian Formalist theories of literature and it became a central concept in the practice and theory of the theatre of Bertolt Brecht. The Russian Formalists conceived of *ostranenie* (the devices and processes of "making strange") as one of the quintessential tasks of aesthetic operations. The aim of this artificial estrangement was primarily to alert the spectator/reader to a different perception of the world, to rupture the rote repetitions of everyday speech, and to renew the senses by estranging them from their conventional representations. But estrangement also meant to alert the spectator/reader to the formal devices and material tools of language as integral elements in the processes of meaning production. Following their own principles and inherent logic, they might even supersede meaning's more traditional elements such a narratives, semantics, or referents in the world of objects. Brecht's *theory or effect of estrangement* transfers the concept from linguistic analysis to the social and political situation of the subject. Throughout his work, Brecht attempted to define viewer participation as active transformations of those cognitive and behavioral structures that have become *naturalized*, as Roland Barthes would later say, and that are invisible to the subject. Estrangement in Brecht therefore means in fact the exact opposite of *alienation*, since one of the tasks of *estrangement* is precisely to resituate the subject in a comprehension of the social and political determinism that suddenly appears as "made" rather than as "fate" and therefore encourages the spectators of Brecht's plays to take the matter of political change directly into their own hands.

facture/faktura

These two terms are intricately related, yet they demarcate a significant shift in the evaluation of artisanal competence and artistic skills in the execution of painting and sculpture. While *facture* played a great role in judgments concerning painterly techniques until the end of the nineteenth (already challenged by Seurat's mechanical facture in divisionism), if not until the beginning of the twentieth century, its status as criterion vanished with the rise of collage aesthetics in Cubism. But even during the time of its validity, *facture* underwent dramatic changes: from the conception of painting as an act of manual bravura, and a display of virtuosity and skills, to the modernist insistence (beginning with Cézanne and culminating in Cubism) on the almost molecular clarity in making every detail and passage of painterly execution transparent in terms of its procedure of production and placement. With the rise of collage aesthetics, a painting became an object, rather than a substratum of illusionistic and perspectival conventions, and to the degree that it aspired to become an object of contemporaneity, it subjected itself to an aesthetic that mimicked manufacturing and industrial montage, all the way denigrating the supposedly hallow grounds of artisanal painting. Thus *facture* now came to mean the degree with which the painterly or sculptural object foregrounded its status and condition of having been *fabricated*, self-reflexively revealing the principles of its own making, and the processes of its production (rather than pretending to have emerged from transcendental inspiration or supernatural talents). The artists emphasizing *facture* in this way is engaged in demythifying the creative process and the artistic object itself, as much as *facture* makes the object itself transparently contingent, rather than autonomous, let alone transcendental.

fetish/fetishism

In the anthropological sense of the word, a fetish is any object endowed with a cultic value or autonomous power of its own, often construed as a magical or divine force, which, rationally speaking, it does not possess. A term with a complex etymology—it was originally used by Portuguese and Dutch traders to designate things that Africans tribes exempted from trade (irrationally, according to the Europeans)—the fetish came to stand for the lowest form of spirituality in various accounts of religion (e.g., in Hegel); that is, to represent the superstitious vulgarity of a mere thing taken to be a sacred entity. It is this notion of the fetish—of an object overvalued by its producers in a manner that subjugates them in turn to it—that Karl Marx and Sigmund Freud turned to critical advantage. In a famous passage in *Capital* (volume 1, 1867), Marx argued that the division of labor in capitalist production leads us to forget how commodities are made, with the result that we "fetishize" them—endow them with a magical power of their own. And, some decades later, Freud suggested that all erotic life involves some fetishism, some investment of inanimate objects with libidinal energy. In short, both Marx and Freud implied that we enlightened moderns are also, at times, superstitious fetishists. In all three definitions—the anthropological, the Marxist, and the Freudian—fetishism has become a central concept in cultural criticism. It is also a multivalent category of the object that modernists have evoked, again and again, in order to test the given parameters—cultural, economic, and sexual—of the work of art.

Gesamtkunstwerk

A German term, translated as "total work of art," the *Gesamtkunstwerk* was vaunted by the nineteenth-century composer Richard Wagner in order to designate the aesthetic ambition of his grand operas—to subsume all the arts within one musical theater, to make an aesthetic experience so awesome that it might be, if not redemptive, at least ritualistic in its power. Thereafter the notion took on a life of its own (in this sense it became an artistic FETISH), soon central to most projects that claimed a transcendental or totalistic dimension for art, with different arts nominated at different times as the master form that would gather all others under it. Thus, for example, in Art Nouveau, design functioned as this dominant term; in De Stijl, it was the painted panel; in the Bauhaus, it was building (the founding program of the Bauhaus carried on its cover a woodcut of a Gothic cathedral under which all arts and crafts were, allegorically speaking, sheltered). However, because it subsumed all the arts, the *Gesamtkunstwerk* became the enemy of another imperative within modernism, that of "medium-specificity," which defined each art precisely in its difference from all the others. Although the notion of the *Gesamtkunstwerk* now seems archaic, it has hardly disappeared: reborn in happenings and other performances after World War II, it lived on in some spectacles of Nouveau Réalisme and Pop art, and has found a resurgence in much Installation art today.

Gestalt psychology

Emerging in the thirties in the work of Wolfgang Köhler and Kurt Koffka, Gestalt psychology was born as a refutation of Behaviorism, then the reigning theory of human mental development. Behaviorists pictured human and animal behavior as a series of learned, automatic responses to repeated stimuli (such as the bell accompanying the food provided a dog, then triggering salivation in the dog [stimulus/response] even when no food accompanies it). This view of the human condition as entirely passive and, worse, as entirely open to vicious training, worried the Gestaltists, who theorized activity within the human subject—the activity necessary to understanding and responding creatively to its environment. Focusing on the perceptual apparatus with which every human subject is endowed, the Gestaltists refused to grant a merely empiricist view of perception, in which the human eye forms a picture of the world by passively internalizing the visual stimuli that fall onto its retinal field. Instead, the Gestaltists argued that even from infancy the human observer is mastering that field by making inferences in which elements of the retinal pattern are associated with one another to form a "figure," everything around that figure being constituted as a "ground" or background. This actively constituted figure was called a gestalt, or form, which means, in addition, a force of hanging together, for which the Gestaltists' term was "praegnanz." Given the period when Gestalt psychology developed, it is clear that the rise of fascism lent urgency to its teaching.

grapheme
In normal usage, a grapheme is the smallest unit of written language, an element of writing that cannot be decomposed into smaller, meaningful units. Even before it gets down to the job of depicting anything, every linear deposit associates itself to another world of drawing or meaning, whether that be the wooden line of the mechanical draftsman, or the flowing mark of the comic-book illustrator, or the simpering contours of the advertisement illustrator. This associative identification is the work of the grapheme, or the cursive mark within which all drawing is formed.

Hegelianism
This shorthand is intended to signal some of the ideas of Georg Wilhelm Friedrich Hegel (1770–1831), the greatest philosopher of the early nineteenth century. Still important to many artists and critics a century later, Hegel argued that history proceeds in dialectical stages, through contradiction, in a steady progress of *thesis*, *antithesis*, and *synthesis* toward the self-consciousness of *Geist* (Mind or Spirit). For Hegel all aspects of society and culture participate in this march of Spirit toward freedom, and are to be judged according to their contributions to its development. In his scheme, then, there is a natural hierarchy in the arts, from the most material to the most spiritual, from architecture through sculpture and painting (equally based and refined), to poetry and music, all of which culminate in the pure reflections of philosophy. This idealism, with its assurance of artistic refinement and cultural progress, influenced many modernists, especially abstract painters such as Kazimir Malevich and Piet Mondrian, who harbored transcendental aspirations.

hegemony/hegemonic
A term in that appears in the writings of both Lenin and Mao, hegemony is most associated with the thought of the Italian Marxist Antonio Gramsci. In his *Prison Notebooks*, written while jailed by the Fascists, Gramsci argued that modern power is not limited to direct political rule but also operates through an indirect system of social institutions and cultural discourses that promote the ideology of the ruling classes as natural, normal, commonsensical, everyday. Such discursive power might seem more benign than direct subjugation, but it is also more subtle, and opposition to it must be rethought accordingly: "revolution" consists, then, not only in the transfer of control over politics and economics, but also in the transformation of forms of consciousness and experience. In this redefinition of politics as a struggle for hegemony, art and culture gain in importance; they are no longer seen as "superstructural" effects of the economy alone. The revision implies—at times romantically—that political change can be effected through critical interventions into art and culture.

hermeneutics
Derived from the Greek word meaning "to interpret," hermeneutics referred at first to the exegesis of The Bible considered as a historically sedimented text that is not to be read literally. By extension, hermeneutics has come to designate any method of interpretation that seeks the meaning of a text beyond its letter. We owe to the German philosopher Wilhelm Dilthey, at the end of the nineteenth century, the first investigation of the relationship between history as a scholarly practice and hermeneutics. Arguing that there is a radical difference between the human sciences, whose facts can be apprehended only through interpretation, and the natural sciences, whose facts can be empirically verified, he directly contradicted the positivist view according to which the ideal model of knowledge is physics. Dilthey's investigation of history, his analysis of how facts are deemed historical and are causally linked, led him to the formulation of what he called the "hermeneutic circle": in order to interpret a document we need to have a prior understanding not only of its whole but also of the culture to which it belongs (or of the genre of which it is only an example, or of the intention of its author), yet our understanding of this larger context depends upon our knowledge of similar documents.

iconic
The American philosopher Charles Sanders Peirce, anxious to analyze the activity of signs, felt the need to separate the profusion of signs into a manageable number of related types. The three kinds he isolated for this purpose were: symbols, icons, and indexes. Arguing that each of these types bore a different relation to its referent (or the thing for which it stood), he taught that symbols have a purely conventional (or agreed upon) relation, for which an example would be the words of a language; indexes, on the other hand, have a causal relationship, since they are the precipitates or traces of an engendering cause, the way footprints in the sand or broken branches in the forest are traces of the being that passed by; thirdly, the icon's relation is neither causal nor conventional but resemblant; it looks like its referent either by sharing its shape (the way figures on a map do) or registering its image (the way photographs do). The problem for this tidy semiology (or study of sign-types) is that signs can be mixed rather than pure; photographs are both icons and indexes; and pronouns are both symbols and indexes (the referent of the pronoun "I" being caused by the source of utterance—the speaker—within the flow of speech).

iconography
This approach to the study of images and objects focuses on questions of *meaning* (more than, say, matters of form, style, etc.), for which it often refers to source texts found outside the art work. The term is most associated with the work of the German-born art historian Erwin Panofsky (1892–1968), who proposed iconography as the basic operation of art history soon after his departure from Nazi Germany for the United States in the early thirties. (In those initial years of the academic discipline, iconography offered the advantage of a technique that could be taught and reproduced—professionalized.) Panofsky proposed three levels of meaning within art: "primary or natural subject matter," which can be treated by "a pre-iconographical description" of the work; "secondary or conventional subject matter," which can be related to known themes in the culture at large (this is the work of iconography proper); and "intrinsic meaning or content," which involves "the basic attitude of a nation, a period, a class, a religious or philosophical persuasion—qualified by one personality and condensed into one work" (Panofsky called this level, which recalls the notion of *Kunstwollen*, "iconology"). Iconographic analysis is suited to ancient, medieval, and Renaissance art and architecture, informed as they are by classical mythology and Christian doctrine, more than to modern practices, which often challenged the presumption of an illustrational relation between image and text in different ways (e.g., through abstraction, chance, found or readymade objects).

ideograph
Discarded by most contemporary linguists, who deem it improper, this term was coined in the nineteenth century to designate a symbol directly representing an idea rather than its name (the Chinese characters and Egyptian hieroglyphs were long thought to be pure ideographs, or ideograms, or even pictograms, but we know now that their complex formation is far from entailing the simple one-to-one connection between an idea and its figurative expression). The word ideograph was appropriated by Barnett Newman in 1947 as a means to elucidate the mode of signification that he and fellow artists such as Mark Rothko or Clyfford Still wanted to implement in their art. Opposed to both the model provided by Surrealism (and its symbology derived from Freud) and that offered by abstract art (which he discarded as formalist exercise), Newman looked instead toward the art of Northwest Coast Indians, which he characterized as "ideographic pictures." For the Kwakiutl artist, wrote Newman, "a shape was a living thing, a vehicle for an abstract thought-complex, a carrier of the awesome feelings he felt before the terror of the unknowable." Although ideograph continued to be used by some critics with regard to the pseudo-glyphic marks that filled the canvases of his friend Adolph Gottlieb until the mid-fifties, it disappeared from Newman's vocabulary almost as soon as he had celebrated it. Not only did he realize that a truly ideographic mode of communication would require the elaboration of a code shared by producers and receivers of messages, but by 1948 he no longer wished to represent "pure ideas" in his art, nor did he think it possible.

informe

Georges Bataille, the challenger to André Breton's hold over the Surrealist group of artists and writers, formed his own journal during the twenties and thirties, which he called *Documents*. This journal published a dictionary of definitions for terms such as "spit," "eye," and *informe* (or formless). *Informe*, he wrote, could not have a definition; it could only have a job, since its work is to destroy the universe of classifications by "declassing" language, or bringing it down in the world. In this way, he said, words would no longer resemble anything but would, formless, operate like a spider or spit. Alberto Giacometti, operating in the mode of formlessness, would blur the differences between male and female (on which the concept of gender depends) in a work like *Suspended Ball*.

intertext

In the definition for DIALOGISM, Bakhtin's concept of dialogue was shown to have modified the picture of the structuralist utterance to show how the sender's message is always already affected by the receiver's imagined response. A further modification of that diagram concerns the channel of emission and reception, which the structuralists labeled "contact," as though it were the telegraph wire opened by the utterance. Bakhtin relabeled this channel "intertext" since it is not the neutral connection of "contact" but the universe of associational relationships figured forth by the sender him/herself.

isotropic

Used in physics, this term means "exhibiting the same physical properties in all directions." A body of pure water, for example, is isotropic. The notion has often been used by modernist architects, from the twenties on, to express their conception of space as nonhierarchical, and their desire to create buildings that would have no center nor privileged point (they often drew in isometric projection, a mode of representation in which each of the three directions of space are equally foreshortened). It has also been applied to Jackson Pollock's allover drip paintings.

kitsch

Kitsch is a form of dissembling the nature of the material of which an object is made, a form that is largely a result of industrial production. Thus when the silversmith no longer works his metal by hand into the extrusions and relief that his technique suggests, and the metal is merely stamped by a "die" cut to imprint it, those forms are no longer conceived as respecting the metal's natural resistance to stress, but are made to mimic other patterns, such as floral motifs or the grooves of Ionic columns. It is this aping that came to be called kitsch and that Clement Greenberg named as the natural enemy of the avant-garde, in his "Avant-Garde and Kitsch" (1939). A more violent definition was proposed by Milan Kundera in his novel *The Unbearable Lightness of Being*, when he spoke of kitsch's transformation of disgust into universal approval and thus its dissimulation of the presence, in human life, of shit. Kitsch is thus the witless embrace of cliché as a defense against the weight of human reality. Because of this defense, he writes, "human existence loses its dimensions and becomes unbearably light."

Kunstwollen

A concept developed by the Viennese art historian Alois Riegl, *Kunstwollen* is usually translated as "artistic volition" or "artistic will," and it proposes, in Hegelian fashion, that a distinctive will-to-form, at once spiritual and aesthetic in nature, permeates all aspects of a given culture and/or period—from "low" crafts like textiles (Riegl worked as a curator in the Austrian Museum of Applied Arts) to "high" arts like easel painting. Unlike Hegel, however, Riegl argued that none of these forms or epochs should be denigrated, and his own work concentrated on practices and periods that were long undervalued, such as Baroque group portraiture and "the late Roman art industry." Pitched against the theories of architect Gottfried Semper (1803–79), who privileged the positive roles of material, technique, and function, the idealism of *Kunstwollen*—the implication that one will-to-form animates all products of a period—was attractive to some artists in the early twentieth century, especially ones involved in the Viennese Secession, whose motto encapsulated the *Kunstwollen* idea: "To each Age its Art, to Art its Freedom."

logocentrism/logocentric

In his doctoral dissertation, published as *Speech and Phenomena* (1973), the French philosopher Jacques Derrida examined Edmund Husserl's theory of language, which privileges speech over all other secondary transmission of meaning, such as writing or even memory. Husserl insisted that meaning must be immediate to the speaker, resonating inside his brain even as he or she produces and utters it. All secondary forms drive a wedge into this immediacy, either forcing the meaning to come after its conception—a temporal distancing that Derrida called "deferral,"—or traducing the meaning by differing from it. Derrida's term for this double betrayal is *différance* (spelled with an "a" to make its written form necessary to its reception). Husserl's refusal of writing in the name of speech, or *logos* (here meaning the "living presence" of the word), Derrida termed logocentrism, the ideology of *logos* and the condemnation of the GRAPHEME.

matrix

The gestalt, or figure, depends on its distinctness from its ground. This distinction brings with it the assumption that every figure is separate both from its neighbor and the space in which it exists. In thinking about this order of the visual, the French philosopher Jean-François Lyotard constructed a third possibility, which he called "matrix", to describe a spatiality that is not consistent with the coordinates of external space, and from which the intervals and differences that make the external world recognizable and observable as objects are excluded. As with Freud's conception of the unconscious, the matrix contains incompatible figures that all occupy the same place at the same time, at war both with each other and with conscious experience. The matrix could, thus, be another avatar of George Bataille's concept of the *INFORME*, or formless.

metonym/metonymy/metonymic

A figure of speech by which a concept is expressed through a term referring to another concept that is existentially related to it. The most common form of metonymy is synecdoche, where a part stands for the whole (as in "sail" standing for "ship"), or the whole for a part (as in "China is losing" standing for "the Chinese soccer team is losing"). It was the Russian linguist and poetician Roman Jakobson who established metonymy as one of the two main axes of language (the other being metaphor), which he aligned to Ferdinand de Saussure's opposition of SYNTAGM and PARADIGM, as well as to Freud's opposition of DISPLACEMENT and CONDENSATION. Although he later admitted that the line of demarcation between metonymy and metaphor is sometime loose, Jakobson had recourse to these two concepts throughout his oeuvre about a vast array of phenomena (identifying Surrealism with metaphor and Cubist or Dadaist collage with metonymy, for example). His most explicit elaboration of the opposition between these two axes figures in his study of aphasia (or the incapacity to communicate linguistically), in which he distinguished two kinds of troubles: a patient whose metonymic function is affected cannot combine linguistic terms and construct propositions, while a patient whose metaphoric function is affected cannot choose between words nor relate any homonyms or synonyms.

mimesis/mimetic

The Greek word for "imitation," mimesis comes from the assumption that the imitative double must reproduce a single or simple object that comes before it, which is then duplicated by imitation. In his important essay "The Double Session" (1981), Jacques Derrida questions this traditional concept of representation as imitation by introducing Stéphane Mallarmé's reverie called "Mimique," in which "the false appearance of the present" is used to refer to a mime's performance of ideas that refer to no possible object, such as "she died laughing": a commonplace expression that names something impossible. In this way the mime does not imitate but rather initiates something. As Mallarmé expresses, "The scene illustrates but the idea, not any actual action, in a hymen tainted with vice yet sacred, between desire and fulfillment, perpetration and remembrance: here anticipating, there recalling, in the future, in the past, under the false appearance of a present."

objet trouvé

Along with the readymade, the construction, and the assemblage, the *objet trouvé* or "found object" is a critical alternative to traditional sculpture based in the idealist modeling of the human figure. As practiced by such Surrealists as André Breton and Salvador Dalí, the found object is best defined in contradistinction to the device closest to it in character, the readymade. First proposed by Marcel Duchamp, the readymade is an everyday product of industrial manufacture—a bicycle wheel, a bottlerack, a urinal—that, repositioned as art, questions basic assumptions about art and artist; the readymade tends to be anonymous, detached from subjectivity and sexuality, with little or no sign of human labor. Not so the found object, at least in the hands of the Surrealists, who were drawn to old and odd things, often found in marginal stalls or flea markets, that spoke to a repressed desire within the artist and/or a surpassed mode of production within the society at large. One such object that constellated both kinds of enigmatic impulse was "the slipper-spoon" that Breton found one day in a flea market on the Paris outskirts (he recounts the anecdote in *Mad Love* [1937]). A wooden utensil, of peasant craft, carved with a little boot as its base, the spoon was an outmoded thing that Breton took as a sign of past desire and future love.

Oedipus complex

A fundamental concept in Freudian psychoanalysis, the Oedipus complex is the web of longings, fears, and prohibitions that captivates the psychological life of the young child, male and female. Named after the Sophocles tragedy *Oedipus Rex*, the complex involves a sexual desire for the parent of the opposite sex and a death wish for the parent of the same sex. The complex is most intense from ages three to five, but returns, after the period of sexual latency, at puberty, when it is usually resolved by the choice of a sexual object beyond the family (though this choice can also carry forward the preferences developed within the complex—that is, a man who seeks his mother, a woman her father—in another guise). According to Freud, the son is forced out of the Oedipus complex through the threat of the father—often, literally or figuratively, the threat of castration. The daughter does not face this same threat, and so, for Freud, the Oedipus complex is not so definitively terminated for the girl. As one might expect, this notion interested the Surrealists, and it continues to provoke feminist artists and theorists.

ontology/ontological

Derived from the Greek words *ontos* ("being," as present participle of the verb "to be") and *logos* (study, discourse), ontology is a term invented in the seventeenth century to designate that part of philosophy pertaining to "being qua being," or to the "essence of being," which had constituted the most important part of metaphysics since Aristotle. By extension, the adjective "ontological" means "that which concerns the essence." Clement Greenberg's conception of the history of each art as a quest for its own essence is both a TELEOLOGICAL and an ontological argument.

paradigm/paradigmatic

Although Ferdinand de Saussure used only the adjective form "paradigmatic," the opposition between paradigm and SYNTAGM is central to his linguistics and by extension to SEMIOLOGY as well as to structuralism. Having established that in language "everything is based on relations," Saussure distinguished between two kinds or relations: syntagmatic relations concern the association of discrete linguistic units resulting in elements of discourse (a word like "reread" is a syntagm made of two semantic units, "re," meaning repetition, and "read"; a sentence like "God is good" is a syntagm made of three units); paradigmatic relations concern the associations that are made *in absentia* between each unit of the syntagm and other units belonging to the same system. The word "revolution," for example, "will unconsciously call to mind a host of other words": revolutionary and revolutionize, but also gyration, rotation, turnover, reorganization, as well as evolution, or even any other word ending with the suffix "tion," such as population or argumentation, or beginning with the prefix re, such as reread. The group of these possible associations, which are governed by specific rules (phonetic and/or semantic) but whose number is indeterminate and which can appear in any order (as opposed to the succession of units in a syntagm) is called a paradigm. In recent years, the term has acquired a new meaning in the field of history of sciences, where it was introduced by Thomas Kuhn in *The Structure of Scientific Revolutions*. Almost a synonym of Michel Foucault's concept of *episteme*, it designates the intellectual horizon of a science during a certain period, determining a threshold beyond which it cannot go unless it fundamentally shifts its tenets and methods (the Newtonian paradigm of physics, for example, was definitively superseded by the Einsteinian one).

performative/performativity

In his book *How to Do Things with Words*, the British philosopher John Langshaw Austin (1911–60) divides language into two modes: the constative and the performative, the first a description of things that the structural linguist Émile Benveniste called "narrative" (which uses, he reminds us, the third person and the historical past tense); the second, an enactment of things, as when a judge says "I sentence you to five years in jail," or a person says either "I do" (in a marriage ceremony) or "I promise," Benveniste calling this "discourse" (which uses the first and second person pronouns and the present tense).

phallogocentrism

This feminist coinage complicates the concept of LOGOCENTRISM, developed by the philosopher Jacques Derrida, with the concept of "the phallus," developed by the psychoanalyst Jacques Lacan. If "logocentrism" signifies the persistent privilege given in Western culture to speech, to the "self-presence" of the spoken word (as in the Word, or *logos*, of God), the prefix "phal" suggests that this privilege is supported by the symbolic power accorded, within this same tradition, to the phallus as the prime signifier of all difference—prime because it is taken to signify the fundamental difference of them all, the difference between the sexes. For feminist artists and theorists this privilege is an ideology, however ingrained it might be in subjective and cultural formation, and as such is subject to radical deconstruction.

phenomenology

In the sixties, translation made Maurice Merleau-Ponty's *Phenomenology of Perception* (1945) available to English-speaking artists, and produced a collective meditation on the way the spatial coordinates of vision determine the meaning of objects. Because the individual's body is lived in its orientation to space—its head above, its feet below, its front fundamentally different from a reverse side it cannot even see—that body effectuates a "preobjective" meaning that determines the gestalts the individual must form. Preobjective meaning is, of course, another way of naming abstraction; thus phenomenology was seen as a support for the idea of abstract art.

phoneme

A phoneme is the smallest distinctive unit of articulated speech, an atom of language. Phonemes are vocal sounds that cannot be decomposed into smaller units, but not every such vocal sound, even in articulated speech, is a phoneme. The aspirated sound that necessarily follows the "p" or the "t" in English, for example, is not a phoneme because it has no distinctive (differential) function. The same sound at the beginning of the word "hair" is a phoneme in that it differentiate this word from "heir," from which it is absent.

polysemy/polysemous/polysemic

The polysemy of a word (and by extension of any other kind of signs, including visual ones) is its quality of having several distinct significations. Polysemy is often substituted for *ambiguity,* whose connotation of vagueness it does not share. Many more words are polysemous or polysemic than one is usually aware of (as the consultation of any good dictionary reveals), a fact on which most puns are based.

positivism

It was the French philosopher Auguste Comte (1798–1857) who first used this term, or that of "positive philosophy," to characterize his doctrine as radically opposed to metaphysics. Instead of attempting to discover the essence of things, thought Comte, philosophy should repel all a priori principles and seek to provide a systematic synthesis of all observable (positive) facts. Based on sense-experience, Comte's empirical theory of knowledge stressed that there was no difference in principle between the methods of the social sciences and the physical sciences, a idea that was directly contradicted by Wilhelm Dilthey's discussion of the HERMENEUTIC circle. Although the philosophers and mathematicians of the Vienna Circle grouped around Rudolf Carnap (1891–1970) and Otto Neurath (1882–1945) in the wake of Ludwig Wittgenstein gave a sounder philosophical base to Comte's argument in their logical positivism, the general tenets of positivism have been decried by most thinkers—and certainly all art historians—valued by the writers of the present book.

postcolonial discourse
This interdisciplinary form of critique aims to deconstruct the colonial legacy embedded within Western representations, verbal, visual, and other. Eclectic in its theoretical sources, it draws on Marxist and Freudian methods, especially as inflected by Michel Foucault, Jacques Derrida, and Jacques Lacan; it also elaborates on modes of thought more anthropological in character, such as "subaltern studies" in India and "cultural studies" in Britain. Even as postcolonial discourse works over the cultural-political residues of colonialism, it also seeks to come to conceptual terms with a present in which the old markers of the colonial world—of centers and peripheries, metropoles and hinterlands, within a globe divided up into First, Second, and Third Worlds—are no longer so relevant. Postcolonial discourse was all but inaugurated by Edward Said with his *Orientalism* (1978), a critique of "the imaginary geography" of the Near East, and it was thereafter developed by Gayatri Spivak, Homi Bhabha, and many others.

referent
Within structural linguistics it was important to differentiate the idea to which a sign refers from the object it might name. This is because, as its founder, Ferdinand de Saussure, taught, "meaning is oppositive, relative, and negative." This means that meaning forms around oppositions, which the structuralists call "binaries" or "PARADIGMS," with the meaning of something depending on its contrast to what it is not; "high," for example, differentiating itself out from "low," or "black" from "white." The referent is this "relative and negative" result of opposition—not an object, but a concept.

semiology/semiotics
In his *Course in General Linguistics*, posthumously published in 1916, Ferdinand de Saussure envisioned a "science that studies the life of signs within society," which he called semiology (from the Greek *semeion*, sign). It would "show what constitutes signs, what laws govern them," and these laws would be applicable to linguistics, which it would include as the science of only one particular system of signs, language. At around the same time, and independently, the American philosopher Charles Sanders Peirce developed his own science of signs, which he called semiotics. "Semiology" and "semiotics" are often used interchangeably, though there are major differences between Saussure's enterprise and that of Peirce. Paradoxically, although Saussure stressed that linguistics was only a part of the future semiology, albeit a privileged one, this discipline modeled itself on linguistics when it developed in the postwar period, to the point that the structuralist author Roland Barthes was led in his *Elements of Semiology* (1964) to reverse Saussure's proposal and state that semiology was in fact depending upon linguistics. This assertion fueled, in turn, Jacques Derrida's criticism of semiology as a LOGOCENTRIC discipline. By contrast, Peirce's semiotics, which consists largely of a TAXONOMY of signs from the point of view of their mode of reference, remained much less dependent upon the linguistic model. Peirce distinguished three categories of signs: the *symbol*, in which the relation between the sign and its referent is arbitrary; the *index*, in which this relation is determined by contiguity or co-presence (a footprint in the sand is an *indexical sign* of a foot, smoke an *indexical sign* of fire, etc.); the *icon*, in which this relation is characterized by resemblance (a painted portrait). These categories are somewhat porous (a photograph is both an index and an icon, for example), and although most linguistic signs are *symbols*, certain categories of words are *indexical signs* (the signification of these words, called *deictics,* change according to their context: "I," "you," "now," "here," etc.), while others, such as onomatopoeias (the moo of a cow, the cock-a-doodle-do of a rooster) are *iconic signs*.

signified/signifier
In his desire to stress the immateriality of the referent, Saussure divided the sign into two parts, one the conceptual domain of the signified, or meaning, the other the material domain of the signifier, or signifying deposit, whether written or auditory.

simulacrum/a
A term in ancient philosophy, a simulacrum is a representation that is not necessarily tied to an object in the world. As a copy without an "original"—in the double sense of both a physical referent and a first version—the simulacrum is often used, in cultural criticism, to describe the status of the image in a society of SPECTACLE, of mass-mediated consumerism. So too, in poststructuralist theory, the simulacrum is called upon to question the Platonic order of representation that adjudicates between "good" and "bad" copies according to their relative truth, or apparent verisimilitude, to models in (or, in Plato, *beyond*) the world. One finds this challenge intermittently posed in twentieth-century art, for example, in the fantastic paintings of the René Magritte and in the serial silkscreens of Andy Warhol—images that, even as they appear to be representations, dissolve the truth-claims of most representations. Indeed, the simulacrum is a crucial concept in the understanding of both Surrealist and Pop art, as attested by important texts on these subjects by Gilles Deleuze, Michel Foucault, Roland Barthes, and Jean Baudrillard.

spectacle
Developed in critical debates within the radical European movement the Situationist International (1957–72), "the spectacle" is used to signal a new stage of advanced capitalism, especially evident in the reconstruction period after World II, in which consumption, leisure, and the image (or SIMULACRUM) became more important than ever before in the economies of social and political life. For the lead figure of Situationism, Guy Debord, "the spectacle" is the terrain of new forms of power but, as such, of new strategies of subversion as well, which the Situationists worked both to theorize and to practice. Taken with Marxist notions of "FETISHISM" and "reification," Debord argued in *The Society of the Spectacle* (1967) that the commodity and the image had become structurally one ("the spectacle is capital," he wrote in a famous line, "accumulated to the point where it becomes image"), and that, as a result, a qualitative leap in control had occurred, one that, through consumption, renders its subjects politically passive and socially isolated. The Situationist hope remains that, if power continues to live by the spectacle, it might still be challenged there as well.

sublimation
Within psychoanalysis sublimation remains an elusive concept, never precisely defined by Freud or any of his followers. It concerns the diversion of instincts from sexual to nonsexual aims; these drives are "sublimated"—at once refined and rechanneled—in the pursuit of goals that are more valued, or at least less disruptive, than sexual activity in the society at large: goals of intellect and art (the ones underscored by Freud) but also of law, sport, entertainment, and so on. The energy for this work remains sexual, but the aims are social; indeed, for Freud there is no civilization without sublimation (not to mention repression). However, no firm line exists between the erotic and the aesthetic; and some artists in the twentieth century—Duchamp most famously—liked to point to overlaps between the two. Other artists (e.g., other Dadaists) sought, more aggressively, to reverse the process of sublimation altogether, to break open aesthetic forms to libidinal energies—a strategy sometimes discussed as "DESUBLIMATION."

Symbolic, the
This term has a specific meaning in the psychoanalytic thought of Jacques Lacan that must be distinguished from its general use. In his controversial thought "the Symbolic" represents all phenomena of the psyche that are

structured like a language, not, say, formed as images (he terms this adjacent realm of experience "the Imaginary"); such phenomena include, in part, dreams and symptoms (see CONDENSATION and DISPLACEMENT). In effect, Lacan reread the Freudian conception of the unconscious through the structural linguistics of Ferdinand de Saussure and Roman Jakobson (neither of whom Freud could have known). At the same time Lacan conveyed, through the term "the Symbolic," that these linguistic operations of the unconscious are also at work in the social order at large (here he was influenced by his contemporary, the anthropologist Claude Lévi-Strauss): the human subject is inserted into society as into language, and vice versa. In this sense "the Symbolic" also stands for an entire system of identifications and prohibitions—of laws—that each of us must internalize to become functional social beings at all. According to Lacan, our difficulties with this order are often expressed through neuroses; any outright denial of this order is tantamount to psychosis. Suggestive as this model is to some artists and many theorists, it can also project a profoundly conservative attitude to the social order, which is made to appear absolute.

synchronic
Trained as a comparativist historian of language, the founder of structural linguistics Ferdinand de Saussure realized that in order to study the essential structure of language (at least that common to all Indo-European languages), he had to ignore historical developments and examine the cross-section of a language at any given time, past or present, much as a biologist looks at some tissue under a microscope in order to study its cellular structure. This hypothetical cross-section is called synchronic because all its elements are frozen in time. The opposite of synchronic, in Saussure's terminology, is DIACHRONIC.

syncretism
Derived from a Greek word meaning "union of all Cretans," this term was first coined to characterize the work of Proclus (CE 410–485), the last major philosopher of ancient Greece, who attempted a synthesis of all past philosophies and scientific doctrines. Although it did not have any negative connotations at first, and it can still be used in a positive sense, this word is now most commonly used to describe any incoherent combination of contradictory doctrines or systems.

synecdoche
Speech is understood either as literal or figurative, the figures of speech swerving away from the literal names into imagistic relations for things. In *The New Science* (1725), the Italian philosopher Giambattista Vico wondered how knowledge might be acquired if it were not revealed to man by God. Imagining a caveman, he assumed that his only means to understanding was a comparison of the unknown with the known, which is the savage's own body. Hearing thunder, the savage likens it to what he knows and decides it is a loud voice, this act of likening constituting the poetic form of metaphor. Next the savage wonders about its cause and imagines a very large body producing the voice, this body being, he thinks, that of a god, the notion of cause then constituting the poetic form of METONYMY. Finally the savage wonders why the god should emit the noise and decides this is because the god is angry, the cause or conceptual foundation, constituting for Vico the poetic form of synecdoche. Unsurprisingly, Vico called this progression from the unknown to the known "poetic knowledge." It is poetic knowledge that in turn structures Michel Foucault's influential study of periods of Western historical development, *The Order of Things* (1970), which he identified as separate epistemes. The Renaissance, he taught, imagines knowledge as based on resemblance, or metaphor. The seventeenth and eighteenth centuries, which he called the Classical period, imagines it as identity and difference, or metonymy; while the nineteenth century, during which the modern disciplines are born, imagines it as analogy and succession, or synecdoche.

syntagm/syntagmatic
First defined by Ferdinand de Saussure as constituting one of the most important elements of language, a syntagm is any succession in the spoken chain of a minimum of two semantic units that cannot be replaced or whose order cannot be changed without changing the meaning or the intelligibility of the utterance. Syntagms can be words ("reread" is made of two units, "re" and "read"), phrases ("human life") or whole sentences ("God is good"). Syntagmatic relations, which he opposed to PARADIGMATIC ones, were particularly important for Saussure, whose primary interest was language as a social fact, in that in them the distinction between the collective and the individual use of language is particularly difficult to distinguish. The case is rather simple when it concerns colloquial syntagms (they belong to common use and thus cannot be changed), but the formation of new words (neologisms) is also governed by rules transmitted by tradition, and thus by common use. After Saussure, Roman Jakobson related METONYMY and metaphor, which he saw as the two main axes of language, respectively to Saussure's conception of syntagmatic and paradigmatic relations.

tachisme
A European toned-down version of Abstract Expressionism, *tachisme* (from the French *tache*, meaning "stain," "splash," or "mark") was also referred to as "lyrical abstraction." The main difference between *tachiste* works and their American counterparts is their modest scale and reliance upon the figurative tradition of landscape. Despite the interest expressed by several *tachiste* artists for the automatic method favored by Pollock, their art remained highly composed and as such dependent upon a Cubist conception of the picture as a harmonious totality. SEE *ART INFORMEL*

taxonomy
From the Greek word *taxis*, meaning "arrangement," taxonomy is the practice or principle of classification or grouping. When the eighteenth-century Swedish botanist Linnaeus drew up a graph as a way of sorting out the orders of living beings, he set the large categories (such as "animal") down one side of the table and called them *genus*, and the smaller ones (such as "dog," "cat," etc.) across the horizontal axis, calling them *species*. Such an inclusive graph is a taxonomy.

***telos*/teleology/teleological**
Telos means "goal" or "end" in Greek, and initially *teleology* designated the study of finality. The first major teleological argument, concluding from the regularities in the operations of nature that all things had a purpose in the universe, was elaborated in the Middle Ages as a proof of God's existence. It was then staunchly refuted during the Enlightenment, first by David Hume in his *Dialogues Concerning Natural Religion* of 1779, then by Immanuel Kant in his *Critique of Pure Reason* of 1781. Today the word teleology is used to characterize any theory presupposing or predicting that a process has an end (in both senses of ending and of purpose), or retroactively interpreting a process as geared toward its end. Darwin's theory of evolution, though attacked by the Church upon its inception, is today commonly recognized as teleological, as is Marx's conception of history.

trope
A trope is a figure of speech—a word, phrase, or expression that is used in a figurative way—usually for rhetorical effect. Giambattista Vico's "poetic knowledge" (see SYNECDOCHE) depends on language's figurative potential, its swerve away from the literal into a set of comparisons and contrasts. This swerve is an example of a "trope," the most common of which is metaphor.

zaum
An abbreviation of the Russian word *zaumnoe* (transrational), the term was coined in 1913 by the futurists Aleksei Kruchenikh and Velemir Khlebnikov to refer to the new poetic language they were inventing, replete with new, nonsensical words and nonrepresentational sounds or, in its written form, groups of letters. Arguing that the word-as-such directly affects our senses and has a meaning independently of its ascribed signification, they sought to bypass the rational use of language and underscored the phonetic materiality of linguistic utterances.

further reading

GENERAL: SURVEY AND SOURCE BOOKS

Michael Archer, *Art Since 1960* (London and New York: Thames & Hudson, 1997)

Herschel Chipp, *Theories of Modern Art: A Source Book by Artists and Critics* (Berkeley: University of California Press, 1968)

Francis Frascina and Jonathan Harris (eds), *Art in Modern Culture: An Anthology of Critical Texts* (London: Phaidon Press, 1992)

Francis Frascina and Jonathan Harris (eds), *Modern Art and Modernism: A Critical Anthology* (New York: Harper and Row, 1982)

George Heard Hamilton, *Painting and Sculpture in Europe, 1880–1940* (New Haven and London: Yale University Press, 1993)

Charles Harrison, Francis Frascina, and Gill Perry, *Primitivism, Cubism, Abstraction: The Early Twentieth Century* (New Haven and London: Yale University Press, 1993)

Charles Harrison and Paul Wood (eds), *Art in Theory, 1900–2000: An Anthology of Changing Ideas* (Cambridge: Blackwell, 2003)

David Joselit, *American Art Since 1945* (London: Thames & Hudson, 2003)

Rosalind Krauss, *Passages in Modern Sculpture* (New York: Viking Press, 1977; reprint Cambridge, Mass.: MIT Press, 1981)

Christopher Phillips, *Photography in the Modern Era: European Documents and Critical Writings, 1913–1940* (New York: Metropolitan Museum of Art/Aperture, 1989)

Alex Potts, *The Sculptural Imagination: Figurative, Modernist, Minimalist* (New Haven and London: Yale University Press, 2000)

Anne Rorimer, *New Art in the 60s and 70s: Redefining Reality* (London: Thames & Hudson, 2001)

Kristin Stiles and Peter Selz (eds), *Theories and Documents of Contemporary Art* (Berkeley: University of California Press, 1996)

Paul Wood et al., *Modernism in Dispute: Art Since the Forties* (New Haven and London: Yale University Press, 1993)

Paul Wood et al., *Realism, Rationalism, Surrealism: Art Between the Wars* (New Haven and London: Yale University Press, 1993)

GENERAL: AVANT-GARDE, MODERNISM, POSTMODERNISM

Serge Guilbaut, Benjamin H. D. Buchloh, and David Solkin (eds), *Modernism and Modernity* (Halifax: The Press of the Nova Scotia College of Art and Design, 1983)

Peter Bürger, *Theory of the Avant-Garde* (1974), trans. Michael Shaw (Minneapolis: University of Minnesota Press, 1984)

Douglas Crimp, "Pictures," *October*, no. 8, Spring 1979

Hal Foster (ed.), *Discussions in Contemporary Culture* (Seattle: Bay Press, 1987)

Hal Foster (ed.), *The Anti-Aesthetic: Essays on Postmodern Culture* (Seattle: Bay Press, 1983)

Serge Guilbaut (ed.), *Reconstructing Modernism* (Cambridge, Mass.: MIT Press, 1990)

Andreas Huyssen, *After the Great Divide: Modernism, Mass Culture, Postmodernism* (Bloomington: Indiana University Press, 1986)

Rosalind Krauss, *"A Voyage on the North Sea": Art in the Age of the Post-Medium Condition* (London: Thames & Hudson, 1999)

Craig Owens, "The Allegorical Impulse: Towards a Theory of Postmodernism," *October*, nos 12 and 13, Spring and Summer 1980

Brian Wallis (ed.), *Art After Modernism: Rethinking Representation* (New York: New Museum of Contemporary Art, 1994)

GENERAL: COLLECTED ESSAYS

Yve-Alain Bois, *Painting as Model* (Cambridge, Mass.: MIT Press, 1991)

Yve-Alain Bois and Rosalind Krauss, *Formless: A User's Guide* (New York: Zone Books, 1997)

Benjamin H. D. Buchloh, *Neo-Avantgarde and Culture Industry: Essays on European and American Art from 1955 to 1975* (Cambridge, Mass.: MIT Press, 2000)

T. J. Clark, *Farewell to an Idea: Episodes from a History of Modernism* (New Haven and London: Yale University Press, 1999)

Thomas Crow, *Modern Art in the Common Culture* (New Haven and London: Yale University Press, 1996)

Thierry de Duve, *Kant after Duchamp* (Cambridge, Mass.: MIT Press, 1996)

Briony Fer, *On Abstract Art* (New Haven and London: Yale University Press, 1997)

Hal Foster, *Prosthetic Gods* (Cambridge, Mass.: MIT Press, 2004)

Hal Foster, *The Return of the Real: The Avant-Garde at the End of the Century* (Cambridge, Mass.: MIT Press, 1996)

Michael Fried, *Art and Objecthood* (Chicago: University of Chicago Press, 1998)

Clement Greenberg, *Art and Culture: Critical Essays* (Boston: Beacon Press, 1961)

Clement Greenberg, *The Collected Essays and Criticism*, vols 1 and 4, ed. John O'Brian (Chicago: University of Chicago Press, 1986 and 1993)

Clement Greenberg, *Homemade Esthetics: Observations on Art and Taste* (Oxford: Oxford University Press, 1999)

Rosalind Krauss, *Bachelors* (Cambridge, Mass.: MIT Press, 1999)

Rosalind Krauss, *The Optical Unconscious* (Cambridge, Mass.: MIT Press, 1993)

Rosalind Krauss, *The Originality of the Avant-Garde and Other Modernist Myths* Cambridge, Mass.: MIT Press, 1985)

Meyer Schapiro, *Modern Art: 19th and 20th Century, Selected Papers, vol. 2* (New York: George Braziller, 1978)

Leo Steinberg, "Rodin," *Other Criteria: Confrontations with Twentieth-Century Art* (London, Oxford, and New York: Oxford University Press, 1972)

Anne M. Wagner, *Three Artists (Three Women): Georgia O'Keeffe, Lee Krasner, Eva Hesse* (Berkeley and Los Angeles: University of California Press, 1997)

Peter Wollen, *Raiding the Ice Box: Reflections on Twentieth-Century Culture* (London: Verso, 1993)

GENERAL: THEORY AND METHODOLOGY

Frederick Antal, *Classicism and Romanticism* (London: Routledge & Kegan Paul, 1966)

Roland Barthes, *Critical Essays*, trans. Richard Howard (Evanston: Northwestern University Press, 1972)

Roland Barthes, *Image, Music, Text*, trans. Stephen Heath (New York: Hill and Wang, 1977)

Roland Barthes, *Mythologies* (1957), trans. Annette Lavers (New York: Noonday Press, 1972)

Leo Bersani, *The Freudian Body: Psychoanalysis and Art* (New York: Columbia University Press, 1986)

T. J. Clark, *Image of the People: Gustave Courbet and the Second French Republic, 1848–1851* (London: Thames & Hudson, 1973)

T. J. Clark, *The Absolute Bourgeois: Artists and Politics in France, 1848–1851* (London: Thames & Hudson, 1973)

T. J. Clark, *The Painting of Modern Life: Paris in the Art of Manet and his Followers* (London: Thames & Hudson, 1984)

Thomas Crow, *Painters and Public Life in 18th-Century Paris* (New Haven and London: Yale University Press, 1985).

Thomas Crow, *The Intelligence of Art* (Chapel Hill, N.C.: University of North Carolina Press, 1999)

Jacques Derrida, *Of Grammatology*, trans. Gayatri Spivak (Baltimore: The Johns Hopkins University Press, 1976)

Jacques Derrida, "Parergon," *The Truth in Painting*, trans. Geoff Bennington (Chicago and London: University of Chicago Press, 1987)

Jacques Derrida, "The Double Session," *Dissemination*, trans. Barbara Johnson (Chicago and London: University of Chicago Press, 1981)

Michel Foucault, *The Archaeology of Knowledge* (Paris: Gallimard, 1969; translation London: Tavistock Publications; and New York: Pantheon, 1972)

Michel Foucault, "What is an Author?", *Language, Counter-Memory, Practice*, trans. D. Bouchard and S. Simon (Ithaca, N.Y.: Cornell University Press, 1977)

Sigmund Freud, *Art and Literature*, trans. James Strachey (London: Penguin, 1985)

Fredric Jameson, *The Prison-House of Language: A Critical Account of Structuralism and Russian Formalism* (Princeton: Princeton University Press, 1972)

Richard Kearney and David Rasmussen, *Continental Aesthetics—Romaticism to Postmodernism: An Anthology* (Malden, Mass. and Oxford: Blackwell, 2001)

Sarah Kofman, *The Childhood of Art: An Interpretation of Freud's Aesthetics*, trans. Winifred Woodhull (New York: Columbia University Press, 1988)

Jean Laplanche and J.-B. Pontalis, *The Language of Psychoanalysis*, trans. Donald Nicholson-Smith (New York: W. W. Norton, 1973)

Thomas Levin, "Walter Benjamin and the Theory of Art History," *October*, no. 47, Winter 1988

Jacqueline Rose, *Sexuality in the Field of Vision* (London: Verso, 1986)

Nicos Hadjinicolaou, *Art History and Class Struggle* (London: Pluto Press, 1978)

Arnold Hauser, *The Social History of Art* (1951), four volumes (London: Routledge, 1999)

Fredric Jameson (ed.), *Aesthetics and Politics* (London: New Left Books, 1977)

Francis Klingender, *Art and the Industrial Revolution* (1947) (London: Paladin Press, 1975)

Ferdinand de Saussure, *Course in General Linguistics*, trans. Wade Baskin (New York: McGraw-Hill, 1966)

Meyer Schapiro, *Theory and Philosophy of Art: Style, Artist, and Society, Selected Papers, vol. 4* (New York: George Braziller, 1994)

MATISSE AND FAUVISM

Alfred H. Barr, Jr., *Matisse: His Art and His Public* (New York: Museum of Modern Art, 1951)

Roger Benjamin, *Matisse's "Notes of a Painter": Criticism, Theory, and Context, 1891–1908*, (Ann Arbor: UMI Research Press, 1987)

Yve-Alain Bois, "Matisse and Arche-drawing," *Painting as Model* (Cambridge, Mass.: MIT Press, 1990)

Yve-Alain Bois, *Matisse and Picasso* (New York: Flammarion Press, 1998)

Yve-Alain Bois, "On Matisse: The Blinding," *October*, no. 68, Spring 1994

John Elderfield, "Describing Matisse," *Henri Matisse: A Retrospective* (New York: Museum of Modern Art, 1992)

John Elderfield, *The "Wild Beasts": Fauvism and its Affinities* (New York: Museum of Modern Art, 1976)

Jack D. Flam, (ed.), *Matisse on Art* (Berkeley and Los Angeles: University of California Press, 1995)

Jack D. Flam, *Matisse: The Man and His Art, 1869–1918* (Ithaca, N.Y. and London: Cornell University Press, 1986)

Judi Freeman (ed.), *The Fauve Landscape* (New York: Abbeville Press, 1990)

Lawrence Gowing, *Matisse* (London: Thames & Hudson, 1976)

James D. Herbert, *Fauve Painting: The Making of Cultural Politics* (New Haven and London: Yale University Press, 1992)

John Klein, *Matisse Portraits* (New Haven and London: Yale University Press, 2001)

John O'Brian, *Ruthless Hedonism: The American Reception of Matisse* (Chicago and London: Chicago University Press, 1999)

Margaret Werth, *The Joy of Life: The Idyllic in French Art, Circa 1900* (Berkeley: University of California Press, 2002)

Alastair Wright, *Matisse and the Subject of Modernism* (Princeton: Princeton University Press, 2004)

PRIMITIVISM

James Clifford, "Histories of the Tribal and the Modern," *The Predicament of Culture* (Cambridge, Mass.: Harvard University Press, 1988)

Hal Foster, "The 'Primitive' Unconscious of Modern Art," *October*, no. 34, Fall 1985

Jack D. Flam (ed.), *Primitivism and Twentieth-Century Art: A Documentary History* (Berkeley: University of California Press, 2003)

Robert Goldberg, *Primitivism in Modern Art* (1938) (New York: Vintage Books, 1967)

William Rubin (ed.), *"Primitivism" in 20th Century Art: Affinity of the Tribal and the Modern* (New York: Museum of Modern Art, 1984)

EXPRESSIONISM

Aesthetics and Politics: Debates between Ernst Bloch, Georg Lukács, Bertolt Brecht, Walter Benjamin, Theodor Adorno (London: New Left Review Books, 1977)

Stephanie Barron, *German Expressionism: Art and Society* (New York: Rizzoli, 1997)

Donald Gordon, *Expressionism: Art and Idea* (New Haven and London: Yale, 1987)

Donald Gordon, "On the Origin of the Word 'Expressionism'," *Journal of the Warburg and Courtauld Institutes*, vol. 29, 1966

Charles Haxthausen, "'A New Beauty': Ernst Ludwig Kirchner's Images of Berlin," in Charles Haxthausen and Heidrun Suhr (eds), *Berlin: Culture and Metropolis* (Minneapolis: University of Minnesota Press, 1990)

Yule Heibel, "They danced on Volcanoes: Kandinsky's Breakthrough to Abstraction, the German Avant-Garde and the Eve of the First World War," *Art History*, 12, September 1989

Siegfried Kracauer, *From Caligari to Hitler: A Psychological History of German Film* (Princeton: Princeton University Press, 1947)

Wassily Kandinsky, *Concerning the Spiritual in Art* (1912) (New York: Dover Publications, 1977)

Wassily Kandinsky and Franz Marc (eds), *The Blaue Reiter Almanac* (London: Thames & Hudson, 1974)

Carolyn Lanchner (ed.), *Paul Klee* (New York: Museum of Modern Art, 1987)

Jill Lloyd, *German Expressionism: Primitivism and Modernity* (New Haven and London: Yale University Press, 1991)

Rose-Carol Washton Long, *German Expressionism: Documents from the End of the Wilhelmine Empire to the Rise of National Socialism* (New York: Macmillan International, 1993)

Joan Weinstein, *The End of Expressionism: Art and the November Revolution in Germany, 1918–1919* (Chicago: University of Chicago Press, 1990)

O. K. Werckmeister, *The Making of Paul Klee's Career 1914–1920* (Chicago and London: Chicago University Press, 1988)

CUBISM AND PICASSO

Alfred H. Barr, Jr., *Cubism and Abstract Art* (New York: Museum of Modern Art, 1936)

Yve-Alain Bois, "Kahnweiler's Lesson", *Painting as Model* (Cambridge, Mass.: MIT Press, 1990)

Yve-Alain Bois, "The Semiology of Cubism," in Lynn Zelevansky (ed.), *Picasso and Braque: A Symposium* (New York: Museum of Modern Art, 1992)

David Cottington, *Cubism in the Shadow of War: The Avant-Garde and Politics in Paris 1905–1914* (New Haven and London: Yale University Press, 1998)

Lisa Florman, *Myth and Metamorphosis: Picasso's Classical Prints of the 1930s* (Cambridge, Mass.: MIT Press, 2000)

Edward Fry, *Cubism* (London: Thames & Hudson, 1966)

John Golding, *Cubism: A History and an Analysis, 1907–1914* (New York: G. Wittenborn, 1959)

Christopher Green, *Juan Gris* (New Haven and London: Yale University Press, 1992)

Christopher Green (ed.), *Picasso's Les Demoiselles d'Avignon* (Cambridge: Cambridge University Press, 2001)

Clement Greenberg, "The Pasted Paper Revolution" (1958), *The Collected Essays and Criticism*, vols 1 and 4, ed. John O'Brian (Chicago: University of Chicago Press, 1986 and 1993)

Daniel-Henry Kahnweiler, *The Rise of Cubism*, trans. Henry Aronson (New York: Wittenborn, Schultz, 1949)

Rosalind Krauss, "In the Name of Picasso," *The Originality of the Avant-Garde and Other Modernist Myths* (Cambridge, Mass.: MIT Press, 1985)

Rosalind Krauss, "Re-Presenting Picasso," *Art in America*, vol. 67, no. 10, December 1980

Rosalind Krauss, "The Motivation of the Sign," in Lynn Zelevansky (ed.), *Picasso and Braque: A Symposium* (New York: Museum of Modern Art, 1992)

Rosalind Krauss, *The Picasso Papers* (New York: Farrar, Straus & Giroux, 1998)

Fernand Léger, *Functions of Painting*, ed. Edward Fry (London: Thames & Hudson, 1973)

Patricia Leighten, *Re-Ordering the Universe: Picasso and Anarchism, 1897–1914* (Princeton: Princeton University Press, 1989)

Marilyn McCully (ed.), *A Picasso Anthology: Documents, Criticism, Reminiscences* (Princeton: Princeton University Press, 1982)

Christine Poggi, *In Defiance of Painting: Cubism, Futurism, and the Invention of Collage* (New Haven and London: Yale University Press, 1992)

Robert Rosenblum, *Cubism and Twentieth-Century Art* (New York: Harry N. Abrams, 1960, revised 1977)

William Rubin, "Cezannism and the Beginnings of Cubism," *Cezanne: The Late Work* (New York: Museum of Modern Art, 1977)

William Rubin, "From Narrative to Iconic: The Buried Allegory in *Bread and Fruitdish on a Table* and the Role of *Les Demoiselles d'Avignon*," *Art Bulletin*, vol. 65, December 1983

William Rubin, "Pablo and Georges and Leo and Bill," *Art in America*, vol. 67, March–April 1979

William Rubin, *Picasso and Braque: Pioneering Cubism* (New York: Museum of Modern Art, 1989)

William Rubin, "The Genesis of *Les Demoiselles d'Avignon*," *Studies in Modern Art* (special *Les Demoiselles d'Avignon* issue), Museum of Modern Art, New York, no. 3, 1994 (chronology by Judith Cousins and Hélène Seckel, critical anthology of early commentaries by Hélène Seckel)

Leo Steinberg, "Resisting Cezanne: Picasso's Three Women," *Art in America*, vol. 66, no. 6, November–December 1978

Leo Steinberg, "The Algerian Women and Picasso at Large," *Other Criteria: Confrontations with Twentieth-Century Art* (London, Oxford, and New York: Oxford University Press, 1972)

Leo Steinberg, "The Philosophical Brothel" (1972), second edition *October*, no. 44, Spring 1988

Leo Steinberg, "The Polemical Part," *Art in America*, vol. 67, March–April 1979

Jeffrey Weiss (ed.), *Picasso: The Cubist Portraits of Fernande Olivier* (Washington, D.C.: National Gallery of Art; and Princeton: Princeton University Press, 2003)

Lynn Zelevansky (ed.), *Picasso and Braque: A Symposium* (New York: Museum of Modern Art, 1992)

FUTURISM

Germano Celant, *Futurism and the International Avant-Garde* (Philadelphia: Philadelphia Museum of Art, 1980)

Anne Coffin Hanson, *The Futurist Imagination* (New Haven and London: Yale University Press, 1983)

Pontus Hulten (ed.), *Futurism and Futurisms* (New York: Abbeville Press; and London: Thames & Hudson, 1986)

Marianne W. Martin, *Futurist Art and Theory 1909–1915* (Oxford: Clarendon Press, 1968)

Marjorie Perloff, *The Futurist Moment: Avant-Garde, Avant Guerre, and the Language of Rupture* (Chicago: University of Chicago Press, 1986)

Apollonio Umbro (ed.), *Futurist Manifestoes* (London: Thames & Hudson, 1973)

DADA

Dawn Ades (ed.), *Dada and Surrealism Reviewed* (London: Arts Council of Great Britain, 1978)

Hugo Ball, *Flight Out of Time: A Dada Diary* (New York: Viking Press, 1974)

William Camfield, *Francis Picabia: His Art, Life, and Times* (Princeton: Princeton University Press, 1979)

Brigid Doherty, *Montage: The Body and the Work of Art in Dada, Brecht, and Benjamin* (Berkeley: University of California Press, 2004)

John Elderfield, *Kurt Schwitters* (London: Thames & Hudson, 1985)

Maud Lavin, *Cut with the Kitchen Knife: The Weimar Photomontages of Hannah Höch* (New Haven and London: Yale University Press, 1993)

Robert Motherwell, *The Dada Painters and Poets: An Anthology* (New York: Wittenborn, Schultz, 1951)

Francis Naumann, *New York Dada, 1915–1923* (New York: Abrams, 1994)

Anson Rabinbach, *In the Shadow of Catastrophe: German Intellectuals Between Apocalypse and Enlightenment* (Berkeley: University of California Press, 1997)

Hans Richter, *Dada: Art and Anti-Art* (New York: McGraw-Hill, 1965)

William S. Rubin, *Dada, Surrealism, and Their Heritage* (New York: Museum of Modern Art, 1968)

Richard Sheppard, *Modernism—Dada—Postmodernism* (Chicago: Northwestern University Press, 1999)

DUCHAMP

Martha Buskirk and Mignon Nixon (eds), *The Duchamp Effect* (Cambridge, Mass.: MIT Press, 1998)

Pierre Cabanne, *Dialogues with Duchamp* (New York: Da Capo Press, 1979)

Thierry de Duve, *Kant After Duchamp* (Cambridge, Mass.: MIT Press, 1996)

Thierry de Duve, *Pictorial Nominalism: On Marcel Duchamp's Passage from Painting to the Readymade* Minneapolis: University of Minnesota Press, 1991)

Thierry de Duve (ed.), *The Definitively Unfinished Marcel Duchamp* (Halifax: The Press of the Nova Scotia College of Art and Design, 1991)

Linda Dalrymple Henderson, *Duchamp in Context: Science and Technology in the Large Glass and Related Works* (Princeton: Princeton University Press, 1998)

David Joselit, *Infinite Regress: Marcel Duchamp, 1910–1914* (Cambridge, Mass.: MIT Press, 1998)

Rudolf Kuenzli and Francis M. Naumann (eds), *Marcel Duchamp: Artist of the Century* (Cambridge, Mass.: MIT Press, 1989)

Robert Lebel, *Marcel Duchamp*, trans. George Heard Hamilton (New York: Grove Press, 1959)

Molly Nesbit, *Their Common Sense* (London: Black Dog Publishing, 2001)

Arturo Schwarz, *Complete Works of Marcel Duchamp* (New York: Delano Greenridge Editions, 2000)

MONDRIAN AND DE STIJL

Carel Blotkamp, *Mondrian: The Art of Destruction* (New York: Harry N. Abrams, 1994)

Carel Blotkamp et al., *De Stijl: The Formative Years* (Cambridge, Mass.: MIT Press, 1986)

Yve-Alain Bois, "Mondrian and the Theory of Architecture," *Assemblage*, 4, October 1987)

Yve-Alain Bois, "The De Stijl Idea" and "Piet Mondrian: *New York City*," *Painting as Model* (Cambridge, Mass.: MIT Press, 1990)

Yve-Alain Bois, "The Iconoclast," in Angelica Rudenstine (ed.), *Piet Mondrian* (The Hague: Gemeentemuseum; Washington, D.C.: National Gallery of Art; and New York: Museum of Modern Art, 1994)

Harry Cooper, *Mondrian: The Transatlantic Paintings* (Cambridge, Mass.: Harvard University Art Museums, 2001)

Joop Joosten, "Mondrian: Between Cubism and Abstraction," *Piet Mondrian Centennial Exhibition* (New York: Guggenheim, 1971)

Annette Michelson, "De Stijl, It's Other Face: Abstraction and Cacophony, Or What Was the Matter with Hegel? *October*, no. 22, Fall 1982

Piet Mondrian, *The New Art—The New Life: The Collected Works of Piet Mondrian*, ed. and trans. Harry Holtzman and Martin S. James (Boston: G. K. Hall and Co., 1986)

Nancy Troy, *The De Stijl Environment* (Cambridge, Mass.: MIT Press, 1983)

RUSSIAN AVANT-GARDE, SUPREMATISM, AND CONSTRUCTIVISM

Troels Andersen, *Malevich* (Amsterdam: Stedelijk Museum, 1970)

Richard Andrews and Milena Kalinovska (eds), *Art into Life: Russian Constructivism 1914–32* (Seattle: Henry Art Gallery; and New York: Rizzoli, 1990)

Stephen Bann (ed.), *The Tradition of Constructivism* (London: Thames & Hudson, 1974)
Yve-Alain Bois, "El Lissitzky: Radical Reversibility," *Art in America*, vol. 76, no. 4, April 1988
John Bowlt (ed.), *Russian Art of the Avant-Garde: Theory and Criticism* (London: Thames & Hudson, 1988)
Benjamin H. D. Buchloh, "Cold War Constructivism" in Serge Guibaut (ed.), *Reconstructing Modernism* (Cambridge, Mass.: MIT Press, 1990)
Benjamin H. D. Buchloh, "From Faktura to Factography," *October*, no. 30, Fall 1984
Magdalena Dabrowski, Leah Dickerman, and Peter Galassi, *Aleksandr Rodchenko* (New York: Museum of Modern Art, 1998)
Charlotte Douglas, "Birth of a 'Royal Infant': Malevich and 'Victory Over the Sun'," *Art in America*, vol. 62, no. 2, March/April 1974
Matthew Drutt (ed.), *Kasimir Malevich: Suprematism* (New York: Guggenheim Museum, 2003)
Hal Foster, "Some Uses and Abuses of Russian Constructivism," *Art into Life: Russian Constructivism, 1914–1932* (Seattle: Henry Art Gallery; and New York: Rizzoli, 1990)
Hubertus Gassner, "Analytical Sequences," in David Elliot (ed.), *Rodchenko and the Arts of Revolutionary Russia* (New York: Pantheon, 1979)
Hubertus Gassner, "John Heartfield in the USSR," *John Heartfield* (New York: Museum of Modern Art, 1992)
Hubertus Gassner, "The Constructivists: Modernism on the Way to Modernization," *The Great Utopia* (New York: Guggenheim Museum, 1992)
Maria Gough, "In the Laboratory of Constructivism: Karl Ioganson's Cold Structures," *October*, no. 84, Spring 1998)
Maria Gough, "Tarabukin, Spengler, and the Art of Production," *October*, no. 93, Summer 2000
Camilla Gray, *The Great Experiment: Russian Art 1863–1922* (1962), republished as *The Russian Experiment in Art 1863–1922* (London: Thames & Hudson, 1986)
Selim O. Khan-Magomedov, *Rodchenko: The Complete Work* (Cambridge, Mass.: MIT Press, 1987)
Christina Kiaer, "Rodchenko in Paris," *October*, no. 75, Winter 1996
Alexei Kruchenykh, "Victory over the Sun," *Drama Review*, no. 15, Fall 1971
El Lissitzky, *El Lissitzky: Life, Letters, Texts*, ed. Sophie Lissitzky-Kuppers (London: Thames & Hudson, 1968)
Christina Lodder, *Russian Constructivism* (New Haven and London: Yale University Press, 1983)
Nancy Perloff and Brian Reed (eds), *Situating El Lissitzky: Vitebsk, Berlin, Moscow* (Los Angeles: Getty Research Institute, 2003)
Margit Rowell, "Vladimir Tatlin: Form/Faktura," *October, no.* 7, Winter 1978
Margit Rowell and Deborah Wye (eds), *The Russian Avant-Garde Book 1910–1934* (New York: Museum of Modern Art, 2002)
Margarita Tupitsyn, "From the Politics of Montage to the Montage of Politics: Soviet Practice, 1919 through 1937," in Matthew Teitelbaum (ed.), *Montage and Modern Life, 1919–1942* (Cambridge, Mass.: MIT Press, 1992)
Margarita Tupitsyn et al., *El Lissitzky—Beyond the Abstract Cabinet: Photography, Design, Collaboration* (New Haven and London: Yale University Press, 1999)
Larisa Zhadova, *Malevich: Suprematism and Revolution in Russian Art 1910–1930* (New York: Thames & Hudson, 1982)
Larisa Zhadova (ed.), *Tatlin* (New York: Rizzoli, 1988)

PURISM, PRECISIONISM, NEUE SACHLICHKEIT, AND THE RETURN TO ORDER
Gottfried Boehm, Ulrich Mosch, and Katharina Schmidt (eds), *Canto d'Amore: Classicism in Modern Art and Music, 1914–1945* (Basel: Kunstmuseum, 1996)
Benjamin H. D. Buchloh, "Figures of Authority, Ciphers of Regression: Notes on the Return of Representation in European Painting," *October*, no. 16, Spring 1981
Carol S. Eliel, *L'Esprit Nouveau: Purism in Paris 1918–1925* (Los Angeles: Los Angeles County Museum of Art: and New York: Abrams, 2001)
Romy Golan, *Modernity and Nostalgia: Art and Politics in France Between the Wars* (New Haven and London: Yale University Press, 1995)
Christopher Green, *Cubism and its Enemies: Modern Movements and Reaction in French Art, 1916–1928* (New Haven and London: Yale University Press, 1987)
Jeffrey Herf, *Reactionary Modernism: Technology, Culture, and Politics in Weimar and the Third Reich* (Cambridge, Mass.: MIT Press, 1990)
Anton Kaes, Martin Jay, and Edward Dimendberg (eds), *Weimar Republic Sourcebook* (Berkeley: University of California Press, 1994
Nina Rosenblatt, "Empathy and Anaesthesia: On the Origins of a French Machine Aesthetic," *Grey Room*, no. 2, Winter 2001
Kenneth Silver, *Esprit de Corps* (Princeton: Princeton University Press, 1989)
Terry Smith, *Making the Modern: Industry, Art, and Design in America* (Chicago: University of Chicago Press, 1993)

BAUHAUS
Herbert Bayer, Walter Gropius, and Ise Gropius, *Bauhaus 1919–1928* (New York: Museum of Modern Art, 1938)
Éva Forgács, *The Bauhaus Idea and Bauhaus Politics* (Budapest: Central European University Press, 1995)
Margaret Kentgens-Craig, *The Bauhuas and America: First Contacts 1919–1936* (Cambridge, Mass.: MIT Press, 1996)
Mary Emma Harris, *The Arts at Black Mountain College* (Cambridge, Mass.: MIT Press, 1987)
Margret Kentgens-Craig, *The Bauhaus and America: First Contacts 1919–1936*, trans. Lynette Widder (Cambridge, Mass.: MIT Press, 1999)
László Moholy-Nagy, *An Anthology*, ed. Richard Kostelanetz (New York: Da Capo Press, 1970)
László Moholy-Nagy, *Painting, Photography, Film* (1927), trans. Janet Seligman (Cambridge, Mass.: MIT Press, 1969)
László Moholy-Nagy, *The New Vision* (New York: Wittenborn, Schultz, 1947)
Frank Whitford, *Bauhaus* (New York: Thames & Hudson, 1984)
Frank Whitford (ed.), *The Bauhaus: Masters and Students by Themselves* (Woodstock, N.Y.: The Overlook Press, 1992)
Hans Wingler, *The Bauhaus: Weimar, Dessau, Berlin, Chicago* (Cambridge, Mass.: MIT Press, 1969)

SURREALISM
Dawn Ades (ed.), *Dada and Surrealism Reviewed* (London: Arts Council of Great Britain, 1978)
Anna Balakian, *Surrealism: The Road to the Absolute* (Cambridge: Cambridge University Press, 1986)
Yve-Alain Bois and Rosalind Krauss, *Formless: A User's Guide* (New York: Zone Books, 1997)
André Breton, "Introduction to the Discourse on the Paucity of Reality," *October*, no. 69, Summer 1994
André Breton, *Mad Love*, trans. Mary Ann Caws (Lincoln: University of Nebraska Press, 1980)
André Breton, *Manifestoes of Surrealism*, trans. Richard Seaver and Helen R. Lane (Ann Arbor: University of Michigan Press, 1972)
André Breton, *Nadja*, trans. Richard Howard (New York: Grove Weidenfeld, 1960)
André Breton, *What is Surrealism?*, trans. David Gascoyne (New York: Haskell House Publishers,1974)
William Camfield, *Max Ernst: Dada and the Dawn of Surrealism* (Munich: Prestel, 1993)
Mary Ann Caws (ed.), *Surrealist Painters and Poets: An Anthology* (Cambridge, Mass.: MIT Press, 2001)
Jacqueline Chenieux-Gendron, *Surrealism* (New York: Columbia University Press, 1990)
Hal Foster, *Compulsive Beauty* (Cambridge, Mass.: MIT Press, 1993)
Michel Foucault, *This is Not a Pipe* (Berkeley: University of California Press, 1982)
Denis Hollier, *Against Architecture: The Writings of Georges Bataille*, trans. Betsy Wing (Cambridge, Mass.: MIT Press, 1989)
Denis Hollier, *Absent Without Leave: French Literature Under the Threat of War*, trans. Catherine Porter (Cambridge, Mass.: Harvard University Press, 1997)
Rosalind Krauss, *The Optical Unconscious* (Cambridge, Mass.: MIT Press, 1993)
Rosalind Krauss and Jane Livingston, *L'Amour fou: Surrealism and Photography* (New York: Abbeville Press, 1986)
Jennifer Mundy (ed.), *Surrealism: Desire Unbound* (London: Tate Publishing, 2001)
Maurice Nadeau, *History of Surrealism* (New York: Macmillan, 1965)

MEXICAN MURALISTS
Alejandro Anreus, *Orozco in Gringoland: The Years in New York* (Albuquerque: University of New Mexico Press, 2001)
Jacqueline Barnitz, *Twentieth-Century Art of Latin America* (Austin, Texas: University of Texas Press, 2001)
Linda Downs, *Diego Rivera: A Retrospective* (New York and London: Founders Society, Detroit Institute of Arts in association with W. W. Norton & Company, 1986)
Desmond Rochfort, *Mexican Muralists* (London: Laurence King Publishing, 1993)
Antonio Rodriguez, *A History of Mexican Mural Painting* (London: Thames & Hudson, 1969)

SOCIALIST REALISM
Matthew Cullerne Bown, *Socialist Realist Painting* (London and New Haven:Yale University Press, 1998)
Leah Dickerman, "Camera Obscura: Socialist Realism in the Shadow of Photography," *October*, no. 93, Summer 2000
David Elliott (ed.), *Engineers of the Human Soul: Soviet Socialist Realist Painting 1930s–1960s* (Oxford: Museum of Modern Art, 1992)
Hans Guenther (ed.), *The Culture of the Stalin Period* (New York and London: St. Martin's Press, 1990)
Thomas Lahusen and Evgeny Dobrenko (eds), *Socialist Realism without Shores* (Durham, N.C. and London: Duke University Press, 1997)
Brandon Taylor, "Photo Power: Painting and Iconicity in the First Five Year Plan," in Dawn Ades and Tim Benton (eds), *Art and Power: Europe Under the Dictators 1939–1945* (London: Thames & Hudson, 1995)
Andrei Zhdanov, "Speech to the Congress of Soviet Writers" (1934), translated and reprinted in Charles Harrison and Paul Wood (eds), *Art in Theory 1900–1990* (Oxford and Cambridge, Mass.: Blackwell, 1992)

HARLEM RENAISSANCE
M. S. Campbell et al., *Harlem Renaissance: Art of Black America* (New York: Studio Museum in Harlem and Harry N. Abrams, 1987)
David C. Driskell, *Two Centuries of Black American Art* (New York: Alfred A. Knopf and Los Angeles County Museum of Art, 1976)
Alain Locke (ed.), *The New Negro: An Interpretation* (first published 1925; New York: Atheneum, 1968)
Guy C. McElroy, Richard J. Powell, and Sharon F. Patton, *African-American Artists 1880–1987: Selections from the Evans-Tibbs Collection* (Washington, D.C.: Smithsonian Institution Traveling Exhibition Service, 1989)
James A. Porter, *Modern Negro Art* (first published 1943; Washington, D.C.: Howard University Press, 1992)
Joanna Skipworth (ed.), *Rhapsodies in Black: Art of the Harlem Renaissance* (London: Hayward Gallery, 1997)

ABSTRACT EXPRESSIONISM
David Anfam (ed.), *Mark Rothko: The Works on Canvas*, catalogue raisonné (New Haven and London: Yale University Press, 1998)
T. J. Clark, "The Unhappy Consciousness" and "In Defense of Abstract Expressionism," *Farewell to an Idea* (New Haven and London: Yale University Press, 1999)
Francis Frascina (ed.), *Pollock and After: The Critical Debate* (New York: Harper & Row, 1985)

Serge Guilbaut, *How New York Stole the Idea of Modern Art: Abstract Expressionism, Freedom, and the Cold War* (Chicago: University of Chicago Press, 1983)
Michael Leja, *Reframing Abstract Expressionism: Subjectivity and Painting in the 1940s* (New Haven and London: Yale University Press, 1993)
Barnett Newman, *Selected Writings and Interviews*, ed John O'Neill (Berkeley: University of California Press, 1992)
Francis O'Connor and Eugene Thaw (eds), *Jackson Pollock: A Catalogue Raisonné of Paintings, Drawings, and Other Works* (New Haven and London: Yale University Press, 1977)
Ad Reinhardt, *Art as Art: Selcted Writings of Ad Reinhardt*, ed. Barbara Rose (Berkeley: University of California Press, 1991)
Harold Rosenberg, *The Tradition of the New* (New York: Horizon Press, 1959)
Irving Sandler, *Abstract Expressionism: The Triumph of American Painting* (London: Pall Mall, 1970)
David Shapiro and Cecile Shapiro, *Abstract Expressionism: A Critical Record* (Cambridge: Cambridge University Press, 1990)
Kirk Varnedoe with Pepe Karmel, *Jackson Pollock* (New York: Museum of Modern Art, 1998)

DUBUFFET, FAUTRIER, KLEIN, AND NOUVEAU RÉALISME

Jean-Paul Ameline, *Les Nouveaux Réalistes* (Paris: Centre Georges Pompidou, 1992)
Benjamin H. D. Buchloh, "From Detail to Fragment: Décollage/Affichiste," *Décollage: Les Affichistes* (New York and Paris: Virginia Zabriske Gallery, 1990)
Curtis L. Carter and Karen L. Butler (eds), *Jean Fautrier* (New Haven and London: Yale University Press, 2002)
Bernadette Contensou (ed.), *1960: Les Nouveaux Réalistes* (Paris: Musée d'Art Moderne de la Ville de Paris, 1986)
Hubert Damisch, "The Real Robinson," *October*, no. 85, Summer 1998
Jean Dubuffet, *Prospectus et tous écrits suivants*, four volumes, ed. Hubert Damisch (Paris: Gallimard, 1967–91) and "Notes for the well read" (1945), translated in Mildred Glimcher, *Jean Dubuffet: Towards an Alternative Reality* (New York: Pace Publications and Abbeville Press, 1987)
Catherine Francblin, *Les Nouveaux Réalistes* (Paris: Editions du Regard, 1997)
Rachel Perry, "Jean Fautrier's *Jolies Juives*," *October*, no. 108, Spring 2004
Francis Ponge, *L'Atelier contemporain* (Paris: Gallimard, 1977)
Jean-Paul Sartre, "Fingers and Non-Fingers," translated in Werner Haftmann (ed.), *Wols* (New York: Harry N. Abrams, 1965)

RAUSCHENBERG, JOHNS, AND OTHERS

Russell Ferguson (ed.), *Hand-Painted Pop: American Art in Transition, 1955–62* (Los Angeles: Museum of Contemporary Art, 1993)
Walter Hopps, Susan Davidson et al., *Robert Rauschenberg: A Retrospective* (New York: Guggenheim Museum, 1997)
Walter Hopps, *Robert Rauschenberg: The Early 1950s* (Houston: Menil Collection, 1991)
Jasper Johns, *Writings, Sketchbook Notes, Interviews* (New York: Museum of Modern Art/Harry N. Abrams, 1996)
Branden Joseph (ed.) *Random Order* (Cambridge, Mass.: MIT Press, 2003)
Branden Joseph (ed.), *Robert Rauschenberg*, October Files 4 (Cambridge, Mass.: MIT Press, 2002)
Fred Orton, *Figuring Jasper Johns* (Cambridge: Harvard University Press, 1994)
Leo Steinberg, *Other Criteria: Confrontations with Twentieth-Century Art* (London, Oxford, and New York: Oxford University Press, 1972)
Kirk Varnedoe, *Jasper Johns: A Retrospective* (New York: Museum of Modern Art, 1996)

FONTANA, MANZONI, AND ARTE POVERA

Yve-Alain Bois, "Fontana's Base Materialism," *Art in America*, vol. 77, no. 4, April 1989
Germano Celant, *Arte Povera* (Milan: Gabriele Mazzotta; New York: Praeger; London: Studio Vista, 1969)
Germano Celant, *The Knot: Arte Povera* (New York: P.S.1; Turin: Umberto Allemandi, 1985)
Germano Celant (ed.), *Piero Manzoni* (London: Serpentine Gallery, 1998)
Carolyn Christov-Bakargiev (ed.), *Arte Povera* (London: Phaidon Press, 1999)
Richard Flood and Frances Morris (eds), *Zero to Infinity: Arte Povera 1962–1972* (Minneapolis: Walker Art Gallery; London: Tate Gallery, 2002)
Jaleh Mansoor, "Piero Manzoni: 'We Want to Organicize Disintegration'," *October*, no. 95, Winter 2001
Jon Thompson (ed.), *Gravity and Grace: Arte povera/Post Minimalism* (London: Hayward Gallery, 1993)
Anthony White, "Lucio Fontana: Between Utopia and Kitsch," *Grey Room*, no. 5, Fall 2001
Sarah Whitfield, *Lucio Fontana* (London: Hayward Gallery, 1999)

SITUATIONISM

Iwona Blazwick (ed.), *An Endless Adventure—An Endless Passion—An Endless Banquet: A Situationist Scrapbook* (London: Verso, 1989)
Guy Debord, *The Society of the Spectacle* (1967), trans. Donald Nicholson-Smith (Cambridge, Mass.: MIT Press, 2002)
Ken Knabb (ed.), *Situationist International Anthology* (Berkeley: Bureau of Public Secrets, 1981)
Thomas F. McDonough (ed.), *Guy Debord and the Situationist International* (Cambridge, Mass.: MIT Press, 2002)
Elisabeth Sussman (ed.), *On the Passage of a Few People Through a Rather Brief Moment in Time: The Situationist International 1957–1972* (Cambridge, Mass.: MIT Press, 1989)

POP

Lawrence Alloway, *American Pop Art* (New York: Collier Books, 1974)
Yve-Alain Bois, *Edward Ruscha, Romance with Liquids* (New York: Gagosian Gallery, 1993)
Thomas Crow, *The Rise of the Sixties: American and European Art in the Era of Dissent* (New York: Abrams, 1996)
Hal Foster and Mark Francis, *Pop Art* (London: Phaidon Press, 2005)
Lucy Lippard, *Pop Art* (London: Thames & Hudson, 1966)
Marco Livingstone, *Pop Art: A Continuing History* (London: Thames & Hudson, 2000
Michael Lobel, *Image Duplicator: Roy Lichtenstein and the Emergence of Pop Art* (New Haven: Yale University Press, 2002)
Steven Henry Madoff, *Pop Art: A Critical History* (Berkeley: University of California Press, 1997)
Kynaston McShine (ed.), *Andy Warhol: A Retrospective* (New York: Museum of Modern Art, 1989)
Annette Michelson, *Andy Warhol*, October Files 2 (Cambridge, Mass.: MIT Press, 2001)
David Robbins (ed.), *The Independent Group: Postwar Britain and the Aesthetics of Plenty* (Cambridge, Mass.: MIT Press, 1990)
Edward Ruscha, *Leave Any Information at the Signal* (Cambridge, Mass.: MIT Press, 2002)
John Russell and Suzi Gablik, *Pop Art Redefined* (New York: Praeger, 1969)
Paul Taylor, *Post-Pop Art* (Cambridge, Mass.: MIT Press, 1989)
Cecile Whiting, *A Taste for Pop: Pop Art, Gender, and Consumer Culture* (Cambridge: Cambridge University Press, 1997)

CAGE, KAPROW, AND FLUXUS

Elizabeth Armstrong, *In the Spirit of Fluxus* (Minneapolis: Walker Art Center, 1993)
Benjamin H. D. Buchloh, and Judith Rodenbeck (eds), *Experiments in the Everyday: Allan Kaprow and Robert Watts—Events, Objects, Documents* (New York: Wallach Gallery, Columbia University, 1999)
John Cage, *Silence* (Hanover, N.H.: Weslyan University Press, 1939)
Jon Hendricks (ed.), *Fluxus Codex*. Detroit: Gilbert and Lila Silverman Fluxus Collection, 1988)
Allan Kaprow, *Assemblage, Environments & Happenings* (New York: Abrams, 1966)
Allan Kaprow, *Essays on the Blurring of Art and Life* (Berkeley: University of California Press, 1993)
Liz Kotz, "Post-Cagean Aesthetics and the 'Event' Score," *October, no.* 95, Winter 2001

POSTWAR GERMAN ART

Georg Baselitz and Eugen Schönebeck, *Pandämonium Manifestoes*, excerpts in English translation in Andreas Papadakis (ed.), *German Art Now*, vol. 5, no. 9–10, 1989
Joseph Beuys, *Where Would I Have Got If I Had Been Intelligent!* (New York: Dia Center for the Arts, 1994)
Benjamin H. D. Buchloh, *Gerhard Richter, 18 Oktober 1977* (London: Institute of Contemporary Arts, 1989)
Benjamin H. D. Buchloh, "Gerhard Richter's Atlas: The Anomic Archive," *October*, no. 88, Spring 1999
Benjamin H. D. Buchloh, "Joseph Beuys at the Guggenheim," *October*, no. 12, Spring 1980
Stefan Germer, "Die Wiederkehr des Verdrängten. Zum Umgang mit deutscher Geschichte bei Baselitz, Kiefer, Immendorf und Richter," in Julia Bernard (ed.), *Germeriana: Unveröffentlichte oder übersetzte Schriften von Stefan Germer* (Cologne: Oktagon Verlag, 1999)
Siegfried Gohr, "In the Absence of Heroes: The Early Work of Georg Baselitz," *Artforum*, vol. 20, no. 10, Summer 1982
Tom Holert, "Bei Sich, über allem: Der symptomatische Baselitz," *Texte zur Kunst*, vol. 3, no. 9, March 1993
Andreas Huyssen, "Anselm Kiefer: The Terror of History, the Temptation of Myth," *October*, no. 48, Spring 1989
Kevin Power, "Existential Ornament," in Maria Corral (ed.), *Georg Baselitz* (Madrid: Fundacion Caja de Pensiones, 1990)
Gerhard Richter, *The Daily Practice of Painting: Writings 1960–1993* (Cambridge, Mass.: MIT Press, 1995)
Margit Rowell, *Sigmar Polke: Works on Paper, 1963–1974* (New York: Museum of Modern Art, 1999)

MINIMALISM, POSTMINIMALISM AND POSTWAR SCULPTURE

Carl Andre and Hollis Frampton, *12 Dialogues, 1962–1963*. Halifax: The Press of the Nova Scotia College of Art and Design, 1981)
Gregory Battcock, *Minimal Art: A Critical Anthology* (New York: E.P. Dutton, 1968)
Maurice Berger, *Labyrinths: Robert Morris, Minimalism and the 1960s* (New York: Harper & Row, 1989)
Hal Foster (ed.), *Richard Serra*, October Files 1 (Cambridge, Mass.: MIT Press, 2000)
Ann Goldstein (ed.), *A Minimal Future? Art as Object 1958–1968* (Los Angeles: Museum of Contemporary Art, 2004)
Donald Judd, *Donald Judd, Complete Writings, 1959–1975* (Halifax: The Press of the Nova Scotia College of Art and Design, 1975)
Rosalind Krauss, *Passages in Modern Sculpture* (New York: Viking Press, 1977
Rosalind Krauss, *The Sculpture of David Smith: A Catalogue Raisonné* (New York: Garland Publishing, 1977)
Lucy Lippard, *Eva Hesse* (New York: Da Capo Press, 1992)
James Meyer, *Minimalism: Art and Polemics in the Sixties*. (New Haven and London: Yale University Press, 2001)
Robert Morris, *Continuous Project Altered Daily: The Writings of Robert Morris* (Cambridge, Mass.: MIT Press, 1993)
Mignon Nixon (ed.), *Eva Hesse*, October Files 3 (Cambridge, Mass.: MIT Press, 2002)
Clara Weyergraf-Serra and Martha Buskirk (eds), *The Destruction of Tilted Arc: Documents* (Cambridge, Mass.: MIT Press, 1991)

EARTHWORKS, PROCESS ART, AND ENTROPY

Thomas Crow, *Gordon Matta Clark* (London: Phaidon Press, 2003)
Robert Hobbs, *Robert Smithson: Sculpture* (Ithaca, N.Y.: Cornell University Press, 1981)
Pamela Lee, *Chronophobia* (Cambridge, Mass.: MIT Press, 2004)

Pamela Lee, *Object to be Destroyed: The Work of Gordon Matta-Clark* (Cambridge, Mass.: MIT Press, 2000)
Ann Reynolds, *Robert Smithson: Learning from New Jersey and Elsewhere* (Cambridge, Mass.: MIT Press, 2003)
Jennifer L. Roberts, *Mirror-travels: Robert Smithson and History* (New Haven: Yale University Press, 2004)
Robert Smithson, *The Collected Writings*, ed. Jack Flam (Berkeley: University of California Press, 1996)
Eugenie Tsai (ed.), *Robert Smithson* (Berkeley: University of California Press, 2004)

CONCEPTUAL ART
Alexander Alberro and Blake Stimson (eds), *Conceptual Art and the Politics of Publicity* (Cambridge, Mass.: MIT Press, 2003)
Benjamin H. D. Buchloh, "Conceptual Art 1962–69: From an Aesthetics of Administration to the Critique of Institutions" *October*, no. 55, Winter 1990
Ann Goldstein (ed.), *Reconsidering the Object of Art: 1965–1975* (Los Angeles, Museum of Contemporary Art, 1995)
Joseph Kosuth, *Art After Philosophy and After: Collected Writing 1966–1990* (Cambridge, Mass.: MIT Press, 1991)
Lucy Lippard, *Six Years: The Dematerialization of the Art Object 1966–1972* (Berkeley: University of California Press, 1973)
Ursula Meyer, *Conceptual Art* (New York: Dutton, 1972)
Kynaston McShine, *Information* (New York: MoMA, 1970)
Anne Rorimer, *New Art in the 60s and 70s: Redefining Reality* (New York: Thames & Hudson, 2001)
Blake Stimson and Alexander Alberro (eds), *Conceptual Art : An Anthology of Critical Writings and Documents* (Cambridge, Mass.: MIT Press, 2000)

INSTALLATION, INSTITUTIONAL CRITIQUE, AND SITE-SPECIFICITY
Michael Asher, *Writings 1973–1983 on Works 1969–1979* Halifax: The Press of the Nova Scotia College of Art and Design, 1983)
Marcel Broodthaers, *Broodthaers: Writings, Interviews, Photographs* (Cambridge, Mass.: MIT Press, 1987)
Daniel Buren, *Daniel Buren: Les Couleurs, Sculptures, Les Formes, Peintures* (Paris: Centre Georges Pompidou, 1981)
Victor Burgin, "Situational Aesthetics," *Studio International*, vol. 178, no. 915, October 1969
Rosalyn Deutsche, *Evictions: Art and Spatial Politics* (Cambridge, Mass.: MIT Press, 1996)
Dan Graham, *Two-Way Mirror Power: Selected Writings by Dan Graham on His Art* (Cambridge, Mass.: MIT Press, 1999)
Dan Graham, *Video, Architecture, Television: Writings on Video and Video Works, 1970–1978* (Halifax: The Press of the Nova Scotia College of Art and Design, 1979)
Hans Haacke, *Unfinished Business* (Cambridge, Mass.: 1986)
Rosalind Krauss, "The Cultural Logic of the Late Capitalist Museum," *October*, no. 54, Fall 1990
Miwon Kwon, *One Place After Another: Site-Specific Art and Locational Identity* (Cambridge, Mass.: MIT Press, 2002)
Jennifer Licht, *Spaces* (New York: Museum of Modern Art, 1969)
Brian O'Doherty, *Inside the White Cube: The Ideology of the Gallery Space* (Berkeley and Los Angeles: University of California Press, 1999)
Birgit Pelzer, Mark Francis, and Beatriz Colomina, *Dan Graham* (London: Phaidon Press, 2001)
Erica Suderburg (ed.), *Space, Site, Intervention: Situating Installation Art* (Minneapolis: University of Minnesota Press, 2000)
Marsha Tucker, *Anti-Illusion: Procedures/Materials* (New York: Whitney Museum of American Art, 1969)
Fred Wilson, *Mining the Museum* (Baltimore: Museum of Contemporary Art, 1994)

PERFORMANCE AND BODY ART
Sally Banes, *Democracy's Body: Judson Dance Theater, 1962–1964* (Durham, N.C.: Duke University Press, 1993)
RoseLee Goldberg, *Performance Art: From Futurism to the Present* (London and New York: Thames & Hudson, 2001)
Amelia Jones, *Body Art: Performing the Subject* (Minneapolis: University of Minnesota Press, 1998
Paul Schimmel and Russell Ferguson (eds), *Out of Actions: Between Performance and the Object: 1949–1979*. Los Angeles: Museum of Contemporary Art, New York, 1998)
Amelia Jones and Andrew Stephenson (eds), *Performing the Body/Performing the Text* (London and New York: Routledge, 1999)
Kristine Stiles, "Uncorrupted Joy: International Art Actions," in Paul Schimmel and Russell Ferguson (eds), *Out of Actions: Between Performance and the Object 1949–1979* (London: Thames & Hudson, 1998)
Frazer Ward, "Some Relations Between Conceptual and Performance Art." *Art Journal*, vol. 56, no. 4, Winter 1997
Anne Wagner, "Performance, Video, and the Rhetoric of Presence," *October*, no. 91, Winter 2000

FEMINISM, POSTCOLONIAL ART, AND IDENTITY ART
Homi Bhabha, *The Location of Culture* (London: Routledge, 1994)
Judith Butler, *Gender Trouble: Feminism and the Subversion of Identity* (New York: Routledge, 1989)
Judy Chicago, *Beyond the Flower: The Autobiography of a Feminist Artist* (New York: Viking, 1996)
Douglas Crimp (ed.), *AIDS: Cultural Analysis/Cultural Activism* (Cambridge, Mass.: MIT Press, 1988)
Douglas Crimp and Adam Rolston (eds), *AIDS DEMOgraphics* (Seattle: Bay Press, 1990)
Joanna Frueh, Cassandra L. Langer, and Arlene Raven (eds), *New Feminist Art Criticism: Art, Identity, Action* (New York: HarperCollins, 1994)
Coco Fusco, *The Bodies That Were Not Ours* (New York: Routledge, 2001)
Thelma Golden, *Black Male: Representations of Masculinity in Contemporary Art* (New York: Whitney Museum of American Art, 1994)
Stuart Hall and Mark Sealy, *Different: Contemporary Photography and Black Identity* (London: Phaidon Press, 2001)
Mary Kelly, *Imaging Desire* (Cambridge, Mass.: MIT Press, 1997)
Lucy R. Lippard, *Get the Message? A Decade of Social Change* (New York: Dutton, 1984)
Lucy R. Lippard, *The Pink Glass Swan: Selected Essays in Feminist Art* (New York: New Press, 1995)
Jean-Hubert Martin et al., *Les Magiciens de la terre* (Paris: Centre Georges Pompidou, 1989)
Kobena Mercer, *Welcome to the Jungle: New Positions in Cultural Studies* (New York: Routledge, 1994)
Linda Nochlin, *Women, Art and Power: And Other Essays* (New York: Harper & Row, 1988; and London: Thames & Hudson, 1989)
Roszika Parker and Griselda Pollock, *Framing Feminism: Art and the Women's Movement 1970–85* (London: Pandora, 1987)
Griselda Pollock, *Vision and Difference: Femininity, Feminism, and Histories of Art* (New York: Routledge, 1988)
Helaine Posner (ed.), *Corporal Politics* (Cambridge, Mass.: MIT List Visual Arts Center, 1992)
Catherine de Zegher (ed.), *Inside the Visible: An Elliptical Traverse of 20th-Century Art* (Cambridge, Mass.: MIT Press, 1994)

PHOTOGRAPHY, FILM, VIDEO, AND THE PROJECTED IMAGE
Dawn Ades, *Photomontage* (London: Thames & Hudson, 1976)
Carol Armstrong, *Scenes in a Library: Reading the Photograph in the Book* (Cambridge, Mass.: MIT Press, 1998. Grove Press, 1959)
Béla Balázs, *Theory of the Film: Character and Growth of a New Art* (London: D. Dobson, 1952)
André Bazin, *What is Cinema?* vol. 1, trans. Hugh Gray (Berkeley: University of California Press, 1967)
Roland Barthes, *Camera Lucida: Reflections on Photography*, trans. Richard Howard (New York: Hill and Wang, 1981)
Roland Barthes, "The Photographic Message" and "The Rhetoric of the Image," *Image/Music/Text* (New York: Hill and Wang, 1977)
John Berger, *Another Way of Telling* (New York: Pantheon, 1982)
Stan Brakhage, *The Essential Brakhage* (Kingston, N.Y.: McPherson & Company, 2001)
Benjamin H. D. Buchloh, "Allegorical Procedures: Appropriation and Montage in Contemporary Art," *Artforum*, vol. 21, no. 1, September 1982
Noel Burch, *Theory of Film Practice*, trans. Helen R. Lane (New York: Praeger, 1973)
Stanley Cavell, *The World Viewed: Reflections on the Ontology of Film* (Cambridge: Harvard University Press, 1971)
Mary Ann Doane, "Information, Crisis, Catastrophe" in Patricia Mellencamp (ed.), *Logics of Television: Essays in Cultural Criticism* (Bloomington: Indiana University Press, 1990)
Sergei Eisenstein, *Film Form: Essays in Film Theory* (San Diego: Harvest Books, 1969)
Robert Hirsch, *Seizing the Light: A History of Photography* (Boston: McGraw-Hill, 2000)
Chrissie Iles, *Into the Light: The Projected Image in American Art, 1964–1977* (New York: Whitney Museum of American Art, 2001)
Friedrich Kittler, *Gramophone, Film, Typewriter* (Stanford: Stanford University Press, 1999)
Elizabeth Ann McCauley, *Industrial Madness: Commercial Photography in Paris 1848–1871* (New Haven and London: Yale University Press, 1994)
Beaumont Newhall, *The History of Photography: From 1839 to the Present* (Boston: Little, Brown and Company. 1999)
Erwin Panofsky, "Style and Medium in the Motion Pictures" (1974), in Gerald Mast and Marshall Cohen (eds), *Film Theory and Criticism: Introductory Readings* (London: Oxford University Press, 1974)
Christopher Phillips, *Photography in the Modern Era: European Documents and Critical Writings, 1913–1940* (New York: Metropolitan Museum of Art, 1989)
Naomi Rosenblum, *A World History of Photography* (New York: Abbeville Press, 1984)
"Round Table: Independence in the Cinema," *October*, no. 91, Winter 2000
"Round Table: The Projected Image in Contemporary Art," *October*, no. 104, Spring 2003
Allan Sekula, "On the Invention of Photographic Meaning," *Artforum*, vol. 13, no. 5, January 1975
Allan Sekula, "The Traffic in Photographs." *Art Journal*, vol. 41, no. 1, Spring 1981
P. Adams Sitney, *Modernist Montage: The Obscurity of Vision in Cinema and Literature* (New York: Columbia University Press, 1990)
P. Adams Sitney, *The Avant-Garde Film: A Reader of Theory and Criticism* (New York: New York University Press, 1978)
P. Adams Sitney, *Visionary Film: The American Avant-Garde, 1943–2000* (Oxford: Oxford University Press, 2002)
Abigail Solomon-Godeau, *Photography at the Dock: Essays on Photographic History, Institutions, and Practices* (Minneapolis: University of Minnesota Press, 1991)
Susan Sontag, *On Photography* (New York: Farrar, Straus, Giroux, 1977)
John Tagg, *The Burden of Representation: Essays on Photographies and Histories* (Amherst, Mass.: University of Massachusetts Press, 1988)
Matthew Teitelbaum (ed.), *Montage and Modern Life: 1919–1942* (Cambridge, Mass.: MIT Press, 1992)
Alan Trachtenberg (ed.), *Classic Essays on Photography* (New Haven and London: Leete's Island Books, 1980
Malcolm Turvey, "Jean Epstein's Cinema of Immanence: The Rehabilitation of the Corporeal Eye," *October*, no. 83 (Winter 1998)
Dziga Vertov, *Kino-Eye: The Writings of Dziga Vertov* (Berkeley: University of California Press, 1984)
Jonathan Walley, "The Material of Film and the Idea of Cinema: Contrasting Practices in Sixties and Seventies Avant-Garde Film," *October*, no. 103, Winter 2003

selected useful websites

Listed below is a small selection of the many websites devoted to modern and contemporary art. Each contains links to other related websites for those wishing to continue their study and research.

GENERAL INFORMATION, RESEARCH PORTALS, AND LINKS

http://americanhistory.si.edu/archives/ac-i.htm Largest source in the United States of primary documentation on the visual arts

http://artcyclopedia.com Links to websites by artist and movement

http://the-artists.org Links to art works, essays, artists' biographies, portraits, and websites, and museums

http://witcombe.sbc.edu/ARTH20thcentury.html Links to art works, essays, artists' biographies and websites, and museums

http://www.abcgallery.com "Olga's Gallery"—brief histories of movements, artists' biographies, images of art works, with extensive links to other websites

http://www.artic.edu/webspaces/arthi/research.html

http://www.art-online.com Links to contemporary art galleries, libraries, and image banks

http://www.bc.edu/bc_org/avp/cas/fnart/links/art_19th20th.html Extensive links to websites by movement, period, and artist

http://www.boisestate.edu/art/artinflux/intro.html Extensive links to websites devoted to theory, theorists, methodology, artists, artists' groups, and museums

http://www.huntfor.com/arthistory Links by artist and movement

IMAGE BANKS

http://www.guggenheimcollection.org Visual archive of the Guggenheim holdings

http://www.photo.rmn.fr Visual archive of the French national holdings of modern and contemporary art

http://www.videomuseum.fr Visual archive of modern and contemporary art, including new media

(also see "Museum and Institutions of Art" below)

MUSEUMS AND INSTITUTIONS OF ART

http://www.artic.edu Art Institute of Chicago

http://www.cnac-gp.fr/ Centres Georges Pompidou, Paris

http://www.documenta.de Documenta

http://www.guggenheim.org Solomon R. Guggenheim Museum, New York

http://www.metmuseum.org/ Metropolitan Museum of Art, New York

ttp://www.mcachicago.org/ Museum of Contemporary Art, Chicago

http://moma.org Museum of Modern Art, New York

http://www.nga.gov/home.htm National Gallery of Art, Washington, D.C.

http://www.sfmoma.org San Francisco Museum of Modern Art

http://www.stedelijk.nl/ Stedelijk Museum, Amsterdam

http://www.tate.org.uk Tate

http://www.whitney.org Whitney Museum of American Art

(also see "General information, research portals, and links" above)

ARTISTS' AND MOVEMENTS' WEBSITES

http://www.artsmia.org/modernism "Milestones in Modernism 1880–1940"—brief histories and images by movement

http://www.iniva.org/harlem/ Institute of International Visual Arts—Harlem Renaissance archive

http://www.lib.uiowa.edu/dada/index.html International Dada archive

http://www.moma.org/brucke/ Museum of Modern Art, New York—Die Brücke archive

http://www.okeeffemuseum.org/index1.html Georgia O'Keeffe Museum

http://www.tamu.edu/mocl/picasso Online Picasso Project—extensive archive of works by date

http://www.usc.edu/dept/architecture/slide/babcock Cubism archive

(also see "General information, research portals, and links" above)

ONLINE DICTIONARIES AND GLOSSARIES

http://www.artlex.com Basic dictionary of terms

http://www.arts.ouc.bc.ca/fina/glossary/gloshome.html "Words of Art" glossary of terms

http://www.groveart.com Authoritative dictionary of art and artists; over 45,000 articles on the fine arts, decorative arts, and architecture; written by over 6,000 international scholars; over 130,000 art images, with links to museums and galleries around the world (subscription)

ONLINE JOURNALS AND PUBLISHERS

http://mitpress.mit.edu/catalog/item/default.asp?tid=18&ttype=4 *October* journal—selected articles from past issues

http://www.artforum.com *Artforum* magazine—selected articles from past issues; links to modern and contemporary art galleries

http://www.caareviews.org College Art Association—extensive archive of reviews of books and catalogues

http://www.cia.edu/administrative/academicaffairs/library/cai.asp Extensive list of modern and contemporary art exhibition catalogues

http://www.thameshudson.co.uk Extensive range of books on modern and contemporary art; links to related websites

http://www.uchicago.edu/research/jnl-crit-inq/ *Critical Inquiry* journal—selected articles from past issues; links to websites of critical interest

picture credits

Measurements are given in centimeters, followed by inches, height before width before depth, unless otherwise stated.

p.5 (left) Ernst Ludwig Kirchner, *The Street, Dresden*, 1908. Oil on canvas, 150.5 x 200 (59¼ x 78⅞). Museum of Modern Art, New York. © Dr. Wolfgang & Ingeborg Henze-Ketterer, Wichtrach/Bern; **(center)** Franz Marc, *The Fate of the Animals*, 1913. Oil on canvas, 194.3 x 261.6 (76½ x 103). Kunstmuseum, Basle; **(right)** Kazimir Malevich, *Warrior of the First Division*, 1914. Oil and collage on canvas, 53.6 x 44.8 (21⅛ x 17⅝). Museum of Modern Art, New York; **p.6 (left)** Gustav Klutsis, *Let us Fulfill the Plan of our Great Projects*, 1930. Photomontage. Russian State Library, Moscow; **(center)** Karl Blossfeldt, *Impatiens Glandulifera; Balsamine, Springkraut*, 1927. Silver salts print. Courtesy Galerie Wilde, Cologne; **(right)** Barbara Hepworth, *Large and Small Form*, 1934. Alabaster, 23 x 37 x 18 (9 x 14 x 7). The Pier Gallery Collection, Stromness. © Bowness, Hepworth Estate; **p.7 (left)** Wolfgang Paalen, *Ciel de Pieuvre*, 1938. Fumage and oil on canvas, 97 x 130 (38¼ x 51⅛). Private Collection, Courtesy Paalen Archiv, Berlin; **(center)** Franz Kline, *Cardinal*, 1950. 197 x 144 (77½ x 56¾). Private Collection. © ARS, NY and DACS, London 2004; **(right)** Ellsworth Kelly, *Colors for a Large Wall*, 1951. Oil on canvas, mounted on 64 joined panels 243.8 x 243.8 (96 x 96). Museum of Modern Art, New York. © Ellsworth Kelly; **p.8 (left)** Morris Louis, *Beta Kappa*, 1961. Acrylic resin on canvas, 262.3 x 429.4 (103¼ x 173). National Gallery of Art, Washington, D.C. © 1961 Morris Louis; (center) Mario Merz, *Objet Cache Toi*, 1968–77. Metal tubes, glass, clamps, wire mesh, neon, 185 x 365 (72⅞ x 143¾). Courtesy Archivo Merz, Turin; **(right)** Bernd and Hilla Becher, *8 Views of a House*, 1962–71. Black-and-white photographs. Courtesy Sonnabend Gallery, New York; **p.9 (left)** Chris Burden, *Trans-fixed*, 1974. Performance, Venice, California. Courtesy the artist; **(center)** Laurie Anderson, performance still of *United States*, 1978–82. Courtesy of Canal St. Communications; **(right)** Rachel Whiteread, *(Untitled) House*, 1993. Destroyed. Commissioned by Artangel. Sponsored by Beck's. Photo Sue Ormera. Courtesy Rachel Whiteread and Gagosian Gallery, London; **p.10** Wassily Kandinsky, final study for the cover of the Blaue Reiter *Almanach*, 1911. Watercolour, India ink and pencil, 27.6 x 21.9 (10⅞ x 8⅝). Städtische Galeries im Lenbachhaus, Munich. © ADAGP, Paris and DACS, London 2004; **p.11** Marcel Duchamp, *Sixteen Miles of String*, 1942. Installation at 'First Papers of Surrealism' exhibition orgnaised by Marcel Duchamp and André Breton for the Coordinating Council of French Relief Societies, New York, October 14 – November 7, 1942. Vintage silver-gelatin print, 19.4 x 25.4 (7⅝ x 10). Philadelphia Museum of Art: Gift of Jacqueline, Paul and Peter Matisse in memory of their mother Alexina Duchamp. © Succession Marcel Duchamp/ADAGP, Paris and DACS, London 2004; **Introduction 1: 1 •** Museum Folkwang, Essen; 2. Museum of Modern Art, New York. © DACS 2004; 3. Collection William Rubin, Bronxville, New York. © ADAGP, Paris and DACS, London 2004; 4. Galerie Krikhaar, Amsterdam. © Karel Appel Foundation/DACS, London 2004; 5. Courtesy Ydessa Hendeles Art Foundation, Toronto; 6. © DACS, London/VAGA, New York 2004; 7. © Lee Miller Archives, Chiddingly, England, 2004. All rights reserved; **Introduction 2: 1 •** Photo Akademie der Künste der DDR, Berlin. © The Heartfield Community of Heirs/VG Bild-Kunst, Bonn and DACS, London 2004; 2. From Szymon Bojko, *New Graphic Designs in Revolutionary Russia*, Lund Humphries, London, 1972. Lissizky: © DACS 2004; 4. Martha Rosler, © Martha Rosler, 1969–72. Courtesy the artist and Gorney Bravin & Lee, New York; 5. Photo Dave Morgan, London. Courtesy Lisson Gallery, London; 6. Courtesy the artist. © DACS 2004; 7. Photo Reiner Ruthenbeck. Courtesy Konrad Fischer Galerie. © Gerhard Richter; **Introduction 3: 1 •** Kunstmuseum, Basel. Gift of Raoul La Roche, 1952. © ADAGP, Paris and DACS, London 2004; 2. Musée Picasso, Paris. © Succession Picasso/DACS 2004; 3. Pablo Picasso, Museum of Modern Art, New York. Gift of the artist. © Succession Picasso/DACS 2004; 4. Haags Gemeentemuseum. © 2004 Mondrian/Holtzman Trust. c/o hcr@hcrinternational.com; 5. Private Collection. © 2004 Mondrian/Holtzman Trust. c/o hcr@hcrinternational.com; **Introduction 4: 1 •** Städtische Kunsthalle, Düsseldorf. Photo © Gilissen. © DACS 2004; 2. © ADAGP, Paris and DACS, London 2004; 3. Museum of Contemporary Art, Chicago, gift of Susan and Lewis Manilow. © Estate of Robert Smithson/VAGA, New York/DACS, London 2004; 4. © the artist; 5. © 1981 by The University of Chicago; © 1981 by Continuum.;6. Courtesy the artist and Metro Pictures; **1900: 1 •** Photo Dr F. Stoedther; **4 •** Leopold Museum, Vienna; **5 •** Photo Jörg P. Anders. Nationalgalerie Staatliche Museen Preussischer Kulturbesitz, Berlin. © DACS 2004; **1900b: 1 •** Baltimore Museum of Art, The Cone Collection – formed by Dr. Claribel Cone and Miss Etta Cone of Baltimore, Maryland. 50.422. © Succession H. Matisse/DACS 2004; **2 •** Iris & B. Gerald Cantor Collection, Beverly Hills, California; **3 •** Musuem of Modern Art, New York. Lillie P. Bliss Bequest. Photo Soichi Sunami. © Succession H. Matisse/DACS 2004; **4 •** Museum of Modern Art, New York. Gift of Stephen C. Clark. © ADAGP, Paris and DACS, London 2004; **5 •** Museum of Modern Art, New York. Gift of Mrs. Simon Guggenheim Fund. © Succession H. Matisse/DACS 2004; **6 •** Museum of Modern Art, New York. Gift of Mrs. Simon Guggenheim Fund. © Succession H. Matisse/DACS 2004; **7 •** Museum of Modern Art, New York. Gift of Mrs. Simon Guggenheim Fund. © Succession H. Matisse/DACS 2004; **8 •** Museum of Modern Art, New York. Gift of Mrs. Simon Guggenheim Fund. © Succession H. Matisse/DACS 2004; **9 •** Museum of Modern Art, New York. Gift of Mrs. Simon Guggenheim Fund. © Succession H. Matisse/DACS 2004; **10 •** Baltimore Museum of Art, The Cone Collection. © Succession H. Matisse/DACS 2004; **1903: 1 •** Private Collection. © ADAGP, Paris and DACS, London 2004; **2 •** Private Collection; **3 •** Albright Knox Art Gallery, Buffalo, New York, A. Conger Goodyear Collection, 1965; **4 •** Kunstsammlung Nordrhein-Westfalen, Dusseldorf. © Dr.

Wolfgang & Ingeborg Henze-Ketterer, Wichtrach/Bern; **5** • The Baltimore Museum of Art, The Cone Collection, formed by Dr Claribel Cone and Miss Etta Cone. © Succession H. Matisse/DACS 2004; **1906: 1** • Musée d'Orsay, Paris. © Succession H. Matisse/DACS 2004; **box** Roger Fry, *Self-Portrait*, 1918. Oil on canvas, 79.8 x 59.3 (31⅜ x 23⅜). By permission of the Provost and Fellows of King's College, Cambridge. Photo Fine Art Photography; **2** • San Francisco Museum of Modern Art. Bequest of Elise S. Haas. © 2004 Succession H. Matisse/DACS 2004; **3** • Statens Museum fur Kunst, Copenhagen, J. Rump Collection. © Succession H. Matisse/DACS 2004; **4** • National Gallery of Art, Washington D.C. © Succession H. Matisse/DACS 2004; **5** • The Barnes Foundation, Merion, Pennsylvania / The Bridgeman Art Library, London. © Succession H. Matisse/DACS 2004; **1907: 1** • Museum of Modern Art, New York, Lillie P. Bliss Bequest. © Succession Picasso/DACS 2004; **2** • Metropolitan Museum of Art. Bequest of Gertrude Stein, 1946. © Succession Picasso/DACS 2004; **3** • Offentliche Kunstsammlung, Kunstmuseum, Basel. © Succession Picasso/DACS 2004; **4** • Photographed for Gelett Burgess, 1908; **5** • Musée Picasso, Paris. © Succession Picasso/DACS 2004; **6** • Sergei Pankejeff, sketch from *The Wolf-Man & Sigmund Freud*, ed. Murial Gardiner, Hogarth Press, 1972, p.174; **7** • The State Hermitage Museum, St. Petersburg. © Succession Picasso/DACS 2004; **1908: 1** • Städtische Galeries im Lenbachhaus, Munich. © ADAGP, Paris and DACS, London 2004; **2** • Städtische Galeries im Lenbachhaus, Munich. GMS 153. © ADAGP, Paris and DACS, London 2004; **3** • Museum of Modern Art, New York. © Dr. Wolfgang & Ingeborg Henze-Ketterer, Wichtrach/Bern; **4** • Kunstmuseum, Basel; **5** • © Wyndham Lewis and the Estate of the late Mrs G. A. Wyndham Lewis by kind permission of the Wyndham Lewis Memorial Trust (a registered charity); **1909: 2** • Civica Galleria d'Arte Moderna, Milan. © DACS 2004; **3** • Albright-Knox Art Gallery, Buffalo, New York, Bequest of A. Conger Goodyear and Gift of George F. Goodyear, 1964. © DACS 2004; **4** • Museum of Modern Art, New York. Acquired through the Lillie P. Bliss Bequest; **box** Edward Muybridge, *Movement Phases of a Galloping Horse*, 1884–5. Collotype print; Étienne-Jules Marey, *Investigation into Walking*, c. 1884. Geometric chronograph (from original photograph). Collège de France Archives, Paris; **5** • Peggy Guggenheim Collection, Venice; **6** • Mattioli Collection, Milan. © DACS 2004; **7** • Galleria Nazionale d'Arte Moderna, Rome. Isabella Pakszwer de Chirico Donation. © DACS 2004; **8** • Pinacoteca di Brera, Milan. Photo © Scala, Florence/Courtesy of the Ministero Beni e Att. Culturali 1990. © DACS 2004; **1910: 1** • The State Hermitage Museum, St. Petersburg. © Succession H. Matisse/DACS 2004; **2** • The State Hermitage Museum, St. Petersburg. © Succession H. Matisse/DACS 2004; **3** • The State Hermitage Museum, St. Petersburg. © Succession H. Matisse/DACS 2004; **4** • St. Louis Art Museum, Gift of Mr & Mrs Joseph Pulitzer. © Succession H. Matisse/DACS 2004; **5** • The State Hermitage Museum, St. Petersburg. © Succession H. Matisse/DACS 2004; **6** • Musée de Grenoble. Gift of the artist, in the name of his family. © Succession H. Matisse/DACS 2004; Pablo Picasso, *Apollinaire blessé (Apollinaire Wounded)*, 1916. Pencil on paper, 48.8 x 30.5 (19¼ x 12). © Succession Picasso/DACS 2004; **1911: 1** • Art Institute of Chicago. Gift of Mrs. Gilbert W. Chapman in memory of Charles B. Goodspeed. © Succession Picasso/DACS 2004; **2** • Kunstmusuem, Basel. Donation Raoul La Roche. © ADAGP, Paris and DACS, London 2004; **3** • Museum of Modern Art, New York. Nelson A. Rockefeller Bequest. © Succession Picasso/DACS 2004; **4** • Museum of Modern Art, New York. Nelson A. Rockefeller Bequest. © Succession Picasso/DACS 2004; **5** • Musée Picasso, Paris. Photo © RMN – R. G. Ojeda. © Succession Picasso/DACS 2004; **1912: 1** • Private Collection. © ADAGP, Paris and DACS, London 2004; **2** • Musée National d'Art Moderne, Centre Georges Pompidou, Paris. Gift of Henri Laugier. © Succession Picasso/DACS 2004; **3** • Musée National d'Art Moderne, Centre Georges Pompidou, Paris. Gift of Henri Laugier. © Succession Picasso/DACS 2004; **4** • Mildred Lane Kemper Art Museum, Washington University in St. Louis. University Purchase, Kende Sale Fund, 1946. © Succession Picasso/DACS 2004; **5** • Musée National d'Art Moderne, Centre Georges Pompidou, Paris. Gift of Henri Laugier. © Succession Picasso/DACS 2004; **6** • Marion Koogler McNay Art Museum, San Antonio. © Succession Picasso/DACS 2004; **7** • Photo Pablo Picasso. © Succession Picasso/DACS 2004; **8** • Guillaume Apollinaire, *'La Cravate et la Montre'*, 1914. From *Calligrammes: Poèmes de la paix et de la guerre, 1913–16, Part I: Ondes.* Paris: Éditions Gallimard, 1925; **1913: 1** • Private Collection. © DACS 2004; **2** • Národní Galerie, Prague. © ADAGP, Paris and DACS, London 2004; **3** • Philadelphia Museum of Art, The Louise and Walter Arensberg Collection. © ADAGP, Paris and DACS, London 2004; **4** • Solomon R. Guggenheim Museum, New York. © 2004 Mondrian/Holtzman Trust. c/o hcr@hcrinternational.com; **5** • © L & M Services B.V. Amsterdam 20040801; **6** • © L & M Services B.V. Amsterdam 20040801; **7** • © L & M Services B.V. Amsterdam 20040801; **8** • Museum of Theatrical and Musical Arts, St Petersburg; **1914: 1** • Philadelphia Museum of Art, The Louise and Walter Arensberg Collection. © Succession Marcel Duchamp/ADAGP, Paris and DACS, London 2004; **2** • Whereabouts unknown. © DACS 2004; **3** • Photo State Film, Photographic and Sound Archive, St Petersburg. © DACS 2004; **4** • Hessisches Landesmuseum, Darmstadt. © Succession Marcel Duchamp/ADAGP, Paris and DACS, London 2004; **5** • Photo Tate, London 2004. © Succession Marcel Duchamp/ADAGP, Paris and DACS, London 2004; **1915: 1** • Museum of Modern Art, New York; **3** • State Russian Museum, St Petersburg; **4** • Stedelijk Museum, Amsterdam; **5** • Museum of Modern Art, New York; **1916a: 2** • Musée National d'Art Moderne, Centre Georges Pompidou, Paris. © ADAGP, Paris and DACS, London 2004; **3** • Private Collection. © DACS 2004; **4** • Kunstmuseum, Bern, Paul Klee Stiftung. © DACS 2004; **5** • Collection The Israel Museum, Jerusalem. Gift of Fania and Gershom Scholem, John and Paul Herring, Jo Carole and Ronald Lauder. Photo Collection The Israel Museum / by David Harris. © DACS 2004; **1916b: 1** • Metropolitan Museum of Art, New York. © ADAGP, Paris and DACS, London 2004; **2** • Museum of Modern Art, New York. © ARS, NY and DACS, London 2004; **3** • Museum of Modern Art, New York. Reprinted with permission of Joanna T. Steichen; **4** • Museum of Modern Art, New York. © ARS, NY and DACS, London 2004; **5** • © 1971 Aperture Foundation Inc., Paul Strand Archive; **6** • Philadelphia Museum of Art, The Alfred Stieglitz Collection. © ARS, NY and DACS, London 2004; **1917: 1** • Rijksmuseum Kröller-Müller, Otterlo, The Netherlands. © 2004 Mondrian/Holtzman Trust. c/o hcr@hcrinternational.com; **2** • Rijksmuseum Kröller-Müller, Otterlo, The Netherlands. © 2004 Mondrian/Holtzman Trust. c/o hcr@hcrinternational.com; **3** • Gemeentemuseum Den Haag. © 2004 Mondrian/Holtzman Trust. c/o hcr@hcrinternational.com; **4** • Stedelijk Museum, Amsterdam. © 2004 Mondrian/Holtzman Trust c/o hcr@hcrinternational.com; **5** • From *L'Architecture Vivante*, Autumn 1924. The British Architectural Library, RIBA. © DACS 2004; **1918: 1** • Philadelphia Museum of Art, Walter and Louise Arensberg Collection. © Succession Marcel Duchamp/ADAGP, Paris and DACS, London 2004; **2** • Museum of Modern Art, New York. Katherine S. Dreier Bequest. © Succession Marcel Duchamp/ADAGP, Paris and DACS, London 2004; **3** • Museum of Modern Art, New York. © DACS 2004; **4** • Yale University Art Gallery, New Haven, Connecticut. Gift of Katherine S. Dreier. © Succession Marcel Duchamp/ADAGP, Paris and DACS, London 2004; **5** • Private Collection, Paris. © Succession Marcel Duchamp/ADAGP, Paris and DACS, London 2004. © Man Ray Trust/ADAGP, Paris and DACS, London 2004; **box** Man Ray, *Rrose Sélavy*, c. 1920–1. Silver-gelatin print, 21 x 17.3 (8¼ x 6¾). Philadelphia Museum of Art. The Samuel S. White 3rd and Vera White Collection. © Man Ray Trust /ADAGP, Paris and DACS, London 2004. © Succession Marcel Duchamp/ADAGP, Paris and DACS, London 2004; **1919: 1** • Musée Picasso, Paris. © Succession Picasso/DACS 2004; **box** Pablo Picasso, *Portrait of Sergei Diaghilev and Alfred Seligsberg*, 1919. Charcoal and black pencil, 65 x 55 (25⅝ x 21⅝). Musée Picasso, Paris. © Succession Picasso/DACS 2004; **2** • Private Collection. © Succession Picasso/DACS 2004; **3** • © ADAGP, Paris and DACS, London 2004; **4** • Musée Picasso, Paris. © Succession Picasso/DACS 2004; **5** • Yale University Art Gallery, New Haven, Connecticut. Gift of Collection Société Anonyme; **1920: 2** • Staatliche Museen, Berlin. © DACS 2004; **3** • Musée National d'Art Moderne, Centre Georges Pompidou, Paris. © ADAGP, Paris and DACS, London 2004; **4** • Photo Akademie der Künste der DDR, Berlin. Grosz © DACS, 2004. Heartfield © The Heartfield Community of Heirs/VG Bild-Kunst, Bonn and DACS, London 2004; **5** • Musée National d'Art Moderne, Centre Georges Pompidou, Paris. © ADAGP, Paris and DACS, London 2004; **6** • Akademie der Kunst, Berlin. © The Heartfield Community of Heirs/VG Bild-Kunst, Bonn and DACS, London 2004; **7** • Russian State Library, Moscow; **1921: 1** • National Museum, Stockholm. © DACS 2004; **4** • Museum of Modern Art, New York. © DACS 2004; **5** • A. Rodchenko and V. Stepanova Archive, Moscow. © DACS 2004; **1922: 1** • © DACS 2004; **2** • Paul Klee-Stiftung, Kunstmuseum, Berne (inv. G62). © DACS 2004; **3** • Private Collection. © ADAGP, Paris and DACS, London 2004; **4** • Sammlung Prinzhorn der Psychiatrischen Universitätsklinik Heidelbert; **5** • Lindy and Edwin Bergman Collection. © ADAGP, Paris and DACS, London 2004; **1923: 2** • Bauhaus-Archiv, Museum für Gestaltung, Berlin. © DACS 2004; **3** • President and Fellows, Harvard College, Harvard University Art Museums, Gift of Sibyl Moholy-Nagy. © DACS 2004; **4** • Bauhaus-Archiv, Museum für Gestaltung, Berlin. © DACS 2004; **5** • © Dr Franz Stoedtner, Düsseldorf; **6** • Barry Friedman Ltd, New York; **7** • Bauhaus-Archiv, Museum für Gestaltung, Berlin. Brandt © DACS 2004; **1924: 1** • Photo Per-Anders Allsten, Moderna Museet, Stockholm. © DACS 2004; **2** • Museum of Modern Art, New York. © ADAGP, Paris and DACS, London 2004; **3** • Museum of Modern Art, New York. Given anonymously. © Salvador Dalí, Gala-Salvador Dalí Foundation. DACS, London 2004; **4** • Collection Jose Mugrabi. © Successió Miró – ADAGP, Paris, DACS, London 2004; **5** • © Man Ray Trust/ADAGP, Paris and DACS, London 2004; **box** Man Ray, cover of *La Révolution surréaliste*. Black-and-white photograph. © Man Ray Trust/ADAGP, Paris and DACS, London 2004; **6** • © Man Ray Trust/ADAGP, Paris and DACS, London 2004; **7** • Private collection, Paris. © ADAGP, Paris and DACS, London 2004; **1925a: 1** • © FLC/ADAGP, Paris and DACS, London 2004; **2** • Musée National d'Art Moderne, Centre Georges Pompidou, Paris. Photo © CNAC/MNAM Dist. RMN/ © Jacqueline Hyde. © FLC/ADAGP, Paris and DACS, London 2004; **3** • Museum of Modern Art, New York. Mrs Simon Guggenheim Fund, 1942. © ADAGP, Paris and DACS, London 2004; **4** • Museum of Modern Art, New York. © ADAGP, Paris and DACS, London 2004; **5** • Léger © ADAGP, Paris and DACS, London 2004; **7** • © DACS 2004; **1925b: 1** • Nationalgalerie, Berlin. © DACS 2004; **2** • Kunstsammlung Nordrhein-Westfalen, Düsseldorf. © DACS 2004; **3** • Private Collection. © Christian Schad Stiftung Aschaffenburg/VG Bild-Kunst, Bonn and DACS, London 2004; **4** • Musée National d'Art Moderne, Centre Georges Pompidou, Paris. © DACS 2004; **5** • Museum of Modern Art, New York, Purchase 49.52. © DACS 2004; **1926: 1** • Ronald S. Lauder. © DACS 2004; **2** • Stadtbibliothek Hannover, Schwitters Archive. © DACS 2004; **3** • Stedelijk van Abbe Museum, Eindhoven, The Netherlands. © DACS 2004; **4** • Stedelijk van Abbe Museum, Eindhoven, The Netherlands. © DACS 2004; **5** • © DACS 2004; **1927a: 1** • Los Angeles County Museum of Art, purchased with funds provided by the Mr and Mrs William Harrison Collection. © ADAGP, Paris and DACS, London 2004; **2** • Musée National d'Art Moderne, Centre Georges Pompidou, Paris. © ADAGP, Paris and DACS, London 2004; **3** • Private Collection. © ADAGP, Paris and DACS, London 2004; **1927b: 1** • Philadelphia Museum of Art. © ADAGP, Paris and DACS, London 2004; **2** • Musée National d'Art Moderne, Centre Georges Pompidou, Paris. © ADAGP, Paris and DACS, London 2004; **3** • The Musée National d'Art Moderne, Centre Georges Pompidou, Paris. © ADAGP, Paris and DACS, London 2004; **4** • National Gallery of Art, Washington D.C. Given in loving memory of her husband, Taft Schreiber, by Rita Schreiber, 1989. © ADAGP, Paris and DACS, London 2004; **5** • The Musée National d'Art Moderne, Centre Georges Pompidou, Paris. © ADAGP, Paris and DACS, London 2004; **1927c: 1** • Mildred Lane Kemper Art Museum, Washington University in St Louis. University Purchase, Bixby Fund, 1952; **box** Alfred Barr 'The Development of Abstract Art' chart prepared for the jacket of the catalogue *Cubism and Abstract Art* published by the Museum of Modern Art New York, 1936; **2** • The Newark Museum, New York. ; **3** • Whitney Museum of American Art, New York; **4** • Museum of Modern Art, New York; **5** • Whitney Museum of American Art, New York, Purchase 41.3. © Estate of Stuart Davis/VAGA, New York/DACS, London 2004; **6** • Metropolitan Museum of Art, New York, Alfred Stieglitz Collection 1969 (69.278.1). © ARS, NY and DACS, London 2004; **1928: 1** • © DACS 2004; **3** • Kunsthandel Wolfgang Werner KG, Bremen; **4** • Sprengel Museum, Hanover. © DACS 2004; **5** • Muzeum Sztuki, Lódz, Poland. Photo Mariusz Lukawski; **6** • Muzeum Sztuki, Lódz, Poland. Photo Piotr Tomczyk; **1929: 2** • Photo © The Lane Collection; **3** • Kunstbibliothek Preussischer Kulturbesitz, Berlin; **5** • © Albert Renger-Patzsch-Archiv/Ann und Jürgen Wilde, Köln/VG Bild-Kunst, Bonn and DACS, London 2004; **6** • Bauhaus-Archiv, Museum für Gestaltung, Berlin. © DACS 2004; **7** • Courtesy Galerie Wilde, Cologne; **1930a: 1** • Sammlung Ann und Jürgen Wilde, Zülpich, Köln/Zülpich. Estate Germaine Krull, Museum Folkwang, Fotografische Sammlung, Essen; **2** • Lotte Jacobi Collection, University of New Hampshire; **3** • Museum Folkwang, Essen; **4** • Museum für Moderne Kunst, Frankfurt am Main. © Gisèle Freund/Agency Nina Beskow; **5** • Lotte Jacobi Collection, University of New Hampshire; **1930b: 1** • Museum of Modern Art, New York. Purchase. © Succession Miró, DACS, 2004; **2** • Alberto Giacometti Foundation, Zurich. © ADAGP, Paris and DACS, London 2004; **3** • Private Collection, Paris. © Man Ray Trust/ADAGP, Paris and DACS, London 2004; **4** • Musée National d'Art Moderne, Centre Georges Pompidou, Paris. ESTATE BRASSAÏ – R.M.N. – © CNAC/Mnam.Dist RMN-Jacques Faujour; **5** • Manoukian Collection, Paris. © Salvador Dalí, Gala-Salvador Dalí Foundation, DACS, London 2004; **1931: 1** • Collection Lucien Treillard, Paris. © Man Ray Trust/ADAGP, Paris and DACS, London 2004; **3** • Photo Per-Anders Allsten, Moderna Museet, Stockholm.

© DACS 2004; **4** • National Gallery of Art Washington, D.C. © ADAGP, Paris and DACS, London 2004; **5** • Collection Robert Lehrman, Washington, D.C. © The Joseph and Robert Cornell Memorial Foundation/VAGA, New York/DACS, London 2004; **1933: 1** • © DACS 2004; **2** • Photo Bob Schalkwijk, Mexico City. © 2004 Banco de México, Diego Rivera & Frida Kahlo Museums Trust. Av. Cinco de Mayo No. 2, Col. Centro, Del. Cuauhtémoc 06059, México, D.F.; **3** • Mexican Electricians' Syndicate, Mexico City. Courtesy of Laurence P. Hurlbert, Middleton, Wisconsin. © DACS 2004; **4** • © 2004 Banco de México Diego Rivera & Frida Kahlo Museums Trust. Av. Cinco de Mayo No.2, Col. Centro, Del. Cuauhtémoc 06059, México, D.F.; **1934a: 1** • © DACS 2004; **2** • Historical Museum, Moscow. © DACS 2004; **3** • Tretyakov Gallery, Moscow. © DACS 2004; **4** • Tretyakov Gallery, Moscow; **1934b: 1** • Père Lachaise Cemetary, Paris. Frantisek Staud/www.phototravels.net. © Tate, London 2004; **2** • Birmingham Museums & Art Gallery. © Tate, London 2004; **3** • Photo Tate, London 2004. Photo David Quinn; **4** • Photo Tate, London 2004. Reproduced by permission of the Henry Moore Foundation; **5** • The Pier Gallery Collection, Stromness. © Bowness, Hepworth Estate; **1935: 1** • Museum of Modern Art, New York. Mr. and Mrs. John Spencer Fund. © DACS 2004; **2** • Die Photographische Sammlung/SK Stiftung Kultur – August Sander Archiv, Köln/VG Bild-Kunst, Bonn and DACS, London 2004; **3** • Die Photographische Sammlung/SK Stiftung Kultur – August Sander Archiv, Köln/VG Bild-Kunst, Bonn and DACS, London 2004; **5** • Philadelphia Museum of Art, Walter and Louise Arensberg Collection. © Succession Marcel Duchamp/ADAGP, Paris and DACS, London 2004; **1936: 1** • Courtesy the Dorothea Lange Collection, Oakland Museum of California; **2** • Library of Congress, Washington, D.C., LC-USF342-T01-008057; **3** • Library of Congress, Washington, D.C., LC-USZ62-103098; **4** • Archives Photographiques, Paris; **5** • Library of Congress, Washington, D.C., LC-USZ62-34372; **1937a: 1** • Photo Bildarchiv Preussischer Kulturbesitz, Berlin; **2** • The Merrill C. Berman Collection. © Schawinsky Family; **3** • Nuremberg, Grounds of the Reichsparteitag, Breker Museum/Marco-VG; **5** • Museo Nacional Centro de Arte Reina Sophia, Madrid. On permanent loan from the Museo Nacional del Prado, Madrid. © Succession Picasso/DACS 2004; **1937b: 1** • Photo Tate, London 2004. © Angela Verren-Taunt 2004. All Rights Reserved, DACS; **2** • Hamburg Kunsthalle/bpk, Berlin. Photo Elke Walford. © ADAGP, Paris and DACS, London 2004; **3** • Felix Witzinger, Switzerland/The Bridgeman Art Library, London; **1942a: 1** • Private Collection, Courtesy Paalen Archiv, Berlin; **2** • Estate of William Baziotes, Collection Mary Jane Kamrowski. Pollock: © ARS, NY and DACS, London 2004; **3** • Formerly collection Simone Collinet, Paris. © ADAGP, Paris and DACS, London 2004; **4** • The Solomon R. Guggenheim Museum, New York. © ADAGP, Paris and DACS, London 2004; **5** • Albright-Knox Art Gallery, Buffalo, New York. Gift of Seymour H. Knox, 1956. © ADAGP, Paris and DACS, London 2004; **6** • Collection Seattle Art Museum. Gift of Mr and Mrs Bagley Wright. © ADAGP, Paris and DACS, London 2004; **1942b: 2** • Morton Neumann Collection, Chicago. © ADAGP, Paris and DACS, London 2004; **3** • © Succession Marcel Duchamp/ADAGP, Paris and DACS, London 2004; **4** • Courtesy Mrs Frederick Kiesler, New York; **5** • Philadelphia Museum of Art, Gift of Jacqueline, Paul and Peter Matisse in memory of their mother Alexina Duchamp. © Succession Marcel Duchamp/ADAGP, Paris and DACS, London 2004; **1943: 1** • Collection Schomburg Center for Research in Black Culture, The NY Public Library, The Astor, Lenox and Tilden Foundations, New York. Courtesy of the Meta V. W. Fuller Trust; **2** • © Donna Mussenden VanDerZee; **3** • The Gallery of Art, Howard University, Washington D.C. Courtesy of the Aaron and Alta Sawyer Douglas Foundation; **4** • National Museum of American Art, Smithsonian Institution. Museum purchase made possible by Mrs N. H. Green, Dr R. Harlan and Francis Musgrave. © Lois Mailou Jones Pierre-Noel Trust; **5** • The Metropolitan Museum of Art, Arthur Hoppock Hearn Fund, 1942, 42.167. © ARS, NY and DACS, London 2004; **6** • The Estate of Reginald Lewis. Courtesy of landor Fine Arts, Newark, New Jersey. Photo Frank Stewart; **7** • The Gallery of Art, Howard University, Washington D.C. © DACS, London/VAGA, New York 2004; **1944a: 1** • Private Collection. Photo Instituut Collectie Nederland. © 2004 Mondrian/Holtzman Trust. c/o hcr@hcrinternational.com; **2** • Private Collection, Basel. © 2004 Mondrian/Holtzman Trust. c/o hcr@hcrinternational.com; **3** • Phillips Collection, Washington D.C. © 2004 Mondrian/Holtzman Trust. c/o hcr@hcrinternational.com; **4** • Kunstsammlung Nordrhein-Westfalen, Dusseldorf. © 2004 Mondrian/Holtzman Trust. c/o hcr@international.com; **5** • Museum of Modern Art, New York. Given anonymously. © 2004 Mondrian/Holtzman Trust. c/o hcr@international.com; **1944b: 1** • Musée National d'Art Moderne, Centres Georges Pompidou, Paris. © Succession H. Matisse/DACS 2004; **2** • Musée National d'Art Moderne, Centre Georges Pompidou, Paris. © Succession H. Matisse/DACS 2004; **3** • UCLA Art Galleries, LA. © Succession H. Matisse/DACS 2004; **4** • Private Collection. © Succession Picasso/DACS 2004; **5** • Musée National d'Art Moderne, Centre Georges Pompidou, Paris. © ADAGP, Paris and DACS, London 2004; **6** • Musée National d'Art Moderne, Centre Georges Pompidou, Paris. © ADAGP, Paris and DACS, London 2004; **7** • Private Collection. © DACS 2004; **1945: 1** • Indiana University Art Museum, Bloomington, Indiana Photo Michael Cavanagh, Kevin Montague, IUAM #69.151. © Estate of David Smith/VAGA, New York/DACS, London 2004; **2** • Museum of Modern Art, New York. Mrs Solomon Guggenheim Fund. © ADAGP, Paris and DACS, London 2004; **3** • Musée Picasso, Paris. Photo © RMN Béatrice Hatala. © Succession Picasso/DACS 2004; **4** • Private Collection. Photo David Smith. © Estate of David Smith/VAGA, New York/DACS, London 2004; **5** • Private Collection. Photo Robert Lorenzson. © Estate of David Smith/VAGA, New York/DACS, London 2004; **6** • Photo Shigeo Anzai. © Sir Anthony Caro; **7** • Whitney Museum of American Art, New York Gift of the Albert A. List Family 70.1579a–b. © ARS, NY and DACS, London 2004; **1946: 1** • Solomon R. Guggenheim Museum, New York. © ADAGP, Paris and DACS, London 2004; **2** • The Menil Collection, Houston; **3** • Galerie Limmer, Friburg im Breisgau. © ADAGP, Paris and DACS, London 2004; **4** • Musée d'Art Moderne de la Ville de Paris. © ADAGP, Paris and DACS, London 2004; **5** • Musée National d'Art Moderne, Centre Georges Pompidou, Paris. Photo Jacques Faujour. © ADAGP, Paris and DACS, London 2004; **1947a: 1** • © DACS 2004; **2** • © The Josef and Anni Albers Foundation/VG Bild-Kunst, Bonn and DACS, London 2004; **3** • Photo Tim Nighswander. © The Josef and Anni Albers Foundation/VG Bild-Kunst, Bonn and DACS, London 2004; **1947b: 1** • Nina Leen/Getty Images; **2** • Art Institute of Chicago, Mary and Earle Ludgin Collection. © Willem de Kooning Revocable Trust/ARS, NY and DACS, London 2004; **3** • Private Collection. © Dedalus Foundation, Inc/VAGA, New York/DACS, London 2004; **4** • Museum of Modern Art, new York. Bequest of Mrs. Mark Rothko through The Mark Rothko Foundation Inc. 428.81. © 1998 Kate Rothko Prizel & Christopher Rothko/DACS 2004; **5** • Private Collection. © ARS, NY and DACS, London 2004; **1949: 1** • Museum of Modern Art, New York. Sidney and Harriet Janis Collection Fund (by exchange). Photo Scala, Florence/The Museum of Modern Art, New York. © ARS, NY and DACS, London 2004; **2** • Photo Tate, London 2004. © ARS, NY and DACS, London 2004; **3** • Photo Musée National d'Art Moderne, Centre Georges Pompidou, Paris. © ARS, NY and DACS, London 2000; **4** • Museum of Modern Art, New York. © ARS, NY and DACS, London 2004; **5** • Metropolitan Museum of Art, George A. Hearn Fund, 1957 (57.92). © ARS, NY and DACS, London 2004; **1951: 1** • Museum of Modern Art, New York. Courtesy of The Barnett Newman Foundation. © ARS, NY and DACS, London 2004; **2** • Museum of Modern Art, New York. Courtesy of The Barnett Newman Foundation. © ARS, NY and DACS, London 2004; **3** • Courtesy of The Barnett Newman Foundation. Photo Hans Namuth. © Hans Namuth Ltd. Pollock © ARS, NY and DACS, London 2004; **4** • Courtesy of The Barnett Newman Foundation. © ARS, NY and DACS, London 2004; **5** • Collection of David Geffen, Los Angeles. Courtesy of The Barnett Newman Foundation. © ARS, NY and DACS, London 2004; **1953: 1** • San Francisco Museum of Modern Art, purchased through a gift of Phyllis Wattis. © Robert Rauschenberg/VAGA, New York/DACS, London 2004; **2** • Collection of the artist. © Robert Rauschenberg/VAGA, New York/DACS, London 2004; **3** • Private Collection. © Ellsworth Kelly; **4** • Museum of Modern Art, New York. © Ellsworth Kelly; **5** • Marx Collection, Berlin; **1955a: 1** • Photo Hans Namuth. © Hans Namuth Ltd. Pollock © ARS, NY and DACS, London 2004; **2** • Hyogo Prefectural Museum of Modern Art, Kobe. Courtesy Matsumoto Co. Ltd; **3** • Courtesy Matsumoto Co. Ltd; **4** • © Makiko Murakami; **5** • Photo Guy Brett. © Cultural Association 'The World of Lygia Clark'. © ADAGP, Paris and DACS, London 2004; **6** • Clark Family Collection. Photo Marcelo Correa. Courtesy Cultural Assosication 'The World of Lygia Clark'. © ADAGP, Paris and DACS, London 2004; **7** • Clark Family Collection. Photo Marcelo Correa. Courtesy Cultural Assosication 'The World of Lygia Clark'. © ADAGP, Paris and DACS, London 2004; **1955b: 1** • Photo Galerie Denise René, Paris; **2** • Photo Tate, London 2004. The works of Naum Gabo © Nina Williams.; **3** • Private Collection. © ARS, NY and DACS, London 2004; **5** • Collection the artist. Photo Clay Perry; **1956: 1** • Photo Tate, London 2004. © Eduardo Paolozzi 2004. All Rights Reserved, DACS; **2** • Private Collection. © Richard Hamilton 2004. All Rights Reserved, DACS; **3** • © The Estate of Nigel Henderson, courtesy of the Mayor Gallery, London; **4** • © The Estate of Nigel Henderson. Courtesy of the Mayor Gallery, London; **5** • Courtesy of Richard Hamilton. © Richard Hamilton 2004. All Rights Reserved, DACS; **6** • Kunsthalle, Tübingen. Prof. Dr. Georg Zundel Collection. © Richard Hamilton 2004. All Rights Reserved, DACS; **1957a: 1** • Musée Nationale d'Art Moderne, Paris, Centres Georges Pompidou, Paris. Jorn © Asger Jorn/DACS 2004; **2** • Musée d'Art Moderne et Contemporain de Strasbourg, Cabinet d'Art Graphique. Photo A. Plisson. © Alice Debord, 2004; **3** • Installation at Historisch Museum, Amsterdam. Photo Richard Kasiewicz. © documenta Archiv; **4** • Courtesy Archivio Gallizio, Turin; **5** • Courtesy Archivio Gallizio, Turin; **6** • Collection Pierre Alechinsky, Bougival. Photo André Morain, Paris. © Asger Jorn/DACS 2004; **7** • Collection Pierre Alechinsky, Bougival. Photo André Morain, Paris. © Asger Jorn/DACS 2004; **1957b: 1** • Photo Tate, London 2004. © ARS, NY and DACS, London 2004; **2** • Modern Art Museum of Fort Worth, Texas, Museum Purchase, Sid W. Richardson Foundation Endowment Fund. © Agnes Martin; **3** • The Greenwich Collection Ltd. © Robert Ryman; **4** • Stedelijk Museum, Amsterdam. © Robert Ryman; **1958: 1** • Museum of Modern Art, New York. Gift of Mr & Mrs Robert C. Scull. Photo Scala, Florence/Museum of Modern Art, New York 2003. © Jasper Johns/VAGA, New York/DACS, London 2004; **2** • Museum of Modern Art, New York. Gift of Philip Johnson in honour of Alfred Barr. © Jasper Johns/VAGA, New York/DACS, London 2004; **3** • Collection the artist. © Jasper Johns/VAGA, New York/DACS, London 2004; **4** • Whitney Museum of American Art, New York. Gift of Mr and Mrs Eugene M. Schwartz. © ARS, NY and DACS, London 2004; **5** • Menil Foundation Collection, Houston. © ARS, NY and DACS, London 2004; **1959a: 1** • Galerie Bruno Bischofberger, Zurich. © Fondazione Lucio Fontana, Milan; **2** • Musée National d'Art Moderne, Centre Georges Pompidou, Paris. © Fondazione Lucio Fontana, Milan; **3** • Private Collection, Milan. © Fondazione Lucio Fontana, Milan; **4** • Archivio Opera Piero Manzoni, Milan. © DACS 2004; **5** • Herning Kunstmuseum, Denmark. © DACS 2004; **1959b: 1** • Photo Charles Brittin. © The Wallace Berman Estate. ; **2** • Photo of *CHILD* courtesy of Bruce Conner. Museum of Modern Art, New York, gift of Philip Johnson; **3** • Photo © MUMOK, Museum Moderner Kunst Stiftung Ludwig, Vienna; **4** • Museum Moderner Kunst, Vienna. © Nancy Reddin Kienholz; **5** • Museum Ludwig, Cologne. © Nancy Reddin Kienholz; **1959c: 1** • Private Collection. © ADAGP, Paris and DACS, London 2004; **2** • Kunsthaus Zürich. Alberto Giacometti Foundation. © ADAGP, Paris and DACS, London 2004; **3** • Purchased with funds from the Coffin Fine Arts Trust; Nathan Emory Coffin Collection of the Des Moines Art Center, 1980. Photo Michael Tropea, Chicago. © Estate of Francis Bacon 2004. All rights reserved, DACS; **4** • Hirshhorn Museum and Sculpture Garden, Smithsonian Institution, Gift of Joseph H. Hirschhorn, 1966. © Willem de Kooning Revocable Trust/ARS, NY and DACS, London 2004; **1959d: 1** • Courtesy Michel Brodovitch; **2** • Courtesy Laurence Miller Gallery, New York. © Helen Levitt; **3** • Courtesy Baudoin Lebon, Paris; **4** • © Weegee (Arthur Fellig)/International Centre of Photography/Getty Images; **5** • Museum of Modern Art, New York. © 1971 The Estate of Diane Arbus; **6** • Courtesy Pace/MacGill Gallery, New York. © Robert Frank; **1960a: 1** • Photograph © David Gahr, 1960. © DACS 2004; **2** • Photo Jean-Dominique Lajoux. Copyright Christo 1962; **3** • Photo Andre Morain. Collection Musée National d'Art Moderne, Centre Georges Pompidou, Paris. Courtesy Ginette Dufrêne, Paris. © ADAGP, Paris and DACS, London 2004; **4** • Musée National d'Art Moderne, Centre Georges Pompidou, Paris. Villeglé © ADAGP, Paris and DACS, London 2004. Hains © ADAGP, Paris and DACS, London 2004; **5** • Museum of Modern Art, New York. Photo Scala, Florence. The Museum of Modern Art, New York 2003. © DACS 2004; **6** • © ADAGP, Paris and DACS, London 2004; **1960b: 1** • Yale University Art Gallery, New Haven. Richard Brown Baker bequest. © ARS, NY and DACS, London 2004; **2** • The Solomon R. Guggenheim Museum, New York. © 1959 Morris Louis; **3** • National Gallery of Art, Washington, D.C., Gift of Marcella Louis Brenner. © 1961 Morris Louis; **4** • Des Moines Art Center, purchased with funds from the Coffin Fine Arts Trust, Nathan Emory Coffin Collection of the Des Moines Art Center, 1974. © Kenneth Noland/VAGA, New York/DACS, London 2004; **5** • Collection the artist, on loan to the National Gallery of Art, Washington D.C. © Helen Frankenthaler; **1960c: 1** • Private Collection. © The Estate of Roy Lichtenstein/DACS 2004; **2** • Scottish National Gallery of Modern Art, Edinburgh. © The Estate of Roy Lichtenstein/DACS 2004; **3** • Musée National d'Art Moderne, Centre Georges Pompidou, Paris. © James Rosenquist/VAGA, New York/DACS, London 2004; **4** • The Eli and Edythe L. Broad Collection. © Ed Ruscha; **5** • Whitney Museum of American Art, New York, Purchase, with funds from the Mrs Percy Uris Purchase Fund 85.41. © Ed Ruscha; **6** • Private Collection. © The Estate of Roy Lichtenstein/DACS 2004; **1961: 1** • Photo © Robert R. McElroy/VAGA, New York/DACS, London 2004. © Claes

Oldenberg and Coosje van Bruggen; **2** • Research Library, Getty Research Institute, Los Angeles (980063). Photo © Robert R. McElroy/VAGA, New York/DACS, London 2004. ; **3** • Courtesy Research Library, Getty Research Institute, Los Angeles (980063). Photo © Sol Goldberg; **4** • Photo Martha Holmes. © Claes Oldenburg and Coosje van Bruggen; **5** • Whitney Museum of American Art, New York. 50th Anniversary Gift of Mr. and Mrs. Victor W. Ganz 79.83a–b. Photo Jerry L. Thompson, New York. © Claes Oldenburg and Coosje van Bruggen; **1962a: 1** • Courtesy the Gilbert and Lila Silverman Fluxus Collection, Detroit. Photo George Maciunas; **2** • Courtesy the artist; **3a** • Photo © dpa. © Nam June Paik; **3b** • Courtesy Museum Wiesbaden. © Nam June Paik; **4** • Courtesy Gilbert and Lila Silverman Fluxus Collection, Detroit. Photo George Maciunas; **5** • Courtesy Gilbert and Lila Silverman Fluxus Collection, Detroit. Photo Paul Silverman; **6** • Courtesy Robert Watts Studio Archive, New York. Photo Larry Miller; **7** • Courtesy Gilbert and Lila Silverman Fluxus Collection, Detroit. Photo R. H. Hensleigh; **8** • Courtesy Gilbert and Lila Silverman Fluxus Collection, Detroit. Photo R. H. Hensleigh; **1962b: 1** • Courtesy Gallery Kranzinger, Vienna; **2** • Courtesy Hermann Nitsch. Photo L. Hoffenreich. © DACS 2004; **3** • Scottish National Gallery of Modern Art, Edinburgh. © the artist; **4** • © The artist; **5** • Courtesy the artist. Photo Werner Schulz. © DACS 2004; **1962c: 1** • Photo Cathy Carver © Dia Art Foundation. Estate of Dan Flavin. © ARS, NY and DACS, London 2004; **2** • Formally Saatchi Collection, London. © ARS, NY and DACS, London 2004; **3** • Courtesy Paula Cooper Gallery, New York. © Carl Andre/VAGA, New York/DACS, London 2004; **4** • Photo Tate, London 2004. © Carl Andre/VAGA, New York/DACS, London 2004; **5** • © Sol LeWitt. © ARS, NY and DACS, London 2004; **6** • Collection Neues Museum Weimar. © Sol LeWitt. © ARS, NY and DACS, London 2004; **1963: 1** • Museum Ludwig, Cologne. © Georg Baselitz; **2** • Collection Verlag Gachnang und Springer, Bern-Berlin. © DACS 2004; **3** • Sammlung Ludwig, Museum of Modern Art, Vienna. © Georg Baselitz; **1964a: 1** • Photo Heinrich Riebeshl. © DACS 2004; **2** • Photo Heinrich Riebesehl. © DACS 2004; **3** • Museum Schloss Moyland, Bedburg-Hau. Collection van der Grinten, MSM 03087. © DACS 2004; **4** • Photo Walter Klein, Düsseldorf. Museum Schloss Moyland, Bedburg-Hau. © DACS 2004; **5** • Hessisches Landesmuseum, Darmstadt. © DACS 2004; **1964b: 1** • Dia Art Foundation, New York. The Menil Collection, Houston. © The Andy Warhol Foundation for the Visual Arts, Inc./ARS, NY and DACS, London 2004; **2** • Photo Tate, London 2004. © The Andy Warhol Foundation for the Visual Arts, Inc./ARS, NY and DACS, London 2004; **3** • The Menil Collection, Houston. © The Andy Warhol Foundation for the Visual Arts, Inc./ARS, NY and DACS, London 2004; **4** • © The Andy Warhol Foundation for the Visual Arts, Inc./ARS, NY and DACS, London 2004; **1965: 1** • Art © Judd Foundation. Licensed by VAGA, New York/DACS, London 2004; **2** • © ARS, NY and DACS, London 2004; 3. © ARS, NY and DACS, London 2004; **1966a: 1** • Collection Hirshhorn Museum and Sculpture Garden, Smithsonian Institution, Washington D.C., Joseph H. Hirshhorn Purchase Fund, Holenia Purchase Fund, and Museum Purchase, 1993. Courtesy Sperone Westwater, New York. © ARS, NY and DACS, London 2004; **2** • Collection Jasper Johns, New York. © Succession Marcel Duchamp/ADAGP, Paris and DACS, London 2004; **3** • Philadelphia Museum of Art. Gift of the Cassandra Foundation. © Succession Marcel Duchamp/ADAGP, Paris and DACS, London 2004; **4** • Philadelphia Museum of Art. Gift of the Cassandra Foundation. © Succession Marcel Duchamp/ADAGP, Paris and DACS, London 2004; **1966b: 1** • Museum of Modern Art, New York. Photo © Estate of Peter Moore/VAGA, New York/DACS, London 2004. © Louise Bourgeois/VAGA, New York/DACS, London 2004; **2** • Courtesy Cheim & Read, New York. Photo Rafael Lobato. © Louise Bourgeois/VAGA, New York/DACS, London 2004; **3** • Courtesy the artist; **4** • National Gallery of Australia, Canberra. © The Estate of Eva Hesse. Hauser & Wirth Zürich and London; **5** • Daros Collection, Switzerland. © The Estate of Eva Hesse. Hauser & Wirth Zürich and London; **1967a: 1** • © Estate of Robert Smithson/VAGA, New York/DACS, London 2004; **2** • Collection of Geertjan Visser. Courtesy Sperone Westwater, New York. © ARS, NY and DACS, London 2004; **3** • Courtesy Gagosian Gallery, London. © Ed Ruscha; **4** • Private Collection. © ARS, NY and DACS, London 2004; **5** • Courtesy the Estate of Gordon Matta-Clark and David Zwirner, New York. © ARS, NY and DACS, London 2004; **1967b: 1** • Courtesy Archivo Merz, Turin; **2** • Photo Claudio Abate. Courtesy the artist; **3** • © the artist; **4** • Installation of 12 Piedi at Centre Georges Pompidou, Paris, 1972. Photo © Giorgio Colombo, Milan; **5** • Courtesy the artist; **6** • Galleria Civica d'Arte Moderna e Contemporanea di Torino – Fondazione De' Fornaris. Courtesy Fondazione Torino Musei – Archivio Fotografico, Turin; **7** • Photo the artist; **8** • Collection Annemarie Sauzeau Boetti, Paris. © DACS 2004; **1967c: 1** • No 58005/1–4, Collection Manfred Wandel, Stiftung für Konkrete Kunst, Reutlingen, Germany. ; Courtesy François Morellet. © ADAGP, Paris and DACS, London 2004; **2** • Photo Moderna Museet, Stockholm. © ADAGP, Paris and DACS, London 2004; **3** • Private Collection. Photo André Morain. © ADAGP, Paris and DACS, London 2004; **4** • © Photo CNAC/MNAM Dist. RMN; **5** • © D.B. © ADAGP, Paris and DACS, London 2004; **1968a: 1** • Courtesy Sonnabend Gallery, New York; **2** • Courtesy Sonnabend Gallery, New York; **3** • Courtesy the artist and Marian Goodman Gallery, New York; **4** • Museum of Modern Art, New York. The Fellows of Photography Fund. © DACS 2004; **5** • © DACS 2004; **6** • Courtesy Monika Sprueth Gallery/Philomene Magers. © DACS, London 2004; **1968b: 1** • Courtesy Gagosian Gallery, London. © Ed Ruscha; **2** • Museum Ludwig, Cologne. Courtesy Rheinisches Bildarchiv Cologne. © Sol LeWitt. © ARS, NY and DACS, London 2004; **3** • Museum of Modern Art, New York. © ARS, NY and DACS, London 2004; **4** • Musée Nationale d'Art Moderne, Centre Georges Pompidou, Paris. © ARS, NY and DACS, London 2004; **5** • © ARS, NY and DACS, London 2004; **6** • Courtesy Lisson Gallery, London; **7** • Collection Van Abbemuseum, Eindhoven, The Netherlands. © ARS, NY and DACS, London 2004; **8** • Courtesy of John Baldessari; **1969: 1** • Formerly Saatchi Collection, London. © ARS, NY and DACS, London 2004; **2** • Courtesy the artist. Photo © Estate of Peter Moore/VAGA, New York/DACS, London 2004; **3** • Museum of Modern Art, New York. Courtesy the artist. Photo © Estate of Peter Moore/VAGA, New York/DACS, London 2004; **4** • Art Institue of Chicago, through prior gifts of Arthur Keating and Mr. and Mrs. Edward Morris. © The Estate of Eva Hesse. Hauser & Wirth Zürich and London; **1970: 1** • Photo © Estate of Peter Moore/VAGA, New York/DACS, London 2004; **2** • Drawing by Lawrence Kenny. Courtesy the artist; **2** • Photo Frank Thomas. Courtesy the artist; **2** • Photo Frank Thomas. Courtesy the artist; **3** • Solomon R. Guggenheim Museum, New York (Panza Collection). Courtesy the artist. Photo © Estate of Peter Moore/VAGA, New York/DACS, London 2004; **4** • © Estate of Robert Smithson/VAGA, New York/DACS, London 2004; **1971: 1** • Musée National d'Art Moderne, Centre Georges Pompidou, Paris. Courtesy the artist. © DACS 2004; **2** • © D.B. © ADAGP, Paris and DACS, London 2004; **3** • Collection Daled, Brussels. Courtesy of the artist. © DACS 2004; **1972a: 1** • Collection Benjamin Katz. © DACS 2004; **1** • Collection Benjamin Katz. © DACS 2004; **2** • Collection Anne-Marie and Stéphane Rona. © DACS 2004; **3** • Galerie Michael Werner, Cologne. © DACS 2004; **4** • Ruth Kaiser, Courtesy Johannes Cadders. © DACS 2004; **5** • Municipal Van Abbe Museum, Eindhoven. © DACS 2004; **6** • © DACS 2004; **7** • © DACS 2004; **1972b: 1** • Museum Ludwig, Köln. Courtesy Rheinisches Bildarchiv, Köln (Cologne) ; **2** • Courtesy the artist. © DACS 2004; **3** • Art Institute of Chicago, Barbara Neff Smith Memorial Fund, Barbara Neff Smith & Solomon H. Smith Purchase Fund, 1977.600a-h. Courtesy Sperone Westwater, New York; **4** • Courtesy the artist. © DACS 2004; **5** • Collection Kunstmuseum, Bonn. © DACS 2004; **6** • Collection Speck, Cologne. Copyright the artist; **1973: 1** • Photo © Estate of Peter Moore/VAGA, New York/DACS, London 2004. © Nam June Paik; **2** • Courtesy Electronic Arts Intermix (EAI), New York; **3** • Courtesy Electronic Arts Intermix (EAI), New York; **4** • © ARS, NY and DACS, London 2004; **5** • Courtesy Electronic Arts Intermix (EAI), New York; **1974: 1** • Photo Erró. Collection the artist. © ARS, NY and DACS, London 2004; **2** • Photo by Minoru Niizuma. © Yoko Ono; **3** • Photo Bill Beckley. Courtesy the artist; **3** • Photo Bill Beckley. Courtesy the artist; **4** • Photo Kathy Dillon. Courtesy the artist; **5** • Courtesy the artist; **6** • San Francisco Museum of Modern Art. © ARS, NY and DACS, London 2004; **1975: 1** • © Judy Chicago 1972. © ARS, NY and DACS, London 2004; **2** • Philip Morris Companies, Inc. Faith Ringgold © 1980. ; **3** • The Brooklyn Museum of Art, Gift of The Elizabeth A. Sackler Foundation. Photo © Donald Woodman. © Judy Chicago 1979. © ARS, NY and DACS, London 2004; **4** • Photo David Reynolds. Courtesy the artist; **5** • Courtesy of the Estate of Ana Mendieta and Galerie Lelong, New York; **6** • Arts Council of Great Britain. Courtesy the artist; **1976: 1** • Photo E. Lee White, NYC, 1978. Courtesy the artist and The Kitchen, New York; **2** • Photo © Christopher Reenie/Robert Harding; **3** • Permanent collection the Chinati Foundation, Marfa, Texas. Photo Florian Holzherr. Art © Judd Foundation. Licensed by VAGA, New York/DACS, London 2004; **1977: 1** • Courtesy the artist; **2** • Courtesy the artist and Metro Pictures; **3** • Courtesy the artist and Metro Pictures; **4** • Courtesy the artist and Metro Pictures; **5** • Courtesy Ydessa Hendeles Art Foundation, Toronto; **1980: 1** • Courtesy the artist and Gorney Bravin and Lee, New York. © Sarah Charlesworth, 1978; **2** • Courtesy Barbara Gladstone Gallery, New York; **2** • Courtesy Barbara Gladstone Gallery, New York; **2** • Courtesy Barbara Gladstone Gallery, New York; **2** • Courtesy Barbara Gladstone Gallery, New York; **3** • Courtesy the artist; **4** • Courtesy Sean Kelly Gallery, New York; **1984a: 1** • Courtesy the artist; **2** • © ARS, NY and DACS, London 2004; **2** • © ARS, NY and DACS, London 2004; **3** • Collection the artist. Fred Lonidier, Visual Arts Department, University of California, San Diego; **3** • Collection the artist. Fred Lonidier, Visual Arts Department, University of California, San Diego; **4** • Courtesy the artist and Gorney Bravin & Lee, New York. © Martha Rosler, 1967–72; **5** • Courtesy the artist and Christopher Grimes Gallery, Santa Monica, CA; **6** • © Martha Rosler, 1974–5. Courtesy the artist and Gorney Bravin & Lee, New York; **6** • © Martha Rosler, 1974–5. Courtesy the artist and Gorney Bravin & Lee, New York; **1984b: 1** • Collection Mrs. Barbara Schwartz. Photo courtesy Gagosian Gallery, New York; **2** • Photo Jenny Holzer. © ARS, NY and DACS, London 2004; **3** • Courtesy Canal St. Communications; **1986: 1** • © Jeff Koons; **2** • Courtesy the artist and Jay Jopling/White Cube (London). © the artist; **3** • Courtesy the artist; **4** • Courtesy the artist; **5** • © Barbara Bloom, 1989. Courtesy Gorney, Bravin + Lee, New York; **1987: 1** • Courtesy of Group Material; **2** • Collection of Ulrich and Harriet Meyer. Photo James Dee. © DACS, London/VAGA, New York 2004; **3** • © Krzysztof Wodiczko. Courtesy Galerie Lelong, New York; **4** • The New York Public Library; **box** Richard Serra, *Tilted Arc*, 1981 (destroyed). Cor-ten steel, 365.8 x 3657.6 x 6.4 (144 x 1440 x 2½). Federal Plaza, New York. Photo Ann Chauvet, Paris; **5** • The Werner and Elaine Dannheisser Foundation, New York. © The Felix Gonzalez-Torres Foundation. Courtesy of Andrea Rosen Gallery, New York; **6** • The Werner and Elaine Dannheisser Foundation, New York. On long term loan to the Museum of Modern Art, New York. © The Felix Gonzalez-Torres Foundation. Courtesy of Andrea Rosen Gallery, New York; **7** • Philadelphia Museum of Art. Courtesy the artist; **1988: 1** • Museum of Modern Art, New York. Photo Axel Schneider, Frankfurt/Main. © Gerhard Richter; **2** • Museum of Modern Art, New York. Photo Friedrich Rosenstiel, Cologne. © Gerhard Richter; **3** • Städtische Galerie im Lenbachhaus, Munich. © Gerhard Richter; **4** • Courtesy the artist; **1989: 1** • Courtesy the artist; **2** • Photo Dawoud Bey. Courtesy Jack Tilton/Anna Kustera Gallery, New York; **3** • Courtesy Jack Tilton Gallery, New York; **4** • Courtesy Marian Goodman Gallery, New York; **5** • Courtesy Gavin Brown's Enterprise, New York; **1992: 1** • Courtesy of Documenta Archiv. © DACS 2004; **2** • Courtesy the artist and Metro Pictures Gallery, New York; **3** • Courtesy Galleria Emi Fontana, Milan. Photo Roberto Marossi, Milan; **4** • Courtesy the artist. Photo Nina Möntmann; **4** • Photo courtesy De Vleeshal, Middelberg, American Fine Arts, Co., New York and Tanya Bonakdar Gallery, New York; **1993a: 1** • Collection Alexina Duchamp, France. © Succession Marcel Duchamp/ADAGP, Paris and DACS, London 2004; **2** • Courtesy the artist. © ARS, NY and DACS, London 2004; **3** • Courtesy James Coleman and Marian Goodman Gallery, New York. © James Coleman; **4** • Courtesy the artist and Metro Pictures Gallery, New York; **5** • Courtesy the artist and Metro Pictures Gallery, New York; **1993b: 1** • Private Collection. Courtesy of the Paula Cooper Gallery, New York; **2** • Arts Council of England, London. Photo Edward Woodman. Courtesy the artist and Jay Jopling/White Cube (London). © the artist; **3** • Courtesy the artist; **4** • Commissioned by Artangel. Sponsored by Beck's. Courtesy Rachel Whiteread and Gagosian Gallery, London. Photo Sue Ormera; **1993c: 1** • Courtesy the Paula Cooper Gallery, New York; **2** • Courtesy the artist and P.P.O.W. Gallery, N.Y.; **3** • Courtesy Sean Kelly Gallery, New York; **4** • Photograph. © Rotimi Fani-Kayode/Autograph ABP; **5** • Courtesy Stephen Friedman Gallery, London; **6** • Courtesy the artist and Brent Sikkema, NYC; **7** • Courtesy the artist and Hauser & Wirth. Photo courtesy Gagosian Gallery, New York; **8** • © 2004 Glenn Ligon; **1994a: 1** • Courtesy Sonnabend Gallery, New York; **2** • Collection of the artist. Photo Ellen Page Wilson, courtesy Pace Wildenstein, New York. © Kiki Smith; **3** • Courtesy the artist and Matthew Marks Gallery. Photo K. Ignatiadis for Jeu de Paume; **4** • Courtesy the artist; **5** • Private Collection/Courtesy Jablonka Galerie, Cologne. Photo Nic Tenwiggenhorn, Düsseldorf; **1994b: 1** • Solomon R. Guggenheim Museum, New York. © Sol LeWitt. © ARS, NY and DACS, London 2004; **2** • Courtesy Regen Projects, Los Angeles; **3** • Courtesy the artist; **4** • Courtesy the artist; **1998: 1** • Photo Florian Holzherr. © James Turrell; **2** • Courtesy the artist. Photo © 1997 Fotoworks Benny Chan; **3** • Courtesy Lisson Gallery, London; **4** • Courtesy David Zwirner, New York; **1999: 1** • Courtesy the artist and Marian Goodman Gallery, New York; **2** • Courtesy the artist and Jay Jopling/White Cube (London). © the artist; **3** • Collection the artist. Courtesy Monika Sprueth Gallery/Philomene Magers. © DACS, London 2004; **2003: 1** • Courtesy the artist and Corvi-Mora, London; **2** • Courtesy the artist and Stephen Friedman Gallery, London; **3** • Courtesy Marian Goodman Gallery, New York; **4** • Courtesy the artist, Frith Street Gallery, London and Marian Goodman Galleries, New York and Paris

index

Page numbers in *italics* refer to illustrations